DONALD /
P.O. BOX 279
ELLENSBURG WASH 98926

A DICTIONARY OF
CHRISTIAN THEOLOGY

A
Dictionary
of
Christian
Theology

edited by
ALAN RICHARDSON

THE WESTMINSTER PRESS
Philadelphia

STANDARD BOOK No. 664–20860–6
LIBRARY OF CONGRESS CATALOG CARD No. 69–19153

PUBLISHED BY THE WESTMINSTER PRESS ®
PHILADELPHIA, PENNSYLVANIA

PRINTED IN THE UNITED STATES OF AMERICA

PREFACE

Theology is a subject of immensely wide range. It is bound up with the long history of ideas, especially those of Western civilization, upon which it has exercised a powerful influence. In this new age of rapid world-wide communication these ideas are disseminated to every part of the globe, and they have not remained unaffected in the process. The roots of Christian theology lie deep in the civilizations of the ancient world, particularly those of Israel and Greece. Since the days of the early Church the Christian proclamation has engaged in dialogue with non-Christian ways of thinking, and Christian theologians have constantly been driven to define their standpoint either in terms of or in opposition to the philosophical presuppositions of their environment. Especially is this true since the days of the Enlightenment (*c.* 1650–1780), when new forms of secular and non-religious thinking about man and the universe were developed. Today it is patently true that theology is being done in dialogue with, or sometimes in reaction from, the various modes of philosophical and scientific thinking which prevail in our time.

It is with the theological issues of today that this Dictionary is primarily concerned. But, since it is impossible to understand an idea or a doctrine without some understanding of how it came to be what it is, considerable attention has necessarily been given to the history of Christian ideas and of the words in which they are expressed. Emphasis is laid upon developments of thought rather than upon biographical details or events of church history; these matters can be investigated by the student who consults the magisterial *Oxford Dictionary of the Christian Church*, edited by F. L. Cross (1957). The main thrust of this Dictionary is in the interlocking areas of theology and philosophy. Limitations had necessarily to be imposed upon the scope of this already large volume, and some fields of Christian thought and practice have had to be treated more sketchily in order that the main doctrinal and philosophical themes could be dealt with more adequately. The *Theological Word Book of the Bible* (1950), under the present editor, has already covered the biblical groundwork, and therefore biblical words are considered here chiefly in respect of their role in the development of Christian theology. *A Dictionary of Christian Ethics* (1967) has recently appeared, edited by John Macquarrie, and it is unnecessary to repeat here what has there been so comprehensively treated. Even so, there remain important areas of Christian thought and practice which have had to be given less attention than their importance and interest required. Liturgiology, if it were to be adequately treated, would demand a dictionary at least as large as this one. Similarly, although it is hoped that this volume may be helpful in the dialogue with other religions, it was necessary to restrict its scope to specifically Christian theology: a dictionary of the comparative study of religion would require an even larger volume.

Preface

The contributors to this Dictionary are drawn from several different Christian traditions. While it is hoped that a high degree of objectivity has been maintained in matters of scholarship and verifiable historical fact, it is inevitable and indeed desirable that in an enterprise of ecumenical co-operation of this kind each writer should present the subject from his own point of view. Many theological issues are being vigorously debated at the present time and new positions are being taken up. Divisions between theological attitudes today often do not correspond to the traditional denominational alignments of former years. In order that the situation of present-day theology might be clearly seen, no attempt has been made to achieve a unified outlook; the agreement *in necessariis* among such a varied body of contributors, drawn from both the Old World and the New, is both a result and an expression of the ecumenical understanding of our age. It is hardly necessary to add that each writer is responsible for his own contribution and not for the views expressed by any other writer. This should be borne in mind especially in connection with articles dealing specifically with questions at issue in contemporary theological debate.

It is hoped that this Dictionary will be found useful by several types of reader. The theological student will be able to look up many words which are new to him or which puzzle him in the course of his studies. The working minister who wishes to keep abreast of contemporary theological thinking will be enabled to do so, especially if he makes use of the bibliographies appended to the main articles. The layman who recognizes his responsibility in theological matters, which ought not nowadays to be regarded as a professional clerical specialism, will be helped in making his opinion (which must be an *informed* opinion) heard in the counsels of his church. The philosopher, who knows that both in history and today the mutual interaction of philosophy and theology has been of immense importance in the evolution of ideas, will be able to acquaint himself with the theological aspects of the on-going dialogue. Finally, anyone who wishes to understand the civilization and culture which have played so large a part in shaping the modern world can find in this volume an outline of the Christian contribution to the situation which has evolved out of the toils and conflicts of the past and will be helped to estimate its role in the shaping of the future.

The thanks of the editor are warmly extended to all the contributors without whose unselfish co-operation this project could not have been carried through.

ALAN RICHARDSON

CONTRIBUTORS

JAMES ATKINSON *Professor and Head of the Department of Biblical Studies, University of Sheffield; Canon Theologian of Leicester.* Articles on Atonement and Redemption, e.g. **Atonement; Cross; Redemption; Salvation**

JAMES BARR *Professor of Semitic Languages and Literatures, University of Manchester.* **Semantics**

JOHN BOWDEN *Editor and Managing Director, SCM Press, London.* **Jesus of History**

B. C. BUTLER *Auxiliary Bishop of Westminster.* **Vatican Council II**

REGINALD CANT *Canon of York.* Articles on Anglicanism, e.g. **Anglican Communion; Anglo-Catholicism; Doctrine of Development; Thirty-Nine Articles of Religion**

J. G. DAVIES *Professor of Theology and Director of the Institute for the Study of Worship and Religious Architecture, University of Birmingham.* Articles on Ecclesiology and Ministry, e.g. **Apostolic Succession; Ascension of Christ; Church; Consecration; Ecclesiology; Ministry; Ordination**

A. O. DYSON *Chaplain, Ripon Hall, Oxford.* **Teilhard de Chardin**

A. RAYMOND GEORGE *Principal, Richmond College, Richmond, Surrey.* **Methodism**

ROBERT T. HANDY *Professor of Church History, Union Theological Seminary, New York.* Articles on American Theology, e.g. **Empirical Theology; Niebuhr; Pragmatism; Tillich**

A. T. HANSON *Professor of Theology, University of Hull.* Articles on Eschatology, e.g. **Christian Hope; Eschatology; Heaven and Hell; Invisible Church; Time and Eternity**

R. P. C. HANSON *Professor of Christian Theology, University of Nottingham.* Articles on Tradition, e.g. **Authority; Canon; Notes of the Church; Rome, Roman Catholicism; Tradition**

JOSEPH HAROUTUNIAN *Professor of Systematic Theology, Divinity School, University of Chicago.* **Spirit, Holy Spirit, Spiritism**

GEORGE S. HENDRY *Professor of Systematic Theology, Princeton Theological Seminary, Princeton, New Jersey.* **Christology**

R. W. HEPBURN *Professor of Philosophy, University of Edinburgh.* Articles on Philosophy, e.g. **Descartes; Hume; Metaphysics; Scepticism; Spinoza**

Contributors

WILLIAM HORDERN *President, Lutheran Theological Seminary, Saskatoon, Saskatchewan.* Articles on **Creation; Doctrine of Man; etc.**

R. M. C. JEFFERY *Faith and Order Secretary, the British Council of Churches.* Articles on **Ecumenical Movement; Religious Liberty; Reunion of the Churches; Theology of Mission**

DANIEL JENKINS *Reader in Religious Studies and University Chaplain, University of Sussex.* **Culture**

A. R. C. LEANEY *Reader in Theology, University of Nottingham.* **Gnosticism**

GORDON LEFF *Reader in History, University of York.* **Nominalism-Realism; Thomism**

JOHN MACQUARRIE *Professor of Systematic Theology, Union Theological Seminary, New York.* **Barth; Schleiermacher**

JOHN T. MCNEILL *Professor Emeritus of Church History, Union Theological Seminary, New York.* Articles on Protestant Reformation, e.g. **Calvin; Luther; Protestantism; Reformation, Reformation Theology**

DAVID A. MARTIN *Reader in Sociology at the London School of Economics and Political Science, University of London.* **Sociology of Religion**

E. L. MASCALL *Professor of Historical Theology at King's College, University of London.* Articles on Eucharistic Theology and Mariology, e.g. **Blessed Virgin Mary; Eucharist; Liturgical Movement**

SIMON MEIN, SSM *Warden, Kelham Theological College, Kelham, Newark, Nottinghamshire.* **Benediction, Blessing**

T. H. L. PARKER *Vicar of Oakington, Cambridge.* Articles on Predestination and Free Will, e.g. **Conversion; Predestination; Providence**

NORMAN PITTENGER *King's College, Cambridge, formerly Professor, General Theological Seminary, New York.* **Process Theology**

NORMAN W. PORTEOUS *Professor Emeritus of Hebrew and Semitic Languages, University of Edinburgh.* **Old Testament Theology**

ALAN RICHARDSON *Dean of York.* Articles on Revelation and a wide range of other subjects including, e.g. **Apologetics; Augustinianism; Being; Christian Initiation; Creed(s); Death of God Theology; Doctrine of Holy Scripture; Hermeneutics; Miracle; Problem of Evil; Problem of History; Religious Experience; Religious Language; Revelation; Theology of Prayer; Worship**

JAMES RICHMOND *Senior Lecturer in the Department of Religious Studies, University of Lancaster.* Articles on German Theology (Modern), e.g. **Crisis Theology; Demythologizing; Existentialism; Liberal Protestantism, Liberal Theology**

N. H. G. ROBINSON *Professor of Divinity, University of St Andrews.* Articles on the Doctrine of God, e.g. **Attributes of God; God**

DOM PLACID SPEARRITT *Monk of Ampleforth Abbey, York.* Articles on Mediaeval Theology, e.g. **Dionysius the Pseudo-Areopagite; Neoplatonism**

ALBERIC STACPOOLE, OSB *Monk of Ampleforth Abbey, York.* Articles on Mediaeval Theology, e.g. **Abelard; Analogy of Being; Anselm; Duns Scotus; Neo-Scholasticism, Neo-Thomism**

PATRICK THOMPSON *Senior Lecturer of Theology, Hull University.* **Orthodoxy (Eastern)**

E. J. TINSLEY *Professor of Theology, University of Leeds.* Articles on Vision of God, e.g. **Asceticism; Eckhart; Imitation of Christ; Monachism, Monasticism; Mysticism; St John of the Cross**

H. E. W. TURNER *Professor of Divinity, University of Durham.* Articles on the Doctrine of Trinity, e.g. **Cappadocian Fathers; Modalism; Monarchism; Trinity**

P. S. WATSON *Professor of Systematic Theology, Garrett Theological Seminary, Evanston, Illinois.* Articles on Law-Grace, e.g. **Faith; Grace; Justification; Law; Righteousness; Sanctification**

ABBREVIATIONS

AV	Authorized Version of the Bible (1611), known also as King James Version
BCP	Book of Common Prayer (1549, 1552 and 1662)
CDT	*A Catholic Dictionary of Theology,* eds. H. F. Davis, A. Williams, I. Thomas, J. Crehan, 1962–
CE	*Catholic Encyclopedia,* 15 vols + index, 1907–14
CH	*Church History*
CR	*Corpus Reformatorum,* Ioannis Calvini Opera quae supersunt omnia, eds. G. Baum, E. Cunitz, E. Reuss. Brunsvigae, 1863–
DCE	*A Dictionary of Christian Ethics,* ed. John Macquarrie, 1967
DHGE	*Dictionnaire d'Histoire et de Géographie Ecclésiastiques,* eds. A. Johnson and others, 20 vols + index, 1937, and Supplement, 1944
DNB	*Dictionary of National Biography*
DS	*Dictionnaire de Spiritualité,* eds. M. Viller, sj, and others, 1937–
DTC	*Dictionnaire de Théologie Catholique,* eds. A. Vacant, E. Mangenot and E. Amann, 1903–50
EA	Martin Luther, *Sämmtliche Werke,* Erlangen, 1826–
EB	*Encyclopaedia Britannica*
EC	*Enciclopedia Cattolica,* eds. P. Paschini and others, 1949–54
ER	*Ecumenical Review*
ERE	*Encyclopaedia of Religion and Ethics,* ed. James Hastings, 1921–
ET	English translation
EVV	English versions of the Bible
ExT	*Expository Times*
IDB	*Interpreter's Dictionary of the Bible*
JEH	*Journal of Ecclesiastical History*
JR	*Journal of Religion*
JTS	*Journal of Theological Studies*
KJV	see AV above
LXX	Greek Translation of the Old Testament (Septuagint)
NEB	New English Bible (1961)
NED	*A New English Dictionary on Historical Principles,* ed. J. A. H. Murray, 10 vols, 1888–1928, and Supplement, 1933
NT	New Testament
OT	Old Testament
PG	*Patrologia Graeca,* ed. J. P. Migne, 1857–66
PL	*Patrologia Latina,* ed. J. P. Migne, 1844–64
PQ	*Philosophical Quarterly*

Abbreviations

PS	The Parker Society for the Publication of the Works of the Fathers and Early Writers of the Reformed English Church, 1840–
Q Met	*Quaestiones Metaphysica*
RB	*Revue Biblique*
RSV	American Revised Standard Version of the Bible (1946 and 1952)
RV	Revised Version of the Bible (1881, 1884)
RVV	Revised Versions: the above two Versions
SCG	*Summa Contra Gentiles*
SJT	*Scottish Journal of Theology*
TDNT	*Theological Dictionary of the New Testament,* ET of *TWNT,* trans. and ed. Geoffrey W. Bromiley, 1964–
TWBB	*A Theological Word Book of the Bible,* ed. Alan Richardson, 1950
TWNT	*Theologisches Wörterbuch zum Neuen Testament,* ed. Gerhard Kittel, ET: *TDNT*
UN	United Nations
ZAW	*Zeitschrift für die alttestamentliche Wissenschaft*

A DICTIONARY OF
CHRISTIAN THEOLOGY

A Priori, A Posteriori

A priori (Latin, meaning 'something prior' or 'going before') is used in philosophy of that which precedes or is independent of sense-experience, as opposed to *a posteriori*, that which follows upon or is known from sense-experience (or by reasoning from what is already given). *See* **Religious** *A Priori*.

Abelard, Peter

Peter Abelard (or Abailard, 1079–1142), was born at Nantes of Breton parents. He studied under Roscelin, with whom he disagreed on the Trinity, under William of Champeaux, with whom he disagreed on Universals and extreme Realism, and under Anselm of Laon, with whom he disagreed on exegetical method. He set up his own brilliant school in Paris (St Geneviève), lecturing on dialectic and later on theology. His tragic love for Heloise, niece of Fulbert, Canon of Notre-Dame, caused him to flee Paris in 1118. He became a monk of St Denis, but was summoned in 1121 to the Council of Soissons to defend his *Summi Boni* on the Trinity, which was condemned and burned. He established an oratory near Troyes, 'The Paraclete', and in 1125 became Abbot of St Gildas in Britanny, returning to teach in Paris in 1136. Arnold of Brescia, to be condemned with him, was among his pupils. St Bernard (q.v.) accused him of heresy and in 1140 the Council of Sens condemned him – six bishops signed the recommendation to the pope – on the basis of a list of propositions supposedly taken from Abelard's writings (though modern scholarship shows them to be grievously inaccurate): these were provided by St Bernard, who preferred this means to open dialogue. Louis VII and Theobald Count of Champagne were present. Innocent II confirmed the findings, Abelard's works were publicly burned and he retired broken to Cluny, where he died in 1142 in the care of Abbot Peter the Venerable.

Abelard never completed his widely ranging works, but revised and rewrote as his thoughts and his disciples' promptings suggested; so that he never reached a final view or definitive exposition of any doctrine: after him, his followers took his studies further still. His influence lay not in the synthesis of his thought (for the *summae* were to come later) but in the brilliance of his handling of particular problems. He brought the full power of reasoning logic to areas of the faith like the Trinity, which had till then been held too sacred for such treatment. In discussing the Trinity, he seems to have confused essential attributes with Persons; in the incarnation, he denied Christ's substantial reality as man.

His extant works are (1) *Summi Boni* (*de Unitate et Trinitate Divina*, 1120); a reply to Roscelin's extreme realism. In discussing universals, he raised the old logical arguments to a new epistemological level; (2) *Theologia Christiana* (1124); drawing on the Fathers, a defence of the above, which had been condemned at Soissons; (3) *Introductio in Theologiam* (1138); a further development of the above, moving towards the *summa* style, for which it stood as an early model. Its threefold division was faith/hope; morals and charity; sacraments; (4) *Sic et Non;* 158 theses with relevant quotations from scriptural, patristic and conciliar sources, set out without glossing their contradictions. Here was a technique for proper use of source material, a model used afterwards by the canonists; (5) *Scito te ipsum* (Ethics); important on morals and penance, where he brought out the importance of love rather than fear as a motive. He stressed, as the whole morality of acts, intention based on purity of heart and conscious responsibility; (6) *A Commentary on Romans*; this contains his doctrine on original sin, condemned at Sens by St Bernard. His atonement doctrine stressed the exemplary value of Christ's sufferings, but little else; (7) *Corpus of Logic* and other philosophical writing, especially the *dialecta*; (8) *Dialogue between a Jew, a Philosopher and a Christian*; (9) *Historia Calamitatum*; his apology for his life; and *Letters* to Heloise; (10) Several *Hymns* of high artistic value, especially his *Planctus*. There also remain several minor commentaries. For Abelard's view of atonement, *see* **Atonement** (6, *d*).

E. Gilson, *Heloise et Abélard*, 1938; M. D. Knowles, *The Evolution of Mediaeval Thought*, 1962; J. R. McCallum, *Abelard's Christian Theology*, 1948; A. V. Murray, *Abelard and St Bernard: A Study in Twelfth Century 'Modernism'*, 1967; J. G. Sikes, *Peter Abailard*, 1932; Helen Waddell, *Peter Abelard*, 1934; F. C. Copleston, *A History of Philosophy*, II, 1950, pp. 136–55; Johan Huizinga, *Men and Ideas*, 1960, pp. 178–95; Dom Jean Lecleucq, 'Les Fames Successives de la Lettre-Traité de St Bernard Contre Abélard', *RB*, LXXVIII, 1–2 (1968), pp. 87–105; L. Minio-Palluelo, *EB*, I, 1964 ed., pp. 40–41; E. Portalié, *DTC*, I, cols. 62–73, E. Vacandard, *DHGE*, cols. 71–91; M. E. Williams, *CDT*. I, pp. 6–8.

ALBERIC STACPOOLE, O.S.B.

Absolute

As an adjective, 'absolute' has meant in philosophy 'unconditioned', 'independent', 'free from contingency', 'necessary'. As a substantive, 'the Absolute' has played important, if obscure, roles in speculative metaphysics, particularly in post-Kantian idealism. To Hegel (q.v.), the Absolute is not a transcendent deity, existing independently of the world, but it is reality considered as a whole and as aware of itself. It is in individual finite minds that reality reaches self-awareness, in art, religion, and most notably in the systematic activity of the philosopher as he seeks to understand the cosmic process as a whole. Nature, from this viewpoint, becomes the necessary objective condition for the appearance and life of spirit, and thus for the goal of self-awareness. Aristotle had spoken of God as self-aware, self-contemplating: but Aristotle's God, unlike Hegel's Absolute, had a centre of consciousness distinct from the consciousness of finite minds such as our own. Hegel was not content to define the Absolute as 'infinite substance' (compare Spinoza, q.v.); it is also Subject and Spirit.

Idealists have differed considerably in their conceptions of the Absolute. To Bradley (q.v.), for instance, the Absolute was the totality of things, in which is reconciled or harmonized whatever in the world of appearance is contradictory and incoherent. In itself, the Absolute is inaccessible to our understanding, though we may have hints and clues in our experience. (Contrast Hegel, to whom the 'contradictory' phases in the world's processes are *retained* in the life of the Absolute, as phases necessary to its development.)

The Absolute is a prime example of a concept that can be elucidated only within the context of a metaphysical system as a whole: the existence or non-existence of an Absolute cannot be verified or falsified like that of a material object by observation or experiment, and the accusations of logical positivism that *therefore* the Absolute is a meaningless notion were unjustified. Real logical difficulties do, however, arise in theories that speak of the Absolute as Mind – but not this or that particular mind, or as 'containing', including' particular finite minds, or as seeing how an Absolute could be both 'perfect' in some sense and yet 'contain' the minds of very imperfect beings within it. At the root of many doctrines of the Absolute are *epistemological* arguments, claiming that all reality is in a sense mental or mind-dependent. But although to conceive an entity as existent is necessarily to conceive it as it would be apprehended by a subject, yet it is a hazardous inference to conclude that therefore to exist is to be the object of a knowing mind. Lastly, the onus falls heavily on the proponent of a theory of the Absolute to justify his claim that the world is more rational and less fragmentary than it appears to ordinary experience – indeed, that it is rational and complete in the highest degree.

F. C. Copleston, *A History of Philosophy*, VII, 1963; A. C. Ewing, *Idealism: a Critical Survey*, 1934.

R. W. HEPBURN

Absolute Dependence, Feeling of

This definition of religion is to be found in *The Christian Faith* (1821–2) of F. D. E. Schleiermacher (1768–1834), German Protestant theologian. According to Schleiermacher, this feeling (or awareness) is universally present in humanity, and manifests itself in the positive world-religions, of which Christianity is the supreme but not the only example. *See* **Liberal Protestantism; Schleiermacher, F. D. E.**

JAMES RICHMOND

Absolution. *see* Worship.

Acceptance, Assent, Assurance

It was usual in mediaeval theology to distinguish three elements in faith: *notitia* (understanding), *assensus* (assent) and *fiducia* (trust). The first two deal with understanding and assenting to the propositional truths of revealed theology (*see* **Revelation**). *Fiducia* was the final act of faith: believing what the Church teaches because God has revealed it. It could mean in effect submission to the teaching of the Church. This mediaeval conception of the nature of faith is largely intellectualist or rationalistic: as A. N. Whitehead declared, the Middle Ages were not so much the Age of Faith as the Age of Reason. At the Reformation a conception of faith more in line with that of the NT was recovered: faith was *trust* in the act of God in Christ and personal commitment to Christ as the sole bringer of truth and salvation. It was belief in a Person, not in a proposition (*cf.* the important distinction between 'belief in' and 'belief that'), although, of course, it implied believing in propositions when the believer came to think out the meaning of his belief. For Luther the fiducial element in faith became once again primary, as it had been for St Paul, and it was no longer understood as submission to the Church's teaching or even as the acceptance of revealed doctrine (John Baillie). But later Protestant orthodoxy tended to revert to the conception of faith as assent to correct doctrinal propositions. A threefold division of faith was generally recognized, assent, acceptance and assurance. Intellectual *assent* to propositions sometimes became almost as dominant as it was in Roman teaching. At the other end of the scale *assurance* was made by certain sects the essential element in faith: certitude concerning one's personal salvation was demanded of all believers but was not so easily professed by the more humble of them. But other theologians taught that *acceptance* was the normal mode of faith for holy and humble men of heart. Assent was not enough: the devils and the unregenerate could assent to the propositions of theology (James 2.19). Assurance was too much and it might lead to overconfidence and pride. Acceptance, the grateful trusting in God's promised salvation in Christ, was the characteristic attitude of the Christian believer.

Note. Paul Tillich uses the word 'acceptance', as he uses many other Christian terms, in a sense foreign to its Christian meaning. With him acceptance is something which *we* accept, and apparently this requires courage, but it is a courage beyond the confidence based on personal encounter with God. The 'God of theism' is transcended in Tillich's philosophy, and faith becomes 'the state of being grasped by the power of being'. Whether this language means anything at all is doubtful, but it is certain that it does not mean what Christian language about faith has always meant. *See* P. Tillich, *The Courage to Be,* 1952, ch.VI. *See also* **Faith.**

John Baillie, *The Idea of Revelation in Recent Thought,* 1956, ch. V.

EDITOR

Accident(s)

For Aristotle, whose thought has been influential in the formation of the classical Christian doctrine of God, an accident is a characteristic (e.g. sunburned) which may belong to a particular type of subject (man) but need not do so. Accordingly for the Christian conception of God there are no accidents in the divine nature. Rather 'in God's nature there is nothing which is not God himself' (H. Heppe, *Reformed Dogmatics,* 1861, ET, 1950, p. 57).

N. H. G. ROBINSON

Activism. *see* Quietism.

Actus Purus. see Being; God (7).

Adiaphora

A Greek word meaning 'things indifferent'; it refers to matters not regarded as essential to faith which might therefore be allowed, if the 'weaker brother' found them helpful. In particular the Adiaphorists were those Protestants who with Melanchthon held certain Catholic practices (e.g. confirmation, veneration of saints) to be tolerable for the sake of unity; controversy continued over what were adiaphora until the Formula of Concord (1577, q.v.). Generally speaking the more rigid forms of Protestantism, including the English Puritans, tended to hold that everything not explicitly allowed in the Scriptures was forbidden; while others (e.g. Anglicans) regarded many traditional practices, though without scriptural warrant, as adiaphora.

EDITOR

Adoptianism, Adoptionism

The Adoptianist heresy broke out in Spain in the eighth century and was condemned at a Synod in Rome convened by Pope Leo III in 799; it reappeared in more moderate forms later in the Middle Ages, when Abelard and others revived similar views. The Adoptianists held that Jesus, *qua* human, was 'adopted' by the Word and thus incorporated into the Godhead: Jesus *as man* is the adopted Son of God. Harnack (q.v.) in his *History of Dogma* (ET, 1894–9) used the term of a heretical tendency in early Greek theology, which suggested that Christ was a man on whom divine qualities were conferred. When the term is thus used (somewhat anachronistically) of early Christian thought, it is usually spelt 'Adoptionism'. The Ebionites, Paul of Samosata, Theodore of Mopsuestia and the 'Antiochene School' in general exemplified this type of christology. In modern times certain Liberal Protestant theologians have found the theory attractive, holding that it safeguarded the real humanity of Christ as over against the Alexandrian type of orthodox christology. The objection to any extreme form of Adoptionism is that, if God had to wait until a man good enough to be adopted as his Son happened to appear, the central affirmation that God *sent* his Son into the world to redeem and save it would have to be abandoned. And then the love of God towards sinful men would become questionable (*cf.* John 3.16). There is a world of difference between the view (which came naturally to the Greeks) that a man became God and the NT proclamation that God became man.

D. M. Baillie, *God Was in Christ,* 1948, esp. pp. 129 ff.; A. Grillmeier, *Christ in Christian Tradition,* ET, 1965, pp. 90–101, and the standard histories of doctrine.

EDITOR

Agape

Agape (Greek: love) is a solemn meal held in the early Church in connection with the Eucharist (q.v.). It may well have originated in the separation from the original eucharistic meal of everything except the two acts connected with the bread and the cup to which at the Last Supper Christ gave new significance as his *anamnesis* (q.v.); and the cause of the separation may have been abuses of the type referred to in I Cor. 11 which were likely to occur when Gentile Christians took part in a sacred meal of Jewish origin unfamiliar to them. It is not always easy to distinguish between references to the Eucharist and references to the Agape in early writings such as the *Didache.* Probably practice as regards the Agape varied considerably from place to place. As a meal specifically connected with the Eucharist it seems to have become extinct by the end of the seventh century, but it has been revived in recent years by some proponents of the Liturgical Movement (q.v.) in the form of a breakfast after the Eucharist.

E. L. MASCALL

Aggiornamento

Aggiornamento is an Italian word which can mean 'adjournment' (i.e. postponement of an event) or 'bringing things up to date'. It is, of course, in this second sense that the word is nowadays used in theological discourse. It was the innovating pontificate of John XXIII which gave currency to the word, after he had made clear his urgent desire for

what he called an *aggiornamento,* or a bringing up
to date, of historic Catholicism. Perhaps the word
is used in its untranslated form by English writers
through their natural dislike of such words as
'modernizing' in view of their unhappy association with the modernist movement in the Roman
Church at the beginning of this century. *See*
Modernism; Vatican Council II.

EDITOR

Agnosticism

An agnostic is a person who holds that we do not,
or cannot, have adequate grounds for either
affirming or denying the existence of God. Such
knowledge is out of reach, either because of
certain insuperable limits of the human intellect,
or because the evidence does not appear strong
enough to support theistic belief or atheism (the
term 'agnostic' originated as a coinage of T. H.
Huxley). The theme of the limits of reason is developed most memorably in Kant's first Critique,
The Critique of Pure Reason (1781). We are constantly tempted, Kant argued, to apply concepts,
which are both intelligible and indispensable in
ordinary reasoning, to the very different task of
talking about the sum of things, or about the
cause of all things. Where speculation outsoars
any possible human experience, we delude ourselves that we can gain reliable insights. This
aspect of Kant's thought was in striking accord
with the tone of David Hume's. Nineteenth-
century agnostics like J. S. Mill and Leslie
Stephen saw challenges to theism not only in these
philosophical difficulties but also in the application of scientific methods and attitudes to theological issues.

A substantial measure of agnosticism is, however, compatible with religious belief. Like Kant
himself, a writer might turn from theoretical
argumentation for God, and seek to develop
instead a *moral* argument, or some variant of that
(e.g. H. L. Mansel, *The Limits of Religious
Thought,* 1858). More generally, to admit any
place for *mystery* within Christian theology (and
it is surely impossible to eliminate it) is to confess
that some agnosticism about the attributes of
deity, the nature of a hereafter, etc. is essential to
Christian belief.

Recent philosophical critiques of theism have
tended to deny *meaning* and *logical coherence* to
theistic concepts rather than concern themselves
with evidence or arguments. On a logical positivist view (q.v.) agnosticism is not a tenable
position, since it is as meaningless to say 'I don't
know whether God exists' as to affirm confidently
that he does or does not exist. But the positivist
accounts of meaning, and of theological concepts
in particular, were grossly oversimplified accounts. To explore and analyse their actual complexity is to be shown that there is indeed scope
for an agnosticism of meaning as well as of
evidence and argument. *See also* **Scepticism.**

R. W. HEPBURN

Albertus Magnus, St (Albert the Great)

A leading theologian, Albert (1200–1280) taught
at Cologne, where St Thomas Aquinas was his
pupil. He encountered Averroism (q.v.) in Paris
(*c.* 1245) and later wrote against it (1256). Nevertheless he defended Aquinas at Paris in 1277, when
the latter's Aristotelian re-interpretation of the
Christian faith was under attack from many
quarters, including the Dominican Order to
which they both belonged. His somewhat inchoate
thought pre-figures Aquinas' clear and developed
system of natural and revealed theology.

EDITOR

Alexandrian Theology. *see* Origen; Clement of Alexandria; Christology (4).

Allegory

Allegory is a method of interpreting Scripture
whereby the text is made to yield a meaning which
is other than its literal or surface or historical
meaning. Palestinian rabbinic Judaism practised
a rudimentary and cautious type of allegorizing on
the text of the Pentateuch in order to reconcile
inconsistencies and remove absurdities in the text,
and the Dead Sea Scrolls show that the Qumran
covenanters used similar restricted allegorizing
techniques. The writers of the NT followed these
examples, as can be detected in such passages as
Gal. 4.21–26; I Cor. 9.8–10; Heb. 7.2 (the last
being an example of allegorizing names, which is a
well-attested rabbinic practice). This sort of
allegorizing can be traced in early Christian
literature up to the third century. But with the
Christian Platonists of Alexandria, Clement and
Origen, a new type of allegorizing, derived from
pagan Hellenistic literature through Philo, appears. The technique of allegorizing certain
authoritative and sacrosanct works of literature
or of myth, such as the poems of Homer or the
traditional legends about the Greek gods, had
gradually been developed, beginning with Plato,
had been greatly advanced by the Stoics, and
brought to a considerable degree of facility by an
author of the first century AD called Heracleitus
Ponticus. Philo took over this technique in order
to apply it to the Pentateuch, with the intention of
shifting the emphasis in interpretation of the
Torah from its literal meaning to philosophical or
psychological meanings. His allegory was in fact
anti-historical, designed to divorce the passage
allegorized from its historical background and
context and cause it to yield general truths of
philosophy, morality or psychology. This technique the Christian Platonists of Alexandria took
over in their turn and employed to extract
general truths of philosophy, morality and
Christian doctrine very freely from all parts of
Scripture. Origen professed to follow a threefold
method of interpretation, seeing in most passages
a literal meaning, in very many a moral meaning
as well, and in some a spiritual (i.e. doctrinal or

mystical or philosophical) meaning as well as the others. But he did not consistently keep to this pattern. Allegory of this sort, once introduced, overshadowed the earlier, more pedestrian, Jewish kind of allegory, and played thenceforward a very important part in Christian exegesis of Scripture. Though allegory helped the Church to retain the OT in spite of the sharp and often penetrating criticism of the Gnostics, it cannot be said to have been a wholesome influence by and large. Later writers were rather more restrained than the Christian Platonists, especially the Antiochene school, but allegory became in the early Middle Ages even more developed, and by the period of the great scholastic writers had been codified into no less than five 'senses'. The Reformers tended to discourage (though they did not wholly reject) allegory, and since the rise of historical criticism it has been seen to be wholly valueless, except perhaps when employed with conscious piety in the liturgical use of the Psalms.

Typology, which has its roots in a purely Jewish background (rabbinic literature and Dead Sea Scrolls), is much more widely used than allegory in the NT. It is the comparison of an event or series of events in the past with an event or series of events in the present or immediate future. The events connected with Moses, or those connected with Adam, are compared with the events connected with Christ (Heb. 3.1–6; II Cor. 3.12–17; Rom. 5.12–21; I Cor. 15.45–49, etc.); the first Passover is compared with Christ's atoning death (I Cor. 5.6–8); and the experiences of Israel in the wilderness are compared to the experience of worshipping Christians (I Cor. 10.1–11). This type of scriptural exegesis has from the beginning always been used in Christian literature, spirituality and worship, and has contributed richly to Christian thought and life throughout the history of the Church. As it entails a correlation of event with event, and involves no divorcing of passages from their context, it has survived more successfully the advent of historical criticism, but it can very easily lapse into fantasy and a purely subjective interpretation.

J. Daniélou, *From Shadows to Reality*, 1960; R. M. Grant, *The Letter and the Spirit*, 1957; R. P. C. Hanson, *Allegory and Event*, 1959; G. W. H. Lampe and K. J. Woollcombe, *Essays on Typology*, 1957.

R. P. C. HANSON

Anabaptists

The name, meaning 'rebaptizers', is used comprehensively for a number of related sects that emerged at the Reformation era, marked by numerous departures from Nicene orthodoxy and traditional views of the sacraments. The origins of the movement are obscurely but traceably linked with certain pre-Reformation enthusiastic and apocalyptical groups, but the Anabaptist brotherhoods of Switzerland and Germany arose in the wake of the first stage of the reforms of Luther and Zwingli. They took their ground on Scripture, but,

employing both mystical and quite literal interpretations, deduced from the text a variety of doctrines. The principle of believers' baptism, with the corresponding more or less absolute rejection of paedobaptism, was generally asserted. Some Anabaptists affirmed the sleep of the soul from death to the resurrection; others became anti-trinitarian. The mediaeval and early Protestant assumption of a church-state system was repugnant to them; and with this was associated their unqualified repudiation, defended from the Sermon on the Mount, of all participation in war and in secular government. Their effort was to establish and by discipline to maintain a church 'without spot or wrinkle' of baptized and regenerate saints. Their discipline included excommunication and 'avoidance' of offenders on action of the local group. The wide circulation of preaching leaders, whose travels were either voluntary or forced by persecution, secured some intercourse among the groups, but the authority acquired by individuals claiming revelation resulted in diversity and led to many schisms. While pacificism prevailed, there were notorious incidents of fanatical violence. Amid continuing persecution the values of the movement were largely perpetuated by the work of Menno Simons (d. 1561). Recent scholarship has brought considerable revision of earlier harsh judgments of the thought of many Anabaptist leaders.

F. H. Littell, *The Anabaptist Doctrine of the Church*, 1952; G. H. Williams, *The Radical Reformation*, 1962; G. H. Williams and A. M. Mergal, eds., *Spiritual and Anabaptist Writers*, 1957.

J. T. MCNEILL

Analogue

This word is nowadays used to signify something which bears a real analogy to something other than itself, even though the latter cannot be known directly by us. For instance, human fatherhood might be held to be an analogue of an aspect of transcendent or divine being, so that it could be appropriate to speak of the Fatherhood of God. *See* **Psychological Analogy; Social Analogy; Thomistic Analogy.**

Analogy of Being, *Analogia entis*

From the Greek *analogia*, 'proportion', analogy is the recognition of true relationships. It is a method of predication where recognizable concepts relative to a known object are applied to an object not properly known in virtue of a real similarity: the objects are called 'analogues'.

Used in theology with God as the datum, it is a relation of similarity between created and uncreated being which cannot be broken down into more simple terms. Being is not, as in a genus, subject to differentiation: so man's being, if it is analogically comparable at all, involves being-like-God, just as his nature involves contingent dependence on God. Man is the *imago Dei* (Gen. 1.27) where other creation bears the *vestigium Dei*

(Rom. 1), and these are not by participation (which would be pantheism), but by analogical relation. The relation is operative one way only, from inferior dependent being to supreme Subsistent Being; for God's nature is not enriched by creation, nor would it be affected by creation's obliteration – God remains essentially untouchable, dwelling in light inaccessible.

The relation of similarity, not being univocal (for therein lies the error of 'anthropomorphism', q.v.), carries with it the counterpart of dissimilarity – of which the Fourth Lateran Council (1215) remarked: 'between Creator and creature there cannot be seen so great a likeness, that there is not also seen an even greater difference'. Nevertheless, total dissimilarity would leave us with mere symbolism, which is barren and fails to reflect a true analogical likeness.

Aristotle's best known example of analogy is this: 'As sight is in the body, so is understanding in the soul, while each is in fact disparate' (*Nicomachean Ethics*, 1096 b. 28). It is a four-term analogy which differentiates between relations of dependence. Aquinas commented: 'one term can be applied to different objects where their difference is not complete, but allows of some part in common.' The common point may be in the beginning or end, or a matter of quality or quantity, or the goodness of proper function – 'good things are called good rather according to this analogy, that as sight is the good of the body, so is understanding the good of the soul'. Where Aristotle emphasized the four-term analogy of proportionality, Plato preferred the three-term analogy of attribution, the middle term being participation in being. Aristotle never tried to extend analogy to being, and appeared to see it as a mode of understanding rather than a mode of reality.

It was the Platonic analogy of being, not the Aristotelian analogy of knowledge, which proved most useful to Christian thought. God was seen as knowable by man in three ways: by negation, by causality, and by the analogy of man's image and likeness (Cistercian spirituality gave these two words separate meanings). While the cause is never exhausted in the effect (and with God, cause remains unchanged by its effects), it is also true – and presumed to be so of God, if man is to understand him at all – that cause produces like effect, in that *agere sequitur esse*: it is from God's created effects that we may come, invoking the analogy of being, to some understanding of his uncreated nature.

But in a sense, both forms of analogy are needed together, for in that both God and his creatures share being as a common term, there is an analogy of participation (or attribution); while in that God's being is his very nature by absolute identity (his essence is to exist) and a creature's being is contingent, there is an analogy of proportionality. It is supremely inadequate in that ultimately God is not relatable to his effects, for the Infinite differs from the finite absolutely: but to overstress this would be to deny man any knowledge of God at all. Aquinas acceded an

analogy of participation (the three-term analogy of being): 'created being . . . in so far as it comes from God, shares in his likeness and so leads us towards assimilation to him' (*de Veritate* 18.2.5): but he finally prefers the four-term analogy of proportionality in that 'God is differently related to being than is any creature, for he is his own being, a property which belongs to no creature'. See also **Psychological Analogy; Social Analogy; Thomistic Analogy; God (7); Language, Religious.**

C. Fabro, *Participation et Causalité selon St Thomas d'Aquin*, 1961; L. B. Geiger, *La Participation dans la Philosophie de St Thomas*, 1942; E. Gilson, *Being and Some Philosophers*, rev. ed. 1952; G. Klubertanz, *St Thomas and Analogy*, 1963; H. Lyttkens, *The Analogy between God and the World*, 1952; E. L. Mascall, *Existence and Analogy*, 1949, 1966; R. L. Patterson, *The Concept of God in the Philosophy of Aquinas*, 1933; G. B. Phelan, *St Thomas and Analogy*, 1948; M. Pontifex and I. Trethowen, *The Meaning of Existence*, 1953; J. H. Crehan, *CDT*, I, 1962 pp. 70–80.

ALBERIC STACPOOLE, OSB

Analytical Philosophy

Under the heading 'analytical philosophy' come a number of significantly differing philosophical programmes – those notably of Bertrand Russell, G. E. Moore, the Logical Positivists, Ludwig Wittgenstein, John Wisdom, J. L. Austin and Gilbert Ryle. They can be loosely grouped together as 'analytical' philosophers, in that none of them sets out to construct a metaphysical system which (like Bradley's or Leibniz's, e.g.) would show up the everyday world as 'appearance' only, and locate Reality in an altogether different mode of being. They seek rather to clarify the knowledge we do in fact have, to give minute accounts of the concepts we actually use, to show how paradox and perplexity frequently arise from failure to understand how language works in detail.

That is not to say that none of these philosophers (or their followers) can be called a metaphysician. Russell's Logical Atomism is certainly a metaphysical theory. According to it, analysis breaks up the complex claims we make about things, persons, abstractions, into their simplest 'atomic' constituents. It was hoped that the formal logic developed by Russell with A. N. Whitehead would be able to show how – with the aid of logical connectives like 'if', 'or', 'not' – the rich and complex statements of ordinary language could be built up from these atomic statements. Russell saw, moreover, that the grammar of our ordinary language could not be counted on to coincide with the logical requirements of meaningful discourse. His analyses were therefore calculated to reveal the logical structures that language normally conceals.

G. E. Moore, however, had a different conception of analysis, clarificatory rather than metaphysical. Although we indubitably know that, for example, time is real, that I have a body, it is another matter to describe precisely in what this knowledge *consists, how* I know these things. To elucidate this is the task of analysis. The statements of paradoxical metaphysicians – that 'time is unreal', that 'to be is to be perceived' – despite their gross erroneousness are useful signposts to the complexities and the pitfalls in the exploration of these problems.

The analytic method of the Logical Positivists was aggressively hostile to metaphysics as such. (*See* **Positivism**.) It sought to show that metaphysical or theological claims were only apparently meaningful; that, admitting of no verification in terms of observations, they were really vacuous or no more than emotive. More constructively, Logical Positivists sought to analyse and clarify the distinctive structure of scientific language.

Wittgenstein's enormously important contribution to the development of analytical philosophy falls into two phases. The early Wittgenstein (*Tractatus Logico-Philosophicus*, 1922) pursued a 'reductionist' analysis in some respects like Russell's, and saw the proper task of language as the 'picturing' of facts. The later Wittgenstein denied that language has the single, simple function of describing the world of facts: the illusion that it has such a single function has itself produced a great deal of philosophical muddle. Rather, the many and mutually irreducible functions of language serve a multitude of different human purposes. It is the task of analysts to identify and discriminate these functions, or 'language-games'. It is their task also to locate the sources of our particular philosophical perplexities, and to trace in detail the particular conceptual confusions out of which they arise.

This still gives little indication of the diversity of types of current analytical philosophy. J. L. Austin, for instance, pursued exceptionally minute investigation into ordinary language, both for its intrinsic worthwhileness, and for the light that might be shed on philosophical problems through a much-sharpened awareness of how our linguistic tools actually work.

A very recent tendency to be noted is a movement, by a few philosophers, away from piecemeal, minute analysis of a limited group of concepts, and towards a new interest in systematic philosophy (e.g. P. Strawson, S. Hampshire). While 'analytic' would be a misleading word for such ventures, the type of philosophy being produced is none the less profoundly influenced by the insights of analytical philosophy.

R. W. HEPBURN

Anamnesis

1. In St Paul's account of the institution of the Eucharist (I Cor. 11.23 ff.; *cf.* Luke 22.19), Jesus is recorded as having the twofold instruction 'Do this for my *anamnesis*'. *Anamnesis* has been variously translated as 'remembrance', 'commemoration', 'recalling' and 'memorial'. Most Protestant writers have interpreted the term as signifying either an act of psychological remembrance on the part of the worshippers or the per-

formance of a solemn ceremony of commemoration (*cf.* the service at the Cenotaph in Whitehall on Remembrance Sunday). Catholics have seen in the sentence a more concrete and objective reference, and it has been widely argued that the Hebrew notion behind the Greek term signifies a bringing into the present of a chronologically past act with all its original efficacy, a literal 're-calling' in the sense of 'calling back'. This view has also been defended at length by the Protestant religious Max Thurian of Taizé (*The Eucharistic Memorial*, I, 1960, II, 1961, passim; *cf.* J. J. von Allmen, *Worship: its Theology and Practice*, 1965, p. 34). J. Jeremias (*Eucharistic Words of Jesus*, 1966, pp. 159 ff.) has adopted the translation 'Do this that God may remember me', but has not been generally followed. In any case, the command of Jesus is not simply to 'do this', but to do it 'as his *anamnesis*' (*cf.* G. Dix, *The Shape of the Liturgy*, 1945, ch. 4).

2. The mention of the passion, resurrection and ascension of Jesus in the canon of most eucharistic liturgies occurs after the account of the institution. In the Roman canon it is the section beginning *Unde et memores ...* In the Book of Common Order of the established Church of Scotland, there is an anamnesis *before* the institution-narrative.

E. L. MASCALL

Anaphora

Anaphora (Greek: lifting up *or* offering) is the name given to the central and essential part of the eucharistic rite which, in its classical forms, consists of the great eucharistic prayer of consecration (*see* **Eucharist, Eucharistic Theology**) and culminates in the communion. The view that there was one primitive form of words for the anaphora has been abandoned, but it seems clear that the general form of a prayer which thanked God for his work of creation and redemption and made specific reference to the institution of the Eucharist by Christ was universal. The anaphora begins, after a mutual salutation of priest and people, with an exhortation to lift up their hearts and an appropriate reply, after which the thanksgiving proper begins. The interruption of the prayer of thanksgiving by the singing of the *Sanctus* (the angelic hymn 'Holy, Holy, Holy . . .'), has resulted in the 'preface' or part of the prayer which preceded the hymn being considered as separate from the rest of the prayer, with a great loss of understanding of its structure and character. (In the West the term 'canon', which corresponds to the Greek *anaphora*, has thus come to denote only the post-*Sanctus* part of the prayer; and the preface itself has tended to lose its character as a thanksgiving for creation and redemption and to become a general act of praise into which, in the West, commemorations of the seasons and feasts of the Church's year have been inserted.) The *Sanctus* does not occur at all in the earliest known eucharistic prayer, that of the *Apostolic Tradition* of Hippolytus of Rome, which, if genuine, dates from *c*. AD 200; some scholars have suggested that in its origin the *Sanctus* was a triumphal ending to the Prayer and not an item within it, but this remains debatable (L. Bouyer, *Eucharistic*, passim). The *Sanctus* is followed by a memorial of the redemptive work of God in Christ and an account of the institution of the Eucharist itself, after which there follows (in the Eastern liturgies) an Epiclesis (q.v.), and concluding intercessions, prayers for communion and a doxology. Variations from this general form as well as insertions into it may be found, but the main outline of the anaphora is more or less constant. For the historical details of the development and inter-relations of the various anaphoras (which are matters of vigorous controversy among professional liturgiologists) and for their classification into various families, specialized works of liturgiology must be consulted.

In the Latin Church the Roman anaphora, whose history is itself a subject of some dispute, has almost universally supplanted all other forms, though recently (1968) three additional canons have been composed and authorized. In the Eastern Orthodox Church there are still in regular use the two anaphoras traditionally ascribed to St Basil the Great and St John Chrysostom. In the lesser Eastern Churches a wide variety are found. As would be expected from its origin the eucharistic prayer is normally addressed to God the Father, though in the East the trinitarian controversies resulted in a partial reorientation of the prayer to the Triune Godhead, and it is possible to find anaphoras which are addressed to the Son and even to the Blessed Virgin Mary. Misunderstanding of the original structure of the eucharistic prayer in the sixteenth century, combined frequently with an assumption that the words of Christ recorded in Scripture form a full account of the rite of the Last Supper, resulted in the production of 'reformed' liturgies whose defects are only now beginning to be corrected. The classical pattern of the eucharistic prayer, for all the accidents which have occurred to it in the course of its history, is modelled on the theological truth of all Christian existence, being directed to the Father through the Son and in the Holy Ghost.

L. Bouyer, *Eucharistie*, 1966.

E. L. MASCALL

Anathema

The literal meaning of this Greek word is 'suspended', and it was used for the Hebrew *cherem*, 'under the ban', 'accursed' (*see* Alan Richardson, 'Devote, Accursed, Ban', *TWBB*). Sentence of anathema was pronounced against heretical doctrines from the fourth and fifth centuries in the Church, and also against heretics. Anathematization became from the sixth century more severe than excommunication, since the latter usually meant only excommunication from public worship and the sacraments.

Angel, Angelology

The word 'angel' is from Greek, 'messenger'. The biblical literature exhibits a rich variety of conceptions of these superhuman beings (*see* J. N. Schofield, 'Angel', *TWBB*). In the NT they are found, on the one hand, as divine messengers (Luke 1.26; 2.9) or ministers (Mark 1.13; Heb. 1.14), and, on the other hand, as among the demonic world-rulers (*see* **Powers**); St Paul knows of no 'good' angels. How far they were understood as representing poetic ways of speaking of the divine action in revelation is much debated among NT scholars. – In mediaeval theology, through the combination of biblical literalism with Greek philosophical speculation (Aristotle held that the planets were superhuman, living beings), angelology, the 'science' of angels, was greatly elaborated; the various ranks of angels were held to constitute an essential link in the Great Chain of Being (*see* **Dionysius the Pseudo-Areopagite**). In recent theology angels have occupied little attention, being generally regarded in Protestant circles as a pre-scientific way of speaking about natural or human (rather than supernatural) phenomena. K. Barth, however, has given them more serious consideration than other theologians. One might ask (though Barth might regard the question as illegitimate, being metaphysical) whether it is reasonable to suppose that there are no higher intelligences than ourselves in the universe until we reach the level of God. Roman Catholicism, while recognizing the traditional teaching about angels, has not in recent times made any notable doctrinal pronouncements on angelology. The belief that the Christian is surrounded by a great company of heavenly helpers, whether mythological or not, has undoubtedly been a great source of comfort and strength to many generations of believers.

EDITOR

Anglican Communion

This is the name given since the nineteenth century to the group of autonomous episcopally governed reformed churches which are in communion with and accord a primacy of honour to the see of Canterbury. The group includes a few missionary dioceses and other areas still separately under the jurisdiction of Canterbury or of one of the other member churches. Their common standards are the Bible and the Nicene Creed, their bishops claim to be in apostolic succession derived through the English episcopate of the sixteenth century, their worship is liturgical, based on the Prayer Books of 1549 and 1552, and for the most part in the languages of their countries. The conscious effort to combine varied elements of Catholic and Protestant traditions and the tolerance of wide varieties of belief and practice have made sometimes for weakness, sometimes for progress, in ecumenical endeavour. There are some three hundred and forty-five dioceses grouped in eighteen national churches or regional provinces. All the diocesan bishops assemble at ten-yearly intervals for the Lambeth Conference. After the 1958 Conference efforts were made to enter into closer relationship with other independent episcopal churches, and a meeting of heads of some of these bodies was held at Canterbury in 1964. A quickened sense of unity and mutual responsibility within the Anglican communion was experienced at the Anglican Congress held at Toronto in 1963.

H. Johnson, *Global Odyssey*, 1963; J. W. C. Wand, ed., *The Anglican Communion*, 1948.

R. CANT

Anglo-Catholicism

The name sometimes describes those in the Church of England from the conservative Henricians onwards who have accepted Catholicism without the pope. Its use is more usually confined to the successors of the Oxford Movement (q.v.) in the nineteenth and twentieth centuries. Anglo-Catholics are not tightly organized in one party, although there are societies such as the Church Union which exist to maintain their principles, and voting on controversial issues in the convocations is often organized on party lines. Anglo-Catholics profess the faith of the Church before the schism between East and West and, in the main, though not uncritically, are receptive to modern developments in the Roman Catholic Church. In speaking of the Church they more naturally think of Rome and the Orthodox than of Protestantism, and for their inspiration they look to the Fathers, the Caroline Divines (q.v.) and contemporary Catholicism rather than to the Reformers. In worship they are content for the most part to use the text of the Book of Common Prayer, but supplement it, often from Roman sources, and adapt Roman or mediaeval ceremonial to it. The theology of the Oxford Movement was fundamentalist, but Anglo-Catholicism was strongly influenced towards the end of the nineteenth century by liberal criticism (*see* **Liberal Catholicism**) and later by Roman Catholic modernism. The collections of essays, *Lux Mundi* in 1889 and *Essays Catholic and Critical* in 1926 (qq.v.) mark significant stages in the reconciliation of Anglo-Catholic orthodoxy with modern thought. Their great stress on the incarnation kept them in the tradition of Richard Hooker and the Caroline Divines (qq.v.) in spite of a divergence from them in devotional practice, e.g. in the importance attached to the daily celebration of the Eucharist. It also encouraged an active interest in social reform, and since the 1880s many Anglo-Catholics have both studied the implications for society of Christian belief and have supported left-wing movements. In this and in the acceptance of biblical criticism the influence of Charles Gore (q.v.) was one of the greatest importance. They have done much to enrich the devotional life of the Anglican communion through founding religious orders, encouraging retreats, private confession and the practice of the spiritual life generally as taught in the post-Tridentine Roman Church. Much Anglo-

Catholic teaching has permeated the Anglican communion, and many practices that a century ago were regarded as unusual are now widely acceptable. In recent years new emphases within Roman Catholicism itself have modified Anglo-Catholicism, and the revival of biblical theology (*see* **Hoskyns, Sir Edwyn**) and the liturgical and ecumenical movements have brought Anglo-Catholics and other churchmen closer together.

F. L. Cross, *Darwell Stone*, 1943; W. L. Knox, *The Catholic Movement in the Church of England*, 1923; R. Lloyd, *The Church of England in the Twentieth Century*, rev. ed., 1966.

R. CANT

Angst

This term is best translated by the English 'dread'. In existentialist thought, it is the most fundamental affective state of human existents, disclosing man's precarious position between possibility and freedom, between what he is (facticity) and what he is obliged to become. See **Existentialism; Phenomenology.**

JAMES RICHMOND

Anhomoeans

The term applied to the extreme Arians (Aetius, Eunomius) who held that the Son was 'utterly unlike the Father'. The view was carried in some cases to the point at which the Son could not even know the Father. Since they lacked a common *Ousia* (substance), the sole relationship between them lay in the divine will. The dialectical approach of the Anhomoeans justified the criticism of Theodoret that they converted theology into technology, a barren exercise in the manipulation of logical categories. See also **Homoeans; Homoeousians.**

H. E. W. TURNER

Animism

The name given to the belief that inanimate natural objects (trees, stones, waterfalls, etc.) are inhabited by spirits or demons, which thus become specially numinous (q.v.) or ominous in character and must be treated with respect by those who approach them. This belief is widespread among primitive peoples of all ages and parts of the world. Remnants of it are to be found in the OT (e.g. Gen. 19.26; 28.22) in the opinion of many scholars. Often legends or myths are attached to the places where the spirits are believed to dwell. Traces of animistic attitudes may perhaps still survive in popular beliefs concerning sacred places to which the name of some saint has become traditionally attached.

EDITOR

Annunciation of the Blessed Virgin Mary

It is the announcement by the angel Gabriel to Mary that she had been chosen to be the virgin mother of the Son of God (Luke 1.26–38). It is celebrated liturgically in East and West on 25 March.

E. L. MASCALL

Anointing

The custom of anointing with oil objects and persons to set them apart as sacred is very ancient and is found in many religions. It is observed in the Roman Catholic Church and in the Orthodox Churches. *See also* **Chrism; Unction; Initiation, Christian.**

Anselm, St

St Anselm (1033–1109) was born near Aosta in Piedmont and entered (*c.* 1060) the Abbey of Bec in Normandy, where he became a monk and student under Lanfranc of Pavia, who was then Prior. In 1063 he succeeded Lanfranc as Prior, and in 1078 he succeeded as Abbot of Bec. After two periods of fifteen years as Prior and Abbot, he was elected in 1093 Archbishop of Canterbury, and this too lasted fifteen years until his death. King William Rufus picked a quarrel with his new Archbishop over feudal dues, the recognition of Urban II, and papal rights in England: Anselm was virtually driven into exile from 1097 until Rufus' death in 1100. While in France and Italy, Anselm attended papal councils at Clermont, Bari and the Lateran and spoke with the leading canonists and Gregorian churchmen; and thus, when Henry Beauclerc succeeded to the English throne and recalled the Archbishop of Canterbury, he had become a firm adherent to the doctrine of refusing lay investiture. Anselm refused to renew the homage he had paid to Rufus, or to consecrate bishops invested by Henry I. The king proved intransigent, and during 1103–7 Anselm voluntarily continued his exile on the Continent, working for a proper reconciliation of Church and State in England, which came with the Council of London in 1107. An agreement was reached which stood as a model for the later Council of Worms in 1122, which marked the end of the Investiture quarrel: prelates were to be invested with their *spiritualia* by the pope or metropolitan after being invested with their *temporalia* by prince or monarch. It was a formula with little meaning, which satisfied churchmen and laymen alike, and brought co-operation. Anselm returned to Canterbury, consecrated all outstanding bishops to their neglected sees, called reforming synods, set up a structure of church discipline and enforced clerical celibacy.

His central tenet was *fides quaerens intellectum,* a theological view borrowed from Augustine, his principal source. 'I do not seek to understand so that I may believe; but I believe so that I may understand. For I believe this also that "unless I believe, I shall not understand"' (LXX, Isa. 7.9): *Proslogion I.* His interest was not in the act of coming to faith, but in the nature and meaning of well-founded faith: 'we must try to understand what we believe'. 'If he can understand, let him thank God: if he cannot, let him rather bow his head in adoration than lower his horns to start tossing': *Incarn. Verbi I.* He believed that faith and reason should not be separated, but that reason should be the servant of faith.

More than half of the bulk of his writing was done in the decade following his appointment to Canterbury. His work was usually polished and finished, leaving little to be edited. (1) *de Grammatico*; an introduction to dialectics, drawing on Aristotle's so-called *logica vetus*; (2) Prayers and Meditations: twenty-two of which are genuinely Anselmian, written during his Bec years; (3) *Monologion* (1076–7); meditations on the existence of God, on the Trinity, and on man's power to know and love the Three Persons; (4) *Proslogion* (1078), containing his famous ontological proof of God's existence; he is a pioneer of arguments for the existence of God (*see* **God (5)**; **Five Ways)** and the essence and attributes of God; (5) *de Veritate* (1080); (6) *de Libertate Arbitrii* (1084); (7) *de Casu Diaboli* (1088); (8) *de Trinitate et de Incarnatione Verbi* (1094), written to refute the trinitarian heresy of Roscelin: touches on the difference between faith and reason, nature and person. Here he laid the ground for subsequent scholastic methods of discussing the Trinity and the incarnation, later incorporated into Council dogmas; (9) *Cur Deus Homo?* (1098, many times translated), a novel and classic exposition of the scholastic atonement doctrine (*see* **Atonement**); it is probably the first treatise on the subject; (10) *Meditatio Redemptionis Humane* (1099); a devotional summary of the above; (11) *de Conceptu Virginale et Originale Peccato* (1100), a complement to *Cur Deus Homo?*; (12) *de Processione Spiritus Sancti* (1102); this defends the insertion of *filioque* into the Nicene Creed. Anselm had defended this publicly at the Council of Bari before a Greek delegation; (13) *Epistola de Sacrificio Azymi et Fermentali* (1106); (14) *de Sacramentis Ecclesiae* (1107); (15) *de Concordia* (1108); a discussion of God's foreknowledge and grace and our free will; (16) *de Anima* (1109), projected, discussed on his deathbed; (17) 450 *Letters* spread over his life. *See also* **God (5); Atonement.**

K. Barth, *Anselm: Fides Quaerens Intellectum,* ET, 1960; G. Bosanquet, ed., *History of Recent Events in England,* I–IV, 1964; M. J. Charlesworth, *St Anselm's Proslogion,* 1965 (with Gaunilo's reply, and the author's reply to Gaunilo); F. C. Copleston, *A History of Philosophy,* II, 1950, pp. 156–65; Eadmer, *Historia Novorum in Anglia,* I–VI; *Vita Anselmi,* ed. M. Rule, Rolls Series, 1884 (Latin); E. R. Fairweather, ed., *A Scholastic Miscellany: Anselm to Ockham,* 1956 (selections in English); D. P. Henry, *The Logic of St Anselm,* 1967; J. McIntyre, *St Anselm and his Critics: a Re-interpretation of Cur Deus Homo,* 1954; M. Rule, *The Life and Times of St Anselm,* 1883; F. S. Schmitt, OSB, ed., *Sancti Anselmi Opera Omnia,* I–VI, 1938–61; R. W. Southern, ed., *The Life of St Anselm,* 1962 (Latin/English); *St Anselm and his Biographer,* 1963; R. W. Southern and F. S. Schmitt, *The Memorials of St Anselm,* 1968 (principally a text and apparatus of the *Miracula* and *Dicta Anselmi,* Br. Academy); L. Bainvel, *DTC,* I, cols 1327–60; D. P. Henry, 'St Anselm's *de Grammatico*', *PQ,* X (1966), 45–66;

M. Mähler, *DS*, I, cols 690–96; P. Richard, *DHGE*, III, cols 464–85; E. A. Sillem, *CDT*, I, pp. 99–103; W. R. W. Stephens, *DNB*, I, pp. 482–503.

ALBERIC STACPOOLE, OSB

Anthropology. *see* Man, Doctrine of.

Anthropomorphism

As the Greek compound word implies, an image of man is taken to represent God, and so anthropomorphism means making God in man's own image. Such a procedure was ridiculed by the rationalistic Greeks, as when, for instance, Xenophanes said that if oxen and lions could paint, they would represent their gods in the form of oxen and lions. Fifty years ago it was commonly said that many parts of the OT contained childish anthropomorphic notions about God, especially the opening chapters of Genesis. Today there is widespread acceptance of the view that the poetic and parabolic language of Genesis represents a very highly developed way of conveying profound existential and religious truth in story form, so that people at any stage of cultural development, except perhaps that of supercilious sophistication, can apprehend it vividly. Anthropomorphism, unless it were poetic symbolism, would violate all the principles of theological propriety which have been established since the Middle Ages, because it would involve the univocal attribution to God of properties which pertain to a lower order of existence, namely human nature. *See also* **Language, Religious; Symbol, Symbolic Theology.** For a consideration of the nature of religious language in Genesis *see* Alan Richardson, *Genesis I–XI* (Torch Commentaries), 1953.

EDITOR

Antinomianism

The view that the gospel renders obedience to the law (*nomos*) unnecessary and even damaging to one's hope of salvation. Since we are justified by faith in Christ and not by works of the law (Gal. 2.16), why should we bother to do them? Is not Christ the end of the law (Rom. 10.4)? Were not the representatives of the law the chief enemies of Christ (Mark 2.1–3.6)? And are not all who rely on works of the law under a curse (Gal. 3.10)? Are they not cut off from Christ and fallen from grace (Gal. 5.4)? Such arguments St Paul had to meet, so did Luther and Wesley. It is not difficult to see that they rest on a confusion of thought, by which obedience to the law (q.v.) is equated with legalism (q.v.). Yet the antinomians have a point. The gospel itself, as Wesley saw, is 'within an hair's breadth' of antinomianism. For if where sin increased, grace abounded all the more (Rom. 5.20), why should we not continue in sin that grace may abound (Rom. 6.1)? If we are not under law but under grace, why should we not sin (Rom. 6.15)? The answer is, of course, that grace sets us free from sin as well as from the law. *See* **Freedom.**

G. Huehns, *Antinomianism in English History,* 1951.

P. S. WATSON

Antiochene Theology

Antiochene theology is the type of thought represented by the theologians of the Antiochene school during the fourth and fifth centuries, e.g. Diodore of Tarsus (d. *c.* 390), Theodore of Mopsuestia (c. 428) and Theodoret of Cyrrhus (d. *c.* 458). Within the limits of orthodoxy it was rationalist, moralist, cautious about the use of allegory and preferred in Christology a separation of the natures of Christ verging towards Nestorianism. *See also* **Christology (4).**

R. P. C. HANSON

Anxiety. *see* Angst.

Apocrypha

The Apocrypha denotes those books regarded as sacred by Greek-speaking Jews at the time of our Lord, and then extant in Greek, but not included in their canon by Aramaic-speaking Jews at that time. They comprise I and II Esdras, Tobit, Judith, Additions to Esther, the Wisdom of Solomon, Ecclesiasticus, Baruch, the Letter of Jeremy, the Prayer of Azariah and the Song of the Three Young Men, Susannah, Bel and the Dragon, the Prayer of Manasses, and I and II Maccabees. Because they all appeared in the LXX, they were all accepted as part of the Bible by all Christian authors up to the fourth century. Jerome in producing the Vulgate translation of the Bible (*c.* 400), since he had been in touch with the Hebrew canon, put them in a separate, inferior category, and there were a few other authors who regarded them as in some sense inferior. But the Eastern Church up to the end of the Patristic period and the Western Church up to the Reformation accepted them as generally on a level with the other books of the OT. At the Reformation, however, all the reformed traditions demoted them either to a position of being equivalent to ordinary literature (Westminster Confession) or to the status of being useful for examples of morals, but not for doctrine (Geneva Bible, Thirty-nine Articles). In contrast, the council of Trent declared their full canonicity. Many Protestant churches still totally omit them from Bible-reading and lectionaries.

With the disappearance of the traditional doctrine of inspiration, however, it has become increasingly difficult to justify this omission of the Apocrypha. As far as witnessing to God's activity towards his chosen race goes, many of the books of the Apocrypha have as much claim to be included in the OT canon as have books of a similar genre of literature already in the canon; *cf.* Ecclesiasticus with Proverbs, Tobit with Jonah, Judith with Esther. Not all the books of the Apocrypha were originally written in Greek; much of the original Hebrew of Ecclesiasticus, for instance, has recently been discovered. Our understanding of the Jews' knowledge of God would be impoverished did we not possess the witness of Hellenistic Judaism given by this last book and the Wisdom of Solomon.

L. H. Brockington, *Critical Introduction to the Apocrypha*, 1961; B. M. Metzger, *An Introduction to the Apocrypha*, 1957.

R. P. C. HANSON

Apocryphal Gospels, Acts, etc.

Many alternatives to the canonical Gospels, Acts and Epistles were produced in the earlier Christian centuries by heretical sects (especially Gnostic) which desired to possess a NT more in line with their own peculiar doctrines than were the books accepted (or gradually becoming accepted during the period of the development of the canon of the NT) by the catholic churches. Generally speaking the apocryphal writings add little to our knowledge of the historical Jesus or of his apostles, though here and there a saying may have the ring of authenticity or an incident be based upon an older tradition. It has often been remarked that a perusal of the NT apocryphal writings, of which many specimens survive, confirms the judgment that the canonical Gospels and Acts are soberly based upon historical foundations. English translations may be found in M. R. James, *The Apocryphal New Testament*, 1924; E. Hennecke, W. Schneemelcher, R. Wilson, *New Testament Apocrypha*, 2 vols., 1962, 1965.

EDITOR

Apollinarianism. *see* Christology (4).

Apologetics, Apologists, Apology

The Greek word *apologia* means a defence, the reply to the speech of the prosecution (*cf.* Acts 26.2; I Peter 3.15). Apologists are Christian thinkers who are ready to defend their faith when it comes under attack, and they must do so in the thought-forms of their day. This is a dangerous enterprise, because the apologist is tempted to go too far in the direction of his opponents' categories in order to present his case the more persuasively. The apologists of the early Church (*c.* AD 120–220), such as Aristides, Justin Martyr, Tatian, Athenagoras, etc., had to correct misrepresentations of the Christian faith and life and to present Christianity to the educated men of their day in the general context of the prevailing Stoic philosophy. Centuries later Aquinas (q.v.), who is probably the greatest apologist the Church has ever produced (*cf.* his *Summa contra Gentiles*), had to defend the faith against the new Aristotelian philosophy, interpreted in a materialistic way by Arabic philosophers like Averroes, which was seeping into the universities of Christendom (then a small island surrounded by the great sea of Islam) and which was making the traditional Augustinian-Platonic philosophy seem old-fashioned. He did this so successfully that his new

apologetic became a dominant force for centuries in the Western Church. In times when the Christian faith is not under intellectual pressure there arise no great apologists; but by the eighteenth century, under the attack of deists (q.v.) and rationalists, there was need for an apologist to present the case for the defence, and Bishop Joseph Butler (q.v.) wrote his famous *Analogy of Religion* (1736). Since that age the Christian faith has been under constant attack. In our own times theologians have had to meet considerable intellectual opposition. Karl Barth and his school refuse to make any kind of apology for the faith on the ground that faith has nothing to do with human reason and philosophy, and therefore apology is a form of un-faith (yet in a sense this is an apologetic position, one which having declared total war demands unconditional surrender). Rudolf Bultmann, on the other hand, has gone to extreme lengths in meeting the categories of modern thought (in his case, the existentialist philosophy of Martin Heidegger), but he does not regard his aim as primarily apologetic but as the restatement of the NT *kerygma* (q.v.) in modern terms. Many other theologians have tried to defend the Christian faith against the attacks of empiricist philosophers. The danger of going too far in the direction of one's opponents' categories is in many cases clearly illustrated. The study of Christian apologetics is in our time a most necessary theological discipline, for apologetics is that branch of Christian theology which is concerned with the defence of faith in Christ's revelation. It is only from the careful study of the history of apology that we can properly understand the nature of the Church's apologetic task today. That task is a never-ending one, because thought-forms change from age to age. When our contemporary empiricist vogue has become a museum-piece, new launching-sites for the attack upon Christian faith will be found. There can be no final apologetic.

John Baillie, *Our Knowledge of God*, 1939; A. B. Bruce, *Apologetics*, 1892; Alan Richardson, *Christian Apologetics*, 1947.

EDITOR

Apophatic Theology. *see* Dionysius the Pseudo-Areopagite.

Apostasy

It means the deliberate disavowal of belief in Christ made by a formerly believing Christian. The most famous apostate was probably the Emperor Julian (332–363).

R. P. C. HANSON

Apostle, Apostolate

An apostle is one who has been sent with authority to act on behalf of the one who has sent him. Within the NT the term is used of Jesus himself (Heb. 3.1), of his twelve intimate associates – their number, corresponding to that of the patriarchs, suggests that they were intended to be the priest-rulers of the New Israel – and of others either authorized directly by God, e.g. Paul (Gal. 1.1), or by a local church, e.g. Barnabas (Acts 13.2 f.). The general use has been maintained so that, e.g. Boniface (680–754) can be styled the 'apostle of Germany', but the term is more frequently restricted to the Twelve and Paul. Debate has centred upon the relationship between the apostles, in this confined sense, and bishops and has therefore tended to concentrate upon discussion of apostolic succession (q.v.). *See* J. Y. Campbell, 'Apostle', *TWBB*.

J. G. DAVIES

Apostolic Fathers

For some three hundred years this title has been used for the writers of the immediate post-NT period: Clement of Rome, Ignatius of Antioch, Hermas, Polycarp, Papias and the authors of the Epistle of Barnabas, the Epistle to Diognetus, the Second Epistle of Clement (not by Clement of Rome) and the Didache. *See* J. B. Lightfoot, *The Apostolic Fathers* (one vol.), Greek and English Texts, 1891; C. C. Richardson, trans. and ed., *Early Christian Fathers*, 1953. *See also* **Patristic, Patrology.**

EDITOR

Apostolic Succession

Apostolic succession relates to the view that episcopacy is derived from the apostles (q.v.) by continuous succession. It received considerable emphasis in the second century when the Church was faced with Gnosticism, in opposition to the novel ideas of which it was maintained that orthodox Christians were secured by a threefold cord to their apostolic origins: by the apostolic scriptures, by the apostolic rule of faith and by the apostolic succession. There were, however, two conceptions of apostolic succession – the one asserted a succession from office holder to office holder, the other of consecrated to consecrator, the former being the interpretation advanced first in time.

The primitive and primarily historical understanding of succession was to the effect that it involved succession to a particular chair, to the bishopric of a particular church and not simply to the possession of episcopal Orders. The bishop of any community had been put in possession of the *cathedra*, teaching chair, in succession to a predecessor who in his turn had been the recognized holder of the chair and so on back to the foundation of the community. If the church had been founded by an apostle, then there was a direct formal connection between its episcopate in any age and the apostles in the first days after Pentecost; if the church was the offshoot of another, then the daughter church could trace its succession back by way of its own bishops and those of the mother church to the apostles. So the church of Canterbury today can trace its succession back from archbishop Ramsey to archbishop Fisher to archbishop Temple and so back to Augustine and from Augustine to Gregory who sent him and

from Gregory back to Peter and Paul. Such office holders are in the succession of the apostles although not the successors of the apostles, that is, each bishop is not another apostle or member of the apostolic college.

The appeal of the second-century Church was thus not in terms of a single line of succession. Indeed it would be more correct to speak in this connection of apostolic successions. Bishops were placed in the apostolic succession only in relation to the church over which they presided; hence succession from the apostles was not a personal possession of the bishop. This understanding explains the emphasis laid in the early Church upon the installation of the bishop; so, for example, Eusebius, referring to the succession at Jerusalem, speaks of James who 'was entrusted with the throne of the episcopate', and of Symeon who was found 'worthy of the throne of the community in that place', while of Fabian of Rome he says that he was 'placed . . . on the episcopal throne' (*Historia Ecclesiastica*, ii. 1.2; iii. 11; vi. 29.4). Nevertheless attention has also to be paid to the manner in which these successors were installed. This was the task of other bishops who would seem to have laid their hands upon a new candidate (*see* **Consecration**) after he had been lawfully chosen by a particular community to occupy the vacant *cathedra*. The imposition of hands therefore was in part a ratification of the choice of the local community and an act of authorization whereby the bishop became not so much a bishop of the Church at large as the acknowledged head of the local community.

The second or sacramental concept of apostolic succession is first hinted at by Hippolytus at the beginning of the third century. Laying on of hands is now regarded as imparting a special gift to the consecrated possessed by the consecrating bishops in virtue of their succession to the apostles, and further the bishop is regarded as a bishop of the whole Church. It would follow from this that if at any point in the line of consecrations there had been a break the succession would be destroyed. This indeed was contended against the validity (q.v.) of Anglican Orders in the seventeenth century on the basis of the spurious Nag's Head story to the effect that Matthew Parker (archbishop of Canterbury, 1559–75) had not been validly consecrated.

The sacramental concept was given greater precision at the end of the fourth century by Augustine of Hippo. In the face of schism (q.v.) and in order to smooth the way to unity, he argued that baptism performed in separated bodies was valid and that re-baptism, if and when schismatics returned, was wrong. He then extended this to cover schismatic ordinations, so that a man validly ordained retains unimpaired the peculiar gift conveyed to him by the sacramental rite. This teaching was refined by the scholastic theologians who submitted that Holy Orders (q.v.) confers an indelible character (q.v.), namely, the *potestas ordinis*, the power belonging to the Order, and in the case of bishops this *potestas* enables them to confer Holy Orders upon others, and this power is never lost even if a bishop be excommunicated. Hence in terms of apostolic succession what is transmitted by this succession is the indelible *character* of the episcopate.

The question of apostolic succession is an important one in reunion discussions at the present day, although it cannot be isolated from the consideration of episcopacy (q.v.) or of the nature of schism (q.v.). Thus the Church of Rome contends that only those who are in communion with the pope are within the Church, but admits that Christians outside that Body possess true Orders and true Sacraments. So, according to Roman theologians, this is the position of the Eastern Orthodox Church but not of the Church of England. Anglicans, on the other hand, many of whom regard apostolic succession, either in the first or second sense, as essential for the Church, are not prepared to surrender what they believe they possess in order to unite with other Christian bodies, e.g. the Methodists or Presbyterians, who are deemed not to have preserved it. At the same time, if the authoritarian view be accepted, it has to be acknowledged that in a divided Church no group has preserved the apostolic succession unimpaired because the authorization can only be a matter of degree, that is, divided Christendom sets limits to the authority given. For apostolic tradition, *see* **Tradition.**

K. E. Kirk, ed., *The Apostolic Ministry*, 1946; O. C. Quick, *Doctrines of the Creed*, 1938, pp. 330–41; C. H. Turner, 'Apostolic Succession', *Essays on the Early History of the Church and the Ministry*, ed. H. B. Swete, 1921, pp. 95–214.

J. G. DAVIES

Apostolicity

Apostolicity is one of the four marks of the Church listed in the Nicene Creed. The term, as used, for example, by Tertullian at the end of the second century, indicates that the Church was built upon the foundation of the apostles (Eph. 2.19 f.) and maintains their doctrine and practice. 'Therefore the churches, although they are so many and so great, comprise one primitive (*prima*) Church, founded by the apostles, from which they all spring. In this way all are primitive and all are apostolic' (*de Praes.* 20). Augustine employed the term against the Donatists, arguing that they were in schism (q.v.) and outside the Church which itself is apostolic in so far as it possesses the apostolic writings and doctrine and can trace its existence by way of the apostolically founded churches back to the apostles (*see* **Apostolic Succession**).

The notes of the Church, including apostolicity, were not generally discussed until the Reformation, when Roman theologians, like Augustine before them, used them to differentiate between the true Church and other bodies claiming to belong to it. So they argued that the Church of the Apostles is identifiable by possessing the apostolic succession, by its communion with the pope as the heir of Peter, the prince of the apostles, and by its continuity of doctrine. The opposing Protestants accepted the term in the sense of 'primitive' and therefore free from the real or supposed corruptions that had been introduced in the centuries following the apostolic age. Apostolicity is also being used in current discussion with reference to participation in the mission (q.v.) of the Church.

D. Stone, *The Notes of the Church*, 1910.

J. G. DAVIES

Apostolicum

Apostolicum is a title used frequently by continental writers for the Apostles' Creed. *See* **Creed(s).**

Apotheosis

The Greek word for 'deification' – e.g. of Caesar, whether during or after his life-time. In Greek patristic and later mystical theology it was sometimes affirmed that, through union with God in Christ, the Christian himself partakes of the divine nature (*cf.* II Peter 1.4); but this particular term is generally avoided, owing to the strong awareness of the distinction between the Creator and the created.

Appropriation

Appropriation is a linguistic procedure whereby an attribute which properly belongs to the whole Godhead is assigned pre-eminently to one Person, not because it is his exclusive property but because it has a greater resemblance to his properties in particular. This resemblance must be clear and not arbitrary and is the better if it is based upon Scripture. Thus Augustine appropriated unity to the Father, equality to the Son and connection (as the bond of love between the Father and the Son) to the Spirit. Other examples are power, wisdom and goodness (Aquinas); unity, truth and loving-kindness (Bonaventura); origin (*principium*), wisdom and virtue (Calvin). Another form of appropriation (based upon Rom. 11.36) distinguishes the prepositions which can be properly applied to the activity of the three Persons, from whom (*ex quo*) of the Father, through whom (*per quem*) of the Son, and in whom (*in quo*) of the Spirit. The same technique can be applied to the external operations of the Trinity. Creation may be appropriated to the Father, redemption to the Son and sanctification to the Spirit, provided that it is remembered that the whole Trinity is involved in the work of each Person (*see opera ad extra*).

H. E. W. TURNER

Aquinas. *see* Thomism; God (6,7); Averroism; Apologetics.

Arianism. *see* Christology (4); Trinity, Doctrine of the.

Aristotelianism

By one of the most extraordinary and important developments in the history of European ideas the thought of the Greek philosopher Aristotle (384–322 BC) underwent a remarkable revival in the twelfth and thirteenth centuries in Western Europe. This was largely due to the 'Arabian' philosophers (*see* **Averroism**), who interpreted his thought in a materialistic direction. Mediaeval Jewish thought was also influenced by this revival (*see* **Maimonides, M.**). After centuries of the domination of Christian philosophy by Platonic thought-forms (*see* **Neoplatonism; Augustinianism**), the 'new logic' of Aristotle swept through the universities of Christendom, notably Paris and Oxford. The achievement of St Thomas Aquinas was to show that the human reason, as represented by Aristotle (known simply as 'the Philosopher'), was not inimical to Christian faith but was able to build up a natural theology (q.v.) upon which the truths of revelation would form a superstructure that completed our knowledge of God. *See* **Thomism; God (6, 7); Nominalism-Realism.**

W. D. Ross, *Aristotle: Selections,* 1934; A. E. Taylor, *Aristotle*, 1943; and the standard histories of Greek Philosophy.

EDITOR

Arminianism. *see* Predestination (1).

Ascension of Christ

The ascension of Christ has been understood traditionally as his taking up into heaven at the conclusion of his earthly ministry. This definition immediately raises the question of demythologization (q.v.), for it appears to rest upon a three-storeyed cosmology with heaven as a place located somewhere above the earth. Recognition of this problem, however, has not had to wait for the studies of R. Bultmann (q.v.). So, for example, an early eighteenth-century writer was prepared to argue that the ascension did not involve transportation to a localized heaven but transference to a new condition of being, which 'far better becometh the Divine Residence than the Top of our Atmosphere'. As far back as the third century, Origen rejected interpretations of the ascension in spatial categories, considering it to be more concerned with spiritual exaltation than with physical motion. Even Luke's description (Acts 1.9), which is the only one contained in the NT, is probably not to be taken literally. The cloud into which Jesus is received is not a cloud of our atmosphere at all but the vehicle of the divine presence, and Luke was thus affirming, by the use of this imagery, that the ascension was no more nor less than the entry of Christ into the divine glory. Expressing his theological ideas concretely, according to the Hebrew pictorial way of thinking, Luke had little alternative but to depict this as a taking up into heaven. Whether or not he understood this to involve a movement in space cannot now be determined; here fact and interpretation

are so closely wedded as to be inseparable. Indeed any certain historical knowledge of the circumstances of the ascension, as of those of the resurrection, is not obtainable.

Contemporary debate is also concerned with the possibility of distinguishing between the ascension and the resurrection. There are those who refuse to differentiate between them, declaring that the resurrection of Jesus means simultaneously his exaltation; while there are others who maintain that the two cannot be identified. This latter group affirms that it is one thing to say that Christ is risen, meaning that death and corruption no longer hold him, and quite another to say that he has ascended, meaning that he is not only alive but sovereign. These scholars rest their case in part on the linguistic grounds that *anistemi* and *egeiro* can refer only to a recall to life, i.e. to resurrection, while *hypsoo* and *anabaino* indicate a further stage, i.e. ascension. *Anastasis* precedes *anabasis* and so, however intimately the two are connected, they are not the same. Assuming that the ascension is distinct, since otherwise there is no point in attempting to understand it in itself, consideration has to be given to its theological meaning. As a preface to such a consideration, however, it must be emphasized that within the NT itself there is no single uniform concept.

A priori it is conceivable, in view of the acknowledged differences between the apostolic writers, that references to the ascension may take a variety of forms. In particular the Lucan and Johannine views appear to be in contrast. Luke sees the ascension as the termination of the resurrection appearances, but in the Fourth Gospel most of the appearances are not only post-resurrection but also post-ascension (John 20.17 implies that the ascension is about to take place; John 20.26 ff. implies that it has taken place). A similar view to that of John is represented by Paul, who lists his own experience on the Damascus road as a resurrection appearance (I Cor. 15.8), while in Acts this is clearly post-ascension. To recognize this is to acknowledge that the frequent modern emphasis upon the finality of the ascension may well be misplaced; to interpret it primarily as the last of a series is probably to be guilty of an error. No longer can it be regarded as a mere appendage, as no more than an imprimatur which adds nothing to what has already been accomplished. It has to be understood as part of the redemptive act; together with the crucifixion and the resurrection it belongs to the salvation-occurrence.

In terms of the 'classic' theory of the atonement, it marks the overthrow of the demonic powers and the triumphal procession of the victor; in relation to the sacrificial theory, it is to be understood as the means of the offering to the Father of that perfect humanity that was slain upon the cross. It consummates the reconciliation of man and God, which is effected by God putting himself in man's place at the incarnation and by man being put in God's place at the ascension. It is this act that allows Christians to proclaim the lordship of Christ.

The ascension is the necessary precondition of the giving of the Holy Spirit. It is the watershed between the mission of the Son and the mission of the Spirit. The Spirit, however, is an eschatological phenomenon; his outpouring is a sign of the end-time; he is the first-fruits of the final consummation, and consequently the ascension, in the words of K. Barth, 'is the beginning of this time of ours'. This means that we live in the period of mission, the period between the ascension and the *parousia*, and our entrance upon this eschatological dimension is marked by the ascension. It therefore determines the eschatological reference of the Church's life in mission.

By living in the tension between the 'already' of the ascension and the gift of the Spirit and the 'not yet' of the consummation, Christians are enabled to live by faith and hope. Without this withdrawal of Christ from the realm of the visible, there would be little occasion for faith in him; but this faith is inseparable from hope which, in the words of John Calvin, 'is the anchor of the soul which presses into the innermost sanctuary, but only because Christ has gone before'. Consequently the ascension must be understood to lie at the basis of the sacraments through which we participate here and now in the glorified humanity, which is the humanity of him who is to come.

In relation to this humanity, the ascension must also be understood as the occasion when, having been subject to the normal conditions of growth and development, it reached its maturity and in indissoluble unity with the Godhead entered upon a new mode of being and was liberated from its previous limitations. In effect the ascension is the revelation of what God has eternally purposed for mankind; it both demonstrates and effects the summit of the evolutionary process. Here is seen man's final goal, now attainable by all men because it has been revealed and attained by Jesus, who has trodden the whole path of human destiny.

If these last statements approximate at all to theological truth, then they provide some answer to those who would dismiss the ascension as other-worldly, as concerned with some world other than the' one in which we live and move. Just as the incarnation is the humanization of God for the sake of the humanization of man, so the ascension raises the fundamental question of the true man. As the basis of the sacraments, as the foundation of faith and hope, the ascension is essentially related to the present time of eschatological mission and this concerns the exaltation of man to that maturity which is embodied, shown forth and available in and through the exalted Christ. The ascension is the divine *ecce homo*, as part of the salvation-occurrence. To live the life of Christ now – a life of liberation and maturity – is to share in his ascended life; under the power of his Lordship, it is to serve God in our fellow men.

The ascension, in the words of Barth, reveals that 'here an ultimate and supreme thing comes into action, behind which there is no other reality'. This is why many of the patristic writers regarded Ascension Day as the crown of all Christian feasts. According to Augustine: 'This is that festival which confirms the grace of all the festivals together, without which the profitableness of every festival would have perished. For unless the Saviour had ascended into heaven, his Nativity would have come to nothing . . . and his Passion would have borne no fruit for us, and his most holy Resurrection would have been useless.'

According to Eph. 4.10, Christ ascended 'that he might fill all things', i.e. he ascended that he might enter into royal relations with the whole cosmos; he was exalted that he might fill the universe with his divine activity as sovereign and as governor, thereby claiming it as his rightful possession.

J. G. Davies, *He Ascended into Heaven*, 1958; C. F. D. Moule, 'The Ascension – Acts 1.9', *ET*, LXVIII (1957), pp. 205–9; A. M. Ramsey, 'What was the Ascension?', *Studiorum Novi Testamenti Societas, Bulletin* II, 1951.

J. G. DAVIES

Ascetical Theology

Ascetical theology is concerned with the Christian life from the beginnings up to the lower reaches of contemplation. It is a systematic analysis of the life of grace under the Spirit in terms of the discipline and endeavours required of the ordinary believer to purify himself of self-reference. This discipline has been analysed in a threefold way. There is first of all the way of purgation, a basic stripping of the self from excessive attachment to personal wants; secondly the way of illumination during which the believer is conformed to the image of Christ by the practice of the virtues; and thirdly the unitive way in which the believer has a profound awareness of union with God. At the latter point ascetical theology merges into mystical theology. *See* **Mystical Theology.**

F. P. Harton, *The Elements of the Spiritual Life*, 1932; K. E. Kirk, *The Vision of God*, 1931; M. Villier, SJ, ed., *Dictionnaire de spiritualité ascetique et mystique*, 1932– .

E. J. TINSLEY

Asceticism

It is a term used to cover all those exercises and forms of discipline which are believed to be necessary to the Christian *in via*. Negatively it concerns forms of renouncing things which in themselves are good and proper, in the interests of greater order, control and simplicity. Positively, asceticism is regarded as a necessary preparation for the higher reaches of the spiritual life, particularly the dimension of contemplation (*see* **Mystical Theology**). Theologically, asceticism is regarded as a necessary feature of the Christian life as an imitation of Christ (*see* **Imitation of Christ**).

Ascetical practices in the OT are the exception rather than the rule, a close grip on the doctrine of creation preventing the Hebrews from accepting a thorough-going world-renouncing asceticism such as became a characteristic of some Hellenistic religions.

In post-biblical Judaism this feature of the OT became still more prominent, the rabbis insisting that man was to enjoy the fruits of created existence and that not to do so constituted blasphemy. This essentially non-ascetical attitude of the Hebrew tradition is prominent in regard to sex and marriage (*see* **Celibacy**).

There are both 'world-renouncing' and 'world-affirming' elements in the practice and teaching of Jesus. His attitude seemed ambivalent and he was himself aware of the irony of this (Matt. 11.17–19; *cf.* Luke 7.31–34). The ascetical note in the teaching of Jesus does not spring from any metaphysically dualistic or gnostic view of the material or of the sexual (*cf.* Mark 7.15 f.). He believed a man must be alert to recognize the signs of the kingdom, and ready to act on them, and this, he indicated, would often involve painful renunciation. The asceticism of Jesus was empirical and practical, not metaphysical or dualistic, and was orientated towards the eschatological character of the kingdom.

In the NT, as a whole, the 'flesh' is something that can be defiled (and it is all too likely that it will be!) but it is not in itself defilement. It is redeemable, and while Paul may use terms which are capable of thorough-going dualistic interpretations, he does not himself use them dualistically. Nevertheless, there are features of the NT which can be detached from the whole and used in a one-sided way. The history of Christian ascetical teaching shows only too clearly how this happened. A NT tension which is eschatologically based was changed into a dualism which is metaphysically based.

In the patristic period, Christian asceticism centres upon the ideals of martyrdom and celibacy, which as substitutes for martyrdom, were regarded as the high peaks of the Christian ascetic endeavour. The primary motivation behind patristic notions of asceticism was the imitation of Christ. This ideal underlay both forms of monasticism (*see* **Monachism**) whether solitary or communal. The eremite particularly was seen as an imitator of the lonely Christ, travelling along the path which led mankind back to the lost paradise.

The Middle Ages saw further development of the ascetical ideal and its full articulation in terms of monasticism. There was a marked development of ascetical discipline: the use of the hair shirt, iron girdles, flagellation and so on (*see* **Discipline**), and the ideal of the imitation of Christ was actualized in the practice of pilgrimage. More and more Christian ascetical devotional practice was centred on the humanity of Christ, particularly the sufferings of Christ, and there are some curious examples of attempts literally to mimic the sufferings of the historical Jesus, as, for instance, Henry Suso.

The Reformation and the Renaissance saw a marked reaction against the Christian ascetical ideal. A strong polemic against monasticism is to be found in the works of Martin Luther, mainly on the ground that it produces a doctrine of justification by works, and similar reservations are to be found in John Calvin.

This suspicion of the monastic ideal and of the asceticism associated with it remained a feature of Puritan thought (*see* **Puritanism**). A reaction in favour of the mediaeval type of asceticism is to be found in counter-Reformation writers.

The problems which arise for the modern Christian concerning asceticism can be tabulated as follows:

(1) What is the meaning of asceticism, mortification and so on in the modern, technological and 'affluent' society? Here it is important to remember that the Christian ideal of poverty is not to be confused with destitution. Traditional Christian ascetical teaching has a good deal to say, which is still relevant, on the necessity for simplicity and austerity in the midst of wealth and plenty. Greater demands are made on inner austerity in modern society, and traditional ascetical teaching is relevant also in the stress which it puts on the need for meditation and contemplation. It is just these features of Indian religions like Buddhism which attract many in the West.

(2) There is the problem of the relationship between Christian ascetical attitudes and aesthetics. This can best be focused in the attitude of Christians to the arts. What is the place of the enjoyment of creation in the Christian ideal? The voice of a writer like Thomas Traherne, writing in exultation over a created life, is not a common voice in Christian history, and yet even the most austere mystics, like St John of the Cross, will inculcate detachment from what he calls creatures and created existence, not in order to despise creation but in order to have a keener eye for its grateful enjoyment.

(3) This leads to the third point as to whether Christian asceticism is conditioned by a metaphysic of dualism or by an eschatology. There can be no dispute that an asceticism which is based upon a dualistic conception of the inherently evil character of matter is incompatible with the Christian religion. On the other hand, Christian eschatology prevents the believer committing himself entirely to time and creation.

Dom Anselme Stolz, *L'Ascèse Chrétienne*, 1948; Blackfriars, *Christian Asceticism and Modern Man*, 1955.

E. J. TINSLEY

Assumption of The Blessed Virgin Mary

The definition, by Pope Pius XII on 1 November 1950 in the bull *Munificentissimus Deus*, that 'the immaculate Mother of God, Mary ever Virgin, the course of her earthly life having finished, was taken up, body and soul, into the glory of heaven' only gave dogmatic status to a belief which from the sixth century or earlier had become general in both Eastern and Western Christendom. It is certainly not explicit in the earliest Christian writers and the legends giving detailed accounts of the Assumption are of no authority, historical or doctrinal, except perhaps for the bare existence of the belief. The definition has thus raised difficult problems about the relation of definability to antiquity of belief which cannot be discussed here. The liturgical celebration of the Assumption or of the Death of the Virgin first appears in Palestine in the fifth century; it was introduced into the West just before AD 700. The Eastern liturgical texts are far more exuberant and explicit in their descriptions of the Assumption than the Western, though in the East the Feast is still called the 'Falling-asleep' (*Koimesis, Uspenie*); it is kept on 15 August.

The definition makes no reference to the disputed question whether the Blessed Virgin died before her Assumption and if so how long after her death her Assumption took place. Recent writers have stressed that the basic meaning of the dogma is that Mary is now where all Christians will be after the general resurrection; *see, for example,* K. Rahner, *Theological Investigations,* I, 1961, ch. 7. *See also* M. Jugie, *La Mort et l'Assomption de la Sainte Vierge: Etude historico-doctrinale,* 1944, for an exhaustive account of the origin and development of the belief down to 1944. For a shorter discussion *see* H. S. Box, 'The Assumption', *The Blessed Virgin Mary,* ed. E. L. Mascall, 1963.

E. L. MASCALL

Athanasius. *see* Christology (4); Trinity, Doctrine of the.

Atheism

As we understand the term today, atheism is a modern phenomenon. The Greek word 'atheist' (used in the NT only at Eph. 2.12) did not mean one who denied the existence of God or the supernatural, but rather one who refused to venerate the popular civic or imperial deities and thus was suspected of political deviationism (*cf.* the case of Socrates). Thus, the early Christians were often accused of atheism. It would be meaningless to speak of atheism in a polytheistic age or in the context of Buddhism, where the biblical idea of a creating and ruling deity is entirely absent. Atheism in the sense of the denial of God's existence is a modern phenomenon, intelligible only in a theistic context; it made its appearance in a serious sense during the period of the Enlightenment (q.v.). It is melancholy but salutary for Christians to reflect that the major atheistic movements of the modern age, from the rationalism of the Enlightenment to the anti-religious zeal of Marxist-Leninism, are the bitter fruit of the Church's reluctance to embrace new ways of thought or of her compromise with effete and repressive social systems. Christians must always regard atheism as a divine judgment upon their own sins and failures. There are many who today think themselves atheists and who deny Christ's

revelation, as they have misunderstood it, for Christ's sake, though they do not know this. Doubtless such considerations are relevant in the strange case of some contemporary thinkers, who consider themselves to be theologians, who yet advocate varieties of religious atheism, e.g. Paul van Buren, *The Secular Meaning of the Gospel,* 1963, and perhaps Paul Tillich, or the so-called 'Death of God' theologians (q.v.).

Alan Richardson, *Religion in Contemporary Debate,* 1966, ch. 3; for the historical aspect *see* C. B. Upton, 'Atheism and Anti-theistic Theories', *ERE,* II, pp. 173–83.

EDITOR

Atonement

1. *Origins and Meaning of the Word.* The English word 'atonement' is derived from the words 'at-one-ment', to make two parties at one, to reconcile two parties one to another. It means essentially reconciliation. In modern usage it has come to have a more restricted meaning, namely, the *process* by which the obstacles to reconciliation are removed. In current usage, the phrase 'to atone for' means the undertaking of a course of action designed to undo the consequences of a wrong act with a view to the restoration of the relationship broken by the wrong act.

This is the meaning which the word 'atonement' carries in a religious or biblical context: to speak more precisely, it means the work of Christ culminating at Calvary. The term occurs frequently in the KJV of the OT as the rendering of the Hebrew root *kaphar* but only once in the NT (Rom. 5.11), where it translates the word *katallage* which means here 'reconciliation'. In the RV and in modern versions the word is rendered 'reconciliation', which means that the word atonement does not appear in modern English versions of the NT at all. Nevertheless, though the word is not there, the idea is expressed in many forms. It is this fact of the various biblical images used to explain the atonement which gives us the seeming theological complexity of the several 'theories of the atonement' (*see below,* 6 [*a*]–[*d*]).

2. *Atonement as God's Work in Christ.* Two points should be borne in mind in discussing the atonement. First, we cannot as creatures explain the Creator and his work. Any explanations of God and his activity which we attempt are only analogies or parables. We see the facts of his activity and experience them and certainly know them: creation, forgiveness, new life in Christ and so on, but when it comes to explaining them, we falter and grope and fall back on human experience and human imagery, such as release from slavery, washing away of defilement, reconciliation of the alienated, forgiveness. Not one of these 'theories', nor even the sum of them, does justice to the fact of God's work in Christ, yet they all help towards a deeper understanding of it. One theory has dominical authority, another NT authority, an-

other patristic authority; we should never set one theory against another, or superior to another, but rather seek to hold Christ's, the patristic, and the biblical metaphor together, not as of equal authority, but as aids to understanding the work of Christ over and beyond them, for it is this to which they point, and this which gives them authority and meaning. It is this and not theories that we are actually describing.

Secondly, and more important, any doctrine of the atonement which does not begin with the fact of God's love and mercy is doomed from the start. All those modern emphases which 'begin at the other end' (to use the contemporary jargon), namely with man's needs and purposes, the integration of broken personalities, adjustment to society and so on, end with an idolatrous human projection of God made to meet the demands for reconciliation as they themselves formulate them and not as the God and Father of our Lord Jesus Christ meets them (John 3.16; Rom. 5.8; 8.32; Eph. 2.4 f.; I John 4.9 f.). It is of the initiative of God that the Bible speaks. It is God's plan and purpose of love. Any suggestion of a just God being constrained by a compassionate, suffering Son should be resolutely avoided. The glorious anthem that peals from the Bible is of the wondrous love and mercy of God, which, while we were still sinners, sought (and seeks) us out. Before this truth we halt stunned. We stand before an ultimate of revelation, a point beyond which we cannot think. Nevertheless, it would do less than justice to this biblical concept of the love of God, if we did not realize the inadequacy of the word love and stand in awe and fear of it. We cannot explain this love of God, but we ought never to forget that it means a love which we may largely experience as the wrath (*see below*), and it is a love that is predestinating and elective with the mighty purpose of adoption and the re-creation in Christ of a new Israel for God's purposes. All sentimental or emotional understanding of the love of God must be resolutely eschewed in favour of a biblical realism at once sternly forbidding yet invitingly kind. The Bible assumes the need for some kind of atoning action if a man is to be restored to a right and proper relationship with God. It everywhere teaches that man is a sinner wholly estranged from God, that his sin caused and causes the alienation, and that this alienation must be remedied and removed before a true relationship can be created. It further argues that this restoration is wholly of the sovereign mercy of God, free and undeserved, and that nothing a man is or has can do anything to effect this relationship.

Throughout the centuries theologians (Athanasius, Augustine and the Schoolmen, in particular) have discussed the mystery of why God should have chosen the path of incarnation, crucifixion and resurrection, to mend this broken relationship. To speculate in this way is not very profitable; but, assuming the fact of the incarnation and moving forward from there, certain corroborative truths emerge. The first is that the sovereignty and omnipotence of the transcendental God are clearly preserved as an ontological reality. Secondly, his grace and mercy are thereby safeguarded and established. These are the only bases for the gospel of redemption to a lost and sinning mankind. There could be none other. Further support emerges on continued reflection. It is utterly clear that all the events of the OT go in a straight line, through Christ, of the nature of a graph $y = mx$. All the promises are fulfilled in him (II Cor. 1.20). This means the entire history of the OT people as God worked out his purposes in and through them – the law, the sacrificial system, the temple, the synagogue, the tradition – culminate in Christ, the God-man.

The Christ event enables a man to see that there was no other way to effect atonement, there was no other Person, no alternative means. More is at stake than forgiveness alone, for the OT showed the forgiveness of God. That something more was justification, that man should be set in a working relationship with God, the righteous one. In a sense, forgiveness is negative but justification is positive: forgiveness means remission but justification a new relationship. Only the Son of God made flesh could qualify in his righteousness, sinlessness and obedience. Christ is the new Adam of a renewed race, which, sinners, though they are, have been begotten of Christ into a new people, acceptable in a righteousness which is Christ's and which he imparts.

There is another sense in which only the incarnation could effect an adequate atonement. Man as a sinner in relation to God experiences the annihilating reaction of God's wrath against his sin. Not that the wrath is in God, God is always and only pure love. The wrath is in us and is the inevitable reaction of a righteous God who appears as an enemy to our sin and self-centredness. His 'hostility' is his work to wear down our sin and self-centredness, to break the sinful self in order to make a new self. Only Christ can free a man from the natural consequences of the wrath, for Christ effected reconciliation while we were enemies (Rom. 5.10), and this reconciliation frees us from the tyranny of sin.

A further consideration of this mystery is that the incarnation in order to effect atonement had to issue in Calvary. Just as Christ in his obedience resisted all temptation to use his divine nature to ease his hunger and thereby make the incarnation less real, so the Father in the final agony could not allow the cup to pass from the Son (Matt. 26.39). The little word *dei* ('it had to be') runs through the Gospel narratives as a deep and disturbing diapason (Mark 8.31; 9.12; Luke 24.7; John 3.14; Acts 4.12, to instance a selection). So great, so deep, so irresistible and invincible is the Father's purpose to redeem us and give us his kingdom, that God carried through our redemption at this awful cost. When we stand before a love as wide as heaven's arch, that stretches from horizon to horizon as a brilliant rainbow of mercy, the heart is compelled to worship in amazement and awe. To put this fact another way: man being what he is, a frail and finite sinner, God being what he is, the eternal righteous one, could there have been any other way of atonement than in the person and work of Jesus Christ?

3. *Biblical Explanation of Atonement.* The best beginning to understand the atonement is with the Bible, principally the OT preparation and the life and ministry of Jesus, paying particular attention to the kind of category and description Jesus used of himself and the Apostles used of him.

(*a*) *Christ as Obedient Servant.* First, there is the category which underpins all others, the sense in which Christ described himself as the servant and minister of God. All his time, all his thought, all his purpose, were circumscribed in total obedience to the will of the Father as his servant. His last act at the last Supper was to wash the disciples' feet to remind them that he was but a servant. Perhaps the great breakthrough of the Reformation should be seen when Luther called the Augustine monks assembled at Heidelberg, 1518, to set aside the mediaeval *theologia gloriae* (theology of glory) in favour of a *theologia crucis* (theology of the cross), to think not of the Christ of glory but of the suffering, emaciated 'worm on the cross, fly-ridden, derelict, broken and rejected', to use Luther's own words. Luther at once recalled individual men to the terrifying cost of Christ's obedience, and the Church away from her idea of herself as *domina* (mistress) to the fact that she was *ancilla* (servant).

Christ was the first to associate messiahship with the Isaianic prophecies of the suffering servant (Isa. 52.13–53.12), but it is important at once to say that he is the servant of God (*Ebed Yahweh*), not of man (Isa. 42.1, 19). Christ himself said this expressly (John 6.38; *cf.* 4.34, 10.17, 10.18). Paul says the same (Phil. 2.7–8): Christ's final act of redemption on the cross is referred to as an act of obedience, and it is also argued that it is by Christ's obedience that we are made righteous (Rom. 5.19). This obedience should not be thought of as a human, unquestioning, slavish obedience of a mechanical or automatic kind. It was deeply personal, creative, costly and developing. Christ *learned* true obedience in costly and painful suffering. Though he was a Son, yet he learned obedience by the things which he suffered (Heb. 5.8). From the boy in the temple learning from and listening to the fathers who were later to crucify him, he waited on God in a growing and discerning obedience. He was made perfect as the captain of men by obedience at whatever cost obedience demanded, or was yet to demand (Heb. 2.10; 5.9). All this Christ learned in increasing obedience through the temptation in the wilderness to the agony of Gethsemane.

(*b*) *Christ as Sacrifice.* The second category is that of sacrifice (I Cor. 5.7; Eph. 5.2; Heb. 7.27; 8.3; 9.14, 23, 25, 26, 28; 10.10, 12, 14, 26. *See* particularly Heb. 13.10–13, where Christ's work is interpreted in terms of sacrifice). The purpose of the OT sacrifices, the sin offerings particularly,

was to make opportunities for the people to expiate their sin, a theme referred to in Heb. 9.6–15, 23, 24; 13.10–13. The OT sacrifices are sometimes described as works salvation, but it might do the system more justice if we were to see it as a scheme not to attain God's favour but to retain it. In this context it should be borne in mind that the sacrificial system was not a humanly devised cogitation but a God-given dispensation. The incarnation meant (among other things) that in God's own good time he had fulfilled this provisional dispensation in Christ (Heb. 1.1–12). While it is true that the OT sacrifices were typological of the sacrifice of Christ, it is equally true to say that the sacrifice of Christ was the archetype after which these were fashioned; they were patterns of the heavenly and figures of the true (Heb. 9.23 f.). In this one act of Christ was perfected the whole anticipatory history (Heb. 10.14). A consequence of this is the idea that Christ is the eternal heavenly high priest (Heb. 5.10), but unique in that though he was the priest he was also himself the freely offered sacrifice (Heb. 7.27; 8.3; 9.14, 25; 10.5–9) and in this way purged our sins. (*See further under* 6 [*d*].)

(*c*) *Christ as Propitiation.* Related to this category is the one of propitiation. There has been considerable debate on the suitability of this word. It is strongly maintained that a better word would be expiation, for it is not a case of an angry God whom we must propitiate, but rather of our own sin and guilt which we must expiate. If the atonement springs from the love and mercy of God, how can we appropriately speak of propitiating him? This argument is broadly true, but the word propitiation need not be ruled out, for it safeguards a truth. The love of God was never under question. What is being maintained is that sinful man experiences this same love as hostile wrath, and it is at this point that Christ's obedient sacrifice of love may not inappropriately be called a propitiation of our sins. The point merits further exploration, if not for its unpopularity, then for its importance. When Christ undertook the work of atonement he bore our sins in that he was condemned as a sinner and died the worst death of the worst sinner. Calvin stressed that though Christ died as the worst of sinners facing condemnation and death, yet the highest court of the land had pronounced him innocent. He died an innocent man, though outwardly condemned. He faced the consequences of sin he never committed and endured the wrath he had never earned, an innocent man; and yet this pleased the Father (John 10.17; *cf.* Isa. 53.10: 'it pleased the Lord to bruise him'). Love and wrath are not contradictory, love and hatred are. By long training in obedience and suffering the Son was able to face judicial wrath, though it meant in judgment and death being forsaken by God (Matt. 27.46; Mark 15.34); he entered our experience to the full. He faced the wrath and judgment that are ours, not his, and in this sense Christ may be described as a propitiation. *Hilaskomai* (Luke 18.13; Heb. 2.17), *hilasterion* (Rom. 3.25), and *hilasmos* (I John 2.2;

4.10) are all cognate words whose root meaning in classical Greek is propitiate or appease. At the same time in the LXX, a much better guide for our purposes, the word does not carry the meaning of appeasement. In Luke 18.13 it means 'be merciful to' and expresses God's attitude to a penitent sinner. In Heb. 2.17 the object is not God but the sins of the people and therefore means expiation. C. H. Dodd has argued with some force that such is its NT meaning. *Hilasmos* can mean propitiation but does not imply this necessarily. For instance, in Ps. 130.4 the Hebrew word for forgiveness is rendered by *hilasmos*, where there is not the slightest implication of propitiation. There is a little more controversy round the word *hilasterion* (Rom. 3.25). Some commentators take it as an adjective referring to Christ and meaning reconciling. Others, in the sense of a noun meaning propitiation, but more generally, expiation. Others take it as 'the mercy seat', referring back to the place in the Holy of Holies where God appeared to declare forgiveness to his people. This is the meaning in Heb. 9.5. The mercy seat is now fulfilled in Christ, and it is at his cross that men find the assurance of the forgiveness of their sins.

(*d*) *Christ as Reconciliation.* When the sinner's wrong relation to God is thought of in terms of an estrangement or alienation from God, the biblical category is reconciliation – we are reconciled to God (Rom. 5.10), and God reconciles us to himself (II Cor. 5.18 f.; Eph. 2.16; Col. 1.20–22). It is nowhere stated that God is reconciled to us. This has caused many scholars to take the view that reconciliation applies to man's alienation and not God's. This view may represent something less than the whole truth. It is true that man is estranged from God owing to his sin, but it is equally true that this incurs the wrath of God and God's alienation. Our sin estranges us from God, but his holiness alienates him from us and positively expresses itself in hostility in the wrath. Reconciliation is more than a mere subjective change in us, and can be explained not in psychological categories but in theological. In other words, the word reconciliation is less about man and more about God.

Two Pauline passages support this emphasis: Rom. 5.8–11 and II Cor. 5.18–21. The first passage argues that Christ died for us *while we were yet sinners*, i.e. when we were in our sinful state, when we were estranged from him. It is about God and the Gospel, not about any change in us: the statement is still true, whatever our reaction. It hinges round God, not man's change of heart. This view is supported by II Cor. 5.19. God was in Christ reconciling the world to himself, not imputing their trespass unto them. It is clear that both passages are emphasizing the objective activity of God not the subjective activity of the human mind. The thought is pursued to the end of the chapter where the graphic phrase is used that Christ was made sin for us, who knew no sin; that we might be made the righteousness of God in him (II Cor. 5.21). Nothing could be more objec-

tive than the stark statement that Christ was made sin, though, of course, it is balanced with the subjective change in us, 'that we might be made the righteousness of God in him'. It is equally clear in Rom. 5.11 that when Paul speaks of 'receiving the reconciliation', he is not speaking about a penitential change of heart in us, but rather of a new relationship created and sustained by God in and through Christ. He is speaking of a gift bestowed and received, a status newly established. This new relationship God sustains (II Cor. 5.19). What is prior is the reconciling action God has already taken; the penitential change of heart is a consequence of this work. The primary meaning of reconciliation is God's action to provide for the alienation from God consequent on man's sin. There is a secondary derivative sense in which the word reconciliation may be understood, namely, the restoration of fellowship with God, which is a consequence of that prior action.

(*e*) *Christ as Redemption.* The OT is steeped in the language of redemption. It runs through the Pentateuch in the language of the great deliverance from the house of bondage, right through all the historical books, the Psalms and the Prophets (*see* **Salvation** where this theme is developed). It is thought of not only in terms of past event and present, but also in terms of the future, when the Redeemer will come to Zion (Isa. 59.20).

In the NT Christ's work is viewed not only as deliverance from bondage. Christ actually uses the term ransom (*lutron*) (Matt. 20.28; Mark 10.45) of himself. *Lutron* was the price paid to buy a slave from his bondage. It is to be noted that this 'price' was related to the 'cost' of the cross, and it is in this context that reference is made to his blood (I Cor. 6.20; 7.23; Eph. 1.7; Col. 1.14; I Peter 1.18 f.; Heb. 9.12, 15; Rev. 5.9). Christ's phrase has given its name to one of the theories of the atonement (discussed under 6 [*c*]). Too much emphasis should not be placed on what is but a vivid contemporary metaphor.

Paul analyses the meaning of redemption in Rom. 5–8. Having shown what it means to be justified by faith in Rom. 1–4, he examines this idea as freedom from the bondage of four tyrants: freedom from wrath (Rom. 5), from sin (Rom. 6), from law (Rom. 7), from death (Rom. 8). He argues that God has set man at peace with him through Christ, and that he no longer needs to fear the wrath, for in this new relation created by Christ he is at peace with God (Rom. 5) and cannot any longer fear wrath which he knows as love. In Rom. 6 Paul argues that a man in Christ is likewise free from the tyranny of sin. He has died to sin and lives to God in Christ, a servant of righteousness and no longer a slave to sin. The third bondage is slavery to the law (Rom. 7), from which a man is delivered by the Gospel of grace. The Law serves to convince a man that he can never keep it and therefore by the law is condemned to death: grace enters to deliver him from this death, for he now walks not under the old covenant of the law but in the liberty of the Spirit in the new covenant of grace. The last enemy to be destroyed is death (Rom. 8). In Christ man is an adopted son and faces not death but eternal glory in Christ. He is now with Christ, and no experience, no person, no event, not even death itself, shall separate him from the love of God which he experiences in Christ. Paul sums up the whole meaning of redemption as being freed from the bondage to the four tyrants, wrath, sin, law and death.

(f) *Christ as Victor over the Devil.* More difficult to categorize is the bondage of Satan, the prince of darkness, the god of this world who has us all in his power. This category is frequent in the Gospels, but more particularly in the Epistles where the victory over Satan won by Christ comes to expression (John 12.31; Col. 2.15; Eph. 6.12; Heb. 2.14; I John 3.8). Satan is seen as the epitome of all hostile powers. Satan's role is seen as the liar or deceiver, the prince of this world. This biblical theme of redemption has played a continuing part in doctrinal history. It was central to Augustine's theology in the fifth century, and played the leading part in the great debate between Erasmus and Luther in the sixteenth century. Erasmus argued for the freedom of the will in his book *de arbitrio libero,* an attack on Luther's Augustinian theology. Luther argued in his *de servo arbitrio* that the natural man was in total bondage to his own interests, and had to be freed objectively by 'a stronger than Satan'. Luther based his work on the teaching of Christ and Paul. The atonement understood as Christ's victory over the devil has played a definitive part in redemptive theology. (*See* 6[b].)

4. *The Perfect Remedy.* In the matter of Christ's atoning work there is an unmistakable note of finality, of completeness, of something unrepeatable, done once for all time: 'for by one offering he hath perfected for ever them that are sanctified' (Heb. 10.14). Christ was once offered to bear the sins of many (Heb. 9.28). He was the only High Priest who could do this (I Peter 2.24). As there is a note of finality, so is there a note of accomplishment and efficaciousness about the work of Christ, a note which was struck by Christ's last word from the cross (John 19.30). When he had by himself purged our sins, he sat down on the right hand of the majesty on high (Heb. 1.3). Not only did he reconcile us to God but he guarantees the final end of our salvation (Rom. 5.9 f.; 8.32, 38 f.). The redemption he obtained is an eternal redemption (Heb. 9.12), a work he achieved at the cost of his life (Acts 20.28). He fulfilled all righteousness (Matt. 3.15) and became the author of eternal salvation (Heb. 5.9). There is a guarantee concerning the end, as the thrice repeated pregnant and prominent phrase echoing like a refrain in John 6 testifies: 'and I will raise him up at the last day' (vv. 39, 44, 54).

5. *Universal or Limited?* It would be false to the evidence to argue that Christ made atonement for all men, though some evidence for universal atonement may be adduced. It is incontravertible that there is the strongest evidence against universalizing the doctrine to mean that all men (or beings) will be saved (Origen speculated that even the Devil would be converted in the end, so great was his faith in the love and mercy of God). In Eph. 5.25–27 and in Rom. 8.29–34 the work is clearly limited to the elect, to the justified, to the Church. If this be established as basic it will be seen that the passages quoted in favour of universalism are best understood within a limited ambit clear from the context. For instance, the 'universal' statement of John 3.16 is found restricted to 'whosoever believeth'. Likewise, the 'universal', 'all' of II Cor. 5.14 f. is found on closer examination to refer not to all men but to those who die in Christ. The atonement is universal in that it is freely offered to all without distinction, but the mystery of divine election cannot at the same time be overlooked. It should be remembered that it is not a human prerogative to restrict: ours is only to declare the love and mercy of God in his atoning work in Christ.

6. *Theories of the Atonement.* How have theologians understood and expounded this evidence? Before we go on to consider the classical expositions of the doctrine of the atonement made by the theologians down the centuries, it is important to say that the doctrine of the atonement is one element in the whole Christian doctrine of salvation which embraces not simply the theological exposition of God's redeeming action in Jesus Christ, which is strictly speaking the doctrine of atonement, but an eschatology which includes judgment and resurrection. (*See* **Salvation**.)

The various theological theories in which the Church has expressed its theology of the atonement are quite simply various answers made by different theologians in different ages to the question: How did Christ effect this great change in man's relation to God of which Christian life and faith are the evidence? Four main theories have presented themselves down the ages: (1) The subjective or moral or exemplarist theory; (2) The classic or dramatic theory; (3) The juridical theory; (4) The sacrificial theory. No one theory should be allowed to be seen as antagonistic to another. In a very real sense they all belong to catholic truth; each expresses an element of the truth uniquely its own, and the wise man would seek to reconcile them knowing that no one theory, nor any combination of them all, is sufficient to contain the fullness of the reality.

(a) *The Exemplarist Theory.* The first theory is associated with Peter Abelard (1079–1142) (q.v.). Abelard's theory starts from his doctrine of sin which he understood to mean contempt for God's will. Consequently his whole stress was on intention rather than commission or even omission. This view led him to an exemplarist theory of the atonement according to which the suffering Christ was a supreme example. Christ brought the message of divine forgiveness, and his whole life revealed the love of God in a way which stirs men's hearts to fresh repentance. Hastings Rashdall (1858–1924) in his Bampton Lectures *The Idea of Atonement in Christian Theology* (1919) upheld this Abelardian or exemplarist theory with considerable energy, arguing that it isolated the central truth, attested to in the Fathers, that the atonement was a revelation of the love of God, intended to call forth an answering love in man.

Of course the theory is true, but two grave reservations may be made. Is it a matter of *hoc significat* or *hoc est*? If Christ's work only symbolizes or signifies the love of God, it shows only what the OT had already long taught. There must be a sense in which it *is* God's act, an act of power which changed things, not a revealing gesture of what was already true. The second objection would be that neither psychological nor theological evidence convinces us that a declaration of this kind releases a sinner from the power and enslavement of sin save in a very limited field.

(*b*) *The Classic or Dramatic Theory.* This theory was revived by Luther (1483–1546), as Gustav Aulén (1879–   ) has convincingly argued in his book *Christus Victor* (ET, 1931). It means essentially that Christ did battle with the Devil and defeated him once and for all. The victory has already been won, and Christian men now enjoy the fruits of that victory in sure and certain hope of life with Christ forever. This view had been expressed rather crudely in patristic times, even to the extent of describing Christ as the worm on the hook which finally caught Satan. Christ's vivid metaphor of ransom (Mark 10.45) has even been developed as if the life of Christ were the price agreed on as a ransom (to whom?) to secure man's freedom from bondage to Satan. Nevertheless, apart from crudities, an essential truth is captured here, and the vigour and vitality of Luther's theology spring from this buoyant sense of being on the winning side and knowing what the final outcome of his life in Christ will be. It ensures the important sense that the atonement is throughout God's work and not ours, and that God's purpose of love was to reconcile the world to himself. Any theory, like any parable, cannot carry more than its prescribed load, and critics of this theory too often raise foolish questions and knock them down. Within its own limitations, this patristic theory, a development of ideas found in the NT, expounded in the mediaeval period and vigorously freshened by Luther, belongs to catholic interpretation on the atonement and cannot be jettisoned without loss. Christ's work was a mighty victory: we share his cross but in sure and certain hope of the resurrection.

(*c*) *The Juridical Theory.* This theory is associated with Anselm (1033–1109) (q.v.), who argued the doctrine in terms of the satisfaction due to the outraged honour of God conceived as man's feudal overlord. Anselm made an abiding contribution to atonement theology in his work *Cur Deus Homo?*, in which he interpreted the doctrine in terms of the 'satisfaction' or 'juridical' theory. He argued strongly against the long prevalent view that Christ's death was a ransom paid to the Devil, the price demanded to release man from Satan who held man in his grip. He took the view that the ransom was paid not to the Devil but to God, whose pure majesty had been outraged by the sin of man his creature. The juridical view means essentially that Jesus Christ, as man, bore the penalty for human sin, and offered satisfaction for it in our stead. It lays too much emphasis on the part played by Christ's manhood, and if the theory is not interpreted in the light of the dramatic theory, the whole idea of the atonement as an act of God proceeding from God's love may be obscured.

There are further difficulties in applying the notion of penal substitution to Christ's atoning death. In what sense was Christ's voluntary suffering the same suffering which a sinner must face, unless he is relieved by Christ in faith, and what is the connection? Is there in fact any real substitution in the simple sense of that word, in which (say) a man may send a substitute to a meeting? Christ endured for us and on our behalf, though not strictly instead of us, what we could never have endured for ourselves. Substitution-language is really talking about the love of God, which was willing to endure to the uttermost the terrible consequences of sin which in justice belong to man as sinner and not to God. When a man realizes that another bears the sufferings justly his own, he is moved to penitence. Justice is satisfied, but love triumphs in that the sinner is relieved from the condemnation which strict justice demands to a new life in grace: the gospel fulfils the law. The full majesty of God's justice is vindicated yet forgotten in the cry '*O felix culpa!*'

(*d*) *The Sacrificial Theory.* This is the only theory to have a systematic exposition in the NT, namely in Hebrews. There is an inescapable impression that Hebrews played a more important expository role among the Fathers than it has done in later times. It is worth removing two stumbling blocks. First, the OT sin-offering never meant the propitiation of God by the killing of a victim in the offerer's stead. The point of sin-offerings was expiation rather than propitiation, whereby the sinner offered a 'sinless' victim as his representative rather than as his substitute. It was expiation of sin rather than propitiation of God. Secondly, there is a remote austerity about the author of Hebrews, a kind of archaic Jewishness, unlike Paul with his gushing doctrines of love, mercy and grace, and this has served to alienate him from church doctrine and tradition. It is not sought to reinstate him here, but rather to do full justice to his work, a canonical part of the NT. It could be explained that the real intention of the sacrifices for sin were the offering of an unstained, unblemished, sinless and pure animal life to God in death, so that man's defilement may be removed to enable him to commune with the pure and righteous God. These were offered strictly in accordance with God's expressed will through his chosen priesthood.

Objections to this 'threshold' theology spring readily to mind. An animal is hardly 'sinless'.

The only sacrificed life which could avail is one that has conquered sin and temptation. The blood of bulls and goats could never really cleanse the human heart. The OT dispensation is but a plea, a cry from the heart met in a preparatory and provisional way. Further, an animal is compelled to die and is never free to offer itself. The real sacrifice must be freely offered in perfect obedience to God. Priest and victim must be the same person. Also, just as the true sacrifice cannot be sub-human, as an animal is, it cannot be super-human as a god, so to speak: the true sacrifice must have conquered temptation and sin in man's own nature. The perfect priest and perfect victim must be fully human to avail anything for man.

Where these objections are expressed, as they are in the previous paragraphs, as leading questions, it is seen at once that the Epistle shows the perfection and finality of Christ's atoning work on an OT basis. He is the priest-victim appointed by God for us. He was a man as we are, tempted, yet without sin. He was not compelled to die (John 10.17 f.) but voluntarily died in utter obedience to the Father. His death is the all sufficient sacrifice which has passed through death and reigns eternally. His blood may be sprinkled on our sin-stained souls so that we, washed clean, may move into the presence of God.

Reflection will show how much theology is held in this one view, how many objections validly met. It delivers us from any subjective view and maintains the objective view of Christ doing what we could never do. It saves from the danger of substitutionary language. It symbolizes in dramatic, historic type how his sprinkled blood restores us to a communion with God wherein we follow the Author, Pioneer and Finisher of our faith, the heavenly high priest active now on our behalf. We have communion as men with his perfect humanity, the high priest who has won through to heaven. We miss in Hebrews the liberating power of the Pauline theology, no longer bound to place or time, and we find him anchored to the old Jewish rite. These objections can be easily met if the suggestion were adopted that the author of Hebrews was writing to supplement the Pauline theology as well as to argue that the same God who gave the sacrificial systems had given the supreme sacrifice in Christ. The writer might have prevailed in a Jewish *milieu* where Paul might not.

7. *Conclusion.* As indicated above, the truth lies less in one theory, perhaps not in their sum, but rather in the illuminating cross-light they shed on a profound mystery. The juridical and the sacrificial theories flood-light the classical theory revived by Luther that Christ once for all finally routed the powers of evil and delivered man from their tyranny. Together, these three high-light that great principle which Abelard so characteristically maintained, that the Cross is the supreme demonstration of God's love for man. *See also* **Representative; Salvation.**

Gustav Aulén, *Christus Victor*, ET, 1931; *Faith of*

the Christian Church, 1960; Karl Barth, *Church Dogmatics*, IV: *The Doctrine of Reconciliation*, 1, 2, 3. 1–2, ET, 1956; Emil Brunner, *The Divine Imperative*, ET, 1937; *The Mediator*, ET, 1934; McLeod Campbell, *The Nature of the Atonement*, 1856; Sydney Cave, *The Doctrine of the Work of Christ*, 1941; R. W. Dale, *The Atonement*, 1876; James Denney, *The Death of Christ* (revised Tasker), 1951; Leslie Dewart, *The Future of Belief*, 1966; P. T. Forsyth, *The Work of Christ*, 1910; R. S. Franks, *The History of the Doctrine of the Work of Christ*, 2 vols., 1918; E. M. B. Green, *The Meaning of Salvation*, 1965; L. W. Grensted, ed., *The Atonement in History and Life*, 1929; F. C. N. Hicks, *The Fulness of Sacrifice*, 1930; Leonard Hodgson, *The Doctrine of the Atonement*, 1951; Geoffrey Lampe, 'The Atonement', *Soundings*, ed. A. R. Vidler, 1962; J. Scott Lidgett, *The Spiritual Principle of the Atonement*, 1901; John Macquarrie, *Principles of Christian Theology*, 1966; R. C. Moberly, *Atonement and Personality*, 1901; Leon Morris, *The Apostolic Preaching of the Cross*, 1955; *The Cross in the New Testament*, 1965; J. K. Mozley, *The Atonement*, 1909; W. J. Phythian-Adams, *The Way of Atonement*, 1944; O. C. Quick, *Doctrines of the Creed*, 1938; *The Gospel of the New World*, 1944; Hastings Rashdall, *The Idea of the Atonement in Christian Theology*, 1919; H. Maynard Smith, *Atonement*, 1925; Vincent Taylor, *The Atonement in New Testament Teaching*, 1940; *Forgiveness and Reconciliation*, 1941; *Jesus and his Sacrifice*, 1937; L. S. Thornton, *The Atonement*, 1937; Paul Tillich, *Systematic Theology*, II, 1957.

JAMES ATKINSON

Attributes of God

The article on God (q.v.) describes the classical Christian doctrine as consisting of a speculative method and a concluding concept; and it notes widespread departures from both sides of this position in modern Protestantism. So far as the divine attributes are concerned, a similar situation is to be observed.

1. In the classical teaching a distinction can be drawn between what might be called the metaphysical and the religious attributes (respectively, what can be known by the way of negation and what can be known by the way of analogy, or, as in earlier orthodox Protestant theology, the incommunicable and the communicable attributes). The attributes constitute the divine essence which in turn is one with the divine existence. 'In God's nature there is nothing which is not God himself' (H. Heppe, *Reformed Dogmatics*, 1861, ET, 1950, p. 57). The plurality of the attributes does not infringe the divine unity but derives from the limited powers of human comprehension.

Chief among the metaphysical attributes are God's aseity or independence (which points to the fact that, unlike everything else, God has his existence from himself), his simplicity (which denies any composition or plurality in the divine nature), his infinity which includes both his eternity (the absence of any temporal limitations) and his immensity or omnipresence (the absence of any spatial limitation), and his immutability which includes his impassibility (which both point to the fact that, for the classical conception, God is pure actuality, entirely devoid of any mere potentiality).

The religious attributes are perfections of intelligence, will and life; and the most important of these are omniscience, omnipotence, freedom, holiness, righteousness, goodness and love, along with the fact that as life God is the source of life to all others. Omniscience is the perfection of the divine intelligence whereby God knows himself and all things without exception or deficiency. Omnipotence is God's absolute power to do anything that is possible and is accordingly the perfection of his will; but the perfection of the divine will is seen also in God's 'freedom, holiness, righteousness, goodness and love.

2. Where the speculative method is discarded or rejected, a different classification of attributes suggests itself, and the attributes themselves tend to be understood in somewhat different ways. This does not mean the elimination of metaphysics, but it does mean that what metaphysical propositions remain are, as it were, the metaphysical overtones of basically religious affirmations rather than a controlling metaphysical centre in relation to which the declarations of faith must be deemed merely analogical in the sense of being more or less equivocal. Thus faith, thinking about its Object, may well have something to say about the divine aseity, simplicity and infinity; but it will have said other things first. At least it will speak from the beginning within a context of grace, and its classification of the attributes will not therefore put certain abstract metaphysical concepts in a decisive position of dominance. For example, one such classification is into attributes of holy love (wisdom, faithfulness, justice and grace) and attributes of absolute personality (omnipotence, omniscience, omnipresence and eternity). (*See* John Dickie, *The Organism of Christian Truth*, 1931, pp. 86 ff.)

Further, the treatment given to individual attributes may well vary in its emphasis. Thus, some modern theologians have insisted that, if truth is to be fully served, the traditional teaching regarding the divine impassibility cannot stand without considerable modification (*see* L. Hodgson, *For Faith and Freedom*, I, 1956, pp. 78 ff.; and D. M. Baillie, *God was in Christ*, 1948, pp. 198 f.). Again, another theologian of the modern period has complained that the treatment of omnipotence by St Thomas as an abstract ability to do everything was misleading and the source of many 'curious, fanciful questions' discussed at length by St Thomas, whereas, seen as God's absolute power over the creation, almightiness appeared as an idea both more biblical and closer to the central affirmations of faith (*see* E. Brunner, *Dogmatics*, I: *The Christian Doctrine of God*, ET, 1949, pp. 248 ff.). Similarly, omnipresence may be seen in this context, not just negatively as an absence of spatial limitation, but positively as standing for the fact that God can reveal himself, that he can be savingly present to his children, through absolutely everything that he has made.

N. H. G. ROBINSON

Augsburg Confession

This is the basic Lutheran confession of faith. It was read before the Imperial Diet of Augsburg on 30 June 1530. In compiling it Philip Melanchthon made use of certain statements by Luther and articles adopted by Lutherans in previous conferences at Marburg, Schwabach and Torgau. The Preface and Epilogue are by Gregor Brück, chancellor of Saxony. There are twenty-one concise doctrinal articles with a summary of these (xxii), followed by seven that are more extended and argumentative describing abuses of the papal church that have been corrected in the Reformation. The document is a frank presentation of the essential tenets of Lutheranism, expressed with moderation and in a tone of hope for Christian reunion. The original text, handed to the Emperor, is not extant. Numerous slightly variant editions were soon printed, some by Melanchthon himself. In 1540 his celebrated *Confessio Augustana Variata* materially altered the article (x) on the Lord's Supper. Whereas former editions stated that the body and blood of Christ 'are truly present and distributed', the *Variata* reads: 'are with the bread and wine truly shown forth (*exhibeantur*)'. This form was in general use until 1561 but was abandoned in the anti-Melanchthon reaction of that time.

Deutsche Evangelische Kirchenausschuss, *Die Bekenntnisschriften der evangelisch-lutherischen Kirche*, 2 vols, 1930; M. Reu, *The Augsburg Confession*, 1930; P. Schaff, *Creeds of Christendom*, III, 1919.

J. T. MCNEILL

Augustinianism

St Augustine of Hippo (AD 354–430), a North African, was baptized on Easter Eve, 387. Before that he had sampled the various philosophies and religions of the age. It has been truly said that he was the first great Christian philosopher and, with the exception of Boethius (q.v.), the last for a number of centuries (D. J. B. Hawkins). In him many of the currents of the thought of the ancient world flow together; from him stem many of the characteristic ideas of mediaeval thinking. Plato, mediated to him largely through the Neoplatonists (q.v.), was the dominant philosophical influence upon him and through him dominated Christian philosophy until the thirteenth century. He accepts the Platonic view of the soul as governing the body but rejects Plato's doctrine of the soul's pre-existence. The soul participates in the divine Ideas; God is the illumination of the soul, as light is of the bodily eye. Discourse with other souls does not impart ideas; it stimulates the divinely illuminated intellect to see what is in fact already present to it. This ability to see by the divine light is a natural human faculty in the sense that all men have an original capacity for it. The intelligible realities (*cf.* Plato's Ideas or Forms), or universals, through which the individual existents known through our sense-experience are identifiable by us, have a prior existence in God, and hence we perceive with the eyes of our souls those necessary connections, laws and regularities of nature (as well as truths of logic and mathematics) without which rational knowledge would be impossible.

All this, says Augustine, can be learned from the philosophers. It is, as we might say, a kind of natural theology (q.v.) which not only Christians can discover for themselves, because all men have access to the divine Light. Yet in another sense the term 'natural theology' is inappropriate, since it suggests that men can discover truth without the aid of divine illumination. Augustine denies that men can know truth or beauty or goodness without the illumination of him who is the Source of all Truth and Beauty and Goodness. He would have rejected (had he known it, which is doubtful) the Aristotelian doctrine that our knowledge of universals is derived from generalizing from sense-experience. In this matter he differs from St Thomas Aquinas, who accepted the Aristotelian view and maintained the distinction between natural and revealed theology. But that was after the rediscovery of Aristotle (largely through the efforts of the Arabian philosophers) in the twelfth and thirteenth centuries (*see* **Averroism; Thomism**). For Augustine there is strictly no 'natural theology', if the term is taken to refer to an unaided knowledge of truth or of God. However, the distinction between Augustine and Aquinas should not be pressed too far, because Augustine is an unsystematic writer and Aquinas does not appear to be aware that he is disagreeing with him and always refers to him with respect. But there is an indubitable difference of emphasis between the two, corresponding closely to the difference between Plato and Aristotle: in each case the latter thinker would be inconceivable without his predecessor. It is appropriate, however, to speak of Augustine as the exponent of general and special revelation (*see* **Revelation**) and of Aquinas as the exponent of natural and revealed theology.

But if all men have access through divine illumination to knowledge of the truth, what in Augustine's view becomes of a special Christian revelation? In a striking passage he tells us that he had learned about God and the Logos from the philosophers, but one thing he had not found in them: that the Word (*Logos*) became flesh and dwelt among us (*The City of God*, xii. 14). Through the special revelation in the Scriptures Augustine discovered history, and his *The City of God* presents us with a profound philosophy of history. Greek and Roman historiography had succumbed to irrationalism, to belief in Fate, Luck and the Roman *Fortuna*. But Rome had been sacked by Attila the Goth in AD 410 and the Vandals were besieging Hippo when Augustine was on his death-bed. He formulates a theology of history based upon the biblical teaching concerning God's judgment on Babylon and Jerusalem, and in so doing he is the first to draw together a universal history which includes Israel, Babylon, Greece and Rome. He sees history as a tale of two cities, the earthly and the heavenly: the *civitas terrena* was appointed by the beneficent providence of God, who disposes of the kingdoms of the earth, as the *milieu* out of which the reborn citizens of the *civitas Dei* might be recruited. Rome had fallen, not because her citizens had abandoned *Fortuna* in favour of the oriental Jehovah, but because as 'the great western Babylon' she had failed to provide the justice and order which the divine providence had decreed for the earthly city. Augustine finally overcame the cyclical view of history and so managed to rid Europe of the ancient superstition which prevented the Greeks from developing a genuine tradition of historiography. He did this by developing the implications of the Gospel (*cf.* Rom. 6.9): it would be absurd to believe that Christ would die again when the wheel of history had come full circle.

Augustine's thought was profoundly biblical (he wrote commentaries and preached many sermons on the books of the Bible). For him the Scriptures constitute a special revelation which avails where the reason of the philosophers fails to impose order upon a restless and fallen humanity. Faith in Christ is the one thing which enables men to understand the world, and themselves within it, on a rational and secure basis. 'Understanding is the reward of faith. Therefore do not seek to understand in order to believe, but believe in order that you may understand (*crede ut intelligas*); for unless you believe, you will not understand' (*In Joan. Evang.*, xxix. 6). This he says over and over again in many different ways. The reason of the philosophers, though valid as far as it goes and made possible only through divine illumination, falls far short of that ultimate divine wisdom which comes by the scriptural revelation and which brings life and understanding to those whom faith has liberated.

As bishop and pastor of his flock in turbulent times, Augustine was caught up into all the controversies of his day. His ardent African temper perhaps led him on occasion to exaggerate his views and to act impulsively. His desire to protect his flock and safeguard its unity brought him into conflict with Donatism (q.v.). His strong sense of the prevenient grace of God led him into controversy with Pelagianism (q.v.) and into the kind of overemphasis upon predestinarian views (*see* **Predestination**) which has brought much criticism upon him in later times. On all subjects he held strong views, to which he gave powerful expression (*see*, e.g. **Trinity**). His influence stretched across the Middle Ages to St Anselm (q.v.) and to St Bonaventura (q.v.), who defended Augustine's view against the 'new theology' of his contemporary Aquinas. Yet Aquinas himself considered St Augustine as his teacher. The Reformers returned to him for instruction and inspiration; and Augustine's conception of the relation of faith to reason ('general and special revelation' – though Augustine did not use these terms) is widely accepted in its essential principles by theologians of the twentieth century (e.g. John Baillie, H. R. Niebuhr, etc.). *See also* **God (4); Grace; Revelation; Trinity; Predestination.**

There is a vast literature on every aspect of St Augustine's life and work. There are also many translations of his works. *See* for an excellent selection E. Przywara, *An Augustine Synthesis*, 1945, or vols. VI, VII and VIII of *The Library of Christian Classics*, ed. by J. Baillie, J. T. McNeill and H. P. van Dusen, 1953, 1955 and 1956 respectively; *The Confessions* in the Penguin Classics, 1961; *The City of God* in the Everyman series, 1945. Useful introductions will be found in G. Bonner, *St Augustine of Hippo: Life and Controversies*, 1963; Peter Brown, *Augustine of Hippo*, 1967; J. Burnaby, *Amor Dei*, 1938; M. C. D'Arcy, C. Dawson *et al., A Monument to St Augustine*, 1934; For Augustine's view of the relation of faith and reason *see* Alan Richardson, *Christian Apologetics*, 1947, chs. V, VI and X; for his theology of history *see* Alan Richardson, *History Sacred and Profane*, 1964, ch. 2. For the background of his ideas *see* C. M. Cochrane, *Christianity and Classical Culture*, 1940.

EDITOR

Aulén, Gustav

Gustav Aulén (1879–   ), Lundensian theologian and Swedish bishop, made a distinctive contribution at Lund where he was a leader in the *Motivsforschung* school which saw Christian truth behind a doctrine, not the form in which it had been preserved. In his Olaus Petri Lectures on the atonement (1930) he developed this theme and argued with conviction that the classical doctrine of the atonement, developed by Luther, was essentially the victory of Christ over the Devil and the powers of darkness. (*See* **Atonement** 6 [*b*]). The book was published in an abridged form in English under the pregnant title *Christus Victor* (1931).

JAMES ATKINSON

Authority

It is useful to divide authority into external and internal authority. External authority is that attaching to a person as an official or to an office as an office. When someone obeys a policeman who asks him not to park his car in a certain place it is not the intrinsic conviction of the policeman's words that count but his holding office as a guardian of the law. Internal authority is the authority residing in convincing argument or weighty moral or spiritual example or experience. If a woman buys a produce advertised on television, for instance, it is the authority of the words and actions of the advertiser which has moved her. The authority of a bishop is an example of external, and the authority of a writer or a saint is that of internal, authority.

In the NT almost all authority is internal. The ultimate authority (which is the word of God) is expressed through preaching or through miraculous occurrences, or found in meditation or prayer or inspired vision and dream or in reading the (OT) Scripture. Even the twelve apostles do not hold authority because they have been invested with an office, but because they are in a position to witness to what Christ did in the days of his flesh and to his appearances as risen Lord. But as the Church gradually became a fixed and relatively uniform institution, official, external, authority inevitably came to play a greater and greater part. By the fourth century Christian writers are appealing to earlier authors as 'the tradition of the Fathers' – having regard rather to who they were than to what they said. This century also sees the advent of decisions of councils, which, once made, naturally have external authority attaching to them as expressing the judgment of the whole church or of a large part of it. As the centuries passed more and more external authorities came into being. Fathers, doctors, councils, popes, and the origin and extensive growth of a codified Canon Law assisted this development. By the end of the Middle Ages the Church was supported by a vast system of external authority.

But the advent of the Reformation with its emphasis upon the response of the individual in faith to the demand of the word of God, and the divisions of the Church which resulted from it, assisted by the many impulses created by the Renaissance towards individualism and the rejection of established authority in metaphysics and theology, gradually brought about an entire change of attitude towards authority in the minds of Christians. Today the pendulum of opinion has swung to the other extreme. Internal authority is now widely regarded as the only authority in matters religious. The pronouncements of Fathers, councils and popes are regarded as purely historical (i.e. as witnessing to the state of opinion in their own periods) or are simply judged on their own merits according to contemporary criteria. In this sense it could be said that reason is the only authority recognized now, but this would be to use the word 'authority' in a quite different sense. *Reason* is the means whereby we reach religious convictions, not the matter which affords the material for making our judgments. All Christian traditions (certainly including the Roman Catholic) have in theory recognized this, at least as far as allowing that a man must always follow the authority of his own conscience in making moral decisions. In fact the question of reason or conscience as authority parallel with Scripture, tradition, etc. can only be raised in a situation where external authority is regarded as the norm.

Judged by modern conceptions of authority, then, the authority of Scripture will not be that of an inerrant oracle delivering equal truth in all its parts nor the authority of the Church that of an autonomous institution under no responsibility to refer to the sources of its doctrine, but the Bible will be considered as the unique witness to the acts of God in history by which he makes himself known to all men and demands their response, and the Church as the organ chosen by God to point to the Bible, to preach it, teach it, and to order its life by the light of the Bible. The authority of the Bible does not lie in the book itself but in the subject to which it witnesses, and the authority of the Church lies ultimately in the Word of God whom it obeys and whose witness it finds in the Bible. The old maxim 'the Church to teach and the Bible to prove' is no less true today than it ever was. In the barest terms, the Church, and the Church alone, has authority to offer to everybody the opportunity of being convinced by the authority of the Bible. But once this position is understood, it must be pointed out that it is impossible and indeed disastrous to attempt to exclude external authority altogether. Every organization claiming to be the Church, or to have any association with the Church, or to represent the Church, even partially and locally, must wield administrative and executive authority in some form and must claim in some sense to wield it in the name of Christ. Again, the collective experience of the Church, either in forming and holding to fundamental dogmas of the Christian faith tested by centuries of discussion and worship, or in learning moral and spiritual wisdom through a continuous history of prayer, worship and practice, still forms a very impressive argument not easily overthrown when rightly understood and handled.

Two more forms of authority must be mentioned. One is the authority of scholarship. To this, fluctuating and subjective though it be, the Church and its theologians must pay full and respectful attention, without elevating it to a position of ultimate authority. The development of historical, literary and linguistic studies in the last two centuries has made this essential. The other is the authority of religious experience. In one sense this must be decisive for every individual, because the personal, existential nature of Christian belief in God implies prayer and worship. And properly handled (e.g. by P. T. Forsyth or F. Von Hügel) this aspect of Christian truth can become a strong argument. But it never can stand alone because of its subjective nature. If religious experience is our sole authority then the experience of a Joseph Smith, a Bernadette Soubirous or a Mrs Eddy is as authoritative as that of an Augustine or of a John of the Cross. The authority of religious experience must be supported and balanced by that of Scripture and tradition. Authority for the Christian is a combination or harmony of several forms of authority, all fused in faith.

J. H. Newman, *An Essay in Aid of a Grammar of Assent*, 1870; J. Oman, *Vision and Authority*, 1902; Alan Richardson and W. Schweitzer, eds., *Biblical Authority for Today*, 1951; J. M. Todd, ed., *The Problems of Authority*, 1962; R. R. Williams, *Authority in the Apostolic Age*, 1950.

R. P. C. HANSON

Autopistic

The Greek word from which this word is derived means 'self (evident) faith'. It refers to the claim of K. Barth and other theologians that faith must shine by its own light, since there is no brighter with which to corroborate it. According to Barth the divine revelation must create in man the power by which it can be received, since man is himself incapable of perceiving the truth by his own natural capacities. In other words faith (like revelation) is a gift of God and its happening is sheer miracle. Biblical support for this kind of view might be sought in the Johannine conception of Christ as the True Light, without which men are blind. Even so, the conception should doubtless be synthesized with its apparent antithesis, Bultmann's assertion of the necessity of pre-understanding (q.v.).

EDITOR

Averroism

The importance of the mediaeval 'Arabian' scholars and philosophers must not be underestimated in the history of European thought. Avicenna (980–1037), a physician at the Persian court, with his Neoplatonist and Aristotelian teachings, exercised considerable influence on the earlier Schoolmen (*see* **Scholasticism**). But it was Averroes of Cordova (1126–1198) whose commentaries on Aristotle caused consternation through the dissemination of Aristotelianism among the students of the University of Paris and elsewhere. He interpreted Aristotle in a materialistic way, denying such doctrines as the providence and indeed the personality of God, the immortality of the soul, etc. Siger of Brabant (1235–1282) was the leading exponent of Averroism in Paris. Albertus Magnus (q.v.) wrote a refutation of Averroism in 1256, and in 1257 Aquinas began his *Summa contra Gentiles* directed chiefly against the Averroistic interpretation of Aristotle. The pope had forbidden the study of Aristotle, but this did not deter Aquinas from his great apologetic work of re-interpreting the Christian faith in terms of the 'new' logic of Aristotle. Though condemned by his own Dominican Order, Aquinas had successfully done the work of an apologist, showing that the new thought of his age could become the vehicle of Christian understanding, and in due course he was recognized as 'the Angelic Doctor'. In order to appreciate the magnitude of his achievement we must recognize that in his day the new Averroistic philosophy threatened the Christian faith just as the mighty military and economic forces of Islam threatened the small island of Christendom which it encircled from Spain, through Sicily, North Africa and the Balkans almost to the gates of Vienna. *See* **Apologetics; Thomism.**

S. J. Curtis, *Short History of Western Philosophy in the Middle Ages*, 1950, ch. VII.

EDITOR

Baptism, Theology of. *see* Initiation, Christian.

Baptists

The Baptist churches arose in England during the development of Puritanism (q.v.). Baptists differed from other separatists in their adoption of believers' baptism. Prior to the 1640s, the mode of baptism was affusion, thereafter immersion. Thomas Helwys, who had felt Mennonite influence at Amsterdam, founded in London the mother church of the General (Arminian) Baptists, 1612. Later from a Southwark centre several churches of Particular (Calvinist) Baptists arose; these jointly issued a confession in 1644. Only in 1891 were the two branches united in the Baptist Union of Great Britain and Ireland. Unlike the Anabaptists, Baptists have generally taken a positive attitude to the state and the political vocation; but they have also asserted strongly the right of conscience, and their writers have included pioneers in religious toleration and liberty. The autonomy of the local church is watchfully maintained, but not to the exclusion of a connectional element. The names of William Carey and Adoniram Judson are sufficient to suggest the prominence of Baptists in the inception of modern missions. In the USA Baptists early became numerous through active frontier preaching, and their laymen have held some prominence in religious, political and business life. Baptist churches have arisen widely in European countries, throughout the British Commonwealth, and in the major nations of Asia and Africa. The Baptist World Alliance was formed in 1905.

H. Davies, *The English Free Churches*, 1952; R. G. Torbet, *A History of the Baptists*, 1950; A. C. Underwood, *A History of the English Baptists*, 1947.

J. T. MCNEILL

Barmen Declaration

Barmen Declaration is the doctrinal proclamation issued by the German Confessional Church at the First Synod of Barmen (29–30 May 1934), which denied, against the teachings of the German National Christians, the existence of subordinate revelations apart from God's unique revelation in Jesus Christ. *See* **Barth, K.**; **Crisis Theology.**

JAMES RICHMOND

Barth, Karl

Karl Barth (1886–   ) was born at Basel, Switzerland, and has become the most celebrated Protestant theologian of this century. After studying at Berns and then in Germany, he held several Swiss pastorates in the period before and during World War I. It was while he was pastor in the industrial town of Safenwil that he composed his *Römerbrief*, a commentary on Romans published in 1919 and one of the turning-points in the history of modern theology. He then taught theology in several German universities, and was Professor at Bonn when Hitler came to power in 1933. Barth was one of the leading spirits behind the declaration of Barmen (1934) and the struggle of the 'confessing Church' against the encroachments of the Nazi state. He was dismissed from his chair in 1935, and the same year became professor at Basel, where he continued to teach until his retirement in 1962.

Barth's commentary on Romans, both the first edition of 1919 and even more markedly the new edition of 1922, was a kind of manifesto of revolt against the liberal theology that had prevailed during the preceding century. Barth had been reading his Bible in his Swiss parish, and found that when Paul is allowed to speak for himself, he sounds many themes that were muted in the liberal theology – themes like the sovereignty of God, the finitude and sinfulness of man, God's priority in grace and revelation, the eschatological character of the NT message as it proclaims a new age in contradiction to the present world. Furthermore, the optimistic promises of liberal theology had not been fulfilled. Europe was in crisis, and it was clear that the Kingdom of God was not just the next step in man's progressive march. Liberal theology had domesticated God into being the patron saint of human institutions and values, but now there was a call to remember what Kierkegaard had named the 'infinite qualitative difference' between man and God.

There is no doubt that the time was ripe for Barth's message and that it supplied a needed corrective. However, as Barth himself has been ready to admit, that message was presented in a one-sided and exaggerated way (perhaps only so can a message get across). The later Barth has modified many of his early statements, and indeed some critics have claimed that the massive *Church Dogmatics* represent a retreat from his early insights into a new scholasticism. Nevertheless, there are some positions to which Barth has remained firmly attached, even when he has qualified the more extreme forms in which they have been stated. (1) There is the preoccupation with revelation. The central concept in Barth's theology is the Word of God, a Word which encounters us in threefold form as the incarnate Word, the Word of Scripture and the Word of proclamation. (2) Correspondingly, there is a depreciation of natural theology. There is no way for man's mind to rise to the knowledge of God. Whatever ideas of God man may form are merely idols and are condemned by the true knowledge of himself which God gives in his Word. It should be added, however, that even revelation is also a veiling, and that the idea of the hidden God is influential in Barth's thought. (3) A sharp distinction is made between revelation and religion. The latter is man's idolatrous attempt to grasp at God, and Barth's understanding of religion in this pejorative way makes it impossible for him to allow that there is any common ground of truth between Christian faith and the great world religions. (4) All of these points are rooted in the great distance which Barth set between God and man. There is strong emphasis on the transcendence of God, and in the early writings there was strong depreciation of the 'natural' man. To some extent Barth's more recent teaching on what he calls the 'humanity' of God and his stress on the incarnation has softened the sharpness of the early writings. But it would be going much too far to say that Barth's theology is humanistic. Actually, it was its very transcendent character that allowed it to exert a strengthening influence among those who stood against Hitler.

Barth's many insights continue to be important, but his extreme revelationism and his over-emphasis on the transcendence of God have fallen out of favour. Yet when these are taken away, what happens to his theology as a whole? It is perhaps significant that most advocates of the 'death of God' point of view (q.v.) have been disillusioned Barthians.

Karl Barth, *Anselm: Fides Quaerens Intellectum*, ET, 1960; *Church Dogmatics*, ET, 1936–62; *The Epistle to the Romans*, ET, 1933; *The Knowledge of God and the Service of God*, ET, 1938; Hans Küng, *Justification: The Doctrine of Karl Barth and a Catholic Reflection*, ET, 1964.

JOHN MACQUARRIE

Baur, Ferdinand Christian

Baur (1792–1860), German theologian and founder of the 'Tübingen School', is commonly regarded as a biblical and historical scholar over-influenced by philosophical presuppositions; it is supposed that his work was fatally biassed as a consequence of his Hegelianism. More recent research, however, is showing this verdict to be a gross over-simplification. Despite the inadequacy of the results obtained by Baur, he can be seen to be a pioneer in the use of the historico-critical method and as such one of the most important figures of the nineteenth century. *See also* **Tübingen School.**

Peter C. Hodgson, *The Formation of Historical Theology, A Study of Ferdinand Christian Baur*, 1966.

JOHN BOWDEN

Baxter, Richard

Richard Baxter (1615–1691), eminent Puritan preacher and author, never attended a university but was tutored by the celebrated John Owen and other scholars and made good use of self-directed reading. In 1638 he was ordained by the bishop of Worcester but was drawn to the Non-conformists. In 1641 he began a highly fruitful pastorate at Kidderminster during which he formed an association of the ministers of Worcester of different persuasions. During the Civil War he served temporarily as a regimental chaplain in the Parliamentary army. At the Restoration he declined the offer of the bishopric of Hereford. In Charles II's reign he suffered harsh prison terms but was not entirely silenced. His fervid eloquence and

persuasive voice combined with an extraordinarily ready mind to make him an effective preacher. He wrote diffusely and with ease. It was said that 'he could accommodate himself to all capacities', but his books of scholarly quality are not so well known as those of devotional and practical content. In the latter class are *The Saints' Everlasting Rest, The Reformed Pastor* and *The Christian Directory*. The first of these is a widely read household book of devotion, the second a still valued guide to the duties of ministers, and the last an ample and discerning work on Christian casuistry. Ecclesiastically he was increasingly liberal and charitable. Classed as a presbyterian, he declared himself a 'true Catholic' and constantly sought pacification and co-operation among denominations. A warm defender of the authority of the Bible, he nevertheless acknowledged verbal errors in some passages. His doctrine of election is without the corollary of reprobation and bears certain resemblances both to Arminianism and to the 'hypothetic universalism' of the Saumur school. In politics he advocated 'a mixt government or limited monarchy', and he severely rebuked Cromwell for his part in the execution of Charles I. His aim was a 'Christian commonwealth' in which piety would be fostered and vice suppressed. At the Restoration he tried to revive the proposal of his deceased friend, Archbishop Usher, for a modified episcopacy, and with like futility presented his *Reformation of the Liturgy* (the 'Savoy Liturgy'), which relies on biblical phrases and is thought to reflect his own practice in the pastorate.

H. Davies, *The Worship of the English Puritans*, 1948; F. J. Powicke, *A Life of the Reverend Richard Baxter*, 1924; R. Schlatter, *Richard Baxter and Puritan Politics*, 1957; J. M. L. Thomas, ed., *The Autobiography of Richard Baxter*, 1925.

J. T. MCNEILL

Beatific Vision

Beatific vision is the name used traditionally for the vision of God as he is, which will be the joy of the redeemed in heaven: man's *summum bonum* or ultimate fulfilment for which he was created. It will be enjoyed *in patria* (i.e. in heaven), but cannot be attained *in via* (i.e. during man's earthly pilgrimage, although it was held by some later mediaeval theologians that the beatific vision had been vouchsafed to certain favoured mortals in this life, especially Moses, St Paul and St Thomas Aquinas. *See also* **Vision of God.**

Being, Becoming

In early Greek philosophy being was contrasted with becoming or change (*cf.* Parmenides and Heracleitus respectively). Being, as such, is that which cannot change: that which is perfect could only change for the worse, which, of course, perfect being logically could not do. Yet the world which we know does change, despite Parmenides' view that change is only an illusion. The world must therefore contain degrees of being or perfection (the idea of the 'Great Chain of Being' is older than Plato). Plato conceived of reality as consisting of the Ideas, i.e. the essences or perfect forms of the things which actually exist and in which they 'participate' more or less imperfectly (e.g. any triangle that can be drawn on paper must necessarily be imperfect, since a line is that which has length but no breadth). In Aristotelian metaphysics, however, actuality is realized potentiality (e.g. an oak-tree is an acorn which has realized its potentiality). An existent is what it is by virtue of its potentiality, (e.g. the potentiality of an acorn is different from that of a tadpole). Change (becoming) is thus the realization of potentiality. The absolutely real is that which has totally realized its potentiality, i.e. the Actuality of all existence, or God. (But it is debatable whether Aristotle's God, having no potentiality of the kind which all other existences have, could be said to exist, since existence involves potentiality. Aristotle's God was 'thought thinking about itself'.)

Although throughout the earlier mediaeval period St Augustine's Platonic view of essences was dominant, in the thirteenth century the rediscovered metaphysics of Aristotle became in the thought of Aquinas (1225–1274) the basis of the 'natural theology' of the high Middle Ages (see **God [7]**). God was pure actuality, having no unrealized potentiality; therefore he was changeless and unchangeable. He is also *necessary* being; all other beings are *contingent* upon his will, creativity, etc. To use a slogan of some contemporary theologians, God is not a being but Being-itself (*ipsum esse*). He is the only existence who can say with perfect propriety, 'I am.' Being is his *métier*. His essence and his existence coincide. He exists by his own pure act (*actus purus*); his essential activity consists in being himself.

It has often been remarked that the identification of the God of Greek philosophy with the living, personal God of the Bible, the Lord of history, is the most astonishing occurrence in the whole history of ideas. It is also a very difficult identification to maintain, though Ex. 3.14 made the matter easier for the mediaevals by supplying a proof-text. It could further be said that, in some sense, the holding together of these two contrasted ideas of God constitutes both the permanent task and the culminating problem of Christian theology as such. When, on the one hand, God's essential being is denied, as in much Protestant theology with its anti-metaphysical bias, God tends to become one being among other beings and eventually becomes only a way of speaking about man's existence or human ideals; he thus becomes increasingly incredible and dispensable. When, on the other hand, he is thought of as Being-itself, as with Tillich, he becomes 'the God beyond the God of theism' and disappears in the shadows of pantheism or in the obscurities of philosophical speculation.

The problem may be stated thus: Being is the most abstract of all possible ideas: the God of the Bible is the most living and personal of all conceivable realities. How are the two conceptions to be held together? Perhaps the answer is that the mystery (not problem) of God's being is beyond the range of human conceiving. This must undoubtedly be true, if God is *God;* nevertheless some things can perhaps be said. For one thing, as both Aquinas and Barth would have agreed, God has come forth out of his mysterious hiddenness and graciously revealed himself to those who will hear his word. Further, as most theologians (but not Barth) would agree, God has left traces of his handiwork in the things which he has made, especially in man, made in his image (*see* **God [6]; Revelation**). The debated question today is how we can understand any analogies which would make the likeness between God and man (Being and beings) credible.

Some contemporary theologians see in Heidegger's analysis of existence a way of speaking validly about God's existence and men as 'existents' (*see* **Dasein**); time, which is the 'horizon' of any understanding of being, may be the appropriate analogy for understanding the relation between being (God) and being (men), since the latter transcend time as mere successiveness. This philosophy reverses the Greek attitude which regards time and change as illusory; man *qua* existent, like being (God), takes time into himself. Man, too, not only is but has the power to 'let be' or to create, which is an ontological way characterizing the love of God, since love is essentially a 'letting be' of others. Love is thus the true analogue of being as such. Thus, J. Macquarrie: 'Being is the letting-be that creates, sustains and perfects the beings; and we find the model to this ultimate mystery in creative, disinterested love' (*God-Talk*, p. 227). Another type of philosophical theology which today seeks to reconcile being and becoming in an intelligible synthesis is that known as Process Theology (q.v.). Both these types of theology are instances of the current tendency to move away from the classical Greek conceptions of the 'real' as changeless, eternal substance towards a more dynamic (perhaps Hebraic) idea of being as activity. But some will claim that this is already provided for in the traditional idea of God as *actus purus*, in which being is itself activity, or, to put it in another way, the concept of being properly includes activity and creativity, a creativity which produces more beings but not more being.

Austin M. Farrer, *Faith and Speculation*, 1967; *Finite and Infinite*, 1943; *A Science of God*?, 1966; J. Macquarrie, *God-Talk*, 1967, ch. 10; *Studies in Christian Existentialism*, 1965, esp. chs. 5 and 6; E. L. Mascall, *He Who Is*, 1943.

EDITOR

Benediction, Blessing

These words are in common use in Jewish and Christian writings in theological and devotional contexts. In Christian usage, the word blessing is common in the context of worship and appears often in the doxologies of hymns, but it is also used as a 'shorthand' term in situations that are believed to result from the saving activity of God. J. Montgomery's hymn, 'Hail to the Lord's anointed' speaks of the ruling Christ as 'All-blessing and all-blest' which sounds well, but suggests problems. For example, is the word blessing used in the same way on both occasions in that line? For the answer we must look at the Hebrew usage. There the main word is *barak*. It appears often in the passive form, 'blessed by the Lord' (Gen. 9.26, etc.),but it is also used in the active of God blessing men or things, and (derivatively) of men blessing other men and also God.

The origins of ideas about blessing lie far back in the primitive religion of the Hebrews. Blessing seems fundamentally to be connected with the production of fertility. In its most primitive usage it is possible that the root *brk* meant not to worship but to fertilize (*see* R. B. Onians, *The Origins of European Thought*, 1951, pp. 481 ff.). Certainly the same root in Hebrew means both 'to bless' and 'knee', and there is some evidence that in primitive thought the knee was regarded as the seat of fertility.

Arguments based on etymologies are often suspect, but it is clear that in the OT the word *barak* is very often connected with the fertility of animals, crops and men (Gen. 22.17). This may be its oldest use.

It may be, too, that the rather odd usage found in Hebrew and Christian writings whereby God blesses men and nature in general (i.e. makes them fruitful) and also man blesses God (i.e. gives him thanks and praise) has its roots in the fertility religions of the ancient Middle East. At this fairly primitive level there was something like a co-ordinate relationship between the people on the one hand and the gods and the land on the other. If such ideas ever had a place in Hebrew religion, there is not much sign of them left in the OT.

The idea that the 'blessedness' of the people and land depends entirely on a right relationship with Yahweh remains (Hag. 2.18 f.), but the battle with the fertility religions had been won by the time the OT was in process of writing (Hos. 2.8 shows it in progress, 'She did not know it was *I* who gave her the grain') and all that remains of man's part in 'blessing' God is to give thanks for the great gifts that God gives his people whom he has elected. Man can no longer be thought of as in some way enabling Yahweh to bless by co-operating in a fertility ritual.

1. *Blessing and Election.* In the patriarchal narratives in their final form, there is a close connection between the idea of God's blessing and his election of Israel.

Abram is chosen and at once blessed (Gen. 12.3). The birth of Isaac is seen by the writer to rest on the blessing of Sarai by Yahweh (Gen. 17.16), and the blessing is handed on not to Esau but to Jacob (Israel). Again the odd incident of the crossing of Jacob's hands in Gen. 48.14 suggests the idea that the blessing or choosing of

Yahweh does not necessarily 'move' according to rule, but by his will. By this time the OT writers do not regard the blessing as the handing on of natural rights, but of the divine promise (*see* W. Vischer, *The Witness of the Old Testament to Christ*, 1949, p. 159).

This shows considerable development of the more primitive idea of God's action in blessing being confined to the promotion of fertility and planty, though the continuation of the basic element of 'peace' is evident. It seems that the liturgical blessing played a large part in the later cultus. The place where Yahweh is worshipped is *the* place where his blessing is received (Ex. 20.24), and this is mediated liturgically by the priestly blessing to which there are several references in the OT (e.g. Deut. 10.8; Num. 6.23 ff.).

2. *The State of Blessedness.* A further word appears in the OT which is often translated 'blessed'. It is *ashre*, a sort of exclamation meaning 'O how happy' (the man who . . .). It is very common in the Wisdom writings and is used to express joy of a specifically religious type. It may be said to be the state of those who, being in the right relationship with Yahweh, receive his blessing. Perhaps the clearest example of this is seen in Ps. 144.12–15. There we are given a comprehensive picture of the blessing of God producing great plenty, and the Psalm ends, 'Happy (*ashre*) the people to whom such blessing fall! Happy the people whose God is the LORD!'

God's blessing brings prosperity which is to be 'happy', but above all the chief happiness of Israel is that 'God is with' them, and this once more emphasizes the connection between God's blessing and his electing of Israel. So it follows that even misfortunes can be a blessing if seen as the action of God in correcting a man – 'Blessed is the man whom thou dost chasten, O LORD' (Ps. 94.12). This is a late development in OT aphorism, 'Prosperity is the blessing of the Old Testament; adversity the blessing of the New.' Still, it remains true that the main idea of blessing in the OT is one of well-being. It is therefore surprising that the word blessing is not found very frequently in eschatological passages in the OT, though the ideas connected with it certainly are (*cf.* Joel 3.18). It is very common for commentators to speak of an 'age of blessing' when referring to typical Hebrew eschatological expectations, and in the non-canonical writings the word is often used in this context. On the whole, the tenor of the apocalyptic writings is to look for blessing in the future, and the writers of these books outdid each other in delineating the forms that God's blessing would take.

3. *Benedictions.* In the period immediately preceding the NT the range of ideas connected with blessing was limited largely to the second OT usage noted above. In the rabbinic writings, blessing is above all the offering of thanks to God. One of the Tractates of the Talmud is entitled

Berakoth ('Blessings') and is largely a collection of prayers to be used before reading the Torah, as grace before a meal, and in many everyday situations, for example, on seeing the first tree in blossom. Though the concept of blessing has here become limited, nevertheless, the idea that man depends on God at all points for his life and gifts is once more emphasized, and this (though in a very formalized way) is expressed by the requirement that at every point man, so completely dependent on God, should acknowledge this by the saying of a blessing (i.e. the offering of thanksgiving). The rabbinic teaching about the liturgical blessings given by the priests is of interest because it goes out of its way to make it clear that God alone blesses; any notion of a priest of the 'mysteries' is excluded. Commenting on Num. 6.23 the rabbis said 'the priests spread out their hands to indicate that God stands behind them' (quoted in C. F. G. Montefiore and H. M. J. Loewe, *A Rabbinic Anthology*, 1938, p. 154). The Aaronic blessing is also treated in one of the fragments found at Qumran (the *Formulary of Blessings*), and again the implication is that the priest declares God's willingness to favour his people (*see* T. H. Gaster, tr., *The Scriptures of the Dead Sea Sect*, 1957, pp. 97–101).

The blessings connected with a meal have a special place and are of importance for our understanding of the Christian development of the idea of blessing. The opening phrase of the table blessing was fixed, but it seems that there was room for individual variations (*see* Montefiore and Loewe, *op cit*, p. 131).

4. *The NT and After.* The writings of the NT seem everywhere to take the theology of blessing suggested in the OT for granted, though it is clear that the writers believe that God's blessing has now been given in a new way.

Paul's use of the Genesis passage dealing with the blessing of Abraham is of central importance. The blessing given to Abraham has come to fruition in the work of Jesus, the Christ, and now men are blessed 'in Christ' (Gal. 3.8 ff.; Rom. 6.4 ff.). This view, however, is not confined to St Paul. It is implied in Heb. 6.17 and by Luke in Acts 3.25, and the Matthean genealogy points to the same idea when it traces Jesus' descent from Abraham. Thus the connection between God's blessing and his election, which is already seen in the OT, is made quite explicit in the teaching of the NT which centres upon the idea of God's decisive action in Jesus Christ. Round him the new community is gathered and shares in the promised blessings of the messianic age already (Eph. 1.3, 14), and it is to be the means by which the blessing of God is made available for all men (Eph. 1.10).

Of all the 'blessings' in the NT, the words of Jesus at the Last Supper have had the most important influence on Christian thought and usage. Here we find overtones of the idea of the messianic banquet which is to be shared by the followers of Jesus and here the simple table blessing of Judaism has been filled with pregnant new meaning. In general, the words *eulogein* and *eucharistein* are used in Greek to express the idea of blessing/thanksgiving and both these appear in the synoptic accounts of the Last Supper (and the feeding miracles). In the end, however, the central service came to be called the Eucharistia and not the Eulogia, and by the time of Justin martyr we find the odd coining, the nuance of which can only be translated 'thanksgivingized bread'! (*eucharistetheis artos*). This is because the Christian Eucharist is not thought of in the NT as just a fellowship meal on perhaps the *Chabburah* pattern. It has a special meaning and place because it is a sharing in the messianic age even now, and it is a sharing in the risen life of Christ. The cup is the seal of the New Covenant, by which God has elected the followers of Jesus, and this covenant is proclaimed at every Eucharist. The blessing/thanksgiving which Jesus made at the Last Supper is made in the church, but includes a thanksgiving for the risen life. The OT concept of Yahweh blessing us through his gifts is still there, but this is the thanksgiving *par excellence* because it is a thanksgiving for the gift of the Risen Lord. Moreover, it is the Risen Lord who is the host at each Eucharist, and the blessing is his word of power, as in the miraculous feedings. Certainly the Eucharist became more than a fellowship meal with a solemn blessing to God as John 6 indicates, and it may be that some of the older uses of *barak* lie behind this development. God alone blesses *things* in the OT and God in the Person of his Son does this in the context of the Eucharist, and the construction of Mark 8.7 (*eulogesas auta*) is quite exceptional since *God* is the object of the normal table blessing.

The patristic writings continued the ideas found in the Bible. Origen commenting on Rom. 9.14 points out that both God and men bless, but the former bestows a gift, whereas the latter offer thanks and praise. The emphasis throughout is on the fact that all comes from God, creation, preservation and redemption. Within the church, this is often centred on the liturgical action of the Eucharist, but the sacramental nature of God's grace is witnessed to by the development of all sorts of blessings of food, household goods, religious objects and medicines. Strictly understood such blessings are an offering of thanksgiving to God for these gifts, but in fact it cannot be doubted that it has often been supposed that something is 'done' to them by blessing them. Little support can be found for this in the Bible or patristic writings.

5. *Conclusion.* Blessing above all comes from God. It is, perhaps, one of the widest of terms for describing the attitude of God to man and their proper response to him. But it is not just an idea. God's blessing operates through his chosen ones as well as by his direct control of the universe. It is seen acting pre-eminently in the salvation-history of the chosen people, first Israel and then the Church, and each stage of that history is marked by a new imparting of God's blessing.

In the final stage of that history, the blessing of God is given through the Person of Christ, and the 'blessedness' of Christians is to be 'in Christ' even though this may bring persecution and death. The Christian may already experience the blessing of God, but as with so many other terms in the NT, the final blessing lies in the future, and this is expressed, not surprisingly, by the Seer of the Apocalypse: 'Blessed are those who wash their robes, that they may have the right to the tree of life and that they may enter the city by the gates' (Rev. 22.14).

SIMON MEIN, SSM

Benefits

In the OT the word 'benefits' connotes the gifts and favours of God to man (II Chron. 32.25; Pss. 68.19; 103.2), and it was a natural transition for the word to pass over into the NT as the summing up of Christ's atoning work (I Tim. 6.2) in the sense of reconciliation as the end of creation, the final proof of the mercy of God. It has come to mean in liturgical and theological language a synonym for Christ's redemptive work. Melanch-thon's statement is typical of the thought of the Reformation: *hoc est Christum cognoscere, bene-ficia eius cognoscere* ('to know Christ is to know his benefits').

JAMES ATKINSON

Berkeley, George

Along with Locke and Hume (qq.v.), Berkeley (1685–1753) ranks as one of the most important British Empiricist philosophers. From another point of view, he counts also as the first thorough-going Idealist in modern philosophy.

Berkeley's thought can best be approached by way of his criticism of Locke's theory of know-ledge. Locke's view of perception had been that material substances, acting upon our sense-organs, produce our perceptual experiences ('ideas'). Although substance itself is unknow-able, it has to be posited as the necessary bearer of qualities. Qualities, Locke believed, must be *in* something, but (once that is said) the 'something' cannot be at all further characterized. Berkeley saw this view of substance as quite incoherent and meaningless: among other difficulties, it seemed impossible to make sense of the claim that sub-stance 'bears' or 'supports' qualities – none of the meanings of these words seemed to meet the case. In fact, said Berkeley, the notion of material sub-stance can be altogether dispensed with: for if we ask what does our experience really entitle us to postulate, the complete answer is 'ideas' and minds entertaining them. For the visible and tangible world to exist is for certain concatena-tions of perceptions to occur. *Esse est percipi* (to be is to be perceived). That does not mean that objects cease to exist when no human percipient is perceiving them. God perceives them; and Ber-keley's distinctive argument to God's existence turns precisely on the need in his system for such an All-perceiver and for a Cause of our ideas.

Berkeley did not see his thought as revolution-ary or as overturning our ordinary view of the world. It certainly did not deny (*pace* Dr Johnson) that objects have the solidarity, impenetrability or any other of the perceptual qualities we normally attribute to them. What Berkeley tried to con-struct was a metaphysical theory that would at once do justice to our ordinary experience, and secure a firmer foundation for religious belief and, in general, for belief in the primacy of mind or spirit. Critics have nevertheless objected that Berkeley's account *is* defective, in that it fails to deal adequately with the difference of logical level between statements about 'ideas' or perceptions and statements about objectively existing entities. The latter are not 'built up' out of the former in any straightforwardly additive way.

Berkeley's thought has a marked resemblance to more recent phenomenalistic philosophy, which analyses material objects in terms of 'sense data'. An important difference, however, is that while Berkeley's analysis is in terms of actual per-ception (if not by men, then by God), the pheno-menalist account is in terms of actual and possible hypothetical experiences. (For phenomenalism, the claim 'This is an apple' is equivalent to a long list of statements, not only about what an obser-ver is seeing, tasting, 'now', but also about what observers *would* see, etc., if . . .). Both Berkeley's concept of 'idea' and the phenomenalist's term 'sense-datum' have come under critical fire, as containing unclarities and confusions.

George Berkeley, *The Principles of Human Knowledge* (Everyman or Fontana); G. J. War-nock, *Berkeley*, 1953; H. B. Acton, 'Berkeley', *EP*.

R. W. HEPBURN

Bernard of Clairvaux

St Bernard (1090–1153) was born at Fontaines, near Dijon in Burgundy, of noble parents. In 1113 he entered the Cistercian monastery of Cîteaux with a number of his kinsmen, including his brother. In 1115 Abbot Stephen Harding sent him as founder-Abbot to Clairvaux (Valley of Light), third daughter-house of Cîteaux. In 1128 he acted as secretary to the provincial Council of Troyes, obtaining recognition of the new Rule of the Knights Templar, which he may have drafted himself. In 1130 the new pope, Innocent II, was challenged by an Italian anti-pope, Anacletus. Bernard successfully championed the papal cause over eight years, which brought him fame and power and privileges to his abbey. He refused the Archbishopric of Genoa and others later. In 1140 Bernard confronted Abelard (q.v.) at the Council of Sens and procured his condemnation on charges of heresy, together with Arnold of Brescia. During the next decade, he earned for himself the soubriquet 'Hammer of Heretics' for attacking Henry of Lausanne in Languedoc, the Albigensians, and Gilbert de la Porrée. In 1145 the Cistercian Bernard Paganelli of Pisa became Pope Eugenius III. Bernard, a close friend, advised him in many ways, and wrote his five books *de Consideratione* to him over the years. In

1146, at Eugenius' request, Bernard preached the Second Crusade through France and Germany, to the accompaniment of miracles. Bernard died in 1153, shortly after the death of Eugenius. In 1173 he was canonized.

St Bernard's mentality was patristic (he was sometimes called 'the last of the Fathers') in a coming age of scholastics: nevertheless there are signs of scholastic method in his writings. He was not a great thinker or theologian, but was rather an outstanding monk, moralist and mystic, who had unusual insight into the psychology of the human soul and a tenderness of heart and compassion for weakness which counteracted his own fierce asceticism. He appears to have had (from where?) a working knowledge of the Greek mystical tradition as in Gregory of Nyssa and Dionysius the Areopagite (q.v.).

His extant writings are: (1) *de Gradibus Humilitatis et Superbiae* (1124), his first work; (2) *Homiliae quattuor super 'Missus Est'* (1125); (3) *in Laudibus Virginis Matris* (1126), where he implicitly denies the doctrine of the Immaculate Conception; (4) *Apologia* (1127) addressed to William of St Thierry 'in which I have treated of some of our (Cistercian) observances and those of Cluny'; (5) *de Moribus et Officio Episcoporum* (1127), *tractatus* to Archbishop Henry of Sens; (6) *de Gratia et Libero Arbitrio* (1127), to William of St Thierry, a discussion of grace and free will according to the principles of St Augustine; (7) *ad Milites Templi de Laudibus Novae Militiae* (1128–36), to Hugh de Payns, Grand Master and Prior of Jerusalem; (8) *de Diligendo Deo* (1126–41), his theme is *causa diligendi Deum, Deus est; modus, sine modo diligere;* (9) *Sermones super Cantica* (1135–53), eighty-six sermons on the Song of Songs, never finished; (10) *de Conversione* (1140), a long sermon to the clergy of Paris; (11) *Capitula Haeresum P. Abaelardi;* Ep. 190 (Ben. ed.) *ad Innocentium II contra Capitula Errorum Abaelardi* (1140), not in Scott-James, cf. *Patrologia Latina*, ed., J. P. Migne, vol. 182. 1053; (12) *de Consideratione* (1145–53), five books addressed to Pope Eugenius III; (13) *de Praecepto et Dispensatione* (1148), a discussion of the abbot's power to dispense from certain precepts of the Rule; (14) *Vita S. Malachiae* (1152); concerning the Archbishop of Armagh who in 1141 asked Clairvaux to make a white monk foundation in Ireland, and who in 1148 died en route to Rome at Clairvaux. Bernard recounts several miracles about him, though never about himself; (15) seventeen Sermons *per annum* (*de tempore, de sanctis, de diversis*); (16) 479 Letters (in B. Scott-James' estimation; some claim up to 530). *See also* **Sacred Heart.**

E. C. Butler, *Western Mysticism*, 2nd ed. 1929; E. Gilson, *The Mystical Theology of St Bernard*, 2nd ed., ET, 1955; J. Leclercq, *St Bernard*, Maîtres Spirituels series, 1966; J. Leclercq, H. M. Rochais and C. H. Talbot, eds., *Sancti Bernardi Opera*, I-IV, 1957–66, unfinished; A. V. Murray, *Abelard and Bernard: a Study in Twelfth Century 'Modernism'*, 1967; A Priest of Mt. Melleray,

Sermons on the Canticles, ET, 1920; B. Scott-James, *The Letters of St Bernard of Clairvaux*, 1953; *The Life of St Bernard of Clairvaux*, 1958; E. Vacandard, *Vie de St Bernard, Abbé de Clairvaux*, 2 vols., 4th ed., 1920; G. Webb and A. Walker, *St Bernard of Clairvaux; the Story of his Life as Recorded in the Vita Prima*, ET, 1960; W. W. Williams, *Grace and Free Will*, 1920; *of Conversion*, 1938 (trans. of the Anchin MS, with notes); *St Bernard of Clairvaux*, 2nd ed., 1952; W. W. Williams and B. R. V. Mills, *Selected Treatises: de Diligendo Deo/de Gradibus*, 1926 (this and *Sancti Bernardi Opera* are in Latin, but both have been translated by E. G. Gardiner in 1915 and a Religious of C. S. M. V., Wantage in 1950, and by F. Mills in 1929); J. M. Canivez, *DHGE*, VIII, cols. 610–44; B. Scott-James, *CDT*, I, pp. 260–3; E. Vacandard, *DTC*, II, cols. 761–88.

ALBERIC STACPOOLE, OSB

Beza (De Bèze), Theodore

Theodore Beza (1519–1605), Reformed Church leader and theologian, came of a prosperous Burgundian family and was tutored by Melchior Wolmar in the classics before entering on the study of law at Orleans (1535–9). Disinclined to the legal profession, he turned his attention chiefly to literature. He held ecclesiastical benefices but in 1544 was secretly married; the union was publicy confirmed on his going to Geneva. A serious illness was the occasion of his conversion and avowal of the Reformed faith in 1548. His first stay in Geneva was from October 1548 to November 1549. He then became professor of Greek in the academy headed by P. Viret in Lausanne. When Bernese pressure upon the Lausanne church and academy became intolerable, Beza led a migration of the ministers and teachers to Geneva where he at once received the professorship in Greek (1558). He was Calvin's choice as rector of the newly instituted Academy of Geneva (1559), and was chiefly instrumental in the success of this institution as an international school of theological and classical learning. His relations with Calvin were close, and he undertook numerous missions to France and Germany as agent of the Geneva church. Notable are his efforts to secure rights for the Reformed in France, 1560–3. At the Conference of Poissy (1561) he ably represented the Reformed cause and was thereafter permitted to preach widely in France and to advise the imperilled churches. He helped to procure the Edict of January 1562, which allowed the Reformed a limited freedom to worship and hold synods. After the outbreak of civil war Beza acted as civilian adviser and treasurer of Condé's army and at the Battle of Dreux (19 December 1562) tried to rally the defeated Huguenots. The pacification of March 1563 gave him opportunity to return to Geneva. In 1571 he attended synods at La Rochelle and Nismes, and in 1586 negotiated vainly with Lutheran theologians at Montbeliard. He published his early poems entitled *Juvenilia* in 1548, with a dedication to Wolmar, and his interest in poetry was never discontinued. His translation of the Psalms was largely used in the Genevan Psalter. His *Abraham's Sacrifice*, first enacted by his students (1550), reflects elements both of Greek tragedy and of the mediaeval mystery play. His *Life of Calvin* (1565), written with affection and reverence, is highly valuable though not fully accurate. His *Icones* (1580) is an invaluable record of portraits with brief sketches of Reformation personalities. In *De hereticis a civile magistratu puniendis* (1554) he holds the Christian magistrate obligated to punish heretics. In his *Tractationes theologiae* (3 vols., 1570), in which was included the *Summa totius Christianismi*, he expounded his supralapsarian interpretation of election and the *ordo salutis*. Most of his treatises are contained in *Theodori Bezae opera*, 3 vols. 1582.

Correspondance de Théodore de Bèze recueille par Hippolyte Aubert, 1960 (IV, 1965, to 1563); F. Gardy, *Bibliographie des oeuvres théologiques, littéraires, historiques et juridiques de Théodore de Bèze*, 1960; P. F. Geisendorf, *Théodore de Bèze*, 1949.

J. T. MCNEILL

Bible. *see* Scripture. Doctrine of Holy.

Biblical Theology

This expression has latterly been used to denote so many different things that it has become a source of confusion; anyone using it should state clearly what he means by it. Among its various connotations four may be distinguished:

(1) A descriptive ('presuppositionless') science which seeks only to clarify the themes and ideas encountered in the Bible or in the different books or portions thereof. (2) The attempt to articulate the theological significance of the Bible as a whole (an almost impossibly difficult task and a highly personal one, but nevertheless one which must be made by anyone who believes that the Bible has a meaning for himself). (3) The attempt to build a complete system of theology out of the biblical materials and nothing else, which (in theory, at least) should result in equating biblical exposition with the whole of dogmatics: Karl Barth has essayed this task more consistently than any other theologian in our time. (4) That kind of exposition of biblical books, texts or words, which is based upon the presupposition that there is a common biblical (or Hebraic) viewpoint which is shared by the various authors of the scriptural writings.

Probably it is this fourth connotation which is chiefly in mind when the expression 'biblical theology' is used today – especially by its critics. After several decades of analytic criticism, which has dissected the Bible into many separate elements, a reaction set in during the 1930s and a new emphasis upon the unity of the biblical outlook and ideas found favour in many quarters. The original contributors to G. Kittel's *TWNT*

(1933 and following) are sometimes named as the chief proponents of biblical theology in this sense; others who have insisted upon the distinctiveness of Hebraic thought are also included in this 'school', e.g. T. Boman, *Hebrew Thought Compared with Greek* (ET, 1960). Recently a critical attitude towards their standpoint has appeared, as in the writings of James Barr (*Biblical Words for Time*, 1962; *The Semantics of Biblical Language*, 1961). The question, however, remains, whether there can be a completely presuppositionless interpretation of any historical documents (as tended to be assumed by those who regarded biblical theology as a purely descriptive science). The scrutiny of presuppositions or of interpretative principles is obviously most important in any discussion of biblical theology, whatever is intended by that term, and therefore the consideration of the subject in Barr's *Old and New in Interpretation* (1966) is to be welcomed. *See also* **Old Testament Theology; New Testament Theology.**

In addition to the works cited, *see also* G. Ebeling, *Word and Faith*, ET, 1963, esp. essay III; James D. Smart, *The Interpretation of Scripture*, 1961.

EDITOR

Bibliolatry

Bibliolatry is a term used pejoratively for theories of biblical inspiration which assert the inerrancy of the Bible and demand the submission of the human reason to the literalist interpretation of it ('a paper pope'). Derived from the Greek, the word means 'bookworship' (*cf.* idolatry, Mariolatry, etc.).

Binitarianism

Binitarianism is the term applied by historians of doctrine to tendencies to phrase the doctrine of the Trinity in twofold rather than threefold terms. Such tendencies were not regarded as incompatible with the use of the threefold formulae of the religious tradition. In the pre-Nicene period much binitarian language was accidental, resulting from the consideration of the problem from the viewpoint of the relation between the Father and the Son. Thus the Logos conception proved capable of absorbing the operations both of the Son and of the Spirit. Heretical forms of binitarianism were also current: (1) A group of heretics in the second and third centuries (*see* **Monarchianism**) maintained two entities in the Godhead, the Father and the Son or the Spirit or Melchizedek. (2) In fourth-century Egypt the Tropici (of uncertain doctrinal affiliation but possibly Arian) denied the divinity of the Spirit on exegetical grounds. Against them Athanasius wrote the *Letters to Serapion*. (3) Later in the century the Macedonians (q.v.) or Pneumatomachi (Fighters against the Spirit) arose in Constantinople and probably elsewhere. They were *Homoeousians* (q.v.), tolerably orthodox with regard to the Son, but refused to extend a similar treatment to the Spirit. Against their argument from tradition Basil wrote his treatise on the Holy Spirit. Other criticisms are found in Gregory of Nazianzus and Didymus. *See* **Trinity, Doctrine of the.**

H. E. W. TURNER

Bishop

The title bishop, which derives from the vulgar Latin (*e*) *biscopus*, in turn coming from the Greek *episcopos*, an overseer, is used of a particular office within the Church. The origins of the bishop's role are obscure (*see* H. J. Carpenter, 'Minister, Ministry', *TWBB*), but in the second century he emerges as the one charged with the spiritual welfare of his flock, as the chief liturgical minister who presides at the Eucharist, ordains, absolves, controls finance and settles matters of dispute.

With the increase in the number of congregations it became necessary either to have more bishops or to delegate some of their functions. Each of these expedients was adopted in different areas. In Syria and parts of Asia Minor each country church was provided with a resident staff supervised by *chorepiscopoi* or itinerant bishops answerable to the bishop of the nearest large city. In North Africa a bishop of full rank was appointed wherever a Christian community existed. Elsewhere the second of the possible courses was followed: so in the districts around Alexandria the villages were entrusted to presbyters under the supervision of the bishop of Alexandria, and it was this practice that was most widespread in Western Europe, where the bishop retained as his exclusive right only the power to confirm and ordain.

Upon the cessation of hostility between Church and State with the conversion of Constantine, the bishop began to play a part not only in ecclesiastical matters but also in secular affairs, his powers of jurisdiction being recognized by imperial decree. Further development of his position came in the fifth century with the disappearance of the western empire, two factors in particular having considerable influence: first, the previous urban civilization was now replaced, after the incursion of the barbarian tribes, by a predominantly rural system which centred in local proprietors living upon their estates, and second, legacies and grants of land to the Church placed the bishops in the position of being themselves landlords and hence leaders of the local community in civil no less than in ecclesiastical affairs. Here lay the origin of the later system of feudal prelacy, so that in the Middle Ages the bishop was as much a man of the State, often employed on State business, as he was of the Church; indeed he tended to become more of a civil servant or temporal lord than a shepherd and overseer of his people.

It is this development that in part explains the opposition of a number of Protestant Churches to the idea of episcopacy (q.v.) at the Reformation, and it is also in part the reason why to this day in England twenty-six Anglican bishops have seats in the House of Lords. It scarcely needs emphasizing that these duties are not of the essence of a bishop's office, and that when episcopacy is under discussion in schemes of reunion, the pattern that has emerged out of mediaeval western Europe should not be regarded as one that must be perpetuated, the bishop being ideally no more and no less than the chief shepherd, the guardian of orthodoxy and the centre of unity.

A. G. Hebert, *Apostle and Bishop*, 1963; K. E. Kirk, ed. *The Apostolic Ministry*, 1926; W. Telfer, *The Office of a Bishop*, 1962.

J. G. DAVIES

Black Rubric

The practice of kneeling to receive Holy Communion was strongly criticized by those Reformers who thought it more consistent with a true understanding of the Sacrament to sit, as at a meal. In the second English Prayer Book, 1552, kneeling was prescribed, and the Black Rubric was a notice inserted only three days before publication which dissociated the practice from any suggestion of adoration of the consecrated elements. The rubric which had the authority only of the royal council was removed by Elizabeth and reinserted, emended so as no longer to appear to deny a real presence, in the 1661 revision.

F. Procter and W. H. Frere, *A New History of the Book of Common Prayer*, 3rd impression, 1905 and often reprinted.

R. CANT

Blessed Virgin. *see* Mary, the Blessed Virgin.

Blessing. *see* Benediction.

Blood of Christ

The word 'blood' in the OT, apart from the everyday physiological meaning, is generally associated with the idea of death, violent death in particular. Certain scholars have urged (Milligan, Westcott, Hicks, Vincent Taylor, to name but a few) that the term means life rather than death, thereby emphasizing that the central idea of sacrifice is the offering up of life, a view that is by no means universally accepted. When the word 'blood' is associated with atonement, or with the cultus, the prime emphasis is on death not on life, or if with life, it is a life offered in death. Similarly in the NT, the word 'blood' is mostly indicative of violent death. Associations with sacrifice are confined to the Epistle to the Hebrews. Other references refer mainly to Christ's death, in particular the death of the cross (Rom. 5.9 f.; Col. 1.20; Eph. 2.13; I John 5.6; Rev. 1.5). It is difficult to come to any other conclusion than that these passages mean the death of Christ on the cross within a framework of salvation doctrine. It is not certain what the scholars mentioned above are arguing when they write that in the death of Christ his 'life' was 'liberated' and 'made available' for man. If by that is meant that the life of the Risen Lord is true life because his death is in it, that is true, but this subtlety, even when true, must not be allowed to becloud the plain fact that Christ laid down his life in sacrifice on the cross. In fact, the phrase 'the blood of Christ', like the word 'the cross', is nothing but a pregnant phrase for the death of Christ in its salvation meaning.

There is a finality and a once-for-all-ness about this death. It is the blood of the New Covenant (Matt. 26.28; Mark 14.24; Luke 22.20; I Cor. 11.25; II Cor. 3.6; Heb. 9.15 etc.), foretold by Jeremiah (Jer. 31.31). It further connotes at once both the fulfilment of the old covenant and its cessation. Jesus is both sacrifice and high priest in one, God's servant whose blood has everlasting atonement for all, and who has sealed the covenant relationship between God and his people for ever. The power of Jesus' blood to effect salvation comes to expression in several forms in the NT: it cleanses from sin (I John 1.7; Heb. 9.14; Rev. 1.5; 7.14): it sanctifies (Heb. 10.29); it offers forgiveness (Eph. 1.7); it re-establishes the people of God (Eph. 2.13); it redeems (Rev. 5.9). Already in the NT the blood is associated with the Holy Communion (I Cor. 10.16; 11.26), but not in any *ex opere operato* sense. It is always bound up with ideas of repentance (Rom. 3.25; 5.9; Col. 1.20–23), confession of sin (I John 1.7–10), and turning to God in faith (Heb. 10.19). *See also* **Atonement; Eucharist; Precious Blood.**

JAMES ATKINSON

Boethius, Anicius Manlius Torqvatus Serverinus

Boethius (*c.* 480–524) was a Christian thinker of noble family and considerable culture. His father, two of his sons and he himself were all consuls in Rome, and it was his honesty in the face of political corruption as much as his non-Gothic and Christian principles that brought him into conflict with his former friend Theodoric. While in prison awaiting execution he composed his best-known work, *De Consolatione Philosophiae*.

His learning was encyclopaedic in scope. He wrote on music, astronomy, arithmetic, geometry, rhetoric and logic. He proposed to translate the works of Plato and Aristotle, and to demonstrate the harmony between their philosophies. Some of his translations of and commentaries on Aristotle's logical treatises and Porphyry's *Isagoge* provided the standard texts for the Middle Ages. Among his *opuscula sacra* is a book in defence of Chalcedonian christology; and the *De Trinitate* was also to become a textbook in the mediaeval universities.

The *De Consolatione Philosophiae* has enjoyed a wide popularity. King Alfred, Chaucer, and Queen Elizabeth I are numbered among its translators. An investigation by the light of natural reason – thus not a specifically Christian book – into the motives that should console us in adversity, the work is divided into three sections. First (i.1–5), Boethius expounds the afflictions that have befallen him; secondly, (i.5–iii.12), philosophy proposes her consolations; thirdly,

(iv–v), there is a series of objections and replies, mostly concerned with providence and free-will. Philosophy's arguments are three, of increasing weight: (1) ii.1–3: Boethius has enjoyed more good than evil at the hands of fortune; (2) ii.5–iii. 1: what he has lost in his disgrace was potentially more evil than good; (3) iii.1–12: Boethius is now for the first time free to recognize his true happiness, since he is liberated from the false security of wealth, dignity, power, glory, bodily delights and all deceptive goods. God, the *summum bonum*, is the ultimate end of all things, and final happiness lies in meditating on the truth that all things are made by him, governed by him, and must return to him. The general judgment of Boethius' achievement is that he was eclectic, to be esteemed more as a transmitter of ancient ideas than as an original or synthetic thinker. *See also* **Soul.**

Opera, PL, vols. 63, 64 (some spurious): *Philosophiae Consolatio*, ed. L. Bieler (Corpus Christianorum, Series Latina 94), 1957; ET of *Theological Tractates* (and *Consolatio*) by H. F. Stewart and E. K. Rand (Loeb Classical Library), 1918; H. M. Barrett, *Boethius*, 1940; M. Cappuyns, 'Boèce', *DHGE*, ix, cols. 348–80.

DOM PLACID SPEARRITT

Bonaventura, St

Bonaventura (1221–1274), an Italian scholar and teacher of great influence, Minister General of the Franciscan Order, defended the traditional Augustinian theology against the new Aristotelian theological synthesis propounded by his almost exact contemporary St Thomas Aquinas. He held that human knowledge, even as propounded by the ablest expositor of it (universally held to be Aristotle, 'the Philosopher'), was darkness as compared with the divine illumination of the souls of Christians. *See* **Augustinianism; Thomism.**

E. Gilson, *The Philosophy of St Bonaventure*, ET, 1938.

EDITOR

Bonhoeffer, Dietrich

Bonhoeffer (1906–1945), German pastor, teacher and theologian, was closely associated during the 1930s with the German Confessional Church's struggle with the Nazi State; he was arrested by the Gestapo in 1943 under suspicion of being implicated in a plot against Hitler's life and was executed at Flossenburg in 1945. The author of an important *Ethics* (ET, 1955), and of certain influential books dealing with the spiritual life (e.g. *Life Together, Temptation*), his work has become extremely well-known internationally through the impact of certain fragmentary passages of his posthumous *Letters and Papers from Prison*, in which he discusses the possibility of a 'non-religious interpretation of biblical concepts', of a 'worldly Christianity' which can wholly dispense with all 'religion' as a precondition of biblical faith. (Hence it is not entirely inaccurate to describe him as the main figure behind the 'religionless

Christianity' programmes.) His later work has given rise to a world-wide discussion and controversy. His ideas were widely disseminated as a result of the publication of J. A. T. Robinson's *Honest to God* (1963). *See* **Crisis Theology; Religion.**

D. Bonhoeffer, *Letters and Papers from Prison*, rev. and illus. ed., 1967; R. Gregor Smith, ed., *World Come of Age*, 1967.

JAMES RICHMOND

Bradley, F. H.

F. H. Bradley (1846–1924), who spent his entire career as a Research Fellow at Merton College, Oxford, was one of the most brilliant British philosophers of the nineteenth century and an important, if unconventional, representative of the Idealist philosophical movement (q.v.). Bradley was severely critical of what he saw as the unsatisfactory mixture of philosophy and associationist psychology prevalent in the 'empiricism' of his time. His *Ethical Studies* (1876) revealed him as a trenchant critic also of utilitarianism, and although the influence of Hegel was plain in his work, he yet diverged from Hegel's opinions at significant points.

Appearance and Reality (1893) was his *magnum opus*. In it, Bradley sought to make evident a concealed self-contradictory quality in all ordinary modes of thinking, particularly where *relations* are concerned. Space, time, causality are all infected. It followed, for Bradley, that whatever Reality was, it could not be this conflict-ridden and fragmentary world of ordinary experience. Absolute Reality must have the unity, the harmoniousness and completeness that the world of Appearance signally lacks. Bradley's Absolute cannot be identified with the God of traditional theism: for since theism cannot give an intelligible account of God's relation to the world, God must belong to Appearance rather than to Reality.

Bradley's thought, though as a whole uncongenial to current philosophical styles, contains numerous individually valuable arguments and insights. It has influenced in a broader way a few recent writers in the philosophy of religion (e.g. C. A. Campbell, *Selfhood and Godhood*, 1957).

R. Wollheim, *F. H. Bradley*, 1959; H. B. Acton, 'Bradley', *EP*.

R. W. HEPBURN

Broad Church.
see Latitudinarianism.

Brownism

The name was loosely applied to an aggressive separatism in the latter part of the reign of Elizabeth I with some reference to Robert Browne (d. 1633) and probably to an earlier figure, John Browne, chaplain to the Duchess of Suffolk and a member of the Plumbers' Hall group suppressed in 1567. Robert Browne, having studied at Cambridge under the devout puritan Richard

Greenham, for his separatism 'saw the inside of thirty-two prisons'. He organized a covenanted congregation at Norwich, which migrated with him to Middleburg in 1581. There he published in one volume three short works (1582) to urge a strictly scriptural reform 'without tarrying' for authorization, and to describe his ideal of a church of believers, democratically governed and supported voluntarily. Browne's shifting opinions brought him back to Anglicanism with a recantation (1585). But many others, chiefly Cambridge men, had begun to express similar ideas of reform and to organize small worshipping groups in London and Norwich. Henry Barrowe, whose adherents were called Barrowists, enlarged on Browne's conceptions with an even more emphatic rejection of Anglicanism. Under the antiseparatist law of 1593, Barrowe, John Greenwood, and John Penry were executed (April and May 1593), leaving many sympathizers. Francis Johnson, Henry Ainsworth and John Robinson came to effective leadership of the increasing groups of separatist exiles in Holland. To these the name 'Brownist' was often applied, though in general they emphatically repudiated it; as did also the Independents (q.v.) of the 1640s.

R. Browne, *A Treatise of Reformation without Tarrying for Anie*, 1582, reprinted, 1903; C. Burrage, *The Early English Dissenters*, 2 vols., 1912; M. M. Knappen, *Tudor Puritanism*, 1939; F. J. Powicke, *Robert Browne*, 1910.

J. T. MCNEILL

Brunner, Emil

Brunner (1889–1965), Swiss Protestant dialectical theologian, for many years was Professor of Dogmatics at Zürich. His thinking was marked by its divergence from that of K. Barth on the issue of natural theology. Brunner held, despite Barth's sharp opposition, that there was a certain very limited knowledge of God available from creation, especially from the 'orders of creation', of which the family is the main example, and that such natural knowledge was a prerequisite of Christian ethical thinking. In his work (e.g. *The Divine-Human Encounter*, ET, 1944, and *Dogmatics*, 3 vols., ET, 1949–52). Brunner used Buber's *I-Thou* category as a model for expressing and understanding the believer's relationship with God. Brunner held it to be the theologian's duty to enter into dialogue with the secular world and with representatives of the non-Christian religions, and he himself occupied an academic position in Tokyo for some years. *See* **Barth, K.; Buber, M.; Crisis Theology; Dialectical Theology.**

JAMES RICHMOND

Buber, Martin

Buber (1878–1965), Jewish Hasidic religious thinker, whose epoch-making *I and Thou* (1923) has deeply influenced much Western philosophy, theology, education, psychiatry and sociology, sharply distinguishes between the two 'primary words' of human existence; *I-It* and *I-Thou*; while the first of these concerns only our experiencing and using of things, our observations, objectification and manipulation of spatio-temporal objects and processes, the second of these (by far the more significant) concerns the whole of our being, referring to the sphere of mutuality and dialogue in which is constituted our genuine, real life. It is through the latter rather than the former that we reach and have communion with God, the 'eternal Thou'. Buber's influence can be discerned in the writings of J. H. Oldham, John Baillie, H. H. Farmer, Karl Heim, Emil Brunner, Friedrich Gogarten, Paul Tillich, Karl Barth, Reinhold Niebuhr, Jacques Maritain, Gabriel Marcel and Rudolf Bultmann.

M. Buber, *I and Thou*, 1st ed., ET, 1937; 2nd ed. (with a postscript by the author), ET, 1958; M. L. Diamond, *Martin Buber: Jewish Existentialist*, 1960; Maurice S. Friedman, *Martin Buber: the Life of Dialogue*, 1955; R. Gregor Smith, *Martin Buber*, 1966.

JAMES RICHMOND

Bucer (Butzer), Martin

Martin Bucer (1491–1551), Strasbourg Reformer and ecumenical theologian, at fifteen became a Dominican at Schlettstadt and was later removed to Heidelberg where in 1518 he heard and conferred with Luther. Leaving the Dominicans, he was employed as a chaplain and preacher until excommunicated for having married. He then went to Strasbourg and joining the reforming leaders there, Matthew Zell and Wolfgang Capito, soon became the foremost figure in the advance of the Reformation in Alsace and Upper Germany. He was the principal compiler of the Tetrapolitan Confession presented to the Emperor at Augsburg, 1530. He was compromised by association with the bigamy of Philip of Hesse (1540). A marked feature of his reforming interests was his zeal for Christian unity. He was associated with Melanchthon in the formulation at Cassel, December 1534, of a statement on the Lord's Supper which led to the Wittenberg Concord of May 1536. By his correspondence, notably with the Czech Brethren 1540–2, he exercised an international influence, and this was only enhanced through his forced departure from Strasbourg under the pressure of Charles V's *Interim* of 1548. He then accepted an invitation to England from Archbishop Cranmer. During the last two years of his life he lectured in Cambridge and was the most influential of Cranmer's foreign advisers. His Strasbourg Liturgy, in its revision of 1537, was largely imitated by Calvin, whose Strasbourg period (1538–41) was spent in close association with Bucer. He was joint author with Melanchthon of the *Consultatio* of Hermann of Cologne (1543), a liturgy used by Cranmer in preparing the Book of Common Prayer, and Bucer's advice entered into the 1549 revision of the Prayer Book. His students and close associates at Cambridge included the later archbishops Parker and Grindal and many who, like Bradford and Hooper, had to do with the beginnings of Puritanism.

Among his writings are: *Das ym selbs niemant sonder anderen leben soll* (1523), ed., H. Strohl, French trans., 1949; English trans., P. T. Fuhrmann, *Instruction in Christian Love*, (1952), a simple and persuasive treatise on faith and service; *Von der wahren Seelsorge* (1538); *Ein summarischer Begriff der Christliche Lehre* (1548, ed., F. Wendel, with French trans., 1951), and *De regno Christi* (1550, first published in Bucer's *Scripta Anglicana*, 1577), a work of wide range in which a covenant concept of the Church is so related to the State that there emerges a 'Christian commonwealth' obedient alike to the Decalogue and the Gospel. Specific measures of moral and educational reform for the English nation are proposed.

J. Courvoisier, *La notion d'église chez Bucer*, 1933; C. Hopf, *Martin Bucer and the English Reformation*, 1946; W. Pauck, *Das Reich Gottes auf Erden: Utopie und Wirklichkeit*, 1928; B. Thompson, 'Bucer Study since 1918', *CH*, XXV (1956), 63–82.

J. T. MCNEILL

Bullinger, Heinrich

Heinrich Bullinger (1504–1575), Swiss Reformer and successor of Zwingli, was the fifth son of the dean of Bremgarten, who also joined the Reformation. At twelve he was sent to the Latin school at Emmerich in Cleves, and later at Cologne (1519–22), was instructed in scholastic writings. From Gratian and Lombard he was led back to the Church Fathers; but finding that Origen, Chrysostom, Ambrose, Jerome and Augustine rested their theology upon the Scriptures, he became an intensive student of the Bible and read with approval treatises of Luther and Melanchthon. Appointed to teach in the Cistercian house at Cappel he formed connections with Zwingli (1523) and won the monks to the Reformation. His marriage with Anna Adlischweiler, a former nun, took place in 1528. On Zwingli's death, 1531, Bullinger, now aged twenty-seven, succeeded him as People's Priest in Zurich. In the critical situation he showed high qualities of leadership, and his influence was a steadying and inspiring factor not only in the churches of German Switzerland but in other countries. From England students and exiles in large numbers came to Zurich, imbibed his teaching, admired the vigour of his administration, and in many instances shared the generous hospitality of his home. John Hooper, though ten years older than Bullinger, became his disciple. Such eminent Elizabethan churchmen as John Jewel, Edmund Grindal and John Parkhurst were deeply indebted to him. Others of his English pupils, such as Thomas Sampson, were among the forerunners of Puritanism. The 'prophesyings' suppressed by Elizabeth were imitations of the 'Prophezei' developed under his supervision in Zurich. His *Decades* (Latin, 1549–51), five series of ten long theological sermons each, a work in part dedicated to Edward VI, became in English translation

under Archbishop Whitgift a prescribed text for
ministers who had not a master's degree. He
joined with Calvin in the Consensus of Zurich,
1549, which affirms that in the Lord's Supper we
receive Christ spiritually, and Christ makes us
participants with him. Towards the Lutherans he
was more guarded than Calvin, especially after
Luther's final attack on the Zwinglians (1544). He
wrote voluminously, under about 150 titles, and
his correspondence was extensive. His theology is
well summarized in the Second Helvetic Confession (1566), of which he was the author.

F. Blanke, *Der junge Bullinger*, 1942; A. Bouvier,
*Henri Bullinger, réformateur et conseiller oecu-
ménique . . . d'après sa correspondance*, 1940; G.
W. Bromiley, ed., *Zwingli and Bullinger*, 1953; F.
Gulley, 'The Influence of Henry Bullinger and the
Tigurine Tradition upon the English Church of
the Sixteenth Century', microfilmed Ph.D. dis-
sertation, Vanderbilt University, 1961.

                                            J. T. MCNEILL

Bultmann, Rudolf

Bultmann (1884–   ), German New Testament
scholar and systematic theologian. *See* **Demythologizing; Existentialism.**

Ian Henderson, *Rudolf Bultmann*, 1965; C. W.
Kegley, ed., *The Theology of Rudolf Bultmann*,
1966; Walther Schmithals, *An Introduction to the
Theology of Rudolf Bultmann*, ET, 1968.

                                          JAMES RICHMOND

Bushnell, Horace

Horace Bushnell (1802–1876), New England Congregational minister and theologian, is usually
considered the father of liberal theology in
America. A graduate of Yale, both college and
divinity school, he reacted against the combination of New England Edwardsean and Scottish
Common-Sense theology as taught by Nathaniel
W. Taylor (q.v.), and instead was attracted by the
romantic idealism of Coleridge. His pastoral
ministry was spent at one church – North Church
in Hartford, Connecticut, where he served from
1833 until his retirement because of ill health in
1859. Here he worked out his theological method
of comprehensiveness, whereby he endeavoured
to find a larger truth to comprehend the partial
truths in the conflicting opinions of theological
parties. He was critical of the system of revivals
which then played so important a part in American church life, insisting that 'the child is to grow
up a Christian, and never know himself as being
otherwise'. In the 1840s he published his arguments for 'Christian nurture' in several forms; an
enlarged and revised *Christian Nurture* appeared
in 1861. It was to play a large role in the development of the religious education movement.

His basic theological book, *God in Christ* (1849),
was in part the product of a moving personal
spiritual experience. In a 'Preliminary Disserta-
tion on Language' he analysed the way language
conveys spiritual truth – not precisely, but
through images, analogies, and paradoxes. He

presented an 'instrumental' view of the Trinity,
defended a 'moral influence' theory of atonement
which had an objective as well as a subjective side,
and endeavoured to minimize the role of dogma
in church life so that the deeper spirit of Christianity might be apprehended by heart as well as head.
God in Christ proved to be a highly controversial
work, but many who were troubled by the in-
roads of scientific thinking on faith found it an aid
to faith. Bushnell's most comprehensive apologetic work was *Nature and the Supernatural* (1858),
in which he declared that nature and supernature
are not antithetical but together are co-factors in
the one system of God. Bushnell's influence was
carried especially by his published sermons and
addresses, on which the liberals were to draw extensively. In his last years, Bushnell returned to
the doctrine of the atonement; his efforts were
finally gathered in an influential two-volume
work, *The Vicarious Sacrifice* (1877).

Bushnell's work prepared the way for the reception of both Schleiermacher and Ritschl in
America. His theological efforts tended to be one-
sided, but by the close of the nineteenth century
his was the most conspicuous theological influence in American Protestant thought. It contributed to the rise of liberal theology and the
social gospel (q.v.).

Mary A. Cheyney, ed., *Life and Letters of Horace
Bushnell*, 1880; H. Shelton Smith, ed., *Horace
Bushnell*, 1965.

                                        ROBERT T. HANDY

Butler, Joseph

Joseph Butler (1692–1752), Bishop of Durham,
was renowned during his lifetime and for more
than a century afterwards for his magisterial reply
to the arguments of the deists (q.v.) entitled *The
Analogy of Religion, Natural and Revealed, to the
Constitution and Course of Nature* (1736). Like
most eighteenth-century churchmen he was himself half a deist, believing that reason could establish the truth of God's existence as the Moral
Governor and Author of Nature, and that
'natural religion is the foundation and principal
part of Christianity'. But he wrote to defend the
biblical revelation against the attacks of the deists.
He agrees with them that revelation, contained in
propositions written down in the Scriptures, is full
of ambiguities and obscurities, but he urges that
so also is the Book of Nature, in which the deists
put their trust. There is thus a real analogy between the two 'Books'. His argument might be
somewhat unkindly summed up by saying that the
illegibility of the hand-writing in both Books
creates a presumption of their common authorship. In this world probability is the guide of life,
and the rational man will accept the greater
probability, however slight: it is more probable
that the scriptural revelation was in fact given by
God. Butler, like his opponents, had no inkling of
the modern critical understanding of the Bible.
The revolution in historical thinking had in his day
hardly begun. For this reason his arguments in *The*

Analogy often seem to us quaint and irrelevant.

Nevertheless his insistence upon reason as a foundation of Christian thinking has its supporters in our time (*see*, e.g. David Jenkins, *Guide to the Debate about God*, 1966, ch. II); Butler's type of argument goes right back into the Christian tradition in maintaining that any reasonable man would have to admit that there is a strong case for the truth of Christianity in the light of the evidence which reason presents to us. However that may be, Butler's enduring fame among the immortals was earned by his work as a moral philosopher, which is represented chiefly by his *Fifteen Sermons Preached at the Chapel of the Rolls Court* (1726).

C. D. Broad, *Five Types of Ethical Theory*, 1930; Ninian Smart, *Historical Selections in the Philosophy of Religion*, 1962, ch. 12; W. R. Sorley, *A History of English Philosophy*, 1920, ch. VII.

EDITOR

Calendar, Liturgical

OT religion differed from the religion of the peoples who surrounded Israel not least in that its yearly rhythm of festivals was based not upon the annual cycle of nature but upon historical events considered as the saving acts of God in Israel's history. Instead of the winter solstice, the harvest, etc., and the general rhythm of spring, summer, autumn and winter, the great Hebrew festivals commemorated such historical events as the Exodus from Egypt (Passover), the Giving of the Law or the Desert Sojournings, even though these celebrations contain aboriginal elements of nature-religion (*see* C. R. North, 'Sacrifice', IV, *TWBB*). Indeed, the dating of the Passover by the moon points to the nomadic origins of the original Hebrew calendar. The earliest Christian festivals (or feasts), Easter and Pentecost, are Christianized versions of the Jewish Passover and Pentecost and are still regulated according to the moon's seasons. The study of the relation of the earliest Christian calendars is too complicated to discuss here; the main point to be noticed is that the Christian Year, like the Jewish, is based upon the recital of the *Heilsgeschichte* (q.v.): it commemorates the coming of Christ and his future coming (Advent), his birth (Christmas), his baptism (Epiphany, q.v.), his desert fast (Lent), his suffering (Passiontide), death (Good Friday), and resurrection (Easter) and the giving of the Holy Spirit (Pentecost). To this basic pattern many accretions (Saints' Days and other Holy Days, etc.) have been added over the centuries. Today there is much discussion (especially at the ecumenical level) of the revising and pruning of the Church's calendar. Such a revision would also necessarily involve a new lectionary (i.e. table of readings from the OT and NT) for all the days of the Christian year. It is obviously desirable, if it could be achieved, that all the Churches should keep the same dates and read the same scriptural passages rather than go their own ways. A suggestive beginning, resulting from the joint labours of scholars of ten British denominations, has been made in *The Calendar and Lectionary* (ed. R. C. D. Jasper, 1967). 'The great liturgical tradition of the west,' say the authors, 'is not self-justifying. It must be brought to the bar of Scripture, theology and the wholeness of tradition.'

G. Dix, *The Shape of the Liturgy*, 1945, ch. XI; A. A. McArthur, *The Evolution of the Christian Year*, 1953.

EDITOR

Calvin, John

Calvin (1509–1564), leader of the Reformation in Geneva and pre-eminent among Reformed theologians, was the son of a notary with advantageous connections, Calvin in boyhood received benefices which provided for his schooling. At fourteen he was sent to the University of Paris, where his brilliant gifts were developed under the influence of scholars who represented both the methods of scholasticism and the new humanist learning. By a decision of his father he gave the years 1528–31 to legal studies at Orleans and Bourges, incidentally acquiring Greek. But he turned from a legal career to pursue a passionate interest in Greek, Latin and Hebrew, taking advantage of the new foundation of the Royal Lecturers in Paris. Little beyond conjecture is known about his religious attitudes before his twenty-fifth year (1533–4). His statement made in 1558: 'God by a sudden conversion subdued my heart to teachableness' almost certainly refers to an experience of this period. In the spring of 1534 he visited Jacques Lefèvre, the inspirer of a French Christian humanist movement in which some of Calvin's friends were active, and then journeyed to Noyon and resigned his clerical benefices (4 March). None of his writings prior to this is convincingly Protestant, while everything that he wrote thereafter is unambiguously so.

Calvin's conversion involved an unreserved commitment to the intense study of the Bible as the source of authority for the Church and for the Christian life. It meant a rejection of the old Order of the Church under the papacy but therewith a devotion to the Holy Catholic Church which is invisible and to the work of Church reform that would follow a pattern based on Scripture. The rich resources of learning, and the scholarly habits previously acquired, became a priceless asset in the formulation and communication of theological thought. His conversion, though scantily documented, must be regarded as a transforming experience that was essential to the making of the Calvin of history. With singular constancy he pursued through later years the direction then taken.

A period of withdrawal in Basel bore fruit in the *Christianae religionis institutio*, 1536; later progressively enlarged editions to 1559 bore the title *Institutio Christianae religionis*. He was soon drawn from the retirement he loved to bear a heavy load of practical duties in Geneva and to stand in the embattled line of the Reformation in Europe. At the price of great effort amid tasks of teaching, preaching, counselling and controversy, he maintained a high standard of excellence in his writings with respect to knowledge, argumentation and style. While we find in his pages some deplorable lapses into vituperation, any extensive reading of his works will make us aware of his animating sense of the living and ever-present God, who commands his adoration and his service, the Creator of all things, the source of all truth and of man's powers of thought, the Redeemer and inspirer of his elect. This lofty conception of deity, divinely revealed in Holy Scripture, is in accord with the evidence of the created world. Calvin without embarrassment appropriated the traditional doctrine of the Trinity. On the Person of Christ he is in full accord with the Chalcedonian formula, and he finds scriptural warrant for the Western 'filioque' teaching. He lays emphasis on the Spirit's inspiration of the Scripture and the secret witness (*testimonium internum*) by which the Spirit makes effective for the devout reader the message of Scripture.

The whole of the canonical Bible is linked together by the analogy of faith, so that the OT is freely employed to support the Gospel. 'Moses' only intention,' he declares, 'was to call all men straight to Christ . . . Without Christ the law is empty and insubstantial . . . The Scriptures should be read with a view to finding Christ in them' (*Commentary on St John*, 5.38, 39, trans. T. H. L. Parker). The ceremonies of the old covenant were types or foreshadowings of the realities of the Gospel and are discarded, having no function, since the full light of Christ has shone. While he takes pains to state in detail the advance beyond the OT made in the NT, yet his principle of interpretation assures a firm view of the unity and continuity of Scripture.

The question whether Calvin affirms a natural theology has been vigorously answered in the negative by Karl Barth. If natural theology implies the ability of man, unaided by grace, to know God through the created world, Calvin repudiates it. But if it means that to the Christian mind aided by the 'spectacles' of Scripture, observation of the created world provides an enhancement (in Brunner's language *Erganzung*, supplement) of the knowledge that is explicitly scriptural, the term cannot be fairly excluded. Innumerable statements of Calvin show him to have been intensely appreciative of the evidence of God's glory in the beauty, power and orderliness of the universe. He likes to say that man has been placed in this most glorious theatre of the world to be a spectator of God's works. He recognizes an awareness of divinity (*divinitatis sensus*) natural to the human mind, and in fallen man's darkness some remaining sparks of light, whose feeble glow is, however, wholly insufficient to afford an adequate knowledge of God.

Calvin's early casual interest in predestination gave place in controversy, and under increasing influence from Augustine and Bucer (qq.v.), to the full-fledged doctrine of double predestination which has sometimes been regarded as the heart of his theology. Though he shudders at the decree of reprobation, he holds it an unavoidable inference from Scripture. The efficacy of election is such as to exclude a lapse from the state of salvation. Calvin warns against speculation on the mystery of election, but it clearly entails repentance, faith and sanctification. Holiness is not sought in detachment but in the society of believers and in active pursuit of the daily calling which is accepted as a station appointed by God. The inculcation of a personal and social piety is linked with a high doctrine of the Holy Catholic Church and of the (two scriptural) sacraments. The holy mystery of the Lord's Supper requires that it be protected from profanation, and here lies the basis of the discipline by which the Reformed Church is historically characterized.

For Calvin's works, the series, *Joannis Calvini opera quae supersunt omnia,* ed., G. Baum and others, 59 volumes, 1863–1900, is now being enlarged by the collection, mainly of sermons, *Supplementa Calviniana,* ed., Erwin Muhlhaupt and others, 1961– ; *Calvin: Institutes of the Christian Religion,* ed., J. T. McNeill, trans., F. L. Battles, 1960; E. A. Dowey, *The Knowledge of God in Calvin's Theology,* 1952; W. Niesel, *The Theology of Calvin,* ET, 1956; F. Wendel, *Calvin, the Origins and Development of His Religious Thought,* ET, 1963.

J. T. MCNEILL

Calvinism

The term is used historically, apart from its application to Calvin's own teachings, in two senses. (1) It signifies the doctrines emphasized by seventeenth-century Calvinist scholars, especially the 'five points of Calvinism' affirmed by the Synod of Dort (q.v.). (2) It is applied broadly to the churches which took their rise under Calvin's influence, and to their impact upon society and culture. Inherent in Calvinism in the latter sense is a certain dynamic quality which is still in process of interpretation.

J. W. Beardslee, ed., *Reformed Dogmatics,* 1965; J. H. Bratt, *Rise and Development of Calvinism,* 1964; W. Hastie, *The Theology of the Reformed Church in Its Fundamental Principles,* 1904; H. Heppe, *Reformed Dogmatics,* ET, 1950; G. L. Hunt, ed., *Calvinism and the Political Order,* 1965; J. T. McNeill, *The History and Character of Calvinism,* 1967.

J. T. MCNEILL

Cambridge Platonists

The seventeenth century was a time of strident theological controversy, but in most countries there were groups of moderate men who sought to stand aside from the battle. One of these was a group of Cambridge theologians linked by friendship and residence in the same university during the middle years of the century. They are of great intrinsic interest, and their subsequent influence was considerable. The most important of them were Benjamin Whichcote (1609–1683), Nathaniel Culverwel (fl. 1640–50), John Smith (1618–1652), Ralph Cudworth (1617–1688) and Henry More (1614–1687).

They were influenced both by Francis Bacon and by Descartes, and believed strongly in the capacity of the human reason to assess the truth of religion, but their conception of reason was itself almost mystical. 'The spirit in man is the candle of the Lord.' They were as much in debt to Plotinus as to Plato and there was a warmth in their piety which was lacking in the deists who succeeded them. Their exaltation of reason as well as the reaction against dogma after the Civil War did, however, encourage the vogue of deism towards the end of their time. But for the Cambridge men God is to be sought within, and may be found by all. Heaven is first a temper, then a place, and he who leads a good life enjoys it already. Their passionate defence of toleration caused them to be nicknamed the latitude men, but they are not to be confused with the latitudinarians (q.v.) of a later day. Their teaching has considerable relevance to the modern debate about God.

E. T. Campagnac, *The Cambridge Platonists*, 1901; H. R. McAdoo, *The Spirit of Anglicanism*, 1965; F. J. Powicke, *The Cambridge Platonists*, 1926.

R. CANT

Campbell, Alexander

Alexander Campbell (1788–1866), principal founder of the Christian Churches, or Disciples of Christ, was born in Ireland, studied a year at the University of Glasgow, and emigrated to America in 1809. His father, Thomas, had already broken with Seceder Presbyterianism to found a fellowship seeking the union of all Christians on the basis of the Bible. Alexander took leadership in the movement, which then for nearly twenty years was in association with the Baptists. But tension arose, and by 1832, merging with other 'Christian' groups, especially that under the leadership of Barton Stone, the Campbellites emerged as a separate denomination. Campbell's theological position was promulgated through the journals he edited, *Christian Baptist* (1823–30) and *Millennial Harbinger* (1830–66), through five celebrated debates, and through a statement of theological principles, *The Christian System*, first published in 1836. He advocated reformation of the church by the restoration of primitive Christianity, and the union of all Christians on a biblical, non-credal basis. He founded Bethany College in 1840 and served as its president for two decades.

Royal Humbert, ed., *A Compend of Alexander Campbell's Theology*, 1961; Robert Richardson, *Memoirs of Alexander Campbell*, 2 vols., 1868–70.

ROBERT T. HANDY

Campbell, John McLeod

John McLeod Campbell (1800–1872), Scottish clergyman and theologian, achieved fame for his preaching the doctrine of the 'assurance of faith' combined with a universalist and unlimited atonement. These doctrines gave rise to intense opposition from his Presbyterian compatriots, and in 1831 he was tried for heresy and deposed by the General Assembly. He continued a successful independent ministry. His view was that it was the spiritual essence and nature of the sufferings of Christ rather than their penal character which constituted their value for atonement when Christ defeated sin by the sacrifice of himself, a view expressed in his major work *The Nature of the Atonement* (1856). The dangers inherent in taking a too narrowly defined and exclusive view of the atonement are discussed under **Atonement.**

JAMES ATKINSON

Canon

The word 'canon' comes from an Egyptian word meaning a reed used for measuring, and in the ancient world it was used in a great variety of meanings, for example, rule, standard, ethical norm, list, rent paid for land to the Roman Emperor, ecclesiastical law. In the Middle Ages it was used to describe secular clergy who lived together in a group observing a certain rule, and from this derives its modern use as an ecclesiastical title. The word is not used for the list of authoritative Scripture until the *Festal Letters* of Athanasius in the fourth decade of the third century, but the concept of a list of authoritative writings connected with the new dispensation given in Christ can be found long before that date. The list of writings of the OT had always been relatively fixed in the Christian Church, for the vast majority of Christians accepted the Apocrypha (q.v.) as part of the Bible. But it was only gradually and in a piece-meal fashion that the canon of NT Scripture grew up. It is probable that a nucleus of the later NT was widely acknowledged as early as between 120 and 130, consisting perhaps of the Synoptic Gospels, ten Pauline letters, Hebrews and perhaps Acts. The Fourth Gospel began to be widely known between 140 and 160 but was not fully recognized as authoritative till the time of Tatian, Theophilus of Antioch and its great champion Irenaeus (c. 135–199). The recognition of the Pastoral Epistles, of I Peter and of Revelation was achieved perhaps a little earlier than this. The acceptance of the other books (Jude, II Peter and the Johannine Epistles) was only effected slowly by a process lasting into the fourth century. The Western Church had considerable doubts about Hebrews during the third century and the Eastern Church about Revelation during the third and early fourth centuries. The discovery of the Gnostic *Gospel of Thomas* and *Gospel of Truth* (both of which in their original form probably pre-date Marcion's activity) has badly shaken the theory of A. Harnack (till then almost universally accepted) that Marcion's treatment of the Gospels and Epistles forced the Church to form the canon of Scripture. Even up till the fourth century the limits of the canon were regarded by all as fluid. The Codex Alexandrinus and the Codex Sinaiticus include in their NT other works besides those which we now call canonical, e.g. Hermas' *Shepherd* and the *Epistle of Barnabas*. The early Christian Fathers, such as Clement of Alexandria, Tertullian and Origen, do not regard the NT canon as a hard and fast line, but quote quite freely apocryphal gospels and apocryphal sayings attributed to Jesus. During the second half of the second century references to the inspired nature of the NT Scriptures appear and by about 250 most of them are regarded as enjoying divine inspiration of much the same kind as the OT Scriptures were thought to possess.

It was under the guidance of the Holy Spirit that the Church gathered together a collection of documents authoritatively witnessing to the advent of Jesus Christ and to the significance which was attached to him in the earliest period of the Church's existence. But the nature of the documents themselves, as well as the manner in which they were canonized, make it very difficult, if not impossible, to describe each of these documents as possessing some quality of inspiration lacking in other Christian documents. There is, for instance, no obvious quality of inspiration present in II Peter but lacking in *I Clement* or the letters of Ignatius, which, incidentally, are earlier than II Peter. If the NT is regarded as a collection or corpus made in order to give witness, this difficulty disappears. As a collection it is unique and irreplaceable, even though some parts of the collection may have much less value than others. For the same reason it would be pointless to attempt to add to or to subtract from the NT canon.

The canonical hours or services appointed for particular times and days were those officially ordered by ecclesiastical or monastic authorities. A canon was (and is) a person who lived according to the rule of the institution to which he belonged, e.g. a Cathedral Chapter or a Collegiate Church. From the earlier Middle Ages women who had taken religious vows were sometimes styled 'canonesses'. *See also* **Canon Law.**

F. V. Filson, *Which Books Belong in the Bible?*, 1957; R. P. C. Hanson, *Tradition in the Early Church*, 1962; F. G. Kenyon, *Our Bible and the Ancient Manuscripts*, 4th ed. rev., 1939; A. Souter, *The Text and Canon of the New Testament*, 2nd ed. rev., 1954.

R. P. C. HANSON

Canon Law
The corpus of legislation ordered by ecclesiastical authority for the regulation of the Church's life (especially in the Roman Catholic Church; in the Church of England the canons or regulations passed by the Convocations of Canterbury, 1604, and York, 1606, are at present undergoing revision by the Convocations). The assumption underlying the making of canon law is that ecclesiastical authority, while able to enact laws for the Church's government, cannot abrogate laws not of its own making, such as natural law (*Jus Naturale*) or divine law (*Jus Divinum*). *See also* J. Macquarrie, 'Canon Law', *DCE*.

EDITOR

Canonization
Canonization is in the pre-Reformation Church and in the Roman Catholic Church since that time, the process of declaring someone a 'Saint' (in the post-NT meaning of the word), to be recognized and venerated as such throughout the whole Church.

Cappadocian Fathers
A group of Fathers, all Cappadocians by birth and Bishops of the places combined with their names, Basil of Caesarea (*c.* 330–379), Gregory of Nazianzus, later of Constantinople (329–389), and Gregory of Nyssa (*c.* 330–395). They were right-wing Origenists or Co-ordinationist Pluralists and became the leaders of the Nicene reaction. They played a major part in the reconciliation of the *Homoeousians* (q.v.) and in the development of the doctrine of the Holy Spirit. Their chief opponents were Arians, Macedonians and Sabellians (qq.v.). Cappadocian orthodoxy was ratified by the Council of Constantinople (381) of which the Creed was especially akin to their teaching in the article on the Holy Spirit. *See* **Trinity, Doctrine of the.**

H. E. W. TURNER

Caroline Divines
The Caroline Divines were a group of learned high-church Anglican theologians who flourished in the seventeenth century, especially, but not only, in the reigns of Charles I and Charles II. The upheavals of the Reformation had partly subsided, and the Elizabethan settlement had secured a relative peace for the church; but the period was still one of political and religious controversy, and those who defended the settlement were aware of being attacked on two sides. 'The Church of England,' said Archbishop Laud, 'is in hard condition. She professes the ancient Catholic faith, and yet the Romanist condemns her of novelty in her doctrine; she practises Church government as it hath been in all ages and in all places . . . yet the Separatist condemns her for antichristianism in her discipline . . . She is between these two factions, as between two millstones.' Later, Anglicans were to congratulate themselves a little smugly on their *via media* between Rome and Geneva, like Bishop Simon Patrick, who approved of the 'virtuous mediocrity' of his church's worship, 'between the meretricious gaudiness of the church of Rome and the squalid sluttery of fanatic conventicles'. But Patrick was a latitudinarian, and Anglican theology was already entering a new phase. The sense of danger which Laud expressed, however, caused the Carolines to lean more heavily on

royal support than was good for them, and they were enthusiastic preachers of the Divine Right of Kings (q.v.). Under the Commonwealth they had opportunity to reflect on the true basis of church authority, and Herbert Thorndike (1598–1672), for example, wrote on the supranational character of the Church. But in the main their exaggerated respect for the Stuart dynasty and their fear of Rome and of Dissent were an unhappy legacy for Anglicans.

They shared with the Puritans a profound regard for the authority of the Bible, but objected to a literalism which sought an unchangeable pattern for worship and morals in it. This is illustrated in the controversy over the keeping of the sabbath. The Carolines appealed to tradition and reason for approval of Sunday games. Much of their writing was occasional, in that it was called forth by the needs of controversy or apologetic. Like the Puritans they admired Calvin, but refused to go all the way with him, and for pastoral reasons did not care to preach on such disturbing topics as predestination and assurance. For this reason their critics dubbed them 'Arminians'. They venerated the patristic writers more than they did Calvin, and no generation of Anglican clergy since has known this literature so well, regarded it so highly or quoted it so freely. The influence of the Greek Fathers is particularly notable in their expression of a eucharistic theology closely related to the incarnation. Their teaching on the sacraments was high, and manuals of devotion show with what reverence the Holy Communion was received. One of the most popular of these books to survive to modern times is *The Rule and Exercise of Holy Living* (1650) by Bishop Jeremy Taylor (1613–1657). This high theology was reflected in the arrangement of the interior of their churches which they favoured, with the altar at the east end of the chancel, protected by communion rails, and in the use of a moderate ceremonial. Like the Puritans they were deeply concerned with moral theology, and produced books of 'casuistical divinity' of great usefulness. The practice of private confession, though strongly recommended by many of them, had largely vanished, and the discussion of cases of conscience in sermons and books partly filled the gap. Robert Sanderson (1587–1663), bishop of Lincoln, was one of the best moral theologians of the century. They were staunch supporters of episcopacy, some holding it to be strictly necessary, others willing to grant that national churches which lacked it might be true, though imperfect, churches. They admired and loved the Book of Common Prayer, and many led lives of great personal devotion. Theologians, statesmen, poets and many ordinary church people, clerical and lay, were nourished by this tradition. Among them may be mentioned Lancelot Andrewes, Lord Clarendon, George Herbert, John Evelyn and Margaret Godolphin. Izaak Walton's *Lives*, published between 1640 and 1678, give an attractive if slightly tendentious account of some of them. Towards the end of the century a change came over Anglican theology. More stress was placed on the proofs of revealed religion than upon its dogmatic content, and piety became more humdrum and moralist. The leaders of the Oxford Movement (q.v.) consciously sought to revive the teaching of the Caroline Divines.

C. F. Allison, *The Rise of Moralism*, 1966; P. E. More and F. L. Cross, *Anglicanism*, 1935.

R. CANT

Cartesianism. *see* Descartes, R.

Casuistry

Casuistry means the application of moral principles to particular situations or to individual circumstances. The necessity for it arises from the fact that it is never possible to frame a general ethical principle which will be relevant to all the circumstances of the individual practitioner. The rise of formal casuistry in the Christian Church begins with the development of the practice of private penance from the seventh century onwards, and by the Middle Ages the Christian Church possessed a fully articulated volume of casuistical analysis of human conduct. Some features of this body of casuistical theory have been responsible for the term 'casuistry' coming to have a pejorative meaning, but important theological issues are nevertheless at stake: nothing less than the doctrine of the incarnation and its implications, particularly the implications of a doctrine of the incarnation which is interpreted in terms of kenosis (*see* **Christology [5]**). This latter involves for the believer a continual exposing of himself to the ambiguity and imperfections of finite existence as a way of doing homage to the manner of the incarnation itself. An impatience with the particularities and partialities of finite existence is the mark of a gnostic turn of mind, and casuistry is involved in any tradition which is willing to take human existence in all its finitude seriously and sacramentally.

J. C. Ford and Gerald Kelly, SJ, *Contemporary Moral Theology*, 1960; K. E. Kirk, *Conscience and its Problems*, 1927.

E. J. TINSLEY

Cataphatic Theology. *see* Dionysius the Pseudo-Areopagite.

Catechesis, Catechumens

Catechesis means instruction, and comes from the same root as the phrase 'you have been informed' of Luke 1.4. It became a technical term for instruction ('catechism') given to candidates for baptism ('catechumens') for some period before the administration of the sacrament. The courses of instruction of several early Church Fathers (e.g. Cyril of Jerusalem) have survived. Catechetical theology is the theology of such elementary instruction, and a catechism is a set form of instruction, usually of the type of questions and answers, used in many different denominations since the Reformation. *See also* **Initiation, Christian.**

R. P. C. HANSON

Catholicism

The phrase 'the Catholic Church' first occurs in Ignatius (*Smyrn*, 8.2), about AD 112, when it probably means not merely 'the universal Church' but 'the Church which has the wholeness of doctrine', in contrast to narrower sects. Thereafter the word in ecclesiastical usage usually has both meanings. The Church is catholic because it is universal, it includes people of all races and ranks, it exists in every place in the world, but also it has a wholeness of doctrine and of life and worship denied to other Christian or would-be Christian bodies who are partial in scope and provenance, and in doctrine are defective and one-sided. In the ancient Church it is often used of the Great Church, the majority Church, the Church of the great sees, such as Jerusalem, Antioch, Alexandria and Rome, and often, too, of the Church supported by the Roman Emperor, in contrast to local sects not in communion with the great sees, commanding only a minority of numbers, and usually in open or tacit opposition to the imperial government. Thus the Catholics are contrasted with the Donatists (virtually confined to Roman Africa, even though sometimes out-numbering the Catholics there), the Novatians (who existed only in small numbers and in a few cities), the Apollinarians, the Eunomians, etc. Catholic Epistles in the NT are letters addressed to the whole Church (e.g. I John, James, Jude), not to particular churches or individuals. As the Church spread over almost the whole of the known world, the geographical sense faded into the background and the doctrinal sense became predominant. The Western mediaeval Church certainly regarded itself as Catholic in doctrine, recalling the proud words of St Augustine *securus iudicat orbis terrarum* ('the whole world can confidently decide [against the Donatists] that it is right'), and the canon or rule for identifying true doctrine of Saint Vincent of Lerins (ob. before 450), *quod semper, quod ubique, quod ab omnibus* ('*what* [has been believed] *always, everywhere and by everybody*'). But it was also Catholic as affecting every side of life, the physical, the intellectual, the moral, the political, the aesthetic, the economic, and as penetrating the whole of society. The use of the word was greatly sharpened by the Reformation, when in opposition to the churches which claimed to be Reformed and renewed the church of the Counter-Reformation claimed to be Catholic, embodying the whole of Christian doctrine and life in contrast to the one-sided representations of it by the Reformed bodies which were essentially local, like the Church of England and the Church of Scotland, or followers of a single Reformer, like the Lutherans, Calvinists and Zwinglians. The word 'catholic' inevitably took on a certain partisan air, so that it could be applied in such curious combinations as 'Catholic statesmen',

'Catholic armies', 'Catholic intrigues', or else, in more recent history, it could be used to describe a surprising number of activities such as 'Catholic courtship' or even 'Catholic sport'. But at its best Catholicism can imply a noble concept, the ideal of the Church which embraces the fulness of Christianity, building through its age-long majestic pondering a consistent edifice of dogma, law and tradition, and expressing its Catholicity, its fulness of Christian understanding and faith, in a deep and varied cultus, devotion, sanctity and pattern of individual behaviour, whose serene and firmly-based comprehensiveness puts to shame the narrowness and shallowness of its Protestant counterparts. Catholicism in this sense is an integration of faith, life and worship which alone represents the fulness of Christianity, for it is expressed by the Church which alone is Catholic, complete, integral, true.

But for certain Protestant writers who have employed the technique of historical criticism the word 'Catholicism' is one of reproach. It means the corruption and adulteration of true, original Christianity which took place early in the history of the Church and transformed the Christian faith by a process of legalizing and stereotyping from its original charismatic, personalist, grace-controlled character (Sohm), or by a process of Hellenization from its original gospel of the Fatherhood of God and the brotherhood of man (Harnack), or by an abandonment of the eschatological conviction (Werner), or by a surrender to 'Gnosticism' (Subilia). For these writers Catholicism means syncretism, involvement in unnecessary and alien metaphysical systems, or the invasion of intellectual worldliness. Their incapacity to agree upon the nature of original Christianity, however, weakens their case. If we are not sure what is the norm, we are not in a strong position to accuse Catholicism of having deviated from it. More serious is the charge that it is impossible to apply the Vincentian canon. The concept of *quod semper, quod ubique, quod ab omnibus* is an empty one, for there never has been such a consensus, either in space or time. What Irenaeus, Tertullian and Hippolytus believed about the Trinity, for instance, is inconsistent with the classical fourth- and fifth-century definitions of this dogma, and the interpretation of *homoousios* (q.v.) by Athanasius was inconsistent with that of his younger contemporary Basil. Again, however we define Catholicism, it seems impossible to reconcile the very latest example of Catholic dogma (the Assumption, 1950, q.v.) with it, unless we say that what the Roman Catholic Church defines as Catholic dogma must be so because the Roman Catholic Church defines it.

Much of this criticism of the traditional concept of Catholicism must be accepted. Catholic doctrine has not grown in a steady, consistent line of uninterrupted organic growth. Newman's assumption that the biological analogy was valid is unjustified. The true picture should be one of a continuous engagement of the Church with the sources of Christian truth, following a varied course of advance and retreat, success and vicissitude, constant discovery and constant reexamination and restatement. The Church has learnt from heretics, from non-Christians and from prophetic voices outside its formal structure, such as those of Søren Kierkegaard, Martin Buber and Simone Weil, and must always be prepared to review the bases of its own thought. The dogma of the Assumption may represent the end of one line of inauthentic speculative development rather than the crown of the evolution of Catholic dogma. But when all these concessions have been made it is still true that there is such a thing as a central Catholic tradition of doctrine which alone represents the fulness of Christian truth as it has been known and believed, understood and practised by the Church through the ages. This tradition is not, however, the monopoly of any one Christian body. On the contrary it is a tradition which at once gives to all Christian bodies a certain basic unity in spite of their divisions and is being gradually made more real as they approach closer to each other through the Ecumenical Movement (q.v.). Catholicism is both already present in a fragmented mode (paradoxical though this may appear) and yet to be realized through – and only through – the contribution of all. *See also* **Rome** (for Roman Catholicism); **Peter; Papacy; Tradition; Infallibility; Orthodoxy.**

K. Adam, *The Spirit of Catholicism*, 1934; E. L. Mascall, *Christ, the Christian and the Church*, 1946; F. D. Maurice, *The Kingdom of Christ*, 1838; V. Subilia, *The Problem of Catholicism*, 1964; N. Zernov, *Eastern Christendom: The Church of the Eastern Christians*, 1961.

R. P. C. HANSON

Celibacy

The subject of celibacy provides a good illustration of the tension between the Hebraic-Jewish ancestry of Christianity and the strong influence of Hellenistic Gnosticism and dualism. The Jewish non-ascetical attitude is especially prominent in regard to sex and marriage. The Hebrews and Jews never accepted a thorough-going gnostic or Manichaean attitude to the human body or to sexuality. Although OT apocalyptic was dualistic in one sense (the contrast between 'this age' and 'that age') the doctrine of the resurrection of the *body* prevented any tendency towards metaphysical dualism. In the Hebraic tradition therefore a large place is given to married love and the family, and celibacy is deprecated (*see* G. Montefiore, *The Synoptic Gospels*, 2nd ed., 1927, p. 265).

There is some evidence that in the period between the Testaments, Jewish tradition was already being affected by gnostic and dualistic notions from Hellenism. Speculation about the fall of man, its cause and its consequences, produced a tendency towards a form of sexual asceticism which was to elevate the ideal of celibacy (*cf.* Eccles. 25.24).

Nevertheless, the main rabbinical tradition remained hostile to the notion of celibacy. The theological basis for this was the rabbinical interpretation of the idea of the image of God. This was taken to be the male-female relationship and therefore the rabbis prohibited celibacy as an ethical ideal because it was a denial of the image of God.

In the early Church the Jewish background of Christianity gradually lost influence in this field and the Hellenistic dualistic approach became predominant. Sexuality and even marriage were regarded as unfortunate consequences of the fall and best avoided for those who would aspire to the perfect life. Whereas the imitation of God in Jewish tradition insisted upon marriage as a way of doing homage to the image of God in man, in the Christian tradition the imitation of Christ had the opposite result. More and more the imitation of Christ was regarded as a literal endeavour to mimic the state of Christ and consequently Christ's own unmarriedness was taken as the model for the Christian aspirant. Next to martyrs, celibates and virgins were regarded as imitators of Christ *par excellence*, and the Church in the West came to adopt celibacy as the rule for the clergy.

H. R. Niebuhr and D. D. Williams, *The Ministry in Historical Perspectives*, 1956; M. Thurian, *Marriage and Celibacy*, 1959.

E. J. TINSLEY

Chalcedon, Chalcedonian Definition. *see* Christology (4).

Channing, William Ellery

William Channing (1780–1842), American Unitarian leader, found guidance and direction from the Scottish common-sense philosophy while a student at Harvard, from which he graduated in 1798. After serving as tutor in Virginia, he resolved to enter the Congregational ministry, was ordained in 1803 and called to serve the Federal Street Church in Boston. He soon became the main spiritual and intellectual force in the liberal party, in 1819 preaching at Baltimore a sermon, 'Unitarian Christianity', which gave Unitarianism a platform and rallying point as it was splitting from Congregationalism to become an independent denomination. The sermon was based on the conviction that the Scriptures are the records of God's successive revelations to mankind, particularly of the last and most perfect revelation of his will by Jesus Christ, and are to be studied carefully and with full use of human reason. It found that the distinguishing doctrines of Unitarianism were five: the unity of God, the unity of Jesus Christ and his inferiority to God, the moral perfection of God, the meditation of Christ by his teachings, example, sufferings, death, resurrection and continual intercession, and the nature of Christian virtue as fundamentally a moral affair. The basic theological point at issue between

Unitarianism and orthodoxy concerned the nature of man; Channing believed in the 'essential sameness' of man and God, and therefore in man's perfectibility. Through his preaching and writing, and participation in humanitarian and re-formed movements for peace, temperance and the abolition of slaves, Channing's influence reached far beyond Unitarianism. In many ways a pro-duct of Enlightenment motifs in religion, especi-ally as made available through common-sense realism, he also sensed and spoke to the romantic and individualist currents of his day.

David P. Edgell, *William Ellery Channing: An Intellectual Portrait*, 1955; Robert Leet Patterson, *The Philosophy of William Ellery Channing*, 1952.

ROBERT T. HANDY

Character

1. Sacramental character is the special effect predicated of baptism, confirmation and holy orders. It is regarded as a supernatural and in-delible mark impressed upon the individual re-cipient which cannot be effaced either by sin or apostasy. Foreshadowed by the concept of the 'seal' (*cf.* Eph. 1.13) or identification mark, the idea was given currency by Augustine, who dis-tinguished between the grace conveyed and the character imprinted by a sacrament. He conten-ded, in his debate with the Donatists, that bap-tism is valid even when administered in schism but conveys no benefit; it is not necessary to repeat it when the schismatic returns to the Church, but it is only then that it fructifies. He was also prepared to extend this idea to ordination, in an effort to smooth the path for returning Donatists.

The concept of character was developed by the Scholastics, for example, by Scotus, who main-tained that it was a kind of quality and, on the basis of Aristotle's categories of quality, that it was something akin to the genus of quality called power. This teaching was endorsed by the Council of Florence (1438–45) and solemnly defined by the Council of Trent (1545–63): 'If any one shall say that in three sacraments, namely baptism, confimation and holy orders, there is not a character impressed upon the soul, that is a cer-tain spiritual and ineffaceable mark (*signum*), whence these sacraments cannot be repeated, let him be anathema' (Conc. Trid. Sess. ult., can. 7).

Acceptance of the indelible character of holy orders has issued in the phenomenon of *episcopi vagantes* (wandering bishops). Since the character cannot be lost, even a bishop who has been ex-communicated by the Church retains the episco-pal 'character' and therefore can and does ordain.

Most Christian Churches would acknowledge the indelible character imparted in baptism, in the sense that it is an unrepeatable act, the princi-pal exception being the Baptists who, rejecting infant and insisting upon believers' baptism, would re-baptize. But many Christians would not accept the indelible character of orders – such a view is repudiated, for example, by the Eastern

Orthodox Churches – on the grounds that ordina-tion conveys authorization rather than an imprint, and hence if a person ceases to be competent to perform the function for which he was given authority, say, by excommunication, he forfeits his orders.

2. Moral character was regarded by some in the patristic period as being directly related to the administration of the sacraments. The Donatists, following Cyprian in part, maintained that the validity of the sacraments depended upon the worthiness of the minister. Hence they contended that episcopal consecrations performed by a *traditor*, that is one who had handed over the Scriptures in the Diocletian persecution and had thereby revealed his apostasy, were unacceptable. Optatus of Milevum, writing c. 366, argued against this on the grounds that the sacraments derive their validity from God and not from the person administering them. It is this latter view that has generally prevailed, as otherwise, since a person's moral character is only fully known to God, no one would ever know whether a baptism or a celebration of the Eucharist had or had not been impaired by the unworthiness of the minister.

B. Leeming, *Principles of Sacramental Theology*, 1960, pp. 129–282.

J. G. DAVIES

Chardin. *see* Teilhard de Chardin, P.

Charisma, Charismatic

Charisma (Greek) means 'gift' or 'gift of grace'. St Paul writes about the different kinds of gifts which the Holy Spirit imparts to those who are baptized (I Cor. 12.13 in its whole context). He clearly prefers 'spiritual gifts' (e.g. those enumera-ted in Gal. 5.22 f.), or the 'greater gifts' (I Cor. 12.31), namely, faith, hope and love, to the more 'showy' gifts such as 'speaking with tongues' (*see* **Glossolalia**). In modern theological usage, how-ever, a 'charismatic man' is one who manifests unusual powers of divination, healing, enthusiasm (q.v.), miraculous works and the like. *See* **Spiritual Gifts**.

EDITOR

Chiliasm

The word (from Greek *chilioi*, a thousand) is thus the equivalent of **Millennialism** (q.v.), the belief that Christ will reign on earth for a thousand years before the final consummation of all things (*cf.* Rev. 20.1–5).

Chrism

From Greek *chrio*, to anoint, the word is used of the holy oil which is used in the three sacraments which confer a character: baptism, confirmation and ordination (according to Roman Catholic and Eastern usage). Chrism is also used at other solemn ceremonies of dedication (of altars, chur-ches, etc.). The Church of England retained anointing at the coronation of the monarch (*cf.*

'the Lord's Anointed' in the OT). Protestant churches have discarded it, although undoubtedly ancient, chiefly because of the obscurity of its symbolism and its lack of NT authorization.

EDITOR

Christendom

The word means 'the Christian world'. It is strictly applicable only to that period of the Middle Ages when the Church could enforce obedience to its discipline both in belief and in practice. Its zenith was the pontificate of Gregory VII (1021–1085), who wrote to the nations to remind them that from the time of St Peter the See of Rome had been their overlord, and who humbled the Emperor at Canossa. The disintegration of Christendom began at the close of the Middle Ages with the rise of nationalism, the Reformation and the inevitable secularization of society which followed the Renaissance (see Secular, Secularization). The Reformers themselves hardly foresaw the break-up of Christendom which was to come, for even in the Protestant countries the reception of the sacraments was still enforced by the magistrates, and heresy and even dissent were offences against the State. But the mediaeval ideal of Christendom – one Church, one State – could not survive the attainment of freedom by men come of age at the Renaissance and the Age of Enlightenment (q.v.). The French Revolution heralded the secular State. The newly independent colonies in America set up a constitution which strictly separated Church and State. Only the reactionaries, to the immense disservice of the Christian cause, tried to keep the civil and lay society in tutelage to the hierarchy of the Church. 'Christendom' was a magnificent ideal, and its realization in mediaeval Europe created a great civilization in the lands which the barbarian invaders had despoiled. But it could not last, for it was not the answer to the human quest for freedom. Today it lingers only as a memory. Its passing did not solve the problems of humanity; it only created new ones. In current usage 'Christendom' is a somewhat vague expression denoting a longed-for state of Christian civilization (q.v.), rather than a present reality to which Christians can point or perhaps even a hope to which they dare to aspire. See also Christian Civilization.

EDITOR

Christening

From Anglo-Saxon cristnian, the word is more popular in general English usage than 'baptism', with which it is almost synonymous. It carries, however, an overtone of 'naming with a Christian name', and in vulgar speech 'to christen' often means to name or to nick-name, without religious reference. See Initiation, Christian.

Christian, Christianity

The name 'Christians' seems to have arisen as a nickname (cf. 'Methodists', 'Quakers') for an unpopular sect (Acts 11.26; cf. 26.28; I Peter 4.16;

Tactius, xv, 44). It eventually took the place of such other designations as 'disciples', 'brethren', 'saints', or 'those of the Way', and became generally used by Christians themselves. It differentiated them from pagans and Jews, as now it differentiates them from Muslims, Buddhists, Hindus, etc. Today it is a generic description of all Christian churches and sects, though in the nineteenth century some Unitarians rejected it. The name of Christ (as distinct from the reputation of the Church) has become so revered in Western civilization that many people who hold no definite Christian beliefs would be offended if they were told that they or their actions were unchristian. But while 'Christian' is thus held to apply to certain ethical standards of behaviour, 'Christianity' remains a synonym for the Christian religion as distinct from other religions or philosophies of life (e.g. humanism, Marxism, etc.).

EDITOR

Christian Civilization

When the Roman civilization of western Europe was destroyed by the invading barbarians (Rome itself was sacked by Attila the Goth in AD 410) the Church became the custodian of civilized values. A Christian culture was developed (e.g. at York in the days of her great native scholar, Alcuin, c.735-804) but it was often again extinguished by fresh waves of invaders. Eventually western Europe was Christianized and civilized, and since the Church alone produced the 'clerics' (men of education), churchmen inevitably became leading figures in the State as well as in the Church. During the high Middle Ages (the age of 'Christendom', q.v.) a fine civilization, governed by law and unified by a common language (Latin), was developed. During the eighteenth century (and among some nineteenth-century writers, such as Macaulay) it was fashionable to belittle the achievements of the Middle Ages (in Gibbon's phrase, the age of 'barbarism and religion'). The Romantic Movement reversed this assessment, and 'Gothic' was no longer a term of abuse but of adulation. Today we are able to make a fairer judgment. We know now that the mediaevals knew much more about mechanics and astronomy than used to be supposed, and that the foundations of modern science were laid in the later Middle Ages. Copernicus, Kepler and Galileo were not a new race of men but the thinkers in whom the work of their predecessors culminated. Renaissance scholarship was the flowering of many years of growth. When the shackles of Aristotelian dogma had been broken off, the scientific and humanist implications of the Christian theological world-view could be gradually developed, as they have been, up to the point of our own world of technological and critical achievement. It has taken many centuries for the understanding implicit in the Christian worldview (a God of reason and order, a doctrine of creation which excluded belief in Fate, Chance, etc., a sense of purpose in history, etc.) to develop, and we are still only at a partial stage of its development. Christian ethical ideals, including justice between nations and races, the rights of individuals, etc., are still far from universal acceptance, but the Christian conception of educational opportunity is demonstrated by the enthusiasm of almost all nations for universities, schools, etc. Health and hospitals are still the concern of the churches and of no one else in several parts of the world. But certain of the long-range benefits of Christian civilization, such as modern scientific technology, agriculture and medicine, are blessings which the whole world is ready to accept, though their source in the Christian civilization of Europe is generally forgotten. How long these achievements will remain a blessing and not be turned to a curse – for the instruments of war, exploitation and oppression are powerfully reinforced by modern science – remains a question of great urgency. The divine command to 'possess the earth and subdue it' (Gen. 1.28) is fulfilled in civilization only when men do not usurp the place of God and use his gifts for their own aggrandisement. *See also* **Culture.**

Eric Ashby, *African Universities and the Western Tradition*, 1964; John Baillie, *What is Christian Civilization?* 1945; T. S. Eliot, *The Idea of a Christian Society*, 1939; A. T. van Leeuwen, *Christianity in World History*, 1964; Stephen Neill, *Colonialism and Christian Mission*, 1966; Max Warren, *Social History and Christian Mission*, 1967.

EDITOR

Christian Science

The 'discoverer and founder' of Christian Science was Mary Baker Eddy (1821–1910), who grew up in New England at the time when transcendentalist thought was widespread. After a fall on the ice in 1866, she claimed that by a remarkable healing experience she was led to the discovery of how to be well and how to cure others. Interpreting the Bible from this perspective, she published in 1875 the first edition of what later became *Science and Health with Key to the Scriptures*. The book was to go through many revisions and it remains, together with the King James (Authorized) version of the Bible, the central authority among Christian Scientists. Also in 1875 the first Christian Science society was organized; in 1879 'The Church of Christ (Scientist)' was chartered with headquarters in Boston. The 'Mother Church' continues as the world headquarters of the movement; other Christian Science churches are branches. There are no ordained clergy, but 'readers' conduct services, while 'practitioners' treat those seeking cure by prayer.

Christian Science rests on the premiss that God is all in all, God is divine Mind. Mind (synonymous with Spirit), Soul, Life, Truth, Love, Principle, is all that exists. Mind's expression of itself is man, who as the idea and image of God is immortal and perfect. Spirit being all, matter is unreal illusion and is nothing. Inasmuch as evil has to do with matter, it too, along with disease, sin and death, is unreal. Death is an illusion of mortal sense, and may continue to appear until destroyed by spiritual sense. Sin is belief in the real existence of other minds than the divine Mind. Sickness too is false belief; suffering exists only in the mortal mind. To the Christian Scientist, healing is a religious function, for disease and illness as delusions of the human mind can be destroyed by the prayer of spiritual understanding. The faith of Christian Science is claimed to be not *primarily* to heal physical disease but to regenerate human thought through spiritual understanding.

Charles S. Braden, *Christian Science Today*, 1958; Sibyl Wilbur, *The Life of Mary Baker Eddy*, 1907.
ROBERT T. HANDY

Christology

1. *Introduction.* Christology means 'the doctrine of Christ' and, as such, it could be applied to the entire inquiry into the significance of Christ for faith. Conventionally it has been restricted to that branch of the inquiry which addresses itself to the person of Christ, as distinct from his work, which is the subject of soteriology (*see* **Atonement**). It is widely recognized in modern theology that the division is artificial and academic, and repeated attempts have been made to overcome it; the most successful is probably that of Karl Barth in *Church Dogmatics IV: The Doctrine of Reconciliation* (*see below*). But while it is clearly impossible to separate the person of Christ from his work, it is convenient for purposes of inquiry to distinguish the question, who he is, from the question, what he does.

Christology is the attempt to clarify the elemental confession of Christian faith, that Jesus is the Christ (Acts 2.36; 5.42; 9.22; 18.5, 28, etc.), or that Jesus Christ is Lord (I Cor. 12.3; Phil. 2.11; Acts 16.31). It must be distinguished from the answers which have been given to the general question presented by Jesus of Nazareth as a phenomenon of world history. As such, he has been accounted for in a variety of ways – a Jewish rabbi, a moral teacher, an ideal figure, a religious genius, a revolutionary, a deluded fanatic, etc. These descriptions resemble the varied answers which were reported by his disciples, when Jesus himself asked them, 'Who do men say that I am?' (Mark 8.27); and, like those answers ('John the Baptist', 'Elijah', 'one of the prophets'), they are not without some grains of truth. All of them fit the figure of Jesus to some degree. But they are answers given by spectators from a stance of neutrality and detachment; they are what 'men' say. And when he had heard them, Jesus turned to his disciples and said, 'But who do you say that I am?' and received from Peter the answer, 'You are the Christ' (Mark 8.29). This answer was not the product of reflection in the phenomenon of Jesus, but confession of faith elicited by personal encounter with the reality of Jesus.

The Gospel narratives frequently show how encounter with Jesus had the effect of confronting men with the question of his person. Indeed, the question is a central motif of the Gospels. Jesus' first appearance at the beginning of his public ministry had the immediate effect of raising the question: 'Who is this that teaches with authority?' (*cf.* Mark 1.27), 'Who is this that forgives sins?' (*cf.* Mark 2.7), 'What manner of man is this that even the winds and the sea obey him?' (*cf.* Mark 4.41). At what was unmistakably a point of decisive import in his career he himself confronted his disciples with the question, 'Who do you say that I am?' (Mark 8.27–29), and the importance of the question is indicated, not merely by the manner of his response to Peter's confession of faith, as reported by Matthew (16.18), but by its immediate effect; for it served as a catalyst to precipitate the division between those who were for him and those who were against him (*cf.* John 6.66–69). From this point the career of Jesus moved into an increasingly critical phase, which culminated in his trial before the Jewish and Roman authorities; and there the crucial question was, 'Who is he?' (*cf.* Mark 14.61). The Evangelists plainly mean to convey that this was the intended effect of his appearance, in the sense that there could be no real encounter with Jesus Christ unless men felt themselves confronted with this question in a decisive way. This is illustrated at a pathological level in the behaviour of the demons who impulsively blurt out the secret (*cf.* Mark 1.24), and it is made very explicit in the Fourth Evangelist's statement of his own purpose: 'these are written that you may believe that Jesus is the Christ, the Son of God, and that believing you may have life in his name' (John 20.31).

Objection has sometimes been made to the christological inquiry on the ground that it distracts faith from its proper object, which, as Melanchthon once said, consists in the 'benefits' of Christ, not his 'natures', and that it leads into dangerous bypaths of speculation. The answer to these objections is not to deny that the christological inquiry may be dangerous to faith, but to point out that the refusal of the christological inquiry may be equally dangerous, if not more so. If the classical christology of the ancient Church looks like a rampage of the Greek speculative intellect on the simplicities of the faith, closer examination will show that it is a determined attempt, with the very tools provided by the Greek intellect, to protect the faith against its rampages. The aim of the christological inquiry is to concentrate faith on its proper object. It is not a substitute for faith. It belongs to the indigenous impulse of faith to seek understanding and clarification of itself and to distinguish itself from spurious counterfeits.

The question is: What is the meaning of faith in Christ? The question can be divided into two parts or stages, according as it is viewed from the angle of faith or from the angle of Christ. When it is looked at from the angle of faith, the problem that presents itself is that of the relation of faith in Christ to faith in God. This is the trinitarian problem which is technically distinguished from the christological problem and usually treated separately (*see* **Trinity**). Both are concerned with the question, who Christ is. But the former considers it as the question of his relation to God, who is the sole and proper object of faith; the latter, assuming the answer given to the first, namely, that he is *homoousios* ('the same in being') with God (so that faith in Christ coincides with faith in God), proceeds to ask how he, who is so defined, could come among us men, as one of ourselves. The doctrine of the Trinity serves to clarify the christological affirmation of the divinity (or deity) of Christ. It affirms that in Jesus Christ (as in the Holy Spirit) it is God himself who is present and active: '*God* was in Christ reconciling the world to himself' (II Cor. 5.19). Christology shifts the focus to Jesus Christ. It inquires how it is *in Jesus Christ* that God is present and active with us. The inquiry thus becomes centred on the relation between the divine and the human in this person.

2 *The Question of Method.* Since faith speaks of Christ as a real man and, at the same time, as one in whom God is present and active among us, two possible methods of approach to the christological problem suggest themselves; we may seek to move from the human to the divine, or, from the divine to the human. Of course, the question applies only to the method of the inquiry. So far as the order of the reality is concerned, there can be no question that the movement with which christology is concerned proceeds in the direction from God to man: 'The Word became flesh' (John 1.14). But it does not follow that in our efforts to understand the movement our thought can proceed in the same direction.

The classical christology followed the downward or 'deductive' method. It began from the eternal Godhead of the Son (as that was established in the doctrine of the Trinity), then went on to speak of the incarnation and the humanity of the incarnate. In so doing it faithfully reflects and celebrates the downward movement of the grace of God in his condescension to us. But it obscures the fact that we know God only as we encounter his presence in Christ here below. In its laudable concern to safeguard the priority of God and the prevenience of grace, it tends to set up an abstract God-in-himself apart from God-with-us, and to convey the impression that his coming to us in Christ is, somehow, incompatible with his divine majesty and glory – in other words, it tends to set up a God whose grace is a miracle to himself as well as to us. Moreover, the classical christology in assuming that the divinity could be taken as the given starting-point of thought had difficulty in establishing an adequate concept of the humanity. The orthodox doctrine of the incarnation as the assumption of humanity by the divine Word (Logos), or the eternal Son, made the divinity dominant over the humanity, which was reduced to a passive or instrumental role. Despite verbal safeguards against it, it encourages the persistent bias towards monophysitism, which is reflected in the accompanying notion of salvation as the deification of man.

The alternative, or 'inductive' method, which holds that, 'the way to the knowledge of Jesus leads from the human Jesus to the Son of God and to the Godhead' (E. Brunner, *Dogmatics* II: *The Christian Doctrine of Creation and Redemption*, 1952, p. 322), has been advocated by a number of theologians from Luther onward, and has been increasingly popular since the Enlightenment. Here it is the humanity that is regarded as given and unquestionable, and the divinity that is problematic. The basic assumption, however, is that there is some kind of continuity between them which makes it possible to ascend in thought from the humanity to the divinity. In the nineteenth and early twentieth centuries this continuity was often looked for in an ethical direction. Many theologians, who were profoundly influenced by Kant, believed it was imperative to transpose all theological doctrines from a metaphysical to an ethical key, and the most notable of these, Ritschl and his followers, propounded a christology according to which the human Jesus has for us the *value* of God. The period was marked by a general shift of interest from the Christ of the classical christology to the human figure who is portrayed in the Gospels, and some were even led to the position that, given 'the Jesus of History', christology could be dispensed with altogether.

Both those who advocated the inductive method in christology and those who believed that the Jesus of history could serve as a substitute for christology assumed that it is possible to extract from the Gospels (especially the Synoptics) a picture of the man Jesus of Nazareth as he was, *before* a christological superstructure had been set up over him. More recent study of the forms of the Gospel narratives has shown that these are not historical records of a pre-christological Jesus, but testimonies written from the standpoint of a confessed faith in Christ as the incarnate and risen Lord. The 'Jesus of history' is a phantom who cannot be reconstructed from the narratives. 'The telling of the story of Jesus was christological through and through from the start' (D. M. Baillie, *God was in Christ*, p. 60).

Both the deductive and inductive methods are unsatisfactory. Both assume that either the divine or the human is given to us in isolation and that we can proceed in thought from one to the other. But in so doing they both abandon the actual situation in which the christological inquiry arises. That is the situation of encounter with Christ in the confession and preaching of the Church. But the Church does not proclaim one side of Christ and leave us to find the other by our own ingenuity; it proclaims the whole Christ, divine and human, and invites us to put our faith in him. It is this Christ who is the proper object of faith, and christology is theological reflection on it.

The situation has its paradigm in the encounter of Christ with Peter at Caesarea Philippi (Mark 8.27–29), or with Thomas after Easter (John 20.24–29). It is re-created in the preaching of the Apostles (the *kerygma*), of which the NT writings are the deposit, and in the preaching of the Church today. All preaching has the character of witness to Christ (Acts 1.8), and it is commissioned with the promise that Christ himself confronts men in the preached word and calls them to faith. It is the risen and living Christ who is encountered in preaching and who calls forth the confession of faith.

But how is the risen and living Christ related to the figure of whom we read in the pages of the NT? Or, to rephrase the question: How does the Christ who 'suffered under Pontius Pilate' enter into the confession of faith? The question has been raised with urgency by the work of Rudolf Bultmann. Bultmann has emphasized the fact that the Christ to whom faith responds is the Christ who is proclaimed in the preaching of the Church (the 'kerygmatic Christ'), rather than the Christ of whom we read in the Gospels, but he virtually discounts the latter as irrelevant to faith. He makes frequent appeal to Paul's statement in II Cor. 5.16: 'Even though we once regarded Christ from a human point of view, we regard him thus no longer', and he interprets this to mean that the risen Christ, rather than the historical, is the subject of evangelical preaching; only the fact that he once was 'in the flesh' is important, not the details (of which in any case, Bultmann holds, practically nothing can be established with certainty). Bultmann is right in his positive emphasis: preaching is not the reporting of historical facts, which, however important, belong to the past; it is the proclamation of the living Christ who is himself present in the preached word. But he ignores the fact that the living Christ who is present in preaching is identical with the Christ who performed his finished work once for all in history for the salvation of the world, and that the *kerygma* also includes reports of these historical events. Paul, who emphasizes the actuality of the *kerygma* (I Cor. 1.21; II Cor. 5.19b–20), relates on a number of occasions to traditions which he had received (I Cor. 11.23; 15.3). And, in addition, the Church saw fit at an early date to canonize the Gospels, which, while they are testimonies of faith, at the same time preserve these traditions.

The preaching of the risen and living Christ cannot be, and was not intended to be, dissociated from the tradition of the historical. The identity of the risen Christ with the crucified was integral to the *kerygma* itself. Faith had from the first a vital interest in the historical facts.

This is not to say that faith is bound up with the validity of the historical documents, still less that faith itself can validate them. The historical documents must be studied by the critical methods of historical research. At the same time, critical study of the documents would be unscientific if it disregarded the faith which brought them into being; for that is itself an historical fact. When this is borne in mind, the possibility of a radical discordance between the faith and the history may be discounted. Indeed, when the documents are studied in full recognition of the faith, of which they are the fruits, it may then appear that details, which lack objective historical certainty, have an authenticity of another kind as testimonies to encounter with Christ, in much the same way as anecdotes about a great figure, like Abraham Lincoln, may, though apocryphal, shed light on what he meant to those who met him.

3. *The Christology of the NT.* If the christological problem be understood in the strict sense as that of the *relation* between the divine and the human in the person of Jesus Christ, the NT contains nothing that bears directly upon it. The Church itself did not become fully aware of the problem until several generations after the apostolic age, and it was not in possession of conceptual tools, with which it could approach it, until the problem of the Trinity had been settled in the fourth century. The NT provides merely the data of the problem in the form of affirmations of the presence of divinity and humanity in Christ; and these affirmations are usually made separately; rarely are they combined. The most notable exceptions are Gal. 4.4; Phil. 2.5–11 and John 1.14; for the most part the NT points to the two sides separately. (The material is very extensive, and here it can only be briefly and summarily reviewed. For a full treatment *see* O. Cullmann, *The Christology of the New Testament,* 2nd ed., 1964.)

The human side is everywhere present in the NT. Everything that is said in the NT, the Epistles as well as the Gospels, and the Fourth Gospel as well as the Synoptics, points to one who was unquestionably a man. It is an all-pervasive assumption, and seldom becomes explicit. There was no need to insist on it; for everybody knew it. Paul was only summarizing what everybody knew when he said that Christ was 'born of woman, born under the law' (the two essential marks of man in the Jewish world, Gal. 4.4); he did not need to elaborate on it. Only in some of the latest writings of the NT is there evidence of an incipient reluctance to accept the fact that Christ was human, and then it becomes a matter of dogmatic insistence (I John 4.2 f.). For the most part the NT accepts and asserts the manhood of Christ with an ingenuous freedom (e.g. I Tim. 2.5).

From the standpoint of a later stage of thought, to which the humanity has become a problem, it is possible to look back over the NT documents, especially the Gospels, and to discern in the picture of Jesus drawn there many traits of his real humanity, not merely his human birth and growth and his subjection to the conditions of creatureliness, but his hunger, his thirst, his weariness – in other words, his liability to all the ills that flesh is heir to, including the last enemy, death. It is the picture of one who was 'made like his brethren in every respect', one thing alone excepted, he was 'without sin' (Heb. 2.17; 4.15).

Jesus' chosen self-designation, 'Son of man' (it is never applied to him by others), has often been thought to be his way of affirming his humanity, but this view has now been abandoned. It is true

that in the OT 'son of man' is equivalent to man, with perhaps an added suggestion of the lowliness of man in comparison with the majesty of God (Ps. 8.4; Ezek. 2.1, etc.). But in Jewish apocalyptic literature it had acquired messianic overtones, as appears from its use in Dan. 7.13, where the one who is to be given the everlasting kingdom is described as 'like a son of man'. It is generally thought that the passage in Daniel is the source from which Jesus derived the name, and there is an evident allusion to it in his statement before the high priest (Mark 14.62) as in other sayings about his coming in glory (Mark 8.38; 13.26; Matt. 24.27, etc.). Thus the name on the lips of Jesus may have been a veiled or cryptic attestation of his messiahship, which he was so markedly reluctant to acknowledge openly (Mark 8.30, etc.). It is used also with reference to his present authority on earth (Mark 2.10, 28). The most unusual feature of Jesus' use of the name is its association of it with his humiliation and suffering (Matt. 8.20; Mark 8.31; 9.31; 10.33, etc.). These two aspects of his Son-of-manship, its present lowliness and its triumphant future manifestation, correspond to the two aspects of the kingdom of God which he proclaimed, its hidden coming in the present and its visible coming at the end. The sequence of these two stages in the mission of the Son of man was later reflected in the christological doctrine of the states of humiliation and exaltation.

The divine side is attested, indirectly for the most part, by the ascription to Christ of various titles which, in effect, make him 'equal with God' (John 5.18; Phil. 2.6). Of these 'titles of dignity' the most important are Christ, Lord, and Son of God.

(*a*) *The Christ.* The Christ or the Messiah was a title of significance primarily to Jewish Christians, since it identified its bearer as the fulfiller of the hope of Israel, the one through whom Israel's destiny in the purpose of God should be realized. The messiahship of Jesus, however, is not presented in the NT as the fulfilment of the specific messianic predictions which occur in the OT; for in his fulfilment of them the messianic expectations of the OT were radically transformed.

Messiah, which means the anointed, is the title of a king in the OT, and it indicates that the king is the charismatic agent or vice-regent of God, who alone is strictly king of his people (Judg. 8.22 f.; I Sam. 8.7). The title is applied to Saul (I Sam. 12.3), to David (I Sam. 16.6), and even to Cyrus, the Persian king, when he is used as an instrument of God's purpose for Israel (Isa. 45.1). It is given to the high priest (Lev. 4.3–5), but never to the prophet (unless this is implied in Isa. 61.1). The messianic expectation played a relatively small part in Israel while the monarchy still endured, but it become more prominent after the destruction of the kingdom and it was focused mostly on a kingly figure of the house of David who would restore the kingdom (Micah 5.2), though occasionally upon a priest (Zech. 3).

It was the kingly aspect that dominated the popular messianic expectation at the time of

Jesus and made his ostensible messianic pretension so offensive; for his outward mien was so unkingly that his claim to be the Messiah, if ever he made it, seemed downright blasphemous (Mark 14.61–64). The interpretation of Christ as the high priest of the eschatological age is made only in Hebrews (esp. 9.23–28). In the Gospels the description of Christ as a prophet appears to belong to popular judgment (e.g. Matt. 21.46) rather than to the confession of the disciples (Mark 8.28 f.); but in Peter's sermon in Solomon's portico he appears to be identified with the (eschatological) prophet of Deut. 18.15 (Acts 3.18–26; cf. 7.37), and if this is correct, a prophetic view of messiahship belongs to the earliest tradition of the apostolic preaching (Luke 24.19; John 6.14; 7.40).

The offices of prophet, priest and king explicate the meaning of the messiahship of Jesus who realizes in himself the full significance of all three. All were officers of the covenant between God and his people, and to this end they were all endowed with his Spirit (if not all anointed with oil). Thus the expected renewal of the covenant involved a reinstitution of the offices, and this took place in Jesus. Jesus as the Christ fulfils the office of the prophet because he brings – rather, because he is in his own person – the final and decisive declaration of the will of God to his people (Acts 3.26). Jesus as the Christ fulfils the office of the priest by the priestly offering of himself as sacrifice for the removal of sins and by thus laying the foundation of a new and everlasting covenant (Mark 14.58; Matt. 26.68; Heb. 13.20). Jesus as the Christ fulfils the office of the king, as by his resurrection he is raised up to reign and thereby raises his people, not only to new life in obedience to God (Rom. 6.4–14), but also to share in his royal rule (I Peter 2.9; Rev. 5.10), until he returns in glory to execute judgment (Matt. 25.34, 40; Acts 10. 42; 17.31).

(b) *The Lord* (*Kyrios*). This title was of more significance to Gentile Christians who were not familiar with the messianic hope of the OT. The title of the Christ was not, of course, repudiated, but for Gentiles it became a proper name and lost its significance as an index of the place of Christ in saving history. But the loss was not so serious, because Christ in fulfilling the hope of Israel transformed it so radically that the discontinuity was as great as, if not greater than, the continuity; and in a way the title of Lord expressed this.

The title of Lord was in common use in the Gentile world, in which, as Paul says, there were 'many lords' (I Cor. 8.5). But it was not adopted from Gentile sources. It was taken from the OT where it was used by the LXX to render the Hebrew title for God. To apply it to Christ was in effect to equate him with God, as may best be seen in Thomas's confession of faith, 'My lord and my God' (John 20.28). And the formula, 'Jesus Christ is Lord', which appears to have been the earliest recognizable confession of the Church (Phil. 2.11; I Cor. 12.3), was equivalent to an affirmation of the divinity (deity) of Christ, especially as attested by his resurrection (Rom. 10.9) and exaltation (Phil. 2.9).

(c) *Son of God*. This title is more decidedly personal than the other two, which could be understood in a functional sense, as pointing to the action of God in this man. Son of God points to the relation of this man to God in his being, and thus it speaks more emphatically than the others of the unique place which Christ holds in Christian faith. For what Christians believe is not merely that God acted in this man, even if the action was decisive and conclusive. This would leave only a difference of degree, and not of kind, between Christ and others in whom God also acted in the course of saving-history. For such men who served as instruments of God's action in history the descriptive category is 'man of God', and the paradigm is Moses (Deut. 33.1). But Christ is more than the man of God; he is the Son of God. His relation to God is more than functional, it is ontological. There is more than divine action in him; there is divine being. This is the essential difference between Christ and all who preceded him; this is the point at which his continuity with the past becomes radical discontinuity; this is what makes his coming definitive. The point is made in terms of the difference between prophets and the Son in Heb. 1.1–3, and in terms of the difference between a servant and a son elsewhere in the same Epistle (3.1–6) and in several other places (Gal. 4.1–7; Mark 12.1–11). The son stands in a much more intimate relation to the father than a servant does; the Son is 'in the bosom of the Father' (John 1.18); something of the Father's very self is in the Son.

⌐ The NT nowhere states categorically that Christ ⌐
is God. It is true that there are a number of pas- |
sages which can be – and have been – taken to
imply, if not to affirm, an identification of Christ
with God; but in some the text is uncertain (John
1.18; I Tim. 3.16), and in most the interpretation
is in doubt (John 1.1; Acts 20.28; Rom. 9.5; Titus
2.13 – in the last two passages the uncertainty
stems from the absence of punctuation from the
original manuscripts). The NT speaks of Christ
being 'equal with God' (John 5.18; Phil. 2.6),
being 'in the form of God' (Phil. 2.6) being 'one
with God' (John 10.30; 17.21), but it stops short
of saying that he 'is God'. If the title Son of God
indicates a 'unity' between Christ and God, this is |
not quite the same as an identity. ⌐

4. *The Christological Problem in the Ancient Church.* The concurrence of dogmatic and historical elements in faith in Christ made it almost inevitable that christology should become a problem. As was noted above, the Christ to whom faith responds is the Christ who is presented in the *kerygma*, and that is the exalted Christ, the living and present Lord. But this Christ cannot be divorced from the Christ who occupied a place on the stage of history, who lived and died and was raised again by God. Faith must have a kind of stereoscopic vision, so to speak, in order to bring the dimension of historical depth into the picture

of the kerygmatic Christ; it must unite the Christ who is present in the Spirit with the Christ who suffered in the flesh. The task of christology is to articulate this dual vision of faith. It has proved, however, to be an inordinately difficult problem to hold the two sides of the picture in focus. There has been a persistent tendency to focus attention on one side of the picture and allow the other to fade into obscurity.

From earliest times there has been a reluctance to accept the full implications of Christ's involvement in historical existence. A late NT writing speaks of people who refused to 'confess that Jesus Christ has come in the flesh' (I John 4.2). Their reluctance stemmed from a Greek view of historical existence ('flesh') as the sphere of corruption and unreality, participation in which would be derogatory to the divine. Moreover, if Christ came to deliver us from the world of flesh, these people argued, his involvement in it can only have been apparent, not real. They received the name of *Docetists* (from the Greek word, *dokein*, to appear), because, while they were unable to deny the historical side of the picture altogether, they reduced it to dissimulation by an ideal being.

Docetism is the simplest solution of the christological problem. Although it was rejected dogmatically, the motive behind it is persistent and has reasserted itself in various ways. Docetism tends to cling to the Christ of popular belief, who is often a divine being walking the earth in disguise. His humanity is not indeed denied, but divinized in such a way as to remove him from real contact with our humanity. Popular piety has found it difficult to take the flesh of Christ seriously; it tends to construe the incarnation as a theophany.

If Docetism reflects the effect of Hellenistic thinking on christology, *Ebionitism* reflects that of Jewish. The origin of the name is doubtful, but it probably comes from a Hebrew word meaning 'the poor' (*cf.* Rom. 15.26 'the poor among the saints at Jerusalem'). The Ebionites, who, originating east of the Jordan and surviving through the earlier centuries of the Christian era, rejected the Pauline interpretation of the Gospel and practised strict obedience to the Law of Moses, held firm to the authentic manhood of Christ, and it is the divinity that they whittled away. They did not deny it, but they construed it as a special dignity which was conferred upon him in virtue of his moral and religious pre-eminence – some said it was the Christ who descended on Jesus at his baptism. The Ebionite conception was that of a deified man.

Both Docetism and Ebionitism presupposed a view of the transcendence of God, derived in the one case from Platonism and in the other from tendencies in late Jewish thought, which virtually set up an antithesis between God and the world of men and precluded any union between them except at the cost of some dilution of either the human or the divine. The Church made it difficult for itself to overcome this prejudice because in its first efforts to articulate the meaning of its faith in

Christ it had recourse to the concept of the Logos. The concept of the Logos (reason or word), which was widely current in the popular thought of the time, has roots in both Platonic and Stoic philosophies, and it carried a variety of meanings. To the philosophically minded it connoted the divine reason which was immanent in the cosmos and in the mind of man; to the more religiously minded it signified the creative agency or power which mediated between a wholly transcendent God and the world of matter. In the latter sense it was introduced into religious thought by Philo of Alexandria. It was first used in a Christian context in the prologue to the Fourth Gospel, not, however, to express an indirect divine immanence but a direct and personal divine incarnation: 'The Word (Logos) became flesh' (John 1.14). The apologists of the second century made extensive use of the concept in commending the Christian faith to the more cultured among their contemporaries, but they stressed the immanentist rather than the incarnational sense and so tended to foster a conception of Christ as a being in whom the divine was immanent in a superlative degree but who was essentially less than God. This was the substance of the Arian heresy, in which Christ was a secondary divine but created being, intermediate between God and the world, and therefore inferior to God. In rejecting Arianism, the Church, which was taught by Athanasius to approach the christological problem from a soteriological perspective, replaced the concept of the Logos with that of the Son and declared that the Son, while distinct from the Father, is *eternally begotten* of him and *homo-ousios* ('the same in being') with him.

The christological problem in the stricter sense was raised when the question was asked how this eternal Son, who was the same in being with the Father, could at the same time be truly man. To Apollinaris of Laodicea it seemed impossible that the humanity of Christ should remain essentially the same as that of all other men if the divine Logos had become the directing principle of his human life. According to the then current anthropology, the directing principle in man is the *nous* (mind). Thus it is the *nous* that leads man into sin. Now if Christ had assumed a human *nous*, Apollinaris thought, he could not have saved us from sin. Apollinaris therefore advanced the view that in the incarnate Christ the place of the human *nous* was occupied by the divine Logos. The incarnate Christ was not then fully man like us, but at best – if we take the trichotomous view of man as composed of body, soul and *nous*, which Apollinaris may be presumed to have held – two-thirds man.

Apollinaris's christology presupposed a peculiar view of salvation, and it was chiefly on this score that his ingenious theory was rejected by the Church. If it seemed to him that the presence of a human mind in Christ would disqualify him from being our Saviour at the point where our sinfulness has its source, most others saw the matter in a different light; to them the presence of a human mind in Christ was the essential condition of his being our Saviour at this point. Gregory of Nazianzus expressed the orthodox attitude succinctly: 'What he did not assume he did not heal' (Epistle 101).

The crucial period in the development of christology in the ancient Church extended from the middle years of the fourth century to the middle years of the fifth, and it was dominated by two opposing strains of thought which emanated from the rival schools of Antioch and Alexandria. The Antiochenes were devoted to biblical exegesis (they were pioneers in this field) rather than to abstract theological thought, and they were concerned for the integrity of the human nature of Jesus, as they read of him in the Gospels. They did not deny the divine, but they so stressed the completeness and integrity of both natures as to intensify the question, which Apollinaris had asked, how two complete entities like two natures could ever be made one. They did not speak of a union(*henosis*) of the two natures, but preferred to call it a combination (*sunapheia*); and they conceived of this so loosely that sometimes they gave the impression they were thinking not only of two natures existing side by side but even of two Sons.

The Alexandrian school, the chief spokesman of which was Cyril, approached the problem from a different standpoint. The background of it was the soteriological thought of Athanasius, in which salvation was conceived in a cultic or sacral sense as the deification of humanity by the communication of divine substance to it. The focus was therefore on the human nature as a substance rather than an agency, and the tendency was, while insisting on its integrity, to assign it a somewhat passive or receptive role in relation to the divine, and even to allow for a communication of the properties of the divine nature to the human (*communicatio idiomatum*). Cyril often spoke of the union of the two natures, somewhat misleadingly, as a 'natural union', and for this and other unguarded phrases his teaching was thought by his opponents to exhibit a dangerous leaning toward monophysitism, that is, the idea that the union of the two natures resulted in a single nature which is divine.

The Alexandrian christology corresponds to the soteriology which lies behind it. Man's predicament is viewed essentially rather than existentially, and his salvation is construed as the impartation of a divine essence which elevates him above the human. The Alexandrian christology tends to become a doctrine of essences.

The decisive encounter between the rival schools occurred when Nestorius, the patriarch of Constantinople and a devoted Antiochene, delivered an attack on the practice of ascribing to the Virgin the title *theotokos* (literally, 'who gave birth to God'). The title, he objected, is improper; for God is not born. What Mary bore was the man who was the bearer or 'temple' of the Godhead. The Antiochenes were fond of talking in this way of Christ as a man in whom God was pleased to dwell as in a temple. They denied a union of natures between the human and the divine, holding such to be impossible, and spoke instead of a union of good pleasure (*cf.* Matt. 3.17). For this they were taken by their opponents to be denying any real union between the two natures and to be teaching a 'duality of Sons': the son who was born of Mary and the Son who is eternally begotten of the Father. Nestorius was charged with this teaching – unjustly, it now appears, in the light of his own *apologia* which came to light only in this century. He was bitterly attacked by Cyril, who, with the aid of Caelestin, bishop of Rome, secured his excommunication and deposition at the Council of Ephesus in 431. The immediate controversy blew over, and a formula of reunion, which cleverly blended the Antiochene position on the duality of the natures with the Alexandrian emphasis on the reality of their union was accepted by Cyril in 433.

Controversy flared up afresh, however, in 448, four years after Cyril's death, when the Alexandrian position was reasserted in an extreme form by Eutyches, who, though he was an archimandrite of Constantinople, was a devoted follower of Cyril. He advanced the view that there were two natures before the incarnation, but after the incarnation one. He was condemned at a Synod at Constantinople, then cleared at the 'Robber-Synod' at Ephesus in 449, and no more is heard of him after that. But in the meantime he had written to Leo, bishop of Rome, who responded in the famous *Tome* (449).

There is little that is original about Leo's christology. It reflects the best thinking of the West, which had already succeeded in large measure in resolving the issues that divided the East. It accepts the Antiochene presupposition of a virtual ontological incongruity between the two natures, and, while affirming their union in the person of the God-man, allows each to retain its integrity and to exercise its characteristic properties; they co-exist in a kind of alternating operation within the unity of the person, who concerts them so effectively that, though there is no real interchange between them, the operation of one may be ascribed to the title of the other. In effect, Leo asserts a functional union.

The controversy was settled at the Council of Chalcedon in 451, which adopted the following 'Definition', that is, authoritative interpretation of the Nicene (or Niceno-Constantinopolitan) Creed:

Following therefore the holy Fathers, we confess one and the same our Lord Jesus Christ, and we all teach harmoniously [that he is] the same perfect in Godhead, the same perfect in manhood, truly God and truly man, the same of a reasonable soul and body; consubstantial with the Father in Godhead, and the same consubstantial with us in manhood, like us in all things except sin; begotten before ages of the Father in Godhead, the same in the last days for us and for our salvation [born] of Mary the virgin *theotokos* in manhood, one and the same

Christ, Son, Lord, unique; acknowledged in two natures without confusion, without change, without division, without separation – the difference of the natures being by no means taken away because of the union, but rather the distinctive character of each nature being preserved, and [each] combining in one Person and *hypostasis* – not divided or separated into two Persons, but one and the same Son and only-begotten God, Word, Lord Jesus Christ; as the prophets of old and the Lord Jesus Christ himself taught us about him, and the symbol of the Fathers has handed down to us' (translation according to E. R. Hardy, ed., *Christology of the Later Fathers*, 1954, p. 373).

The Chalcedonian Definition cannot be called a 'solution' of the christological problem, if by solution is meant an answer to the question *how* the two natures are united. It endorses the position, which was so important to the Antiochenes, that we must not speak of the union of the two natures as a 'natural union', as if the ground or possibility of unification lay in the natures themselves; the unifying factor is the person or subsistence. But how the union takes place – to this the Definition has nothing to offer but the four negative adverbs.

The Chalcedonian formula satisfied neither side completely. The Nestorians disliked it because in their eyes a hypostatic, or personal, union was as good as a natural union, the Monophysites disliked it because to them a hypostatic union was no substitute for a natural union. (They called those who believed in the two natures in the one person of Christ Dyophysites.) Monophysitism proved very stubborn, particularly in Egypt, and yielded neither to political persuasion nor the suggested replacement of the Chalcedonian Definition by a compromise formula, the Henoticon (482), in which the unity of the person was reaffirmed in such a way as virtually to obliterate the distinction of the natures.

Since it was generally agreed that the term 'person' refers to the individual entity and 'nature' to the universal, and that, in accordance with the prevailing Aristotelianism, a universal could exist only in individuation, the formula 'two natures in one person' appeared to postulate a logical impossibility. The formula was retrieved when Leontius of Byzantium propounded the theory that the human nature of Christ had no hypostasis or personal centre of its own (*anhypostasia*) and achieved personalization only in the Logos (*Enhypostasia*). This ingenious theory received official endorsement at the Second Council of Constantinople in 553.

Difficulties were encountered when psychological questions were asked regarding this metaphysically constructed figure. If the person be taken as the subject of experience, it was difficult to resist the inference that the Logos, or the second person of the Trinity, who is equal to God, was the subject of the suffering. This conflicted with the traditional notion of the impassibility of God.

The idea of the divine suffering was accepted in the East, but rejected in the West. A similar problem arose when it was asked whether there was one 'operation' or 'will' in the incarnate Christ, or two. An attempt to conciliate the Monophysites by adopting the formula, 'one divine-human operation' (*Monothelitism*), which had been devised by Sergius of Constantinople, met with stubborn resistance elsewhere, and eventually the position that 'there are two natural operations in him and two wills', the human being always subject to the divine (*Dyotheletism*) was confirmed at the Third Council of Constantinople in 681.

The emergence of these residual questions points to the limitations of the Chalcedonian Definition. If the Definition has been accepted in most of Christendom as the standard of christological orthodoxy ever since, it is not because it put an end to thinking on the christological problem but rather because it indicates how such thinking should begin. For this reason it has often been held up as a good example of the true function of dogma, which is not to prescribe what must be believed, but to define the conditions which must be observed when faith seeks to understand itself, if it is not to lose itself in the course of the quest.

The Chalcedonian Definition has been subjected to much criticism by modern theologians, who complain that the terms it employs are no longer usable. It is true that the terms which are rendered 'nature' and 'person' do not coincide in meaning with their modern English equivalents, but it is doubtful if the Fathers at Chalcedon thought the terms they used were adequate to express the reality of God in Christ. The incarnation is a mystery that defies conceptualization. It was the attempt to express the inexpressible that drove them to paradox. The language of the Definition, however, is not an irresponsible play with paradoxes; it is not an attempt to translate the mystery into intelligible speech. Rather, as it has been said, the Definition is an attempt to bring human speech into the presence of the mystery (O. Weber).

A more specific and frequently expressed objection to the Chalcedonian christology is that it is too static. It fails to give expression to the historical and dynamic aspect of the reality of which it seeks to give account. It suggests that the quest for the self-understanding of faith in Christ can be satisfied by a statement concerning the composition of his person, with almost no reference to the course of his mission. It lends countenance to the impression often given by the Greek Fathers of the ancient Church, that they thought of salvation as something which Christ accomplished essentially by his incarnation, rather than by his atoning death. It ignores a whole dimension of the christological inquiry; for an adequate answer cannot be given to the question: Who is Jesus Christ? without taking into account the history in which he is who he is. In other words, faith's understanding of Jesus Christ cannot be expressed in concepts of being only; it requires also dynamic-historical concepts.

5. *Christology at the Reformation*. The Reformers were content with the classical christology which they had inherited through mediaeval scholasticism. They had no quarrel with the dogma, and no desire to change it. The only change that is discernible is the replacement of the scholastic with a more existential stance – in reality, a reinstatement of the original and authentic stance of the christological inquiry, which is that of encounter with the living Christ as he encounters us in preaching. That is why Luther favoured the method of beginning with the human Christ, because this is where we receive him and the gifts he brings us. Luther was opposed to the kind of theology that presumed to climb up to heaven and scrutinize the divine majesty; he called this a 'theology of glory', and he opposed to it a 'theology of the cross' which was content to begin where God comes to meet us in the lowliness of the humanity of Christ. It is for the same reason that Melanchthon was disposed, if only for a time, to abandon the christological inquiry altogether and focus the attention of faith on the 'benefits of Christ'.

It was in the context of their controversies about the Lord's Supper that the christological question became an acute one for the Reformers. The controversy arose over the manner of Christ's presence in the Supper – all parties were agreed on the *fact* of his presence, the question that divided them was the *how*. This question could not be answered without stirring up subtle and complex christological problems.

Luther insisted on the 'real presence' of the body and blood of Christ in the bread and wine of the Lord's Supper. Body and blood belong to human nature, and human nature, as we know it in ourselves, is subject to spatial circumscription. The body and blood of Christ cannot, therefore, be present on a thousand altars simultaneously, if his human nature is under that same limitation. It must possess the power of ubiquity, whether this be exercised by an act of will at the Lord's Supper only (*Multivolipresence*), as some followers of Melanchthon taught, or whether it be held as a permanent endowment, as Luther himself taught.

Luther invoked the ancient doctrine of the *communicatio idiomatum* to support his contention that the glorified body of Christ participates in the divine attribute of ubiquity or omnipresence, and can therefore be really present wherever the Lord's Supper is observed. Similarly he argued that, when the Creed says of Christ that 'he sitteth at the right hand of God', this does not mean that he is confined to one location in space; for 'the right hand of God is everywhere'.

To Zwingli, who was his chief opponent in the controversy, Luther's christology exhibited a dangerous monophysite tendency. Zwingli allowed the *communicatio idiomatum* only as a loose manner of speaking. He was concerned to maintain the distinction between the human nature and the divine, and he insisted that the human nature, even in its glorified state, retains the essential characteristics of humanity and resides in heaven at a specific location. It is not therefore 'really' present in the Lord's Supper, but only as a subject of recollection. The sharpness of the distinction he drew between the historical Christ and the glorified gave his christology a Nestorian ring, which Luther did not fail to notice.

Calvin differed from both Luther and Zwingli in that he sought the answer to the question concerning the manner of Christ's presence in the Lord's Supper, not in christology, but in the work of the Holy Spirit. It is not then a palpable, objective presence, nor is it merely a subjective presence. It is a spiritual presence, and as such it is the presence of the whole Christ with all his benefits.

In his christology Calvin accepted the *communicatio idiomatum*, but in a dynamic and actual sense; he related it wholly to the mediatorial office of Christ, but not to his person as such. He denied that the divine attribute of omnipresence could be imparted to the human body of Christ; for this would mean that an infinite entity could be contained in a finite vessel, and such a thought is more than paradoxical, it is logically impossible (*finitum non capax infiniti*). Calvin accordingly revived the teaching of several of the ancient fathers that, when the divine Logos became incarnate in the human Jesus, he did not relinquish the divine attribute of omnipresence but continued to fill the whole universe, and thus to be *outside* as well as inside the humanity he had assumed (*Extra Calvinisticum*).

The difficulty in all these constructions points to the inadequacy of the Chalcedonian conceptuality to compass the entire range of the mystery of Christ; for there is an historical dimension to the mystery which cannot be grasped in ontological concepts and categories. It is here that the Reformation made its most distinctive contribution to christology by introducing the doctrine of the two states of Christ, the state of humiliation and the state of exaltation. The doctrine appears to have been originated by Martin Chemnitz, and it was quickly accepted and developed in both Lutheran and Reformed orthodoxy.

The doctrine of the two states was intended to give fuller recognition to the dynamic or historical aspect of the fact of Christ. It was not meant to displace the doctrine of the two natures, but to supplement it in the same way as the side elevation of a building supplements the front elevation. Or, to change the figure slightly, the two-natures christology presents the fact of Christ in cross-section; but the fact of Christ is also a history, or a process, and it is this aspect the doctrine of the two states sought to bring out.

The doctrine of the two states can also be regarded as an attempted answer to a question which the classical christology of the two natures leaves unclear: Who is the subject about whom these statements are made? Is it Jesus of Nazareth who appeared in Palestine during the reign of the Emperor Tiberias and was crucified under Pontius Pilate? Is it the risen and exalted Christ who is seated at the right hand of God? Is it the living Lord who is present with his faithful people in the preaching of the word and the administration of the Lord's Supper? The question lies behind the question which has been raised by Bultmann and is much discussed today concerning the relation of the kerygmatic Christ to the historical Jesus. (*See below,* 6. (*e*) and cf. Wolfhart Pannenberg, *Jesus God and Man,* 1968, §1, 1.) (A further contribution of the Reformation to christology was the doctrine of the three offices of Christ as prophet, priest and king, which was first elaborated by Calvin and which was subsequently adopted in Lutheran and Roman Catholic theology.)

The doctrine finds its main biblical support in Phil. 2.5–11 (perhaps a fragment from an early credal hymn), in which the meaning of Christ for faith is presented in terms of a sequence of two states (or three, if the initial state of equality with God be taken into account). Here Christ is advanced to the dignity and name of Lord by passing through a state of humiliation into a state of exaltation, and the confession that he is Lord is the response of faith to this sequence. Christology is presented as a movement which, if traced in a diagram, would appear as a parabola (E. Brunner).

The doctrine of the two states corresponds much more closely to the manner in which the NT speaks of Christ. The classical christology relies heavily on nouns – and highly abstract nouns at that; but the NT uses mostly verbs (as the Apostles' Creed does also). The doctrine of the two states focuses attention on the 'verbal' aspect of christology.

The verbs, however, bring their own problems, which can be just as intractable as those of the nouns, and which, in fact merge into them. The most persistent problem concerns the transition from the initial state of equality with God to the state of humiliation. Discussion has centred on the meaning of the phrase in Phil..2.7: *heauton ekenosen* (literally, 'he emptied himself').

Two questions have been asked about it: (1) Who is the subject of the statement? Is it the pre-existent divine Son or Logos? Or is it the God-man incarnate? (2) What is the nature of the *kenosis* or self-emptying? Does it connote an abdication or renunciation of divinity or its attributes? Can a real humanity be ascribed to Christ without something of the sort? But how can there be an abdication of divinity if divinity is, by definition, immutable?

It is this last question that dominated men's minds when the problem first engaged serious attention. It was taken for granted that the incarnate God-man, who was assumed to be the subject of the *kenosis,* did not really divest himself of the attributes of divinity, such a thing being considered impossible, but, the suggestion was, he voluntarily renounced the use of them during his life on earth, to resume them only at his exaltation to the right hand of God. The *kenosis* might thus be construed, not as a real self-emptying, but rather as concealment (*krupsis*). This was the

subject of a lengthy controversy among Lutherans in Germany in the seventeenth century.

The *kenosis* idea received a new interpretation in the nineteenth century, when a number of theologians, notably Thomasius in Germany and Bishop Gore in England, propounded the view that the subject of the *kenosis* is the pre-existent divine Son or Logos, and the act of *kenosis* virtually coincides with the incarnation as such: the assumption of humanity by the eternal Son, it was held, involved the renunciation of divinity, or at least of the relative attributes of divinity (omnipotence, omnipresence, omniscience and the like).

The kenoticism of the nineteenth century was more or less contemporaneous with the quickening of interest in the historical Jesus, and it was inspired in part by a desire to give full recognition to the human traits which were found in him and which tended to be blurred when he was viewed through the glass of the classical christology. A question which figured largely in the discussion was the extent of the knowledge of Jesus. Was he omniscient, or was his knowledge limited like that of all other men? It is evident from the Gospels that Jesus was not only ignorant of specific matters (such as the date of the final consummation, Mark 13.32), but that he shared the general outlook and presuppositions of his contemporaries (such as the attribution of sickness to demon-possession). Had he been in possession of all knowledge of all things in heaven and earth, he would not have been human. Ignorance, or limited knowledge, is a mark of authentic humanity. If then the human Jesus is the divine Son of God incarnate, there seems to be no resisting the conclusion that when he assumed humanity he laid aside the divine attribute of omniscience.

The kenotic christology was a sincere and bold attempt to construct a christology which would be consonant with the figure portrayed in the Gospels. There Jesus is portrayed as one who is subject to all the essential limitations of humanity, and who, if he is exceptional, is humanly exceptional – even the miracles, which are ascribed to the divine nature in Leo's *Tome,* and which are popularly understood as demonstrations of divinity, are usually presented in the Gospels as acts of faith on the part of Jesus, and thus, in principle, open to every one (*cf.* Mark 9.14–29).

Nevertheless, the kenotic christology contains difficulties which have generally been considered insuperable. The abstract principle of the immutability of the divine is not now insisted upon, since it is now recognized that the principle is derived from Greek philosophical thought rather than the biblical revelation. Moreover, the classical interpretation of the incarnation as the 'assumption of humanity' by the divine Logos might be viewed as implying a divine mutation. Even so, however, it studiously avoids the conception of a mutation *in* or *of* the divine, and this is what kenoticism seems to do. Kenoticism interprets the incarnation as the transformation of God into man, or the exchange of divinity for humanity, partial or complete. But can God cease to be God?

Or can he continue to be God in the incarnate Christ and at the same time relinquish some of his attributes? Is the Godhead reducible, or divisible?

The manifest difficulties of the kenotic christology have exposed it to severe criticism, and even contempt; it has been called the '*kenosis* of understanding'. But this is hardly fair. The kenotic christology is a serious attempt to grapple with a genuine problem, and however unsatisfactory the solutions it has proposed may be, the problem remains. The incarnation unquestionably involves an element of *kenosis*, and christological thought must continue to strive after its meaning.

6. *Current Trends in Christology.* Much thought has been devoted to the christological problem in the present century, and an adequate survey is far beyond the scope of this article. Mention will be made of only a few of what appear to be the more significant developments, those which have some elements of novelty about them (though none is perhaps completely new), and which either suggest some new and constructive approach to the problem, or call attention to some hitherto neglected aspect of it.

(*a*) *The Trinitarian Christology of Karl Barth.* Barth's christology offers, in effect, a happy escape from the dilemma posed by kenoticism (which is not to suggest that this is how Barth would wish it to be understood). How can true God become true man, given the basic principle of the immutability of the divine? Barth's answer is to repudiate the assumption which has underlain the application of this principle from (at least) the time of Theodore of Mopsuestia down to the earlier phase of his (Barth's) own theological thought, namely, that God is 'wholly other' than man and (ontologically) incompatible with him, and to reinstate in theology the idea which Hegel thought he had derived from theology, namely, that there is a basic unity between God and man and that the purpose of God is the healing of the estrangement which has disrupted it.

Barth presents his thesis in terms of a revised, and indeed revolutionary, interpretation of the doctrine of the Trinity. He sees in the doctrine of Trinity an expression of the fact that the unity of God embraces an inner self-relatedness. In the language of Leonard Hodgson, it is not a unity of the mathematical type, which excludes complexity, but of the organic, which includes it. Thus, while God is eternally one in himself, he is eternally related to himself; he is not merely an I, a solitary, undifferentiated monad, but an I-Thou. The self-other relationship is not, therefore, something new, which he experiences only at the creation of the world, but an outward expression of the inner structure of his own being. But Barth goes further than this. He introduces the new note that the relation within the unity of God is not one of equality or reciprocity, but a relation of first and second, upper and lower, superiority and subordination, majesty and humility, authority and obedience – and all this without prejudice to *homoousia* of classical trinitarianism. It follows

then that the incarnation does not mean the transmutation of God into something other than God; it means 'that God himself becomes a man amongst men in his mode of being as the One who is obedient in humility' (*Church Dogmatics,* IV: *The Doctrine of Reconciliation,* 1, p. 203).

Barth develops his thesis by taking the doctrine of the two states as the framework of his christology and adapting the doctrine of the two natures to it, thus reversing the order which has been customary in Protestant theology. He strongly emphasizes the fact that the reality of Jesus Christ, which it is the task of christology to interpret, is an historical reality, an event, and that, as such, it cannot be captured in the static categories of the two-natures christology. He does not, however, interpret the doctrine of the two states in the traditional way as two successive phases (with all the difficulties to which that gives rise, as has been shown above); he treats them as 'two sides or directions or forms of that which took place in Jesus Christ for the reconciliation of man with God' (*ibid.,* p. 133). He relates them dialectically rather than historically. The humiliation refers to that aspect of Christ in which, as true God, he becomes man and performs his priestly work of atonement, and the exaltation to that in which, as true man, he is raised up and converts man to God, in this performing his kingly work; as true God and true man, he is the witness to the reality of reconciliation in himself and the pledge of its fulfilment in us, and this is his prophetic work.

With this Barth has achieved a brilliant synthesis of the traditional elements of christological doctrine. Brilliant as it is, however, it may be said to follow, with an almost Euclidean necessity from the initial axiom of his thought, namely, the 'humanity of God'. The question is whether this axiom is an implicate of revelation, as Barth claims, or whether it is a speculative idea which is postulated for the purpose of achieving a systematic doctrinal unity, and which is destructive of the very history which it pretends to undergird.

(*b*) *The Paradox Christology of D. M. Baillie.* In his beautiful book, *God was in Christ,* D. M. Baillie developed the thesis that the appropriate conceptual form for the expression of the christological mystery is paradox. To speak of the union of true God and true man in Jesus Christ is to utter a paradox, and the element of paradox can never be eliminated from it without losing the incarnation.

In a sense there is nothing new or original about this. It has been recognized from the first that the christological dogma is paradoxical – the Chalcedonian Definition is a veritable maze of paradoxes – and throughout history there are several who have been particularly sensitive to this – Tertullian, Luther, Kierkegaard. What is novel in Baillie's thesis is the demonstration that the christological paradox does not stand alone, but rather belongs to a constellation of paradoxes which we encounter at various points in the faith. He cites the paradox of creation, which asserts that all things are created *out of nothing,* a position at variance with the world of our experience, in which all things originate out of existing antecedents – and that includes ourselves, who are both created and procreated. There is the paradox of providence, which states that all events stem from first and second, or divine and creaturely, causalities. And above all there is the paradox of grace, which expresses the Christian conviction that everything good we do is the work of God in us, and not our own ('Not I, but the grace of God'). Baillie then suggests 'that this paradox of grace points the way more clearly and makes a better approach than anything else in our experience to the mystery of the incarnation itself; that this paradox in its fragmentary form in our own Christian lives is a reflection of that perfect union of God and man in the incarnation on which our whole Christian life depends, and may therefore be our best clue to the understanding of it . . . If the paradox is a reality in our poor imperfect lives at all, so far as there is any good in them, does not the same or a similar paradox, taken at the perfect and absolute pitch, appear the mystery of the incarnation?' (ibid., pp. 117 f.).

Baillie's thesis has the merit of restoring what is held by many to be the true intent of christological inquiry (as it is illustrated in the Chalcedonian dogma), which is to preserve the mystery of the incarnation, not to solve the problem. The question is whether the concept of paradox is best suited to serve this purpose. A paradox (from the Greek words, para dokein, to appear contrary) means an apparent contradiction. There is no logical distinction between a paradox and a real contradiction; they can be distinguished only by a judgment of fact. One man's paradox is another man's contradiction. It is difficult, therefore, to see what is achieved by the introduction of the concept. It proves nothing – and Baillie would not have claimed that it did. But the form of the argument, consisting as it does in the marshalling of parallels or analogies to the paradox of the incarnation, suggests an apologetic motive, reminiscent of that which inspired Butler's Analogy of Religion (1736). Granted that the Christian faith is full of paradoxes, as Baillie claimed, that does not prove that the particular paradox, with which he was concerned, is not a contradiction.

A more serious objection to Baillie's argument is that in using the Christian experience of grace as a clue to the christological paradox he reverses the priorities. In other words, when he equates the manner (not the degree) of the presence of God in Christ with that of his presence in other men, Baillie undermines the uniqueness of Christ. In the ancient Church there were some among the Antiochenes who held that the union of God with Christ was a moral union, and that it differed only in degree from his union with the saints. But the Church resisted any construction which reduced the difference between Christ and the saints to one of degree, and insisted that the union of God and Christ be expressed in terms of being rather than of disposition or action. God acts in the saints; but 'God was in Christ' (II Cor. 5.19). There is an essential difference between Christ and the rest of us, which is inevitably obscured if he and we are brought under the same concept of grace. We are made sons of God by the grace of adoption, but we receive this grace through him who is the Son of God by nature (John 1.12). We are recipients of grace; he is the donor or mediator of grace (John 1.17).

(c) Christology and Evolutionary Thought. A number of contemporary theologians have seen in the philosophy of process an aid towards christological restatement. The two who have gone furthest in this direction are L. S. Thornton in The Incarnate Lord (1928) and W. N. Pittenger in The Word Incarnate (1959). Although there is an appearance of novelty about this approach, the underlying theological motive is an ancient one. It is a revival of the endeavour, which first found expression in Irenaeus, to interpret the incarnation as the crown and consummation of God's on-going work in creation and so to achieve a closer integration between creation and redemption. The endeavour failed in the ancient Church for lack of an appropriate philosophical framework. The framework of the classical christology was the hierarchical cosmos of Hellenistic philosophy. It made sense to construe christology as an arrangement of substances in the framework of a reality conceived as a structure with a vertical axis. This framework is now obsolete. We no longer think of reality as a cosmos in which the higher is above the lower, but as a process in which the new emerges from the old. The new view of reality, which was powerfully reinforced by the discovery of evolution in the nineteenth century, has been articulated in the philosophy of emergent evolution (C. Lloyd Morgan), and, in a more abstract form, in Whitehead's philosophy of process. Reality is viewed as a process continually moving on to new and higher levels of complexity and value: 'From matter up through life to mind and on to spirit or apprehension of value, there is a continuity of process; yet on the other hand, each higher level is very much more than the mere "resultant" of that which has gone before. Each higher level "emerges" with a genuine element of novelty about it' (Pittenger, op. cit., p. 151).

Now, while philosophers may seek to account for the process in terms of a drive or nisus immanent in it, theologians, who see reality as God's creation, naturally incline to think of a driver rather than a drive, and to ascribe the process to the activity of divine purpose. Pittenger invokes the ancient doctrine of the Logos, which he describes as 'the self-expressive principle of God at work in the whole creation'. The incarnation of God in Christ is then the culmination of the process. In Thornton's view, it does not simply emerge from the process, but represents rather a new act of creation, a new divine intervention in the process. Pittenger holds that in thus construing the incarnation as a new divine act ab extra Thornton has broken the schema of his thought and has imperilled the true humanity of Christ; he himself prefers to think of Christ, not as a 'divine intruder' in humanity, but rather as one who emerges from humanity and 'in whom God actualized in a living human personality the potential God-man relationship which is the divinely intended truth about every man', and so to interpret christology, not as a union of two natures, but as 'the coincidence in him of the divine Self-expression (and thus the Word or *Logos* of God humanwise) and free human response in self-surrender and faith and dedicated love (and thus the limit of human action in its supreme form) . . . he is the fulfilment of man's capacity for God; but first he is the fulfilment of God's purpose in man' (*ibid.*, p. 285).

Interest in this aspect of christology has also been stimulated in Roman Catholic thought by the posthumous publication of the writings of Pierre Teilhard de Chardin, who crowned his scientific investigation of human origins with a vision of the whole cosmic process as one of continuous complexification, converging on the 'Omega point', which coincides with the doctrine of Christ as the centre of the final unification of the cosmos (Col. 1.20; Eph. 1.10). In an essay on christology within an evolutionary world-view Karl Rahner has presented a view of Christ as the appearance in history of one who genuinely emerges from it and who, as at the same time the absolute self-impartation of God, inaugurates in a definitive and irrevocable way the ultimate phase in the process of self-transcendence, which comes to its decisive break-through in man, namely, the self-transcendence of spirit into the life of God.

Cosmic christology (if this line of thought may be so designated for brevity's sake) points to a genuine aspect of the problem. The continuity of the incarnation with God's previous action in the world has been important to Christian faith from the beginning; it is the theme of the prologue to the Fourth Gospel, and other passages, like Heb. 1.1–3. But when the continuity is looked for in the process of evolution, there is a danger that the purposive activity of God in his creation will be too unequivocally identified with it, and that, even when room is left for the emergence of novelty, the radically re-creative aspect of the work of God in Christ, will not be recognized. Although, as Rahner points out, the Scotist view that the incarnation was part of God's purpose for the fulfilment of his creation from the beginning, and was not made necessary only by the fall, has not been declared heretical, it does tend to diminish the gravity of evil (Teilhard has often been criticized for a defective view of evil). There is a discordance between the divine purpose and the life of man, and the presence of the Logos in the world is like a light shining in darkness (John 1.5). So if there is continuity between creation and incarnation, there is also discontinuity. Christ does emerge from the process; as the son of Mary he is continuous with the whole race of mankind from Adam (Luke 3.23–38). But he is also the second Adam, a new divine creation, a new be-

ginning of mankind (Col. 1.18), whom God inserts into the process (and to some this is the significance of the virgin birth). He is the fulfilment of man; he is also the Saviour and Judge of man.

(*d*) *Christology and Psychology.* Early attempts to explore the psychology of the incarnate Christ in the period following Chalcedon were rendered abortive by the dominance of ontological categories in christology. The spectacular developments which have occurred in the study of psychology during the present century have raised the question whether a more fruitful and constructive approach is possible with the tools that are now at our disposal. A first suggestion has been offered by W. R. Matthews in his essay, *The Problem of Christ in the Twentieth Century* (1950).

An earlier attempt to transpose christology from an ontological to a psychological key was made by Schleiermacher (to whom Matthews pays due tribute). Schleiermacher equated the divinity of Christ with his superlative 'God-consciousness'. 'God-consciousness' is common to all men, and so the possession of it marks Christ as a true man; but his 'God-consciousness' was so absolutely powerful and unbroken as to constitute 'a veritable being of God in him'.

In treating consciousness as the distinctive quality of personality, Schleiermacher was still standing in the Cartesian tradition, although his concept of consciousness had romantic and mystical overtones which are absent from the rationalism of Descartes' *res cogitans.* But what the psychology of the twentieth century has brought to light is that consciousness is only like the exposed part of the iceberg and beneath it lie the hidden depths of the unconscious, by which much of our behaviour is influenced.

Matthews thinks that the idea of the unconscious – and especially C. G. Jung's idea of the racial unconscious – may assist our understanding of the humanity of Christ (when we think of it as experience rather than as 'nature'). How did Christ participate in the common experience of humanity? 'If . . . the hypothesis of the racial unconscious is confirmed by psychological investigation, we shall have a strong suggestion on empirical evidence that our normal way of thinking about humanity is too individualistic and that our separateness is true only on the level of consciousness, while, below the level, we are linked together. Humanity may, after all, be more than an abstract general term. If we all partake in the same racial unconscious, a new meaning lights up the phrase 'in Adam all die' (*ibid.*, p. 50). Matthews suggests that the idea of the *libido* as the basic and comprehensive drive in personal life may help us to unravel the very complex question of the relation of Christ to sin, if we think of the *libido* as morally neutral, and not itself sinful, although it is infected by sin and furnishes the occasion for sin. It forms the substratum of a genuine human experience in Jesus as in other men; but, whereas it drives all other men into sin, for him it provided the material on which he learned obedience.

Matthews also suggests that the concept of pattern, as it has been developed by modern psychology, may help us to understand the divinity of Christ. It has always been notoriously difficult to conceive how two substances could be united, especially two substances with such widely differing properties as divine nature and human nature, but if we think of persons as moving patterns of behaviour events (primarily of willed actions), identity of pattern can be exhibited on widely different scales, and thus 'there is no contradiction or absurdity in holding that the moving pattern of the will of God could be also the moving pattern of the behaviour events which constitute the temporal and historical aspects of a human life'. A life of which this was true would be 'God manifest in the flesh'. So, when Jesus said, 'My meat is to do the will of him that sent me and to finish his work . . . ' 'that would be something more than a forcible metaphor; it would be an almost exact statement of fact. The pattern of the Father's will, on this hypothesis, is the essential reality of the temporal personality of the Son. It is his life; without it, or departing from it, he would cease to be himself (*ibid.*, pp. 70–71).

Attractive though they sound, it is doubtful if these suggestions do more than set ancient problems in a new light. The relation of temptation to sin has always been a difficult problem, but it is not apparent that the concept of the *libido* contributes materially to its solution, or, indeed, that it adds anything but a new term to what was already known to Augustine. And the suggested interpretation of the divinity of Christ encounters the same difficulty as inheres in all attempts to amend the ontological conceptuality of the classical dogmas.

(*e*) *Existentialist Christology.* In the existentialist christology of Rudolf Bultmann and his followers the classical christology with its ideas of incarnation and resurrection is regarded as a 'mythological' expression of the significance of Christ for faith, which is essentially a new self-understanding by believers and, as such, does not involve objective information about the historical Jesus. Bultmann's concentration on the *kerygma* is claimed to be a reproduction in different language of the Lutheran concentration on justification by faith alone (*sola fide*) as the sum of the gospel; faith alone, according to Bultmann, means that faith has its ground in itself and not in history. On the other hand, his reduction of christology to statements regarding the 'significance' of Christ is regarded by some critics as a variation on the one-time view of Melanchthon ('To know Christ is to know his benefits') and of the Ritschlian theory of value-judgments; and his position on the christological irrelevance of knowledge of the historical Jesus is suspected of being a sophisticated modern version of docetism. Some of Bultmann's pupils have moved from this position and have inaugurated a 'new quest of the historical Jesus', with inconclusive results thus far. The question of the relation of *kerygma* and history, which Bultmann has raised, sets the christological problem in a new perspective.

7. *Conclusion.* Christological thought is fluid at the present time, and no one can predict what course it will take in the future. There is fairly general agreement that the classical dogma, which served its purpose in its time, is no longer adequate, not because the answer it gives to its own question is wrong, but because the question presupposes a frame of reference which has now been abandoned. More is involved than the replacement of the conceptuality of Chalcedon, which is so often complained of. A major task is the re-examination of the question how the christological inquiry arises from the christological confession (Sellers) and a reformulation of the problem in terms of its indigenous structure and context.

D. M. Baillie, *God was in Christ*, 1948; K. Barth, *Church Dogmatics*, I: *The Doctrine of the Word of God*, 2, 1956; IV: *The Doctrine of Reconciliation*, 1, 1956; C. E. Braaten and R. A. Harrisville, *Kerygma and History*, 1962; O. Cullmann, *The Christology of the New Testament*, 2nd ed., 1964; P. T. Forsyth, *The Person and Place of Jesus Christ*, 1909; C. Gore, *Dissertations on Subjects Connected with the Incarnation*, 1895; E. R. Hardy, ed., *Christology of the Later Fathers*, 1954; J. N. D. Kelly, *Early Christian Doctrines*, 1958; H. R. Mackintosh, *The Doctrine of the Person of Christ*, 1912; W. R. Matthews, *The Problem of Christ in the Twentieth Century*, 1950; W. Niesel, *The Gospel and the Churches*, 1962; Wolfhart Pannenberg, *Jesus God and Man*, 1968: W. N. Pittenger, *The Word Incarnate*, 1959; Karl Rahner, 'Christology within an Evolutionary View of the World', *Theological Investigations*, V, 1966, pp. 157–92; R. V. Sellers, *The Council of Chalcedon*, 1953; *Two Ancient Christologies*, 1940; L. S. Thornton, *The Incarnate Lord*, 1928; P. Tillich, *Systematic Theology*, II, 1957.

GEORGE S. HENDRY

Church

Various factors have combined at the present day to make the doctrine of the Church (*see* **Ecclesiology**) a centre of theological discussion. These factors may be defined as the emergence of Biblical Theology, the Ecumenical, the Missionary and the Liturgical Movements (qq.v.).

Biblical Theology, which seeks to understand the Bible as a whole and to present its inner unity amidst diversity, has compelled scholars to recognize that its authors did not write as individuals in isolation, but as members of the chosen people for the chosen people. Immediately numerous questions arise: What is it that constitutes the chosen people? What is the nature of their election? How are we to understand the covenant which unites them to God and to one another? What, in other words, is the meaning of the Church? The Ecumenical Movement, with its vision of *one* Church of Christ according to the will of God, has equally brought the same final question before Christians, while the Missionary Movement has raised, first, the practical issue of how the preaching of the Gospel can be effective when it is performed by representatives of apparently contending Christian bodies and, second, the theological issue of unity as the will of God. The Liturgical Movement, with its stress upon the corporate nature of worship, upon devotion as an act of the whole Body and not that of a mere collection of individuals, praying separately as best they can, has also focused attention upon the nature of the Church.

This revived ecclesiology has resulted in a flood of critical studies, from both Roman Catholics and Protestants, which have laid bare some fundamental issues, although no general consensus is yet to be found upon their resolution. The basic question remains: Granted the agreement that the Church is a fundamental fact in the Christian revelation, what exactly is the Church? Is it, for example, an extension of the incarnation? In what sense is the Pauline description 'the Body of Christ' to be understood? There are those who contend that the Church cannot be regarded as the extension of the incarnation since Christ was sinless and the visible Church clearly is not. It is possible that this may be resolved by acknowledging that the Church is an extending of the incarnation; it is both holy and sinful and still has to attain 'unto the measure of the stature of the fulness of Christ'. The difference of view relating to the Body of Christ may be expressed by saying that some interpret this as a simple metaphor, and others believe that it refers to an organic reality. It may be suggested that this debate should take greater note of the Hebraic outlook of Paul. The Hebrew, unlike the Greek, is not interested in things in themselves but only in things as they are called to be. He is not concerned with an object as such but with what it becomes in relation to its final reference according to the divine purpose. The meaning of an object therefore does not lie in its analytical and empirical reality, but in the will that is expressed by it. Hence Jesus could say of a piece of bread: 'This is my body.' The bread does not cease to be bread, but it becomes what it is not, namely, the instrument and organ of his presence, because through his sovereign word he gives it a new dimension. Hence, too, Paul could say of a collection of money: 'This is the *koinonia*' (Rom. 15.26). The money does not cease to be money but it becomes what it is not, namely, the means of furthering the *koinonia* of Jew and Gentile, because its nature lies in the divine intention that is realized through it. Similarly the Church is the Body of Christ because its true nature rests upon its relation to God's purpose. Understood in this way the opposition between metaphor and non-metaphor is seen to be an unreal one. Paul, a Hebrew of the Hebrews, regards the Church as the organ of Christ's presence uniting his members to himself and in him to one another. Just as the body is not only the sign of a man's presence but also the organ, because a man has not a body but is a body, so the Church is the sign and organ of Christ's presence.

Present-day ecclesiology also involves a close study of the relationship of Church and ministry (q.v.) and of the Church to the kingdom of God. This latter issue arises from the observation that the kingdom receives a primary emphasis in the preaching of Jesus but has little direct attention paid to it in the rest of the NT. The tendency in past ecclesiology has been to equate the kingdom of God on earth with the Church; the tendency today is to see the Church as the instrument of the kingdom. Yet another aspect of the doctrine of the Church is its relationship to the world, arising in part from the study of mission (q.v.) as a theological concept and the recognition of the need for the Church to be open to the world which is God's creation.

Underlying all these questions is the further one: What is the basis of ecclesiology? In the past it has been usual to find this in christology, but it is now being recognized that this is insufficient; the doctrine of the Church must also be founded upon pneumatology. The true nature of the Church is then revealed by that which has been accomplished through Christ and that which is being and is yet to be accomplished through the Spirit; the latter is founded upon the former which is its objective condition. From the christological aspect the Church is static, built upon an unshakable foundation; from the pneumatological the Church is dynamic, stretching out to its final destiny, to the union of each human person with God. Hence the Church has both an organic and a personal character, an accent of necessity and of freedom, of objectivity and subjectivity; it is a reality both immovable and defined and also a reality to come. Hence the double polarity of the Church, with its twofold reference to Christ and to the Spirit. The Church *is* the Temple of the Presence; it *is* the Body of Christ; it *is* the Bride of Christ; yet the Temple has still to be built together, the Body has still to be built up, the Bride has still to become wholly one with her divine Bridegroom. Failure to appreciate this double polarity of the Church is in part responsible for the distinction between the visible and the invisible Church, of which the NT knows nothing. But it is aware of a tension between the present blessings and the final consummation, between the kingdom as a present reality and its complete realization at the end of all things. Ceaselessly the Spirit continues his work of transforming the individual components of the Church of God, building the Temple together, building up the Body, but this is not a question of quantity or of size, it is a question of quality, of progressive sanctification by the Holy Spirit of the individual cells which are incorporated to form the Temple or the Body or the Bride of Christ.

In the preceding paragraphs the main emphasis has been ontological, i.e. the basic theological problem is understood as the quest for a metaphysical definition of what the Church *is*. There is, however, a strong current in contemporary theological thought which seeks to understand the Church functionally, and this has some affinity with the concept of the Body of Christ discussed above. From this perspective the basic theological problem is understood as the quest for a definition of the role or function of the Church in relation to God's purpose for the world. This approach opens new possibilities for ecclesiology. See also **Invisible Church.**

J. G. Davies, *The Spirit, the Church and the Sacraments,* 1954; F. W. Dillistone, *The Structure of the Divine Society,* 1951; E. Mersch, *The Whole Christ,* 1949; J. E. L. Newbigin, *The Reunion of the Church,* 1948; L. S. Thornton, *The Common Life in the Body of Christ,* 2nd. ed., 1964.

J. G. DAVIES

Circumcision. *see* Initiation, Christian.

Clapham Sect

This was the name popularly given to a group of well-to-do and influential Anglican Evangelicals (q.v.) who lived around and worshipped in Clapham parish church at the turn of the eighteenth century. J. Venn was rector of Clapham from 1792-1813 and one of the leaders, but the others were laymen, perhaps the most outstanding of them being William Wilberforce. They interested themselves in the abolition of the slave trade and of slavery itself, in missionary work overseas and in the task of encouraging and, to some extent, through legislation, of imposing higher moral standards on the people at home. It has been said that they worked with, rather than for, the poor, thinking that there were good grounds in religion and reason for the different orders of society to be kept in their places. They were influential within their own class, and the high seriousness and sense of responsibility which were typical of the nineteenth-century English upper classes at their best were largely their work, as was the popular image of mid-Victorian England as Bible-reading, sabbatarian, puritanical, disciplined and serious.

F. K. Brown, *Fathers of the Victorians,* 1961; E. M. House, *Saints in Politics: the Clapham Sect and the Growth of Freedom,* 1960.

R. CANT

Clement of Alexandria

Little is known of Clement's life. He taught in Alexandria from about 190 to 202, when the persecution of Septimus Severus caused him to leave Alexandria. He is known later to have visited Antioch and to have been dead by 215. His chief work is a trilogy consisting of the *Protreptikos,* a book which attacks pagan religion and demonstrates the superiority of Christianity, the *Paidagogos,* intended to be an introduction to Christian faith and life, and the *Stromateis,* which professes to set out Christian doctrine in a more advanced form. A sermon of his on the incident of the rich young ruler (known as *Quis Dives*) and some minor works survive too. Clement's chief distinction lies in having been the first unequivocally to welcome contemporary Greek philosophy as

an ally of Christianity, instead of viewing it with suspicion, as had most Christian writers before him. He was deeply influenced by the thought of the Alexandrian Jew Philo, and reflects to some degree that writer's penchant towards Platonism and Stoicism. Clement's mind is a wide-ranging one, immensely well-stocked with knowledge of Greek literature and myth, comprehensive rather than precise, and his thought is loose and unsystematic. The concept of the Logos is central to his thought, but it is the cosmological rather than the soteriological function of the Logos that interests him. The Logos not only taught and guided the men of the OT, but also revealed himself in some way to the Greek philosophers, and indeed to anybody who has ever discovered truth at any time. Clement can quote Homer as readily as Isaiah in order to establish Christian doctrine and in a famous passage suggests that philosophy was to the Greeks what the Law was to the Jews. But both revelations are inferior to the manifestation of the Logos in Christ, who has now come to enlighten all men in a new way. Clement's attitude to Gnosticism is curious, not to say equivocal. He claims that the Christian is the true Gnostic; he insists that the Church's Rule of Faith must be followed; but he betrays a knowledge of and even sympathy for Judaeo-Christian near-Gnostic speculations and traditions which sort ill with his profession of orthodoxy. His is an enigmatic figure, standing between the religion of primitive, fundamentally Jewish, Christianity and the more sophisticated faith of Origen.

E. F. Osborn, *The Philosophy of Clement of Alexandria,* 1957; R. B. Tollinton, *Clement of Alexandria,* 1914.

R. P. C. HANSON

Clergy, Clerical

The term is derived from the Greek *kleros,* meaning one's 'portion', 'inheritance' or 'lot' (it literally means 'lot' in Act 1.26, at the election of Matthias; *cf.* Mark 15.24). NT examples are Acts 1.17; 8.21; 26.18; Col. 1. 12. In the OT Israel is frequently spoken of as Yahweh's *kleros,* inheritance (e.g. Deut 4.20). In this biblical sense the whole Church is God's *kleros;* the whole Christian body could thus have been spoken of as God's 'clergy' or as his 'laity' (q.v.). But in I Peter 5.3, the presbyters are exhorted not to lord it over their *kleroi,* i.e. the pastoral spheres allotted to them individually within the whole *kleronomia* ('inheritance') of Christ. It is from this latter use that *clericus, clergy,* etc. are derived, though not found in this sense before Tertullian. After the Middle Ages, when the clergy were almost the only literate men, the words 'clerical' and 'clerk' acquired their present non-ecclesiastical significance, as the 'clerics' themselves became secularized. But the words 'clergy', 'clergymen' and 'clerk in holy orders' were retained (in England properly for the ministers of the Established Church) as denoting the ordained ministry of the churches.

EDITOR

Coinherence

Coinherence (Latin: *circumincessio, circumin-sessio*; Greek: *perichoresis*) is the doctrine denoting the mutual indwelling or interpenetration of the three Persons of the Trinity whereby one is as invariably in the other two as they are in the one. Based on John 10.28–38 and adumbrated, for example, by Novatian, the doctrine became important from the fourth century onwards as the reciprocal of the *Homoousios*. Each person belongs to the others (Athanasius, Cyril of Alexandria). It is especially important for the Cappadocian Fathers (q.v.) with their strong pluralism. As three sciences interpenetrate each other and the omnipresent God permeates the universe, so much the more each Person interpenetrates the others. In the West it is emphasized by Hilary and Augustine. Each Person is the mirror of the others (Hilary). Each Person is relative to the others; the Spirit is the bond of love (*vinculum amoris*) of the Father and the Son (Augustine). The key to the doctrine is mysticism rather than the logic of the divine relations. The term *perichoresis* does not occur before Maximus the Confessor (seventh century) and it is then applied to the reciprocal action of the two natures of Christ. Its transference to Trinitarian doctrine is completed by John of Damascus. The idea expressed in similar words from the same root is familiar in earlier times (Irenaeus, Cappadocians). In modern Trinitarian theology it is used both by monists (Barth) and pluralists, for whom it is of even greater importance.

H. E. W. TURNER

Coleridge, S. T.

Coleridge (1772–1834) became famous as co-author with Wordsworth of the collection of poems, *Lyrical Ballads* (1798), which is usually held to mark the beginning of the Romantic Movement in English literature. The son of an Anglican clergyman he went through many phases of religious experience which makes him at once one of the most interesting and most seminal (in J. S. Mill's word) thinkers of the nineteenth century. He was one of the first Englishmen to come under the influence of Kant, and this led him to see the deficiencies both of popular deism and of the prevailing orthodox apologetic against it. He suspected the validity of metaphysical argument for religious truth, and stressed the importance of moral experience and the practical effects of belief upon life. 'The Bible *finds* me at a deeper level than any other book.' This for him was the most convincing proof of its inspiration, and this line of argument recurs in Christian apologists for more than a century.

He denied that there was any contradiction between science and religion, and in a later generation it was those who regarded him as their master who most successfully weathered the storms of the Darwinian debate. He welcomed the beginnings of biblical criticism, and adumbrated an historical interpretation of gradual revelation

in the biblical text. He believed that Christians could and should unite on the basis of a few common beliefs. Church and State were complementary to each other, but he distinguished between the 'national church' whose task was civilization in its widest sense, and which was indeed a broad church, including all learned men, and the Christian church which was spiritual and supranational. Coleridge exercised great influence through lectures and friendships, as well as by his books. The most important religious writings were *Aids to Reflection* (1825) and *Confessions of an Enquiring Spirit* (1840). Broad Churchmen, Liberal Anglicans (q.v.) and F. D. Maurice (q.v.) were among those deeply influenced by him.

F. R. Leavis, ed., *Mill on Bentham and Coleridge*, 1959; C. R. Sanders, *Coleridge and the Broad Church Movement*, 1942; B. Willey, *Nineteenth Century Studies*, 1949.

R. CANT

Communicatio Essentiae

Communicatio essentiae is the doctrine that the Son receives his essence from the Father and the Spirit his essence from the Father and the Son, though this takes place within the single essence of God. This is an inference from the *Homoousios*, the Divine Monarchy (*see* **Monarchianism**) of the Father considered as the Fount of the whole Trinity and the relations of origin (*see* **Generation; Procession[s]**). Calvin argues vigorously against the view that the Father is the *essentiator* of the Son and the Spirit and claims that the essence of God belongs to the one true God alone (and not, therefore, of sole right to the Father and by derivation from him to the Son and the Spirit). His frequent use of *autotheos* of the Son or his reference to his *autousia* was sharply criticized by contemporary Roman Catholic theologians as a denial of the 'God from God' of the Nicene Creed and of the Eternal Generation of the Son by the Father. Calvin, however, denied neither and did not maintain the heresy called 'Auto-theism' (the view that Christ was God *a se ipso, non a Patre*). Christ may be said to be from another either by production or by communication of essence. In his repudiation of the former view (an extreme type of Subordinationism) he used language which might appear to exclude the latter, which he clearly accepted. Bellarmine held that Calvin here errs not in judgment but in form of words. Calvin's followers were more guarded: 'We do not deny that the Son received his essence from the Father but we deny that his essence is generated.' This is in line with the Scholastic maxim, *Essentia nec generat nec generatur* (an essence neither generates nor is generated). Karl Barth (following Calvin) treats the doctrine with great reserve on different grounds. The relations of origin are attempts to express the ineffable (a view for which he can cite good patristic precedent). He can accept the *communicatio essentiae* as a statement of the dependence of God's existence as Son and Spirit upon his existence as Father (*see* **Person[s]**; **Modes of Being**), but hesitates on the question of origin. The Father is the presupposition or ground of the Son and the Spirit. This is bound up with the doctrine of the Divine Persons as modes of being or 'styles' of God's being God.

The phrase *communicatio essentiae* safeguards the monarchy of the Father as the source of the whole Trinity. If, however, communication is glossed by production or the essence shared by the Son and the Spirit regarded as subordinate because it is derived, it might lead to subordination-ism. Calvin's exaggerated protest against such misunderstandings was intended to safeguard the full divinity of Christ, not to deny his relation or origin to the Father.

H. E. W. TURNER

Communicatio Idiomatum

'The sharing of the attributes or properties' is a christological term used to describe the transference of epithets appropriate to the human or the divine nature of Christ either to each other or to the total unitary subject of the incarnation. It had a long history in patristic christology with a notable example in the *Tome* of Leo. The principle was set against a tight doctrinal background in Alexandrian christology but was deeply suspect (though not completely excluded) by Antiochene christologians. The controversy over the title *Theotokos* (Mother of God) between Cyril of Alexandria and Nestorius centred on the legitimacy of this principle. Monophysitism gave it an ontological ground, Nestorianism, with its sharp separation of the two natures, went even further than Nestorius himself in its repudiation. In Reformation times the Lutheran doctrine of the Eucharist demanded the transference of the attribute of ubiquity from the divine to the human nature of Christ. The principle of the *communicatio idiomatum* was therefore invoked and interpreted as a real participation in attributes. This clearly tended towards Eutychianism, and Melanchthon abandoned the attempt to clarify the doctrine of the eucharistic presence in this way. The Reformed tradition which (unlike Luther) held that the finite could not contain the infinite regarded the principle as valid as a turn of speech but not as describing a real transference or sharing of qualities.

H. E. W. TURNER

Communicatio Operationum

Communicatio operationum (participation in operations) is the term used in second generation Lutheranism by Chemnitz to express and to delimit the realist interpretation of the *communicatio idiomatum* (q.v.).

H. E. W. TURNER

Communion in the Eucharist

The reception of the eucharistic elements by clergy and laity in the eucharistic service is called communion. Originally universal at all celebra-

tions of the Eucharist, the communion of the laity became very infrequent though attendance at the Liturgy every Sunday remained general. Various reasons have been suggested, such as (1) emphasis on the sacredness of the presence of Christ as God, resulting from the Arian controversy; (2) the note of dread which entered the Liturgy in order to discipline the influx of half-converted pagans into the Church after the official establishment of Christianity; (3) the 'clericalization' of the Church and the loss by the laity of their sense of membership of the Body of Christ. The *minimum* of one act of communion a year, laid down by the Fourth Lateran Council in 1215, still applies in the Roman Church in spite of the recent development of frequent, and even daily, communion. The Church of England in the sixteenth century raised the minimum from one to three. Attempts in the reformed Churches to insist upon the laity communicating whenever present at the Eucharist had the unforeseen result that, instead of communion becoming more frequent, the celebration of the sacrament became extremely rare. In recent years there has been, in almost all parts of Christendom, a welcome movement towards more frequent communion, which has gone with a recovered sense by the laity of their membership of Christ's Body, the Church.

From the eleventh or twelfth century onwards in the Latin Church communion has been received under the species of bread alone by all except the celebrating priest, though since the Second Vatican Council communion in both kinds has been restored on an increasing number of occasions. All the reformed Churches, including the Anglican, normally give communion in both kinds. The Eastern Orthodox and Byzantine uniate Churches place the consecrated host in the chalice and communicate the faithful thence in both kinds by means of a spoon.

The emphasis laid by the Reformers on the act of communion has tended to overshadow the Godward aspect of the Eucharist to such an extent that, as, for example, in the Anglican Churches, the whole service has often come to be known simply as 'the Holy Communion'.

E. L. MASCALL

Communion of Saints

Communio sanctorum first occurs apparently in a sermon of Nicetas of Remesiana (d. *c.* 414), where it is treated as a masculine plural. The phrase is not actually used in the NT, though the conception is there of course, e.g. Col. 1.12. Compare also I John 1.3 f., where we find the true NT emphasis that the communion of saints is based on their communion with the Father through the Son. In II Cor. 13.13 we are reminded that this communion is in the Spirit. There is not much light to be found in the NT on the question of how faithful Christians who have died are joined in communion with Christians on earth. All are in Christ. The practice, attested in Corinth, of being baptized for the dead (I Cor. 15.29) would seem to imply that what we do on earth can affect them, but it is an obscure passage. The Book of Revelation shows us the martyrs worshipping God in heaven; in 6.9 they cry out for judgment on those who have murdered them, which presupposes a knowledge of what is happening on earth.

It is no coincidence that the book in the NT which is most concerned with martyrdom contains these passages, for it is in connection with local saints, mostly martyrs, that we find the first examples of requests for the prayers of the saints. These occur in the third century, mostly on tombs or in the catacombs. Invocation of the Blessed Virgin Mary is very rare until well after AD 300. The earliest known prayer to her occurs in a third-century papyrus: 'Under the shelter of thy mercy we take refuge, O Mother of God; lead our prayer not into temptation, but deliver us from evil, thou who alone art chaste and beloved.' The practice of invoking the saints became officially countenanced during the fourth century. The first known introduction of an invocation of St Mary into the liturgy occurs about 480. Gregory the Great offers us a good example of the theological justification which was provided for the practice of invocation of the saints: 'The saints inwardly see the brightness of Almighty God, and therefore we cannot believe that they are ignorant of anything outward' (*Moralia in Job*, 12.12). At the Second Council of Nicea in 787 an attempt was made to define the various degrees of reverence 'which ought to be paid to God and the saints respectively. The final schema ran thus: to God alone must *latreia* be offered; to the Blessed Virgin *hyperdouleia* may be rendered; to the saints *douleia*, and to icons *proskynesis*.

The veneration of saints would seem at first sight to be an issue between the Catholic and the reformed which cannot be resolved. There are certainly features in connection with the veneration of saints which responsible Catholic theologians would not claim to defend, such as the making of specific requests to them – frequent as this practice is in popular devotion. The following sentence occurs in S. Bulgakov's *The Orthodox Church* (1935): 'It is naturally necessary for us to hide ourselves in awe before the Judge of all, and here we take refuge beneath the protection of the Virgin and the saints' (p. 142). This sentiment could easily be paralleled in the piety of the Counter-Reformation. It is doubtful if the theologians of the *aggiornamento* would readily endorse such a suggestion.

It is possible, however, that the concept of *comprecation* may provide at least a means of mutual comprehension. Cyril of Jerusalem (d. 386) writes: 'We make mention of those who have fallen asleep before us, first of patriarchs, prophets, apostles, martyrs, that God would at their prayers and intercessions receive our supplications.' This is explained by Max Thurian in the following terms in *The Eucharistic Memorial* (ET, 1961): 'There is a theological necessity to recall the saints in the liturgy of the Church. They are a reminder of the mediation of Christ in the universal Church of all time. The Son of God has willed to be present in the incarnation to men by the mediation of his humanity. The risen Christ has willed to leave certain signs which recall and realize this mediation . . . The saints are therefore the signs of the presence and of the love of Christ . . . It is thus that in the ancient Church prayer for the apostles, prophets, and martyrs became after their death a prayer *with* them in the communion of saints on behalf of the whole Church' (cf. p. 23). Compare also a Roman Catholic theologian, Fr B. Häring: 'The prayer dialogue with the saints, by comparison with our direct adoration of God, is a prayer only in an analogical sense. It is communication corresponding to the communion of saints' (*The Law of Christ*, II, p. 534). But if there is to be genuine mutual comprehension on this issue there is much questioning of popular devotion still to be undertaken.

D. Bonhoeffer, *Sanctorum Communio*, ET, 1963; S. Bulgakov, *The Orthodox Church*, ET, 1935; B. Häring, *The Law of Christ*, ET, 1963; Daniel Jenkins, *The Gift of Ministry*, 1947; Max Thurian, *The Eucharistic Memorial*, ET, 1961.

A. T. HANSON

Comparative (Study of) Religion

Comparative (study of) religion is the study and comparison of the world's religions. Two difficulties are encountered in its pursuit. First, its immense scope and complexity involve the necessity of a knowledge of several languages if it is to be more than superficial. Secondly, since religion is an existential involvement, it cannot adequately be studied at a distance or from the outside; only an empathetic living within a religious culture, a knowing from the inside, can enable the study to be more than merely academic. Yet it is obviously desirable that, as the world becomes increasingly unified, some understanding of religious cultures other than one's own should be acquired. Furthermore, the study is important in the history of ideas. An interest in other religions than Christianity began to arise with the widening of horizons during the period of the Enlightenment (q.v.), and the study was pressed forward during the time of the dominance of the Liberal Theology (q.v.) which followed (*see* **Religionsgeshichtliche Schule**).

L. Aletrino, *Six World Religions*, 1968; G. Appleton, *On the Eightfold Path* (Buddhism), 1961; A. C. Bouquet, *Comparative Religion* (Penguin), 1941; A. Cohen, *The Natural and the Supernatural Jew*, 1966; R. Hammer, *Japan's Religious Ferment*, 1961; E. O. James, *Comparative Religion*, 1938; L. Sherley-Price, *Confucius and Christ*, 1967; J. W. Sweetman, *Islam and Christian Theology*, 1967; J. V. Taylor, *The Primal Vision* (African Religion), 1963.

EDITOR

Concomitance

Concomitance means literally companionship. According to Catholic theology, in the Eucharist the bread becomes Christ's body and the wine becomes his blood *ex vi sacramenti*, that is, in virtue of Christ's own words 'This is my body' and 'This is my blood', repeated by the Church in obedience to Christ's command. On the other hand, Christ being now risen and glorified, there can be no real separation of his body from his blood, such as took place on the Cross, nor can there be any real separation of his soul from his body or of his manhood from his Godhead; various theories are held as to the way in which the Eucharist 'represents' the death on the cross, but it is agreed that Christ is not put to death in the Mass and that it is the living, not the dead, Christ who is there present in the fulness of his being, truly God and fully man. It is therefore held that, although under the species of bread only Christ's body is present *ex vi sacramenti*, all the other constituents of his divine-human being are present *ex naturali concomitantia;* and similarly for the species of wine. It follows that the whole Christ is received by a communicant under either species, and the doctrine of concomitance has therefore been used to justify the mediaeval and modern Western practice of communion under the species of bread alone. Some such view, however, seems inevitable for anyone who believes in the real presence of Christ in the eucharistic elements but does not believe that there is in the Eucharist a literal repetition of Christ's death (*see* **Immolation**). The teaching of St Thomas Aquinas on the subject will be found in *Summa Theologica*, 3. 76.

E. L. MASCALL

Concord, Formula of

This long document closes the series of Lutheran confessions which comprise the Book of Concord. Compiled in 1577 by Jacob Andreae of Tübingen and others on the basis of previous statements, especially the Book of Torgau of 1576, it was approved by the German Lutheran states in 1580, and published at Dresden. Its terms are framed with intent to correct extreme positions taken in theological controversies within Lutheranism that had preceded. The document is in two parts, the brief *Epitome* and the amplified *Sana, plana ac perspicua repetitio et declaratio* which consists of an introduction and twelve articles. The unaltered Augsburg Confession (q.v.) as shown to Charles V in 1530 is expressly approved, as is also Melanchthon's Apology for the Confession, though without his name. Luther is frequently quoted with reverence; his two Catechisms are 'the Bible of the laity'. Original sin corrupts man's nature utterly; man's will is entirely hostile to God and incapable of good until renewed by the Holy Spirit. The doctrine of justification *sola fide* is inferred from Pauline phrases. Good works are not the cause of salvation, but follow from true faith. Explicit Lutheran definitions of the Lord's Supper, the Person of Christ, the descent into Hell, predestination, and other points of doctrine, are set forth, and a number of the more active sects of the time are condemned. The doctrine of the *communicatio idiomatum* (q.v.) as applied to the Lord's Supper is the subject of an appendix.

Concordia Triglotta, German, Latin, English, ed. F. Bente and W. T. Dau, 1921 and 1955; Deutsche Evangelische Kirchenauschuss, *Die Bekenntnisschriften der evangelisch-lutherischen Kirche,* 2 vols., 1950; P. Schaff, *Creeds of Christendom,* I, 1919 (critical analysis), III (text of *Epitome*), 1919; T. G. Tappert, ed., *The Book of Concord,* 1959 (complete translation with informative notes).

J. T. MCNEILL

Confession(s), Confessionalism

1. Confession is an acknowledgment of sin made in general terms at a public service of worship or with reference to the penitent's own personal sin(s) in private ('auricular') confession to a priest. In either case confession is usually followed by the pronouncement of absolution.

2. In the ancient Church *confessio* meant the profession of faith made by a martyr (or 'confessor', who had withstood persecution for his faith) (*cf.* I Tim. 6.13; II Cor. 9.13). The word thus came to mean a firm declaration of religious convictions with or without reference to persecution. (The word is also used of the tomb or shrine of a martyr or confessor; e.g. the *confessio* of St Peter in the Vatican.) It could also have a still more general sense, namely the biblical sense of *praising* God, e.g. St Augustine's *Confessions,* in which Augustine blesses God for his conversion.

3. From this second sense of *confessio*, the declaration of what is believed, arises the use of the term in the churches of the Reformation during the sixteenth and seventeenth centuries for their credal statements ('confessions') or professions of faith as over against Rome. They were not intended as alternatives to the ancient ecumenical creeds (the Apostles' or the Nicene) but rather as statements of how the traditional creeds ought to be understood. Their aim is to make clear what is meant by proclaiming that 'Jesus is Lord' and to show that this affirmation can be made only in the light of the doctrine of justification by faith. They were confessions of the Church rather than of individual theologians. The earliest of them was the Augsburg Confession (1530); among the latest is the Westminster Confession (1643), which became the formulary of the Church of Scotland in 1689. The decrees of the Council of Trent (1545–63) may be thought of as a 'confessional' reply of the Roman Church to the principles of the Reformation as enunciated in the various Protestant Confessions. Although the Anglican communion is often regarded as one of the 'confessional' churches, this view is not strictly correct. The Thirty-nine Articles are not a confessional statement in the above sense; they were not so much the work of theologians defining a confessional position as of statesmen attempting to reconcile conflicting confessional points of view

in the interests of a comprehensive church unity; and in any case they are not binding through the various provinces of the Anglican communion. It should be added that the Declaration of Barmen (1934) is not strictly a 'confession' in the above sense, since it does not seek to distinguish one *church* from another but rather Christian faith from its denial. For confession of sins *see* **Worship.**

H. Bettenson, *Documents of the Christian Church*, 1943; A. C. Cochrane, *Reformed Confessions of the 16th Century*, 1966; G. S. Hendry, *The Westminster Confession for Today*, 1960; B. J. Kidd, *Documents Illustrative of the Continental Reformation*, 1911.

EDITOR

Confirmation. *see* Initiation, Christian.

Congregationalists, Congregationalism

The essential principle of Congregationalism is the autonomy of the worshipping congregation to the exclusion of any deciding authority outside it, whether exercised by synods or by individual officers. This polity is held to be in accord with the practice of first-century Christianity. Many sects before and during the Reformation were so organized, and in some cases a covenant was used to bind the members of the group. As early as 1550 separatist and autonomous congregations began to appear in England, and with the Elizabethan settlement of religion these became numerous. Brownists (q.v.) and Independents (q.v.) with variations held the same principle. After the Cromwellian period, when Independent ministers held parish appointments, Congregationalism gradually emerged in its real character as nonconformist. The Savoy Declaration (q.v.) of 1558 gave tentative form to Congregationalist principles of faith and order, and approved the Westminster Assembly's doctrinal statements; but it never became an operative constitution. Under the Heads of Agreement of 1691 Congregational and Presbyterian ministers joined in acts of ordination. In America the Cambridge Platform of 1648 was a Congregationalist constitution somewhat affected by Presbyterian concepts, as when it states (14) that synods 'if not absolutely necessary to the being are necessary to the well-being of churches'.

G. G. Atkins and F. L. Fagley, *History of American Congregationalism*, 1942; D. T. Jenkins, *Congregationalism, a Restatement*, 1954; A. Peel, ed., *Essays, Congregational and Catholic*, 1931; W. Walker, *Creeds and Platforms of Congregationalism*, 1893.

J. T. MCNEILL

Conscience

The conscience refers to the ability of man to judge the ethical status of his actions. It implies a 'law written on the heart' as opposed to external controls of behaviour. It has sometimes been assumed that the conscience is the only criterion of the goodness of an action as is expressed in the popular slogan: 'Let your conscience be your guide.' Christian thought rejects this viewpoint. Paul said that although he knew nothing against himself, his clear conscience did not mean that he was innocent (II Cor. 4.4). It is the will of God, not the conscience of man that is the final judge. Only in so far as the conscience is illuminated by Christ is it reliable. Christian faith gives man an uneasy conscience in so far as it convicts him of sin before God. Freedom from this uneasiness is to be found through God's forgiveness rather than through man's own attainments. Many theologians have seen the conscience as a mark of the image of God within man. Even Luther, who believed that the image of God was lost in man's fall, found the law and the uneasy conscience a point at which the gospel becomes relevant to man. *See also* **Man, Doctrine of.**

WILLIAM HORDERN

Consecration

Consecration is the action of solemnly dedicating someone, as in the case of bishops, or something, as in the case of churches, to a sacred or religious purpose.

1. *Consecration of Bishops.* In the early Church bishops were elected by the people and consecrated by a fellow-bishop or bishops laying his or their hands upon them, following apostolic precedent (Acts 6.6), and uttering prayer, which commented upon the action and revealed the belief that something was conveyed thereby, for example, according to Hippolytus, 'the high-priestly Spirit'. There was little elaboration of this ritual until the Middle Ages, except that according to the *Apostolic Constitutions* one of the bishops is to 'elevate the sacrifice upon the hands of him that is consecrated' – this seems to be an imitation of the OT custom at the consecration of the high priest (Lev. 8.27) – and deacons are to hold an open Gospel book upon the candidate's head, this latter prescription entering the West through its inclusion in the fifth century *Statuta ecclesiae antiquae*.

In the developed mediaeval rite two strands, at first distinct, were combined, namely, the Roman and the Gallican. As an example may be cited the sequence of actions in the *Ordo Romanus* XXXVB, produced c. AD 1000: (*a*) An examination of morals and doctrine. (*b*) The dressing of a candidate in vestments. (*c*) The imposition of the Gospel book – a Gallican feature. (*d*) Prayers. (*e*) The consecration proper, with an anointing of the head in the midst of the accompanying prayer – this unction is a Gallican practice no doubt influenced by Lev. 8.12. (*f*) The anointing of the hands, a Merovingian usage borrowed from the ordination of priests. (g) The anointing of the thumb with which the bishop will give his blessing – probably of German origin and possibly influenced by Lev. 8. 23. (h) The tradition of instruments, including the blessing of the ring and the placing of it on the finger, and the blessing and presentation of the pastoral staff. (i) The kiss of peace. A similar order is found in a twelfth-century Roman pontifical with the giving of a Gospel book inserted after the tradition of instruments.

It will be noted how a number of ancillary ceremonies, of a symbolic character to express the meaning of the rite, have been added to the primitive laying on of hands, which nevertheless remains the essential element, although in 1439 Pope Eugenius IV declared that the tradition of instruments was the essential matter of the sacrament, a view widely accepted by Latin theologians until the seventeenth century.

The Orthodox Churches have retained much of the primitive simplicity but with some additions; for example, the Armenians have borrowed the anointing of the head and hands from the Roman rite, while the Byzantine order includes a giving of a pastoral staff.

The aim of the Reformers was to simplify the mediaeval rite and to emphasize the essentials as they discerned them in the NT, namely, prayer and the laying on of hands. Hence in the Anglican Ordinal of 1550 the imposition of hands is given prominence; the laying of the Bible on the neck and the presentation of the pastoral staff were retained until 1552 when the former was changed into the giving of a Bible and the latter was entirely omitted. The Church of England has, however, preserved what must be deemed essential, but the validity of its consecrations has been questioned on the grounds of defective intention (see **Orders**) and upon its disputed retention of the apostolic succession (q.v.).

2. *Consecration of Churches.* Solomon's dedication of the temple (I Kings 8.63) provided the model for the consecration of churches by Christians. No special ritual, however, was at first devised, and as late as the sixth century at Rome consecration was affected simply by celebrating the Eucharist in the new church in which relics had previously been deposited.

By the eighth and ninth centuries a fairly elaborate ritual had been developed, of which there were two distinct forms, the Roman and the Gallican, the former being based upon funerary rites and the latter upon the rites of Christian initiation. (1) *Roman.* The central idea of this rite was the preparation of the tomb of the patron saint, represented by his relics, and his conveyance to and enclosure within it. The main elements were: (a) The carrying of the relics in procession. (b) The entrance of the bishop and his associates into the new building to prepare the mortar for sealing the altar stone and to wash the altar with exorcized water. (c) The exit of the clergy. (d) The re-entrance of all, the anointing of the four

interior angles of the cavity in the altar, the deposition of the relics, the sealing of the stone and its anointing at the centre and four corners. (e) The blessing of the building and its vessels and of a lighted taper with which all the church lights were kindled. (f) The Mass. (2) *Gallican.* The central idea of the rite was the washing and anointing of the church, corresponding to baptism and confirmation by unction. The main elements were: (a) The entrance of the bishop. (b) The tracing by the bishop of the letters of the alphabet with his staff upon the floor in two diagonal lines crossing in the centre of the church. This ceremony corresponds to the ancient Roman method of taking possession of a piece of land and marking out its boundaries. The Roman surveyor traced two transverse lines and connected them to form the perimeter; similarly the bishop marks the area which is to be Christ's by tracing the sign of the cross, while the entire alphabet was an expansion of the alpha and omega. (c) The preparation by the bishop of lustral water. (d) The sprinkling of the altar. (e) The sprinkling of the church. (f) A prayer of consecration, eucharistic in character. (g) The anointing of the altar. (h) The anointing of the church walls. (i) The blessing of the objects used in worship. (j) The deposition of the relics. (k) The lighting of the lamps. (l) The Mass.

As with the consecration of bishops so here the two strands fused in the later Middle Ages, although the modern Roman rite has most affinities with the Gallican usage.

In the Orthodox Churches the rite centres in the consecration of the altar and while the walls are sprinkled and anointed this is understood primarily as an extension of what has been done to the altar. Within the Anglican communion forms for consecration were not produced until the seventeenth and eighteenth centuries. In England itself there is no agreed order, each diocese producing its own, but in Scotland, the USA, Canada and South Africa authorized forms are included in the Book of Common Prayer.

The theological rationale underlying these practices combines various factors. There is the idea that the building is thereby liberated from demon possession; there is the belief that that which was previously profane is now made holy, and there is the concept that it is set apart henceforth for 'sacred uses' for ever. Each of these views is open to adverse criticism and it may be better to understand consecration today as primarily an act of thanksgiving whereby the relationship of the building to the divine purpose is explicitly affirmed, i.e. by consecration a church is dedicated as the instrument of the mission of God; its nature is not altered but its function declared.

W. K. Lowther Clarke, ed., *Liturgy and Worship,* 1943, pp. 626–87; J. G. Davies, *The Secular Use of Church Buildings,* 1968, pp. 249–64; R. W. Muncey, *A History of the Consecration of the Churches and Churchyards,* 1930.

J. G. DAVIES

Consecration, Eucharistic

Eucharistic consecration applies to the solemn act of 'making holy' of the bread and wine in the celebration of the Eucharist. Catholic theology in both East and West sees this as consisting of the conversion of the bread into Christ's body and of the wine into his blood, but, whereas in the West the essential words in the rite by which this conversion is effected are held to be the dominical words 'This is my body' and 'This is my blood', in the East, while the dominical words are held to be obligatory, the conversion is associated with the invocation of the Holy Spirit (*see* **Epiclesis**). Many Protestants who deny a real presence in the elements (Luther did not; *see* **Consubstantiation**) would nevertheless hold that the elements acquire a genuine if undefined sacred character, as set apart from any common use, but others would deny that they acquire any such character and would indeed hold that the word 'consecration' cannot be properly applied to them.

E. L. MASCALL

Consubstantiation

Consubstantiation is the name commonly applied to the view of the eucharistic presence held by Luther. In contrast to the mediaeval doctrine of transubstantiation, according to which the substance of the bread and of the wine were changed into the substance of Christ's body and of his blood respectively, Luther taught that the substance of the bread and the wine remained but that the substances of Christ's body and blood were respectively united to them.

E. L. MASCALL

Contemplation

A level of prayer which exponents of Christian spirituality (q.v.) consider may be reached by natural means but which at its higher stages may be assisted by divine grace and may pass into mystical experience (*see* **Mysticism**). Meditation is a lower form of prayer (sometimes curiously called 'mental prayer', perhaps in contrast to spiritual prayer, i.e. Spirit-assisted prayer). It usually consists in devotional reflection upon a scriptural passage with a view to deepening understanding and strengthening resolve. In non-Christian religions many techniques of meditation (or 'transcendental meditation') are advocated by spiritual directors (such as the Indian *gurus*). St Ignatius Loyola's *Spiritual Exercises* are probably the best known Christian writings on meditation. The Contemplative Orders (e.g. Carthusian, Carmelite) devote their lives chiefly to Contemplative Prayer. A question to be asked from the biblical standpoint is whether there can be any 'natural' prayer, whether Christian or not, which is not prompted or assisted by the operation of divine grace.

Bede Frost, *The Art of Mental Prayer*, 1931.

EDITOR

Contingency

In the senses most relevant to the philosophy of religion, an event or an entity may be called 'contingent', if it could have *not* happened or *not* existed; if it is conditional (or dependent) on some other event's occurring or some other entity's existing. The argument to God *e contingentia mundi* (an important form of the cosmological argument) claims that all things cannot be contingent and that one being – God – must be 'necessary'. But what exactly can 'necessary' mean here? Some critics of the argument (e.g. Hume) have denied that the existence of any being is necessary; and have claimed that no *contradiction* at any rate is ever involved in denying the existence of anything. 'God does not exist' could be contradictory only if the concept of God itself included 'existence' as one of its essential constituents. That the concept *does* include 'existence' is essential, and much disputed, claim of the *ontological* argument. 'Existent' has a very different logic from 'omniscient' or 'all-loving'. Unlike these, it does not describe or characterize: and thus it is hard to see how it could play the role the argument requires it to play.

The contingent-necessary distinction can, however, be interpreted in more ways than one. 'A sense of contingency' may be a sense of dependence, derivativeness or creatureliness. With these as starting-points an argument may be attempted to God as Cause or Creator and Sustainer. Alternatively, step-by-step argument may be by-passed in favour of an alleged direct 'insight' or 'intuition' of God as the source of our contingent being. Each path has its pitfalls. In the first case the concept of 'cause' is strained to the limits of meaningfulness, and perhaps beyond them. In the second, the problem is how to test whether or not there is a genuine cognitive act, or only the appearance of one, in an experience that may be predominantly emotional.

R. W. HEPBURN

Conversion

The NT uses one word (*strepho*, with its prepositions *epi* and *apo*) to denote both a physical turning and a change of attitude towards God. Thus in John 21.20 Peter, standing with Jesus beside the lake, *turns round* and sees John. On the other hand, when the gospel was preached to the Greeks in Antioch, many of them *turned* to the Lord. The Vulgate translated this by the word *converto* and, on the one occasion when the noun is used ('reporting the conversion of the Gentiles', Acts 15.3), by the word *conversio*, from which comes our English 'conversion'.

Yet theologians cannot be said to have shown much liking for the word. They noted that it was not one of the great biblical terms and that it was an image that left much to be desired on account of its ambiguity.

Augustine prefers the verb, though even this he uses sparingly. When he writes of his own 'conversion', the noun does not appear at all. At the end of the account, however, he puns on the verb: 'For thou hast converted me to thee, so that I should seek neither wife nor any hope of this age . . . and thou hast converted [my mother's] mourning into joy far more abundant' (*Confessions* viii 12.30). In his narrative he also uses the verb in reference to St Antony. His own conversion he describes in terms of illumination. Elsewhere in the *Confessions* he prefers the synonym 'change' (*mutare*) (x, 36.58), and when he uses the word 'convert' it is in quite a different context, the difficult passage on the Creation (xiii. 2.3 and 5). The reader is here referred to the quotations of Augustine given in the article on predestination (q.v.). To summarize: (1) Faith is the gift of God. (2) Repentance and faith are the temporal outworking of the eternal election of God. (3) No merits precede repentance and faith. (4) The electing God gives to his Son those whom in eternity he has chosen. And to these we may add: (5) It is by the preaching of the gospel that men come to faith.

It was, in effect, on the concept of the nature of conversion that Pelagius attacked Augustine. By thinking in terms of man's capability, willing and being, Pelagius saw conversion as an orientation that man was in a position to effect, though the original capability was God's gift. Mediating theologians like John Cassian tried to cover the division by the use of the word 'co-operate': 'the grace of God co-operates with our will and helps it in all things' (*Collatio* xiii. 13). In this controversy Augustine was adjudged the winner, but the prize was awarded to the compromisers.

Western mediaeval theologians used the word and even the noun more freely. It now bears various meanings. It signifies the entering upon a monastic life, with the thought of a conversion from the world to religion. It is used as a technical philosophical term for a change of substance, particularly in the Eucharist. But it is also used for the turning of a man to God. It will be found frequently in Bernard of Clairvaux, for example, in this sense. Aquinas, on the other hand, chooses to speak of 'justification' – e.g. 'the justification of the ungodly' (*Summa Theologica*, 1.113).

The Reformers were shy of the word. The index to the Erlangen edition of Luther's works, for example, gives only four instances of 'conversion' (*Bekehrung*), but a very large number of 'repentance' or 'penitence'. He uses the verb actively: 'to convert sincerely and with complete seriousness, and to become another man, although the flesh and the outward man does not cease to strive and lust in a contrary direction' (EA, xxxviii, p. 339). Here 'convert' means to turn in another direction. Soon after in this context, he again identifies conversion with a change (*Veränderung*). But what he is chiefly concerned to bring out is that conversion is the work of the Holy Spirit. Against Erasmus on free-will he presses that the commands to turn in the OT (and especially Jeremiah) do not imply that repentance and turning (i.e. conversion) are in man's power (*The Bondage of the Will*, trans. J. I. Packer and O. R.

Johnston, 1957, pp. 157 ff.). On the contrary, 'He who is converted to faith, cannot say anything different than that the Holy Spirit comes when he will, and at what place he will, and to what person he will, and also at what time it pleases him' (EA, XLVI. p. 294). Repentance is viewed, not as a single act, but as the process of a life-time. It is on this note that he opens his attack on indulgences: 'Our Lord and Master Jesus Christ, in saying "Repent ye, etc.", meant the whole life of the faithful to be an act of penitence' ('Ninety-five Theses', *Documents of the Christian Church*, ed., H. Bettenson, 1943, p. 260).

Calvin is also not much given to the word, though there is a remarkable passage where he uses it in Sermon 170 on Deut. 30.6–10. Because we are enemies of God by nature, we have to be converted before we can hear God, observe his law and be subject to him. God must change us at the root, or we shall never bear good fruit. 'Now this word *Conversion* means that a man, instead of having his back turned to God, turns his face to him. It is as if Scripture speaks of a changing, as also it is said that we must be renewed' (CR, XXVIII, pp. 569–70). Elsewhere renewal is sharpened to resurrection: 'Observe from this that conversion is, as it were, resurrection from eternal death. For it is all up with us so long as we are turned away from God. Converted, we are reconciled and freed from death. Not that our repentance earns God's favour; but because it is in this way that the Lord raises us from death to life' (*Commentary on Isaiah*, 19.22. CR, XXXVI, p. 347). This is not, of course, effected by man's own power. He is converted 'not by his own will, but by the secret operation and impulse (*instinctu*) of the Holy Spirit' (*Praelection on Jeremiah*, 31.19. CR, XXXVIII, p. 673). We may even find Calvin preaching as if he believed that conversion is inevitably a single event. 'But now, as for us, we have the Gospel, we see that this is the opportune time, that this is the day of salvation, that this is God's acceptable time. Let us therefore make haste. Let us enter in while the door is open; while the way is clear let us advance along it. Let us not delay. For if God sees that we despise his grace, he can easily enough withdraw it, as also he threatens to do. Let us not therefore put off until tomorrow following where God calls us' (*Sermon*, 148, on Deut. 26.16. CR, XXVIII, p. 287). But he can also say: 'men never so repent as not to have need of the continuing help of God. For we are renewed from day to day, and little by little we renounce the desires of our flesh. We do not put off the old man in one day . . . We are converted to God (as I have said) gradually and by sure degrees; for penitence has its own increases (*progressus*)' (*Praelection on Jeremiah*, 31.18. CR, XXXVIII, p. 671).

In Bullinger, who by 'repentance' in the title of his sermon *Of Repentance, and the Causes thereof* (Decade 4, Sermon 2. PS, III, pp. 55–114) means 'a converting or turning to the Lord, for the acknowledging of sins, for the grief conceived for sins committed, for mortification, and the beginning to lead a new life; and finally for the change, correction, and amendment of the life from evil to better: that which we Germans call *Bekeerung* (*Bekehrung* – conversion), *Enderung* (*Änderung* – change), oder *Besserung* (amendment)' (PS, III, p. 56), we may probably trace the beginning of the Protestant scholastic *ordo salutis* (stages of salvation). In its later developed form the *ordo salutis* (with some variations) became *vocatio* (calling), *illuminatio* (enlightening), *conversio*, *sanctificatio*, and *unio Christi* (*see* H. Heppe, *Reformed Dogmatics,* 1934, ET, 1950, chaps. XX-XXII). We have here a symptom of that over-occupation with man that led at last to the resolving of theology into psychological categories. Although the scholastic method of precise and apparently cold analysis was abhorrent to the pietists, the two movements were treading the same path, not only in 'subjectivism' (a charge more to be levelled at the pietists than at the schoolmen, in whom this is, generally speaking, still only a tendency, an unheeded early warning), but also in the separating off of 'conversion' as an event in itself and on its own. We arrive at the pietist view of conversion as a necessarily instantaneous event. John Wesley held this originally, under the influence of Jacob Boehme, but he was to modify it when he learned from experience 'the irreconcilable variability in the operations of the Holy Spirit in the souls of men' (*see* A. S. Yates, *The Doctrine of Assurance,* 1952, p. 57). Like the Reformers, to whom he regarded himself as very close on this particular doctrine, he is not over-much given to the use of the word 'conversion'. But as a synonym he prefers, not repentance, but 'new birth'. This is nearer to Calvin's concept of conversion as resurrection. And we may note that both these aspects, death-resurrection and death-rebirth, are mirrored in baptism, the sacrament of conversion.

We may conclude with a brief examination of the language. (1) *Conversion.* It signifies a turning from sin and the rule of the devil to God. (2) *Repentance.* If used as commonly for the renunciation of sin, it is negative and needs to be supplemented by *faith* towards God. But in its NT signification, the dominant thought is reorientation. It is thus very close to converting or turning. (3) *Regeneration*, or *being born again.* The image expresses both a completely new beginning and also the entry into a family (*cf. adoption,* which, however, would be very rarely used as a synonym for conversion). The distinction made by William James between once-born and twice-born Christians is a pretty epigram but poor theology. The NT knows only twice-born Christians. It has unfortunately been seized upon by those who would have Christ to be a teacher, example, or leader, rather than the Redeemer. (4) *Change.* If used in conjunction with regeneration, this will mean primarily a change in status in the sight of God and cognately a change in attitude towards God. In the modern usage (e.g. by the Oxford Group Movement), it denotes a moral and psychological change. (5) *Deciding for Christ.* Here the weight

lies on an act of will by which a man determines to go over to the side of Christ. It has obvious affinities with existentialism, but is older than it. The father of existentialism, Søren Kierkegaard, would no doubt have thought it shallow. (6) *Accepting Christ.* This most interesting phrase was obviously thought at one time to be an accurate description of conversion, and also to be comprehensible to hearers, for it was in great vogue. It has now become so obscure, even to a sympathetic critic, that one finds difficulty in fixing meaning to the words. The full expression is: 'Accepting Christ as your personal Saviour'. If this meant: 'Accept with your whole being the fact that Jesus Christ is the Saviour of you personally in virtue of his death and resurrection' it would be following in the tradition of the NT, Augustine and the Reformers. If, however, it means (as one suspects it does), 'Accept Christ into your heart that he may become your personal Saviour', the notion is closer to the Roman Catholic doctrine of infused grace.

It would seem that the time is overdue for the Church to examine her doctrine of conversion carefully, and therefore in the process to subject her language about it to the test of theological inquiry.

T. H. L. PARKER

Coronation Rite

The present form of the English coronation rite goes back to the coronation of king Edgar in 973. It is set in the context of the Eucharist, and consists of three parts – the monarch's promises and the people's acclamation; the anointing; and the vesting with the regalia, the coronation and enthronement. The influence of the Reformation is seen in the presentation of the Bible, but in its main structure and contents the service is mediaeval.

What does the rite do to the monarch? It does not make him a king, for his accession dates from the death of his predecessor. It was held in the thirteenth century that the anointing was a sacramental act conferring the sevenfold gift of the Holy Spirit, but it is difficult to see how this differs from confirmation. English kings have not exercised either liturgical or priestly functions, and at the Reformation a careful distinction was made between the power of jurisdiction in ecclesiastical matters and the power of order, *potestas ordinis*. In modern times the rite is interpreted both as the personal dedication of the monarch at the beginning of his reign and a public and solemn acknowledgment on the part of the nation that all earthly power depends upon God.

E. C. Ratcliff, *The English Coronation Service,* 1936.

R. CANT

Corpus Christi

Corpus Christi (Latin: The Body of Christ) is a feast observed in the Western Church on the Thursday after Trinity Sunday in honour of the

Holy Eucharist and in commemoration of its institution. Originating in the visions of a nun at Liège in the earlier part of the thirteenth century, it was officially established by Pope Urban IV in 1264, and its observance became universal throughout Western Christendom. The Office and Mass for the Feast were composed by St Thomas Aquinas and contain several magnificent hymns. The most spectacular feature of the Feast is the solemn procession of the Sacred Host.

E. L. MASCALL

Corredemptrix, Co-Redemptrix

It is a title that has been widely applied to the Blessed Virgin Mary to indicate the part played by her in the redemption of the world by her Son; it does not occur in the catalogue of titles applied to her in the Constitution on the Church of the Second Vatican Council (n.62). It has been argued, as by R. Laurentin (*Le Titre de Corédemptrice*, 1951), that the supersession by it of the earlier title *Redemptrix* was deliberately intended to indicate the subordinate character of Mary's role; *cf.* the description in II Cor. 6.1 of all Christians as 'co-operators' (*Synergountes*) *with* Christ, where the prefix clearly implies not an equal but a subsidiary agency.

E. L. MASCALL

Cosmogony

Cosmogony is derived from a Greek word implying the brining forth of the universe (Greek: *kosmos*); the term indicates the theory of the origins of the physical universe. It is used of the mythological-metaphysical speculations of primitive peoples (e.g. the Egyptian generative world-egg or the Hindu tortoise supporting the elephant) and especially of the early Greek philosophers (Thales' view that the world was made of water, and so on). Plato's *Timaeus* is probably the most influential cosmogony ever written; it dominated European thought until the rise of modern science. The term is also used of the *speculative theories* of modern scientists themselves concerning the beginning and the end of the physical universe, e.g. whether it originated at a moment of 'creation' between twenty and sixty thousand million years ago, when a superdense primeval atom disintegrated, or whether the universe is in a steady state, while within it there is a continuous creation of matter and stars and galaxies are evolving and disappearing throughout infinite time. These speculations in no way involve theological doctrines, such as the creation of the world by God, since science involves a resolute methodical atheism (q.v.) and cannot answer theological questions. Christian theology for its part is indifferent as to which of the two hypotheses mentioned is correct (or neither of them), because nowadays it is not supposed that there is a revealed cosmogony in the Bible which may be proved or disproved by scientific research. *See also* **Cosmology.**

A. C. B. Lovell, *The Individual and the Universe*, 1958, ch. VI; E. L. Mascall, *Christian Theology and Natural Science*, 1956.

EDITOR

Cosmology

There is no very clear distinction between cosmogony (q.v.) and cosmology (literally, 'talking about the ordered universe'; the Greek *kosmos* carries the meaning of an ordered whole, even a thing of beauty). It may be said that in general usage cosmology is wider than cosmogony and embraces it. The word may be used in three ways. (1) It may be considered a part of metaphysics, as it was in the Age of Enlightenment (q.v.), dealing with the totality of things, or with such questions as whether a creative mind could be inferred from the ordered universe (*cf.* the 'cosmological argument'; *see* **God** [6]). This usage is less common today. (2) It may be used of the discussion of contemporary scientific theories of the universe, e.g. 'steady state' theories or the theory of the 'expanding universe'. In this sense it is used more frequently than 'cosmogony'. (3) In theological discussion it usually refers to the world-view of a particular age, e.g. the Ptolemaic cosmology. It is not generally understood that the Bible itself has no one cosmology but several. The Hebrews were not interested in such matters and borrowed their cosmological ideas from their contemporaries, such as the Babylonians or the Greeks. Nor is it generally recognized that the so-called cosmology of the three-storey universe is not that of the Bible but that of the late mediaeval world-view. This was a synthesis of Greek and biblical ideas, but it owes more to the Aristotelian-Ptolemaic theory of the universe than it does to the Bible. Such is the mental furniture which 'modern' men and women are today slowly discarding, two centuries or more after the disintegration of the mediaeval world-view at the period of the Enlightenment (*see* **Fides Historica)**. It is not the biblical cosmology which requires demythologizing, because such cosmological ideas as we meet with in the Bible are merely forms of communication or symbols rather than pieces of information about the structure of the universe. It is because rationalistic biblical critics have read their Western literalism into the symbolic language of the Bible that it has appeared to them necessary to set up a highly elaborate procedure for demythologizing elements of the Bible which were not mythical but symbolical in character. *See also* **Cosmogony; Symbolism.**

Alan Richardson, *History Sacred and Profane*, 1964, ch. 2.

EDITOR

Counter-Reformation

The phenomena usually treated under this head include much more than the reactions within Roman Catholicism to the Protestant Reformation. Out of Spanish mystical piety came the work of Ignatius Loyola (d. 1556) and the world-wide missions and educational efforts of the Jesuit

Order. Numerous other Orders, chiefly in Italy, engaged in work of clerical reform, preaching, hearing confessions and service to the poor. A large body of controversial writing reaffirmed against Protestantism scholastic doctrines and papal authority. Paul III (1534–49) was the first of a series of reforming popes. Under him the Council of Trent (q.v.) began its sessions. It was to meet intermittently over a period of eighteen years (1545–63) and to produce documents that formed a new basis for the modern advance of the Church. Among the representative writers of the Counter-Reformation may be named: John Fisher, bishop of Rochester; John Eck, John Cochlaeus, Josse Clichtove, Alfonsus de Castro, Melchior Cano, and at the later stage Cardinal Carlo Borromeo, chief author of the Catechism of Trent (1564), Philip Neri, founder of the Oratory (1564) and the learned Caesar Baronius, author of the *Ecclesiastical Annals.*

E. M. Burns, *The Counter-Reformation,* 1964; B. J. Kidd, *The Counter-Reformation,* 1933; Many representative sources are in the series, *Corpus Catholicorum: Werke katholischer Schriftsteller im Zeitalter der Glaubensspaltung,* ed., J. Greving and A. Ehrhard, 1919– .

J. T. MCNEILL

Covenant

The idea of the covenant relationship between God and Israel is utterly basic to the theology of the OT. The thought was basic for Christ, too. He took the idea and fulfilled it, and his apostles (and the NT writers) both used it and developed it. (So basic is the word to biblical theology that under the titles of the Old Covenant and the New Covenant it provides the name of the collection of writings we call the Bible.)

The covenant with Israel stemmed from the sovereign, gracious, freewill of God; this divinely originating move and no other constituted Israel as the People of God. God on his part was always sure and steadfast, utterly unchangeable (Ex. 34.6), and demanded of the patriarchs Abraham, Isaac, Jacob, as they renewed it, utter faithfulness on their part. A highly significant development arose with the prophets who restlessly began to seek for and hope for a different and better covenant, a true faithfulness. They pictured this in all kinds of symbols: a better marriage (Hos. 2.22); as idealized in a more faithful servant of a different kind (Isa. 42.18 ff.; 52.13 ff.); a new covenant written on the heart (Jer. 31; Ezek. 36–7). This prophetic hope is of considerable importance to the Christian interpretation of covenant, and is not always given its due weight. (*See* **Recapitulation.**)

The crucial transition between the OT idea at its height in the prophets and in Christ's use of the word is made at the Last Supper (Mark 14.22–5 and parallels), an idea strikingly fulfilled by Paul who spoke of Christ's death sealing the new covenant (I Cor. 11.23–25). The solemnity of the hour stresses the importance of the thought, which may appropriately be described as Christ's last word. This new covenant is incontrovertibly associated with Christ's death and with the forgiveness of sins. Whereas under the old covenant men offered their own imperfect righteousness and their faulty allegiance in exchange for the promises and mercies of God, under the new covenant men without claim or merit are freely forgiven by God in Christ, who at the cost of supreme sacrifice reconciles men to God. All the hopes and ideals of the old covenant simply melt into the grandeur of such a conception of the new covenant. Here is the entire Gospel: here is perfect atonement. God is finally proved gracious, and the New Israel is restored in a new relationship and with the new commission of offering this gospel to the entire world. For biblical references *see* J. O. Cobham, 'Covenant', *TWBB. See also* **Initiation, Christian.**

JAMES ATKINSON

Covenanters

The 'godly band' by which the Protestant Scottish lords agreed to defend the adherents of the Reformation (1557) has been called the first national covenant. More truly national was the covenant of 1581 reaffirming the Confession of Faith of 1560 which had the authority of both the General Assembly and the King and was renewed in 1590 and in 1596. The name 'Covenanters', however, became the designation of those who subscribed, first in Greyfriars Church, Edinburgh, the Covenant of 1638, protesting the prayer book prescribed by Charles I. The treaty known as the Solemn League and Covenant of 1643 extended to England the principle of a covenant for the establishment of Presbyterianism, and in the Westminster Assembly the concept was strongly asserted by the Scottish commissioners, especially George Gillespie and Samuel Rutherford. After the defeat of Presbyterianism in England and the suppression of the Scottish Assembly by Cromwell, many Scots still ardently affirmed the principle of a religiously covenanted nation and held the previous covenants to be perpetually binding. Under Charles II they gathered in conventicles led by their 'outed' ministers but suffered under increasingly drastic penal laws enforced by dragoons. The 'killing time' ended, except for the execution of notable individuals, under James II. The struggle is a significant part of the background of the Revolution of 1688.

T. R. Barnett, *The Story of the Covenants,* 1928; J. Barr, *The Scottish Covenanters,* 1946; G. D. Henderson, *Religious Life in Seventeenth-Century Scotland,* 1937; J. C. Johnston, *The Treasury of the Covenant,* 1887.

J. T. MCNEILL

Creation

The Apostle's Creed begins by confessing faith in 'God, the Father Almighty, maker of heaven and earth'. Belief in God as the Creator is central to

Christian faith. The Bible begins with the Genesis story of creation, and most of the Bible presupposes that the world is the creation of God. Langdon Gilkey does not overstate the case when he says: 'The idea that God is the Creator of all things is the indispensable foundation on which the other beliefs of the Christian faith are based.' When early Gnosticism argued that the God who created the world is not the same God who redeems men, the Church had to repudiate this view as a major perversion of the whole Christian faith.

The Hebrew people came to a belief in creation neither through a philosophical analysis of the origin of things nor through a search for a First Cause. On the contrary, they found God as he acted in history and it was because they were convinced that God is the Lord of all nations that they were led to see that he is the Creator. The Christian doctrine of God as Creator is not a cosmological theory. Rather, as Luther expressed it in his *Small Catechism*, God's creation means 'that God has created me and all that exists; that he has given me and still sustains my body and soul, all my limbs and senses, my reason and the faculties of my mind . . .'. In short, the doctrine of creation is a confession of a man's absolute dependence upon God.

In recent centuries there have been a number of debates between natural science and theology about creation. These debates became most heated when science accepted the hypothesis of evolution. Evolutionary theory seemed to conflict with the Genesis account of creation. Furthermore, science claimed to be able to explain all events by reference to a purely natural sequence of cause and effect, without any need of the 'hypothesis' of God. This scientific challenge to the doctrine of creation has been met in two quite different ways. One group of thinkers has tried to demonstrate that the biblical account of creation can be harmonized with scientific views. Another group has denied that there could be any conflict between science and theology because the two disciplines are not dealing with the same kind of question or explanation.

The first approach, adopted by fundamentalists and conservative Christians, begins by showing the rather amazing parallel between the order of the appearance of life forms as depicted in Genesis and the order described by modern science. Where contradictions do appear, it is argued that scientific conclusions are continually changing so that if the Bible agreed completely with today's science, it would no doubt be in disagreement with tomorrow's science. At certain points this approach reinterprets the Bible. For example, where Genesis refers to creation in six days, it is pointed out that a 'day' in Genesis does not necessarily mean a period of twenty-four hours, it may mean an indefinite period of time. This approach does not have a wide theological following today.

The second approach has been developed during the last two centuries. Often it is expressed by saying that science deals with the 'how' and theology with the 'why' of events. Typically this approach points out that a scientific explanation must be in terms of causal relationships within the natural order. Scientific explanation occurs when it is possible to demonstrate the continuing patterns of events and to describe them within general laws and hypotheses that have been found to hold true in general. By its very nature science cannot explain the completely unique or solitary event and it does not explain in terms of free actions or purposes. Because theology speaks of creation as an unique event, performed through God's free decision for his purposes, creation is in principle beyond scientific study.

The attempt to interpret the theological doctrine of creation as an explanation that cannot conflict with science is attacked by various forms of positivism which insist that the only explanations that are possible or meaningful are those made by science. But developments in recent philosophy have cast doubt on this viewpoint. Contemporary Anglo-Saxon philosophy has demonstrated that man 'plays many language games'. That is, different forms of discourse are used for different purposes and thus there are different legitimate ways of explaining events. Thus philosopher Gilbert Ryle points out that even if the day comes when physics has answered all questions of physics, we must remember that not all questions are questions of physics. Ryle illustrates his point by a reference to a game of billiards. No movement of a billiard ball breaks any of the laws of mechanics and thus the whole of a billiards game can be explained in terms of mechanical laws. But such an explanation, although complete in itself, does not satisfy us. To understand a billiards game we must also explain it in terms of the rules of billiards and the strategies or purposes of the players.

In light of such understanding of different forms of explanation, the theologian argues that the theological explanation which speaks of God as the Creator is not meant to answer the kind of question that science answers. Genesis does not provide a hypothesis that would explain the causal sequence of the origin of the universe or which could be put into competition with scientific theories. The biblical doctrine of creation is compatible with all scientific theories of how the universe developed. In terms of Ryle's billiards illustration, Genesis contributes nothing to our knowledge of the mechanical laws involved but it does reveal who the 'player' is and something of his 'strategy'. That is, the doctrine of creation is a doctrine that deals with the purposes behind the universe. The Christian claims to have no revelation about how the universe has developed; that is a question for science to answer, but he does believe that he has a revelation from the One whose purpose lies behind its development.

This general theological approach divides into two wings. One group argues that while theology does not give a scientific answer, it does give an answer to metaphysical questions. This line of thought is well represented by Thomism which identifies God, the Creator, with the metaphysical concept of the First Cause (*see* **God** [6]). Whereas science cannot locate a First Cause, rational thought is none the less able to demonstrate that, of necessity, there is a First Cause. This metaphysical conclusion justifies us in accepting the biblical revelation in which the First Cause reveals his true nature.

The use of metaphysical arguments to defend theological language about creation is under considerable suspicion today. Contemporary philosophy has directed a devastating attack upon all metaphysical thinking. But perhaps more important is the fact that a significant group of theologians has denied that it is possible to identify the biblical God with any philosophical First Cause. To think of God as the First Cause runs almost inevitably into one of two dangers. It may so emphasize the analogy between the First Cause and other causes that it loses sight of God's transcendence and sees him as a part of the universe. On the other hand, it may defend God's transcendence by asserting the radical difference between the First Cause and all other causes, but then the analogy becomes so strained that it is debatable whether it is any longer meaningful to speak of the First Cause as a 'cause'. Because of such problems, this wing of theology denies that man can gain any metaphysical knowledge of God by philosophical methods. Instead, it asserts that our knowledge of God as Creator is dependent upon revelation alone.

1. *Continuing Creation.* Christians do not think of creation as being simply an event in the past. Deism taught that God had created the world, somewhat as a watch-maker manufactures a watch, which then runs independently of its maker. Against such a view Calvin speaks for the traditional Christian position when he says: 'To represent God as a Creator only for a moment, who entirely finished all his work at once, were frigid and jejune. . . .' The universe, the Christian believes, continues to depend upon God's creative power for its existence at all times.

On the other hand, the Christian doctrine affirms that the created universe does have a real existence separate from God. It has its own laws of operation as a result of God's creative action. Although the universe remains within God's Providence, the events within it cannot be simply identified with God's action. This is true both of the natural forces which operate according to their created laws and of man who has been created with freedom so that he is capable of acting contrary to the will of God.

2. *Ex Nihilo.* One of the distinctive features of the Christian doctrine of creation is the affirmation that it is *ex nihilo*, that is, God creates it 'out of nothing'. The actual term 'out of nothing' does not appear in the biblical references to creation. It probably appears for the first time in the Second Book of the Maccabees but it has been held consistently in Christian theology.

The concept of *ex nihilo* is not intended to provide a positive description of God's creative activity, it is rather a denial of opposing views. It denies the Platonic view that God created the world out of pre-existing matter and ideas. This means that Christianity denies all forms of ultimate dualism. God alone is responsible for the existence of all that is. This makes it impossible for the Christian to locate the source of evil in matter and hence in the body of man as did Neoplatonism. To the Christian the material world is good. Various attempts through the centuries, beginning with Gnosticism, to see the 'nothing' as an ominous kind of something which opposes God are hence contrary to Christian faith. On the other hand, the doctrine of creation out of nothing also denies that the world is either God or an emanation from God. As a result Christianity rejects all forms of pantheism.

Creation out of nothing is a doctrine that arises from out of the unique Judaeo-Christian understanding of God. Biblical monotheism is not simply a matter of believing in one God instead of several. It arises from an understanding of the biblical God as being radically different from other concepts of gods. The biblical God is not limited by anything beyond himself, except for those areas of his own creation where he willed to limit himself. The biblical God is truly Lord of all.

Creative activity as we find it in man is sometimes seen as analogous to God's creative activity. But creation out of nothing places a wide gulf between the creativity of God and of man. The most creative acts of man are always a restructuring of the environment given to man. God alone may create out of nothing.

K. Barth, *Church Dogmatics*, III: *The Doctrine of Creation*, 1, 1958; E. Brunner, *Dogmatics*, II: *The Christian Doctrine of Creation and Redemption*, 1952; L. Gilkey, *Maker of Heaven and Earth*, 1959.

WILLIAM HORDERN

Creationism

Creationism is the official Roman Catholic doctrine which teaches that each individual soul is created by God at the moment of the individual's conception. Creationism developed to replace various alternative theories of the soul's origin. Some early Christians accepted the Platonic view of the pre-existence of each soul. Others accepted the view that the soul is an emanation from God himself. Tertullian developed a view, known as traducianism, which argued that the soul is a human substance that comes into existence through the procreative action of the parents. Traducianism could interpret original sin, therefore, in terms of an actual biological inheritance transmitted from Adam through one's parents. Augustine accepted the view that original sin and guilt are inherited through human procreation but he did not accept the hypothesis of traducianism.

Aquinas explicitly taught creationism. Luther leaned towards traducianism and Calvin towards creationism.

WILLIAM HORDERN

Creed(s)

In OT religion there are no creeds that correspond to the Christian creeds. The Israelites (or the Jews of NT times) were not united by means of a common system of doctrine. There were sects in Judaism (e.g. Pharisees, Sadducees, etc.), but they were not nonconformist; they all worshipped in the Temple. What the Jew recited daily was the *Shema* (the word means 'hear' and it is the first word of Deut. 6.4: 'Hear, O Israel: The Lord our God is one Lord, and you shall love the Lord your God with all your heart . . .'). The form of the Shema is not a *credo* but a command. The Jew's faith was something which he did, and when he confessed it he made an act of obedience. Orthopraxis (i.e. right behaviour) rather than orthodoxy (right opinion) was important in his eyes. The common allegiance expressed by the Shema did not excommunicate heretics but rebuked the disobedient.

Christianity began life as a Jewish sect (*cf*. Acts 28.22). Why then did it become necessary to develop a doctrinal creed or creeds? The answer must have something to do with the fact that, having spread into the Greek world, the converts from paganism required (as a born Jew never did) instruction in a faith which was not that of his fathers. The disputations and permissive atmosphere of the Hellenistic world made it necessary (as it never was in Judaism) to insist upon the affirmation of truths which certain parties had denied. Thus, we are not surprised to find that the earliest Christian creeds are baptismal creeds: the instructed catechumen, when he was baptized, confessed his faith in a personal affirmation. Doubtless this affirmation was in the earliest days very short and simple: 'Jesus is Lord' (*cf*. I Cor. 12.3), 'Jesus Christ is the Son of God' (Acts 8.37, RV margin only); the NT at Matt. 28.19 seems to give us an early trinitarian baptismal formula. There are also in the NT other passages which read like early credal formularies (e.g. I Cor. 8.6). Different local churches seem to have used different credal forms, but eventually the Old Roman Creed developed into the creed which we call the Apostles' Creed, which was doubtless helped to attain universality by the legend of its apostolic composition.

Besides the baptismal creeds there were also the conciliar creeds, i.e. creeds drawn up by ecumenical councils to refute heresy. The most famous of these is the Nicene Creed, or more correctly the Niceno-Constantinopolitan Creed, because it consisted of the original creed of the Council of Nicea (AD 325) as confirmed and expanded by the Council of Constantinople in 381. This creed was the Catholic response to the Arian heresy (q.v.). Conciliar creeds originally began with the words 'We believe' instead of the 'I believe' of the baptismal creeds.

Along with the Apostles' Creed and the Nicene Creed there stands in the West the so-called Athanasian Creed (which, unlike the Nicene Creed, has nothing to do with Athanasius). It is not, however, ecumenical in the sense that the others are, because it was composed in Latin and has never been used in the East. It seems to belong to the period of the Apollinarian controversy (q.v.). It is used in the Roman, Lutheran and Anglican communions, but with decreasing regularity, because its language is not readily intelligible today and also because of its anathemas or so-called 'damnation clauses' (*see also* **Orthodoxy**).

In churches where traditional liturgical rites are used the Apostles' and Nicene Creeds are said or sung (with more or less elaborate musical settings) as acts of praise during worship. Like the *Te Deum* they recite the acts of God for our salvation. In this sense they resemble certain of the Psalms or those 'confessions' of the OT in which the faithful Israelite recited the wonderful works of God for his salvation (e.g. Deut. 26.1–11; Josh. 24.1–14; Pss. 105; 106). Instructed church-goers, who understand their historical background and the poetic-symbolic character of their words, can join whole-heartedly in the recitation of these ancient creeds.

Yet it must be admitted that the ancient creeds are better as hymns of praise than as formulations of doctrine for the use of Christians today. As long ago as the orthodox Protestant theologians of the seventeenth century they were criticized as dealing with matters only on the periphery of the Gospel (e.g. the virgin birth or the descent into hell) while neglecting the all important theme of justification by faith. The truth is that every age requires its own contemporary formulation of the faith; the faith can never be captured in any set of propositional forms which shall be valid for every age. The Reformers found it necessary not indeed to re-place the creeds, but to re-interpret them in the various Confessions (q.v.) with which they sought to answer the questions that confronted their own generation. But these works, as Oscar Cullmann has pointed out, tended to involve an exegesis of the whole Bible. They would be unsuitable as 'symbols' (q.v.) or watchwords of the unity of the faith down the ages, and they have never inspired the great religious composers to set them to music for choral or congregational recitation. The traditional creeds, if understood historically and used in the tradition of liturgical worship, have great value as an expression of the unity of the faith, linking ancient and modern believers in a communion of saints which knows no limitations of space and time. *See also* **Orthodoxy**.

O. Cullmann, *The Earliest Christian Confessions*, ET, 1949; W. A. Curtis, *A History of Creeds and Confessions of Faith*, 1911; Alan Richardson, *Creeds in the Making*, 1935.

EDITOR

Crisis Theology

Crisis theology is the title of that type of theology initiated immediately after the first World War by several theologians under the leadership and inspiration of Karl Barth (1886–). The term 'crisis' may be legitimately interpreted in several ways. First, as indicating the critical point in an illness; Barth and his colleagues were convinced that nineteenth century anthropological, immanentist, optimistic theology had shown itself to be dangerously unhealthy by the second decade of the twentieth century, and that the time was now ripe for a new, healthy and vigorous type of theological thought. Secondly, the term may usefully be taken as referring to the *critical* times through which Christian theology was passing, in the light of the approval which had been given by distinguished German liberal theologians to the German government's war policies in 1914. But, most significantly of all, the term 'crisis' refers quite literally to the *judgment* (Greek: *krisis*) of God emphasized by Barth and his fellow crisis theologians in their new theological emphasis, a judgment regarded as falling uniformly and severely upon all merely natural and human endeavours and enterprises, including moral and religious ones. The main influences upon Barth are usually taken to be the Pauline writings of the NT, the thought of the sixteenth-century Reformers (of Calvin especially), and the writings of certain nineteenth-century critics of bourgeois liberal Christianity, most especially Kierkegaard and Dostoievsky. In the early years of his new theological programme Barth was closely associated with other theologians, for example, with Eduard Thurneysen, Friedrich Gogarten and Paul Tillich.

Crisis theology (sometimes known as *dialectical* theology, q.v.) made rapid progress towards becoming continental theological orthodoxy during the 1920s and particularly during the 1930s, and its influence soon came to be felt strongly in Britain and in the USA. Two episodes in the career of crisis theology in the 1930s deserve brief mention here. First, it made a significant contribution to the cause of the German Confessing Church in its struggle for doctrinal purity and autonomy against the so-called 'German Christians' (q.v.), that section of German Protestantism which was prepared to synthesize Christian doctrine with German National Socialist racist ideology. The strong influence of crisis theology can be clearly seen in the teaching of the Declaration of Barmen (q.v.) (May 1934), which, over against the doctrine of the German Christians, explicitly denied the existence of 'subordinate revelations of God' (e.g. in history, nature or race), apart from God's only and sufficient revelation in Jesus Christ as witnessed to in the Church by Holy Scripture. Secondly, there was the celebrated dispute between Barth and Emil Brunner in 1934, over Brunner's suggestion that there was a limited place in Christian theology for natural theology, a suggestion that evoked from Barth his celebrated pamphlet *Nein! Antwort an Emil Brunner* (*No! An Answer to Emil Brunner*), in which Barth reiterated the fundamental negative tenet of crisis theology that there was absolutely no 'point of contact' (German: *Anknüpfungspunkt*) between human nature and God's revelation, and hence that *all* natural theology is an impossibility.

The *direct* influence of crisis theology has declined gradually since 1945, although it has left a deep mark on postwar theology in continental Europe, in Britain and in the USA. One theologian, Dietrich Bonhoeffer (1906–1945), for example, whose work lies at the centre of contemporary theological debate, was decisively influenced in his formative years by crisis theology; his later revolutionary views (as expressed in his *Letters and Papers from Prison* [illus. and rev. ed., 1967]) are almost unintelligible if they are interpreted in isolation from this seminal influence. See **Barmen Declaration; Barth, K.; Bonhoeffer, D.; Brunner, E.; Dialectical Theology; Gogarten, F.; Liberal Protestantism; Neo-Orthodoxy; Nygren, A.; Point of Contact.**

H. R. Mackintosh, *Types of Modern Theology*, 1937 and 1963; J. Macquarrie, *Twentieth-Century Religious Thought*, 1963; James Richmond, *Faith and Philosophy*, 1966; S. P. Schilling, *Contemporary Continental Theologians*, 1966; Paul Tillich, *Perspectives on Nineteenth and Twentieth Century Protestant Theology*, 1967.

JAMES RICHMOND

Criticism, Biblical

The development of the historical criticism of the Bible in the nineteenth century caused widespread alarm among Christian people (*see* Essays and Reviews). The word 'criticism' was misunderstood, and it was feared that sceptical thinkers were venturing to criticize or pass judgment upon God's word in the Holy Scriptures. In fact, the word had been a technical term among scholars for centuries. An *apparatus criticus*, which included variant readings in the MSS., had been usual since 1550, when R. Stephanus' Greek NT printed a critical apparatus for the first time. This kind of critical reconstruction of the text is known as *lower criticism*. It is thus distinguished from *higher criticism*, the application of modern literary and historical critical methods to the study of the Bible. *Source criticism* refers to the investigation of the sources (e.g. the J [Jahvist] source in Genesis, or the Q source in the Synoptic Gospels). *Form criticism* is the name given to the method of assessing the historicity, provenance, etc. of biblical passages by means of a careful analysis of their forms, thus determining whether they belong to a recognizable group. The method was first developed in OT studies by H. Gunkel and was then applied by M. Dibelius, R. Bultmann, K.-L. Schmidt and others after first World War to the study of the Synoptic Gospels with a view to reconstructing the oral traditions which lay behind the written records. *See also* **History, Problem of.**

Most introductory text-books contain accounts of the critical method and its development. For an historical survey *see* Stephen Neill, *The Interpretation of the New Testament, 1861–1961*, 1964; S. L. Greenslade, ed., *Cambridge History of the Bible: the West from the Reformation*, 1963, chs. VII and VIII; W. G. Kümmel, *Introduction to the New Testament*, ET, 1966, a work of considerable detail. Perhaps the most useful general introduction is Robert M. Grant's *Historical Introduction to the New Testament*, 1963. For form criticism *see* M. Dibelius, *From Tradition to Gospel*, ET, 1934; R. Bultmann, *History of the Synoptic Tradition*, ET, 1963; for a general introduction *see* Vincent Taylor, *The Formation of the Gospel Tradition*, 1933.

EDITOR

Cross, Theology of the

Crucifixion was a Roman and not a Jewish punishment. There was always the remote possibility that a Jewish felon, on the rare occasion of a capital offence, could have his body impaled on a stake and exhibited to the public by way of a deterrent, but it was the corpse that was impaled, never the living man, and the corpse had to be taken down before sunset. Certain scholars (e.g. Paul Winter, C. K. Barrett) argue with some justification that Christ was executed by the Romans rather than by the Jews. This does not alter the fact that crucifixion ruled Christ out utterly as any kind of Messiah for the Jew (Deut. 21.33; Gal. 3.13), apart from their earlier rejection of him on religious and theological grounds.

Christ saw his cross as a victory and not a defeat (Mark 8.31; John 19.30), and both Paul and the early preachers in Acts proclaimed this fact as the victory over the powers of darkness (Col. 2.15; Acts 2.36, etc.). Nevertheless, the cross remained a theological difficulty for the Jew and a cultural offence to the Greek (I Cor. 1.23 f.; Gal. 5.11). Yet it was in this cultural situation that the preaching of the cross fired the imagination and stirred the will of the ancient world and became the power of God unto salvation. It was the very ignominy of public crucifixion undeserved, the agony of such pure innocence undergoing this bitter, degrading humiliation, that served to bring in high relief the love of God which could choose to take this way of redemption. At once the single word cross became a synonym and designation for the way of atonement God had chosen to reconcile lost man to himself (Col. 1.20; II Cor. 5.19), as well as the means of the creation of a common brotherhood for divided and alienated mankind. To Paul the word 'cross' meant the saving Gospel (I Cor. 1.18), and it was the touchstone of his message and mission (I Cor. 2.2). Here was the foolishness of God proved wiser than the wisdom of men (I Cor. 1.24 f.; II Cor. 13.4). The cross was the only way through an impasse created when the righteous God meets unrighteous man, who, in his wilful disobedience to the revealed, righteous will of God, earns the curse and hostility of God. This same God in Christ faced the full fury of sin and unbelief in its onslaught to destroy him. Though righteous and innocent he took the punishment for sin and unbelief and was treated as the worst sinner. He defeated sin by never succumbing to it, and thereby overcame death and mortality. As the willing victim he destroyed the curse by taking it on himself, thereby defeating a hitherto invincible power, and in breaking this power he released men from its bondage and tyranny into a new and eternal freedom. In fact, the cross might be described as a simpler word for atonement.

It was precisely at the point of his theology of the cross that Luther broke away from scholasticism to his evangelical theology. In 1518, when he faced his triennial chapter of the Augustinians at Heidelberg, Luther attacked the Aristotelianism of scholasticism and commended his Augustinian and biblical theology. He opposed the *theologia gloriae* (theology of glory) of his day in favour of a *theologia crucis* (a theology of the cross), a phrase he coined at that time. The *theologia gloriae* argued that a true knowledge of God could be obtained from a study of nature and tended to think of Christ in his divinity, an image of splendour and glory and worship. This Luther reversed. He argued that a proper knowledge of God could be found in the incarnation only (*deus incarnatus, deus revelatus*), and that God in his essence and purity was an unknown and hidden God (*deus incognitus, deus absconditus*), a view that has affected German theology profoundly ever since, not least Karl Barth's. Further, when Luther spoke of incarnation, he directed all his thinking to the weakness and powerlessness to which Christ submitted himself rather than to his majesty and power. He went further and taught that the hiddenness of God lay in the reversal of values the cross revealed, of life through death, of victory through sacrifice, of light through darkness, of power through weakness, the foolishness of God being wiser than the wisdom of man. Every theological revival in history has had the theology of the cross as a basic element.

The cross has also played a role in religious symbolism. The signing of the forehead with the cross can be traced back as far as Tertullian (c. 160–c. 220). As a mark it appears in the catacombs by about the fourth century. The progress from the cross to the crucifix took longer. Sozomen (early fifth century) speaks of the cross on the altar, but the crucifix proper with the dead Christ appears only in the eleventh-twelfth centuries (earlier than that Christ was portrayed alive). Helena, the mother of Constantine, visited the Holy Land in 326 and, according to fourth-century traditions, is reputed to have found there the true cross on which our Lord was crucified. A large part of this is said to have been distributed throughout the world in the form of small relics, the remainder preserved in a silver casket. The veneration of this cross is mentioned in the pilgrimage of Etheria (fourth century), the first known reference to the custom. This relic is reputed to have fallen into the hands of the Persians but was recovered by Emperor Heraclius in 629.

In Roman Catholic circles a rite of veneration occurs on Good Friday, using either relics or images, a ceremony which involves creeping to it, kissing it, saying prayers and singing hymns. Roman Catholic theologians assert that such practices have Christ and his redeeming love as their object and are not idolatrous. Aquinas thought the practice idolatrous (*Summa Theologica*, 3.1. q.25, a.4), and a number of modern theologians are of the same opinion. Certainly all the Reformers of the sixteenth century attacked the practices with energy. Similar rites occur on 3 May, its supposed invention (i.e. discovery), and on Holy Cross Day, 14 September, the Feast of the Exaltation of the Cross, the anniversary of the recovery by Heraclius in 629. *See also* **Atonement.**

JAMES ATKINSON

Cult, Cultus

From Latin *cultus*, worship (*colo*, to till the ground, cultivate, worship). Cult (or the Latin form cultus) is used especially of the rites and ceremonies of worship associated with a system of religious belief, whether Christian or non-Christian. 'Culture' is used in a wider or more secular sense of the whole intellectual, artistic and moral achievement of a society or an epoch; religion would thus be considered as a normal ingredient of culture, perhaps in some instances (such as the Christian Middle Ages) as its most important ingredient. *See* **Culture.**

EDITOR

Culture

If human culture is understood as a corporate undertaking in which men succeed in establishing a distinctive style of living based on common values, it can be seen that much of what is distinctive in Christian faith emerges from its dialogue with it. This dialogue is inherent in their relationship and takes place not only between Christians and those who do not share their faith but also among Christians themselves. This was clearly and self-consciously grasped from the beginning of the Christian story. The first account of creation in Genesis can be legitimately thought of as the imposition by God of an order, which implies a cultural pattern, upon primeval chaos. The earth is separated from the shapeless waters. The creatures are distinguished from each other, named and set in relationship. Man is given dominion. Yet we are immediately confronted with the second account, in which man, dwelling in the Garden, is seduced through the woman from that obedience to God from which he derives his dominion and surrenders himself to the serpentine power of the world about him, whose independent existence is not explained and which offers him an apparent freedom to manage his own life without reference to God. The result is that he is cast out of paradise and his work now becomes not the enjoyment and celebration of God's gifts but a painful struggle for survival.

This two-sided attitude to culture expresses itself throughout the OT. Babel, the representative institution of the religion and culture of the ancient Middle East, is confounded. Zion, the true city of God, is contrasted with Babel, but Zion herself also quickly becomes ambiguous. When, through the Exodus and the discipline of the Torah, Israel is able to settle in the promised land, she becomes vulnerable to the cultural complacency which besets all settled societies. This complacency was, to some extent, the consequence of her success, just as the desire to have a king and to have a glorious temple to house the traditionally mobile ark of the covenant were partly the fruit of a genuine desire to serve and magnify God. Yet the danger, which the great prophets saw so clearly, was that the life of Israel should become an end in itself and her faith turned into a self-enclosed culture-religion. The essence of that faith lay in her dependence on her Lord and her continual openness to fresh disclosures of his will from the One who is only really known in the commitment of venture into the unknown. Once that openness was lost, Israel had no barrier against cultural assimilation to the nations around her and no distinctive purpose and no power of self-criticism. This is the point of the insistence on the jealousy of God, of the eloquent rhetoric of Deuteronomy about the dangers of prosperity and of the denunciations and lamentations of the great prophets. Israel can enjoy the Law and the cultus and the kingship, but only if she realizes their relativity to the will of a God who stands over against her and who may at any time ask her to forsake them and to go on her travels again. It was their realization of this which made the prophets see the Exile, not as the catastrophe which it otherwise would have been, but as a corrective punishment, designed to recall Israel to the terms upon which she could alone keep covenant with God.

It is facts like these which give substance to the contention of the writer to the Hebrews that the men of faith of the OT sought a city with truly durable foundations, which they never identified with the earthly Jerusalem. They always strove to realize what Abraham was made to see at the beginning of their history, in the great story of the sacrifice of Isaac, that the way of life for Israel consisted always in being prepared to lose her life and that she must always love her Lord even more than the precious gift of the community of Israel which she has received from him as the fruit of the covenant.

This prophetic interpretation is intensified and fulfilled in the experience of Jesus. The cultural anthropologist would describe him as a man who was fully identified with the community of Israel. He grew up in obedience to the Law, a member of the house of David, and, as the story of the temptations implies, he discovered and defined his own task through sustained meditation upon the meaning of the tradition of Israel. Yet all this led him to reject the cultural forms through which Israel expressed her distinctive identity in his time, which, in its turn, meant his complete repudiation by the official representatives of Israel. It was not simply that he preached that the Sabbath was made for man and not man for the Sabbath, which meant that the Law must be seen as relative to man's highest good, which always has to be freshly defined; it was much more that he wanted Israel to see that the way in which she now thought of herself had become the greatest barrier to entry into the kingdom of God.

This is the point of Jesus' much misunderstood teaching about the rich man and the kingdom. The rich man is primarily Israel herself, blessed in the things of God – the Law, the cultus and the promised land. But these very fruits of past faith produced a self-sufficiency which prevented her from seeing her real relation to God and discerning his will for her present situation. This was why the spiritually impoverished publican was in a more hopeful situation. Jesus believed himself called to be the true representative of Israel, the one who was most conscious of her richness, who found that he could only fulfil the vocation of Israel by becoming poor. In becoming accursed for his brethren's sake, he accepted God's rejection of the empirical form of Israel's life and trusted in God's ability to establish a new way of life for his people. His death and resurrection are the exemplification of the truth proclaimed in the Sermon on the Mount which says that it is only as we first seek God's kingdom and his righteousness that the good fruits of human culture will be added to us and which concludes with the warning that only the house built on the rock of the faith celebrated in the Beatitudes, with their transvaluation of human values, is able to endure when the storms come.

Paul, who was also acutely conscious of what was involved for Christian faith in its break with the cultural tradition of the old Israel, underlined the fact, in Galatians and elsewhere, that the possession of the gifts of the Spirit means a rejection of the old patterns and a new outburst of cultural creativity, which must at all costs reflect the freedom of the Spirit. He was, however, so conscious of the imminence of the End and, in his later writings, was so caught up in turbulent events, that he had little incentive to deal with the kind of problem which arose when the rich community life of those who dwelt together in the mutual dependence and the *agape* which he described in classic terms became sufficiently articulated to have a well-defined cultural pattern of its own. Persecution prevented this from being a very living issue for the other NT writers also, except partly in the Pastoral Epistles and I Peter, but as the Church established itself in the world, and particularly in the post-Constantinian era, it became more and more inescapable. So pervasive, in fact, has it become that, in his well-known book *Christ and Culture*, Richard Niebuhr was able to distinguish five different types of attitude towards human culture which have received sig-

nificant expression in the history of the Church. He describes them as those respectively of Christ against culture, of the Christ of culture, of Christ above culture, of Christ and culture in a relationship of paradox, and of Christ as transformer of culture.

Niebuhr sees Tertullian and Tolstoi as the chief historical exemplars of the first attitude, which emphasizes the opposition between the claims of Christ and those of all forms of human culture. These Christians, it is asserted, do not see it as part of their responsibility to try to build a stable order of society in accordance with the divine command for the ordering of human life. Their duty is to withdraw into a community of their own, in which they do their best to minimize their earthly desires and reduce their contacts with those outside the saved community as much as possible. To possess many material goods or to exercise secular power is a form of disobedience.

The second attitude moves in the opposite direction, rejecting the first attitude as both inconsistently impracticable and unworthy, a denial of the promise of the gospel. Christ is the supreme example of universal human goodness and the fulfilment of cultural aspiration. This attitude is exemplified in different ways by Gnosticism in the early centuries, by Abelard in the Middle Ages and, in particular, by Schleiermacher and the whole liberal theological movement which has become widespread in modern Protestantism. All who share this attitude take a positive view of human cultural achievement but believe that it cannot be true to its best ideals except through obedience to Christ.

The third attitude, that of Christ above culture or, better, of Christ and culture in synthesis, has affinities with but also important points of difference from the second. It sees a clear distinction between the spirit of Christ and that of culture but does not believe that their relationship needs to be one of opposition. When culture fulfils its proper role, their relationship is complementary and a synthesis between them is possible. This is the attitude which has, perhaps, won most favour in the course of Christian history and it has inspired notions of Christendom and 'Christian civilization'. Its outstanding representative is the Roman Catholic Church in the Middle Ages, with Thomas Aquinas as its intellectual exponent. Clement of Alexandria in the ancient world and Bishop Butler in modern Anglicanism (Niebuhr might also have added Richard Hooker) are also good examples of synthesists. Those who hold this view lay great stress on the importance of law, which they see as natural law rather than revealed Torah, although with the recognition of a close relationship between the two. This law all men can see, but it is qualified and illuminated by the light of the gospel.

The fourth attitude, which sees Christ and culture standing in a relation of paradox, is exemplified by such great figures as Paul himself, Luther and Kierkegaard. Like those who see Christ and culture in opposition, they are acutely conscious of the distinctive character of the claim of Christ, but they accept realistically their inescapable involvement in the life of human culture, because they are men among men. They take both faith and culture too radically to find it possible to achieve a stable synthesis of them. They have to follow Luther's paradoxical injunction, *Pecca fortiter*, participating fully in human culture, conscious of its ambiguity, yet recognizing the inescapability of commitment and trusting to the forgiving mercy of God, which will open up the way of obedience to them in forms which cannot be foreseen. The tension in which men stand between the will of God and human culture cannot be relaxed except eschatologically, but this does not encourage a defeatist attitude in relation to the cultural possibilities of life on this earth. On the contrary, it encourages vigilance and self-criticism and stimulates creativity.

The last attitude is the conversionist one, which sees Christ as the great transformer of culture. Human culture on its own stands opposed to Christ, as part of a fallen world, but he gives men power to remove the threat to his lordship which all culture contains and to establish it on a different basis. Augustine, Calvin and, in modern times, F. D. Maurice are held to be representative conversionists. The world of culture has its demons, but they can be exorcized, and something like a new Christendom becomes a possibility, not through synthesis but through radical transformation.

While these five attitudes can be distinguished in history and it is helpful to see an otherwise almost intractably complicated story in their terms, it must be remembered both that these attitudes cannot in practice be so sharply distinguished from each other and that they are much more clearly exemplified by outstanding theologians and churchmen than by ordinary church people. Thus, while the first and the last two have a powerful impact and very considerable indirect influence, they have never been anything like as widespread as the second and the third. It is obvious that to maintain a consistent attitude of opposition to the ordinary life of the world is very hard, and all kinds of compromises will have to be made. To live in the situation of paradox as between Christ and culture is possible only to people of quite exceptional independence and insight, who are always few and far between. The whole drive of cultural achievement is, quite properly on its own terms, to reduce the tension and to try to make life in the tents of our earthly pilgrimage as comfortable and self-sufficient as possible. This means that, to the extent that men of faith live successfully in the paradox, they become rich, like the old Israel, and they, or still more their children, develop a synthetic or a cultural Christianity. Thus, Lutheranism, which, originally developed a theology of the orders of creation on the basis of a theology of paradox, quickly found itself subtly giving a much more positive status to such orders as the State and the family and thus transforming itself into a form of conservative culture-Protestantism.

A similar danger confronts the 'conversionist' in his attitude towards culture. The transformation of culture into the image of Christ is authentic only when it carries with it a prophetic challenge and risk. But when the transformation takes place in a particular situation, it is natural that it should lead to celebration and enjoyment, which in their turn lead to a relaxation of tension and an emphasis on consolidation of hard-won gains. This is why the transformationist's vision of the kingdom of Christ must always be radically eschatological, making him dissatisfied with his best achievements and acutely aware of the relativity of all earthly forms. Otherwise, to the extent to which he is serious, he cannot escape the dangers of theocracy, where men are set in the place of God, and this in its turn leads to a form of culture-Christianity, which may be repressive or 'soft-centred' according to circumstances. Christian experience through history suggests that a healthy relation cannot exist between faith and all forms of culture, including 'Christian' culture, without a measure of tension.

It is important to bear in mind the complicated history of the relation of faith to culture and the various attitudes which have seemed right at various times when we come to consider the current theological discussion inspired by the ideas of Dietrich Bonhoeffer, those of 'secularity', 'coming of age' and 'speaking to man in his strength'. To take a positive view of 'secularity', the recognition, that it is in this world and no other that we have to work out our present Christian obedience, can be seen as an act of faith in the transforming power of Christ. We should rejoice in man's strength and not feel under the necessity of trying to demonstrate to him that it is really weakness in order to make room for God. Like the riches of the Bible, this strength should be gratefully accepted as a gift from God, together with the freedom for creative action which it makes possible.

But the Bible and history make abundantly clear to us the perils of riches, and they are perils which are particularly acute in the modern world. If it is true that man has 'come of age', he has done so, Christians believe, only 'in Christ'. His power of self-direction is not, therefore, something which he can take for granted as a natural right, but a gift which has constantly to be renewed and which prompts him to choose one course rather than another. When, as the fruit of faith, men succeed in establishing a new cultural pattern, they are in danger, as we have seen, of slipping out of the situation of tension in which Niebuhr's 'paradoxical' school sees them to stand and of ignoring the perpetual challenge and risk of which his 'conversionists' are aware. When this happens, they are in danger of creating a new form of cultural Christianity or, at best, of achieving a new Christian synthesis which fails to do justice to the radicalism of the Christian claim. This is why the Church always needs to recall itself to the significance of the cross and resurrection of Jesus Christ and to see that all human culture, including

'Christian culture', has always to be revalued anew in their light.

W. Leibrecht, ed., *Religion and Culture*, 1959; H. Richard Niebuhr, *Christ and Culture*, 1952; Paul Tillich, *Theology of Culture*, ed., Robert C. Kimball, 1959.

DANIEL JENKINS

Cyprian, St

Cyprian (d. 259) was bishop of Carthage from 248 to 259, having been converted from paganism about two years before his consecration as bishop. In 259 he was martyred in the persecution directed by the Emperor Valerian. His period in the see of Carthage was marked by a number of events and controversies which called forth both his powers as ruler and counsellor of his flock as well as his capacities as a writer – the persecution under Decius, the Novatianist schism and the conflict with Stephen bishop of Rome over the re-baptism of heretics. One of his chief works, *De Lapsis* (*On those who have Lapsed*), was occasioned by the difficult situation created by the demand for re-admission to the Church of those who had lapsed during the Decian persecution, and the other, *De Catholicae Ecclesiae Unitate* (*On the Unity of the Catholic Church*), by the schisms in both Carthage and Rome which were part of the aftermath of that persecution. He wrote several minor works and a great number of letters, about seventy of which have survived to give us invaluable glimpses both into his thought and into the day-to-day working life of his north African see. Cyprian was not primarily a theologian but a pastor, an ecclesiastical statesman and an administrator. His concept of the role of the bishop was to be very influential in later Western thought, and indeed his ideas were determinative for the whole mediaeval concept of the Christian ministry. The bishop was the God-given ruler, shepherd and priest (a combination of the Roman magistrate and the OT priest), who governed his see, in consultation with his presbyters, independently of any other bishop, who offered sacrifice (the Eucharist) as the OT priest had done, and whose person was sacrosanct, as his had been. His office had been directly instituted by the apostles who were the first bishops. Cyprian's eucharistic theology (Christ is offered by the celebrant, and the bread and wine are his body and blood) laid the foundations of Western mediaeval eucharistic thought. In Cyprian's view the bishops of the Church had a common responsibility to God for the Church, and their unity was symbolized by the primacy in honour of the see of Peter. No bishop had jurisdiction over any other, and in his controversy with Stephen, whose practice of admitting heretics without re-baptizing them he strongly condemned, he always allowed that the pope had a right to his own opinion (*cf.* his well-known sentiment *salvo iure communionis diversa sentire*, 'allow diversity of opinion as long as communion is unbroken').

E. W. Benson, *Cyprian, his Life, his Time, his Works*, 1897; S. L. Greenslade, ed., *Early Latin Theology*, 1956, pp. 113–74.

R. P. C. HANSON

Cyril of Alexandria, St

St Cyril (d. 444) closely follows Athanasius and the Cappadocian Fathers in trinitarian theology. The doctrine of the Holy Spirit forms the subject of the ninth anathema against Nestorius, in which he describes the Spirit as belonging to or having the properties of the Son. In other passages Cyril's terminology varies between Procession 'from the Father through the Son' (the normal Eastern formula) and 'from the Father and the Son' (the Western description of Double Procession). No doctrinal difference is probably intended. *See also* **Christology** (4).

H. E. W. TURNER

Cyril of Jerusalem, St

Representative of non-party orthodoxy in the Arian controversy, Cyril (c. 315–386) was banished from his see in 357 for two years for his opposition to Arianism and later suspected by the Nicenes for his dislike of the *Homoousios* as a man-made term, though he finally accepted it. In his Catechetical Lectures (*c.* 350) Cyril maintained the full divinity of the Son and his Eternal Generation from the Father interpreted as a once for all act rather than as an eternally continuous process. The controversial *Homoousios* is avoided. His discussion of the Holy Spirit is notable for the period. While plainly holding his divinity, Cyril concentrates on his operations as described in Scripture.

The theory of F. J. A. Hort that the Nicaeno-Constantinopolitan Creed (C) represents substantially the Jerusalemite Creed submitted to the Council of Constantinople (381) as a test of Cyril's orthodoxy has failed to maintain itself. The Creed of Jerusalem can only be inferred from his writings and contains significant differences from (C). Nor is the historical situation implied by the theory probable.

H. E. W. TURNER

Damnation

The verb 'damn' (from Latin *damno*, to condemn) can be used in a non-religious sense (e.g. Alexander Pope, 'Damn with faint praise . . .'). 'Damnation' is the equivalent of the modern 'condemnation' and is usually used in the religious sense of divine condemnation to hell, punishment, etc. Certain dominical (q.v.) words (e.g. Matt. 25.46; Mark 9.43–8), if taken literalistically and also authoritatively, imply the eternity of damnation, but since the mid-nineteenth century the traditional doctrines of eternal punishment have been questioned (e.g. by F. D. Maurice, q.v.). *See also* **Heaven and Hell.**

EDITOR

Dasein

Dasein is a word used by M. Heidegger to denote human existence, i.e. man, not as an isolated individual nor yet as mankind in general, but as he finds himself in the world into which he is 'thrown' and there 'abandoned for death'. The word is made up of the German *da* and *sein* and literally means 'being there'. *Dasein* is contrasted with *Vorhandenheit*, the kind of being which belongs to things 'present-to-hand' of which we have no inward or personal awareness and to which we have only an external relatedness. The one thing man indubitably knows is his own thereness-in-the-world; he also knows that one day he will no longer be 'there', i.e. will no longer exist, for existence as we directly know it consists in our being there-in-the-world. This knowledge has an ontological as well as an existential dimension, for we take cognizance of our thereness, or of our involvement in being.

EDITOR

Deacon

A deacon is a member of one of the Orders (q.v.) of ministers or officers in the Church. The origin of the diaconate in the apostolic age is obscure (*see* H. J. Carpenter. 'Minister, Ministry', *TWBB*), and although Acts 6.1–6 was regarded by the patristic writers as the record of its institution this is very questionable. From the outset, however, the deacon was the bishop's right hand man (Phil. 1.1) and during the period of the early Church assisted him in all matters relating to the oversight of the Christian community. His duties were: (1) administrative: he collected alms and was responsible for Church funds; (2) pastoral: he informed the bishop of those who were sick and visited them himself, ministered to the confessors in prison, sought out offenders and reproved them; (3) liturgical: he kept the men's door at the Eucharist, from the fourth century replaced the lector as the reader of the Gospel, dismissed the catechumens and penitents, brought up the offerings and administered the chalice.

Although the diaconate was originally conceived in terms of function and its members therefore were normally appointed for life, it gradually hardened into an office and became a grade in an ascending hierarchy. Hence whereas initially it was possible for a deacon to become a bishop without having been a priest, in time he had to advance through all the Orders, and so Ambrose of Milan, who at the time of his election was not even baptized, underwent initiation and on successive days was made deacon, ordained priest and consecrated bishop, that is, he obtained his Orders *per saltem*, in jumps.

In the Middle Ages the deacon lost most of his administrative and pastoral duties and became mainly a liturgical minister on the way to the priesthood. This is generally the position in the West at the present day, so that, for example, in the Church of England the diaconate normally lasts only one year, being a period of probation before ordination to the priesthood. In the Reformed Churches, however, the deacon has no liturgical duties, Calvin having recognized two classes, those who administer alms and those who care for the sick, but among the Baptists and Congregationalists deacons help the minister in the distribution of the Eucharist.

Because of the necessity of *diakonia* (deaconing or service) to the life of the Church, there is an equal need for a particular ministry to embody this responsibility in order to recall the Church to service and to develop the life of service in the world. The diaconate therefore is or should be a ministry with a special character of its own and should not be regarded, as is often so, as an auxiliary function of a ministry that is set over it. Its distinctive character, however, is not to be recovered merely by a return to patristic practice, although this may assist in providing hints towards development.

J. G. Davies, 'Deacons, Deaconesses and the Minor Orders in the Patristic Period', *JEH*, XIV (1963), 1–15.

J. G. DAVIES

Deaconess

A deaconess is a member of an Order of women, which seems to have come into existence in the third century, having been developed in the East from the active widows to perform a ministry to women. Her duties were: (1) pastoral: she had to visit sick women in those heathen households where a deacon might not fittingly enter; (2) liturgical: she administered the pre-baptismal unction to women candidates; she gave instruction to women after baptism; she kept the women's door at the Eucharist and carried the reserved sacrament afterwards to sick women. The purpose and function of the Order, as understood in the patristic period, was clearly expressed by Epiphanius:

Although there is an Order of deaconesses in the Church, yet it is not for priestly service, nor to undertake anything of the sort, but on account of the modesty of the female sex with a view to either the occasion of Baptism, or of inspection of illness, or of suffering and when the woman's body is bared, so that it may not be seen by the men officiating, but by the deaconess, who is directed by the priest to see to the woman when her body is bared (*Adv. Haerr.* iii. 2.79).

In the nineteenth century the Order, which had fallen into abeyance in the early Middle Ages – it was abrogated by councils at Epaon (517) and Orleans (533) but is found in some centres as late as the eleventh century – was revived in the Church of England, the Church of Scotland and by the Methodists. The functions of a deaconess, however, are not clearly defined and while, in the Church of England, she is admitted by the laying on of episcopal hands and acquires a lifelong status, it is by no means evident what the extent and limitations of her ministry are. The circumstances that operated in the patristic period to bring about the inauguration of the order – the seclusion of women and their nakedness at baptism – no longer obtain in the West. Whether there are modern circumstances which require such an order is something that needs investigation.

Church of England, *The Ministry of Women*, 1919; J. G. Davies, 'Deacons, Deaconesses and the Minor Orders in the Patristic Period', *JEH*, XIV (1963), 1–15.

J. G. DAVIES

Death

Paul says that with sin death came to all men (Rom. 5.12). As a result, Christians traditionally believed that man was created immortal but lost his immortality as a result of his fall into sin. Consequently, it was logical for Anselm to argue in his *Cur Deus Homo* that Christ, being without sin, did not need to die. When Christ none the less voluntarily chose to die it was a vicarious acceptance of God's judgment upon the sin of the world. Aquinas argued that Adam was created with a supernatural power that would have preserved his immortality but he lost this power when he fell. Although God's grace brings man the forgiveness of his sins and the hope of glory, it does not remove the need for death that came with sin. The Reformers generally accepted the view that death is the result of sin.

Among modern theologians the relationship between sin and death has been questioned. We are aware today that whatever else he may be, man is a part of nature, an animal, and we know that death held sway among the animals before man sinned. Consequently it would appear that man dies because he is a finite creature and not because he is a sinner.

Despite this modern understanding, several contemporary theologians note that there is a deeper relationship between sin and death than appears on the surface. As Reinhold Niebuhr points out, man fears death in a way that animals do not. If we examine the NT treatment of death, it is evident that it frequently speaks of the living as being dead in sin (e.g. Eph. 2.1). Thus Niebuhr argues that the ideal possibility is that man, in perfect faith, would not fear death because of his assurance that neither life nor death is able to separate him from the love of God (Rom. 8.39). But sinful man, lacking faith, must approach death in fear. Thus Paul is correct in saying that the 'sting of death is sin' (I Cor. 15.56). Along the same lines, Emil Brunner argues that the result of sin is not that men die but that they die as they do with fear, agony and anxious uncertainty about what may lie on the other side of death.

This scheme has been developed most fully by Karl Barth. Death, Barth argues, as we see it in Christ's crucifixion, can be seen as neither natural nor as a result of God's good creation. The Bible sees death as an enemy to be dreaded. This becomes more evident in the NT than in the OT for it links death to the threat of hell, the final separation from God. It teaches that death is to be feared for it means the final facing of God in the knowledge that we are sinners. And yet, notes Barth, the whole Bible recognizes that God is the limit of death. It is God, not death, that we need to fear.

When Christ voluntarily accepted his death, Barth argues, he took upon himself the full condemnation of sin, he revealed the full meaning of man's death under the judgment of God. But because Christ bore his death, we are delivered from the second death – the death that means ultimate separation from God. The Christian knows that he has died already with Christ, but he also knows that Christ arose so that the second death has been defeated. This means that the Christian can now see his death as a finite creature, which he must still die, as no more than a symbol of what death would be without Christ.

Such interpretations help us to understand the Christian dialectic about death. On the one hand, death to Christianity is not, as in some philosophies, a friend or man's brother in disguise. It is an enemy to be feared and defeated. On the other hand, the Christian knows that the grave has lost its victory and he can know joy even in the face of death because he knows that he who dies will live again (John 11.25). *See also* **Hope, the Christian.**

WILLIAM HORDERN

Death of God Theology, The

In the ancient Church a theology of the death of God was put forward in the school of thought known as modalism (q.v.) towards the end of the second century AD. Praxeas, who belonged to this school, taught that at the incarnation the Godhead was emptied into the person of Christ without remainder; it was God the Father who came down into the Virgin's womb and was born as the Son, proceeding from himself. It was the Father who suffered and died: hence the nickname 'patripassian'. In recent times an extreme form of this type of theory has been put forward by certain 'radical' (q.v.) theologians, notably T. J. J. Altizer, who asserts that God died when Christ died on the cross; his death was an act of self-annihilation, of total self-emptying (*kenosis*). Christ was not resurrected, ascended or glorified, and hence 'the radical Christian' can rejoice in the death of God because he perceives the forward movement of the Spirit and knows Christ as a secular presence in a world which is now happily rid of the traditional Christian conception of God as an almighty Creator, reigning in transcendental glory, a distant king and final judge. But Altizer, despite his emphatic assertions that God's death was a real historical event, does not really believe that God died. Nor did Praxeas. Praxeas taught that God raised himself from the tomb (which he could hardly have done if he had died) and thereafter existed as Spirit. Altizer teaches that God changed himself from his pre-incarnate form, ceasing to be a remote, transcendent, impassible, self-sufficient being, and becoming wholly immanent in the world, a secular presence among us, estranged from himself and now involved in all the sinful ambiguity of the secular order.

Between Praxeas (whose illogicality was disposed of by Tertullian and Hippolytus) and Altizer there has intervened the period of nineteenth-century romanticism, in which visionaries like Blake and Nietzsche sought artistically to create meaning in a world left meaningless as a result of the destruction of the traditional Christian world-view by the rationalism of the Enlightenment. In America especially, and in pietistic circles in Europe, the effects of rationalism have only recently shattered the simplicities of traditional evangelical religious belief and habits, so that a romantic awareness of man's nothingness has created a religious mythology based upon the non-event of the death of God, which offers a means of the aesthetic savouring of nihilism. To be told that we must respond authentically to the absurd, i.e. to the situation of man in the world, knowing that he must live without God, without values or meaning, is itself the naive reaction of delayed-action European romanticism, which shirks the hard discipline of the search for a rational theology.

The theme of the death of God begins with J. P. F. Richter (d. 1825), better known as Jean Paul, and his 'Speech by the Dead Christ . . . that there is no God' – a description of what it would feel like to be an atheist. The theme (*etsi Deus non daretur*) fascinated the minds of the romantics. Modern science had achieved its successes by interpreting nature *as if there were no God*, and human life must likewise now be lived on this same supposition. The discovery of the truth that God is not, a 'need-fulfiller' or 'problem-solver' is still in the twentieth century apparently a principal cause of the success of the death of God theology among those who have had no adequate training in philosophical theology. (Bonhoeffer discovered this truth at the end of his life, but whether he would have remained content with aesthetic romanticism had his life not been cut short we shall never know.) As early as 1802 Hegel had spoken of the Good Friday experience of the death of God as the basic religious awareness of modern times. In his philosophy the god-forsakenness of the world is a necessary element in the dialectical process, though it is not the final word. For Kierkegaard contempt for outward things as godless, meaningless and absurd goes hand in hand with the existential inner life of subjective piety. For Nietzsche God is dead and men have killed him; they must therefore themselves be gods or supermen. Man takes charge of history, which now he builds on the corpse of God; the cross is the symbol of man's victory over God. In Feuerbach and Marx all the attributes which metaphysics has attributed to God are now attributed to man and theology has become anthropology. The death of God results in the deification of man, of the absurd, the nothing.

Today there are those who speak of the death of God as 'a cultural fact' (e.g. G. Vahanian). They mean only that modern secularized men have lost

all experience of God or all awareness of transcendence. This may or may not be true, but it is an assertion to be investigated by psychologists and sociologists; the statement is not theologically interesting and has little relevance to the question of the existence of the living God. The biblical writers were well aware of how easy it is to forget God. But perhaps there is some significance in the fact that, though God is said to be dead, he is nevertheless a very lively subject of popular interest, if we may judge by the number and circulation of books and articles which are nowadays being devoted to the post-mortem.

T. J. J. Altizer, *The Gospel of Christian Atheism*, 1967; T. J. J. Altizer and W. Hamilton, *Radical Theology and the Death of God*, 1966; T. W. Ogletree, *The 'Death of God' Controversy*, 1966; D. Sölle, *Christ the Representative: an Essay in Theology after the Death of God*, ET, 1967; G. Vahanian, *The Death of God*, 1961.

EDITOR

Dedication

The solemn setting apart for sacred use of churches (often dedicated in the name of a saint or in a divine name), altars and other objects of religious use is called dedication. The giving of a name (as in the case of a church or chapel) is often associated with the act of dedication. In denominations which do not practice infant baptism (*see* **Christening; Initiation, Christian**) a service of dedication of a new-born child is sometimes held, at which the child receives his Christian name.

EDITOR

Deism

In the eighteenth century rationalism reached its most extreme form in the type of thought which came to be known as deism. The period of the Enlightenment (q.v.) justly earned for itself the title of 'the Age of Reason'. The deists held that reason itself was capable of demonstrating the propriety of believing in God as 'the Intelligent Author of Nature' and 'the Moral Governor of the World'. There was no need of any divine revelation. Newton's mathematically ordered heavens published in every land the works of an almighty hand, as Joseph Addison declared in his Ode in *The Spectator*. Sir Isaac Newton himself believed strongly in the mysterious revelation to be sought in the Scriptures, and spent much more time studying his Bible than he spent looking through his telescope. So also the other Englishman, whose thought along with Newton's dominated the eighteenth century, John Locke, held that revelation was necessary to supplement man's reason, but he felt it necessary to argue that belief in the scriptural revelation was rationally justifiable (*cf.* his *Reasonableness of Christianity*, 1695). From Locke's position, which was accepted by most leading churchmen, it was easy to take the step which led to deism: if revelation were only an alternative method of establishing truths which could be perceived by reason, might not rational men, 'come of age', dispense with revelation altogether? Matthew Tindal, a clergyman who remained a Fellow of All Souls until his death in ripe old age, published his *Christianity as Old as the Creation* (1730) with the aim of proving that revelation was superfluous; he cleverly gave it a subtitle which was a quotation from Thomas Sherlock, the conservative Bishop of London: *The Gospel a Republication of the Religion of Nature*. This was the book which Bishop Joseph Butler (q.v.) had chiefly in mind when he wrote his magisterial reply, *The Analogy of Religion* (1736). The defect of the deists' arguments, which was equally shared by their opponents, including Butler, was their total lack of any sense of historical development. Because they had no glimmer of historical understanding, it was hardly surprising that the Bible should be compared unfavourably in content, clarity and style with the 'natural revelation' (i.e. rational argumentation) of Newton's *Principia Mathematica* (1687). The arguments of the 'orthodox' refuters of deism were even more inept than those of the deists themselves. The emergence of a genuine historical consciousness towards the end of the eighteenth century and its propagation in the nineteenth century have rendered both sides of the argument nothing more than museum-pieces today.

Nevertheless the old deistical notions about a God 'up there', controlling the universe from outside it like some almighty invisible Clockmaker, have survived in the inherited theological furniture of the twentieth century. The historical and critical attitude towards revelation has not yet thoroughly penetrated into the minds of the majority of uninformed Christian folk. Bishop J. A. T. Robinson's *Honest to God* (1963) seems to have created a sensation, in part at least, because it attacked residual deistic ideas about God which were widely believed to be both orthodox and biblical. Similarly the assaults of the empiricist or linguistic philosophers of our day upon belief in God seem to be directed against a deistical notion of a 'metaphysical' God, whose existence could be demonstrated by reason alone; this is doubtless why David Hume is regarded among them as an important contributor to the debate about God. But Hume, though he wrote history, had no more sense of historical development in the Bible or in the history of religion generally than had the deists: and still today the significance of an historical revelation (as contrasted with metaphysical reasoning) is hardly perceived among his admirers. Deism is dead but the corpse stinks.

Many of the deists passed over into pantheism or sheer atheism. John Toland's *Christianity not Mysterious* (1696) proved to be only a step on his road to pantheism. Locke's disciple and close friend, Anthony Collins, moved from deism to the denial of Christianity altogether; ever since the publication of his *Discourse of Free-thinking* (1713) the word 'free-thought' has been synonymous with scepticism and atheism in the English vocabulary. Others, such as Thomas Woolston, mounted bitter attacks upon the Christian faith.

Disbelief in a God who so loves mankind that he has actually revealed himself to men must inevitably lead to the denial of the existence of a God of love. The Christian faith stands or falls with the belief in revelation. The movement from deistical to sceptical notions, which characterized the thought of some eighteenth-century intellectuals ('men of enlightenment'), is being reproduced at the level of popular theology today.

Alan Richardson, *History Sacred and Profane*, 1964, Appended Note I; W. R. Sorley, *A History of English Philosophy*, 1920, ch. VII; Leslie Stephen, *History of English Thought in the 18th Century*, 3rd ed., I, 1949.

EDITOR

Demiurge

In his myth of the creation of the world Plato in the *Timaeus* spoke poetically of the Creator as a craftsman (in Greek, *demiourgos*). The Greek Fathers naturally (though hardly accurately) hailed Plato as the Greek Moses (Moses, of course, was assumed to be the author of Genesis). Hence the word passed into Greek Christian usage as the equivalent of 'Creator'. But it fell into disrepute as a consequence of its having been adopted by the Gnostics (q.v.) as the designation of the inferior deity who had made the world and had made it badly.

EDITOR

Demonic, Demons, Demonology

In pre-scientific ages belief in demons or devils was widespread; they were evil spirits, minions of their Lord, Satan, and were useful in explaining phenomena of which no rational account could be given. We find little reference to them in the OT, but by NT times belief in them was almost universal both among Jews and pagans. 'The whole world and the circumambient atmosphere were filled with devils . . . every phase and form of life were ruled by them. They sat on thrones, they hovered around cradles. The earth was literally a hell, though it continued to be a creation of God. To encounter this hell and all its devils, Christians had command of weapons that were invincible' (A. Harnack, *Expansion of Christianity in the First Three Centuries*, I, 1904, pp. 160 f.). Jesus cast out many demons: today we would de-mythologize the stories of his exorcisms in the Gospels, though we would not thereby necessarily deny the historical truth of the stories, namely, his power to restore sanity to the mentally deranged. But, as Harnack says (*ibid.*), 'it was as exorcizers that Christians went out into the great world, and exorcism formed one very powerful method of their mission and propaganda'. They seem to have regarded the idols of pagan worship as demons (I Cor. 10.20 f.). Classical literature is full of stories of prophets (or more usually prophetesses) as inspired by a god or demon, but it is doubtful how seriously such 'enthusiasm' (q.v.) was taken by philosophers; how far, for instance, did Socrates believe in his *daimon* or how far was it merely a way of speaking of an inspiration which he felt to come from outside himself?

The realm of evil in the crudely realistic (object-ivized, q.v.) sense of the ancient religious writers must today be demythologized, but the question whether evil influences come from outside our-selves, and even from outside the society around us, remains an important theological issue. Some recent writers (esp. P. Tillich) have used the word 'demonic' to signify those powers or influences which are not evil in themselves but which, when diverted from their proper ends, become destruc-tive of human life and its possibilities ('the de-monic character of modern industry', etc.). But, though it may indicate an important aspect of modern life, the use of the word 'demonic' is still semi-mythological, pointing perhaps to a reality of evil (the corruption of the good) which per-vades human existence.

'Demonology' is the study of men's beliefs about evil spirits or forces throughout history and today (anthropological studies). It is a very vast and complex subject. See also **Powers; Evil, The Problem of; Spirit** (2).

A. von Harnack, excursus on 'The Conflict with Daemons', *The Expansion of Christianity in the First Three Centuries*, I, 1904, pp. 152–80.
                                                                                            EDITOR

Demythologizing

Demythologizing is the English translation of the German term *Entmythologisierung*, the method of interpreting the NT proposed by the German theo-logian and biblical critic Rudolf Bultmann (1884–) in his essay 'New Testament and Mythology', first published in 1941. Since the second World War both NT scholarship and systematic theology have been much concerned with the nature and implications of Bultmann's proposals. To 'demy-thologize' is to translate the 'mythological' dis-course of the NT (and hence of doctrine, worship, preaching, etc.) *absolutely* into the discourse of human existence. Bultmann has put forward a formal definition of 'myth': 'Mythology is the use of imagery to express the otherworldly in terms of this world and the divine in terms of human life, the other side in terms of this side.' But he apparently uses the term in a wider sense than his formal definition would allow, as a col-lective label for various forms of theological dis-course which he regards as problematical. For example, myth occasionally denotes the 'object-ifying' talk about God; as when God is presented in discourse as a cosmic power or force disrupting the ordinarily stable structures or processes of nature, a disruption depicted as a publicly ob-servable event. Sometimes it is employed to indicate the expression of the gospel in terms of an outmoded cosmological theory; or in terms of a dated theological world-view, for example, that of Gnosticism or of Jewish apocalyptic. Certainly at times myth signifies the various elements in theological language which in his view have been rendered unacceptable by the insights of modern

science for which he has a high respect. Myth is problematical for Bultmann because he holds that it represents a false stumbling-block for modern secular man; behind Bultmann's demythologiz-ing proposals stand strong *apologetic* motives. The myth must first be dealt with so that the mean-ing and relevance of the gospel for the life of contemporary man can be made clear.

To demythologize means to translate the mythological language exhaustively into existen-tial (or anthropological) terminology. That that is possible, according to Bultmann, is because of his insistence that in the myths of Scripture the narrators intended to portray above all else the ways in which they understood their own exist-ence rather than objective reality. To demy-thologize (or, we might say, 'existentialize') them means for Bultmann to interpret them existenti-ally, in the light of the portrayal of human exist-ence which we find in the analysis of the various modes of man's life in the work of the German philosopher of existence Martin Heidegger (1889–). If we approach the biblical text with questions derived from these analyses, it is claimed, we can obtain answers which are immensely relevant for the self-understanding of contemporary man. These answers are determinative for the Church's understanding of its own teaching, and hence for its proclamation of the gospel to the world. Accordingly Bultmann has tried to give a syste-matic existential interpretation of the NT, with special emphasis upon the Pauline and Johannine anthropology, notably in the two volumes of his *Theology of the New Testament* (ET, 1952, 1955) and in other related works.

Bultmann's demythologizing proposals and the systematic theology which has grown up around them have of course given rise to immense con-troversy and to a considerable body of theological literature, both in attack and in defence of his theological standpoint. For detailed knowledge of the issues at stake, reference must be made to the texts given in the bibliography; all that can be attempted here is to indicate several essential features of the debate. Since Bultmann is an apologist, a philosophical theologian, the debate has naturally very largely been concerned with the perennial question about how far it is proper to allow Christian theology to be influenced by or interpreted in the light of current philosophical movements (*see* **Existentialism**). Within the de-bate itself, it has on the one hand been argued that Heidegger's thought is so incompatible with Christian thought that grave distortion is inevit-able, and on the other that Heidegger's Christian background makes his philosophy ideally suitable for the understanding and communication of the Christian gospel. It is likely here that the truth lies somewhere between these two extremes.

The main problem inherent in Bultmann's de-mythologizing proposals are connected with his insistence that the translation of mythological into existential discourse must be absolute or ex-haustive; that is, that after demythologizing has been completed there should be no non-existential remainder. It has been widely and vigorously argued that a completely demythologized Christianity would be a contradiction in terms, and that on (at least) two grounds. (1) First, it is argued, that to translate Christian discourse exhaustively into existential terms would be to overlook the strong *ontological* element in such discourse. The traditional Christian doctrine is concerned not merely with God as he is in his relationship with man (the *existential* aspect of God), but also with God as he is *in himself*, apart from man and human experience, in his transcendence (the *ontological* aspect of God). By insisting that all valid discourse about God should be fundamentally and exclusively existential, it is argued that Bultmann comes perilously close to transforming Christianity into a philosophical way of life which has little reference to objective reality as such. Similarly, it may be argued that in Bultmann's view there is a dangerous dichotomy between man and nature. (2) It is argued that a complete demythologization would be to disregard the *past* (historical) element in the Christian faith. A completely demythologized (i.e. existentialized) Christianity would also be a completely de-historicized one. If all valid theological statements were existential or anthropological ones, there would seem to be no room for purely historical ones, a position which is quite unacceptable to those who hold that an essential part of the fabric of Christian belief concerns certain crucial events and happenings of the past. Hence, those who have been most critical of the fundamental assumptions of Bultmann's demythologizing proposals have demanded that a comprehensive Christian theology should incorporate not only existential elements but also ontological and historical ones. With reference to the historical aspect of Christianity, it is interesting to note that certain of Bultmann's former pupils at Marburg (e.g. Ernst Käsemann and Ernst Fuchs) have attempted to supplement his theological approach by giving a more positive place to the historical element in their versions of Christian theology.

The defenders of Bultmann may argue that his position is neither an arbitrary nor an irresponsible one. In many respects his theology represents the systematic, apologetic fusion of some of the most significant theological and philosophical trends and movements of recent decades. Within its structure may be traced, for example, themes derived not only from the theological revolt initiated after first World War by Karl Barth, but also from that nineteenth-century theological tradition of which Barth was so critical; as well as themes derived from twentieth-century existentialist thought and from form-critical research. As a theologian, Bultmann has shown himself to be fully aware of the complex issues involved in the contemporary debate about the *secularization* of the modern world. He has also been deeply influenced by modern studies in the philosophy of history. Both his critics and disciples have demonstrated that he is deeply conscious of how modern thinking and living have been conditioned by the rise of modern science.

Since Bultmann's theology is such a complex and many-sided whole, and since the demythologization proposals are related in a complex manner to the several themes which constitute Bultmann's entire theological structure, a final estimate of these proposals would be dependent upon a most careful philosophical and theological sifting of these various themes. To say this is only to say that a critical examination of Bultmann's demythologization programme must be simultaneously a critical investigation of many of the significant areas of modern theological thought which engross contemporary theologians. That is, the demythologization controversy is a door which leads into a house built by biblical critics, philosophers, philosophical theologians, historical theologians and historiographers. *See also* **Existentialism.**

H. W. Bartsch, ed., *Kerygma and Myth*, I, 1953; II, 1964; R. Bultmann, *Jesus Christ and Mythology*, ET, 1960; John Macquarrie, *An Existentialist Theology*, 1955; *The Scope of Demythologizing*, 1960; L. Malevez, SJ, *The Christian Message and Myth*, 1958.

JAMES RICHMOND

Depravity

Depravity is the term used generally in theology to describe the condition of man after the fall. The concept is made necessary because the Christian believes that God created man good and destined him for a life of love towards both God and his fellow men, but it is obvious that man does not normally live such a life. Even theologians who have denied that Adam's fall corrupted later generations and who have denied the doctrine of original sin have been forced none the less to admit the strange fact that the line of least resistance for man never leads into the paths of righteousness.

It has been widely debated in Christian history as to how depravity passes from generation to generation. One line of Christian thought has followed Augustine in claiming that depravity is inherited biologically through one's parents. Many modern theologians have argued that it is transmitted through social influence. The patterns of society become corrupted and the child, born into these patterns, is corrupted by this environment. This theory has been strengthened by depth psychology which reveals how parental influence and the general social environment of a child is able to distort his personality at an early age. Most contemporary theology is not so much concerned with how depravity is transmitted as it is concerned with how it may be overcome. *See* **Man, Doctrine of.**

WILLIAM HORDERN

Descartes, René

René Descartes (1596–1650) counts as certainly the greatest French philosopher, and as in many respects the founder of modern philosophy. His ideal of system and rigour, his determination to secure his thought by working back to indisputable first principles, the importance he gave to epistemological questions and his according of certainty to a private and inner self-awareness – these have shaped the course of three-hundred years of philosophical reflection. A scientist and mathematician, he sought to work out a view of nature (a *geometrical* nature) that would make intelligible and metaphysically well-based the aims of the new science. At the same time he was a defender of a Catholic belief in God and immortality, and sought to make room for the autonomy of spirit, an autonomy that might well seem threatened by the very success of scientific explanations in terms of physical mechanisms, matter in motion.

In the search for certainty, Descartes argued, whatever *can* be doubted *ought* to be doubted. Is there any limit to what can be doubted? There is: my own existence is apparent to me even in the act of doubting. It cannot itself be subject to doubt; for doubting is a kind of experiencing or thinking, and if I think I must exist. Descartes goes further: he takes it as proved that I exist as a 'thinking substance'.

What is there about '*Cogito ergo sum*' that entitles me to trust in its certainty? I apprehend or intuit it with clarity and distinctness. But can I then generalize from this and affirm the truth of all propositions that are clearly and distinctly conceived? No, because there is at least a theoretical possibility that I might sometimes be deceived. I can make clarity and distinctness general criteria of certain truth only if I am assured that deception is ruled out – and only the existence of a perfect, non-deceiving God could rule it out.

Now I am aware of myself as limited, imperfect, and I have the idea of God as perfect and unlimited. Such an idea could not emanate from myself. Its source can be no other than God himself; no lesser cause would be adequate to account for it. When we speak of God, we speak of a being perfect in every way. So, since deception goes with *im*perfection, it cannot be attributed to deity. What we conceive as clear and distinct can therefore be relied upon as true.

From Descartes' day onwards critics have accused him with some reason of arguing in a circle. The proof of God's existence is needed in order to justify the criteria of clarity and distinctness. But does not Descartes use these very criteria in the course of his proof of God? For the principles involved in the proof are certainly not immune to doubt.

Descartes propounds a further argument for God – the Ontological Argument. Existence, it is claimed, is *essential* to the idea of God as 'perfect being. In this, God is quite distinctive: with other beings it is possible to settle their essential characteristics without thereby settling the question: Does such a thing exist or not? Existence being, to Descartes, a 'perfection', we are unable to conceive of God as lacking it.

Descartes is now in a position to reassure himself about the reality of the external world. Systematic deception being ruled out, we may take the impressions of our senses to be indeed due to the impact on us of a world outside us, extended in space and existing in its own light. This is the only reasonable way of interpreting our experience of our own bodies and our sense of passivity under sensation. Any other account would make God out to be a deceiver.

Descartes has developed his thought in a radically dualist manner. Although in one strict sense only God counts as 'substance' – being alone completely self-sufficient, Descartes applied the term in a secondary sense to *thinking substance* and to *extended substance*; and neither of these could be reduced to the other. The first is soul or mind, non-extended, self-aware and free: the other is the field of geometrical properties, amenable to the investigation of the sciences; and into it God puts a constant amount of motion.

If this dualistic theory preserves the distinctiveness of spirit or mind, it produces intractable problems over the relation between the two substances. They are so defined in fact as to make unintelligible any claims that they interact; and yet body does act upon mind, and mind upon body. The Occasionalists, Spinoza and Leibniz, made various attempts to escape from this impasse. (*See* **Spinoza, B.; Leibniz, G. W.**) Indeed, attempts are still being made in the twentieth century.

René Descartes, *Descartes: Philosophical Writings,* trans. and ed. G. E. M. Anscombe and P. T. Geach, 1954; *The Philosophical Works,* trans. E. S. Haldane and G. R. T. Ross, 2 vols., 1911–12; N. Kemp Smith, *New Studies in the Philosophy of Descartes,* 1952; *Studies in the Cartesian Philosophy,* 1902.

R. W. HEPBURN

Descent into Hell, The

There are only two places in the N T where Christ's descent into hell is absolutely explicitly referred to, and one of these has often been interpreted differently. These are I Peter 3.19 f.; 4.6 and Eph. 4.9 f. The author of I Peter certainly represents Christ as preaching to the spirits that are in prison, whether this means those who died in the Flood or the rebellious angels. The author of Ephesians very probably refers to Christ's triumph over the elemental spirits in his interpretation of Ps. 68. But there are several other passages in the N T where Christ's presence among the dead, or his victory over the realm of the dead, is at least alluded to; compare Matt. 27.52; Luke 23.43; Acts 2.27, 31; Phil. 2.10; I Tim. 3.16; Rev. 5.13. The main emphasis in the N T references is on the completeness of Christ's victory by means of the cross and resurrection. The I Peter passage introduces another motif: the doctrine of the descent helps to answer the question: 'what of those who have died before the incarnation?' This is undoubtedly how we should interpret the article in the Apostles' Creed, 'He descended into hell'.

Owing to Augustine's failure to distinguish between Hades (the place of the dead) and Gehenna (the place of punishment), theologians in the West have occasionally interpreted the descent into hell as meaning that Christ underwent the punishment, or at least the experience, of condemned sinners. Calvin is the most famous exponent of this view, and Karl Barth has adopted a modified form of it. But there is no justification of this in Scripture. Apart from Barth, modern theologians have tended to adopt one of three methods of dealing with this late comer to the Creed. They can reject it altogether: for example, F. W. Beare calls it 'a fantastic dream'; or they may follow the main NT tradition and say that it underlines the completeness of Christ's victory; or they may take it as emphasizing that Christ really died as man, as contrasted, for instance, with the Muslim claim that he never really died. This last is no doubt legitimate, but has no more claim to scriptural support than Calvin's interpretation. The suggestion found in I Peter that the descent gave an opportunity for those who died before Christ to hear the gospel is rather too mythological for modern minds, but it may be regarded as a hopeful symbol of the destiny of those who have died without ever having heard the good news of Christ. Some means must be found for safeguarding the insight that the generations before Christ were not deprived of the gospel.

Commentaries on I Peter, especially those by E. G. Selwyn (1946) and F. W. Beare (1947). Since E. H. Plumptre's *The Spirits in Prison* (1871), no single book of the subject in English has appeared but the following is relevant: H. A. Blair, *The Creed Behind the Creeds*, 1955.

A. T. HANSON

Determinism. see Providence.

Deus A Se

Latin: 'God (as he is) in himself', i.e. in the mystery of his inner being, which cannot be apprehended by human reason; as contrasted with *deus pro nobis* (q.v.), God as he has made himself known and available to man through his saving revelation.

Deus Pro Nobis

The phrase means 'God on our behalf' or 'God for us', and in addition to the Pauline sense of God identifying himself with man for the purpose of man's redemption here on earth and in eternity (Rom. 8.31), it has the clear reference to what is generally called the substitutionary theory of the atonement. The idea goes back to Christ himself, 'The Son of Man . . . came not to be served but to serve, and to give his life as a ransom for many' (Mark 10.45). The significance lies not only in the word ransom but in the 'for many' (*anti pollon*). The meaning of *anti* is 'instead of' and cannot

properly be escaped or explained away. The thought is echoed in I Tim. 2.6 with its use of *antilutron* and perhaps also in Titus 2.14, where the verb *lutro* occurs. The idea of substitution is discussed in **Atonement** (6 [*b*, *c*]). It can hardly be doubted that Isa. 53, and indeed the 'servant' passages generally, have had considerable influence on the interpretation of Christ's death as a substitution (*see* **Atonement** 3 [*a*], 6 [*c*]). The doctrine was preserved in the mediaeval theories of atonement and further underwent a strong revival under Luther. Barth's energetic maintenance of the idea, which was actually a revival of Luther's theology, has had considerable influence on contemporary theology. The doctrine has always been an essential plank in the militant evangelical platform, and has had a not inconsiderable influence in existentialist circles, particularly in Germany. *See* **Atonement** (3 [*d*], [*e*]).

JAMES ATKINSON

Development, Doctrine of

Before the eighteenth century Christians were united in believing the Christian faith to be unchanging. If a new heresy arose they could appeal to antiquity; if a heresy were discovered in antiquity they inquired what was universally believed; if a new case arose upon which Christians had not yet decided, the opinions of all could be collected and collated. This in short was the Vincentian Canon (*see* **Catholicism**). Protestants might believe that Catholics had corrupted or unlawfully elaborated the faith; Catholics could retort that Protestants had diminished or falsified it. Both agreed that its essence was unchanging. With the dawn of the modern historical outlook and the comparative study of different periods of Christian history it became apparent that although Christians could still speak of an unchanging gospel they could not mean by this exactly what their ancestors had done. There had been development, and the question was how to distinguish true from false.

There was one notable exception to this attitude in the Spanish schoolmen of the sixteenth and seventeenth centuries who maintained that there could be a logical explication of revealed truth which was itself true, and binding on the faithful even before it had been proclaimed by authority. Thus the idea of a development which rendered explicit what had always been implicit in the original deposit of faith was already advanced among Catholics. With the dawn of the modern comparative and historical outlook and particularly when ideas of evolution in the sphere of biology began to be put forward the idea of a development in theology like the organic growth of life itself became feasible. J. H. Newman (q.v.) took up this argument and expressed it brilliantly and with great feeling in his *Essay on the Development of Christian Doctrine*, written in his last months as an Anglican, 1845. His purpose was to explain to himself and to his public why he could now accept teaching and practices in contemporary Roman Catholicism which clearly were not in the Bible or the early Church. His most daring assertion of the principle of growth was his admission that Nicene orthodoxy could not be proved from Scripture (a view offensive to most Protestants as well as Catholics of the time). In his book Newman was concerned to propose tests whereby true growth could be distinguished from false. The notes of genuine development of an idea were preservation of its type, continuity of its principles, power of assimilation, logical sequence, anticipation of its future, conservative action upon its past and its chronic vigour.

This apologetic was received with dismay by some Roman Catholics and was vigorously attacked by Bishop Browning in the USA but has since received a modified acceptance. Indeed the interpretation of tradition which has enabled the Mariological dogmas of the Immaculate Conception and the Assumption to be proclaimed owes something to this doctrine of development. In a different sense the doctrine is used by modernist and liberal theologians to explain and to justify considerable modifications of Christian doctrine in the light of modern scientific knowledge and history. *See also* **Tradition**.

Owen Chadwick, *From Bossuet to Newman*, 1957.

Devil. *see* Satan; Powers; Evil, The Problem of; Demonic.

Dialectical Theology

Dialectical theology is an alternative title for crisis theology (q.v.). Rejecting the classical Catholic threefold method of gaining knowledge of God (the *via Affirmativa*, the *via Negationis*, and the *via Eminentiae*), Karl Barth and his colleagues insisted that the only valid theological method was the *via Dialectica*; this was the method of statement and counterstatement, of 'yes' and 'no', of paradox, in which polar pairs (whose unity cannot be thought) are held together only in the response of God-given faith – finite and infinite, time and eternity, wrath and grace. God thus transcends rational comprehension and, it must be stressed, dogmatic formulation. It follows from the *via Dialectica* that it is impossible to identify divine truth with a set of dogmatic propositions, God's Word with a written theology. *See* **Barth, K.; Crisis Theology**.

JAMES RICHMOND

Didache, The

A short manual written in Greek called 'The Teaching of the Lord through the Twelve Apostles' was discovered by Bryennios, an Orthodox prelate, in Constantinople in 1875 and published in 1883. The manuscript of it dated from 1056, but scholars have everywhere assigned the work to a very early period, ranging from AD 60 in parts of it and the rest between 70 and 80 (Audet) to the end of the second century (Vokes). It consists of two parts, one of them a discourse called 'The Two Ways' (the ways of life and of death), other versions of which can be found in the *Epistle of Barnabas* and in Hermas' *Shepherd*, and which appears in an earlier form to have influenced the *Manual of Discipline* among the Dead Sea Scrolls. The rest of the Didache consists of regulations, ordinances and suggestions concerning baptism, fasting, prayer, the Eucharist and the ministry. The tone of the Didache is intensely Jewish, and the work clearly belongs to the Judaeo-Christian phase of the early Church's thought and life. Baptism is to be by the triple formula akin to that of Matt. 28.19. The Eucharist is described as 'spiritual food' and a 'pure sacrifice', and though the Lord's Prayer is given elsewhere it is not associated with the Eucharist, nor is the narrative of the institution of the Eucharist mentioned. Some scholars have thought that the two different eucharistic passages refer to the Eucharist and the agape. Bishops (probably equated with presbyters, who are not mentioned) and deacons are mentioned, and even more space is devoted to Christian prophets, who are somewhat curiously described as 'your high-priests'. The christology of the Didache is primitive; there is no Logos-doctrine, and a favourite description of Jesus is 'thy (i.e. God's) holy Child (*pais*)'. On the whole scholars today would agree that the work probably has a Syrian provenance, and its date might be tentatively conjectured to be about 100.

L. W. Barnard, *Studies in the Apostolic Fathers*, 1966; F. E. Vokes, *The Riddle of the Didache*, 1938.

R. P. C. HANSON

Dilthey, Wilhelm

Dilthey (1833–1911), German neo-Kantian philosopher, for many years was Professor of Philosophy at Berlin. Through his sharp distinction between the 'sciences of man' and the 'natural sciences' Dilthey opened up the way towards modern studies in the philosophy of history (and thus also towards the modern historical understanding of Christianity), in which his position is not unlike those of the philosophers B. Croce (1866–1952) and R. G. Collingwood (1889–1943). Beneath and underlying empirical historical events and processes there is, Dilthey insisted, a universal *humanitas* which can only be grasped by the interpreter in a process of 're-living' or 're-experiencing' (German: *nacherleben*). Thus history is basically the story of man, his inner life, experience and thought. Dilthey's work has also significantly influenced modern theological hermeneutics.

H. A. Hodges, *Wilhelm Dilthey: An Introduction*, 1944; *The Philosophy of Wilhelm Dilthey*, 1952; H. P. Rickman, *Meaning in History: W. Dilthey's Thoughts on History and Society*, 1961.

JAMES RICHMOND

Dionysius the Pseudo-Areopagite

Dionysius (Denis) the pseudo-Areopagite (c. 500) was probably a Syrian monk who wrote in Greek, between about AD 480 and 530, treatises on the *Divine Names, Mystical Theology*, the *Celestial Hierarchy*, the *Ecclesiastical Hierarchy* and ten *Epistles*. It is not certain that he claimed to be the real Dionysius converted by St Paul in the Areopagus (Acts 17.34): the sub-apostolic trappings – addressing the writings to St Timothy and St John, description of the eclipse at Christ's crucifixion, etc. – seem to be a literary device. References to a master, Hierotheus, who ranks in authority only after St Paul, and other probably conscious inconsistencies, suggest that the author did not intend his literary personality to be taken too seriously. Studies of his post-Chalcedonian christology, his description of monastic rites, his eucharistic liturgy, and especially his dependence on the Neoplatonist philosopher Proclus (d. 485), have converged to place him fairly accurately at the end of the fifth century. The first commentaries and Syriac translations of his work were written about 530.

Denis was probably the coiner of the word 'hierarchy', which he defined as 'a sacred order and knowledge and operation tending to the analogous imitation of God according to the enlightenment given by him'. It is correlative with 'thearchy', God considered as the source of our sanctification. The order of the hierarchies is appointed by God, to the best advantage of all participants, and according to their free response. The motive dynamism in their operations is love. The knowledge of God and of Christ for which the hierarchies exist is received from above and passed on to others still in need of enlightenment. The triple process of purification, illumination, and perfection by which this is done, was later to be elaborated into the 'three ways' of the spiritual life, the *via purgativa, via illuminativa*, and *via unitiva*. The eminently 'co-operative' character of the threefold division finds expression in Denis' arrangement of the scriptural angels into nine choirs: Seraphim, Cherubim and Thrones; Dominations, Virtues and Powers; Principalities, Archangels and Angels.

The ecclesiastical hierarchy is neither purely intellectual like the angelic, nor purely symbolic like the Mosaic, dispensation. It consists of liturgical symbols intended to raise our minds to the contemplation of the divine realities. Hence the 'sacraments' are not treated as entities, but as dynamic symbolic activities. The Eucharist is above all the rite of union and communion. Bishops, priests and deacons have as their principal functions perfecting, illuminating, and purifying respectively. The 'contemplative order' is precisely the 'holy people', i.e. those who have received Baptism. Monks are distinguished by their search for or attainment of unification.

The two *Hierarchies* are part of Denis' cataphatic or positive theology, which states what can be affirmatively predicated of God. It includes also some missing or probably never-written treatises, notably the *Symbolic Theology* to explain such terms as 'lion' and 'rock' applied to God in Scripture. The *Divine Names* sets out to discuss the 'intelligible' names that can be attributed to the divine unity. God is known from his creatures, his processions *ad extra*. He creates freely and intelligently; creatures participate in his exemplar ideas of them. The principle of the processions is God's goodness: *bonum est diffusivum sui*. The first gratuitous gifts of God are being, life, and understanding; and the creature's return to God is according to its analogous participation in his own being, life and intelligence. Both the exitus from God and the reditus to him are motivated by love.

Cataphatic theology needs, however, to be complemented by negative or apophatic theology, in which we acknowledge that God surpasses human predication. Hence in the *Mystical Theology* it is asserted that God is not goodness, being, or anything else visible or intelligible. Indeed he transcends both affirmation and negation, and is to be attained ultimately not in intellectual contemplation, but in an ecstasis of love, where union with God, 'deification', takes place in 'unknowing'.

The influence of Denis has been comparatively slight in the East; even for Maximus the Confessor, John Damascene and Gregory Palamas, he is only one authority among many. The Western scholastics and mystics were more enthusiastic, though even there his 'apostolic' authority was less significant than the elements of doctrine drawn from him. St Thomas relies on him particularly for the exitus-reditus structure of the Summa, the *bonum diffusivum sui* principle in creation, the theology of evil, the intellectual nature of angels, and in his respect for negative theology. The Victorines, the Rhineland and Flemish mystics, the author of the *Cloud of Unknowing* and St John of the Cross are all disciples of Denis in spirituality.

Text is found in *PG*, III; Critical edition of *Celestial Hierarchy* (Sources Chrétiennes, 58), 1958; *The Works of Dionysius the Areopagite*, 2 parts, trans., J. Parker, 1897, 1899; *Dionysius the Areopagite on the Divine Names and the Mystical Theology*, trans., C. E. Rolt, 1920; *The Mystical Theology and the Celestial Hierarchies*, with commentaries by the editors of the Shrine of Wisdom, 1949; *The Divine Names . . .* , trans., the editors of the Shrine of Wisdom, 1957; R. Roques, *L'univers dionysien*, 1954; R. Roques, *et al*, 'Denys l' Aréopagite', *DS*, III, 1957, cols. 245–429; A. H. Armstrong, ed., *The Cambridge History of Later Greek and Early Medieval Philosophy*, 1967, ch. 30.

DOM PLACID SPEARRITT

Disciplina Arcani

Disciplina arcani is the practice of keeping the rites and some of the doctrines of the Church secret so that they are divulged only to communicants and not to catechumens or pagans. There is no satisfactory evidence for this practice until the fourth century, when it was occasioned partly by imitation of the mystery religions and partly by the increased interest in Christianity taken by pagans.

R. P. C. HANSON

Discipline

Discipline is a term used in the Christian tradition in four main senses: (1) It can be used of the way of life which is prescribed by the Church and embodied in various regulations and rules, especially as these are backed, as they often have been, by the power of the state. (2) It is used as a term covering all those forms of asceticism and mortification which one associates, for instance, with the monastic tradition (*see* **Monachism**). (3) Arising out of this, discipline is used in a quite precise and technical sense for the scourge, a kind of whip of knotted cords, used in monastic practices of discipline. (4) Discipline is used, in a way which is closely akin to the first sense, of a way of life prescribed by the church and enforced upon its practitioners. Examples of this are the discipline laid upon the life of the Christian community by Calvin in Geneva, and the discipline, in the same way, of the Scots Presbyterians.

E. J. TINSLEY

Dispensation

The term is derived from Latin *dispenso*, to weigh out, to administer as a steward. In theological usage it is the system established by God to regulate men's obedience towards him in matters of religion and morality, e.g. 'the Mosaic dispensation' or 'the dispensation of Law' (the Old Covenant) as contrasted with 'the dispensation of Grace' (the New Covenant of Jesus Christ). From at least the fifth century 'dispensations' were licences granted by a bishop or other ecclesiastical authority permitting some act which would in the absence of such dispensation be illegal according to canon law (q.v.).

EDITOR

Disruption

The Scottish Disruption of 1843 culminated an era of antagonism between the Moderates, whose church policy was that of acquiescence in the demands of the state, and the rising party of the Evangelicals who resented state encroachment upon church autonomy. Interpretations of the Patronage Act of 1712 virtually annulled the right of the people to call ministers. The General Assembly's Veto Act of 1834, against intrusion by a patron of a pastor not approved by the heads of families, was followed by the 'Ten Years' Conflict', a time of much litigation and public controversy. The Veto Act and other measures of the Assembly were held invalid in the Scottish Court of Session (1838, 1842). Led by Thomas Chalmers, Robert Candlish and William Cunningham the Assembly put forth the 'Claim of Right' (1842),

upholding on historical and theological grounds the deciding power of parishioners; this was summarily rejected by Parliament. The Evangelicals, rather than yield the right of call, to them essential, resolved to sever their connection with the established Kirk. When the Assembly met in St Andrews Church, Edinburgh, 18 May 1843, the retiring moderator, David Welsh, read a protest declaring it impossible in the circumstances to hold a free Assembly, then led about half the members in impressive procession out of the church through the streets to Tanfield Hall. There, with Chalmers as moderator, the Free Church of Scotland was formed.

T. Brown, *Annals of the Disruption*, 1884; R. Buchanan, *The Ten Years' Conflict, Being the History of the Disruption of the Church of Scotland*, 2 vols., 2nd. ed., 1884; G. D. Henderson, *Heritage, a Study of the Disruption*, 2nd. ed., 1943; H. Watt, *Thomas Chalmers and the Disruption*, 1943.

J. T. MCNEILL

Dissent, Dissenters. *see* Nonconformity.

Docetism. *see* Christology (4).

Doctrine

The word is derived from the Latin *docere*, to teach, and means 'teaching'. Christian doctrines are those which are held in common (though perhaps in distinctive expressions) among the great historic traditions or confessions of Christendom; contrasted with these there are the doctrines distinctive of the separate traditions, e.g. Protestant doctrines, Reformed doctrines, and so on. The Roman Catholic Church still promulgates dogmas (q.v.), which are regarded as authoritative and binding upon all the faithful. Non-Roman theologians usually prefer to speak of doctrines rather than dogmas; they tend to restrict the latter term to the official pronouncements of the undivided Church of the first five centuries in its ecumenical councils. (But they nevertheless speak of 'dogmatics' as the study of Christian doctrines.) Instead of dogmatic affirmations the Churches of the Reformation have 'confessions' (q.v.): they confess what they believe from the heart rather than submit to an imposed external doctrinal statement (dogma). Thus, they might speak of the dogma of the Trinity or the incarnation, but not of (say) a Lutheran dogma of the Lord's Supper; they would speak of a distinctively Lutheran *doctrine* of the Lord's Supper. Anglicans claim to hold no distinctively Anglican doctrines which are not the doctrines of the whole Church: *quod semper, quod ubique et quod ab omnibus* (the Vincentian Canon). In the past doctrinal differences have divided the churches, but in these ecumenical times since the second Vatican Council the words of G. Ebeling would find general agreement: 'Only a doctrinal difference as to what makes the Church its true self can have divisive significance for the Church, and only in face of doctrinal differences which are in fact dividing the Church can there be a definition of what has to rank in the strict sense as church doctrine' (*Word and Faith*, ET, 1963, p. 189).

EDITOR

Dogma

The Greek word dogma meant either (1) a decree or order issued by authority (*cf.* Luke 2.1; Acts 16.4; 17.7; Eph. 2.15; Col. 2.14; of these five NT uses, Acts 16.4 is the only one which speaks of dogmas or ordinances imposed by apostolic authority) or (2) an opinion. In the latter sense it meant originally a doctrine which seemed good to this or that philosophical school, the implication being that it was incapable of either logical or empirical verification. The word soon acquired a definite and distinctive theological meaning in the Church, and one which combined both of these original meanings. Dogmas were the decrees of the ecumenical councils of the Church, usually formulated to correct teachings put forward by heretics. A dogma is thus quite simply a church definition. Today Christendom as a whole may be said generally to accept the dogmas formulated by the ecumenical councils of the ancient and undivided Church, even though it would be generally admitted that the dogmas need re-interpreting in the light of modern understanding, since the ancient Greek philosophical modes of expression in which they were formulated are largely unintelligible to twentieth-century men. The Roman Catholic Church has continued until this century to promulgate dogmas, but the Churches of the Reformation make use of Confessional Statements (*see* **Confession[s]**) and speak of doctrine (q.v.) rather than dogma. Since the Enlightenment the words 'dogma' and 'dogmatic' have often been used in a pejorative sense as indicating an authoritarian, unreasoned and even obscurantist attitude of mind.

EDITOR

Dogmatics, Dogmatic Theology

These terms refer to the scholarly and systematic study of Christian doctrine or of the official dogmas of the Church. Before the Age of Enlightenment (q.v.) it was assumed by Catholic and Protestant alike that the Bible was the source-book of divinely revealed truth; but since the Bible itself did not systematize the various truths which it contained, it was necessary for the Church's theologians to perform this task. (*See also* **Systematic Theology.**) This was the function of the dogmatician or dogmatic theologian. But with the rise of the critical-historical method of biblical research in the period after the Enlightenment there appeared a widening gap between the biblical scholars and the dogmatic theologians. The former were deemed to follow a strictly scientific and uncommitted line of approach; the latter were spinning unscientific theories ('mere dogma') out of their heads. (*See* **Hermeneutics.**) Karl Barth, whose *Church Dogmatics* is the most

impressive dogmatic treatise of the twentieth-century, remains so aloof from the work of the 'scientific historians' as to be quite indifferent to their conclusions about the historical Jesus ('chasing the ghost of the historical Jesus in the vacuum behind the New Testament'); for him revelation is sheer miracle and shines by its own light, and biblical research is irrelevant to it. But today among the existentialist theologians there is a new movement, called the 'new hermeneutics', which regards interpretation or hermeneutics (q.v.) as being the proper task of the biblical scholar as such, and thus the dogmatic theologian is in danger of losing his job. In England, however, there is a call for the critical study of the truth and adequacy of doctrinal statements, i.e. for doctrinal criticism comparable to biblical criticism; this demand is understandable against the background of the long British tradition of philosophical theology and in a country in which specialization (as among biblical, dogmatic and philosophical theologians) has not been so markedly developed as on the European Continent. *See also* **Philosophical Theology; Systematic Theology; Hermeneutics.**

The latest and perhaps the best history of dogma during the early period is the English edition of A. Grillmeier, *Christ in Christian Tradition from the Apostolic Age to Chalcedon*, 1965. There is no comparative and critical study of dogmatic systems as such, but each dogmatic theologian usually includes a critique of his predecessors and contemporaries in his introductory material (*see* e.g., J. Moltmann, *Theology of Hope*, ET, 1967). For the meaning of 'doctrinal criticism' *see* the essay of that title in *Prospect for Theology*, ed. F. G. Healey, 1966.

EDITOR

Dominical

'Pertaining to the Lord' (Latin *Dominus*), e.g. the dominical sacraments, i.e. those instituted by Christ (baptism and the Lord's Supper).

Donatism

A schism in the north African Church in the fourth and fifth centuries originating in the rejection of Caecilian as Bishop of Carthage (consecrated AD 311) on the grounds that he had been consecrated by a defector (*traditor*) during Diocletian's persecution. The quarrel against the Catholics was sustained by north African nationalism and led to violence and state intervention. The theological issues raised concerned the unity of the Church and the validity (maintained by the Catholics) of sacraments celebrated even by unworthy ministers; Augustine maintained the Catholic principle that the true minister of the sacraments was Christ himself.

W. H. C. Frend, *The Donatist Church*, 1952; S. L. Greenslade, *Schism in the Early Church*, 1953.

EDITOR

Donum Superadditum

The concept *donum superadditum* (supernatural or additional endowment), suggested by Athanasius and most fully developed by Aquinas, distinguishes between certain natural endowments that man has from God and which he retains after the fall and the supernatural or additional endowments which he lost in the fall. The *donum superadditum* included the powers that enabled man to know God, to live according to God's will and thus to retain immortal life. When these powers were lost in the fall, man's natural powers of reason, conscience, etc. were weakened but not destroyed. As such they are the image of God within fallen man. Fallen man thus still has the power to practice the natural virtues of prudence, justice, courage and self-control but he has lost the ability to attain a vision of God or to live the Christian virtues of faith, hope and love. Fallen man can regain these lost abilities only through the grace that comes to him through the sacraments of the church.

The Protestant Reformation generally denied any distinction between natural and supernatural endowments. The fall, it declared, resulted in the corruption of the whole of man and not in his loss of supernatural endowments. Calvin, in his *Institutes*, ii. 2, came as close to the concept of the *donum* as did any Protestant. He argued that certain natural talents of man had been corrupted by sin but that certain 'celestial' talents were totally lost. Thus sinful and fallen man still retains an ability for political order and general reason and Calvin suggests that in such areas Christians can learn from pagan philosophy. But in coming to know about God and the way of salvation, Calvin found that 'the most sagacious of mankind are blinder than moles'. In this way Calvin could argue that even sinful man is able to live on a level above the animals but he cannot, by his own efforts, do anything to aid his own salvation. *See also* **Man, Doctrine of.**

WILLIAM HORDERN

Dort, Synod of

The Synod, 13 November 1618 to 9 May 1619, was convened by the States General of the Netherlands to end the bitter doctrinal controversy over Arminianism. Episcopius, the successor of Arminius (d. 1609) and his adherents were summoned to appear not as members but as offenders. The Five Points of Arminianism that had been formulated in the Remonstrance of 1610 were condemned, and five opposing doctrines, the so-called Five Points of Calvinism, were explicitly stated. These are expounded with learning and precision in four chapters, each with numerous sub-divisions. The titles are: (1) Of Divine Predestination; (2) Of the Death of Christ and the Redemption of Man thereby; (3) Of the Conversion of Man, his Conversion to God and the Manner thereof; (4) Of the Perseverance of the Saints. The supralapsarian view of election advocated by Francis Gomarus, outstanding opponent of Arminius, was not affirmed. The position is infralapsarian: the decree of election is subsequent to the fall, but it is founded not upon foreseen faith but upon God's good pleasure. Christ's atonement is limited to the elect. Man is so corrupted by the fall that he is unable of himself to turn to God. The elect are preserved in a state of grace. Representatives from England, the Palatinate, Hesse, Nassau, Bremen, Emden, and the Swiss cantons were present. The Decrees of Dort were widely approved by the Reformed Churches.

Acta synodi nationalis . . . Dordrechti habitae anno MDCXVIII et MDCXIX, 1620; *Articles of the Synod of Dort and Its Rejection of Errors*, trans. from the Latin by Thomas Scott, 1841; D. Nauta, *Het Calvinisme in Nederland,* 1949.

J. T. MCNEILL

Double Procession (Holy Spirit)

The doctrine that the Holy Spirit proceeds both from the Father and the Son (credally expressed in the *Filioque*, q.v.) is a marked feature of Western theology (Augustine) which always held firmly to the Unity of the Godhead and emphasized the relations between the Persons. The East preferred the doctrine of the single Procession from the Father, which seemed to secure better the Unity of the Godhead on the pluralist premises. They endeavoured to express the operation of the Son with regard to the Spirit either by the use of an additional verb (send, receive from) or by a change of preposition (proceeding from the Father *through* the Son). *See* **Trinity, Doctrine of the.**

H. E. W. TURNER

Dualism

Any philosophical theory is dualistic, if it argues that there are exactly two irreducibly different constituents of the world. The best-known form of dualism is probably the Cartesian bifurcation of reality into material substance and mental substance. The term can be applied also to philosophies which are dominated by some contrast between two principles or modes of being, for example, between the mutable world of 'becoming' and the eternal world of 'being'. A religion can be termed dualistic, if it claims that there are two divine powers or principles in opposition (e.g. Zoroastrianism; Manichaeism).

In a great many philosophical quandaries, a dualism can appear to offer a solution: but it may in fact create as many new problems as it seems to solve. Define mind and body as belonging to utterly distinct, mutually incompatible realms of being, and at once the question arises, how are these substances to interact, as mind and matter undoubtedly do interact? The problem, so stated, is intractable; since by definition no common ground exists between the substances that could make interaction intelligible.

R. W. HEPBURN

Duns Scotus, Johannes

Duns (*c.* 1264–1308) was probably born in Berwickshire (so Fr Balic) and in 1279 he entered the Franciscan friary of Dumfries. He was ordained in 1291 and in 1293 was sent to Paris to study for four years. From 1297 to 1300 he lectured on the *Sentences* of Peter Lombard (q.v.) at Cambridge. In 1300–1 he lectured on the *Sentences* at Oxford and produced his so-called *Opus Oxoniense* or *Ordinatio*; and in 1302–3 he lectured on the same at Paris. He refused to support Philip the Fair against Boniface VIII and was exiled back to Oxford; but he returned to Paris in 1304, where he received his doctorate and acted as *magister regens* till he was transferred to Cologne in 1307. He died in 1308 at Cologne. His epitaph reads: *Scotia me genuit, Anglia me suscepit; Gallia me docuit, Colonia me tenet.*

Many works previously thought authentic are now proving spurious or by his direct disciples, notably *de Rerum Principio* and possibly the *Theoremata* and *de Anima*. The authentic works are listed and discussed by Fr Balic in *John Duns Scotus, 1265–1965*, 1–27 and *Some Reflections*, 29–44. They are all of a technical nature – *ordinationes, reportationes, quaestiones, collationes, quodlibeta, lectura, tractatus*: of these it is important to make this distinction, that an *ordinatio* was written or accurately dictated by the master, while a *reportatio* was only a student's account of a delivered lecture. His main *summa* now carries the name *Ordinatio* and is based on his commentary on Peter Lombard's *Sentences*.

Scotus' special interest lies in his differences from Aquinas (*see* **Thomism**), who usually follows Aristotle. The main disagreements are as follows: (1) Aquinas believed in the primacy of knowledge and intellect: 'the pursuit of wisdom is the most perfect, the most sublime, the most useful and the most agreeable of human pursuits' (*SCG* 1.1): Scotus followed the Franciscan doctrine of the primacy of love and the will. This has its dangers, for from it one can say that God's actions are not determined by wisdom but by spontaneous volition, good and bad being merely the reversible fiat of a Creator. This borders on blind dynamism, and removes God from being knowable by his creatures by analogy (q.v.). However, he agrees with Aquinas that revelation never contradicts reason: as God, *qua* Love, liberally bestows goodness, so his will operates in an infinitely rational way, determining ends first and then in proper sequences all that is ordered to those ends. His revelation, natural and positive, is a totally rational act of a super-loving will. (2) Aquinas held that transcendental predicates – *ens, unum, verum, bonum, pulchrum* – are analogous. Scotus held that they are univocal. He especially argued that the notion of being is univocal, for otherwise we cannot know God: *Deus non est a nobis cognoscibilis naturaliter, nisi ens sit univocum creato et increato* (*Ordinatio*, 1, 3, 3, 9). So also with 'good' and 'true'. Aquinas insisted on analogical likeness, and an absolute exclusion of univocal likeness, for the Creator cannot be compared with the creature, being infinite, perfect, subsistent Pure Act. (3) Aquinas accepted hylomorphism, i.e. the doctrine that a being might be expressed as two principles of the one essence – matter and form. Scotus accepted this too, but failed to see that the principle was inseparably contributive to a single being (*ens*): he allowed the possibility of separate existence of matter or form, believing that a distinction *in intellectu* corresponded with a distinction *in re* (a mistake made also by Descartes). If this were so, the result would be a plurality of forms – a spiritual and a corporeal form. (4) Aquinas accepted that form was the principle of universality and matter of individuation; and that the intellect knew the form as being universal: for him, singulars, as individual, were unintelligible. Scotus held the opposite: *Si singulare est unum quid, est per se intelligibile* (*Q. Met.* 7. 13.23). For him the intellect knows particulars by a confused intuition of what he called 'thisness' (*haecceitas*), which is a property of all singular objects (the property not lying in the individuation of matter). Where for Aquinas knowledge of the universal was prior, for Scotus knowledge of the singular was prior. (5) Aquinas saw a radical distinction between the mode of sense perception and the mode of intellection, while the object of both is one and the same, namely, *quidditas rerum sensibilium*. Scotus saw no such fundamental distinction of modes: for him intellection was like sense perception in that it was the perception of spiritual realities in the external world – so he found himself positing 'quasi-subsistent universals' in reality. He slid into a sort of Neoplatonist hinting that redeemed man would be released from the limitation of Aquinas' *quidditas* imposed by original sin: he believed in different kinds of objects, instead of different orders of knowing. (6) Aquinas rejected the doctrine of the Immaculate Conception (q.v.) of the Mother of Christ. Scotus was the first outright champion of that doctrine, and his influence led to the definition in 1854. His principle was this: that if Scripture or tradition will countenance it, *videtur probabile quod excellentius est attribuere Mariae.* (7) Aquinas held that the incarnation occurred as a direct response to the fall. Scotus and the Franciscans contended that it would have occurred anyway, since it is the first and absolute act *ad extra* of God as infinite Love. Christ then is necessarily the exemplary and final cause of mankind, without regard to the fall.

Whereas Thomism was taken up by the Dominican order, the Scotist doctrine was adopted by the Franciscans, even to this day.

C. Balic, ed., Critical ed. from MSS by the Scotist Commission, Rome, 6 vols. so far, 1950–   ; Evan Roche, ed., *De Primo Principio*, rev. text and trans., 1949; A. Wolter, ed., *A Treatise on God as First Principle*, 1966 (with two related questions from an earlier commentary on the Sentences); C. Balic, *John Duns Scotus: Some Reflections on the Occasion of the Seventh Centenary of his Birth*, 1966; E. Bettoni, *Duns Scotus: the Basic Principles of his Philosophy*, ET, 1961; F. C. Copleston, *History of Philosophy*, II, 1950, pp. 476–551; E. Gilson, *Jean Duns Scotus: Introduction à ses Positions Fondamentales*, 1952; C. R. S. Harris, *Duns Scotus*, 2 vols., 1927, rep., 1960; P. E. Longpré, *La Philosophie du Bl. Duns Scotus*, 1924; J. K. Ryan and B. M. Bonausea, eds., *John Duns Scotus, 1265–1965*, 1965; A. Wolter, *Duns Scotus: Philosophical Writings*, 1962; *The Theologism of Scotus*, Franciscan Stud. VII, 1947; C. Balic, *DS*, III, cols. 1801–18; *EB*, 1964 (a very good note); *EC*, IV, cols. 1982–90; J. H. Crehan and G. Reidy, CDT, II, pp. 199–201; P. Raymond, *DTC*, IV, cols. 1865–1947.

ALBERIC STACPOOLE, OSB

Dyotheletes. *see* Christology (4).

Dysteleology
The word is derived from Greek *dys*, bad, *telos*, an end: evidence of disharmony or purposelessness in creation. *See* **Teleology; Evil, Problem of.**

Ebionitism. *see* Adoptianism; Christology (4).

Ecclesiology
Ecclesiology is a term that was first used in the nineteenth century of the science of church building and decoration; it is now commonly applied to the doctrine of the Church.

1. *Ecclesiology as the Science of Church Building and Decoration.* The nineteenth century ecclesiologists considered, in the words of Pugin, that 'there should be no features about a building which are not necessary for convenience, construction, or propriety'. They thus, in this particular, anticipated the modern functional approach to architecture according to which the primary basis for any plan should be an analysis of the purposes for which a building is to be used. This analysis, however, involves facing fundamental theological questions: What is the Church? What is a church? What is worship? What is the Eucharist? What is baptism? etc. Only when a full doctrinal study of the Christian community, its role, its activities and the relationship between its members, for example, between clergy and laity, has been undertaken can an adequate brief be formulated. Ecclesiology in this sense has therefore an essential theological aspect.

2. *Ecclesiology as the Doctrine of the Church.* Ecclesiology in the current sense of the study of the doctrine of the Church must be deemed to begin with the NT, wherein numerous images are employed, for example, the messianic community, the Body of Christ, the Bride of Christ, the Temple of the Tabernacling Presence etc. (*see* R. H. Fuller, 'Church, Assembly', *TWBB*).

In the decades succeeding the apostolic age there was little immediate development in ecclesiology, the apologists, for example, contenting themselves with reproducing the NT images, although Irenaeus, in his fight against Gnosticism, laid particular stress on the apostolic succession (q.v.) as a guarantee of the purity and authenticity of the Church's teaching. The Church is the repository of truth and is regarded as the New Israel which has inherited the promises God made to the Old; it is essentially one, called into existence by God and guided by the Spirit.

At the beginning of the third century the Alexandrians, Clement and Origen, with their Platonic and spiritualizing sympathies, tended to distinguish between the visible Church and the invisible or heavenly Church, the former being the organized community, empirically discernible, and the latter the ideal to which eventually will belong all those who attain perfection on earth.

In contrast to this was the teaching of Cyprian, whose views were to dominate the West until Augustine. With his practical and even legalistic approach, Cyprian laid stress upon the oneness of the Church, arguing that the episcopate provided the God-given principle of unity. Hence the criterion of membership was submission to the bishop, opposition to whom meant that a person was either in heresy or in schism (q.v.) and therefore outside the Church. Further, according to Cyprian, salvation is not obtained apart from the Church because 'he cannot have God for his Father who has not the Church for his mother' (*de Unit.* 6). Cyprian's was a clear-cut conception but it had undoubted weaknesses. While it safeguarded the Church against external schism by simply treating schismatics as apostates, it provided no solution if groups of bishops failed to agree and such a situation could be exacerbated by his insistence on the autonomy of each bishop within his own diocese.

It was not until the end of the fourth century that the Donatist controversy compelled first Optatus and then Augustine to reconsider ecclesiology, but in the East no such problem presented itself, and therefore there was a tendency to reproduce only the time-honoured commonplaces about the Church, so that, for example, from the writings of Cyril of Jerusalem it is evident that he had not considered the problems involved in the Church's existence. Nevertheless there was an implicit consensus that the Church is the Body of Christ, common to such men as Athanasius, the Cappadocian Fathers and Cyril of Alexandria.

Optatus emphasized the factors that enable the true Church to be recognized and these, in his view, were two: its possession of catholic sacraments and its catholicity, that is, its extension throughout the world. Augustine laid less stress on the first of these but certainly brought the second into the forefront of the debate against the Donatists. He further, like Cyprian, regarded the episcopate as the focus of unity but, unlike Cyprian, was prepared to allow that the Church is a mixed community of both good and bad. He was also influenced, like the Alexandrians, by Platonism to posit a distinction between the visible and the invisible Church, the latter consisting of the good both inside and outside the visible Church. His developed predestinarianism, towards the end of his life, led him also to declare that the invisible Church consists of the fixed number of the elect known only to God. One other aspect of Augustine's ecclesiology is worthy of note: his teaching, most clearly formulated in his sermons, that the Church is the *totus Christus*, that is, the whole Christ. 'Christ with all his members is one, just as a head with its body. But what is this body save the Church? As the apostle Paul says: "Now ye are the body of Christ, and severally members thereof . . . " The whole therefore, i.e. the head and the body, is one Christ' (*Sermo* 144. 4). It was this organic conception of the Church that was to dominate Western ecclesiology through the succeeding centuries until the Reformation.

In one further respect Augustine's ecclesiology was of importance for the mediaeval understanding, which otherwise was little developed beyond his position. In asserting that the unity of the Church is provided by the one episcopate, he also declared that this unity is shown by communion with St Peter's see at Rome. This prominence given to the papacy immediately affected ecclesiology. The zenith of papal claims was reached by Leo the Great (440–61) who contended that: (*a*) Supreme authority had been bestowed by Jesus upon Peter. (*b*) Peter was the first bishop of Rome. (*c*) His authority has been perpetuated in his successors. (*d*) There is a mystical presence of Peter in his see. (*e*) The authority of all bishops, other than that of the bishop of Rome, is not derived immediately from Christ but mediately through Peter. (*f*) While the authority of individual bishops is limited to their dioceses that of the bishop of Rome extends over the whole Church whose government rests with him and of which he is the head. By accepting the concept of collegiality at the Second Vatican Council, the Roman Church today has somewhat modified this position, but the progressive acceptance of these claims meant that ecclesiology came to involve the primacy of the pope, the true Church consisting of those in communion with him. Nevertheless these claims did not pass unchallenged: John Wyclif (c. 1328–1384) and John Huss (c. 1369–1415) both maintained that the primacy of the pope had no basis in Scripture, and the former was prepared to denounce both papacy and hierarchy as anti-Christ. These protests were in some measure anticipations of the Reformation.

Luther's ecclesiology differed from that of the mediaeval theologians in that for him the constitutive element in the Church is the Word of God, which had been neglected by his predecessors for whom the constitutive element was the hierarchy. 'The Word and the sacraments constitute and build the kingdom of Christ', that is, the Church is the realm where Christ reigns. To Luther the Church is the communion of saints and the fellowship of believers; it is the mystical Body of Christ. He would not allow, however, this mystical Body to be identified with the organized Church; the borderlines of inner and external Christendom do not coincide, while the two do belong together; the one cannot be thought of without the other. Only God knows the boundaries around the communion of the faithful, and so the Body of Christ is a hidden Church and therefore an object of faith. This Church lives within external Christendom because the Word and the sacraments are functioning within it, and 'the Church is found everywhere in the world where the gospel and the sacraments are found'.

In Luther's teaching there was a certain tension that was to be resolved in two different ways. This tension arose because his understanding of the Eucharist was taken to point in one direction and his understanding of baptism in another. Laying emphasis upon personal faith, he contended that the Eucharist is for the gathered Church of convinced believers, but he also accepted infant baptism wherein one cannot speak of the personal faith of the baptized. The former stress issued in the idea of a confessing Church, that is, one that consists solely of convinced believers, and the latter in the idea of a territorial Church, that is, one in which the confession is that of the majority in a locality and one to which all may belong by baptism, the minority of dissenters being free to migrate to another area.

Calvin shared Luther's view that the faithful preaching of the Word and the right administration of the sacraments are marks of the Church and he added the exercise of vigilant discipline. He, too, regarded the Church as the Body of Christ and as the creation of the Holy Spirit, being the sphere of the self-revelation of God and of the encounter between Christ and men. But his doctrine of predestination induced him, following Augustine, to distinguish between the visible and the invisible Church, since there could be those elect outside the organized body of Christians; hence his dictum: 'The secret choice of God is the foundation of the Church.'

Both Luther and Calvin were concerned with the unity of the Church and in this are to be distinguished from the Independents who asserted that the only essential outward unity is that of each local congregation and that national churches are undesirable.

In recent times numerous factors have contributed to stimulate a renewed interest in ecclesiology which has become one of the doctrines most studied at the present day. *See* **Church.**

G. Cope, *Ecclesiology Then and Now*, 1964; J. N. D. Kelly, *Early Christian Doctrines*, 1958; W. Niesel, *The Theology of Calvin*, 1956; G. Rupp, *The Righteousness of God*, 1953.

J. G. DAVIES

Eckhart, Meister

The works of Meister Eckhart (c. 1260–1327/8) form a *locus classicus* for the examination of many of the difficulties which are felt about the compatibility of mysticism with the Christian religion: for example, that mysticism is necessarily pantheistic and that it denies the unique place of the historical incarnation and the inviolable character of individual, separate selfhood (*see* **Mysticism**). Many of the issues raised by Eckhart are similar to those posed by some modern theologians, especially Paul Tillich (*see* **Tillich, P.**) whose language about 'Being' and 'The God beyond God' bears a marked similarity to that of Eckhart.

One major difficulty in the study of Eckhart concerns the character of his language. One needs to remember that he is the first considerable writer in vernacular German, and secondly that he is more of a pulpit popularizer of scholasticism rather than a careful and precise theologian. Consequently it is questionable how far his daring metaphorical language ought to be treated as a carefully thought out and precisely formulated theology rather than a rhetoric, often extravagantly employed by Eckhart it is true, which he thought to be appropriate for his work as a preaching friar.

The basic themes of the teaching of Eckhart are as follows:

1. *On knowing God.* For Eckhart there are two stages in the process of knowing God. (*a*) What he calls knowing God 'in a mirror and mystery' and (*b*) knowing God 'by a mirror and light'. Knowledge of God type (*a*) is the result of pursuing the method of the *via negativa* as defined by Augustine and pseudo-Dionysius (*see* **Via Negativa**). Knowledge of God type (*b*) is given to those who as the result of a process of discipline whereby they are freed from the extravagances of self-reference attain union with God and know him 'face to face'.

2. *The Nature of God.* Eckhart is an impenitent intellectualist and comes down heavily on the side of the belief that God is to be conceived as primarily Mind or Intellect rather than Being. God is because he knows. In his argument for this Eckhart is more scientific in his exegesis of Ex. 3.14 than Aquinas. This passage for Eckhart is not a revelation of the nature of God as perfection of Being but an oblique pointer to the fact that what God is can only be deduced from what he wills and does, and in this respect his exegesis is closer to the intention of the Hebrew original.

Eckhart is reluctant to speak of God as Being because this was for him primarily an attribute of the creature, and to speak to God as 'a Being', he believed, would encourage ordinary folk to think of God anthropomorphically; also, one suspects, this preference for the *via negativa* appealed to Eckhart because it allowed an arresting paradoxical language which he preferred for pulpit purposes: 'God does not exist but I exist' and 'I give God existence'.

In his comments on Scripture, Eckhart is more willing to call God Being, and he speaks of Being as the very essence of God. Indeed in his *Opus Tripartitum* Eckhart identifies God with Being (*esse est Deus*). Being can be used of creatures not because they truly are but because they are related to God, who alone truly is. Through creation creatures participate in the divine being.

Throughout his writings Eckhart is speaking of God from two points of view: (*a*) there is God as he is, and (*b*) God as he is known. In (*a*) he is the ineffable mystery above Being. Here Ex. 3.14 is interpreted to mean the concealing of the divine name. In (*b*) he contains all perfection that he creates in creatures, especially Being. Here Ex. 3.14 is interpreted as in Augustine to mean the revelation of the divine name. A good illustration of these two approaches of Eckhart is to be found in his sermon *Quasi stella matutina*:

> Thus when I say that God is not being and that he is above being I have not denied him but rather I have dignified and exalted being in him. If I find copper in gold it is in a medium more precious than itself . . . When we consider God as being we are thinking of him in the keep of his castle where he dwells, for where God is being is, and it is the stronghold of his habitation. Where then is God in his temple? In intelligence? Yes, intellect is the temple of God and nowhere does he shine more holy than there. As sundry authorities say: God is intelligence that lives only in knowledge, apart, alone with himself so that nothing disturbs him as he is there alone in the silence.

3. *The Unity of God.* For Eckhart God is ineffable perfection of oneness in contrast with the multiplicity of phenomena, and he relates this belief to the Christian doctrine of the unity of God in trinity. He distinguishes between Godhead and God. By Godhead he means the ineffable unity, the Godhead, which lies behind the revealed Trinity (God), and we must not, Eckhart insists, identify God as he is revealed to us, known to us, and responded to by us in the Trinity with God in the perfection of his being, the One.

4. *Creation.* Creation for Eckhart involves God conferring himself on his creatures, and his language about the nothingness of creatures in relation to the creator God has led some to think that Eckhart is incurably pantheistic. But when he speaks of creatures as being absolutely nothing, or of existence as being identical with God, he is saying nothing more (of course in his paradoxical manner) than that in comparison with the being of God the existence of creatures is so incommensurate that one can profitably say that God exists and they do not, and when he speaks of existence as being identical with God does he mean any more than that in him we live and move and have our being in a way that we can never be fully conscious of or knowledgeable about?

5. *The Incarnation.* The paradox in the writings of Eckhart is that while on the one hand he seems

to have a certain hesitation or even distrust in his speaking about the incarnation, on the other hand there are very moving passages on the earthly life of Christ. This fact seems to arise from his feeling that excessive devotion to the historical Christ might well keep some of the faithful earthbound, so to speak. For Eckhart, the historical incarnation, the physical birth of Christ and the development of his mission was a reflection in time and history of the eternal nativity of the Son in the human soul. The soul also, for Eckhart, is independent of time, and the perfect counterpart of the eternal generation of the Son is the birth of Christ in the individual eternal soul. The spiritual life of the Christian is, for Eckhart, a process whereby God reproduces in miniature, in time, the incarnation of the Son in Jesus of Nazareth. Our knowledge of the historical facts of Christ is a preparation of our souls for the birth of the Son in them. The *motif* of the imitation of Christ for Christians takes two forms in Eckhart. There is, first of all, the imitation of Christ by 'way of manhood' which includes for Eckhart imitation of the active life of Christ, and this is a way which he believes must be trodden by all Christian believers, and there is second, what he calls the imitation of Christ by 'way of godhead', and this is for mystics only. This latter he saw as an imitation of the trinitarian action of God as revealed in Christ. But there is sufficient stress in the teaching of Eckhart on Christ acting in us through the Spirit to show that he does not conceive of the imitation of Christ as a mere servile imitation, but rather a process of transformation into Christ.

6. *The Divine Spark, the Soul.* Eckhart seems to have believed that there is, in every human being, a divine spark which is uncreated and eternal, and it is this which is at the root of the spiritual life. It is because he seems to have spoken uncompromisingly on occasions about the definitely uncreated character of this divine spark of the soul that he was arraigned for heresy and condemned in Cologne in 1326. Certainly he seems, on occasion, to have used extravagant language which suggests that he took the view that the beginning of the Son in the human soul is strictly like the incarnation, and so just as there is in the Son no human personality, in the human being he seems to have taken the view that the seat of personality is the divine spark.

Finally, it should be noted that Eckhart is a good example of the mystic who places no emphasis on his own particular experiences. It is possible from a close study of his writings to deduce something about the kind of experience which he knew, but at no point is there any explicit reference to it.

Jeanne Ancelet-Hustache, *Meister Eckhart and the Rhineland Mystics*, 1957; R. B.. Blakney, *Meister Eckhart* (a modern translation with introduction and notes), 1941; J. M. Clark and J. V. Skinner, *Meister Eckhart, Selected Treatises and Sermons*, 1963.   E. J. TINSLEY

Economic Trinity

Economic trinitarianism is the theory that the Son and the Spirit have the status not of full *Hypostases* (q.v.) but of economies or functional dispensations of the one God extrapolated for the purposes of creation and redemption. After their extrapolation they became independent internal differentiations. God is therefore one rather than three but became threefold in his dealings with creation. Logically, as Marcellus of Ancyra saw, this should imply a resumption of the monadic isolation of God after the conclusion of the economy. The theory is obviously monist in emphasis and differs from modalism (q.v.) merely in assigning a more permanent existence to the divine plurality. Some sources attribute to Sabellius (q.v.) terms characteristic of economic trinitarianism.

Traces of this view in the early Church were widely claimed by F. Loofs, though his interpretation of the evidence is too optimistic. The distinction drawn between the immanent and uttered Logos by Theophilus of Antioch, which contrasts sharply with the more pluralist Logos conception of other apologists, may tell in this direction. Traces are also discernable in Novatian and Tertullian. Paul of Samosata (q.v.) probably, and Marcellus of Ancyra (q.v.) certainly, held economic views.

Prestige held that the word 'economy', at least in the West, had nothing to do with extrapolation but merely pointed to a structured or organic monotheism. But the lexicography of the word strongly suggests a functional sense, and its abandonment in trinitarian contexts at a later date suggests growing hesitation over its use. In post-Nicene theology it is increasingly used of the incarnation as the greatest of the dispensations of God, and this is the level to which it properly belongs.

The root objection to this theory is that it makes God dependent for one element in his being upon his relationship to creation. It confuses an unfolding purpose with an unfolding Being. The former is orthodox and necessary, the latter neither. *See* **Modalism; Essential Trinity.**

F. Loofs, *Paulus von Samosata*, 1924; G. L. Prestige, *God in Patristic Thought*, 1936, pp. 97–111; A. E. J. Rawlingson, *Essays on the Trinity and the Incarnation*, 1928, pp. 258–67.
H. E. W. TURNER

Ecstasy

By ecstasy is meant an overwhelming and coercive experience wherein the sense of individual separate selfhood is transcended, the primary tense dimensions of time, past, present and future, are blended in an overwhelming sense of the eternal now, and there is an unforgettable experience of serenity, of well-being, of joy. This seems to be the raw material the interpretation of which will vary according to the religious, or philosophical, presuppositions of the person concerned. In religion this experience is closely associated with mysticism (*see* **Mysticism**), the apex of the ascetical discipline being ecstasy. In the Christian tradition, ecstasy is associated both with the prophet and the mystic, and there has been a good deal of discussion as to whether the prophetical experience differs in any way from that of the mystic. Furthermore the question arises whether there is any relation between the prophetical and the mystical experience and that of the poet. What is the difference between ecstasy and poetic inspiration?

The immediate occasion of the ecstatic experience is very varied: sexual and parental love, aesthetic experiences in literature, drama, poetry, music, some natural scene, mountain, lake etc., and in all cases there is a profound, unmistakable experience of oneness, of unity, of being part of a larger living whole. In the mystical tradition there is strong emphasis that the experience of ecstasy is not to be sought for its own sake; the experience is at God's disposal and man must not behave as if it could be induced. For all practical purposes it is wise to take these experiences, if they come, as testing points rather than well-merited awards.

The difference between the prophetic, the aesthetic and the mystical experience is perhaps best determined by a consideration of what is the end-product in all three cases. In the aesthetic experience the end-product (poem, symphony, etc.) is part of the experience. In prophetical ecstasy the experience leads to the address to the people, and in relation to that mission the experience occupies a subordinate position. In mystical experience the end-product seems to be the experience itself, although the mystic is driven to say something about the experience while emphasizing the hopeless inadequacy of any language which he may choose to try and describe it.

Ecstasy, then, in Christian thought and practice takes on the character of a sign. In itself it is not indisputably from God or from men, but retains an ambiguous character which summons man to a decision of faith.

W. R. Inge, *Christian Mysticism*, 7th ed., 1933; William James, *The Varieties of Religious Experience*, 1902; K. E. Kirk, *The Vision of God*, 1931; Marghanita Laski, *Ecstasy*, 1961; J. H. Leuba, *The Psychology of Religious Mysticism*, 1925; Evelyn Underhill, *Mysticism*, 12th ed., rev., 1930; R. C. Zaehner, *Mysticism, Sacred and Profane*, 1957.

E. J. TINSLEY

Ecumenical, Ecumenical Movement, Ecumenism

The word 'ecumenical' comes from the Greek *oikumene* which means 'the inhabited earth'. It is one of the words used in the NT for the 'world' and can mean the inhabitants of the world. It was also used of the whole known world, which meant the Roman Empire. In current theological thinking the word 'ecumenical' is used to describe that concern among Christians for the unity of the Church and the unity of all things in Christ. The Ecumenical Movement needs to be seen not just in terms of the movement towards Christian Unity but also as part of the wider movement proceeding throughout the whole of creation to manifest the unity of all things. Mission and unity are interdependent. The proclamation of the gospel to the whole of creation is part of the process of summing up all things in Christ; and the unity of the Christian Church is central to the process and makes the proclamation of the gospel effective. It was the missionary expansion of the nineteenth century which gave birth to what is now called the Ecumenical Movement, which is generally reckoned as having had its starting point at the Missionary Conference at Edinburgh in 1910; but it must not be forgotten that there have always been those within the Christian Church who have sought to establish, maintain or extend the unity of all Christian people.

The Ecumenical Movement begins and ends in God. The oneness of God is an essential aspect of the biblical revelation. Man's unity with God was broken by the one man Adam, and is restored in the one new Man, Jesus Christ (I Cor. 15.22). This restored relationship with God in Christ is demonstrated in the oneness of those who accept the new relationship by faith through their participation in the Church, and so share in the oneness of God through communion with him and with one another. It is here that the doctrine of the Trinity is important. In the same way as the persons of the Trinity, though they are one, show no confusion of persons, the union of Christians with each other and with Christ does not deny or destroy the diversity and uniqueness of every individual. The very diversity of mankind is the essential prerequisite of unity. It is the interdependence of mankind which reveals true unity. Hence within the Church there are many 'gifts' (*charismata*) and ministries which together make up the unity of the Church (I Cor. 12.4–30). Division and divisive factors are the result of sin. The divisions of Christendom and the bitter divisions within the human race are the effects of man's sin. They are the results of man's refusal to accept the lordship of Christ over all creation and oneness in him.

It is contended by Pierre Teilhard de Chardin and others that the whole creation is slowly moving towards the unity of all things in Christ. The whole movement towards one world and the new interdependence brought about by technology and the discoveries about the nature of man and his evolution are given as evidence of this. The role of the Church would be seen as forwarding this unity by leading men into union with God. Such a view is to be welcomed for its optimism but is regarded with suspicion by some as being too universalistic and as not giving a proper place to the redemptive work of Christ.

The establishment of the World Council of Churches in 1948 was a major event in the history of the Ecumenical Movement. It has been the servant of the Ecumenical Movement and has done much to promote concern for unity throughout Christendom. It must be remembered that the World Council of Churches is not the Ecumenical Movement. The Ecumenical Movement is all those who are working for the unity of Christians and of humanity and is not by any means limited to those churches who belong to the World Council of Churches. The ways in which the Ecumenical Movement is forwarded may be summarized as follows:

1. *Prayer for Unity.* For many years the churches have prayed for unity, but it was the work of the Abbé P. Couturier to bring prayer to the centre of the Ecumenical Movement. Prayer itself is an expression of the unity of God and man. Unity without the holiness which comes from union with God would be a very unstable and shallow phenomenon. The Vatican decree on Ecumenism regards common prayer as that part of *'communicatio in sacris'* which is suitable to all Christians of whatever denomination. Thus common worship, even if it does not go as far as sharing in the Eucharist (*see* **Reunion**) is a valuable means of expressing the unity which already exists between Christians through their common allegiance to Christ. The fact of all Christians seeking a deeper unity with God through prayer is bound to encourage unity among all Christians.

2. *Mutual 'Diakonia'.* The mutual help and service which Churches can give to one another is a practical expression of unity. It is necessary because it is an act of love, which is the fruit of the Gospel, but restores the God-given unity of the Church by this 'realized ecumenism'.

3. *Joint 'Diakonia' to the World.* The concept of the Servant Church gains considerably when the whole Church serves the world and not as separate Christian communities. This kind of service may take many and various forms. The 'Life and Work' movement, which was one part of the early Ecumenical Movement, has done a great deal to develop the idea of Christian service to society. The Christian witness in matters of social justice, world affairs, personal relationships, education and human rights has been considerable and co-operation in this sphere is helping to bring unity to mankind as well as to the churches.

4. *Joint Action for Mission.* Co-operation and planning in the preaching of the Gospel is a central part of the Ecumenical Movement (*see* **Mission**). The growth of the missionary movements led the churches to see the scandal of competing with one another in preaching the Gospel. Mission comity, the dividing up of areas between the churches, was one way of dealing with this problem and it soon led to an awareness that this was not enough and that organic union was the only solution. In the meanwhile a great deal can be done by co-operation in mission.

5. *Mutual respect and avoidance of Proselytism.* The recognition of other Christian bodies as having ecclesial reality by the Roman Catholic Church (*see Constitution on the Church* and *Decree on Ecumenism*) has helped to make this much more of a practical reality. But the proper definition of a Church still remains the central problem of ecclesiastical ecumenism. The Decree on Ecumenism recognizes that a common worship of the triune God, the centrality of Scripture, the acceptance of baptism and the Eucharist and the demonstration of faith in public and private worship are signs of the Church which all share. On this basis real dialogue and mutual respect can be developed.

6. *Discussion of matters of Faith and Order.* 'Faith and Order' has been a major aspect of the work of the World Council of Churches. This is concerned not just with seeking ways of church union (*see* **Reunion**) but also in seeking together a common mind on matters of theology. Like inter-church *Diakonia*, inter-church theological discussion becomes a form of realized ecumenism where churches learn from one another the theological insights and values of other Christians. Thus a unity of theological thought with all its diversity is being sought and gradually achieved. For this, however, there must be a willingness to listen and to understand the theological position of others. It also means that the claim of any Christian or of any church to possess the whole truth must be resisted. The unity of God is far greater than can be fully possessed or understood by man.

7. *Dialogue.* This word may sum up the means by which ecumenism may proceed. True dialogue needs to be based on the following principles:
  (a) Honesty by both partners, which implies that each accepts the integrity of the other's position.
  (b) A common basis. Without some basis dialogue is impossible.
  (c) An understanding of one's own position.
  (d) An attempt really to understand the other person's position.
  (e) The willingness to listen to each other.
  (f) Penitence for one's own failures.
  (g) A willingness to change; dialogue has little point without this.
  (h) Personal encounter; dialogue cannot be impersonal.
Dialogue is the basis of all ecumenism, both ecclesiastical (to achieve union) and secular (to seek the unity of mankind in Christ). See **Mission.**

It will be seen from this that renewal is an essential element in ecumenism. The Ecumenical Movement has always been related both to mission and to renewal. The organic union of the Church without mission and without the right priorities would be stagnation. The churches need one another so that they may be renewed effectively to preach the gospel in the modern world. Churches which open themselves to each other to seek unity are far more likely to be renewed than those which do not, because through the dialogue their own position is questioned and their own understanding enlarged.

One question which has always concerned the World Council of Churches is its own ecclesiological nature. It is not a 'super-church'; it does not have its own ministry or sacraments. Nor is it to be equated with the Ecumenical Movement, which is something much wider than its own membership. It is probably best described as a servant of the Ecumenical Movement; and as it fulfils this role it does in some ways foreshadow the Coming Great Church. It does this in so far as its Basis expresses an essential confession of faith. Its conciliar structure may be in embryo the conciliar structure of a united world church. But it is not and must not be seen to be a church in any real sense of the word. The Basis of the World Council of Churches reads as follows:

> The World Council of Churches is a fellowship of Churches which confess the Lord Jesus Christ as God and Saviour according to the Scriptures and therefore seek to fulfil together their common calling to the glory of the one God, Father, Son and Holy Spirit.

This Basis was adopted at the New Delhi Conference in 1961. It owes its origin to the Basis of the Young Men's Christian Association of a much earlier period. The more evangelical churches of Christendom regard it as too inclusive and too vague and open to a very wide interpretation. They would rather see something far more specific. Yet for other parts of Christendom (e.g. The Religious Society of Friends) it is far too exclusive and specific. The World Council of Churches is regarded by some as betraying the essentials of the Christian faith and by others as not expressing it fully enough. How far can the ecclesiastical Ecumenical Movement go? The World Council of Churches Basis provides a clue but is not enough in itself. Clearly there are many groups on the edge of Christendom which cannot be included, and the Church needs still to preserve itself from heresy, but there is a great deal of difference between recognizable heresy and a variety of interpretations of the Christian faith which do not lead to heresy. This is a problem which requires very considerable discussion.

The development of Regional and National Councils of Churches has enabled the churches to come together at a more local level to discuss matters of concern to them. One of the main problems in planning joint ecumenical action is the problem of overlapping boundaries and jurisdictions. Such matters are better discussed locally and can lead to the setting up of new structures for the Church.

One problem, to which the World Council of Churches has given some consideration, is that of institutionalism. This arose out of the earlier debate about the so called 'non-theological factors' in preventing church union. The way the churches are organized, the role of leadership, how authority is exercised, the growth of bureaucracy in the churches are issues which deeply affect the way churches behave towards one another. And as these are human factors, which affect every organization, they are also factors in the way the World Council of Churches acts towards the churches. Thus they are matters which need to be kept continuously under review; because they are concerned with the Christian doctrine of man and society, they need careful theological understanding. If the World Council of Churches and other ecumenical bodies are to be seen as the servants of ecumenical dialogue, then this may sometimes require a servant who will draw the attention of the participants to issues which they have neglected or avoided.

Paul Tillich (*Systematic Theology*, III, 1960) has pointed out the paradoxical nature of the Ecumenical Movement. Even if a united world church came into existence, he argues, new divisions would occur. The role of the Ecumenical Movement is to overcome the divisions which have become obsolete. This view makes us face the realities of the creative tensions which must exist within any kind of unity. It has become an axiom of the Ecumenical Movement that unity does not imply uniformity; diversity is essential for unity. The polarities of division and unity are not just limited to the Church; they are inherent in any form of human unity. The role of the Church is to demonstrate to the world that the ambiguities of unity can be held together, so that the way to true human unity may be made manifest. On the way to this goal the Ecumenical Movement will take into account the dialogue between religions, the relationships of East and West, the growth of new nations, the tensions between races and cultures, and the search for political responsibility. For nothing is outside the scope of the summing up of all things in Christ.

N. Goodall, *The Ecumenical Movement*, 1964; B. Lambert, *Ecumenism*, 1967; B. Leeming, *The Vatican Council and Christian Unity*, 1966; A. van Leeuwen, *Christianity and World History*, 1964; E. Molland, *Christendom*, 1959.

R. M. C. JEFFERY

Edwards, Jonathan

Jonathan Edwards (1703–1758), Congregational minister and theologian, was one of the greatest intellects in American history. Grasped by the vision of the universe as an interdependent, unified system of being, he asserted a 'consistent Calvinism' utilizing the discoveries of Lockean psychology and Newtonian science. Laying the foundations of his theological work while student and then tutor at Yale, he began to publish while in the pastorate at Northampton, Massachusetts (1727–50). Four major motifs characterize his theological work.

First, he was a defender and critic of religious revivals. Himself a central figure in the Great

Awakening, he distinguished between true re-vivalism and false in *Some Thoughts Concerning the Present Revival of Religion* (1742) and in *A Treatise Concerning Religious Affections* (1746), in which he declared that religion is primarily a matter of the affections. Truly spiritual and gracious affections arise only from special in-fluences of the Spirit in the souls of the saints, the elect. Second, Edwards was a champion of the purification of the Church, especially in *Qualifica-tions Requisite for Full Communion* (1749), in which he insisted that full standing in the visible Church should be restricted to truly gracious persons – visible saints. This was not accepted by his congregation. He was dismissed, and the next year settled as missionary to the Indians at Stock-bridge, where he was to do some of his most sig-nificant writing. Third, he defended Calvinism against Arminianism, in his famous *Treatise on the Will* (1754), in which he argued that if a man is free to do as he wills he is then responsible for his acts, even though he may not be free to will as he wills, and in *The Great Christian Doctrine of Original Sin Defended* (1758), in which he dis-cussed the imputation of Adam's sin to all man-kind on the basis of a divinely constituted per-sonal identity between Adam and his posterity. Fourth, Edwards planned a massive systematic work, but, accepting the presidency of Prince-ton, he journeyed there in 1758 only to die from the effects of a smallpox inoculation. Some frag-ments of the projected work were posthumously published as *Two Dissertations* (1765). 'The Nature of True Virtue' is a theologico-philo-sophical discussion of the love of God; 'Concern-ing the End for which God Created the World' is a scriptural and philosophical analysis of the work of God in creation.

Besides these and other published treatises and sermons, Edwards left many unpublished writ-ings and notes. As the founder of 'New England Theology' (q.v.) he exerted great influence on the history of American theology.

Conrad Cherry, *The Theology of Jonathan Ed-wards: a Reappraisal*, 1966; Douglas J. Elwood, *The Philosophical Theology of Jonathan Edwards*, 1960; Perry Miller, *Jonathan Edwards*, 1949.

ROBERT T. HANDY

Elder

The word elder, derived from the Old English, is synonymous with presbyter (q.v.), derived from the Greek. In contemporary usage, however, the two words tend to be distinguished, a presbyter being an ordained minister of word and sacra-ments and an elder being a layman set apart by ordination to assist the presbyter in his adminis-tration and government of the church. This differentiation corresponds in the Presbyterian Churches to the two types of elder defined by Calvin: (1) Teaching elders, that is, presbyters with pastoral functions, and (2) ruling elders, that is, elders with administrative functions.

In the *Book of Common Order of the Church of Scotland* the duties of elders in the second sense are listed as follows: 'to set the example of a virtuous and godly life, and of regular attendance at public worship; to take part with the Minister in administering the care and discipline of the parish; and to represent their brethren in Pres-byteries, Synods, and General Assemblies, when commissioned thereto'. The office of elder, some-what similarly conceived is also found in Christian bodies other than the Presbyterian, for example, the Disciples of Christ and the Moravians.

Whether or not Calvin's distinction has any NT basis may be questioned, but as a means of allowing the laity a greater part in church affairs the eldership may be said to have much to com-mend it. For bibliography, *see* books listed under **Bishop**.

J. G. DAVIES

Election. *see* Predestination.

Elkesaites

Elkesaites, a Jewish Christian sect, came into being towards the end of the first century AD. Their provenance, practices and teaching were similar to those of the Ebionites (q.v.), but their doctrine of Christ's person was more docetic (q.v.). Their claim that their revelation (the Book of Elkesai) was delivered to them by an angel ninety-six miles high places them among the more colourful deviationists from the orthodox de-velopment of Christian thought.

Empirical Theology

Empirical Theology in America emerged in the early twentieth century as part of the general movement of theological liberalism within Pro-testantism. The empirical theologians were at-tempting to answer the challenges of atheism and humanism on the common ground of human experience and scientific knowledge. Both his-torical-critical and systematic-constructive meth-ods were employed. The empirical theologians were basically apologists, for they sought to re-interpret Christian theological symbols so as to make them intelligible and effective in a scientific-industrial age, but they did this in such a way as to set them well towards the theological left. They were influenced by the philosophical work of Peirce, James and Dewey (*see* **Pragmatism**), and by the rigorous insistence on empirical data so important in various schools of historical and sociological inquiry.

A major centre of empirical theological thought was at the Divinity School of the University of Chicago under the administration of Shailer Mathews (1863–1941). After graduating from Colby College and the Newton Theological Institute, Mathews was not ordained, but con-tinued study in history and political economics in Germany. In 1894 he began his career at the divinity school in the field of NT history, later shifting to historical and systematic theology. He served as dean from 1908 to retirement in 1933. A leader in the application of social historical analysis to Christian life and doctrine, he avoided any appeal to religious authority but insisted on a fully scientific, rigorously empirical, inductive method in the theological disciplines. In *The Atonement and the Social Process* (1930) he demonstrated how theological positions are influenced by the cultural and political settings of the time of their expression. In *The Growth of the Idea of God* (1931) he insisted that the starting point for religion is 'a relationship with the universe described by the scientist', and defined God as 'our conception, born of social experience, of the personality-evolving and personally responsive elements of our cosmic environment with which we are organically related'.

Henry Nelson Wieman (1884–) was the other major figure of the 'Chicago school'; his approach was primarily systematic-constructive, under the influence both of the empiricism of Dewey and of the metaphysics of Whitehead (q.v.). After graduating from Park College and San Francisco Theological Seminary, he studied in Germany and then completed a doctorate at Harvard (1917). Ten years later he joined the Chicago faculty, in search of a theocentric as against an anthropocentric religion. In such early books as *Religious Experience and Scientific Method* (1926) and *The Wrestle of Religion with Truth* (1927), he maintained that God must be known as is any other object in experience, by means of scientific observation and reason. Following the clue of defining God as the source of values disclosed in experience, he came to characterize God as a delicate system of complex growth, that is, as the development of meaning and value in the world. His major work, *The Source of Human Good* (1946), asserted that his religious thought was within the Christian tradition, and developed certain christological, eschatological and ecclesiological positions. 'Salvation through Jesus Christ' was presented as 'a transformation in the life of man which is accomplished not by human intelligence and purpose but by certain happenings in history centering in the man Jesus'.

Douglas Clyde Macintosh (1877–1948), born in Canada, educated at McMaster University, received his doctorate at Chicago in 1909, and began a lifetime of teaching at Yale Divinity School the same year. As philosopher of religion, Macintosh insisted on a solid empirical basis for assertions. His *Theology as an Empirical Science* (1919) was a classic statement of the empirical movement. But Macintosh also allowed room for a realm of 'over-beliefs', which are not determined by evidence gathered through scientific methods but by what we need to believe in order to live as we ought. Such beliefs, however, should be reasonable and consistent with what we learn by empirical approaches. Holding to a position of 'moral optimism', he defended an understanding of God as a supreme personality of intelligence and goodness, and argued for personal immortality.

In 1931, Macintosh edited and contributed to an important volume, *Religious Realism*, which sought to resist the romantic subjective tendencies of earlier liberalism. His procedure involved proving the existence of God in essentially that religious sense in which the term has been used throughout history, 'and proving this by a new and regenerating experience'. To this symposium, intended to affirm the objectivity of a divine ground of faith, Wieman also contributed, as did E. W. Lyman.

Eugene W. Lyman (1872–1948) was educated at Amherst and Yale, and after study in Germany, he began a teaching career that climaxed in a professorship (1918–40) in the philosophy of religion at Union Theological Seminary, New York. In an early systematic book, *Theology and Human Problems* (1910), Lyman interpreted James' pragmatism as a way of bringing the objective truths of science and philosophy into a creative relationship with the equally valid truths of moral and religious experience. In his *magnum opus, The Meaning and Truth of Religion* (1933), Lyman argued for the realistic trend then current in the philosophy of religion, indicating that in 'intuition' the depths of reality are really presented. Intuitions are not self-validating, he affirmed, but need careful synthesizing and rigorous testing by scientific and other appropriate means. Intuitions are 'perceptive', 'synthetic', and 'creative'; they discover truth while reason tests and establishes truth. As with most empirical theologians, Lyman was concerned about the social order, and sought to bring religious resources to bear on the problems of modern living.

The empirical movement in American theology exerted influence on many thinkers who never fully accepted its tenets, among them such figures as John C. Bennett, Robert L. Calhoun and Walter M. Horton. The realistic movement in the 1930s tended on the whole to provide a transition to neo-orthodox trends, and empiricism in theology fell under sharp attack, especially from Reinhold and H. Richard Niebuhr (q.v.).

Kenneth Cauthen, *The Impact of American Religious Liberalism*, 1962; Sydney E. Ahlstrom, 'Theology in America: A Historical Survey', and Daniel D. Williams, 'Tradition and Experience in American Theology', *The Shaping of American Religion*, eds., J. W. Smith and A. L. Jamison, 1961, pp. 232–321, 443–95.

ROBERT T. HANDY

Encratites

Encratites is a general name (under variant forms) given by patristic writers (e.g. Irenaeus, q.v.) to various groups of extreme ascetic and heretical sects, such as Ebionites, Gnostics, Docetists (qq.v.). It was in these 'encratite' groups that the Apocryphal Gospels (q.v.) circulated and perhaps were written.

Encyclopaedists, The

The immense success of the *Dictionnaire historique et critique* of Pierre Bayle (1647–1706), which was published in the Netherlands in 1695–7 and went through many editions after its author's death, doubtless inspired the writing of the French *Encyclopédie* between 1751 and 1780, from which the contributors to it derived their title of Encyclopaedists. Under the editorship of Denis Diderot the work became the repository of all the sceptical and advanced ideas of the French Enlightenment (q.v.). The last seven of its thirty-five volumes were published in Amsterdam (as Bayle's *Dictionary* had been) in order to escape censorship. The group of like-minded thinkers were also known as *les philosophes*, although they were not philosophers in the strict sense; philosophy for them meant the ideas and ideals of the 'men of enlightenment'. Nor were they scientists, although their association with the secretary of the Académie des Sciences, the long-lived Fontenelle (1657–1757), lent to them something of the prestige of science. They were literary men who popularized scientific ideas, and it may be said that they invented the 'conflict' between science and religion. The real scientists of the age were, like Newton, religious men. Nor were they historians, though they utilized history, as Bayle had done, for their attack upon the idea of revelation and upon social institutions. Their teaching was one of the factors which led to the French Revolution, though they were mostly aristocrats who would have been horrified at the result. Many of them believed in 'natural religion' (*see* **Deism**); a few might be classed as agnostics or atheists; but all believed strongly in the power of the human reason. The Encyclopaedists and their associates are collectively very important for the study of the history of ideas, though individually they were neither original nor profound – unless, perhaps, Voltaire is included in the group. They are theologically important because they were among the first to publicize the difficulties which inevitably arose as a result of the breakdown of the traditional conception of revelation (q.v.).

For the theological implications of this aspect of eighteenth-century thought *see* Alan Richardson, *History Sacred and Profane*, 1964, ch. 3. *See also* the bibliography under **Enlightenment.** For a perhaps unduly sympathetic survey of the period *see* Peter Gay, *The Party of Humanity*, 1954 (USA), 1964 (London).

EDITOR

Enhypostasia

Enhypostasia is the doctrine that the *hypostasis* (i.e. person) of the Godhead, which was incarnate in Christ, included all the attributes of human nature as perfected, and that therefore the one person of Christ, though divine, is fully human. In the patristic age the doctrine was advocated by St John of Damascus (d., c. 749) and in the present century by H. M. Relton in *A Study in Christology*, 1917. *See* **Christology** (4).

Enlightenment, The

This is the name given to the period, usually reckoned from about 1650 to 1780, which witnessed the final disintegration of the mediaeval world-view and the gradual secularization of thought and of institutions in western Europe. Its German name is *Aufklärung* (French: *L'illumination*). It is also known as 'the Age of Reason'. Progressive thinkers spoke of themselves as 'enlightened', although in reality their age was one of half-seeing: the Newtonian scientific revolution was accomplished, but the fruition of the even more significant historical revolution did not occur until after the period had closed. Hume, Voltaire and the *philosophes* (q.v.) wrote history, but they were not historically minded in the modern sense. Hence many of their intellectual objections to Christianity arose out of their failure to understand the scriptural revelation historically in an age when it was becoming increasingly difficult to accept the literal truth of the Bible. Thus the period was one of acute crisis for theology, and it is true to say that for many in our own age the crisis of the eighteenth century remains. Men 'come of age' set themselves free from the dogmas, morals and inherited institutions of the past; and for the first time since Constantine the Church and the Christian faith were openly abused and derided. The task of the reconstruction of a theology of revelation was entirely beyond the orthodox opponents of deism (q.v.), since they were as deficient in historical understanding as were the deists and sceptics. Indeed, it is true to say that this task still awaits completion in our own times. *See also* **Revelation**.

There is an enormous literature on the thought of this period. Special mention may be made of G. R. Cragg, *The Church and the Age of Reason*, 1960; Peter Gay, *The Enlightenment*, 1967; Paul Hazard, *European Thought in the 18th Century*, ET, 1954; D. G. James, *The Life of Reason*, 1949; Leslie Stephen, *History of English Thought in the 18th Century*, 3rd ed., 1949; and Carl Becker's provocative and witty *Heavenly City of the 18th Century Philosophers*, 1932. The theological issues arising from the crisis of thought in the age of Enlightenment are dealt with in Alan Richardson, *History Sacred and Profane*, 1964, where a full bibliography is given.

EDITOR

Enmity against God

Christian theology speaks of sin, not simply in terms of disobeying the law but as a revolt against God. Man, in his pride, desires to take that place in his own life that God ought to have. Enmity to God is thus expressed in putting oneself at the centre of life instead of letting God be at the centre. *See also* **Man, Doctrine of.**

WILLIAM HORDERN

Enthusiasm

From a Greek word literally meaning 'possessed by a god', the word came in the eighteenth century to signify undue religious emotionalism or fanaticism, things much disapproved in the Age of Reason. For an evaluation of enthusiasm in relation to the work of the Holy Spirit see **Spirit** (5, [*d*]).

R. A. Knox, *Enthusiasm, a Chapter in the History of Religion*, 1950.

EDITOR

Epiclesis

The petition in the Anaphoras (q.v.) of the Eastern Church for the descent of the Holy Spirit upon the eucharistic elements to change them into the body and blood of Christ is known as epiclesis. This petition, which comes after the dominical words of institution, is commonly held by Eastern Orthodox Churches to effect the transubstantiation (q.v.). The view, formerly widely held, that an epiclesis was an invariable feature of primitive liturgies is now virtually abandoned, but the origin of the epiclesis is obscure and is much debated by liturgiologists. In the 1549 Prayer Book Cranmer inserted an epiclesis (of the Spirit *and the Word*) before the dominical words, but it was omitted in 1552 and 1662. Under the influence of the older view, an epiclesis in the Eastern position has been made a feature of a number of Anglican revisions of the eucharistic rite, including the proposed rite of 1927–8, but not in that temporarily authorized for the Church of England in 1967.

E. L. MASCALL

Epicureanism

Epicureanism was a philosophy widely current in the Roman Empire before, during and after the NT period (*cf.* Acts 17. 18). Founded upon the teaching of Epicurus (342–270 BC), it accepted the theory of the Greek Democritus that reality consisted in the swirling movements of particles of matter in motion. At death the human soul disintegrates and there is no immortality. Epicurus conceived of this teaching as a real liberation from the fear of Hades and of the revenge of the gods upon human beings who had failed to satisfy their demands for craven flattery. Epicurus and his followers did not deny the existence of the gods (they were made of very refined atoms); they taught that the gods in their state of bliss were totally uninterested in the doings of the human race. Nor did the Epicureans teach the kind of vulgar hedonism (q.v.) which has so unfairly been attached to their name. They held, indeed, that pleasure was the chief end of human life, but not in the sense of merely sensual pleasure. The principal virtue was prudence, because without wisdom and self-control true happiness or pleasure could not be attained or sustained. The Roman poet Lucretius at the end of the first century AD gave memorable expression to the Epicurean attack upon superstition (i.e. religion) in his philosophical poem *De Rerum Natura*. It will be readily apparent from the above brief description of the Epicurean philosophy why it did not exert any influence upon the development of Christian thought comparable to that of Stoicism (q.v.).

C. Bailey, *The Greek Atomists and Epicurus*, 1928; R. D. Hicks, *Stoic and Epicurean*, 1910; A. E. Taylor, *Epicurus*, 1910.

EDITOR

Epiphany

1. The Greek word means 'manifestation'. In polytheistic religion nature is full of local manifestations of the gods. In popular Greek religion a deity might manifest himself in a 'divine man' – a prince (e.g. Antiochus Epiphanes), a miracleworker (Simon Magus, Elymas), and so on. In Greek philosophy epiphany-religion is the foundation of a natural theology which discerns manifestations of the eternal present (or of the divine) in all things. But in biblical religion direct epiphanies of God are spoken of with reticence, though they do occur, as notably at the burning bush (Ex. 3.2). Usually God manifests himself in the paradoxical act of veiling himself, supremely of course at the incarnation. It is true to say of the Bible in general that such manifestations as are vouchsafed in history are by way of *promise*: not until the final Epiphany of Christ at the end of history can we speak of 'epiphany' in any fulfilled sense.

2. Epiphany is a feast of the Church (January 6), originating in the East where it celebrated the nativity of Christ (i.e. his 'manifestation' to mankind) or, more usually, his baptism. It was introduced into the West in the fourth century, but there it lost its connection with the baptism and became the feast of the manifestation of Christ to the Gentiles, celebrating the visit of the Magi (Greek: *magoi*, sages), assumed to be the first Gentile believers. (But there is nothing in the story in Matt. 2.1–12 to indicate that the wise men from the East were not Jews of the Dispersion.)

EDITOR

Episcopacy

Episcopacy may be used either of the office of a bishop (q.v.) or of the system of church government which comprises three major orders (q.v.) – bishop, priest and deacon. As a system of church government it was repudiated at the Reformation by a number of Protestant Churches, partly on the grounds of its corruption and of its transformation into prelacy and partly on the less certain grounds of its lack of justification from the NT.

Its preservation, within the apostolic succession (q.v.), is claimed by the Roman, Old Catholic, Eastern Orthodox, Oriental and Anglican Churches. It is also accepted by certain members of the Lutheran family of churches, although in Sweden the historic succession was retained, while in Denmark, Finland, Norway and Iceland the first consecrations were by simple priests. The Moravians have also a priestly origin for their episcopacy, while their bishops are excluded from governing, their authority being confined to ordination. Episcopacy also found a place in American Methodism, Thomas Coke, who had been ordained 'superintendent' by John Wesley and others in 1784, regarding himself as a bishop and duly consecrating Asbury as such; Methodist bishops are, however, regarded as elders (q.v.) but with the additional function of ordination.

In contemporary discussion concerning re-union, episcopacy inevitably becomes a centre of debate. There are those who maintain that it is of the *esse* of the Church, that is, it is of the Church's essential being without which it would not exist; there are those that regard it as of the *bene esse*, that is, beneficial to the Church but not necessary for its being; finally there are those who hold it to be neither necessary nor beneficial. Most Christians, however, would agree that *episcope*, in its original sense of oversight, is essential to the Church, but they differ as to who may be said to exercise it. So, for example, Methodists in England locate *episcope* in their annual conference, while those churches that have the historic episcopate see the bishops as the sole organs duly authorized to exercise it. It is doubtful if those churches who have retained it will be prepared to give up episcopacy to achieve reunion, and it is to be noted that in all recent schemes, for example, in South India, Ghana and Australia, episcopacy has a place on the grounds that 'as a personal expression of the oversight that is Christ's, it is essential to the life of the Church'.

C. Jenkins and K. D. Mackenzie, eds., *Episcopacy Ancient and Modern*, 1930.

J. G. DAVIES

Epistemology

Epistemology or theory of knowledge is a part of philosophy that has great relevance to the theologian. It explores problems about knowing, believing, doubting, proving, about the probable and the improbable: the justification of claims to know, to be sure, to have good grounds; and the counter-claims of sceptics.

Epistemology has been dominated, and in a measure retarded, by the dispute between empiricism and rationalism. Each of these views champions one of the two most obvious sources of certainty, the testimony of incontrovertible 'experience' and the demonstrations of pure 'reason'. The empiricist sees our knowledge of the world as based ultimately on what is taken in by the senses. Yet it must be admitted that even the simplest statement about a material object refers to a great deal more than to momentary sense-impressions. We can 'build up' our picture of the world only by *interpreting* the sense-impressions by means of a rich and complex set of concepts and principles (such as cause-effect), which are themselves very different from sense-impressions, and do not have the immediacy and certainty that experiences of pure sense-impressions might be argued to have. But the rationalist

is in no better state. To secure his sort of certainty (mathematical and logical certainty), he really must remain within a circle of concepts, symbols and rules of inference. He cannot retain the certainty, if he makes any claims about what exists: He must work with 'if . . . , then's'.

As so often in philosophy, it is the exclusiveness and the over-generality of these rival views that distort the map of knowledge and belief. It would be impossible for us to know the world without senses; and yet (as Kant, notably, saw) without 'pure concepts of the understanding' sense-impressions by themselves could not furnish us with an ordered, structured world of experience. Neither sense nor reason provides an infallible source of knowledge of nature. Rather, we interpret the data of the senses, and submit our interpretations to checking and testing procedures, procedures that we constantly try to make more rational and discriminating.

If we agree that epistemological questions cannot be answered by reference to a single source of all knowledge, but are complex, we will go on to analyse and to compare a wide variety of *different* sorts of knowledge, belief, etc., probing the risks of error and illusion, seeking to understand and assess the problematical and complicated cases in the light of the basic and simpler ones.

Let us briefly apply some of these observations to philosophy of religion, particularly to the question of God's existence. Once again a radical empiricism is quite unable to produce a plausible case for theism. No conceivable set of sense-impressions could *by themselves* justify the bold claim that an object of experience was *infinite* (not just 'very great'), *eternal* (not just long-lasting), *omniscient* (not just knowing a great deal), etc. But at the rationalist extreme are arguments like the Ontological, that may fail to emerge from the circle of concepts and justify their application to what *is*.

Suppose a theologian wants to say that men 'encounter God' in an *I-Thou* relationship. To examine this claim from an epistemological viewpoint, he will compare it carefully and minutely with encounter-claims of a less problematic kind – including face-to-face meetings with visible and audible persons. He will seek to estimate the possibilities of illusion, any risks of conceptual confusions, when the one encountered is said to be as different from the other objects of our encounters as God differs from man.

If our ultimate ground for knowledge of God is to be *revelation*, we have once more to resist the temptation to take revelation as the name of yet another infallible source of certainty. Who and what *do* the revealing? What grounds have we for trusting them? On what rests their claim to authority? If on alleged *historical* data, then how well-based are these data? And so on: analysing, interrogating, appraising.

R. M. Chisholm, *Theory of Knowledge*, 1966; A. Woozley, *Theory of Knowledge*, 1949.

R. W. HEPBURN

Erastianism

Thomas Erastus, or Lüber (1524–1583), was professor of medicine at Heidelberg and a Zwinglian. He opposed the power of the elders of the newly reformed church government of Heidelberg to excommunicate without permission of the lay ruler. His theses were published in England in 1589 and found many sympathetic readers. The party of Erastians which emerged at the Westminster Assembly in 1643 went further than Erastus in denying the right of the Church to any independent self-government. It is in this wider sense that the word has passed into the language.

The word is almost invariably now a pejorative term, in spite of the fact that a good case can be made for a measure of state control over ecclesiastical authority in order to ensure toleration and justice. This modern usage reflects a general suspicion among Christians in the mid-twentieth century of the intentions of the omnicompetent state, and a renewed understanding of the ultimately inalienable authority of the Christian Church to express its faith and order its discipline.

J. Lecler, *Toleration and the Reformation*, 2 vols., ET, 1960.

R. CANT

Erigena, John Scotus

John Scotus Erigena (c. 810–c. 877), an Irish scholar, was head of the palace school of Charles the Bald, in Paris. Apart from controversies with Gottschalk on predestination and Paschasius Radbertus on the Eucharist, he made translations from the Greek of pseudo-Dionysius and others. In his main work, *De Divisione Naturae,* book i he considers God as creator, using both the negative and the affirmative theological methods. Book ii concerns the exemplar ideas by which God creates. Book iii deals with creation, man and the fall, and books iv and v are on God as final cause, on Christ and the sacraments as our means of return to God. Condemned after 350 years (Paris 1210, Sens 1225), he has been accused of rationalism, pantheism, and agnosticism; but clearly these suspicions do not take sufficient account of his intellectual environment.

Opera, PL 122; A. H. Armstrong, ed., *The Cambridge History of Later Greek and Early Medieval Philosophy,* 1967, ch. 34, 'Johannes Scottus Eriugena'; M. Cappuyns, *Jean Scot Erigène,* 1933, reprinted 1964; I. P. Sheldon-Williams, 'A Bibliography of the Works of Johannes Scottus Eriugena', *JEH,* X (1959), 198–224: F. Vernet, 'Erigène', *DTC* V, cols 401–34.

DOM PLACID SPEARRITT

Eschatology

It is significant that the word 'eschatology' first occurs apparently in 1844, where it is used in a disparaging sense. This is because the traditional account of Jesus' career and teaching really had no place for eschatology, except as a description of what is yet to happen at the end of human history. Traditional Christian theology, proceeding on the assumption that Jesus throughout his time on earth had divine foreknowledge of all events, relegated all his references to the future into one of three categories: some of his prophecies referred to his presence with the Church from the time of Pentecost onwards (e.g. Mark 9.1); some referred to the fall of Jerusalem (e.g. Luke 21.20); and some to his final coming in glory (e.g. Matt. 24.37 ff.). This scheme worked well enough when applied to all the teaching attributed to Jesus in the Gospels, since this is no doubt the significance it bore for those who recorded it. But it only applied in a very unsatisfactory way to the strong expectation of an imminent *parousia* which runs through most of Paul's Letters. Already as early as the time of the writing of II Peter (which we take to be c. AD 120) we can see the embarrassment caused by this expectation (*see* II Peter ·3.3–9). Traditional theology could only answer the complaint that the *parousia* (coming) had not arrived as expected by saying that, since we do not know the day or the hour, it might occur at any time, probably would occur very soon, and that we must live as if it would take place immediately.

The rise of the critical study of the NT, which only began to affect English theology in the second quarter of the nineteenth century, altered all this. Once you have abandoned the belief that Jesus knew all about the future by means of a divine foreknowledge, you are at once faced with the question: What precisely did he mean by the kingdom of God? The kingdom obviously plays an essential part in his thought; if you cannot necessarily assume that he had in mind the Christian Church as it actually developed in history, what did he have in mind? The first attempts to answer this question (mostly emanating from Germany) were based on the assumption that it was possible to penetrate behind the dogmatic constructions of the early Church in order to find and vindicate 'the Jesus of history', the real human figure with his original teaching. In the course of this attempt the kingdom tended to be represented as a largely immanental one, a spiritual condition available to those who associated themselves with Jesus or who accepted his teaching about God. The eschatological traits, the prophecies about future woes, the descriptions of the coming world cataclysm, all these were usually dismissed as the products of the fervent apocalyptic atmosphere in which the early Christians moved. Thus eschatology, along with christology and the doctrine of the Church, appeared to be part of the dispensable wrapping in which the Jesus of history was encased.

Between 1901 and 1906 Albert Schweitzer may be said to have placed a bomb under this imposing structure. In two books he effectively argued his thesis that critical scholarship is bound by its own premises to give to the eschatological teaching of Jesus not a peripheral, but a central position. He maintained in fact that Jesus' eschatology is the key to a right understanding of his life; only by means of a consistent application of the eschatological category can we understand Jesus at all. Jesus, says Schweitzer, came in order to proclaim the approaching eschatological climax. He originally believed that by sending out the Twelve he would bring the crisis to its consummation. When this failed to happen, Jesus decided that he must deliberately take upon himself the apocalyptic woes and offer himself as the ransom which would enable God to grant the New Age. He went up to Jerusalem, therefore, with one aim only, to die in order that history might end, and God's great act of consummation might take place after his death. His cry on the cross leaves us doubtful whether he maintained this conviction to the very end. Schweitzer insists that, with the collapse of the attempt to rediscover 'the Jesus of history', critical scholarship is left with only two alternatives: either to accept his theory of consistent eschatology, or to relapse into almost total scepticism about the life and significance of Jesus.

Schweitzer's thesis has had a lasting effect on the study of the Gospels. Nothing can be quite the same as it was before. But this does not mean that his theory is universally accepted in all its details today. He put too much emphasis on contemporary Jewish apocalyptic; his disparagement of the value of rabbinic sources has not been justified; the Qumran documents have shown us how much more complicated were the various messianic expectations than Schweitzer realized. In the 1930s C. H. Dodd restored the balance to a considerable extent by his concept of 'realized eschatology'. Beginning from the undeniable fact that in Acts and the Pauline Letters the kingdom is represented as something which is very much present in power already, he argued that much of Jesus' teaching suggests a kingdom that is already accessible. He therefore claimed to be reasserting Jesus' central emphasis when he said that with Jesus the kingdom in all essentials had come already. Jesus brought the kingdom and was the kingdom; the whole complex of events comprising Jesus' ministry, teaching, death, and resurrection themselves constitute the coming of the kingdom. Concentrating mainly on the implications of 'the parables of the kingdom', he argued that Jesus was not greatly concerned with the future, and suggested that some at least of the apocalyptic prophecies attributed to him in the Gospels are the product of the early Church.

Since them various mediating positions have been taken up. The clearest in English is set forth in a book, *The Mission and Achievement of Jesus* (1954), by R. H. Fuller where he makes out a strong case for what might be called 'inaugurated eschatology': Jesus saw the kingdom as connected with his ministry, but not as being fully revealed and operative till after the great crisis which his death and subsequent vindication were to bring about. The attempt to decide what was Jesus' teaching about the kingdom is, of course, inextricably bound up with the whole problem of the historical Jesus. It may be said generally that

the more radical form critics, whose foremost representative is still Rudolf Bultmann, much though they insist on the impossibility of recovering many authentic details about Jesus' life and teaching, tend to accept the validity of Schweitzer's thesis, inasmuch as they agree that in Jesus' mind there was to be no interval between his death on the one hand and the full consummation of the New Age on the other. They do not believe that Jesus foresaw an era in which the Church was to live and develop in the midst of an on-going world. It should also be noted that C. H. Dodd's thesis has had some recent defenders among British scholars: T. F. Glasson and J. A. T. Robinson have both written books in which they maintain that Jesus was not expecting an immediate and supernatural return from the heaven after his death.

In one sense Schweitzer's diagnosis may be said to have been justified: he said that the choice was between consistent eschatology and scepticism. But it is scepticism that has been winning the field, to judge by present trends in the study of the Synoptic Gospels. As more and more of the material in the Synoptic Gospels is being attributed to the early Church rather than to Jesus himself, it becomes easier and easier to relegate to the same source the eschatological sayings attributed to him. This does not mean, however, that a non-eschatological message of Jesus emerges, but that we are precluded from ever discovering what his message was, since we cannot hope to penetrate behind what the early Church said it was. The logical (and absurd) conclusion is a Jesus who (for reasons which we can never hope to discover) was the cause of an outbreak of extensive eschatological expectation among the first Christians. More hopeful as far as positive conclusions are concerned is the general recognition among scholars that the theology of the NT is based upon a realized eschatology. Whatever their expectations about the future, the writers of the NT proclaim their message on the assumption that the all-important event has happened; we are they 'upon whom the end of the ages has come' (I Cor. 10.11); we have 'tasted the powers of the age to come' (Heb. 6.5). This conclusion is already having a reinvigorating effect on the theology of the Church and the sacraments, and should begin to affect the theology of the ministry.

In the meantime a substantial part of Christendom, that part which is often described by the epithet 'conservative evangelical', continues with the concepts and expectations of traditional theology, deliberately eschewing all critical speculations. One of the consequences, however, of the divorce between traditional theology and critical thought is that the former is more vulnerable than it was to adventism. Theologians and others have always been prone to the conviction that they could calculate the exact time of the *parousia*, but up till the rise of critical thought adventist speculations were to some extent checked by the disapproval of the majority of Christian scholars, whom the adventists themselves still regarded as orthodox. Now that the bond of orthodoxy no longer links catholic and evangelical to the same extent, the conservative evangelical is more strongly tempted by adventism. Sects now flourish which originated in a claim to know the time of the *parousia*, and then, when that claim proved to be mistaken, adapted their theology to a 'spiritual' advent. This is true of both Seventh Day Adventism and the Jehovah's Witnesses. Naturally the cataclysmic possibilities latent in the atom bomb have produced a strong conviction among some Christians that we really have now reached the age when the *parousia* is very close. Along with adventism often goes Millenarianism (Chiliasm), the belief in a thousand year reign of Christ and the redeemed on earth in the future. It seems probable that Millenarianism, basing itself on one distinctive element in Jewish apocalyptic thought, originated in Asia Minor. It is represented in the Book of Revelation, in Papias, and in Irenaeus. It is an element in the NT which modern critical theology has not attempted to incorporate, and is therefore left to the adventists and literalists to expound. The same could be said of the antichrist, who plays some sort of part in Paul's thought, and a much more profound one in the Apocalypse. Adventist speculation has never lacked a contemporary figure with which to identify him, whether Mahomet, the pope, Napoleon, or Hitler. Here, however, modern critical theology has occasionally attempted a reinterpretation. As long as it is realized that antichrist is not exhausted in any one historical individual, but is to be found in various forms in every generation, there is no reason why this compelling symbol should not play a fruitful part in Christian theology.

C. H. Dodd, *The Apostolic Preaching and its Development*, 1936; R. H. Fuller, *The Foundations of New Testament Christology*, 1965; *The Mission and Achievement of Jesus*, 1954; T. F. Glasson, *His Appearing and His Kingdom*, 1953; *The Second Advent*, 1945; J. Moltmann, *Theology of Hope*, ET, 1967; J. A. T. Robinson, *In the End God*, 1950; A. Schweitzer, *The Quest of the Historical Jesus*, ET, 1910, 1954.

A. T. HANSON

Essays and Reviews

This is the title of a volume of essays (1860) by seven distinguished contributors, all members of the Church of England. The general tone was 'liberal' and the essayists not only asked for but actually assumed freedom of inquiry in biblical research and dogmatic interpretation. The work aroused strong feelings; 11,000 clergymen signed a protest, and the case came before the Judical Committee of the Privy Council. Benjamin Jowett's essay on 'The Interpretation of Scripture' attracted the most attention. One of the contributors, Frederick Temple, later became Archbishop of Canterbury. To us today the positions taken up by the essayists would seem mild and conservative, but the incident is a landmark in the

development of English religious thought in the nineteenth century.

The subject may best be studied in biographies of the contributors, e.g. Geoffrey Faber on *Jowett*, 1958, V. H. H. Green, *Oxford Common Room* (Mark Pattison), 1957; *cf. also* such historical surveys as S. C. Carpenter, *Church and People, 1789-1889*, 1933.

EDITOR

Essays Catholic and Critical

This volume of essays by fourteen Anglican scholars, two of whom later became bishops (A. E. J. Rawlinson, K. E. Kirk), was published in 1926. The writers belonged to the school then known as Anglo-Catholic, a term much less frequently heard today. Their object was to show that the methods of biblical and historical criticism were not in conflict with but rather supported the doctrines of the historic Catholic faith as over against the reductionist or negative conclusions drawn by modernist and liberal protestant scholars. *The Riddle of the New Testament* (1931), written by one of the contributors, Sir Edwyn Hoskyns (with F. Noel Davey), combines a radical critical position with a fully Catholic standpoint. The group stood in lineal succession to Bishop Gore and the other contributors to *Lux Mundi* (1889) (q.v.): since the days of Pusey and the original leaders of the Oxford Movement, Anglo-Catholic theology has not usually been anti-critical or obscurantist.

EDITOR

Essence. *see* Substance.

Essenes

An ascetic Jewish community existing between the second century BC and the second century AD. Their code of belief and practice was akin to Pharisaism, but much more rigid. They seem to have had their principal centre near the Dead Sea (Qumran), and their connection with the Dead Sea Scrolls is probable. So little is known about them that speculations concerning their influence upon John the Baptist (to say nothing of Christ himself) and upon (e.g.) the Fourth Gospel should be treated with caution. *See* A. Dupont-Sommer, *The Jewish Sect of Qumran and the Essenes*, ET, 1954, and the literature about the Dead Sea Scrolls generally.

EDITOR

Essential Trinity

Essential trinitarianism is the doctrine that God is in himself and independent of his relations with creation – one God, Trinity in Unity, Unity in Trinity. God reveals himself in a threefold manner, causes himself to be experienced in three ways, because he is eternally and intrinsically Trinity. Another way of describing this view is to speak of an immanent Trinity.

Historically this was the result of a long process of development in which alternative theories were explored (*see* **Economic Trinity; Modalism; Subordinationism**) and proved the only view capable of supporting both the biblical data and the church's worship which bore testimony to a co-worshipful and conglorifiable Trinity. It is, therefore, the classical view and still holds the field. It was defended by Aquinas on the ground that in God all relations are immanent (a realist doctrine of relations) and by Barth for the reason that in God Act and Being are one. As the explication of the biblical data, the implicate of religious experience and the richest and most coherent evocation of the mystery of the Being of God it still maintains itself against alternative theories of a reductionist type.

L. Hodgson, *The Doctrine of the Trinity*, 1943; C. Welch, *The Trinity in Contemporary Theology*, 1953.

H. E. W. TURNER

Eternal, Eternity. *see* Time and Eternity.

Eucharist, Eucharistic Theology

Certainly since the beginning of the second century (as, e.g. in the Letters of St Ignatius of Antioch) and possibly in the NT itself (*cf.* I Cor. 14.16) the word *Eucharistia* (thanksgiving) was used by Greek Christian writers to denote the rite which Jesus instituted at the Last Supper and which became the central observance of the Christian Church. Whether the Last Supper was in fact a passover meal is disputed by biblical scholars, but there is little doubt that the accounts of the institution of the Eucharist given in the Synoptic Gospels and in I Cor. 11 are not meant as a complete description of the rite but simply record, as handed down in the liturgical traditions of the various churches, certain words which Jesus added to the accepted forms of blessing bread at the beginning, and a common cup at the end, of a solemn Jewish meal. Those words consist of (1) a declaration that the bread was his body and that the wine was his blood of the (new) covenant (or that the cup of wine was the cup of the [new] covenant in his blood), and (2) a command to 'do this' as his *anamnesis* (q.v.) or 'memorial'. Whether or not the Greek words translated 'do this' have a sacrificial meaning, the reference to the blood of the covenant seems clearly to echo, in a new context, the 'blood of the covenant' in the sacrifice offered by Moses in Ex. 24, while the notions of covenant and sacrifice are raised to the new and more genuinely religious level foretold in Jer. 31.31 ff. and fulfilled by Jesus in his own person in his death on the cross. Furthermore, whether or not the Last Supper was in fact the passover meal, it seems clear that at it Jesus solemnly consecrated himself as the true paschal lamb, by whose blood the people of God were to be saved, and his death on the morrow as the true act of deliverance which had been foreshadowed by the Exodus from Egypt, commemorated each year in the passover ceremonies.

It is essential to note that the Jewish method of blessing food or drink was by giving thanks to God for it and naming him over it; only after this recognition of him as its maker and therefore its owner was it considered to have been set free to be used for human purposes. Thus the one Hebrew word *berachah* is translated by the two Greek words *eucharistia* (thanksgiving) and *eulogia* (blessing), and the fact that in all the primitive liturgies the bread and wine are consecrated by a prayer of thanksgiving bears witness to the essentially Jewish origins of the Christian Eucharist. In the *anaphora* or *canon* the eucharistic elements are both offered and consecrated by the process of giving thanks. (Subsequent forgetfulness or ignorance in Gentile circles of the significance of this Jewish conception of blessing by means of thanksgiving has led to considerable misunderstanding of the nature of the eucharistic action and also to the mutilated liturgies produced by the Reformers in the sixteenth century.) From the earliest times the Eucharist has been seen as the 'pure offering' to be made 'in every place' according to the prophecy of Mal. 1.11. Christ who, in the language of the Book of Common Prayer, made on the cross, 'by his one oblation of himself once offered, a full, perfect and sufficient sacrifice, oblation and satisfaction for the sins of the whole world', has left the Eucharist with his Church as his perpetual *anamnesis*.

At the time of the Reformation Protestants commonly believed that Roman Catholic theology held that the Eucharist either repeated the sacrifice of the cross or else performed some further sacrificial function that the cross had been unable to perform, and mediaeval devotion and practice certainly gave some colour to this impression, though whether mediaeval *theology* taught anything like this has been disputed (*cf.* e.g. Francis Clark, *Eucharistic Sacrifice and the Reformation*, 1960). In consequence Protestantism in general denied altogether the sacrificial character of the Eucharist, while Roman Catholic theologians of the Counter-Reformation tended to seek for some element in the action of the Mass which could be interpreted as the equivalent of an actual immolation; thus we get the notion that, by his confinement in the host, Christ is rendered impotent and immobile. The Council of Trent, however, while insisting that the Mass is 'a truly propitiatory sacrifice', refrains from defining the relation between the Mass and the cross beyond saying that Christ 'left a sacrifice whereby that bloody sacrifice which was to be enacted once on the cross might be represented and its memory remain until the end of the world'. We may compare the statement of the Anglican Catechism that the sacrament of the Lord's Supper was ordained 'for the continual remembrance of the sacrifice of the death of Christ and of the benefits which we receive thereby'. And, while the Anglican Article XXXI declared that 'the sacrifices of Masses, in which it was commonly said that the Priest did offer Christ for the quick and the dead to have remission of pain or guilt were blasphemous fables and dangerous deceits', on the ground that there is no other satisfaction for sin but the offering of Christ on the cross, many of the Anglican divines of the sixteenth and seventeenth centuries were ready to admit that the Eucharist is a sacrifice, if 'sacrifice' is qualified by such adjectives as 'commemorative' or 'representative'. Clearly a great deal depends on what is meant by such adjectives, and this is not easy to determine. At the height of the Middle Ages St Thomas Aquinas had been content to say that the Mass is a 'sort of representative image' (*imago quaedam repraesentativa*) of the passion and that it is 'the same' (*non aliud*) as Christ's sacrifice because it is its 'commemoration' (*Summa Theologica*, 3. 83.1 and 22.3). However, the fact remains that, while Catholics have emphasized the sacrificial character of the Eucharist, Protestants in general have vehemently denied it. It is thus all the more striking that in recent years there has been a remarkable rapprochement on this question; this has been due to movements on both sides. On the Catholic side the significant works are M. de la Taille's *Mysterium Fidei* (1915), A. Vonier's *Key to the Doctrine of the Eucharist* (1925), E. Masure's *The Christian Sacrifice* (*Le Sacrifice du Chef*, 1944) and *The Sacrifice of the Mystical Body* (1954, the latter stimulated by Pope Pius XII's encyclical *Mediator Dei* of 1947) and C. Journet's *La Messe, Présence du Sacrifice de la Croix* (1958), works which, while not on the surface stating a common position, certainly converge towards a synthesis. On the Protestant side we have J. D. Benoit's *Liturgical Renewal* (1958), D. M. Baillie's *Theology of the Sacraments* (1957), O. Cullmann and J. Leenhardt's *Essays on the Lord's Supper* (1958), Geddes MacGregor's *Corpus Christi* (1959), M. Thurian's *Eucharistic Memorial* (I, 1960, II, 1961), G. Aulén's *Eucharist and Sacrifice* (1958) and R. Prenter's *Skabelse og Genlösning* (German trans: *Schöpfung und Erlösung*, I, 1958, II, 1960). And among Anglicans there was F. C. N. Hicks, with his ponderous but influential work *The Fullness of Sacrifice* (3rd. ed., 1946). The later phases of this movement have been reinforced by the massive liturgical research of such scholars as G. Dix (*The Shape of the Liturgy*, 1945) and J. A. Jungmann (*The Mass of the Roman Rite*, 2 vols., 1951–5 [*Missarum Sollemnia*] and *The Early Liturgy*, 1960). It will be instructive to see how this rapprochement has come about.

In the first place, there has been, largely as a result of the studies of historians and anthropologists, a widening and deepening of the whole idea of sacrifice. The tendency to identify sacrifice simply with the destruction of the victim, in virtual isolation from its antecedents and its setting, which was strongly marked in the Middle Ages and became dominant in post-Reformation thought, both Catholic and Protestant (*cf.* the French school of spirituality, with its stress upon 'annihilation', *anéantissement*), has given place to an understanding of sacrifice as consisting essentially in the offering of God's creatures to him, in order that they may be transformed by his acceptance of them and may find in him their true end; God is not to be thought of as glorified by the destruction of his creatures or as taking pleasure in it. To give one example, in the Jewish sacrifices the properly priestly and sacrificial act was the giving of the victim's life to God, its killing being only the way in which that life was released and the means by which it was wholly withdrawn from use by man in order to be wholly transferred to God.

Secondly, while full recognition is made of the fact that in a fallen and sinful world death is inevitably involved in the transference of the victim to God, sacrifice is now seen as embracing in its scope the whole course of the victim's life from the first moment of its existence onwards; thus the sacrifice of Christ, while reaching its supreme moment of self-abandonment on the cross, began when the eternal Word took flesh in the womb of his virgin mother and has become an enduring achievement in his ascension into heaven where 'he ever liveth to make intercession for us'.

Thirdly, with the recovery of the sense of the Church as the Body of Christ and of the unity of Christ with his members (*totus Christus membra cum capite*), the eucharist has come to be seen as renewing and developing the baptismal incorporation of Christ's members into him and as maintaining the unity of the Church as his Body, rather than as simply reproducing his individual self-offering. Thus to the question which has caused so much dispute among Christians: 'Is anything offered in the Eucharist, and if so who offers what?' the all-inclusive answer is not just 'Jesus offers himself' or 'Jesus offers us' or 'We offer Jesus' or 'We offer ourselves' or 'We offer bread and wine', but 'The Whole Christ offers the Whole Christ', an answer which can be seen to include, in their right places and proportions, all the others.

This movement of broadening may be considered to have begun in the Roman Catholic Church with the great work *Mysterium Fidei* by the Jesuit theologian de la Taille, completed in 1915. For de la Taille, a sacrifice consists of three elements, namely, a ritual oblation, an immolation and a divine acceptance, which, in the case of the one effective sacrifice, that of Christ, are realized respectively at the Last Supper, on Calvary and at the ascension. The Mass is not a new immolation, but it is a new oblation, an *oblatio hostiae immolatae*, made after the immolation, the Last Supper being an *oblatio hostiae immolandae*, made before. (A similar view was held by the Anglican lay theologian Sir Will Spens.) While avoiding any suggestion that the Mass repeats the slaying of Christ, this view is open to the opposite objection that it makes the Mass not a complete sacrifice, but only part of one. Abbot Anscar Vonier, in *A Key to the Doctrine of the Eucharist*, introduced a new consideration into the debate. For him, the fundamental fact about the Eucharist is that it is a *sacrament*, that is to say a *sign*, though it is a sign of a very special and indeed unique kind, which by the sheer agency of its God-conferred sacramental character makes present and effective that which it represents. Sacramental efficacy is entirely *sui generis*: the body and blood of Christ are present in the Eucharist in virtue of the sole fact that Christ has made the species of bread and wine the sacramental signs of them, and no further explanation is needed. This notion of presence in virtue of sacramental causality, which Vonier applied to the body and blood of Christ as *objects*, has much more recently been applied by Charles Journet to the sacrifice itself as an *action*, in *La Messe: Présence du Sacrifice de la Croix*; the Mass is not another sacrifice than that of the cross, but another presence of the same sacrifice, and this presence subsists in view of the sacramental character – the character as a *sign* – which Christ has given to the eucharistic action. Much the same view had been already developed, with considerable reference to anthropological data and against a much wider background, by Eugène Masure in *The Christian Sacrifice* and *The Sacrifice of the Mystical Body*: each Mass is not a fresh event in Christ's biography, but a sacramental presence of his sacrifice in its entirety.

Mention should also be made of the rather different train of thought which is due to Dom Odo Casel of Maria Laach, for whom the Eucharist, and indeed the whole sacramental system, were the fulfilment of the partial and obscure intuitions of the ancient mystery religions. Casel was accused, perhaps unfairly, of approximating to the view, held by certain liberal scholars in the early part of this century but now almost universally abandoned, which held that Roman Catholic sacramentalism was simply an infusion into primitive Christianity of notions altogether foreign to it and derived from the mystery-religions of the Roman Empire. A more judicious and better informed application of his approach has been made by other Roman Catholic scholars, such as Louis Bouyer and Hugo Rahner, who, without detriment to the unique character of the sacrifice of Christ and of the Christian sacraments, have seen these as fulfilling and not just as contradicting the aspirations and insights of human religion in general.

While there is much divergence of outlook among Roman Catholic theologians today about the nature of the eucharistic sacrifice, their almost universal refusal to admit that it either repeats or supplements the sacrifice of Christ, and their emphasis upon it as perpetuating throughout the ages in the life of the Church the one sacrificial act of Christ in all its efficacy, mark a very notable development in eucharistic theology and one of ecumenical significance. A similar judgment holds in general for the movement from the Protestant side which is manifested in the books mentioned earlier in this article, though here again some have been ready to go further than others. It is noticeable that Calvinists have found it easier to make this movement than Lutherans, for whom Luther's abhorrence of anything that 'smelt of oblation' is still very influential. One of the most

hopeful lines of further advance may come from the recognition, both on anthropological and on theological grounds, that the notions of a sacrifice and of a sacred meal, so far from being mutually exclusive, may well imply each other.

As regards the eucharistic presence, rapprochement has been much less evident. In spite of the thoroughly realistic language about the presence which is found in the Fathers (for whom such terms as 'type' and 'figure' commonly connote signs of a present reality and not of an absent one), Protestantism in general has seen the presence of Christ as operative in the *action* of the Eucharist rather than as in any way identified with the eucharistic *objects*, the bread and wine. Luther's doctrine that the body of Christ is present *with* the bread, and his blood *with* the wine ('consubstantiation'), has not had a large following, even among Lutherans. In consequence, while the Roman Church has adhered firmly to the doctrine of transubstantiation, promulgated at the Fourth Lateran Council in 1215 and reaffirmed by the Council of Trent in 1551, Protestantism has tended either to 'receptionism' (i.e. the doctrine that Christ's body and blood are received by the devout communicant at the same time as the bread and wine but are in no real sense identical with them) or to a doctrine of 'real absence' which makes the act of communion a simple consumption of bread and wine, in obedience to the Lord's command, as a memorial of the Last Supper and a demonstration of the communicant's faith in the saving work of Christ. The Anglican formularies, while ruling out this last view (which is commonly ascribed to Zwingli and by many to Cranmer), are not altogether explicit as between receptionism and the doctrine of a real, though 'spiritual', presence in the elements. However, even here the tension between Catholics and Protestants has been to some extent eased, largely owing to the common recovery of a recognition that the Eucharist is not simply a means of sanctification or an expression of the devotion of the individual communicant, but is concerned with the maintenance and edification of the Church as the people of God. A renewed emphasis is placed upon the dual reference of the phrase 'the Body of Christ' as it is used, for example, by St Paul and St Augustine, to signify both the eucharistic bread and the Church: 'The bread which we break, is it not a participation (communion) in the body of Christ? Because there is one loaf, we who are many are one body, for we all partake of the same loaf' (I Cor. 10.16 f.); '. . . without discerning the [Lord's] body' (I Cor. 11.29); 'You are on the table, you are in the chalice' (Augustine, *Serm*. 229); 'The mystery of yourselves is laid upon the table of the Lord, the mystery of yourselves you receive' (Augustine, *Serm*. 272). This conviction of the corporate nature of the Eucharist has never been lost in the Eastern Church, in spite of the fact that there the communion of the laity became as infrequent as in the West. But even in the West it was never altogether absent: St Thomas Aquinas in the thirteenth century was simply following Peter Lombard in the twelfth, when he wrote that the *res* – the ultimate effect or reality signified – in the eucharist is 'the unity of the mystical body' (*Summa Theologica*, 3. 73.3, etc.). And even in the 'bad period' of the nineteenth century M. J. Scheeben was making the same point in his *Mysteries of Christianity* (ET, 1946). There is in any case a general recognition that the presence is for the sake of the sacrifice and not vice versa; that is to say, that it is not because something is done to Christ in the Eucharist that the Eucharist is a sacrifice, but it is because the Eucharist is essentially identical with the sacrifice of Christ that Christ, as priest and victim, must be present in it. However, there is not yet anything like agreement between Catholics and Protestants as to the relation of the presence of Christ to the Eucharistic elements. Perhaps the problems of the sacrifice and of the presence will find their ultimate solution together. For if the Eucharist is the offering of the Whole Christ by the Whole Christ, that is to say, if in the Eucharist Christ offers to the Father his Body and its members in their union with him as their Head, then the purpose of the eucharistic presence is not to scatter Christ over a multitude of altars or to divide him up among a number of communicants but to gather the scattered multitude of the faithful into him. The key may then lie in the reminder which is given by St Augustine and others of the Fathers, and which was so inspiringly recovered by R. I. Wilberforce in the middle of the last century, that, unlike ordinary food which is assimilated into the eater, the divine food of the Eucharist assimilates the eater to itself.

A further emphasis has appeared in recent years, especially in those circles which have been affected by the Christian social movement initiated by F. D. Maurice in the nineteenth century and carried on by Charles Gore and his successors. The elements of bread and wine, it is pointed out, are not mere fruits of nature but are the products of human industry working upon those fruits. In their presentation to God, to be transformed by his acceptance and returned to man as his supernatural food, there is an offering to God of all the vast range of human activity, with all the toil and sweat, the pain and joy, the love and hate, the holiness and the sinfulness, much of it having no conscious reference to God or to Christ, that have been involved in the manufacture of the elements and the bringing of them to the Church's altar to be offered to God in union with the one effectual sacrifice of the incarnate Son. The notion has been given an external expression, sometimes perhaps an unbalanced one, in some circles affected by the Liturgical Movement and such bodies as the *Jeunesse Ouvrière Chrétienne*, but it clearly represents a profound truth about the nature of the Eucharist, a truth which the early Church made explicit in its consciousness that when it offered the Eucharist it was bringing before the throne of the Father the needs and the achievements of the whole human family, that 'one human race' in

which, in the words of St Irenaeus, 'the mysteries of God are fulfilled' (*Adv. Haer.*, v. 36.3). This in no way contradicts, but rather confirms, the eschatological character which the Eucharist had for the primitive Church, for which it was an anticipation of the return of Christ in glory and of the final transformation of the created universe. It would be difficult to find a nobler statement of the nature of the Eucharist than that which is given by St Augustine in the tenth book of his great work on *The City of God*:

That whole redeemed community which is the congregation and society of the saints is offered as a universal sacrifice to God by that High Priest who has also offered himself in suffering for us in the form of a servant, that we might be the body of so great a Head (x, 6).

In the nature of the case it is impossible to draw a sharp line between eucharistic theology in the strict sense and other branches of theology, such as ecclesiology and liturgiology. It might in fact be argued that the recent revival of interest in liturgical matters has almost resulted in the appearance of a new branch of study which might be called 'liturgical theology', in which the liturgical material which has come down to us is considered not primarily for its historical and literary interest but for the light which it throws upon the Church's understanding of the sacred rite which lies at the heart of its life and thought. An example of this may fittingly conclude this article.

At the Last Supper the new rite instituted by Christ consisted of two parts, containing four and three acts respectively and separated by the whole of the intervening meal. At the opening of the meal Jesus (1) took, (2) blessed, (3) broke and (4) distributed the bread; at the end of the meal he (5) took, (6) blessed and (7) distributed the wine. No doubt this pattern persisted for some time after the ascension whenever the Church celebrated the Lord's *anamnesis*. When, however, the whole of the meal except the two parts to which the Lord had given the new significance became a separate observance (*see* **Agape**), the rites of the bread and the cup were brought into immediate juxtaposition and were no longer separated by the interval of time that would be occupied by a somewhat leisurely meal. In consequence the two rites were dovetailed into each other and the original 'seven-action' rite was superseded by the 'four-action' rite which is exemplified by every known early liturgy. In this the celebrant (1) takes both bread and wine, (2) blesses them both, (3) breaks the bread and (4) distributes both. These correspond to the four stages which we now know as (1) the offertory, (2) the canon, (3) the fraction and (4) the communion. The first of these stages, it should be noted, consists of the taking of the elements by the celebrant; the bringing of them to him for this purpose in a solemn way may indeed be made into an impressive addition to the service, but it is a preliminary to the eucharistic rite and not a part of it. It corresponds to the preparation of the upper room for the Last Supper rather than to anything that our Lord himself did at the meal; a misunderstanding of this by some enthusiastic members of the Liturgical Movement (q.v.) has led to an exaggerated emphasis being ascribed to a so-called 'offertory procession'. In contrast, many liturgical theologians would hold that the essential actions of the Eucharist are not four in number but only two, namely, the 'blessing' and the 'distribution', the 'taking' being simply a convenient preliminary to the former of these, and the 'breaking' to the latter. In this way the significance of the 'blessing' as being, according to its Jewish origin, a 'thanksgiving' is fully brought out: there is one great Prayer which offers by consecrating and consecrates by offering and does both by giving thanks.

Furthermore, while the bread at the beginning of the meal was blessed with a very brief formula of thanksgiving, the cup at the end was blessed with a much longer utterance, which thanked God not only for the gift of wine but for the great acts of redemption by which he had brought the Jews out of bondage, made them his people, sealed with them a solemn covenant and given them a law by which they were to live. For Christians these great acts of Jewish history were only foreshadowings of the greater act by which Jesus the Messiah had wrought an even greater deliverance by the shedding of his own blood. It was therefore inevitable that when the members of his body met to 'do *his anamnesis*', they would include in the prayer a thanksgiving for his redemptive death and resurrection and, especially in view of the fact that it was correct practice in performing any Jewish rite to make mention of the divine command which authorized it, it was equally inevitable that the prayer would include a reference to the words by which, at the Last Supper, Jesus had transformed a Jewish table-ceremony into the *anamnesis* of the redemption of the human race. It was not quite so inevitable that this reference would be made by an actual quotation of the Lord's words, and there have survived a few early eucharistic prayers in which such a quotation is not found, though the reference itself is clear. In actual fact, the incorporation into the prayer of a narrative of the institution became all but universal, but when the significance of consecrating by thanksgiving had been forgotten or had never been understood, it led to a very strange result. The recitation of the narrative, which by origin was only one item, albeit a very significant item, in the second of the four actions which composed the liturgy, was taken to be the whole essential eucharistic rite, and the manual acts corresponding to the four actions tended to be fully or partially transferred to it or duplicated in it. This reached its climax in most of the reformed liturgies of the sixteenth century in which practically the whole of the eucharistic prayer was scrapped except the narrative of the institution. But this was only the logical working out of an interpretation of the rite which had been taken for granted for centuries. However much it may be regretted, it was not a sheer perversion; for it was the words

which at the Last Supper the Messiah added to the official Jewish formulas that provided his Church with an *anamnesis* of the world's redemption and not merely a form for saying grace at meals combined with a patriotic prayer-meeting for Jews. *See also* **Liturgical Movement; Liturgiology.**

In addition to the books mentioned above, the following may be noted as dealing with various aspects of eucharistic doctrine: J. J. von Allmen, *Worship: its Theology and Practice*, 1965; L. Bouyer, *Eucharistie*, 1966; *Life and Liturgy*, 1956; *Rite and Man*, 1963; Y. Brilioth, *Eucharistic Faith and Practice, Evangelical and Catholic*, 1930; O. Casel, *The Mystery of Christian Worship*, 1962; C. W. Dugmore, *Eucharistic Doctrine in England from Hooker to Waterland*, 1942; *The Mass and the English Reformers*, 1958; C. Gore, *The Body of Christ*, 1901; M. Hurley, ed., *Church and Eucharist*, 1966; E. L. Mascall, *Corpus Christi*, 2nd ed., 1965; J. I. Packer, ed., *Eucharistic Sacrifice*, 1962; J. M. Powers, *Eucharistic Theology*, 1968.

E. L. MASCALL

Eudaimonism, Eudemonism

The latter is the more common English form of the word, which derives from the Greek *eudaimonia*, lit. 'the well-being of the spirit (soul)'. As used by modern philosophers eudemonism is the theory of ethics which teaches that happiness or contentment is man's highest good. The word, however, goes back to Aristotle, who taught that *eudaimonia* was the criterion and end of right conduct. For St Thomas Aquinas (*see* **Thomism**) *beatitudo* or blessedness consists in the vision of God (*see* **Beatific Vision; Vision of God**). This view has been questioned by more recent theologians on the ground that any form of cultivation of one's own spiritual life, or the making of one's own blessedness the goal of ethics, is a form of selfishness which leaves no room for the love of God for his own sake or for the love of our fellow creatures as man's chief ethical end. *See*, e.g., A. Nygren, *Agape and Eros*, new ET by P. S. Watson, 1953.

EDITOR

Euhemerism

The theory of Euhemerus (c. 315 BC), a Sicilian Greek philosopher, that the traditional (Homeric, etc.) beliefs about the gods originally developed from legends and traditions about human heroes of distant ages. The ancient Christian apologists (e.g. Lactantius, AD 240–320) were quick to seize upon this convenient explanation of the origins of Greek religion.

Eutychianism. *see* Christology (4).

Evangelicals, Evangelicalism

Early Methodism contained a tension within itself between the Calvinism of Whitfield and the 'Arminianism' of the Wesleys. There soon appeared also a disagreement over church order between those who wished to work within the parochial framework and those who were willing to disregard it. The Evangelicals were those priests and lay people who remained within the Church of England after both Methodism and the Calvinist Lady Huntingdon's Connexion had severed their links with it. Anglican Evangelicals, however, then and now have felt a deep kinship with all reformed churches, inclining more naturally to those in the Calvinist tradition, and thinking of themselves as the closest disciples of the Reformers to be found in the modern Anglican communion. In many ways they resemble most closely the pietist movements within the reformed churches. In the nineteenth century they were less noticeable for intellectual vigour than for missionary enthusiasm at home and overseas. They defended a biblical literalism with unbending logic, and took little save hostile notice of contemporary scientific or philosophical thought. In the twentieth century a strong school of liberal evangelicalism has arisen.

An important group in their earlier history was the Clapham Sect (q.v.). At a slightly later period their leader was Charles Simeon, vicar of Holy Trinity Church, Cambridge, 1783–1836, whose influence was powerful in the university and in the mission field. He was one of the founders of the Church Missionary Society in 1797, and was instrumental in sending many evangelical missionaries to India. The moral earnestness and the scriptural preaching of Newman were at first welcome to Evangelicals but very soon they were offended by the progress of the Oxford Movement and became bitterly opposed to what they held to be its Romeward direction. In the Gorham controversy over baptism they criticized the belief in baptismal regeneration. Lord Shaftesbury carried on the interest of the earlier generation in social reform, and was responsible for many humane laws on behalf of mine and factory workers and other victims of bad social conditions. Evangelical piety consisted in regular Bible reading, the strict observance of Sunday and the conscientious discharge of the duties of one's station in life. The revived popularity of early communion services was one of the fruits of the movement. The simple fundamentalist faith of the early Evangelicals exercised a great attraction for many different types of English-speaking Christians in the nineteenth century, and the considerable numbers who attend revivalist missions today attest its continuing appeal.

G. R. Balleine, *A History of the Evangelical Party in the Church of England*, 1908; C. H. E. Smyth, *Simeon and Church Order*, 1940.

R. CANT

Evangelism. *see* Mission, Theology of.

Evil Spirits. *see* Demonic; Powers; Spirit (2).

Evil, The Problem of

The 'problem of evil' is raised by the opening words of the Apostles' Creed: 'I believe in God, the Father, Almighty . . .' If God loves as a father loves his children, and if he is also omnipotent, why does he permit suffering and other forms of evil in the world? If God is good, he cannot be almighty; if he is almighty, he cannot be a God of love. This is a problem only for believers in a personal God (Jews, Christians and Muslims). For others evil is no problem: it is simply 'the way things are', although it would be possible to press them about 'the problem of good' – why certain things should appear more valuable than other things, if all things are simply the way they are. Where then does the illusion of value come from? Attempts at a solution of the problem of evil may be divided into four types.

1. *Evil as Non-being.* The 'perennial philosophy' (q.v.) from Plato through Neoplatonism to St Thomas Aquinas held that evil was non-being. God is *ens realissimum*, the source of all perfection; below him in the Great Chain of Being there stretch orders of being each less perfect and therefore less real than the one above it (*cf.* Aristotle's gradation from Form to Matter). As God is absolute reality and absolute perfection, so at the other end of the Chain evil is absolute imperfection and therefore absolutely non-existent. Various stages of perfection correspond to their equivalent degrees of being. Evil is nothing in itself; it represents only an absence of good. There is therefore in fact no problem of evil at all. Since every degree of perfection is necessary to the fulness of perfection as a whole, every form of imperfection in creation must necessarily exist, and the justification of its existence is that without it the wholeness of perfection could not be; but absolute imperfection cannot (logical 'cannot') exist. Various forms of idealistic philosophy of the Hegelian type similarly regard evil as an illusion, or at least as necessary to the perfection of the whole. The notion is sometimes given an aesthetic expression. The dark colours in a picture are necessary to the artistic perfection of the whole work; if we could but 'stand back from the canvas', we would realize that what looks like an ugly smudge seems thus only because of our bad perspective. Or again, the profundity of tragic beauty could not be experienced unless evil in defeat encompassed also the destruction of the good: not only is an Iago necessary in 'Othello' but the very imperfection of Othello's love is necessary to the tragic defeat of evil. Life is tragedy or tragi-comedy; it is not melodrama, in which the unsullied good comes into conflict with the wholly bad and defeats it. – The difficulty with this kind of 'solution' to the problem of evil is that it requires a long period of philosophical training before it can be appreciated, and in the twentieth century the philosophy involved does not seem so self-authenticating as it did in former centuries. It would be difficult to bring comfort to

a bereaved parent or an incurable invalid by means of an explanation of the degrees of being and of perfection.

2. *Dualism.* The above type of solution to the problem of evil is offered by philosophical monism. Another explanation is given by dualistic or pluralistic philosophies, which in some way limit the omnipotence of God. Zoroastrianism in ancient Persia envisaged the world as the scene of a struggle between light and darkness, good and evil. Crude dualism, however, is philosophically unsatisfactory, because there cannot (logical 'cannot') be two ultimate principles of reality. Similarly Satan cannot help to provide a philosophical explanation: how did the Serpent get into the Garden of Eden, after God had seen that the whole creation was 'very good'? Speculation about a 'pre-mundane fall' (q.v.) – a rebellion of angelic beings in heaven before the creation of the world – is unlikely to commend itself to thoughtful people in the age of demythologizing. No exception need be taken to the ancient symbolism, revived by Luther, of Christ's defeat of the powers of evil; indeed, the *Christus Victor* concept is rooted in the NT and in the ancient Fathers (*cf.* G. Aulén, *Christus Victor*, ET, 1932). But this is not a philosophical explanation of evil; it is rather an affirmation that Christ has defeated evil and that we also can overcome in Christ. Christ came not to explain evil but to defeat it (*cf.* A. N. Whitehead, 'The Buddha gave his doctrine; Christ gave his life'). Pluralistic philosophies are no more intellectually satisfying than is dualism. A limited God, who is himself struggling not only *pro nobis* but *cum nobis* against the forces of disorder in the universe, satisfies neither the reason nor the religious awareness of thoughtful Christians (e.g. H. G. Wells, *God the Invisible King*, 1917; William James, *A Pluralistic Universe*, 1909). Theories of a limited God, who is himself in process of overcoming the disorder of the universe of which he is himself a part, are again receiving favourable attention from some theologians (*see* **Process Theology**), but they seem to others more akin to gnostic speculation or sheer mythologizing than to the historic tradition of biblical and Christian thought. It would seem that the denial of the omnipotence of God does not offer a convincing solution of the problem of evil.

3. *Despotism.* In contrast to the views which limit the omnipotence of God are the views which emphasize it strongly. Such views are based on oriental conceptions of sovereignty. (The Greek *despotes*, master, owner, lord, does not necessarily imply 'tyrannical'.) What the Sultan wills is right, is law, simply because he wills it; he does not have to conform to any objective law or right external to himself. This, indeed, is not the Hebraic view of kingship; in Israel the king was judged entirely by his obedience to the divine will. Nor is it the OT view of God's sovereignty, since his sovereignty is identical with his righteousness (*cf.* Gen. 18.25). Yet in the OT there are found

metaphors of God's sovereignty which imply an almost arbitrary despotism, e.g. the potter and the clay, Isa. 45.9; 64.8; Jer. 18.6; and in Rom. 9.20 f. Paul states one side of the paradox of man's relationship to God. The most grossly oriental conception of the Godhead remains in Islam, in which an enervating fatalism is based upon the doctrine of 'the will of Allah'. Within Christianity Calvinism has most strongly asserted the sovereignty of God and has developed the consequent doctrine of predestination (q.v.). Karl Barth, while he modifies the harshness of the predestinarian teaching, nevertheless sternly refuses to discuss the problem of evil. If God is God, how can we dispute his wisdom in making things as they are? The clay can have no just grievance against the potter. If God decrees from eternity that this man shall be saved and that one damned, his decree is just because he is God, and what God decrees is automatically right. Hence there can be no such thing as a problem of evil: 'whatever is is right' because God wills it. This kind of attempt to solve the problem of evil by denying its existence is unlikely to appeal to thoughtful people today. For one thing, it loses sight of the fatherhood of God behind his sovereignty, whereas the essence of the problem is how to reconcile the fatherhood with the omnipotence. Secondly, the idea that a thing is right because God wills it rather than that it is willed by God because it is right will appear offensive to the moral sense of most Christians today.

4. *The Moral Theory.* In contrast to the view that God's power is subject to limitation and also to the view that it is absolute and constitutes right and wrong by decree there stands the mediating view that God's power is limited by his own character of righteousness, truth and love. According to this view God is not limited by anything external to himself (as in dualism or pluralism) but he is limited by the essential character of his own being. He cannot will the irrational or the morally wrong, because his nature is truth and righteousness. Because he is *God*, he cannot will two and two to be five; because of the nature of goodness (which is his own nature) he cannot create beings who are instantly free and good. This is because value to be valuable must be freely chosen; as every teacher knows, outward obedience can be enforced by iron discipline, but it is not genuine goodness. Goodness to be good must be freely chosen; value must be freely loved in order to be attained. God in creating mankind (and perhaps the whole evolutionary process which preceded it) desired to bring into existence beings who could freely choose the true, the beautiful and the good, and above all who could freely return the love which he had lavished upon them. The creation of a world in which this end was possible necessarily involved three things, which together constitute the problem of evil: (*a*) Pain; (*b*) Suffering, and (*c*) Moral Evil. (*a*) The *biological* utility of pain is obvious: if the child did not hurt his hand when he touched the fire, he would

quickly perish. There is also undoubtedly a corresponding *spiritual* utility of pain, which when bravely born results in the formation of noble character. But against this it must be remembered that there is a great deal of physical suffering in the world which is not ennobling but on the contrary would seem to be soul-destroying and meaningless. (*b*) Suffering is wider than pain, though pain is often involved in it. It is probably the *irrationality* of much of the suffering in the world which causes moral revulsion – earthquakes, pestilences, famines, infants born deformed, insanity, etc. Undoubtedly character is formed in the struggle to overcome suffering; yet it is unconvincing to argue that a lot of people are starving or stricken simply in order that others may have the opportunity of character-forming unselfish relief-work. Even so, it is hard to see how distinctively human values could emerge in a world in which suffering did not exist. There is something in the insight that, if this world were created to be 'a vale of soul-making' (Keats) or 'a school of manhood' (Streeter), it serves its purpose fairly well. The insight is an ancient one (*cf.* e.g. Wisdom 3). If this world is a preparation for a future life, the problem of suffering is immediately alleviated (*cf.* Rom. 8.18). Nothing but the hope of 'the glory which shall be revealed' can make bearable the thought of the infinite wastage, suffering and pain of the centuries of evolution which had to pass before man as a free moral agent could exist: 'with a great sum I obtained this freedom'. (*c*) It is in moral evil that the problem of evil culminates – man's rejection of God and the divine law in order to put himself in God's place and create his own right and wrong. The parable of Gen. 3 (the Fall) succinctly delineates, though it does not explain man's predicament as a fallen creature. The problem of evil is ultimately the problem of man's existence. As such it requires indeed a rational explanation, if that is forthcoming, and men will for ever go on searching for explanation because they are themselves rational beings. But while rational explanation can perhaps give us a glimpse, as through a mist, of the outline of an answer to the problem, it is possible for the Christian to understand existentially his own situation as in rebellion against God and yet as redeemed by God. He knows that he is himself the problem of evil and also that through the unmerited grace of God the problem has been solved in his existence. This is not indeed the kind of solution which can be explained philosophically to an interested intellectual, because it can be understood only in Christian faith and life. The ultimate solution of the problem of evil must lie in the fact that the God who created the world is also the God who has redeemed it; the Creator is himself in Christ the bearer of all creation's sin and suffering as he is the bringer of the redemption that shall be. But only the Christian can know that Christ has explained evil in the act of defeating it.

A. M. Farrer, *Love Almighty and Ills Unlimited*, 1962; John Hick, *Evil and the God of Love*, 1966; C. S. Lewis, *The Problem of Pain*, 1940; B. H. Streeter, *Reality*, 1926; W. Temple, *Mens Creatrix*, 1917; F. R. Tennant, *Philosophical Theology*, II, 1929.

EDITOR

Ex Opere Operato

The phrase, *ex opere operato* (*Latin:* through the performance of the work) contrasted with *ex opere operantis* (through the work of the performer), is used by Catholic theologians to signify that, in the words of the Anglican Article XXVI, 'Sacraments . . . be effectual, because of Christ's institution and promise, although they be ministered by evil men.' Although its meaning is often misunderstood, the purpose of the phrase is simply to emphasize that sacraments are primarily the acts of God and not of men; it does not deny the fact that the grace given in a sacrament will only be morally effective in the life of the recipient if he has the right dispositions and co-operates with it.

E. L. MASCALL

Exegesis

The Greek verb behind this noun means to direct, to expound or interpret. (Eisegesis, a word sometimes used by way of contrast, would mean reading a meaning *into* a text instead of reading the meaning from it.) In traditional usage hermeneutics (q.v.) lays down the general rules of interpretation (of Scripture, etc.), while exegesis is concerned with their actual application to a given text. The manner in which the exegete interprets the scriptural text will be governed by his presuppositions; thus, in the ancient Church there were those who favoured the literal method of interpretation and those who favoured the allegorical (q.v.). By the high Middle Ages it was generally agreed by exegetes such as Peter Lombard or Thomas Aquinas that the method of interpretation was fourfold: literal, figurative (or allegorical), moral and anagogical (i.e., spiritual or supernatural). At the Reformation the interpretation of Scripture according to the dogmas of the mediaeval Church was replaced by the principle that Scripture must be interpreted by Scripture alone (*scriptura interpres scripturae*), but this, it might be argued, was only the substitution of one set of dogmatic principles of interpretation for another. The rise of modern historical biblical criticism (q.v.) since the later eighteenth century has, of course, altered both the traditional Catholic and Protestant ways of exegesis, but it has not succeeded in finding an objective or 'scientific' process of exegesis which is entirely independent of the personal beliefs and standpoint of the exegete. Reason and tradition – historical critical method and the *communis sensus* of the mind of the Church down the ages – have still their part to play in the work of scriptural exegesis, and the insight of the individual exegete in relating the word once written in a past historical epoch to the needs and situations of his own day remains indispensable. *See also* **Hermeneutics.**

F. W. Farrar, *History of Interpretation*, Bampton Lectures for 1885–6, 1886; W. Sanday, *Inspiration*, Bampton Lectures for 1893, 1893; Beryl Smalley, *The Study of the Bible in the Middle Ages*, 1941; J. D. Smart, *The Interpretation of Scripture*, 1961, esp. ch. II.

EDITOR

Exemplarism

That view of the atonement, called also the 'subjective' or 'moral' theory, associated with Abelard and H. Rashdall in the mediaeval and modern periods respectively, which holds that the value of Christ's atoning work lies in the moral and exemplary character of his love and self-surrender, stirring the imagination and will to repentance and holiness. *See* **Atonement** (6 [*a*]).

JAMES ATKINSON

Existentialism

This term is best taken as descriptive of a certain *type* of philosophical thinking rather than as the name of a unified *school* of philosophical thought. Although it is not uncommon to find theologians such as St Augustine and Pascal, and novelists such as Dostoievski and Kafka, classified as existentialists, it makes for clearer understanding if the term is reserved for those philosophers who have been influenced by and whose thinking stands in continuity with the thought of the Danish religious thinker Søren Kierkegaard (1813–1855). Although, as has been said, existentialists do not form a single school, and, as we shall see, existentialist thought is reconcilable with a wide variety of theological (and anti-theological) positions, there are sufficient themes common to existentialist thinkers to enable us to characterize the existentialist *standpoint as a whole*.

In general, existentialist thinkers have on the whole rebelled against many of the main trends of Western philosophy, especially in so far as this has been influenced by the thinking of 'the Father of Western philosophy', René Descartes (1596–1650). In so far as Western philosophy has concerned itself with the objective exploration of 'beings-in-general' and with the essential categories applicable to these, it has been held by most existentialists to be gravely defective. This is so for two reasons: first, in investigating 'beings-in-general' it has tended to ignore the reality and problematical nature of truly personal existence; and second, in so far as it has attempted to grasp human being by those categories applicable to non-human being it has been gravely erroneous, since this approach overlooks the immense differences between human and non-human being. This second error was, *par excellence*, the error of Descartes and his school. Existentialists can therefore be described as *anti-positivistic* in standpoint; they radically disagree with the positivist tradition that the methods of the empirical sciences are our only means of acquiring knowledge, precisely because these sciences are unable to grasp the reality of human existence, which requires radically different techniques for its elucidation.

Existentialists have accordingly placed a heavy stress on *subjectivity* (*cf.* Kierkegaard's celebrated aphorism: 'Truth is Subjectivity'). By this stress existentialists do not wish to relinquish the claim to *objective* truth, but rather to emphasize, first, that the only route to such truth in the sphere of human existence is through the human *subject's* own personal participation in being from, so to speak, the inside; and second, that man's knowledge of being must begin with his own personal being, since man himself is the only element in being which possesses self-understanding and hence understanding of being in general. But existentialists have deliberately refrained from giving detailed, concrete descriptions of what human existence involves, confining themselves to formal analysis of the structure of such existence. (The technical philosophical way of putting this is to say that they give *ontological* but not *ontic* descriptions.) They have done so because they hold that existential characteristics and possibilities are uniquely grouped in unique personal subjects and thus evade detailed analysis and description. The German philosopher of existence Martin Heidegger (1889–) thus isolates two categories of human existence – *Jemeinigkeit* (*my* existential characteristics and possibilities are inalienably and uniquely *mine*), and *Geworfenheit* (I am *thrown* [German: *geworfen*]) into existence at a certain point in space and time, and therefore my existence has a unique *givenness*, a uniqueness which transcends general analysis, description and prescription).

Nevertheless, certain very general descriptions of human existence are not out of the question. Generally speaking, existentialists would assent to, in some sense or other, the proposition, 'existence precedes essence'. By this is meant that man, unlike natural things, objects and organisms, does not have his essential nature given to him as an already realized possibility (or as a possibility whose realization is inevitable), but that man's essential nature is one from which in his actual existence he is separated, one that as yet lies before him, yet to be laid hold of, grasped or realized. Hence the denial by existentialist thought that human essentiality can be grasped and communicated by the natural sciences (e.g. biology, physiology, psychology) or by the human or social sciences (e.g. anthropology, sociology). Rather, such essentiality can only be described as future existential possibility.

Closely linked with the claim that 'existence precedes essence' is the concept of what we might describe as 'fallenness'. By this is meant that empirical human existence is in greater or lesser degrees estranged from or fallen away from its true, genuine or authentic nature. Thus Heidegger speaks of 'inauthentic' existence, in which man flees from responsibility for his own self by sinking himself in the average or the typical, or by understanding his being purely by the categories of the sciences. The Jewish personalist philosopher Martin Buber (1878–1965) speaks of man's sinking himself in the world of *It*, the world of objects, ideas and instruments, thus cutting himself off from the maturation of his personal being which is possible only in *I-Thou* relationships. Karl Jaspers (1883–) speaks of man's immersion of himself in the world of objectifiable things, an immersion which separates man from transcendent life. The French Catholic existentialist Gabriel Marcel (1889–) speaks of man's overindulgence in the attitude and activity of egocentric 'having', at the expense of the mutual, reciprocal, communal activity of 'being'.

Conversely, all of these thinkers speak of the possibility of the transition from false to genuine modes of existence. Hence Heidegger speaks of man's transition to authentic existence. Buber holds that real personal being is possible through 'turning' from over-indulgence in *It*-relations to openness towards the *Thou* which alone constitutes man's true and essential being. Jaspers speaks of the achievement of a 'philosophical faith' in which man is linked to his genuine, transcendent self, and to God. Marcel points to the reality of personal existence which can come about through man's 'engagement' of himself to communal life and to God.

Generally speaking, in existentialist thought we also find importance being ascribed to the cognitive value of certain subjective affective dispositions, states and moods. It is denied by existentialists that such feeling-states are merely subjective or arbitrary; rather it is asserted that they point to or bring to light certain aspects or dimensions of being which might otherwise be overlooked or ignored. Here might be cited the celebrated example of Jean-Paul Sartre's analysis of nausea (*La Nausée*), in which he tries by a series of evocative descriptions to communicate the feeling subject's convictions about the futile nature of much human existence and the ridiculousness of the world. But much more fundamental to existentialist thought is the great attention paid to the cognitive status of *Angst* ('anxiety' or 'dread'), considered as an essential part of the structure of human existence. Anxiety is considered to be a fundamental part of humans because it is not evoked by this or that object or state of affairs within the world, but by the total situation of human being as such, disclosing man's awful freedom and responsibility as a being flooded by dissatisfaction with the empirical self he has become and by the awareness of the true, genuine self that he might become through the realization of his existential possibilities.

The roots of the significance attached to these affective cognitive states appear to be twofold. First, there is the obvious influence of the brilliant analyses of anxiety and dread worked out by Kierkegaard in his *The Concept of Dread* (ET, 1944) and *The Sickness Unto Death* (ET, 1941). Kierkegaard's work here has been both philosophically and theologically influential. Second, there is the philosophical method of *pheno-*

menology, pioneered by Heidegger's teacher, the German philosopher Edmund Husserl (1859–1938), a method which was adapted and developed by Heidegger in his work. Husserl attempted to work out a philosophical method which was purely descriptive, in which an attempt was made to elucidate and analyse the knowledge of pure universal essences which are inalienably present to human consciousness. According to Husserl, accurate description and analysis are possible only if certain techniques are employed in order to remove those *particular* (as contrasted with *universal*) elements which obscure and distort these essences. The phenomenological analysis of 'anxiety' or 'dread' which we find in Heidegger's work is a result of his application of the phenomenological method to human existence.

It follows from what we have said that by and large existentialist thinkers have been highly critical of much in our modern and contemporary civilization and culture. In the sphere of civilization they have protested vigorously against contemporary mass-society, with its dreadful potentialities for obscuring or denying the reality of personal existence; they have criticized modern society's frightful abuse of mass-communication and its over-employment of modern man in industrial techniques which dehumanize and depersonalize him. They have laid bare the impersonality and anonymity of much modern life, and have warned us of the grave dangers to humanity implicit in totalitarian and collectivist societies. Martin Buber's *I and Thou* (ET, 1937) and Karl Jaspers' *Man in the Modern Age* (ET, 1933) are notable examples of existentialist writings which are critiques of modern civilization. In the sphere of culture, existentialists have protested against the sinister qualities of modern 'scientism', the idolization of science as the main (or the only) source of our knowledge about the world, a procedure which overlooks the significance of personal being within reality as a whole. Heidegger's *Being and Time* (ET, 1962) can aptly be regarded as partly, at least, a critique of certain basic and insidious errors implicit in the history of modern thought and culture.

It goes without saying that the debate about the relationship between the philosophy of human existence and Christian theology is an immensely complicated one, bristling with disagreements and difficulties. The nature of this relationship can naturally be investigated fully in the context of the work of a theologian who has systematically tried to link existentialist thinking with Christian thought; for example, in the context of the work of Paul Tillich or Rudolf Bultmann. But certain general remarks can be made here. First, certain theologians have been highly critical of the attempts to synthesize Christianity and the philosophy of existence. Certain conservative Protestant theologians have protested against the attempt, not infrequently on the grounds that to interpret Christianity in the light of *any* secular philosophy whatever must lead to distortion and impoverishment of the former. This is so, for example, of Karl Barth's criticisms of both Tillich and Bultmann. Sometimes there is combined with this type of objection the argument that existentialism is only a single cultural aspect of twentieth-century gloom and despair, understandable enough in the light of the century's frightful political and international history.

More specifically, hostile critics have tried to argue that existentialism is fundamentally humanistic, if not atheistic. They have pointed, for example, to Sartre's insistence that existentialism is fundamentally an expression of a humanism which has no room whatever for transcendence (*see* Sartre's *Existentialism and Humanism*, ET, 1948). Much has also been made of Heidegger's leaving of the question of God open; it can be objected that Heidegger allows that man's transition from inauthentic to authentic existence is possible without any dependence upon grace, a position which is basically hostile to the Christian understanding of human nature. More specifically still, it can be argued that a careful examination of the *content* of fundamental existentialist categories such as inauthenticity, authenticity, fallenness and the like, demonstrates that this does not at all correspond with the *content* of their allegedly Christian counterparts. Again, critics can point out that when a theologian attempts *radically* and *thoroughly* to synthesize Christianity and existentialist philosophy (a good example of which would be Professor Fritz Buri of the University of Basel), he may very well end by denying both divine transcendence and the idea of the special, particular action of God. Other criticisms of existentialist theologies may take up and develop the theological consequences of radical subjectivism, irrationalism and anthropocentricity.

On the other hand, existentialist theologians have had much to say in reply and defence. As apologetic, mediating theologians they have deplored the attempt to make theological constructions in isolation from and independently of contemporary philosophy. In particular, they have been able to argue that the philosophy of personal existence is a much more apt vehicle for conveying the meaning of Christian doctrine than, say, contemporary Anglo-Saxon empiricism or positivism. This is so, it can be argued, because most existentialist thinkers have been in greater or lesser degree influenced by Christian traditions; there is no denying the Protestant Christianity of Kierkegaard or the Catholicism of Marcel; Heidegger's anthropology has been deeply coloured by theologians like St Augustine, Duns Scotus, Luther and Kierkegaard; the effect of the biblical tradition on Jaspers is clear. Gross distortion, it has been insisted, can be guarded against and avoided. Existentialism represents a salutary corrective against a shallow utopian optimism based on the idolatry of science or a belief in inevitable technological progress. This debate is intrinsically of the first importance, because to engage in it enables us to perceive more clearly the inner nature both of Christian theology

itself and also its relation to contemporary civilization, culture and thought. *See* Angst; Buber, M.; Demythologizing; Hamann, J. G.; I-Thou; Jaspers, K.; Kierkegaard, S.; Phenomenology; Sartre, J-P.

H. J. Blackham, *Six Existentialist Thinkers*, 1952; F. Copleston, SJ, *Contemporary Philosophy*, 1956; M. King, *Heidegger's Philosophy*, 1964; J. Macquarrie, *An Existentialist Theology*, 1955; *Studies in Christian Existentialism*, 1966; D. E. Roberts, *Existentialism and Religious Belief*, 1957.

JAMES RICHMOND

Exorcism. *see* Demonic; Spirit (2); Initiation, Christian.

Experience, Religious

Many millions of people of all cultures and in all ages have had an experience which in some sense can be described as religious, ranging from an awareness of the numinous (q.v.) to ecstasy (q.v.) or beyond that to fully developed mysticism (q.v.). Yet despite this the argument from religious experience to the existence of God was not developed by Christian theologians until the later eighteenth century (the Romantic period). This was doubtless because rationalism in theology was dominant from the scholastic period to the close of the Age of Reason (c. 1780). It is true that certain elements in Protestantism, like evangelical sects today, laid considerable emphasis upon the necessity of the individual's experience of conversion, salvation, etc., and upon the inward assurance of the divine grace (*cf.* the Tate and Brady hymn: 'O make but trial of his love, Experience will decide . . .'). But this evangelical stress upon the inward experience of salvation was not developed into a rational argument for the truth of the Christian proclamation. In the evangelical theology of the dialectical theologians (q.v.) of this century the notion of such an apologetic argument (like the appeal to mysticism) is sternly rejected.

However, by the end of the eighteenth century the rise of biblical criticism (q.v.) had destroyed the notion of the infallible authority of the Bible, as at an earlier date the Reformation had destroyed (outside Catholicism) the notion of the infallible authority of the Church. The authority of the Christian experience of God thus came naturally to take the place of the discredited authorities of Church and Bible, and the stress upon experience (artistic, religious, etc.) was highly congenial to the Romantic temperament. Schleiermacher (q.v.) defined religion as the *feeling* of absolute dependence, which is expressed in different ways, all partially valid, in different religions, but which finds its highest expression in Christianity. Barth has called the nineteenth century 'the century of Schleiermacher': his successors developed and refined his teaching in various ways. Ritschl (q.v.) held that religion was not reducible to other forms of experience and that faith does not consist in the apprehension of metaphysical truths or historical facts but in value-judgments (e.g. the divinity of Christ) which are subjectively apprehended as true. Herrmann (q.v.) even excluded personal religious experience from the religious life, insisting that the historical Christ is important for us only in respect of his ethical value. Herrmann's disciples, Barth and Brunner, brought the nineteenth-century theology of religious experience to an end by returning to the Reformation principle of the Word of God in the Scriptures, albeit in a novel mode. But another of his disciples, Bultmann, translated Herrmann's subjectivism into the new mode of existentialist subjectivism.

In Britain a characteristic theologian like John Baillie (also a pupil of Herrmann) did not find it necessary to choose between reason and experience, or between subjectivity and authoritarianism (*see* bibliography below). The almost universal sense of the presence of God was for him an object of rational reflection in an age dominated by empiricism in philosophy; it was not something which could be accepted only after rational argument had been forsworn. Many Anglo-Saxon theologians have acknowledged the indubitable fact of the religious experience of mankind and of Christians in particular, not making it the key factor in theological explanation nor yet denying that it possesses any significance for Christian belief or apologetics. The question is how much significance is to be attributed to it. Baillie himself persuasively developed the thesis that many people have an experience of the divine action or grace within their own lives, but they have not recognized it for what it is. It has also been argued that the scientist's sense of obligation to discover truth and proclaim it; the artist's urge to create beauty, and the reformer's devotion to the cause of social betterment are all evidences of the pressure of the divine upon men's lives, even though the particular agent concerned might consider himself an atheist. This does not mean that 'the good pagan' is really a crypto-theist at heart, but that in spite of his avowed unbelief he nevertheless testifies by the integrity of his behaviour to the reality of the source of all truth, beauty and goodness which Christians know as God (*see* **Revelation**). This line of thought approaches quite closely the moral argument (q.v.) for the existence of God.

Nevertheless such considerations do not add up to a compelling argument for the truth of the Christian claim, still less to any kind of proof. Like the more traditional arguments for the existence of God, they serve to interpret the Christian's own beliefs and experiences and to assure him that his faith is not irrational or lacking empirical evidence. At best they can only arrest the attention of the thoughtful unbeliever and make him reconsider his own experience. The truth would seem to be that the evidence of religious awareness is ambiguous. By its very nature it is subjective and therefore notoriously open to misinterpretation. It may be pointed out that experience of the moral pressures upon our consciousness may be socially conditioned, that the sense of the holy is as strong among primitive animists (*see* **Animism**) as among devout Christians, and that mystical experience is common to Jews, Muslims, Buddhists, etc. as well as to Christians and that, so far from corroborating Christian dogmas, it yields no conceptual framework of doctrine and is usually interpreted in terms of the mystic's own religious and cultural background. Furthermore, states of ecstasy (or self-transcendence) can be induced by fasting, techniques such as Yoga and by drugs (*see* **Psychedelic Experience**). Finally it is to be noted that the Bible itself places little emphasis upon subjective experiences (though prophetic visions, such as Isa. 6.1–8, are regarded as a frequent means of the reception of divine revelation); the main thrust of the Bible is that 'faith comes by hearing' (Rom. 10.17 in its context), i.e., as the result of the proclamation of God's action in Christ. It is impossible to translate 'religious experience' into NT Greek.

There is an immense literature on this subject written from every point of view. *See esp.* John Baillie, *Invitation to Pilgrimage*, 1942; *Our Knowledge of God*, 1939; H. D. Lewis, *Our Experience of God*, 1959; J. Macquarrie, *Studies in Christian Existentialism*, 1965, esp. ch. 3; Alan Richardson, *Christian Apologetics*, 1947, ch. 5.

EDITOR

Expiation. *see* Atonement (3*[c]*.

Faith

1. *In Catholic Theology.* 'Faith' in Catholic theology means mental assent to divinely revealed truth, that is, to 'the faith' of which the Church is the custodian and interpreter. The mind is prepared for such assent by a rational perception of the intrinsic credibility and the sufficient attestation of the articles of faith, and is then moved to give its assent to them by an act of the will in voluntary submission to the authority of God. It cannot directly perceive their truth, which is above reason, but it can see that they are credible (as not being contrary to reason) and that there are adequate grounds for affirming them to be of God (and therefore true, since God cannot lie). For the average man, no doubt, both their credibility and their status as revealed are sufficiently attested by the authority of the Church; but for those who can follow them there are rational arguments (philosophical and historical) for the existence of God, the fact of revelation, and the infallibility of the Church as witness to the revelation. It is therefore no leap in the dark when a man proceeds to the act of faith, saying in effect: 'I see that this doctrine is credible; I see good reason to hold that God has revealed it; I will therefore believe it because God has revealed it.'

Such an act of faith, presupposing trust in the

veracity of God and a knowledge of what he has revealed, might conceivably (though improbably) be made by the unaided powers of man's mind and will. But as a purely natural act it would avail nothing towards his salvation, for which supernatural acts are necessary. The act of faith must therefore be both inspired and assisted by divine grace, in order that it may be raised to the supernatural level of an 'infused virtue' (*see* **Infusion**). Since, however, grace is never lacking, even non-Catholics and non-Christians (provided they do not resist it) may attain to some measure of supernatural faith; and for any deficiency in this they may be excused on the ground of 'inculpable ignorance'. There is, moreover, an important distinction to be drawn between 'explicit' and 'implicit' faith. The act of faith, as an act of submission to the authority of God, implies in any one instance the readiness to submit in every instance; hence it embraces implicitly all the truths that God has revealed, although it is and can be directed explicitly only to those known at the time. As to how much must be known and explicitly believed (as necessary to salvation), opinions differ; but it is commonly held that the two truths mentioned in Heb. 11.6 – namely, that God exists, and that he rewards those who seek him – represent the absolute minimum.

2. *In Classical Protestant Theology*. 'Faith' in classical Protestant (as in modern biblical) theology means obedient trust or trustful obedience towards God as he is revealed in his Word. It is a response to the divine grace revealed in that Word, as it was variously spoken to the fathers by the prophets (Heb. 1.1), found incarnate expression in the Son (John 1.14), and is addressed to us now by the Holy Spirit through the word and sacraments of the gospel.

The object of faith is not here a set of doctrinal propositions, but the personal reality of God in Christ; and faith itself is understood essentially in terms of personal relationship. For although the gospel cannot be proclaimed without the use of propositional statements, what the gospel calls for is not simply assent to certain propositions, but faith in Christ and in God through him. After all, as both Luther and Wesley point out (with reference to James 2.19), even the devil can believe in the sense of assenting to true statements concerning God and Christ. But truly to believe the gospel is to have faith in God through Christ – such faith that we look to him for all good and for help against all evil, and are ready to do or endeavour to do whatever he may command. It is analogous to the confidence a man may have in another man. In so far as I have confidence, for example, in my doctor, I take him at his word when he assures me I am going to get well, and I take both his advice and his medicine even when they are unpalatable.

My confidence in my doctor rests, of course, on what I know of him, whether from my own observation or the testimony of others. What I know, however, is not here primarily a matter of factual information, since there are people who 'inspire confidence' even on first acquaintance – while others gain our confidence only slowly, if at all. Just so, God in Christ 'inspires confidence', though not immediately or equally in everyone, and in some not at all; and hence faith itself can be understood as a gift and work of the Holy Spirit. As to why the Spirit does not evoke the response of faith in all who hear the gospel, and as to the possibility of salvation for those who never hear it – these questions have been variously answered in the history of Protestant thought, and sometimes much too confidently answered. But in general Protestantism has been more concerned with a right understanding and faithful proclamation of the gospel than with such questions, the answers to which are best left in the hands of God.

The use of the arguments of natural theology (q.v.) as preambles to faith is uncongenial to classical Protestantism. Although Luther himself was prepared to use all the arguments he could muster in defence of the Christian position against Jews, Turks and Infidels, he regarded them as worse than useless 'in the matter of justification', that is, where the personal relationship to God was concerned. Such arguments tend both to compromise the Protestant emphasis on salvation by grace through faith alone, and also to devalue the content of revelation by equating it with 'revealed truths' that are supplementary to their own 'rational truths'. This has in fact happened in some phases of Protestant thought, with unfortunate results for faith. A distinction has been drawn between faith as correct belief (the emphasis of orthodoxy) and faith as heartfelt trust (the emphasis of Pietism), and controversy has arisen as to the relative importance of each, as well as to the relation of faith (in either sense) to ethical obedience or good works. Such problems are almost inevitable whenever the primary object of faith is other than the personal reality of God in Christ; for there is no faith without an object of faith, and the nature of the object determines the character of the faith itself.

D. M. Baillie, *Faith in God and its Christian Consummation*, 1964; R. McAffee Brown, *The Spirit of Protestantism*, 1961; R. Bultmann, *Faith*, 1961; G. Ebeling, *The Nature of Faith*, 1961; G. Forell, *The Protestant Faith*, 1960; K. E. Skyddsgaard, *One in Christ*, 1957; G. D. Smith, ed., *The Teaching of the Catholic Church*, 2 vols., 1948; P. Tillich, *The Dynamics of Faith*, 1957.

P. S. WATSON

Fall. *see* Man, Doctrine of.

Festivals. *see* Calendar.

Feuerbach, Ludwig Andreas

Ludwig Feuerbach (1804–1872), German Hegelian philosopher and theologian, took as his starting-point Hegel's teaching that the divine is immanent and attains to self-consciousness in the human. But, rejecting the notion of divine transcendence, he insisted that the 'divine' was merely a this-worldly *aspect* or *dimension* of the human, limited to the sphere of man's as yet unfulfilled potentialities. Hence, for Feuerbach, theology was to be translated into anthropology; all statements about God were to be translated into statements about man. Feuerbach's influence on subsequent nineteenth-century theologians was marked, and on thinkers like K. Marx and F. Engels considerable.

L. Feuerbach, *The Essence of Christianity*, ET, 1957.

JAMES RICHMOND

Fichte, Johann Gottlieb

Johann Fichte (1762–1814), German Absolute Idealist philosopher, identified the Absolute Ego of ethical idealism with God. He conceived of reality as a moral order in which a moral struggle between inner freedom and that which limits it goes on continually. Fichte, together with Goethe, Schelling and Hegel, contributed enormously to nineteenth-century immanentist theology.

JAMES RICHMOND

Fideism

The word was coined in the nineteenth century, probably by A. Sabatier and his modernist circle of Protestants in Paris, to denote the view that (as Kant has demonstrated) reason could not prove the truths of religion and that therefore believers could rely upon faith, which was a kind of religious experiencing. Dogmas were only the symbolic expression of religious feelings; this view stands in the general succession from Schleiermacher (q.v.) and Ritschl (q.v.). 'Fideism' has continued to be used especially by theologians of the Thomist tradition as a pejorative term for subjectivist theories which are based upon religious experience and which undervalue reason in theology.

EDITOR

Fides Historica

Fides historica is an expression denoting the conventional or inherited ideas of one's social group, family, etc., as distinct from a living, personal faith of one's own. Such a faith is not really faith at all in the Christian sense; it is 'historical', i.e. a past or dead faith, not a present, existential one. It is the conglomeration of half-remembered teaching from childhood, uncriticized metaphysical notions, ill-digested traditional materials – the three-storey universe, the images of Adam and Eve, the Last Judgment, the Great Assize and the whole late mediaeval cosmological-metaphysical world-picture – all of which is rapidly being dissolved by the changing climate of opinion without need of help from the so-called 'new' or 'radical' theologians. What is commonly spoken of on the mass-media as the decline of religious faith in recent times is really the gradual disappearance of *fides historica*, the inherited religious-ideological mental furniture of the nominally Christian multitudes, not the disappearance of faith in the Christian sense of the word.

Alan Richardson, *Religion in Contemporary Debate*, 1966, ch. 6.

EDITOR

Filioque

Filioque is the Western insertion in the article on the Holy Spirit in the Nicaeno-Constantinopolitan Creed, 'Who proceedeth from the Father *and the Son*', to express the doctrine of the Double Procession of the Spirit (q.v.). While the underlying theology had deep roots in the West from Augustine onwards and had formed part of official documents from the fifth century, the intrusion into the Creed is first evidenced in France in Carolingian times. Widely accepted in the West, it was only later received at Rome. This has been bitterly resented in the East both on canonical and doctrinal grounds. *See* **Trinity, Doctrine of the; Spirit.**

H. E. W. TURNER

Final Perseverance

Final Perseverance means continuing in grace, and dying in a state of grace. It is common Christian teaching that to be in a state of grace now (present salvation) is no guarantee that one will continue in it (perseverance) or die in it (final perseverance) and so attain to eternal life and blessedness (final salvation). In the Catholic view, perseverance is impossible without the special help of God, and final perseverance is a special gift of his providence. It is indeed so much his gift and so little in our own power that no man can be sure of it without a special revelation, which is very rarely given. In Calvin's view, final perseverance depends on an irresistible operation of God's grace, which is given only to the elect. But the elect can be sure of their election – each only for himself, of course – precisely as a result of this operation of grace. In Wesley's view (which repudiates Calvinistic election and the irresistibility of grace) some few persons do receive a special assurance of their final salvation. All, however, can have an assurance of present salvation, and on the basis of this they can rightly have confidence that he who has begun a good work in them will carry it to completion (*cf.* Phil. 1.6).

G. C. Berkouwer, *Faith and Perseverance*, 1958.

P. S. WATSON

Five Ways

The name is commonly given to St Thomas Aquinas' five 'proofs' of the existence of God. These are treated under **God** (6 and 7) and **Thomism.** *See also* E. G. Jay, *The Existence of God: a Commentary on St Thomas Aquinas' Five Ways of Demonstrating the Existence of God*, 1946; J. Maritain, *Approaches to God*, ET, 1955, ch. 2.

Foreknowledge

Implicit in the traditional belief in divine omniscience is the corollary that God knows in advance everything that will happen in the future. If this is the case, then it follows that human freedom of the will is an illusion: if God now knows what decisions I will make tomorrow or next year, then it is already predetermined how I will act. The problem has long been discussed by theologians and philosophers. Generally speaking, theologians have been more ready to accept the deterministic view than have philosophers of religion. Perhaps the solution of the problem is to be found in the steady refusal to deny either God's foreknowledge or man's free-will. If this seems a paradox, it is not without parallel in normal human relationships. The fact that I know what decision my friend will make tomorrow when he is confronted by a certain choice does not mean that he is predetermined to make it. I know what choice he will make because I know my friend, his character and his thoughts; he is predetermined only by factors internal to his own inner being, such as the character which has been formed by many previous choices, and so on. I could, of course, be wrong in my conviction of what he will do, because no man can ever know even his most intimate friend with complete knowledge. But God's knowledge is not limited as human knowledge is. We can be free in the sense that our decisions are our own and are not forced upon us (like those of a computer) by anything outside ourselves; and yet God, to whom all hearts are open and from whom no secrets are hid, knows the outcome of all human choices until the end of history. *See also* **Providence; Predestination** (1).

D. M. Baillie, *God Was in Christ*, 1948.

EDITOR

Forgiveness

Forgiveness is the act whereby an injured party allows the party responsible for the injury to go free. The O T clearly teaches that God is a gracious and forgiving God (*see* N. H. Snaith, 'Forgive, Forgiveness', *TWBB*). The thrust of the N T doctrine is that not only does God not demand a prior reparation from the offender before he restores him to his friendship, but actually takes upon himself the act of reparation, so that the sinner may be restored to the true relationship of sonship, man's real destiny. Paul argues that this doctrine of the pure love of God is the moment of truth for Christian thinking and living (Rom. 5.5–8), a thesis argued with conviction by Anders Nygren in his work *Agape and Eros* (ET, 1953). It is sometimes argued that forgiveness is conditional upon repentance, the change of mind and intention demanded of the sinner. It is surely not right to use the word 'conditional' in relation to God's love, which is wholly unconditional, free and unmerited. Better to say that this teaching of God's love calls out repentance from the human heart as the sun brings new life out of a plant. The doctrine

should be safeguarded from any idea that repentance is the human contribution to the bargain. We are not talking of a new kind of fellowship consequent upon human action, of the kind a treaty between nations provides, but of a new kind of fellowship created by God, individually, personally and decisively, unmerited and undeserved. A condition seems indicated in the Lord's Prayer, 'Forgive us our trespasses as we forgive them that trespass against us' (Matt. 6.12; Luke 11.4), a view enforced by the striking parable of the Unmerciful Servant (Matt. 18.23–35) and the teaching of Jesus (Mark 11.26). Again the word condition is dangerous. What is being said is that the terms forgiveness and repentance are meaningless to the natural man; in fact they offend his proper sense of justice (*see* the parable of the Labourers, Matt. 20.1–16). It is when he sees the incredible message of God's reconciling love in Christ that his heart is moved to repentance towards God and forgiveness towards his brother. We should resist the prevalent psychological attempts to explain the divine relationship as consequent upon human thoughts, feelings and acts, by means of biblical teaching.

H. R. Mackintosh, *The Christian Experience of Forgiveness*, 1927.

JAMES ATKINSON

Form Criticism. *see* Jesus of History (7).

Foundations

Published in 1912 this book of essays by Anglican theologians in the University of Oxford was 'a statement of Christian belief in terms of modern thought'. B. H. Streeter's essay on the historic Christ expressed a somewhat sceptical mood, and William Temple described the 'formula of Chalcedon' as 'a confession of the bankruptcy of Greek theology'. The underlying philosophy of the essayists was optimistic and immanentist. It has its place in the succession of influential symposia which includes *Essays and Reviews* (1860), *Lux Mundi* (1889), *Essays Catholic and Critical* (1926) and *Soundings* (1962) and which both reflected a prevalent mood and helped to influence the future. *Foundations* evoked a brilliant satire from the pen of R. A. Knox in a poem entitled *Absolute and Abitofhell*, and a more sober criticism in *Some Loose Stones*.

J. K. Mozley, *Some Tendencies in British Theology from the publication of Lux Mundi to the present day*, 1951.

R. CANT

Free Thinking, Freethought. *see* Deism.

Freedom

Freedom is the ability to make one's own choice between different possibilities and to decide for oneself how to act or what attitude to adopt in any given situation. Such freedom or self-determination is ordinarily and rightly attributed to every normal human being (*see* **Free Will**).

Nevertheless, there is a profoundly important sense in which human beings are not free – just because and in so far as they are *self*-determined. They have not the freedom with which Christ came to set men free, the freedom of divine love and grace (qq.v.) which he both exemplifies and gives. For everything Christ did for us men he did freely and of his own accord, even to the laying down of his life. He was not obliged to do it, but he did it in free and willing obedience to his heavenly Father, and in free and unconstrained love for mankind. The Father's sending of him into the world, moreover, as well as his own fulfilment of his mission in the world, was motivated by nothing else but divine love. It was God's own love that was in Jesus Christ our Lord, and it was a love wholly undeserved by those to whom it was given. God's love is free, entirely independent of the merits or demerits of men. God therefore both wills and acts freely; he does not simply react, as we so commonly do.

For us, as our Lord points out (Matt. 5.43–48; Luke 6.27–36), it is natural to love those who love us, and to do good to those who do good to us – or who we hope will do good to us in return. We naturally salute our brethren – those who have some ties of kinship with us, of family, nationality, race, or religion – and when God commands us to love our neighbours, we naturally think this means our friends and excludes our enemies. As for loving people enough to die for them, why, as St Paul says, we would not ordinarily give our lives even for a just and upright man, though we might conceivably for one who was good and lovable (Rom. 5.6–8).

By contrast, the Son of God gave his life for sinners and his enemies. And those to whom he gives power to become children of God (John 1.12) also love their enemies. They do good to those who hate them, bless those who curse them, pray for those who abuse them. They give and lend to those who have no claim upon them, expecting nothing in return. They take after their heavenly Father, who makes his sun shine and his rain fall on the just and the unjust, and is kind to the ungrateful and the wicked. In other words, they share in the freedom of God himself, the freedom of grace and self-forgetful, self-sacrificing love for others. Such is the glorious liberty of the children of God.

But such freedom we human beings do not normally and naturally possess. We are not born with it, and if we ever attain to anything like it, we do so by the grace of God alone. We are born self-centred, self-important, self-concerned, and we grow up self-indulgent or self-righteous or both – apart from the grace of God. Therefore we are not by nature free, but slaves of self-will. This is very plain when we follow our own inclinations without even asking about duty and the will of God. It is less plain but just as true when we do our duty in spite of contrary inclinations. If we do

it with a calculating eye to our own interests, as judging it to be 'the best policy'. And it remains subtly true even if as individuals we give ourselves in self-sacrificing devotion to the selfish cause of our own class or nation, race or creed. Still we fall short of the freedom of that love which 'seeketh not its own' (I Cor. 13.5).

R. E. Davies and R. Newton Flew, eds., *The Catholicity of Protestantism*, 1950; R. T. Osborn, *Freedom in Modern Theology*, 1967; P. S. Watson, *The Concept of Grace*, 1960.

P. S. WATSON

Freedom of the Will, Free Will.
see Providence.

Friends, Society of

The Society of Friends is the religious body founded by George Fox (1624–1691) in an age in which religious intolerance led to their persecution and inured them to 'sufferings'. They constituted a 'way' rather than an 'orthodoxy', a friendship-group rather than a church. Dispensing with the outward forms of religion (e.g. sacraments, creeds, liturgies), they nevertheless adopted very formal manners of speech, dress, etc. in daily life. Their distinctive doctrine, if they had one, was that of the Inner Light (q.v.), but this was interpreted in a strongly christological sense. Their personal integrity eventually led to their being universally respected and trusted, and this in turn led them to success in various fields of commerce, etc. They have earned for themselves a great reputation for social concern in such matters as prison-reform (Elizabeth Fry, 1780–1845), elementary education (Joseph Lancaster, 1778–1838), philanthropy, international relief-work, ambulance service in war (the Friends are resolutely pacifist, slum-clearance, etc. The theological problem which they pose for 'orthodox' Christians is raised by their *doing* the work of Christ while conventionally Christian people are content with formal church-observances, saying 'Lord, Lord' but doing little for those in whom Christ suffers amidst all the miseries of a hungry and war-ridden world: 'By their fruits you shall know them.' Their witness to the whole Church of Christ might be summed up in the phrase, 'Orthodoxy is not enough'. The term 'Society of Friends' was not used until the nineteenth century; the name 'Quakers' is said to have been given to them by Justice Bennet in 1650 because George Fox had bidden him to tremble at the Word of the Lord. But there existed a religious sect which had been called 'Quakers' before that date. The early Friends themselves attributed the name to the trembling which sometimes came upon them in their religious meetings.

The classical exposition of Quaker belief in the earlier period is Robert Barclay's *Apology for the True Christian Religion, as the same is set forth and preached by the People called in Scorn*

'Quakers', 1678. *See also* W. C. Braithwaite, *Beginnings of Quakerism*, 1912; R. M. Jones, *Faith and Practice of the Quakers*, 1927; *Quakers in the American Colonies*, 1911. For a recent presentation *see* Harold Loukes, *The Quaker Contribution*, 1965.

EDITOR

Fulfilment. *see* Promise.

Fundamentalism

Although this term is frequently used as a synonym for the theory of the verbal (or 'plenary') inspiration and inerrancy of the Bible, it properly denotes a whole body of evangelical doctrine of a strictly conservative type. The word took its origin from a series of tracts issued from the USA under the general title of 'The Fundamentals'. The first appeared in 1909. They were written by eminent evangelical leaders and theologians (including B. B. Warfield, James Orr, H. C. G. Moule and G. Campbell Morgan); they expounded conservative views, such as the substitutionary theory of the atonement, the imminent return of Christ, the reality of eternal punishment, the necessity of conversion and of personal assurance of salvation, as well as the doctrine of the verbal inerrancy of scripture. Probably the latter doctrine became chiefly associated with the word because all the other doctrines could be demonstrated only by the literalist interpretation of certain biblical texts. In general fundamentalism is akin to pre-Enlightenment evangelical theology, but it differs significantly from that theology by its deliberate rejection of the methods and conclusions of post-Enlightenment biblical-historical criticism, which the earlier theologians had not rejected because they knew nothing of them. In this sense fundamentalism may be said to be a radically different theology from that of the older evangelical position. *See* Inspiration; Scripture, Doctrine of Holy.

Charles Gore, *The Doctrine of the Infallible Book*, 1924; J. I. Packer, *'Fundamentalism' and the Word of God*, 1958; Alan Richardson, 'The Rise of Modern Biblical Scholarship and Recent Discussion of the Authority of the Bible', *The Cambridge History of the Bible*, ed., S. L. Greenslade, II, 1963.

EDITOR

Generation

The term, Generation (Greek: *gennesis*; Latin: *generatio*), has been increasingly used from the time of Origen to express the relation of the Son to the Father. Its scriptural basis lies in the correlation between the Father and the Son in the Gospels (particularly the Fourth Gospel). Origen interpreted the Generation of the Son as an eternally continuous act, though Cyril of Jerusalem (q.v.) preferred to interpret it as a single event before time. The Arians took the basic biological analogy

behind the word with deadly metaphysical seriousness in their clichés, 'There was a time when the Son was not' and 'for Isaiah too was older than his son'. For them the distinction between the Ingeneracy of the Father and the Generation of the Son excluded the ascription of full Divinity to the Son. The Cappadocian Fathers employed the term as the differentiating particularity of the Son. *See* Ingeneracy; Procession(s).

H. E. W. TURNER

German Christians

German Christians were those members of the German Protestant churches who, taking up an extremely anti-Judaistic theological attitude, synthesized Christian theology with German National Socialist racialist ideology prior to and during the second World War. *See* Crisis Theology; Barmen Declaration.

K. Barth, *The German Church Conflict*, ET, 1965; A. S. Duncan-Jones, *The Struggle for Religious Freedom in Germany*, 1938.

JAMES RICHMOND

Glossolalia

Glossolalia, a Greek word, literally 'speaking with tongues', refers to the type of ecstatic utterance of meaningless syllables under the excitement of powerful religious emotion. It has been (and is) a feature of religious (esp. revivalist) activities at many periods of Church history. Sometimes the practice of 'speaking in an unknown tongue' has been encouraged for its own sake, but St Paul deprecates this attitude (I Cor. 14). Nevertheless he still appears to think that the phenomenon is a genuine manifestation of the presence of the Holy Spirit, although he tries to regulate the practice of it in the interests of orderliness and he urges his converts to seek the more important spiritual gifts of faith, hope and charity (I Cor. 13.1, 13). The investigation of the subject belongs primarily to the psychology of religion; in their evaluation of glossolalia theologians will bear in mind that it is a phenomenon to be found in other religions than the Christian. *See also* Pentecost.

EDITOR

Gnesio-Lutheranism

The Gnesio- (sincere) Lutherans defended the doctrine of ubiquity in the Eucharist, a position developed by John Brenz and strongly contended for by Jakob Andreae and Mathias Flacius Illyricus. Opposing were the followers of Melanchthon, the Phillipists, also dubbed Crypto-Calvinists. A number of other points of doctrine, including oral manducation and *communicatio idiomatum*, were much stressed by some of the Gnesio-Lutherans, notably Flacius, their ablest controversialist, the learned editor of the *Magdeburg Centuries*. Shortly after Melanchthon's death (1560) numerous doctrinal statements were drawn up and locally adopted by the opposing sides. In 1574 the Phillipists in Wittenberg were imprisoned by the elector Augustus, leaving the Gnesio-Lutherans triumphant. The controversy had its echoes in the Syncretistic Controversy of the seventeenth century in which George Calixtus reflected Melanchthonian liberalism and Abraham Calovius and others defended rigid Lutheran dogmas.

O. Ritschl, *Das orthodoxe Luthertum im Gegensatz zu der reformierten Theologie*, 4 vols., 1908–27.

J. T. MCNEILL

Gnosticism

1. *Definition*. Gnosticism is a term describing systems of belief which claimed to impart a special knowledge (Greek: *gnosis*) of God, of his relation to the world and to men, and of redemption, whose possession intellectually and spiritually enlightened the initiated and thus guaranteed the salvation of their souls.

2. *Origins*. The OT Daniel, gifted with superiority over ordinary mortals, foretells the future and offers hints to the 'wise' whom he commends. These are the *maskilim*, the instructed or initiated. In the *Rule* of Qumran, the *maskil* is a similarly instructed person able to expound both a doctrine about the structure of the universe and rules closely connected with it which the Qumran sect demanded of its adherents. Men's dispositions, even their physical characteristics, are determined by the stars, that is, the state of the universe, when they are born as well as by the proportions of the *spirit of truth* and of the *spirit of perversity* which entered into their composition. Here is reflected the influence of astrology probably ultimately derived from Babylon, and of a dualism found indeed in the OT but with probable affinities with Persia. The intertestamental *Book of Jubilees* and parts of the composite *I Enoch* show close connections with Qumran and on the other hand with Greek influences, including Pythagoreanism. It is uncertain whence derives their solar calendar regulating worship designed to reflect exactly the movement of the cosmos as well as to commemorate God's historical acts and to obey his Law revealed on Sinai. Christian literature reflects these elements in its parent Judaism when I John 4.6, for example, speaks of a spirit of truth and a spirit of perversity. A complementary process is seen in the Hellenization by the Septuagint of Hebraic devotion to the Law: if Ben Sira identified Wisdom with Law, the Codex Alexandrinus assimilates both to the concept of Light (Ecclus. 45.17) and the Septuagint transforms a phrase in Hos. 10.12 into 'enlighten yourselves with the light of knowledge (*gnosis*)'. The idea of light or enlightenment, divinely granted, illuminating or enlarging an implanted spark in the candidate for salvation, was to become fundamental to gnostic systems; it developed from the basic human experience of the alternation of day and night which relatively early were associated with good

and evil respectively in both Iranian dualism and in post-exilic Judaism, so that both for Qumran and the NT the saved and lost may be respectively Sons of Light and Sons of Darkness (War Scroll passim; John 3.19; 12.36; 17.12; Acts 26.18; II Cor. 6.14; Eph. 5.8; I Thess. 5.4 f.; I Peter 2.9).

Other streams of thought which flowed into the pool where later gnostic teachers fished, swam or drowned, rise in Egypt, bringing the Isis and Osiris myth of great antiquity discussed by Plutarch, and the Hermetic writings now dated in the second or third centuries AD. The latter, produced in Egypt, were part of the flood from the thought-world of Hellenism, which contributed in these and other works in sometimes garbled form the ideas of Plato, the Stoics and Pythagoreanism. Cumont, perhaps wrong in overlooking the early origins and gradual growth of 'pregnostic' or 'gnostic' ideas, and in dating Gnosticism exclusively to the Christian era, usefully emphasizes the importance of the old native gods in the Roman Empire. By the time of the Severi 'all forms of paganism were received and retained while the exclusive monotheism of the Jews kept its adherents, and Christianity strengthened its churches and fortified its orthodoxy, at the same time giving birth to the baffling vagaries of gnosticism'.

3. *Gnosticism and the NT*. There is no certain evidence for developed gnostic systems created and taught by leaders whose names they often bear until the days of the early Church; but Reitzenstein, and later Bultmann, and other scholars have argued that already before NT times there was a system of *gnosis*, knowledge of the heavenly origins of one's self and of the way of redemption out of this world for the 'spiritual' or 'pneumatic' man, redemption not only of the individuals possessing their sparks of light but also through these the redemption of the Primal Man of whom they are the broken pieces, a redemption to be wrought by the descent into this fallen world of another man of light sent by the highest god. This view is reached by assembling material from separated passages in the NT and constructing a system to which they are held to refer. The Corinthian correspondence of Paul may serve as one example: I Cor. 6.12 ff.; 8.1 ff., reflect the personal power bestowed by *gnosis*, I Cor. 7 the ascetic tendency of the system, I Cor. 15 the Corinthian gnostic denial of a physical resurrection on the basis of believing the only true resurrection to be a 'spiritual' resurrection and consequent illumination which they already possessed. II Cor. 10–13 (in the view of W. Schmithals revealing the sole opposition to Paul) is concerned with proof of pneumatic excellence, implying that adversaries were gnostics. Paul indeed holds fast to the Christian conception of *gnosis* as God's gracious 'acknowledgment' of man rather than man's 'knowledge' of God, but his position approached the gnostic outlook. Hence the absolute use of *gnosis* in I Cor. 8.1, 7, 10 f.; 13.8; II Cor. 8.7. Against this we must urge that Paul devalues *gnosis* in I Cor. 8.1; 13.8, 12 and the

letter to the Colossians argues against angel-worship, asceticism, calendar observance and 'philosophy' (an incipient pre-gnostic system derived from Essenes?) with incisive rational power from an orthodox Christian point of view, though it may be true that Paul's and others' argument is disposed in relation to 'gnostic' (i.e. 'pre-gnostic') positions, as, for example, in the eloquent Eph. 3.19.

The Johannine literature poses the problem differently. The author of the Gospel and the First Epistle is clearly anti-gnostic (e.g. I John 2.18 ff.; 4.2) but does he protest too much (I John 1.1–3)? He avoids the term *gnosis* but 'to know' rightly seems a way of expressing the state of redemption (John 17.3). For Bultmann indeed the Gospel is based on the gnostic redeemer myth of the man of light. Yet the thought of the Gospel can be as clearly explained as Judaism in contrast with Hellenism without the supposition of a system otherwise not known to exist. Elsewhere in the NT some early gnostic notions are vigorously opposed, as in I Tim. 1.4, 6 f.; 6.4, 20 f.; II Tim. 2.14, 16, 23; 4.4; Titus 3.9; II Peter 1.16; 2.1–22; Jude 10 ff.; again, newly-discovered gnostic works from the second century do not present us with any traces of Bultmann's reconstructed system.

4. *Gnosticism and Apocryphal Works.* Early tributaries to the great river of later Gnosticism can be discerned among the apocalyptic literature in the Apocrypha and Pseudepigrapha of the OT. Later gnostic works sometimes took the form of an apocalypse: the medium used by an author of a book like Daniel or *I Enoch* for revelations of things to come lent itself readily to revelations of invisible heavenly realities. R. M. Grant has argued indeed that things to come, when they failed to arrive, were transformed into things as they are in another world. The cosmology and angelology of *I* and *II Enoch*, of *Jubilees* and the Dead Sea Scrolls may therefore be prototypes of features in later fully-developed gnostic systems. Such features include the Four Lights from the Four Angels governing the four seasons, the Seven Spirits corresponding to the days of the week (in Tobit, the *Testament of Levi*, Enoch literature, Revelation and the gnostic *Apocryphon of John* from Nag Hammadi) and thirty aeons from the thirty days of the month in the solar calendar, probably assimilated to other powers which governed the heavenly bodies in *I Enoch* and *Jubilees* who make up the Pleroma ('fulness' or assembly of Powers making up the content of deity) in the later system of Valentinus.

Again, a particular type of mystical speculation, centred upon the creation narrative and the opening of the book of Ezekiel, was practised by some rabbis of the NT period. Such developments and speculations are psychologically intelligible after the cruel disappointment in AD 70, 115 and 135 of Jewish apocalyptic hopes. Samaria, no less than Judea devastated by Roman armies, seems to have been the source of less austere speculations of a gnostic character, though the figures of Dositheus, Simon Magus with his mistress Helena and Menander are obscured by legends. Simon (Acts 8.9 ff. and the *Ps.-Clementine Homilies*), early established as the father of gnosticism viewed as a system deliberately hostile to the Church, maintained this position in the minds of the orthodox until well on in the mediaeval period.

5. *Main Gnostic Works.* Simon was reputed to have been the author of a *Gospel of the Four Points of the Compass*, interesting in view of the contention of Irenaeus (c. 130–200) against gnostics that there cannot be more nor less than the four Gospels since there are four points of the compass and four winds from the four quarters of the world; but the work is, like some others receiving passing mention, unknown and may not ever have existed. For an extant early work of true gnostic character which, according to Irenaeus, was intended to be a kind of fifth Gospel we must turn to the Valentinian *Gospel of Truth* which promises joy to those whom the Father of truth has granted to know him by the power of the Logos. There were many other gnostic Gospels, the *Gospel of Eve* known only in a citation of Epiphanius (c. 315–403), and a number which are extant, often taking the form of a dialogue of the risen Christ with the apostles in which he reveals all the mysteries of salvation. Such are the *Sophia Jesu Christi*, the *Dialogue of the Redeemer*, the composite *Pistis Sophia* in which the risen Saviour spends eleven years with his disciples before revealing in the twelfth the last mystery of all, the envelopment of the world in light, and the *Two Books of Jeû*. The place of origin of these was certainly Egypt. The apostles are natural authorities to claim for works conveying gnostic revelations, and a number of 'Gospels' may have been ascribed to them corporately, although references to such works are obscure; one *Gospel of the Twelve Apostles* may be identical with the Gospel of the (Jewish Christian) Ebionites, another with the Gospel of the Manichaeans, although Manes may himself have written his own *Living Gospel*. We are on firmer ground with Gospels ascribed to individual apostles; possessing since 1947 the *Gospel according to Thomas* (more fully, Didymus Judas Thomas) in a Coptic version, parts of the Greek version of which, it now appears, were known in earlier discovered Sayings on papyri from Oxyrhyncus. The work announces itself as 'the secret words which the living (i.e. risen) Jesus spoke and Didymus Judas Thomas wrote' and consists of usually cryptic sayings some of which have manifest connections with sayings and parables in the Synoptic Gospels, constituting in the view of some scholars evidence of an independent tradition of the sayings of Jesus, although the form in which they appear almost always betrays obvious gnostic influence. Its original form probably dates to the early third century, and seems to have been composed from previously existing collections of 'sayings'. The *Gospel of*

Philip appears next in the Coptic manuscript, its Greek original being of uncertain date, perhaps as early as the second century. The author echoes the canonical Gospels of Matthew and John and to a lesser extent Luke, as well as other parts of the NT including Paul, whom he sometimes quotes. The work is distinguished by poetic feeling, and, like other gnostic works, considerable psychological insight expressed in strange terms. For this Gospel the great mystery is the bridal chamber, the sphere of union with heavenly reality. It contains an isolated reference to Philip the apostle, perhaps the origin of the title in the colophon of our manuscript, although a passage in *Pistis Sophia* represents Jesus revealing secrets above all to Philip, Thomas and Matthew, the last being named in a manuscript of the *Book of Thomas the Athlete* as the scribe for Thomas. Irenaeus is the earliest authority for a non-extant *Gospel of Judas*, belonging to the Cainites, but the *Apocryphon of John* is one of the major works surviving virtually intact. It claims to be by John, son of Zebedee, and the record of a vision in which Christ revealed to him a whole system of cosmology and redemption; it was known to Irenaeus and therefore dates from not later than the middle of the second century. The *Gospel according to Mary*, probably composite, is of similarly early date; in it Mary Magdalen comforts the apostles on the departure of the risen Lord and imparts a doctrine of the soul's attainment to peace, claimed to be a revelation to her from Christ. The apocryphal *Gospel of Peter*, whose existence was attested since Serapion (c. 200) and known from a fragment found at Akhmim in 1886, represents not so much gnosticism as the tendencies which produced it.

Founders of gnostic schools other than Valentinus have had 'Gospels' attributed to them; among them are Basilides and Marcion, but it is doubtful whether Basilides wrote one and Marcion merely produced his own edition of Luke.

The principle that Jesus revealed secret knowledge to the apostles produced books other than Gospels ascribed to them: in the *Acts of John* dependent on the Apocryphon, the pneumatic Christ appears to his apostle on the Mount of Olives while the crucifixion takes place in the ignorant and wicked Jerusalem below – a paramount example of the docetic division of Christ and Jesus which we meet in Basilides and elsewhere, and whose main tendency was to consider the humanity and sufferings of the earthly Lord as apparent only ('docetic' comes from the Greek for 'to seem'). In the *Apocryphon of James* Jesus calls on the disciples to be ready for martyrdom, which is ordained for them by God. Gnostic elements were probably present in the *Preaching of Peter*, but both these works are more obviously Jewish (non-Pauline) Christianity than gnostic. The *Acts of Thomas*, certainly gnostic, makes Thomas the twin brother of Jesus and not only receiver of his revelation but sharer in his work as redeemer. Like the original *Gospel according to Thomas* probably from Syria, it is a romantic story of a hero's wanderings in a wonderland. It contains two songs, a wedding song and the *Hymn of the Pearl*.

6. *Main Gnostic Systems and Themes.* Gnostic systems are usually based on the conception of an inconceivable ineffable God at an immeasurable spiritual remove from the cosmos, superior to the God of this world; the existence nevertheless in the natural man of a spiritual (pneumatic) as well as a psychic and material element; and a redeemer from above who is to illuminate and liberate this element so that it may rise (literally and metaphorically) above the cosmos and flesh in which it is imprisoned. Between the ineffable God and man there is therefore room for an infinite variety of beings (the Pleroma). The systems of Saturninus and of Basilides, early enough to be known to Irenaeus, illustrate these points and incidentally our uncertainty about the teaching of those gnostics for knowledge of whom we must rely on Christian opponents since their own works are not extant. According to Irenaeus Basilides conceived of the chain of being as: Ungenerated Father – Logos – Understanding – Sophia and Power – Powers, principalities, angels who made the first heaven. Other heavens, totalling 365, took their origin from these. The angels who control the last heaven made the world, their chief being the God of the Jews. The Ungenerated Father sent his firstborn Mind (Christ) to free those who believe in him from the power of those who made the world. He did not suffer, but Simon of Cyrene was crucified instead. Mind ascended to the Father. If this is not the system of Basilides, it may well be taken as a typical system known to Irenaeus. According to Hippolytus (c. 170–236) Basilides taught an infinitely complicated system, given here as an example of gnosticism in free speculative flight, especially since a philosophical basis can be clearly detected in the three orders of being and their relation and lack of relation to one another. A non-existent God made a non-existent universe out of the non-existent, giving substance to a seed or mixture of seeds having within it the whole semination of the universe. This is, at the same time, the creation of light. Man originates from and is illuminated by that seed which also contained a Triple Sonship sharing the nature of the non-existent God. One Sonship flew up to the Non-existent. Another, united with the Holy Spirit, ascended to the first Sonship and the Non-existent but could not keep the Holy Spirit, who brought down to the formless and distant place where man is, a 'perfume' from the Sonship, and was set as a firmament between the supermundane and the cosmos. The third Sonship remained in the mixture of seeds from which was now begotten the Archon of the cosmos who went up to the firmament, ignorant of anything beyond it, though wisest and best of all below except the Sonship in the seeds, of whose superior quality he was also ignorant. From the materials below him this Archon or Demiurge now begot a Son wiser than the Demiurge himself, who indeed worked in him and advised him. He was seated at the right

hand of the Archon, his sphere being called the Eight. Then another Archon arose from the seeds, greater than anything except the first Archon and his Son, and similarly made for himself a Son wiser than his father. This Archon's place is called Seven and in this space are all beings who are born naturally. The Third Sonship had yet to be revealed and restored above the dividing Spirit. This is the 'revelation of the sons of God' (Rom. 8.19), and for it the gospel came into the cosmos. It really came even though nothing came down from above and the Sonship did not leave the Non-existent. The Archon of the Eight then learned that he was not the God of all, who the Non-existent is, and other truths of the supermundane. The Archon of the Seven was then illuminated by him and from the Seven the light came down upon Jesus, son of Mary ('Holy Spirit will come upon you', Luke 1.35). The cosmos waits for the Sonship left below to be purified and to follow Jesus by ascending. Then the creation will obtain mercy, which means that everything will remain within its own spatial and natural limits. In ignorance of possibilities outside, it will desire nothing impossible, so avoiding suffering. This is the restoration of all things. The Gospel is the knowledge (gnosis) of the supermundane which the great Archon did not possess. After Jesus came into existence everything happened as in the Gospels: the bodily part of his being suffered, the psychic part rose again and was restored to the Seven, another part to the Eight. The Third Sonship was purified through him and ascended to the blessed Sonship.

Of other gnostics known to Irenaeus, Carpocrates (and his son Epiphanes, as we learn from Clement of Alexandria) inclined to a practice of licence based on a law of nature; like Carpocrates, Cerinthus taught that Jesus was son of Joseph and Mary and regarded 'the Christ' as descending on Jesus at his baptism and withdrawing from his passion. Irenaeus connects the Nicolaitans (Rev. 2.6, 15) with Nicolaus of Acts 6.5 but some other early writers disagree. Our knowledge of them is negligible. Cerdo is most important as he is regarded by Irenaeus as the teacher of Marcion, famous for hating the God of the OT and regarding the God who was the Father of Jesus as opposed to the former. He therefore desired the Church to reject the OT and formed his own canon of the NT and indeed his own version of the scriptures of which he approved. Saturninus and Marcion saw the flesh as evil and taught celibacy, apparently blaming the creator God for making man male and female. Tatian, famous as the composer of the Diatessaron, a harmonization of the four canonical Gospels, was also an ascetic, perhaps wrongly reported to be a gnostic and credited with being founder of the Encratites, this term being more accurately applied to several groups of ascetic Christians on or beyond the fringe of orthodoxy.

Irenaeus uses the *Apocryphon of John* as a source for the Barbelo-Gnostics who believed in a never-ageing Aeon called Barbelo, whose rela-

tion to 'the unnameable Father' is something like that of Wisdom in Jewish literature to God; but as in all gnostic systems the Aeons, or heavenly beings between the absolute God and this world, are numerous, though not as many as the 365 in Basilides. In the *Apocryphon*, Seth, the son of Adam and Eve, and his descendants are blessed ones; a group of gnostics traced their descent from him and are known as the Sethites. For them the serpent (Ophis), instrumental in giving man knowledge, was really Sophia. Ophites is an alternative title of the sect, to whom, incidentally, the Nag Hammadi library may have belonged. Opposition to the God of the OT recurs in the *Cainites* who sympathize with his victims (such as Esau, Korah and the Sodomites) and rejoice in breaking his laws. Their opposition is positive: Judas brought about the mystery of the betrayal because he alone possessed knowledge of the wisdom in such figures. Another group who have in common with them their veneration of the serpent are the *Naassenes* (Hebrew: *nachash*, a serpent).

Valentinus was great enough to found a school; his *Gospel of Truth* known of through Irenaeus, has appeared at Nag Hammadi and reveals a deeper interest in psychology than in the cosmology which forms its background. The state of ignorance delivers a man over to the terrors of his unconscious. 'But when morning comes, he knows that the fear was nothing. Thus they were ignorant of the Father; he is the one whom they did not see.'

Ptolemaeus succeeded Valentinus in the west about 160, attempted to derive the school's system from the Fourth Gospel (whose first exegete he was), and in his *Letter to Flora* implied that it was in the apostolic tradition and had divine authority. It is roughly of the same kind, though more complicated, as that of the earlier gnostics such as Basilides. Theodotus, known from excerpts made by Clement of Alexandria, became the leader of the eastern branch of the school. Marcosians were followers of a Valentinian, Marcus.

Of the same school was Heracleon whose commentary on early chapters of the Fourth Gospel was largely quoted by Origen who himself was deeply influenced by Gnosticism, like his predecessor Clement who indeed regarded the Christian as 'the true gnostic'.

Whatever the truth about the existence of Gnosticism before Christianity the forms in which we know it are almost always recognizable as Christian deviations. The Mandaeans, a gnostic sect originating from east of the Jordan at a date much debated (first or second century or not before 400?) and still surviving near Bagdad, probably derive from Christianity in spite of their hostility to it; though the prominence given, in their *Ginza* and other writings, to John the Baptist and to the necessity for frequent baptism has supported a claim that their origin is pre-Christian. Their teachings are like Manichaean dualism: man's soul, imprisoned in the body and persecuted by demons, will be freed by the redeemer, Manda da Hayye, that is, the personified *Knowledge of Life*.

Manes (c. 215–275) similarly taught the necessity for the release of light imprisoned in man, and enjoined a severe asceticism. The acute dualism and hatred of the physical body characteristic of developed Manichaeism were well known to Augustine.

7. *Sources*. For long Irenaeus was our chief and somewhat biased informant about early Gnosticism, filled out sometimes by quotations in other Fathers; in the nineteenth century Coptic texts from Egypt became known: the Codex Askewianus of the *Pistis Sophia* and Codex Brucianus containing two books of the *Mystery of the Great Logos* (i.e. probably the *Books of Jeu*) and a Sethite work; in addition the Berlin Papyrus (Pap. Berol. 8502) containing the *Gospel of Mary*, the *Apocryphon of John* and the *Sophia Jesu Christi*, and the *Acts of Peter* which is not gnostic. The second and third reappear in the thirteen codices containing forty-nine works discovered at Nag Hammadi in Egypt in 1945. This great discovery, of as great importance for the history of the Church as that of the Dead Sea Scrolls in 1947 for late Judaism, revealed many other gnostic works, e.g. the *Epistle of the Blessed Eugnostus, the Dialogue of the Saviour*, two *Revelations of James*, the *Gospel of Truth*, the *Epistle to Rheginos on the Resurrection*, a treatise on the Three Natures, the *Gospels of Thomas* and *Philip*, the *Book of Thomas*, the *Threefold Discourse of the Threefold Protennoia, Revelation in the form of an Epistle, Paraphrase of Shem* (Sethite), *Revelations of Peter* and *of Dositheus* (or, for the last, *The Three Pillars of Seth*) and *of Paul*, and *of Adam to his son Seth* and *of the Great Seth* and the *Authentic Address of Hermes to Tat*.

Books about this hoard are a good introduction to Gnosticism; e.g. the paperback by R. M. Grant and D. N. Freedman, *The Secret Sayings of Jesus*, 1960, is an illuminating edition of the *Gospel according to Thomas* with discussions of its ancestry and meanings. W. C. van Unnik has described the whole collection in *Newly Discovered Gnostic Writings*, 1960; R. McLachlan Wilson has discussed *The Gnostic Problem*, 1958, with great caution; his recent American lectures are being collected and published under the title *Gnosis and the New Testament*, 1968; R. M. Grant has provided *Gnosticism, An Anthology*, 1961, and *Gnosticism and Early Christianity*, 2nd ed., 1966; and H. Jonas treats main ideas in *The Gnostic Religion*, 1958.

A. R. C. LEANEY

God

1. *Introduction*. The Christian understanding, knowledge and doctrine of God may most conveniently be gathered from the creeds and confessions of the Christian Church. Thus the Apostles' Creed, which is an expansion of the old Roman creed and has yet proved itself serviceable to the contemporary Ecumenical Movement and which again and again in the history of theology has provided the text and ground-plan of more elaborate expositions of Christian faith, declares its belief in 'God the Father almighty, creator of heaven and earth'. Although more extensive creeds such as that commonly called the Nicene (more correctly, the Niceno-Constantinopolitan) are manifestly concerned to define as explicitly as possible specifically Christian belief, not simply in God, but in God in Christ, they none the less affirm a basic belief in 'One God the Father almighty, maker of heaven and earth, of all things visible and invisible'. (This interest is not, of course, entirely absent from the Apostles' Creed, which in describing God as Father probably means the Father of all men, the Father of our Lord Jesus Christ, and indeed the Father and Creator of the universe; but a distinction can be drawn between creeds which in origin sought to summarize faith and creeds designed as tests of orthodoxy.) According to the Thirty-nine Articles of the Church of England, 'there is but one living and true God, everlasting, without body, parts or passions; of infinite power, wisdom, and goodness; the Maker and Preserver of all things both visible and invisible'. The Augsburg Confession declared that 'there is one Divine essence which is called and is God, eternal, without body, indivisible, of infinite power, wisdom, and goodness'; while the Westminster Confession held that God 'hath all life, glory, goodness, blessedness, in and of himself; and is alone in and unto himself all-sufficient, not standing in need of any creatures which he hath made, nor deriving any glory from them, but only manifesting his own glory, in, by, unto, and upon them: – he hath most sovereign dominion over them, to do by them, for them, or upon them, whatsoever himself pleaseth'. Again, the Profession of the Tridentine Faith (*Professio Fidei Tridentina*), sometimes called the Creed of Pope Pius IV, re-iterated in its first article the whole of the Niceno-Constantinopolitan Creed.

Such credal affirmations, however, are very summary statements indeed and each arose out of a particular historical situation. In certain respects therefore they are like the intermittent ripples that appear here and there on the surface of the stream, and in order to grasp more adequately the Church's thought and conviction in their fulness and continuity it is necessary to take into account also the underlying currents and cross-currents of theological opinion, and, no less, the source of the Church's life and thought in the religion of the Bible.

2. *Biblical Faith in God*. To begin at the beginning is to begin with that complex of events and messages which arose within a particular strand of history and which are recorded together in the Scriptures of the OT and NT. Even a long familiarity cannot finally obscure the grandeur and profundity of the Jewish religion and the Christian faith in which it culminated; and the develop-

ment of thought and belief which is here involved is on any reckoning a most remarkable one. Its distinctive note is sometimes said to be that of monotheism; and certainly, while in this respect it may not claim to be absolutely unique, since there are adumbrations of a practical and ethical monotheism in the great poets of ancient Greece and of a speculative but still largely ethical monotheism in the philosophy which flourished on that same soil, these foreshadowings are as fumblings in the dark, productive of 'imperfect and partial conceptions which seem to show glimpses of the truth rather than attainment' (A. C. Headlam, *Christian Theology*, 1934, p. 157), which do not share the firmness of apprehension characteristic of Hebrew-Christian religion.

Monotheism, however, is not by itself the distinctive stress of biblical religion. One theologian has even said that 'monotheism is neither a characteristically Christian view nor even a biblical one, save as an inference derived from the truth that God is the Lord' (E. Brunner, *Dogmatics*, I: *The Christian Doctrine of God*, 1949, p. 137). Not even the characterization of biblical religion as ethical monotheism adequately grasps its peculiar outlook. It is rather as if the unity of God cannot be affirmed without attracting to God alone all the hopes and fears of all mankind. For the Bible the divine unity is not an abstract speculative principle so that its first implication is that polytheism is an error. Rather the divine unity already means that God alone is the ultimate authority in human life and the ultimate refuge amid all the perils of historical existence. The worshippers of idols are not only in error – the falseness of their gods means also, inseparably, that the claims of these gods are a pretence and their promises illusory. It is as if the Bible declared, in one and the same breath, that God is one, that he is holy and just and good and that he is love. Even so, we have missed the essential part if we do not think of God as active. He is the Creator and in his loving-kindness he takes the initiative. He chooses his own people out of all the families of the earth and they in turn look for the coming of the Messiah. Accordingly this outlook finds its fulfilment in the new covenant and specifically in what the NT calls 'the grace of our Lord Jesus Christ'.

Such is the origin of the Christian doctrine of God, the source from which the stream of Christian thought takes its rise; but a conception of God which could be expressed, with its own adequacy, in the simple words of the prayer 'Abba, Father', was to be the subject of an extensive and often debatable elaboration as the Church, under the inherent pressures of its historical situation, sought both to articulate more fully the saving truth of the gospel and to repel insidious but serious error. Moreover, although it may seem a far cry from the Sermon on the Mount to the findings of the Council of Nicea or the Chalcedonian Definition (q.v.), it is important to remember, on the one hand, that the intellectual demand for systematic elaboration was legitimate and inevitable, and, on the other hand, that for the most part the work of elaboration was regarded by those who performed it as precisely that, a work of elaboration and not of fresh construction, and that, further, it was often undertaken with an acute sense of man's unworthiness for the task, in the very spirit of the prayer 'Abba, Father' and in a context of worship and mystery.

3. *The Hebraic and the Greek Confrontation*. If it was the Hebrew religion which culminated in the work of Christ which provided the Church with the substance of its faith and of its knowledge of God, that religious tradition did not supply the intellectual concepts and categories for the systematic articulation of this knowledge. These were, however, available in the Greek philosophical tradition; and if the philosophy of ancient Greece failed to become an alternative and rival to the monotheistic faith of Israel it did contrive to become at least the handmaid of Christian theology. If Christ conquered the ancient world in the sphere of religious faith, it was Greek philosophy which had prepared men's minds for the theological task of understanding, so far as possible, the redemptive reality by which they had been apprehended. This is what happened. One might even say, this is what had to happen; nothing else is conceivable. Yet from a much later perspective two opinions have been held of the process, for some see in the philosophical constructions of ancient Greece something hardly less than a *praeparatio evangelica*, a preparation for the gospel, while others see in them the source of a radical distortion of Christian faith, the Hellenization of the gospel.

Whatever be the truth in the area covered by these conflicting verdicts the fact remains that Greek philosophy provided the instrument with which Christian theology set about its task, and, in particular, what is sometimes called 'the Platonic-Aristotelian philosophy' (W. R. Matthews, *God in Christian Thought and Experience*, 1930, p. 100). Even so, although the philosophical influence can thus be indicated by a single comprehensive title, it would be misleading to assume either that this philosophical influence was itself a single stable and unchanging factor, or that its effect on the Christian understanding of God was a solitary and permanent achievement. On the contrary, so far as the latter is concerned, a distinction may be drawn between the concept of God on the one hand and the method by which it is reached on the other; and it was in the former direction that first of all the influence of Greek thought made itself felt explicitly and extensively, and this especially in the form it assumed in certain aspects of Platonism and in Neoplatonism.

4. *The Augustinian View*. One of the key figures in this connection was undoubtedly St Augustine; and it is important to realize that, although in the modern period many Christian thinkers have been attracted to the teaching of Plato and have made frequent use of it, it was not in exactly the

same way that St Augustine found it congenial. Rather it was through the Neoplatonist Plotinus that Platonism came into St Augustine's theological outlook. Every student of Greek philosophy knows that one of the distinctive Platonic doctrines was that of the forms or ideas, the thesis that beyond the world of sensible objects there is a world of unchanging essences, more real than the world of sensible objects, and indeed through participation in which sensible objects have whatever reality they do possess and knowledge of them is possible to the limited extent that such participation is possible. Moreover, supreme among the ideas or forms, according to Plato, is the idea of the Good. No doubt it is tempting to regard the Good as divine, although in fact Plato does not seem ever to have identified God and the Good (in spite of the *Republic*, 517). On the contrary in book x of the *Laws* he spoke of God as a divine soul who is the self-moved mover and the cause of the basic and regular movements of the heavenly bodies. God in this sense is not the Good but has knowledge of it and indeed seeks its realization in all his causal activity; and it is this Platonic God who has appealed strongly to many Christian thinkers in the modern period, in spite of the fact that on this statement of the case the Good is metaphysically independent of God and in the *Timaeus* is even represented as superior to God. It was not, however, this Platonic God who directly attracted the mind of St Augustine but rather the teaching of Plato as seen through the eyes of Plotinus. According to Plotinus God is identical with the Good, not a divine Soul, but the source of all being and knowledge, of whom properly nothing at all can be predicted (for otherwise his unity would be destroyed), but rather from whom everything else derives as regards both its essence and its existence. This relationship of one-way dependence was called emanation, and although the idea of emanation has been termed a 'Neoplatonic theory of causality' (A. E. Taylor, 'Theism', *ERE*, XII, p. 266) it was such that it did not imply antecedence in time and was in fact consistent with belief in the eternity of the world; hence one distinguished Catholic philosopher can say that 'the world of Plotinus and the world of Christianity are strictly incomparable' (É. Gilson, *God and Philosophy*, 1941, p. 49). Yet it was in terms of the former that St Augustine had to give expression to his firm grasp of the latter and in doing so he inevitably gave to it what may be called an 'essential' rather than an 'existential' slant. Thus the divine is identified with pure being and is marked by immateriality, intelligibility, immutability and unity. This does not mean that St Augustine's grasp of the Christian faith was any less firm. He could wage unremitting warfare against Pelagianism as others had fought the Arian thesis; he could provide the distinctively Christian doctrine of the Trinity with something like a completed statement, and he could supply what was to prove in due course an important warrant of the Protestant Reformation. But it did mean that in the permanent background of the Church's thought there was a conception of God which was in certain respects, some would hold, basically alien to the Christian faith, which led, for example, to St Augustine's privative view of evil and which identified the sphere of the divine with that of the true, immutable, unchanging and timeless, in almost unrelieved contrast with the realm of change and decay.

Moreover, in the shadow of this conception of God there is the other topic already distinguished, the question of method, in particular the attempt to prove or demonstrate by rational argument the existence of God. There can be no doubt that St Augustine was one of the very great figures in the history of Christianity, and it is remarkable how many diverse and sometimes mutually conflicting movements can with more or less justice claim something of his authority. Perhaps not the least noteworthy of such facts in the field of thought is that two famous arguments, St Anselm's ontological proof of the divine existence and the *cogito ergo sum* of Descartes, had what one writer has called both their 'material' and their 'formal preformulation' in St Augustine (Benjamin B. Warfield, 'Augustine', *ERE*, II, p. 222). The self and God, these were indeed the great objects of all St Augustine's intellectual life: '*Deum et animum scire cupio. Nihilne plus? Nihil omnino*' (*Soliloquies* i. 2. 7). So far as the divine existence is concerned the core of the type of argument favoured by St Augustine himself involved an ascent (which was also an escape) from the changing world of sensible things to the possession of truth in the mind and a further ascent (which was, however, a fulfilment rather than an escape) from this truth to Truth itself, its one and only possible source, the unchanging Truth which is God. If such an argument were treated as a self-sufficient exercise and a detached demonstration, it might not seem entirely satisfactory, for if one begins by positing Truth as the only possible source of truths one would then be making no advance to argue from truths to Truth and the attempt to do so might well appear as circular. In the case of St Augustine, on the other hand, it must be recognized that again and again he emphasized that man's mind is so darkened by sin that he could not of himself make the ascent to Truth, and that accordingly he consistently taught that man can learn only by grace and must believe in order that he may understand. Thus M. C. D'Arcy can quote St Augustine as holding that no-one can 'become fit to discover God unless he shall have first believed what he is later to come to know' (*De Libero Arbitrio*, 11.2.6, quoted in *A Monument to St Augustine*, 1934, p. 166); and there is no doubt that the constant conjunction of this teaching alongside a proposed rational demonstration of God's existence sets up a tension which is not readily resolved, which in fact it may not be possible to resolve so long as the priority of intellect is taken for granted.

5. *The Ontological Argument.* Be that as it may, it

is a fact that some six hundred years after St Augustine's death another saint, Anselm (1033–1109), was to be found teaching the same view that in order to understand one must believe (*credo ut intelligam*), and also insisting that one can none the less by reason demonstrate the existence of God – by the famous ontological argument. The ontological argument is St Anselm's argument and, ever since St Anselm devised it, it could scarcely have had a more chequered history. St Thomas Aquinas, who was not averse to rational demonstrations of the divine existence, who on the contrary gave definitive and classical form to the natural theology of which proofs of God's existence are a fundamental and substantial part, none the less rejected this one. Yet in the sphere of philosophy it re-appeared in the work of René Descartes and was later rejected by Immanual Kant; but, curiously enough, it has re-appeared in the troubled state of the philosophy of religion at the present time.

The ontological argument reflects the general type of argument favoured by St Augustine; but, as St Anselm formulated it, it takes its start neither from sensible things nor from the possession of truth, any truth, in the mind, but from a concept or definition of God. According to Anselm, God is that than which nothing greater can be conceived; and, therefore, Anselm concludes, God must exist, since if he did not exist, he would not be that than which nothing greater can be conceived. God, not existing, might have all conceivable forms of greatness but he would still fall short in respect of greatness of the same God having all these forms of greatness and, into the bargain, existing. Consequently, if God is that than which nothing greater can be conceived, existence cannot be taken away from him, he must exist.

As already indicated, opinions have varied widely on the validity of this argument. In Anselm's own life-time it was pointed out by Gaunilo of Marmoutiers that if a lost island is said to be wealthier and better than any inhabited island the argument would be invalid which sought to suggest that this lost island must exist, on the ground that otherwise it would not really be richer than all inhabited islands. Centuries later, Kant was to use a somewhat similar argument concerning not an imaginary island but an imaginary hundred dollars. But Anselm had already pointed out in reply that his demonstration is not applicable to a whole class of concepts but to the one unique concept to which his definition of God refers, and certainly no critical assessment of the ontological argument has really reckoned seriously with it if it does not take account of the peculiarity of the concept of God. Thus A. E. Taylor has argued that everything turns upon the correct answer to the question whether we really have any such concept as that described by St Anselm, whether the words 'that than which nothing greater can be conceived' have any meaning ('Theism', *ERE*, XII, pp. 268 f.); while others have insisted that the

concept of God is such that if there is no logical defect in it, God must exist, whereas if there is a logical defect in the concept God cannot exist (*cf.* C. Hartshorne in Sidney Hook, ed., *Religious Experience and Truth*, 1962, p. 213). Moreover, when the ontological argument is confronted on this more profound level it becomes apparent that the verdict depends to some extent on the presupposition entertained regarding the function and competence of reason and logic. If the function of reason is to order and so to comprehend the reality that confronts man in experience (which may in turn be narrowly or broadly conceived), then reason may indicate that something cannot be but not that something must be, whereas if reason is also such that it has its own opening upon reality, either through some power of intellectual intuition distinguishable from experience no matter how broadly conceived, or because reality is not just constructed on rational lines but is itself of the very stuff of reason, this restriction would not apply. To accept the ontological argument involves the defence of one or other of these two possibilities covered by the latter main alternative; and neither is easy. On the other hand, if one were confronted by God in his self-revelation as the one who exists out of himself of sheer necessity and who conveys existence to everything else, one might well have a concept of God of which the ontological argument is perhaps a clarification. It is clear, however, in that case, that one's belief in the existence of God does not rest ultimately upon a demonstration but on the revelation.

Even if the ontological argument as a piece of pure reasoning is of questionable validity, it did, however, give shape and substance to a natural theology, a theology based on reason independently of all revelation; and it was this that in the thirteenth century was re-fashioned and given its completed form by St Thomas Aquinas. Indeed it was not only natural theology but the entire contribution of Greek philosophy to Christian thought which received definitive expression from the Angelic Doctor of the thirteenth century. It is important to realize, however, that what did receive definitive expression in this way was something for which the pattern had already been set, in the shape of a speculative method and an abstract conclusion. This seems to the present writer to remain basically true whether one minimizes or magnifies the change that was then taking place. It also seems to remain basically true whatever verdict we may reach on this development, whether we agree with Benjamin B. Warfield's criticism that the whole history of the Church of Rome 'since the second Councll of Orange (529) has been marked by the progressive elimination of Augustinianism from its teaching' ('Augustine', *ERE*, II, p. 220) or with Étienne Gilson's thesis that 'Saint Augustine . . . had reached . . . the limit of Greek ontology itself' and that 'a new and decisive progress in natural theology was made only through Aristotle and Thomas Aquinas' (*God and Philosophy*, p. 62).

6. *The Cosmological and Teleological Arguments.*
The change of emphasis which made itself felt at
this time was a change from essence to existence,
from the sphere of 'what' to the sphere of 'that',
and, consequently, so far as the proofs of the
divine existence are concerned, a change from *a
priori* argument to *a posteriori* argument, from
arguments taking their rise in ideas and concepts
to arguments taking their rise in facts and things.
For Aristotle the supreme reality was not a static
essence, no matter how remote, no matter how
abstract, but an act of thinking, a pure act of self-
thinking; and what St Thomas Aquinas did was to
transpose this teaching from the key of knowing
or thinking to that of existence. This may well
seem a radical transposition, and there is no doubt
that St Thomas was enabled to make it only in the
light of what he had learned from the biblical
revelation and in particular from the name by
which God had made himself known to Moses,
namely, 'He who is' (Ex. 3.14). Yet once the
transposition has been made the resultant insight
is deemed able to stand upon its own feet as a
properly rational theology. As one modern follower of St Thomas has expressed it, it is 'difficult
for us to see that "it is" ultimately points out, not
that which the thing is, but the primitive existential act which causes it both to be and to be precisely that which it is. He who begins to see this,
however, also begins to grasp the very stuff our
universe is made of. He even begins obscurely to
perceive the supreme cause of such a world' (É.
Gilson, *God and Philosophy*, pp. 69 f.).

The recognition of what the same writer elsewhere calls 'the radical primacy of existence over
essence' (*The Christian Philosophy of St Thomas
Aquinas*, 1924, p. 34) to such an extent that, as has
just been quoted, the act of existence or the existential act causes anything 'both to be and to be
precisely that which it is', moves the attention
from ideas to sensible objects and paves the way
for an *a posteriori*, as distinct from an *a priori*,
proof of the divine existence. As a matter of fact
St Thomas offered not one but five proofs of the
existence of God, known as the Five Ways of St
Thomas; but by and large they cover much the
same ground as the argument provided by Plato
in the *Laws*, xii, and are in turn comprehended by
the two lines of proof which theology has come
traditionally to distinguish as the *cosmological*
argument and the *teleological* argument. The
latter argues from the evidence of design in the
universe to an originating intelligence, and this is
what St Thomas also does when, from the orderliness of the universe, he infers the existence of a
supreme intelligence whom everyone understands
to be God. Different writers may look in different
directions for the evidence of order and design.
One theologian has commented that 'Paley,
writing as late as 1802, says, "For my part, I take
my stand in human anatomy." And Plato, writing
about 350 B C, may be taken as saying only that he,
for *his* part, takes his stand in mathematical
astronomy' (J. Baillie, *The Interpretation of Religion*, 1929, p. 78). Others have taken their stand

elsewhere, for example, in the varied field of
entomology; but perhaps the distinctive feature
of the Thomist form of the argument is that here
the final appeal is to order over the whole extent of
the universe. Indeed, although basically it is the
same argument, the difference between these two
forms of it, that which appeals to order over the
universe at large and that which looks to order in
some more limited and compact sphere, points to
the proper assessment of the argument; for the
choice of a restricted sphere where order can be
detected and explored in detail is always somewhat
arbitrary, whereas the orderliness of the whole is
rather a postulate than an attested fact. Accordingly, the argument has at the most a fairly high
degree of probability, and it functions more
readily as the articulation of a belief in God than
as a demonstration *de novo*. By itself it may raise
a question and suggest an answer without creating
a conviction.

Three of the remaining four ways of St Thomas
clearly cover the ground of the cosmological
argument which infers from the causal series a first
and uncaused cause. This is precisely what St
Thomas argues in respect of three features of anything to be found in the causal series, the fact that
it may be in motion for which it cannot account,
the fact that it falls within this series, and the fact
that in or out of the series it enjoys only a contingent existence and does not exist out of itself.
In all three respects it is either assumed or affirmed
as a self-evident truth that an infinite regress in the
series of causes is not possible, and consequently
it is concluded that at the beginning of the series
there stands a first and unmoved mover, a first and
uncaused cause and an absolutely necessary
being, whom in each case, St Thomas affirms, all
men understand to be God.

The fourth way of St Thomas is rather more
difficult to understand, and there are in fact considerable differences between the two expositions
of it which Aquinas gives in the *Summa contra
Gentiles* and in the *Summa Theologiae*. The
aspect of sensible objects from which this proof
takes its start is what is called 'the degrees of
being', and this in itself is not easy for a modern
reader to grasp, because the idea brings under one
category and into one class 'real' qualities and
normative ones, and treats both as somehow
residing in the object or even thinks of the object
as having these qualities by participation (a
Platonic idea) in their supreme form. If, however,
we can think of reality in this way, we can, St
Thomas would say, further infer the existence of a
supreme cause in which all being and perfection is
to be found. It is true that not only is this a more
difficult argument but also it is one which can
quite readily be interpreted as if St Thomas were
arguing from the perfection of essence or being to
existence in a way reminiscent of the ontological
argument of St Anselm. However, we probably
keep much more closely to the mind of St Thomas
himself if we think of all five arguments as taking
their rise in sensible objects, as employing the
Aristotelian analysis of causation in terms of

material, moving, formal and final causes, and as arguing that, since an infinite regress is not possible, each type of cause must lead us to the thought of God, who into the bargain must be further deemed self-existent or else the causal series could never get under way. Thus when set against the Aristotelian fourfold analysis and Aquinas' own concept of, and emphasis upon, existence, the five ways can be seen to form a unity which subsequent reflection has broken up into two main arguments, the cosmological and the teleological.

This is not the only view of the inter-relationship of the five arguments in Aquinas, but it is interesting to note that the distinguished student of St Thomas, Étienne Gilson, rejects the view that 'there are not five proofs of God's existence, but only one divided into five parts'. Rather he holds that 'the structure of the five proofs of St Thomas is identical, even that they form one whole and reciprocally complete one another'; and he says that 'the multiplication of convergent proofs cannot be considered a matter of indifference. Each different approach discloses to us a different aspect of the divine causality' (*The Christian Philosophy of St Thomas Aquinas*, p. 67). It is, however, no less important to see that the validity of this unified fivefold argument depends on the correctness of Aristotle's fourfold analysis of the causal nexus and the distinctive emphasis upon existence imparted by St Thomas himself.

7. *The Thomistic View.* On the face of it a philosophy of existence such as St Thomas Aquinas favoured is more congenial to the modern mind than the kind of philosophy of essence that lay behind the Christian thought of St Augustine, and its conception of causality seems nearer to the Christian belief in creation than is the idea of emanation inherent in Neoplatonism. St Thomas, however, meant a great deal more by existence than appears at first sight. It is tempting to think that, since we know what we mean when we say that a tree exists, we must know what we mean when we say that God exists, even if we realize that unlike the tree God exists out of himself and so necessarily; but if we mean by God's existence the existence of something else over and above all mundane existing things, we have not properly grasped what St Thomas really means. To put it thus is to imply a distinction between what God is and his self-existence, whereas it is precisely this distinction that St Thomas rejects when he says, *Deus est suum esse*; or, as he has been expounded, 'like whatever exists, God is by his own act-of-being; but, in his case alone, we have to say that *what* his being is is nothing else than that by which he exists, namely, the pure act of existing' (*ibid.*, p. 91). In other words, God is 'an act of existing of such a kind that his existence is necessary'; and as such he is the source of everything both in respect of what it is and in respect of the fact that it is. Moreover, for St Thomas this conclusion of natural theology that God is 'nothing else than . . . the pure act of existing' is confirmed by God's revelation of himself in scripture where in reply to Moses he names himself as 'He Who Is' (Ex. 3.14); and so a link is forged between natural and revealed theology.

Since the 'what' and 'that' of God's being are identical, since God is nothing but what has been called a pure act of existing, theology is compelled to speak of the *simplicity* of the divine nature, and by that it means to do justice to the purity of the act and therefore to the total lack of composition, division and qualification in the divine nature. To say anything more of God than that he is to misrepresent him by denying his simplicity. Yet theology is bound to try to say more, although this it can do only if it is prepared to follow what was called the way of negation, that is, by saying what God is not. Accordingly theology can and must deny of the divine being all the imperfections of creaturely reality and so speak of God's perfection. The idea of degrees of being or perfection is not an easy one for the modern mind and it may well seem that to eliminate all the varied content of creaturely existence is to end with the most abstract and nearly empty of ideas, the idea of pure being. Some Thomists would admit that their view 'can appear as the emptiest . . . of philosophies', but they would also argue that to follow Aquinas faithfully in his interpretations of the identification of the 'what' and the 'that' of God from the side of the 'that', in contrast to its interpretation in Augustinianism from the side of the 'what', is to turn it at once into the fullest of philosophies. Moreover, to say that God is marked by simplicity and perfection in this sense is to say that he is infinite, omnipotent, immutable, eternal, and one. Indeed all these characteristics are but hedges to secure and safeguard the purity and uniqueness of his existential being.

On the other hand, sensible things are God's effects and the nature of these effects should tell us something positively about God. Yet care must be exercised in claiming any knowledge of God in this way. Even if we consider the chief perfections to be found in the universe, that is, in the sphere of God's effects, such perfections as intelligence, will and life, we cannot simply and naively attribute these to God. They are God's effects and not God himself. On the other hand, according to St Thomas, we can affirm these perfections of God in an eminent and inconceivable way, that is, in a way and degree which does not conflict with the simplicity of the divine nature or the identity of essence and existence in God. When we thus predicate perfections of God, we do so not univocally but equivocally, yet in a way which, as St Thomas says, is not altogether equivocal; and the knowledge of God we thus have St Thomas calls analogical. Moreover, these attributes of intelligence, will and life, analogically predicated of God, include what on a mere matter of fact level would come first to mind, the goodness of God and the love of God. God's goodness is his perfection, and his love is his willing of the good; and both are identical with his pure act of being.

8. *Reformation Views*. It would be too much to say that this conception of God is not a specifically Christian one. On the contrary two facts must be noticed, first, that this conception provided the philosophical sub-structure on which were raised the specifically Christian doctrines of christology (q.v.) and the Trinity (q.v.); and, secondly, that the conception itself was developed under the guidance of the biblical revelation, especially that of the OT and, in particular, of Ex. 3. On the other hand, in order to appreciate the full effect of the Reformation on this sphere of Christian belief, it is necessary to keep in view the complete development in this direction. It is true that the Council of Trent was content to reaffirm the Niceno-Constantinopolitan Creed, and that the doctrine of God was not made a matter of dispute by the Churches of the Reformation. None the less there was an underlying process of shaking loose which is evidenced by an elusive but real change of atmosphere. Thus, while the Augsburg Confession continues to speak of a 'Divine essence', the Scots Confession, 1560, is content to declare that 'we confess and acknowledge only one God to whom only we must cleave, whom only we must serve . . .', adding the attributes 'eternal, infinite, unmeasurable, incomprehensible, omnipotent, invisible'; and, although the Westminster Confession extends considerably the list of attributes, each is attested by a scriptural reference. It is noteworthy, too, that in none of these documents is the simplicity of the divine being mentioned. The affirmations tend to be more directly biblical and not to depend so clearly on the systematic presuppositions of a given philosophy.

There is then a recognizable change of atmosphere; but the completed mediaeval doctrine of God contained not only a certain conception of God but a well-established speculative method, a natural theology, and here the beginnings of drastic change can be observed. It is true that even John Calvin retained a natural theology as something 'not to be controverted'. He retained it, however, only to secure man's responsibility for his total sinfulness and depravity, and, so far from being expounded in detail as an independent theme worthy of elucidation, it became nothing more than a thoroughly obscured natural knowledge, and even natural sense, of God. For neither Calvin nor Luther was God basically an abstract essence or a pure act of existing. For the latter he was fundamentally our heavenly Father and for the former our sovereign Creator. Moreover, under this silent untrumpeted revolution, this *fait accompli*, one may not be wrong in detecting another, radical but as yet only implicit. This was an instinctive decision in favour of the priority of will in contrast to the prevailing assumption in both Augustinianism and Thomism of the priority of intellect.

None the less what was implicit did not immediately become explicit. Instead, the age of the Reformers was quickly followed by the development of a Protestant scholasticism in the seventeenth century in which natural theology came once again into its own. Even as late as the second half of the nineteenth century, in the influential theological work of Charles Hodge and his son A. A. Hodge, a place was found for the various proofs of the divine existence. The latter, for example, even included the ontological argument in the form given to it by Descartes, although assigning it only a very ambiguous validity as enhancing the credibility of other arguments. More generally, Hodge held that the various arguments gave '*confirmatory* evidence that God *is* and *complementary* evidence as to *what* God is'. It is noteworthy, too, that Hodge gave importance to the topic known as the evidences of Christianity, by which he meant a rational proof that the God whose existence has already been proved is likely to reveal himself and that this revelation is to be found in the pages of the OT and NT. Thus, the logical continuity of the theological system is maintained in this strand of post-Reformation theology, and the arguments from the occurrence of miracles in connection with the biblical revelation, from the fulfilment of prophecy therein, from 'the miraculous harmony of all the books', and from the moral character and spiritual power both of Christianity and of Christ take the place of Ex. 3.14 ('He Who Is') in providing the link between what can be learned by reason and what is taught by revelation.

9. *Kant and the Moral Argument*. It is impossible in the space of this survey even to mention every school of thought relevant to the topic, such as the teaching of the Cambridge Platonists and the work of the Deists (qq.v.), both in the eighteenth century. Any selection presupposes a fallible judgment. On almost any reckoning, however, the contribution of Immanuel Kant in the same century must receive attention, in the last resort on the ground that, if indeed in the Reformation there was a radical, but as yet implicit revolution in the silent affirmation of the priority of will over intellect, this affirmation was made explicit by Kant, not in the sense of pragmatism, but in that of Kant's famous principle of the primacy of the practical reason. Kant's contribution was both massive and varied, and for this reason estimates of it are apt to be widely diverse. It may be that some degree of objectivity can be achieved if the two main sides of his philosophical system are kept in view. On the speculative side (which made contact not only with Protestant scholasticism but with the whole history of theology), it is well to recall that, at an earlier stage of his own career, Kant had believed in the possibility of natural theology and favoured an argument which curiously combined elements of both the ontological and the cosmological proofs and which, according to Kant, justified belief in a supreme being and creator 'one, simple, immutable, and eternal'. He even allowed a certain validity to the teleological argument in proving the Creator 'one, wise, and good', but held that the evidence of order was not sufficient to justify the traditional

concept of God. All this, however, came before the development of his distinctive critical philosophy. In this, on the speculative side, Kant maintained that in principle there are three types of theistic argument, the ontological (which is based on ideas and takes no account of what exists), the cosmological (which makes use of the fact that something does exist), and the teleological (which takes some account of what it is that does exist), of which he dismissed the first as an illegitimate attempt to move directly from what is intelligible to what actually exists. It is, however, the remaining two arguments which constitute the real strength of speculative theism. Both employ the category of causality, and it is against this common element that Kant concentrated his attack. According to him the category of causality is imposed upon experience by the human understanding and is therefore applicable only to the world of appearance as it presents itself to us in our experience. It may not conceivably be given an application, as in the two arguments, which would transcend the limits of that world and lead to affirmations concerning reality itself.

This is the basic contention in Kant's demolition of natural theology and the speculative method in theology; but the odd thing about this 'demolition' is that, widely as the conclusion has been accepted, the premise on which it was based has been no less widely rejected. Kant's radical separation of a world of appearances or of experience from a real world of things in themselves simply will not do, especially when it means a similar separation between the real 'I' and the empirical 'I'; and yet the rejection of this division has not led to the reinstatement of speculative theism. The criticism of the causal argument can be stated independently of the distinction between appearance and reality; and then it affirms that, while it is legitimate and significant to inquire of anything within the causal series or system what its cause is, it is not legitimate and significant to make the same inquiry regarding the casual series or system itself.

This odd state of affairs draws attention to the massive complexity of Kant's thought and if he denied what he called knowledge he did so to make room for what he called faith and so to give substance to his principle of the primacy of the practical. In other words, if he rejected the three speculative theistic arguments, he immediately replaced them by what has come to be called the *moral* argument. For Kant the complete good was one in which virtue received its due reward of happiness and yet the good will must act virtuously whatever the consequences. This is the antinomy at the heart of the moral life of men, that morality shines out most clearly when it suffers the persecution of fate, and yet no less clearly these things ought not so to be. To this antinomy there is only one solution, the postulate by the practical reason of a God, wise and holy, who ordains the complete good. In more general terms, the situation in which the claim of morality is not vindicated is, it

is argued, morally intolerable, and is, on Kant's interpretation, an absurdity of the practical reason in which it would be illogical to rest.

Kant's rejection of a speculative natural theology, then, has gained a much wider acceptance than the argument with which he supported it, and, in turn, his moral argument has also had a wider influence than the severely rational interpretation of morality which makes it most convincing. As a matter of fact, although all the credit cannot by any means be given to Kant, the theistic outlook which the moral argument suggests has had an even wider effect than the argument itself; and a belief in God as the supreme being, personal, all-wise, all-holy, and all-loving, established itself as the form of theism characteristic of the later nineteenth century and the early part of the twentieth. It may be that this outlook can claim a longer lineage than has so far been suggested and that it can find its ancestry in Greek philosophy; but, if so, it is in the Platonism of the *Laws*, not in Neoplatonism nor in the teaching of Aristotle nor in the so-called 'existentialism' of Aquinas. Even so it has acquired a wealth of content in the interval, to be measured by the difference between the divine soul and the Personal Spirit or Absolute Person. Into the bargain it has received powerful reinforcement from a contemporary movement wherein supremely revelation has come to be conceived in terms not of propositions or divinely guaranteed information but, precisely, of a unique person.

10. *Developments since Kant.* If, however, in the Christian thought of God the absolute has taken the place of the one that is marked by utter simplicity, it has brought its own peculiarly difficult problems and especially the question of immanence and transcendence; but it has done so not by itself but in conjunction with a changed view of the universe. No longer does the latter appear as a panorama of diverse existents, each perhaps possessing what reality it has by virtue of its participation in some eternal and unchanging form. No longer does it appear as a vast collection of different classes of different objects. Rather it confronts modern man as a process, and if he is a theist he finds the origin of the process in God; but then the question faces him whether God transcends the process or is wholly immanent within it. It is well known that Hegel developed the thought of Kant in the latter direction, and the movement of absolute idealism, which had studied long in the school of Hegel, exercised a wide influence on the Christian thought of God. On the other hand, the Christian mind, the more it is governed by the fact of revelation rather than by the logic of philosophical presuppositions, does not readily rest in any such thesis. As one theologian has put it, 'To adopt the hypothesis that the process of nature in all its range is to be accounted for by the intelligent purpose of mind is Theism . . . Yet there are still ambiguities. Is this mind, which pervades, sustains, and directs the whole, so entirely expressed in it, as to have its whole

being in it or is it something over and above all that the Process contains or ever could contain? Plainly it is immanent; is it also transcendent?' (William Temple, *Nature, Man and God*, 1934, p. 257). To this question the writer found himself bound to give an affirmative reply.

The twentieth century has made its own distinctive contribution to this development in the Christian thought of God, a contribution which, without achieving anything like finality, is definitive of a phase in that development; and those who see the situation in this light would probably agree that it is largely the work of one man, Karl Barth. The traditional view posited, as we have seen, both a speculative method and a set of conclusions; and, since the end of the fifth century, through the writer known as the pseudo-Dionysius, this view has been associated with the threefold way of knowing, the way of negation, the way of analogy (*eminentia*) and the way of causality, although so far as the divine nature as distinct from the divine existence is concerned, the last of these has played little part as an independent avenue. Accordingly the knowledge of God as understood by the traditional system can be expressed in the words, 'We learn what God is, partly by removing from the idea we form of him all perfections which belong to creatures, partly by attributing to him, in a more excellent form, all the perfection we find in them' (W. E. Addis and T. Arnold, *A Catholic Dictionary*, 15th ed., 1951, p. 373). Now in a sense, but in a very different one, Barth has his way of negation and his way of analogy. They are, however, ways which have their origin in God's condescension rather than in man's searching aspiration. The element of negation consists in the negation of all natural man's understanding and especially his natural theology. 'This negation,' Barth has said (*Church Dogmatics*, I: *The Doctrine of the Word of God*, 2, 1956, p. 260), 'the negation of man through God's eternal grace and mercy, is only the obverse of his position as a child of God, as a member of the covenant between God and man'; and he has claimed that the *Theological Declaration* of the Synod of Barmen in 1934 was 'the first confessional document' to make this clear (*Church Dogmatics*, II: *The Doctrine of God*, 1, 1957, pp. 172 ff.). On the other hand, there is still a place for analogy, but it is not the traditional analogy of being (*analogia entis*) but the analogy of faith (*analogia fidei*). What this means is that, not directly, but through his works of mercy, God has allowed man to know him and has permitted him to see him through his Word and through it alone; but this human knowing and seeing and apprehending always fall short of what is truly given to man. 'This being known, the divine possibility, even in the Christian remains distinct from the human possibility of knowing: the latter cannot exhaust the former; the resemblance, the analogy remains' (*op. cit.*, I, 1, p. 279); but by the nature of the case it is the analogy of faith, not 'an already existent analogy' but 'an analogy to be created by God's grace, the analogy of grace and

faith' (op. cit. II, 1, p. 85). Moreover, this means that the Christian knowledge of God is not one for which the trinitarian aspect is a further instalment. Rather it is knowledge of God which from the beginning is the knowledge of God as 'Lord, Creator, Reconciler and Redeemer' (*ibid.*, II, 1, pp. 79 ff.). More than that, while this theological approach can speak of the divine simplicity, it rejects the traditional idea and declines to allow it to be 'exalted to the all-controlling principle', holding that it led, not to the abandonment of biblical themes, but to an improper hesitation in their affirmation (*ibid.*, II, 1, pp. 327 ff.). In place of the idea of simplicity appropriate to the idea of God as pure being it speaks of 'the multiplicity, individuality and diversity of the divine perfections' in the inviolable unity of the divine being. Similarly another traditional attribute, the divine incomprehensibility, changes its status, achieving, however, in this case an unprecedented status and indeed 'a basic and determinate position' (*ibid.*, II, 1, pp. 184 ff.).

Many would admit that Barth has brought to completion a phase or rather a strand in the post-Reformation thought of God; and yet finality cannot be claimed for his massive contribution to theology even in its broad outlines. For one thing, in comparison with not a few contemporary articulations of the Christian doctrine of God, Barthian theology in its closely related concepts of God and of revelation stands out as affirming the transcendence of God to the extreme detriment of his immanence. In the second place, in close relation to this theology, in certain cases virtually out of it, there has arisen what is sometimes called 'the new theology' (q.v.), in which in general the immanence of God is vigorously reaffirmed to such an extent that, according to some interpreters, the recognition of transcendence has become highly ambiguous. Sometimes God seems to be pushed over the edge of what is knowable as the unknown Cause of identifiable effects (Rudolf Bultmann); sometimes he is identified with the power of being itself (Paul Tillich). Indeed, not merely in a reaction provoked by Barthianism but also independently, under the influence of such movements as empiricism and linguistic analysis, existentialism, secularism and 'process' philosophy, theology appears to be entering a new phase in which diverse lines of thought sometimes tend to converge towards a position marked, curiously, in respect of the doctrine of God, by something like elements of negation and analogy. The negation is to be found in the radical elimination of all metaphysical structures, whether erected by reason or by revelation, while the element of analogy is to be seen working in quite the opposite direction from the usual one, in that traditional formulations are seen as metaphorical or symbolical representations of human and historical possibilities. Thus the second half of the twentieth century has witnessed the appearance of such titles as *The Secular Meaning of the Gospel, The New Essence of Christianity*, and even *The Gospel of Christian Atheism*.

It ought also to be noticed, however, that if in these changing emphases of modern religious thought the slogan 'the death of God' has even been heard, it has not meant the end of the old theology; and indeed the Thomist outlook has shown itself capable of adaptation to certain pervasive presuppositions and approaches of modern thought. One of these characteristically modern ways of thinking is that which substitutes apprehension for argument, and monstration and manifestation for demonstration; and it is precisely this change that Thomism has proved itself capable of making in the hands of some of its contemporary expositors. For example, it has been argued (cf. E. L. Mascall, *Existence and Analogy*, 1949) that the five ways of St Thomas are not really five separate proofs of the divine existence – otherwise it is difficult to see why, if valid, they do not prove the existence of five separate beings – but rather five ways of looking at the world around us, five aids in jockeying for a position and perspective, so that we see finite being as totally incapable of accounting for its own existence, so that indeed we apprehend God over the horizon of the finite world as the One who not only exists out of himself but accounts for the existence of everything else. Moreover, on this view, the primacy of intellect over will is once again posited, God is understood basically as the self-existent One, and a revised natural theology is enabled to make contact with the God of revelation through the OT name of God, 'I am that I am' or, as it is philosophically translated, 'He who is'.

11. *Conclusion*. This summary account of the movement of Christian thought around the concept of God is not intended to yield conclusions, but it does underline certain basic questions, the question of method which involves the question of the primacy of intellect or will; the resultant concept of God; and, finally, the question of the relationship and the connection between reason and revelation – or between revelation and will. Historically different answers have been given to each of these questions, and this in the course of a highly complex movement of human thought from the primitive witness of Scripture, 'Abba, Father', to the much more sophisticated theological dictum that 'God cannot be expressed but only addressed' (M. Buber, *I and Thou*, 1937, pp. 127, 133). *See also* **Attributes of God; Personality of God; Revelation.**

J. Baillie, *Our Knowledge of God*, 1939; E. Brunner, *Dogmatics*, I: *The Christian Doctrine of God*, 1949; H. H. Farmer, *The World and God*, 1935; É. Gilson, *God and Philosophy*, 1941; H. Gollwitzer, *The Existence of God*, 1965; E. L. Mascall, *He Who is*, 1943; W. I. Matson, *The Existence of God*, 1965; W. R. Matthews, *God in Christian Thought and Experience*, 1930; S. M. Ogden, *The Reality of God*, 1967; W. Temple, *Nature, Man and God*, 1934.

N. H. G. ROBINSON

God of the Gaps, The. *see* Science and Religion; Methodical Atheism.

Godparent. *see* Initiation, Christian.

Gogarten, Friedrich

Friedrich Gogarten (1887–1967), German Protestant theologian who, while beginning his career as a Dialectical theologian with K. Barth and E. Thurneysen, and while remaining loyal to many of the central tenets of the Dialectical school, has progressively broadened in his philosophical and cultural interests. He has been influenced to a large extent by Buber's *I-Thou* philosophy, and in 1953 he defended certain aspects of Bultmann's demythologizing programme in his *Entmythologisierung und Kirche* (ET *Demythologizing and History*, 1955).

JAMES RICHMOND

Good Works

It is common Christian teaching that men are not saved *by* good works but *for* them, and that they cannot do truly good works unless they are in a state of grace (cf. Eph. 2.8 ff.).

The Catholic view is that men can do something to prepare themselves for the reception of grace, and that having received it they can perform good works by which they can merit more of it, until finally they merit eternal life and the blessedness of heaven. Moreover, to be truly good, the works must be done with this end in view. The thought of the beatific vision need not be the conscious motivation of each particular act, but it must be the underlying motivation of the total activity of the agent. When it is, then each and every morally right action can be a meritorious good work. There is, however, a difference in value between different kinds of works, some being more meritorious than others. The 'religious' vocation of the monk, for example, rates more highly than the secular occupations of the father of a family.

Protestantism rejects, of course, the whole conception of merit (q.v.). It also denies the goodness of acts performed with an eye to one's own advantage, even when it is as highly spiritual an advantage as the beatific vision; and it repudiates the notion of any difference in religious value between different sorts of works. Instead, it asserts that truly good works are motivated by loving gratitude to God for the gift of his saving grace. They are performed in willing obedience to the vision God has given us of himself in Christ, not in order to win any advantage for oneself, but solely to please God. There are, moreover, innumerable good works lying around, so to speak, waiting to be done in the world – from sweeping floors to governing states, from bringing up children to tending the sick, or to preaching the gospel – and it is for such works that we are saved.

K. Barth, *Church Dogmatics*, IV: *The Doctrine of Reconciliation*, 2, 1958; A. Richardson, *The Biblical Doctrine of Work*, 1952; A. Ritschl, *The*

Christian Doctrine of Justification and Sanctification, 1958; S. I. Stuber, *Primer on Roman Catholicism for Protestants*, 1965; H. Thielicke, *Theological Ethics*, I, 1966.

P. S. WATSON

Gore, Charles

Charles Gore (1853–1932) records that at the age of eight or nine he came across a book which prescribed 'confession and absolution, fasting, the Real Presence, the devotion of the Three Hours, the use of incense etc., and I felt instinctively and at once that this sort of sacramental religion was the religion for me'. He was consistent in his sacramental devotion and in his strict discipline through all his life as Oxford don, founder of a religious order (the Community of the Resurrection, Mirfield), bishop (successively of Worcester, Birmingham and Oxford) and in retirement. His theology, however, changed, and his essay on the Holy Spirit in *Lux Mundi* (q.v.) which he edited marked the abandonment of Tractarian conservatism for the new biblical criticism. Later he aroused much controversy by his statement of a kenotic theory of the incarnation. In his Bampton Lectures of 1891 and subsequent discussions his intention actually was to rebut the extreme exponents of this theory, and to defend the Chalcedonian position, but he realized that he was departing from conventional language in maintaining that it does not do simply to juxtapose the omniscient Godhead with the limited manhood; the Son must be thought of as personally living, praying, thinking, speaking, acting – even working miracles – under the limitations of manhood. In *The Ministry of the Christian Church* (1888) he upheld conservative views of apostolic succession and the dominical institution of episcopacy. In *The Body of Christ* (1901) he tried to express a doctrine of the real presence in the Eucharist while avoiding transubstantiation. He always had great concern for the social applications of the gospel, preached the need for disestablishment of the Church of England, and for church reform. His last major work was a fine and very influential apologia, *The Reconstruction of Belief* (published separately in three parts 1921–4 and together in 1926).

L. Prestige, *The Life of Charles Gore*, 1935.

R. CANT

Gorham Controversy

The Book of Common Prayer taught the doctrine of baptismal regeneration and the necessity of the sacrament for all. The subtle point had been left undefined whether the efficacy of baptism depended on prevenient grace or solely upon the sacramental act. The question became of great interest with the preaching by evangelicals of rebirth as the consequence of conversion, itself caused by divine grace. High church divines asserted more strongly that regeneration always accompanied baptism. G. C. Gorham (1787–1857), a Cambridge evangelical clergyman, was subjected to a prolonged examination on the subject by Bishop Philpotts before his institution to a living in the diocese of Exeter. When the bishop refused to institute on the ground that Gorham's teaching was contrary to the articles and formularies of the Church of England, Gorham instituted proceedings against him in the provincial ecclesiastical court, and in 1849 judgment was given against Gorham. The court held that regeneration at and through baptism was the church's doctrine, and that the articles were to be interpreted in the light of the Prayer Book (in this case the words of the baptismal service). Gorham appealed to the Judicial Committee of the Privy Council which since 1833 had been the ultimate court of appeal from the provincial church courts. This was the first case in which matters of clerical liberty in interpreting doctrine had been brought before it, and so it aroused great feeling at the time and was regarded as a precedent afterwards. The court refrained from pronouncing on the truth or error of Gorham's teaching, but decreed that it was not inconsistent with the declared doctrine of the Church of England. The judgment concerned itself more with the particular question of prevenient grace than with the more general one of the necessity of sacraments. The judgment caused much dismay among high churchmen, and was the occasion of the secession of Manning to Rome. Later, however, high churchmen as well as others were to benefit from the principles enunciated whereby some latitude of interpretation of doctrine was safeguarded.

J. C. S. Nias, *Gorham and the Bishop of Exeter*, 1951.

R. CANT

Gospel

The English word is derived from the Anglo-Saxon *godspell*, 'God-story', and is used to translate the Greek *euangelion*, 'good tidings'. The theological use of the word is controlled by its biblical usage, beginning with the Greek OT (e.g. Isa. 61.1). The word is used in the NT for the good news of the kingdom of God, proclaimed by Jesus himself (e.g. Mark 1.15), and for the apostolic proclamation of the good news about Jesus, especially his resurrection from the dead (e.g. Rom. 1.1–5). For the biblical meaning *see* Alan Richardson, 'Gospel', *TWBB*; *see also* **Kerygma**.

EDITOR

Grace

1. *General Meaning*. In general grace (Latin: *gratia*; Greek: *charis*; Hebrew: *chen*) means favour freely shown, especially by a superior to an inferior. In the NT, it denotes primarily the favour and kindness of God, freely shown to men in the incarnate life and atoning death of his Son (II Cor. 8.9; Phil. 2.6 ff.). This is a stupendous example of favour freely shown by a superior to an inferior. For if as God's creatures we might reasonably expect him to show some favour to us, yet as sinful, ungodly creatures and enemies of

God (Rom. 5.6–10) we could deserve nothing but his utmost disfavour. Nevertheless, 'God so loved the world that he gave his only Son . . . not to condemn the world, but that the world might be saved through him' (John 3.16 f.). That is grace. It is the redemptive activity of divine love.

To describe this activity of God's love as grace is to emphasize the freedom of it. For grace, as St Augustine says, is not grace unless it is *gratis*. (*a*) God's love is free in that it is unmerited. God is not moved to love us by our virtues, nor does he withhold his love from us because of our vices. He loves us freely, regardless of our deserts. Naturally he wants us to be good and not bad – just as human parents who love their children want them to be good – and he therefore disciplines us, sometimes severely; but that is because he loves us, not in order that he may be able to love us. (*b*) God's love is free in that it is unrestricted. It is not directed only to his chosen people, Israel, but to all mankind and everyman. When God chose Israel to be his own peculiar people (*see* **Predestination**), this was not an act of favouritism. He chose Israel for salvation, certainly, but also to be the bearer of salvation to the world – a task which involved a good deal of suffering.

Why he chose Israel rather than any other people, we do not know; but we do know it was not for any virtue or worthiness of theirs (Deut. 7.7). It was an act of pure grace – which again and again they repaid with ingratitude and disobedience, as the prophets repeatedly complain; and for this, too, they had to suffer. God's love is no easy-going sentimentality. It finds expression in judgment and chastisement as well as mercy and deliverance, in wrath (q.v.) as well as grace. But wrath, in Luther's phrase, is God's 'strange work' (*opus alienum*) in contrast to his 'proper work' (*opus proprium*) of grace, which is the most characteristic expression of his love.

This divine love, active throughout the history of ancient Israel, finds its supreme manifestation in the grace of our Lord Jesus Christ. It is active also among us today, as it has been throughout the history of the Christian Church, wherever the gospel of Christ is proclaimed by preaching, teaching and sacrament. Indeed, the proclamation of the gospel is itself an act of grace, that is, of God himself in his grace (I Cor. 15.10; II Cor. 5.18 ff.). Hence the spoken words and sacramental acts through which it is proclaimed are called *means of grace*, as being instruments and vehicles whereby God's redeeming love is brought home to us, offered and given to us, if only we will receive it.

To those who do receive it, the grace of God means first and foremost the forgiveness of sins and a new standing with God (justification). They enter into a relationship with God which is determined solely by his grace, and in which they can be described as in a *state of grace*. This same grace then becomes a power in their lives, producing a new outlook, attitude, spirit and temper like God's own (sanctification). At the same time, their eyes are opened to see God's grace manifested in the world around them, as Christ did. For it is a sign of his grace when God 'makes his sun rise on the evil and the good, and sends rain on the just and on the unjust' (Matt. 5.45). It is a sign that God distributes his gifts, not according to the deserts of men, but according to his own will of love. God *is* love (I John 4.8, 16), and his love for us does not depend on what we are but on what he is. Hence, as Luther puts it: Sinners are not loved because they are lovable, they are lovable because they are loved.

2. *Usage in Protestantism and Catholicism.* In Protestantism, grace has mainly been understood in terms of God's goodwill or favourable regard, communicated primarily by the spoken word, and with the accent on the forgiveness of sins and the restoration of the sinner to favour with God. In Catholicism, the main emphasis has been on grace as a power, conveyed primarily through the sacraments, and often described in terms suggestive of a metaphysical substance, not to say quasi-physical force. Again, in the Protestant view, grace is received and operates through faith alone, to the total exclusion of man's works and merits, whereas in Catholic thought, faith and works belong together both as regards the initial reception and the subsequent increase of grace. The exclusive connection of grace with faith (q.v.) is one of the most important points of difference between Protestantism and Catholicism, since in the latter, grace is always more or less bound up with merit (q.v.).

Both Catholic and Protestant theologians attach various adjectives to grace, apparently implying that there are different kinds of grace; but the intention is rather to describe different operations or effects of grace, of which the following are among the more important.

(*a*) *Actual Grace.* Catholic: a supernatural help given by God to enable a person to avoid sin or to perform some particular action which tends towards his salvation; it is a gift internal to the person and of a transient nature.

(*b*) *Habitual Grace. See below, Sanctifying Grace.*

(*c*) *Irresistible Grace.* A term associated particularly with St Augustine and John Calvin. Both held that grace might work effectively in a man, producing faith and the fruit of the Spirit, without being any guarantee of his ultimate salvation; for unless he was among the elect, that is, predestined to eternal life, he could fall away from grace. In fact, even the elect themselves would fall if God's grace did not work irresistibly to give them final perseverance (q.v.).

(*d*) *Prevenient Grace.* The activity of God's grace preceding or going before (archaically: 'preventing') any movement of man towards God or goodness. This is vividly symbolized in infant baptism, where God acts towards the infant that has no awareness even that God exists. Opinions differ as to the extent and the means of this activity, but there would be widespread agreement today: that it is universal, God seeking everywhere to move sinners to repentance, draw unbelievers to faith, and quicken the conscience of both Christians and non-Christians; that it may operate through outward means (e.g. the words and actions of other persons), or by some more direct influence on a man's interior life; and that it does not operate coercively or irresistibly.

(*e*) *Sanctifying Grace.* Catholic: a supernatural quality added to the soul, uniting it to Christ and making it acceptable to God (*see* **Justification** [3]), by producing in it a new 'habit' (*habitus*) or disposition, giving it powers of supernatural action in the form of 'infused virtues' (*see* **Infusion**), and directing its activities to their true end, the Vision of God. Protestant: the work of the Holy Spirit in the justified believer, purging him of sin and effecting his sanctification (q.v.).

(*f*) *Sufficient Grace.* Catholic: a grace which gives the power to do a thing, but which is not made use of. (Where it is made use of it is called Efficacious Grace.) Sufficient Actual Grace (*see above*) is given to all men, though how it is given we may be content not to know. Even the worst of sinners have sufficient grace to enable them to repent, and the heathen have sufficient grace to enable them to make the minimal act of faith that is absolutely necessary for salvation (*see* **Faith** [1]).

D. M. Baillie, *God Was in Christ*, 1948; J. Daujat, *The Theology of Grace*, 1959; H. D. Gray, *The Christian Doctrine of Grace,* 1949; D. Hardman, *The Christian Doctrine of Grace*, 1947; K. E. Skyddsgaard, *One in Christ*, 1957; C. R. Smith, *The Bible Doctrine of Grace*, 1956; G. Smith, ed., *The Teaching of the Catholic Church*, 2 vols., 1948; P. S. Watson, *The Concept of Grace*, 1960; W. T. Whitley, ed., *The Doctrine of Grace*, 1932.

P. S. WATSON

Grosseteste, Robert

A scholar primarily, Grosseteste (c. 1175–1253) taught during 1224–35 at the Franciscan house of studies at Oxford, where his close friend was Adam Marsh, with whom he went to the Council of Lyon in 1245; here he also knew Simon de Montfort. In 1235 he became bishop of Lincoln, the largest diocese in England, which included Oxford. He carried out severe reforms: Matthew Paris called him 'the bishop to whom quiet is a thing unknown'. In 1250 he visited Rome, making a famous oration *de corruptelis ecclesiae* against the system of provisions to foreign benefices.

He was a leading scientist (mathematics, optics, astronomy), with Roger Bacon as a pupil, and also an important translator from Greek and commentator (especially upon Aristotle's *Ethics* and Physics and the works of Dionysius the Areopagite). His theology included studies of the soul, intelligence, free will, potency/act, causality, truth. Franciscan in view, he taught the primacy of will over intellect (*see* **Duns Scotus**). In *de Luce* he followed Augustine and the Neoplatonists in a metaphysic of light, which the gothic cathedral builders were quick to use: he called light the nearest thing to pure form – *corpus spirituale, spiritus corporalis.* His pastoral writing covered confession and purgatory, the Eucharist and devotional works. It was his use of Augustinian Neoplatonism, Aristotelianism and Christian Revelation together as a synthesis, which made his work remarkable.

D. A. Callus, ed., *Robert Grosseteste, Scholar and Bishop*, 1955; F. C. Copleston, *History of Philosophy*, II, 1950, pp. 228–32; A. C. Crombie, *Robert Grosseteste and the Origins of Experimental Science, 1100–1700*, 1953; H. R. Luard, *Roberti Grosseteste Epistolae*, 1861 (with a good preface); J. R. H. Moorman, *Christian Life in England in the Thirteenth Century*, 1955; D. E. Sharp, *Franciscan Philosophy at Oxford in the Thirteenth Century*, 1930; F. S. Stephenson, *Robert Grosseteste*, 1899; S. Hamilton Thomson, *The Writings of Robert Grosseteste*, 1940; D. A. Calus, *Oxoniensia,* X (1945), 42–72; A. C. Crombie, *EB,* 1964; A. Gatard, *DTC,* VI, cols. 1885–7; H. R. Luard, *DNB,* VIII, pp. 718–21.

ALBERIC STACPOOLE, OSB

Grotius, Hugo (Huig van Groot)

Hugo Grotius (1583–1645), precocious student at Leyden and Orleans, at seventeen took a doctorate in law and became an advocate. He wrote numerous Latin poems and plays, of which *Adamus exsul* (1601) is best known. His employment on embassies began when he was fifteen. At eighteen, taking a lively interest in religious affairs, he resolved to write 'nothing that is not Catholic and ecumenical'. In Netherlands disputes he favoured Arminianism and Oldenbarnevelt's pro-Arminian policy, and on that stateman's execution Grotius was imprisoned, 29 August 1618. His wife (Marie Reigersberg) devised his escape from Loevestein Castle, 22 March 1621. He spent most of his later life in Paris, where he served as Swedish ambassador, 1634–44. His writings show both scholarship and originality. The *De jure belli et pacis* (1625) remains a fundamental text for international law. The earlier *De veritate religionis Christianae* (1622) ably asserts the historic validation of Christianity and its superiority to other religions. He entertained ambitious schemes for Christian unity, best exemplified by his *Via et votum ad pacem ecclesiasticam* (1642).

W. S. M. Knight, *Life and Works of Hugo Grotius,* 1925; R. W. Lee, *Hugo Grotius*, British Academy Proceedings XVI, 1930; F. Blanke, 'Hugo Grotius und die Einigung der christliches Kirchen', *Reformatio,* 1953, pp. 595–609.

J. T. MCNEILL

Guilt

The term 'guilt' may be used in different contexts with important differences in meaning. Governmental authorities define guilt rather precisely in terms of legal codes and apportion punishments to correlate with the seriousness of the crime and the amount of responsibility involved. Ethical guilt is not synonymous with legal guilt. We often judge a man to be ethically guilty even when he is legally innocent. A man is normally judged ethically if, through his free choice, he violates a moral law that he knows. Another dimension of guilt occurs in personal relationships where a man violates a relationship with another person and experiences guilt in terms of estrangement from the other. This differs from either ethical or legal guilt. An alcoholic drinks from compulsion and not from free choice so that, ethically speaking, we could say that he is not guilty. But such a man experiences guilt as estrangement from his wife and children because his action has broken·the harmony of his relationships with them.

Theological discussion needs to notice the different meanings of the term guilt. In theology guilt has a connotation that is more analogous to guilt in personal relations than it is to guilt in either ethical or legal contexts. Before God man experiences guilt in the form of his estrangement from the righteousness of God. He knows himself to be unworthy of fellowship with God. Man's problem is not primarily the fact that he has broken God's laws so it is useless for him to plead that his sins have been 'small ones'. His primary guilt lies in the fact that he is a prodigal in a far country. His guilt can only be removed when the Father's forgiveness receives him home as a son. Jesus equated the guilt of a man who has lust in his heart with the guilt of a man who actually commits adultery (Matt. 5.28). To understand this, we must see that Jesus is speaking theologically. Ethically and legally, of course, there is a vast difference between the guilt in the two cases. Jesus' point is that both men are equally alienated from God.

When Protestantism rejected the Catholic distinction between mortal and venial sins, it was thinking in exclusively theological terms. Protestants recognize that particular sins may differ in terms of their seriousness if weighed legally or ethically. But in so far as guilt means a separation from God, all sinners are equally guilty (*see also* **Mortal Sin**).

In the history of theology it has been widely held by both Catholics and Protestants that each child inherits Adam's guilt. Where this is held, baptism is often seen as necessary to remove the inherited guilt. If a child dies unbaptized it may be impossible for him to go to heaven. This doctrine has been widely rejected in modern theology. In society a man does share the guilt for crimes committed by his social group, but it is never just to hold a man guilty of what happened before he was born. Today Protestants and Catholics are almost unanimous in rejecting the view that Jews living today are guilty of crucifying Jesus. Increasingly theologians who defend the doctrine of original sin are desirous of dividing between inherited guilt and sin. Man may inherit the nature and/or the situation in which sin is inevitable, but he does not become guilty until he acts to alienate himself from God.

With the rise of modern psychotherapy the term guilt has taken on further connotations and new problems have been raised for theology.

Psychotherapists tend to concentrate upon feelings of guilt which can be a cause of psychological illness. Such guilt-feelings are not necessarily correlated to objective guilt. Whereas one man may be guilty without feeling guilty, another man may have a deep feeling of guilt without in fact being guilty. Various areas of tension have arisen between theology and psychotherapy. Theology is criticized by psychotherapists for creating unwarranted guilt-feelings that lead to illness. Psychotherapy is charged by theology with undermining ethical concern by easing the guilt-feelings of the guilty. Further conversation between the two disciplines is necessary. Theology needs to learn more about the psychological dynamics of the one who feels guilty. Psychotherapy needs to be reminded that other persons are involved in all situations where there is guilt. See *also* **Man, Doctrine of.**

G. Aulén, *The Faith of the Christian Church*, ET, 2nd ed., 1961, ch. 32; R. C. Johnson, *The Meaning of Christ*, 1966, ch. 3; R. Niebuhr, *The Nature and Destiny of Man*, I, 1941, chs. 8–9.

WILLIAM HORDERN

Hagiography, Hagiology

Hagiography, Hagiology are derived from the Greek words *hagios*, 'holy', 'saint', *grapho*, 'to write', and *logia*, 'discourse'. These words connote the writing of the lives of the saints and the study of them. This was a considerable industry from early times until the close of the Middle Ages; legendary and indeed totally fictitious elements abounded, until in the seventeenth century a critical attitude began to develop among the Bollandists (the Jesuit editors of the *Acta Sanctorum*, so called after the originator of the series, John van Bolland, 1596–1665). *Foxe's Book of Martyrs* (1563) might be regarded as a kind of Protestant hagiography; but in general Protestants detested the cult of the saints, whom they generally regarded as dead Roman Catholics.

EDITOR

Hamann. Johann Georg

Johann Georg Hamann (1730–1788), German philosopher of religion, was a contemporary and friend of I. Kant at Königsberg. Hamann, having rejected Kant's rationalistic and moralistic account of religion, made ideas such as 'encounter', 'immediacy' and 'experience' central in his religious thought. Hamann's thinking was especially influential upon S. Kierkegaard (1813–1855), who quotes his writings with approval. See **Kierkegaard, S.A.**

R. Gregor Smith, *Johann Georg Hamann: A Study in Christian Existence*, 1960.

JAMES RICHMOND

Harnack, Adolf von

Harnack (1851–1930), German ecclesiastical historian and systematic theologian, was one of the most distinguished members of the Ritschlian theological school. In his celebrated works on early Church history. Harnack applied the Ritschlian presupposition that from earliest times Christian dogma had been affected and infected by alien Greek metaphysical thinking, to its great detriment. As a typically nineteenth-century liberal theologian he delivered and published a set of lectures on basic Christianity (*Das Wesen des Christentums*, 1900; ET, *What is Christianity?*; trans. T. B. Saunders, Harper Torchbooks ed., 1957), in which he stressed the ideas of the divine fatherhood, the universal human brotherhood, and man's duty to his neighbour, while, in Ritschlian fashion, depreciating the ontological elements in Christian teaching. *See* **Liberal Protestantism; Ritschl, A.; Jesus of History, The.**

JAMES RICHMOND

Healing. *see* Spiritual Healing.

Heaven and Hell

In the NT spatiality is by no means an essential feature of heaven. The pictures of heaven which we meet in Revelation are pictures, not photographs. The writers of the NT were familiar, of course, with contemporary Jewish speculations about the various heavens existing above the earth: Paul refers to 'the third heaven' in II Cor. 12.2, and in Eph. 4.10 Christ is described as having ascended 'far above all the heavens'. But the very fact that he has ascended far above them suggests that he has thereby transcended space; and in Eph. 2.6 Christians are described as having been already made to sit with Christ 'in the heavenly places'. If therefore we can in some sense be in heaven already before we experience physical death, we have no reason to be troubled as to whether heaven is a place or a state. Heaven in the NT is in fact the consummation; and because of the highly eschatological nature of NT thought, the consummation is in some sense already beginning to be experienced.

This profound and sensitive conception of heaven was not maintained in the ensuing centuries of the Church's existence. Once Christians began to look forward to a long period of history lying before the Church, the temptation to map out what came increasingly to be regarded as 'the future life' grew very strong indeed. Augustine in *The City of God* mentions certain 'secret havens and abodes' where the souls of the faithful departed await the last judgment (xii.9); traditional mediaeval theology held that some souls, having been cleansed made to of their sins in purgatory, have already reached heaven, though they still await their bodies. When we add that the exceptions to this condition are Enoch, Elijah, and the Blessed Virgin Mary, we realize that we are already in the realm of mythology, not to say fantasy. Modern theology envisages heaven as the natural consummation of the Christian life, not as the carrot held before the donkey to persuade him to stumble onwards. The Marxist accusation that Christ-

ianity preaches 'pie in the sky when you die' may have been true of certain forms of Christianity in the past, but is certainly not true now. On the contrary, we suffer from a silence in the pulpit on the subject of heaven. Perhaps it may come into its own again by means of the liturgical revival. Charles Wesley's fine conception of the Eucharist as 'the antepast of heaven' is better appreciated today than when he wrote, and liturgiologists confirm that this was an important element in the primitive Eucharist.

The NT witness on the subject of hell is more ambiguous. The pictures of the lake of fire in Revelation are certainly symbolical, but we do find the phrase 'eternal punishment' in Matt. 25.46. Whether Jesus himself actually used this phrase may be doubted, and in any case the punishment seems to be one which belongs to this aeon. Even in the Apocalypse, at the very end of the age, when God is all in all, there are no more obstacles to his reign, which would seem to carry the implication that hell also has ceased to exist. It is noteworthy that in the NT we do not find hell fire to be a part of the primitive preaching. The author of the Epistle to the Hebrews comes near to attempting to frighten people into the kingdom – or rather frighten them from falling away from it; *see* Heb. 2.1 – 3. There are also some indications in the NT that the ultimate fate of those who refuse God's offer of salvation may be annihilation rather than eternal punishment, e.g. II Thess. 2.8. In any case the symbols for hell are taken from contemporary Jewish thought; the Jews in their turn seem to have based their speculations on the substitution of Gehenna for the pre-exilic *She'ol* (the place of the dead); and Gehenna is surely a place of destruction rather than of unending torment.

It was no doubt inevitable that the images of fire, worm, and grinding of teeth which we meet in the NT should have been understood in a literal sense by later ages. Christians were, after all, chiefly marked off from competing purveyors of religion in the ancient world by their emphasis on the importance of moral choice. We find Augustine devoting a distressing amount of space in *The City of God* to proving that the fire of hell is something physical or quasi-physical. The Scholastics distinguished two elements in the pains of hell, *poena damni*, which was the sense of separation from God, and *poena sensus*, which was some sort of external agent of torment. Till very recently the fear of hell was considered a perfectly respectable inducement towards conversion. One of the spiritual exercises of Ignatius Loyola consists largely of an imaginative reconstruction of the conditions of penal fire, etc. The weakening of belief in the verbal inspiration of the Bible has meant that hell fire has largely disappeared from the theological scene. This is not all gain: the NT language about hell is symbolic, but symbolic of what? Most modern theologians would say that hell means simply separation from God. It is not a punishment which God arbitrarily inflicts; it is what we do to ourselves. From this it follows of course that hell (like heaven) begins in this life.

Indeed there are traces of this belief in the NT, e.g. John 3.36. Throughout his period on earth each man is either moving towards life or towards death, and judgment is in that sense already begun the moment we are born. But as long as we are on earth the process is reversible. This would seem to imply that final loss, not eternal punishment, is the fate of those who ultimately refuse. It is very remarkable that an atheist writer, Jean-Paul Sartre in his play *No Exit*, has probably come as near as any modern theologian to a representation of hell that does justice to NT insights.

Just as the sharp lines and clear contrasts of the literalistic doctrine of hell have been softened and blurred by the necessity of adopting a critical approach to the Bible, so also with the doctrine of judgment. We have suggested that judgment is always taking place; thus both death itself and the last judgment must be looked on as a process by which an already existing state of affairs is fully and ultimately revealed, rather than as acts of forensic conviction and sentencing. Once again we find that the modern attitude enables us to recover an essential insight of the NT. Compare John 3.19: 'And this is the judgment, that the light has come into the world, and men loved darkness rather than light, because their deeds were evil' – a classic passage for the exposition of realized eschatology in the sphere of judgment. But when we go on to ask 'Are there many that shall be saved?', we get no clearer answer from the NT than the disciples did from their master. There runs through the entire NT a strong strain of predestinarian belief, as evident (if we follow D. E. Nineham) in Mark as in John. And it should hardly be necessary to point out how deeply this strain of thought has influenced the theological development of the West. Whether we turn to Augustine or Aquinas or Calvin, we can scarcely avoid the conclusion that in their view only some are predestined to eternal life, and that the rest are predestined to eternal loss. It is difficult to resist the conclusion that the NT on the whole is not on the side of universalism, the belief that ultimately all men will be saved. There are some witnesses on the side of universalism, it is true, notably the author of the Pastoral Epistles, one of whose great virtues is his emphasis on the universality of salvation. From the time of Origen at least, universalism has always had its defenders in the Church, and it must never be treated as a heresy. Ultimately of course the most honest thing is to admit agnosticism as to whether all men are to be saved or not. Christians are not committed to the belief that all the heathen are doomed to perish, despite the considerable part which this belief played as a motive for the missionary activity of the last century. The one important point to hold on to is that, whether in this life or the next, God as revealed in Christ is the ultimate norm by which men will be judged. *See also* **Wrath of God.**

John Baillie, *And the Life Everlasting*, 1934; A. T. Hanson, *The Wrath of the Lamb*, 1957.

                                                    A. T. HANSON

Hedonism

Hedonism is the doctrine that pleasure, and only pleasure, is intrinsically good. To the hedonist, therefore, the goal of moral endeavour is the increase of pleasurable experience and the decrease of painful and unpleasant experience. If we ask, '*Whose* experience?', different answers are given by different types of hedonist. The *egoistic hedonist* argues that the object of concern should be the agent's own well-being. The *psychological hedonist* argues that every man is so constituted – psychologically and physiologically – that he *can* desire only his own individual pleasure. *Altruistic hedonism* claims, in contrast, that all duties are duties to increase the happiness of others: and *universalistic hedonism* (or 'hedonistic utilitarianism') holds that our duties are to increase the general happiness – that is, with respect both to self and to others.

The hedonist does not regard himself as committed to a policy of 'eat, drink and be merry'. As Bentham's 'felicific calculus' insisted, it is not merely the intensity of pleasure that needs to be considered, but also such factors as likely duration, 'propinquity or remoteness' and fecundity. J. S. Mill wished further to distinguish pleasures of higher and lower quality. Critics have questioned whether hedonism can make this distinction consistently – without, that is, introducing supplementary and non-hedonistic criteria. (For a very subtle and sophisticated defence of a hedonistic utilitarian position, *see* H. Sidgwick, *The Methods of Ethics*, 1874.)

A thoroughgoing hedonist may attach value to things other than pleasure, for example, knowledge, freedom, justice; but only in so far as they are instrumental to pleasure. The debate over hedonism is, therefore, in part a dispute whether these goods have instrumental value only, or are desirable *independently* of their tendency to produce pleasure.

The psychological hedonist, in arguing that no action can be performed unless the agent sees in it the prospect of pleasure, may be guilty of an important confusion. It is one thing to desire something, for example, a meal, and another thing to desire the pleasure of eating the meal. Clearly, all desire is not for pleasure in the latter sense. Again, the satisfying of my desire to know something may bring me pleasure, but I may have sought the knowledge for its own sake and not at all for the pleasure.

The literature on hedonism is vast: good discussions (with references) can be found in J. Hospers, *Human Conduct*, 1963; P. H. Nowell-Smith, *Ethics*, 1954; G. H. von Wright, *The Varieties of Goodness*, 1963.

                                                    R. W. HEPBURN

Hegel, Georg Wilhelm Friedrich

Hegel (1770–1831), German metaphysician, tried to comprehend within one system the whole of reality (defined as the rational) and all human knowledge; within this system he stressed such ideas as becoming, development, and process, but he emphasized above all else unity and comprehensiveness. His effect on subsequent nineteenth-century theology was great; among the more conservative Hegelian theologians were A. E. Biedermann (1819–1885) and P. K. Marheineke (1780–1846), but his ideas were developed in a more radical direction by D. F. Strauss (1808–1874) and L. A. Feuerbach (1804–1872) (qq.v.). His influence on British thought was most marked in the British Absolute Idealist tradition. See **Baur, F. C.; Feuerbach, L. A.; Liberal Protestantism; Tübingen School.**

JAMES RICHMOND

Heidegger, Martin

Martin Heidegger (1889–), German existentialist philosopher, is a significant figure in contemporary theology, for his philosophical categories have been used by R. Bultmann in his interpretation of the NT. See **Demythologizing; Existentialism; Hermeneutics.**

JAMES RICHMOND

Heidelberg Catechism

This important Reformed Church statement of doctrine was framed by Zacharias Ursinus and Casper Olevianus apparently with the co-operation of the whole theological faculty of Heidelberg in 1562. The German text with a preface by the Elector Frederick III was adopted by a synod at Heidelberg, 19 January 1563. It was designed to serve as a guide to preachers as well as a manual of instruction and confession of faith. The first personal pronoun, usually in the singular, is employed in each answer, enhancing the tone of Christian commitment and devotion. Part I is entitled 'Of Man's Misery', Part II (questions 12–85) 'Of Man's Redemption', and Part III (86–129) 'Of Thankfulness'. The principal topics of theology are expounded in Part II, which includes the Apostles' Creed as 'the articles of our catholic undoubted Christian faith' (23). The interpretation of the Creed shows the influence of Calvin. Thus the Lord's Supper makes us partakers of Christ's true body and blood through the working of the Holy Ghost, and the Descent into Hell is explained as Christ's 'unspeakable anguish on the Cross and before'.

In Part III, thankfulness is the heartfelt joy with which we do good works in response to divine grace. This section traverses the Ten Commandments and the Lord's Prayer. For use in sermons the Catechism was published with fifty-two portions marked for the annual round of Sundays. It came into general use in the German Reformed Church and was adopted in some churches of Hungary, Poland and the Swiss cantons. In 1591 it was by royal authority printed in English for the Church of Scotland.

B. Thompson, H. Berkhof, E. Schweizer and H. C. Hageman, *Essays on the Heidelberg Catechism,*

1963; T. F. Torrance, *The School of Faith,* 1959.

J. T. MCNEILL

Heilsgeschichte

The term, a German word, literally meaning 'salvation-history', was coined in the eighteenth century and used in the nineteenth century by certain theologians who rejected Schleiermacher's attempt to rest theology upon religious feeling and emphasized the primacy of the biblical historical revelation. Today it is used of two quite opposed theological views (hence the confusion over the meaning of the term). (1) Barth and his followers conceive of the events of sacred history, such as incarnation, redemption, etc., as taking place in a supra-historical sphere, inaccessible to secular historical research and known only to faith. This conception enables them to be quite indifferent to the question of the historicity of the events recorded in the Gospels and provides an escape from the pressures of positivistic historicism (*see* **History, Problem of**). The critics of this view regard it as a kind of twentieth-century docetism (q.v.). (2) The other view (held by Oscar Cullmann and others) insists that the total history of revelation and salvation is connected with real events in actual history, of which Christ is both the centre and the culmination. From all the variety of individual NT elements there emerges one picture of the Christ-event from pre-existence to *parousia*. This view does not make the Christian religion dependent upon the vicissitudes of historical research; it is faith in Christ which makes sense of the witness of the biblical records, and faith is essential to the right understanding of their historical content. The stress is upon the acts of God in history.

O. Cullmann, *Christ and Time,* ET, 1951; *The Christology of the New Testament,* ET, 1959; *Salvation in History,* ET, 1967; W. Pannenberg, *Jesus God and Man,* ET, 1968; Alan Richardson, *The Bible in the Age of Science,* 1961, ch. 6; G. Ernest Wright, *God Who Acts: Biblical Theology as Recital,* 1962.

EDITOR

Heim, Karl

Karl Heim (1874–), German systematic theologian, in trying to interpret the Christian Faith in the light of modern science, has utilized Buber's distinction between *I-Thou* and *I-It*, in which man is related to other persons and to objects respectively; Heim speaks of these as 'spaces', but adds to them a third, the 'supra-polar space', in which man is related to God.

JAMES RICHMOND

Hell. *see* Heaven and Hell.

Henotheism

The Greek form of the more familiar **Monotheism** (*see* **God**).

Herder, Johann Gottfried

J. G. Herder (1744–1803), philosopher of history
of the German Enlightenment (*Aufklärung*), is
significant for modern theology in two ways: first,
he analysed historical process as analogous with
scientific process, thus stimulating interest in the
philosophy of history, and evoking in opposition
to his own views an understanding of history as
concerned essentially with *human* freedom, decision and action; secondly, he advocated critical,
scholarly and historical study of the scriptures
which, he insisted, was quite compatible with the
acceptance of orthodox Christian beliefs. He thus
occupies a place in the development of modern
critical biblical scholarship.

R. G. Collingwood, *The Idea of History*, 1946.

JAMES RICHMOND

Heresy. see Orthodoxy.

Hermeneutics

The word is derived from the Greek *hermeneus*, an
interpreter, which in its turn is derived from
Hermes, the divine messenger of the gods and
patron of eloquence (called Mercury by the
Romans). Hermeneutics is thus the science and
art of interpretation, especially of ancient writings,
which were held to contain divine truth. In the
ancient world it was held that the men of old time
stood nearer to the source of truth than later
generations can hope to do, and therefore what
has been handed down from their 'treasury' is
worthy of special veneration and careful explication (*cf.* Plato, *Philebus* 16 c, 5–9; *Phaedrus* 274c,
1; Aristotle, *Metaphysics* 1074 b, 1). In the golden
age near the beginning of the world-cycle men
stood nearer to the gods and were in a position to
hand down the unsullied truth; but their words
must be rightly interpreted. The Christian Church,
of course, naturally took over this assumption; it
fitted in well with the doctrine of the faith once
delivered to the saints, the sacred history written
down in Scripture by the prophets and apostles
who stood so near to God. It was therefore of the
utmost importance to discover and apply the
correct principles for the interpretation (or
exegesis) of Scripture; and thus hermeneutics became a very important part of the study of
theology. The various methods of interpreting
Scripture – the literal, the allegorical, the analogical, the anagogical (or spiritual, mystical) – all
had to be carefully assessed and employed
according to the rules of this or that school of
interpretation. So things continued until the
Enlightenment, or later in conservative quarters.

With the rise of the critico-historical method of
scriptural investigation in the nineteenth century
an entirely new aim was set before biblical
scholars: to understand what the writer was saying against the background of his own unsophisticated and pre-scientific times. The idea that
because the writings were ancient they were therefore nearer to the divine truth was now held to be

the reverse of the facts. Exegesis became more a
matter of relating the scriptural sayings to their
historical background and less a matter of asking
about their truth as revelation. This latter question
was left to the dogmatic theologian; it did not
concern the biblical scholar as such, since any
preoccupation with the question of the truth of the
Scriptures *for us* would compromise the scientific
integrity of his research. One of the characteristic
features of the Liberal Protestant era was the gap
which had opened between the biblical exegete
and the dogmatic theologian.

The New Hermeneutics. In recent years, however, a revival of interest in biblical hermeneutics
has been stimulated in the existentialist theology
of Rudolf Bultmann and his school. Gerhard
Ebeling and Ernst Fuchs have followed further in
the direction pointed out by Martin Heidegger
than Bultmann himself was prepared to go. For
Heidegger language is not a game which we play,
making up the rules as we go along; it constitutes
our humanity, which he defines as the place where
'being' speaks. Language is prior to humanity,
because it fashions human understanding. Man's
existence is defined by his linguisticality. Language is the instrument through which 'being' itself communicates with our existence and imparts
understanding. Man's existence becomes 'authentic' when in his linguistic responsibility he becomes the mouthpiece ('voice') of 'being'. Hence
the poet becomes the true priest of mankind,
because through him the word of 'being' is
mediated. The mythology of Hermes as the herald
of the gods, like so much of the Greek poetic
mythology, is full of meaning for Heidegger.

If we substitute for Heidegger's romantic
notions about the poets the theme of the authentic
voice of prophecy in the biblical sense, we can see
how the new hermeneutics can develop: the
authentic word of the past, which in happening
once became an event which shaped the course of
history, can become through the interpretative
work of the 'hermeneut' a word-event again
today. The word-event which happened long ago
and in happening became the text can challenge
the existence of the interpreter himself and then
the existence of those to whom he interprets the
text. This involves something more than the
understanding of the words of (say) Amos in
their historical context; it means letting the word
of Amos speak to our existence in our own historical context. Thus, in the hands of Fuchs a theology
of the word of God may open up lines of advance
in the 'new quest of the historical Jesus' by showing how the authentic words of Jesus are identifiable with his actions. When the hermeneutical
task is conceived in this way, the interpreter of
Scripture becomes himself 'a learner in the language school of faith': the critico-historical
biblical scholar and the dogmatic theologian are
one and the same person. In the words of Ebeling,
'The hermeneutic task consists for theology in
nothing else but in understanding the *Gospel* as
addressed to *modern* man.' It is not sufficient to
demythologize the gospel; it must be made to

speak in terms of the existential situation of the men of today. Thus, the hermeneutic task is basically the same activity as that of the preacher; both presuppose historical, critical scholarship of the highest quality *and also* insight into our existential situation in the modern world. Scholarship is only the threshold of interpretation, but without it we cannot properly begin the task of translating the word of understanding which once happened into word-events today, so that the word which once was event before it became 'text' may be liberated from imprisonment in the letter and become word-event again. This is the task of hermeneutics and of preaching; it is the task of theology as such. If this conception of the nature of hermeneutics is accepted, it is clear that hermeneutics will have become the whole of dogmatics, while historico-critical scholarship will be merely ancillary to hermeneutics. *See also* **Dogmatics.**

Carl E. Braaten, *History and Hermeneutics,* 1968; R. Bultmann, 'The Problem of Hermeneutics' (1950), *Essays Philosophical and Theological,* ET, 1955, ch. 12; G. Ebeling, 'Word of God and Hermeneutics' (1959), *Word and Faith,* ET, 1963, ch. 11; E. Fuchs, 'What Is Interpreted in the Exegesis of the New Testament', *Studies of the Historical Jesus,* ET, 1964, ch. 5; J. Macquarrie, *God-Talk,* 1967, ch. 7; J. M. Robinson and John B. Cobb, eds., *The New Hermeneutic,* 1964.

EDITOR

Hermetic Literature

A collection of Greek and Latin writings representing a noble religious philosophy of the Hellenistic period (the chief work is the 'Poimandres'), fusing together Platonic and Stoic teachings with oriental elements. The writings were ascribed to Hermes Trismegistus, a name for the Egyptian god Thoth. The best introduction to the subject will be found in C. H. Dodd, *Interpretation of the Fourth Gospel* (1953), pp. 10–53. W. Scott's four-volume *Hermetica* (1924–36) is for scholars only. Critical text ed. by A. D. Nock and A. J. Festugière, with French trans., *Corpus Hermeticum,* 4 vols., 1945–54.

EDITOR

Herrmann, Wilhelm

Wilhelm Herrmann (1846–1922), probably the most distinguished German systematic theologian of the Ritschlian school, insisted, like Ritschl, that Christian theology is concerned only with those value-judgments (judgments of moral worth) attached by the Christian community to the facts of Jesus accessible to us by historical research. Herrmann exhibited, like most Ritschlians, anti-mystical and anti-metaphysical tendencies in his strongly moralistic theology. He exercised a strong influence as a teacher and writer of international repute at Marburg from 1879 until 1922. *See* **Kaftan, J.; Liberal Protestantism; Ritschl, A.**

JAMES RICHMOND

Heterodox

From Greek *heteros*, other, and *doxa*, opinion. Contrary to the received opinion; unorthodox. *See* **Orthodoxy.**

Hierarchy

From Greek *hieros*, 'sacred' and *arche*, 'rule': the ordered levels of authority in the structure of the Church. The word has been used in this sense from the patristic period. The Roman Catholic, Eastern Orthodox and Anglican Churches have retained the threefold Order of bishops, priests and deacons. But the Roman Church has a distinctively elaborate hierarchial structure, and in common usage 'the hierarchy' refers to the higher levels of jurisdiction in that Church, the papacy, cardinals, legates and vicars apostolic on the one hand, and the episcopate on the other. *See also* **Dionysius the Pseudo-Areopagite.**

EDITOR

Hippolytus, St

It is now generally (though not universally) agreed among scholars that the man called Hippolytus (c. 170–c. 236) mentioned as a presbyter and martyr in the Liberian Catalogue c. 255 and described in an inscription by Pope Damasus as a Novatianist priest was in fact a presbyter of the church of Rome who in 217 set himself up as anti-pope to Pope Callistus (217–22) and continued his schism under Popes Urbanus (222–30) and Pontianus (230–5), but was probably reconciled to Pontianus before they both died in the Sardinian mines to which they had been relegated in the persecution of Maximin (235–8). A mutilated statue of this Hippolytus, now in the Lateran Museum in Rome, was dug up in the garden of a villa in Rome in 1551. His main work was a 'Refutation of All Heresies' which has been identified with a work originally attributed to Origen and called the *Philosophumena*, which survives in large part in the original Greek and forms one of the chief sources of our knowledge of Gnosticism. In this work Hippolytus bitterly attacks Popes Zephyrinus (198–217) and Callistus, accusing them of surrendering to the heresy of Sabellius, and Callistus in particular (whose career he sketches in lurid and probably exaggerated detail) of extending the opportunity of pardon and communion to categories of sinners to whom the Church had hitherto closed its doors. His own christology is very defective, and owes much to the 'economic trinitarianism' of Justin Martyr and some of the other Apologists. Hippolytus was a prolific writer and several of his minor works have survived in whole or in part, including an interesting fragment of a treatise against Noetus and a *Commentary on Daniel.* He also composed a scheme for calculating Easter. His *Apostolic Tradition,* an account in outline of the rites and customs prevailing in the church of Rome in Hippolytus' youth, is of the greatest interest to scholars, and especially to liturgiologists, but the state of its text, which survives in Greek fragments, Latin fragments and versions in several other tongues, is so uncertain as greatly to reduce its value and to render appeals to its evidence for liturgical purposes in many cases very conjectural.

English translations of a reconstruction of the *Apostolic Tradition*, with notes, have been produced by B. S. Easton (1934) and G. Dix (1937).

R. P. C. HANSON

History, Problem of

The revolution in historical thinking took place a century or more after the scientific revolution was accomplished: Sir Isaac Newton had no understanding of modern historical methods and attitudes. To him and to his contemporaries the Bible was still a book of oracles. It was not until the time of the Göttingen historians (J. C. Gatterer, J. S. Semler, etc.) in the latter half of the eighteenth century that the combination of literary and historical criticism was genuinely achieved (i.e. of lower and higher criticism) and the development of modern critico-historical methods began in earnest. (Modern historical method, as we now know it, was developed in its first stages largely by theologians and biblical scholars.) In the nineteenth century these methods were widely employed in all fields of historical research and western man became genuinely historically minded. The consequences for theological thinking were far-reaching. The whole conception of biblical revelation had to be revised and the work of reconstruction is still in process (*see* **Revelation**). Even today many remain unaware that the historical revolution is of greater significance for human self-understanding than the scientific revolution itself. It is impossible today to comprehend the significance of theological ideas without some knowledge of the development of historiography, i.e. the history of historical thinking and writing. The subject is closely bound up with the history of theology itself. We now understand (as previous ages did not) that an institution, an idea, or a theological viewpoint cannot be understood without knowing how it came to be what it is. It is in this respect that theology and all the human sciences differ most markedly from the natural sciences, though even in this field there is a growing recognition of the importance of the history of science; but this is a 'humane' study (*see* **Humanism**).

Because of its long start and the prestige which natural science had acquired, many nineteenth-century thinkers (Auguste Comte, H. T. Buckle, etc.) supposed that history should and could be scientific in the manner of the natural sciences. This notion (that *all* knowledge, including historical knowledge, is of the same type as in the natural sciences) is often called positivism (the word was invented by Comte). It is also often called historicism (*Historismus*, 'scientific history'), but this term is used in so many different senses that it would be wise to abandon it altogether. It remained the dominant theory of

history until at least about the 1930s (*cf.* J. B. Bury's famous phrase, 'history is a science, no less and no more', Inaugural Lecture at Cambridge, 1902, 'The Science of History'). According to this rationalist view, the historian collected facts, which might then be processed in the form of generalized laws by social scientists, etc.; it was Hume's theory of history, though he happily forgot about it when he was writing his history. Because history was thus regarded as a closed system of causes and effects, many of the dominant theologians of the first half of the twentieth century believed it to be necessary to dissociate divine revelation (or, if they did not use such language, the truth about man's existence) from real history altogether, i.e., the history with which historians deal every day. Karl Barth, Emil Brunner, Rudolf Bultmann, Paul Tillich and many others have in their various ways sought to disengage theology from history, because the positivist view of history was taken by them very seriously. Much confused thinking has been caused by the fact that the Germans have two words for 'history' – *Historie*, the mere historical facts, and *Geschichte*, the significantly historical (*see Heilsgeschichte*).

Long before the 1930s, however, some thinkers (Wilhelm Dilthey, R. G. Collingwood, etc.) had become dissatisfied with positivist notions about history, and since that decade historians themselves as well as students of the critical philosophy of history have largely abandoned it. Historical method, it is recognized, is quite different from the method of the natural sciences; generalization is not relevant in history in the same way as in natural science, and other methods are available to historians which are not available to natural scientists, namely, human or existential methods (it is more conceivable, for instance, why Caesar crossed the Rubicon than why lemmings rush to destruction in the sea or why sub-atomic entities behave as they do). In view of the very great changes which are today coming over the whole field of historiographical thinking, it is unlikely that the solutions proposed by the theological giants of the recent past will continue to be acceptable when the problems of a revelation in history or of miracles, and so on, are reconsidered by a new generation of theologians. However that may be, because Christianity is an historical religion, a faith which sprang out of actual situations in real history, it is obvious that theologians will have to come to grips with the problem of the nature of historical thinking, if they are to make a significant contribution to the development of thought in the later decades of this century. *See also* **Jesus of History, The.**

The problem of history is discussed at length in Alan Richardson, *History Sacred and Profane*, 1964, where the significance of contemporary historiographical thinking is considered in relation to current theological issues, such as revelation, the resurrection of Christ, miracles, etc.; a full bibliography is also given. For a general introduction *see* Herbert Butterfield, *Man on his Past: the Study of the History of Historical Scholarship*, 1955. For Bultmann's view *see* his *History and Eschatology*, 1957.

EDITOR

Hodge, Charles

Charles Hodge (1797–1878), American Calvinist theologian, was a graduate of both the college and the seminary at Princeton (1815–19), and studied in Germany under Tholuck, Hengstenberg and Neander. He taught a lifetime at Princeton Theological Seminary, first as Professor of Oriental and Biblical Literature (1822–40), then as Professor of Theology (1840–78). Hodge defended strict Calvinism on the basis of the Bible, which he understood to be fully inspired and inerrant. He distinguished sharply between revelation and inspiration; the former he regarded as consciously received from outside, while the latter operates in a continuous and plenary way without the recipient's being aware of it. Inspiration guided the biblical writers into all truth, not only concerning moral and religious matters but also extending to scientific, geographical and historical facts. Hodge vehemently opposed the negative conclusions of the higher criticism; the alleged discrepancies in Scripture he located in the errors of the transcribers, but insisted that the original text was in all points reliable. His theology was developed inductively from the biblical source, for 'the Bible is to the theologian what nature is to the man of science'. He worked within the framework of the Westminster Confession, but was much influenced by the Calvinistic scholasticism of seventeenth-century Holland and Switzerland (especially by Turretine and the Helvetic Consensus) and by eighteenth-century anti-deistical apologetics. His theological voice was very important in the USA, particularly in his own Presbyterian Church, especially through the famous *Biblical Repertory and Princeton Review*, which he founded in 1825. His mature position, the classic expression of 'Princeton theology', was published in full in the massive, three-volume *Systematic Theology* (1871–2).

A. A. Hodge, *The Life of Charles Hodge, DD., LL.D., Professor in the Theological Seminary, Princeton, NJ*, 1880.

ROBERT T. HANDY

Höffding, Harald

Harald Höffding (1843–1931), Danish neo-Kantian philosopher, claimed, with justification, to derive his ideas from Kant. He distinguished carefully between science and religion: while science attempts to *explain* the various parts, aspects and processes of the world, it falls short of and lacks the ability to provide a final and comprehensive explanation of the world *as a whole*, and, more significantly, cannot take account of human *values*. But religion, through its dogmas, cults and myths is comprehensive in so far as it gathers up, integrates and conserves the *values* which con-

stitute the world, fosters the moral life and produces highly developed moral personalities.

Harald Höffding, *Philosophy of Religion*, ET, 1906.

JAMES RICHMOND

Holy Ghost

In sixteenth- and seventeenth-century English the word 'ghost' (from Anglo-Saxon *gast*; *cf.* German *Geist*) meant 'spirit' (whether of God or of a man) and had not yet been restricted (as normally in current usage) to the sphere of the preternatural or 'spooky'. It is retained in liturgical worship which follows traditional forms, e.g. *The Book of Common Prayer* (1662), but it is being increasingly abandoned in favour of 'Spirit'. *See* **Spirit.**

Holy, Holiness, The Holy

The holy is closely associated in meaning with the 'numinous' (*see* **Numinous**) and the idea of the sacred. Strictly speaking the holy refers to those 'numinous' aspects of experience which promote either religious or aesthetic responses: the sense of awe and mystery and the feeling of unease, if not downright fear. One particular reaction to the numinous, the setting aside of particular spaces or particular periods of time, is spoken of as the sacred. The sacred place or building is sacred because, in view of some experience which may have taken place there, it has come to be regarded as having in a sacramental way the power to suggest and point to the holy itself. For the non-religious person all space, for example, is homogeneous. For the religious person certain spaces break this homogeneity and give him a fixed point of orientation by which he is enabled to interpret the whole of space in a religious way, as containing sacramental resources to point to the transcendent. The creative use of sacred space is regarded as a holy undertaking because in its reduction of what is potentially chaotic to order and significance man is engaged in the imitation of the creative work of God himself. The sacred building becomes holy because it is one of the means whereby man engages in the imitation of the holiness of God through his creative activity as pro-creator.

The idea of the holy expressed in sacred places, sacred times and so on is necessary to human experience if it is to remain loyal to the limited and partial possibilities of finite existence. Impatience with the particular holy place, the particular holy act, is a symptom of an incipient Gnosticism which attempts to jump out of the necessary restrictions of finitude. Christian holiness, therefore, is rooted in the particular, finite 'mystery' (*see* **Mystery**) of the incarnation of 'Christ in us' (II Cor. 13.5). The mystery of Christian existence for St Paul turns on the fact that the life of the Christian is nothing less than the life of Christ himself, lived out through the action of the Spirit.

Mircea Eliade, *The Sacred and the Profane*, 1959;

O. R. Jones, *The Concept of Holiness*, 1961; R. Otto, *The Idea of the Holy*, 1923.

E. J. TINSLEY

Holy Spirit. *see* Spirit.

Homiletics, Homily

The Greek word *homilia* meant 'intercourse', 'converse', 'dealings with others', and so it came to mean a conversational exposition, e.g. of a passage of Scripture which had been read. The custom of commenting upon the lections would have been taken over by the early church from the synagogue. The earliest homilies known to us are those of Origen. The Christian homily followed the scriptural text as a commentary does, and so differed from the *sermon* (Greek: *logos*, Latin: *oratio*) which usually assumed a freer and more rhetorical form. Ancient and early mediaeval *homiliaria*, collections of homilies for reading at Matins according to the church calendar, are numerous. In the Church of England the Book of Homilies (part 1, 1547; part 2, 1562) was issued for reading in churches to ensure a measure of sound doctrinal unity in an age of upheaval and also to remedy the deficiencies of those who were unskilled and unlearned in the difficult art of sermon-making.

Homiletics is that branch of theology which traditionally has dealt with the rules for the construction of sermons. This subject used to be taken with great seriousness (let anyone who has access to a library glance through the 478 pages of A. Vinet, *Homiletics, or the Theory of Preaching*, ET, 1853). Today, though many lectures on the art of preaching are given and published, it would seem that no rules (beyond a few obvious 'don'ts') can be formulated, and that the most acceptable and effective preachers are usually quite incapable of transmitting the secret of their power to their hearers. Perhaps the most helpful instruction that can be given to preachers is to ask the deeply theological question of what one thinks one is doing when one is preaching. *See* **Preaching; Hermeneutics.**

EDITOR

Homoeans

The term was used to describe the conciliatory Arians whose watchword, that the Son was *Homoios* (like the Father), was adopted in a series of formulae of the years 359–360 as the official ecclesiastical policy of the Emperor Constantius. *See* **Trinity, Doctrine of the; Anhomoeans; Homoeousians.**

H. E. W. TURNER

Homoeousians

Homoeousians were the middle party between the full Nicenes and the conciliatory Arians (*see* **Homoeans**), otherwise called the Semi-Arians or Semi-Nicenes. Under their leader, Basil of Ancyra, they proposed the term *Homoiousios* (of like substance with the Father) to describe the status

of the Son. *See* **Trinity, Doctrine of the; Anhomoeans; Homoeans.**

H. E. W. TURNER

Hooker, Richard

Richard Hooker (c. 1554–1600) was the greatest theologian of the Elizabethan Church of England, and contributed more than any other single writer to mark out a distinctive Anglican position, with his triple appeal to Scripture, tradition and reason. His work was polemical, in that it was designed to rebut the criticisms of the Church Settlement by Calvinist Puritans, but it has an enduring value. After teaching at Oxford he became Master of the Temple and an influential London preacher. He developed his teachings in his *Treatise of the Laws of Ecclesiastical Polity*, the first four books of which came out in 1593, the fifth and longest in 1597 and the last three at intervals after his death. He criticized the Puritan view that the Bible contained an exact and unalterable pattern of church government, and that Scripture was the only authority for a Christian man, and agreed with Erastus (q.v.) in resisting the right of lay-elders to excommunicate. He devoted the first book to a discussion of law itself, which is the expression of divine reason and in whose hierarchy state law has its place. He tried to allow for some development and change in church institutions, and in this context saw the justification for the Anglican form of church order. In the fifth book he treated of the church and sacraments, linking both very closely to the incarnation. His eucharistic teaching was a variant of receptionism – the consecrated elements are not naked signs but effect what they signify and unite the communicant to Christ. In breadth of mind and beauty of language he stands out among contemporary theologians, and his influence over later Anglicans was great and various. His cool appeal to reason, and his ironic dissection of the mind of fanaticism (in his preface to the book) appealed to the eighteenth-century deists; his appeal to tradition provided high churchmen with a valuable argument; and King James II claimed that it was his reading of Hooker that converted him to Roman Catholicism.

F. Paget, *An Introduction to the Fifth Book of Hooker's Treatise of the Laws of Ecclesiastical Polity*, 1907; L. S. Thornton, *Richard Hooker*, 1924; B. Willey, *The English Moralists*, 1964.

R. CANT

Hope, The Christian

Hope is a word which figures prominently in the NT, and in the great majority of cases it means the hope of life continuing after physical death. This hope is based primarily on the fact that Christ rose from the dead, and indeed this is the specific ground alleged for the Christian hope throughout the NT; *cf.* I Cor. 15.19: 'If for this life only we have hoped in Christ, we are of all men most to be pitied.' Of course this hope is not entirely exhausted in the mere fact of the empty tomb, as if it was simply a question of whether the tomb was or was not found to be empty, with no other possible consideration. Through the NT the hope of life eternal is based quite as much on the present experience of the risen Christ as on the actual proof that he rose on the third day. Indeed the NT writers would not have understood our modern tendency to separate the evidence for Christ's resurrection from the experience of his risen power in the on-going life of the Church. The two are intimately connected, and one cannot be understood without the other.

We are, however, fortunate in having what we do not have in a great many other matters of interest to Christians, clear evidence about Jesus' own teaching on this subject. In Mark 12.18–27 we actually find Jesus' proof that 'the dead are raised'. Jesus would have accepted this belief in any case, in common with the great majority of Jews who did not belong to the Sadducaean party; but he does in fact provide us with a proof text, Ex. 3.6: 'I am the God of Abraham, and the God of Isaac, and the God of Jacob.' This is no rabbinic quibble, but a serious argument from the unity of religious experience: if God revealed himself to the patriarchs, gave them promises, made covenants with them, it is wholly out of character that he should have let them just be annihilated at death. In other words, those who know anything of communion with God in this life cannot believe that this communion will be destroyed for ever at death. The God whom we know in OT and NT alike is not that sort of God. He does not have dealings with the living, only in order to let them die eternally.

The Christian hope has always been a hope in the resurrection of the dead, not in a Platonic type of immortality. Undoubtedly the conception of resurrection of the body as against natural immortality of the soul was taken over from Judaism. Judaism came to this belief relatively late in its history; it is very doubtful whether before the exile there is any belief in anything beyond death except She'ol (the place of the dead). Belief in the resurrection of the dead was greatly fostered by the experience of the persecution of Antiochus IV, the Seleucid ruler (175–63 BC): devout Jews argued that men and women who had died rather than betray the Torah simply could not be permitted by God to remain in the gloomy underworld of She'ol. The only writer in the NT who makes any attempt to answer the question 'How are the dead raised?' is St Paul (I Cor. 15.35). His answer (inevitably obscure) is to be found in I Cor. 15 and II Cor. 5, but it is plain that he does not believe in the resurrection of this flesh; had he understood our modern physics, he would not have been concerned with what happens to the material elements which compose our bodies. It is very likely that his thought on this subject followed the same lines as the Jewish apocalyptic tradition, which pictures the blessed dead as receiving bodies of light. This is probably what is intended by the 'white robe' of Rev. 6.11 (cf. also Rev. 3.4 f., 18). When Paul speaks of 'a spiritual body' in I Cor. 15.44, he does not mean a body

made of spiritual matter, but a body belonging to the realm of the Spirit, that supernatural realm into which we are introduced by our baptism; and baptism means being buried with Christ and rising with him. Because of the fairly consistent expectation of the *parousia* prevalent throughout the NT, there is not very much interest shown in the conditions of the life after death. But it is a fair summary to say that in its foundation documents the Church had a doctrine of the resurrection that was distinguished on the one hand from the notion of the natural immortality of the soul as the non-material element in man (which was the prevailing doctrine in Greek thought), and on the other from a belief in the resurrection of *this* flesh that would carry with it all sorts of restrictions and safeguards about the correct mode of disposing of the corpse.

But the Church, in the West at least, soon departed from Pauline doctrine. We find Tertullian arguing passionately that when Paul says 'flesh and blood cannot inherit the kingdom of God' (I Cor. 15.50), he is not denying the physical resurrection of the flesh. Augustine in *The City of God* carefully defends a literal physical resurrection, with all sorts of speculations as to how difficult cases will be dealt with, cannibalism for example. He bequeathed to the mediaeval Church a fundamentally Platonic doctrine of the natural immortality of the soul, together with a more-than-Jewish literalism about the resurrection of the physical elements composing the body. An index of this is the disappearance of cremation, which had been the common way of disposing of the corpse over large parts of the Roman Empire. Cremation has only been re-introduced into the West since the nineteenth century. The Reformation made no difference here: the common expectation was that in the general resurrection at the end of the world all the dead would find their souls reunited with their bodies, raised from the grave for that purpose. Then would follow the general judgment.

As was inevitable, the emergence of the critical approach to the Bible, and the revolution in theology which this entailed, have demanded a new consideration of the content of the Christian hope. In certain directions this has been a gain: sensitive Christians (e.g. Bishop Synesius in 410) have always experienced difficulty in defending the doctrine of the literal resurrection of the flesh. They need no longer defend it. Again, it could be said that Paul at least has been vindicated, and has been cleared from the imputation of holding a doctrine of the literal resurrection of the flesh. Paul's doctrine of a 'spiritual body' is more congenial to the present age than Augustine's account of a physical resurrection. It is also surely a gain that the doctrine of the natural immortality of the soul should have been shown to belong to the school of Plato rather than of Christ. Eternal life is the gift of God, not something which we inherit anyway. On the other hand it has become increasingly difficult to say anything meaningful about the nature of the life to come. It is quite true that, when we try to describe that life, we must use the language of symbol, for we have no other language that we can use. The question is: does the symbol convey any real meaning? Modern psychology has long ago dispensed with the body-soul dichotomy on which so much of the old-fashioned language was based. What can we put in its place? The most frequent answer has been in effect to say that when we speak of the resurrection of the body we mean the continuance of the personality. This of course has its own difficulties: 'personality' is a word that has no generally agreed connotation. Perhaps the best account that can be given is one which proceeds by the *via negativa*, a method sometimes employed in other branches of theology also. When we confess the resurrection of the body, we do not mean the resurrection of the physical elements which compose the flesh; we do not mean a re-absorption into the infinite; we do not mean the continued existence of one element in human nature which is indestructible. We mean the enjoyment by the human personality of that communion with God which can be partially experienced here, in conditions which make a much closer communion possible, but which do not obliterate the distinction between the creature and the Creator.

The Christian hope is therefore based on an act of religious faith and cannot be either proved or disproved by any empirical observation. William Temple and John Baillie were right in insisting that psychical research had nothing to do with the Christian hope. From this it follows that Christians ought to believe in the life everlasting, in precisely the same sense in which they ought to trust in Christ in this life. The Christian hope is not hope in a divine transformation scene which alone enables us to tolerate life in this vale of tears. It is the inevitable consummation of the life lived in Christ on earth. We come back always to Jesus' words: 'He is not the God of the dead, but of the living.' It is absurd and inconsistent to claim to believe in Christ and in Christianity and at the same time to profess agnosticism about, or lack of interest in, the life to come. Any system of Christian theology that is ambiguous or agnostic about the Christian hope is to that extent deficient in its presentation of the true Christian faith.

As long as Christians looked on the Bible as a document containing guaranteed information about matters not otherwise accessible to human inquiry, it was natural that they should attempt to piece together from the Scriptures some picture of what the condition of the faithful departed is. It must be confessed that the Bible, not really being this sort of volume, did not supply any very coherent answer. Some passages (e.g. I Thess. 4.13–16) speak of Christians falling asleep; others again, such as Rev. 6.9–11, give us a picture of the souls of the martyrs at rest. The great roll-call of the heroes of Israel in Heb. 11 conveys the impression that the faithful under the old dispensation existed in some intermediate state until the coming of the Christian era should permit them with us to be perfected. Throughout the Apocalypse the one activity in which the blessed dead are constantly engaged is worship. As we have already noted, the language of symbol is the only language we can employ here, and in it the note of glory recurs again and again. In Rom. 5.2 and Col. 1.27 the hope of glory is held up before Christians as their ultimate aim. That this glory should be expressed in terms of light, radiance, visible splendour was natural and inevitable; and this language has persisted through the ages. A very modern example occurs in a prayer composed in March 1963 by the late Pope John XXIII for the beatification ceremony of Louis Maria Palazzolo. It begins: 'O blessed Louis Maria, now shining in eternal light . . .' In the earliest age of the Church the blessed dead were thought of as enjoying rest and refreshment, but from the time of Augustine onwards in the West the element of purgatorial discipline becomes much more obtrusive. Augustine himself is by no means dogmatic on the subject of purgatory. In *The City of God*, xxi 26, he mentions the theory that the spirits of the dead will be purified by fire between death and the last judgment, and he comments: 'I do not reject this theory, for it may be true.' The *Dialogues* of Gregory the Great gave great impetus to the mediaeval doctrine of purgatory, purporting as they do to give real-life stories about men and women who have experienced the life after death. But the doctrine was not officially formulated till the Council of Florence in 1439. The East never officially accepted it, despite the temporary and partial adherence of the Eastern delegates to that Council. The abuses of the doctrine of purgatory were violently denounced by the Reformers; and the Council of Trent was very moderate in its formulation of the doctrine, being content with saying 'that there is a purgatory and that souls there detained are helped by the intercessions of the faithful, but most of all by the acceptable sacrifice of the altar'. If Roman Catholic theologians today are content with this, and are ready to regard as optional and dispensable all the practices and beliefs that go beyond this, there may well be a prospect of agreement with other Christians. Compare this sentence from F. J. A. Hort: 'though little is said directly [sc. in the NT] respecting the future state, it seems to me incredible that the divine chastisements should in this respect change their character when this visible life is ended. Neither now nor hereafter is there any reason to suppose that they act mechanically by an irresistible natural process, irrespectively of human will and acceptance.'

It has been rightly claimed that, 'except in modern Protestantism, prayer for the dead, inherited from Judaism, has been a universal Christian custom'. The practice does not require specific scriptural warrant, least of all from II Macc. 12.39. It is surely a necessary corollary of the doctrine of the communion of saints.

The doctrine of metempsychosis has never been anything but an alien intruder within Christianity. In the West it seems to have originated in the Orphic mysteries, and ever since has haunted certain Christian thinkers. Of these the greatest is Origen, who no doubt received it as part of his legacy from Platonism. Its proper home is India, where, under the more exact name of *janmāntara*, or succession of births, it has always formed a necessary part of Hindu theology, or rather a necessary part of Hindu theodicy, for it is by this means that apparently innocent suffering is explained. Hindus sometimes claim that Mark 9.11–13 shows that *janmāntara* was part of Jesus' teaching; but this goes far beyond the evidence. In fact Christians cannot accept the notion of successive rebirths because they believe in only one rebirth, the rebirth through baptism into the new life of Christ.

John Baillie, *And the Life Everlasting*, 1934; Jürgen Moltmann, *Theology of Hope*, ET, 1967.
                                                                    A. T. HANSON

Hoskyns, Sir Edwyn

Through his teaching at Cambridge from the end of the first World War till his death and by his writings, particularly an essay in *Essays Catholic and Critical* (1926) on 'The Christ of the Synoptic Gospels' and his book (with a pupil, F. N. Davey) *The Riddle of the New Testament* in 1931, Hoskyns (1884–1937) had a great influence on the scholarly interpretation of the NT in English-speaking countries, and may rightly be regarded as a seminal thinker in this branch of theology. He shook the ascendancy and popularity of liberal and modernistic attitudes, and helped to restore the confidence of a rising generation of scholars in the inherent authority and the unity of the Bible. The effect of his teaching was to make it possible to maintain that the rigorous use of the critical method of studying the NT itself disturbed the current assumption that there was an unbridgeable gap between the Jesus of the Gospels and the Christ of later theology. He sought, with success, to show that in every stratum of NT material there were to be found the same mysterious claims which were intelligible only if the attempt was made to understand them in their own terms. He stressed the unique importance of the OT background to primitive Christianity, and the close connection of Christ with the church. By translating Karl Barth's *Römerbrief* (*Commentary on Romans*) in 1933 he introduced many English readers to a new and exciting continental theology, and was responsible for initiating a fruitful union between it and certain strands in Anglo-Catholicism (q.v.). His posthumous *Fourth Gospel* (1940, with Davey) had an invigorating effect on Johannine studies.

E. C. Hoskyns, *Cambridge Sermons*, ed. C. H. E. Smyth, 1938; *We are the Pharisees* ... with a preface by F. N. Davey, 1960.
                                                                    R. CANT

House-Tables. *see* Vocation.

Humanism

In its original and proper sense the word meant education based on the Greek and Latin classics (*cf.* 'humane studies', 'the humanities', *litterae humaniores*, or the chairs of Humanity, i.e. Latin, in the Scottish universities). This usage is closely related to the ancient secondary meaning of the Latin word *humanitas* ('the human race') as denoting the distinctively human or moral attitude of one human being to another: kindness, philanthropy, courtesy, civilized behaviour (contrast 'inhuman'); thus it came to be an equivalent of the Greek *paideia*: polite education, high culture. Without this European tradition of humanity the higher life, culture, scholarship and the university tradition itself could not have been born in the Middle Ages. The recovery of a genuinely humanist attitude at the Renaissance (as over against the scholastic dogmatism of the narrower kind of Aristotelian theology) made possible the rise of critical studies and indeed the modern scientific movement itself. From Petrarch (1304–1374), 'the first modern man', to Erasmus (1467–1536), 'the European man', a remarkable succession of scholars recovered the spirit and the treasures of ancient culture and a whole new system of education and free inquiry was gradually developed. If in an age of immense concentration upon science and technology we neglect the humane tradition and undervalue the study of the humanities, we shall forfeit the inestimable riches of our inheritance, including academic freedom, and become the automated people of a totalitarian state. The Christian humanism of the later Middle Ages and of the Renaissance has proved to be the only foundation of personal and academic liberty in the modern age.

In recent times, however, the word 'humanism' has been put to a different use. It is true that in Renaissance humanism there had been among extreme thinkers an element of anti-religious bias, but it was not until the nineteenth century that the word was used for belief in man's self-sufficiency in conscious opposition to belief in God. Auguste Comte adopted the word in connection with his 'religion of humanity'. He also invented the word positivism, and today the word 'humanism' is being increasingly used for that kind of anti-historical positivist view which looks to the scientific intellect rather than to historical, moral and religious insight for progress in human affairs. This type of thought is the lineal descendant of eighteenth-century rationalism, but, because that word (since Marx and Freud) is no longer viable currency in modern thought, another had to be found. Today there are many kinds of latter-day humanists: some who stress the moral values of human life and are deeply concerned for human rights and dignity: others whose mainspring seems to be the hatred of everything associated with the Christian religion. Walter Lippmann's *Preface to Morals* (1929) introduced the term 'scientific humanism' to denote a philosophical attitude based upon science and morals without religion. Jean-Paul Sartre has proposed an existentialist humanism (*L'existentialisme est un humanisme*, 1946; ET, *Existentialism and Humanism*, 1948). C. H. Waddington has attempted to show that ethics can be based upon scientific knowledge (*Science and Ethics*, 1942). Organized neo-humanism is represented in Britain by the Rationalist Press Association Ltd, which publishes a monthly magazine, *The Humanist* (incorporating the secularist periodicals of a former age, *Literary Guide* and *The Rationalist Review*), and also *The Rationalist Annual* (formerly *The Agnostic Annual* founded in 1883 by Charles A. Watts). There are so many different kinds of neo-humanist today that it is impossible to characterize them otherwise than negatively: they have in common a rejection of the Christian faith, whether that rejection be regretful or spiteful, but also a rejection of nihilism and of all kinds of moral irresponsibility. Meanwhile Christians will be unwilling to surrender their old and honourable title of humanist. *See also* **Secularism.**

R. W. Hepburn and others, *Objections to Humanism*, 1964; Alan Richardson, *University and Humanity*, 1964.

EDITOR

Hume, David

In the philosophy of David Hume (1711–1776) British Empiricism of the eighteenth century received its fullest development. Indeed, twentieth-century empiricists, despite many divergences from Hume, still take their bearings from him more than from any other single writer. It was his chief aim to extend scientific method to the study of human beings, their intellectual powers and limitations, the life of the emotions, their moral and political judgments. His main philosophical writings are *A Treatise of Human Nature* (1739–40), *An Enquiry concerning Human Understanding* (1748), *An Enquiry concerning the Principles of Morals* (1751), and *Dialogues concerning Natural Religion* (posth. 1779).

A scientific philosophy must be an experience-based philosophy. Experience, to Hume, derives in the last analysis from 'impressions' directly presented to the mind. 'Ideas' are less vivid copies or images of impressions. That is to say, all explanations and definitions of concepts must end in reference to what is immediately given. We should ask of any speculative idea (like 'substance' or 'soul'), from what impressions is it derived? If from none, it will be an empty and bogus idea, however venerable. A view of material substance as an unknowable 'substratum' had clearly to be rejected by Hume, and an account of 'spiritual substance' – as in George Berkeley (q.v.) – could fare no better, since in the case of the self, too, Hume was committed to an analysis in terms of impressions and derivative ideas. With this minimal apparatus Hume had great difficulty in accounting plausibly for personal identity and memory.

The relation of cause and effect is both crucial to scientific explanation and everyday life, and is at first sight difficult to accommodate to Hume's theory. Causality seemed to be a matter of necessary connections between events; and although it is not so hard to see how there can be such connections among propositions in logic and among mathematical ideas, it was repugnant to Hume that one event could 'imply the existence of any other'. What causes what, we discover by experience alone. Hume's definition of 'cause' runs as follows: '*an object, followed by another, and where all the objects similar to the first are followed by objects similar to the second*', or '*where, if the first object had not been, the second never had existed*'. The element of 'necessity' is produced subjectively, from our experience of constant conjunction between events: it is in fact nothing but a 'determination to carry our thoughts from one object to another'. The 'necessary connection' is not a rational or a metaphysical one. There are other very important places in Hume's philosophy where a rational or metaphysical account is abandoned. We believe in the continuing existence of unobserved objects, for instance; and this is the work of memory and imagination building upon 'impressions' that show coherence and constancy. The result is an ineradicable 'natural belief' in objects as independently existing. If philosophy cannot provide a firmer and a rational basis to this belief, neither does Hume see it as undermining the belief, any more than he sees his explanation of causality as explaining causality away. In these respects Hume was no sceptic – although sceptical of rationalist philosophical *theories*. The same can be said of his moral philosophy. Hume denied that moral judgments are fundamentally the product of reason: there is a place for reason and reasoning in investigating the situation in which we have to act and the likely effects of actions, but moral judgment itself consists basically of feelings of approbation and disapprobation. Moral sentiment is a 'disinterested' sentiment: 'utility' is an important touchstone of moral evaluation – though not the *sole* touchstone: virtues can be 'natural' (e.g. benevolence) or 'artificial' (e.g. justice).

In the philosophy of religion Hume can be called 'sceptical' with much more propriety. In the first place, given his theory of the self, he could scarcely advance arguments for the immortality of the soul. Secondly, in the *Dialogues* the character who puts forward distinctively Humean arguments ('Philo') powerfully assaults the traditional arguments of natural theology. In the *Enquiry concerning Human Understanding* also Hume included critical studies of argument to God and of miracle. To argue from features of the natural world to the existence of God is to infer a cause from various effects. But we are not entitled, in this kind of arguing, to posit in the cause qualities other than those we see in the effect: not entitled, therefore, to claim that God has moral qualities which nature itself does not display. 'Let your gods, therefore, O philosophers, be suited to the present appearances of nature.' For these and other reasons presented in detail in the *Dialogues*, natural theology can reach a conclusion no more exalted than this – '*that the cause or causes of order in the universe probably bear some remote analogy to human intelligence*'.

When, Hume asks, would it be reasonable to accept someone's testimony that a miracle had occurred? He answers, only 'if the falsehood of his testimony would be more miraculous, than the event which he relates'. There is inevitably a conflict in the evidence between the weighty testimony of normal experience and a particular testimony of the miraculous: and Hume in fact argues that 'no human testimony can have such force as to prove a miracle, and make it a just foundation for any . . . religion' (*An Enquiry concerning Human Understanding*, X, II, §98).

The critiques of Hume and Kant together constitute the most serious challenge to natural religion in modern times, and have implications that extend widely into theological reasoning in general. Twentieth-century analytical philosophy has revised and restated many of Hume's arguments on these and other topics, sifting the logical from the psychological, refining many of his particular analyses, in the light of advances in logic and the theory of knowledge.

R. W. HEPBURN

Huss, John

John Huss (Jana Hus, c. 1371–1415) inherited from his widowed mother habits of piety and study, but his higher education was delayed by the necessity of doing menial tasks for a living. Having studied theology at Prague he was ordained, 1401, and held the half-yearly rectorship, 1402; in that same year he also became director of the Bethlehem Chapel. This institution for vernacular preaching represented the reformed movement started by Conrad Waldhauser, John Milic, and the learned Matthew of Janov to whose biblical theology Huss was especially indebted. He became increasingly familiar with the writings of John Wyclif (q.v.); but J. Loserth's thesis that Huss was a mere disciple and copyist of Wyclif has been rejected in later research, notably by M. Spinka. He quoted Wyclif freely where he approved him, but wide differences from Wyclif appear. His spirited refusal at his trial to call Wyclif a heretic was a factor in his condemnation. Enmity against Huss arose from his vigorous attacks upon clerical offences, fraudulent miracles, and papal indulgences, and also through the shifty behaviour of Zbynek, archbishop of Prague, in relation to the policy of King Wenzel (Vaclav) on the papal schism. In 1412 he was excommunicated and forced to leave Prague. He welcomed the summons to the Council of Constance, though he made his will before going, not trusting the Emperor Sigismund's safe-conduct. Arriving 3 November 1414, he was promptly imprisoned. He was called upon to recant many opinions, alleged to have been drawn from Wyclif, that he emphatically said he had never held. On 6 July 1415, still testifying to the truth of his teachings, he was burned at the stake. Besides

numerous informing letters, Huss left a considerable body of writing. Important are the following: *De corpore Christi* (1406), the vernacular treatise *Exposition of the Faith* with additions on the Decalogue and the Lord's Prayer; *The Postil* (selected sermons); *On Simony* (a translation of which is included in *Advocates of Reform from Wyclif to Erasmus*), a severe arraignment of clerical abuses; and *De Ecclesia*. All but the first of these belong to the period between his excommunication and his journey to Constance, 1412–4. On the Eucharist he is no Wyclifite: he continued in Constance to affirm transubstantiation. His doctrine of the Church stresses the headship of Christ: Peter was not a potentate but excelled in faith, humility and love. A pious pope may be Christ's vicar; an evil pope is the vicar of Anti-Christ. Simony, which is 'an evil consent to an exchange of spiritual goods for non-spiritual' is illustrated from the warnings of Gregory and other Church fathers. Simoniacs may include popes, bishops, monks, priests and laymen such as unscrupulous patrons of churches and parents who send their children to school in order that they may become rich. Like Wyclif and Matthew of Janov, Huss rested the cause of reform on the Scripture and felt himself in agreement with Augustine.

John Huss, *De Ecclesia*, ET, 1915; M. Spinka, *Advocates of Reform from Wyclif to Erasmus*, 1953; *John Huss and Czech Reform*, 1941; *John Huss and the Council of Constance*, 1965.

J. T. MCNEILL

Husserl, Edmund

Edmund Husserl (1859–1938), German philosopher, was the founder of the modern school of philosophical phenomenology, whose aim has been to analyse the fundamental structures of consciousness. Husserl's long-term effect on philosophy and theology has been considerable; it is evident in the work of the philosopher M. Heidegger, the theologians R. Otto and M. Scheler (qq.v.), and the French school of phenomenology, whose most distinguished representative was M. Merleau-Ponty. *See* **Existentialism; Otto, R.; Phenomenology; Scheler, M.**

JAMES RICHMOND

Hylotheism

The belief that matter (Greek *hyle*, wood, matter) is divine, or that God is material substance.

Hymnary, Hymnology

From the earliest times hymns, perhaps originally of Jewish origin (*cf.* Mark 14.26), were sung by Christians (*cf.* Eph. 5.19, the Magnificat, etc.). In the Western Church the *Hymnarium* was the liturgical book containing the sacred poetry (hymns) of the Divine Office (q.v.) ordered for the particular seasons of the liturgical year (*see* **Calendar**). Hymnology is the study of the history and contents of hymns.

J. Julian, *A Dictionary of Hymnology*, rev. ed, 1907.

EDITOR

Hypostasis

Unlike *Ousia* (q.v.) this term (in the doctrine of the Trinity) had a more popular background. In secular usage it could connote a statue, camp, or sediment or dregs of wine. Hope draws its *hypostasis* from faith, rivers from rainfall. It could be used either in a passive sense (substratum) or more actively (that which gives support). These two senses taken together serve to explain its use as equivalent to *Ousia*. But its use to describe a statue could also suggest a meaning ultimately of even greater importance, that which stands up by itself, hence a concrete, objective, externally presented individual.

In trinitarian usage it was not at first distinguished from *Ousia*. Thus Origen can as easily say that the Father and the Son are two entities in *Hypostasis* though one in harmony or agreement, as that the Son differs from the Father in *Ousia*. The anti-Arian anathema attached to the Creed of Nicea attacks those who say that the Son is of a different *Ousia* or *Hypostasis* from the Father. Epiphanius (fl. c. 360) asks the Arians whether they do not know that the two terms are identical in meaning.

A curious phrase occurs at the beginning of the Draft Creed of the Council of Sardica (343) which speaks of the one *Hypostasis* of the Father, the Son and the Holy Spirit which the heretics call *Ousia*. The Council met to rehabilitate Marcellus of Ancyra (q.v.) and was proposed by Ossius of Cordoba (among others). The phrase is usually explained as the equivalent of the Western *una substantia* but it may perhaps represent the highwater mark of trinitarian Monism. The tailpiece 'which the heretics call *Ousia*' is not the least of its difficulties and might appear to exclude the *Homoousios* by implication.

Later in the period the Cappadocian Fathers (q.v.) clarified trinitarian terminology by distinguishing carefully between *Ousia* and *Hypostasis*, restricting the latter to that wherein the Godhead was three. The term was important for what it excluded, the notions of the Persons either as modes or economies. True, at one stage, Arius had spoken of his three tritheistically conceived entities (*see* **Tritheism**) as three *Hypostases*, but in Cappadocian usage this was counterchecked by an equally strong emphasis on the *Homoousios*. In this sense an early application in Origen who defined rational beings as logical *Hypostases* was important. The three Persons of the Trinity could, therefore, be so described by virtue of their concrete objectivity. It is perhaps significant that in modern times Karl Barth, who offers a different interpretation of the word Person, dislikes both the term and the concept which it implies.

H. E. W. TURNER

Hypostatic Union. *see* Christology (4).

I-Thou. *see* Buber, M.; Heim, K.

Iconoclasm

Iconoclasm is the policy of breaking, or suppressing the use of, images, either painted or carved, in Christian devotion or worship. It was ardently pursued by several Byzantine emperors in the eighth century, but the use of images was allowed by the Second Ecumenical Council of Nicea (787), and the veneration of icons has always played a large part in Orthodox devotion.

R. P. C. HANSON

Idealism

Idealism is a rather wide and vague term, whose philosophical and theological meanings should be distinguished from its everyday usage, where it refers to the possession of high moral ideals or to the conviction that morally laudable states of affairs are practically realizable. In philosophy, *idealism* may mean the view that reality is (relatively or absolutely) *mind-dependent* (as in the thought of Bishop George Berkeley, 1685–1753), or to the view that man possesses *a priori* (or innate) knowledge (e.g., the knowledge of universals, as in Plato), or to the view that a sharp distinction should be drawn between *appearance* and *reality* and that the contradictions inherent in the realm of *appearances* are reconciled in a perfect and all-inclusive Absolute which alone is to be accounted *real* (as in the thought of F. H. Bradley, 1846–1924). In speculative theology, idealism may mean the view that reality is *one* (as contrasted with *plural*) and ultimately spiritual in character, or that there is significant continuity between our highest aims, insights and aspirations on the one hand and the nature of God on the other. Frequently theological idealism makes a sharp distinction between man and nature and sometimes between body and soul.

'Idealism', *The Concise Encyclopaedia of Western Philosophy and Philosophers*, ed., J. O. Urmson, 1960, pp. 190–3.

JAMES RICHMOND

Ideologists, Ideology

The word 'ideology' originally meant the philosophical study of the origin and nature of ideas. It became especially connected with the school known as 'the ideologists of Paris' (Condorcet, etc.) in the eighteenth century, which held that all ideas are derived from sensations, a view which had affinities with the teaching of Thomas Aquinas and John Locke. It thus had no pejorative meaning, until Napoleon began to use it derisively of the impractical ideals of visionaries and utopians, who had not realized that power, military and economic, was the only thing that mattered. The word never recovered its original innocence. According to the economic interpretation of history, intellectual life is only the by-product of economic development (*cf.* Karl Marx: 'The mode of production of the material means of existence conditions the whole process of social, political and intellectual life. It is not the consciousness of men that determines their existence, but, on the contrary, it is their social existence that determines their consciousness.' [preface to the *Critique of Political Economy*]). Men's philosophical and political views, their morality and religion, are all determined by their class or position in society. While admitting that all our thinking is to some extent the rationalization of our social or class consciousness, it may be asserted in reply that the awareness of our proneness to ideological influences helps us to think rationally and enables us to escape from the mesh of our social conditioning. (After all, Marx himself was a bourgeois.) Today the word 'ideology' has become so widely and vaguely used as to be almost worthless. It is useful only if it is strictly confined to those concealed mental processes of which we are ourselves unaware; in this sense ideology is to be distinguished from a considered philosophy or ethic, which has been subjected to critical scrutiny. The Christian faith, which has persisted through many changing forms of society, ancient, mediaeval and modern, cannot intelligently be described as an ideology. Its origins were in actual historical events, not in the subconscious aspirations of a depressed social class, even if at various times in Christian history a considerable ideological element has been present in the conventional religious forms of the day.

Karl Mannheim, *Ideology and Utopia*, 1936; Alan Richardson, *Christian Apologetics*, 1947, ch. 3.

EDITOR

Idolatry

From the Christian perspective idolatry may be defined as a worship of a god that man creates instead of worshipping the God who created man. Or, as Paul Tillich puts it, it is being ultimately concerned with that which is not ultimate. In biblical times idolatry was associated with pagan religions and graven images. But through its history Christianity has recognized that man's idolatry takes more subtle forms. Thus John Wesley could say, 'We have set up our idols in our hearts; . . . we worship ourselves, when we pay that honour to ourselves which is due to God alone. Therefore, all pride is idolatry . . .' *See also* **Man, Doctrine of.**

WILLIAM HORDERN

Imago Dei. see Man, Doctrine of.

Imitation of Christ

The imitation of Christ as a Christian ideal has played an important role both in Christian ethics (*see* E. J. Tinsley, 'Imitation of Christ', *DCE*) and

spiritually (*see* **Mysticism; Monachism, Monasticism**).

It is possible to trace in the development of the gospel tradition about Jesus a growth of the idea of the imitation of Christ. The Gospels are allegories in the sense that they are about discipleship at the same time that they are about Christ, and are an important monument to the belief that the pattern of the life of Jesus mattered very greatly to early Christian believers.

But does this belief have a foundation in the thought of Jesus himself? There seems to be reliable evidence that Jesus saw his task as an enactment of the way of Israel which he believed had been outlined in certain key parts of the OT. This outline Jesus took as the God-given model for his own mission: the way of the Son of Man in which he believed had had to go was indicated to him by the Father in God's summons to Israel to walk in the way of the Lord.

In the Pauline literature the life of Christ is something which the apostle believes can be seen being lived out by the operation of the Spirit in the lives of Christians. This is what he calls the mystery of 'Christ in you' (II Cor. 13.3,5). The new and better 'way' which is Christ himself is to be discerned in the lives of Christ's followers (I Cor. 13). Paul does not shrink from exhorting his readers to imitate him in so far as he is showing marks of the Lord Christ (such as self-abnegation, obedience, charity); but there is no suggestion in Paul that the imitation of Christ is some kind of endeavour literally to mimic the historical Jesus. It is primarily a work of the Spirit who is seeking to mould Christians into conformity with Christ, the model, the image of God, and the principal thing to be imitated is the self-giving and self-abnegation displayed in the process of incarnation as such, and in the historical Jesus.

The lack of interest in the historical Jesus in the early Church prevented an immediate development of the idea that the imitation of Christ was some kind of literal mimicry. The emphasis in the early period was on self-abnegation as the essence of the *imitatio Christi* and this was to be expressed in martyrdom or its equivalent.

Developments in the Middle Ages (liturgical mysticism and devotion to the sacred humanity of Jesus) produced a notion of the imitation of Christ as a literal archaeological reproduction of the historical Jesus. Examples of this are to be found in Bernard of Clairvaux's meditations on the 'states' of the sacred life and, of course, in Francis of Assisi where there is the idea of a literal attempt to reproduce the Christ of the past. The most thorough-going attempt at literal mimicry was probably the point-by-point imitation of the 'stations' in the Lord's life in the liturgy of the Mass where every movement came to be interpreted as a miming of some phase of the Lord's life.

Luther was greatly influenced by such mystics as Bernard of Clairvaux and writings like the *Theologia Germanica* and Thomas à Kempis. But he soon came to react violently against them, for two main reasons: first, he was repelled by the puerilities and extravagances of some of the Schwärmerei groups (as, for example, when he found old folk playing hoops in the street because it said in the Gospel 'except you become as little children you cannot enter the Kingdom of Heaven'); and secondly, he became convinced that the whole idea of the imitation of Christ concealed a doctrine of works. He believed that it became inevitably some kind of exercise to emulate Christ which a man could set about by his own efforts. Consequently he came to dislike the term *imitatio* and preferred *conformitas*, and his view on the whole subject is epigrammatically expressed in his famous saying (in his *Commentary on Galatians*) '*Non imitatio fecit filios, sed filiatio fecit imitatores*'. In Calvin, remarkably, there is a prominent place given to the ideal of the imitation of Christ, and the Christian's mystical union with Christ is worked out in a way which does full loyalty to the NT material.

Two developments in the modern period are notable: (1) First of all, that of S. Kierkegaard, particularly in a work like *Training in Christianity*. Three aspects of Kierkegaard's treatment of the theme are of special interest: (*a*) the distinction which he makes between 'admiration' of Christ and 'imitation' of Christ, (*b*) the relationship between the idea of the imitation of Christ and the doctrines of atonement and grace, and (*c*) the relationship between the imitation of Christ and mysticism indicated in Kierkegaard's idea of 'contemporaneity with Christ'. (2) Since the work of Rudolf Bultmann in his *The History of the Synoptic Tradition* (1921) and that of the form critics generally, NT scholars have been sceptical about the possibility of recovering the historical Jesus, and this has made the older form of the ideal of the imitation of Christ unfashionable. Nevertheless, the imitation of Christ remains in these circles an ideal for the Christian and in the work of some of the followers of Rudolf Bultmann (particularly G. Ebeling and E. Fuchs) it consists of the Christian saying, like Christ, an affirmative to God. 'What came to expression in Jesus', says Ebeling, 'was faith', and the Christian act is, in fact, to say, like Jesus, 'Yes' to the Father in a way that involves total commitment.

Among the issues of theological importance in any study of the ideal of the imitation of Christ are the role of the Holy Spirit in conforming Christians to the image of God which is Christ, and the doctrines of the Church, the sacraments and grace.

E. J. Tinsley, *The Imitation of God in Christ*, 1960.

E. J. TINSLEY

Immaculate Conception of the Blessed Virgin Mary

The definition by Pope Pius IX on 8 December 1854 in the bull *Ineffabilis Deus*, that 'the Blessed Virgin Mary, in the first moment of her conception, by a singular grace and privilege of Almighty God, in virtue (*intuitu*) of the merits of Jesus Christ the Saviour of the human race, was pre-

served immune from every stain of original guilt', gave dogmatic force to a belief which, though it had been a matter of vigorous controversy during the Middle Ages, had become universal in the Roman communion. From at least the seventh century the perfect sinlessness of Mary had been accepted in both East and West, but most of the great schoolmen of the Middle Ages (e.g. St Bernard, St Albert, St Bonaventura, St Thomas Aquinas, but not Duns Scotus) denied that she was conceived without original sin, while generally holding that she was freed from original sin before her birth. The opposition gradually diminished, largely through a distinction being drawn between the physical union of the parental germ-cells and the infusion of the soul into the embryo, and through agreement that the immaculate conception did not mean that Mary was not redeemed but rather that she was redeemed by Christ in anticipation of his atoning death. Protestants have generally, but not universally, rejected the doctrine; Roman Catholics for the last few centuries have universally accepted it. It is doubtful, however, how many of either have clearly understood it. It is frequently confused by the uninstructed with the quite different doctrine of the virginal conception of Jesus. It does not mean that Mary was conceived without the sexual union of two human parents; it is perhaps most simply stated as the belief that Mary received, at the moment when her soul was infused into her body, the graces that Christians normally receive at baptism. Since 1854 Eastern Orthodox theologians have commonly rejected the doctrine, often on the ground that it detracts from the merit of Mary's actual sinlessness; before 1854 many of them accepted it. In any case, the Orthodox Church lays great stress on the complete purity of Mary, whom it describes liturgically as 'immaculate' (*achrantos, prechistaya*); some of its theologians have suggested that the basic divergence between East and West on the question is due to a different understanding of the nature of original sin, the East thinking of it more in terms of disability and the West more in terms of guilt (*cf*. J. Meyendorff, *A Study of Gregory Palamas*, p. 234). The Anglican Bishop Ken (1637–1711) taught it in the stanza:

The Holy Ghost his temple in her built,
Cleansed from congenial, kept from mortal
    guilt;
And from the moment that her blood was fired
Into her heart celestial love inspired.

The Feast of the Conception of the Blessed Virgin Mary appeared in the East in the seventh century and spread to the West; it had established itself in England in the first half of the eleventh century, but its diffusion throughout Europe was slow. St Thomas Aquinas, writing c. 1272, says that, although the Church of Rome does not keep it, some other churches do, and therefore its celebration is not to be entirely reprobated (*Summa Theologica*, 3.27, 2.3). It was officially adopted for the Roman Church in 1476, imposed on the whole Western Church in 1708, and the adjective 'Immaculate' was added to the title after the promulgation of the dogma in 1854. It appears without the adjective in the Calendar of the Church of England Prayer Book. It is kept on 8 December. *See also* **Mary, The Blessed Virgin; Duns Scotus.**

An admirable account of the doctrine in every aspect, historical, dogmatic, liturgical, iconographical etc., written with complete objectivity, will be found in the American symposium *The Dogma of the Immaculate Conception*, ed. E. O'Connor, 1958. *Cf. also* H. S. Box, 'The Assumption', *The Blessed Virgin Mary*, ed. E. L. Mascall, 1963; K. Rahner, *Theological Investigations*, I, 1961, ch. 6.

E. L. MASCALL

Immanence. see God; Transcendence.

Immolation

In classical usage, *immolatio* (from *mola* – meal, flour) originally referred to the sprinkling of a sacrificial victim with meal as a preliminary to its slaying, but was transferred to the slaying itself and was adopted in this latter sense into Christian theology, in which it is virtually identical in meaning with *mactatio*. Its primary Christian application is to the death of Christ upon the Cross, but it is also used in Catholic theology to describe the offering of Christ in the Eucharist; this had led to the accusation on the part of Protestants that Catholics believe in a literal slaying of Christ in every Mass. It is, however, noticeable that St Thomas Aquinas, while giving an affirmative answer to the question 'whether Christ is immolated in the celebration of this sacrament' (*Summa Theologica*, 3.83.1) amplifies this assertion by saying that the Mass is a 'sort of representative image' of the passion of Christ, this latter being the 'true immolation' and that in the Mass 'we are made partakers of the fruits of the Lord's passion'. He illustrates this by a remark from St Augustine that it is customary to apply to pictures the names of their subjects, so that one may point to a picture and say 'That is Cicero'. For further discussion of the relation between the Eucharist and the cross, *see* **Eucharist, Eucharistic Theology.**

E. L. MASCALL

Immortality. see Soul.

Imputation

To impute something to someone is to count it for or against him, to reckon it to his credit or discredit. The theological use of this idea derives from St Paul's argument that just as Abraham's faith was reckoned (*or* imputed) to him as righteousness (Gen. 15.6) so the faith of Christians is imputed to them (Rom. 4.3, 9, 22; Gal. 3.6), or so God imputes righteousness (Rom. 4.6, 11) and

does not impute but forgives sin (Rom. 4.7 f.; II Cor. 5.19) to those who have faith.

Luther made use of this idea in opposing his doctrine of justification to the Scholastic doctrine. The latter taught that men are justified by 'faith furnished with love', and that both the faith and the love are supernatural virtues imparted to the soul by an infusion (q.v.) of divine grace, whereby every stain of sin is removed and men are made acceptable to God. Luther, to whom this smacked of legalism (q.v.), held by contrast that men are justified by 'faith alone', i.e. faith in Christ alone, which is imputed to them as righteousness, or on account of which Christ's righteousness is imputed to them and their sin is not imputed. For faith is no mere abstract notion, but a living relationship in which the believing soul is united to Christ as closely as a bride to a bridegroom (who are bound to one another for better, for worse), and because of this bond the believer, sinful though he is and unacceptable in himself, is accepted by God for Christ's sake. It is as when human parents accept for their son's sake a daughter-in-law otherwise unacceptable to them, making her as lovingly welcome into the family as if she had all his right to belong to it.

Admittedly, this means that God accepts the sinner while he is still sinful, not first (as in the scholastic doctrine) purging him of sin. But it does not mean that the justified believer can remain unaffected by his new relationship to God. The purging begins from the first moment of his acceptance, since Christ with whom he is united by faith is present and active through the Holy Spirit in his heart and life, ceaselessly working to eradicate sin. Hence, Luther can say that 'justification is a kind of regeneration to newness of life'. In subsequent Protestantism, however, justification as the imputation of righteousness and non-imputation of sin came to be interpreted forensically, as simply a verdict of acquittal, from which the renewal of life by the gift of the Spirit was held sharply distinct.

P. S. WATSON

Independents, Independency

These terms came into general use during the Puritan Revolution to designate the party opposed to the state-connected Presbyterian Church projected by the majority in the Westminster Assembly. The New England leader, John Cotton of Boston, in *The True Constitution of a Particular Visible Church* (1642), first formulated the Independent position. The *Apologetical Narration* presented to the Assembly by the Five Dissenting Brethren in February, 1644, rests partly upon Cotton's treatise and expressly approves the New England church polity. The church officers are pastors, teachers, ruling elders, and deacons. Church discipline is exercised by the elders within each congregation; but a particular church may be after trial excommunicated by neighbouring ones. Synods are held in respect, but the subordination of the Presbyterian structure of jurisdiction, with its provision for provincial, national and ecumenical synods, is wholly rejected. Although the *Narration* did not espouse the principle of toleration, members of the Independent party argued for toleration of a variety of sects as they lent their support to Cromwell in his rise to power. John Goodwin, from an essentially Independent position, became about 1646 a powerful exponent of liberty of conscience. Cromwell's policy placed the Independent ministers in the (for them) incongruous position of a state-supported clergy. *See* **Congregationalism; Savoy Declaration.**

B. Hanbury, *Historical Memorials relating to the Independents or Congregationalists*, 3 vols., 1834–44; G. Yule, *The Independents in the English Civil War*, 1958.

J. T. MCNEILL

Index

Index (in full, *Index Librorum Prohibitorum*) means the list of books which the Roman Catholic Church forbids its members to read or possess. It has been periodically added to since 1557, but recently its authority has been greatly reduced by limiting its scope to general categories of literature rather than lists of particular books.

R. P. C. HANSON

Induction

An inductive argument claims to give *probability, likelihood,* to its conclusions. The premises do not logically necessitate the conclusion – as they do in a valid *de*ductive argument. That is to say: if the conclusion of a deductive argument is denied, while the premises are affirmed, the result is illogic, contradiction. In an inductive argument it may be unreasonable or 'against all experience' to deny the conclusion; but it can be done without contradiction. The study of induction in a wide sense of the word has been the study of scientific method, the justification of inferences from observations and experiments to laws of nature. Checks need to be devised for eliminating irrelevant factors in would-be causal explanations; hypotheses must be submitted to stringent testing. In some fields of investigation (though by no means all) techniques can be worked out by which we may calculate the exact degree of probability that is given to a particular claim by the evidence adduced for it. Probability-theory thus constitutes an important part of mathematical logic.

J. S. Mill's *A System of Logic*, 1843, contains a classical study of inductive method. More recent contributions include R. B. Braithwaite, *Scientific Explanation*, 1953; W. Kneale, *Probability and Induction*, 1949; G. H. von Wright, *The Logical Problem of Induction*, 1941.

R. W. HEPBURN

Indulgences

An indulgence is a remission granted by the (Roman Catholic) Church of the temporal punishment which often remains due to sin after its guilt has been forgiven. Temporal punishment is punishment on earth or in purgatory as distinct from eternal punishment, which is remitted by the absolution from guilt.

In the early Church satisfactions (*see* **Penance**) imposed for grave sins were very severe; but gradually a system of commutation of penalties was evolved to deal with cases of special hardship. From this, the idea of indulgences seems to have developed. An indulgence may be partial, remitting some portion of the penalties due, or plenary, remitting the whole. It is *not a pardon of sin*, still less a permission to commit sin, and it is of no avail apart from confession and absolution. In the Middle Ages, however, it came to be popularly understood as a 'full remission of sins' and an 'absolution from penalty and guilt'. The latter phrase appeared in the indulgence letters offered for sale in connection with the Jubilee Indulgence of the year 1300, which entitled each purchaser to a plenary indulgence once in his lifetime. Theoretically, all the letter intended was to give its purchaser permission to choose any confessor he wished, and to authorize the latter to absolve him from all his sins, including those otherwise reserved to higher authority. But in practice, indulgence letters generally became known as pardons, and the mendicant friars who peddled them as pardoners. The sale of indulgences became a prime means of financing the Church.

The theology of indulgences presupposes that unless satisfaction is made for sin, the sinner must be punished either on earth or in purgatory. Satisfaction may be made either by the sinner or on his behalf – the latter being made possible by the communion of saints, in which all Christians are united with Christ and with one another as members of his Mystical Body. Within this Body the superabundant merit of Christ and the superfluity of merit acquired by the saints form a spiritual treasury for the benefit of the whole Body. On this treasury, the Church, as possessing the power of the keys (*see* **Keys, Power of**), is able to draw unceasingly in order to furnish satisfaction for the sins of Christians. It has at its disposal expiatory acts which the solidarity of the Church renders of value to any Christian to whom they are applied. It can even offer to God satisfaction on behalf of souls in purgatory – an idea which led in mediaeval times to the belief that the mere purchase of a 'pardon' was sufficient to free a soul at once from purgatory.

It was the marketing of an indulgence that led to the publication of Luther's famous *Ninety-Five Theses* in 1517, which launched him on his reforming career. Luther's attack was provoked, not only or primarily by the sordid commercialism of the indulgence traffic, but rather by its disastrous spiritual effects, which he observed in the course of his work as a pastor. When a pardon could be bought for a few pence, what call was there for contrition and amendment of life? When grace was so cheap, how could men take seriously either the law or the gospel of God? – The abuses connected with indulgences were too glaring to be denied, and the Council of Trent (Sess. XXV) reformed the practical use of them, while the Protestants rejected them entirely, along with the sacrament of penance with which they are bound up. The conditions required for obtaining an indulgence today are these: the recipient must be in a state of grace, must have the intention of gaining an indulgence, and must perform the prescribed works. Indulgences gained by the living are certainly effective, as having the force of an authoritative decree. The effect of those applied to souls in purgatory is not so certain, since the Church's disciplinary authority does not extend so far; but as they are backed by expiation officially offered by the Church from her treasury of merits, they are more certain than the private intercessions of the faithful.

J. M. T. Barton, *Penance and Absolution*, 1961; G. Smith, ed., *The Teaching of the Catholic Church*, 1956; S. I. Stuber, *Primer on Roman Catholicism for Protestants*, 1965.

P. S. WATSON

Infallibility

Infallibility is the quality of being divinely preserved from error. It is equivalent to inerrancy, though the use of the latter word is usually restricted to its reference to the Bible. The general infallibility of the Church in its enunciation of dogmas pronounced or endorsed by General Councils, or in its holding and teaching of the basic Christian truths, has for a long time been held by Roman Catholics, by the Eastern Orthodox Church, and since the Tractarian Movement by many Anglicans (in spite of Article XIX of the Thirty-nine Articles, which does not formally contradict this belief). In 1870 the first Vatican Council of the Roman Catholic Church defined the infallibility of the pope as an expression of the infallibility of the Church: it declared that when the pope speaks *ex cathedra*, when he defines a doctrine concerning faith or morals to be held by the universal Church, he is then 'endowed with that infallibility with which the Divine Redeemer has willed that his Church should be equipped', and it added that such decisions are 'of themselves – and not by virtue of the consent of the Church – irreformable.' Theologians of other traditions have attacked this dogma, usually on two main grounds. First, there are plain historical instances of popes making errors while apparently defining faith or morals to be held by the universal Church. In particular Pope Liberius (352–66), under pressure from an Arian Emperor, signed a document whose exact form is unknown but which was certainly Arian in content, and excommunicated the orthodox Athanasius. Pope Vigilius (537–55) issued a Constitution in the form of a definition, and containing the phrase 'we ordain

and decree', on the subject of the disputed Three Chapters, which he explicitly revoked some months later, declaring that he had been deceived by the devil. Pope Honorius I (625–38) gave his opinion, when asked for it by Sergius, Patriarch of Jerusalem, in favour of Monotheletism, 'we confess one will of our Lord Jesus Christ'. Pope Martin I at a Lateran Synod in 649 condemned this view, and the sixth General Council, the third of Constantinople, in 680 endorsed this condemnation, anathematizing Honorius by name. Secondly, it is denied that our Lord did endow, or desire to endow, his Church with infallibility. Indeed, it is held that a desire for infallibility is incompatible with the true nature of Christian faith. It argues a false desire for security and even an unconscious fear and unbelief which take the form of an exaggerated profession of certitude. Perhaps very recent theologians might argue that the quality of infallibility is meaningless apart from individual statements which can only be judged true or false on their own merits.

The Roman Catholic reply to these arguments has usually taken the form of examining each apparent papal error and attempting to show that the pope was not in each case defining faith as universal teacher for the benefit of the whole Church. The tendency on the part of Roman Catholic writers since 1870 has also been to restrict drastically the area of the pope's infallibility. He is not held to be infallible, for instance, in the introduction to his actual definition, nor in the reasons which he gives for his definition, nor in the arguments which he actually depends upon to reach his definition. They also tend to define infallibility as little more than the ordinary certitude which anybody possesses when he becomes convinced of moral or spiritual truth. If this last line were developed it is possible that the two sides might come closer together.

H. Burn-Murdoch, *The Development of the Papacy*, 1954; B. C. Butler, *The Church and Infallibility*, 1954; J. H. Newman, *An Essay in Aid of a Grammar of Assent*, 1870; G. Salmon, *The Infallibility of the Church*, 1923 (latest unabridged ed.).

R. P. C. HANSON

Infant Baptism. *see* Initiation, Christian.

Infusion

Infusion means pouring in. The NT speaks of God's love as 'poured into' men's hearts by the Holy Spirit (Rom. 5.5), and of the Spirit himself as 'poured out' upon men (Acts 2.17, 33). Hence, where divine grace is thought of essentially in terms of a supernatural power or force, it is not unreasonable to speak of it as 'infused' or poured into the human soul. This idea is uncongenial to Protestantism, but quite natural in a Catholic context. Here it is held that an infusion of sanctifying grace (*see* **Grace** [2]) at baptism effects the regeneration of the baptized, making him a partaker of the divine nature, so that he is a child of God, not simply by adoption, but by kinship. Or it can be said that a new, supernatural 'habit' or disposition is infused into the soul, making it acceptable to God, and equipping it with the 'infused virtues' which make it capable of supernatural acts of faith, hope and charity. These things are called 'infused' as being produced directly in the soul by God, not acquired by any natural activity of man. Their infusion, however, neither destroys nor displaces man's natural powers, but rather supernaturalizes them, on the principle that grace perfects nature.

P. S. WATSON

Ingeneracy

Ingeneracy (Greek: *agennesia;* Latin: *innascibilitas*) is the term used increasingly from the fourth century to express the differentiating particularity of the Father. The Arians regarded this characteristic as the sole authentic mark of Deity and therefore rejected the full divinity of the Son and the Spirit. The Cappadocian Fathers drew a sharp distinction between 'uncreated' and 'unbegotten' (*agenetos, agennetos*), two very similar adjectives often confused in the earlier period. The former was the Universal of Godhead, the latter the characteristic of the Father. While in fourth-century polemical theology the negative term Ingeneracy was indispensable, the more positive word Paternity was equally widely used. Aquinas, however, classifies the two terms differently. Paternity is a relation, Ingeneracy (which denotes the absence of relations) is a notion. *See* **Generation; Procession(s).**

H. E. W. TURNER

Initiation, Christian

From apostolic times the initiation of new members into the Church has been by baptism (*cf.* Acts 2.38, 41). For biblical practice *see* R. R. Williams, 'Baptize, Baptism'; 'Laying on of Hands', *TWBB*. Theologically baptism signifies what God has done for our salvation through Christ (Jesus connected his own baptism by John Baptist with his death and rising again) and also what God does for men individually and corporately through the mediating work of Christ. Baptism, like the other dominical sacrament, the Lord's Supper, is a proclamation of Christ's death and resurrection and is thus closely bound up with preaching. It is (not merely represents) a dying to self and a being reborn (in Latin, *regeneratio*) to a new life in Christ. The going down into the waters symbolizes a burial and the coming up from the waters a resurrection (*cf.* Rom. 6.3–11). There is thus a new creation (II Cor. 5.17); a new person is made. Hence the practice of taking a new name (a 'Christian name'): a man's proper name is not his surname, which is generic, but his Christian name, which is his own.

Baptism is thus an eschatological event: even though a baptized person still has a physical death to die, death has no power over him; he is already risen with Christ (*cf.* Col. 2.12; 3.1) and even now

shares Christ's heavenly reign. The Holy Spirit is given in baptism, and the NT knows of no water-baptism which is not a baptism into the Spirit (*cf.* I. Cor. 12.13). The Spirit in the NT always represents the in-breaking power of the Age to Come and is essentially an eschatological agent. The Spirit is the 'earnest' of that which is to come, and the baptized already possess and perceive in themselves the 'first-fruits' of the Spirit of God, the Spirit of the End-time. The Spirit unites us with God in the resurrection-body of Christ, which is the Church. This means, of course, that we are united with one another; the Church is the fellowship or communion of the Holy Spirit, the anticipation on earth of God's Kingdom of heaven. Already here below the baptized join with angels and archangels and with all the company of heaven in praising the name of God.

As we are born into a natural family on earth, so at baptism we are reborn ('regenerated') into the family of our heavenly Father. We partake of the family meal at the Table of the Lord and are fed with the Bread from heaven; in the patristic Church, and normally ever since that time, admission to the Holy Communion is reserved for the baptized. This is not only because the partakers of the Holy Communion need careful instruction in what they are doing (the catechumens, or candidates for baptism, have traditionally been baptized only after a careful period of preparation) but also because the Church is the royal priesthood (*see* **Priesthood of all Believers; Laity**) which offers up the Christian sacrifices through Jesus Christ. The admission of unbaptized persons would change the character of the central act of Christian worship. Baptismal creeds (*see* **Creed[s]**) were from the earliest times designed for recitation by the persons to be baptized. The profession of faith in Christ or in the triune God in the presence of witnesses was required of the candidate for baptism (*cf.* I Tim. 6.12). Jesus himself had made his 'good confession' before Pontius Pilate (I Tim. 6.13) on the eve of his baptism in the waters of death. His death is to be understood as the baptism of the whole human race, of which he is the Representative (q.v.); but individuals must be baptized into him, or into his death, in order that they may appropriate to themselves the fruits of his redemption. In the early Church catechumens who were martyred in the persecutions before they could be baptized were judged to have been baptized in their death, if they had died making profession of the name of Christ (*see* **Martyr**).

The baptism of Christ and of the Christian is a recapitulation and fulfilment of the history of Israel. At the exodus from Egypt Israel was baptized and saved by passing through the waters of the Red Sea (*cf.* I Cor. 10.2), understanding little of what was happening; but at the Covenant-making at Sinai, having been instructed by Moses, Israel's promise was ratified (*cf. below*, 'confirmation'): 'All that Yahweh has commanded we will do and be obedient' (Ex. 24.7 in its context). This has long been regarded as the prototype of infant-baptism (*see below*) in the Church: *cf.* Hos. 11.1, 'When Israel was a *child*, then I loved him, and called my son out of Egypt.' The baptism of Jesus by John in the river Jordan was regarded as the fulfilment by Christ ('the New Israel': 'my beloved Son', Mark 1.11) of the OT pattern of salvation. Jesus, too, goes into the Wilderness after his baptism, and is tempted as the Old Israel had been. The messianic Son recapitulates the history of Israel, the disobedient son, but is not vanquished by the Tempter. He makes a New Covenant with a New Israel, which is ratified in his own blood. The baptism of the individual into the Church, which (like the baptism of Christ in his death) is once-for-all, unrepeatable, is commemorated every time the Lord's death is shown forth in the Eucharist. The two sacraments of baptism and the Lord's Supper are thus indissolubly connected.

Christian baptism is not entirely parallel to circumcision among the Jews. Circumcision was the sign of God's Covenant with Abraham (Gen. 17.10), not of the deliverance at the Red Sea and the Sinai Covenant. It was the token of descent from Abraham, i.e. of Israelite nationality; a proselyte converted to Judaism would have to change not only his religion but his nationality. Into the New Israel people of all nations were baptized (Matt. 28.19), and females were baptized as well as males (*cf.* Gal. 3.28). A characteristic of Christian baptism is its universality. Nevertheless, as circumcision was the 'seal' of the Covenant with Abraham, baptism was the 'seal' of the New Covenant of the Messiah. Nor is Christian baptism strictly comparable with the baptism of John, though the element of the confession of sins is common to both: each is 'a baptism of repentance', and indeed the washing away of sins is strongly emphasized in the traditional forms of Christian baptism. Rigorists in the ancient Church maintained that post-baptismal sin could not be forgiven, at least in certain forms (*cf.* Heb. 6.4–8, and *see* W. Telfer, *The Forgiveness of Sins*, 1959). The great difference between John's baptism and Christian baptism was that the latter was baptism in Holy Spirit; according to the Christian tradition John had prophesied a coming messianic baptism with Holy Spirit and with fire (Matt. 3.11, etc.). Doubtless John was referring to the fires of judgment, but the Church considered the prophecy to have been fulfilled by the tongues of fire at Pentecost (Acts 2.3 f.); this was the baptism of the apostles, who had not (we may suppose) been baptized with water. Not only was baptism held by the early Church to be a washing away of sins, an enlightenment of the heart (*cf.* Heb. 6.4; 10.32; Eph. 1.18; 5.8), the way to sanctification and justification (I Cor. 6.11), and the sealing by the Holy Spirit till the day of redemption (II Cor. 1.22; Eph. 1.13; 4.30): it was also the exorcizing of evil spirits. It is possible that (as Cullmann has suggested) St Mark's story of the Epileptic Boy (9.16–29) has baptismal undertones. The Book of Common Prayer of 1549 contained a prayer of exorcism in the Baptismal Office.

From NT times the laying on of hands has been associated with baptism (*see* R. R. Williams, 'Laying on of Hands', *TWBB*). The history of this practice is so confused that no theological conclusions can be drawn from it. From the earliest times the bishop would appear to have been the minister of baptism and the laying on of hands (or confirmation, as the ceremony is now usually called). The two acts of baptizing and confirming seem originally to have been performed in immediate succession: in a missionary situation the catechumens would be mostly adult. As the number of church members swelled, the bishop could not be present at every baptism and he would lay on hands later at a convenient season. When during and after the third century the practice of baptizing infants had begun, it became normal in the West to postpone confirmation until the candidates were old enough to ratify on their own behalf the promises which their sponsors or 'Godparents' had made on their behalf. But in the East hands were laid on the infant at his baptism, the bishop's part having been performed from a distance and consisting in the blessing of the oil with which the infant was anointed (*see* **Unction**). In Lutheran and some other Protestant churches which practice infant baptism, the parish clergyman is the minister of confirmation. Disagreement within the same church is sometimes found concerning the nature of the gift received through the laying on of hands. Thus among Anglicans some regard the gift of the Spirit as being imparted in confirmation (K. E. Kirk, A. J. Mason, F. W. Puller, L. S. Thornton, G. Dix), while others insist that the Spirit is given in baptism (D. Stone, G. W. H. Lampe). In the case of adults the problem hardly arises, because baptism and the laying on of hands may be administered together; it becomes more acute when baptism in infancy is separated by several years from confirmation. Even so, the problem is an unreal one; it has been created by the unbiblical disjunction of the total act of Christian initiation into two separate acts, or separate sacraments. When this disjunction occurs in theology as well as in time, there is no solution for a problem which is entirely of artificial manufacture.

Infant baptism (*paedobaptism* in its Greek form) has been practised by the Church in an unbroken tradition from the third century until the Reformation, when the Anabaptists (q.v.) and later the Baptists (q.v.) renounced the practice and proclaimed the necessity of 'believers' baptism.' The churches of the Catholic tradition and many Protestant confessions (including the Lutheran and the Presbyterian) have retained the practice of infant baptism. In recent years much has been written on the question of the propriety of infant baptism. Some eminent NT scholars hold that in the NT, even in the Gospels, there is evidence of and authority for the practice of infant baptism (Cullmann, Jeremias); others dissent from this view (K. Aland, G. R. Beasley-Murray). The propriety of infant baptism, however, cannot be determined by research into NT texts; it must be accepted or rejected upon strictly theological considerations. Obviously an important factor in judging the issue will be the weight which is given to tradition in the interpretation of Scripture: the extreme Reformation sects held that what was not explicitly enjoined in Scripture was forbidden. Since they held that there was no scriptural sanction for the baptism of infants and also that the profession of personal faith was demanded in Scripture from those who were to be baptized, the latter must be old enough to understand what they were doing and saying. Doubtless laxity in the administration of confirmation and the reduction of the rite to a matter of mere formality and social conformity led to the insistence upon the necessity of personal faith and of conversion-experience in the light of the rediscovery of the doctrine of justification by faith. A principle of great theological importance was involved, namely, the biblical emphasis upon personal faith in Christ on the part of those coming to baptism. On the other hand, no great matter of principle is involved in the manner of baptizing – whether by total immersion or by sprinkling or by pouring water on the head. While it may readily be granted that immersion best symbolizes the dying and rising again with Christ, the mode of baptism is agreed by most theologians to be a matter of indifference. Much depends upon climate, as Calvin himself noted. Theologians of all schools, however, would agree that the confession of personal faith is not a matter of indifference.

How, then, can the baptism of infants be justified? It can be justified only if baptism and confirmation are looked upon as together making up the one act of Christian initiation, even though they are separated in time by months or years. Baptism in infancy, if it is not followed at the age of discretion by a personal confession of faith (whether accompanied by the laying on of hands or not), is not Christian initiation in the NT sense; a good work has been begun but has not been completed. Nor will confirmation administered conventionally as a social custom fulfil the NT requirement, for then the 'faith' of those confirmed will not be personal commitment to Christ in his Church but mere *fides historica* (q.v.). Indiscriminate confirmation, like indiscriminate baptism, sets up grave pastoral problems for churches in ages in which everyone is conventionally baptized and confirmed, as is being increasingly recognized now that convention no longer requires conformity to Christian institutions in lands which were once 'Christendom' (q.v.).

Infant baptism, understood as the first part of the whole action of Christian initiation, symbolizes an essential NT truth. Faith is the response to God's saving act in Christ, not the condition of it. I have not decided to believe and therefore be baptized: when I was weak and helpless, God chose me (as he chose Israel in Egypt). My faith is God's gift; it is called into being by the knowledge that God through the mediation of my parents or Godparents (since God uses human agents to baptize as well as to preach) has called me to be his son. I am not justified by my faith (always a fragile thing); I believe because I am justified by God's action in Christ. 'You have not chosen me, but I have chosen you' (John 15.16): this is the truth enshrined in the symbolism of infant baptism. The important thing in baptism is what God does, not what we do, whether we are infants or adults. Faith is the response of a child to the loving call of one who would otherwise have been a stranger (*cf.* Mark 10.13–16; also 9.36 f.). Infant baptism signifies that most mysterious yet central doctrine of biblical faith, the mystery of the divine election (q.v.). I do not know why of all people God chose me; I only know that I was brought to the font by God's grace working through others, and that I must respond in humble gratitude to the love which he has offered to me in my baptism. Christ's death upon the cross was indeed in some mysterious way the baptism of the whole human race, but it was the result of their unbelief, not of their believing. It created the faith of those who believe. Similarly the baptism of the individual *theologically* precedes the awakening of faith and is not the consequence of it. Hence the theological propriety of infant baptism. In a word, the faith by which we are justified is not our achievement but God's gift. Infant baptism is a symbol of the doctrine of justification by faith properly understood. If we are asked what is the 'grace' (or gift of the Spirit) conferred on the baptized infant and how it differs from that given through the laying on of hands (or at a service of admission to adult church-membership), we may reply that it is not the theologian's duty to debate or decide speculative questions to which answers are not forthcoming from scriptural revelation (or from the confused tradition about such matters); it is enough for us to know that at each stage of the life of the baptized person, God's grace is sufficient for him.

There is 'one baptism' (Eph. 4.5). This truth has been practised among all the churches, although certain evangelical sects (such as the Anabaptists or 're-baptizers') have not followed the general custom. Churches do not re-baptize those who have been baptized by a minister or layman of other denominations. The validity of lay baptism, at least in cases of urgency, is recognized. The acceptance of baptism by other churches is an ecumenical fact of great importance, since it implies that in some sense baptized Christians of all denominations are 'in Christ'. Where it is uncertain whether baptism has indeed been administered, 'conditional baptism' is generally practised, using some such formula as 'If thou hast not already been baptized, I baptize thee . . .' In the earliest days of the Church, it appears that baptism was often administered 'in the name of Christ', but since the beginning of the second century baptism has been normally in the threefold name (*cf.* Matt. 28.19). In the baptism of every Christian each person of the Trinity (q.v.) is involved: the new Christian becomes a son in the family of the universal Father, a new man through the saving and regenerating work of Christ, and a participant in the gifts of the Holy Spirit.

K. Aland, *Did the Early Church Baptize Infants?* ET, 1963; K. Barth, *The Teaching of the Church regarding Baptism*, ET, 1948; G. R. Beasley-Murray, *Baptism in the New Testament*, 1962; O. Cullmann, *Baptism in the New Testament*, ET, 1950; G. Dix, *The Theology of Confirmation in relation to Baptism*, 1946; W. F. Flemington, *The New Testament Doctrine of Baptism*, 1948; J. Jeremias, *Infant Baptism in the First Four Centuries*, ET, 1961; G. W. H. Lampe, *The Seal of the Spirit*, 1951; A. J. Mason, *The Relation of Confirmation to Baptism*, 1890; M. Perry, ed., *Crisis for Confirmation*, 1967; Alan Richardson, *Introduction to the Theology of the New Testament*, 1958, ch. 15; J. Schneider, *Baptism and Church in the New Testament*, ET, 1957. A booklet published by the Church of Scotland's Panel on Doctrine, *The Doctrine of Baptism*, 1962, presents an excellent summary in twenty pages.

EDITOR

Inner Light

The idea of faith as an enlightening of the eyes of the heart is a very ancient one (*cf.* Eph. 1.18). Illumination in this sense was considered to be a consequence of baptism. In modern times, when rationalism (q.v.) in theology was fashionable, the Cambridge Platonists spoke of reason as 'the candle of the Lord'. But the expression 'inner light' was used, especially by the Society of Friends, of the Christian's inward assurance or experience of salvation, and this is what is usually understood by it. The doctrine may be interpreted in such a way as to avoid the charge of ontologism (q.v.). *See* Harold Loukes, *The Quaker Contribution*, 1965, ch. III. *See also* **Assent.**

EDITOR

Inspiration

Although it has been much used in theological discussion, this is hardly a biblical word (only at II Tim. 3.16 in A V, and this is altered in R V: the meaning is that God breathes life into the dead letter of scripture and makes his word live in our hearts: *cf.* Gen. 2.7; Wisd. 15.11). Pagan ideas of the divine *afflatus* were not uncommon in the early Christian centuries (*see* Alan Richardson, 'Inspire, Inspiration', *TWBB*): the normal biblical way of referring to the divine imparting of truth is by means of the metaphor of God's speaking his word. Since the nineteenth century the idea of inspiration has played a considerable part in the discussion of the nature of biblical revelation; it is congenial to romantic and liberal notions of man's relation to God. The term 'verbal inspiration' has been used of the literalist theory of scriptural inerrancy (*see* **Fundamentalism**). These theories go far beyond the biblical conception as expressed (e.g.) in II Peter 1.21, that prophetic men 'spoke from God, being moved by

the Holy Spirit'. *See also* **Witness of the Spirit.**

S. L. Greenslade, ed., *Cambridge History of the Bible: the West from the Reformation*, 1963, ch. VIII; W. Sanday, *Inspiration* (Bampton Lectures for 1893).

EDITOR

Insufflation

Insufflation is a blowing or breathing upon a person or thing to symbolize and/or effect the giving of the Holy Spirit (*cf.* John 20.22) and the expulsion of evil spirits. In the primitive and mediaeval periods insufflation was a feature of exorcism, of the rites of the catechumens and, from thence, of baptism; it also forms part of the blessing of the font and of the chrism or holy oil. It remains a feature of Roman Catholic ritual and is found in some Eastern rites, particularly those that have undergone Latin influence, e.g. the Maronite.

J. G. DAVIES

Intercession. see Prayer, Theology of.

Invincible Ignorance

This term appears primarily in Catholic theology but the concept is widespread in Christian thought. Christians believe that Christ offers salvation for man, but all men do not hear about this salvation and often they hear it in a form that makes it unpersuasive or even unacceptable. Some Christians have been prepared to argue that all who are ignorant of the gospel are thereby doomed to eternal damnation. But this is difficult to justify in the light of God's love and justice as revealed in Christ. The concept of invincible ignorance is used to describe any ignorance of Christ and his way of salvation for which the ignorant one is not responsible. Unlike wilful ignorance, invincible ignorance does not lead to damnation.

WILLIAM HORDERN

Invisible Church, Visible Church

In the NT there are two distinct traditions concerning the question whether the Church is visible or not, the Pauline and the Johannine. Paul in all his Letters assumes that the membership of the Church is pretty clearly ascertainable: he writes to 'the Church of God which is at Corinth', and he continues to treat his readers as the Church in Corinth even while he rebukes them for sins quite inconsistent with their Christian profession. Likewise in Phil. 3.12–14 he envisages the possibility of his ultimately failing to attain salvation even though he had preached to others. Thus Paul believes in a Church which is visible, whose membership can be known, and from which it is possible to fall. On the other hand John (and his disciple who wrote the Johannine Epistles, assuming that they are not from the same hand) seems to hold the view that apostasy is a sign that the apostate has never really belonged to the Church. This is implied in what is said about Judas (*see* John 6.70 f.; 13.11, 18; 17.12). He is 'a son of perdition', and Jesus knew he was predestined to treachery. This becomes explicit in I John 2.19. Behind this lies the assumption that a member of the Church cannot fall from grace, and the corollary holds that the Church is invisible, as its membership can be known to God only.

The Alexandrian theologians tended towards a doctrine of an invisible Church; Origen, with his universalist convictions, held that the Church mystically comprises all humanity. Augustine was faced with the problem of reconciling his strict views on predestination with the sacramental functioning of the historical Church. His solution was to insist on the principle that the true Church consisted of those who were genuinely devout Christians, and was therefore invisible as being known only to God (*see* **Predestination**); but he added that this invisible fellowship is only to be found within the – visible – historical Catholic Church. In *The City of God* we find a passage which adumbrates the later mediaeval distinction between the Church militant on earth (Augustine would say 'on pilgrimage'), expectant in purgatory, and the church triumphant in heaven (*see The City of God*, xii. 9; *cf.* Rev. 7.9–11). In the West the emphasis which later came to be laid on the power of the keys belonging to the pope meant that the doctrine of the Church as a visible organization was much more to the fore.

It is remarkable that both Luther and Calvin resisted the temptation to call to their aid a doctrine of a purely invisible Church, despite the fact that they had to find an ecclesiology that would justify them in breaking with the Church as visibly organized. It is true that Luther distinguishes a spiritual, inner Christendom from the man-made, external Christendom, but he does not want to divorce the two. The true Christendom (which is known only by faith) exists inside the external Christendom. Luther also gives the seven external marks by which we can perceive where the Church is on earth. These are: (1) the preaching of the word: 'Where you hear or see this Word preached, believed, confessed, and acted on . . . there there must be a true *ecclesia sancta catholica*' ('On the Councils and the Churches'); (2) baptism; (3) the Lord's Supper; (4) the keys, i.e. the administration of churchly discipline; (5) the calling of ministers; (6) prayer and public worship; and (7) 'possession of the Holy Cross', that is, suffering. Thus, though Luther refused to identify the true Church with the organized institution, he did not maintain a doctrine of a purely invisible Church.

Calvin's doctrine of the Church closely follows Augustine's. The elect of God are a small number in the midst of a huge multitude, so 'only to God is knowledge of his Church to be allowed, a Church whose foundation is his hidden election' (*Institutes*, iv. 1.2). But this does not mean that we can ignore the visible Church: 'As it is necessary for us to believe in the invisible Church which is apparent only to the eyes of God, so we are commanded to respect that Church which is called the Church on the human plane, and enjoy its communion' (*ibid.* 7). We can know this visible Church by the preaching of the word and the celebration of the sacraments, and he even cites the example of the Corinthian Church to prove that a Church with serious moral faults was not repudiated by Paul. To this visible Church are the keys committed; indeed for the exercise of the Church's discipline a doctrine of a visible Church is essential. It is obvious that the teaching of both Luther and Calvin has influenced the wording of the nineteenth article of the Thirty-Nine Articles of the Church of England, which defines the visible Church as 'a congregation of faithful men, in which the pure Word of God is preached, and the sacraments be duly administered according to Christ's ordinance'.

The theologians of the Liberal school on the whole sat loose to a doctrine of a visible Church, but in the last fifty years two new movements have compelled theologians to re-examine their doctrine of the Church. The first is the rise of the 'biblical theology' (q.v.) inspired by Karl Barth. Barth has himself condemned what he calls 'an ecclesiastical docetism' which tends to 'magnify an invisible fellowship of the Spirit and spirits' at the expense of the visible Church (*Church Dogmatics*, IV: *Doctrine of Reconciliation*, 1, ET, 1956, p. 653). He insists that the Church is at one and the same time both visible and invisible. There is not some other invisible Church different from the visible Church, but 'the living community of the living Lord Jesus Christ calls for the perception of faith, and is accessible only to this perception and not to any other' (*ibid.*, p. 656). In thus insisting that the Church is not invisible but that it requires faith to see it, Barth seems to be harking back to Luther. But he insists that the unity of the Church must be shewn forth visibly; it is no use retiring into 'the unity of an invisible Church' (*ibid.*, pp. 676–8).

The second new feature is the Ecumenical Movement (q.v.); the urge to unity can only be based on belief in a visible Church. Thus the whole Ecumenical Movement is instigated by the conviction that the Church about which we read in the NT must be in some sense identified with the visible, empirical Church as we know it. The process of discussion and preparation of schemes for union has necessarily involved taking very seriously the visibility of the Church. Most union schemes begin from the assumption that the unity of the visible Church springs from our common baptism. Recently there has been a new attempt by Roman Catholic theologians to frame a doctrine of the Church beginning from this point rather than from the denominational structure. But the Ecumenical Movement has also had the effect of drawing together those who regard the visible Church with suspicion and who lay their main emphasis on an invisible fellowship of 'real Christians'. Thus we find most schemes for union opposed by a combination of extreme Evangelicals and liberal Protestants, who have in common only belief in an invisible, rather than a visible, Church. To them are generally joined militant denominationalists who are willing to identify their church with *the* Church. *See also* **Church.**

St Augustine, *The City of God* (many versions); Karl Barth, *Church Dogmatics*, IV: *The Doctrine of Reconciliation*, 1, ET, 1956; John Calvin, *Institutes* (many versions), iv; E. Mersch, *The Whole Christ*, ET, 1949; L. Newbigin, *The Household of God*, 1953; *Reunion of the Church*, 1948.

A. T. HANSON

Invocation of Saints

Devotion to the Saints (*see* **Canonization**) increased after the fourth century until it was generally taught (as by Leo the Great, d. 461) that their intercession at the throne of grace could and should be invoked on behalf of the living and the departed. The Reformers abolished the practice in the Protestant churches, not merely because of the superstitions which had grown up around it in the Middle Ages, but more especially because it obscured the truth of the doctrine of the one Mediator (I Tim. 2.5).

EDITOR

Irenaeus, St

Iranaeus (c. 130–c. 200) was bishop of Lyons (Lugdunum) from c. 178 to c. 200. He had come earlier in his life from Asia Minor (perhaps from Smyrna, where he says that he knew its bishop Polycarp) to Rome, and later was a presbyter of the church of Lyons. He was in Rome on a deputation to the bishop Eleutherus when fierce persecution broke out in the churches of Lyons and Vienne (177) which resulted in the death of the then bishop of Lyons, Pothinus. Irenaeus succeeded him as bishop, and lived to at least 190, when he wrote a letter to Victor, bishop of Rome, about the Quartodeciman controversy, and probably longer. Two of his works have survived, the *Adversus Haereses*, his *magnum opus*, a treatise in five books against all heresies existing in his day, extant in a Latin translation and in several considerable fragments of the original Greek, and the *Demonstration of the Apostolic Preaching*, a smaller book written probably towards the end of Irenaeus' life, and extant only in an Armenian version. Irenaeus' thought marks a distinct advance upon the theology of the sub-apostolic period and of most of the Apologists. He is convinced of the necessity of believing in God both as creator and as redeemer, in opposition to the Gnostics (the constant target of his attack) who tended to separate the creation of the world from God's direct agency, or even to regard it as a mistake or a fault. Irenaeus teaches an 'economic Trinity' no less than the Apologists; for him the Logos only became an independent hypostasis for purposes of creation and redemption. But his thought is centred on the incarnation more than that of any non-Scriptural writer before him. This is particularly evident in his doctrine of 'recapi-

tulation', whereby Christ retraced all the stages of Adam's experience and all the process of Adam's transgression, at each stage and each act obeying where Adam had disobeyed, and in his great principle that Christ 'became what we are that he might make us what he is'. Irenaeus also stressed the succession of bishops as teaching organs in their sees reaching back to the apostles and the continuity of the rule of faith as a way to bring tradition to support Scripture.

J. Lawson, *The Biblical Theology of St Irenaeus*, 1948; G. Wingren, *Man and the Incarnation*, 1959.

R. P. C. HANSON

Jansenism

This movement, so called because of its origins in the teaching of Cornelius Otto Jansen (1585–1638), bishop of Ghent and later of Ypres, developed in France after c.1640 and persisted through the eighteenth century. It maintained an extreme form of St Augustine's doctrine of grace, conceived as irresistible, and also a severe moral rigorism. Hostile to the Jesuits, it opposed *probabilism*, the view that when the rightness of a course of action is in doubt, it is lawful to pursue a probable opinion in favour of liberty, even though the opposed opinion in favour of the law is more probable: as against *probabiliorism*, which maintains that such a course may be pursued only if the libertarian opinion is *more probable* than the opinion in favour of the law. That such matters could excite controversy and even promote schism seems in our altered climate of opinion almost incredible. But in the seventeenth century the nuns of the Convent of Port-Royal (SW of Paris) were caught up into the controversy, refusing to subscribe to the papal condemnation of Jansenism. Blaise Pascal (1623–1662), whose sister became a nun of Port-Royal, wrote his *Provincial Letters* in defence of the movement. A further papal bull (*Unigenitus,* 1713) condemned Jansenism; its supporters, being persecuted in France, migrated to the Netherlands. Eventually the Dutch Jansenists opted for schism and chose for themselves a bishop of Utrecht (1723). This was the origin of the Old Catholics, though they have been joined by other groups of formerly Roman Catholic churches since that date. *See* **Old Catholics; Pascal, B.**

N. J. Abercrombie, *The Origins of Jansenism*, 1936; J. Paquier, *Le Jansénisme*, 1909.

EDITOR

Jaspers, Karl

Karl Jaspers (1883–   ), German philosopher of existence, began his career as a psychiatrist. Jaspers sharply distinguishes between the subject-matter of science (the world of objects) and the sphere of human *existence*. Within the latter he stresses human finitude and what he calls limit-

or border-situations (German: *Grenzsituationen*). In such situations (e.g., of dread, guilt, death, etc.) there is the possibility of the disclosure of *transcendence*, a concept in Jasper's thought which possesses striking resemblances to the Hebrew-Christian notion of God. But Jaspers is careful to distinguish his position from that of the biblical tradition by criticizing the latter's *exclusiveness*; he holds that the possibility of the disclosure of transcendence belongs to the structure of human existence as such, and is not confined to any one religious tradition or any one set of historical events. Jaspers' *philosophical faith* has deeply influenced the work of his colleague in the University of Basel, the theologian Fritz Buri (1907–), who has constructed a 'theology of existence' which is strikingly similar to the philosophy of Jaspers.

H. J. Blackham, *Six Existentialist Thinkers*, 1952, ch. III.

JAMES RICHMOND

Jerome

Jerome (c. 342–420) was the greatest biblical scholar in the ancient Church. He was born at Strido near Aquileia and had a varied career as hermit, priest, scholar, spiritual director of noble and wealthy Roman women, and monk. He had studied at Rome and then travelled in the East and visited Chalcis in the Syrian desert, Antioch and Constantinople before he returned to Rome (382–5) to become secretary of Pope Damasus. He then visited Antioch again, Egypt and Palestine, before settling finally in a monastery at Bethlehem where as well as directing the affairs of his community he could oversee the development of the convent there which some of his women devotees had founded and joined. His chief work was the production of a new Latin translation of the whole Bible, later known as the Vulgate, which he had finished by about 400. He was one of the best Hebrew scholars in the ancient Church, if not the best, and his translation has the great advantage of being made for the most part direct from the Hebrew instead of from the LXX. But in some of his versions of the Psalter (for he produced more than one) and in several of the books of the NT, Jerome's translation was rather a revision of an existing Latin translation than a translation *de novo*. Realizing as he did the importance of the original Hebrew, Jerome was led to distinguish sharply between those books of the OT which were extant in Hebrew and those extant only in Greek, the Apocrypha, and was one of the first Christian writers to do so. Jerome was of a passionate and quarrelsome disposition and was incapable of controlling the violence of his pen when engaged in the many controversies which marked his career. The two main conflicts in which he played a prominent and aggressive part were concerned with Origenism, a type of thought which he had favoured in his youth but which he later attacked, and with asceticism, to which he attributed an exaggerated value in controversy

with two writers, Helvidus and Jovinian, who had criticized it. His other main works, besides biblical commentaries, were a series of biographies of famous Christians (*De Viris Illustribus*) and his letters, which throw important light on Christianity in Rome during the second part of the fourth century.

S. L. Greenslade, ed., *Early Latin Theology*, 1956, pp. 281–400.

R. P. C. HANSON

Jesus of History, The

1. *The Problem*. The phrase 'Jesus of history' ('historical Jesus') is an odd one; its very character suggests that it arose in a situation of controversy. For 'Jesus of history' is evidently contrasted with a Jesus who is not 'of history'; the obvious alternative would seem to be Jesus as presented in Christian tradition from the NT onwards (*see* **Christology**). The first appearance of the phrase 'Jesus of history' – and, indeed, of the term christology – is to be found in the context of the thorough-going critique of the Christian tradition in all its aspects launched at the Enlightenment (q.v.). Behind it was a conviction that there were elements in the Church's picture of Jesus which, when examined critically, would prove to be later embellishments; their removal would reveal a figure different from, perhaps even contradictory to, the main lines of that picture. In subsequent writing, 'Jesus of history' has become a convenient shorthand term for 'Jesus as he comes to be known by strictly historical methods', and because historical knowledge of a figure of the past is regularly taken to be 'real' knowledge, the 'historical' Jesus in this sense has often been understood to be the 'real' Jesus – Jesus as he really was. While the phrase *can* be understood in strictly neutral terms, both these connotations, the contrast between the historical Jesus and the Church's Christ and the historical Jesus as the 'real' Jesus, are frequently to be noted.

As both the understanding of the nature of the evidence for the life and work of Jesus and the understanding of historical criticism itself have changed considerably over the past two centuries, the full significance of the phrase and the problems which it raises can best be shown by a survey of its use over this period.

2. *The Sources*. Despite the meagreness of the extra-biblical evidence for Jesus (Tacitus, Suetonius, Josephus, Talmud) and the problem, in some cases, of its authenticity, there is no reason to doubt that Jesus existed. When we add to this evidence the material contained in the NT, and note the character of the controversies carried on in the early centuries after Jesus' death (the fact of Jesus' past existence is taken for granted by all sides), we have sufficient grounds for ruling out the possibility of Jesus having been a purely mythical figure. On the other hand, none of the evidence outside the Gospels tells us much about what Jesus said or did that can be said to have in-

dependent historical value. Consequently, while the background to the age in which Jesus lived may be increasingly illuminated by further discovery and research, unless we are given any authentic new material bearing *directly* on the life of Jesus, historical investigation into his career is dependent on the interpretation of the Gospels, which, by their very nature, present exegetical problems of the utmost complexity. Early investigations, to which we now turn, were inevitably vitiated by insufficient knowledge of the historical background and a failure to realize the interpretative problems.

3. *The 'Quest of the Historical Jesus'*. The first period of critical study of the figure of Jesus takes its title from Albert Schweitzer's classic account, published in English as *The Quest of the Historical Jesus*. For Schweitzer, the beginning of the 'Quest' is marked by the work of Hermann Samuel Reimarus (1694–1768), a teacher of oriental languages in Hamburg. Seven sections of a long criticism of Christianity by Reimarus were published after his death by Gotthold Lessing (1729–1781) as the *Wolfenbüttel Fragments*. In the longest of them, 'On the aims of Jesus and his Disciples', Reimarus claimed to be distinguishing what Jesus really said and taught from the (false) account of the apostolic writings. The substance of his argument was that Jesus was a traditional Jew persuaded that he was the long-foretold Messiah. At first Jesus' disciples believed his claims, but after his death they revised the whole story of his career and made the earthly kingdom into a heavenly one. Similarities between Reimarus' theory and that of Schweitzer (*see below*) led Schweitzer to view Reimarus as a great pioneer. The truth, however, is not so simple nor are the similarities quite as striking in context as Schweitzer makes out. The work of Reimarus is hardly yet historical reconstruction. The rest of his writing shows him to have been preoccupied with the conflict between reason and Christianity in all its aspects; in this he was strongly influenced by English Deism (q.v.); for the most part, his arguments reflect standpoints developed from the beginning of the eighteenth century. The same thing specifically applies to his study of Jesus; rationalist views show through again and again, and the features of the work which so impressed Schweitzer are not least born of the necessity of reconciling the Gospels with convictions held on other grounds. If, however, Reimarus represents little advance beyond his English predecessors, he is significant in that the form of his work and the way in which it was presented raised the question of the person of Jesus in Germany in a way which could not be ignored.

The case of Reimarus illustrates the disadvantage of the wholesale use of the title 'The Quest of the Historical Jesus'. It is difficult to know just where 'historical' is the proper adjective to begin to apply. Enlightenment historiography, with its recurrent inability to see figures of the past other than as eighteenth-century men in different garb, leads readily to quite unhistorical accounts, which explain the unusual in terms of misunderstanding or deception. This feature has a long-term influence.

In the period immediately following Reimarus, we see a heightened interest in the miraculous – the unusual in the extreme – an element in which the Gospels are seen to be rich. Some lives of Jesus, notably that by H. E. G. Paulus (1761–1851), are no more than a collection of explanations of the miracles without any interconnecting links; here, too, possible individual explanations are heaped up at the expense of general historical probability.

As much is pointed out by David Friedrich Strauss (1808–1874), in his first *Life of Jesus*, published in two volumes in 1835–36. Strauss, too, lacked a historical sense and did not construct a coherent 'life' of Jesus; like his rationalist predecessors, he was concerned to criticize individual points of the Gospel narratives. He differed from them, however, in his introduction and widespread use of the category of myth. The category of myth is carefully explained, and positive and negative criteria are given: it contradicts natural, historical and psychological laws, being poetic narrative which expresses religious concepts, deriving from Christian experience, the OT and elsewhere. By examining the Gospels in the light of this approach, Strauss was able to play off the earlier rationalist approach against the traditional orthodox approach and found both wanting. Despite his explanation of the term myth, Strauss gives the impression of using too loosely and too enthusiastically an imprecise concept; it can be employed as a blunt instrument to suppress almost any unwelcome opposition. Consequently, Strauss's results are overwhelming negative. On the other hand, his shortcomings should not obscure Strauss's positive contribution: his use of myth introduced a new and important element into the discussion and showed up the inadequacies of previous work – nor was his scepticism entirely unjustified.

The contribution of Strauss, however, like that of his great teacher F. C. Baur (1792–1860), the first theologian seriously to come to grips with the beginnings of Christianity in historical terms, was a considerable time in bearing fruit. For the moment it was neglected, even (paradoxically enough) by Strauss himself in his second *Life of Jesus* (1864). By far the most dominant feature in the area with which we are concerned during the latter half of the nineteenth century was the wealth of 'Lives' of Jesus which attempted to present a coherent picture of him by removing features regarded as inauthentic and supplying material to fill the many gaps in the Gospel narratives. The opportunities for selectivity and elaboration are considerable, and inevitably there are numerous lives written to further specific ideals and numerous examples of sheerly bad historical writing. Details are available in Schweitzer's book. Even among the best writing, however, an important trend is to be noted. The early lives which presented a coherent picture of Jesus, e.g. K. F. Bahrdt's *Explanation of the Plans and Aims of Jesus* (1784–92) and K. H. Venturini's *Non-supernatural History of the Great Prophet of Nazareth* (1800–02), were predominantly concerned with criticism and explanation of events in Jesus' life; later work was concerned rather with Jesus as a *personality*. Reconstruction of Jesus' teaching, his conduct, his inner development and his impact on his contemporaries was a means of arriving at this personality. Side by side with the open claim that the historical method was neutral and discovered facts (*see* **History, Problem of**), ran an idealist view of history for which personality was all-important. Man was seen to be a partner in the movement towards the divine goal of the historical process, and shared in this movement by making himself open to spiritual power. From time to time great individuals appeared, who embodied this power to a supreme degree. Chief among these was Jesus, on whom God brought his fatherly goodness to bear, revealing the infinite value of the human soul.

In theory, the great liberal systematic theologians, Albrecht Ritschl and Wilhelm Herrmann (*see* **Liberal Theology**), and the liberal historian Adolf von Harnack, set out to maintain a distinction between fact and value, between history and faith. It was, however, more difficult, particularly for lesser lights, to maintain in practice. As a result, the work of reconstructing an historical Jesus became fatally entangled with a second task, the construction of a figure considerable enough to replace the Christ of the Church's tradition as an object of faith. Two representative works to be seen against this background are E. Renan's *Life of Jesus* (1863) and J. R. Seeley's *Ecce Homo* (1865): there are many, many, others. Believing that they knew the main lines of what the figure of Jesus would embody when he was 'discovered', historians projected what they were looking for on to the lay-figure of Jesus, whether there was support in the Gospels or not. When Schweitzer came to write his book, it was therefore an easy task for him to demonstrate that the 'liberal' lives of Jesus were no more than mirror-reflections of the views of nineteenth-century man.

4. *Jesus in his Time.* Johannes Weiss (1863–1914), pupil and son-in-law of Ritschl, influenced by developments in the study of late Judaism and the world of Jesus' time, represents another step forward in the discussion. In his short monograph *Jesus' Preaching about the Kingdom of God* (1892), Weiss established on an exegetical basis that Jesus was a prophetic Jewish figure, using the thought-patterns of his own time, proclaiming a kingdom of God which was imminent, but had not yet come. Weiss's view was popularized and developed by Schweitzer later; the result was a figure alien to the modern world, even a figure to whom Schweitzer believed that contemporary Christianity could not subscribe. In this, too, he resembled Johannes Weiss: Weiss recognized the

gulf between the 'eschatological' Jesus and the theology of his master, Ritschl. Having come to this point, however, both Schweitzer and Weiss turned their back on the question of the significance of the Jesus they had found: given, in effect, a choice between him and their cherished nineteenth-century ideals, they both unhesitatingly chose the latter.

5. *Source criticism.* An account of the nineteenth century lives of Jesus is liable to give a misleading impression of critical study unless it also calls attention to the specialist groundwork of the period which formed the basis for later developments. The 'Lives' of Jesus marked a point at which NT study was presented to the more general public; they represent for the most part a 'secondary' literature, one stage removed from the solid work being done on the NT: an indication of this is the number of insignificant names which fill Schweitzer's survey. It is plain that the motives behind the 'Quest' were important and honourable; its execution left much to be desired. As we saw earlier, a presentation of the life of Jesus is dependent on the Gospel evidence and demands an extremely careful assessment of it. Many of the nineteenth century 'Lives' were written without sufficient attention being paid to these sources, even when conclusions were available.

Up to the eighteenth century, the four Gospels were harmonized, i.e. dovetailed together to form a single picture of Jesus. A first step beyond this treatment was taken by J. J. Griesbach (1745–1812), who in 1775 published the text of Matthew, Mark and Luke in parallel, together with the relevant material from John. This procedure alone made it quite clear that there was a special relationship between the first three Gospels ('Synoptic Gospels'), whereas John occupied a different role. In the early period, the question whether John or the Synoptic Gospels came first was an open one. A number of writers, including Schleiermacher, favoured John because of the lesser degree to which the miraculous appeared in his work; it was Strauss who was instrumental in pointing out the secondary nature of the Fourth Gospel. Griesbach himself had argued that Matthew was the earliest of the Gospels we have, and this position was favoured by F. C. Baur and the Tübingen school (it is still defended by some Roman Catholic scholars and has at least one notable Protestant scholar as its champion today). In 1838, however, C. H. Weisse argued that Mark was the first of our Gospels, and after a period during which his work was almost forgotten, his theory was revived in 1863 by H. J. Holtzmann (1832–1910). Taken further by scholars in Germany and, most notably, in England, this theory won almost universal acceptance and became the foundation-stone for the later 'lives' of Jesus. Mark, it was believed, offered a reliable chronological framework on the basis of which the life of Jesus could be portrayed. Whereas confidence in Marcan priority continued, the latter assumption was soon, however, to be challenged.

6. *The 'Historic Christ'*. As we have seen, it was assumed, whether explicitly or tacitly, by those who used historical criticism to construct a picture of Jesus that this 'Jesus of history' was the 'real' Jesus. This fundamental assumption was vigorously challenged by Martin Kähler (1835–1912) in a lecture, first published in 1892, entitled *The So-called Historical Jesus and the Historic, Biblical Christ*. The subtle distinction between 'historical' and 'historic' indicates the degree of sophistication now reached in reflection upon history and historical method. Kähler uses the word 'historical' (*historisch*) in the sense, mentioned above, of 'what is discovered by the method of the historian'; on the other hand, a person or event is 'historic' (*geschichtlich*) by virtue of the effect he or it has on the future.

Given the choice between the 'historical Jesus' and the 'historic Christ', it is clear, Kähler argues, which is the 'real' Christ. Even more forcibly than Schweitzer, and, of course, before him, Kähler argued that the quest of the 'historical Jesus' was a blind alley; indeed, the historical Jesus only served to conceal the living Christ. Kähler commended the quest as a protest against abstract dogmatism, but now it had immodestly gone too far. He unerringly points to the weaknesses: inadequate sources which appear in two basic forms with substantial differences; no certain eye-witnesses; an 'almost incomprehensible' carefreeness in transmission; the material subservient to the evangelists' purpose. (In much of this Kähler is reminiscent of Strauss, to whom in fact he refers.) It is therefore impossible to write a life of Jesus, let alone to 'psychologize' him. Not that this would be possible anyway, for Jesus is different from us *in kind*. This introduces Kähler's positive argument, which moves between two poles. The Christ of the Bible (not just the earthly career of Jesus, but the Lord risen, ascended and proclaimed) evoked in the past and still evokes the confession 'Christ is Lord'; that Christ is Lord is also confirmed by the present experience of the believer. The way in which each of these aspects confirms the other is sufficient to give the believer his certainty. After all, only a few specialist scholars have the training to carry on the work of historical criticism and their work spans barely a century; what of the countless others who still know Jesus?

Kähler's arguments raise important questions to which they do not provide completely satisfactory answers; in fact, some of them are still being discussed today. In a remarkably prophetic way he points to future developments, even in the realm of detailed criticism, in which he himself was not versed.

7. *Form criticism*. In answer to the objection that the picture of Christ on which he relied would itself also turn out to be an arbitrary figment of the imagination, Kähler pointed to the way in which the Gospels offer a series of 'sketches' – examples of how Jesus customarily acted – each one reflecting the full person of the Lord. These 'sketches' were next to occupy the attention of NT critics. This new study did not spring directly from Kähler's work, but from various hints already offered by NT scholars and more particularly from work pioneered in the OT field in the 'history of forms' (*Formgeschichte*), now commonly known as 'form criticism'. In the NT, as in the OT, form criticism was an attempt to trace the history of the biblical material before it was written down. It was based on the recognition that the traditions of a community are shaped and stylized according to its life and needs – various settings and purposes giving rise to quite specific forms. The critic looked for the *'Sitz im Leben'*, the setting in the life of the community, for the sermon he studied. The undifferentiated use of the term 'form critic' can, however, be misleading, particularly in the NT field, as the three pioneers, whose work appeared independently and almost simultaneously, differed considerably in their approaches. Karl Ludwig Schmidt (1891–1956), in his *The Framework of the Story of Jesus* (1919), examined the framework of Mark and the other Synoptic Gospels and discovered from the details it contained that, far from being original, it represented an attempt on the part of the evangelists to impose an order on material which reached them with no fixed chronological sequence. Connecting links were given to them only towards the end of the Gospels, in the passion narrative. On the basis of increasing information about the situation of the early church, Rudolf Bultmann (1884–   ) in *The History of the Synoptic Tradition* (1921) and Martin Dibelius (1883–1947) in *From Tradition to Gospel* (1919) examined the individual units (pericopes) of which the Gospels were now seen to be made up. Bultmann subjected the Gospel material to a thorough analysis and concentrated his attention on the pericopes themselves; Dibelius made an imaginative attempt to picture the life of the community and to see from that the way in which the Gospel material might have arisen. Inevitably, in either case the argument was a circular one, by the very nature of the evidence; furthermore, there was considerable divergence on points of detail, again because of the sparsity of the sources. Nevertheless, some general conclusions of agreed importance began to emerge. The material available to the evangelists had been preserved and shaped in the worshipping life of the Christian community, with the consequences that entails: a public setting, selection of material to suit the community's ends in its preaching and teaching, and a neglect of the information which the modern historian would most like to have. Moreover, the Gospels, too, made up of this material, are themselves written from faith to faith, to meet specific needs in the churches of their origin (further investigations of the Gospels *as a whole* along these lines, described by the neologism 'redaction criticism' (*Redaktionsgeschichte*), have done much to illustrate the considerations which might have motivated the evangelists in their work, but cannot concern us here). The significance of all this is plain, and remains despite any

particular criticisms. The framework of Mark, the backbone of the nineteenth century 'Lives', no longer sustains the weight placed on it; and because of the process through which the Gospel tradition has passed, the historicity of its details can be asserted *confidently* only where their origin cannot be explained in the life of the church. In establishing facts about the life of Jesus, the burden of proof is on the would-be biographer, and the problems now involved might well suggest that to write a 'Life' of Jesus is *impossible*.

8. *Kerygmatic theology*. Kähler's stress on the 'Christ of faith' was also taken on and intensified immediately after the first World War (again not directly) in the theology represented by Karl Barth (q.v.; *see also* **Dialectical Theology; Crisis Theology**). In reaction to the main trends of nineteenth-century theology, Barth, beginning with his explosive *Commentary on Romans* (1919), turned his back on previous views of the continuity between human personalities and God to emphasize the discontinuity between God and man. This emphatic assertion of the 'otherness' of God brought with it an assertion of the 'otherness' of the Bible and a consequent tension with historical criticism. For Barth, the all-important thing was the *Word* conveyed in the Bible, a Word which could not suffer questioning, but demanded obedience. Whatever the background which leads up to Barth's theology, *in* that theology, there is no question that here is a course dictated by the rigours of criticism; Barth's position would, he himself argues, hold even if there were no problems of critical interpretation. During this period, much of the systematic theological writing of Bultmann is virtually indistinguishable from that of Barth, and he agrees on the points just made: the Word, the *kerygma* (q.v.), which is the proclamation of Jesus Christ, demands unquestioning obedience. It carries its own legitimation, and, even if there were every chance of success in historical terms, to attempt to legitimize it by historical criticism would be to deny faith. On this basis, to look for a 'historical' Jesus as the nineteenth century did is not only impossible, but *illegitimate*.

9. *Rudolf Bultmann*. Because of his prominent position in both form criticism and kerygmatic theology, Bultmann has in many quarters become an embodiment of historical scepticism, just as he has become a focal point for most recent study. The *reasons* for Bultmann's position, and hence its significance for the possibility of historical knowledge about Jesus, are not always, however, seen sufficiently clearly. Despite claims to the contrary, Bultmann's views on the impossibility and illegitimacy of a 'quest of the historical Jesus' are not interdependent. His reasons for finding such a quest illegitimate are, as we have seen, a consequence of his *theological* position: his close link with Barth and, equally important, his Lutheran heritage with its *sola fide* (q.v.). His reasons for finding the quest impossible are *his-*

torical and *critical*, and are based on exegetical work completed before his close contact with Barth. The acceptance or rejection of kerygmatic theology does not therefore affect the historical difficulties which Bultmann raises.

In this latter field, there is more to Bultmann's position than is usually allowed. He was much influenced by the *Religionsgeschichtliche Schule* (q.v.) and took over from it a number of theories about the nature of early Christianity which have since been seriously questioned. There is, however, no unanimity in the way in which this questioning has developed; some conclusions have been more positive than those of Bultmann, others considerably more radical. All in all, the scene represents changes which might have been expected after the research and discoveries of two generations into the problems which Bultmann opened up but no clear step forward. As will be seen, the questions raised by him are still the ones which await an answer today.

Once Bultmann's theological concern is allowed for, his most vigorous statements appear in a different light. Like his contemporaries in form criticism, Bultmann believed that important things about Jesus' work and person could in fact be known – Bultmann, Schmidt and Dibelius each devoted an entire book to Jesus. After his constant distinction between *kerygma* and historical research and refusal to allow the use of the latter to legitimize the former, Bultmann's polemic is directed against the nineteenth-century concern for the 'personality' of Jesus and the 'psychological' approach to him. Once these attempts are renounced, Bultmann allows that a picture can be drawn of Jesus as a messianic prophet, a teacher with traits of a rabbi, who consorted with the outcast, healed the sick and cast out demons, and made a last decisive journey to Jerusalem (*see Jesus and the Word*). His call to decision with respect to his own person even 'implies a christology'.

The fact remains, however, that for Bultmann all this is of subsidiary interest. For the Christian, for Paul and John, it is necessary to know only 'that' Jesus once existed. The *kerygma* needs no firmer basis.

10. *The 'New Quest of the Historical Jesus'*. Whereas the concern of nineteenth-century scholarship was generally, as we have seen, to establish the *difference* between the Jesus of history and the Christ of tradition, as a result of the work of Kähler and Bultmann the central question has now changed. It is now one of the continuity between the activity of Jesus and the preaching of him in the early Church. Precisely what was there about Jesus which led the Church to proclaim him as the Christ? Bultmann, as we have seen, does not completely neglect this question, but because he regards it as unimportant and, in some contexts, improper, he relegates it very much to the background. More than a generation later, when Bultmann's own work was in essentials complete, and his pupils had risen to occupy distinguished

academic posts in Germany, several of them in different ways expressed their dissatisfaction at this state of affairs, and set out to take investigations further. Their various writings have been said to add up to a 'new quest' of the historical Jesus.

The title can easily mislead. First, it properly refers to a small group of NT theologians whose work is only relatively different from that of their teacher. The important points at which they agree with Bultmann far outweigh those at which they disagree. Secondly, the 'new quest' is not necessarily a dominating concern of these writers, all of whom are active in a far wider field of NT theology. It is one question among many. Thirdly, the use of a single title suggests, once again, a unity where there is considerable diversity. There are notable differences between the viewpoints of Günther Bornkamm (1905–), Ernst Käsemann (1906–), Ernst Fuchs (1903–), Hans Conzelmann (1915–) and James M. Robinson (1924–), whose names usually appear in this connection. A degree of confusion has been caused by the fact that the Baedeker to the 'new quest', James M. Robinson's *A New Quest of the Historical Jesus*, which was instrumental in giving the term currency in the English-speaking world, exists in two versions, English and German, with not insignificant differences. Failure to distinguish Robinson's personal position from that of the scholars he describes can also be misleading.

In Germany, two of the most important works to mark the new trend were Ernst Käsemann's lecture, 'The Problem of the Historical Jesus', given in 1953 and published a year later (ET in *Essays on New Testament Themes*, 1964, pp. 15– 47) and Günther Bornkamm's book *Jesus of Nazareth*, published in 1956 (ET, 1960). In these very different studies, two points are agreed and stressed: on the one hand, it is quite impossible to write a 'Life' of Jesus, as the necessary material is simply not available. On the other hand, however, it would be quite fatal if scepticism were to lead us to a complete disengagement of interest from the earthly Jesus. The question of what can be known about Jesus is an extraordinarily difficult one – but that does not mean that no attempt can be made to answer it. The change is thus one in *theological* position; it is a reaction to Bultmann's real or supposed views about the *legitimacy* of going back behind the Church's *kerygma*. The minor degree to which the *critical* position has changed can easily be seen by a comparison between the factual material about Jesus in Bultmann's *Jesus and the Word* and that in Bornkamm's *Jesus of Nazareth*. In these terms the latter represents virtually no advance over the former. But whereas Bultmann is saying *vis à vis* the nineteenth century. 'We *only* know this', Bornkamm is saying *vis à vis* Bultmann 'We know *all* this'. In *intention*, then, these writers do represent a change in perspective, but at present there are not sufficient agreements in their work to suggest whether their contribution will mark a substantial advance.

The possibility of such a substantial advance is claimed by James M. Robinson himself in his account of the 'new quest'. In his view, we may be more optimistic about having knowledge of Jesus because of a change in the understanding of history brought about by the work of Dilthey, Croce, Collingwood and others. Whereas the historians of the nineteenth century were concerned with facts – names, places, dates, events, sequences – this new view of history is aware of a deeper plane. It sets out to grasp the act of intention, the commitment, the meaning for those involved, behind the external events. It is concerned with the 'selfhood' of those involved. And material about the 'selfhood' of Jesus is precisely what we have in the Gospels. Through this we *can* know Jesus.

Now it is true that there have been important changes in the understanding of history over the last century, and these are relevant for an understanding of Christianity as a whole. It is doubtful, however, whether they affect an understanding of Jesus in the way which Robinson describes. For this kind of historical understanding needs as its basis a framework of concrete events – places, dates, sequences – and this is precisely what we lack. It is difficult enough to 'understand' a Luther or a Newman, with all the copious material available – how can this be possible in the case of Jesus? The examples given by Robinson (and by Ernst Fuchs, who is the most akin to him of the German scholars) of this new interpretation look remarkably like the earlier quest in a new form – with the difference that the liberal Jesus has been exchanged for the Jesus of existentialism.

11. *Conclusion.* The preceding survey has inevitably been concerned almost exclusively with the German theological scene, as it is there that the important questions have been raised either first or in their most pressing form. English scholars, on the other hand, have acquired a reputation for being sceptical about form criticism and naively more optimistic about the possibility of historical knowledge about Jesus. While this characterization is hardly a completely apt one – there is a line of distinguished, if not always prolific, English scholars who have been well aware of the force and significance of the arguments outlined above – it at least indicates the reluctance of much of English theology to take to heart the problems we have seen. These problems are fundamental problems of method and cannot be countered by superficial criticism of detail or vague statements along more positive lines. It *may* be the case that more positive presentations of Jesus may be made in the future, but unless they can adequately counter the difficulties typified first in Schweitzer, and then in Bultmann and his successors, they will be little improvement on what has already emerged. Indeed, the disappointing aspect of recent NT study has been the failure on the part of those dissatisfied with the conclusions of Bultmann and his followers to put forward an adequate alternative in terms of method.

What, then, are the prospects? The importance of historical study of Jesus should now be clear. In many ways it represents biblical criticism at its best, not shrinking from putting to itself the most difficult and far-reaching questions. The attempt to regard this study as unnecessary and illegitimate will surely be seen in time to have been conditioned by a particular theology and a particular situation and to have done less than justice to the concerns which arise as a result of man's rationality. Furthermore, this study has ruled out the two extremes of total scepticism and total credulity about the Gospel tradition. The future lies in the many possibilities offered in the difficult middle ground.

Which of these possibilities may be fruitful can only be seen by constant deployment of hypotheses, testing them against the available evidence in the light of past attempts. To take a single example: there is clearly a need to go beyond the position which would see as authentic words and actions of Jesus only those which cannot be attributed to the interests of the early Church. But given the activity of the early Church in the preservation of Jesus' words and actions, can other criteria be more than tentative in the extreme? Arguments about the Gospel tradition are inevitably circular and there are many imponderables; variety, controversy and uncertainty thus seem inevitable features of the study of the Jesus of history for the foreseeable future.

If this is so, it becomes increasingly necessary for there to be a heightened awareness of the place of historical criticism within Christian theology. What is the relationship between the competence of historical criticism and the practice of Christianity, between the historian and the believer? Confusion between these two roles has been a recurrent theme in this article, from the liberals to the 'new quest'. While NT theologians continue their work on the Gospels and their environment, it is therefore necessary for others to ask about the nature of the 'Christ' whom the Church worships and proclaims, to examine critically with all the means at their disposal the use of this word in all its varied settings. Claims are made here – resurrection, exaltation, lordship, atonement – which have implications far beyond the historian's competence.

(H. G. Reimarus), *Zur Geschichte und Litteratur aus den Schätzen der Herzoglichen Bibliothek zu Wolfenbüttel*, Vierter Beytrag von Gotthold Ephraim Lessing, and, *Von dem Zwecke Jesu und seiner Jünger. Noch ein Fragment des Wolfenbüttelschen Ungenannten*, in *Gotthold Ephraim Lessings sämtliche Schriften*, ed. K. Lachmann, 1897, vol. 12, pp. 303–428 and vol. 13, pp. 221–327, partial ET in: *Fragments from Reimarus*, ed. Charles Voysey, 1879; D. F. Strauss, *Das Leben Jesu, kritisch bearbeitet*, 2 vols., 21837, ET *The Life of Jesus Critically Examined*, 3 vols., 1846; Martin Kähler, *The So-called Historical Jesus and the Historical, Biblical Christ*, ET, 1964; Albert Schweitzer, *The Quest of the Historical Jesus*, ET,

31954; Rudolf Bultmann, *Jesus and the Word*, ET, 1958; Günther Bornkamm, *Jesus of Nazareth*, ET 1960.

Recent discussions of the question are available as follows: W. G. Kümmel, *Das Neue Testament, Geschichte der Erforschung seiner Probleme*, 1958; H. Conzelmann, 'Jesus Christus', *Die Religion in Geschichte und Gegenwart*3, III, 1959, cols. 619–653; J. M. Robinson, *A New Quest of the Historical Jesus*, 1959; Heinz Zahrnt, *The Historical Jesus*, ET, 1963; Carl E. Braaten and Roy A. Harrisville, eds., *The Historical Jesus and the Kerygmatic Christ*, 1964; G. Ebeling, 'The Question of the Historical Jesus and the Problem of Christology', *Word and Faith*, ET, 1963, pp. 288–304; C. F. D. Moule, *The Phenomenon of the New Testament*, 1967; N. Perrin, *Rediscovering the Teaching of Jesus*, 1967; F. G. Downing, *The Church and Jesus*, 1968. Further references to the vast literature on the subject will be found in all these latter books.

JOHN BOWDEN

Jewel, John

During a brilliant career at Oxford John Jewel (1522–1571) came under the influence of Peter Martyr Vermigli, with whom he formed a lasting friendship. On the accession of Queen Mary he was expelled and escaped death by subscription to Roman doctrines. Still in great danger, he fled to Frankfurt where he publicly repented of his lapse. Joining Peter Martyr at Strasbourg, he presently accompanied the latter to Zurich and resided with him there, engaged in intense study, for nearly four years. Early in 1559 he returned to England and on 21 January 1560 was consecrated Bishop of Salisbury. His letters to Martyr and Heinrich Bullinger (q.v.) give some record of the events in which he then participated. On Palm Sunday he delivered his famous 'challenge sermon' at Paul's Cross, charging the Roman Church with twenty-seven errors, chiefly on the Eucharist, contrary to scripture and the Fathers. His *Apologia Ecclesiae Anglicanae*, 1562 (rendered into English by Lady Bacon), presented at a critical moment a powerful defence of the Anglican position against Rome. A controversy followed with his former schoolmate John Harding, then at Louvain. Jewel suffered from lameness and increasingly from illnesses, but tenaciously pursued his diocesan and scholarly labours until his death. His *Defence of the Apology* features patristic support for Reformation doctrines. His other writings include *An Exposition of 1 Thessalonians*, a letter to his Italian friend Scipio on the Council of Trent, a tract against the Puritan Thomas Cartwright, and numerous sermons. He exercised an influence on Richard Hooker who called Jewel 'the worthiest divine that Christendom hath bred for some hundreds of years'.

Jewel's Works are in the Parker Society series. *See also* J. E. Booty, *John Jewel as Apologist of the Church of England*, 1963; W. N. Southgate, *John*

Jewel and the Problem of Doctrinal Authority, 1962.

J. T. MCNEILL

John of the Cross, St

St John of the Cross (1542–1591) is the greatest systematic writer on mysticism in the Christian tradition and a good example of the close relation between poetry and mysticism. *The Ascent of Mount Carmel* is a commentary on his poem 'On a Dark Night', but while the poem is concerned with what mystics call illumination and union the prose commentary on the poem deals entirely with the initial stage of purgation. The theme of book i is mortification, or as St John calls it 'the night of the senses' in which through the action of the grace of God man can succeed in 'voiding himself of all his desires'. The climax of this process comes when the soul discovers that it 'covets nothing, nothing wearies it when it is lifted up, and nothing oppresses it when it is cast down, for it is in the centre of its humility'. The second and third books describe the more drastic process of purgation in what John calls 'the night of the spirit'. The clearest description of this process of self-stripping are to be found in the intended continuation of *The Ascent of Mount Carmel, The Dark Night of the Soul*. Book ii begins with an exposition of the virtue of faith which John equates with the second night and then goes on to discuss the progress from meditation to contemplation. He then deals with the 'detachment of the understanding' and here he gives an extensive treatment of the question of visions, locutions and other forms of supernatural revelation. Book iii deals mainly with the purgation of the memory and will, but John also discusses the devotional use of images, the furnishing of oratories, the celebration of religious festivals, the abuse of ceremonial and the qualities of a good sermon, and the treatise suddenly breaks off in the middle of a sentence. In *The Ascent of Mount Carmel* he has been concerned with what he calls the active night of sense and of spirit, in other words with ascetical theology (*see* **Ascetical Theology**). In *The Dark Night of the Soul* he describes what he calls the passive night of the sense and of the spirit, *see particularly* i.8 and ii.5.

The Spiritual Canticle and *The Living Flame of Love* describe the highest flights of the mystical experience, the state of illumination, what John calls the spiritual betrothal with the Word, the Son of God, and *The Living Flame of Love* is concerned particularly with the state of mystical union.

There are some initial difficulties in appreciating John of the Cross:

1. *His austere teaching on detachment.* This sounds like advocating the complete extinction of every kind of natural desire or feeling. There must first, he says, be detachment from spiritual things, and at a certain stage this means the abandonment of all intellectual activities. But there are passages which suggest that what John

has in mind is the kind of distancing and extinction of personality which T. S. Eliot speaks of as the vocation of the poet: 'he will find greater joy and recreation in creatures through his detachment from them, for he cannot rejoice in them if he looks upon them with attachment to them as to his own. Attachment is an anxiety, that like a bond ties the spirit down to the earth and allows it no enlargement of heart. He will also acquire in his detachment from things a clear conception of them, so that he can well understand the truths relating to them both naturally and supernaturally' (*Ascent of Mount Carmel*, iii.20). 'And this is the great delight of this awakening: to know the creatures through God and not God through the creatures; to know the effects through their cause and not the cause through the effects; for the latter knowledge is secondary and this other is essential' (*The Living Flame of Love*, stanza 4).

2. *Absorption mysticism.* It is often suggested that in John of the Cross the soul is represented as being lost or absorbed into the being of God in the higher reaches of the mystical life. He certainly uses language to stress the intensity of the sense of union in mystical experience, but nevertheless an analysis of his imagery shows some care to avoid the suggestion of pantheistic experience. One can contrast the favourite figures of salt dissolving in water or of rivers flowing into the ocean which one finds in pantheistic mysticism with the imagery which John uses: married love, the two candle flames, the window and the ray of sunlight, the log of wood in the fire. The latter image, which might seem to come nearest to implying loss of personality, is used by John in a way which makes clear that he regards the soul in the highest reaches of mystical experience as nevertheless retaining its separate individuality. 'When a log of wood has been set upon the fire it is transformed into fire and united with it; yet, as the fire grows hotter the wood remains upon it for a longer time, it glows much more and becomes more completely enkindled until it gives out sparks of fire and flame' (*Living Flame of Love*, Prologue 3).

3. *The spirituality of John of the Cross and 'otherworldliness'.* In the life of prayer and contemplation John speaks of creatures as guides in our journey to Christ. His essential attitude is made clear in the distinction which he makes between the two ways of knowing the created world: 'morning knowledge' and 'evening knowledge'. In 'morning knowledge' we know creation through God, in 'evening knowledge' we know creation according to our natural lights, that is, apart from its source and ground in God. The ascent of the soul to the life of God is not by means of by-passing the natural or ignoring it or despising it but precisely through it. The necessary safeguard he states in *The Ascent of Mount Carmel*, iii.24:

I wish therefore to propose a test here whereby it may be seen when these delights of the senses aforementioned are profitable and when they are not. And it is that whensoever a person hears music and other things, and sees pleasant things, and is conscious of sweet perfumes, or tastes things that are delicious, or feels soft touches, if his thought and the affection of his will are at once centred upon God and if that thought of God gives him more pleasure than the movement of sense which causes it, and save for that he finds no pleasure in the said movement this is a sign that he is receiving benefit therefrom and that this thing of sense is a help to his spirit.

John of the Cross, St, *Complete Works*, ed., E. Allison Peers, 3 vols., 1934–5; E. W. Trueman Dicken, *The Crucible of Love*, 1963; E. Allison Peers, *Spanish Mysticism*, 1924; *Spirit of Flame*, 1943; *Studies of the Spanish Mystics*, 2 vols., 1927–30.

E. J. TINSLEY

Judgment, Last Judgment. *see* Heaven and Hell; Time and Eternity; Wrath of God.

Jung, Carl Gustav

C. G. Jung (1875–1961), Swiss psychoanalytic scholar who, while remaining agnostic about the existence of the transcendent, held religion in very high esteem because of its great psychotherapeutic value, and formulated an interpretation of religious symbols and myths in terms of archetypes belonging to the collective subconscious.

JAMES RICHMOND

Justice

Justice (Latin: *justitia*, Greek: *dikaiosune*) is one of the moral virtues. It is a disposition of the soul according to which we have a constant will to render to, and preserve for, every man his due. *See also* **Righteousness.**

P. S. WATSON

Justification

1. *General Meaning.* Justification is making or being made just or righteous; showing or being shown to be in the right (or at least blameless); putting or being put right with God. Both Catholic and Protestant teaching is that man is not by nature righteous, but sinful. Hence, he is not in a right but a wrong relation to God, and he cannot put himself right. He can only be put right by finding pardon and acceptance with God through God's grace. As to how this comes about, Catholic and Protestant views differ.

2. *Protestant Interpretation.* In classical Protestant theology, man is justified by 'faith alone' (*sola fide*), or more precisely, by grace alone through faith alone in Christ alone. The word 'alone' is meant to exclude all thought of sinful man's doing or deserving – all 'works' and 'merits' of his – as in any way motivating his justification.

Admittedly, to have faith or to believe is something man does, and it is in a sense a condition of his justification; but it is so only in the way that holding out one's hand to receive a gift is a condition of receiving it. The gospel tells us there is free pardon for our sins and full acceptance with God for us on the sole basis of God's grace in Christ. To believe this is to confess that we are sinners, and that God in his grace accepts even us, sinners though we are. Faith is our acceptance of God's pardon and acceptance of us, whereby alone we are pardoned and accepted, that is, justified.

But the word 'alone' is not meant to exclude all human activity. For although Luther, for example, maintains that 'faith alone justifies, without any, even the smallest works', yet he heartily agrees with St James that 'faith without works is dead' (James 2.26). Hence he strongly attacks two misinterpretations of *sola fide*. First, there are those who conceive of faith as an inward disposition, a 'quality in the heart', on account of which God will forgive their sins and treat them as righteous, while they neglect or even refuse to seek God where he may be found, namely, in the outward means of grace, the word and sacraments of the gospel. They are in effect turning faith into a human 'work' and despising the works of God. Then there are those who neglect or even reject love and good works as the necessary fruit of living faith. Against these, Luther insists that 'justification is a kind of regeneration to newness of life' – naturally, since it means entering into a new relationship of trust and obedience towards God (*see* **Faith** [2]). Hence, while 'faith alone justifies, yet faith is never alone'; it is never without love and the works of love. Indeed, 'where there is not love, neither is there faith, but mere hypocrisy'. (*See also* **Simul Justus et Peccator**.)

In Protestantism after Luther, however, justification came to be thought of simply as the forgiveness or non-imputation of sin, while renewal of life through the Holy Spirit (sanctification) was a quite distinct and even separate gift. In consequence, the proper relation and proportion between these two aspects of salvation has not always been maintained.

3. *Catholic Interpretation.* In Catholic theology, justification is not by 'faith alone', but by 'faith furnished with love' (*fides caritate formata*). (This is understandable in the light of the Catholic definition of faith (*see* **Faith** [1]). The Reformers themselves denied that a man could be justified by that sort of faith 'alone'.) Faith, however, is 'the beginning, foundation and root of all justification' (Trent, Sess.vi, cap.vii.); and to the act of faith a man is led and drawn by the grace of God. That is to say, he is enabled to believe what has been divinely revealed, particularly the doctrines of redemption and the forgiveness of sins, and thus believing to hope in God and to love him, and hence to turn his heart in penitence away from sin. He is then ready for the gift of sanctifying grace (*see* **Grace** [2]). whereby his sin is not only

forgiven but purged away, so that he is made acceptable to God. This gift is imparted initially through baptism, and if afterwards it is lost, it can be restored through the sacrament of penance (q.v.). Baptism and penance are justifying sacraments, which do not presuppose like the other sacraments that the recipient is in a state of grace. Both presuppose faith, however, and in the case of infant baptism, the faith of the Church deputizes for that of the infant. Infants stand in need of the justifying gift of sanctifying grace no less than adults who have lost it through committing mortal sin, for no one is born with it, owing to its having been lost to all mankind through Adam's fall. It has, however, been retrieved through Christ and is available now to men through the Church and its sacraments.

The necessity for justifying faith to be 'furnished with love' is explained on the ground that, while God certainly forgives the penitent sinner, he does not and cannot accept him and enter into fellowship with him in his sinful state. It is unthinkable that the Holy One should countenance the unholy, or the Righteous One the unrighteous. Hence, in justifying the sinner, God makes him just or righteous. He does not simply impute righteousness to him, allowing him to remain sinful, but he imparts to him the love which is the fulfilling of the law, and which therefore makes him acceptable to God.

G. Aulén, *The Faith of the Christian Church*, 2nd ed., 1961; R. E. Davies and R. Newton Flew, eds., *The Catholicity of Protestantism*, 1950; Hans Küng, *Justification*, 1964; G. W. H. Lampe, ed., *The Doctrine of Justification by Faith*, 1954; G. Smith, ed., *The Teaching of the Catholic Church*, 2 vols., 1948; V. Taylor, *Forgiveness and Reconciliation*, 1952; P. S. Watson, *The Concept of Grace*, 1960.

P. S. WATSON

Kaftan, Julius Wilhelm Martin

Julius Kaftan (1848–1926), German Ritschlian systematic theologian, although like Ritschl beginning his theological system with 'value-judgments' (German: *Werthurtheile*), proceeded to base 'being-judgments' (*Seinsurtheile*) upon these. That is, he was the most conservative of the Ritschlian theologians, attempting to work out the *ontological* and *metaphysical* implications of a morally-based faith. *See* **Harnack, A. von; Herrmann, W.; Liberal Protestantism; Ritschl, A.**

Julius Kaftan, *The Truth of the Christian Religion*, 2 vols., ET, 1894.

JAMES RICHMOND

Kairos

An important word in the Greek NT, it means 'the appointed time in the purpose of God' (e.g. Mark 1.15, 'the *kairos* is fulfilled'). Paul Tillich (q.v.) has given it prominence in his theology, in which it appears to mean those crises or turning-points in history which demand specific existential decision while the opportunity is still present; the coming of the Christ is the unique example of such *kairoi*.

Kant, Immanuel

Immanuel Kant (1724–1804), German philosopher. *See* **Liberal Protestantism; Metaphysics.**

Keble, John

Keble (1792–1866) carried the high church tradition of the Caroline Divines (q.v.) into the nineteenth century and, through the influence which he exercised in Oxford in the 1820s and 1830s upon J. H. Newman (q.v.) and R. H. Froude, may be reckoned to be the chief begetter and, by his consistent tenacity after Newman's conversion to the Church of Rome, the nursing father, with Pusey, of the Oxford Movement (q.v.). He provided the occasion for the beginning of the movement by his measured attack on the Erastianism of the government in 1833, but his greatest personal contributions to English religion were his volume of verse, *The Christian Year* (1825),which invested the Prayer Book with a new romantic appeal, the example of his own holiness and the encouragement which he gave to the revival of religious orders in the Church of England.

G. Battiscombe, *John Keble; a study in limitations*, 1963.

R. CANT

Kenosis, Kenotic Christology. *see* Christology (5).

Kerygma

This is a Greek word meaning 'the thing preached', 'proclamation'. It occurs eight times in the NT, twice of the proclamation of Jonah. The remaining six occurrences refer to the apostolic proclamation of the death and resurrection of Jesus Christ (*see* Alan Richardson, 'Preach', *TWBB*; C. H. Dodd, *The Apostolic Preaching*, 1936). In recent theological discussion the term has been given wide currency by R. Bultmann who distinguishes between *kerygma* and myth (*see* **Demythologizing**). Much of the proclamation of the apostles is regarded by Bultmann as myth, and hence he has proposed an existentialist *kerygma* which differs markedly from the apostolic preaching and the historic Christian faith; his *kerygma* is, in fact, 'another gospel', not the historic gospel of the resurrection of Jesus Christ from the dead. Much confusion is caused by investing NT words with new philosophical meanings. *See Kerygma and Myth*, ed. H. W. Bartsch, ET, I, 1953; II, 1964.

EDITOR

Kerygmatic Theology. *see* Jesus of History (8).

Keys, The Power of The

This is a phrase taken from Matt. 16.19 to denote the authority to excommunicate from, and to admit to, the Church's fellowship, and generally to exercise the jurisdiction of the Church. Roman Catholics believe that the power of the keys was given by Christ peculiarly (though not exclusively) to Peter and to his successors as bishop of Rome, and that therefore ultimate authority and jurisdiction throughout the Church belongs to the pope as of right. This is one of the points on which Luther challenged the papacy most sharply. For example, in his 'Appeal to the Ruling Classes of German Nationality' he writes: 'It is plain enough that the keys were not given to St Peter only, but to the whole Christian community.' But none of the Reformers, not even the Anabaptists, wished to abolish the power of the keys. The only question was, how, and by whom, should it be exercised? It has been left to modern Liberal Protestantism to present the image of a completely voluntarist Church, where the Church claims to exercise no authority whatever, and where in consequence the power of the keys is left in the hands of each individual Christian to use as his own conscience directs. In fact such an arrangement is only possible in a 'Christendom' or 'post-Christendom' situation where the Church is divided into a number of voluntary societies. Among the younger churches, where Christians are a small minority in a non-Christian society, the power of the keys is necessarily exercised by every church. Though few Christians outside the Roman Catholic Church would yearn for the autocratic, centralized discipline of Rome, the question of how the Church's authority should be exercised is a pressing one today. It requires more fundamental consideration than it has yet received.

Robert Adolfs, *The Church Is Different*, ET, 1966; Y. Congar, *Power and Poverty in the Church*, 1964; F. W. Dillistone, *The Structure of the Divine Society*, 1951.

A. T. HANSON

Kierkegaard, Søren Aabye

Kierkegaard (1813–1855), Danish religious thinker and philosopher, is generally considered to be the founder of modern existentialist philosophy. Kierkegaard repudiated the classical Western philosophical tradition (as represented especially by the system of Hegel), because of its alleged inability to comprehend the existing subject and its obsession with objective things-in-themselves. Announcing his radical allegiance to the principle 'truth in subjectivity', Kierkegaard made profoundly accurate analyses of human existence (paying particular attention to the concepts of sin and dread), attacked Hegelian philosophy, and launched a vigorous onslaught on Western Christendom as represented by the Danish Established Church, with its obsession for objectively 'proving the truth' of Christianity (apart from its inward appropriation by the subjectively existing believer), and its ignoring of the importance of the uniquely existing individual. Kierkegaard's influence on twentieth-century thought has been both wide and deep; not only did his thinking decisively influence the early thinking of Karl Barth and members of his school, but modern continental existentialism in all its forms acknowledges Kierkegaard both as founder and patron saint. *See* **Existentialism; Heidegger, M.; Jaspers, K.; Marcel, G.; Sartre, J-P.**

M. Channing-Pearce, *Søren Kierkegaard: A Study*, 1946; Louis Dupré, *Kierkegaard as Theologian*, 1964; H. R. Mackintosh, *Types of Modern Theology*, 1937 and 1964; Paul Sponheim, *Kierkegaard on Christ and Christian Coherence*, 1968; Paul Tillich, *Perspectives on Nineteenth and Twentieth Century Protestant Theology*, 1967.

JAMES RICHMOND

Kingdom of God. *see* Eschatology.

Kings, Divine Right of

In many different cultures rulers have been regarded as in some sense sacred personages, although this has not always been inconsistent with criticism of them or their deposition. The first Christian Roman emperors inherited such a tradition and only partly modified it. They noted that in the OT kings had been anointed and had led both church and state: that Jesus had enunciated the principle 'Render unto Caesar . . .' and that Peter and Paul had counselled obedience, the latter asserting that the secular power enjoyed divine sanction. Most conscientious rulers, kings or not, presumably believe that they govern by divine permission, and that their responsibility is undertaken towards God as well as to their people; and most Christians believe it to be their duty to obey all just laws and to reflect very seriously before disobeying unjust ones. There is, however, a difference between this attitude and the belief that grew in the Middle Ages and came to full expression in the seventeenth century that hereditary monarchs govern by divine right and in a sense represent God to their people; have the power of healing and possibly a quasi-sacerdotal character (*see* **Coronation Rite**) and that their subjects have in no case the right of active resistance. The more theologically minded supporters of these beliefs in seventeenth-century England saw in them the proper scriptural substitute for the vacuum left by the rejection of the papacy, and always maintained that the king was under the law of God; others saw in them a convenient justification for absolute monarchy. They were vigorously criticized and, in the event, successfully repudiated in the name of religion and of constitutional precedent. The issue, however, is not dead. Modern dictators have ascribed their rise to power as part of an inevitable historic process which it is wicked and futile to resist, so claiming in fact if not in name a divine right; and the attitude of Christians to the state must still be ambivalent, on the one hand seeing it as sanctioned by God and on the other as capable of becoming a substitute for him.

J. N. Figgis, *The Divine Right of Kings*, 2nd ed., 1914.

R. CANT

Knox, John

At St Andrew's University John Knox (c.1513–1572) felt the influence of the eminent John Major. He became a priest and an apostolic notary, but in 1545 he joined George Wishart who had returned from Zurich and Cambridge to preach the Reformation in Scotland. After Wishart's burning, March 1546, and the murder of Cardinal Beaton, Knox was with the defenders of the Castle of St Andrew's, and thereafter spent nineteen months as a French prisoner and galley slave. On his release he reached England where he spent five active years, 1549–54, chiefly in Berwick and Newcastle but on occasion in London and elsewhere. He made his influence felt in the declaration in the Prayer Book of 1552 that kneeling in the Eucharist is not an act of adoration of any bodily presence. He joined the Marian exiles in 1554, met Calvin in Geneva, participated in the Prayer Book controversy among the Frankfurt refugees, and became minister of the English congregation in Geneva. In 1556 his work there was interrupted while he returned to Berwick, where he was married, and to Scotland, where he preached openly. After his final return to Scotland, in May 1559, his resourceful leadership was largely instrumental in bringing the nation to the acceptance of the Reformation (1560). He continued to wield paramount influence for another decade. Theologically Knox is not among the great men of the period. His strength lay rather in effective exhortation and prompt action. As a follower of Wishart, his Protestant beginning was Zwinglian, but he moved into fairly close agreement with Calvin. Politically he is as close to his teacher, Major, as to Calvin, but expressed his views with a passionate zeal of his own. In his long work, *On Predestination, an Answer to an Anabaptist* (1559), he is careful to guard free will and moral responsibility within the framework of divine predestination. His position is judged by J. S. McEwen as 'on the whole, infralapsarian'. Typical of his controversial writing is the *Answer to a Scottish Jesuit* (James Tyrie), 1572. But his most important work is the *History of the Reformation in Scotland*, written 1559 to 1571, which preserves indispensable data presented with vehement partisanship in a lively and readable style. More than fifty letters of advice from his hand are extant, written to his anxious-minded mother-in-law, Mrs Bowes, and to reforming friends in England.

John Knox, *History of the Reformation in Scotland*, ed., W. C. Dickinson, 2 vols., 1949; *The Works of John Knox*, ed., D. Laing, 6 vols., 1846–64; J. S. McEwen, *The Faith of John Knox*, the

Croall Lectures, 1960, 1961; G. MacGregor, *The Thundering Scot. A Portrait of John Knox*, 1957.

J. T. MCNEILL

Koinonia

The Greek word for 'fellowship', 'communion': e.g. 'the fellowship of the Holy Spirit' (II Cor. 13.14; Phil. 2.1).

Krauth, Charles Porterfield

C. P. Krauth (1823–1883) was a leader of the confessional resurgence in American Lutheranism. After service as pastor and editor, he became in 1864 Professor of Systematic Divinity at the new Lutheran seminary in Philadelphia, which had been organized to counter the influence of the 'American Lutheranism' of Samuel Simon Schmucker (q.v.). He was a central figure in the General Council, founded in 1867 as a national Lutheran body in opposition to the more liberal General Synod. In 1871 he published what is generally considered the most important Lutheran doctrinal work of native American authorship – *The Conservative Reformation and Its Theology*. Here he argued for a conservative interpretation of the Reformation against revolutionary radicalism and for a strict interpretation of the historic confessions. He put special emphasis on original sin, the person of Christ, baptism, and the Lord's Supper – the four central doctrines of the 'conservative Reformation'. He wrote many other theological and philosophical works, for he also became Professor of Philosophy (later Vice-Provost) at the University of Pennsylvania.

Adolph Spaeth, *Charles Porterfield Krauth*, 2 vols., 1898–1909.

ROBERT T. HANDY

Laity, Lay

These words are derived from Greek *laos*, 'people'. In the NT *laos* is used of the members of the Church as the people of God. But the idea is taken over from the OT, in which Israel is the covenanted people of God. According to the OT prophetic understanding God chose Israel not for privilege but for service; her special function was to bring the knowledge of God to the Gentiles, i.e. to non-Israelite peoples. Israel was to be a priest-nation to the Gentile world (*cf.* Ex. 19.4–6); the doctrine of the priesthood of the laity was written into the Covenant of Sinai. Every Jew was to be a priest to ten Gentiles, according to the vision of Zech. 8.23. This prophetic hope of the OT was not fulfilled until the coming of Jesus and his Church, which became a people of mission, a light to the Gentiles, the new royal priesthood and people of God's own possession (I Peter 2.9 f.).

Thus, in the NT the whole Church corporately was priestly, offering up to God the sacrifices which were now acceptable to him through Jesus

Christ – worship, works of charity, almsgiving, etc. As yet no *sacerdos* (q.v.) had appeared to take over and absorb the priestly function of the *laos* itself, although there were regular offices performed by those to whom they were assigned (not all members had the same office; I Cor. 12). Every member of the NT *laos* was endowed with his appropriate gift of the Spirit for his own ministry. But after NT times the clergy (q.v.) became increasingly removed from the laity, and during the Middle Ages an elaborate hierarchical (q.v.) structure of priestly (and other) offices was developed, with the result that the laity came virtually to be regarded as having no priestly or ministerial function at all. Thus, 'lay' came to mean 'non-professional' or 'non-qualified' as in ordinary speech today, when, for instance, a clergyman in a discussion of legal issues among lawyers might describe himself as a 'mere layman'. Before the Reformation the 'clerics' were the professionals, in the State as well as in the Church, since they were the 'educated classes'. During the process of secularization (q.v.) which set in after the renaissance period the word 'lay' became almost a synonym for secular (*cf.* French *laïque*). The NT conception of the whole Church as the laity (*laos*) of God had become entirely obscured.

The churches of the Reformation took certain steps to remedy this situation, and Luther's teaching on the vocation of the Christian man made it clear that one could serve God in other ways than in Holy Orders or in a religious community. But generally the distinction between the ordained ministry and the laity remained (despite such developments as those of 'elders' or 'local preachers' in some denominations); even though the theological distance between minister and layman was lessened, the sociological distinction remained. The minister was the 'professional' and the layman's duty, even where he appointed and controlled the minister, was that of seeing that he was duly paid and housed. The absorption of all, or nearly all, ministry in the Church by the professionals was doubtless primarily a sociological feature of bourgeois Christianity, but it tended to obscure the NT conception of the ministry of the laity as a whole.

In recent decades, as a result largely of the new understanding of the Bible and also of the Liturgical Movement (q.v.), the central importance of the laity and of lay ministry in the Church has been rediscovered. To these influences should be added ecumenical thinking about Christian vocation under the leadership of J. H. Oldham, W. Temple, etc. The 'Life and Work' Conference at Oxford, 1937, and the Second and Third Assemblies of the World Council of Churches (Evanston, 1954 and New Delhi, 1961 respectively) gave considerable attention to the vocation of the laity. The Roman Catholic Church has also been engaged in new thinking on this subject in recent years. The place of the laity, not only in the work of mission (q.v.) and of witness to Christian belief and standards in the workaday world, but also in the liturgy itself is today a leading theme of discussion and action

throughout the Christian world. In particular, the theological training of the laity for a proper understanding of its true nature and role is widely emphasized. There seems a good prospect of realizing again in the life of the churches the concept of *laos* which is found in the NT.

S. C. Neill and H. R. Weber, eds., *The Layman in Christian History*, 1963; J. H. Oldham, *Work in Modern Society*, 1950; J. H. Oldham and W. A. Visser 't Hooft, *The Church and its Function in Society*, 1937; Alan Richardson, *The Biblical Doctrine of Work*, 1952; *Introduction to the Theology of the New Testament*, 1958, ch. 13; G. Wingren, *The Christian's Calling: Luther on Vocation*, ET, 1958; World Council of Churches, *Evanston Speaks*, Report of the Second Assembly of the World Council of Churches, 1954, section VI; *The New Delhi Report*, The Third Assembly of the World Council of Churches, 1962, pp. 202–7.

EDITOR

Language, Religious

There have been two periods in the history of Christianity at which the problematic character of religious language has been seriously investigated by theologians faced with a demand from philosophy for its clarification. The first was in the Middle Ages, the second is in our own century. The same basic question gave rise to both discussions. If all our knowledge comes to us by way of the five senses (a proposition held as firmly by Aquinas as by our contemporary empiricist philosophers), how then can we speak about God, who is not an object of sense-perception? In the mediaeval period the question was how one could go beyond the *via negationis* and say anything positive about God. If God can be described only by negatives (e.g. incorporeal, infinite, impassible, invisible, etc.), can we be said to have any knowledge of God at all? Accordingly there was developed the *via eminentiae* by which it could be asserted that every characteristic of finite being, because it was being and to that extent real and possessing some degree of perfection, must bear some correspondence to infinite being, i.e. God. That is to say, God (who is *ens realissimum* and *perfectissimum*) must contain in a supremely *eminent* way the qualities or degrees of being (or perfection) manifested in every finite being. This is the argument from **Analogy** (q.v.). Thus, when we say that God is 'Father', we do not mean that God is the begetter of mankind (or of the universe) in the same sense that men beget children; but we do mean that there is a genuinely analogical relationship between God's Fatherhood and human fatherhood, and the element of identity in this relationship is what constitutes the essential nature of fatherhood as such. Hence it is possible according to the presuppositions of mediaeval philosophy to speak meaningfully about God. Although those presuppositions are not ours, mediaeval thinking about the analogical character of religious language is very instructive, since it is obvious that all our language about

God must be analogical (unless, as some would claim, the concept of being is the sole literally true concept which applies unequivocally to God). Much of the recent discussion about demythologizing has been confused because the analogical character of religious language has not been understood. Analogical language does not require to be demythologized, and the NT writers were surely speaking analogically or symbolically and knew that they were not speaking literally in many places where modern western critics attribute to them a crude literalism.

In the twentieth century two philosophical pressures have brought the problematic character of religious language to the forefront of attention. The first is the existentialist philosophy (especially of Martin Heidegger), with its emphasis upon the priority of language as creating and constituting *Dasein* (humanity). This question is discussed under hermeneutics (q.v.). In the Anglo-Saxon world an entirely different philosophical movement, linguistic analysis (*see* **Analytic Philosophy**) has compelled theologians to show in what sense talk about God, or religious language in general, can be said to have any meaning. Religious concepts (such as God) must be reckoned meaningless, it is argued by the new empiricism (as it was argued by David Hume two centuries ago), unless empirical verification can be established for them. Certain theologians, overawed by the uncompromising severity of the empiricists, have capitulated and have admitted that the word 'God' is meaningless (e.g. P. van Buren, *The Secular Meaning of the Gospel*, 1963), thus joining up with those existentialist theologians who (as R. Bultmann himself would not) regard all religious terms, including 'God', as merely mythological ways of expressing man's understanding of his own existence. Another way of answering the empiricist argument is to reply that there is an *experience* of God (q.v.) in human life, not only in mysticism (q.v.) but also in our everyday experience of grace; there are, moreover, in human experience intimations of the transcendent (q.v.) which cannot be dismissed as illusory. (It has also often been pointed out that the dogma that nothing can be known to be true which is incapable of empirical verification is itself incapable of empirical verification.)

Karl Barth has taken a strikingly original line as regards the problem of religious language. He dismisses the *analogia entis* (or *via eminentiae*) as quite incapable of bridging the infinite gulf between the created and the Creator, and also the reductionist conclusions of both the existentialist and the neo-empiricist theologians. Instead of the analogy of being he asserts the *analogia fidei* or *analogia gratiae*. God of his sheer, uncoerced grace gives to men faith by which the truth of revelation is perceived. No analogical reasoning could ever have bridged the gulf, but the grace of God works the miracle, so that by faith the creature actually knows the Creator. In other words, God confers upon human language the capacity to speak meaningfully about him, but

this speaking will always be a speaking from faith to faith, never a speaking which moves on the plane of human philosophical discourse. This cutting of the knot of the problem of religious language is unlikely to satisfy either philosophers or philosophical theologians, but it at least calls attention to an enduring element in the biblical and Christian tradition, namely, that our knowledge of God (which in this context must mean our capacity to speak meaningfully about him) is never a human achievement but always a divine gift. *See also* **Analogy; Symbolism; Revelation; Hermeneutics; God.**

K. Barth, *Church Dogmatics*, II: *The Doctrine of God*, 1, 1957; J. Macquarrie, *God-Talk*, 1967; E. L. Mascall, *Words and Images*, 1957; Ian T. Ramsey, *Religious Language*, 1957.

EDITOR

Laodicean

The word is sometimes used as meaning 'lukewarm' in matters of faith or religion. The usage derives from Rev. 3.15 ff.

Lapsarian Controversy

Theories as to the relationship of predestination to the fall provided a point of amicable controversy between the holders of the high doctrine of predestination (q.v.) in the seventeenth and eighteenth centuries. Supralapsarianism taught that the man whom God had in mind when he determined his future state was man still to be created and still to fall. Infra (or sub) lapsarianism, however, regarded him as man already created and fallen. There was no disagreement on the eternity of predestination, as if the one placed the decree in eternity and the other only after the creation and fall. For both views the decree was determined in eternity and therefore before man existed. The difference lay in whether God was contemplating man as he intended to create him or as if he were created and fallen. On the whole, Infralapsarianism has been regarded as the more orthodox view.

For the theological implications, *see* Karl Barth, *Church Dogmatics*, II: *The Doctrine of God*, 2, ET, 1957, pp. 127–45; Heinrich Heppe, *Reformed Dogmatics*, ET, 1950, pp. 157–62.

T. H. L. PÁRKER

Latitudinarianism

This term was used by their opponents to describe the views of those seventeenth-century Anglican divines who preferred 'reason' to authoritarian direction, whether in matters of dogma or of ecclesiastical polity. They included those who inclined to Arminianism (*see* **Predestination** [1]) in theology and the Cambridge Platonists (q.v.). They were the precursors of the more thoroughgoing rationalism of the eighteenth century (*see* **Deism**), and they have had their counterparts in the Church of England in each succeeding age. In the nineteenth century the contributors to *Essays and Reviews* (1860, q.v.), and indeed all who were in sympathy with the liberal attitude of Thomas Arnold and his friends, could be said to be their spiritual descendents. In their day, however, they were usually known as Broad Churchmen (in contradistinction from the High Churchmen of the Oxford Movement and from the Low Church evangelical party). In the twentieth century the attitude has been known as 'modernist' or 'liberal'.

EDITOR

Latria

It is derived from Greek *latreia*, service of the gods. Distinctions have been traditionally made by theologians in the degree (or kind) of worship which is appropriate for different objects of veneration. Thus *latria* (in church Latin) is the supreme adoration properly offered to God alone. *Hyperdulia* represents the degree of veneration uniquely given to the Blessed Virgin Mary. *Dulia* (from Greek *douleia*, service; *cf. doulos*, slave) is an inferior kind of veneration, such as that paid to saints and angels.

EDITOR

Law

Law is an expression of the will of God in the form of commands and prohibitions. In the Bible, it refers most commonly to the Mosaic law, centring in the Decalogue and contained in the Pentateuch. This was originally understood as 'instruction' (*torah*) given by God to his chosen people for their good, which they would willingly observe out of loving gratitude for his grace in choosing them and establishing his covenant with them. But its observance came to be thought of less as their grateful response to him and the keeping of their part in the covenant, than as the means of securing his gracious regard for them and ensuring their claim to a part in the covenant. In post-exilic Judaism, conformity with the requirements of the law became the way of salvation. By strict observance of the law, men would be holy and righteous as God is holy and righteous, in order to pass the test of his judgment and merit a place in his everlasting kingdom. The law became in fact the mediator between man and God.

In the Gospels, Christ displays a dual attitude to the law, now quoting and obeying it as divinely authoritative, now criticizing and even disregarding it on his own authority. This can be understood in the light of the fact that he has come into the world to 'fulfil' the law. He fulfils it, first, by his teaching and example, whereby he discloses its inner meaning in terms of the double commandment of love (Matt. 22. 34–40). Love like his, expressed in utter trust and obedience towards God as his heavenly Father and in utterly selfless service to his fellowmen, even though it leads to the cross – this is what the law essentially demands. Hence he affirms its divine authority, hence also sets it aside or re-interprets it whenever its literal observance would inhibit the exercise of such love.

Considered simply as teacher and example, however, Christ stands over against us, in judgment upon us; for who among us *so* obeys God's law, who is *thus* holy and righteous? Yet at the same time he stands with us in mercy; for the love he preaches and practises is directed precisely to us. In spite of our lovelessness, our distrust and disobedience towards God and our self-seeking and self-righteous attitudes towards our fellows, he loves us with God's own love. Thus the will of God expressed in the law expresses itself also as gospel, as grace, when God in Christ shows towards us the love he cannot find in us. In this way, the law is both fulfilled and – just therefore – abolished as the way of salvation. Christ is in both senses the end of the law (Rom. 10.4). He, and not the law, is the Mediator between God and man.

Nevertheless, the law still stands as an expression of the will of God; and according to both Catholic and classical Protestant teaching all men have 'by nature' some knowledge of it, though this is obscured by sin (*see* **Natural Law**). What this means is that God's law is written in life before it is ever written anywhere else, and particular formulations of it (such as the Decalogue or the Golden Rule) arise out of the realities of human existence. For God and our God-given neighbours are there, making ceaseless demands on us just by being there, so that we cannot escape them even if in our sinfulness we are blind to their true meaning. The particular content of these demands varies, of course, with the varying relationships and circumstances of life; yet through them all with unvarying constancy runs the ultimate demand for love. Love therefore, as Luther says, 'is the queen and mistress of all laws', so that no law, whether civil, ecclesiastical, or even moral, can be or remain valid any longer than it serves in one way or another the purposes of love.

The law, however, was never in any of its forms intended as a way of salvation. For although as an expression of the will of God it is 'holy and just and good' (Rom. 7.12), yet it is powerless to produce what it essentially demands. Its particular provisions may control men's conduct, so that they behave decently, and it is very necessary that this should be so; but no law can make men love. Instead, as St Paul says, the law reveals – and even increases – our sinfulness (Rom. 3.20; 7.13). Just in so far as God's will stands over against us as law, it is plain proof that we are sinners; for 'the law is not made for a righteous man' (I Tim. 1.9). If we were righteous, i.e. in true harmony with the will of God, we should not encounter his will as law at all. His commandments would rather be 'instructions' which we should gladly welcome and willingly carry out. As it is, the law rather increases sin, by provoking our self-will to assert itself, whether in the rebellious self-indulgence of vice and crime, or in the calculating self-righteousness that characterizes so much of our religion and virtue.

The best the law can do for us is to bring home to us our sinfulness – our failure to fulfil it in love – and so prepare us for the remedy offered in the gospel. It thus becomes our 'tutor to bring us to Christ' (Gal. 3.24) and his love. For men cannot love unless they are loved – modern psychiatry has rediscovered what Christian faith has always known. But even when they are loved, it does them little good unless they believe they are loved – as can be seen in ordinary human relationships. Hence the gospel calls us, not to do, but to believe. And the law itself might well encourage us to believe; for the fact that God commands us to love is testimony to his own eternal nature of love.

G. Aulén, *The Faith of the Christian Church*, 1961; C. H. Dodd, *Gospel and Law*, 1950; T. E. Jessop, *Law and Love*, 1940; H. Kleinknecht and W. Gutbrod, *Law*, 1962; G. Wingren, *Creation and Law*, 1961.

P. S. WATSON

Laying on of Hands. *see* Initiation, Christian.

Lectionary. *see* Calendar, Liturgical.

Legalism

In ethics, legalism is the idea that strict conformity to prescribed rules of conduct is the hallmark of moral goodness, even though the claims of compassion or even commonsense are thereby inhibited. In theology, it is the idea that man's fulfilment of God's law is the indispensable foundation of man's standing with God. It makes no difference whether the requirement of the law is understood in terms of outward conduct or inward motivation, or whether the fulfilment is brought about by man's unaided efforts or by the assistance of divine grace. The point is that the religious relationship is governed by the law (q.v.).

P. S. WATSON

Leibniz, Gottfried Wilhelm

The theological significance of Leibniz (1646–1716), German philosopher, is threefold: first, his monadological view of the universe found its key and completion in the concept of God; second, his *Theodicé* was a profound and subtle defence of the view (later popularized in an inferior form by Christian Wolff, 1679–1754) that, given the character and ultimate purposes of the Creator, this world is 'the best of all possible worlds'; third, his philosophical system contained versions of the classical theistic demonstrations, including an extremely important reformulation of the ontological proof for the existence of God. Leibniz's natural theology, through the work of various commentators and popularizers, became an essential part of eighteenth-century European Christian rationalism. *See* **Pre-Established Harmony.**

JAMES RICHMOND

Lessing, Gotthold Ephraim

Lessing (1729–1781), German poet, critic and writer, was one of the principal philosophers of the German Enlightenment (*Aufklärung*). Lessing's influence on nineteenth-century German Protestant theology was considerable, owing to his conception of religion as intramundane progressivistic morality, finding its fulfilment in the age of Enlightenment itself. Lessing initiated a European controversy by publishing the so-called *Wolfenbüttel Fragments*, posthumous writings of H. S. Reimarus (1694–1768), which violently attacked the historical reliability of the Synoptic Gospels. Lessing's celebrated aphorism, 'the accidental truths of history can never become the proof of the necessary truths of reason', has been much discussed by subsequent theologians (e.g. Søren Kierkegaard) and philosophers of history.

H. Chadwick, *Lessing's Theological Writings*, 1956.

JAMES RICHMOND

Liberal Catholicism

The appeal to reason and respect for sound learning which were characteristic of classical Anglican divinity were severely tested in the nineteenth century when biblical criticism and scientific knowledge appeared to question the foundations of traditional Christianity. Among the various attempts to come to terms with modern thought liberal catholicism was among the most interesting and courageous. It sought to retain the credal orthodoxy of the earlier centuries, while allowing full authority to the 'assured results' of criticism. This type of theology is seen at its best in *Lux Mundi* (q.v.) and in *Essays Catholic and Critical* (1926, q.v.). The chief objection made to this approach was that the criticism was not radical enough, and that their theory of development did not allow any room for the Reformation. In the thirties this type of theology was under something of a cloud, but its virtues are better appreciated today.

A. M. Ramsey, *From Gore to Temple*, 1960.

R. CANT

Liberal Protestantism, Liberal Theology, Liberalism

These are somewhat vague terms descriptive of certain dominating trends in nineteenth- and early twentieth-century theology. Liberal theologians claimed freedom in two directions: first, from traditional dogmas and credal formulations; second, in the handling of historical texts and sources. They claimed that theology must be formulated in the light of advancing knowledge in philosophy, the sciences and other disciplines, and accordingly tried to be astringent critics of what they considered to be theological and ecclesiastical obscurantism. Historically the roots of nineteenth-century theological liberalism are to be found in post-Renaissance science and in the critical philosophy of the Enlightenment, of which that of Immanuel Kant (1724–1804) was both typical and influential. The effects of Kant's thinking on theology were twofold: first, his attack on metaphysical thinking cast doubt upon the validity of traditional natural theology, of which the classical demonstrations of God's existence and of personal immortality were an integral part; secondly, his attempt to establish man as a thinking and moral creature, transcendent over nature, was immensely influential in nineteenth-century theological circles. Partly as a result of his work, the demonstrative, metaphysical approach to theology was gradually abandoned in favour of one emphasizing man's transcendent status and unique inner awareness.

Nineteenth-century theological liberalism's greatest debt was probably to the thought of the German systematic theologian F. E. D. Schleiermacher (1768–1834), who, having rejected speculative natural theology, sought to base Christian belief upon the universal, trans-subjective awareness of God rooted in man's inner aesthetic and religious response to reality as a whole. Man's 'feeling of absolute dependence' was for Schleiermacher the essence and basis of religion in general and Christianity in particular. Parallel, in a sense, to Schleiermacher's teaching was the idealistic philosophy of G. W. F. Hegel (1770–1831), stressing the rationality of reality and that process whereby immanent Absolute Spirit attained to self-awareness in human thinking, ideas which were to be immensely influential upon subsequent theological enterprises. The overall effect of the thought of Hegel and Schleiermacher was to give nineteenth-century German Protestant theology a strongly anthropological character and to emphasize a firm continuity between human thinking and feeling on the one hand and Christian revelation on the other.

Within the context of liberal theology the other dominant influence was the system of Albrecht Ritschl (1822–1889) and his school. Reacting sharply against contemporary naturalism, positivism and determinism, and against the influence of all metaphysical thinking upon theology, Ritschl, influenced by neo-Kantian idealism, sought to base Christian theology upon the 'purely factual' historical basis of the N T, in which is portrayed in archetypal form 'man's supremacy over nature'. Jesus, whose being is threatened by hideously hostile forces, trusts absolutely in God's love and power; in so doing, he reveals man's true response to God, revealed as unqualified love and grace. Jesus is thus considered within Ritschlianism to be Archetypal Man and also the unique revelation of God. Upon this basis, Ritschl erected his theology of 'value-judgments'; contemporary man, understanding himself as threatened by blind, mechanistic, impersonal nature (as portrayed by nineteenth-century naturalism) can be delivered from this situation only by the work of Jesus mediated to him by the Christian Church. Man can attain to religious

knowledge only through the awareness of the 'value' or 'worth' imparted to his life by God through Jesus. There is no religious knowledge apart from this value-knowledge; there are no valid religious propositions apart from these value-judgments of faith. Those who are delivered from the threat of nature by the work of Jesus form, in community, the Kingdom of God, a social entity destined gradually to redeem and transform ethically the society in which it is set. Ritschl's basic theological ideas were developed in various directions by such theologians as Adolf von Harnack (1851–1930), Wilhelm Herrmann (1846–1922) and Julius Kaftan (1848–1926).

The roots of nineteenth-century liberalism are also to be sought in the development of the literary and historical criticism of the Bible. Briefly, by this is meant the application to the biblical sources of those techniques which were applied to non-biblical materials, in order that they might be 'objectively' interpreted in the context of the historical circumstances in which they originated. In practice, the tendencies were to isolate the biblical materials from later, especially Greek, philosophical 'accretions'; to regard them as literary and historical creations rather than as the numinous sources of unquestionable sacred doctrine; and frequently to interpret them in the light of fashionable contemporary philosophies, for example, Hegelianism.

In the light of this analysis of the origins of nineteenth-century liberalism, it is possible to attempt a characterization of it. First, liberalism exhibited a tendency to regard Christianity as not distinctively and exclusively unique, but rather as one 'religion' among others, and sometimes as one cultural movement among others. This was clearly an implication of Schleiermacher's theological method (adopted by later theologians), which defined first a universal religious awareness and only then dealt with Christianity as the highest but not the only form of this. This liberal tendency found its most extreme expression in the views of the so-called History of Religions School (*Religionsgeschichtliche Schule*), whose leader was Ernst Troeltsch (1865–1923). In its studies this school directed attention to those common features which Christianity shared with other religions; Troeltsch even admitted that it was conceivable that Christianity might be superseded as the highest form of religion.

Secondly, in trying to deal with, for example, the Gospel narratives 'scientifically' and 'objectively', critics such as H. E. G. Paulus (1761–1851) and D. F. Strauss (1808–1874) tried in a rationalistic manner to make apparently miraculous events accord with the laws of nature, as these were understood by nineteenth-century science. The result was a radical 'desupernaturalization' of these narratives. Linked with this tendency was another; namely, the tendency to distinguish sharply between the 'natural facts' of the Gospel stories and later legendary or 'mythical' accretions. Strauss's *Life of Jesus* (*Das Leben Jesu*) was a classic example of this kind of attempt.

Thirdly, there was a strong tendency to apply to Christian sources (the Bible, the history of dogma and the Church) the presuppositions and categories of contemporary philosophical movements. The influence of Romanticism on Schleiermacher is marked; the influence of Hegelianism on Strauss and F. C. Baur (1792–1860) is even more obvious; and, as we noted, Ritschl was heavily influenced by anti-naturalistic and anti-positivistic philosophy of a neo-Kantian type. It has been widely maintained by certain twentieth-century theologians that such philosophical influences produced varying degrees of distortion and impoverishment of the theological materials. Such distortion and impoverishment are most clearly seen in the work of Strauss and Baur.

Fourthly, in the highly critical atmosphere of nineteenth-century intellectual life, theologians tried to define the perennial 'essence' (German: *Wesen*) of the Christian Faith. By the end of the century this had hardened into the distinction between the religion *of* Jesus (often regarded as simple, ethical, practical Galilean) and the religion *about* Jesus (often regarded as Paulinist, Hellenistic, metaphysical, miraculous, supernaturalistic). Celebrated attempts to isolate and analyse Christianity's timeless essence were Ludwig Feuerbach's *The Essence of Christianity* (1841) and *The Essence of Religion* (1845), and Adolf von Harnack's *What is Christianity?* (*Das Wesen des Christentums*, 1900). Ritschl, through his rejection of all metaphysics in theology, and by his attempt to base Christianity upon 'purely historical' facts to which we attach moral and spiritual values, also contributed strongly to this tendency. In practice, over-concentration upon Christianity's perennial essence led to the well-known liberal distrust of traditional creeds and dogmas. It also contributed to the fundamental lack of awareness in liberal theology of the basically 'kerygmatic' character of the NT writings, of the insight that they represent an inseparable unity of fact and interpretation.

Fifthly, much liberal theology tended to overlook the 'historic eventfulness' of Christianity as a happening in which God had acted, radically altering the entire human situation. Christianity, as we have noted, was regarded rather as the supreme concrete expression of those religious drives and insights which permeated *all* history as such. Christianity's 'uniqueness' tended to be located, not in its historic eventfulness, but in the uniquely sublime teaching (about God, man and man's relationships with his fellows) and moral example of Jesus, and in the unique effect of these upon the progress and welfare of human society. In this sense it can be said that Christianity's uniqueness consists in the timelessness and unchangeability of its teaching rather than in the unique historicity of its central events.

The sixth and final characteristic of liberal theology is to be found in its attitudes to sin and salvation. Human sinfulness was not uncommonly regarded as a (merely negative) lack of knowledge or insight, or a dulled spiritual awareness. Correspondingly salvation tended to be regarded as a filling of this lack by inspiration, information, correction or even education. Typical of this teaching was the Ritschlian conception of sin as a confused misunderstanding based upon man's ignorance of God's true nature. It is therefore not accidental that the typically nineteenth-century liberal doctrine of the atonement tended to be of the exemplarist, moral-influence type. It is notoriously difficult to judge how far liberal theologians were influenced here by the nineteenth-century faith in human progress, whether linked with contemporary economic utopianism or with Hegelianism, and how far their well-known participation in schemes for social, political and educational reform was motivated by their theological convictions.

The revolt against nineteenth- and early twentieth-century theology was initiated and carried through by the Swiss theologian Karl Barth (1886–   ), strongly influenced by the Danish religious thinker Søren Kierkegaard (1813–1855), and by the writings of the sixteenth-century Reformers, Calvin particularly. Over against liberalism, Barth denied that Christianity is one religion among others, stressing rather that it concerns only God's unique self-revelation. He has vigorously tried to free Christianity from philosophical influences; he has stressed the centrality and the kerygmatic character of the biblical writings, the radical discontinuity between God and human nature, and has made much of the concepts of crisis, judgment and grace. Above all, against liberalism he has taught God's unqualifiable and indissoluble *subjectivity*: it is God who acts upon and towards man and not vice-versa.

It is rather unfortunate that in the present century there has taken place what R. R. Niebuhr has called a 'Barthian captivity' of the history of modern Christian thought. This is due largely to the immense influence exercised by Barth's *Die protestantische Theologie im 19. Jahrhundert*, Zürich, 1947, eleven chapters of which have been translated into English and published as *From Rousseau to Ritschl* (1959, in USA under the title *Protestant Theology*). Consequently too many have become acquainted with the nineteenth-century liberal tradition through the rather hypercritical accounts of it given by Barth and Emil Brunner (1889–1966). This has been unfortunate because it has obscured the positive, apologetically valuable aspects of the liberal tradition.

In the 1960s there are signs of a renewed and more objective interest in the liberal tradition of the last century. Furthermore, the highly influential contemporary theologies of Rudolf Bultmann (1884–   ) and Paul Tillich (1886–1966), in so far as they have been intended to be mediating, apologetic systems, and in so far as they have been attempts to interpret theological materials in the light of modern philosophy and science and to stress a certain continuity between God and human nature, may be taken as partly continuous with the liberal tradition described above. Since both Tillich and Bultmann were closely associated with Barth's theological revolution of half a century ago, they have tried to avoid the excesses into which the older liberalism fell; but it is only fair to add that their critics frequently bring against them the criticisms which were brought against their theological predecessors in the second decade of the twentieth century. *See also* **Kant, I.; Schleiermacher, F. D. E.; Hegel, G. W. F.; Absolute Dependence; Ritschl, A.; Harnack, A. von; Herrmann, W.; Kaftan, J. W. M.; *Religionsgeschichtliche Schule*; Troeltsch, E.; Strauss, D. F.; Baur, F. C.; Feuerbach, L. A.; Barth, K.; Kierkegaard, S.; Bultmann, R.; Tillich, P.; Jesus of History, The.**

Karl Barth, *From Rousseau to Ritschl* (USA: *Protestant Theology: From Rousseau to Ritschl*), 1959; Hugh R. Mackintosh, *Types of Modern Theology*, 1937 and 1964; John Macquarrie, *Twentieth-Century Religious Thought*, 1963; Richard R. Niebuhr, *Schleiermacher on Christ and Religion*, 1965; B. M. G. Reardon, *Liberal Protestantism*, 1968; James Richmond, *Faith and Philosophy*, 1966; A. R. Vidler, *The Church in an Age of Revolution*, 1961.

JAMES RICHMOND

Liberty, Religious

The basis of the Christian gospel is the freedom of the people of God. God delivered his people from bondage and in the process made them a nation. When they slipped back into the bondage of idolatry or into captivity, or into being overrun by enemies, God sent his prophets to proclaim deliverance, or 'liberty to the captives' (Isa. 61.1.f.). As the history of Israel developed, the deliverance of God was seen to be related to the individual's relationship with God, rather than being related to the saving act of God in history. (This tension between individual and corporate liberty can be seen in all discussions about religious liberty.) The expectation of God's deliverance later became an eschatological one – the deliverer (the Messiah) would come and set his people free and bring in the New Age.

Jesus Christ claims that he has come to bring deliverance to the captives (Luke 4. 16–22) and the Gospels show him doing this in his exorcisms, healing, serving and preaching. Above all, the NT sees Jesus as the Christ, who had come to set God's people free and overthrow the powers, which held man in bondage, by his redeeming activity. Jesus is the liberator, the pioneer who leads his people into the promised land (Heb. 4.1–11). Jesus sets man free so that man can freely respond to his fellow man and to God with his whole being in love. If this freedom is to be complete it involves every aspect of human life, personal and social, interior and exterior. This does not mean either antinomianism or political anarchy. Christian freedom involves Christian responsibility. Freedom is not simply freedom 'from', but also freedom 'for'; for the gospel, for the service of man, for the love of the brethren, for the worship of God. Moreover, Christians are

called upon to use their freedom for the maintenance of government and the State (Rom. 13.1–10). This, of course, raises great problems for the Christian of every age living under oppressive and dictatorial governments, which clamp down on religious liberty and other human rights.

Freedom returns to the world in Jesus Christ and remains with the Christian and the Church through his Spirit; where his Spirit is, there is liberty (Rom. 8.2; II Cor. 3.17; Gal. 5.1). To be a free man is to be possessed by the Holy Spirit and the freedom of Christ shows itself in the distinctive marks of the fruits of the Spirit. These lead to order, not to chaos.

In so far as the Church continues the work of Christ, it shares in the freedom of Christ. The whole ministry of the Church of God therefore requires a certain measure of freedom within which to proclaim and live the gospel. While outward liberty may not be necessary for the existence of the Church, it certainly is necessary for its full life and well-being. It is part of the proclamation of the gospel to be concerned with religious liberty for all men. It is in the interests of the gospel for Christians to support a society where freedom, with the proper limitations, is guaranteed to all men.

The biblical pattern is one in which the initiative always lies with God and not with man. It is God who acts and God who calls and God who gives the grace for man to respond through the indwelling of the Spirit. The freedom of man is also a gift of God, which he needs to make a free response to God.

Man as created in the image of God is born to be free. The dignity of every man demands freedom. Religious freedom is an essential part of human and civil rights. The role of the Church therefore involves ensuring the freedom of individual rights as an end in itself. This principle is now contained in the Universal Declaration of Human Rights of the UN, Article 18 of which reads:

Everyone has the right to freedom of thought, conscience and religion; this right includes freedom to change his religion or belief, and freedom, either alone or in community with others and in public or private, to manifest his religion or belief in teaching, practice, worship and observance.

The question of religious liberty concerned the Church from very early in its life, both in its own relation with alien governments and in dealing with heretics within the Church. It is on this matter that differences of opinion within the Church can be seen from this early time. Some like Athanasius, Hilary of Poitiers (*Contra Arianos vel Auxentium*, Migne x, 610) and Lactantius (*Divina Institutio*, Migne vi, 1061) reject the idea of the use of force to put down heretics. It was Augustine of Hippo who argued that liberty goes only with truth and that it was justifiable to employ the force of the state to put down heretics. People should not have the right to choose error, for such a choice is not freedom but bondage. False religions should be exterminated; they lead people not to freedom but slavery. More than this, error ought to be put down, because error is harmful to man and society, the occasion of sin and injurious to the rights of others.

This view inevitably implies a certain doctrine of the State. It was a view which could be supported in a 'Christendom' situation where the state was seen as an arm of the Church. The free exercise of religion is not tolerated because the Church has the truth and the task of the state is to help the Church to ensure that the truth is accepted and observed. This view of freedom is far too idealized and does not allow for changes in views of government, nor for the growth in understanding the importance of the individual. While true freedom may be to choose only the good, the risk must always be open for people to choose the bad; individual responsibility demands it. This attitude is not capable of adaptation according to changing historical situations. We no longer live in the 'Christendom' situation in which it originated.

Another view of liberty allows for the risk that man may choose the bad and argues that since this is a risk which God takes there is no reason why man should not take the same risk. Man needs freedom to enable him to respond freely to God. The task of government is to allow man as much freedom as is consistent with the freedom of others. Religious freedom may therefore be defined as follows: (1) It is concerned not only with the inner freedom in Christ (Gal. 5.1) but also with the outer freedom of the individual within society. (2) Religious freedom must be granted by governments. (3) There is a distinction to be made between freedom of conscience and freedom of religious exercise. The rights which religious liberty involve in society include the following: (1) the right to freedom of conscience; (2) the right of religious expression and public witness; (3) the right of proclaiming the social, political and economic implications of faith; (4) the right to freedom of association for worship and mutual edification; (5) the right to express the faith in service to the community; (6) the right of national and international freedom of movement for missionaries and the material required for the proclamation of faith; and (7) the right of a recognizable relationship with the state.

The social implications of all this will be seen to be very considerable, and the Christian community in many places may have to fight to obtain them. It is clearly the task of the Church to gain whatever of those freedoms it can and when this is not possible to make the best of any situation. But too self-conscious a clamouring for rights will have the wrong effect. Religious liberty must be seen to be exercised in a responsible way. Churches find themselves as majority churches supported by the state, as minority churches which are tolerated in secular states and also as minority churches in situations where the Government is opposed to Christianity. Each of these situations will require different approaches by the Church. The liberty which the churches require must be shown to respect the liberty of others. For the Christian must also recognize his responsibilities as a man in society. These include his responsibilities to his fellow men in respecting their freedom; to society in playing his role within it; and to the state in furthering its purposes of order and justice. There may sometimes be a tension between these responsibilities and the Christian right of religious liberty. Furthermore, the Bible and experience should not lead us to expect that the Christians will always be accepted; they may well be persecuted and rejected. Even under persecution the Church should ask for religious liberty for all men. It should do so not for itself but for the benefit of the state. For it is a Christian task to support the state and this may mean at times criticizing the state.

Isolated churches do not, however, stand alone. The Church is also supra-national. The existence of the World Council of Churches can make a real difference to churches struggling to claim religious liberty. An international ecumenical community can help to encourage the development of religious liberty at an international level. The World Council of Churches' statement on 'Christian Witness, Proselytism and Religious Liberty', which was commended to the member churches for consideration in 1960 (see ER, XIII, 1, October 1960), points to principles on these matters. These can be used by the member churches to develop a consistent attitude to liberty throughout the world. This has now spread further to the Declaration of the Second Vatican Council on Religious Freedom. This Declaration marks a development in Roman Catholic thinking on this subject (this it admits) and is clearly influenced by the thinking of the World Council of Churches. There is therefore a chance of a consensus of Christian opinion on the subject of religious liberty emerging in the near future.

A special problem of religious liberty arises in countries where there is an established church which regards its position as a national church as giving it some kind of responsibility and right to exercise pastoral care over everybody in the country. This is justified as an expression of the catholicity of the Church. Problems arise when a national church is believed by some to be failing in its obedience to the gospel and other churches either are asked to come in and preach the gospel or a schism takes place. At what point does the authority of the national church cease to be real because of its failure to be the Church? In general it seems that it is far more important to accept the principle of co-operation than for national churches to appeal to their historic authority. The basis of toleration between Christian churches must always be that of Matt. 7.12. On this basis true religious freedom is guaranteed to all Christians and also to everyone else.

We now live in a world where most states claim to be secular. The Church can no longer expect the state to uphold the truths of the Christian religion. Rather the Church must show the significance of the Christian faith through its participation in the secular state and through its concern for the human rights of all. Such concern will include the requirements of religious liberty. In some places Christianity is seen to threaten national solidarity and in such situations some liberties may be limited and Christians will have to accept these limitations. Indeed some writers have gone so far as to suggest that such limitations signify the judgment of God on the Church for communicating the truths of the gospel in an alien and uncharitable manner. Certainly self-examination should be an essential part of the consideration of the reasons for oppression.

If the Church is going to affirm religious liberty as the basis of human rights, then it must show the same type of tolerance within itself. If it is to do so, it must refuse to use force against heretics. It must keep clear the distinction between faith and knowledge, allow its members to pursue the truth, and allow for tensions and differences of outlook among its members. The question how far such allowance should go is part of the ecumenical debate. How much agreement on the Christian faith is required for divided churches to unite? How far must any individual be expected to hold the complete faith of the Church to which he belongs? Certainly there must be some agreement; otherwise such membership is dishonest. Moreover the acceptance of a faith implies some acceptance of the *authority* of the Church in matters of doctrine. There must be some agreement about what are the essentials and what is less essential in the membership of the Church, and variety is needed to prevent the Church becoming stagnant.

There are still many points in the debate on religious liberty which need considerable clarification. Can the state have any competence in matters of religion? What is the relationship between freedom of conscience and social religious liberty? Religious liberty needs always to be examined within a specific historical and social context. As this is always changing, the questions need to be kept continuously under review. The way does now seem open for a united Christian approach to this topic. This will be very welcome: the maintenance of religious liberty may be important for the freedom of all mankind. A state which will not allow religious liberty is liable to limit other freedoms as well.

C. de Albornoz, *The Basis of Religious Liberty*, 1963; J. Courtney Murray, *The Problem of Religious Freedom*, 1965; Vatican II, *The Declaration on Religious Freedom with Commentary* by E. McDonagh, 1967; World Council of Churches Report 'Christian Witness, Proselytism and Religious Liberty', *ER XIII*, 1 (October 1960).

R. M. C. JEFFERY

Limbo

From Latin *limbus*, a hem or edge: the notion that persisted from the early Middle Ages, that there must be some place where after death souls (e.g. those of unbaptized infants) undeserving of condemnation or of the beatitude of heaven could enjoy their natural state of happiness in eternity. There were many different forms of the notion.

Liturgical Movement

The Liturgical Movement is a movement which began in the Roman Catholic Church in the last century but has affected almost all branches of Christendom; its purpose is to restore to the laity an intelligent, active and intimate participation in the public worship of the Church, and especially in the Eucharist. It is usually held to have begun with the labours of Abbot Prosper Guéranger of Solesmes, under whose encouragement his abbey became a famous centre for the scrupulously exact and reverent performance of the Roman rite and for the recovery of the allegedly (though disputedly) authentic form of the traditional plainchant of the Church. Later critics have accused Dom Guéranger of unscholarliness, antiquarianism and romanticism, but this is the common lot of pioneers and there is no doubt that the later development not only of Solesmes but also of such monastic houses as Maredsous and Maria Laach as great and popular centres of liturgical activity and pilgrimage ultimately derive from Guéranger's work. In more recent years the Movement has spread out into the parochial and missionary spheres and has led to pressure not merely for the scrupulous observance of the Roman rite in the form which it has come to take as a result of mediaeval and post-mediaeval developments, but for a radical reform of the rite itself in order to bring it into line with primitive and pre-mediaeval liturgical understanding and practice and with the pastoral and evangelistic needs of the present day. This resulted in such forms as the 'dialogue mass', in which the people joined in all the responses, and also in the widespread custom by which, while the priest at the altar performed the rite in Latin, a vernacular version was simultaneously and audibly read in the body of the church. The Movement has had its main success in France, Germany, Belgium and Holland and in parts of the mission fields; it has made slower impact in Italy, Spain, England, Ireland and the United States, though everywhere there has been a vigorous body of supporters. The attitude of the hierarchy has on the whole been cautious, as has that of the curial authorities in Rome, but it must not be forgotten that the strong encouragement of frequent communion by Pope Pius X and the universal permission for evening masses and for considerable modification of the fast before communion by later popes have immensely stimulated participation in the Eucharist by the laity. However, the strength of the Movement has recently shown itself in a quite remarkable way, in the constitution on the Sacred Liturgy of 1963, which was the first concrete achievement of the Second Vatican Council. The working out of the practical details of the liturgical reforms are left to the discretion of the various national and other local groups of bishops guided by the various needs and opportunities which confront them, but the Constitution is uncompromisingly explicit upon the aims which are to be pursued. The laity are given a full, active and intelligent share in the Liturgy as members of the Body of Christ; there are to be radical simplifications and modifications in the existing rite to meet the local situations, and there has been a greatly extended, and indeed almost complete vernacularization of the text. And behind this there lies, not a mere motive of practical expediency, but a recovered understanding of the nature of the Church as the Body of Christ, sharing in his redemptive activity and commissioned to bring the whole human race within its sphere. The Constitution on the Liturgy is far more than a set of directives for reforms in liturgical practice; it is beyond dispute the finest *theological* statement of the nature of the Church's life as arising out of the creative and redemptive activity of God that has yet been produced and it provides a striking proof that the Liturgical movement is neither an antiquarian fad nor a go-getting gimmick but a remarkable efflorescence of the Church's true nature as the Body of Christ. There is indeed a close connection between the Liturgical Movement itself and developments in ecclesiology and eucharistic theology (qq.v.).

The influence of the Liturgical Movement has not been confined to the Roman communion. Introduced to the notice of Anglicans in 1935 by Fr Gabriel Hebert's striking book *Liturgy and Society*, which was followed by the symposium called *The Parish Communion* in 1937, the Movement has obtained a firm hold in a large number of parishes. In many of these the established pattern of Sunday morning worship, consisting of a plain celebration of the Eucharist at 8.00 a.m., followed at 11.00 a.m. by either Morning Prayer or a Solemn Eucharist at which only the celebrant communicated, has given way to a 'Parish Eucharist' or 'Parish Communion' at 9.15 or 9.30 a.m., at which practically all those present receive communion. This has often been accompanied by ceremonial developments intended to stress the corporate nature of the sacrament; the two most notable of these are the 'westward position' of the celebrant, who faces the people across the altar throughout the service, and the 'offertory procession', in which the people or their representatives bring up the bread and wine to the altar before the anaphora. Sometimes the service is followed by a 'parish breakfast', which is intended to reproduce the character of the primitive Agape (q.v.). Some of these ceremonial developments have been defended as revivals of primitive practice by arguments which not all historians are able to accept, but their real justification must be sought on pastoral and educative grounds, as is shown by the fact that there are many primitive practices which no one would contemplate reintroducing. There is also a danger of stressing the activity of the people in the Eucharist to the point of obscuring the fact that the Eucharist is primarily the act of God and not of man; however,

the more perceptive members of the Movement are well aware of these dangers and take safeguards against them. There is no doubt that the Movement has revivified many parishes; it has shown its power especially in new and growing centres of population. It has also done a great deal to bridge the gap between the 'Catholic' and 'Evangelical' parties in the Church. In Protestant bodies, both on the Continent and in Britain, the Movement has made itself felt in an increased demand for communion and a deepened understanding of the corporate nature of the sacrament.

One effect of the Movement is that liturgical revision, in which almost all Christian bodies except the Eastern Churches are now engaged, is concerned far less with modernizing the language and brightening up the services, and far more with the production of liturgical forms which will more adequately express the true nature of the Church and the sacraments. The experience of the Liturgical Commission of the Church of England has shown that the rank and file of the clergy and people are not always ready to move as fast in this respect as the theologians and liturgists would desire. *See also* **Eucharist; Eucharistic Theology.**

Apart from those mentioned above the following books may be consulted: J. J. von Allmen, *Worship: its Theology and Practice*, 1965; J-D. Benoit, *Liturgical Renewal*, 1958; L. Bouyer, *Life and Liturgy*, 1956; G. Dix, *The Shape of the Liturgy*, 1945, esp. ch. 1–6, 9–11 and 16 (some of Dix's views have been disputed, but his book remains as the most inspiring treatment in existence of the nature of the Liturgy; its publication brought interest in liturgiology to life when it had for long been relegated to the remotest academic circles); Caryl Micklem, ed., *Contemporary Prayers for Public Worship*, 1967; L. Sheppard, ed., *True Worship*, 1963; M. Thurian, ed., *Eucharist at Taizé*, 1962.

E. L. MASCALL

Liturgical Worship

Liturgical Worship is worship according to prescribed ritual (*see* **Worship**), as contrasted with 'free' (i.e. without fixed forms) worship or private prayer. The expression is used of services such as the Canonical Hours or (in Anglicanism) of Matins and Evensong, but it is perhaps chiefly used of the Eucharist (q.v.), which is often called 'the Liturgy' because it is the chief act of Christian worship. See **Liturgy; Worship; Office, Divine.**

Liturgiology

Liturgiology is the name commonly used to denote the historical and theological study of the liturgy (q.v.).

E. L. MASCALL

Liturgy

In the narrow sense the word (Greek: *leitourgia*, a public work) is used as a synonym for the Eucharist as the Church's corporate and official act of worship *par excellence*. In a wider sense it covers all the Church's public formal worship, in contrast to the private devotions of individual Christians and less formal public services such as prayer-meetings, though the line cannot be very sharply drawn. It is used in the wider sense in the *Constitutio de Sacra Liturgia* issued by the Second Vatican Council at the end of 1963.

E. L. MASCALL

Locke, John

John Locke (1632–1704) was the first great figure of modern British empiricism. Locke sought to assimilate the philosophical implications of the new science of his day, and in particular to analyse the human mind afresh, its powers and limitations. His chief work, *An Essay Concerning Human Understanding*, published in 1690, gave to modern philosophy its central concern with theory of knowledge. All our awareness, Locke argued, is of 'ideas', and all ideas are ultimately derived from 'experience' – either from sense-experience or from 'reflection' (awareness of our own minds in action). None of these ideas is 'innate': the theory of innateness is redundant.

A material object is known to us as a constellation of ideas – a particular shape, size, colour, etc. Locke considered that of these qualities some must be deemed to be 'in' the object itself – the primary qualities ('solidity, extension, figure, motion or rest, and number'); and the others – though their appearance to us as sounds, colours, smells, tastes is due to the 'powers' of the object – are not in the object itself (secondary qualities). The qualities of bodies required a substratum (substance) in which to inhere. Substance is 'the supposed but unknown support of those qualities . . . which we imagine cannot subsist . . . without something to support them'.

All these arguments had plausibility, but the theory as a whole stands open to grave objections, despite its attempts to be faithful to experience, commonsense and science. If all we are aware of are ideas, we have really no authority to posit a substratum which 'supports' them. How also can we compare our ideas with their objects and tell which ideas resemble qualities in bodies and which do not? Locke's central concept of 'idea' is itself ambiguous, in ways that are damaging to his whole enterprise. For instance, we may have ideas *of* sensible qualities (the two being distinguished), but the sensible qualities are also spoken of by Locke as ideas themselves, and ideas include not only the impressions of the senses (in their particularity) but also general notions.

Locke's political philosophy is expounded in his *Second Treatise of Government* (also 1690). Locke used the traditional account of a 'state of nature', a state that passes into civil society by way of a 'contract'. The state of nature was by no means as chaotic and amoral as Thomas Hobbes imagined it, but it was only in organized society that our rights and liberties could properly be secured. The conception of government as having to fulfil a *trust*, and the emphasis throughout upon the consent of the citizen to submit to law and to majority government produced a theory of *limited* government, with division of power.

Mention should also be made of Locke's *The Reasonableness of Christianity* (1695). Though not itself deistic, this work exerted an important influence in subsequent controversies over deism. There was a place in Locke's thought for revelation; but reason, he claimed, sits in final judgment.

John Locke, *An Essay Concerning Human Understanding*, ed. and abr. A. D. Woozley, Fontana Library, 1964; R. I. Aaron, *John Locke*, 2nd. ed., 1955; D. J. O'Connor, *John Locke*, 1952; I. T. Ramsey, *Locke's Reasonableness of Christianity*, 1958.

R. W. HEPBURN

Logic

Logic can claim to be both the most technical, specialized branch of philosophy and the branch that has more general relevance to other disciplines than any other part of philosophy. Its breadth can be seen in its concern with the structure of argument as such. It can be defined as the systematic study of argument, the methods to be used in distinguishing correct from incorrect – valid from invalid – patterns of reasoning. Reasoning is investigated also by psychology, but as a human activity, a process, a series of events – talk, inward musings, 'dawnings' and doubtings. The logician is primarily interested in the reliability or unreliability of inferring such and such a conclusion from such and such premisses.

The degree of development and specialization logic has now attained is a relatively recent phenomenon, our own century having seen an enormous extending of logic as traditionally conceived, and an equally great effort to give all possible rigour to logical systems. The traditional Aristotelian logic was not able adequately to analyse the logic of propositions – where the elements of the arguments are not 'terms' but complete propositions. Stoic logicians had in fact worked on the logic of propositions, but traditional logic failed properly to incorporate their researches. Only recently, too, philosophers and mathematicians have elaborated theories about the foundations of mathematical reasoning. The augmented field of logic includes such topics as the nature of definition, types of proposition, the study of forms of argument (among which the syllogism retains a place, although among many other forms), methods of testing deductive arguments for validity, the reducing of a logical system to its formal essentials – displaying its axioms and rules of inference. Again, 'modal' logic investigates arguments which turn upon words like 'must', 'may', 'cannot'; arguments about what is possible, impossible or necessary.

Logic is by no means confined to the study of deduction alone. In *inductive* inference no contradiction is produced if the premisses of an argument are affirmed and the conclusion denied. Yet, of course, there are good and bad, better and worse, arguments here, too. This is the field of 'reasonable', 'probable' inference, where a claim can be supported by evidence more or less weighty, more or less flimsy. (*See* **Induction**.) Inductive logic has been developed, historically, as the analysis of scientific canons of reasoning, although the extent to which science requires inductive arguments is itself debated today by some philosophers of science. (*See*, for instance, Karl Popper, *The Logic of Scientific Discovery*, 1959).

'Philosophy of logic' is the study of higher order questions like 'What are propositions?' 'What do we mean by "truth", "validity", "probability", "logical necessity"?' It includes the study of 'meaning' in general, the problems of how logic and metaphysics are related: what assumptions, if any, the logician makes about the world, and what implications, if any, his studies have for our overall view of the world.

At what points, finally, does the study of logic bear most directly upon the conduct and assessment of theological argument? In so far, of course, as logic deals with the conditions for any consistent discourse and correct argumentation, it bears on it at *every* point. From a contradiction, e.g., any proposition whatever may be deduced, however absurd or palpably false. The theologian needs to develop, therefore, a logic that will give a satisfactory account of any apparent contradictions he finds himself moved to affirm. This is an arduous task: renaming the problem-cases 'paradoxes' will do only as a first move.

Again, the traditional theistic arguments have involved a great deal of very complex logic. The dispute over the ontological argument (q.v.), for instance, is largely a dispute over the logical nature of the words 'exist', 'existent'. Do they function as predicates: does 'existent' figure among the perfections – so that to omit existence from the account of God's qualities would count as failure to conceive of God as the 'greatest conceivable being'? Or is 'existent' of an entirely different order from all predicate-words? The cosmological argument (q.v.) speaks of God as 'necessary being': does 'necessary' here mean 'logically necessary' (i.e. does the denial of God's existence involve contradiction)? If so, the ontological argument and its difficulties return once more. If 'necessary' is used in some other sense, there needs to be a logical analysis of that sense, and its relation to other senses of the word.

The study of religious language (q.v.) raises many more logical cruces. If language about God is analogical or symbolical or in some other way 'oblique', we need (as part of a theory of meaning) an account of how this language operates, how it can be kept from extravagance or emptiness, of how the symbols refer to the God they ostensibly are *about*. Claims about God's infinity bring logical problems of their own. Expressions that normally are perfectly comprehensible may become logically perplexing if 'infinite' or 'infinitely' are prefixed to them. How far are analogies from the mathematics of infinite series illuminating or misleading? The complexity and obscurity of many of the notions a theologian deals with, the way in which they hover on the borderline between sayable and unsayable, and vanish into mystery – all this makes the pursuit of logical rigour and precision a most difficult task for the theologian; but, for the very same reasons, a most necessary task also.

I. M. Copi, *Introduction to Logic*, 1953; G. B. Keene, *Language and Reasoning*, 1961; S. Toulmin, *The Uses of Argument*, 1958.

R. W. HEPBURN

Logical Positivism. *see* Positivism.

Lombard, Peter

Born in Lombardy, Peter Lombard (c. 1100–c. 1160), styled *Magister Sententiarum*, studied at Bologna, Rheims, Paris; he followed Abelard's (q.v.) lectures and later employed his method to good effect. In 1148, he was at Rheims for the examination of the supposedly heretical Gilbert de la Porrée; here he was in company with Robert of Meulun and they were called *magistri scholares*. He also knew the canonist Gratian and followed his method as in the *Decretum*. In 1159 he was appointed Bishop of Paris. Attacked after his death by Joakim of Flora and others, he was entirely vindicated at the 1215 Fourth Lateran Council.

His principal work is 'The Sentences' or *Sententiarum libri quattuor*, 1148–51. A collection of sources, it deals successively with the Trinity, providence, evil; creation, sin and grace; the incarnation, the redemption, the virtues and the commandments; the sacraments (where he establishes the seven for the first time) and the four last things. It draws on many sources, especially Augustine, and less so Hilary of Poitiers and John Damascene, the Greek Father (who was hardly known in the West till Grosseteste's translations). The work steered a safe, unoriginal middle course between the two prevalent tendencies, recourse to speculation and to authority; he was as contemptuous of the *garruli ratiocinatores* as of those who lived under the wing of another. His method was developed into the great *summae* in the next century, notably of St Thomas Aquinas (*see* **Thomism**), who began, as Duns Scotus (q.v.) and many others did, with a *Commentary on the Sentences*. His distinction between sacrament and sacramental, and his doctrine of causal efficacy of the sign (*sacramentum*) were of special influence.

F. Protois, *Pierre Lombard, Évêque de Paris*, 1880; J. de Ghellinck, *CE* XI. pp. 768–9; *DTC* XII (2), cols. 1941–2019, (with long bibliography); Migne, *PL* 191–2; 'Sentences' in *Opera S Bonaventurae*, Quaracchi I–IV, 1882–9; *Repertorium Commentariorum in Sententiae Petri Lombardi*, 2 vols. 1947; 'Livres des Sentences: Petri Lombardi libri IV Sententiarum, studio et cura PP. Collegii S. Bonaventurae in lucem editi', Quaracchi, F. Stegmüller, ed., 2 vols, 1916.

ALBERIC STACPOOLE, OSB

Lord's Supper, The

The Lord's Supper is the common title for the Eucharist among Protestants; it is taken from I Cor. 11.20. In view of the separation of the Eucharist from the Agape (q.v.) it is at least arguable that the name 'Lord's Supper' is more appropriate to the latter than the former. In the 1549 and subsequent English Prayer Books it is used as the first of alternative titles for the Eucharistic service. *See also* **Eucharist, Eucharistic Theology.**

E. L. MASCALL

Lotze, Rudolf Herrmann

While being, like Kant, a firm admirer of the methodology of the natural sciences, and holding that philosophy receives its starting-point from them, Lotze (1817–1881), German neo-Kantian philosopher, nevertheless taught that a comprehensive and unified picture of reality is possible only through the interpretative power of mind and the unique *values* which are innate in mind (in his *Mikrokosmos*, 1856–64). Lotze was from 1864 until 1881 a colleague at the University of Göttingen of A. Ritschl (1822–1889), and it was from Lotze that Ritschl derived his theory of knowledge based upon *value-judgments*. *See* **Herrmann, W.; Kaftan, J.; Ritschl, A.**

JAMES RICHMOND

Love

Love is the essential characteristic of the divine nature (I John 4.8, 16), from which all Christian love is derivative (4.19). The originality of the NT teaching is shown by its use of a word (*agape*) which is hardly found previously, except in a few instances in LXX. *Agape* (q.v.) is the love which loves despite even the repulsiveness of its object (man the sinner) and is contrasted with *eros*, which is the love that is elicited by the attractive qualities of the loved one. 'Charity', derived from Latin *caritas*, is used in the older EVV of the NT, but is replaced by 'love' in RVV because of the unhappy patronizing overtones it had acquired during the industrial era. ('The unemployed want justice, not charity.') The word 'care' (from Anglo-Saxon *caru, cearu*, sorrow), in the sense of solicitude for others, is often a useful modern equivalent for the hackneyed and ambiguous 'love': to *care* for the aged, the afflicted, the hungry, etc. is what is involved in love, which is not a mere disposition but is essentially an activity. ['Care' in one of its original meanings, namely, self-distress, anxiety (*Angst*), which figures prominently in existentialist philosophy, is not in any sense an equivalent of love.] The systematic study of love in Christian thought is undertaken in A. Nygren's *Agape and Eros*, new ET by P. S. Watson (1953). *The Mind and Heart of Love* by M. C. D'Arcy, SJ (1945) may also be recommended among recent studies. *See also* **Agape.**

EDITOR

Luther, Martin

Luther (1483–1546), educated at the University of Erfurt and in the monastery of Augustinian Hermits there, while young, was familiar with mediaeval theology. As a professor in Wittenberg he struggled through a time of deep anxiety concerning his own salvation. When he fully yielded to the Pauline teaching of justification by faith he felt as if the gate of heaven had been opened to him. His lectures on Romans (1515–6) bring to expression the elements of this doctrine. The Reformation controversy began at the point where this conviction was brought to bear on the practice of indulgences. As his theology was widened in controversy he still kept the emphasis on justification by faith. With intensity and mounting force, and with constant reference to Scripture, he challenged the constituent elements of scholastic theology and ecclesiastical claims to authority. The papacy itself was soon involved, and all the pressure it could employ was insufficient to silence him. From 1517 to 1530, protected at Wittenberg by the Electors of Saxony, Luther and his associates through teaching, preaching and writing, wrought a vast and lasting change in the religious scene. The wide response to his daring course of thought and action was made possible by previous widespread dissatisfaction with the old order. The new invention of the printing press, called by him 'God's latest and best work to spread the true religion', gave to a man of Luther's gifts a protean power to alter the motivating beliefs of millions. He wrote in Latin and German, and translations spread his message beyond the readers of these languages to most parts of Europe. The foundation of his new theology was laid in five brilliant treatises published between May and November, 1520: the *Treatise of Good Works; The Papacy at Rome; Address to the German Nobility; Babylonish Captivity of the Church; Freedom of a Christian Man.* From the Ten Commandments, the stress in good works is laid on wholesome social behaviour and useful tasks. The Church is seen not as a hierarchical structure but as a spiritual community. Those in political authority are summoned to aid in reform by means of a series of councils. The sacraments are expounded from the NT, and are to be released from the captivity in which they have been held under the papacy. The doctrine of the priesthood of all believers is strongly presented in the last two treatises mentioned. The most impressive, and the least controversial of the five is the *Freedom of a Christian Man*, which manifestly reflects his experience of emancipation through faith. The Christian is 'the most free lord of all', in union with Christ partaking of Christ's kingship, and of his priesthood in virtue of which Christians share with each other the things of God. So also the Christian is 'the most dutiful servant of all', helping others without hope of reward and joining in mutual service even to the extent that we become 'Christs one to another'.

These early treatises present simply and powerfully the doctrines most emphasized throughout his later writings. He had already made himself a biblical scholar, and he constantly challenged his opponents to meet him on the ground of Scripture. A great deal of his life work had to do with the translation and interpretation of the Bible. He could count on the fact that the authority of Scripture was a common presupposition in theology. But among the clergy there had long prevailed a strong sense of peril in placing it in the hands of laymen. To Luther Scripture-testimony rather than tradition or scholastic opinions was the sufficient test of all doctrines, and laymen were not only to be instructed in the Bible but also to read and meditate upon it for themselves. If he speaks of the Bible as the Word of God he does not mean that all parts of it are in equal degree divine utterances. Out of proportion to other passages, the words of Jesus in the Gospels, the Epistles, Romans, Galatians, Ephesians, I John and I Peter, with many of the Psalms and certain chapters of Isaiah, contributed to his thought, since in them he recognized most readily a revelation of Christ. The OT is a book of law and the NT a proclamation of grace, yet the former is not to be lowly esteemed. The key is in John 5.39, 'Search the scriptures because . . . they . . . bear witness to me.' Accordingly Genesis is 'almost a gospel book' and in the Psalter the Holy Ghost composed 'a short Bible'. A certain antagonism appears between Scripture and reason. In his repudiation of reason as a means of knowing God he thinks of reason as wayward and egocentric and intolerant of the unknowable, in opposition to faith for which God is both known and unknown, *revelatus* and *absconditus*.

Luther's doctrine of the Church has negative and positive aspects. He gives habitual expression to his intense dissatisfaction with prevailing conditions and with the whole system of ecclesiastical thought and practice associated with the papal hegemony. Obedience to popes and bishops is not required where they are disobedient to God's Word. The true Church is in essence not any visible entity but the invisible society of the true Christians which, however, presses towards visibility in the preaching of the Word and the administration of the sacraments. Among these he gives to penance a place subordinate to the two NT sacraments. The satisfactory works of penance are worthless by comparison with the spirit of repentance and the renewal of man's life by faith. On the Eucharist he abandons transubstantiation and rejects the Zwinglian conception of a spiritual presence of Christ's spatially absent body. The bodily presence is emphasized, but the miracle does not occur in the hands of the priest; it becomes real to the worshipper through the Scripture passages in the rite, such as 'This is my body', 'This is my blood . . . shed for many for the remission of sins'. The sacraments express and enhance that holy communion of saints in which the Church consists.

Martin Luther, *Werke, Kritische Gesammtaus-*

gabe, 69 vols. published, 1883–   ; *Luther's Works*, ed., J. Pelikan, 1952–   , in progress, to be completed in 55 vols.; R. L. Bainton, *Here I Stand; A Life of Martin Luther*, 1950; E. M. Carlson, *The Reinterpretation of Luther*, 1948 (on Swedish interpreters); V. H. H. Green, *Luther and the Reformation*, 1964; G. Rupp, *The Righteousness of God: Luther Studies*, 1953; E. G. Schwiebert, *Luther and his Times*, 1950; E. Seeberg, *Die Lehre Luthers*, 2 vols. 1917–20.

J. T. MCNEILL

Lutheranism

Contrary to Luther's wishes, his followers came to be called and to call themselves 'Lutherans'. The term 'Lutheranism' is used to refer to the doctrines adopted and authoritative in Lutheran Churches, and as a general term for these Churches in their entire extent. The early expansion of Lutheranism through Sweden, Denmark and Norway left in these lands national Churches that have endured in strength. Swedish Lutherans have been particularly active theologically during the present century. German and Scandinavian Lutheranism has accompanied the spread of the peoples of these countries throughout the New World, while modern missions have planted many Lutheran congregations also among the peoples of Asia and Africa. In general the Lutheran Churches have entered on an era of unification. The Lutheran World Federation, founded in 1947, cultivates world unity and mutual aid among its fifty or more member Churches. The original 'Luther Country' lies within East Germany, and there the people are traditionally strongly Lutheran. In Sweden theology has been advanced by the 'Lundensian School' led off by Nathan Söderblom and presently represented by Anders Nygren and Ragnar Bring. The Swedish writers have furnished an extensive re-interpretation of Luther with emphasis on the social implications of his teaching. Front rank German Lutheran theologians include Rudolf Bultmann, Werner Elert and Paul Althaus. Denmark in the last century had the contrasted thinkers N. F. S. Gruntvig and Søren Kierkegaard, and recently Regin Prenter in Denmark and Eivind Berggrav in Norway have extended the study of important aspects of Luther's thought. *See also* **Augsburg Confession; Concord, Formula of.**

W. Elert, *The Structure of Lutheranism*, ET, 1962; J. Pelikan, *From Luther to Kierkegaard, A Study in the History of Theology*, 2nd ed., 1963.

J. T. MCNEILL

Lux Mundi

This volume of essays edited by Charles Gore (q.v.) in 1889 marked the acceptance by a section of Anglo-Catholicism (q.v.) of the higher biblical criticism and of idealistic philosophy. It was the production of a group of Oxford friends, accustomed to leisurely theological discussions at country reading parties. It was a serious and very influential attempt to present the Catholic faith, as received in the Church of England by the disciples of the earlier Tractarians (q.v.), in meaningful relation to the intellectual and moral problems of the end of the nineteenth century. Notable among the contributions were Scott Holland's essay on 'Faith', and Gore's on 'The Holy Spirit and Inspiration'. All the essayists were agreed that Jesus Christ was the light of the world, but were prepared to admit that the church was often responsible for mistakes and prejudices, and that a first condition of right interpretation of the truth was an appreciation of the times they lived in. Theology should take a new development, but no development would be true if it did not preserve the type of the Christian creed and the Christian church. The standpoint of the essayists was neither that of pure liberalism nor of the 'development' exemplified by Rome. The book made a distinctive and important contribution to the theological debate of the time.

L. E. Elliott-Binns, *English Thought, 1860–1900*, 1956.

R. CANT

Macedonianism. *see* Pneumatomachi.

Maimonides, Moses

Moses Maimonides (1135–1204), a Jewish philosopher and learned Talmudic scholar, born at Cordova, who wrote in Hebrew and Arabic. In view of the prominence given by the Arabian philosophers to the new Aristotelianism (*see* **Averroism**) he devoted much effort to the task of showing how human reason (represented by Aristotle) supplemented the truths of the Jewish revealed theology and did not contradict it. Maimonides was in fact doing for Jewish theology what St Thomas Aquinas was later to do for Christian theology. *See* **Thomism**.

EDITOR

Man, Doctrine of

1. *Introduction.* When the Psalmist asks, 'What is man?' (Ps. 8.4), he asks a question that is universal. Implicitly or explicitly every man has an anthropology by which he lives. The Christian doctrine of man has shared many of these common human concerns but it is distinguished by its conviction that the true understanding of man is to be found only in terms of man's relationship to God as revealed in Christ.

The Christian doctrine of man begins with the doctrine of creation. Man is created by God from the dust (Gen. 2.7). This means that man is seen as an animal among the animals. He is an appropriate object of study for various natural sciences. He is created to be a part of God's total cosmos. There have been times, particularly under the influence of Neoplatonism, when Christian thought has de-emphasized the body and even

deplored it as the source of sin. But Christian thought always has returned to the recognition that the body, as God's creation, is good (Gen. 1.31).

Because man is created to be a creature within God's world, the Bible blesses marriage and the rearing of children (Gen. 1.28; 2.24; Matt. 19.3–9). The NT frequently uses marriage as a suitable analogy for the relationship between Christ and his church (e.g. Mark 2.18–20; Eph. 5.23–33; Rev. 19.7–9; 21.2, 9). The bodily needs of man are recognized as legitimate when Jesus feeds the hungry multitudes (Mark 8.1–9) and calls men to feed the hungry and clothe the naked (Matt. 25.35 f.). Finally, the Christian hope for life after death is described in terms of the resurrection of the body, a concept that is not compatible with the view that the body is evil.

2. *Imago Dei.* Man is a part of God's total creation but he is also unique. In the earliest creation story this is symbolized by God's breathing into man's nostrils the breath of life (Gen. 2.7). In the later creation story we are told that God created man 'in his own image' (Gen. 1.27). The concept of the *Imago Dei* (image of God) has played a prominent role in the Christian doctrine of man. It is agreed that the image of God distinguishes man from the rest of creation. Man has been given 'dominion' over creation (Gen. 1.28). But the Bible does not define clearly the nature of God's image or where it is found and through Christian history there have been different interpretations of it.

A few theologians have located the *imago*, at least partly, in the fact that man stands erect. The vast majority of theologians, however, have agreed that the *imago* is not to be found in any aspect of man's physical form. A major problem, however, arises when we ask whether or not man lost the image of God in the fall. If fallen man retains the *imago*, even if only in a distorted form, then it is possible to identify it with some features that can be found in all men. If, on the other hand, the *imago* was totally lost in the fall, it can be found now only in redeemed man or perhaps only in Jesus Christ.

Theologians who see the image of God within man after the fall have located it primarily in man's reason but they have also found aspects of it in man's moral nature, his thirst for God and in his creative abilities. Rational man, they argue, is the image of God because he can think God's thoughts after him. Traditionally 'reason' has meant more than the word usually means today. Thus Augustine saw the image of God, not in man's abstract reasoning faculties, but in his power to use his reason to obtain knowledge of God. Traditionally an important part of man's reason was located in his ability to distinguish good from evil. Theologians often have found evidence of the *imago* in man's uneasy conscience which reveals that, even as a sinner, man has some awareness of the good.

Basic to the argument of those who find the

imago in fallen man is the claim that if man had lost the image of God he could no longer be a sinner. The mere animal cannot sin. Sin implies the intelligence and freedom involved in responsibility. Thus Aquinas argued that if man were not rational, he could not sin. While these theologians in no sense deny the radical sinfulness of man, they insist that God's image remains within the sinner.

Mediaeval theology developed the distinction between the natural powers of man and the *donum Superadditum* (supernatural endowment, *see also* **Donum Superadditum**). Aquinas taught that Adam was originally created with a supernatural endowment which enabled his reason to be subject to God, the lower powers subject to his reason and hence his body was subject to his soul. In the fall man did not lose the image of God that is found in his reason but he lost this supernatural endowment.

Against this mediaeval position, Luther declared that man lost the image of God when he fell. He argued that the image of God is not a set of static qualities but the complete orientation of life towards God. God's image appears only in the man whose life reflects the will and love of God. The *Formula of Concord* made this the Lutheran Confessional position.

Calvin leaned towards the Lutheran view but conceded that the divine image was not utterly annihilated in the fall. However, he affirmed, it was 'so corrupted that whatever remains is but horrible deformity'. The later Reformed tradition drew a distinction between a 'broader' and a 'narrower' sense of the image of God. In the narrow sense the image of God was man's original righteousness wherein he lived in conformity to the will of God. In this sense the *imago* was lost in the fall. But in the broader sense the *imago* refers to those aspects of man which make him human and distinguish him from the beasts. In this sense the *imago* is not lost, although it is deformed.

Karl Barth, in his *Church Dogmatics*, reinterprets the *imago*. Like Luther, Barth denies that the image of God can be found in any static quality or faculty of man. Barth denies that there is any analogy between the being of creation and the being of the Creator. Barth does find, however, an analogy of relationship between God and man. He takes very seriously Gen. 1.26, 'Let *us* make man in *our* image' and Gen. 1.27, 'male and female he created them'. As the trinitarian God is not alone within himself, so God created man male and female that man might not be alone. As male and female, mankind is capable of covenant relationship.

Because, for Barth, the *imago* is to be found in relationships and not in something that man possesses, it remains a hope and a promise that God makes to man. God promises to bind man to himself in a covenant. In Christ the *imago* is made manifest as Christ calls his bride, the Church, into covenant fellowship with himself. Thus, to see the true image of God we must look not at men but at Jesus Christ and his congregation.

Emil Brunner also sees the image closely related to relationships. God willed a creature who could love and be loved. Because this kind of relationship requires freedom, Brunner believes that it is necessary to see the *imago* in both a formal and a material aspect. The formal aspect, which man cannot lose without ceasing to be man, lies in the structural aspects of human nature such as man's freedom and his being as 'subject' or 'person'. This distinguishes man from the lower creation and constitutes him as human. On the other hand, the material image of God is found in that answer of man to God that is in conformity with God's will, the answer of reverent, grateful love. In the material sense, the image of God has been lost, and is only restored through God's work in Christ. True humanity thus does not arise from the development of man's natural capacities but through man's accepting the grace of God. Brunner claims that the concept of the formal image is taught in the OT and the material image in the NT.

Brunner's formal-material distinction bears considerable similarity to the Reformed tradition's concept of the broader and narrower concepts of the *imago*. The main difference would appear to be Brunner's insistence that the basis of the *imago* is always relationship. Even the formal image cannot be identified with something that man possesses, it consists of his standing responsible before God even when he stands as a sinner.

It is obvious that in the discussion of the *imago* two analogies of the concept have been held. On the one hand, the *imago* may be thought of as an image, such as Caesar's, which is stamped on a coin. With this analogy in mind, we seek the image in some faculties of man and we argue that if the image had been obliterated, man would no longer be man and thus he could not even be a sinner. On the other hand, the *imago* may be thought of as the image that is reflected in a mirror. Although the mirror remains a mirror, it no longer reflects our image if we do not stand in front of it. According to this analogy, the *imago* is a matter of relationship and hence it is completely lost when man no longer reflects God in his life.

In the theological debate those who have argued that the *imago* remains in fallen man have not usually denied the radically sinful state of fallen man, although in some cases man's possession of the image after the fall has been used to deny the seriousness of man's sinful state. On the other hand, those who have argued that the *imago* is lost have not denied that man remains man after he falls. In many cases the debate as to whether the *imago* is lost or only marred is a debate over how the term 'imago' is to be defined. It is noteworthy, however, that the Bible gives little basis for identifying the *imago* with any faculties that man possesses. Those who locate the *imago* in terms of the relationship with God seem to stand on the more solid scriptural ground. As such, we can say that being created in the image of God means that man was created for the purpose of a covenant relationship with God. When man falls out of this relationship, we can speak of his still bearing the *imago* only in a forced sense, if at all.

3. *Original Sin and the Fall.* Man, created in the image of God for fellowship with God, has fallen from his destiny. He has become a sinner. This is a basic theme of Christian anthropology.

In the early history of the Church, the story of Adam and Eve was taken as a historical account of the first man and woman. Because they disobeyed God's command, they were driven from the garden. In their disobedience all men fell into 'original sin'. One line of thought, represented by Augustine, saw this original sin as being biologically transmitted to later generations through the sexual procreation of the human race. This inherited sin meant that man is born both guilty and with a corrupted nature that is prone to sin. Another line of thought, represented by the Westminster Confession of Faith, has seen Adam as the federal representative of the human race who acted on behalf of the future generations of man. Thus a man's sinful state consists in his sharing of the guilt for Adam's sin, the corruption of his own nature and the actual transgressions which he commits as a result of his corruption.

Nineteenth-century biblical criticism discredited the historical nature of the Adam and Eve story. At the same time the wide acceptance of the evolutionary hypothesis led to the view that man had progressed from his primeval state instead of falling from a higher one. Nineteenth-century theology tended to see man, not as a sinner, but as an essentially good creature who was destined to become better. The doctrines of the fall and original sin have been revived in the twentieth century. Few theologians today accept the view that guilt can be inherited (*see* **Guilt**). But theologians are widely agreed that the state in which we find man is out of harmony with God's will and purpose for him. The universality of sin remains a fact even if we no longer think in terms of Adam's fall. Today theologians point out that 'Adam' is the Hebrew word for a human being or mankind collectively. There seems to be a legitimate reason to interpret the Genesis account as a teaching about man as such and not as the history of the first man.

Contemporary theology has rediscovered deep relevance in the traditional Christian analysis of sin. In the Genesis story of the fall, Adam and Eve are persuaded to defy the command of the Lord by a twofold argument. First, the word of God is questioned when, contrary to what God has said, the serpent says that if they eat the forbidden fruit, they 'will not die' (Gen. 3.4). Secondly, the serpent argues that if they do eat it, 'your eyes will be opened, and you will be like God, knowing good and evil' (Gen. 3.5). Theology sees here the basis of sin as unbelief and pride. Man's sin begins when he doubts God's word (unbelief) and culminates in his attempt to make himself like God (pride). Instead of accepting his status as a child of God, man tries to take God's place, for to know

good and evil as God knows them is to know them as the one who creates the difference between them. Instead of obeying God's will, man attempts to be his own master. Fallen man is 'man in revolt'.

The Christian understanding of sin makes it necessary to distinguish between sin as a state and sins as individual actions. Sin is the prideful state in which man revolts against God and makes himself the measure of all things. From this state of sin the various sins flow in the form of unethical and immoral actions. Man is not a sinner because he commits the various sins but he commits the sins because first of all he is a sinner. The term 'original sin' comes to mean not the historically first act of sin but the logically first sin. Sin's beginning is not when man commits his first unethical act but when he separates himself from God by his unbelief and pride.

The irony of man's revolt against God is that he begins by declaring his freedom from his Creator but he ends by falling into servitude to a variety of idols of his own creation. As Luther said, man must worship and if he does not worship God he will worship the devil. Modern theology has found vivid examples of such idolatry in twentieth-century totalitarianism, nationalism, racism and other ideologies of man's creation to which he becomes a slave (*see also* **Idolatry**).

The Protestant Reformers repudiated the mediaeval idea that in his fall man lost his supernatural endowment but retained his natural faculties relatively undistorted. The Reformation declared that man is 'totally depraved' (*see* **Depravity**). This grim sounding phrase was never intended to mean that natural man is incapable of doing good. Those who defended total depravity, such as Luther, Calvin and Wesley, were always careful to point out that natural man is capable of many ethically good actions. He can be a respectable citizen and a good neighbour. What they did affirm was that there is no aspect of man, such as his reason, which has remained unaffected by his sin. Furthermore, as Luther made clear, the law is truly fulfilled only in love. A man may keep the law and perform good acts for a variety of selfish reasons. In such a case despite the correctness of the actions, the motivation of the man is depraved (*see also* **Justification; Law; Good Works**).

In his prideful revolt from God, man is in bondage to sin. Because he is 'curved in on himself', man cannot deliver himself from this sinful state. Any act that man performs to free himself from his self-centredness is an act of the self and thus re-enforces his self-concern at a new level. As Barth, Reinhold Niebuhr and others have made clear, religion and morality themselves can become the occasion of a new pride in which man thanks God that he is not as others. Although Catholic and Protestant theologies have differed as to what place 'good works' have in man's salvation, they both agree that man cannot save himself by his own efforts.

4. *The Second Adam.* Christian faith views the

reality of sin with realism, but not with despair. As Barth says, we cannot say that man is fallen completely away from God. This is not because man retains some redeeming elements of goodness but because God refuses to abandon his prodigal sons. The Bible is the story of God's continual search for sinful man. He calls Abraham to be the founder of a nation through whom all men may be blessed (Gen. 22.18). Finally, God sent his Son in whom man is reconciled to God and delivered from sin.

Christ is the second Adam (Rom. 5.12–21). In Christ the Christian finds not only the revelation of God but also the revelation of the true nature of man. Christ, the second Adam, is man as man was created to be. He lives his life before God saying, 'Not my will, but thine, be done' (Luke 22.42). Where man fell by trying to become equal with God, Christ '. . . though he was in the form of God, did not count equality with God a thing to be grasped, but emptied himself, taking the form of a servant . . . he humbled himself and became obedient unto death . . .' (Phil. 2.6–8).

Christians seldom have been content to see Christ as only an example. In fact, as an example he drives men to deeper despair because those who would try to imitate Christ on their own power must fail. In fact, the Christian doctrine of the fall of man does not rest on the Genesis story of Adam but upon this acceptance of Christ as the revelation of the true man. If Christ is man as man was meant to be, then man as we find him in ourselves and others is a fallen creature.

The Christian believes that Christ is his saviour because he reconciled man to God. In Christ there is atonement for sin and a new life (see **Atonement**). Christ is the Mediator through whom God brings forgiveness to man (see **Mediator; Forgiveness**). Through Christ man is justified, that is, brought again into the Father-son relationship with God for which he was created (see **Justification**). In this relationship man finds the power for a new life (see **Sanctification**). Freed from his rebellion against God, man is freed to love his neighbour. Man finds this relationship with God through the Church which Christ called into being (see **Church**).

In the resurrection of Christ, the Christian finds the promise that he is destined for eternal life with God. Although theologians have debated whether the immortality of the soul or the resurrection of the body is the more adequate symbol, Christians have been almost universal in confessing faith in 'the life everlasting' (see **Soul**).

Upon certain points in the doctrine of man, Christians have never agreed. From an early time there was disagreement as to the nature and degree of man's freedom. Pelagius stands at the head of a long series of theologians who have argued that if man lost his freedom in the fall, he cannot be considered a sinner since sin presupposes the freedom not to sin. Pelagius thus argued that Adam's fall ruined himself only. Outside of the bad example set by Adam, later generations were as free as Adam to choose to do good. Pelagius obviously overemphasized man's freedom when he asserted that in each decision man remains completely free. This overlooks the power of habit in human nature. Many of his followers, therefore, would concede that a man through habitual sinful choice may lose his freedom not to sin. But they continue to insist that originally, at least, each man has the power of free choice.

The opposition to Pelagius, begun by Augustine and continued through Luther and Calvin down to Reinhold Niebuhr and Karl Barth, argues that Pelagianism is a too 'moralistic' view of sin. It sees sin as a series of relatively isolated immoral actions and fails to see that basically sin is a separation from God. As such, sin is in many respects like an illness from which man must be delivered. Until man is freed by grace he cannot choose the good. This raises the dilemmas of predestination. Does God choose to save some and to damn others? Wesley tried to solve this problem by arguing that God gives all men prevenient grace which does not save them but which gives them freedom to choose salvation (see also **Predestination; Grace**).

A similar debate revolves around the question of whether man can know that he is a sinner apart from grace. One side has argued that even man apart from God has knowledge of the law, he knows that he sins. Without a knowledge of the law, man could not be considered to sin since sin implies a knowledge of a law which is disobeyed. Others feel that this is also a 'moralistic' view of sin. The very essence of sin, they argue, is found in the complacent conscience of man. They would argue that, although natural man may know that he commits immoral actions and even that he is out of harmony with his neighbours and himself, this is not to know that he is a sinner. To be a sinner is to be out of the intended relationship to God. Man can only recognize this when, confronted by God in Christ, he learns his true status before God.

K. Barth, *Christ and Adam*, 1956; E. Brunner, *Man in Revolt*, 1939; R. Niebuhr, *The Nature and Destiny of Man*, 2 vols., 1941–3.

WILLIAM HORDERN

Manichaeism

The term is derived from Manes (styled in Latin, Manichaeus, AD 215–275), a Persian, who founded the religion, which spread rapidly to the West. For nine years before his conversion St Augustine himself was a Manichee. Manichaeism was an extreme variety of Persian dualism (*cf.* Zoroastrianism, by which it was regarded as heretical). Because matter itself was held to be evil, an extreme asceticism was practised by its adherents.

F. C. Burkitt, *The Religion of the Manichees*, 1925.
EDITOR

Marcel, Gabriel

Gabriel Marcel (1889–   ), French Roman Catholic philosopher, is sometimes given the title 'existentialist'. He has formulated the illuminating concept of 'mystery' (which he distinguishes sharply from 'problem') as that which can be grasped only through existential participation (which he distinguishes sharply from 'objective observation'). A parallel distinction to that between 'mystery' and 'problem' is that between 'being' and 'having'. It is only through grasping 'mystery' and participating in 'being' that man attains to his true existence, in relation to both God and human community.

JAMES RICHMOND

Marcellus of Ancyra

Marcellus (d. 374), called 'the scandal of Nicea', was a firm anti-Arian and a strong champion of the *Homoousios*. He was expelled from his see in 336 for his trinitarian opinions; but he was accepted as orthodox in the West at Councils held at Rome (340) and Sardica (343) on acceptance of the Old Roman Creed (R) and on the charitable ground that his heretical opinions were mere speculations. If the West recalled his services to the *Homoousios*, the East remained more critical, and until his death the question of his ecclesiastical status divided the Nicene parties of East and West. Significant fragments of his writings are preserved by Eusebius of Caesarea in refutation of his opinions. Initially God was a Monad, including within himself both the Son and the Spirit. At creation he became a Dyad with the extrapolation of the Son and, finally, a Triad at the Insufflation (John 20.22). This can be explained by the fact that this incident, not Pentecost, is the earliest instance of the conferment of the Spirit in the NT. Thus, we have a clear and precisely dated form of economic trinitarianism (*see* **Economic Trinity**). The expansion of the Godhead depends upon the economies of creation and redemption. The unique feature of his theology (following his exegesis of I Cor. 15.28) is the resumption of the Godhead into monadic isolation after the conclusion of the economy. The whole process is comparable to the dilation (*diastole*) and contraction (*systole*) of the human heart. For him, then, trinitarianism becomes a divine episode, a rhythmic heart-beat in the divine life. Marcellus stands to the monist tradition as Arius to the pluralist, a warning that its basic insights needed to be supplemented by other approaches.

H. E. W. TURNER

Marcionism

Marcion (d c.160) rejected the OT on the ground that the Demiurge or Creator-god of the Jewish religion of Law was utterly incompatible with the God of Love revealed in Christ. He found it necessary also to re-edit St Luke's Gospel, which, along with the ten Epistles of St Paul (excluding the Pastorals), constituted his canon of Holy Scripture. In modern theological discourse the term 'Marcionite' is used somewhat loosely to describe interpretations of Christianity which are judged to undervalue or to misunderstand the place of the OT in the elucidation of the Christian revelation, e.g. Bultmann's assertion that 'for the Christian faith the Old Testament is not in the true sense God's Word'. *See* B. W. Anderson, ed., *The Old Testament and Christian Faith*, 1963.

E. C. Blackman, *Marcion and his Influence*, 1948; J. Knox, *Marcion and the New Testament*, 1942.

EDITOR

Martyr, Martyrology

The secular meaning of the Greek word 'martyr' is a witness, one who bears testimony (*cf.* Acts 1.8, 22). When before the conversion of Constantine Christians endured severe persecution, the word in Christian usage came to be used only of those who had witnessed to their faith by having died for it. A candidate for baptism who had thus died before he could be baptized was considered to have been baptized by the baptism of blood, and so validly baptized (*see* **Initiation, Christian**). Martyrologies, or records of martyrs, were very popular in the Middle Ages as edifying reading, when martyrs were held to take precedence over other saints. Tertullian (d. 220) is often cited as the author of the saying that 'the blood of the martyrs is the seed of the Church'; what he actually said was: 'The more you cut us down, the more we grow; the seed is the blood of Christians' (*Apol.* 50).

EDITOR

Mary, The Blessed Virgin

The references to Mary in the NT are few in number, but they are significant as showing her intimate, but subordinate and unobtrusive, cooperation in the redemptive work of her Son. It is noteworthy that in the account of the annunciation (Luke 1.26–38) Mary's free and willing consent, expressed in the sentence 'Behold the handmaid of the Lord; be it unto me according to thy word', is the climax of the narrative. In her virginal conception and motherhood of the divine Word and the few but important recorded events of his childhood (Matt. 1.18–2.23; Luke 1.26–2.52), in her presence at the wedding at Cana (John 2.1–12), in her standing by the cross (John 19.25–27) and in her union in prayer with the apostles between the ascension and pentecost (Acts 1.14), Christian devotion has found much material for meditation and amplification.

The earliest theological interpretation of the role of Mary in the work of salvation appears to be that which sees her as the second Eve, who by her obedience reversed the disobedience of the first Eve; as early as the second century this is found in Justin Martyr (*Tryph.* 100), Irenaeus (*Contra Haer.* 3.22) and Tertullian (*De carne Chr.* 17). It becomes universal and in the Latin-speaking West gives rise to the pious pun which sees the name *Eva* reversed in Gabriel's greeting

Ave; this appears in the ninth-century hymn *Ave Maris stella* in the stanza *Sumens illud Ave/Gabrielis ore/Funda nos in pace/Mutans Evae nomen.* The definition by the Third Ecumenical Council (Ephesus, AD 431) that Mary is *Theotokos* (Mother of God) was directed primarily against the christological errors of the Nestorians, who were believed to hold that Mary gave birth to a mere man, with whom the Divine Word came into a purely moral union; the word *Theotokos* occurs in Cyril of Alexandria and the Cappadocian Fathers and was admitted, though grudgingly, by Nestorius himself. The emphasis implied by the term upon the organic part played by Mary in the incarnation and upon the fact that she was not merely a passive aperture for the entry of the Divine Word into the world gave a great impetus to devotion to Mary herself. Belief in her perpetual virginity, her absolute purity and sinlessness, her physical reception into heaven (*see* **Assumption**) and her freedom from original sin (*see* **Immaculate Conception**), though this last was, even in the West, a matter of long controversy, have marked the development of Mariological doctrine and have become surrounded by a mass of speculation, pious romancing and devotion of very varied value. A full and very impartial account of this is given in the two volumes of Hilda Graef's *Mary: A History of Doctrine and Devotion* (I, 1963, II, 1965). Judgment upon the doctrines themselves, for those outside the Roman communion, will probably largely depend upon the weight that is felt to pertain to beliefs which, while clearly not explicitly held from the beginning, established themselves as virtually universal throughout Christendom. In quite another category is the doctrine of Mary's virginal conception of her Divine Son (commonly, though not quite accurately, known as the Virgin *Birth*); this, explicitly affirmed in two places in the Gospels (Matt. 1.18–25; Luke 1.26–38) of obviously independent origin, and affirmed in the Catholic Creeds, has been part of the Church's belief and preaching from primitive times. It does not imply any slur upon sexual union as such, but is thoroughly coherent with the conditions of the incarnation, which involves not the procreation of a new human person but the taking of a complete human nature by the pre-existent Son of God. Modern proposals to retain the credal formula 'conceived by the Holy Ghost, born of the Virgin Mary', while giving it an entirely new interpretation (as by T. Boslooper in *The Virgin Birth*, 1962, where it is proposed to understand it as meaning merely that God has acted in history and that monogamous marriage is civilization's most important social institution), raise questions about the limits of both orthodoxy and semantic plasticity which cannot be discussed here.

In mediaeval, and still more in Counter-Reformation, Catholicism Marian devotion developed a note of tenderness and intimacy which is extremely moving; it produced many of the loveliest hymns, both Latin and vernacular. It also led to aberrations and loss of balance, which many Roman Catholics are eager to discountenance; these seem largely to be due to a tendency to isolate particular elements of the Christian faith and to lose their true proportion in the organic context of the whole, which has affected christological, no less than Marian, theology and devotion. In the official liturgical texts of Western Catholicism much more restraint and conservatism have been shown. In Eastern Orthodoxy, on the other hand, the Liturgical texts have given to Marian devotion the most exuberant and flamboyant expression (such a service as the Lenten *Acathist*, with its almost incessant acclamations 'Hail, Bride unwedded' is typical), and popular devotion is no less intense than in the West; miraculous icons of the *Theotokos* take the place of miraculous statues. The tendency towards dogmatic definition has, however, been less evident in the East, though the place assigned to Mary in theological speculation has been, if anything, higher (*cf.*, e.g. V. Lossky, 'Panagia', *The Mother of God,* ed. E. L. Mascall, 1949, pp. 24 ff.; *The Mystical Theology of the Eastern Church,* 1957, pp. 193 ff.). Protestantism and Anglicanism have, with a few striking exceptions, ignored the Lord's mother almost completely, though under the impact of the Oxford Movement, Marian devotion has shown a striking recovery within Anglicanism, of which the restoration of the shrine of our Lady at Walsingham as an active centre of pilgrimage in 1921 is the most notable manifestation. The extraordinary seventeenth-century work of baroque devotion *The Female Glory*, which bore the imprimatur of Archbishop Laud of Canterbury, and some well-known verses of Bishop T. Ken (1637–1711) provide other, but very rare, Anglican examples. It is arguable that the adoptionist tendency of much modern Protestant christology has been at least partly due to a loss of the sense of the uniqueness of Mary as the one woman in all human history who has conceived in her womb the Eternal Word and has given human nature to the Son of God.

Until quite recently twentieth-century Roman Catholic Marian theology and devotion seemed to have embarked on an ever accelerating course, and it was remarked that those Roman Catholics who were most conservative in all other respects, both doctrinal and practical, seemed the most ardent advocates of development and innovation in Marian matters. Typical of this tendency (though traceable back to the three rules of appropriateness, comparativeness and similitude of such a late mediaeval nominalist as Gabriel Biel [c. 1420–1495; *cf.* H. A. Oberman, *The Harvest of Mediaeval Theology,* 1963, pp. 304 ff.]) are the four principles laid down by Fr G. M. Roschini: (1) *singularity*: the Blessed Virgin Mary has privileges which can apply to no other creature; (2) *propriety*: all perfections belong to her which have some basis in revelation and are not contrary to faith and reason; (3) *eminence*: all privileges granted to any other saint must have been in some way granted to her; (4) *analogy*: she has been granted privileges analogous to all the privileges that have been granted to the humanity of Christ (cf. G. Miegge, *The Virgin Mary*, 1955, pp. 21 ff.). By the time of the Second Vatican Council, however, a reaction against this extreme deductive movement in Mariology had clearly set in. By a small majority it was decided by the Council not to issue a separate Mariological document, but to attach to the Dogmatic Constitution on the Church a final chapter entitled 'The Blessed Virgin Mary, Mother of God, in the Mystery of Christ and the Church', thus keeping Mariology in a firm organic relation with christology and ecclesiology; it was also stated that there was no intention of setting out the doctrine of Mary in its fulness or of settling points still disputed among theologians. This chapter, while repeating in so many words, though without further comment, the operative clauses of the definitions of the immaculate conception and the assumption, and while approving the titles of Advocate, Auxiliatrix, Adjutrix and Mediatrix as applied to Mary (the much discussed term 'Corredemptrix' is noticeably not included), explicitly asserts that 'this practice is so understood that it represents no derogation from, or addition to, the dignity and efficacy of Christ the one Mediator' (n. 62), and stresses Mary's real, though entirely subordinate and dependent, share in Christ's redemptive work. This is seen simply as a supreme example of the way in which, according to Catholic belief, God's primary causality stimulates, and does not exclude, the activity of his creatures (n.62, para. 2). Though, like other human beings (but in an exalted way peculiar to her unique vocation) she is a co-operator in Christ's mediatorial work, she is herself one of the redeemed; she is herself a member of the Church, though a chief and unique member (n.53). Both exaggerations and understatements about Mary are forbidden, as are sterile, transitory emotion and idle credulity in devotion (n.67).

The declaration by Pope Paul VI on 21 November 1964 (the day of the promulgation of the Constitution on the Church) that Mary is 'Mother of the Church' is thus in line with the Constitution itself and does not represent a new attempt to exaggerate her status. The essential unity of Mary with the Church may be seen as a natural outcome of the early identification of the type of the Second Eve with both Mary and the Church (Mary as the mother of the Second Adam, and the Church as his bride), an identification which some scholars, as well as many devotional writers, have seen typologically signified in the Woman of Rev. 12 (cf. E.C. Hoskyns, 'Genesis I-III and St. John's Gospel', *JTS*, April 1920, pp. 210 ff; A. M. Farrer, 'Mary, Scripture and Tradition', *The Blessed Virgin Mary*, ed., E. L. Mascall, 1963 p. 51). In this connection, it is important to remember that the Christian Church is the fulfilment of the Jewish Church, as the people of God and the true Zion. Mary in her ecclesiological reference is thus seen as the embodiment of the OT type of the Virgin Daughter of Zion. This theme has been worked out not only by Roman

Catholic Mariologists such as Hugo Rahner (*Our Lady and the Church*, 1961), O. Semmelroth (*Mary, Archetype of the Church*, 1964), E. Schillebeeckx (*Mary, Mother of the Redemption*, 1964) and L. Bouyer (*Woman and Man with God*), but also by Eastern Orthodox such as V. Lossky (*op. cit.*; *cf.* various liturgical allusions), Anglicans such as L. S. Thornton ('The Mother of God in Holy Scripture', *The Mother of God*) and Protestants such as M. Thurian (*Marie Mère du Seigneur, Figure de l'Eglise*; ET: *Mary, Mother of our Lord*). The figure of the praying woman (*orante*) in early Christian art has also been taken as having a dual reference to Mary and the Church. Clearly, such a line of thought can become over-elaborate and fanciful, but at its best it holds Mariology firmly in the context of Scripture, the incarnation and the Church. Its furtherance might lead to a rapprochement between Protestant and Catholic thought comparable with that which the reinvestigation of the notion of sacrifice has produced in the case of the Eucharist. A hopeful sign of such a rapprochement is provided by an article by G. A. F. Knight entitled 'The Protestant World and Mariology', *SJT*, March 1966, pp. 55 ff. The symposium by a group of Anglicans entitled *The Blessed Virgin Mary* (ed. E. L. Mascall, 1963) is notable specially for the essays by J. de Satgé, 'Towards an Evangelical Re-appraisal', and A. M. Allchin, 'Our Lady in Seventeenth-century Anglican Devotion and Theology'.

The term 'Mariology' to denote theology about Mary should be carefully distinguished from 'Mariolatry', which means giving to Mary the honour due to God (*latreia*). The common distinction between *dulia*, the honour due to saints in general, and *hyperdulia*, the supreme degree of it due to Mary, is not mentioned by the Second Vatican Council and seems to be falling into disuse.

Since the middle of the nineteenth century, there have been a number of alleged appearances of the Blessed Virgin, mainly to children or young people: La Salette (1846), Lourdes (1858), Fatima (1917) and Beauraing (1932) are the best known; earlier appearances are also recorded. The attitude of the ecclesiastical authorities towards these has been extremely reserved, even in the case of Lourdes, which has become a great centre of pilgrimage, largely for the sick. The problem of assessment is obviously extremely difficult and delicate.

The formal denotation of Mary in Western Catholicism is 'Blessed Mary the Virgin' (*Beata Maria Virgo*) or 'Mother of God' (*Mater Dei, Genetrix Dei*). In Eastern Orthodoxy it is 'Mother of God' (*Theotokos, Bogoroditsa*). However, in the West the term *Deipara* is also found, and in the East every *icon* of the *Theotokos* bears on her halo the contraction MPΘY (for *Meter Theou*); there is no theological implication in the difference of usage. It is difficult to find a liturgical English equivalent for *Theotokos*. 'Godmother' is misleading. 'Godbearer', 'Bearer of God' and 'Birthgiver of God' are hardly English. In addition, 'bearer' is ambiguous, as 'bear' can mean either 'give birth to' or 'carry'; in the latter sense the Nestorians applied the term 'Godbearer' (*theophoros*) to Jesus himself. As it is common in English to describe a woman who gives birth to someone as the latter's mother, the obvious equivalent of *Theotokos* would seem to be 'Mother of God'. It was made quite plain in the fifth century that the term *Theotokos* did not imply that Mary was the source of Christ's Godhead, but that she gave human nature and human birth to the pre-existent Son of God. *See also* **Immaculate Conception of the Blessed Virgin Mary; Virgin Birth.**

Among earlier works, A. T. Wirgman, *The Blessed Virgin and all the Company of Heaven* (1905) is a mine of material. Of more recent works, that of H. Graef mentioned above and D. Attwater, *A Dictionary of Mary* (1956), are specially useful.

E. L. MASCALL

Mass

Mass (Latin: *missa*) is the usual name for the Eucharist in Western Catholicism. Its origin is somewhat obscure, but it is usually thought to be derived from the utterance *Ite, missa est* ('Go, you are dismissed') by the deacon at the end of the Eucharist. It was retained as an alternative title for 'the Supper of the Lord and Holy Communion' by Cranmer in the Prayer Book of 1549.

E. L. MASCALL

Materialism

Materialism is the philosophical doctrine that the only existents are material substances. Mental phenomena, consciousness, sensation, feeling are explained as modifications of material substance – without the introducing of distinctive mental or spiritual substances.

The theory is an ancient one. Democritus (fifth century BC) and Epicurus (fourth-third century BC) were early speculative atomists. The greatest materialist philosophy is certainly that of Thomas Hobbes (1588–1679): important also are d'Holbach (*System of Nature, 1770*), Büchner (*Force and Matter*, 1855), and the Darwinian contribution, notably in *The Descent of Man* (1871). Marxism considers itself a form of materialism ('dialectical materialism'). In the twentieth century materialism can be found – not always, or often, so named – in 'naturalistic' and 'physicalistic' theories. Physicalism, for example, was a development within Logical Positivism (*see* **Positivism**), in which the unity of science was secured by construing statements about experience as shorthand for statements about behaviour.

Materialism can be held in a variety of ways; as an *a priori* speculative theory, as an inference about the world based on the success of the physical sciences, or as a methodological rule – that one should always look for a physical explanation of any phenomenon, and treat no other sort of explanation as ultimate; that man should not be seen as *over-against* nature but as a *part* of nature.

The ethical and religious implications of materialism are not so obvious as often supposed. First and foremost, there is no logical relation between materialism as a philosophical theory and materialism in the sense of the pursuit of wealth, luxury and sensual indulgence. Clearly the materialist proper is committed to no denigrating of the cultural, of moral and aesthetic value. Even if, e.g., aesthetic experience is a function of material processes in our bodies, that is not to depreciate it *qua* experience, nor does it obliterate the difference between valuable and valueless experiences. The materialist may argue that his awareness of human potentiality together with our vulnerability as organisms can inculcate respect and compassionate concern for the individual.

But how far, if at all, can a Christian theology be sympathetic to materialism? There are indeed materialistic elements in Hebraic thought (the role of 'heart', 'reins', 'bowels' in OT psychology); and an account of the after-life may be more clearly meaningful in terms of a resurrection of the body than of disembodied survival. But it is most doubtful whether Christianity is compatible with any full-blooded materialism; the irreconcilable point comes with the doctrine of God, of which no consistently materialistic version seems possible.

For a recent materialistic philosophical theory, *see* J. J. C. Smart, *Philosophy and Scientific Realism*, 1963.

R. W. HEPBURN

Maurice, F. D.

Maurice (1805–1872) was the son of a Unitarian minister and member of a family saddened by religious divisions. He at first refused to subscribe to the Thirty-nine Articles (q.v.), but in 1830 at the age of twenty-five he decided to join the Church of England and was ordained four years later. He was much influenced by the writings of S. T. Coleridge. In 1836 came his best remembered book, *The Kingdom of Christ*, addressed nominally to a Quaker, and expounding a definite and dogmatic theology based upon Scripture and tradition, but making a real attempt to meet questioners on their own ground. He was very ready to admit whatever of value other positive teachings contained, whether Quaker, orthodox Protestant or Unitarian. The signs for him of the kingdom were the sacraments of Baptism and Eucharist, the creed, liturgy, Bible, episcopate. The book contains his famous denunciation of theological parties, including the 'no-party' party. He was to become a controversial figure, but his book was in intention and in recent years has turned out to be in effect eirenical. The progress towards visible unity owes much to the revived interest in his theology. Maurice's strong belief in the incarnation and the visible church led him to take up the cause of social reform, and he was allied with Charles Kingsley in the origins of Christian socialism and in the organization of working men's education. A celebrated controversy which cost him his professorship at King's College, London was set off by his *Theological Essays* in 1853 in which he denied the popular view of everlasting punishment. 'Eternity' in relation both to life and to death was not to be equated with 'everlastingness'. Most of his published writings were originally sermons or lectures. Among the most important are several commentaries, more useful for their theological insight than for critical knowledge, and a restatement of the doctrine of the atonement in *The Doctrine of Sacrifice*. The cross is the revelation of the eternal nature of God and expresses the true principle that man is made in God's image. Maurice himself was a disciple of Coleridge (q.v.) and he transmitted his influence to a later generation of the disciples of the Oxford Movement (q.v.).

A. M. Ramsey, *F. D. Maurice and Modern Theology*, 1949; A. R. Vidler, *F. D. Maurice and Company*, 1966.

                                                        R . CANT

Mediator, Mediation

A mediator is one who stands between two parties and whose function it is to reconcile. In the context of atonement theology the word is used of the work of Christ reconciling man to God. St Thomas Aquinas describes the function as one which conjoins and unites. This office is proper to Christ as a man (*cf.* I Tim. 2.5), but as the man endowed with the fulness of grace owing to his divinity (*Summa Theologica*, 3a, q. 26, a.2). If it is proper to Christ it is also unique to him, for God was in Christ reconciling the world to himself (II Cor. 5.19).

Though Christ is the sole mediator, it is worth considering the antecedents of the word, and also its subsequent extra-biblical developments (largely illegitimate). Mediation in the OT was essentially of two kinds, prophetic and priestly. The prophet's mediatorial work was essentially that of revealer, interpreter and teacher: the priest's, that of intercessor and reconciler. The prophets explained God and his ways, the priests sought reconciliation with God for a wayward people. These roles are not mutually exclusive but are supplementary to one another, and may even be embodied in a single person, e.g. Ezekiel. The NT gathered all this up into the person and work of Christ. He is not only prophet and priest but God-man, the only Mediator, able to act and speak on behalf of God to man, able to reconcile sinning man to God (John 1.18; 14.9; Heb. 1.2; 2.17; 9.14 f.; I Tim. 2.5).

Protestant theology (following Calvin and Reformed theology) has long been accustomed to think of the mediatorial work of Christ under the categories of prophet, priest and king (the *triplex munus*). This is perfectly valid, but the divisions should not be rigidly categorized. It is the one Person fulfilling these offices (as any ordinary father provides a home for his son, but may help him with his Latin homework, or to mend his bicycle). The offices of Christ interpenetrate: he is the King in the Kingdom of Heaven, he is the Prophet who reveals God, he is the Priest who intercedes to God for sinful man. He is these all the time, and at any one time may function in any combination of these offices. Because of his Kingship, appointed of God, he is both Prophet and Priest. His prophetic ministry subsists not only in what he said and what he did but also in who he was. His words were a revelation of divine truth as was his entire ministry, culminating in his death, resurrection and ascension. 'He that hath seen me hath seen the Father' (John 14.9–11). His priestly function is equally sharply defined in the NT (Hebrews). It is important for a full grasp of the meaning of mediator to appreciate that the NT represents man's separation from God as not fully amenable to a prophetic ministry: the alienation is one of sin and guilt, a distance that can be bridged only by Christ's propitiation as the Priest and not simply by his teaching as a Prophet.

The subject of the mediatorial work of Christ became a divisive element between Protestants and Roman Catholics, but the two positions are nevertheless essentially the same. The Council of Trent declared, 'We were saved through the merits of one Mediator, our Lord Jesus Christ' (Sess. 5. Can. 31), a position carefully safeguarded also in Protestant confessions and liturgies at the time, and a view maintained by contemporary Roman Catholic theologians. Difficulty arises because Rome has qualified this position by allowing a kind of secondary order of mediators comprising the priesthood on earth, and angels, saints and the Virgin Mary in heaven. The priest is represented as a mediator on three main grounds: (1) that he is the appointed representative of the Church apart from which there is no salvation; (2) that he has power to offer propitiation for all venial sins in the sacrifice of the mass; (3) that he has the right and power to offer absolution. Protestants would counter these by arguing for (1) a larger doctrine of the Church, (2) Christ's sacrifice not the priest's, and that (3) forgiveness is God's and that a priest is no more an intercessor than a layman is. In other words, there is only one Sacrifice, one Mediator. Protestants dismiss the intercession of saints, angels and the Blessed Virgin Mary as extra-biblical, and they set Christ in the centre as our only Mediator. It could appropriately be added that the modern Ecumenical Movement is fast drawing the sting from these debates and is bringing many Roman Catholics to reassert the sole mediatorship of Christ, based as it is on the NT. *See also* **Atonement** and the bibliography to that article.

                                                JAMES ATKINSON

Mediatrix

The movement in the Roman Church for a dogmatic definition that the Blessed Virgin Mary is Mediatrix of All Graces reached its climax in the later years of Pope Pius XII (1876–1958). Much less has been heard of it recently, though the bare mention of the title, with cautious approval, occurs in the Marian chapter of the Constitution on the Church of the Second Vatican Council (n.62). Much difficulty was experienced by theologians in framing an acceptable agreed definition of the doctrine. *See also* **Mary, the Blessed Virgin.**

E. L. MASCALL

Meditation. *see* Contemplation.

Melanchthon, Philip

Philip (Schwarzerd) Melanchthon (1497–1560) was Luther's chief associate and one of the most learned of theologians. He was a nephew of the humanist John Reuchlin who directed his early studies at Tübingen. At twenty-one, already an accomplished classicist, he joined the Wittenberg faculty, where he attracted many students to the study of Greek. He soon attained a mastery of the debated topics in theology and supported Luther in controversies over justification and papal authority. In 1521 he published the first edition of his *Loci communes rerum theologicarum*, an invaluable summary of Reformation doctrines. While on most points he was in full accord with Luther, he tried, directly and through friends, to induce him to moderate his controversial vehemence. At the Marburg Colloquy (1529), however, he was more firmly opposed to Zwingli than was Luther himself. He was the primary author of the Augsburg Confession (q.v.) and to meet criticism he wrote the *Apology for the Confession*, a vigorous affirmation of Lutheran positions. Essentially a truth-seeker he did not flinch from altering his opinions as new insights came to him. Thus in the 1535 edition of the *Loci* he admits a co-operation of man's will in salvation, employing Chrysostom's phrase: 'God draws him who is willing.' And his 1540 edition of the Confession (the *Augustana Variata*) shows an approach to Calvinism on the Lord's Supper. His willingness to make concessions to Roman Catholics on the issue of ceremonies led to the 'Adiaphoristic Controversy' in which he was under attack. More interested in truth and peace than in personal vindication, he took little trouble to defend himself. His expectation of the approaching end of the world may have affected his attitude in this. His services to educational reform in Germany, and to patristic and classical scholarship, were important. His influence waned during his lifetime, and it is only in our century that his work has begun to be adequately esteemed.

His *Opera* fill vols. I-XXVIII of the *Corpus Reformatorum*, ed. Bretschneider and Bindseil, 1884–1850; C. L. Manschreck, *Melanchthon, the Quiet Reformer*, 1958; R. Stupperich, *Melanchthon*, ET, 1965.

J. T. MCNEILL

Mercersburg Theology

Mercersburg Theology arose in the 1840s at the theological seminary of the German Reformed Church in Mercersburg, Pennsylvania. Positively, it was a restatement of classical German Reformed theology, ecclesiology and liturgy, informed by the currents of romanticism and idealism; negatively, it was a reaction against the revivalism then so strong in American Protestantism. Its conspicuous leaders were two: Philip Schaff (1819–1893), Swiss-born, German-educated professor at Mercersburg for two decades, author of *The Principle of Protestantism* (1845); and John Williamson Nevin (1803–1886), graduate of Union College and Princeton Seminary, professor at the seminary, 1840–1853, and author of *The Anxious Bench* (1843), a spirited attack on the system of the revival in favour of the system of the catechism. In articles in the *Mercersburg Review* and in his greatest work, *The Mystical Presence* (1846), Nevin emphasized the objective and organic aspects of the Christian tradition, and stressed the 'spiritual real presence' of Christ in the Lord's Supper. The Mercersburg theology did not make much impression on the church of its time, except in liturgy, but it foreshadowed aspects of twentieth-century neo-orthodoxy and ecumenicity.

James H. Nichols, ed., *The Mercersburg Theology*, 1966; *Romanticism in American Theology: Nevin and Schaff at Mercersburg*, 1961.

ROBERT T. HANDY

Mercy

Applied to God, this word refers essentially to his work, not only in creation, revelation and the providential care of man, but more particularly in the redemption of man through our Lord Jesus Christ. It invariably connotes the idea of the free, gracious love of God, unmerited and undeserved, shown in Christ for us men and for our salvation. For biblical data *see* N. H. Snaith, 'Mercy', *TWBB*; *see also* **Atonement** (*2*); **Forgiveness; Redemption.**

JAMES ATKINSON

Merit

According to Catholic teaching, nothing that man does or can do by his own merely natural powers is meritorious in the sight of God. There is no merit without grace. Yet with the help of grace, if he will but co-operate with it, man can merit not only more grace but eternal life and blessedness. And this he must do if he is to be saved, for there is no salvation without merit. Both the possibility and necessity of merit are held to be established by NT teaching about rewards and punishments to come and the judgment of men according to their works. A distinction must be drawn, however, between two levels of merit. No man merits (for example) the 'actual grace' which first enables him to prepare himself for justification, nor is his co-operation with it meritorious in the strict sense of the term. But when a man does what he can, it is 'congruous' or fitting that his efforts should be rewarded. Hence we may speak of a 'merit of congruity' (*meritum de congruo*). In this qualified sense a man may be said to merit the sanctifying grace which is essential to his justification, although this grace is strictly speaking merited by no man, but has been merited for all men by Christ alone. Once he is justified, however, and thus in a state of grace, it becomes possible for a man to perform truly meritorious acts, whereby he quite strictly deserves and becomes entitled to the eternal reward. Here we must speak of the 'merit of worthiness' (*meritum de condigno*). What is more, it is possible for a man to go beyond what is strictly required of him, and to perform 'works of supererogation' whereby he acquires more merit than he needs for his own salvation. This the saints have done; and their superfluity of merit, joined with the superabundant merits of Christ, goes to form a Treasury of Merit, on which the Church can draw for the benefit of those who are deficient in merit (*see* **Indulgences**).

In Protestant teaching, by contrast, the concept of merit has no place – unless with regard to the merits of Christ. The Reformers denounced it on the ground that: (1) Man as a creature owing all that he is and has to God, can never establish a claim upon God or put God in his debt. Least of all can he perform 'works of supererogation', for there simply are no such works (Luke 17.10). (2) The promises of reward in Scripture are given out of pure grace, and the goodness or righteousness of those who receive them is the effect of grace alone. (3) The rewards promised are to be understood as consequences of, not motives for, well-doing. To take them as motives is to foster a mercenary, self-seeking spirit that corrupts both religion and morality. (4) A good man does good works, loves and serves God and his neighbour, not in order to secure any reward, but simply because he is good and wants to do nothing else. Just as to be honest means to act honestly regardless of whether honesty is the best policy or not, so to be good and godly means to love and serve God and one's neighbour regardless of heaven and hell.

P. S. WATSON

Messiah. *see* Christology (3).

Metaphysics

Metaphysics is the most ambitious part of the philosophical enterprise, and (for that reason) the part which is most easily brought into suspicion of over-pretentiousness and neglect of the limits of reason. Metaphysicians have seen their work as the construction of a science of 'being', as the penetration beyond 'appearance' to 'reality'. They have aimed at the systematic presentation of a vision of the world as a whole – one which often, though not always, has involved the overthrowing of everyday habits of thought and imagination – for example, Berkeley's polemic against the existence of 'material substance', and Schopenhauer's doctrine of the cosmic 'will'.

Against all inferrings of unobserved entities, all claims to uncover a more 'ultimate' reality than that revealed to experience, the following criticism is often levelled: 'science, and science only, can give information about the world, about *what*

is. The only instrument for extending knowledge is disciplined observation.'

Nevertheless, to be aware of the great *diversity* of types of thinking that have been called 'metaphysical' should be enough to produce caution in face of attempts to discredit metaphysics as such. If we ask, 'what features do all metaphysical theories have in common?', we shall be able to say little more than – 'system', a striving after totality, comprehensiveness, the synoptic view. Thereafter the road forks into what has been called the 'transcendent' type of metaphysics and the 'immanent' type. Transcendent metaphysics believes that it *is* possible to argue to what lies, and must lie, beyond experience: to Platonic 'forms' or an immortal soul-substance, to God as First or Final Cause. Immanent metaphysics denies that such inferences are legitimate; and finds less ambitious work to do, in the mapping of the limits of reason, in giving a philosophical analysis of the basic concepts we do in fact use in articulating, giving structure to, our experience of the world. More strongly (and putting the point in a way reminiscent of Kant, whose doctrine this is), metaphysics may be able to show why certain concepts are indispensable, *if we are to have any experience of a world at all*; that is, it charts the conditions of the possibility of any experience. It plots also the conditions that make possible particular bodies of knowledge, as to Kant, e.g. geometry is made possible because of the *a priori* nature of space. On the other hand, concepts like cause, effect, substance, which are indispensable conditions of any experience, are, on a Kantian view *no more than* that – they cannot legitimately be disengaged from this experience-ordering role and used speculatively out of relation to any possible experience. So, for instance, we cannot speak of 'completing' the regress of causes, and reaching a cause of the universe as a whole: we cannot argue to an immortal soul from the unity of the self which is again a condition of experience.

Immanent (or descriptive) metaphysicians of the mid-twentieth century are not sympathetic to Kant's claim that a single list of categories can be rigorously deduced once-for-all. There is more sympathy for a view like R. G. Collingwood's that the absolute presuppositions of an age may differ from those of another period: finality here may be a will-o'-the-wisp. It is still arguable, however, on Kant's side, that without certain quite basic concepts, we should be unable to make those distinctions (between self and others, subjective and objective, etc.) that make possible our very status as experiencers and reasoners.

Among other accounts of immanent metaphysics under current discussion, the following may be mentioned: metaphysics as 'ways of seeing' the world, the disclosing of arresting and illuminating aspects of the familiar, aspects normally veiled through some recalcitrant feature of our language, or the bias of ordinary interests. The paradoxical nature of many metaphysical statements can be interpreted as a summons to notice the neglected aspect. Again, although a metaphysical claim (e.g. 'every event has a cause') can neither be verified nor falsified, and hence is not an empirical or scientific statement, it can have a regulative, controlling function upon the forming of scientific hypotheses. It may forbid the construction of some theories and encourage the search for explanations of particular, favoured kinds. If our metaphysical statement is 'Nature is a teleologically ordered system', the quest for evidence of design and adaptation will be fostered. Likewise, if the metaphysician says 'Every mental event is correlated with a set of physical events', a distinctive sort of investigation, psychological and physiological, is favoured.

It might be thought that such a programme for metaphysics involves the abandoning of 'ontology', the study of what can properly be said to *be*. Is not the ontological replaced by the conceptual? Not really: for ontological judgments are reflected in judgments about concepts: which concept has priority over which; which concept is to be analysed in terms of what other concepts; which are to be taken as primitive. Furthermore, even avowedly anti-speculative philosophies have *implied* ontologies (e.g., 'ultimately there are only sense-data').

Does the Christian theologian need metaphysics? Is theology essentially a metaphysical enterprise? Many theologians have wanted to answer No. What they mean is that Christianity is not a world-view established, if at all, by speculation; that natural theology is discredited and that its arguments could *at best* lead to a god of the philosophers, not the living God of Christianity. The work of the metaphysician must be done by reason and reasoning: but the work of the theologian relies crucially on faith as well. Metaphysics concerns the *abstract*, rational insights into the timelessly true: Christian theology in contrast deals with the concretely historical and the revealed.

This is, however, a misleading over-simplification. The theologian is obliged not only to expound the content of revelation, but also to justify his claim that the revelation is from and about *God*. He must be able to make sense of the statement that the historically concrete, revealing events (say, of the NT story) reveal a God who also transcends the world and all its particularities, who is eternal, not temporal . . . and so on. But this once more is the problem – the *metaphysical* problem – of transcendence in general, of relating the finite to the infinite, the conditioned to the unconditioned.

If this metaphysical task is altogether rejected by the theologian, the only account of Christianity that is still open to him is an account in terms of a pattern of human living, here and now. The Scriptures will be taken as 'parable' – in a very wide sense of the word, delineating a way of life, but in no sense revealing or referring to the transcendent, or indeed to a hereafter. Theology becomes 'anthropology'.

Considering how drastically attenuated a theo-

logy this would be, it does seem essential to the Christian theologian not to repudiate metaphysics. As this article has indicated, philosophers have been working upon revised and reconstructed forms of metaphysics in very recent years. Yet the theologian must be cautious in judging whether any of these cope with his own central problems, since those reconstructed forms have tended to be predominantly of the descriptive or 'immanent' variety.

For an interesting and clearly presented account of metaphysical problems, an account which employs the distinction between 'transcendent' and 'immanent' metaphysics, *see* W. H. Walsh, *Metaphysics*, 1963.

R. W. HEPBURN

Metempsychosis

The word is derived from Greek *meta*, denoting change, *en*, in or into, and *psyche*, soul: another term for the doctrine of reincarnation (q.v.). *See also* **Hope, The Christian.**

Methodical Atheism

The progress of modern science was achieved by the crucial recognition that God must not be used as a term of explanation in science. Science by its very nature must employ 'methodical atheism', i.e. commit itself to the principle *etsi Deus non daretur* ('as if there were no God'). The scientists of the early years of the Royal Society (founded 1662) – Boyle, Newton, etc. – did not understand this principle and frequently called in God when their scientific explanations proved inadequate. Thus Newton supposed that certain irregularities in the heavens, which he could not bring under his mathematical formula, must be due to the direct intervention of God. But Laplace (1749–1827), the greatest theoretical astronomer since Newton, solved the mathematical problem which had defeated Newton. This doubtless gave rise to his famous but apocryphal remark, 'I have no need of that hypothesis': he would not use God as a short-cut in scientific problems. Laplace was, of course, entirely right. The recent discoveries of some of the so-called 'new theologians' about the 'God of the gaps' show that even today there are theologians who have not yet learnt the meaning of methodical atheism in science. It is a confusion of thought to imagine that, because science *qua* science must employ this method, scientists must therefore be atheists or that methodical atheism in science involves its exponents in atheistic philosophy. *See also* **Science and Religion.**

EDITOR

Methodism

The word 'Methodism' was used as a nickname of a religious society in Oxford, also known as the 'Holy Club', to which John and Charles Wesley belonged. They both subsequently experienced a decisive turning-point in their lives, often called their evangelical conversion. John Wesley wrote of this experience, which he had on 24 May 1738, 'I felt my heart strangely warmed. I felt I did trust in Christ, Christ alone for salvation: and an assurance was given me that he had taken away *my* sins, even *mine*, and saved *me* from the law of sin and death.' Thereafter he won converts by his preaching, and gathered them in societies; he also organized a body of preachers in connection with himself. These were all popularly known as Methodists. In America they organized themselves as a church in 1784: in England they separated themselves from the Church of England only in gradual stages, of which the most decisive was in 1795. They have spread widely and experienced various divisions and reunions. They now consist of a group of autonomous churches, to which are attached various missionary districts, which are themselves rapidly becoming autonomous. Some Methodist churches have been merged in united churches. Methodists now claim to be one of the largest, though also one of the youngest, of the world confessional groups. They are loosely held together by the World Methodist Council. Their theological outlook, largely derived from the Wesleys, is Arminian. There have been movements which have adopted a Calvinist theology, and yet shared some of the general characteristics of Methodism, but this article deals only with the main non-Calvinist stream.

Methodism claims to be a scriptural church, holding the Catholic faith and loyal to the Protestant Reformation. Like many other churches, it claims to hold no distinctive doctrines but simply the true Christian faith without addition or subtraction. Yet it often qualifies this by acknowledging that it has doctrinal emphases. Its doctrinal standards vary slightly from one country to another, but usually include John Wesley's forty-four sermons and his Notes on the NT, and sometimes include also the Twenty-five Articles, his abridgement of the Thirty-nine Articles of the Church of England. Methodist theology is, however, enshrined in a more popular form in the hymns of Charles Wesley.

John Wesley was a many-sided character. A presbyter of the Church of England, he had read widely the Greek and Latin Fathers, the Schoolmen, and other Roman writers, and both Anglican and Puritan divines. He was deeply influenced by personal contact with Moravians, and his 'evangelical conversion' occurred while he was listening to a reading from Luther. He had some links with English Dissent; as his followers became separated from the Church of England, they claimed that they were a third type, neither Anglican nor Dissenting, but later they came to be classified among the English Free Churches and their equivalents in other countries.

Interpretations of John Wesley's theology and of Methodist theology generally have thus varied as different writers have laid the emphasis on one or other of these affinities. Wesley believed in experimental, or, as we should now say, experiential, religion. He thus reacted against the intellectualism of the Enlightenment, though the appeal to empirical evidence was in harmony with that spirit. It is sometimes said that in his emphasis on experience he anticipated the theology to which Schleiermacher gave expression, but to him experience was 'the appropriation of authority, not the source of authority' (C. W. Williams, *John Wesley's Theology Today*, p. 33). In harmony with classic Protestantism, he acknowledged the final authority of Scripture.

Some see Wesley as a great Protestant, a belated English equivalent, as some say, of Luther. Among these some lay emphasis on his pure Lutheranism; others regard him as a pietist, though the Moravianism by which he was influenced was itself not identical with the Pietism of Halle. Those who regard him as a pietist emphasize his stress on experience, his emphasis on such doctrines as that of the new birth, and his gathering of his followers into small groups each of which might be described as *ecclesiola in ecclesia*. There are others again who, underestimating his Arminianism, regard him as having close links with Calvinism, in reaction against the humanistic element of the High Church Arminianism of the Church of England in his day. But others, who lay less stress on the experience of 1738, regard him as reacting against Reformed views and mediating between Protestantism and Catholicism.

Methodists hold the great doctrines of the faith in a form common to most Christians. They believe in such doctrines as the Holy Trinity, the deity of the Lord Jesus Christ, the universality of sin, the atoning work of Christ, and the future life, though in our own day, as in almost all churches, some would express these in more conservative and some in more radical terms. They lay especial stress on the doctrines, dear to Protestants, of the supremacy of Scripture, salvation by grace through faith, and the priesthood of all believers. They further emphasize those doctrines which relate to the work of the Holy Spirit in applying salvation to the heart of the believer, particularly the new birth. They stress the duty of personal evangelism. They are far removed from antinomianism, for they emphasize the importance of holiness, both individual and social.

Those who speak of distinctive emphases in Methodism usually enumerate three.

1. All men can be saved. The offer of salvation is universal (which is to be distinguished from universalism, the view that all men will accept it, which is held by some but by no means all Methodists). This is the Arminian doctrine as opposed to the Calvinist doctrine of predestination or election. The fallen state of man is offset by preliminary or prevenient grace (q.v.), which operates to some extent in all men and leads them towards conversion. Thus no man will be condemned except by his own fault.

2. All men can know that they are saved. This is the doctrine of assurance, an assurance of present salvation, not the Calvinist doctrine of guaranteed perseverance to final salvation. This assurance is given by the witness of the Spirit (Rom. 8.16). Towards the close of his life John Wesley, though still holding that this was the

common privilege of believers, abandoned the view that it was essential to salvation. Those who emphasize the experimental aspect of Methodist theology regard this as the major contribution of Methodism, but this doctrine has not been greatly developed.

3. All men can be saved to the uttermost. This doctrine is variously known as entire sanctification, scriptural holiness, Christian perfection, or perfect love.

All these doctrines have been attacked from outside Methodism. Charges have been brought not only of pietism, but of synergism, Pelagianism, 'Popery', and 'justification by feeling', and Methodism has been described as a perfectionist sect, all in pejorative senses. Such criticisms usually disregard the precision which John Wesley and others introduced into their expositions. The doctrine of perfection especially has always been carefully qualified; and although it is not now so much preached as formerly, it has permanently contributed a distinctive ethos to Methodism, 'the optimism of grace', which sees salvation not primarily in forensic or imputational terms but as a transforming power which has visible ethical results.

Methodist ecclesiology has evolved but slowly, though Methodism has always emphasized fellowship and given a large role to the laity, particularly in many countries as preachers and leaders of classes (i.e. sub-pastors). Methodists, having become independent of the Church of England, have had to evolve a system of ecclesiastical practices to match their claim to cherish a place within the catholic church. In America this process began earlier than it did in Great Britain. In both countries the development has been largely pragmatic, and its theological implications are only now being fully realized and investigated. The polity in America, and in churches derived from America, is episcopal (though with no claim to 'apostolic succession' in the usual sense of the words); in Britain and churches derived from Britain, it is largely presbyterian. In both countries ministers are ordained by prayer with the imposition of hands.

Methodists attach importance to the means of grace. They have simple evangelical preaching-services, and also make some use of liturgical forms derived from the Church of England. They observe the two Gospel sacraments, Baptism and the Lord's Supper. John Wesley retained the baptism of infants, with which he associated a mystical washing away of sin: he thought that children subsequently lapse into sin and thus need the new birth. He thus virtually combined traditional and pietist teaching, though without distinguishing very clearly the various meanings of regeneration. Methodists still practise infant baptism, and are beginning to use the word 'Confirmation' to describe a later stage of entry into the Church. The eucharistic doctrine of the Wesleys, found chiefly in their *Hymns on the Lord's Supper*, is a subject of much controversy, and is said by some to point to a reconciliation between 'Catholic' and 'Evangelical' views. Until recently Methodists have tended towards liberal Protestant views on these subjects, but recently under the influence of the Ecumenical Movement they have paid more attention to the sacramental elements in the teaching of the Wesleys.

Wesley's Standard Sermons, edited and annotated by E. H. Sugden, 2 vols., 1921; W. R. Cannon, *The Theology of John Wesley*, 1946; Rupert Davies and Gordon Rupp, eds., *The History of the Methodist Church in Great Britain*, I. 1965; John Deschner, *John Wesley's Christology*, 1960; Harald Lindström, *Wesley and Sanctification*, 1946; Colin W. Williams, *John Wesley's Theology Today*, 1960.

A. RAYMOND GEORGE

Millenarianism, Millennianism

A doctrine derived from Jewish apocalyptic speculation (esp. by way of Rev. 20.1–7) and held by certain heretical sects and some orthodox theologians in the early Church, according to which there would be a thousand-year (millennium) reign of the saints before the return of Christ. It was revived by Anabaptists and others after the Reformation and has been held tenaciously by Adventists and other evangelical sects until the present day. The rise of modern historical criticism (q.v.) has, however, made this kind of biblicist speculation impossible for theologians who do not reject its methods and results. *See also* **Eschatology.**

EDITOR

Ministry

The ministry of the Church has always been regarded as one with that of Christ, and the ministry within the Church as the organ of his continuing ministry. The fundamental characteristics of this, as they are expressed in the NT, are authority, mission, service, preaching, teaching and oversight (*see* H. J. Carpenter, 'Minister, Ministry', *TWBB*).

Historically these functions came to be performed through the three main orders (q.v.) of bishop, presbyter and deacon, and the relationship of this ministry to the Church did not become a vital theological issue until the Reformation. Two opposed positions have been adopted with regard to this issue which may be called the utilitarian and the organic and may be illustrated by the use of analogy. The utilitarian view considers the ministry much as one may regard a man's clothes, that is, he needs them, and some kinds are more convenient than others, but those that are suitable for one occasion may not be on another and hence he may change them depending upon circumstances, for example, a difference in climate or occupation. If this be applied to the ministry, then it leads to the assertion that while some forms of outward order are necessary there is no one form which ought to persist; variation at different times and places may be and frequently is necessary. Hence for Episcopalians or Presbyterians to declare that there is one form of the ministry for all time is simply not true.

The organic view takes the different analogy of the relationship between a man and his body. From the Hebrew standpoint a man *is* his body, which may develop and grow but presents a constant structure, a persisting unity and a living continuity. A radical alteration of form would involve a maiming or mutilation and therefore an injury to the man himself. A man may change his clothes but he cannot change his body without ceasing to be himself. If this be applied to the ministry, then it is that that enables the living organism of the Church to be identified, to preserve its continuity of life and its unity, breaks in which have taken place but are comparable to lesions in a body and not to a change of clothes. Those who hold this view regard order (q.v.) as a question of the Church's very existence or *esse*.

Arguments for and against these two different positions continue; the utilitarian is certainly persuasive but it may be doubted how far it can find a basis in the NT, where matters of external polity and organization are not treated simply as questions of expediency, and further it has to justify itself against the historical fact that it was scarcely thought of before the Reformation. At the same time it has to be recognized that the organic view can be held in different forms. Roman theologians have tended to separate the ministry from the Church in the sense that they regard the former as primary and standing over against the latter; hence possession of so-called valid orders, in the Roman sense of orders within the apostolic succession (q.v.) sacramentally interpreted and conveying an indelible character (q.v.), is regarded as guaranteeing whether or not a particular group of Christians is within the Catholic Church. This is to provide the Church with a ministry, as it were, *ab extra*, and it conflicts with the exact analogy of a body which is not something other than the man himself–a man *is* his body. Orthodox theologians on the other hand regard the ministry as an organ of the body which, while essential to the proper functioning of the body, cannot operate apart from it. This is a variation of the organic view that would be acceptable, for example, to many Anglicans.

Whichever position be adopted, it is clear from the history of the Church that the ministry can become deformed, and this may be noted in particular in reference to clericalization. In the early Christian centuries the emphasis was upon the variety of operations within the one Church, all being necessary for the harmonious conduct of its life. Gradually, however, the ministry began to be set over against the Church, with the idea of function subordinated to that of office and privilege, so that the people of God became dominated instead of guided by the clergy. This may be illustrated from the development of eucharistic worship which, while initially corporate with everyone having a part to play and each as important as the other, became something done by the priesthood alone in the presence of a passive congregation or even apart from any congregation. Thus the idea of the Church as the *laos* or people of God was compromised and the non-ordained became known as the laity and as inferior members of the body. This deformation of the ministry into an exercise of dominant authority is now being challenged strongly as the idea of the ministry of the laity is gradually recovered. *See also* **Laity.**

C. Gore, *Church and Ministry*, 1936; H. Kraemer, *A Theology of the Laity*, 1958; R. C. Moberly, *Ministerial Priesthood*, 1910.

J. G. DAVIES

Miracle

In NT times, when every village had its miracle worker, miracles were not necessarily regarded as proof of divine attestation of the teaching or character of the miracle-worker. Only after the Stoic conception of natural law had permeated Christian thought was it held that miracles possessed evidential value. For St Augustine a miracle was not something contrary to nature but only to what is known of nature (*The City of God*, 8). During the Middle Ages it came to be held by theologians that supernatural truth must be attested by miracle, since it would be irrational to believe what cannot be demonstrated by reason without some miraculous divine attestation. Aquinas considered that the fact that Mohammed did not attest his supposed revelation by means of miraculous signs was proof of the inferiority of Islam to Christian faith (*Contra Gentiles*, i, 6). This belief in the necessity of miracle for the attestation of religious claims continued until long after the Reformation among Catholics and Protestants alike (*cf.* R. Hooker, *Laws of Eccles. Polity*, vii, 14). As late as the eighteenth century Bishop J. Butler upheld the argument that the biblical miracles demonstrated that the Law of Moses and the Gospel of Christ were 'authoritative publications of the religion of nature' (*Analogy*, 2. 1, 7). It would be irrational to accept the 'mere word' of Christ unless his authority were demonstrated by miraculous evidences.

Since miracles had thus for so long been regarded as evidence for Christian belief, it was inevitable that in the age of Enlightenment (q.v.) they should be attacked by the deists (q.v.) and rationalist philosophers. David Hume in his famous essay 'Of Miracles' (*Enquiry concerning Human Understanding*, X) argued that a miracle is a violation of the laws of nature and therefore that which never happens in the common course of nature. A few rationalist philosophers still support his argument. It may be noted, however, that Hume's definition of miracle is much less perspicacious than Augustine's, and also that if one defines a miracle as that which never happens, the discussion is precluded quite apart from a consideration of the evidence. Today it would be more generally agreed that laws of nature are not logically necessary laws, but generalizations which tell us what normally happens, not what *must* happen. In other words, whether an event happened must be decided by an examination of historical evidence, not by *a priori* dogmatism.

During the nineteenth century a heated debate continued between the rationalists (e.g. H. E. G. Paulus, d. 1851, whose preposterous explaining away of the Gospel miracles was untouched by any historical awareness or even by a sense of humour) and the champions of traditional orthodoxy (e.g. J. K. Mozley's Bampton Lectures for 1865). It was only during the process of the development of critical and historical biblical research over the last hundred years or so that the old intransigent rationalism and orthodoxy could be tempered by common sense, though representatives of the older pre-critical attitudes are still with us. One of the principal results of our modern historical-mindedness has been the recognition that the miracle stories of the Gospels, as we now have them, were written to inculcate truths of Christian faith and conduct rather than to give us eye-witness accounts of what happened. In other words, the theological motives underlying the miracle stories must be understood before we can begin the discussion of whether they were founded upon fact, and if so, upon what facts. The process of critical examination which is involved is a delicate enterprise, and no general or blanket formula can be devised (e.g. complete 'demythologizing', q.v.) to cover all the miracle stories, since they collectively involve many different types and motives. Before we can begin profitably to discuss 'what happened', we must first try to understand how the stories were intended to be received by the original hearers. The inquiry must therefore begin with historical, critical and, above all, theological exegesis, before the question of actual historical happening can be approached. It is inevitable that the interpreter's own personal beliefs about the universe and human destiny will be involved in his conclusions.

Then comes the question of philosophical understanding. Bishop Butler's contemporary successor in the see of Durham, Ian T. Ramsey, has done constructive work upon this aspect of the problem to which his great predecessor gave so much thought. Nothing could better illustrate the difference between the outlook of the eighteenth century and our own than a comparison of the thought of the two bishops about miracles. Miracles are no longer seen as divine authentications of super-rational or (in Butler's case) rational beliefs; they are rather the complex of historical circumstances or incidents with which a new insight into truth is inextricably bound up. They are 'disclosure situations' in which truth is personally apprehended in a new way. Of course, the expression of this insight-event will be determined by the thought-forms of the writer's own period, whether the first century or any other. The work of interpretation, as in all historical reconstruction, is never-ending. But it is the insight into or disclosure of the truth, rather than the details of the stories by which it is conveyed, that constitutes the miracle: the revelation of truth, as a personally apprehended or appropriated concern, is

what constitutes the essence of miracle. Revelation as such is miraculous; the opening of the blind eyes and the unstopping of the deaf ears is always a divine work and is in the profoundest sense miraculous.

Roman Catholic orthodoxy claims that miracles still take place within the Roman Catholic Church, as in every previous Christian century, and certain places (notably Lourdes) are associated with miraculous healings. The absence of miracles in Protestant churches is often remarked as an evidence of the lack of the fulness of the Church. *See also* **Resurrection of Christ; Revelation.**

C. S. Lewis, *Miracles*, 1947; Ian T. Ramsey, *Miracles: an Exercise in Logical Mapwork*, 1952; *Religious Language*, 1957, esp. pp. 144–50; Alan Richardson, *Christian Apologetics*, 1947; *History Sacred and Profane*, 1964; *The Miracle Stories of the Gospels*, 1941; F. R. Tennant, *Miracle and its Philosophical Presuppositions*, 1925. For a recent Roman Catholic exposition *see* Louis Monden, *Signs and Wonders*, ET, 1966.

EDITOR

Mission, Theology of

The search for an adequate theology of mission – evangelism – has been one of the main concerns of the churches in recent years. The great missionary expansion of the nineteenth century was based upon the desire of Christians to fulfil the great commission of Jesus (Matt. 28.18–20). This was itself an innovation. The Reformers, with the possible exception of M. Bucer (*Von der waren Seelsorge*, 1538), regarded the great commission as ceasing to have effect when the apostles died. Such a view was never held by the Roman Catholic Church, but it very often expresses mission in terms of pastoral care. Notable exceptions to this can be seen in the work of Francis Xavier and his followers (Matteo Ricci, Roberto Di Nobili) in Asia in the sixteenth and seventeenth centuries.

For the purpose of this article the word *evangelism* is regarded as synonymous with the word *mission*. Literally the word means the preaching of the gospel. A distinction needs to be made between evangelism and 'revivalism', which is the preaching of the gospel to revive the faith of Christians, whereas evangelism has a much wider connotation. A useful distinction between mission and evangelism can be made if evangelism is used (as it sometimes is) to describe the methods and techniques of mission, thus leaving the word mission to be used theologically, but not all would accept such a distinction.

Mission is an activity of God and has its origin in the Holy Trinity. The God of the Bible is a sending God, he sends messengers, prophets and leaders to his people. Finally he sends his Son to bring in the *malkuth* (Kingdom), the active reign of God to man and to the world. Jesus brings in the kingdom by his preaching, exorcism and healing. He comes to bring *shalom* (peace), which implies righteousness, justice, fellowship, wholeness and harmony of life. The whole activity of God in creation and redemption has a missionary aspect. Mission is also an eschatological event which takes place in the interim between Pentecost and the *parousia*. Therefore mission is seen in every person of the Trinity, for only there is *shalom* demonstrated completely. God the Father shows his mission through his sending activity to man and by his perpetual working in creation. (The missionary is the one who allows himself to be 'God's fellow worker', I Cor. 3.9.)

God the Son is the expression of God's sending activity towards man. In him the perfect sonship with the Father is made available to all men. The barriers are broken down and the reconciliation of all things is achieved. The sending mission of Jesus does not begin with the great commision after the resurrection but with the sending out of the apostles and the seventy to proclaim the imminence of the kingdom (Mark 6.7–13; Luke 10.1–20). These passages look back to the Passover of the Israelites. In mission, the disciples were to go out like Israel travelling light, moving quickly and with similar urgency. But the real mission can only begin in the power of the risen Christ. It is through Jesus' gift of the Holy Spirit (John 20.21–23) that the new creation and the new age is really brought into being.

The Holy Spirit is central to the mission of God. The missionary activity of the early Church began with Pentecost. Often the missionary aspect of the Holy Spirit has been neglected and when this has happened the Spirit becomes an individualized concept. The Spirit is seen as justifier and sanctifier but not the sender of men. The Holy Spirit is seen as a builder of the Church and the edifier of the faithful, not as the sender of the faithful in mission; yet that was the chief effect of the pentecostal event. Mission is to be seen as an activity of God, ratified in the sending of his Son and activated through his Spirit. There is therefore a missionary dimension to the whole of Christian theology.

The mission of God is world centred and not Church centred. It is the way in which God is to pour out his Spirit 'on all flesh' (Acts 2.17). The gospel is to be preached to all creatures, and the arena of God's mission is the world (John 3.16). It is therefore argued by some that the proper theological progression in thinking about mission is *God-world-Church* and not the progression *God-Church-world*. The Church is the instrument of God's mission but it is not the theme of the mission. Against this it is argued by others that this makes too little of the role of the Church and that the biblical pattern is that God works through his chosen people to the rest of the world. It is clear that in the pattern of both creation and redemption God is concerned for the whole world. God acts not only through his people; his redemptive activity is wrought through those outside the covenant. Sennacherib and Cyrus are seen as the instruments of God (Isa. 10.5, 44; 44.28; 45.1), though not in the same way.

The theology of mission has been described in various ways:

1. *Mission as Response*. Mission is the Christian response to a loving and sending God. The mission belongs to God, he takes the initiative. In the Bible the sending and redeeming God demands a response from man in mission (Isa. 6.1–8; John 20.21–23). Mission is the response of the Christian community to the gospel.

2. *Mission as Dialogue*. The way of dialogue is the way of openness to others and of personal encounter (*see* **Ecumenical Movement, Ecumenism**). The missionary has been described as a man who crosses frontiers with the gospel. These frontiers are not just geographical; they may be social, racial, cultural or political ones. The missionary who goes out in dialogue needs to be aware that Christ has gone before him and that he breaks down the barriers between men (Eph. 2.11–16). In dialogue the Christian and non-Christian seek on the basis of their shared humanity to find the true meaning of life, which the Christian believes is in Jesus.

3. *Mission as Translation*. God's revelation of himself in Jesus Christ was a process of translation into the terms which men could understand. The whole process of *kenosis* (Phil. 2.5–11) is a process of translation into the terms which men could understand. So the missionary activity of man in response to God's mission may be seen in terms of the translation of the gospel into the language of the people to whom it is preached. This is a very risky undertaking, but one which is necessary in mission. Translation requires not only an understanding of the gospel but also a full understanding of the language and culture of the people to whom the gospel is to be preached. Here the principle of indigenization becomes important. This has been described as 'mission as it relates to culture'. As Christ is the Lord of all history, so the Christian faith must express itself in transforming the values and patterns of the indigenous cultures. There are great dangers of indigenization ending in syncretism on the one hand, or in denying the transforming power of Christianity on the other; but the gospel must be translated if it is to be properly understood. Nor is the process of translation and indigenization related only to preaching; it has to show itself in the way churches grow and develop. The 'Three self principle' – self-government, self-support and self-propagation – first formulated by Henry Venn in the nineteenth century, was a very important concept in the growth of the Church during the ages of missionary expansion. Many think that it has now served its purpose. Autonomy is not sufficient, nor does it express the true partnership and interdependence which is a great basic truth of the universal Church.

4. *Mission as Service*. The mission of God is expressed in the Servant Christ (John 13.1–16; Phil. 2.5–11), and so in a servant Church the Christian gospel becomes fully credible when it expresses itself not just in words but in loving action and service. Much of this service is simple

and unspectacular, but its essential basis is that it must be the disinterested service of direct love. Such is the pattern of Christ; he loves and serves whether people respond or not. Christian service to the world is participation in the mission of God which he fulfils by showing his love to the world by sending his Son.

5. *Mission as Presence.* It is the promise of God to his people that he will be present with them (Ex. 3.1–14; 33.12–19; Matt. 1.23; John 1.14; Rom. 8). Man cannot escape the presence of God (Ps. 139.7–12). In St John's Gospel, as in the great commission, presence and witness are closely linked. The role of mission is to reveal the God who is already present. The word 'presence' is preferred to 'mission' by some because it does not imply confrontation over against others in the world. The Christian will seek to fulfil the mission of God by being 'present' in different situations and not basically by preaching within it. There are dangers in this, for the need for proclamation and the awareness of being over against the 'world' are essential biblical insights. But the concept of mission as presence is also biblical and should have its place in a theology of mission.

6. *Mission as Fulfilment.* The ultimate aim of mission lies in the Godhead, for its aim is nothing less than the unity and reconciliation of all creation in Christ (Eph. 1.9 f.; Rev. 21.1–5) and of Christ in the Father (I Cor. 15.20–28). So mission is concerned with the realization of the potentialities of the whole of creation, which will finally come with the *parousia*. The aim of mission, as Karl Barth has pointed out (*Church Dogmatics* IV: *The Doctrine of Reconciliation,* 3, p. ii), is not personal salvation (which may be seen as a form of selfishness and which makes Christ the means and not the end of mission) but the consummation of all creation in Christ. This must not be interpreted as denying the place of personal salvation in the Christian mission; it is one of the means whereby we share in the eschatological event of the Kingdom. The mission of God therefore moves through the whole of history and back to God.

In a consideration of the theology of mission there is present the tension between Church and mission. This tension appears already in the NT; the post-Pauline Epistles show a picture of a church concerned to defend the faith against heretics and to build up the people, rather than one which is open to all and always going out in mission, which was more typical of the earliest Christianity. This division has continued in the Church, so that some people have seen the role of mission as that of preparing for the Church, so that when a Church is established the role of mission ceases. The need is seen to be to establish the Church as a Christian presence in every place. While this may be a factor in mission, such a view regards mission as an instrument of the Church rather than the Church as an instrument of mission. The mission of God is wider than the Church. The resurrection stories (Mark 16.20; Matt. 28.19 f.; John 20.21–23) reveal that mission is prior to the Church and not subject to it. The role

of the Church is to participate in the mission of God; the defence against heresy and the building up of the faithful are to enable the mission to be manifested. Paul Tillich sees the role of mission as helping to make manifest the latent Church which already exists in every society.

If mission is central to the life of the Church, then Christian congregations need to be missionary congregations and not merely concerned with the pastoral care of the faithful. Since the apostolate is part of the whole life of the Church, it is important that mission and worship should be related to each other. The God we worship is a sending God, and therefore we need to relate worship to the missionary movement of God to man. The inward emphasis of worship as building up the Body of Christ needs to be supplemented by an equally essential outward emphasis in worship. Baptism is not simply incorporation into the life of Christ; it is a commitment to the missionary life which is Christ's. The Eucharist also has a mission-context. As reconciliation is the context of mission, so the Eucharist embodies the pattern of reconciliation. As the Eucharist is an eschatological event (I Cor. 11.21), so it participates in the eschatological event of mission. The Eucharist builds up the people of God for mission. All the elements of Christian worship have a mission-dimension.

The role of the missionary response of the Church is a universal one. There are not missionary areas and non-missionary areas; the whole world is the arena of God's mission, and all God's people are to participate in it. This means that:

1. Mission is also in depth as well as in breadth. There is always more of every person to be converted to God and to his mission.

2. Mission is the main cause of the Ecumenical Movement (*see* **Ecumenical**). The gospel of peace and reconciliation is not easily preached by a divided church. Because the mission is the mission of the one God, the Christian response requires that it is one Church which participates in one mission.

3. Mission is a community activity. It is not an individual activity but one in which all share and help one another. The term 'missionary' has come to be used for those who go overseas in the service of the gospel. This is acceptable so long as it is realized that all are to share in mission and that the 'missionary' is simply emphasizing the partnership of all Christians in mission, regardless of race or culture.

One of the main problems of missionary activity has been that 'missionaries' have not always demonstrated partnership, but dominance and paternalism also. The whole question of 'sending' and 'receiving' churches is a delicate one. The mission of the Church can often be marred and stultified by the wrong attitude from sending churches. A further problem here is that of the membership of churches in world confessional bodies (*see* **Reunion**), which may militate against the growth of a truly indigenous Christianity, unless the world-confessional bodies explicitly understand that their work is to help new member churches to do so.

The whole emphasis on the universality of mission has been made much clearer by the realization that the whole world is now one world as a result of the technological developments of recent years. The world is now one interdependent society. Some regard this as one of the fruits of God's mission, as part of the process of the drawing together of all things in Christ which began with the resurrection. Certainly the influence of Western Christianity on the rest of the world, through exploration, colonization, education and technological advance, has been considerable, and could not have been so without the Christian Church.

One factor which is of importance is the effect of the Christian mission and the Christian presence not only on the world but on the Church and Christian theology itself. It was J. Weiss (*Earliest Christianity*, II, 1937, pp. 442–4) who pointed out that the very success of the mission of the early Church means that the theology of the N T will not be entirely adequate for any future generation. The presupposed conditions of Pauline theology (e.g. a Jewish or a pagan society) no longer exist for most modern men, who are influenced either directly or indirectly by the Christian mission. It is this fact, along with the requirements of a theology of mission, which makes a continuous reconsideration and restatement of the Christian gospel a necessity.

R. Allen, *Missionary Principles*, 1964; J. Blauw, *The Missionary Nature of the Church*, 1952; J. G. Davies, *Worship and Mission*, 1966; F. Hahn, *Mission in the New Testament*, 1965; A. Harnack, *The Expansion of Christianity*, 1904.

R. M. C. JEFFERY

Mithraism

Mithras was a Persian sun-god, whose cult invaded the Greek-speaking world in the centuries before Christ and eventually reached Rome a decade or two after Christianity had arrived there. It was popular with the Roman army, and hence the memorials of Mithraism may still be seen as far north as Hadrian's Wall. Its sacramental system had sufficient in common with the Christian rites and ceremonies for Tertullian to be driven to argue that they were plagiarized versions of the Christian sacraments, while in more recent times some *religionsgeschichtliche* (q.v.) scholars, actuated by motives precisely opposite to those of Tertullian, claimed that Mithraism was one of the oriental mystery-religions (q.v.) from which early Catholicism had borrowed several features of its cultus. According to the cult-legend of Mithraism Mithras had overcome and sacrificed the bull from which all living creatures were descended. The *taurobolium*, or bath of bull's blood, used in the initiation-rites of various mystery-religions (especially Attis and Cybele) can be shown to have any connection with Christian baptism only by

means of the more eccentric ingenuities of scholarship.

L. Patterson, *Mithraism and Christianity*, 1921; W. J. Phythian Adams, *Mithraism*, 1915.

EDITOR

Modalism

Modalism is one of the extreme limits of the doctrine of the Trinity (*see* **Tritheism**), emphasizing the unity of the Trinity at the expense of the plurality. The term is derived from the status of modes or manifestations assigned to the three Persons. The *one* God is substantial. the three differentiations adjectival. Its aim was to assert the unity of Father and Son in redemption; its defect was the failure to provide for the immanent stability of God and therefore ultimately for his divinity.

Modalism was an Asiatic movement (Noetus of Smyrna), from there transferred to Rome where it made a determined attempt to capture the Church (Noetus, Epigonus, Cleomenes, Callistus). It spread to Africa where Praxeas was opposed by Tertullian (q.v.) and to Libya (Sabellius). Basil still regarded Modalism as theologically dangerous in the second half of the fourth century.

It made a strong appeal to the Church's instinctive monotheism and basic religious concerns. It turned into a theological theory early religious forms of expressing the unity of the Father and the Son in the work of redemption (Ignatius 'the passion of my God'). It sought to provide within the limits of a single theory both for the unity of God and the divinity of Christ, two facts which the Church found it difficult to hold together. From the inference that the Father suffered as the Son (Noetus) is derived the nickname Patripassian (q.v.). Early Modalists phrased their doctrine in a twofold manner (Father and Son) in line with much contemporary Church thinking (*see* **Binitarianism**), but on their premises three modes presented no more difficulty than two. Sabellius (q.v.) introduced this, possibly with other refinements, into the doctrine in the third century.

Tertullian's charge that modalism offered 'a turncoat Deity' (*Deum esse verspipiellem*) and Basil's more sophisticated criticism that the modalist God 'metamorphosed himself to meet the changing needs of the world' are both relevant. Modalism offered a Trinity of manifestation, not even a Trinity of economy (*see* **Economic Trinity**), still less a Trinity of being (*see* **Essential Trinity**).

H. E. W. TURNER

Model

This word has recently been introduced into theology from the language of scientific theory and it has been given wide circulation especially by I. T. Ramsey. In the nineteenth century scientists thought of their models as replicas or copypictures of what they were designed to represent (e.g. atoms). Today it is recognized that such things as atoms cannot be pictured at all; yet models (e.g. of a mathematical type) are used which can help us to a far better understanding of atoms and hence to harness atomic energy. This means that models which 'work' must give some disclosure of the 'real' nature of atoms, which yet in their essential being remain a mystery. Ramsey suggests that there are parallel models in theological investigation and that they too give us some disclosure of the real, even though the reality itself remains mysterious. John McIntyre has discussed at length the use of models in christology.

John McIntyre, *The Shape of Christology*, 1966; Ian T. Ramsey, *Models and Mystery*, 1964.

EDITOR

Modern Churchmen

At the beginning of the twentieth century the influence of the German theologian A. von Harnack became increasingly felt in England, especially by the heirs of the Broad Church school. They suspected metaphysical propositions and dogmatic formulations concerning Christ, regarded the essence of Christianity as consisting in the teaching of Jesus about the Kingdom, the fatherhood of God and the brotherhood of man. T. R. Glover's *The Jesus of History* (1917) puts this point of view devoutly and persuasively. Some theologians who were anxious to reconcile Christianity with modern thought sought to establish a modern christology, among them B. H. Streeter, but they failed to command assent. This Liberal Protestantism was vulnerable to the radical criticisms of A. Loisy, under whose influence a more Catholic type of Modernism appeared in England, represented at its best by Sir Will Spens, *Belief and Practice* (1915). Among the later Modern churchmen were W. R. Inge, a famous preacher and writer on the life of devotion, H. Rashdall, a philosophic theologian who wrote significantly on the incarnation and the atonement (an exemplarist theory). The society which eventually became the Modern Churchmen's Union was founded in 1898 and one of its outstanding leaders was H. D. A. Major. In the middle twentieth century the annual meetings of the Union evinced a more churchly interest in theology, and became important platforms for considered liberal presentations of the faith.

R. D. Richardson, *The Gospel of Modernism*, 1933; *The Modern Churchman* (periodical), 1911–

R. CANT

Modernism

This is the name of a movement within the Roman Catholic Church around the turn of this century. Accepting biblical criticism and adopting a highly critical attitude towards Christian origins, the modernists held that Roman Catholic dogmas and liturgical forms were only symbolically true (hence the Roman Catholic suspicion of symbols while strongly supporting analogy, q.v.), but that

they nevertheless had a high moral value and were effective in bringing men into touch with supernatural reality. The leading figures were the Abbé A. Loisy (1857–1940) in France and the priest George Tyrrell (1861–1909), a native of Dublin who taught in England, with the layman Baron F. von Hügel (1852–1925) on the outskirts of the controversy which ensued. Modernism was condemned by Pope Pius X's encyclical *Pascendi* in 1907. In the Church of England certain churchmen called themselves 'modernists' during the first three or four decades of this century. Most of them belonged to the Modern Churchmen's Union (which from its founding in 1898 until 1928 was called the Churchmen's Union) which publishes *The Modern Churchman*. Its aim was to promote liberalism in theology, but in other regards its standpoint was conservative (politically and in its antidisestablishmentarian attitude regarding the Church of England). With the general decline of theological liberalism the term 'modernist' became unfashionable and nowadays left-wing theologians prefer to speak of 'radical theology' (q.v.).

E. W. Barnes, *Should Such a Faith Offend?* 1927; A. R. Vidler, *The Modernist Movement in the Roman Church*, 1934; *The Modern Churchman*, XI (1921/22): addresses at the Girton Conference in September, 1921.

EDITOR

Modes of Being

The phrase 'modes of being' was introduced into theology by Basil in contrast to 'modes of revelation' which he used to describe modalism (q.v.). It is normally used in connection with the characteristic particularities of the three Persons (*see* **Ingeneracy; Generation; Procession**) to express the internal relations within the Trinity. The transition to the meaning 'mode of existence', the characteristic style of being God the Father, the Son and the Spirit was an easy one. It is contrasted with *Ousia* by Amphilochius of Iconium and combined with (and therefore not identical with) *Hypostasis* (q.v.) by Maximus the Confessor. It is a corollary of but not a substitute for *Hypostasis*.

Karl Barth has revived the phrase in his definition of Person as mode of being (*Seinwesen*) but with a different emphasis. Both Basil and Barth reject the modalist interpretation but, while Basil stresses the full, objective and independent status of the hypostases, using the phrase to describe their relations, Barth seems anxious to avoid the use of Person as unduly tritheistic and to substitute 'modes of being' as a weaker equivalent.

H. E. W. TURNER

Monachism, Monasticism

Monachism (from Greek *monachos*, monk) or monasticism (from *monos*, alone) is a central ideal in both the Christian and the Buddhist religions. In Christianity it has retained this position in both its Western and Eastern forms. In both the Buddhist and the Christian religions human perfection takes the form of the monastic ideal, and in both religions also the dominant form of the monastic life has come to be that of the community. Historically speaking, however, the solitary form of the monastic life, eremitism, was in Christianity the original. In later systematization the eremitic ideal, the life of the solitary monk was thought to be dependent upon a preliminary phase in which the ascetic lived in community. Semitic religions, both Judaism and Islam, have remained on the whole antipathetic to the monastic ideal. Where monasticism does occur in the Jewish tradition, for example, at Qumran, it is very likely that this is an instance of Judaism being influenced by Hellenistic practices.

The question of the motives behind the early forms of Christian monasticism is complicated. No doubt there were social and political motives, as has frequently been pointed out. Nevertheless, there can be no doubt that the main motivation was theological. The writings of early Christian ascetics show quite clearly the place they gave to the ideal of man as a pilgrim, a *peregrinus*, on his way back to a lost paradise, gradually through grace recovering the lost perfection and virtue of Adam. Here the motivation of the imitation of Christ was powerful, Christ as the new Adam being the model for the monk (*see* **Imitation of Christ**). In the case of eremitism, the motivation of the imitation of Christ was blended with the motivation of the imitation of God. The solitary monk was, through grace, being approximated to the image of the simplicity and unity of God. His very solitariness and his liberation from the passions gave his life a symbolic character as a pointer to the ineffable unity and simplicity of God.

A further motivation is of course the ideal of perfection (*see* **Perfection**), this being interpreted as detachment from the world to be expressed in surrender of material possessions in poverty, surrender of personal will in obedience, and surrender of sexual life in celibacy.

While monasticism has remained central to the outlook of both Eastern Orthodox and Western Catholic Christians, Protestantism has never been unreservedly sympathetic. This is because of its rooted conviction that behind the theory and practice of monasticism there lies inevitably concealed a denial of the doctrine of justification by faith. Monasticism is believed inevitably to run the risk of ending up as a doctrine of salvation by works, by *ascesis*. Recently, however, there have been signs of a more accommodating attitude towards the monastic ideal. This is strikingly illustrated by the foundation of the monastic community at Taizé by members of the Calvinistic Reformed Church.

The history and practice of monasticism raise a number of permanent issues for the Christian Church. Has the monk a permanent, abiding, symbolic significance for the Christian believer? (*See* **Ascetism**.) Is there a permanent necessity for such a movement of withdrawal to balance the commitment and involvement of the Christian in practical affairs? Is the correct formula the one

suggested by Dr A. R. Vidler in his book *Essays in Liberality* (1957) that the rhythm of the Christian attitude to the world is first, affirmation, because this is a created universe, second, negation, because this creation is tainted by evil and sin, but third, affirmation again, because of the belief that this universe is redeemable, that it has in fact been redeemed in principle by the action of God in Christ? It is difficult to conceive how the necessary eschatological perspectives of Christian belief can be preserved and expressed without something very like a monastic movement.

But when this has been said, there remains a basic problem concerning monasticism, namely, whether it contains a latent Prometheanism. The nature of this particular misgiving has been well expressed by Karl Barth (*Church Dogmatics*, IV: *The Doctrine of Reconciliation*, 2, 1958, p. 17):

> For is there any relationship of man with man whose structure may try to imitate that between God and man institutionally? Is there any authority of man which can represent to other men the authority of God institutionally? Is there a real obedience, not of works only, but of the heart which men can feel bound to render to other men institutionally? In a relationship between sinful men will not this necessarily mean that the majesty of God is obscured, that a burden is laid upon both those who have to command and those who have to obey, which neither can bear? Will not the attempt to actualize institutionally, a representation of the *communio sanctorum*, inevitably result in an illusion which does injury to God and falsely exalts one man and falsely debases another?

Over against this it ought to be said that the institutionalizing of such relationships, which certainly is the basis of the monastic rule of St Benedict, for example, is the measure of the realism which the Christian ought to be prepared to face as a means of giving concrete expression to his homage to Christ. There is already evidence in the NT that St Paul, for instance, sees the relation between the Christian believer and the apostolic minister as the concrete (institutional) means whereby the Christian makes a reality for himself his relationship to the Lord Christ. This concrete institutionalizing and sacramentalizing of the believer's relation with Christ, with all the risks that it inevitably involves, is the price which a religion based upon the historical incarnation, and willing to take the realistic implications of that incarnation seriously, must be prepared to take.

One final reservation about the monastic ideal has to be made. It is unfortunate that the emphasis upon celibacy in the traditional formulations of the monastic ideal has led to the ready acceptance that the married relationship is inevitably inferior, and that the highest reaches of Christian discipleship are only open to those who are celibate. The argument for this position is usually based upon St Paul's assertion that the married person is inevitably inward looking, absorbed in caring for the needs of his partner, whereas the unmarried person is necessarily liberated from such self-concern for the service of God. This is unsatisfactory as a matter of psychology, since celibacy can, by its very nature, enhance a tendency to introspection and self-reference, and a married relationship can have as one of its first results liberation from self-gratification, See **Celibacy.**

P. F. Anson, *The Call of the Cloister*, 2nd ed., 1964; L. Bouyer, *The Meaning of the Monastic Life*, 1955; K. E. Kirk, *The Vision of God*, 1932; T. Merton, *The Silent Life*, 1955.

E. J. TINSLEY

Monarchianism

The term is used to describe two trinitarian heresies of the second and third centuries which took as their starting point the unity of God. The word derives from the Greek word *monarchia*, the sole rule of God or one sole originating principle in God. The formula 'monarchy in triad' is an early expression for unity in Trinity. Outside trinitarian contexts it expressed Christian monotheism against gnostic or Marcionite dualism. Within the doctrine of the Trinity it could refer either to a strong concentration on the unity of God or to the derivation of the whole Godhead from the Father as its origin or as the fount of deity. The former harmonizes with a monist starting point; the latter, as in Origen and the Cappadocians, is compatible with pluralism.

Its application to the two heresies arises from the former sense. (1) Dynamic monarchianism was held by the two Theodoti, Artemon (or Artemas) and possibly Paul of Samosata. But the description is probably inaccurate since, according to the sources, the first three affirmed two entities within the Godhead (the Father and the Son or the Spirit) without any special emphasis either on the Unity of the Godhead or their relation to each other. The inclusion of Paul of Samosata (q.v.) in this group is doubtful. All members of this group held that the divine rested upon the man Jesus as a power (*dynamis*). The description 'Dynamic Binitarian' is therefore preferable. (2) Modalist monarchianism (Noetus, Praxeas, Sabellius) certainly has a monarchian character. It started from the unity of God and reduced the plurality to the status of modes. *See* **Modalism; Patripassianism; Sabellianism.**

J. N. D. Kelly, *Early Christian Doctrines*, 1958, pp. 115–23.

H. E. W. TURNER

Monism

The speculative mind tends to be dissatisfied with a multiplicity of 'fundamental' substances, attributes and modes of explanation. This craving for unity is most completely realized in a philosophical monism – a reduction of substances, or attributes to a single substance or single attribute. An example of a one-*substance* theory is that of Spinoza, who named his single substance 'Deus sive Natura'. As an example of a one-*attribute* theory, materialism holds that substances, however numerous, are of one and only one *kind*. *See also* **Dualism; Pluralism.**

R. W. HEPBURN

Monolatry

Monolatry is the worship of one divine being as contrasted with the belief that there is only one God (monotheism; *see* **God**). Thus in the earlier stages of their existence the Israelites were monolatrist; they worshipped only Yahweh, but did not deny the existence of the gods of the Ammonites, Moabites, etc. *See* **Latria.**

Monophysitism. *see* Christology (4).

Monotheism. *see* God (2).

Monothelitism. *see* Christology (4).

Montanism

Montanism is a fervent apocalypticist movement of a type which has become familiar in more recent ages of the Church. It looked for the immediate fulfilment of the prophecy concerning the pouring out of the Spirit in the last days (Joel 2.28–32; *cf.* Acts 2.16–21) and it regarded the utterances of its own prophets and prophetesses as the first installment of this consummation. Its name is derived from Montanus, who began his revivalist preaching in Phrygia in the latter half of the second century. It was condemned by Pope Zephyrinus before the end of that century, but by this time it had spread to various churches, including the African, where it won a notable convert in Tertullian. Ascetic in character, it upbraided the churches for their laxity and lack of zeal. Such movements have frequently put to shame the 'respectable' churches in many periods of history; they raise the question why it is that odd or exaggerated opinions always seem to engender more enthusiasm and missionary fervour than do the more normative forms of Christian belief.

EDITOR

Moral Theology

Moral philosophy is concerned with reflection upon the problems raised by human morality. Such problems are, for example, how ought men to behave, what is the good life, and moral philosophy seeks to clarify and evaluate the moral judgments of human beings.

In the broadest sense moral theology is the study of human conduct in relation to the tenets of some theological belief. Christian moral theology is, therefore, the study of Christian conduct and is therefore sometimes known as Christian ethics. In the development of the Christian Church, however, moral theology soon came to acquire a distinctive character which separates it from Christian ethics. This distinctive character K. E. Kirk defines as follows: 'Moral theology is concerned not so much with the highest standards of Christian conduct (that is perhaps the special province of Christian ethics) as with the *minimum* standard to which conduct must attain if it is to be adjudged worthy of the name Christian at all' (*Study of Theology*, 1939, p. 363). Moral theology in this sense in some Christian churches (especially the Church of Rome) consists to some large extent of reproducing the precepts of canon law (*see* **Casuistry**).

K. E. Kirk, *Some Principles of Moral Theology*, 1949; R. C. Mortimer, *The Elements of Moral Theology*, 1947; H. Waddams, *A New Introduction to Moral Theology*, 1964.

E. J. TINSLEY

Mortal Sin

In Catholic thought a distinction is made between mortal and venial sins. A mortal sin is one that separates a man from God so that if one dies with a mortal sin unforgiven he receives eternal damnation. The sacramental grace of the Church provides forgiveness for mortal sins. Venial sins are either sins that are in themselves less serious or sins that, although mortal in nature, have been committed in passion or ignorance. Penance by the sinner can remove the guilt of venial sins and even after death such guilt can be removed in purgatory.

This is a point at which Luther and Calvin broke decisively with Catholic thought. They understood sin as basically unbelief and pride, that is, sin is the state in which man lives separated from God. The problem of sin is the problem of the total orientation of one's life, a man either lives 'in sin' or 'in Christ'. Where sin is so seen, the distinction between greater and lesser sins becomes irrelevant. The cure for such sin can never be found in the sinner's penance but only through God's forgiving love welcoming his prodigal home. *See also* **Guilt; Man, Doctrine of.**

WILLIAM HORDERN

Mystery

The meanings to be attached to the word 'mystery' depend upon whether one is considering it in its biblical or in its Hellenistic background. In Hellenistic mystery religions, the mystery is a secret rite or ritual, a kind of password, through the knowledge of which a person is initiated into the immortal life of one of the gods. This is the meaning of the term 'mystery' in the Hellenistic mystery religions. In the biblical literature, however, the word 'mystery' is used in a distinctive way, for two main things. First, for the plan of God, the purpose of God in history, his eternal purpose and sovereignty; and second, for the thing or the situation which is the medium by which the secret plan of God is disclosed. It is with these meanings that the NT speaks of Christ as the mystery of God. By that is meant that he is the perfect, the unique

medium by which the plan of God in history has been disclosed: Christ is the open secret of God, the open mystery of God.

In the Hellenistic tradition the mystic is the person who, having got possession of the secret ritual or the secret password, is thereby initiated into a new experience of oneness with the life of the god. In Christian mysticism there is no question of any secret ritual or password. The mystic is one who by his close attention to the mystery-situation, the particular person of Christ, for instance, realizes through this agency his oneness with the Father.

Odo Casel, *The Mystery and Christian Worship*, 1962; M. B. Foster, *Mystery and Philosophy*, 1957; A. Plé and others, *Mystery and Mysticism* (a symposium), 1956; Hugo Rahner, *Greek Myths and Christian Mystery*, 1963.

E. J. TINSLEY

Mystery Religions

'Mystery religions' is a term which relates to that form of religion which is associated particularly with the Hellenistic world from roughly about the time of the conquests of Alexander the Great onwards (latter part of the fourth century BC). These religions were enormously popular at the time of Christ, and it is easy to trace in the NT the influence of the vocabulary of these religions. One could also point to such early Christian Fathers as Clement of Alexandria and Origen as Christians who were willing to think of their religion as a greater and newer form of mystery religion.

The mystery religions were essentially religions of redemption, offering to those initiated into them release from the tragedies and limitations of human existence. This release was obtained by a process of initiation whereby, after long and arduous purifications, the initiate was taken up into the life of the god of the particular religion and thus attained immortality. *See also* **Gnosticism.**

S. Angus, *The Mystery Religions and Christianity*, 1925; H. A. A. Kennedy, *St Paul and the Mystery Religions*, 1913.

E. J. TINSLEY

Mystical Theology

In theological textbooks Christian spirituality is divided into ascetical and mystical theology. Mystical theology is used as a term to describe the analysis and systematization of mystical experience. The mystical experience is the datum out of which is constructed the framework of mystical theology. 'Mystical theology' as a term was first used by Dionysius the Areopagite (sixth century, AD) in his book, *The Mystical Theology*. As used by Dionysius 'mystical theology' means knowledge of God by way of mystical experience, rather than the theorizing about the experience. St Teresa of Avila used the term 'mystical theology' with the same kind of meaning in chapter ten of her *Life*. Here she speaks of 'such feeling of the presence of God as made it possible for me to doubt that he was within me. I believe,' says Teresa, 'that this is called "mystical theology".'

Anselme Stolz, *Théologie de la Mystique*, 1947.

E. J. TINSLEY

Mysticism

Great care is required in defining the meaning of the term 'mysticism'. A common tendency, especially in German reformed theology, has been to equate mysticism with Neoplatonism (or Neoplatonism as popularized by Dionysius the Areopagite) and then to insist on the incompatibility of mysticism with the Bible and the Christian religion. Another common practice is to use the word 'mysticism' in such a way that it covers not only religious experience in general but all kinds of awareness of transcendental reality. The most satisfactory procedure is to examine accounts of mystical experience, and see if there is a common pattern. When this is done the main characteristics of mysticism seem to be: (1) there is a profound, compelling, unforgettable sense of union and unity; (2) the successive character of time is transcended in an awareness of simultaneity; (3) the experience is not felt to be a mere subjectivity; it is rather a disclosure, what Julian of Norwich called a 'showing', or what William James called a 'neotic' experience; (4) there is always a sense of enhancement of joy, exultation, a suffused sense of well-being, and (5) there is also an overwhelming sense of 'presence', of the utter nearness of the transcendent.

The early Christian use of the term 'mystical' suggests that mystical experience was always associated with something concrete and factual, with what was called 'the mystery'; which could be, for example, either the written words of Scripture or the action of the liturgy. To see in them not only symbols but the reality symbolized is what has been called 'mystery-mindedness'. This is what the early Fathers of the Church meant by 'mysticism': the 'sign', the concrete event or situation, or piece of Scripture, and thing signified were taken as inseparable. This patristic type of mysticism is a genuine mysticism and at the same time is completely compatible with Christian belief in an historical incarnation.

As well as this kind of mysticism, which is biblically based, there is a strong current of Neoplatonism in the early Church which interpreted mystical experience along different lines. This type of mysticism stemmed from a metaphysics which was reluctant to ascribe significance to what was finite, material and bodily, and consequently denied the necessary place of the 'mystery' in mysticism. Mysticism thus came to be used, not for the whole complex of sign and things signified, but for the thing signified only. Hence mysticism now meant a knowledge of reality apart from the symbolic image or sign. Mysticism therefore amounted to an unmediated experience of external verities, a heightened state of awareness and direct experience of God, an ecstatic sense of

fusion with ultimate reality (*see* **Ecstasy**). The basic structure of 'mystery-mysticism' as seen in the early Fathers and in mystics like Julian of Norwich, is very similar to what Paul Tillich describes as the process of revelation. There are two elements in mystical apprehension as described by Tillich: (1) there is first of all the 'sign-event' which is a real historical happening (or a concrete situation, a particular human relationship, an external object); (2) perception of this concrete particular as a sign is the result of 'ecstasy'. This ecstasy is not a mere experience, nor is it a specially vivid anticipatory realization of some truth which could be reached by discursive reason, or scientific analysis. It is a quite special turn of mind, having its own coercive character.

Hostility to mysticism has risen for a number of reasons. The basic misgivings can perhaps be traced back to Luther, who was, initially, very much influenced by Bernard of Clairvaux and the *Theologia Germanica* (*see* **Imitation of Christ**). The main lines of the indictment against mysticism are: (1) that it really conceals a doctrine of works and is a system of self-endeavour by which one can effect one's own salvation and enlightenment; (2) that it interprets sin not as moral evil, but as either ignorance or imperfection, and redemption is therefore taken to depend not on a divine act of atonement but on some process of illumination, or progressive enlightenment; (3) that it is thought to have a very loose hold on the historical incarnation and its derivatives, the Church and the sacraments; (4) that it is believed to be indifferent to ethics and to hold to a kind of asceticism (*see* **Asceticism**), which is a denial of the Christian doctrine of creation; (5) that it is thought to be incompatible with Christian eschatology because the mystic identifies the beatific vision-to-come with his own mystical experience.

It would not be difficult to refute each of these charges from the works of accredited mystics themselves. On the first charge, for example, it could not seriously be held that a denial of the doctrine of grace is necessarily a feature of mysticism in all its forms. An emphasis on grace is the characteristic of such very different mystics as Henry Suso, Julian of Norwich, St John of the Cross, or St Teresa. Secondly, it would not equally be possible to state categorically that mysticism in all its forms is alien to the Christian doctrine of sin, even including the doctrine of original sin, and the insistence on a divine act of atonement in Christ. Again, illustrations of this could be made from Henry Suso and Julian of Norwich. Thirdly, a marked feature of mediaeval mysticism was its attachment to the liturgy, to the doctrine of the Church, and to its sacramental actions. Fourthly, it is, of course, true that mysticism in many of its forms does insist upon an ascetical discipline, the whole aim of which is to increase the practitioner's detachment from a created existence. In some cases this attitude is influenced by a dualistic denial of the relevance of material existence; but this is an aberration rather than a necessary characteristic of mysticism. Even such a harshly ascetical writer as St John of the Cross will insist upon a discipline by which detachment is reached, but this, he insists, enables the mystic to appreciate the delights of created existence all the more. Then fifthly and finally, with regard to eschatology, it is not at all self-evident that the mystic does identify his own experience with the beatific vision-to-come; on the contrary, the majority-tradition insists that the mystical experience is but a transitory token of what is to come. It could, therefore, more feasibly be argued that the mystic takes his eschatology very seriously indeed; the mystical experience is a particularly acute realization in the present of that which is to come.

There seem to be two main types of mysticism. One, introvertive, where the mystic by turning inwards on his own consciousness and experience, and by stressing the necessity for discarding from his mind all visual or concrete images, comes to realize in a peculiarly coercive way his essential oneness with ultimate reality (*see* **Via Negativa**). But secondly, there is the type of mysticism which is closely akin to the experience of the poet and the prophet: this is a mysticism which is closely linked with the objective experience, or circumstance, with what the early Christian Fathers called the 'mystery'. This 'mystery-minded' mysticism is that which is particularly congenial to the Christian tradition.

J. Dalby, *Christian Mysticism and the Natural World*, 1950; F. von Hügel, *The Mystical Element in Religion*, 1927; T. Hywel Hughes, *The Philosophic Basis of Mysticism*, 1937; Roy C. Petry, ed., *Late Medieval Mysticism*, 1957; A. Plé and others, *Mystery and Mysticism* (a symposium), 1956; W. T. Stace, *Mysticism and Philosophy*, 1961.

E. J. TINSLEY

Myth. *see* Demythologizing; Existentialism.

Natural Law

Along with his concept of natural theology, Aquinas developed the concept of natural law. Man, by his own reason, can gain considerable knowledge of the ethically good without any reference to God's revelation. This knowledge forms the natural law or law of human nature. Natural law is distinguished by Catholics from the theological virtues of faith, hope and charity which are known only through revelation and which can be performed only by one who receives grace. Natural law is the area in which Christian and non-Christian can find a basis for agreement and co-operation in ethical action.

The concept of natural law has gained wide, but not universal, support in secular thought in general and in legal thought in particular. Pro-

testants never have put as much emphasis upon natural law as does Catholicism, and many Protestants have denied the concept. A major problem is that on many important issues, such as birth control, there is no agreement upon what the natural law teaches.

Thomas Aquinas, *The Summa Theologica*, 2.1. 1.90 ff.; Ian T. Ramsey, *Christian Ethics and Contemporary Philosophy*, 1966, ch. 20.

WILLIAM HORDERN

Natural Man

This term is widely used in Christian theology to refer to man who, after the fall, lives outside of the relationship with God for which he was created. The term thus implies that man is 'by nature' a sinner. *See* **Man, Doctrine of.**

WILLIAM HORDERN

Natural Theology; Revealed Theology

Natural theology is traditionally that knowledge about God and the divine order which man's reason can acquire without the aid of revelation. St Thomas Aquinas (*see* **Thomism; God** [6.7]) formulated the distinction between natural and revealed theology clearly and authoritatively, as over against the older Augustinian view that there is no 'unaided' knowledge of God. On the Thomist view reason can assure us that God is and can infer by analogy (q.v.) certain truths about him; but only divine revelation could acquaint us with the truths of revealed theology, e.g. the doctrines of the Trinity, the incarnation, the atonement, etc. The word 'natural' in this connection reflects the ancient Platonic and Stoic conception of the natural as the rational; natural theology is rational reflection on the question of divine existence. *See* **Revelation.**

EDITOR

Naturalism

Naturalism is a term, more frequently met with forty years ago than today, meaning those types of philosophy which assert that the world can best be accounted for by means of the categories of natural science (including biology and psychology) without recourse to the supernatural or transcendent as a means of explanation. It is thus wider than positivism (q.v.), which regards physico-chemical explanation as the valid type of philosophical reasoning. Nor is it restricted to empiricism, for Spinoza was essentially a naturalist. In fact, it covers a wide variety of philosophies, including that of Samuel Alexander (1859–1938); *cf.* his *Space, Time and Deity* (1920). The title of C. D. Broad's *The Mind and its Place in Nature* (1925) illustrates the inversion of the Hegelian idealistic standpoint of the earlier generation, which would have spoken rather of 'nature and its place in Mind'. Naturalism in ethics asserts that 'ought' is reducible to 'is' (with this many theologians would have agreed); G. E.

Moore in *Principia Ethica* (1903) attempted to refute this view, which he called 'the naturalistic fallacy'.

R. G. Collingwood, *The Idea of Nature*, 1945; J. B. Pratt, *Naturalism*, 1939; C. A. Strong, *Origin of Consciousness*, 1918; J. Ward, *Naturalism and Agnosticism*, 1898.

EDITOR

Necromancy

Necromancy is divination or prediction based upon a pretended communication with the spirits of the dead, or, more generally, sorcery and magic (Greek *nekros*, dead). See **Spiritualism.**

Neo-Calvinism. *see* Barth, K.; Crisis Theology.

Neoplatonism

Neoplatonism is a generic term covering the revival of Platonist tendencies in philosophy from the third to sixth centuries A D. The two predominant personalities involved were Plotinus (c. 205–270) and Proclus (411–485). Some regard Plotinus as the real founder of the doctrine; others ascribe the honour to his teacher, Ammonius Saccas (c. 175–242). Another pupil of Ammonius was a certain Origen, who may or may not have been the Christian Alexandrian. Plotinus' immediate disciple, biographer and literary executor was Porphyry (c. 232–303), whose contributions were more scholastic than original. He was the teacher of Iamblichus (c. 250–c. 330), a Syrian who developed the specifically religious elements in the Neoplatonist tradition. In the fourth century Marius Victorinus translated some of Porphyry's and Plotinus' works, and re-established their influence in Rome, so becoming an important mediator in the transmission of Plotinian philosophy to Augustine. Proclus was the last master of the Academy in Athens. On the one hand he was much more scholastic than Plotinus, and on the other hand much more devoted to the quasi-magical practices of theurgy and respectful of the 'inspired' authority of the Chaldean oracles. Certain elements of his synthesis, notably his doctrine of evil, were adopted by Pseudo-Dionysius the Areopagite (q.v.). Practice varies as to the extension of the term 'Neoplatonism'; there is already so much breadth in it, if both Plotinus and Proclus are accommodated, as to make it reasonable to speak also of Christian Neoplatonists. In any case, unless one restricts the term to the philosophy of Plotinus alone, it is necessary to be extremely diffident in presenting any doctrine as characteristic of Neoplatonism.

The common ground among Neoplatonists is a respect for the text of Plato. Ammonius and Plotinus are said to have attempted to harmonize his philosophy with that of Aristotle, but Proclus is less sympathetic towards that project. Plotinus was opposed to Gnosticism (q.v.), which he regarded as a confusion introduced in the name of

religion into philosophical contemplation. He was to some extent influenced by the 'agnostic' tendencies of Indian wisdom, which he knew from researches during an expedition to Persia. The rather purist Hellenism of Plotinus was much modified by Iamblichus and Proclus in their attempts to ally Platonism with pagan mystery religions, whether of Greek, Mesopotamian, or Egyptian origin. Manichaeism (q.v.) was generally regarded as an arch-enemy, its dualist principles being in outright contrariety to the supremacy of the One. The priority of the One over the many can fairly be called the keystone of Neoplatonism. Based on a particular exegesis of Plato's dialogue the *Parmenides*, the doctrine determines both the ontology and the epistemology, and therefore also the soteriology of the Neoplatonists. The One or the Good, being perfect, begets in his own image the *Nous*; the *Nous* in turn begets as the fruit of its contemplation of the One, the *Psyche*, or world-soul. The soul is the efficient cause of the rest of the universe: of other lesser souls, of the heavenly bodies, and of matter. The final cause of all is the One, to which all things return by their conversion in knowledge and desire back to the *Psyche* and the *Nous*. Thus the universe is constituted by the twofold ecstasis in which creatures proceed or emanate from the One, and return to it by conversion. Such is the basic framework of the Plotinian system. Other Neoplatonists elaborate various parts of it more or less extravagantly. Proclus fits in a whole pantheon of mediating deities in groups of threes and nines. Some lesser writers of the school tend to associate evil with the emanation of matter, but Proclus explicitly rejects such a solution to the problem of evil. His doctrine that evil is always a particular parasitic defect in a particular good entity was to be adopted by Thomas Aquinas, through the mediation of the pseudo-Denis. Neoplatonism cannot be called pantheistic without qualification. It insists that all beings participate in the being of the One, who is thus universally present even in matter, but it also maintains firmly the multiplicity of beings at various levels of existence, and the union with the Good which is aimed at is a union of knowledge and love rather than ontological annihilation. The doctrine of the emanation of creatures from the One usually preserves the distinction between the divine nature which does not proceed, and the divine 'workings' or 'energies' which do. Correlative with this is a positive programme of contemplation – more intellectual in Plotinus, more magical in Proclus – culminating in a 'negative' ecstasis in which the transcendence of the One is recognized. Plotinus speaks of a super-intellectual faculty for this last experience; Proclus equates it with the 'flower of the mind', which is one of the sources of the mediaeval theory of the *apex mentis*.

The assertion that the idea of a divine incarnation is incompatible with Neoplatonism is somewhat gratuitous. The apparent pantheism involved in Erigena's theology is not a necessary consequence of Neoplatonist views. Augustine and the pseudo-Denis were both strongly influenced by Neoplatonism, and the traces of the system in mediaeval scholasticism were seriously underestimated until recently. Particularly the mediaeval theories of participation and analogical predication are due to Neoplatonic as much as to 'purely' Aristotelian sources. In the humanist renaissance, Gerson, Ficino and Nicholas of Cusa were among many who drew heavily on Neoplatonism.

Neoplatonists have had a bad press during the intensified anti-hellenist campaign in recent Western theology, but the continued study of the philosophers themselves and of their effects on the classical Christian theologians is achieving a rehabilitation, if not a revival, of their account of the many creatures and the One God.

Proclus, *The Elements of Theology*, ed. E. R. Dodds, 2nd ed. 1963; A. H. Armstrong, *Introduction to Ancient Philosophy*, 2nd ed., 1949, chs. XVI–XIX; ed., *The Cambridge History of Later Greek and Early Mediaeval Philosophy*, 1967, Parts III-VI; E. R. Dodds, *Select Passages Illustrating Neoplatonism*, text, 1924, ET, 1923; W. R. Inge, *The Philosophy of Plotinus*, 1918; T. Whittaker, *The Neo-Platonists*, 2nd ed., 1928.

DOM PLACID SPEARRITT

Neo-Orthodoxy

As used especially by Paul Tillich, this term refers to the deplorable imposition of an out-dated synthesis of theology and secular thought in an altered contemporary situation. It is also used of theologians of the schools of Karl Barth and Emil Brunner (qq.v.) in the sense of their reassertion of the principles of the Reformation in a post-liberal form.

JAMES RICHMOND

Neo-Scholasticism, Neo-Thomism

By this title is meant the revival of mediaeval scholastic method in theology and philosophy during the later nineteenth century as a modern restatement of the *philosophia perennis* (q.v.) which began with Hellenic thought and was brought to a high synthetic perfection by St Thomas Aquinas (*see* **Thomism**) in the fifteen years following 1260. It might be called a philosophy of ultimate causes. It rests on the Aristotelian concepts of form and substance, soul and body, of changing accidents in unchanging essences, of movement from potency to act in expression of an immutable nature (leaving little room for evolutionary theory), of substantial change through dying and birth of offspring. To these are added a Christian sense of God's 'otherness' as pure and perfect Actuality, incapable of change, yet the Author of all change and all creation – which leaves him nevertheless unmoved (*impassibilis*), although placing all created things in contingent dependence upon him. This last concept bears the sense of convergence to finality, that creation is in dynamic process towards an end planned by God, perceived intuitively in a dim way by man's intelligence (not by lesser creation, for only man has intelligence to understand and will to choose); and that this end is creation's proper culmination, its rest and fulfilment. There is an innate optimism in the doctrine, which vaults over the 'random selection' theories of evolution: for God, the beginning and end of the creative process, is also the all-knowing guide. In modern dress, this Scholasticism can digest evolutionary evidence and the dynamic interpretations of substance, the findings of psychology and the more sophisticated laws of ethics. It allows a just balance between rationalism and voluntarism, monism of nature and spiritual dualism (Descartes' 'ghost in the machine').

The leading nineteenth century names in this revival were Sanseverino (d. 1865), Kleutgen (d. 1883), Stöckl (d. 1895) and de San (d. 1904). Leo XIII's encyclical *Aeterni Patris* of 4 August 1879 (the first year of his reign) gave the movement the fullest blessing of the Church of Rome. In 1874 the Accademia di San Tommaso was founded in Rome, and in 1891 the Institut de Philosophie at Louvain under Mgr (later Cardinal) Mercier. Thereafter the movement grew fast and the Leonine editions of the *Summa Theologica* of Aquinas began to appear together with numerous Thomistic reviews. In this century the names of Martin Grabmann, Maurice de Wulf, Père Garrigou-Lagrange OP, Jacques Maritain and Étienne Gilson are outstanding.

M. D. Chenu, *Towards an Understanding of St Thomas*, ET, 1964; É. Gilson, *The Christian Philosophy of St Thomas Aquinas*, 1961; *Histoire de la Philosophie Médiévale*, 2nd ed. 1943, ET, 1955; *Introduction à la Philosophie Chrétienne*, 1960; J. Maritain, *The Degrees of Knowledge*, 1937, 2nd ed. 1959; M. Perrier, *The Revival of Scholastic Philosophy in the Nineteenth Century*, 1909; Josef Pieper, *Scholasticism: Personalities and Problems of Mediaeval Philosophy*, 1960; M. de Wulf, *Introduction à la Philosophie Neoscolastique*, 1904, ET, 1907, Dover ed. 1956; Encyclical *Aeterni Patris* in Blackfriars trans. of St Thomas Aquinas' *Summa Theologica*, 9–33, 1920; M. de Wulf, *CE*, X.746–9.

ALBERIC STACPOOLE, OSB

Nestorianism. *see* Christology (4).

New England Theology

New England theology was the most conspicuous theological movement in American Congregationalism in the last half of the eighteenth and the first half of the nineteenth centuries. Known also as the 'New Divinity', it was founded by Jonathan Edwards (q.v.) and it continued after his death to debate issues he had discussed, such as native depravity, the divine permission of sin, the nature of regeneration, human freedom and responsibility, the nature of virtue, and the relationship of both regenerate and unregenerate to the Church. Some of the leaders of the New England Theology sought especially to continue the Edwardsean tradition, though they felt free to make adaptations and they failed fully to catch the poetical and imaginative power of the master. Joseph Bellamy wrote *True Religion Delineated* (1750), which served for about a century as a practical guide in American Calvinism. Samuel Hopkins, Edwards' literary executor and author of a two-volume *System of Doctrines* (1793), made certain 'improvements' in the New Divinity so that in its strictest form it became known as 'Hopkinseanism'. Jonathan Edwards, Jr, advocated the 'governmental' or 'benevolence' theory of the atonement, while Nathaniel Emmons compiled his sermons into a late expression of New England Theology in two volumes, *System of Divinity* (1842).

The New Divinity was a shaping force in a wider circle of New England theologians, including Timothy Dwight, Leonard Woods, Nathaniel W. Taylor (q.v.), Bennet Tyler and Edwards A. Park. New England Theology was involved in the founding of three theological seminaries: Andover, Yale and Hartford. Especially in the encouragement it gave to revivalism and to missions, it influenced American Protestantism far beyond its own circles.

George N. Boardman, *A History of New England Theology*, 1899; Frank H. Foster, *A Genetic History of the New England Theology*, 1907.

ROBERT T. HANDY

New Testament Theology

The term is used in at least three contrasting ways. (1) It may mean a flat, descriptive ('history-of-religion') science, which attempts to state, compare and contrast the underlying theological standpoint of the various parts of the NT (e.g. the Synoptic, Johannine, Pauline, etc.) without in any way being concerned to discuss their significance for dogmatics or for Christian belief as such. It is based upon the presupposition that an objective or detached attitude can and should be maintained by the scholar. The outcome of such an approach has usually been to dissect and lay bare the various NT components and to leave unasked the question of the meaning of the NT as a whole. (2) It may imply the standpoint, often referred to as 'biblical theology' (q.v.), which is said to assume that there is such a thing as a biblical (or Hebraic) way of thinking which informs the Bible as a whole. (3) The third position is more existential or personal. It is concerned with the question about the meaning and truth of the NT as a whole. What can be learned from the NT about the outlook (or theology) of the men who knew Jesus best and of those who had been of their company – that is, the men of the apostolic age and those who handed on their teaching in the sub-apostolic period, the age spanned by the oral tradition and the written records of the years in which the NT books were produced? The way in which one may

attempt to state the theology of the NT (in this third sense) is by the framing of an hypothesis (whether consciously or unconsciously) and then testing it by continual checking with the NT documents and other relevant evidence from the period. This is in fact the way in which historical-critical interpretation is done nowadays in every field of historical reconstruction. It necessarily involves a personal or subjective element, but this is now seen to be unavoidable, as the illusion of scientific or presuppositionless history recedes (*see* **History, Problem of**). It does not, however, involve an absolute subjectivism or historical relativism, for the pursuit of history as a humane science involves the conviction that one historical interpretation can be rationally shown to be better than another. Each hypothesis must be evaluated by the evidence available. Thus, for example, R. Bultmann's hypothesis that the theology of the NT is a mythological conglomeration of Jewish apocalyptic and Hellenistic gnostic ideas which have somehow coagulated round the name of Jesus of Nazareth, about whom little certain historical knowledge can be attained, must be studied to see whether it gives a rational and coherent explanation of the NT evidence. In this respect it should be compared with other hypotheses, such as that Jesus himself is the prime author of the striking re-interpretation of the OT theology which is found in his own reported teachings and in the NT as a whole (the new covenant, the new Israel, the reinterpreted Messiahship, the reign of God, and so on).

Recent NT theologies include R. Bultmann, *Theology of the New Testament*, ET, I, 1952, II, 1955; Alan Richardson, *Introduction to the Theology of the New Testament*, 1958; E. Stauffer, *New Testament Theology*, ET, 1955; but works on New Testament christology are also relevant, e.g. O. Cullmann, *Christology of the New Testament*, ET, 1959. For general survey, *see* Hugh Anderson, *Jesus and Christian Origins*, 1964.

EDITOR

New Theology, The

The expression was first used in this century of the ferment of ideas which attracted widespread attention through the sermons of R. J. Campbell, minister of the City Temple, London. Preaching rather than the mass media was the usual channel for the communication of new ideas in the first decade of the twentieth century, and Campbell, who was not a trained theologian, disseminated from his pulpit the novelties which seethed in many minds. He also wrote a book entitled *The New Theology* (1907), which had a considerable vogue. Much controversy was stirred up and accusations of heresy were put forward, but Campbell undoubtedly helped many to see the real issues. His emphasis was upon the immanence of God to the virtual exclusion of transcendence, and his teaching seemed to point to pantheism. Notable fellow-Congregationalists such as A. M. Fairbairn and P. T. Forsyth strongly opposed him. Bishop Gore declared that such statements of Campbell's as that 'the real God is the God expressed in the universe and in yourself', or that 'there is no dividing line between our being and God's', left little room for the thought of God as self-complete and beyond and above the universe. Campbell's own position changed in the direction of the historic Christian faith, and in 1916 he was ordained in the Church of England; he eventually became a canon of Chichester.

In more recent times the expression 'new theology' has been associated with the ferment of ideas incoherently articulated in Bishop J. A. T. Robinson's *Honest to God* (1963), which bears obvious resemblances to Campbell's 'new theology'. The immanentist tendency (God as the ground of our being) is equally noticeable. The beneficial and the controversial results of the two works are also roughly parallel, but today the mass media have given the 'debate' a world-wide coverage which Campbell could not have attained. It was said of Campbell by his critics that his new theology was neither new nor theology. It can be said today that there is not and cannot be a *new* theology; there can be only a re-occupying of positions which had once been taken up and subsequently abandoned or forgotten.

David L. Edwards, ed., *The Honest to God Debate*, 1963; J. K. Mozley, *Some Tendencies in British Theology*, 1951; J. A. T. Robinson, *The New Reformation?* 1965; T. F. Torrance, *Theology in Reconstruction*, 1965, esp. essay 15.

EDITOR

Newman, J. H.

J. H. Newman (1801–1890), a leader of the Oxford Movement (q.v.) and later a cardinal of the Roman Catholic Church, came as a child under the Calvinist influences which are reflected in the austere moralism of his earlier preaching. *The Parochial and Plain Sermons* were for the most part delivered while he was vicar of St Mary's, Oxford and before university audiences, and are, both for their intrinsic theological merit and their powerful moral influence upon people who were themselves to be leaders in church and state, among the most important sermons in the English language. His friendship with John Keble (q.v.) and with R. H. Froude and his own patristic studies influenced his mind in a Catholic direction. He wrote the earliest and most forceful of the Tracts for the Times, was chiefly responsible for a series of translations, the Library of the Fathers, and for one of the most useful of compilations of Anglican divinity, the Library of Anglo-Catholic Theology, thus making much of the work of the Caroline Divines (q.v.) available for his generation. In *The Prophetical Office of the Church* (1837) he made a subtle defence of the Anglican *via media* and in *Lectures on Justification* (1838) some trenchant criticisms of contemporary evangelical theology. Already, however, his study of the Donatist schism and the repudiation by the bishops of his attempt in Tract

XC to reconcile the Thirty-nine Articles (q.v.) with the Council of Trent were causing him to be dissatisfied with the Church of England. In 1845 after prolonged travail of spirit during which he wrote his most daring theological work, *An Essay on the Development of Christian Doctrine,* he was received into the Roman Catholic Church. He helped to found the Oratory of St Philip Neri in Birmingham, where he spent most of the rest of his life except for his part in an abortive attempt to found a Roman Catholic university in Dublin. Much of his later life was shadowed by the suspicion in which he was held by the more intransigent members of his church, but he was always a widely influential and respected writer, and through a vast correspondence he touched many minds outside his communion. His answer to Charles Kingsley's attack on the honesty of some moral theologians and, by implication, on Newman's own integrity evoked the most celebrated apologia in English literature (1864). His *Grammar of Assent* (1870) was a significant contribution to the defence of Christian theism and, by putting a case which was very difficult to disprove in logic, took the place of the discredited arguments of an earlier age.

The Letters and Diaries of J. H. Newman, edited at the Birmingham Oratory, 1961–   ; J. Coulson and A. M. Allchin, eds., *The Rediscovery of Newman*, 1967; Meriol Trevor, *Life of Newman*, 2 vols., 1962.

R. CANT

Niebuhr, H. Richard

H. Richard Niebuhr (1894–1962), American theologian, was a native of Missouri and was educated at Elmhurst College, Eden Theological Seminary, Washington University, and Yale University (BD, 1923; PhD, 1924). Ordained to the ministry in 1916, he served as pastor of an Evangelical Church in St Louis, taught at Eden, served as president of Elmhurst, and in 1931 entered upon his work at the Yale Divinity School, where he became Sterling Professor of Theology and Ethics. He interwove theological, sociological and ethical analyses in his lifetime of creative work. As theologian, he wrestled with the problems posed and perspectives offered by such widely divergent figures as Ernst Troeltsch and Karl Barth. Influenced by relativism and existentialism, yet always a convinced churchman, he was a pervasive influence in the renewal of American theology since the 1930s. Deeply concerned with the problem of communication, he characteristically employed dialectical method in theological work. He insisted that theology, 'as disciplined development of the reasoning that permeates faith and as critique of faith, must always participate in the activity of faith, though its ultimate concern is with God'. The 'activity of faith' involves the specific ethical concerns of daily living; Niebuhr conceived of Christian ethics as the effort of the Christian community to criticize its moral action by means of reflection, both as to its past and its present. Yet his contextualist ethics always focused on God – his theology and ethics were cast in a radically monotheistic form.

Richard Niebuhr's impact was made through his many students, through his public lectures and many occasional writings, and through his major works: *The Social Sources of Denominationalism* (1929), *The Kingdom of God in America* (1937), *The Meaning of Revelation* (1941), *Christ and Culture* (1951), *Radical Monotheism and Western Culture* (1960), and *The Responsible Self: An Essay in Christian Moral Philosophy* (1963). He also collaborated in a number of important works: with Wilhelm Pauck and Francis P. Miller, *The Church Against the World* (1935); with Waldo Beach, *Christian Ethics: Sources of the Living Tradition* (1955); and with Daniel Day Williams and James M. Gustafson, the publications of 'The Study of Theological Education in the United States and Canada', *The Purpose of the Church and Its Ministry* (1956), *The Ministry in Historical Perspectives* (1956), and *The Advancement of Theological Education* (1957).

Paul Ramsey, ed., *Faith and Ethics: The Theology of H. Richard Niebuhr*, 1957.

ROBERT T. HANDY

Niebuhr, Reinhold

Reinhold Niebuhr (1892–   ) was the most conspicuous figure in American Protestantism in the second quarter of the twentieth century. After study at Elmhurst College and Eden Theological Seminary, he won two degrees at Yale, where he was influenced by D. C. Macintosh (*see* **Empirical Theology**). For thirteen years (1915–28) he was pastor of Bethel Evangelical Church in Detroit, where he found increasingly irrelevant the 'mild moralistic idealism' of much of American Christianity, and discovered afresh the adequacy of biblical faith for dealing with deeper human problems. Called to teach ethics at Union Theological Seminary, New York, in 1928, he also spent much time in the next quarter-century on university campuses and in political activities. Theological ethics and apologetical theology formed the focal points of Niebuhr's wide-ranging effort to relate Christian faith to the contemporary world by taking both with great seriousness.

Early convinced that liberal theology did not take sufficient account of human sinfulness and pride, especially in their corporate dimensions, his first major work, *Moral Man and Immoral Society* (1932) marked a revolt against the optimistic and individualistic ethics of the Social Gospel (q.v.). In this period Niebuhr drew from the Marxist analysis of society (*see Reflections on the End of an Era*, 1934), and became the central figure in the Fellowship of Socialist Christians. The search for a fully adequate foundation for ethical judgments, however, led him to criticize both liberal and Marxist views of human nature and history on the basis of a deepening appreciation of the profundity of classical Christian (in-

cluding Augustinian) insights into ultimate reality and the human predicament. Although he drew freely on the contributions of scientific and philosophical thinkers, Niebuhr asserted that the 'dramatic-historical' perspective of the Bible, which often can be articulated through tortuous paradoxes and difficult symbols, provides 'a truer view of both the nobility and the misery of man than all the wisdom of scientists and philosophers'. In *Beyond Tragedy* (1937), in his Gifford lectures, *The Nature and Destiny of Man* (2 vols., 1941–43), and in *Faith and History* (1949) his mature theological views were fully elaborated. Meanwhile, he expressed social and political judgments in literally hundreds of addresses, articles and editorials; he became editor of a bi-weekly journal of Christian opinion, *Christianity and Crisis* (1941–   ). Aware of the ceaseless struggle for power among humans, he criticized pacifist analyses of the world situation and encouraged responsible Christian involvement in the tragic power struggles of the time (*see Christianity and Power Politics*, 1940; *Christian Realism and Political Problems*, 1953). He asserts that the final answer to the human problem lies beyond history, which remains morally ambiguous to the end, in a divine redemptive love, revealed in the cross of Christ. So suffering divine love, which is always initiating a reconciliation between God and man, is the final coherence of life.

June Bingham, *Courage to Change: An Introduction to the Life and Thought of Reinhold Niebuhr*, 1961; Gordon Harland, *The Thought of Reinhold Niebuhr*, 1960; Hans Hofmann, *Die Theologie Reinhold Niebuhrs, im Lichte seiner Lehre von der Sunde*, 1954, ET, *The Theology of Reinhold Niebuhr*, 1956; Charles W. Kegley and Robert W. Bretall, *Reinhold Niebuhr: His Religious, Social, and Political Thought*, 1956.

ROBERT T. HANDY

Nietzsche, Friedrich Wilhelm

Nietzsche (1844–1900), German philologist and philosopher, believed that Hebrew-Christian theism had been completely undermined by philosophical and scientific advance (which he expressed by the statement, 'God is dead') and attacked not only the Christian religion but also those moral values and codes derived from it. He believed that 'going beyond good and evil' (as these had for centuries been understood by Christianity) involved the evolution of supremacy and rule by Superman (German: *Übermensch*), an intellectual, spiritual, psychological and physical *élite*, prepared to ignore the values of (a now discredited) religion, and to exercise the 'will-to-power'. Nietzsche's thought, almost unintelligible without a knowledge of nineteenth-century philosophy, especially the work of Schopenhauer and atheistic evolutionary naturalism, remains an important critique of nineteenth-century culture and thought. Its effect on twentieth-century thought (e.g. on the philosophers of fascism) has been considerable. And Nietzsche's terminology at least is discernible in the work of contemporary so-called 'death of God' theologians.

H. J. Blackham, *Six Existentialist Thinkers*, 1952, ch. II; Karl Löwith, *From Hegel to Nietzsche*, 1965.

JAMES RICHMOND

Nihilism

The basic meaning of nihilism, a rather vague and wide term which means literally 'belief in nothing', is probably the rejection of all moral and religious principles, and historically it became current in nineteenth-century Russia, where in revolutionary circles it was almost indistinguishable in meaning from 'anarchy'. Occasionally, especially in Eastern philosophy, it means the denial that anything at all is real. But, especially in more modern and contemporary philosophy, it can refer to a philosophical trend which directs our attention to the cognitive value of affective states such as boredom, cynicism, lack of concern, emptiness, or a trend which warns us of the spiritual dangers attendant upon such states and attitudes.

JAMES RICHMOND

Noetics

The term is derived from Greek *noetikos*, 'intellectual', the name of a group of Fellows of Oriel College, Oxford (including two Provosts), who sought greater freedom of thought and comprehensiveness in the Church of England in the earlier nineteenth century. They inevitably came into conflict with the Tractarians and earlier leaders of the Oxford Movement (q.v.). *See* W. Tuckwell, *Pre-Tractarian Oxford*, 1909.

Nominalism-Realism

The terms nominalism and realism belong properly to the disputes over universals at the end of the eleventh century and the first two decades of the twelfth century. Far from dominating the thinking of the Middle Ages, they are now seen to have been a phase. Although the term nominalism is also frequently applied to the outlook of William of Ockham and his followers in the fourteenth century, this bears no direct relation to the earlier nominalism. As raised at the end of the eleventh century, the problem of universals concerned the status and relation of genera and species to the individuals belonging to them. What was the nature of terms like 'animal' or 'man' and where were they to be found in the world of individual animals and men? Those, like Roscelin of Compiègne (c. 1050–1125), who replied that universals were nothing but names, which consisted in mere sounds (*flatus vocis*), were nominalists. For them only actual individuals were real. Universals were the terms designating them. At the other extreme were those who, like William of Champeaux (1070–1121), endowed universals with an essence of their own and treated them as the foundation of all individual existence. On this view, universals were prior to individuals as the condition of their existence. As upheld in its extreme form by William of Champeaux, a species was at once fully present in each of its individuals and common to them.

Some degree of realism was common to the majority of mediaeval thinkers both before and after the controversy of the eleventh and early twelfth centuries. Without the acceptance of the reality of universals there was no means of theological discourse. As St Anselm – himself among the most outstanding of all realists – who did not directly participate in the dispute, said, 'How would he who does not understand that several men are specifically one man, understand that in the most mysterious of all natures several persons, each of whom is a perfect God, is one God?' To that extent the problem of nominalism and realism was peripheral to the main preoccupations of mediaeval thinkers, certainly until the fourteenth century. Apart from Roscelin, much of the earlier discussion was concerned with different degrees of realism. The origin of the disputes may be seen as springing directly from one of the few surviving legacies of classical philosophy. This centred on the Introductions by Boethius and Porphyry to Aristotle's *Categories*. As concerned with the attributes of substance they invited the very questions of the relation of genus, species and individuals which Porphyry posed. In the climate of growing dialectical awareness which marked the later eleventh century, these questions invited reply. Not only were they among the perennial problems of philosophy; but at that time they offered virtually the only philosophical problem to discuss. The fact that it was treated as primarily a logical one is an indication of the absence of any established body of metaphysics or natural knowledge. This was to come in the second half of the twelfth century with the translation of Aristotle's works together with much of the Greek heritage.

The place of these first disputes between the nominalists and realists is due partly to their novelty as genuinely philosophical discussions, and partly to the prominence which Peter Abelard (1079–1142) gave to them. As the foremost teacher and dialectician of his age he turned his back upon the methods and the solutions of his own teachers, Roscelin and William of Champeaux, openly deriding the latter in his attempts to retain his position of extreme realism. Abelard's own answer to the problem of universals was to treat them as terms without reverting to Roscelin's pure nominalism. On the one hand, he recognized that the attribute of a universal was that it described several individuals; this could only be because it was a term, since 'it is monstrous to predicate a thing of a thing'. On the other, to leave it as a mere word did not explain why it could be applied to certain things and not to others. This took Abelard into the realm of epistemology. He criticized Roscelin for treating logic as if it had only to obey the rules of grammar. What might be grammatically correct could be logically absurd, as, for example, to say that a man is a horse. Terms had to refer to what actually existed to be acceptable. Since universals did not directly correspond to actual things, Abelard sought their validity in describing the state or condition proper to a particular class of individuals. Thus the species 'man' refers not to an essence 'humanity' but to something which shares the state of being a man: it connotes 'to be man'. Accordingly Abelard concluded that the mind reached this universal notion through abstracting it from actually existing individuals. In itself the genus or species did not exist outside the mind; but the mind was able to discover it through individual things. For that reason the universal was known only in a blurred and general way. Unlike, say, the individual tower which was known for itself, the species 'tower' referred to no tower in particular and so lacked the definition which was the property of individual knowledge.

Abelard's solution resolved the dispute. Although limited by his lack of the metaphysical and psychological conceptions which were later to be found in Aristotle's works, he succeeded in overcoming the stark antinomy between individual experience and the mind's constructs. After him, largely owing to the broadening of intellectual activity, the problem no longer existed in the purely logical and philosophical form in which it had been posed by Boethius and Porphyry.

The revival of nominalism with William of Ockham (c. 1290–1349) was of a different order. Its object was not the status of universals as such but the principles of valid demonstration; and it was directed to theological and metaphysical propositions rather than to those of logic. Coming two hundred years after the earlier nominalists Ockham and his followers showed, as we should expect, greater refinement of concepts. Ockham divided knowledge into simple and complex. Simple knowledge consisted either in direct experience of objects encountered through the senses (intuitive) or the images of things in the mind (abstractive). Complex knowledge was the result of the exercise of judgment by which we formulate our simple knowledge into propositions; it constituted knowledge in the strict sense, since it was only thus that we could make our experience intelligible. But conversely, this demanded the safeguard that our propositions were really founded in verifiable experience. Ockham's means to ensure that they were thus verifiable constituted his nominalism. Like Abelard, he held that all universals were merely mental constructs, the mind's response to its experience of individuals existing outside it. But he went further in denying any part to abstraction so that universals could thereby be said to inhere in individuals. On the contrary, Ockham reaffirmed Roscelin's position that only individuals were real. All knowledge, to be valid, had to be verifiable in intuitive experience. Propositions which could not be supported empirically were not strictly knowledge. Accordingly, unlike both Abelard and Roscelin, Ockham was concerned less with the status of universals than with that of our propositions and the prerequisites for demonstrative empirical knowledge. Moreover, again in contrast to the earlier nominalists, he was not disputing with realists in the traditional sense. His opposition to Duns Scotus was over the validity of the metaphysical notion of a common being and of Duns's famous formal distinction which Ockham rejected because it was not founded on a real distinction. At the same time, however, Ockham largely carried further Duns's teaching on God's freedom of will, which reinforced his own stress on individual verification: because God could do anything, there was no ascertainable means of attributing a particular course of action to him. We could only know what was given in experience.

The different import of Ockhamism can be seen in its effects. These lay less in opening up an old philosophical issue than in a radical reassessment of the scope and limits of metaphysics and natural theology. Unlike the earlier disputes over universals, Ockham was concerned with the very status of knowledge; and the conclusions which he drew had lasting impact upon the status of theology. Since God and metaphysics lay outside the scope of verifiable natural experience, what could be said about God was a matter of faith, while metaphysics largely lost their *raison d'être*. Instead of discussing problems concerning the proofs for God's existence or the nature of being Ockhamism accepted the tenets of faith as a matter of belief and confined natural knowledge to what could be known through experience. In doing so it polarized theology and philosophy and largely destroyed the framework of scholasticism (q.v.).

L. Baudry, *Guillaume d'Occam: sa vie, ses oeuvres, ses idées*, 1949; F. C. Copleston, *A History of Philosophy*, III: *Ockham to Suárez*, 1953; E. Gilson, *A History of Christian Philosophy in the Middle Ages*, 1955; J. G. Sikes, *Peter Abailard*, 1932; 'Nominalisme', *DTC*, XI, cols. 717–84.

GORDON LEFF

Non-Being

In classical Christian theology the ancient Greek doctrine of degrees of being (or perfection) was universally accepted. God (*ens realissimum*) alone possessed the fulness of being; all created things possessed only partial being (or perfection). The absolutely evil was the absolutely non-existent. In modern existentialist theology, however, non-being takes on a positively threatening character. Man (*Dasein*, q.v.) is anxiously aware of non-being, because his existence is threatened by it. It is, of course, logically impossible to think of non-being, for how can we think of that which does not exist? Nevertheless according to M. Heidegger (q.v.), although non-being cannot be thought, it can be apprehended through anxiety as a kind of indescribable, ultimate dread. Our lives are bounded by this ever-present threat of non-being. P. Tillich affirms that God is 'the power of being' which overcomes the threat of non-being. There is thus an interesting parallel between the classical Christian-mediaeval conception of evil as non-being and the modern existentialist teaching about the sinister or dreadful character of non-being. But whereas the former is mainly philosophical and intellectual, the latter strictly defies conceptualization and comes to us through 'apprehension' (in both senses of the word).

EDITOR

Nonconformity

Nonconformity is the general name for all those who, in a country which has an Established Church (i.e. one 'established' by State enactment), do not conform to the Establishment but set up dissenting denominations outside it. Hence also the terms 'dissent' (a synonym for 'nonconformity') and 'dissenters'. The alleged disappearance in England of 'the nonconformist conscience', so strong at the end of the nineteenth century, is a subject which falls within the scope of the sociology of religion (q.v.).

Non-Jurors

The passionate belief in the Divine Right of Kings (q.v.) which characterized so many high Anglicans proved a grave embarrassment in 1688 when some of them, whose opposition to the illegal policies of James II had precipitated the revolution, found themselves unable in conscience to take oaths of loyalty to the new monarch while the one they believed to be legitimate was still alive. This difficult situation lasted with diminishing seriousness till the end of the eighteenth century. The first serious consequences were felt in Scotland. Bishops had been restored under Charles II, and a system of church government by bishops in presbytery had evolved which still has some interest for modern reunion schemes. The new government would have been willing to tolerate its continuance provided it could be assured of political loyalty. The bishops' inability in conscience to take the oaths led to the division of the Scottish Church between Presbyterians and Episcopalians with damage to both. In England a minority of bishops, priests and laity, but a minority that included some of the most learned and devout, refusing the oaths were obliged to go into partial schism from the Church of England. This division contributed considerably to the triumph of Latitudinarian theology and Erastian policies (qq.v.) in the eighteenth century, because some of the most churchly minded theologians of the day were unable, through their isolation, to influence the church at large. Among the most notable of the non-jurors were Bishop Ken and William Law, mystical and devotional writer.

J. H. Overton, *The Non-jurors*, 1902.

R. CANT

Notes of the Church

When those who repeat the Nicene Creed in the liturgy declare that they believe in 'one, holy, catholic and apostolic Church' they are exercising a considerable act of faith because the outstanding fact of contemporary Christendom is that the Church is not one, but divided. The two main Christian bodies who believe that the Church can be identified without remainder with an existing Christian denomination – their own – are the Roman Catholics and the Eastern Orthodox. They point out that the NT and the Nicene Creed and the whole of early tradition alike agree that there can be only one Church, that the existence of two true churches together or of a true Church in a divided state is as anomalous as the existence of a squared circle. From this position, they have no difficulty in arguing that theirs must be, among all existing denominations, the only one representing the true Church. But situations can be shown to have arisen long before the Reformation in which it was difficult to determine which was the true Church. There were the Melitian schism at Antioch in the second half of the fourth century, a state of affairs affecting the validity of the orders of such august names as John Chrysostom and Basil the Great; the Great Schism in the Western Church (1378–1414); but above all the schism between the Eastern and the Western Church (generally reckoned to have taken place in 1054). The Eastern Church had, and has, every traditional sign of the true Church, unless communion with the see of Rome is the touchstone of belonging to the true Church, a conclusion supported by neither Scripture nor tradition except for those who approach the question with their minds already made up. It would, on the other hand, be equally absurd to maintain that the Eastern Church alone constitutes the true Church and that the Roman church stands outside it. The 'Branch-Theory', that there are three or four different branches of the one true Church, namely, the Roman, the Eastern and the Anglican, and perhaps some others, publicized, if not invented, by the Tractarians and much canvassed by the later Anglo-Catholic movement, finds few supporters today. The very different and quite widely held Protestant view that a loose federation of 'churches' acknowledging a spiritual unity and refraining from open competition or rivalry, as many denominations do today, is sufficient, is quite unsatisfactory. The unity of the Church demanded by the NT and by the tradition of the undivided Church is deeper than this and certainly includes unity (though not uniformity) in sacraments and ministry.

The Church being holy does not mean that its individual members are all necessarily perfect, personally holy or even good, but that Christ, who forms the Church's unity, lives in his Church by the Holy Spirit and both confers on it a consecration, an apartness from the world, and calls its individual members to holiness. It is Christ who administers the sacraments so that the sin of the ministers of the sacraments does not affect their working. Similarly, the Church is apostolic because it is entrusted with the apostles' gospel and called to the apostles' mission to spread this gospel over the world. Even when the Church is not fulfilling this apostolate properly the apostolic calling and nature of the Church remain, for these are gifts of Christ. Consideration of the holiness and apostolicity of the Church may throw some light upon the thorny question of the Church's unity. The Church is in some sense given, as the gospel and the sacraments are given, not purely human devices, but gifts of God, to be responded to and made actual and effective in the lives of each Christian. Perhaps the unity of the Church is similarly given, at once something which individual Christians do not create (hence perhaps the sense of unity between Christians of different, severed, communions) and something which Christians have to strive to make actual and concrete, as they have to strive to realize holiness and apostolicity.

B. Leeming, *The Churches and the Church*, 1963; E. L. Mascall, *Christ, the Christian and the Church*, 1955; E. Mersch, *The Theology of the Mystical Body*, 1951; L. Newbigin, *The Household of God*, 1953; *The Reunion of the Church*, 2nd ed., 1960; A. Nygren, *Christ and his Church*, 1957.

R. P. C. HANSON

Novatianism

Novatianism was a rigorist schism arising out of the Decian persecution (249–250). Its author, Novatian, was a leading Roman presbyter and an accomplished theologian whose *de Trinitate* represents the Roman orthodoxy of his day. At first prepared to accept tolerant views on the reconciliation of the lapsed, he swung over to rigorism partly owing to disappointment at the election of Cornelius as Pope. Consecrated rival Bishop of Rome, he soon became the focus of conservative disciplinary forces throughout the Church. Apart from Dionysius of Alexandria, who as an Origenist was not in sympathy with Novatian's starting point in trinitarianism, no serious charge was raised against the orthodoxy of the schism. Indeed, Constantine summoned the Novatianist bishop of Constantinople to Nicaea where he assented without difficulty to the anti-Arian decisions of the Council. It was their boast that their churches were completely free of Arian influence. Nicenes and Novatianists suffered together during the Arian controversy and at times seemed on the verge of reconciliation. Socrates, the Church historian, was well informed on Novatianist affairs and might even have been an adherent. Some of its leaders were highly regarded within the Great Church. At least in the larger centres of Christianity the movement seems to have died out by the end of the fifth century. It had made its disciplinary point (however unsuccessfully) and after the achievement of trinitarian orthodoxy had nothing further to offer.

A. d'Alès, *Novatien*, 1924; E. Amann, *DTC*, XI, cols. 826–49.

H. E. W. TURNER

Numinous

Numinous is a term particularly associated with the work of Rudolf Otto, notably in his book *Das Heilige* (1917), ET, *The Idea of the Holy*, (1923). In this book Otto used 'numinous' as a category for distinguishing the particular features of religion. Otto saw the origin of religion in what he called the *mysterium tremendum et fascinans*. By this, Otto meant that particular experience, usually for primitive man some confrontation with natural forces, but for more sophisticated man some depth of personal relationship, where simultaneously one is both attracted and repelled by a sense of awe.

A criticism of Otto's discussion of the numinous has called in question his thesis that this is an experience which is characteristic only of religion, and it has questioned further whether the numinous is as isolated from the moral sense as Otto maintained. It has been argued, perhaps rightly, that the undifferentiated sense of the holy, what Otto called the numinous, is in essence indistinguishable from the root of the aesthetic sense or the moral sense. *See* **Ecstasy.**

O. R. Jones, *The Concept of Holiness*, 1961; Rudolf Otto, *The Idea of the Holy*, 1923.

E. J. TINSLEY

Nygren, Anders

A. Nygren (1890–   ), Swedish dialectical theologian and bishop, was the author of *Agape and Eros*, his *magnum opus*, on the subject of love. Nygren sharply distinguished between these two concepts, *Agape* and *Eros*: while the latter (which can sometimes be very spiritual, as in Platonic philosophy) is characterized by desire and egocentricity, the former is understood by him as theocentric and self-forgetting, and distinguishes Christianity decisively from every form of non-Christian religion, culture and way of life. Nygren's thesis has been much discussed and criticized by twentieth-century theologians. *See also* **Love.**

A. Nygren, *Agape and Eros*, new ET by P. S. Watson, 1953.

JAMES RICHMOND

Objectifying

This word is much used by existentialist theologians. It means 'making an object' out of something which is non-existent except as an imaginative expression of human values or anxieties. R. Bultmann considers that the essence of myth is objectification; in mythology human ideas, fears, hopes, etc., are objectified as divine beings or demons having an existence over against ourselves. He holds that much of the NT is mythological in this sense and must therefore be demythologized, so that its true significance (or existential meaning) can be understood by men who live in a scientific age. Existentialist theologians urge that traditional theology has tended to make

God or his attributes objects which men can conceive, objects of intellectual knowledge or exploration. But, they claim, God is the Subject who can never be made an object of human investigation, because he is not an object in the sense in which everything else in the universe is an object. In its most extreme form existentialist theology regards even God as merely an objectification of human aspirations, but Bultmann himself rejects this conclusion. *See also* **Demythologizing; Existentialism.**

EDITOR

Oblation, Offertory

Strictly speaking, these two words should be identical in meaning, being derived from two different stems of the same Latin verb meaning 'to offer'; in practice they have come to bear slightly different but related meanings. The Offertory is the presentation of the bread and wine for consecration by the celebrant of the Eucharist. In the early Church it was customary in many places for the people to bring up to the altar their own offerings of bread and wine; this 'offertory procession' of the people has been restored in many churches under the influence of the Liturgical Movement (q.v.), and sometimes in a way which makes it appear (which it is not) the most important action of the Eucharist. There is no real connection between the offertory procession of the people and the 'Greater Entrance' of the Byzantine and some Western mediaeval rites (e.g. that of Sarum), which are purely clerical performances. The name 'offertory' is also applied to the anthem traditionally sung while the elements are presented; its use to describe a collection of money is improper and obsolescent.

The word 'oblation', on the other hand, usually in the plural, refers to the gifts which are offered, whether before or after consecration (*see* **Eucharist).** In the primitive Church it was customary to bring other gifts (e.g. oil, grapes, etc.) with the bread and wine; a trace of this probably survives in the passage beginning *Per quem haec omnia* in the Canon (q.v.) of the Roman Mass.

E. L. MASCALL

Obscurantism

Obscurantism is the attitude which desires to hinder the progress of knowledge in order that old beliefs may not be disturbed; the obscuring of the light of new truth in the interest of traditional orthodoxy.

Occam's Razor

Occam's Razor is the principle that beings should not be multiplied unnecessarily (*entia non sunt multiplicanda praeter necessitatem*): simplicity is the ideal of logical thinking. It was enunciated by William of Occam (d. 1349), the controversialist philosopher whose linguistic analysis led him to deny the possibility of proving the existence of God and many other propositions of scholastic philosophy. A native of Ockham in Surrey, his name is properly spelt Ockham in English. *See* **Nominalism-Realism.**

EDITOR

Occasionalism

The Cartesian view of mind and matter considered these as entirely distinct substances, *res cogitans* and *res extensa.* Their essential characteristics were incompatible. A thought, for example, has no spatial dimensions or location. Yet mind does *appear* to interact with body. How can it? Occasionalism was the doctrine that God takes a mental event as the 'occasion' of bringing about a correlated physical event, and vice versa: God himself being in fact the sole cause, and there being really no direct impact of body on mind or mind on body.

Nicolas Malebranche, *Recherche de la Vérité,* 1674; Arnold Geulincx, *Ethics,* 1675; *Metaphysics,* 1691.

R. W. HEPBURN

Ockham, William of. *see* Occam's Razor; Nominalism — Realism.

Odium Theologicum

Hatred (*odium*) generated by theological controversy.

Office, Divine

This is the name used to denote the official regular worship of the Church, with the exception of the Eucharist and such 'occasional' services as Baptism, Marriage and the like. Ideally, the whole Office, which in the West since the end of the fifth century has consisted of the Night Office (Matins) and the seven 'hours' of the Day Office (Lauds, Prime, Terce, Sext, None, Vespers and Compline), should be sung or recited in public, though this has become rare except in monastic communities. Lauds and Vespers (roughly corresponding to Anglican Morning and Evening Prayer) probably originated in the parish churches, the other hours in the religious communities. The Office probably consisted originally almost entirely of Scripture readings supplemented by psalms, but as time has gone on the proportions have become reversed and the scriptural element has become minimal. The fact that the Office remained in Latin when Latin ceased to be the vernacular meant that by the end of the Middle Ages participation in the Office by the laity was practically extinct; their public devotions consisted, apart from attendance at Mass, in such forms of prayer as the Rosary and later of Benediction of the Blessed Sacrament. In the sixteenth-century Anglican Prayer Books the vernacular was restored, the proportion of Scripture to Psalms recovered, and the whole structure much simplified.

The recitation of the Office, in public or in private, is obligatory on all clerics in major Orders both in the Roman and in most parts of the Anglican Church. Attempts to simplify the Roman

Office in the sixteenth century were almost entirely unsuccessful. Fairly considerable changes were made by Pope Pius X in 1911, but it has been left to the Second Vatican Council, in the Constitution on the Liturgy published at the end of 1963, to institute a really radical reform. This involves a much increased use of the vernacular, emphasis on Lauds and Vespers as the primary Hours, shortening and simplification of the Office in general, 'fewer psalms and longer readings' in Matins, and all possible encouragement to the laity to take a full and active part, as members of Christ's Body singing the praises of God.

In the Eastern Churches the structure of the Office has become very different from that in the West, though the pattern of the eight Hours is discernable; the recitation of the Office is not obligatory for the non-monastic clergy. In parish churches such parts of the Office as are celebrated are in a much abbreviated form. *See also* **Opus Dei.**

E. L. MASCALL

Old Catholics

The Old Catholics are a group of churches which broke away from Rome, one of them (in Holland) as early as 1724, the others (in Germany, Austria and Switzerland) after the promulgation of the dogma of Papal Infallibility by the First Vatican Council (1870). They are in full communion with the Church of England (since 1932). *See also* **Jansenism.**

C. B. Moss, *The Old Catholic Movement*, 1948.

EDITOR

Old Testament Theology

The theology of the OT is one of the most controversial branches of the study of the OT today, not so much because there are so many points of detail, more or less important, about which there is disagreement among experts, but because there is fundamental difference of opinion about the actual nature of the discipline itself. In a short article such as this it is obviously impossible to offer even a summary of the subject-matter with which OT theology, on any view of its nature, is concerned. That would have to be so superficial as to be of little value. What is possible and might prove helpful is to consider the nature of the problem associated with the idea of a theology of the OT and certain of the solutions which have been offered, in the hope that the issues may to some extent be clarified, even though no way beyond the present impasse can be found.

Almost all discussions of the problem with which we are concerned refer to the famous distinction drawn by J. P. Gabler in 1787 between biblical and dogmatic theology, according to which the former should confine itself to a description of the religion of the Bible and refrain from passing any normative judgments which would involve trespassing into the domain of dogmatic theology. On this view OT theology would restrict itself to the OT evidence and would resist any temptation to criticize the material with which it dealt even from the point of view of the NT.

Gabler's distinction was a useful one, since it did much to break the stranglehold of dogmatic theology upon the study of the OT and so left scholars free to look at it without preconceived ideas as to what they should find. The result was an increase of interest in OT history and religion and a growing appreciation of the extraordinary variety of points of view to be found in the OT. More and more, however, was interest directed to the history of the development of OT thought, in conjunction with a rearrangement of the literary material. This did not indeed lead to the disappearance of attempts to treat the religion of Israel systematically – the books of G. F. Oehler, H. Schultz and others are proof of the contrary – but, as time went on, the truly theological interest in the OT lessened. The emphasis came to be on religious experience and religious psychology. In particular the Hebrew prophets acquired a new significance and were treated primarily as men of religious genius with a message directed to their own time and only in a secondary way to the future. Concurrent with the interest in religious experience was the intensive study of the literature of the OT, which concerned itself in the first instance with the presumed sources of the existing documents and their relation to each other and later with the even more fruitful form-critical study of the various literary types in the situations which determined their character.

Apart from A. B. Davidson's *The Theology of the Old Testament* which appeared in 1904 and showed genuine theological characteristics and so was prophetic of what was to come, the period of a revived interest in OT theology was inaugurated in 1922 by E. König's *Theologie des Alten Testaments*. There followed a number of articles by prominent OT scholars who concerned themselves with the question of the nature of the discipline, in particular by O. Eissfeldt in 1926 who distinguished sharply between the history of OT religion and OT theology, confining the latter to a study of timeless truths as they were revealed to the men of the OT on the basis of faith, and by W. Eichrodt who adumbrated the views which he subsequently developed on a grand scale in his well-known *Theologie des Alten Testaments* which began to appear in 1933. Of less importance, though deserving of mention, were works by E. Sellin (1933) and L. Köhler (1936). In 1934 and 1942 were published the controversial volumes of W. Vischer, entitled *Das Christuszeugnis des Alten Testaments,* which, inspired as they were by the Dialectic Theology, placed the OT on the same level as the NT by employing the methods of typology and allegory to justify the claim that the OT is from beginning to end direct witness to Jesus Christ and his atoning work. Though undoubtedly a passing fashion of interpretation, this type of theological handling of the OT had its historical importance during the Church struggle in Germany and it did something to conserve a truth about the Bible which should not be overlooked, even though the method by which this was done must be rejected. It represented a gallant, if misdirected, effort to maintain the relevance for Christianity of the O T at a time when the latter was the main target of the attack of paganism on the Christian faith. In 1949 two more O T theologies appeared, the posthumous one of O. Procksch and the original Dutch edition of that of Th.C. Vriezen which subsequently in its German and English editions has played a notable part in the current debate, alongside the work, above mentioned, of W. Eichrodt and the highly original volumes of G. von Rad published in German in 1957 and 1960 and subsequently appearing in English in 1962 and 1965. Eichrodt's great work has also appeared in an English dress (I, 1961; II, 1967). A smaller but admirable work by a French scholar, E. Jacob, was published in French in 1955 and in an English translation in 1958. Though traditional in its arrangement, unlike the works of Eichrodt, Vriezen and von Rad – it adopts like Köhler's book a dogmatic scheme – it is distinguished by a full treatment of the action of God in history which makes the book relevant to the modern debate.

There is, of course, an extensive literature of monographs and articles (for the latter *see*, for example, the volume *Essays on Old Testament Interpretation*, ed. C. Westermann, 1963, translated from the original German, *Probleme alttestamentlicher Hermeneutik*, 1960 and *The Old Testament and Christian Faith*, ed. B. W. Anderson, 1964) dealing with the nature of OT theology and the various conflicting views which have to be taken into account in any thorough discussion of the subject. The names of some of these scholars will be mentioned in what follows, but the aim of the present writer must be restricted to the attempt to clarify a few of the more important issues involved. To attempt to do justice to all those who have contributed in an important way to the current debate would defeat the purpose which this brief article is expected to fulfil. It should perhaps be mentioned here that one of the most useful and balanced discussions of the various issues is given by Vriezen in the first part of his book; he is deeply concerned about the questions of the relevance of the O T to the Christian and of the relation between the Testaments. The expected new edition of his work should put readers still further in his debt.

What is involved in all this discussion can best be appreciated by looking at the works of Eichrodt and von Rad and at the criticisms of von Rad by a scholar who has not yet been mentioned, F. Baumgärtel, whose book entitled *Verheissung* (Promise) was published in 1952 and who may be said to have kept up a running fight with von Rad on certain fundamental issues of biblical interpretation. The recent little book of F. Hesse entitled *Das Alte Testament als Buch der Kirche* (1966) will be found very helpful for an understanding of Baumgärtel's rather involved thought.

It would be a mistake to regard these scholars as being at variance all along the line. Eichrodt, for example, is full of admiration for von Rad's skill in delineating the main features of the various O T 'theologies', those of the Yahwist, the Deuteronomist, the Chronicler and so forth. Similarly Baumgärtel pays generous tribute to the brilliance of von Rad's traditio-historical work. It can be safely asserted that no one can read von Rad's *Old Testament Theology* without being immensely stimulated by his flashes of insight and his original handling and combining of evidence. To neglect reading von Rad's great book is to miss a remarkable and rewarding experience. The very brilliance of his achievement, however, should not blind the reader to certain defects in his thought which are all the more difficult to detect as one is carried away by the beauty of his style.

Eichrodt and von Rad contrast sharply in their methodology. The former, as is well known, lays the emphasis on the underlying unity of the O T. This he demonstrates by the method of the cross-section which brings to light the fundamental and enduring features of O T religion and religious institutions. The central thought is alleged to be that of the Covenant between Yahweh and Israel which eventually broadens into Yahweh's willingness for fellowship with all men. Within this systematic scheme Eichrodt makes full allowance for historical development. There are many who think that Eichrodt has come nearest to producing a theology of the O T which does justice to the nature of the material and to the unity in variety and movement.

Von Rad's main contention, on the other hand, is that the correct way in which to write a theology of the O T is that of reportage, retelling the story of Israel's salvation-history (*Heilsgeschichte*) as it was 'confessed' at the ancient Israelite sanctuaries in credos like those in Deut. 26 and Josh. 24 and subsequently expanded in various ways (*cf*. G. E. Wright, *God Who Acts*, 1952, and, as a contrast, the penetrating criticism of the idea of revelation through history by James Barr in his recent book *Old and New in Interpretation*, 1966). This method results in an elaborate study of Israel's historical traditions which record the varied interpretations of God's dealings throughout the centuries with the people of Israel as put forward by the Hebrew writers. At this point it is important to quote what von Rad actually says about this variety:

> Unlike the revelation in Christ, the revelation of Jahweh in the Old Testament is divided up over a long series of separate acts of revelation which are very different in content. It seems to be without a centre which determines everything and which could give to the various separate acts both an interpretation and their proper theological connection with one another. We can only describe the Old Testament's revelation as a number of distinct and heterogeneous revelatory acts.

One is left wondering how in these circumstances one can speak of revelation at all.

What is perhaps even more serious than this

denial of a fundamental unity in the OT is von Rad's apparent lack of concern at the violent separation he makes between Israel's salvation-history and the actual course of history as it is approximately determined by modern scientific methods of historical investigation. The contrast is pressed by von Rad to such an extreme that it becomes clear that, if he is right, there is simply no historical basis for some of the most important elements in Israelite belief. His extreme scepticism about the role of Moses, which he shares with M. Noth, is a case in point. It is perfectly true, of course, that the modern historian does not, in the character of historian, permit himself expressions of faith regarding the events he is describing. Moreover the biblical evidence for events is to a very large extent cast in the form of witness to God's activity in history. That, however, does not entitle us to conclude that, from the theological point of view, what actually happened is a matter of indifference. For one thing the salvation-history itself, as soon as it was recited, became a part of the actual history of Israel and influential in determining the subsequent course of events in that history. This failure on von Rad's part to realize the importance of actual history is one of the points specially singled out for criticism by Eichrodt, who connects it with von Rad's existentialist approach to the OT (*see* the excursus at the end of vol. I of the English translation of Eichrodt's book). That Eichrodt should do so – probably quite correctly – is nevertheless a little odd, since Baumgärtel, in his criticism of von Rad's use of typology in passing beyond mere description, seems to think that he is lacking in the existential point of view (*see* his detailed criticism of von Rad's work in *Theologische Literaturzeitung*, 86 Jahrgang, Nummer 11 and 12, November and December 1961) contenting himself with pointing out analogies between events (or supposed events) in the OT and the NT and failing to ask the fundamental question of relevance which interests Baumgärtel. Von Rad, he feels, lays himself open to the charge of not really passing beyond mere description and an aesthetic interest in correspondences.

Eichrodt follows a similar line and criticizes von Rad for a typological procedure which compares a NT act of faith with a supposed OT type, the detection of the correspondence being left to the arbitrary choice of the expositor disguised as the expositor's *charisma*. (Baumgärtel declares that what von Rad is really talking about is 'pneumatic exegesis'.) Eichrodt does indeed recognize that there are parallels of structure between the Testaments which lend some justification to the typological procedure and are valuable for elucidating the meaning of religious terms and the significance of religious institutions. Nothing, however, should be allowed to divert us from the recognition that in the OT we have the record of how God worked out the salvation of Israel in the concrete events of history, and how what he accomplished in his dealings with the men of the OT eventually found its fulfilment in Christ. What God was doing in OT times was no mere shadow-

play with no ultimate significance for the actors in the events. Nor have we just a succession of hypotheses without any ultimate ground in history. Rather in all the undoubted variety of the OT we have as centre and focus the purpose of God working itself out in the movement of history.

Part of the trouble with von Rad's thought is that he lays himself open to the charge of inconsistency. When he ostensibly confines OT theology to reportage of the salvation-history of the OT and contrasts it sharply with the actual history in which the modern critical historian is interested, he seems to forget that he himself is employing critical methods in his assessment of the documents and so does not confine himself to reportage. For example he does not accept Deuteronomy at its face value as an address of Moses, but chooses to take up a highly critical position as he determines its place and time of origin. Moreover, when he insists that attention should be confined to the saving acts of God in history and that the history of Israel's faith and piety is irrelevant for an OT theology, he seems to overlook the fact that the very salvation-history of which he speaks is itself an expression of Israelite faith. The divine act and the human response in faith in fact belong together. Von Rad would probably agree that this is so. But then he must recognize the consequences for his theory. Eichrodt and Baumgärtel are at one in criticizing von Rad's over-emphasis on the supposed external facts as if they were not inseparable from the internal facts of faith. By cutting off the 'facts' of the salvation-history both from the actual facts of history on the one hand and from the accompanying faith of those who proclaim them on the other, von Rad is in danger of condemning his salvation-history to the status of myth. Eichrodt's words may be quoted:

> It seems necessary to us to emphasize that the withdrawal from all 'conceptualism' with regard to the activity of God in history ought never to involve isolating this activity in such a way as to ignore the testimony of faith evoked in response to it from the Old Testament Community. It is rather that the latter affords the only legitimate commentary on that activity. It is the interior overmastering of the human spirit by God's personal invasion which in the first place brings to life the Old Testament understanding of history. Here is to be found the decisive inward event, without which all external facts must become myth.

Eichrodt goes on to insist that the divine activity and the human response must be held together in thought.

There is still another feature of his thought in which von Rad lays himself open to criticism, namely, his view that there were actual breaks in the salvation-history when it came to an end and that there was a pause until God intervened with a new creative act. This is really to forget that the salvation-history consists not only in God's positive saving acts towards Israel but also in his negative acts of judgment. In fact the judgments are all part of the one continuous saving act of God. Von Rad indeed is inconsistent in the way in which he writes of the prophetic work of reinterpretation. Sometimes the language he uses seems to imply a complete break with the past – Yahweh's original appointments in election, covenant, law, conquest and monarchy – whereas in another place he admits that there is continuity in the reinterpretation. He cannot have it both ways. After all, the grandiose movement of interpretation and reinterpretation of Israel's tradition, with God's promise always pointing towards the future and ever more complete fulfilments, would seem to imply continuity of purpose amid all the variety. At the same time it may be admitted that there is a relative truth in von Rad's division of the salvation-history into stadia.

Whether or not von Rad is correct in his contention that the events of Israel's history clearly point forward to future fulfilments within the OT period itself and beyond it in Christianity, is a question on which there are strong differences of opinion. It should not be forgotten that to the Jews the OT with its continuation in early Judaism is not a torso requiring the completion given by Christianity. It is only from the point of view of NT faith that the incompleteness of the OT is apparent and Christians should be humbly aware that their faith is challenged by the adherents of a faith which claims the OT as its own rightful property, drawing out its implications in rabbinic thought.

In the last resort, if we leave on one side von Rad's highly original and controversial theory, there are two main views of the nature of OT theology, first that it must restrict itself to being purely descriptive, second that it must include a normative element. In his earliest discussion of the matter (*ZAW* xlvii (1929), pp. 83–91) Eichrodt inclined to the former view, maintaining that the OT theologian must confine himself to historical description, though he went so far as to admit that, for the correct performance of this task, there must be a relation of 'congeniality' between the scholar and his subject matter. It is probable that Eichrodt, while still regarding it as his primary task to demonstrate the unity of the OT system of faith, has moved some way towards the view that it does make a difference to one's assessment of the OT whether one views it in a Christian or a Jewish perspective. The names of R. C. Dentan (*Preface to Old Testament Theology*, rev. ed., 1963) and K. Stendahl (*IDB*, I, pp. 432 ff.) may be cited as examples of scholars who consider that a rigid insistence on the descriptive character of OT theology is required if it is to fulfil its function of acting as a check on dogmatic theology. Von Rad, on the other hand, argues that OT theology is more than a phenomenology of Israelite faith. But then, as we have seen, he seems to find in typology a satisfactory way of indicating the normative relation of the NT to the OT. Baumgärtel regards this as much too vague and arbitrary a procedure for the purpose of making OT theology serviceable to dogmatics.

There must, he thinks, be a much more scientific procedure if OT theology is to be taken seriously.

Though Baumgärtel would not agree with R. Bultmann in the latter's depreciation of the OT history which he dismisses as a history of failure or miscarriage, the two men have this in common, that they draw a very sharp line between Israel's religion and Christianity. The OT, they maintain, is not directly relevant to the Christian. Baumgärtel works out his position as follows. The key-word for the understanding of the Bible, OT and NT alike, is *epangelia*, promise. God's basic promise, which is undoubtedly historical, even though there may be some doubt as to where it is to be pinpointed in history, consisted in his choice of a people for himself. It is expressed in the proclamation of Yahweh as the God of Israel and Israel as the people of Yahweh, and again in the preface to the Decalogue, 'I am Yahweh your God who brought you out of the land of Egypt'. Throughout the OT period this promise is represented by promises, the partial fulfilment of which maintains the life of Israel, so that they are relevant to Israel, but must be kept distinct from the original basic promise which is always valid and does not require fulfilment in the material ways on which Israel ever and again set its heart. This basic promise was confirmed and sealed in Christ, and we are pointed forward to the eschatological fulfilment, when it will become finally manifest that God's purpose in choosing Israel was the salvation of all mankind. As we look back over history we must frankly recognize that there is no possible rational proof that God did make such a basic promise as the inner meaning of history. That has to be accepted by faith. Apart from faith history remains opaque. We can only believe that God is active 'in, with and under' the historical process. But that God did so act in real history and that his promise is still valid is quite essential for Christian faith. This is what we should mean by salvation-history.

What then is our relation to the OT as Christians? Baumgärtel maintains that, as we are not Israel, the partial fulfilments of the promise, which meant so much to Israel, are not directly relevant to us. The OT, however, retains its validity for us by its witness to the basic promise and further by the ambiguous nature of its witness to God's dealings with Israel throughout its chequered history. For the OT possibility of partial appropriations of the promise is still a possibility for us as Christians. The partial witness has a positive side which can help us on our way of faith and a negative side which can warn us of the many possibilities of misunderstanding and error.

It will be clear that this view of Baumgärtel's implies that the OT witness to the promise of God is to be judged by the norm of Christianity, the application of which makes clear the limited and ambiguous character of the OT and enables it to reflect the ambiguous quality in ourselves. The difficulty may be raised that the NT witness to Christ is varied and even contradictory, so that we do not have the unambiguous norm that seems to be required. It may also be objected that a truer view of the relation between the Testaments would recognize that they have a reciprocal influence upon each other, the OT being required to throw light on the NT, just as the latter is required to throw light on the former. It may be suggested, however, that the difficulty is made greater by the tendency to look at it too exclusively from the intellectual point of view as a puzzle to be solved. Christianity is first and foremost a way of life and our Christian judgment is gradually formed by the experience of living it. We learn through our relations with other people, not only with those within the Christian fellowship but also with those outside it, by our ventures of faith, by our failures and betrayals as well as by the times when the Spirit moves us to acts of true brotherhood and loyalty. Perhaps the most helpful way of looking at the whole matter is to remember that the God who made the promise to Israel which was confirmed in Christ is the living God who gives life to his people. The OT with all its limitations bears witness to that communication of life, and we know from our own experience as Christians, both in the Christian fellowship and in our contacts with the world outside, that Christ does indeed communicate the life which is more abundant. With that experience we can enter the world of the OT through its varied literature and, recognizing our kinship with these men of old, of whose faith ours is the fulfilment, discover that their witness, for all its limitations, can guide us into the presence of the living God. Theology is theology and not life, but unless the theologian, and that includes the biblical theologian, keeps close to the source of life and allows his thinking to be enriched by the wisdom which only life can impart, his theology will be defective for the discharge of its critical function.

James Barr in his challenging book, *Old and New in Interpretation* (1966), doubts if there requires to be a discipline called OT Theology, but recognizes that there has to be 'criticism of the aspects of theological currents which lie close to relevance for the Old Testament and . . . the pointing out of ways in which these currents might have to be altered if they are really to do justice to the Old Testament texts' (*ibid*., p. 170). He may be right. Certainly it should be clear from what has been said that the theological task, whatever form its end product should take, can be carried out properly only if thought and life act upon each other. Such thought need not be arbitrary or irresponsible, but unless the biblical theologian is prepared to take some risks he may fail in his task of mediation.

B. W. Anderson, ed., *The Old Testament and Christian Faith*, 1964; R. C. Dentan, *Preface to Old Testament Theology*, 1963; W. Eichrodt, *Theology of the Old Testament*, 2 vols. 1961–67; E. Jacob, *Theology of the Old Testament*, 1958; G. von Rad, *Old Testament Theology*, 2 vols. 1962–65; H. W. Robinson, *Inspiration and Revelation in the Old Testament*, 1946; 'The Theology of the Old Testament', *Record and Revelation*, ed., H. W. Robinson, 1938; Th. C. Vriezen, *An Outline of Old Testament Theology*, 1958; C. Westermann, ed., *Essays on Old Testament Interpretation*, 1963; N. W. Porteous, *Living the Mystery*, 1967; 'The Theology of the Old Testament', *Peake's Commentary on the Bible*, 1962; K. Stendahl and O. Betz, 'Biblical Theology', *IDB*, I, 1962.

NORMAN W. PORTEOUS

Omega, Omega-Point. *see* Teilhard de Chardin, Pierre.

Ontic

The word comes from Greek *on*, 'being', and means 'pertaining to being' or 'reality'. The precise significance of the word can usually be determined only from the context in which a particular theologian or philosopher uses it. Thus, for instance, R. Bultmann (q.v.), adopting the terminology of M. Heidegger (q.v.), argues that what is ontologically a human possibility, i.e. something which it is possible for men to know, is ontically actualized in Christian faith (e.g. the knowledge of the eschatological), that is to say, faith gives us knowledge of what actually is. It is much discussed today whether religious language merely illustrates human attitudes or whether it possesses ontic significance, i.e. refers to what really exists.

EDITOR

Ontologism

Ontologism is the view that we can have a direct knowledge of God in this life through some natural or innate organ of the soul. Many doctrines of an 'inner light' or of 'the divine spark in every man' and many theories of mysticism (q.v.) are akin to ontologism and have more in common with Stoicism and Neoplatonism than with Christianity. The doctrine is condemned as erroneous by the Roman Catholic Church, which has generally held (with Aquinas) that in this life (*in statu viatoris*) all our knowledge, including our knowledge of God, is derived from sense-data and that only in the world to come (*in patria*) shall we know God directly. Protestantism, too, in its classic forms has rejected the doctrine on the ground that the Word of God alone mediates our knowledge of God.

John Baillie, *Our Knowledge of God*, 1939, pp. 166–77; Alan Richardson, *Christian Apologetics*, 1947, ch. X.

EDITOR

Ontology

Ontology, 'the science of being', used to be commonly regarded as a part of metaphysics (q.v.). Today, in an age in which metaphysics is out of favour, ontological knowledge of a non-speculative and non-ratiocinative kind is insisted upon by philosophical theologians of the existentialist school and by certain others. We are directly aware of *being* itself, through our own existence-in-the-world (*see* **Dasein**). Other theologians speak of a 'disclosure' of being (or of the real, or of God) in certain situations in history and in our own lives. These are not to be dismissed as merely emotive or subjective, because they have a cognitive and therefore an ontological content as well as an affective or volitional one. *See* **Metaphysics.**

EDITOR

Openness

Openness is a term much used by existentialist theologians as a demythologized way of speaking of the benefits brought by Christ, who was himself the man supremely open to others. Instead of being 'shut in upon ourselves' we are made open to our world, so that we can be creative in it, open to the possibility of living authentic lives, released from fear and selfishness, open to other people, open to God and especially 'open to the future'. This last term appears frequently in the writings of E. Fuchs, G. Ebeling, etc. 'Openness is constitutive for being' says J. Macquarrie, who sees in the expression a demythologized way of saying that God is light. Heidegger's metaphor of an opening or a clearance in a forest, where light breaks through, is suggestive in this regard. But it may be noted that openness is a metaphor drawn from the material world, and thus is basically impersonal; it is doubtful whether unsophisticated Christians can recognize what is meant by exhortations to be open to the future, etc. On the other hand, the expression 'open-hearted' is well understood.

J. Macquarrie, *God-Talk*, 1967, pp. 208–11.

EDITOR

Opera ad Extra

The distinction between *opera ad intra* and *ad extra* is applied by the scholastic theologians both to finite agents and to God. The former relates to actions considered from the standpoint of the agent himself, the latter with reference to their external effects. With God all his operations can be considered as internal to himself since they depend unilaterally upon his will and character. Some, however, can also be considered as external in relation to their effects. From this point of view we can refer creation to the Father, redemption to the Son and sanctification to the Spirit, provided that we remember that the external operations of the Trinity are indivisible (*opera sacrosanctae Trinitatis ad extra sunt indivisa*) since behind them lies their dependence upon the interior will and character of the One God. While then we can speak of one Person as eminently involved in a given operation, all three Persons are involved in the operation of each. There are no 'blank files' in the *opera ad extra* of the Trinity.

H. E. W. TURNER

Optimism

The term optimism and its antonym, pessimism, have no clearly defined uses in theology. All too often they are used loosely as terms of praise or abuse. What is 'pessimism' to one man is 'realism' to another. The terms appear frequently in reference to the doctrine of man. These who teach original sin and the fall of man often are called pessimists. But it has been argued that the most 'optimistic' of all doctrines is the doctrine that man is a fallen creature because this assures us that man, as we find him, is not man as he was meant to be. Therefore, it gives hope that man does not have to remain as he is.

Reinhold Niebuhr has said that Christianity is provisionally pessimistic but that it is ultimately optimistic. That is, Christianity faces the facts of sin and looks forward to a future where evil will continue to grow with the good. But the Christian believes in the ultimate victory of God over all evil. Karl Barth has argued that Christianity is pessimistic about man but optimistic about God. Man, by his own efforts is a sinner, but man, in the hands of God, is sanctified to a new life.

WILLIAM HORDERN

Opus Dei

Opus Dei is the name of the liturgical forms of worship prescribed for daily use at fixed hours observed as a matter of obligation in monastic communities, cathedrals, etc., or as used daily by priests (and devout laymen) in churches of the Catholic tradition. St Benedict gave the name of *opus Dei* ('the work of God') to his arrangement of the 'offices' (Latin *officium*, 'service', 'function', 'duty'). The earliest 'offices' of the Christian Church were modelled on Jewish examples of fixed hours and days of prayer, fasting, etc. *See* **Office, Divine.**

Order

The question of order has a prominent place in ecumenical discussions. It turns upon the question whether or not the ministry (q.v.) is a necessary function in the Church and is founded upon a divine commission; if it is, then it is clearly essential to the Church; if it is not, then it can scarcely be regarded as a subject of the first importance. According to the latter view order relates to organization which may be changed at different times to suit different circumstances. According to the former view it is a question of doctrine; it is an essential part of the whole sacramental order within which alone the sacraments, in the full and regular sense, can exist; hence to disregard order or to treat it as something separate from faith is to isolate it incorrectly from the overall pattern of structure, belief, etc. which is the Church.

There are therefore two opposed positions: the one sees order in terms of organization, the other in terms of structure; the one understands the reality of the Church as spiritual, the other as sacramental. It is difficult to see how these can be reconciled without some modification on either side, and it is precisely on this that reunion schemes in the past have foundered.

G. Aulén, *Reformation and Catholicity*, 1962, pp. 160–76.

J. G. DAVIES

Orders, Holy

Holy Orders is the term applied to the several offices or ranks within the ministry (q.v.) of the Church. Debate continues as to their number, their differentiation, their necessity and their validity. The Anglican and Eastern Orthodox Churches recognize three Major Orders: bishop, priest and deacon. The Roman Church, since Innocent III in 1207, includes the subdeacon in the Major Orders, and in the Minor Orders the porters, exorcists and acolytes. In the East, since the Trullan Council of 692, lectors and cantors survive, while porters, exorcists and acolytes have been merged in the subdiaconate.

Of the Major Orders the deacon (q.v.) was originally the bishop's right-hand man with administrative, pastoral and liturgical duties. The differentiation between bishop and priest is largely one of function, the former retaining the power of confirmation and ordination, but both are said to share the priesthood, although the bishop's is *primum sacerdotium* and the priest's *secundum sacerdotium*.

The validity (q.v.) of orders is a matter of ecumenical debate, the Roman Church, for example, denying that of Anglican orders on the grounds of defect of intention. The idea of intention relates to the necessity of administering the sacraments with the purpose of doing what the Church does. Unless intention is required, it is argued, the right form of the sacrament may be performed by accident, for example, in religious drama. So the Council of Trent demanded right intention, and it was on these grounds that Leo XIII in 1896 condemned Anglican ordinations.

J. G. DAVIES

Orders, Religious

Religious orders are societies or fraternities living under a rule; they originated in the monastic movement in the early Church. The ideal of a mortified life has never been absent from Christianity since its beginnings and in the second and third centuries many congregations had inner groups of virgins and ascetics. In the second half of the third century a number of men adopted a form of anchoritic life, chief among whom was Antony (251–356), who is usually regarded as the founder of monasticism. This is an oversimplification, since factors were at work other than his influence, e.g. the secularization of the Church, consequent upon the conversion of Constantine, and the economic situation which led many to forsake the world that cost so much. At first monasticism was as it were outside the Church, or at least outside its organized community life. It was a protest of individuals seeking their own sal-

vation. Its primitive eremitical character was changed by the labours of Pachomius (*c*. 296–346) who provided a pattern of ascetical life within a community under a rule. His example inspired Basil of Caesarea (c. 330–379) and later, among the pioneers in the West, John Cassian (c. 360–435) who was to be followed by Benedict of Nursia (c. 480–c. 550). There can be little doubt that these men and women, living under vows of poverty, chastity and obedience, preserved Christian learning and culture and moral ideals throughout the centuries of chaos that followed the collapse of the empire.

Later religious orders were in effect groups living under rules reformed in accordance with the ideals of their founders. So the Cistercians or White Monks were reformed Benedictines, while the Cluniac reform, issuing in the Black Monks, was also Benedictine in character. The Carthusians on the other hand were a contemplative order, founded by Bruno in 1084, while the Franciscans and Dominicans of the thirteenth century were mendicant friars, being religious orders devoted to service and preaching. The Jesuits were a product of the Counter-Reformation and were concerned to support the papacy and catholic teaching and to undertake missionary work among the heathen. Suppressed in England at the Reformation, religious orders were refounded in the nineteenth century while within the Reformed Churches a community was created at Taizé in France.

The main differentiation between the orders is to be found in whether they are contemplative, i.e. given entirely to prayer and without contact with the world, or active, i.e. combining the monastic life with, for example, teaching or nursing. The role of such orders within the Church may be defined as that of intercession, of service and of witness.

P. F. Anson, *The Call of the Cloister*, 1955; *A Directory of the Religious Life*, 1943 (issued by the Advisory Council on Religious Communities under the chairmanship of the Bishop of Oxford, K. E. Kirk).

J. G. DAVIES

Ordination

Ordination is the action of admitting a candidate to the ministry of the Church. It usually relates to the conferring of orders upon priests or presbyters but is frequently applied to the making of deacons.

In the patristic period presbyters were ordained by the laying on of hands, with prayer, of the local bishop and all the existing presbyters, whereas in the case of deacons the bishop alone gave the imposition. An elaboration of this simple rite took place in the Middle Ages so that there was added to the ordination of presbyters the vesting of the candidates, the tradition of instruments, i.e. the presentation of symbols of office being paten and chalice with hosts and wine, the anointing of the hands and a second imposition at the end of the service connected with the final blessing and accompanied by a formula based upon John 20.22. In the case of deacons there was a similar but not so extensive elaboration involving their being vested in dalmatic and stole and their receiving a gospel book.

Among the Eastern Orthodox Churches some have adopted Latin features, e.g. the Maronites have the anointing of hands and the Armenians the tradition of instruments; in general, however, there is a basic common nucleus, namely, a proclamation known as the 'Divine Grace' and the laying on of hands with prayer. The Anglican forms reduced the two impositions of hands to one and eventually confined the tradition of instruments to the delivery of a Bible to a priest and of a NT to a deacon.

Apart from the aberration of Pope Eugenius IV who in 1439 declared that the tradition of instruments was the essential matter, there would now be common agreement upon the necessary features of the rite of ordination as defined in the *Book of Common Worship* of the Church of South India.

(1) The presentation of the candidates to the presiding Bishop, this being the last step in the process of choice of them by the Church; (2) prayer for those about to be ordained or consecrated, that they may receive the gift of the Holy Spirit for their ministry; and (3) the laying on of hands of at least three Bishops (in an episcopal consecration), of the Bishop and Presbyters (in an ordination of Presbyters), or of the Bishop (in an ordination of Deacons). To these have been added an examination of the candidates concerning their beliefs and duties, the delivery to them of the instruments of their office (Bible, pastoral staff), and the giving of the right hand of fellowship. These ceremonies, however valuable for their symbolism, are not essential elements in the rites of ordination.

The doctrinal interpretation of the action admits of a greater variety, but two main positions are held: according to the one ordination is a sacrament whereby something is conveyed; according to the other it is not a sacrament and is primarily an act of authorization. Whether or not it be a sacrament is clearly a question of definition; what is conveyed may be differently described as grace, a gift of the Spirit or a functional gift, together with, according to Roman belief, an indelible character (q.v.) – it is obviously possible not to accept this last item and still to maintain that something other than this is bestowed.

It would appear that from the earliest days Christians have believed in the transmission of something by the laying on of hands. According to the ordination prayer for a presbyter in the *Apostolic Tradition* of Hippolytus, God is asked to 'impart the Spirit of grace and counsel of the presbyterate', and there is a reference to the elders chosen by Moses having been filled 'with thy Spirit'. In the sacramentary of Serapion the petitions are made that 'the Spirit of truth may dwell upon him . . . Let a Divine Spirit come to be

in him . . . Give a portion of Holy Spirit to this man also, from the Spirit of thy Only-begotten.' The basis of this belief seems to have been two-fold: the equation of the Christian ministry with that of the OT and in particular of the presbyters with the elders who received of the Spirit that was upon Moses (Num. 11.17) and the acceptance of the account in John 20.23 as the ordination or consecration of the apostolic ministry. Such an understanding of ordination does not preclude the idea of authorization, but it is possible to accept the latter while repudiating the conception of a gift conveyed.

The view that ordination is primarily authorization and nothing more rests upon the contentions that the basis of belief in the bestowal of a gift is inadequate and that the concept of a gift is imprecise and conflicts with a full understanding of the role of the Holy Spirit. Hence it is argued that the Christian ministry is essentially distinct from that which is described in the OT, that it is illegitimate to transfer ideas about the latter to the former, and that John 20.23 is to be understood as a doublet of Pentecost, when the Spirit was given to the *whole* Church, and not as a prototype of later ordination ceremonies. It is further pointed out that all Christians, by virtue of their initiation, became partakers of the Spirit and that his indwelling presence is revealed by gifts which are not bestowed *ab extra* on separate occasions, sacramental or otherwise, but are forms of his activity. A presbyter or priest, it is said, can scarcely need more for the performance of his functions than that which he already possesses because of his membership of the Church, namely, the Holy Spirit of God.

The corollaries of these two positions, the sacramental and the authoritarian, are that whereas ordination in the first sense is to the priesthood of the whole Church, in the second sense it is only to a ministry to a specific body of Christians and, in the state of divided Christendom, is necessarily limited.

J. G. Davies, *The Spirit, The Church and the Sacraments*, 1954, pp. 165–77; W. K. Firminger, 'The Ordinal', *Liturgy and Worship*, ed. W. K. Lowther Clarke, 1943, pp. 626–82; O. C. Quick, *The Christian Sacraments*, 1941, pp. 123–60.

J. G. DAVIES

Origen

Origen (186–255) is the greatest name among the theologians of the pre-Nicene Church. Born in Alexandria in 186, he early lost his father Leonides, who was martyred in the persecution of Septimius Severus (202–3), and was made head of the catechetical school at Alexandria at a very early age. He quickly made a name for himself as a scholar, teacher and author. In 232 he finally left Alexandria, as the result of a disagreement with the bishop of Alexandria, Demetrius, paid a visit to Athens and then settled in Caesarea in Palestine. Here, except for a three-year visit to Caesarea in Cappadocia caused by the persecution of the Emperor Maximin (235–8), he remained until the outbreak of the Decian persecution (249). He suffered as a Confessor in this persecution, and died (probably in Tyre) in 255. His scholarship gives him a pre-eminence in the ancient Church second only to Jerome's. He learnt Hebrew and consulted Jewish rabbis for points of biblical information. He produced a comparative edition of the Greek OT, called the Hexapla, giving the Hebrew, the Hebrew translated into Greek, and the versions of the LXX, of Aquila, Symmachus and Theodotion. He was very well versed indeed in contemporary philosophy. His greatest work was perhaps the *De Principiis*, or *First Principles*, the first attempt in history to give Christianity a philosophical grounding. But his apologetic work written towards the end of his life (248), *Contra Celsum*, rivals it in brilliance, in erudition and in intellectual grasp. He produced an immense number of commentaries and homilies on books of the Bible, among them commentaries on John, on Matthew and on Romans, and Homilies on Luke and on Jeremiah, and two works on the Song of Solomon, which were the foundation of the subsequent ascetical and mystical interpretation of this work, and minor works on Prayer and on Martyrdom. His scriptural exegesis is marked by an extensive use of allegory in the tradition of Philo.

His thought is deeply influenced by Platonism, and he can be associated with the last great movement of ancient philosophy, Neoplatonism, founded by Plotinus, Origen's younger contemporary. All spirits have existed with God from eternity, though in dependence upon God, and the Fall took place before the world was created (premundane). The material, physical world was made by God as a testing-place or 'approved school' for fallen spirits, who under the direction of the Logos experience it either as human beings or as devils. Indefinite experience of purgation in different states of existence awaits all souls beyond this life, but in the end all, even the devil, will be saved. Origen conceived the useful doctrine of the eternal generation of the Son by the Father, thereby pointing a way out of the unsatisfactory 'economic Trinitarianism' of his predecessors, but though all the members of his Trinity were divine, it was a graded Trinity in which the Son mediated the Father to the created world and the Spirit was the first production of the Son. Origen's Platonism and his use of allegory tended to make him ready to dissolve the historicity of many of the incidents in the Bible such as the story of Adam and Eve in the garden of Eden, but he certainly accepted the historical existence of our Lord.

Origenism means some of the leading ideas of Origen, such as the pre-existence of souls, as developed by his disciples in the third and fourth centuries (notably Evagrius Ponticus) and as attacked by several theologians (notably Epiphanius, Jerome [who had been an Origenist] and Theophilus of Alexandria) at the end of the fourth and beginning of the fifth centuries. The attack was renewed in the sixth century, by the Emperor Justinian, who condemned Origen's doctrines in his Letter to Mennas, Patriarch of Constantinople, and at a Council there in 543 endorsed by Pope Vigilius, and caused them to be condemned by the Second Council of Constantinople (553).

Alexandrian Theology is the type of Platonic thought characteristic of Clement of Alexandria and of Origen, marked by a symbolic interpretation of the physical universe, an intellectualism and a tendency to disparage the concrete, the historical and the material. It can also be used for the christological views taught by the later theologians of Alexandria, especially those of Theophilus, of Cyril and of Dioscoros.

J. Daniélou, *Origen*, 1955; B. Drewery, *Origen and the Doctrine of Grace*, 1960; R. P. C. Hanson, *Allegory and Event*, 1959; J. E. L. Oulton and H. Chadwick, *Alexandrian Christianity*, 1954.

                                                    R. P. C. HANSON

Original Righteousness

Original righteousness is the term used to describe the state in which man was created and remained until he fell. Through the early centuries of Christianity this was believed to refer to a historical time in the history of man. Mediaeval and Reformation theologies give extensive descriptions of the perfections possessed by man at this period.

With the rise of evolutionary theory the concept of original righteousness was thrown into doubt. Liberal theology in the nineteenth century tended to abandon it along with the doctrine of original sin. The first man, liberalism thought, was primitive man. Nevertheless, with J.-J. Rousseau, some liberals thought that primitive man did dwell in a state of idyllic innocence that was unspoiled by the later development of civilization.

In the twentieth century many theologians have restored the concept of original righteousness without identifying it with a historical past. They find the concept necessary to describe the paradoxical aspects of human nature. Man, the sinner, is never content to be simply a sinner. He rationalizes about his conduct and tries to interpret it in a better light. Man cannot accept his sinful state as normal. Thus the concept of original righteousness is used to refer to man's essential nature which is dimly apparent even in his existential state of sin. Reinhold Niebuhr locates original righteousness in the 'perfection before the act'. That is, the self looks out on its world from the perspective of its values and ideals and has a righteousness that is lost when it tries to put its ideals into practice. *See also* **Man, Doctrine of.**

Martin Luther, *Lectures on Genesis, see especially* commentary on Gen. 2.9, 11, 15, 16, 17, 25; Reinhold Niebuhr, *The Nature and Destiny of Man*, I, 1941, ch. 10.

                                              WILLIAM HORDERN

Original Sin. *see* Man, Doctrine of.

Orthodoxy

There are no creeds in the NT, though a concern for sound doctrine is occasionally expressed in it (e.g. I Tim. 6.3; II Tim. 1.13). The earliest Christian creeds are so tenuous as to be quite insufficient as tests of orthodoxy. During the second half of the second century and most of the third it was the rule of faith that expressed orthodox belief, in a fluid and undogmatic way. It was not until the creeds and formulae emerged from the great councils of the fourth and fifth centuries that an orthodoxy defined in words and capable of being forced on believers was widely accepted. The 'Athanasian' Creed (probably fifth-century) exactly expresses this concept when it makes eternal salvation dependent upon a precise and subtle definition of the doctrine of the Holy Trinity. The Eastern Church, learning perhaps by its repeated failure to achieve an advance upon the Chalcedonian Formula, showed no inclination to add extensively to the classical early dogmas. But the Western Church suffered no such hesitation, and continued to develop dogma in a number of directions right up to the Reformation, and, in the Church of the Counter-Reformation, up to the present day (Immaculate Conception, 1854, Papal Infallibility, 1870, Assumption of the Blessed Virgin Mary, 1950). The Easterns reckon seven General Councils, the last in 787; the Roman Catholics estimate twenty-one, the last (Vatican II) having closed as recently as 1965.

But even the 'Athanasian' Creed does not say 'we assent to One God in Trinity' but 'we *worship* One God in Trinity'. The Easterns have always had the conception of 'sobornost', a living unity of faith, conduct and worship which cannot be entirely defined in words. The coming of historical criticism has had the salutary effect of causing Christian theologians of all traditions in the West (though more markedly among Protestants than Roman Catholics) to re-examine Christian dogmas and to realize how much involved are their expressions in particular and accidental circumstances, with a resultant mitigation of a narrowly doctrinaire or arrogantly dogmatic spirit almost everywhere. The essentials of Christianity do not lie in the words of the dogmatic formulae, but in the unchanging reality, only partly apprehensible by the intellect and capable of expression in words, which the transitory and time-bound phrases and thought-forms were trying to express.

Nevertheless, this does not mean that the concept of orthodoxy is meaningless or evanescent. There is a central and consistent tradition of Christian doctrine and practice, very little affected by the extremes of denominational or factional variation, roughly summed up in the doctrines of the Trinity, the incarnation and the atonement, and the use of the sacraments of Baptism and the Eucharist, to deviate from which is not the proper use of the liberty of a Christian man, but self-opinionated refusal to believe and worship with the Church, which is the meaning of heresy. It is this central tradition which provides a common ground for all participants in the Ecumenical Movement today. *See also* **Creed(s)**.

R. P. C. HANSON

Orthodoxy (Eastern)

The word 'orthodoxy' means properly the quality of whatever or whoever is orthodox. Like 'catholicism' or 'christianity', however, it is often applied to the whole body of persons who share this quality. The word 'orthodox' is formed from two Greek words, meaning 'straight' (or 'right', 'correct'), and 'opinion' (or 'view', 'thought'). 'An orthodox', is a right-minded, or right-thinking, person; an orthodox view or practice is one common to orthodox people. In the context of Christianity or Christendom, the word 'Christian' is implied. 'An orthodox' is an orthodox *Christian*. Orthodoxy is orthodox *Christianity* or Christendom. The first use of the word (so N.E.D.) was in contrast to *un*orthodox Christians, i.e. those of the Nestorian or Monophysite churches, sometimes, confusingly, spoken of as 'Eastern' Christianity. Where the word *Eastern* is prefixed, Eastern Orthodox(y) is being contrasted with Western Catholic(ism). Implicit in the words orthodox or Christian thus used is the suggestion: orthodox or Christian 'in the mind of all others thus minded', and the further suggestion: '. . . whom God will eventually show to have been right'.

The term 'Eastern', in this context, originally referred to the Eastern divisions of the Roman empire (as divided in AD 395): the Eastern provinces could be roughly marked out by a great square, the sides running east from near Belgrade, through Bucharest and Sebastopol, to Batum; south from Batum to the gulf of Aqaba; west through Alexandria to Benghazi; thence north through Corfu and Albania, back to Belgrade. (The triangle between the upper Danube and the Adriatic was a frontier province, often re-allocated.)

Greek had been spoken everywhere within this square, and, outside it, at least in southern Italy. Westerners therefore sometimes speak of the Eastern Orthodox as 'Greek Orthodox' or 'Greek Catholic', and even define them as those in communion with the Ecumenical Patriarch (of Constantinople). For the Eastern Orthodox themselves the 'mind of all others like-minded' is defined not locally (no bishop can command all others) nor linguistically (no tongue is privileged), but historically.

The Orthodox Church is the Church of the Seven Councils (Nicea, 325; Constantinople I, 381; Ephesus, 431; Chalcedon, 451; Constantinople II, 553; Constantinople III, 680; Nicea II, 787). The 'feast of Orthodoxy', on the first Sunday in Lent, commemorates the recovery, in 842, of freedom to venerate the sacred images (icons), which the Council of 787 had defined and defended: then 'blessings are invoked upon the champions of Orthodoxy and anathemas upon its foes'. Nicea I gave the Church its universal creed, and asserted the divinity of Christ's person against Arius; Constantinople I completed the creed, against those who denied the personal divinity of the Holy Spirit, and asserted the completeness of Christ's manhood, against Apollinaris; Ephesus condemned Nestorius, asserting against him the unity of Christ's person in his two natures – so that Mary is rightly styled mother of God (*theotokos*): Chalcedon, against Eutyches, asserted that Christ's divine and human natures remain distinct. Constantinople II tried to reconcile those who had rejected the formula of Chalcedon by posthumously condemning some opinions of Origen and some passages of three Nestorian writers. Constantinople III asserted two distinct centres of will and activity in the one Christ; and Nicaea II claimed that the incarnation makes it lawful to depict the manhood of incarnate God, and the figures of those whom God indwells; to worship God, and to glorify his grace, by use of such pictures. This use had been common since 250 and dominant since 400, until the puritan reaction in Asia Minor in the mid-eighth century (*see* **Iconoclasm**).

Though Eastern Orthodoxy meant originally Christianity as received and understood in the Greek-speaking lands of the eastern Roman empire, and the Byzantine emperor continued to style himself 'Prince of the Romans', it has not remained confined to that area. Round the South-eastern and Eastern shores of the Mediterranean, and in Asia Minor, it has dwindled since the coming of Islam, the Arabs in the seventh century and the Turks in the eleventh. Within the 'square' defined above, it has expanded to the north, and far beyond it, to the north-east, in Georgia, Russia and across Siberia. It is still the dominant form of Christianity in Bulgaria, Yugoslavia and Romania. Colonies of Orthodox exist in most European countries, in North America, East Africa and Japan.

Already by 864 Western and Eastern missionaries were competing for the allegiance of the Bulgarian converts. A bishop was sent to Kiev in the same year. A Serbian prince was converted a little later; and prince Vladimir of Kiev, the 'Russian Constantine', in 988. Bulgaria was recognized as an independent Patriarchate in 945 (and again, in modern times, in 1946, after a rift over jurisdiction); Serbia in 1375; Moscow, not till 1589. Peter the Great abolished the Moscow Patriarchate in 1721, and replaced it by a synod, of which only three members were bishops, under a lay procurator. It was not restored until 1917, when an all-Russian council met, under the Provisional Government.

The pioneers of this vast expansion of Orthodoxy within and outside the limits of the Roman Empire, were two Greek brothers, Saints Cyril and Methodius, who invented a modification of the Greek alphabet, and used it to translate scriptures and service-books into the dialect of the Slavs of Macedonia. This Church Slavonic became and remains the language of the Bulgarian, Serbian and Russian churches. The conversion of Romania, where Roman colonists were numerous, was much more gradual, and its language remains an amalgam of Latin with Slavonic. Romania achieved political unity and independence only in 1862, and ecclesiastical independence as late as 1885. Orthodoxy is thus no more coterminous with Slavonic than with Greek speech. Though Serbia and the Romanians resisted Latin attempts to win them over throughout the Middle Ages, Croats, Slovenes, Czechs, Slovaks and Poles became and remain Western, Roman, Catholics.

N. Zernov, in his *Eastern Christendom* (1961, pp. 222–6), gives a useful list of the independent churches which today make up the Eastern Orthodox Church. From the original nucleus within the empire come the Patriarchates of (1) Constantinople (given precedence of honour after Old Rome in 381), (2) Alexandria, (3) Antioch and (4) Jerusalem, the churches of (5) Greece (independent since 1852), of (6) Cyprus (since 431), the monastery of (7) Sinai (since 1782) and the Catholicate of (8) Georgia. From missionary effort in the Middle Ages, and since, come the Patriarchates of (1) Moscow, (2) Bulgaria, (3) Yugoslavia, and (4) Romania, the church of (5) Albania, and those of the Orthodox in (6) Poland and (7) Czechoslovakia. Modern mission churches still dependent on some support from outside are those in Hungary, Finland, China and Japan. Dr Zernov gives rough figures for the membership of these various groups, totalling 150 million, which show that the Greeks outnumber the Arabs by nearly twenty to one, the other Balkan churches outnumber the Greeks by more than three to one, and the Russians outnumber all the rest put together by more than three to two. The Ecumenical Patriarch, now practically a prisoner in Constantinople (Istanbul), has jurisdiction over little more than half a million, including Crete, and the monastic 'republic' of Mount Athos.

The organization of Orthodoxy, by which, within national churches, the bishops and their dioceses are held together, assembled at need, guided and represented (much as the Anglican clergy in England are by a rural dean) by one of their number, normally the bishop of the capital city, styled Metropolitan or Patriarch, goes back to before 'the peace of the Church' under Constantine. The Church then spontaneously followed the provincial divisions of the empire, and the bishop of the chief city of each province spoke to and for any others within it. This was regularized by the great councils. The wider dominance of Rome, Antioch and Alexandria, likewise, was due to spontaneous recognition of their *de facto* pre-eminence. The later inclusion of Constantinople (and eventually of Moscow) was won by diplomatic assertion of an actual shift in the balance of influence: Jerusalem, however, gained Patriarchal status on purely honorific grounds. The same pattern has been followed since.

This modelling of the Church organization on that of civil society, together with Greek willingness (contrasted with Latin refusal) to accept the use of scripture and liturgy in the native language of the barbarian convert peoples, and Turkish insistence on treating their Christian subjects as a separate people, administering and taxing them through their bishops, has had a double result. It effectively identified Church and people through four hundred years of shared servitude; but, on the other hand, besides compromising many of those who had to act as go-betweens, it made it hard for the subject peoples to distinguish in thought between their nationality and their Christianity, or to identify themselves with Christians elsewhere who had not shared their experience. The Patriarchs of Constantinople, in particular, were placed in a false position of influence without power.

The Byzantine empire was an autocracy, and by many of its subject-peoples was felt as a foreign tyranny: they avenged themselves by espousing 'heresy' or by welcoming the Moslem invader. From 1453 till sometime in the nineteenth century the north-west as well as the south-east of the 'square' of the Eastern empire was at the mercy of the Turks: but Russia had already experienced the equally stifling and stultifying rule of the Tartars, from 1240 to 1480; from 1721 to 1917 the Russian church and people were cramped and inhibited by the Germanic St Petersburg bureaucracy; and then, after only the briefest interval, fell under the worse tyranny of Communism, working deliberately, where earlier tyrants had worked only sporadically or inadvertently, for the destruction of religion; a tyranny which, with the second World War, was extended to the only recently freed countries and churches of the Balkans. To keep the faith, at the cost of degradation, deprivation, even martyrdom, has, therefore, so often been all that the Orthodox could do, that it is no wonder if, since the eighth century, scholarship has often been scanty among them, and political and social theory and action minimal, at least till the brilliant outcrop of lay theologians in late nineteenth century Russia, and in the emigration since. Russia has now only two theological academies, and Constantinople one: Greece, only two university faculties or schools of theology. Centuries of oppression, with effective revolt impossible, have bred a temper of passive acquiescence, coupled with inward withdrawal from the State and its alien purposes. This, however, is often combined with ardent patriotism, and with compassion and forgiveness for those who bear the burden of rule. It is only in the light of this long experience of the Orthodox churches that it is possible to understand their attitude to Christian faith and life.

To be orthodox is to share the views and practices of all who are like-minded. This would mean that orthodoxy had no content, unless we start with some one particular set of people. We do. We start with the apostles. But we of the present day, and all the orthodox everywhere, are in touch with the apostles not merely through history and archaeology, but through tradition, the living memory of the Church. And tradition, handing-over, works not only onwards from the

past, but outwards in the present, and on into the future. It is only partially embodied in anyone, or anything, less than the whole Church; not the Fathers only, not the Councils only, not the bishops and clergy, not the theologians only, but all orthodox believers. In the days of the first or second general Councils, it was essential to accept the creed as they proclaimed it, for otherwise you would not be worshipping the God or the Christ or the Spirit the apostles knew. It was essential, but it was not sufficient. So in the days of the third Council, it was essential to retain the creed unchanged, but it was not sufficient – not if you denied to the Mother of the Lord her traditional title. The argument was the same that St Basil (379) had used to defend the personal divinity of the Spirit, when he argued from the customary language of the Church in its prayers.

The obligation to receive the faith as it comes to us from our forbears carries with it the obligation to hand it over to our contemporaries and down to our successors: and this cannot be done without recognizing and meeting the new needs of our day. The Spanish Christians who in the sixth century added to the words of the creed: 'the Holy Ghost who proceedeth from the Father' the further words 'and from the Son' were entitled so to believe, since holy men before them had said the like; and even to exact such a profession from their converts among the local Arians, if it seemed necessary; but not to impose their addition on the rest of the church, without consultation; still less to blame others for failing to do so, or – worst of all – to accuse them of having deleted it. On this offence against brotherhood every attempt to mend the worsening relations between Eastern and Western Christendom in the Middle Ages broke. It was seen as a symptom of the unbrotherly arrogance prompting the ever more peremptory assertions by the popes of their right to supervise all other bishops; and this suspicion, for most Orthodox then and since, was only confirmed by the Crusaders' capture and sack of Constantinople in 1204, and the Western connivance at its final capture by the Turks in 1453.

Fidelity to tradition is ultimately fidelity, in the present, to Christ, the master of the apostles, and himself the revelation of the Father. Freedom within the tradition is the result of the realization that it is the Spirit, the gift of Christ from the Father, who communicates the revelation to the believer and restores in the church the image of God according to the likeness of Christ. To this conviction is owing the welcome given to the new life of monasticism in the third and fourth centuries, and the part it has played in Orthodox prayer and worship ever since. It was and is an escape to freedom, freedom to follow the biddings of the Spirit. Among the Fathers of the Egyptian and Syrian Desert were worked out the principles and practices of the life of devotion which monks have been passing on to laymen ever since. (Every bishop in Orthodoxy must be a monk, and monasteries have been the chief centres of spiritual direction.) The most learned of the Desert

Fathers, Evagrius (346–399), left teaching which was developed by Simeon the New Theologian at Constantinople in the tenth century, and by Gregory Palamas on Mt Athos in the fourteenth, and is exemplified in St Seraphim in Russia in the eighteenth. Solitary prayer is a matter of turning from this world which is passing away: but common prayer, and the sacraments (the mysteries, in Orthodox language) are a matter of greeting the transfigured world which is to be; and here too the Orthodox owe to the monks the bulk of the prayers, the hymns (with their chants) and the icons in which matter and senses are put at the service of the Spirit, so that right belief may be shown forth in right worship.

The Orthodox Liturgy, 1939–1954; *Orthodox Spirituality* by a monk of the Eastern Church, 1945; H. Chadwick, *The Early Church*, 1967; M. Rinvolucri, *Anatomy of a Church: Greek Orthodoxy Today*, 1966; T. Ware (Fr Kallistos), *The Orthodox Church*, 1963; N. Zernov, *Eastern Christendom*, 1961.

                                    PATRICK THOMPSON

Osiander, Andreas

Andreas Osiander (1498–1552) studied at Ingolstadt and was ordained priest. Having joined the cause of Luther he issued in 1552 an improved Latin Bible. At Nuremberg he became celebrated for his controversial sermons and wrote against the Franciscan Kaspar Schatzgeier on the Mass. He was instrumental in the publication of the *De revolutionibus* (1545) of Copernicus for which he wrote an anonymous preface representing its new cosmology as hypothesis only. After the *Interim* of Charles V Osiander went to Breslau and then to Königsberg (1549) where as professor of theology he published three short treatises (1550–1) bearing startling interpretations of Justification: *Whether the Son of God would have been Incarnated if Sin had not entered into the World: Disputation on Justification; Confession of Jesus Christ the only Mediator and of Justification by Faith.* Osiander's life was a succession of controversies, but the term 'Osiandrian Controversy' applies to the disputes that followed these writings. His teaching that Christ imparts to the believer the 'essential righteousness' of his divine nature was generally repudiated in Lutheranism and sharply attacked by J. Calvin, *Institutes*, iii, 11, 5–12.

Concordia Triglotta, German, Latin, English, ed. F. Bente and W. H. T. Dau, reprint Minneapolis, 1955; E. Hirsch, *Die Theologie des Andreas Osiander*, 1919; W. Niesel, 'Calvin wider Osianders Rechtfertigungslehre', *Zeitschrift für Kirchengeschichte*, XLVI, 1927, 410–30.

                                    J. T. MCNEILL

Otto, Rudolf

Rudolf Otto (1869–1937), German Protestant philosopher and theologian, was a pupil and member of the Marburg neo-Kantian philosophical school. His vastly influential classic *The Idea of the Holy* (ET, 1923) attempted to show that at the heart of *all* religion is the inter-subjective experience of the *Mysterium tremendum et fascinans*, which is possible for all humans as such through their possession of an innate 'feeling for the numinous', which Otto held was not unlike one of Kant's *a priori* categories of the mind. Otto was a celebrated student of the thought of F. D. E. Schleiermacher (q.v.) and of oriental religions.

                                    JAMES RICHMOND

Oxford Movement

The Movement, strictly speaking, began with John Keble's (q.v.) Assize sermon in 1833 and ended in 1845 with J. H. Newman's (q.v.) secession to Rome, but its antecedents go back long before the first date, and the consequences are still powerfully felt in western non-Roman Christendom. In origin a protest against the Erastianism (q.v.) of the Church of England it gave fresh life and direction to the dry high church tradition which had persisted from the Caroline Divines (q.v.). Keble's religious poetry (which helped to bring a romantic temper to the interpretation of the Prayer Book) and the influence of his attractive personality prepared the way; Newman's preaching aroused a devoted response from Oxford men who were to become influential in church and state. The publication, largely under the inspiration of Newman, of the *Tracts for the Times* between 1833 and 1840 gave the Movement its popular name and carried its message far and wide over the country. Their leading ideas were sketched out in the discussions among a group of like-minded friends who assembled around Newman at Oriel College, and they were at first written in an urgent compelling style and provided a standard and a battle cry for those who thought the church to be in danger. The danger was conceived of as twofold, the radical attack on the privileges of the established church, and the liberal criticism of dogma. Behind these the Tractarians saw a widespread apathy and mediocrity in Christian life. They summoned men, therefore, first to holiness; reminded the bishops of their spiritual authority which did not depend upon the state (hence their increasing stress on the apostolic succession as the basis of this authority) and all churchmen of the inviolability of catholic truth enshrined in the creeds and conforming to the Vincentian canon. At first the movement aroused a great deal of favourable response, but soon the evangelicals and old fashioned high churchmen became alarmed at what they felt to be the Romewards tendency of some of the leaders, and Newman's secession brought its first phase to an end. Under other leaders, notably E. B. Pusey, its principles were carried all over the Anglican communion. For a description of the consequences *see* **Anglo-Catholicism; Ritualism.**

Owen Chadwick, *The Mind of the Oxford Movement*, 1960; R. W. Church, *The Oxford Move-*

ment, 1891; E. R. Fairweather, ed., *The Oxford Movement*, 1964.

R. CANT

Paedobaptism

From Greek *paidos*, a child, and *baptizo*, to dip, baptize. Hence 'infant baptism'. *See* **Initiation, Christian.**

Paganism

The word is derived from Latin *paganus*, a peasant; *pagus*, a village or rural area; one who is not a Christian, Jew or Muslim (i.e. a worshipper of many gods; idolater). It is said that the word was thus used because the Christianization of the rural areas was inevitably much slower than that of the cities; hence 'countryman' and 'idolater' became synonymous terms. *Cf. also* the word 'heathen' (from Anglo-Saxon *haethen*, lit. 'one inhabiting a heath', a countryman).

Paley's Watch

William Paley (1743–1805), a Fellow of Christ's College, Cambridge who eventually became Archdeacon of Carlisle, was a somewhat unoriginal writer whose books nevertheless became standard texts for generations of students. Chief among them was his *Evidences of Christianity* (1794), an apologetic work in which the arguments for a divine Author of the universe were set out in considerable detail. He was an able mathematician, well versed in the mechanistic views of natural science prevalent in his day. He held that the marvellous construction of an eye or of a butterfly's wing implied the existence of a master-craftsman who had fashioned instruments so perfectly adapted for the function which they were designed to fulfil. If the universe exhibited the mechanical regularity of a watch which kept perfect time, the existence of a divine Watchmaker must be presupposed. However, this version of the argument from design or teleological argument (q.v.) was called in question when Charles Darwin's *Origin of Species* (1859) put forward the hypothesis that the eye or the butterfly's wing could be more adequately accounted for by the principle of natural selection in the course of evolution without recourse to the assumption of a divine Creator. The fittest for their biological purpose would be likely to survive: hence the evolution of species with perfectly adapted eyes, wings, etc. The biological categories thus replaced mechanistic ones, and 'Darwinism' had to be taken into account by theologians of the later nineteenth century. Darwin himself (1809–1882) became increasingly agnostic in religion, but theologians (apart from the vociferous conservatives) did not generally oppose the idea of the evolution of species; their historical and biblical studies were in any case leading them towards the doctrine of progress (or evolution) in

men's ideas of God, from those of primitive religion to the noble ideas of the Hebrew prophets and of the Christian revelation. By the end of the nineteenth century the theme of 'progressive revelation' was much cherished by liberal theologians, especially in Britain. Today there is much discussion among biologists about the adequacy of 'Darwinism' (i.e. in this context the theory of natural selection as against other factors, such as environment), but there is general agreement among scientists and theologians about the fact of the evolution of species, if not about the precise manner of it. Much has happened since Paley's time; yet even if his eye and butterfly's wing have lost something of their apologetic value, his watch still raises a question, though in a less crude form: is it sufficient to say that the mathematical exactitude of the physical universe just 'happened', or that it just happens to be the way things are? Or must we say that a Great Mathematician 'must' have worked out the formulae from 'the beginning'? The question remains.

EDITOR

Palingenesis

From Greek *palin*, again, and *genesis*, birth, origin; hence the word is the equivalent of Latin *regeneration* (*see* **Initiation, Christian**). In secular usage it may mean a transformation or metamorphosis, as of insects.

Panentheism

A Greek compound word meaning 'everything (exists) in God', thus indicating a conception rather different from pantheism, which holds that everything is divine. The word originated with K. C. F. Krause (1781–1832) as a title for his own philosophy. In our day process theology (q.v.) may be said to be panentheistic.

Panpsychism

Panpsychism is the theory that everything in the universe enjoys a measure of psychic life or consciousness, put forward by G. T. Fechner (1801–1887) and other nineteenth-century philosophers. It has received little support from theologians.

Pantheism

This word is said to have been coined by the deist John Toland in 1705; it is derived from Greek *pan*, 'all', and *theos*, 'God'. It denotes the view which is an opposite of deism, namely, that the whole universe is divine. In the East Hinduism is pantheistic (all *life* is especially sacred). In the West Spinoza (1632–1677) with his formula *Deus sive Natura* ('God, otherwise Nature') is the best known philosopher of pantheism, which in his hands is a deeply religious or mystical form of materialism. Mysticism often finds expression in pantheistic language. But for the main line of biblical-Christian thinking pantheism is entirely abhorrent, because it does away with the absolute qualitative distinction between the creature and the Creator.

EDITOR

Papacy

The title 'pope' (papa – father) was in the early Western Church given to any important or outstanding bishop (e.g. Cyprian) and in the Eastern Church it was applied to the bishop of Alexandria. But it gradually became restricted to the bishop of Rome. During the second and third centuries the bishop of Rome exercised considerable moral authority, based partly on the political pre-eminence of his see but more on the fact that both Peter and Paul had been martyred and were commemorated in Rome. He must also by the third century have exerted some executive authority over a large area round the city of Rome itself, for Cornelius in 251 was able to depose the rural bishops who had consecrated his rival Novatian. The jurisdiction of the bishop of Rome over the Western Church, in the sense of his right to hear appeals, as contrasted with his merely occupying a position in which he could be appealed to (which he had long enjoyed), was recognized by the Council of Sardica (343). Thereafter the history of Papal authority in the West is one of increasing claims and increasing power, marked by various milestones represented by Leo I (440–61), Gregory VII (1073–85) and Innocent III (1198–1216). The climax was perhaps reached with Boniface VIII (1294–1303), who in his bull *Unam Sanctam* (1302) declared that both the temporal and the spiritual power were in the power of the Church and the former was subject to the latter, and concluded that it is altogether necessary for the salvation of every human creature to be subject to the Roman pontiff. Boniface VIII was not able to maintain in practice his extensive claims (as Innocent III had been able) and from his reign dates the origin of the gradual erosion and finally the virtual extinction of the Pope's temporal power. But the papacy still maintains its claim to universal spiritual authority and jurisdiction.

The Eastern Orthodox Church has usually allowed the pope primacy and indeed authority over the Western Church. On occasions of extreme pressure (e.g. the Council of Lyons 1274–89, and the Council of Ferrara-Florence 1438–45) its representatives professed themselves ready to admit all the claims of the pope of the period, but these admissions were never consistently endorsed by the Orthodox Church as a whole. The churches of the Reformation began by rejecting the jurisdiction of the pope (for the Reformation was essentially a crisis of authority) but quickly found that his temporal power and all his other claims were bound up with this. The identification of the pope with anti-Christ was first made by the defeated minority movement within the Franciscans in the fourteenth century, but was ardently taken up by most of the Reformed traditions. Though it has appealed in some forms to a few modern theologians (e.g. Reinhold Niebuhr) it is now virtually restricted to extreme and fanatical minority groups. The controversy about the papacy today usually turns on the interpretation of the scriptural evidence about the position of Peter, the relation of Peter to his successors (if any), the subject of authority and the question of infallibility. Most non-Roman Catholic Christians today would find the historical claims of the papacy uncongenial not only on the ground that they cannot find satisfactory support in Scripture and tradition but also because many of them appear to betray a repulsive spirit of self-aggrandisement masquerading under religious pretexts, difficult to reconcile with a proper Christian humility. But two recent developments have tended to modify this attitude. One is the great increase of esteem for the pope simply as a leader of Christian opinion shown ever since the pontificate of John XXIII by the leaders of non-Roman Catholic communions in the last few years, and especially displayed in the new practice of their paying visits of courtesy to the pope. This is to be distinguished from one not inconsiderable section of Anglican opinion which has always shown itself ready to accord to the pope a primacy of honour (but not jurisdiction) as head of the Western Church, much as the archbishop of Canterbury is accorded a primacy of honour in the Anglican communion. The other recent development is the tendency showed in the Second Vatican Council to limit the authority of the pope by emphasizing the relationship of 'collegiality' which all bishops enjoy towards him as a fellow-bishop, without ostensibly affecting his historic claims to be bishop of bishops and to exercise a plenitude of power over all bishops.

H. Burn-Murdoch, *The Development of the Papacy*, 1954; J. Chapman, *Studies on the Early Papacy*, 1928; T. G. Jalland, *The Church and the Papacy*, 1944; B. J. Kidd, *The Roman Primacy to AD 461*, 1936.

                                    R. P. C. HANSON

Paraclete

Paraclete is a Greek word meaning 'defending counsel' (in a lawsuit). It is used as a title of the Holy Spirit in the Fourth Gospel (John 14.16, 26; 15.26; 16.7). The older English versions translated it by 'comforter' (i.e., strengthener, helper), but Vulgate and NEB 'advocate' is the better. The spirit defends the Christian against the accusations of his adversary (i.e. Satan). (*See* NT commentaries.) The idea behind 'comforter' was drawn from the context of the word in the Fourth Gospel: the Spirit would 'console' the disciples after Christ had 'gone away'.

                                    EDITOR

Paradox

A paradoxical statement is one that runs 'against opinion' (Greek: *para* and *doxa*), often one that is *prima facie* self-contradictory or absurd, but which may or may not prove to be so on examination. Among the 'logical paradoxes' are Zeno's arguments against the possibility of motion (e.g: to traverse a distance, half the distance must first be crossed, then half of the remaining distance, and so on, *ad infinitum*. But it is impossible to traverse an infinite number of lengths in a finite time. Therefore motion is impossible). In modern logic great attention has been paid to paradoxes arising out of problems in the logic of classes. A lighthearted one that can be briefly stated is the 'Barber' paradox. Suppose there is a village barber who shaves all those villagers (and those only) who do not shave themselves. Does he shave himself or not? If he does shave himself, then he has to be counted among those who are not shaved by the barber. If he does not shave himself, he belongs to the class of non-self-shavers and thus is one of those whom the barber shaves: i.e., if he does shave himself, he does not; if he does not, he does.

What can be concluded from this sort of paradox? In the Zeno case, not that motion has been proved impossible, for we know well enough that it *is* possible; but that some confusion (about space and time as continua, about finite distance and infinite divisibility) must have entered the argument. So with the Barber: the conclusion must be that there could *be* no person, so described. The philosopher's task is to show how the paradox arises and how it may be dispelled: and he often learns something of importance to logic or metaphysics in the process.

But in philosophy of religion, the situation is rather more difficult. Practitioners of many of the religions claim that their account of the divine must contain paradox – paradox that cannot be eliminated, and which is not the product of logical confusion. Brahman and atman are one: Brahman is both near and far. God is transcendent and yet immanent: eternal, yet active in the temporal world: in some sense personal, yet lacking the finite, limited characteristics that normally make personality intelligible. What attitude is it reasonable to assume to paradoxes like these? Certainly not one of uncritical acceptance; for if an alleged paradox should really be a straight *contradiction*, the theology in which it appears is vitiated. Elementary logic can show that from a contradiction any statement, however absurd, can be derived. And it will always be open to the sceptic to say – as in the Barber case – that if contradictoriness enters the description of the deity, there cannot *be* a deity so described. The theologian's task will be to demonstrate that the paradoxes are not in fact contradictions, that more outrage would be done to his total experience by denying any part of the paradox than by affirming it. This defence cannot be complete unless he also takes issue with the various alternative, naturalistic interpretations, which try to explain why paradoxical language seems forced upon the believer, but explain his experience in non-cognitive terms.

R. W. Hepburn, *Christianity and Paradox*, 1958; J. Wisdom, *Paradox and Discovery*, 1965.

R. W. HEPBURN

Parousia. see Eschatology.

Parthenogenesis

The word is derived from Greek meaning 'birth from a virgin'. The word is used by entomologists of certain reproductive processes of the insect-world, and it has been transferred, somewhat inappropriately, by some writers to discussions concerning the Virgin Birth of Christ (q.v.).

Pascal, Blaise

Pascal (1623–1662), French mathematician and philosopher, won for himself a deserved high place in the history of modern science. After 1654, when he was converted to Christianity, Pascal took a great interest in theological and religious matters. Holding that religious belief can neither be conclusively vindicated nor refuted by rational argument, he advocated 'wagering one's life' on its truth, on the grounds of prudence. He attacked the God of Cartesian functionalism ('the God of the philosophers and men of science') and advocated adherence and fidelity to the God of inner Christian religious experience ('the God of Abraham, of Isaac and of Jacob'). He is occasionally, but rather inaccurately and anachronistically, described as an 'early existentialist'.

JAMES RICHMOND

Pasch, Paschal

Originally a Hebrew word (from Hebrew *pāsach*, to pass over; *cf.* Ex. 12), it is taken over into Greek and Latin as *pascha* as a name for Easter, the Christian Passover (*cf.* I Cor. 5.7 f.). The word has survived in several English dialects in such forms as 'pace-eggs' (Easter eggs). The derivation of *pasch* from the Greek *pascho*, to suffer, is an error, but a felicitous one. From ancient times various paschal ceremonies have been observed in the Western Church, e.g. on Holy Saturday the lighting of the Paschal Candle from the 'new fire' symbolizing the resurrection-light. Baptisms took place at these liturgical celebrations (signifying the being buried with Christ in baptism, Rom. 6.3–5). In modern forms a renewal of baptismal vows on the part of the congregation is often incorporated into the rite. *See also* **Passiontide.**

EDITOR

Passion

In a Christian context, this word applies exclusively to Christ's redemptive suffering, particularly to the last days culminating in his crucifixion. It derives etymologically from the Latin *passio* (suffering) not from the Greek *pascha* (Passover). We have grown accustomed to think of Christ's Passion and suffering, but that should not blind us to the fact of its utter inappropriateness and incongruity to a Greek who could never allow suffering and sympathy and feeling to be associated with God. The very adoption of the word begs the entire work of God's costly redemption of man, and carries the whole connotation of atonement (q.v.). *See also* **Passiontide; Pasch; Passover; Cross; Redemption.**

JAMES ATKINSON

Passiontide

Passiontide, Latin *passio*, suffering (from *patior*, to suffer; *cf.* Greek *pathos*; *cf. also* 'patient', 'passive', 'compatible', etc.), applied to the Passion or Suffering of the crucified Christ. Traditionally Passion Sunday is the fifth Sunday in Lent, when Passion-music (Bach, etc.) is nowadays often rendered. Passion Week begins on the sixth Sunday in Lent ('Palm Sunday') and lasts until Holy Saturday or Easter Eve. Pasch (q.v.) originally combined the commemoration of both the suffering (*passus sub Pontio Pilato*) and resurrection of Christ in the great feast of the Christian Passover. *See also* **Pasch.**

EDITOR

Passover. *see* Pasch; Eucharist, Eucharistic Theology.

Pastoralia, Pastoral Theology

Pastoral theology, or pastoralia, is that branch of theological education which concerns the theoretical and practical training of clergy and ministers for their proper work. It varies considerably in content and emphasis from one denomination to another. It would be generally agreed, at least in principle, that training in the devotional and spiritual life should have a high priority. It includes preparation for the conduct of public worship and the administration of the sacraments, the art of preaching (homiletics, q.v.), the cure of souls, the ministry to the sick, the bereaved and the dying, and nowadays also the practical study of the social agencies, youth work, teaching-methods, industrial relations – and indeed so many other matters in which the minister is likely to be involved that a long and very thorough course of training, including practical work, would be needed if pastoral theology is to be truly effective.

EDITOR

Patripassianism

Patripassianism is a nickname applied to modalism (q.v.) by its opponents taken from a corollary of the doctrine. 'If Christ is God, he must be identical with the Father, and, if he is identical with the Father, then, since Christ suffered, the Father suffered' (Noetus). According to Tertullian, Praxeas maintained that 'the Father was born and the Father suffered'. The term is drawn from Tertullian's charge that Praxeas 'banished the Paraclete (through his opposition to Montanism) and crucified the Father (through his modalist views)'. An improved variant of these modalist statements is also cited by Tertullian, 'the Son suffered, the Father co-suffered' (*patitur, compatitur*); but this is either a mere verbal amendment or shipwrecks the modalist position, since 'What else is compassion but "suffering with"?' (Tertullian). At least at this stage of its development modalism regarded the modes as successive and not simultaneous. The compassion of the Father with the Son (purged of any modalist associations) became orthodox teaching on the subject. *See also* **Death of God Theology.**

H. E. W. TURNER

Patristic, Patristics

The patristic age is in normal theological usage the period from immediately after the NT period to the end of the eighth century (though this date is sometimes extended so far as to include St Thomas Aquinas). 'The Fathers' (*patres*) are all the important theological writers of the patristic age, and patristics is the branch of theology which studies their writings. *See* **Patrology; Apostolic Fathers.**

Patrology

Patrology is the science of studying the writings of the early Fathers of the Church, whose number is generally reckoned to have ceased with John of Damascus (c. 675–749).

R. P. C. HANSON

Paul of Samosata

Paul of Samosata (third century), bishop of Antioch, c. 260, was deposed (not without difficulty) by a Synod composed mainly of Origenist Bishops in 268. His opinions are preserved in scanty fragments, some of doubtful authenticity and most without their context, by opponents often of much later date. Much, therefore, is necessarily uncertain though there are two fixed points, a sharply phrased dualism in christology and his opposition to Origenist views.

Different interpretations of his doctrine of God are current.

1. Some (e.g. R. Seeberg and J. N. D. Kelly) regard him as a strict unipersonalist who denied any personal subsistence to the Word. With this view his christology would be in accord and his monist starting-point in theology is not in doubt. He could speak of the Word as immanent in the heart of God as reason in man, and according to Hilary he used the *Homoousios* in the sense that 'God was unique and solitary to himself'. It is, however, more probable (especially in view of his descriptions of the Word as the utterance or the command of God) that, like the apologist Theophilus of Antioch and some others, he believed that the Word, first immanent within the One God, received a quasi-hypostatic existence in the course of God's operations towards Creation. A view of this kind would explain his intense opposition to Origenism, its pluralist Logos doctrine, its assertion of full independent existence as a *Hypostasis* (q.v.) beside the Father. Possibly a similar controversy arose over the meaning of the *Homoousios*. There are also some fragments which appear to speak of the Holy Spirit as an independent grace or force. This evidence suggests a doctrine more complex and subtle than bare unitarianism.

2. One widely accepted view describes him as a dynamic monarchian or binitarian (*see* **Monarchianism; Binitarianism**). This is confirmed by the

reply of his judges who (in response to a query where he could find communion after his expulsion from the Church) suggested that he might send letters of communion to Artemon or Artemas, a contemporary member of this school. His christology would also harmonize with dynamic binitarian opinions. Two factors, however, tell against this theory, the independent mention of the Holy Spirit besides the Father and the Son in a few fragments and the probability that he held a distinctive view of the relationship of the Father and the Word. Neither has any counterpart in dynamic binitarianism.

3. F. Loofs found in the fragments of Paul of Samosata echoes of Irenaeus and Tertullian and anticipations of Marcellus of Ancyra (q.v.). He saw in Paul of Samosata an economic trinitarian (*see* **Economic Trinity**), maintaining that, while God was initially One, he posited dispensing activities which became independent *Hypostases* during the course of his economy for creatures. With this view what we can learn of his doctrine of the relationship between the Father and the Word would harmonize well enough, and it might possibly explain the two sets of passages which speak of the Spirit, now as a third grace, now as included together with the Word in the Father. We never, however, hear in the fragments of an actual unfolding of the Godhead and the data with regard to the Spirit are too scanty to admit of satisfactory interpretation. This theory must then remain an attractive but unproved possibility.

Paul seems to have enjoyed considerable local support, certainly of a political but probably also of a theological character. After his condemnation his followers appear to have created a schism which lasted until the Council of Nicea.

G. Bardy, *Paul de Samosate*, 1923; F. Loofs, *Paulus von Samosata*, 1924; H. de Riedmatten, *Les actes du procès de Paul de Samosate*, 1952.

H. E. W. TURNER

Paulinism

Paulinism is the term applied to the taking of 'Christianity according to St Paul', and especially his characteristic contrasts between law and grace, faith and works, as the norm of all Christianity, so that other parts of the NT (not to mention later Christian writings) are either virtually ignored or interpreted so as to conform to the Pauline position.

P. S. WATSON

Pelagianism. *see* Predestination (1).

Penance

Penance is one of the seven sacraments of Catholicism, and the means for obtaining remission of mortal sins (q.v.) committed after baptism. It avails of course also for venial sins (q.v.) though these can be remedied by other acts of devotion. The sacrament is held to have been instituted by

Christ when he gave his Church power to forgive or refuse to forgive sins (Matt. 16.19; 18.18; John 20.21 ff.). This power is not the prerogative of all Christians, but only of the priesthood, since it is a judicial power such as can be exercised only by a person in an official position. Even a priest, however, cannot exercise it validly except within the jurisdiction conferred on him by competent authority (usually the bishop), and even then there are or may be certain sins with which he is not authorized to deal, but which are reserved for higher authority.

The constituent elements of the sacrament are, on the part of the sinner, contrition, confession and satisfaction, and on the part of the priest, the pronouncing of absolution. Contrition is necessary, since the impenitent cannot be forgiven. Confession is also necessary, because a judicial sentence can only be pronounced on the facts made known to the judge. It must therefore be as full and circumstantial as possible, and normally it must be made orally and in private to the priest. Satisfaction is an act or acts of atonement, expiation, or making amends – commonly called doing penance – prescribed by the priest in accordance with the Church's rules of penitential discipline. Its value lies, not in the act itself, but in its union with Christ's atonement, which is effected through the sacrament. Failure to perform the satisfaction does not invalidate the sacrament, provided the will to perform it was present when the absolution was pronounced, though culpable failure is sin. The absolution follows on the confession, must normally be spoken by the priest in the presence of the penitent, and may be longer or shorter in form. The shortest prescribed form is: 'I absolve thee from all censures and sins in the Name of the Father, and of the Son and of the Holy Ghost. Amen.' Normally it is accompanied by prescribed prayers.

Classical Protestantism denies the sacramental status of penance, and rejects the idea of satisfaction, but retains confession and absolution. It holds that the power of the keys was given by Christ to the whole Church as part of the ministry of the Word, and while ordained ministers or priests have a special responsibility for it, they have no monopoly of it. This power is exercised, as Calvin says (*Institutes* iii, 4, 14), in three main ways: (1) when a whole congregation joins in the general confession and the minister pronounces absolution in the name of God; (2) when individual offenders, guilty of grave misdoing, confess and are absolved in the presence of the congregation; and (3) when an individual with a burdened conscience makes private confession to the minister and seeks absolution. It can also be legitimately exercised by a Christian layman to whom a brother layman unburdens his soul. As regards the idea of satisfaction, the Reformers repudiated it chiefly because it was bound up with the doctrine of merit and indulgences (q.v.), which cheapened the grace of God and obscured the all-sufficiency of Christ's atoning work. Had it been understood simply as a disciplinary measure to test the genuineness of penitence, and as a deterrent against further sinning, they would have found little reason to object to it.

J. M. T. Barton, *Penance and Absolution*, 1961; R. C. Mortimer, *The Origins of Private Penance in the Western Church*, 1939; B. Poschmann, *Penance and the Anointing of the Sick*, 1964; O. D. Watkins, *A History of Penance*, 1961.

P. S. WATSON

Penitence

Penitence means sorrow for sin. There is a difference, however, between being sorry because our sins have found us out (or because we fear they will), and being sorry because we see how wrong they were and how offensive to God. This recalls St Paul's distinction between worldly and godly sorrow (II Cor. 7.10) and also the distinction so important in Catholic theology between attrition and contrition (q.v.). *See also* **Repentance.**

P. S. WATSON

Pentecost

Originally it was the Jewish Feast of Weeks on the fiftieth day (Greek *pentekoste*) after the Passover; in later Judaism it commemorated the giving of the Law on Mount Sinai. Following the Lucan tradition (Acts 2) it became in Christian usage the commemoration of the gift of the Spirit (seven weeks after Easter) and thus the annual Festival of the Holy Spirit, one of the three great Feasts of the Church. In English-speaking countries 'Whitsunday' is usual instead of 'Pentecost' (from Anglo-Saxon, *hwit*, white); the name is said to derive from the fact that Pentecost was a regular season for christenings, when white robes were worn. There is much discussion among scholars whether the 'gift of tongues' at Pentecost (Acts 2.4–13) was in fact a manifestation of glossolalia (q.v.), or whether the story is a symbolic presentation of the truth that the Holy Spirit overcomes the deepest divisions among men, including that of language.

EDITOR

Perfection

The ideal of Christian perfection is rooted in two NT texts, both of them to be found only in St Matthew's Gospel (5.48 and 19.21). There is no difficulty in relating the theme of Matt. 5.48 to the rest of the teachings of Jesus. He regarded his own life and that of his disciples as involving nothing less than the imitation of the perfection of God, and this latter he undoubtedly interpreted along OT lines meaning 'walking with God', 'fearing God', 'walking in the law of the Lord', 'eschewing evil' and so on. There is good evidence in the NT that Jesus saw his mission as being an actualization of Israel's vocation to walk in the way of the Lord and to obey the great injunction to Israel, 'You shall be holy, for I the Lord your God am holy' (Lev. 19.2). In Matthew 19.21 'being perfect' and 'following Christ' are used synonymously, and Christ himself is spoken of as perfection in Heb. 5.9; Rom. 12.2; 8.29 and Eph. 4.13. Already

in the NT there is evidence of a move in the direction of interpreting the perfection of the Christian disciple in terms of sinlessness. This is evident particularly in the first epistle of St John (3.6, 9). Here it appears to be asserted that sinlessness is a characteristic necessarily of the Christian as redeemed. From this there develop the difficulties, soon experienced in the early Church, of the problem of post-baptismal sin. Many early Christians were shocked at the idea of the possibility of sin after Christian baptism.

The present reality of the Christian's perfection in the NT certainly only has meaning in relation to the perfection of Christ. Christian perfection is a description of the human, finite life, as it is in Christ through the action of the Spirit. In a proleptic sense the Christian is perfect but of course perfection as an absolute quality of the Christian can only be spoken of in an eschatological way.

The Reformers feared that this eschatological tension concerning Christian perfection had been lost sight of during the Middle Ages, so much so that perfection had become a matter of moral endeavour. Consequently the Reformers emphasized perfection not as a moral quality but as a description of the nature of faith.

An important treatment of the Christian ideal of perfection is to be found in John Wesley's work *A Plain Account of Christian Perfection* and *Brief Thoughts on Christian Perfection*. He worked out his thinking on this subject in relation to that of William Law (*see* William Law's *Treatise on Christian Perfection*).

Another important treatment of this ideal is to be found in the works of P. T. Forsyth, for whom the idea of perfection presented in the NT was not a moral endeavour but a right relation with God, through Christ, and this turned on faith.

The idea of Christian perfection focuses clearly the issues between Christianity and humanism. The latter has shown a tendency in its history to base its ideas of perfection on human perfectibility, and in such belief Christians have always seen a latent Pelagianism or 'angelism', the idea that man can attain perfection by some heroic endeavour. It should be noted here that Wesley definitely ruled out the idea of angelic perfection from his thinking.

The saying in Matt. 19.21 has been very greatly influential on Christian thinking concerning the nature of perfection, and more particularly on the formation of the idea of the double standard, the idea that there is one ideal for ordinary practitioners of the faith, but a standard of perfection for the few who are heroic enough to face its demands. Furthermore, a very literal interpretation of the ideal of the imitation of Christ resulted in the exaltation of celibacy (*see* **Celibacy**) as the essence of the Christian ideal of perfection. The ideal of perfection needs, however, to be released from this archaeological, literalistic attempt to mimic the Jesus of history and to be linked, as it is in the Epistle to the Hebrews, with the imagery of the journey, of the way. Perfection is endless self-giving in love, and this for the Christian is Christ himself, and the Christian can be said to be perfect in so far as he participates in the life of Christ, which he does through the action of the Spirit.

R. Newton Flew, *The Idea of Perfection in Christian Theology*, 1934; P. T. Forsyth, *Christian Perfection*, 1899; John Wesley, *A Plain Account of Christian Perfection*, 1765; *Brief Thoughts on Christian Perfection*, 1763; William Law, *A Treatise on Christian Perfection*, 1726.

E. J. TINSLEY

Personalism

Personalism is, broadly speaking, a philosophical standpoint which takes as its starting-point human *personality*, or which finds in such personality the main key to central metaphysical problems. Many personalities have posited a *personal* God as our key to understanding the ultimate nature of the world. While thinkers like M. Buber (1878–1965) and N. Berdyaev (1874–1948) have sometimes been described as 'personalists', the term is best reserved for members and adherents of the Boston (Mass.) school of philosophical personalism, such as B. P. Bowne (1847–1910) and E. S. Brightman (1884–1953).

JAMES RICHMOND

Personality of God

Traditionally personality has been predicated of God in the form of the perfections of intelligence, will and life, although it must be emphasized that the predication has been analogical and equivocal. For a religious outlook not governed by speculative presuppositions, personality is more directly affirmed as lying very near to the core of the Christian idea of God; and yet the characterization of the divine nature in this way is not without its difficulties. In particular, personality as known to us may be held to involve a double dichotomy, that of self and not-self (or environment) and that of 'I and thou', which is highly problematical when the category of personality is applied to God. On the other hand, whatever solution to such problems may be proposed, there remains a central and irresistible drive towards the affirmation of personality. 'Possibly the Godhead is best described as "supra-personal", but impersonal categories are not admissible' (W. R. Matthews, *God in Christian Thought and Experience*, 1930, p. 179). *See also* **Trinity; Person(s)**.

L. Hodgson, *The Doctrine of the Trinity*, 1943; C. C. J. Webb, *God and Personality*, 1918.

N. H. G. ROBINSON

Person(s)

Person(s) is the term used to express the plurality of the Godhead in trinitarian formulae; it came from Latin *persona*, originally an actor's mask or role, then, more widely, one's role or character in life.

In the West it was introduced into trinitarian terminology by Tertullian and incorporated into Western official usage under his influence. In secular language it could be used dramatically of an actor's mask or role, grammatically of the persons of a verb, concretely of a person or human being. The legal sense regarded as decisive by Harnack has, it seems, no special significance. While *persona* could be used to express a manifestation, the sense of a concrete individual came to prevail. Thus, in the *Adversus Praxeam* Tertullian makes the word a plank in his anti-Modalist apologetic. *Persona* in his usage expresses that which differentiates the divine being, *substantia* that which unites it.

With his strong monist inclinations, Augustine is clearly puzzled over the meaning of the word. His use of the psychological analogy (q.v.) clearly points to a doctrine of the personality of God which makes some reinterpretation of the term Person inevitable. Augustine finds this in his doctrine of the Divine Relations which are real, immanent but relative to each other. The definition of Boethius that Person means the individual subsistence of a rational nature (*Persona est naturae rationabilis individua substantia*) passed into general currency in the West and Aquinas (not without difficulty) combines this with the Augustinian theory of the divine relations.

In modern trinitarian usage the term Person can be used either in a monist or a pluralist connotation. The former (using the psychological analogy) speaks of the personality of God and interprets the term Person along the lines of the Augustinian-Thomist doctrine of the divine relations, the latter (using the social analogy) assigns to the term a meaning similar to the Greek *Hypostasis* (q.v.) as inner differentiations of the divine life, distinct but interpenetrating centres of consciousness. Karl Barth, while refusing the use of analogies on theological grounds, exemplifies modern monism. The trinitarian God, the primary implicate of revelation, discloses himself as a Thou. To speak of Person in terms of 'He' is not Trinitarianism but sheer tritheism. Person in the trinitarian sense must, therefore, be interpreted as a mode of being (q.v.), a permanent style of God's being God. Pluralists like C. C. J. Webb claim, however, that even in God the term must have a greater approximation to normal usage. To speak of the Personality of God does not do justice to the trinitarian formula which implies rather Personality in God, leaving the divine unity to be described as supra-personal. The coinherence of the Trinity (q.v.) has, therefore, a special importance in this tradition. Both approaches can be cogently presented and are theologically viable. The knife edge between modalism (charged against monist interpretations) and tritheism (the accusation made against pluralist thinkers both in ancient and modern times) must inevitably beset man's approach to the central mystery of the Trinity so long as he walks by faith.

G. L. Prestige, *God in Patristic Thought*, 1936, pp. 157–96, 242–64; C. C. J. Webb, *God and Person-*

ality, 1918, pp. 35–133; C. Welch, *The Trinity in Contemporary Theology*, 1953, pp. 252–72.

H. E. W. TURNER

Pessimism. *see* Optimism.

Peter Lombard. *see* Lombard, Peter.

Peter, St

The NT clearly accords to Peter a pre-eminent place among the Twelve. All the lists of apostles place him at the beginning; all four evangelists record his being named Cephas by the Lord (Mark 3.16; Matt. 10.2–4; Luke 6.14; John 1.42); three texts in particular have been thought to confer on him particular status, Matt. 16.17–19; Luke 22.31 f.; John 21.15–17. It is very likely that, as Paul states and as Mark, and perhaps Luke, imply, it was to him that the Lord first appeared after the resurrection (I Cor. 15.5; Mark 14.28; 16.7; Luke 24.34). Peter takes the lead in the events narrated in the early chapters of Acts. On the other hand, the capital text Matt. 16.17–19 has been attacked for long by many scholars as inauthentic on the grounds that it contains the suspect word *ecclesia* for 'church', a description of the early Christian community which certainly does not date from the most primitive period, and that this passage appears in no other evangelist; further, the privileges conferred on Peter are given to the other apostles in Matt. 18.18. Matt. 16.17–19 has, however, recently been defended as authentic by some Protestant scholars (e.g. O. Cullmann). Again, though Peter takes the lead in the early days of the Church, later in Acts he appears to lose it to James the brother of the Lord, who presides at the 'Apostolic Council' described in Acts 15, and to Paul. Paul himself clearly reckons Peter among the most important of the Twelve (Gal. 1.18; 2.2, 9) and regards him as the apostle to the Jews *par excellence* (Gal. 2.7–9), yet he was perfectly ready to oppose him upon what he considered a vital issue (Gal. 2.11–14). The NT is silent about Peter's finishing his career in Rome, and scholars are far from unanimous in attributing I Peter to his authorship; it is wholly unlikely that he wrote II Peter, which is probably a late second-century work. But early tradition (represented by *I Clement*, Ignatius, Irenaeus, Papias, Gaius and Tertullian) held that Peter had been martyred on the Vatican Hill in Rome during a persecution by Nero (64) and archaeology has recently supplied confirmation of this tradition by establishing that a memorial shrine commemorating Saint Peter existed on the Vatican Hill, on the site of the present Saint Peter's, as early as 160. It is anachronistic to describe Peter as 'first bishop' of Rome, because the apostles were not bishops and the evidence that they directly instituted monarchical bishops is very uncertain. Christianity certainly reached Rome before Peter did, and perhaps Paul reached it before him too. The discussion whether the traditional Roman Catholic doctrine of the privileges of Peter and his successors can be constructed out of these facts probably depends upon the presuppositions of the reader. But it can be said with confidence that the subject of the position of the apostles, and particularly that of Peter, in the NT has not yet been exhausted by scholarly research, and there is room for modifications of views on both sides.

O. Cullmann, *Peter: Disciple, Apostle, Martyr*, 1953; J. Lowe, *Saint Peter*, 1956.

R. P. C. HANSON

Phenomenalism

Phenomenalism is the epistemological theory that our knowledge cannot go beyond those appearances (*phenomena*) which we apprehend by sense perception, and as such it has much in common with *empiricism*.

JAMES RICHMOND

Phenomenology

Phenomenology is that philosophical discipline which conducts a descriptive inquiry into the most fundamental structure of our experience, into those essences which are most immediately present to our consciousness. See **Husserl, E., Otto, R., Scheler, M.**

JAMES RICHMOND

Philo

Philo was an Alexandrian Jew, an older contemporary of St Paul, known to have been regarded as the leader of the Jewish community in Alexandria during the reign of the Emperor Gaius (37–41) and to have taken part in a deputation sent to protest to that Emperor about the treatment of the Jews in Alexandria by the Greeks. He attempted in his voluminous works, of which about forty survive, all written in Greek, to give a reinterpretation of traditional Judaism in Hellenistic terms. His philosophy is a remarkable combination of Jewish monotheism, Platonic traits such as the doctrine of ideas, and the Stoic concept of the Logos immanent in the world and animating and directing it. He was not a heterodox Jew, and observed and reverenced the Law, but he was anxious to reinterpret it, and while preserving its form to transmute its substance into general philosophical, moral and psychological truths, in accordance with a characteristically Hellenistic Jewish tendency observable in his predecessors, Aristobulus (second century BC) and Pseudo-Aristeas (c. 100 BC). In order to effect this he borrowed and developed from pagan Hellenistic literature the technique of allegorizing a sacred text, and applied it to the OT (mainly the Pentateuch). Philo had no discoverable influence on later Judaism, but had a considerable impact upon Christian thought. Some scholars have discerned the traces of his thought in the Epistle to the Hebrews (though this can be doubted), and still more in the Logos-doctrine of the Fourth Gospel. He may have influenced Justin Martyr and Theophilus of Antioch, but his greatest influence was undoubtedly upon Clement of Alexandria, Origen and Ambrose. This influence mainly appears in the Platonic tendency to see the material or physical world as symbolic rather than real, and to undervalue the historical, the concrete and the particular. He must also be held to be the *fons et origo* of the main stream of traditional Christian allegory.

E. R. Goodenough, *An Introduction to Philo Judaeus*, reprint, 1962.

R. P. C. HANSON

Philosophes, Les. *see* Encyclopaedists.

Philosophia Perennis

Philosophia perennis is a term used to denote that main stream of philosophical thinking which began with Plato (or indeed before him) and continued through the Stoics and some neoplatonists and passed over into Christian thought in the Middle Ages and so into one of the main lines of Christian thinking in the modern age (e.g. William Temple, A. E. Taylor) and indeed into idealistic philosophy and even into the thought of certain neo-humanists (e.g. Aldous Huxley, *The Perennial Philosophy*, 1946). It has also marked affinities with the thought of the orient. According to this stream of thought the values which are sought and found in human existence are clues to the nature of reality as a whole; the natural law, understood by reason, which pervades all things, is evidence of the rationality of the world. The perennial philosophy does not necessarily involve belief in a personal God or in any specifically Christian commitment, but it generally implies a conviction that reality is ultimately friendly to human ideals. *See* **Platonism.**

EDITOR

Philosophical Theology

Philosophical theology is that branch of theology which seeks to give rational expression in terms of the philosophical ideas of the day to belief in Jesus Christ as the supreme revelation of God. It thus differs from the philosophy of religion (q.v.), which does not necessarily start from Christian convictions in its critical examination of religious affirmations and experience. Philosophical theology may be defined in Anselm's phrase as *fides quaerens intellectum*, faith in search of rational articulation. It has recently been fashionable to deny the propriety of philosophical theology on the ground that to attempt to underpin faith with rational argumentation is unfaith (Karl Barth, Emil Brunner); but it may be answered that A. N. Whitehead's insight into the real nature of Christianity is superior to such obscurantism: 'Christianity has always been a religion seeking a metaphysic, in contrast to Buddhism, which is a metaphysic generating a religion.' The philosophical theologian finds an inner compulsion to explain to himself how as a rational person, living in the climate of thought of his own time, he can

profess belief in the Christian revelation. In so far as he feels a compulsion to explain the reasonableness of Christian belief to others he is also an apologist (q.v.). In either case he is compelled to face the difficulties encountered by the Christian believer in the presence of contemporary unbelief. But the philosophical theologian will be ware of compromising his Christian convictions through an excessive desire to come to terms with some fashionable philosophy (e.g. existentialism), since then he might find that the Christian content of his position has been evaporated, as with certain so-called existentialist theologians. Equally he will not confuse philosophical theology with a religious philosophy, such as Tillich's 'System', which uses all the categories and symbols of Christian theology but in an alien and de-Christianized meaning. The disregard of philosophical theology on the Continent of Europe and perhaps in certain quarters in America has manifested itself in a surprising naivety among certain so-called theologians who late in life have suddenly awakened to the seriousness of the rationalist objections to Christian faith (God as the 'problem solver' or 'need fulfiller', 'the God of the gaps', etc.) and have abandoned rational belief in favour of one or other of the many irrationalisms of the present decade. In Britain a long line of hardheaded philosophical theologians has done something to prevent the spread of irrationalism in theology and perhaps even the decay of Christian faith among the more thoughtful elements of society – John Oman, F. R. Tennant, William Temple, A. E. Taylor, C. C. J. Webb, John and Donald Baillie, Ian Ramsey, John Hick, T. F. Torrance and many others. The writings of those named in this list would constitute a suitable bibliography for this article. *See also* **Philosophy of Religion; Apologetics.**

EDITOR

Philosophy of Religion

Philosophy of religion is the logical study of religious and theological concepts, arguments, language: the scrutiny of various interpretations of religious experiences and activities. As the philosopher who practises it need not be committed to the religion he is studying, the philosophy of religion must be distinguished from apologetics. Again, it is not identical with 'natural theology', since the philosopher of religion may concern himself also with the appraisal of alleged revelations. Even if a revelation-centred theology does not formally *argue* to the existence of God, etc., it still must use language, apply concepts – and thus be exposed to problems of meaning and logical coherence quite as much as is natural theology. Philosophy of religion examines the peculiar structure of reasoning within theology, comparing and contrasting it with reasoning in, e.g. the sciences, the arts, historical studies. It tries to appraise the theologian's standard of evidence, his handling of concepts like faith, reason, doubt, commitment, miracle, law of nature, good and evil, life after death. *See also* **Analytical Philo-**

sophy; Epistemology; Metaphysics; Psychology of Religion; Scepticism.

G. L. Abernethy and T. A. Langford, eds., *Philosophy of Religion; A Book of Readings*, 1962; A. Flew and A. MacIntyre, eds., *New Essays in Philosophical Theology*, 1955; John Hick, ed., *The Existence of God*, 1963; *Philosophy of Religion*, 1963.

R. W. HEPBURN

Pietism

Historically speaking, pietism is used in the history of the Christian Church of the reaction in seventeenth-century Germany against a religion which was regarded as having become too formalist and intellectual. This reaction is associated with the names of Spener and Francke. The pietist movement in Germany occupied the position in relation to German church life which, in England, is associated with that of John Wesley and the early Wesleyans; in fact early Methodism was considerably influenced by pietism. German pietism is important because, among other things, it brought back into German Lutheranism the influence of the mystics.

The main features of pietism are: (1) an emphasis on personal religious experience, on conversion of a precise kind often precisely dated; and (2) a kind of Puritanism which led to a distrust of the theatre and amusements.

R. N. Flew, *The Idea of Perfection in Christian Theology*, 1934; A. W. Nagler, *Pietism and Methodism*, 1918.

E. J. TINSLEY

Piety. *see* Perfection; Holiness.

Platonism

Plato (427–347 BC) was the first great European philosopher (unless that honour should be reserved for Socrates, whom Plato uses as the mouthpiece of his own thoughts in many of the *Dialogues*). His influence was profound and lasting. It was strong in the early centuries of the Church. So congenial was his philosophy to those theologians (especially at Alexandria) who were engaged in interpreting Christian faith in terms of contemporary thought that he was regarded as 'a Christian before Christ' or 'Moses speaking Attic Greek.' His idealist (as opposed to materialist) philosophy conceives of the primary realities behind the visible world as consisting in Ideas or Forms (universals) which are eternal, transcending time and space. Actual things (e.g. triangles which we can draw) are only imperfect approximations in the sensible world to the perfect Ideas (e.g. of the triangle, which consists of lines having no breadth and therefore incapable of corporeal actuality) in which they participate. Things are real only in so far as they participate in the Ideas, and thus they acquire their proper degree of perfection in the great chain of being. The myths of Plato (esp. the myth of creation in the *Timaeus*)

could easily be interpreted in a Christian sense. The *Timaeus* was the only dialogue of Plato which was known in the Middle Ages (in a Latin translation) and its influence in the formation of the mediaeval Christian world-view was immense. Christian philosophy remained Platonic in character for most of the mediaeval period, largely as a result of the continuing influence of St Augustine. But in the thirteenth century Platonic thought was eclipsed by the newly discovered philosophy of Aristotle (*see* **Thomism; God**).

The impact of Platonism on Christian thinking can be studied by consulting the following articles: **Clement of Alexandria; Origen; Neoplatonism; Augustinianism; Boethius; Pseudo-Dionysius; Bonaventura, St; Cambridge Platonists.** The best introduction to Plato's own writings will be found in Sir R. Livingstone's *Selections from Plato* (World's Classics), 1940. Introductions to Plato's thought include J. Burnet, *Greek Philosophy*, Part I: *From Thales to Plato*, 1914; G. C. Field, *The Philosophy of Plato*, 1949; R. Klibansky, *The Platonic Tradition during the Middle Ages*, 1939; A. E. Taylor, *Plato*, 1922; *Plato, the Man and his Work*, 3rd ed., 1929.

EDITOR

Plotinus

Plotinus (205–270) was the leading philosopher of the Neoplatonist school. Though an Egyptian, born in Lycopolis, he imbibed a predominantly Hellenic wisdom from Ammonius Saccas, his master in Alexandria for eleven years. Under the patronage of the Emperor Gordian he made an expedition to Persia to acquaint himself with Mesopotamian and Indian philosophies. From 244 until nearly the end of his life, he taught in Rome, and his illustrious pupil Porphyry subsequently arranged his writings into six groups of nine, the *Enneads*. His influence on Christian theology is most evident in St Augustine (q.v.) and in Pseudo-Dionysius the Areopagite (q.v.). *See* **Neoplatonism** for an outline of his teaching.

Opera, ed. P. Henry and H. R. Schwyzer, 1951–   ; *Enneads*, ET by A. H. Armstrong (Loeb Classical Library), 1966–   ; and by S. MacKenna, 3rd. ed., 1962; A. H. Armstrong, *Plotinus*, 1953; A. H. Armstrong, ed., *The Cambridge History of Later Greek and Early Medieval Philosophy*, 1967, Part III: 'Plotinus' by A. H. Armstrong; W. R. Inge, *The Philosophy of Plotinus*, 3rd ed., 1929, 1948.

DOM PLACID SPEARRITT

Pluralism

Pluralism, in the widest sense, is a philosophical theory which claims that there are several mutually irreducible substances; or that there are several mutually irreducible attributes. To label a theory 'pluralist' most usually implies the former – substance-pluralism; but the alternative types need to be carefully distinguished. G. W. Leibniz, for instance, held a pluralism of substance, his 'monads' being individually distinct existences:

but since they all share a common type of existence – a 'spiritual' one, the theory contains a monism, not a pluralism, of fundamental *attributes*. On the other hand, a pantheistic or idealist theory may be monistic with respect to substance (everything is a modification or aspect of one deity, or of the Absolute), but it may grant that attributes are many, even infinite, as in Spinoza's case.

A philosopher who wants to emphasize personal freedom tends to be drawn towards a pluralism in which the histories of individuals are not represented simply as moments in the history of a single substance. For such a representation is seen as making illusory the apparent autonomy of the individuals. In ethics, likewise, a pluralism of duties consists in the denial that all duties stem from a single supreme duty (denying, e.g. that 'benevolence is the whole of virtue'), a pluralism of goods in the denial that good things are of one type only. While such a pluralism guards against the oversimplifying and hence the distorting of moral phenomena, it has to defend itself against the criticism that it makes of morality a disconnected heap of duties and ideals, chaotic and unintelligible. There are parallel difficulties and dangers with metaphysical pluralisms also. They pay admirable respect to the diversity and individuality of things and persons; but they encounter their greatest difficulties just where a monism is more likely to succeed – in showing the possibility of interaction among the diverse elements, in showing how these elements can (in spite of being ontologically quite dissimilar) nevertheless make up a single nature. *See also* **Monism; Dualism; Pragmatism.**

W. James, *A Pluralistic Universe*, 1909; A. M. Quinton, 'Pluralism and Monism', *EB*.

R. W. HEPBURN

Pneumatology

Pneumatology is derived from Greek *pneuma*, spirit: the branch of theology which deals with the doctrine of the (Holy) Spirit (q.v.).

Pneumatomachi

'Pneumatomachi' is the Latin form of a Greek word literally meaning 'fighters against the (Holy) Spirit'. It is used of certain theologians of the fourth century who denied the full divinity of the Holy Spirit (*cf.* the Arians, who had denied the full divinity of Christ). They were condemned at the Council of Ephesus in AD 381. They were said to be followers of Macedonius, and hence are also called Macedonians. *See* the standard histories of doctrine, e.g. J. F. Bethune-Baker, *Introduction to the Early History of Christian Doctrine*, 4th ed., 1929, ch. XIII; *see also* **Spirit.**

EDITOR

Poimandres. *see* Hermetic Literature.

Point of Contact

This term, the literal translation of the German *Anknüpfungspunkt*, gained theological currency especially after the Barth-Brunner debate on natural theology in 1934, when Barth denied, over against Brunner, the existence of any *contact-point* in nature or human nature for God's revelation in Christ. *See* **Barth, K.; Brunner, E.; Crisis Theology; Dialectical Theology.**

JAMES RICHMOND

Pope. *see* Papacy.

Positive Theology

Positive theology is an old term for the branch of theology which deals with historical fact (the historical or scriptural revelation) and church development, customs, enactments, etc., as contrasted with natural or philosophical theology (qq.v.), which professes to deal with the rational basis of Christian belief.

Positivism

Positivism is a type of philosophy belonging to the empiricist tradition, but distinctive in its thoroughgoing repudiation of metaphysics and theology. To the positivist, knowledge can be increased only by observation and experience, never by speculative argument alone. The word 'positive' (probably deriving from a usage of Francis Bacon) is here contrasted with the conjectured: it is associated with the 'given', the data of the sciences.

Certain of the empiricists (e.g. J. Locke and G. Berkeley) were speculative metaphysicians nevertheless: D. Hume's critique of metaphysics, however, was radical, denying that we could have any knowledge of the world that carried the certainty of logical or mathematical demonstration.

Auguste Comte (1798–1857) added to these strands of positivism a 'historical' thesis about three stages of development towards scientific enlightenment: the theological (where explanations refer to the agency of supernatural beings), the metaphysical (where philosophical abstractions replace the gods) and the positive – where speculation 'beyond' the given phenomena is renounced, and the phenomena themselves become the proper objects of investigation. The full development of the study of man was to culminate in a 'religion of humanity'.

In the twentieth century – dating from the 1920s – Logical Positivism has argued that metaphysical disputes may be altogether eliminated, once it is realized that metaphysical claims are quite literally meaningless. A claim is factually meaningful only if it admits of verification or falsification by experience; and metaphysical claims admit of neither. The same applies to the statements of theology. A statement like 'God is love' (as held characteristically by a believer) is compatible with any and every experience that the believer may suffer: it is thus unfalsifiable and without meaning. The fierce criticism which

Logical Positivism met from without was less effective in chastening it than troubles within – problems about the logical (or metaphysical?) status of the verification principle itself, difficulties over the concept of 'experience' ('sense impressions', 'atomic facts', etc.). These perplexities have led to a softening and qualifying of its pretensions. Logical Positivism should not be confused (as still seems to happen) with Analytical Philosophy (q.v.). See also **History, Problem of; Humanism.**

A. J. Ayer, *Language, Truth and Logic*, 1936 and 1946; ed., *Logical Positivism*, 1959.

R. W. HEPBURN

Powers, The

In the NT the 'powers' (*exousiai*) often mean the political authorities of the Roman Empire (Rom. 13.1–7; Titus 3.1). But in accordance with the general outlook of the Graeco-Oriental world these political rulers are linked with the supernatural principalities, powers, angels, spiritual rulers, etc. which God had appointed to govern the universe. Originally they were good, but they became evil and tyrannized the lives of men, who were in bondage to them. Christ, however, had delivered men from the power of darkness (Col. 1.13), and the powers can no longer separate Christians from the love of God (Rom. 8.39). Christ's death and resurrection constituted a victory over the alien powers (Col. 2.15). The deliverance wrought by Christ, who is now set at God's right hand, 'far above every rule, authority, power and lordship' (Eph. 1.21), is often represented in the NT and the Fathers as a victory over the powers. Yet the powers still in this present age retain some of their former potency, and Christians must contend against them (Eph. 6.12). They are still thus 'demonic' in character, i.e. appointed by God to perform certain necessary functions in the ordering of the world and yet still possessing some capacity to frustrate his will: 'the whole world is in the power of the evil one' (I John 5.19). The idols of pagan worship represent the power of these demonic agencies (*cf.* I John 5.21).

The whole subject of the relationship of the powers to the rule of God, to the political authorities and to Satan has been much debated in recent NT scholarship. The important theological question which is raised concerns the reality of the evil which surrounds man-in-the-world. Are 'the powers' merely the result of man's mythologizing objectification (q.v.) of his own fears and frustrations, or is there *evil* outside men, forces in the universe which are superhuman and which despoil human achievements? Is man himself the source of all evil, which can be exorcized by the existentialist *kerygma*, or even by better education, social amelioration, psychological techniques, etc.? Or is evil objectively real? To put the question in another way, is the myth of the powers simply a pre-philosophical error of objectification, or does the NT and patristic language about

the powers, the Devil, etc., represent a poetic way of speaking about evil which exists outside man (or at least outside the individual man as a reality of collective human societies)? Does demythologizing (q.v.) solve the problem of the evil which men have always felt to be pressing in on them from beyond themselves, or does the admittedly mythological language of the NT refer to a constituent element of the world into which man finds himself projected? *See* **Evil, Problem of; Atonement; Angel, Angelology.**

G. Aulén, *Christus Victor*, ET, 1931; R. Leivestad, *Christ the Conqueror*, 1954; Clinton D. Morrison, *The Powers that Be*, 1960.

EDITOR

Practical Theology. *see* Pastoralia, Pastoral Theology.

Pragmatism

Pragmatism made its greatest impact on American philosophical and theological thought in the first four decades of the twentieth century. Often considered to be America's most important contribution to philosophy, it drew heavily on empirical, scientific and evolutionary thought in its reaction to idealism. The ideas of Charles Sanders Peirce (1839–1914) planted the seed of the movement when he affirmed that beliefs are really rules for actions which establish habits; to determine a thought's meaning it is necessary only to determine what conduct it is fitted to produce.

William James (1842–1910), Harvard professor of philosophy who had been educated there in science and medicine, developed this principle of pragmatism as a test of truth. In his definitional work *Pragmatism* (1907) he declared that true ideas are those that can be corroborated and verified, while false ones are those that cannot. Truth is what happens to an idea; an idea is made true by events. Thus the meaning and value of all assumptions and ideas must be evaluated in a radically empirical way by attention to their practical consequences in use. In *A Pluralistic Universe* (1909) James rejected any fixed or static interpretations of the universe to insist on the changing and evolutionary character of reality. He was fascinated by the religious question all his life; in his famous Gifford lectures, *The Varieties of Religious Experience* (1902), he explained that there are certain empirical justifications for religious experiences in the way that the latter enrich life and shape conduct. His was an open, seeking, non-traditional attitude toward religion; his study led him to suggest that the God of the pluralistic universe was finite.

The other great exponent of pragmatism, John Dewey (1859–1952), was much less interested in theological matters. As a religious humanist he argued for the separation of religious values from organized religion in *A Common Faith* (1934). Much of his philosophical work centred on the epistemological problem. In *The Quest for Certainty* (1929) and other writings, he rejected any association of ideas about value with Antecedent Being, insisting that they should be associated always with practical activity. His version of pragmatism was often called 'instrumentalism' or 'experimentalism', and through his many writings in many fields he exerted a wide influence upon the thought of his time.

The impact of pragmatism on Protestant theological and ethical thought was strong, especially in liberalism, at the height of the movement. The 'Chicago school' attempted to express Christian faith in terms of pragmatic and empirical philosophy. The religious education movement drew heavily on pragmatically-based ideas. The rise of realistic and neo-orthodox trends in the 1930s tended to check the influence of pragmatism on Protestant thought and life.

John J. McDermott, ed., *The Writings of William James – A Comprehensive Edition*, 1967; Ralph Barton Perry, *The Thought and Character of William James*, 2 vols., 1935; Herbert W. Schneider, *A History of American Philosophy*, 1946.

ROBERT T. HANDY

Prayer Books of the Anglican Communion

The first reformed Prayer Book was issued in 1549, and the second in 1552. Both owed a large part of their theological outlook and literary grace to Cranmer. Small, but sometimes significant changes were made subsequently, but in the main the book of 1662 follows the lines of the second one, and was the book which Anglicans took with them when they carried their faith overseas to the colonies and trading posts where Anglican chaplains were required in the later centuries. The American colonies separated from Britain after winning the War of Independence, but Anglicans in the USA took steps to maintain their communion with their mother church while continuing to be loyal to their own country. This necessitated some changes in the stated prayers, and led eventually to a conservative revision of the 1662 book. Meanwhile in the Scottish Episcopal Church, under the influence of scholarly Non-Jurors (q.v.), experiments in revision had been taking place, which drew upon the 1549 rather than the 1552 book, and on the rites of the Eastern Orthodox Church. Most subsequent revisions elsewhere in the Anglican communion have followed the same path, notably in re-ordering of the eucharistic rite to allow for an oblationary prayer immediately after the consecration. Some parts of the Anglican communion still use an only slightly amended version of 1662, but the provinces of South Africa and of the West Indies, as well as the church in the USA and in Canada, have made notable revisions. The Church of South India (though not strictly speaking a part of the Anglican communion) deserves special mention in this connection, for one of the most striking results of the union has been the revived interest in liturgy, and

the beginning of a revision likely to be increasingly influential in the Anglican communion and beyond. Whatever varieties in detail the revised books show from each other they are agreed in the effort to use the vernacular in a more modern way while keeping where appropriate as much Cranmerian English as possible; to increasing the element of praise especially in the Eucharist and in modifying the somewhat excessive expressions of penitence of the 1662 book; in modelling the eucharistic rite more closely on the rites of the early Church, and in enriching the calendar. Among the more interesting recent Prayer Books are these: *The Prayer Book as proposed in 1928*, not sanctioned by Parliament but authorized by the bishops and widely, if selectively, used in England; and the recent (1960) revision of the Canadian Prayer Book. In many parts of the Anglican communion a more thorough reform of liturgy than has ever been proposed since the sixteenth century is under consideration. In England, under the authority of the Prayer Book (alternative and other Services) Measure 1965, revised eucharistic rites, known as Series I and Series II, were approved for experimental use in 1967.

W. K. Lowther Clarke, ed., *Liturgy and Worship*, 1932; B. J. Wigan, *The Liturgy in English*, 1962.

R. CANT

Prayer, The Theology of

Since the earliest days of Israelite religion prayer to Israel's God was spontaneous, natural and unaffected, however formalized it may have become in later Judaism. The God to whom Israel prayed was the saving, protecting and judging God of prophetic religion. The Psalms exemplify the direct approach of Israel to God: the Israelite, whether individually or corporately, poured out all his concern to God – for his safety, his harvest, his sins and failures, his joys and sorrows, his thanksgiving and praise. Such spontaneous address was possible only because God was essentially 'Thou', the one who called forth the response of those who knew his name.

Jesus and his disciples inherited this long and rich tradition of personal approach to God. But Jesus added a new intimacy to the prayer of his followers. The OT is certainly familiar with the idea of God as Father of Israel, his 'son' (*cf.* Hos. 11.1), but the prayer of Jesus introduces a distinctively personal relationship, as is instanced by his use of an intimate family-address, *Abba*, 'daddy'. The seven petitions included in the prayer which he taught to his disciples ('the Lord's Prayer') indicate what he considered to be the seven most important things about which Christians should pray. The first three of the petitions concern God's name, God's will and God's reign. Among the other petitions the prayer for God's forgiveness is characteristically made conditional upon the supplicant's own willingness to forgive.

The NT requires and indeed assumes that Christians will pray without ceasing. It also teaches that prayer should be made 'in the name of Jesus', as indeed it is only 'through Jesus Christ our Lord' that Christians have access to God at all. Christian prayer thus contains only those petitions which can be genuinely offered in the name (character, spirit) of Christ, the same Christ who 'at the right hand of God' makes intercession for us. This rules out all selfish requests and every suggestion that prayer is a kind of magic by which God's attention can be caught or his will influenced. The essence of prayer is not asking but offering, not self-seeking but self-dedication: 'not my will but thine be done.'

It is often objected that, if God is a loving father who knows that his children have need of all sorts of things, there is no purpose in intercessory prayer. Yet Jesus himself says 'Ask . . . knock . . . seek' (Matt. 7.7 f.), shortly after saying 'Your heavenly Father knows that you need all these things' (Matt. 6.32). This implies that intercession is not begging for necessities which might otherwise be withheld; in fact, we are not to worry about our own food and clothing. Our prayer should be concerned with God's kingdom of righteousness: with those who suffer from injustice, deprivation, disease, violence. A father expects his children to be concerned, as he is, for other members of his family in distress. He also expects them not merely to speak to him and then leave him to do everything; he desires their active co-operation. If our communion with God is even a faltering reflection of Jesus' own intimate sonship, we shall not be able to prevent ourselves from bringing to our heavenly Father all the concerns which press upon us. If we have the Spirit of Jesus in us, these concerns will be for others rather than for ourselves; but our own personal griefs and problems will, quite naturally, not be excluded from our speaking with God. The Christian will turn spontaneously to God, the Father of Jesus Christ, as the one who is always 'there'.

But can we expect God to interfere with the laws of nature for our or others' benefit when we pray to him (e.g.) for the rain in time of drought? Much depends upon the way in which this question is formulated. The question as posed above implies a deistic conception of God (*see* **Deism**) and is an unreal one for Christians today. We must first clarify our conception of the God to whom we pray. Christian prayer is possible only if we believe in the God whom Jesus called Father, not the clockmaker God of the deists, or the Absolute in whom all differences are reconciled, or the 'problem-solver' or Aladdin's Lamp of popular misconception. If our belief in God is the child-like (not childish) trust in one to whom we can always turn quite spontaneously, there is nothing that can be asked 'in the name of Jesus' about which we cannot pray to God. But will our prayers be answered? Yes, though not necessarily in the way we would have chosen; there is much to be learned from the so-called unanswered prayers of Jesus (e.g. Mark 14.35 f.). Of course, we will pray for deliverance from danger or for rain: the child cries to his father for help, even though he knows that his father is doing the best that can be done in the situation. Christian prayer is possible only where Jesus' own utter trust in the loving Father is present. In this it differs from all other prayer: other religions have developed well-tested methods of contemplation (q.v.) and of mystical identification with what Tillich would call 'the power of being', and these might indeed be valuable accessories to the prayer-life of the Christian. But they do not approach the distinctively Christian continuous intercourse (not merely on formal occasions, whether individual or corporate) with the Father of Jesus, and our Father.

Three other things remain to be said about the theology of Christian prayer. First, Christian prayer is always corporate in character, even when we enter into our private chamber to pray. Even then it is the Church, in heaven and on earth, praying through us. We cannot enter alone into the presence of 'our' Father; God is 'my' God only because he is the God of my fellow-men, and therefore my concerns are his concerns and vice-versa. Secondly, the state of our feelings, when we pray, is unimportant. If we are thinking about what we feel, or are concerned with our own religious satisfaction or enjoyment, we shall not be praying in the Christian sense. If we are preoccupied with psychological problems, such as whether there is anyone there at the other end of the line, we shall not be praying. Prayer is utter dedication and self-forgetting; it should lead to action, not to introspection. Questions about the psychology of prayer are legitimate matters for discussion at the right time and place, but they should not obtrude upon our personal prayer life. Lastly, all men in every age, including our own, at least at certain moments in their lives, spontaneously and yet inevitably experience an urgent desire to pray. This universal compulsion is given its true expression and fulfilment in Christian prayer, in which divine grace perfects the essential nature of man as such. In the last resort men pray because they must, because the need of their hearts will not be repressed without violence to their human nature. *See also* **Contemplation; Worship.**

P. Baelz, *Prayer and Providence*, 1968; F. Heiler, *Prayer*, ET, 1932; J. Jeremias, *The Prayers of Jesus*, ET, 1967.

EDITOR

Prayers for the Dead

Evidence for the practice of offering prayers for the dead from the earliest Christian times can be found in the catacombs and in the writings of the early Fathers. (Those who accept the authority of the Apocrypha [q.v.] can find explicit sanction for the practice in II Macc. 12.40–6.) Those in purgatory (q.v.) are members of Christ's mystical Body, and having not yet attained their final blessedness, may be assisted by the prayers of the Church on earth.

Preaching

In the NT the three verbs used for 'preach' all express the meaning: telling of (good) news to people who had not heard it before, i.e., evangelization (*see* Alan Richardson, 'Gospel' and 'Preach, Teach', *TWBB*). Throughout the NT mission (q.v.) is one of the fundamental marks of the Church, without which it could not be the Church. Today, while the word 'preach' is still used in this sense of evangelizing the heathen, it is much more commonly employed in connection with the preaching of sermons in churches, i.e. to the converted. It is obvious that the word is not then being used in its NT sense. The question arises: Why should the Christian congregation need to be preached to? The answer to this question is that conversion is not a once-for-all occurrence but involves a continuous re-turning to the truth. This is why the Church's most searching, most anxious and most persevering preaching must always be directed to itself (*cf.* I Cor. 9.27). The ministry of the Word is understood in every branch of the Church to be an essential function of ministry as such; and, while it is not co-terminous with preaching (other things belong to it, such as reading the Scriptures in the divine office, catechizing, liturgical recitation or singing of Scripture, e.g. the Psalms), nevertheless preaching (in the sense of the sermon) is and always has been an essential part of the Church's ministry to itself. It is necessary that the preacher should therefore constantly ask himself what he thinks he is doing when he is preaching. Clearly he should not be giving his personal views about current political or social issues – or indeed about any other matters at all, even about current theological debates. Preaching consists in one thing only: the exposition of the Word of God as contained in the Scriptures in such a way as to bring home its saving and liberating truth to the hearers, enabling them to understand that truth in relation to the situation of their daily lives in the world which Christ came to redeem and which those who are in Christ are called to serve. Karl Barth rightly declares that the ultimate purpose of theology is to enable the preaching of the gospel by the Church's ministers to be done the more articulately and effectively; conversely, the Church's proclamation is the material of dogmatics (q.v.). 'The normal and central fact with which dogmatics has to do is, very simply, the Church's Sunday sermon' (*Church Dogmatics*, ET, I: *The Doctrine of the Word of God*, 1, 1956, p. 91). Nevertheless it is not the preacher's learning, oratory or 'personality' which exercises converting power during the preaching of the Scriptures; it is rather that the Holy Spirit uses the words of the preacher to bring home to the hearers the truth of the scriptural message for them (*see* **Witness of the Spirit**). This does not mean that the preacher need not spend hours of prayer and study in the preparation of his sermon; although it is God who gives the increase, the labour of planting and watering must be done by human ministers (I Cor. 3.6). Whereas Barth has affirmed that dogmatics is concerned with preaching, theologians of the existentialist school argue that dogmatics is essentially hermeneutics, i.e. the science and art of scriptural interpretation,

and thus they would be no less eager than Barth to claim that the ultimate purpose of theology is the promotion of sound preaching or proclamation with especial relevance to the existential situation of those who are addressed. *See* **Hermeneutics; Homiletics;** *Kerygma.*

A. B. Come, *An Introduction to Barth's Dogmatics for Preachers*, 1963; G. Ebeling, *Word and Faith*, ET, 1963, esp. ch. XI; E. Fuchs, *Studies of the Historical Jesus*, ET, 1964, esp. ch. II; G. Wingren, *The Living Word*, ET, 1960.

EDITOR

Precious Blood

The allusions of Christ at the Last Supper to the blood of the New Covenant (Mark 14.24;.Matt. 26.28) and to the Paschal Lamb (John 19.36; *see also* 1.29; 1.36), added to the fact that the apostles associate the blood with the passion and death of Christ (I John 1.7; Rev. 1.5; I Peter 1.2, 19; Rom. 3.25; Eph. 1.7; Heb. 9.12), gave rise to the idea that the precious blood is a part of the sacred humanity and is hypostatically united with the second Person of the Trinity. It is argued that this view goes back to Ignatius of Antioch. This idea grew in the Middle Ages into a cult of veneration. There was a fruitless debate in the fifteenth century between the Franciscans and the Dominicans on whether the Blood shed remained united to the Word, the Dominicans arguing for, the Franciscans against. Since Trent (q.v.) referred to the body and blood of Christ as *partes Christi Domini*, it was subsequently argued that the blood shed during the passion was united with the body at the resurrection, save for those few particles which were now holy relics (i.e. the blood that adhered to the spear, the scourging pillar, etc.). Such blood, it is argued, is worthy of worship, and the Roman Church has appointed feasts of the Most Precious Blood (Friday after Lent IV; First Sunday in July). The various fraternities dedicated to this cult devote themselves to meditation on the Passion and concern themselves especially with the conversion of sinners, with the wants of the Church, and with the relief of souls in purgatory. *See also* **Blood of Christ.**

JAMES ATKINSON

Predestination

1. *The Traditional Doctrine.* The traditional doctrine of predestination is basically that of Augustine. His teaching was modified in certain features and sharpened in others by later theologians, but the framework and the terms of reference which ruled the doctrine for fifteen hundred years were laid down by Augustine at the end of the fourth century. We may therefore describe the traditional doctrine by way of Augustine and the changes made by later writers.

Salvation is the gift of God. This theme dominates all Augustine's thinking on the subject. It is true that he consistently allows a place to man's free-will; but that man chooses aright is itself the gift of God. This truth he learned long before the Pelagian controversy, and before he wrote his *Letter to Simplicianus*. At that time I Cor. 4.7 impressed itself powerfully upon him: 'For who maketh thee to differ and what hast thou that thou hast not received? Now, if thou hast received it, why dost thou glory as if thou receivedst it not.' He already held that election was God's act, but 'that even the merit of faith was God's gift, I neither thought of inquiring into, nor did I say' (*Pred. Sts.* ch. 7). Now he learned from I Cor. 4.7 that faith also was the gift of God. Therefore, while we must not forget Augustine's emphasis on the role of the will, it does not affect our present argument that salvation is the gift and action of God. It was God who took the first step by turning to sinful man in mercy, who sent his Son to die and rise again for man's redemption, who sent preachers to declare the redemption of Christ and to call men to repentance and faith, who quickens faith in the Gospel and gives a heart of flesh to repent, who justifies, sanctifies and glorifies man. But we must go further. When did he turn to man in mercy? When did he determine to send his Son? Behind God's redeeming dealings with mankind lies his purpose and determination. The doctrine of predestination affirms that this was no reaction of God when confronted by sin, no *ad hoc* decision, but his eternal purpose, determined freely before and outside time. Moreover, God's mercy is shown, not to mankind in general, but to individual men, so that it is to individuals that God's eternal purpose relates. A man hears the gospel and repents and believes. This is a moment in an eternal history. The call that the man heard and responded to was made in consequence of God's eternal decision for him. And now before him lies the 'inheritance incorruptible and undefiled, reserved in heaven for you who by the power of God are guarded through faith unto a salvation ready to be revealed in the last time' (I Peter 1.4 f.). Thus Augustine will say: 'The Lord knows those that are his. All things work together for good for those alone who are called according to his purpose: the called according to his purpose, not the called simply: not the many called, but few chosen. For whom he did foreknow he also did predestinate to be conformed to the image of his Son, that he might be the first-born among many brethren: and whom he did predestinate, them he also called; and whom he called, them also he justified; and whom he justified, them he also glorified. All things work together for good to those who were chosen before the foundation of the world by him who calleth those things which be not as though they were; to the elect according to the election of grace, who were chosen before the foundation of the world freely, and not on account of any good works foreseen. Within that number of the elect and the predestinated, even those who have led the worst lives are by the goodness of God led to repentance' (*Jul. Pel.* ch. 5).

It was clear to Augustine that the fact that, wherever the gospel is preached, some believe and accept it and some reject it, was to be ascribed to the election of God. 'Many hear the word of truth; but some believe, while others contradict' (*Pred. Sts.* ch. 11). There is thus a division made between men. But why do some believe, others contradict? 'The former will to believe; the latter do not will. Who does not know this? Who can deny it?' But this is not the final answer, for 'in some the will is prepared by the Lord, in others it is not prepared' (*Pred. Sts.* ch. 11). Therefore it is God who makes the division between men, according to his mercy and judgment. That he chooses sinners is an act of mercy; that he leaves sinners to the recompense of their sin is an act of judgment. Both are sinners; the one is not more deserving than the other; both have earned and deserve the judgment of God. 'Therefore what the election obtained, it obtained freely. There preceded none of those things which they might first give, and it should be given them again. He saved them for nothing. But to the rest who were blinded, as is there plainly declared, it was done in recompense' (*Pred. Sts.* ch. 11). The conclusion, to which Augustine was not afraid to go, is that mankind is from all eternity divided into two classes of elect and nonelect. The elect, of whom there are from all eternity a fixed number (known only to God) will in time believe and at last be saved. Nor is it possible that any of them should perish, otherwise God would be mistaken in his foreknowledge. The nonelect are so because God has rejected them on account of their sin, and they are justly, as sinners, condemned to eternal punishment. Yet Augustine does not, strictly speaking, teach a double predestination, putting reprobation into the same category as election, as part of the one decree. Predestination for him means election to eternal life and is therefore opposed to reprobation.

The eternal will of God was regarded as active determination and not as permission or passive foreknowledge. Augustine's earlier position was that God predestined those whom he foresaw would believe: 'I pursued my reasoning to the point of saying: "God did not therefore elect the works of anyone in foreknowledge that he himself would give them, but he elected the faith, in the foreknowledge that he would elect that same person whom he foreknew as one that would believe on him, to whom he would give the Holy Spirit, so that by doing good he might obtain eternal life also." I had not yet very carefully sought, nor had I as yet found, what is the nature of the election of grace which assuredly is not grace if any merits precede it' (*Pred. Sts.* ch. 7). His settled teaching, however, was to regard foreknowledge itself actively as predestination (*Gift Pers.* ch. 47). In other words, God was in no sense a passive spectator before the event, but as the sovereign Lord determined the eternal lot of each man and therefore foresaw how he would deal with each man and what should become of him.

The obvious objection to be levelled against Augustine's doctrine of predestination is the apparent arbitrariness of God's action, in that all men deserved alike of God but he did not treat all alike; the one was eternally, and justly, condemned for his sin, the other eternally, and mercifully, blessed in spite of his sin. In answer Augustine retaliates with the verses, 'Nay but, O man, who art thou that repliest against God? Shall the thing formed say to him that formed it, Why didst thou make me thus?' (Rom. 9.19) and 'O the depth of the riches both of the wisdom and the knowledge of God! How unsearchable are his judgments, and his ways past finding out!' (Rom. 11.33). The will of God in this respect is hidden and unrevealed, and therefore unknowable, 'a gulf of bottomless depth, God's unsearchable purpose' (Hooker, ed. Keble, 1845. II. 556). It is blasphemous temerity to attempt to discover it. Yet Augustine is firm to defend God against the charges of arbitrariness and injustice. That God is merciful even in rescuing one sinner from hell, no-one who accepts the biblical view of sin will deny. But it is also necessary that he shall show his justice, or his righteousness will be impaired. Justice is shown when he leaves sinners to the just recompense of their sin. 'It is therefore settled that God's grace is not given according to the deserts of the recipients, but according to the good pleasure of his will, to the praise and glory of his grace; so that he who glories may by no means glory in himself, but in the Lord who gives to those men to whom he will because he is merciful: if, however, he does not give, he is righteous; and he does not give to whom he will not, that he may make known the riches of his glory to the vessels of mercy. For by giving to some what they do not deserve, he has certainly willed that his grace should be free, and thus genuine grace; by not giving to all, he has shown what all deserve. Kind in his kindness to some, righteous in the punishment of others, and good in respect of all, because it is good when that which is due is rendered; and righteous in respect of all, since that which is not due is given without wrong to anyone' (*Gift Pers.* ch. 28).

But it may well be asked what place Jesus Christ has in Augustine's doctrine of predestination, especially because we shall later find that the most devastating attack made on the traditional doctrine concerns this very point. In the first place, Christ is the 'most eminent', 'most illustrious' example of predestination. This is the theme of chapters 30 and 31 of *Pred. Sts.* and of chapter 67 of *Gift Pers.* Christ was predestinated to be the Son of God, not from any merit in himself but purely by the grace of God. His predestination is the pattern of man's, particularly in that it is by grace. Therefore, 'if any believer wishes thoroughly to understand this doctrine, let him consider him, and in him he will find himself also' (*Gift Pers.* ch. 67). Again, Christ was predestinated that he might be the head of the Church, and that it might be his body. Secondly, through Christ our election is realized. The salvation to which God had predestinated his elect is effected by the sacrifice and resurrection of Jesus Christ and, subjectively, by faith in Christ on man's side. The corollary to this is of very great importance in Augustine. It is that we are elected *into* Jesus Christ. Here the Johannine sayings of Jesus play a

large part: 'All that the Father gives me will come to me' (6.37); 'no one can come to me unless the Father who sent me draw him' (6.44); 'thine they were, and thou gavest them to me' (17.6); 'my Father, who has given [my sheep] to me' (10.29). It is true that Augustine very frequently both quotes Eph. 1.4 and also himself asserts that God elected us in Christ and chose us in accordance with his purpose in Christ, but he does not follow this up or lay the same weight on it as he does on the texts in St John. Election into Jesus Christ means the objective and subjective effectualization of predestination.

Even in its basic form, and before contention had pressed Augustine to strengthen and harden his position, this doctrine had aroused controversy. Pelagius, a monk resident in Rome, was distressed at the moral standards prevalent among Christians. For this he blamed the doctrine of grace, particularly in the form in which Augustine had stated it in his *Confessions* with the epigram, 'give what thou commandest and command what thou wilt'. Pelagius considered this as so putting the emphasis upon the work and gift of God as to destroy man's answerability before God and hence his responsibility for his actions. He put forward in opposition the following scheme: Man's relation to God should be thought of in terms of capability, willing and being (in Latin, *posse, velle* and *esse*). God has endowed man with the *capability* for doing good. But whether he *chooses* to do good depends upon himself; he may go wrong and choose evil, but he has at any rate been given the capability of choosing good. Whether he puts his good will into effect also depends upon himself. This being so, it is easy to take the next step, as Pelagius apparently did, and say that man is able to keep the commandments and to be without sin. Pelagius no doubt believed that he was balancing the claims of God and of man in his theory. God gets his due, because he first gave man the capability. Man gets his due, and is made answerable and responsible. Augustine, however, saw that this was a complete perversion of Christianity; that, instead of the biblical good news that Jesus Christ is the unique Saviour and therefore that salvation is by faith in him, Pelagius was purveying the gloomy tidings that man had to save himself by his good activities. To this moralism and legalism he opposed the doctrine of gracious predestination that we have expounded. The outcome of the controversy was that Pelagius was condemned but that his ideas lingered on down the ages. In an effort to remove both the scandal of Pelagianism and the rigour of Augustine, some theologians taught what is called Semi-Pelagianism. Here far more weight is placed on God's part in salvation and far less on man's; and certainly many of the blatantly unbiblical elements in Pelagianism were corrected. Nevertheless, semi-Pelagianism was still thinking along the wrong lines, was still moralistic at heart, and therefore could not begin to provide a biblical doctrine of predestination and to correct Augustine's weaknesses.

Thomas Aquinas deals with predestination (*Summa Theologica*, 1.23) as a special part of the general doctrine of providence, and it is to providence that he continually recurs. Just as all things are ordered by the providence of God towards their due end, so men are directed towards the eternal life which God in his mercy desires for them. But this directing does not come into being when man comes into being but pre-exists in the mind and will of God. Thomas expresses this pre-existent directing by the very difficult Latin word *ratio*. The Dominican translators of the English version render it in this context as 'type', linking it with the exposition of Plato in 1.15–30. So Thomas defines predestination as 'the type of the direction of a rational creature towards the end of life eternal' (1.23.1). Nevertheless it is clear from his later statements that he does not envisage this type or pre-existent direction as a passive foreknowledge but as an active willing by God of the salvation of those not yet born.

Not all men are predestinated to eternal life. On the contrary, God reprobates some (1.23.3). But, like Augustine, Aquinas places reprobation in a different category from predestination. For him also, predestination is to eternal life. Objection 2 had deliberately related the two: 'If God reprobates any man, it would be necessary for reprobation to have the same relation to the reprobate as predestination has to the predestined.' His reply is that whereas predestination is the cause of both present and future gifts of believers – i.e. grace and glory – reprobation is the cause only of the future lot of unbelievers, eternal punishment, since the sin comes from the free-will of the man who is not given God's grace. For reprobation is God's permissive will, allowing a man to fail to reach the goal of eternal salvation, or put positively, permitting him to fall into sin and condemning him for his guilt.

After this view of the shadow side of the providence of God, Aquinas immediately returns to predestination, which signifies a choice on the part of God (1.23.4). Those who are predestinated are indeed chosen by God for salvation in preference to others. But election, in its turn, presupposes the love of God. The way is now open for the discussion of the question of the cause of predestination (1.23.5). Does God choose those whom he foreknows will merit grace and eternal life? After a short historical survey, he gives his answer. On the one hand, wishing to preserve freewill, and the merit of virtuous acts, he sees predestination as primary and secondary: 'Thus we might say that God pre-ordained to give glory on account of merit, and that he pre-ordained to give grace to merit glory.' On the other hand it must unequivocally be said that predestination had no cause in ourselves; its reason 'must be sought for in the goodness of God'. And we must note that the goodness of God is revealed, not only in predestination, but also in rejection: 'in respect to those whom he predestines, by means of his mercy, in sparing them; and in respect of others, whom he reprobates, by means of his justice, in

punishing them. This is the reason why God elects some and rejects others.'

Predestination infallibly and most surely achieves its end (1.23.6). This does not mean that man's freedom of choice is destroyed and that a necessity of action is laid upon him. Considered from the side of man, it is possible for him to fall away and die in mortal sin. Yet, since providence is infallible and the will of God immutable, it is not possible, granted that a man is predestinated. Therefore, even the number of the elect is settled (1.23.7). This number cannot, of course, be known to us; but it is known to God, not merely because he is omniscient and therefore knows the number of the elect just as he knows the number of grains of sand on the sea-shore, 'but by reason of his deliberated choice and determination'.

If predestination is certain, what place is there for prayer (1.23.8)? Wny pray for one's own salvation or that of others? On the other hand, may we not say that prayer changes the predestination of God? Against these two questions, Scripture both exhorts us to pray and also declares that God's predestination is immutable. Thus this matter must be discussed from two sides. In that God's will is unchangeable, predestination cannot be furthered by prayer. It is not due to prayer that anyone is predestined. But predestination is effected through secondary and natural causes, in such a way 'that whatever helps that person towards salvation falls under the order of predestination'. Prayer (along with other good works) comes in this category of means by which 'predestination is most certainly fulfilled'.

All this, it will be observed, Aquinas has been able to declare without specific reference to Jesus Christ. For this we have to wait until the Third Part of the *Summa*, Question 24, where in four Articles he considers the predestination of Christ. That the Word became flesh was no after-thought of God but the effecting of his eternal predestination. But this must be viewed rather from the side of Christ's human nature than from the divine. Aquinas, it is clear from this section, is thinking of predestination as the decision of the Father taken in respect of realities that exist over against him. Predestination is neither a self-determination of the Father, nor can it be a determination of the Son in himself, for the Son is one with the Father. Hence the predestination that is involved in the incarnation is the predestination of the man to become one with the Word; 'but because grace was not bestowed on the Son of God that he might be man, but rather on human nature, that it might be united to the Son of God, it is more proper to say that *Christ, as Man, was predestined to be the Son of God, than that Christ, as Son of God, was predestinated to be Man*' (3.24.2). Nevertheless, he also admits that the assumption of flesh by the Son of God must be regarded as predestination inasmuch as it was gratuitous (*ibid.*).

The relation of Christ's predestination to our own he describes in two ways. First, it is the exemplar and pattern of ours. Yet not in respect of the act of God's decision, for this embraces both

Christ and us in one. God did not predestinate Christ and us separately and in different ways but in the same way and together, by one act of predestination. Exemplar, or pattern, implies a certain distinction as well as a relationship; it is an analogical term. Hence, Christ's predestination is the exemplar of ours in the effect of predestination, and this in two ways: both he and we are predestinated to certain good ends, he to be the Son of God by nature, we to be the sons of God by adoption; and again, both he and we are predestinated by grace; his flesh had no antecedent merits to demand its assumption by the Word, and we also are made the children of God by grace and not by merits.

But secondly, Christ's predestination is the cause of our own. Once again, not in regard to God's act of decision, for, since this was one act, causality can play no part. But in respect of its effect God determined that our salvation should be achieved through the incarnation, cross and resurrection of Jesus Christ. It is true that he could have determined other means, if Christ had not been incarnate. But in fact, by determining the incarnation he also determined that through this means we should be saved.

We turn to Calvin, with whose name predestination is popularly linked. Yet Calvin himself thought that he was merely reproducing Augustine's doctrine. Not only does he lean heavily on him in the relevant section in the *Institutio* (iii.21–24) and also in *The Eternal Predestination of God* (in which, indeed, he devotes a whole section to an exposition of the master's doctrine), but he even goes so far as to say that he could quite willingly confine himself to copying out Augustine, for this would give his own doctrine also (iii.22.8). Nevertheless he goes beyond Augustine and Aquinas, for he follows post-Augustinian orthodoxy in ascribing election and reprobation to the one predestining decree of God. For the sake of brevity we will expound Calvin's doctrine in the 1559 *Institutio*; but the reader should remember that this is to some extent balanced in his other writings and given a less philosophical form in his commentaries and sermons.

He starts by taking up Augustine's point on the inequality of preaching. The gospel is not preached to all and even where it is preached, it meets with an unequal reception. The reason is to be found in God's will. 'In this diversity the wonderful depth of God's judgment is made known. For there is no doubt that this variety also serves the decision of God's eternal election' (iii.21.1). But this is a subject fraught with difficulty and even danger, for it is hidden within God himself and to inquire into it is to penetrate 'the sacred precincts of divine wisdom' (iii.21.1). The only safe path of investigation is to keep to the Scriptures, where God reveals to us so much of his will as he knows to be good for us. The Word of God will then both enlighten our darkness and restrain our imaginations. Therefore we must keep to the Scriptures alone; but, keeping to them, we must nevertheless enter into the fulness of the Scriptures. Temerity and fear are equally out of place here. This introduction ended, Calvin gives his well-known definition: 'We call predestination God's eternal decree, by which he determined with himself what he willed to become of each man. For all are not created in equal condition; rather, eternal life is foreordained for some, eternal damnation for others. Therefore, as any man has been created to one or the other of these ends, we speak of him as predestined to life or to death' (iii.21.5).

Predestination is seen first, in the election of Israel, the people of God, and secondly, in a choice and rejection within the nation itself, so that, for example, Isaac and Jacob were chosen, Ishmael and Esau rejected. When he comes to the individual elect, whether Jews or Gentiles, Calvin at once refers us to Christ 'in whom the heavenly Father has gathered his elect together' (iii.21.7). Unfortunately, he does not develop this theme. The election of God is free; it is not dependent on human merits, for God's decision precedes all merits: 'When Paul teaches that we were chosen in Christ "before the creation of the world", he takes away all consideration of real worth on our part, for it is just as if he said: Since among all the offspring of Adam, the heavenly Father found nothing worthy of his election, he turned his eyes upon his Christ, to choose as members from his body those whom he was to take into the fellowship of life' (iii.22.1). Nor is election to be regarded as God's foreknowledge of merits, for this would place the cause of election in man and so take it out of the power of God and destroy the freedom of his will. There is certainly a relationship between predestination and the good works of men, but it is one in which God's choice is primary and effective and man's righteousness is secondary and consequent. 'Say: "He chose us because he foresaw that we would be holy", and you invert Paul's order' (iii.22.2). On the contrary: 'he chose us that we should be holy . . . the godly have their holiness from election' (iii.22.2). In any case, God's foreknowledge must not be regarded as passive, as if 'he foreknows, from an idle watchtower, what he does not himself carry out' (iii.22.6), for he 'is not a watcher, but the author, of our salvation' (iii.22.6).

At this point Calvin takes up the Johannine texts that had so influenced Augustine. Some men are already the possession of the Father, in virtue of his choosing them to himself. In due time he gives them to his Son, that they may become believers in him, members of his body. And this, not purely by some transcendental transaction, but by 'drawing' them to Christ: 'the Father's gift is the beginning of our reception into the surety and protection of Christ' (iii.22.7). 'The elect are said to have been the Father's before he gave them to his only-begotten Son' (iii.22.7). Once again, however, Calvin checks himself as he sees the danger of separating Christ and the Father, and insists that the divine elector is the Father and the Son together: 'although Christ interposes himself as the Mediator, he claims for himself in common with the Father, the right to choose' (iii.22.7). Hence 'he makes himself the author of election' (iii.22.7). We might say that these two themes run side by side in Calvin's doctrine, but that the former, that the Father gives his elect to Christ, predominates.

What of reprobation? Calvin's definition, it will be remembered, stated that 'eternal life is foreordained for some, eternal damnation for others' (iii.21.5). There is no question here of a mere taking out of the elect from the mass of mankind and of overlooking the rest. Calvin will certainly speak of 'passing over' and 'setting apart', but he sees the passing over as a deliberate excluding by God, determined in eternity: 'those whom God passes over, he condemns; and this for no other reason than that he wills to exclude them from the inheritance which he predestines for his own children' (iii.23.1). This he determined, therefore, before the sin for which the reprobate would in time be condemned had been committed. More, God willed the fall of man: 'man falls, the providence of God so ordaining' (iii.23.8).

The objections to Calvin's doctrine are obvious and weighty. Does it not make God act arbitrarily and tyrannically? Why should God, who is love, will the destruction of any of his creatures made in his image? Is not man given excuse for his sin? On the other hand, why trouble to lead an upright life and strive after the kingdom of heaven if you are already elect? What is the point of preaching? Those objections which concern God's will Calvin answers summarily, like Augustine, by saying that God's predestining will is secret and unfathomable. We are therefore moving in a sphere where the question 'Why?' is impossible and meaningless in that it demands a will prior or superior to God's will and therefore a God behind God. Nevertheless, he is eager to declare that God's will, although hidden and therefore to be taken on trust, is good and righteous. No man has any just cause for complaint. The objection that man is excusable is difficult to combat, as Calvin admits. The fact that God's judgment is righteous means that, although we do not know the cause, the reprobate is righteously condemned. Therefore, he ought not to look at God's predestination and excuse himself on the grounds of necessity, but he should consider 'the corruption of nature from which it really springs' for 'the only reason for his ruin is that he has degenerated from God's pure creation into vicious and impure perversity' (iii.23.9). Similarly it shows a complete misunderstanding of election to argue that it leads to irresponsibility in believers. On the contrary, says Calvin, the purpose of election is that we shall be holy, and its effect is to humble us and to make us fear and adore God. These are the foundations of a responsible Christian life. In rebutting the objection on preaching he follows Augustine's lead.

The last word is with the Johannine passages. Predestination cannot be treated on its own, isolated from the Christian life, from faith, from spiritual wrestling, from perseverance. Therefore not everything has been said when the definition has been laid down, explained and defended. For election is election *into Christ*. Those whom the Father (and the eternal Son) have chosen, he gives to Christ to be members of his Body. From henceforth Christ is their *patronus*, they are under his care and in his service. In him they are already the elect people of God, knowing God in him; by him they are led into the fulness of truth and blessedness. It is impossible that they should be lost – not out of necessity or because they are strong enough to stand, but because their *patronus* will and can keep them as his own. For this reason, Calvin places assurance, not in an inward conviction of election, but in the objective Christ. He quotes Bernard with pleasure: 'Oh place of true repose! . . . O place in which God is beheld! . . . Here true rest is felt. The God of peace renders all things peaceful, and to behold him at rest is to be at rest.' And where is this place? 'If we seek God's fatherly mercy and kind heart, we should turn our eyes to Christ, with whom alone God's heart (*anima*) is pleased'; 'if we have been chosen in him, we shall not find assurance of our election in ourselves, nor even in God the Father if we conceive him as severed from his Son. Christ, then, is the mirror wherein we must contemplate our own election' (iii.24.5).

Just as Augustine's doctrine provoked the Pelagian controversy, so Calvin's restatement of it, made still more rigid by Beza and by the following generation of 'High' Calvinists, led to the revolt of the Dutch theologian Jakob Arminius (1560–1609), Professor at Leyden. His own teaching was carried further by his followers, the so-called Remonstrants, who in 1610 set forward five theses in opposition to Calvinism: (1) God's eternal decree was to elect those who would believe in Christ and to reject those who were not to believe. (2) Christ died, not for the elect only, but for all men, yet so that only believers benefited from it. (3) Man is impotent apart from the work of the Holy Spirit in renewing him. (4) Although the grace of God is the cause of man's redemption from beginning to end, it is not irresistible. (5) The final perseverance of believers is in doubt. In fact (as the Remonstrants afterwards held), believers might fall from grace entirely and be lost. Arminianism was condemned at the Synod of Dort (1618–19) and high Calvinism reasserted; but, as with Pelagianism, the heretical teaching permeated the Protestant Churches and by the twentieth century had almost entirely prevailed. It demands the same general judgment as does Pelagianism. We may sympathize with rebellion against the Augustinian doctrine of predestination. But none of those who rebelled down the centuries was able to save himself from being pushed into an unbiblical way of thinking. Against predestination they could only oppose, ultimately, non-predestination. *See also* **Lapsarian Controversy.**

2. *Karl Barth*. We have described the traditional

doctrine in its three chief exponents. The Augustinian doctrine held sway from the fifth century onwards. Theologians were either Augustinians, semi-Augustinians or anti-Augustinians. They did not step outside the charmed circle. Nothing new of any significance was added, nothing significantly changed. But since the 1930s there has been a new era in the doctrine. Karl Barth has completely and brilliantly rearranged its conditions of treatment and the relative positions of the component parts. He has been like a landscape gardener at work. There is the same place; it has the same name; the same prominent natural features still confront us. But the whole view has been changed by readjustments, trees planted, undergrowth torn up, a stream diverted, new vistas, a new scene.

He first dealt with the doctrine intensively in a series of lectures in Hungary in 1936. But it is in the greatly expanded and carefully worked out form in *Church Dogmatics*, II: *The Doctrine of God*, 2 (ET, 1959) that we shall now encounter it. The chapter, entitled 'The Election of God', is divided into four sections: 'The Problem of a Correct Doctrine of the Election of Grace'; 'The Election of Jesus Christ'; 'The Election of the Community'; 'The Election of the Individual'.

Note the first title: *The Problem of a Correct Doctrine*. It at once becomes obvious that Barth does not see his way clear before him and that he is unable to ally himself to the traditional doctrine as he would wish to do and as he is nearly always able to do elsewhere. He confesses that he wishes he could write this chapter too within the Augustinian-Calvinist tradition, but he cannot: 'I would have preferred to follow Calvin's doctrine of predestination much more closely, instead of departing from it so radically.... As I let the Bible itself speak to me on these matters, as I meditated upon what I seemed to hear, I was driven irresistibly to reconstruction' (p. x). Even more than this, he finds that he is forced into direct opposition to the tradition: 'We cannot be too soon, or too radical, in the opposition which we must offer to the classical tradition' (p. 13). This causes him much heart-searching. How could these great theologians, Augustine, Aquinas and Calvin, overlook something that, as soon as it is noticed, is so obviously true? In particular, how could Augustine and the Reformers, who placed Christ at the heart of their theology, fail to do him justice at this point? 'It is one of the great puzzles of history that the step which we are now taking ... was not taken long ago' (p. 147).

But characteristically, even while disagreeing, Barth listens carefully to what the traditional doctrine is saying and finds value in its underlying purpose. It was intended to protect and proclaim the freedom, the mystery and the righteousness of God – an intention that Barth makes his own.

He is forced to reject the traditional teaching for one reason only: he thinks the Scriptures point in a different direction. Here is an excellent example of Barth's method. He is reverent and attentive to tradition, but obedient to Scripture

alone. In a sense, all that he does in this doctrine is to treat it in the same way that he does all other parts of theology. Whereas the earlier theologians had in effect set up two sources of knowledge about God's predestination, Scripture and Jesus Christ, Barth works with but one, Jesus Christ as he is witnessed to in Scripture. Theology must consistently start with Christ and not come to him later in its course. And, having started with him, it must continue with him to the end. If this procedure is adopted with predestination, the all-important step is taken at the outset. According to John 1.1 ff. (a passage which once again plays a decisive part in Barth's thinking), Jesus Christ is the Word who was with the Father and who became flesh; or, in the words of later theology, he is God-Man. But in predestination it is God who is the subject, the one who elects and chooses man. Therefore Jesus Christ is the electing God, it is he who chooses man. He is, however, also man. But in predestination it is man who is the object of election. Therefore (*see* e.g. Luke 9.35; I Peter 2.6) Jesus Christ is the elected man, the man who is chosen by God: 'before all created reality, before all being and becoming in time, before time itself, in the pre-temporal eternity of God, the eternal divine decision as such has as its object and content the existence of this one created being, the man Jesus of Nazareth, and the work of this man in his life and death, his humiliation and exaltation, his obedience and merit' (p. 116). Jesus Christ is therefore both the electing God and elected man.

But this means that at one stroke the traditional doctrine of the *decretum absolutum*, the hidden and unrevealed will of God, is destroyed. Who is the God who determines this *decretum*? If he is not the God revealed in Jesus Christ, he is an idol and therefore not God. For the eternal will of God is the eternal will of Christ, who is revealed and not hidden. Nor is it valid to posit another will of God (hidden from us) alongside the will of God revealed in Christ. To do so would be to transgress against the simplicity and unity of God. Therefore the *decretum absolutum* is, as Barth puts it, crowded out by Jesus Christ; no room is left for it. This is why Barth is so fierce against Calvin and accuses him that 'in the last analysis he tore God and Jesus Christ asunder' (p. 111).

Moreover, included in this insight is Barth's criticism that theologians have always been in too much of a hurry to get to man as the object of predestination. Primarily, election is a self-election, a self-determination, on the part of God. God elects not to be alone but to have man as his covenant partner. 'I will be your God: you shall be my people' is a choice of the people only because it is first God's choice to be the God of this people. This is a genuine choice; God chooses this mode of existence and rejects any other. It is a gracious choice; God was not compelled to make it, but chose freely. And again, God's self-election appears in the fact that graciously and freely he chose to become man and to bear man's rebellion and guilt himself. 'In the beginning, before time and space as we know them, before creation, before there was any reality distinct from God which could be the object of the love of God or the setting for his acts of freedom, God anticipated and determined within himself (in the power of his love and freedom, of his knowing and willing) that the goal and meaning of all his dealings with the as yet non-existent universe should be the fact that in his Son he would be gracious towards man, uniting himself with him. In the beginning it was the choice of the Father himself to establish this covenant with man by giving up his Son for him, that he himself might become man in the fulfilment of his grace. In the beginning it was the choice of the Son to be obedient to grace, and therefore to offer up himself and to become man in order that this covenant might be made a reality. In the beginning it was the resolve of the Holy Spirit that the unity of God, of Father and Son, should not be disturbed or rent by this covenant with man, but that it should be made the more glorious' (p. 101).

Since Jesus Christ is the electing God, this finally means that, because Christ is God for us, God taking our side against the forces that enslave and destroy us, the electing God is for us. Thus the existence and death of Christ are the objective guarantees that we are elect.

Jesus Christ is at the same time elected man. This is a concept taken over from traditional christology. But whereas it was said that as man he was one of the elect, Barth corrects this sharply and says that he is *the* elect. It is not as if he were merely one among others, for there are no other elect alongside him, far less apart from him. His election is unique, so that the election of all others is a partaking in his election. Eph. 1.4 ('he chose us in him before the foundation of the world') is the other verse on which Barth lays very great weight. We are not merely elected *through* Christ, as if his incarnation and death were the agency or instrument on account of which we are chosen. We are chosen *in* him; his election includes within itself the election of all others. We should note that, because of his emphasis on this verse, Barth makes no use of the Augustinian and Calvinist insistence on predestination *into* Christ.

The election of Jesus Christ is the type of our election, and this in three ways: First, it is, as the traditional doctrine says, not of merit but of pure grace that he is chosen to be the Son of God. There was nothing that he himself as man could advance by way of merit that would cause the eternal Word to become flesh, taking and sanctifying the flesh of Adam that it should become holy and obedient. We also are chosen by grace and not on account of any merit that we might have.

Secondly, his election was to suffering and death. That the NT understands his suffering as foreordained is abundantly clear. 'This Jesus, delivered up according to the definite plan and foreknowledge of God, you crucified and killed by the hands of lawless men' (Acts 2.23); 'the lamb [that hath been] slain from the foundation of the world'

(Rev. 13.8 AV). The converse is equally true, that his election was to suffering and death. 'Was it not necessary that the Christ should suffer these things and enter into his glory?' (Luke 24.26). Here we meet the 'shadow side' of predestination. To speak of *this* election to suffering is to speak of rejection or reprobation. In the death of Christ the wrath of God against sin was actualized, so that he suffered the rejection of God. Yet it was not he but sinful man who had incurred God's rejection. It is therefore sinful man who should bear the rejection and hear God's 'No'. Jesus Christ, the only begotten who was in the bosom of the Father, who satisfied all God's demands upon him, should hear only God's 'Yes'. But God has chosen man's lot for himself. He therefore transfers the rejection, the reprobation, to Christ. Thus the election of the Son of God is also an election to reprobation. In Jesus Christ is worked out the double predestination of God. The consequence of this is that sinful man is not rejected but accepted. 'The justification of the sinner in Jesus Christ is the content of predestination in so far as predestination is a No and signifies rejection. On this side, too, it is eternal. It cannot be overthrown or reversed. Rejection cannot again become the portion or affair of man. The exchange which took place on Golgotha, when God chose as his throne the malefactor's cross, when the Son of God bore what the son of man ought to have borne, took place once and for all in fulfilment of God's eternal will, and it can never be reversed. There is no condemnation – literally none – for those that are in Christ Jesus (Rom. 8.1)' (p. 167).

Thirdly, in Jesus Christ, that is, in his existence and death and resurrection, there is actualized God's faithfulness to him and his faithfulness to perform the will of God. God, who has chosen him, stands by him at every point, even in the heart of rejection, and finally justifies and proclaims his choice by the resurrection. And on his side, Jesus, trusting in God's faithfulness, walks faithfully in the path set before him, even into the midst of rejection. And his faithfulness is justified by the resurrection. This is the type of man's election. The election of those who are chosen in him consists concretely in their faith in him; that is, they trust in him as the actualization of God's faithfulness to him and his own faithfulness to God. Hence, faith in Jesus Christ is election in him.

Here is destroyed the false subjectivity which is concerned about whether one is elect. The answer is: You cannot know anything about God's will for you except as it is revealed in the one Mediator. He has been chosen for your sake, not for his own. He has suffered the rejection due to you on account of your sin. But you believe in him. You believe that the whole significance of his coming, death and resurrection was the execution of God's eternal will and purpose, and further, that he carried out God's will. Therefore, you are in Christ. That which he is and has done is yours. You have been crucified with Christ and have risen again with him. In other words, your rejection has been actualized in him, and in him you are elect.

We can now see that in his landscape gardening Barth has transformed the scene from severity and even gloom into a place of joyfulness and light. He has brought about a miracle that even Capability Brown could not achieve – he has made the sun shine on the scene. It is only after reading his account of the doctrine of predestination that we are able to appreciate the synopsis with which he prefaces the chapter: 'The doctrine of election is the sum of the Gospel because of all words that can be said or heard it is the best: that God elects man; that God is for man too the One who loves in freedom. It is grounded in the knowledge of Jesus Christ because he is both the electing God and elected man in One. It is part of the doctrine of God because originally God's election of man is a predestination not merely of man but of himself. Its function is to bear testimony to eternal, free and unchanging grace as the beginning of all the ways and works of God' (p. 3).

Abbreviations: Augustine, *Pred. Sts. – On the Predestination of the Saints; Jul. Pel. – Against Julian the Pelagian; Gift Pers. – On the Gift of Perseverance.*

Thomas Aquinas, *Summa Theologica*, 1.23; 3.24; 1911–25; St Augustine, *Anti-Pelagian Works*, ed., Marcus Dods, 3 vols.; K. Barth, *Church Dogmatics*, II: *The Doctrine of God*, 2, 1957, ch. 7; John Calvin, *The Eternal Election of God*, ed., J. K. S. Reid, 1961; *Institutes*, iii. 21–24, 1961; H. Heppe, *Reformed Dogmatics*, 1950, chs. 7–8; P. Maury, *Predestination*, 1960; J. B. Mozley, *The Augustinian Doctrine of Predestination*, 1878.

T. H. L. PARKER

Pre-established Harmony

In Leibnizian metaphysics, the ultimate constituents of the world are *monads* (simple, i.e. indissoluble and indestructible substances), and these are incapable of causal interaction with each other; the monads are, in Leibniz's word, 'windowless'. That they *appear* to interact with each other (e.g. as in the much discussed case of mind and body) is due to a 'pre-established harmony' between them having been instituted by God, their Creator. *See* **Leibniz, G. W.**

JAMES RICHMOND

Premundane Fall

Several times in the history of Christianity theories have appeared which argued that a fall of some angels preceded the fall of Adam. This was taught by men like Irenaeus, Athanasius and Aquinas. The persistence of this theme is strange in light of the fact that there are only a few obscure biblical texts that could support it (e.g. Isa. 14.12; Gen. 6.1–4; II Peter 2.4). The theme has no doubt been attractive as an explanation of the origin of the Devil and the source of man's temptation (*see* **Temptation**). It is interesting that usually the

angelic fall is attributed to pride, the same sin that is seen as man's original sin.

Origen developed the most radical concept of the premundane fall. For him the creation of the temporal world was preceded by the eternal creation of the spiritual world. In the spiritual world the angels were free to choose permanent communion with their Creator and the heavenly angels did this. A number of angels chose evil and became the Devil and his followers. A large number took a middle course, being less virtuous than the good angels and less demonic than the devils. For this latter group the physical universe was created in order that they might win their way back to heaven. Men are the incarnations of these fallen angels. Thus Adam's fall can be explained because he had already fallen from his destiny in heaven before he appeared on earth.

Augustine taught that God's original creation consisted of angelic beings. When, under Satan, a group of the angels revolted against God and fell from heaven, God created the earth and man so that saved men might replace the fallen angels. This view of the premundane fall was presupposed by Anselm in his *Cur Deus Homo?*.

The premundane fall has little significant support in contemporary theology. The concept of angels is not theologically popular at present and even the doctrine of the Devil is seldom discussed. On the other hand, the fall of Satan holds a rather prominent place in popular thought where it owes more to Milton than to either the Bible or traditional theology.

N. P. Williams, *The Ideas of the Fall and of Original Sin*, 1927.

WILLIAM HORDERN

Presbyter

The presbyter or elder (q.v.) had an important part to play in the ministry of the Church, but in the early centuries it is not easy to differentiate his role from that of the bishop. This arises from the fact that, with the sole exception of ordination, a presbyter could perform all the functions of a bishop. Nevertheless he did so only as the bishop's deputy. 'Let that eucharist be considered valid,' states Ignatius (*c.* 114), 'which is under the bishop or him to whom he commits it.' The presbyter did not therefore teach, baptize or celebrate except in so far as he had the bishop's express permission to do so. This liturgical dependence of the one upon the other may be illustrated from an interesting custom which survived in the West until the eighth and ninth centuries, although in the East it dropped out of use by the fourth. This was the practice of conveying a portion of the bread consecrated by the bishop at the eucharist over which he was presiding to be placed in the chalice at each of the lesser Eucharists celebrated by presbyters elsewhere in the same city. This *fermentum*, as it was called, was a token that the bishop was the liturgical minister of his whole local church and that each presbyter was at the same time in union with him and subordinate to him.

The presbyter was then subject to the bishop who could call him to account, whereas he and his fellow presbyters could not censure their superior. At the same time the presbyters did assist in the government of the Church, forming a kind of senate or council under episcopal presidency. It was indeed seldom that a bishop acted without seeking their advice and so in the ordination prayer in the *Apostolic Tradition* the petition is made that the presbyter may be filled 'with the spirit of grace and counsel . . . and govern thy people with a pure heart'. In time presbyters became known as priests (q.v.) so that the second of the major orders (q.v.) in the Anglican, Eastern Orthodox and Roman Churches is the lineal descendant of the ancient presbyter.

Although after the second century presbyters clearly did not have the right of ordination, it was the opinion of John Wesley that this was originally one of their functions in the period of the NT; hence when Methodist presbyters were created this was accomplished by the laying on of hands of other presbyters. *See also* **Elder.** (For bibliography, *see* books listed under **Bishop.**)

J. G. DAVIES

Presbyterianism

The term is used for the principle of church polity in which the substantive ministry is that of presbyters, and is also applied to denote comprehensively all branches of the Reformed Church in which this presbyteral pattern of ministry is followed. The Reformers Zwingli and Calvin, in accord with Jerome and Erasmus, held that bishops were originally elected from the presbyterate and did not constitute a superior order. In Britain post-Reformation disputes sharpened the constrast between episcopal and presbyterian churches, and certain standard-bearers of presbyterianism emphatically rejected all forms of episcopate. The Westminster Assembly's *Form of Presbyterial Church-Government* (1645) states that the church officers appointed by Christ are 'extraordinary as apostles, evangelists and prophets, which are ceased', or else 'ordinary or perpetual as pastors, teachers, and other church governors (i.e. lay elders) and deacons'. In American presbyterianism the statement reads: 'The ordinary and perpetual officers of the Church are Bishops or Pastors; the representatives of the People, usually styled Ruling Elders; and Deacons.' The scriptural word 'presbyter' is commonly used of both pastors and elders when they meet in presbyteries. The general structure of Presbyterian Churches is that of an ascending order of courts judicatory composed of pastors and elders in equal numbers. These are representative ruling bodies, each having powers constitutionally defined. Doctrinally presbyterianism reflects its Calvinist beginnings.

G. D. Henderson, *Presbyterianism*, 1954; L. A. Loetscher, *The Broadening Church: a Study of Theological Issues in the Presbyterian Church since 1869*, 1954; J. Moffatt, *The Presbyterian Churches*, 1928.

J. T. MCNEILL

Pre-understanding

R. Bultmann has introduced this word (German: *Vorverständnis*) into contemporary theological discussion as a first principle of hermeneutics (q.v.). The interpreter of a text must bring to his task an understanding of what it is talking about, i.e., of the human situation of the original author. There must be a living relation between the writer and the interpreter, since otherwise no understanding of what is being said can be reached. If we did not have some pre-understanding of what (e.g.) the biblical text is saying about the human condition, the Bible could not be understood existentially, i.e. in its true meaning both for the existence of the biblical writers and for our existence today. K. Barth denies that such pre-understanding is possible or necessary. *See* **Autopistic.**

EDITOR

Priest

The word 'priest' is a contraction of presbyter, itself derived from the Greek *presbuteros*, but while the latter is usually translated in the English versions of the NT by 'elder', the word priest is reserved as a rendering of *hiereus*. *Hiereus*, however, is used in the NT of the Church as a whole (*see* **Priesthood**) and was not applied to Christian ministers until towards the end of the second century; and it was not until Cyprian (c. 250) that the presbyters of the NT were commonly called *sacerdotes* or priests. Initially the term was generally confined to bishops and would seem to have been applied to them by a doubtful analogy between the OT hierarchy and the Christian ministry; so according to the *Apostolic Constitutions,* bishops 'are your high priests, as the presbyters are your priests, and your present deacons instead of your levites' (2.25). There is no reason to suppose that this parallelism was just fortuitous; rather it would seem to have arisen from the fact that the early Christians searched the OT to find practice and precept to guide the regulation of their affairs, and this naturally led the Church to think of its ministry more and more in sacerdotal terms and to define its functions largely in terms of worship. Hence the presbyters were regarded as *sacerdotes* or priests, but only in that they shared in episcopal *sacerdotium* by delegation.

The increase in the number of Christian congregations, without a corresponding increase in the numbers of bishops, made this delegation the norm, so that presbyters obtained the right, independently of the bishop, to consecrate at the Eucharist and to administer most other sacraments. Thus by the Middle Ages they were regarded as essentially priests and the ultimate purpose of their office was held, e.g. by Thomas Aquinas, to lie in its relation to the Eucharist, and since this was now given an almost exclusively sacrificial interpretation, the office of priest was understood to consist in his ability to offer sacrifice. This was further supported by the practice, which spread in the eleventh century, of ordaining priests who had no benefices and whose role could therefore be no other than liturgical.

The Continental Reformers, who repudiated any idea that the Eucharist was in any sense a repetition of the sacrifice once for all offered on Calvary, rejected the term priest because of its almost exclusive relation to the Mass so interpreted. It was, however, retained in the *Book of Common Prayer*, apparently to emphasize that deacons have no authority to celebrate the Holy Communion.

Although today there is a renewed and indeed transformed ecumenical understanding of the Eucharist as a sacrifice (q.v.), the question remains whether in view of the fact that in the NT it is the Church as a whole that is priestly, it is legitimate to have an order of priests within the Church. It may be argued that it is, as long as the term is not misinterpreted. Just as the fact that Christ is 'the great shepherd of the sheep' (Heb. 13.20) does not preclude the necessity for under-shepherds to tend his flock, so the fact that he is the great High Priest does not necessarily mean that there should be no 'priests' in his community. Furthermore, just as the Old Israel was a royal priesthood and yet possessed its priests and levites, so the New Israel is a royal priesthood and may possess its priestly organs. But the priestly function is not one that anyone possesses in his own right, as his own private property; it belongs to the whole Body. The special priesthood at the Eucharist, for example, is necessary not in order that its members may do something in the stead or for the sake of the whole Church, but that the whole Church may make its offering by and through it. The nature of this priesthood may best be defined as that of organic representation. The priesthood is representative of the Body not in the sense of acting as a delegate but in that it expresses the whole life of the Body in action. So, for example, when the hand picks up an object, its function depends upon its relationship to the whole body from which it draws its life; it is therefore the active representative of the body, but it is not picking up the object instead of the body, it is the body picking up the object. Hence the priesthood is the representative and organ of the whole priestly Body in the exercise of prerogatives and powers that belong to the Body as a whole. It is ministerially empowered to wield, as the Body's organic representative, the powers which belong to the Body, but which the Body cannot wield except through its own organs duly fitted for the purpose. Understood in this way and freed from any association with false ideas of sacrifice, an order of priests seems a logical corollary of the existence of a Church which as a whole is a royal priesthood. *See also* **Sacerdos**.

E. O. James, *The Nature and Function of Priesthood*, 1955; R. C. Moberly, *Ministerial Priesthood*, 1910.

J. G. DAVIES

Priesthood, Priesthood of all Believers

According to the NT the Church is a 'royal priesthood' – this is a theme implicit in several of the Pauline Epistles and explicit in I Peter (2.9 f.) and Revelation (1.6; 5.10). This priesthood is to be understood in terms of election and is a continuation of that of the Old Israel. According to Ex. 19.5 f., 'Now therefore, if you will obey my voice, and keep my covenant, you shall be my own possession among all peoples: for all the earth is mine: and you shall be to me a kingdom of priests and a holy nation.' Hence priesthood and covenant are closely related and the purpose of the latter indicates the function of the former. God's choice of Israel and his covenant relationship were in order that he might use Israel for a universal blessing (*cf.* Gen. 11.3; Isa. 55.3 ff.; 56.6 ff.). The religion of Yahweh was not to be the exclusive privilege of Israel, but was for all mankind, and her election was to be the medium of blessing to all nations. Israel was therefore chosen by God that he might be revealed through her to the Gentiles. In exercising this mission Israel would fulfil the purpose of her election by bringing God to all men and all men to God. Hence the meaning of Israel's priesthood is to be found in the exercise of a mediatorial function *vis-à-vis* God and the world.

The failure of Israel to carry out this mission, culminating in the crucifixion of God's Messiah, did not mean the failure or the alteration of the divine purpose, for that is eternal and the election was made before the foundation of the world (Eph. 1.4 f.) – this mission passes to the New Israel, under the New Covenant, who are God's elect and are to show forth the excellencies of God (I Peter 2.9). So the priesthood of the Church derives from this election in the same way that the priesthood of the Old Israel derived from its covenant with God and it is then a continuation of that of the Old Israel. The link between the two and the continuity were preserved by the person of the Messiah. Not only Israel but the Messiah also is the object of God's election: he is the elect one, the chosen of God (Isa. 42.1; Luke 9.35; 23.35). When Israel rejected Christ, he remained the sole representative of the true Israel – the Son of Man, both in the individual and collective senses of the term. It is in virtue of his messianic office and of the election that involves that Christ is the 'High priest of our confession' (Heb. 3.1); hence the New Israel derives its priestly character from its continuity with the Old through its Messianic Head.

Because the priesthood belongs to the Church as a whole, it is incorrect to speak of the 'priesthood of the laity'; there is a collective priesthood of the *laos* as a whole, and in this all members of the society, whether lay or clerical, share. There exist two opposite tendencies that can issue in a deformation of this view; the priesthood of the Church may be limited to an order of priests (q.v.) within the Church, and alternatively the priesthood of all believers may be so expressed that it means no more than either 'the priesthood of no believers whatsoever' or 'the non-priesthood of all believers'. *See also* **Laity**.

T. W. Manson, *Ministry and Priesthood*, 1958; H. H. Rowley, *The Biblical Doctrine of Election*, 1950.

J. G. DAVIES

Priscillianism

Priscillianism was a fourth- and fifth-century heresy associated with Priscillian, Bishop of Avila (380–1). The Council of Saragossa (380) condemned certain doctrines and ascetical practices probably derived from him but without mentioning his name. From 388 he is described as a Manichaean (an extreme form of dualist). The movement flourished until the first Council of Toledo (400) which condemned Priscillianist Bishops, but it was not finally suppressed until the Council of Braga (563). According to this Council Priscillian taught Sabellian views of the Trinity combined with an Apollinarian type of christology. Since, however, he rejected Patripassianism, accepted the full trinitarian baptismal formula and some of the other condemned opinions that might have passed muster before Nicea, it is still arguable how much of the later heresy goes back to Priscillian himself. A. E. Burn held that the *Quicunque Vult*, which combines trinitarian and christological teaching, was originally directed against Priscillianism. Other heresies (Arianism, Nestorianism and Eutychianism) are, however, also envisaged. The document rather resembles an encyclopaedic rejection of errors than a counterblast to a single heresy. Burn's view is not supported by recent research.

H. E. W. TURNER

Probabiliorism, Probabilism. *see* Jansenism.

Process Theology

Process theology is the name given in the USA (and increasingly elsewhere in the English-speaking world) to that kind of theological reconception which employs the philosophical conceptuality enunciated in the metaphysics of Alfred North Whitehead (1861–1947), the Anglo-American mathematician and philosopher, and Charles Hartshorne (1897–   ), the contemporary American philosopher. The main point of this conceptuality is seen in its insistence on the full significance of evolutionary (or 'processive') views of the cosmos, coupled with its conviction that God is not only supreme cause of all things not himself, but is also supreme affect–in other words, that God is 'bi-polar' rather than simply and solely 'absolute', 'eternal', and 'infinite'. Whitehead's teaching, that God includes both a 'primordial' (or eternal) aspect *and* a 'consequent' (or everlasting) aspect, is developed to show that he is both infinite and unchanging (in respect to his abiding quality as deity, unsurpassable by any-

thing save himself) *and* also related and affected by all that goes on in his creation; hence he is eminently temporal as well as eternal.

Process theologians assert that the universe is changing, dynamic, even living, with a forward-thrust towards the actualization of the potentialities of which it is composed; they believe that God, as the chief (although not the *only*, since in the creation there is a 'radical freedom') principle of explanation, must also be conceived as dynamic and living, open to the creation as it is open to him. It is their contention that such a model for God is truer to the biblical symbols than the 'classical theism' (as Hartshorne calls it) which would pay God what Whitehead styled 'metaphysical compliments' at the expense of the serious use of those biblical symbols. Hence process theologians cannot accept the conventional notion that God's root-attribute is aseity; rather, it is his love, since such relationship with creation as God is seen to maintain is essentially loving, self-giving, affective, and faithful to its undeviating concern for the fullest realization of the good and its readiness to include within itself all the good that is brought about in the world.

In the light of these major assumptions, process theology has attempted to re-interpret the traditional attributes of God. Omnipotence, for example, is taken to mean that God in his faithful love can use all things, even 'the wrath of man', to turn to his praise; but his 'praise' means his satisfaction in the good which is both his *and* his world's. His omnipresence is interpreted as signifying 'panentheism', all events occurring 'in' God, since his knowledge includes them (whether they be actualized or potential; but precisely *as they are*, in actuality or potentiality) and he is operative as chief agency in them all. The analogy suggested for this is the vitalistic one of the mind and body, rather than the workman and his work; the world is God's 'body', since in every part of it he 'dwells' and 'works'.

The conception of God which emerges from such reconstruction has been outlined in some detail in several recent books, more especially those of Schubert Ogden and John Cobb (*see* bibliography below). Whitehead, in *Process and Reality* (now conveniently re-arranged and edited by D. W. Sherburne, in *Key to Process and Reality*, 1966), and Charles Hartshorne, in *The Divine Relativity* (1948) and *A Natural Theology for Our Time* (1967), have provided the philosophical basis; but the two writers just mentioned as well as others in the USA and Britain have sought to stress their particularly Christian application with reference to various theological positions common to all Christians.

With respect to these theological positions, process theologians would regard the Christian Church as itself dynamically 'in process'; it is a living tradition, whose central experience is life in loving relationship with God and men, rather than the communication of propositions or the maintenance of given liturgical practices. The identity of this on-going process (which *is* the Christian tradition) is precisely in the vision of the divine activity in its continuing interpenetration with the world and men, given focus in the event of Jesus Christ as this has been received and understood. Man, too, is seen as a process, in which he is 'being made and being kept human', his existence being with his fellows in community, rooted in history and organic to the whole natural order. In this conceptuality, it is improper to attempt to define man in static terms; he must be seen as 'becoming man', in that his forward-thrust or 'subjective aim' (in Whitehead's phrase) is the making actual of the possibilities which, from a variety of sources and causes, find their concretion in him.

To interpret the significance of Jesus, process theologians suggest that the Whiteheadian notion of 'importance' (that given event or occasion which, by reason of its illumination of the past, its contemporary impact, and its fruitfulness for future development, may be taken as a significant clue or key to the cosmic drive) is of immense help. Jesus is 'important' in that he gathers up what has gone before him, presents himself with tremendous loving power to those who respond to him, and makes possible new and enriched relationships, both with God and with men, in the time after him. The 'work' of Christ – his soteriological function – is the enhancement of the capacity of those who accept him to live in such new and enriched relationships, freeing them from bondage to their past (which yet remains as a constituent in their forward movement), making available to them a more profound 'subjective aim' for actualization, and providing for them a fellowship or communion in which they may effectively 'become' that which by the intention of God they already are: 'sons of God and brothers of Christ'. In this respect, Jesus is seen as being, not the supreme anomaly in the divine-human (and divine-world) relationship, but as the classical instance; by focusing and concentrating, in a given event, the intentional reality of that relationship, God has provided for his children an empowering that is not alien to their condition but rather the completion and correction of that condition.

It should not be thought that because of this stress process theologians minimize the reality of evil and sin in the world and in human experience. On the contrary, they insist that there is always the possibility, in such a world and among men, each with 'radical' freedom, of deviation from the road to true fulfilment. Not only the possibility, however, but also the present fact of evil and sin: hence process theologians have been prepared to accept much of the analysis of the situation made, say, by Reinhold Niebuhr (q.v.). Yet they have thought that it was both more Christian and more intelligible, in a world such as we now know, to speak of this evil and sin in terms of deviation, 'back-water', failure to participate in the purposes of love (which are God's purpose in his world), than in terms of some 'state' into which man has 'fallen' or some radical evil in the world. For to say 'radical', in this context, is (as they see it) to

deny both the goodness of God's creation and the possibilities which are still present and available for man's fulfilment through the working of 'grace through faith'.

The concern for the dynamics of the physical universe and of human personality, the social nature of man and his organic relation to the universe in which he lives, and the interpenetration of mental and physical in human experience, have led process theologians to assert that it is in 'events', rather than in 'things'; in action or activity, rather than in 'substances'; in creation as a continuing process, rather than in creation as a finished product, that we may best interpret the order of nature and human life. At the same time, since God is 'the chief exemplification' (as Whitehead once put it) of the 'metaphysical principles' required to make sense of that with which we are concretely presented in experience, the conception of deity cannot be so entirely different as to contradict all that is thus presented to us. In consequence, process theologians have been attracted to those results of biblical study which emphasize the living God as intimately related to every aspect of creaturely existence and which see the world as 'open' to him and patient of his activity within it. They have also found in contemporary existentialism, with its stress on man's 'subjective pathos' and the requirement laid upon him to 'decide', 'engage himself', make 'commitments', an illuminating insight for which (they think) process metaphysics provides a context. In addition, the view of history as essentially 'the past-come-alive-in-our-present', a view often expressed in modern discussion of the philosophy of history, has been of interest to them; while the findings of the newer 'depth psychologies', putting such emphasis on man's desires and strivings for self-realization, have appeared to confirm their own convictions about the nature of man as 'becoming', his potentialities seeking actualization, and his identity through the 'subjective aim' which possesses him.

In conclusion, we may note that the process theologian feels that his point of departure as well as his constant reference to the concrete experience of men in the world, enables him to escape the 'linguistic veto' which certain types of contemporary philosophy seem to impose on all metaphysical (and theological) statements. The world in which we live, as we experience it, is no meaningless flight of fancy, no absurd leap out of common existence. It includes not only the strictly factual, in the sense of scientifically verifiable, data; but also feeling-qualities, apprehensions and intuitions, poetic insight, and the empathetic identification of man with his natural environment. All this is related to, organic with, indicative of, and significant for the order of things apart from man. Here, process theology believes, is a connection, a reference, and even a verification of the 'religious interpretation' of 'how things go'. Hence such thinkers accept the therapeutic function of linguistic philosophy but refuse to permit such philosophy to confine 'truth' to the tautological, the scientifically verifiable, or the immediately tested. There is more to man and his world than *that*, they say, and it is in no sense 'irrational' or 'nonsensical' to attempt to develop the significance of this 'more'.

Every theology must have some final criterion. Paul Tillich has 'the new being'; biblical fundamentalism had 'the word of Scripture'; liberalism, in the older mode, appealed to 'experience'. Process theology finds *its* criterion in the biblical text, 'God is love', understood in the light of the event of Jesus Christ in whom (for Christian faith) the Love 'which moves the sun and the other stars' was vividly 'enfleshed'. Any theological opinion which cannot express that central affirmation process theologians would reject; it is their belief that the conceptuality which they propose sustains the test. It is also their belief that such a conceptuality makes it possible for Christians today to respond in obedience to the summary of the Law given by Jesus: 'Thou shalt *love* the Lord thy God with all thy heart, soul, and mind; and thy neighbour as thyself.'

J. B. Cobb, Jr, *A Christian Natural Theology*, 1966; P. N. Hamilton, *The Living God and the Modern World*, 1967; Charles Hartshorne, *The Divine Relativity*, 1948; *Man's Vision of God*, 1966; *A Natural Theology for our Time*, 1967; *Philosophers Speak of God*, 1953; Schubert M. Ogden, *The Reality of God*, 1967; Norman Pittenger, *God in Process*, 1967; *Process Thought and Christian Faith*, 1968; A. N. Whitehead, *Adventures of Ideas*, 1933; *Process and Reality*, 1929; *Religion in the Making*, 1926; *Science and the Modern World*, 1925.

NORMAN PITTENGER

Procession(s)

The term Procession is used in Cappadocian theology as the characteristic particularly of the Spirit (*see* **Generation; Ingeneracy**). After a period of search for a suitable category in which the term Generation was explored (Origen notes the difficulty, Arianism assumed the extension of the term to the Spirit), the Cappadocians settled on Procession (John 15.26). In the Johannine passage it may apply to the Temporal Mission of the Spirit; at least it could be readily extended to the Eternal Procession in later doctrinal development. *See also* **Double Procession** (Holy Spirit).

In Thomist theology the word was applied both to the Son and the Spirit in their relation to the Father. Processions are immanent operations since they issue in Persons of the Trinity and remain within the divine Essence. Aquinas relies on John 8.42 for the Procession of the Son and John 15.26 for the Procession of the Spirit. The distinction between the two Processions corresponds to that between intelligence and will. The Procession of the Word is an operation of the divine Intelligence by way of similitude (the Son is the image of the Father) and is called Generation because 'like begets like'. The procession of the Spirit is an act of the divine will by way of impulse and move-

ment. This is implied by the very name Spirit and confirmed by the special relationship of the Spirit to Love which depends upon will and issues in the movement between the Lover and the Loved.

Two corollaries are drawn from this principle: (1) Since Will also implies Intelligence, the Word is involved with the Father in the Procession of the Spirit (*see* **Double Procession** [Holy Spirit]). (2) Since Will and Intelligence exhaust the possible modes of divine operation, there must be two and can only be two divine Processions from the Father.

Thus Aquinas uses the term Procession in a double sense, more widely to include both the Son and the Spirit and more narrowly to cover the specific relation of the Spirit to the Father and the Son (*see* **Spiration**). Patristic and most modern theology prefer the narrower usage.

H. E. W. TURNER

Promise and Fulfilment

Biblical faith is based upon the promises of God in Israel's history and their fulfilment in Jesus Christ. But the NT itself promises a fulfilment in the future. The Hebrews never lost their original nomadic sense of the horizon which must always be sought, even after they had settled in Canaan. 'Nomadic religion is a religion of promise' (V. Maag). There was always the promise of something new to look forward to: a new Exodus, a new Covenant, a new David, a new Zion. So in Christian faith, though all the promises of God are fulfilled in Christ (II Cor. 1.20), there is still a horizon: Christ's resurrection is promise as well as fulfilment. The NT itself foreshadows a new theology of history: the future is the future of Christ: its purpose is mission (q.v.). Some contemporary theologians, following Bultmann (q.v.), have demythologized the Christian hope, so that it has lost its sense of the goal of history; they speak merely of the goal of the individual believer: eschatology is only a way of describing the existentialist liberation from history. Others (notably Jürgen Moltmann, who sets forth a theology for today based upon hope) are seeking to recover the biblical sense of promise and fulfilment in the historical future, which is the future of Christ's unfinished mission. *See also* **Hope; Eschatology.**

J. Moltmann, *Theology of Hope: on the Ground and Implications of a Christian Eschatology*, ET, 1967.

EDITOR

Propaganda

Propaganda is strictly speaking the Roman Catholic Congregation *De Propaganda Fide* founded as a commission in the sixteenth century to disseminate the faith in newly-discovered heathen countries. But the word is now in general use to mean any sort of propagation of religious belief by any denomination or sect.

R. P. C. HANSON

Prophecy

In speaking forth God's word or verdict upon the situation of their own day the OT prophets enunciated truths which long afterwards were seen to be valid for new crises as they arose in history, supremely in the events of Christ's coming and of the crisis of Jerusalem in A D 70: the divine judgment upon the old Israel and the fulfilment of the hope of Israel in the mission of the Christian Church. Though theologians do not nowadays understand the OT prophecies in a literalistic way (as did the ancient Church), they may hold that nevertheless the Holy Spirit spoke by the prophets (Nicene Creed). (The prophets who seem to have constituted an order of ministry in the NT Church, e.g. Eph. 4.11, are in no way similar to the great prophets of the OT.) The important question for today concerns whether or in what sense the Christian Church itself is or should be prophetic. The prophets of Israel spoke about the will of God in the crises of social justice, politics and international affairs in their own times; in so prophesying they re-shaped traditional ideas about God and gave to the world a new understanding of God's character and purpose. Pronouncements by church assemblies today usually lack this kind of prophetic quality; they are cautious, platitudinous and often trail behind the best thinking of secular societies. They do not make the judgment of God real in the affairs of the nations. Perhaps, then, we should look to prophetic individuals to speak God's verdict upon the issues of our time. St Augustine, steeped in the Scriptures, was able in his *The City of God* to interpret the crisis of Rome (sacked by the barbarians in A D 410) in the light of God's judgment upon Jerusalem in the days of Jeremiah or in A D 70. But today theologians do not seem to consider it to be their duty to relate biblical insights to the crises of the twentieth century. There are notable exceptions: Reinhold Niebuhr (q.v.) and perhaps on occasion Karl Barth (q.v.). There was the Confessing Church in Germany under the Nazis. But the chief theological movement of the earlier twentieth century, Liberal Protestantism of the Harnack type, gave its support to the Kaiser's War in 1914 (and thus caused the young Barth to reject that theology); and the dominant existentialist theology of more recent times has turned eschatology into a matter of individual self-understanding (q.v.) in the here and now. Why did not theologians pronounce God's verdict upon (say) the Treaty of Versailles or relate the destruction of Berlin in 1945 to the purpose of God as revealed in the Scriptures? Who is the prophet of the will of God in the crisis of racial conflict in the later twentieth century? Such questions raise serious issues for theology today. But theology has become a respectable academic subject and prophecy in this sense is hardly the province of academics. Prophecy and theology have been separated, and this may be why theology is deemed by so many to be irrelevant to life in the modern world. *See also* **Promise and Fulfilment.**

H. Berkhof, *Christ the Meaning of History*, ET, 1966; J. Moltmann, *Theology of Hope*, ET, 1967; R. Niebuhr, *Moral Man and Immoral Society*, 1932, and other writings.

EDITOR

Propitiation. *see* Atonement (3 [c]).

Proselytism

The word proselyte comes from the Greek word *proselutos* meaning 'one who has come over' and hence a convert to a faith not originally his own. In the NT this means a Gentile who had been won to Judaism by Jewish missionary activity and became a Jew by undergoing circumcision. Proselytism is now used, almost entirely in a derogatory sense, to describe a corruption of evangelism whereby people are compelled or coerced into accepting a new faith. It is used both of people changing their religion and of those changing their denominational allegiance within the Christian faith. While proselytism is difficult to define it is often typified by aggressive self-assertion, destructive attacks on other people's beliefs and practices, the use of various forms of seduction and coercion and attempts to undermine the religious faith of others.

For the Christian, proselytism may be defined as preaching the gospel by methods which are unworthy of the gospel. The call of God requires a free response; for love cannot be compelled, but only freely given. The preaching of the gospel accompanied by any form of compulsion is a denial of this end. As Jesus Christ refused to compel people to follow him (e.g. Mark 10.17–22), so his followers should refrain from compulsion. While most Christians would accept these principles, it does not follow that the Churches have always kept them, or do keep them in practice.

Some attempts have been made in recent years by the World Council of Churches to ensure that the Christian Churches behave decently towards each other (*see* 'Christian Witness, Proselytism and Religious Liberty', *ER*, XIII. 1 [1960]). This has become possible because of the growing understanding and confidence which has developed between the Churches through their membership of the World Council of Churches (though it has spread further than that membership). In some non-Christian countries even simple Christian witness is regarded as proselytism on the grounds that the exclusive claim of Christianity seems to be a form of proselytism as it brings alien elements into a national culture. The syncretistic attitude of Hinduism finds Christianity very difficult to accept at this point.

A definition and condemnation of proselytism as the abuse of religious liberty (q.v.) to coerce people into changing their faith may be acceptable to most Christians, but the implications of this should be clearly understood. It means that no one person has the right to regard his own position as one which others should accept at all costs.

Charity requires that we should seek the truth together and not try to force any one point of view on others. We do not possess the truth; the truth possesses us in Christ. The use of coercion in evangelism is unworthy of the gospel because it implies that the preaching of the gospel is a human matter. It is God, who is the truth, and not man, who leads people to himself. To coerce is to demonstrate a lack of confidence in the power of the Holy Spirit. Moreover, it shows a lack of respect for the uniqueness of every man, which is implicit in the doctrine of creation.

As a result of the psychological study of the techniques involved in some methods of evangelism, some of them may now be open to the objection that they are in fact proselytism. Even when an evangelist may not be aware of the fact, he may be using psychological pressure which is in fact coercion and not proclamation. This matter requires very careful consideration, for if this is the case what is to be said about the 'willing proselyte' who is glad to have techniques of persuasion used on him when otherwise he will not make up his mind?

A similar problem arises with the question of indigenization (*see* **Mission**). At what point does the failure to proclaim the gospel in the culture, language, and thought forms of any society become the coercion of people to accept concepts which they do not understand and cannot themselves express? If this point is reached it is presumably proselytism and not preaching.

These questions require further consideration, but what the Churches can do right away is to work out in detail a series of principles which could be used by them all to prevent proselytism taking place among them. For a bibliography *see* **Liberty, Religious.**

R. M. C. JEFFERY

Prosopon

Prosopon is a term used as an alternative to *Hypostasis* (q.v.) to express the plurality of the Godhead. In secular Greek usage it could mean an actor's role or mask but rarely a concrete individual. In wider theological usage it could express the Hebrew conception of the face of God, his form or manifestation, and in exegetical contexts it could pin-point the application of an OT passage to the richer subject-matter of the Christian revelation. The vice of 'respect of persons' (*prosopolempsia*) castigated by St Paul relates to the treatment of individuals at less than their true worth. In trinitarian usage it enjoyed a vogue among Western writers who wrote in Greek. Here it secured a greater firmness of application possibly as a result of the influence of the Latin *persona*. Early modalists seem to have used the word for the One God and not for his temporary manifestations, though it is possible that at a later stage the word acquired Sabellian undertones. Seldom used at Alexandria (Athanasius uses it only in anti-Sabellian passages), it failed to maintain itself in Eastern theological terminology. The existence of the more adequate alternative *Hypo-stasis* and its lack of metaphysical background militated against its adoption.

The term played its part in the terminological misunderstandings which were resolved by the Council of Alexandria (362). Its use as a translation of the Latin *persona* was suspected (together with the generally monist approach of the West) of Sabellian influence.

In christology it is used by Antiochene theologians (Theodore of Mopsuestia and particularly by Nestorius) to reinforce a somewhat weak theory of the unity of the Person of Christ in preference to the Cyrilline use of *Hypostasis*.

H. E. W. TURNER

Protestant Principle

A phrase sometimes used by Protestant theologians to denote what is considered to be the central affirmation of Protestantism, namely, the doctrine of justification by faith (q.v.), *sola fide, sola gratia.*

Protestantism

The word 'Protestants' was applied in political circles to the Lutheran signatories of the Protest made at the Diet of Speyer, 19 April 1529, against the annulment of that decision of the Diet of 1526 by which, until a Church council should meet, the governments of individual states were to regulate religious affairs. The term was soon applied to Lutherans in general and finally to all adherents of the Reformation including Anglicans and left-wing groups. Few of the many branches of Protestantism have adopted the designation 'Protestant' in their titles. In many minds it bears connotations of controversy and of contrast with 'Catholicism' where this term is made equivalent to Roman Catholicism. In this sense the word becomes a convenience for statisticians. Protestantism has always shown great variety and rapid change. Sharp internal controversies and numerous secessions on points of theology or conscience were long characteristic; but this individualistic trend was indirectly conducive to the liberal recognition of variety. Early in the twentieth century scholars drew a clear distinction between the Old and the New Protestantism. The latter is marked by adoption of the principle of disengagement of the Church from the state together with that of toleration, thus showing the influence or imitation of the opinions of earlier spiritual humanists, Baptists and Independents (qq.v.). These concepts were most effectively written into political theory by John Locke. The New Protestantism has also been profoundly affected by two movements that gained headway in the nineteenth century and are still rapidly advancing, critical biblical scholarship and the physical and biological sciences. Protestant foreign missions were instituted largely on the initiative of individuals, but their vigorous activities led to the enlistment of entire denominations with the growth of a vast network of organization. This century is strongly marked by a movement away from Protestant individualism. The disadvantages of a competing denominational approach to missions became painfully apparent and various plans of co-operation were put into effect, many of which have already resulted in acts of union. The Ecumenical Movement of the past half-century has felt a strong impulse from missions and missionary organization; but it is also a revival of the largely frustrated unitive projects and efforts of the Reformers and their seventeenth-century followers, and has been shared by Eastern Orthodoxy. Ecumenical Protestantism and Orthodoxy are now in friendly contact with Roman Catholicism. This new and somewhat surprising development is thought of by some as prelude to a veritable transformation of Christianity in its structures, worship forms, and functions in relation to the world society and the non-Christian religions.

J. C. Brauer, *Protestantism in America*, 1965; J. Dillenberger and C. Welch, *Protestant Christianity*, 1954; G. W. Forell, *The Protestant Spirit*, 1960; J. S. Whale, *The Protestant Tradition*, 1955.

J. T. MCNEILL

Providence

The word bears two related senses. Etymologically it means foresight. But this is also transferred to the measures used in regard to what is foreseen. Thus, we *provide for* some contingency, or we are *provident* in saving against a rainy day. Of God's providence it means that he foresees the future (not as a passive spectator but as ruling all things) and also that he cares for his creation, providing for its needs and guiding the course it takes.

With this doctrine we are still in the doctrine of creation. Not that providence is the continuation of God's creating activity, for Genesis represents this work as completed (2.2); but it says that God continues to act towards his creation with the same purpose and in the same spirit in which he had created it. At this point it would be all too easy to treat of God the Father and his fatherly care in isolation from the Son and the Holy Spirit, confining the discussion almost entirely to the OT (though with excursions into Matt. 6.25 ff.; Acts 14.15 ff., etc.), and so set up a doctrine of providence unrelated and even antagonistic to the doctrine of redemption.

Therefore, it is necessary at the outset to ask after the identity of the Lord who will provide. If he is the one who is the Creator, it is certainly not sufficient to say that he is God the Father. According to John 1.3, 'all things were made through' the Word of God, 'and without him was not anything made that was made'. And in Heb. 1.2 we are told that it is through his Son that 'he made the worlds'. In providence, therefore, just as in creation, the subject is the triune God whom we know as the incarnate Word, Jesus Christ. Karl Barth has a fine, bold saying here: 'The world came into being, it was created and sustained by the little child that was born in Bethlehem, by the Man who died on the Cross of Golgotha, and the third day rose again' (*Dogmatics in Outline*, 1949, p. 58). Our earthly life is therefore in no different

hands from our heavenly life. It is through Jesus Christ that God mediates to us not only salvation but all the blessings of this life.

We must also try to describe correctly the relationship between created things with the course of their history and God's purpose in Jesus Christ. It would be a travesty of the doctrine to imagine two different purposes of God, one in creating and providing for and the other in redemption. But it is also insufficient to speak of the creation as the theatre of the mighty acts of God in Jesus Christ. It is this also, but not primarily. The aim and end of providence, as of creation, is Jesus Christ himself. Heb. 1.2, already quoted, has first said that God's Son was appointed heir of all things; and to the same end Col. 1.16 f. says: 'in him all things were created . . . all things were created through him and for him. He is before all things, and in him all things hold together.' It follows that we cannot regard creation as an end in itself. Nor can we regard man in general as the crown of the creation, for whom all things exist. The creation was both made and preserved for the sake and glory of Jesus Christ, the true man and the crown of creation. It belongs to him and reaches its true goal in glorifying him.

It is with these two necessary points in mind that we expound the doctrine of providence as the continuing will and activity of God the Creator towards his creation. God's care for his creatures and their physical needs is universal. This is such a commonplace of both OT and NT that Jesus tells his disciples to treat it as something settled and not to give another thought to it (Matt. 6.25–34). Paul assures the Philippians that 'my God will supply every need of yours according to his riches in glory in Christ Jesus' (4.19), and Peter exhorts his readers to cast all their anxiety upon him, 'for he cares about you' (I Peter 5.7).

There is, however, both a direct and an indirect working of God. First, the direct but hidden working whereby God holds all things in being. Moreover, he can, in caring for his creatures, bypass man and his labours when he will. The sabbath rest, when the creation does not collapse because man stops working; the gift of manna in the wilderness; the feeding of the five thousand; all these indicate that it is God's work which is primary and essential and that man's work is only secondary and accidental. Yet because God's work lies behind man's work, it not only relativizes it but also validates it and makes it fruitful. God supplies man's needs ordinarily as and when man works. Men may therefore confidently execute their work, aware, indeed, that it is only secondary and accidental, but knowing that in the Lord it is not in vain.

Providence refers also to God's oversight of history and ruling of natural events. Once again, his oversight is universal in its scope. He does not appear on the scene just at the great crises (Gen. 3; Matt. 1.18; Matt. 28), but continually accompanies history on its course. The rise and fall of dynasties, life and death, poverty and riches, sickness and health, are all in the hand of the Lord.

Natural phenomena are ordered by him. The heavenly bodies move at his command. They themselves do not (as astrology, that perversion of providence, would assert) either control the course of events or contain within their movements the secrets of the future. Foresight and government belong to God and not to any alien power. To speak of God's direct and indirect working in this context would be misleading, for what is less than direct can only be influence or persuasion, and this does not express the biblical view of God's relationship to history. Nor does it do justice to God's continuing care for his creation to say that he sets in motion a train of events, and that because he is the author of event *a*, he is also the author, at a remove, of event *z*. Instead, we should think of God continually accompanying and continually active in the course of history. On the other hand, we must not picture God as the only genuine actor in history, with men as animated puppets, lacking both choice and power of execution. With their strong or their weak wills, their activity or their indolence, their wickedness or their godliness, men live their own lives. God has given to men that they should be human, not divine, and therefore that their actions should be human and thus their own and not his. There is not destroyed man's autonomy or the reality of his actions or his responsibility for them.

Thus a freedom of man is taken for granted. Man chooses between alternatives. He makes plans. He executes his aims. The theological opponents of free will (e.g. Luther and Calvin) have not denied this freedom. Yet even here man is limited. Why is it often so hard to make a choice? What of the successful execution of plans? Alas! it lies not in mortals to command success. Man proposes. Sometimes he is successful, sometimes not. Why not? Humanly speaking because, perhaps, he has undertaken a task too hard for him, or perhaps because his plan conflicts with the plan of someone stronger than he. Nor should we forget the answer of determinism at this point, declaring that man's choice and planning is not free but determined by such factors as heredity, environment and the pressures of society. That cannot be denied. But this is precisely what it is to be a man – to have ancestors, to live in the world and to live in society. All that determinism denies is absolute freedom, and only God is free like this.

In what sense, then, can we speak of God's activities in history? It is not possible to point to one event and call it the work of man and to another and ascribe it to God. Nor can we say that, normally, there are earthly actions of God running concurrently with men's actions. We have to do with only one kind of actions – human actions. Hence in this sense there are normally no earthly actions of God. Yet this is not to say that God is not active on earth. Behind and alongside all human actions stands the activity of God. According to his own eternal purpose he guides and makes his own use of human activity. This does not make human activity divine and therefore holy. It continues in all its humanity to be a source

of pride or shame to the doer of it and it bears the praise or blame that human works deserve. Men act, and must act, in the human freedom that God has given them. It is in that freedom that God claims their obedience. Yet God does not fulfil his purpose only in men's obedient actions, but also in his careless and even downright rebellious deeds.

Not that God cannot and does not by-pass man's activities and act directly in history. The miracle of the birth of Jesus and the miracle of his resurrection from the dead are the open declarations and guarantees of God's continual oversight and ruling of history which is normally hidden. But whether openly or hidden, God is the Lord over history. Step by step on its road from beginning to fulfilment he accompanies it, guiding and overruling. The fulfilment of history, the purpose of creation and providence, is the incarnation, death and resurrection of Jesus Christ. And it is to this end that God shaped the course of events from the beginning. In their relative freedom of choice and action, men intended this or that. In his divine and loving freedom, God brought to pass that which the Gospels witness to.

Finally we may speak of the significance of providence for men themselves. First, we have the assurance that our world and our lives are in the hands of our Saviour and God Jesus Christ. He who has died for us and has borne our flesh into the presence of God is the Saviour and Preserver of our souls and bodies. Secondly, our faith is not split up, so that now we trust in and pray to the Creator and now to the Redeemer. We have all things, both 'spiritual' and 'material', in Jesus Christ. And thirdly, although it is true that God's purpose will come to pass whether men be obedient, or disobedient, yet he desires his will to be done on earth as it is in heaven. His people, who know that the mystery of the creation is unveiled in Jesus Christ, become by their obedient service the instruments whom God uses to effect his purpose.

Karl Barth, *Church Dogmatics*, III: *The Doctrine of Creation* 3, ET, 1961, ch. xi, 48–49; John Calvin, *Institutes*, i. 16–17; H. Heppe, *Reformed Dogmatics*, ET, 1950, ch. xii; C. S. Lewis, *Miracles*, 1947.

                                                        T. H. L. PARKER

Psilanthropism

Psilanthropism, from Greek *psilos*, mere, and *anthropos*, man, is the doctrine that Christ was a mere man and nothing more. Though Eusebius (*Eccl. Hist.*, v, 28.6) knows of someone who held this view in the ancient Church, the term has been used only since the nineteenth century of the denial of the divine nature of Christ.

Psychedelic Experience

The word 'psychedelic' is sometimes said to have been coined at Harvard around 1961–2, but it is probably older. It is derived from Greek *psyche* (mind, soul) and *delo* (to reveal, make clear or bright); it should therefore be pronounced with a long second e. One of the co-authors of the book *The Psychedelic Experience* (1967), Dr Timothy Leary, was Professor of Clinical Psychology at Harvard Medical School. In psychedelic experience there is a heightening or enlarging of consciousness and a transcending of personal identity, space, time and of almost anything that can be described by language. Yoga and various techniques of meditation, fasting, physical exercise and states of mind induced by religious activities are variously mentioned as possible means of inducing the experience. But the subject has doubtless received widespread attention because of its recent association with phantasy-producing drugs, notably LSD – 25. Hence the rapid degradation of the word 'psychedelic' through its use by advertisers who are eager to catch the attention of the masses by means of the latest cults and 'pop' interests (*cf.* 'the season's new psychedelic colours' – usually orange, lime green, yellow and purple). The matter, however, raises important issues for the philosophy and psychology of religion. If the so-called psychedelic drugs can induce states of heightened consciousness, tranquillity, ecstasy, etc., similar to those experienced at the lower levels of mysticism, ought they not to be welcomed as making available to the many what has previously been the privilege of the few? Or are the dangers (at least in the present state of medical knowledge) so great that the immature, with no stable environment of religious community and moral instruction, ought to be protected against all experimentation and even exploitation? (We cannot here consider the question of the use of drugs in general: *see* Arthur McNaughtan, 'Drugs', *DCE*). If experience of a religious nature can be chemically induced, does this demonstrate the futility of any arguments based upon religious experience (q.v.)? If religious experience is something that can be switched on when we feel the need for some fresh stimulus, does not this show that religion after all is only an escape-mechanism from the harsh realities of life? Or are we back at the primitive level of conjuring with superior powers and substituting magic, albeit scientific, for responsible living? Since the drugs can produce hallucinations and mental derangement (as indeed religion may: the line is hard to draw in cases such as that, e.g., of Christopher Smart) as well as religious exaltation, can the difference between madness and mystical bliss be reduced to a matter of fractional variations in the chemistry of the brain? Some of these questions were asked in a powerful and discerning leading article in *The Times* (London) of 15 July 1967, in which it was also suggested that perhaps most people need to be insulated from the divine wind that blows through the universe, just as they are insulated from cosmic radiation by the earth's atmosphere: 'Certain powerful influences, religion, contemplation, green fields, madness and drugs, which operate on the biochemistry of the mind can fracture the protection and expose the human mind to a divine experience. The experi-

ence is one which only humility and spiritual wisdom can properly contain and comprehend.' Since it is certain that research and experimentation (controlled or uncontrolled) will go on in the coming decades, the questions raised by what has now come to be called psychedelic experience will require the serious attention of Christian theologians and church leaders. *See also* **Experience, Religious.**

Jane Dunlap, *Exploring Inner Space, Personal Experiences Under LSD–25*, 1961; Timothy Leary and others, *The Psychedelic Experience*, 1967.

EDITOR

Psychological Analogy

The psychological analogy is the attempt to find an analogy to the Trinity within the individual soul. This analogy goes beyond most of the 'vestiges of the Trinity' (q.v.) which are often extrinsic and even accidental. Augustine, who first used the analogy, offers several variants: *Mens, notitia, amor* (the powers of inward and outward apprehension and the ability to connect the two); *memoria, intellectus, voluntas* (pure consciousness, image and the simultaneous affirmation of the image and its reversion to pure consciousness); *amans, id quod amatur, amor* (love, lover, loved); *esse, nosse, amare* (being, knowledge, love). The distinctions drawn here are often finespun and the basic psychology obsolete. The most successful triad of Love involves the inclusion of an external object. The analogy has a long history (*see* **Thomistic Analogy**) but one modern adaptation by Dorothy Sayers in *the Mind of the Maker* (1941) deserves special mention. Taking the analogy of human creative experience she constructs the analogy, Creative Idea, Creative Energy, Creative Power. The tendency of the analogy (in whatever form) is monist and leads to a unity in Trinity with greater difficulty in analogizing the plurality. The analogy can be used either to illustrate a doctrine already accepted on other grounds or as supplementary and relatively independent evidence pointing towards and helping to formulate the doctrine itself. *See* **Social Analogy; Thomistic Analogy.**

C. Welch, *The Trinity in Contemporary Theology*, 1953, pp. 152–5.

H. E. W. TURNER

Psychology of Religion

The psychology of religion is the systematic study of religious phenomena as forms of human experience; study of the emotions, attitudes, behaviour-patterns, evaluations, which are associated with religious beliefs and practices; the impact of such beliefs upon the development of the personality; the patterns of needs and desires taken account of by particular religions. It investigates conversion-experiences, prophetic and mystical states of consciousness, experiences as of encounter with divine beings, experiences of anxiety and contrition over sinfulness, of guilt and the removal of guilt; religious exaltation and experience of the sacred; alleged cosmic insights or disclosures. It is concerned not only with individual experiences, but also with group psychology, e.g. the pressures, privileges, obligations to be found within religious groups. It aims at the description of religious experience, at its causal explanation, and at bringing out the affinities and differences among religious and non-religious states of consciousness, both normal and morbid.

A difficult, and for the Christian theologian, very important question, is how far, if at all, this study can bear upon the truth of religious claims, how far it can strengthen or weaken the case for theism. A short answer would be that since psychology is primarily a descriptive study rather than an evaluative one, it has no such bearing. In general, it might be argued, to discover what goes on psychologically when someone engages in an activity does nothing towards assessing the truth of any claims he makes while engaged in it. For example: in playing chess or doing arithmetic my experiences, my anxieties and elations, are irrelevant to estimating the correctness or incorrectness of my moves or answers. So too a *causal* account of how I came to the right answers is logically independent of the validity or invalidity of my reasoning-processes. Our religious experiences, then, might well involve a 'projecting' of emotions, which in early childhood were directed towards a parent, towards an allegedly transcendent being; and although this account might be accepted, it would not necessarily oust the belief that this transcendent being actually existed. God might have indeed built in these mechanisms by which belief is aroused and fostered. Such an account would not rule out independent arguments or evidences for belief in God; and on the strength of these the reasonableness of theism would hang. The Freudian type of account, however, *could* be detrimental to Christianity, if the case for belief rested on alleged 'direct experiences' of God themselves and if the account showed how such experiences could be expected to arise naturally, even if no God existed. The analogies which psychology has brought out between some 'revelatory' states of mind and heightened states of awareness under drugs or in mental illness have made it quite clear that such states can give an *illusion* of being cognitive, and are in themselves an unreliable guide to the nature of the world at large.

The psychology of religion, on the other hand, might have a positive contribution to make to the apologetics of a religion (though again not a *decisive* contribution), if comparative studies showed that it was able to produce in believers a particularly harmonious, well-integrated, flexible, morally serious personality. Not decisive, since these happy effects might follow upon delusory beliefs, sincerely held.

A psychologist who writes on the topic of religion comes to it in the course of wider inquiries, and brings to it his general presuppositions and methodological principles, whether hospitable or

inhospitable to religion. A critical study of the literature must therefore be alert to these principles, which will interpret and evaluate the religious phenomena, and must not accept them as so many indisputable data. A detailed consideration of religious experience, particularly the irreducible 'inwardness' of some experiences, is itself able to challenge over-behaviouristic presuppositions and methods in psychology. *See also* **Psychedelic Experience.**

Among important works are the following: G. W. Allport, *The Individual and his Religion*, 1951; S. Freud, *The Future of an Illusion*, 1927; *Totem and Taboo*, 1919; William James, *Varieties of Religious Experience*, 1902; C. G. Jung, *Modern Man in Search of a Soul*, 1933; *The Psychology of Religion*, 1938; R. Otto, *The Idea of the Holy*, 1917.

R. W. HEPBURN

Psychosomatic

The word is derived from Greek *psyche*, soul, spirit, and *soma*, body. It is frequently used today in medical and psychological discussion to express the truth that man is a unity of body, mind and soul. It is recognized that physical ailments can be caused by deep-seated spiritual or mental afflictions (and vice-versa). *See* **Spiritual Healing.**

Punishment

In the preaching of the gospel as well as in the teaching of the doctrine of the atonement the ideas of the punishment of God come to expression, generally conceived as the annihilating reaction of God's wrath meeting man's sin ([the wrath is never in God but in man, *see* **Atonement** 2, 3 [d] [e].) *See*, e.g. Matt. 25.46; II Cor. 5.11; Heb. 10.26–31). The reality of punishment should not be psychologized into the idea of revenge, nor socialized into the idea that punishment is solely reformatory. The wrath of God and divine punishment safeguard both the individual freedom of man as a self-determining agency as well as the fact of evil, at the same time retaining a fundamental hope in God and his ways. The fact that God has sworn in his wrath that those who err in their hearts shall not enter his rest does not prevent our calling upon such men to sing to the Lord and rejoice in the strength of our salvation (Ps. 95). God repudiates man's sin and man's wilful sin draws to itself its own consequences, its appropriate punishment. God at once dissociates himself from man's sin as man goes his own way undergoing pain, rejection and suffering (i.e. punishment and wrath), but associates himself with the sinner in Christ to redeem him from his sin and thereby annul the punishment due. This argues that in spite of our sin God remains eternally good – he is neither embittered by it, nor revengeful on account of it; he destroys the power and guilt of sin by maintaining his mercy while we were yet sinners. This assurance is the crux of the whole doctrine of atonement which the Church is commissioned to proclaim to sinners.

The OT argues a final day of the Lord when the unfaithful will be finally judged, an idea developed by Christ (and later in the Creeds). It is incontrovertible that the NT envisaged a Second Coming and a great Judgment Day, when the end of history was involved, a visible manifestation of the Christ meting out eternal salvation to the faithful, eternal destruction to the rebellious. There is room for a wide variety of interpretation in all this imagery, crying out as it does for demythologization. Nevertheless, it is incumbent on all demythologizers to learn the harder art of re-mythologizing. Christ's words are hauntingly explicit: 'Fear not them which kill the body, but are not able to kill the soul: but rather fear him who is able to destroy both soul and body in hell' (Matt. 10.28). Luke expresses it more strikingly still (Luke 12.4). Christ's concern is that man should realize that 'there is one who searches and judges' (John 8.50), lest the temporal punishment experienced by the sinner as the wrath of God fulfil itself in eternal punishment. *See also* **Wrath; Forgiveness; Atonement** (2, 3 [*d*] [*e*]).

JAMES ATKINSON

Purgatory. see Hope, The Christian.

Purification of the Blessed Virgin Mary

The purification of the Blessed Virgin Mary is the presentation of Jesus in the Temple at Jerusalem by Joseph and Mary in accordance with the Jewish law (Luke 2.22–39). It is celebrated liturgically in East and West on 2 February. The custom of blessing and distribution of candles, inspired by Simeon's words declaring Jesus to be 'a light to lighten the Gentiles', has given the feast the informal name of 'Candlemas'. It is considered to be a feast of Christ as much as of the Blessed Virgin Mary; in the Latin Church the preface of the Nativity is used, not that of the Blessed Virgin Mary. In the Eastern Orthodox Church its primary title is 'The Meeting of the Lord', and in the Church of England 'The Presentation of Christ in the Temple'.

E. L. MASCALL

Puritanism

Many distinct and mutually discordant movements reflecting the influence of their personal founders are embraced within historic Puritanism. Tendencies analogous to Puritanism are easily identified in the teaching and discipline of Stoics, Pharisees, monastic reformers and mediaeval biblical sects. In Tudor England the influence of the continental Protestant refugees Martin Bucer, Peter Martyr Vermigli, John à Dasco and others, and of the writings of Heinrich Bullinger and John Calvin (qq.v.), and the associations formed by the Marian Exiles, contributed notably to the shaping of the Puritan spirit. In the reign of Elizabeth I those who on narrowly scriptural grounds objected to ceremonies and vestments prescribed in

the *Book of Common Prayer* were called 'precisians' or 'puritans', and the word was also applied to opponents of the Anglican episcopate, many of whom shared the same scruples on ceremonial. Many classed as Puritans sought the recognition of their principles within the establishment; others readily formed separatist groups. Theologically Puritanism was far from homogeneous, but the larger segments, Presbyterians, Independents and Baptists, were prevailingly Calvinist. On predestination, a number of outstanding Puritans, such as John Goodwin and Richard Baxter (q.v.), were nearer to the Arminian position. William Perkins (d. 1602) and in the seventeenth century William Ames, John Preston, John Milton, John Bunyan, Richard Baxter and John Owen were among representative Puritan writers on theology and ethics. Puritan piety rested upon scripture and was in only a few instances mystical. It tended to emphasize the experience of conversion, daily self-examination, and a firm and demanding moral code for social and economic life, for which numerous treatises on casuistry were written. Puritan teaching on austerity and industrious pursuit of one's calling as service to God and man has been associated with the rise of capitalism, but can be largely duplicated from typical Anglican writers. The Mayflower Pilgrims were separatists who had been in exile in the Netherlands, while the Massachusetts Bay colony consisted of Puritans who had never broken from the Church of England and refused to be classed as separatists. American Puritanism produced much serious theological writing, culminating in the brilliant and original Jonathan Edwards (d. 1758, q.v.).

P. Collinson, *The Elizabethan Puritan Movement*, 1967; C. H. George and K. George, *The Protestant Mind of the English Reformation*, 1961; W. Haller, *The Rise of Puritanism*, 1938; M. M. Knappen, *Tudor Puritanism*, 1939; J. T. McNeill, *Modern Christian Movements*, 1954; 1968.

J. T. McNEILL

Pyrrhonism

Pyrrho (c. 360–270 BC) was a Greek philosopher about whom little is known but who acquired the reputation of being the founder of absolute scepticism. In the Enlightenment (q.v.) period the word Pyrrhonism was used as a synonym for scepticism. Pierre Bayle called his own view 'historical Pyrrhonism', by which he meant that no philosophical truths could be founded upon historical facts, however certain these were. He nevertheless made full use of historical facts for demolishing every pretension to philosophical or theological knowledge. *See* **Scepticism.**

EDITOR

Quakers. see Friends, Society of.

Quartodecimanism

A second century controversy concerning the date on which Easter should be observed. The Quartodecimans in Asia Minor followed the Jewish rule of celebrating the Passover on Nisan 14 (hence their name), while in the West Easter (the Christian Passover: *see* **Pasch**) was observed on the Sunday following. A Quartodeciman sect was still in existence in the fifth century.

Quietism

Historically this term is used of forms of spirituality (q.v.) which taught the abandonment of all human activity and the utter self-surrender of the will to God, so that the man who achieves this state by means of mental prayer (*see* **Contemplation**) is no longer interested even in his own salvation. As advocated by M. de Molinos (1640–1697) quietism was condemned by Pope Innocent XI in 1687. Today the word is used loosely of forms of Christian spirituality which advocate non-participation by Christians in political and social affairs and their withdrawal to a 'spiritual' area beyond the reaches of worldly affairs. Its opposite, *activism*, a modern word, is used to denote the attitude of those who believe that the Christian's duty is to be fulfilled in the political arena, the market-place, industrial life, etc. and who speak slightingly of prayer, withdrawal and the contemplative life.

EDITOR'

Qumran. *see* Essenes.

Rashdall, Hastings

Rashdall (1858–1924), English moral philosopher and theologian, made three distinctive contributions: his classic *Universities of Europe in the Middle Ages* (1895); an important treatise on ethics, *The Theory of Good and Evil* (1907); his Bampton Lectures on *The Idea of Atonement in Christian Theology* (1919). In the latter work he became the spokesman for the 'modern churchmen', developing the 'subjectivist' or 'exemplarist' or Abelardian theory of the atonement in modern terms (*see* **Atonement** 6 [*a*]). He argued that the Abelardian view was acceptable to reason and conscience alike, and traced it in John, Paul and the Fathers. The main objection to the view is that no mere example, not even Christ's, does full justice either to the NT expressions of the reality of God's saving act in Jesus Christ or to the NT understanding of the stranglehold of sin.

JAMES ATKINSON

Rationalism

The term is used in different senses, of which at least three must be clearly distinguished. (1) In philosophy it is used to denote the view of such thinkers as Descartes, Spinoza, etc., that certain ideas are purely rational ('innate ideas') in origin and do not depend upon sense-experience for their verification; this view is contrasted with empiricism (e.g. of Locke and Hume), which maintains that all our ideas are derived from sense-experience. (2) In theology reason was held by a long succession of thinkers (from Aquinas to the deists) to be a source of the knowledge of God, at least negatively (*see* **Revelation; Deism**), and this view is often called rationalist. (3) In the nineteenth century rationalism became equated with secularism or atheism or agnosticism: *The Rationalist Annual* (formerly *The Agnostic Annual*) is still published by the Rationalist Press Association, London. But nowadays the old-style rationalists usually prefer to call themselves humanists (*see* **Humanism**).

EDITOR

Real Presence. *see* Eucharist.

Realism. *see* Nominalism-Realism.

Reason. *see* Revelation; Deism; Rationalism; Authority.

Recapitulation

The word is the Latin equivalent of the Greek *anacephalaiosis*, a summing up, or summary. The term occurs in Eph. 1.10, where it is stated that God summed up all things in Christ. Irenaeus (c. 130–c. 200) made it especially his own, interpreting the term both as the restoration of fallen humanity to communion with God by the incarnation and as the summing up and completion of the entire *Heilsgeschichte* in the incarnation. This idea was taken up by the Fathers, and its importance in a theology of the atonement will be readily appreciated. The recapitulation in Christ connotes the total work of God for man's redemption. In Christ are summed up the 'sure word of prophecy', which had always looked for a new Messiah, a new redemption, a new exodus, a new covenant, a new inheritance, a new eternal hope. More is being said in this doctrine than that Christ sums up all the prophecies, aspirations, hopes and promises associated with the OT. It means also that none of these ideas of the OT can be appreciated unless they be interpreted 'backwards from Christ'. Recapitulation means the summing up in Christ of God's long and sure purpose of redemption, a dimension meant to include not only the present aeon of incarnation but the eternal aeon of ascension.

JAMES ATKINSON

Reconciliation. *see* Atonement (3 [*d*]).

Redemption, Redeemer

From the Latin *redimere*, this word signifies the buying back, or paying the ransom, of a slave to ensure his freedom (*see* **Atonement** 3 [*e*]; **Salvation** 6). The idea is usually conveyed in the NT word *lutron* (ransom) and its associated word group, sometimes also with the words connected with buying. The biblical usage of these words is in connection with the saving action of God which culminated in the cross.

God had appeared in Israel as the Redeemer of his People (*see* **Salvation**), particularly in the redemption wrought in Egypt commemorated at the Passover, the hour at which Christ's work on the cross culminated. Jesus expressly associated the role of the servant innocently suffering for his people with the idea of ransom, thereby associating permanently the two ideas of sacrifice and redemption (ransom). It is particularly significant that the NT writers do not develop the idea of ransom to explain the cross, but rather developed the idea of the deliverance from bondage which was its result, a freedom which meant a reconciliation with God of slaves who had been freed by him and were now his adopted sons, in the Son who ransomed them. It is of little profit to ask to whom the ransom was paid, for at that point the metaphor breaks down. The early Fathers spoke as if the ransom were paid to the devil who held all souls in bondage, but Anselm (q.v.) found this idea revolting and spoke of a ransom paid to an offended God of righteousness. It is safer to remain on NT ground where it is argued that the slavery from which we are redeemed is the slavery of wrath (Rom. 5; I Thess. 1.10), sin (Rom. 6), the law (Rom. 7; Gal. 3.13; 4.5), death (Rom. 8; II Cor. 1.10) and the power of darkness (Col. 1.23). If these passages are taken together, it will be seen that Paul uses the technical term for redemption as well as other more general words meaning purchase, deliverance, liberation, salvation. The NT carries on the OT usage in this respect by keeping God and his work in the centre and speaking of the victory or deliverance he effected rather than of the payment of ransom. The thought is on the divine love that went as far as the cross (Rom. 5.6–8). (*See* **Atonement** 6 [*b*].)

Redemption by the cross can be understood only in relation to the reconciliation effected by God (*see* **Atonement** 3 [*d*]). The two ideas should be kept in the closest relationship. Reconciliation should not be seen as an outcome of God's redemptive work, for God was reconciling us while we were sinners (Rom. 5.6–8; II Cor. 5.19). If these two ideas go together, it should always be borne in mind that such reconciliation with God cannot be separated from reconciliation with one's fellows (Col. 1.20, 22; Eph. 2.11–18). If it is safer to remain on biblical ground, it is also prudent to consider how the early Fathers thought of the ransom as paid to the Devil and the later as paid to God. It is obvious that the Devil had no right to it, and equally obvious that the Author of such costly redemption could never be bought. Is there a profounder truth baffling them both? Quite certainly in strict justice God could not simply wipe out man's sinful past as if it did not matter. Sin is man's free act. Simply to remove the sin by divine fiat, or even by divine violence, would never restore the true freedom which God is seeking to give the enslaved sinner. A costlier, slower work of reparation (q.v.) is demanded, wherein man would be restored to membership of a new race in Christ. This is what the earlier Fathers mean, and when they referred to the 'worm' Christ, baited on the hook which the Deceiver deceived, snatched at and was caught, they are only expressing more colourfully what Paul said when he wrote that if the powers of this world had really known their business they would not have crucified Christ (I Cor. 2.8). This is what those Fathers who develop the image of the debt to the Devil are really saying in out-dated thought forms. St Anselm, though arguing a contrary truth, was in fact contributing a complementary truth, when he said the ransom was paid to God. Anselm was arguing that the offence to God of man's sin could never be repaired by man. God's honour could never be satisfied, except at one moment, when Christ for us men and our salvation, standing on our side of the line, met as Son of Man the demands of God in true, filial obedience and defeated the tyrants at the cost of the death on the cross. Anselm is only arguing the cost of our redemption. The two arguments may properly be gathered up in the Pauline arguments of Adam and Christ, the death in Adam and the life in Christ (Rom. 5).

There is another level at which these two complementary truths may be welded. Paul argues that redemption is, on the one hand, from the bondage of sin, death and the devil, and on the other, from the curse of the divine Law and the wrath of God. Yet the Gospel delivers us from the judgment *of God* and the curse *of God*. Is there not a sense here in which we are delivered both from the Devil and from God, and both deliverances by God himself? Is this not what the early Fathers and the later Fathers are maintaining in arguing that the ransom was paid to the Devil and to God? They are both emphasizing a truth too precious to jettison. The imagery has been stretched as far as it will go. We see the cost to God; we see clearly that he could not redeem our freedom by destroying it. We at once move into the imagery of sacrifice to break the tension. This is exactly what St Thomas did in developing the idea of the reparatory sacrifice implied in the reconciliatory sacrifice. He argues that Adam had earned our loss, but the New Adam in his passion had saved us by making the reparatory satisfaction for our sin that we ourselves were incapable of making by accomplishing the reconciliatory sacrifice, and finally by redeeming us in this way from the slavery in which our sin had set us (*see Summa Theologica* 3a. q. 48, a 1–4).

JAMES ATKINSON

Reductionist

Reductionist is a term usually used pejoratively to describe those types of theology which attempt to dilute traditional dogmas of the faith or explain them away, as in 'modernist' attempts to minimize the hard core of essential beliefs in order to make them more palatable.

Reformation, Reformation Theology

The sixteenth-century Reformation in Western Christianity was the culmination of countless movements in which discontent was registered, usually with an appeal to Scripture, against beliefs and practices of the mediaeval Church. None of these antecedent movements explicitly generated the Reformation. It was made possible by the peculiar social and educational conditions of the age, the commanding leadership of Martin Luther (q.v.), and the dedicated services of many other gifted and competent scholars, preachers and organizers. Amid general deterioration in the Church, the abuses connected with penance and indulgences offered the point of departure in 1517. Luther was no cynical satirist but a sensitive Christian whose assurance in controversy came from a personal religious experience. John Calvin, Huldreich Zwingli, Heinrich Bullinger and other eminent Reformers were likewise men who had passed through an inward struggle to an earnest and undoubting assurance of a biblical and evangelical faith. The Reformers were also a company of singularly able men, thoroughly versed in the Bible and the Church Fathers and familiar with the writers of pagan antiquity. A sometimes forgotten factor in the advance of the Reformation is the fact that its opponents themselves accepted the authority of Scripture. When they invoked tradition and papal decisions they could always be embarrassed by an argument to the contrary drawn from Scripture. John Eck confessed at Augsburg that the Roman cause could not be defended from Scripture alone. The Bible had been much utilized in mediaeval theology, but in general had been so interpreted as to avoid calling in question prevailing ecclesiastical practice. The Reformation presented the holy writings as the exclusive norm of belief and worship, often utilizing, with critical appreciation, the patristic interpreters in rejection of the scholastics. It is safe to say that the canonical Scriptures had never before been so intensively studied and so exclusively employed as the basis of Christian thought and action, and as presenting a divine challenge to church reform.

The Reformation gained its successes essentially by persuasion rather than force. The power of certain states was, indeed, used in its behalf. But the great powers of Europe, under Hapsburg and Valois rulers, and many of the smaller principalities did what they could to crush it. In England the preaching of the Cambridge evangelicals led by Bilney and the circulation of Tyndale's NT antedated Henry VIII's abolition of the papal jurisdiction and ambiguous course of legislative reform. These early witnesses were in large degree the inceptors of that scriptural and truly religious phase of the English Reformation later represented by Hooper, Latimer, Cranmer, Ridley and Jewel. The view that the Reformation was either a product or a cause of nationalism runs counter to some weighty facts. The formation of territorial and national churches in the sixteenth century may be thought of as culmination of a process already far advanced under the system of papal concordats and through the frequent intervention in church affairs by princes and local governments. International intercourse among the Reformers was constant and none of them wished to circumscribe his religious fellowship to a national church. The works of many early Protestant theologians passed without hindrance from nation to nation in Latin, and not a few of them were promptly rendered into various vernaculars. Flight from repressive governments caused much fruitful dispersion of scholars and teachers and promoted a mutual acquaintance of churches distantly separated. Sixteenth-century Protestantism largely shared a common stock of ideas and beliefs and was disturbed by the same theological discords. National borders did not halt the intercourse of thought. The radical sects with their emphasis on local group authority were nevertheless constantly stirred by visiting teachers from other political areas and made aware of the struggles of their fellow-radicals everywhere. A great mass of correspondence among religious leaders of the era gives evidence that they felt free to advise and consult as Europeans, or, on matters of high moment, as members of the One Holy Catholic Church.

The social and economic impact of the Reformation has been tendentiously interpreted. A substantial development of capitalism took place in the previous era, and the mediaeval Church was deeply involved with the bankers, notably in connection with the indulgence traffic. Economic habits were of course considerably affected by the stress laid upon the lay vocations as a means of a holy service to God and of usefulness to one's fellows, as well as by the abolition of many economically unproductive holy-days. In the Reformed Churches especially thrift became a Christian virtue, but it was approved not as a means of amassing wealth but as a means of helping others. A strict accountability in the use of one's time, as of his worldly possessions, was enjoined and idlers and spendthrifts were disciplined. To relieve unemployment in Geneva Calvin initiated the establishment of new industries. But nowhere was there in the trail of the Reformation an outburst of capitalistic enterprise. The notion of the individualistic accumulation of wealth was habitually rebuked from the pulpit.

With the affirmation of biblical authority there were differences with regard to its application in the field of worship. Lutheranism and Anglicanism admitted a large element of traditional ceremonial not specifically drawn from Scripture. Lutheranism was disturbed at the middle of the sixteenth century by the controversy over adiaphora (q.v.). What was the range of these things neither enjoined nor forbidden, and how far was it permitted to use them in accommodation to Roman Catholic ceremonial? In England the debate between Anglicanism and Puritanism turned in part on the same issue. The vestments John Hooper was required to wear were admittedly 'things indifferent'. 'Why insist upon them?' he asked; 'why make a point of rejecting things indifferent?' was in effect Cranmer's reply. Hooper had been trained in Zurich, where all unscriptural features had been rigidly eliminated from worship. The order of worship used by Bucer in Strasbourg, based upon a drastically altered version of the Mass, was imitated by Calvin, who opposed Melanchthon's wide range of acceptable adiaphora, and essentially observed, with less rigour than Zwinglians and Puritans, the negative Scripture rule. With regard to the ministry, a similar issue can be discerned. But none of the major Reformers adopted either the high presbyterian or the high episcopalian view.

While the entire Bible was their arsenal in assailing the mediaeval system, it was from the Pauline letters that the Reformers drew their most effective arguments. The doctrine of justification by faith is rooted in Paul's thought, as is also that of the priesthood of all Christians. A new stress was laid by all Reformers upon exegetical preaching, and this was received with keen attention by hearers who were themselves devout readers of the text. The lay folk also participated heartily in singing, whether using the spontaneous hymnody of Lutheranism or the versified vernacular Psalms characteristic of Calvinism. In these ways the Reformation brought a new dimension to the religion of the common people. By spreading the Bible to the people, it made every man a potential participant in its Bible-centred theology.

R. L. Bainton, *The Reformation of the Sixteenth Century*, 1952; H. J. Grimm, *The Reformation Era*, 1954; H. J. Hillerbrand, *The Reformation in its own Words*, 1964 (with extensive source selections); K. Holl, *The Cultural Significance of the Reformation*, 1959; *Gesammelte Aufsätze zur Kirchengeschichte*, III, *Der Westen*, 1932; T. M. Lindsay, *A History of the Reformation*, 2 vols., 1906–7, 1950; W. Pauck, *The Heritage of the Reformation*, 1961; P. Wernle, *Der Evangelische Glaube nach den Hauptschriften der Reformatoren*, 3 vols., 1919.

J. T. MCNEILL

Regeneration. *see* Initiation, Christian.

Reincarnation

The doctrine of the transmigration of souls is familiar in the religion of ancient Greece and in the religions of the East, according to which a soul on the death of the body is born again into another body. (Since 1875 the cult of Theosophy, of which the best known leader was Mrs A. Besant, has also included the doctrine in its eclectic system.) The belief in reincarnation, which has probably been held by the majority of human beings who have ever lived, doubtless sprang from an ethical intuition that justice must prevail in the world: a man who had done ill might be punished by being re-born as a woman or even as an animal. It may thus be held to be an expression of the deeply human conviction that there is an ultimate justice even in a world in which the wicked so often prosper and the good so often suffer.

EDITOR

Religion

This is hardly a biblical word at all. It occurs not at all in the English versions of the OT and only about five times in the NT, where it represents different Greek words (*see* Alan Richardson, 'Religion, Religious', *TWBB*). The OT strongly opposes the 'religion' of the surrounding Canaanite peoples and of Assyria and Babylon because of the crudities and immoralities of the worship of the nature-gods (*baalim*). Similarly the NT sees little connection between the revelation in Christ and the pagan religions of the Roman Empire. Karl Barth has good biblical support for his claim that the Christian faith is not one religion among others and for his assertion that Christianity is not a religion at all. Religion for Barth is human piety, human self-justification and human conjecture: faith is that which God creates in us (*Church Dogmatics*, I: *The Doctrine of the Word of God*, 2, 1956, ET, pp. 280–361). He was reacting strongly from the history-of-religions school, which at the beginning of the twentieth century reduced Christianity to a mere specimen of the world-wide phenomenon of religion. It is in the light of Barth's denunciation of religion that Bonhoeffer's plea for 'religionless Christianity', by which he meant unpietistic, unchurchy Christianity, should be understood. Christian faith should manifest itself in the whole life of the world, political, social, etc.; it should not be identified with what goes on in gathered churches at formal hours. But in the English-speaking world this teaching that Christianity is not a religion and that Christians should be non-religious is puzzling to many who meet with it for the first time, because for centuries now the Christian religion has not been distinguished from faith in Christ, and the view that it should be carried by Christian believers into secular life has been a commonplace (*cf.* J. H. Oldham, William Temple, Reinhold Niebuhr and many others). It is unlikely that English usage will change in this respect. To speak of 'the Christian religion' does not suggest that Christianity is only one religion among many or that it is not the ultimate truth about God and man, the fulfilment of the religious aspirations of the whole world. By entering into discussion with men of other religions (Judaism, Islam and the ethnic religions) Christians do not have to compromise their own belief in Jesus Christ as the final revelation of God. The relation of Christianity to the other religions is not simply a matter of academic inquiry (the comparative study of religion, q.v.) but is an existential encounter, in which Christians have something to learn as well as to teach.

The definition of religion in its wider sense is the subject of an enormous literature. From an anthropological and sociological point of view religion could rightly be described as man's response to the exigency of the human condition, in which he is driven to seek security, status and permanence by identifying himself with a reality greater, more worthy and more durable than himself. Such a definition would cover not only the great ethnic religions but also primitive animistic religion, nature religions (fertility cults, etc.), and the ancient mystery religions, as well as such 'religions' of the industrial era as Fascism and Communism. If we define religion in some such way as this, there are probably no 'religionless' men, for the phenomenon of religion is universal. Sophisticated individuals might indeed provide themselves with a philosophy of defiance or of despair when they find themselves alone in a universe which they believe to be hostile or indifferent to human values, but such a philosophy would still be their response to the exigency of the human condition. It is open to Christians to believe that all religion, even in its most distorted and inhuman forms, is man's response, however feeble and unworthy, to the God who has in his wisdom so created us that our heart is restless till it rests in him.

From the vast literature on the nature and significance of religion, three short books may be selected as introductions to the subject: John Baillie, *Invitation to Pilgrimage*, 1942; Daniel T. Jenkins, *Beyond Religion*, 1962; Alan Richardson, *Religion in Contemporary Debate*, 1966 (where references are given to other books).

EDITOR

Religionsgeschichtliche Schule

Religionsgeschichtliche Schule, literally, the 'History of Religions School', was a German theological school of thought, active in the closing decades of the nineteenth century and in the opening decades of the twentieth, which studied and laid theological stress upon parallel developments and common doctrines within Christianity and Judaism, and later, within Christianity and other, mainly middle Eastern, religious traditions. This school, whose viewpoint originated partly in reaction against the christocentric and bibliocentric emphasis of the Ritschlians, counted among its members H. Gunkel (1862–1932), W. Bousset (1865–1920) and W. Heitmüller (1869–1925). Early in his career R. Bultmann (q.v.) was associated with and influenced by some of its adherents.

JAMES RICHMOND

Religious *a Priori*

A term widely used by philosophers of religion to indicate an awareness of the holy or divine; the expression implies that religion is not deduced from any idea or concept of God but arises from man's innate awareness or intuition of the sacred. This understanding of the basis of religion was first clearly formulated by Schleiermacher (q.v.), who considered that all particular religions are different expressions of this fundamental constituent of human nature: 'to feel oneself absolutely dependent and to be conscious of oneself as being in relation to God'. *See also A Priori.*

EDITOR

Reparation

The reparatory satisfaction for our sin that we by ourselves were incapable of making, made by Christ in his passion, when he accomplished the reconciliatory sacrifice, and finally redeemed us from the slavery in which we were set by our sin (*cf. Summa Theologica*, 3a, q. 48, a 1–4). In Roman Catholic devotion the word signifies those prayers, good works, acts of self-denial and the like offered to God and the saints to make good the evil or sacrilege committed by men. *See also* **Redemption.**

JAMES ATKINSON

Repentance

Repentance is a change of mind; a feeling of regret or remorse; a turning away from sin and back to God. The last of these meanings, which is practically equivalent to conversion, is the most characteristic in the Bible. It is also the most characteristic in Protestant thought, for which repentance is virtually an aspect of faith, or at least inseparable from faith. Since faith is directed to the God who justifies the ungodly (Rom. 4.5), that is, pardons and accepts sinners, clearly it presupposes an acknowledgment that one is a sinner and in need of pardon and acceptance (*see* **Justification** [2]). This is much more than a feeling of regret or remorse, although it is commonly accompanied and indeed occasioned by such a feeling. But a feeling of regret or remorse does not necessarily lead to repentance (II Cor. 7.10), nor is the intensity of the feeling a measure of the reality of the repentance. To repent is to accept God's judgment upon us and to confess that in his sight we are sinners, whatever our own feelings in the matter may be. And the genuineness of our repentance is to be measured more by our actions than our professions of penitence. If we truly turn from sin to God, we shall cease to do evil and learn to do well; we shall seek to do no harm but all possible good to others, and we shall not neglect but take every opportunity of using the means of grace which God has provided so that we may seek him where he may be found. *See also* **Penitence; Conversion.**

W. D. Chamberlain, *The Meaning of Repentance*, 1943; W. L. Knox, *Penitence and Forgiveness*, 1953; W. Telfer, *The Forgiveness of Sins*, 1960.

P. S. WATSON

Representative

The word does not occur in EVV of the Bible, but it is nevertheless valuable in interpreting the significance of Christ to contemporary men and women. Christ is our representative in the presence of God; he also represents God to mankind. He is in truth the Representative Man. A representative is not a substitute (an important point to stress in discussions of the Atonement, q.v.). A substitute takes or usurps our place, whereas a representative keeps it open for us, acts on our behalf and causes us to be present where in fact we cannot personally appear. These reflections are well developed in Dorothee Sölle, *Christ the Representative*, ET, 1967, a book which can be welcomed for the freshness of its approach despite its sub-title, *An Essay in Theology after the Death of God*.

EDITOR

Reprobation. *see* Predestination.

Reservation

The practice of keeping the consecrated bread (and sometimes also the wine) for the purpose of receiving communion outside the service of the Eucharist was first mentioned by Justin Martyr, c. AD 155, and until the beginning of the fourth century many more acts of communion must have been made from the reserved sacrament at home than during the Eucharist in church. However, with the establishment of Christianity in the fourth century the normal place of reservation was either the sacristy or somewhere in the body of the church. Reservation was commonly under the species of bread alone as in the Roman Church today, but in the East in the eleventh century the present custom of dipping the host in the consecrated wine and drying it artificially came into use; in both East and West the usual place of reservation is a cupboard ('tabernacle') on the altar, but in the Middle Ages in the West hanging pixes were common and also in some places 'aumbries' (i.e. cupboards) in the wall. There is considerable controversy among liturgical experts about the historical details involved. In the reformed Churches reservation has been practically unknown, but, under the pressure of pastoral needs and for other reasons, the practice of reservation was revived against violent opposition in the Church of England towards the end of the nineteenth century and in many places has become a normal and accepted feature of church life.

The primary purpose of reservation is the provision of communion for the sick and others unable to be present at the Eucharist. In the Western Church, however, the reserved sacrament has become a natural focus of devotion to the sacramental presence of Christ and various forms of expression of this devotion, both private and public, have developed, for example, Benediction with the reserved Sacrament and Processions of the Host (*see* Corpus Christi). These are practically unknown in the East. The increased emphasis upon the Mass itself which has come with the Liturgical Movement (q.v.) and also the introduction in the Roman Church of evening Masses have brought about some diminution in these extra-liturgical forms of devotion.

A. King, *Eucharistic Reservation in the Western Church*, 1965.

E. L. MASCALL

Reserve

Reserve in the communication of doctrine means the practice of withholding profounder and more difficult doctrines from simple believers and divulging them only to the educated or more advanced spiritually. It was first recommended and employed by the Christian Platonists of Alexandria in the third century.

R. P. C. HANSON

Resurrection of Christ

The evidence of Christ's resurrection consists in the coming into being of the Church, if we have regard to the circumstances in which the earthly mission of Jesus ended in disaster. The continued existence of the Church down the centuries bears witness to the truth which it first came into being to proclaim. Every book in the NT bears a testimony to the Risen Lord. The historic faith of the Church has agreed with St Paul: 'If Christ has not been raised, your faith is futile' (I Cor. 15.17). All other Christian doctrines are dependent upon the proclamation of the resurrection: the significance of Christmas lies in the fact that the child who was born is the one whom God raised from the dead; Good Friday is only the anniversary of one more martyrdom, unless he who died is the one who rose again; the institution of the Lord's Supper in the Church would have been unthinkable, had not the Lord been known to the faithful in the breaking of bread.

The willingness of certain influential theologians in our own times to compromise with post-Enlightenment historiography is a sign of the disintegration of contemporary Protestantism. Under the influence of historical positivism, which regards history as a closed system of cause and effect, Rudolf Bultmann has denied that the resurrection of Jesus is an event of history; he has propounded his notion that 'Christ is risen in the preaching' as an alternative to the historic proclamation of the Church. Paul Tillich, who believed even less than Bultmann in the possibility of our knowledge about the historical Jesus, re-interprets the whole idea of the resurrection of Christ (as he re-interprets every other doctrine of the historic faith) in accordance with the requirements of his 'System'. On the other hand, there is the strange phenomenon of Paul van Buren's insistence upon the truth of the resurrection of Jesus, while denying that it can have any significance whatever for our doctrine of God.

Since the years in which Bultmann and Tillich did their formative thinking in the earlier decades of the twentieth century there has been a very considerable movement away from nineteenth-century positivistic conceptions of history among historians themselves. It has become obvious that capitulation to the formerly dominant notion of history as a 'science' was somewhat premature. Even the disciples of Bultmann (such as G. Bornkamm) have not moved far enough in the direction of contemporary historiographical thinking when they assert that the last fact which historians can know is the Easter faith of the disciples (why Easter, if nothing particular *happened* on Easter Day?). The way is wide open for a new approach to the question of the historicity of the resurrection, when the character of contemporary thinking about history has been understood. There is no need to explain away the historic gospel of Christ's resurrection in these later decades of the twentieth century. *See* **History, Problem of.**

Walter Künneth, *The Theology of the Resurrection*, ET, 1965; Alan Richardson, *History Sacred and Profane*, 1964, esp. ch. 6, in which the resurrection of Christ is discussed in the light of contemporary thought about the nature of history.

EDITOR

Resurrection of the Body (of the Dead). *see* Soul.

Reunion of the Churches

The term 'reunion' is used to describe the moves to unite various separated Christian churches. The term is not satisfactory; it implies a going back rather than a moving forward. The unity which the churches now seek will not be that of the early Church (and how much unity there was in the early Church is. open to question; *see* J. Knox, *The Early Church and the Coming Great Church*, 1957). Moreover, because of the pattern of Christian history and the present divisions, a united church of the future is unlikely to be similar to the Church of the past. This article will consider some of the factors in achieving church union (for the wider aspects of Christian unity *see* **Ecumenical, Ecumenism**).

The need for organic church union is generally accepted. There are still some people and churches who consider that a spiritual unity of all Christians is all that is necessary and that the complications of organic union are irrelevant, but there can be no doubt that Jesus Christ wished his Church to be one Church (John 17.21–26; Eph. 4.1–16). Spiritual unity permits subjective interpretations of the faith and allows for private judgment which can take the place of a full expression of the Christian faith, real fellowship and proper church order. The Church needs to be one so that it may reveal the gospel in a way which is visible and understandable to all. This is even more urgent in a world which is increasingly aware of its own oneness and interdependence. Others suggest that 'federal union' is all that is required. This proposes that churches should retain their own polity while being in full communion with each other. But this would not remove the scandal of disunity. The Church needs to be seen to be one in each place; 'federal union' does not go far enough.

Various ideas about and schemes of church union have been put forward in the history of the Church. The twentieth century has seen a great increase in the number of such schemes and unions. This has been mainly due to the missionary expansion of the nineteenth century, which led many to see the scandal of churches competing with each other in pagan lands. The now famous Tranquebar Statement of the South India Christians made in 1919 sums up this concern:

> We face together the titanic task of the winning of India for Christ – one fifth of the human race. Yet, confronted by such an overwhelming responsibility we find ourselves rendered weak and relatively impotent by our unhappy divisions – divisions for which we were not responsible and which have been, as it were, imposed upon us from without: divisions which we did not create, and which we do not desire to perpetuate (G. K. A. Bell, *Documents on Christian Unity*, 1925, pp. 278–81).

It is for this reason that the pressures for Christian unity are coming from the more recently evengelized countries, where the reasons for union are more obvious and the social and historical inhibitions far less than in countries where Christianity has been established for many centuries.

Schemes of reunion may be divided into two categories: (1) *Intra-Confessional Union*. This is the union of churches of the same ecclesiastical polity. These are the easiest type of church union to achieve and have been the most common in recent years. They normally take place in areas where two missions of the same church but from different countries have found themselves working in the same place. (2) *Trans-Confessional Union*. This is the union of churches from different confessional families. Church unions may take different forms. They may be the union of one or more non-episcopal churches (e.g. Presbyterian, Methodist and Congregationalist), or it may be between an episcopal and a non-episcopal church, or between two episcopal churches holding different views of the episcopate. This is made easier if the cultural inheritance is the same (e.g. all the churches having sent missionaries from one country).

It is this second type of union which causes the most theological problems, but there are also relationships between churches which fall short of organic union. Apart from their common relationship in membership of the World Council of Churches (*see* **Ecumenical, Ecumenism**) which implies some recognition of one another as churches, and the relationship resulting from mission comity agreements, these are usually summed up in the term '*communicatio in sacris*' (literally 'communication in holy things').

There are various forms of this: (1) *Taking part in common prayer together*. This level is now accepted by all Christian churches. (2) *Full Communion*. This is the situation which exists between churches of the same confessional families where members of churches freely communicate at each other's churches and accept each other's ministries. A relationship of 'Intercommunion' (*see below*) which has reached this level of interchange (as with the Church of England and the Old Catholic Church) is sometimes also described in this way. (3) *Intercommunion*. This is an agreement whereby members of two different churches may communicate at each other's altars. In some cases this also includes interchangeability of the ministers and in other cases it does not. In some agreements it is little more than an arrangement whereby Christians cut off from the sacrament of their own church are offered hospitality by another. (4) *Open Communion*. This is used to describe the practice of some churches which invite all Christians and sometimes all baptized, communicant Christians to receive communion at their celebrations of the Eucharist regardless of their denominational allegiance.

Full communion is the next thing to organic union and is often what defines a confessional body in union discussions. It is generally agreed that open communion on its own has not furthered the moves towards organic union. There is considerable disagreement whether intercommunion is a means of achieving union or not. Those who think that it is argue that the Eucharist is an essential means of achieving union and that intercommunion expresses the essential spiritual unity of Christians. Moreover the Eucharist is the *Lord's* Supper and it is not for man to make regulations about it. Unity lies in baptism and this is enough to justify intercommunion, for if Christians can hear the Word of God together then they should share the sacrament together. Against this other Christians see the Eucharist as the fruit of union and not a means to it. True fellowship, doctrinal agreement and agreement on what church membership involves is necessary before Christians can share the sacrament of unity. Moreover, it is wrong to conceal the fact the churches are divided. These positions are not fixed and there are many attitudes between them but the true solution lies in organic union.

Some churches are considering the idea of entering into a covenant for union. The idea is that, realizing the problems of establishing an immediate union, churches can commit themselves to a binding covenant to work for a union. This covenant would mean that they would work for union by whatever means are possible and never go back, even if a scheme fails. This kind of covenant is held by some not to end schism but to nullify the effects of schism in such a way as to allow for further '*communicatio in sacris*'. Others doubt the morality of commitment to some undefined union and consider that what the covenant seeks to achieve is more clearly done just by entering into union negotiations.

Schemes of union seek to gain organic union through a threefold unity of doctrine, sacraments and organization. Whatever the union scheme under discussion, there are certain theological problems which occur in such schemes.

The basic problem is inevitably the doctrine of the Church. Agreement on the nature of the Church and how it is to function and be organized is necessary for any union scheme. The question whether historic continuity is necessary is a major area of debate. Hence, while the Roman Catholic and the Orthodox Churches both claim to hold the faith of the apostles, some Churches are in lesser degrees concerned with historic continuity. They are far more concerned with purity of doctrine and can see no point in belonging to a Church which may have historic continuity but lacks the true faith of the Scripture, as they interpret it. The historic episcopate can be seen as a means of retaining the purity of doctrine.

The problem is very much related to the lack of an agreed pattern of church order in the early church and to the fact that most ecclesiastical polities can appeal to some aspect of the NT pattern. What is at issue is the nature of '*episcope*'. While not every church has bishops all, of necessity, have individuals or corporate bodies which exercise 'oversight' over the church at various levels. These people fulfil some of the roles performed by bishops in episcopal churches, though in the days of highly centralized administration some of this oversight is being performed less by bishops than by an ecclesiastical administration. A discussion of '*episcope*' is therefore needed in all churches, episcopal or not. The theories used to justify the episcopate are very often different from the way in which they work out in practice in various churches.

Related to this issue is that of 'collegiality'. This doctrine, as propounded in the Constitution of the Church of the Second Vatican Council, means that the bishops of the Church in conjunction with the pope form a college, which is the foundation of all authority in the Church. Through this doctrine the position of the bishop is changed so that he has a fuller part to play in the government of the Church. The concept as envisaged in the Constitution is essentially hierarchical. The idea of collegiality, together with a stronger emphasis on the role of the laity in the Church, may well play an important part in union schemes.

The whole nature of the ministry of the Church comes into question. Union schemes are showing concern for a renewal of a perpetual diaconate either for catechists or, in Presbyterian polity, to take over the role of the elder. The use of the word 'priest' is also rejected in many schemes, the word 'presbyter' or 'pastor' being substituted in its place. It is recognized that priesthood is something which belongs to Christ and therefore to the whole Church and not just to the full-time ministry, but some are anxious to preserve the word priest, as emphasizing the essential representative and ministerial nature of this ministry.

A common faith for a united Church is generally based upon the acceptance of the supremacy of Scripture, the Apostles and the Nicene Creed and the Declarations of Faith of the uniting churches. The need for continuity in faith as well as in ministry must be recognized, but union schemes have to allow for as much variation of interpretation as that allowed in any one of the uniting churches. This can be obtained where there is agreement on Christian practice in such matters as church membership and the Eucharist. Difficult problems occur when union schemes involve churches who reject the practice of paedobaptism. Should a united church allow a dual practice of both infant and adult baptism? This is usually workable but it does not allow for those baptized in infancy who later wish to be re-baptized, having been convinced that a public confession of faith is an essential part of baptism. Such schemes normally suggest that these matters should be referred to the bishop.

It will be seen that union schemes necessarily imply that there may be a considerable diversity of theological interpretation and practice in a united church. While a common liturgy may be a desirable unifying factor it cannot be regarded as essential. What holds a united church together is its acceptance of common faith and a common form of church government. The government of united churches which involve episcopacy is usually synodical with a moderator elected for a limited period from among the bishops of the church. There would be a general Synod for the whole church and a diocesan synod in every diocese. Those without episcopacy are usually also synodical in character.

So far united churches have generally been seen as the uniting of churches within a given geographical area. Such an approach may enable the united church to be related to the situation in which it is to preach the gospel, and may accept within it certain national and cultural characteristics. This can encourage local leadership. The Church of Christ is not to be seen simply as isolated churches. A united church needs some relation to the churches in other parts of the world, to emphasize the universality of the Christian gospel. Some writers have gone so far as to suggest that local unions are undesirable and that the catholicity of the Church can only be safeguarded through a world-wide unity of World Confessional Bodies. So it is far more desirable, they argue, that the Anglican communion should be united with World Methodism than that their component churches should be engaged in various union schemes in different areas. Apart from the extremely difficult organizational issues this raises theological problems. Central to the Church in the NT is that each church is embodied in a local situation. The catholicity of the Church is concerned more with the universality of its faith than with its geographical application. The principle of the incarnation requires that the Church becomes incarnate as one church in each place. Not all the churches of Christendom are present in every place, and a world confessional union might well submerge the truths which minority churches witness to by their existence. It is necessary that a united church in any one place should be related to and in full communion with churches in other places, even if their form of church union and polity are somewhat different. There is therefore a great need for consultation about church union

with churches other than those directly involved in the discussions. But the idea of united national or regional churches in full communion with each other seems to be a possible solution to the problem. The relationship of united churches to the confessional bodies from which their member churches came also needs serious consideration. It would be wrong for them to be isolated from the rest of Christendom and equally wrong for them simply to continue as if nothing had happened. While world confessional union may be impracticable in most cases, the possibility of ultimate union with the Roman Catholic Church, which is more universal and far larger than any other Church, does not raise this question in a different form and world unity may be a more natural way forward in this case.

Most schemes for church union involve some form of the reconciliation of the churches and their ministries. It is important to see this problem in that order; one of the problems of the Ecumenical Movement has been created by those theologians who seemed to be arguing that the ministry determines the nature of the Church. An effective and truly apostolic ministry is only one sign of the Church. The need for some means of reconciling the churches and making them one has to be seen as concerning the whole Church and not just as a means of reconciling the full-time ministries of the churches. It is on this point that there is very great difficulty. The Church of South India was formed on the basis of a mutual recognition of one another's ministries without any form of laying on of hands and with all subsequent ordinations being episcopal, with bishops consecrated within the historic episcopate. This scheme had its difficulties because it meant that the Church seemed to have two forms of ministry, one episcopally ordained and the other not. Subsequent schemes have proposed a reconciliation through a mutual laying on of hands from the very beginning. The Ghana scheme specifically states that such a service is based upon the mutual recognition of each other's ministries and that it is not ordination. Other schemes are less specific and are to some extent ambiguous. Thus they may be seen as ordination by those who think that it should be. This type of service is best regarded as a prayer to God asking him to make up whatever is lacking in the ministries of all those entering into a united church. It has been compared to the baptism of Jesus by John as being an unrepeatable unique act of identification which cannot be adequately described because it has no precedent. This type of service tends to reflect the theological view of Dr O. C. Quick (*The Christian Sacraments*, 1927, ch. VII) that while the church is divided no ministries are fully valid or complete; but they need not be interpreted in this way.

Whatever form of reconciliation is agreed upon a measure of anomaly and ambiguity is inherent in the situation. A divided Church is the worst anomaly of all.

A. C. Headlam, *The Doctrine of the Church and*

Reunion, 1920; S. Neill, *Church and Christian Union*, 1968; Lesslie Newbigin, *The Reunion of the Church*, 1948; J. I. Packer, ed., *All in Each Place*, 1965.

R. M. C. JEFFERY

Revelation

In the NT 'reveal' and 'revelation' are not used in their everyday sense of 'disclose', 'uncover', but as technical theological terms (*see* G. S. Hendry, 'Reveal, Revelation', *TWBB*; Alan Richardson, *Introduction to the Theology of the New Testament*, 1958, pp. 53 ff.). The NT use is almost entirely eschatological: revelation (*apocalypsis*) is the final unveiling at the end of the age (*parousia*). This does not mean that God has not revealed himself in Israel's history or in Christ; it means that God's revelation (in our modern sense of the word) in history and through the work of the Holy Spirit today is a revelation through faith, as contrasted with *the* revelation at the end of the age, which will be an actual seeing. 'We shall see him as he is' (I John 3.2); 'every eye shall see him' (Rev. 1.7); we shall see 'face to face' (I Cor. 13.12). The mention of revelation in history through the prophets is not entirely absent from the NT, as I Peter 1.12 shows, although the passage as a whole makes it clear that revelation in the absolute sense is still a future event, which will take place 'at the last time' (vv. 5, 7, 13). If is unnecessary to deny a revelation in history (*cf.* F. Gerald Downing, *Has Christianity a Revelation?*, 1964) or to reject the theological practice, which developed in post-NT times, of using the word in the sense of God's manifestation of his character and purpose in the history of his chosen people culminating in Christ. This is the normal usage of the word 'revelation' in theological discussion today.

In the Bible God's characteristic manner of revealing his truth is by his word spoken through the prophets in the events of the biblical history. The word spoken by the prophet, whether it be a word of judgment or of mercy, had a self-realizing efficacy (Isa. 55.11); and it was because Israel had come to know the power of God's word spoken by the prophets in the crises of their history that they eventually came to formulate the doctrine of the creation of the heavens and the earth by the word of God's mouth (e.g. Pss. 33.6, 9; 147.15–20). The word of revelation is none other than that creative word by which the world was made, ordered, preserved and redeemed. Supremely Jesus Christ is God's creative and redemptive word, his word incarnate, and thus the fulness of God's revelation of himself.

It was perhaps inevitable that, after the canon of the NT was closed, revelation should have come to be increasingly thought of as contained exclusively in the written words of the Bible, as the Holy Spirit breathed life into them in the hearts of those who read or heard them (*cf.* **Witness of the Spirit**). It was not, of course, denied that the revelation originally came through God's mighty acts in history, for the Scriptures and the Church alike existed to proclaim those acts (*cf.* Ps. 145.12).

But before the Renaissance, and indeed until the nineteenth century, men were not truly historically minded. They thought in terms of a *written* revelation, and it was inevitable that they should conceive of the task of the theologian as being that of systematizing all the individual texts of the whole Bible in one complete and harmonious *corpus* of truth. The Reformation did not significantly modify this traditional conception of revealed truth. Calvin would have agreed with Aquinas that divine revelation consisted in truth supernaturally communicated to men in propositional form. The Reformers would, of course, have rejected the view that there was a penumbra of revealed truth alongside the Bible in the unwritten traditions of Christ and his apostles, handed down in successive ages in the Church. Even so, Aquinas would have agreed with the Reformers that nothing was to be received as *de fide* which could not be proved out of the Holy Scriptures. The Bible was the only source of our knowledge of revealed truth, and its supernatural authority was guaranteed by miracle and prophecy.

1. *The Knowledge of God, Natural and Revealed.* During the Middle Ages it came to be widely held that there are two sources of our knowledge of God. Natural theology (q.v.) formulated those truths about the divine Being which could be discovered by the unaided powers of the human reason. Such truths were accessible to pagans as well as to Christians; the Platonists and the Stoics, for example, were aware of them. After the days of Albertus Magnus and Aquinas, it was generally conceded that Aristotle was the great master of this type of knowledge of God, and he was often spoken of as 'the Philosopher'. But this 'natural' knowledge of God, it was held, does not give to man all he needs to know and cannot satisfy his deep craving for truth beyond the capacity of the unaided human reason. It is not *saving* knowledge. The full, saving knowledge of God, expressed in such doctrines as those of the incarnation, the Trinity or redemption, can be learnt only from revelation, i.e. from the Scriptures as received by faith and supported by reason (e.g. the arguments from miracle and prophecy). Man is an incomplete being and stands in need of divine grace and therefore of a revelation which supplements and perfects his natural knowledge. At the Reformation some theologians (following Luther) came to minimize the value of natural theology, because they were convinced of the paramount importance of the revealed truth contained in the Bible: 'by faith alone' could easily be held to imply 'by reason not at all'. This attitude has been vigorously reaffirmed in the twentieth century by Karl Barth (q.v.) and his followers, who were in their turn reacting from another post-Reformation development in theology. This latter development took the opposite road from Luther's rejection of reason in order to stress the importance of divine revelation; thinkers like Lord Herbert of Cherbury (1583–1648) took the alternative course of

minimizing the value of revealed theology, because they had come to hold that reason could discover and establish all that men need to know concerning the divine nature and purpose. This line of thought eventually carried rationalism in theology to its ultimate development in the Deism (q.v.) of the Enlightenment (q.v.), according to which revelation was nothing more than a 're-publication of the religion of nature', i.e. of reason. The truly rational man had no need of revelation at all. The possibility and indeed the necessity of providing a natural theology today is a question widely discussed, not only among Roman Catholic theologians; it seems to be increasingly accepted that, if sheer irrationalism is to be avoided, it must and can be shown to be possible to put forward reasonable arguments for the existence of God.

2. *General and Special Revelation.* Without foreclosing the discussion about natural theology many theologians today, who belong neither to the school of Aquinas nor to that of Barth, consider the conception of general and special revelation to be preferable to that of natural and revealed knowledge of God. They hold that there is no such thing as purely natural or unaided knowledge of God or indeed of truth, beauty and goodness. All our knowledge of truth and value is inspired by God, or by his Logos immanent among men. Without the aid of the God of truth, no man would be able to discover or enunciate truth, whether in philosophy or in science or in personal knowledge. Without the inspiration of the Creator of all beauty, no artist or musician or writer would be able to create that which is beautiful or would hate that which is ugly. Without the pressure of the hand of the God of righteousness, no social reformer (be he humanist or Marxist or atheist in his views) would strive for justice among men or attack ignorance, poverty and vice. Indeed, without this God-inspired longing among men of every race and age, civilization itself would disintegrate and mankind would not be genuinely human. This *general* revelation (which is clearly acknowledged in the Bible) is given to men everywhere and makes them truly human. Man, even Hindu man or Communist man or pagan man, could not exist as man apart from the divine grace of general revelation. This general revelation, so far as it goes, is saving revelation, for there is no such thing as a non-saving knowledge of God. But, of course, it is not the complete knowledge of God, for this comes only by his *special* revelation through the prophetic history of Israel and its culmination in Christ. It is only by reason of God's special revelation that the true significance of his general revelation can be understood (*cf.* Acts 17.22-31). Nevertheless we must not despise the grace of God in general revelation. The truths which are contained in the great ethnic religions or the ethical insights of contemporary humanism are genuine disclosures of the God of truth and righteousness, even if in the absence of belief in the special revelation of the biblical history they are not properly understood in their deeper meaning. These truths form a basis upon which a dialogue with men of other faiths may be set up; and where the significance of general revelation is recognized by Christian participants in such discussion, it will be humbly conceded that Christians have something to learn as well as to teach.

It should be pointed out that, though it has been reformulated in the twentieth century (by John Baillie and others), the concept of general and special revelation is older than the mediaeval concept of natural and revealed theology. It is in its essentials St Augustine's doctrine of revelation. It has, moreover, the great advantage of not involving the notion of revelation as consisting in revealed propositions or revealed 'truths'. God has revealed himself in his mighty acts in history, as these have been interpreted by the prophets of the OT and the apostles of the NT. The idea of inerrant propositional truth contained in the Bible did not survive the rise of the critical historical method since the age of Enlightenment. It is only in recent times that the true character of divine revelation as historical has been recovered. By way of action or reaction from the post-Enlightenment confusion, after the traditional conception of an inerrant scriptural revelation had broken down, most of the dominant theologians of the first half of the twentieth century (including Barth, Brunner, Bultmann and Tillich) failed to discover the true *locus* of revelation in real human history and attempted (in quite different ways) to disengage revelation from real history altogether. This attempt has proved unsuccessful and unnecessary. The central feature of the biblical revelation is that it was given in real history, among real men in the crises of their national and individual lives. *See also* **History, Problem of; Natural Theology; Paley's Watch.**

John Baillie, *The Idea of Revelation in Recent Thought*, 1956; *Our Knowledge of God*, 1939; E. Brunner, *Revelation and Reason*, 1946; A. L. Lilley, *Religion and Revelation*, 1932; H. R. Niebuhr, *The Meaning of Revelation*, 1941; Alan Richardson, *Christian Apologetics*, 1947; *History Sacred and Profane*, 1964; C. C. J. Webb, *Studies in the History of Natural Theology*, 1915.

EDITOR

Revivalism

Revivalism in America began with five 'harvests' in the Congregational Church at Northampton, Massachusetts, during the ministry of Solomon Stoddard. It spread through the colonies in the period of the 'Great Awakening', which arose in the 1720s in the Reformed Dutch Church under the preaching of Theodore J. Frelinghuysen. It reached other colonies and communions through such leadership as that of Gilbert Tennant, a Presbyterian; the Anglican itinerant, George Whitefield; and Stoddard's grandson and successor, Jonathan Edwards (q.v.). In its later stages, especially among Southern Baptists and Methodists, the Awakening tended to present

Christian faith in oversimplified and emotional terms.

At the dawn of the nineteenth century came the so-called 'Second Great Awakening'. In both its more orderly, eastern forms and in its extremer western, 'frontier' ways, revivalism eroded traditional patterns of theology and practice for more pietistic, freer styles. Methods of promoting revivals were carefully studied and consciously employed; classical Protestant theologies were modified in the effort to secure converts. Such eastern revivalists as Lyman Beecher and Nathaniel W. Taylor (q.v.) showed this tendency, but the most conspicuous exponent of modern revivalism was Charles Grandison Finney (1792–1875). Converted in 1821, he shortly set out on revivalist tours, and despite lack of formal university or theological training was ordained as Presbyterian (later Congregationalist) evangelist. He systematically developed the techniques of stirring up revivals by such 'new measures' as services at unusual hours, gatherings 'protracted' for many days, inquiry meetings, and 'the anxious bench'. In many writings, especially *Lectures on Revivals of Religion* (1834–5) and *Lectures on Systematic Theology* (1846–7), Finney articulated out of biblical, Calvinist, Methodist, Pelagian and pietist elements a theology designed to get revivalistic results. American Protestantism, confronted with the task of following a rapidly-growing population westward across a continent, generally found revivalism acceptable, though there were such protests as Mercersburg theology (q.v.). Denominations which employed revivalistic patterns most extensively – Methodists, Baptists, Disciples of Christ, and to a lesser degree Presbyterians and Congregationalists – flourished. The nation-wide, seemingly 'spontaneous' prayer-meeting revival of 1857–8 illustrated how deep revivalist theology and practice had shaped American Protestantism.

In the later nineteenth century, hundreds of revivalists itinerated restlessly; most conspicuous among them the Congregational layman, Dwight L. Moody (1837–1899). Early in the twentieth century, William A. ('Billy') Sunday brought modern revivalism to a peak of mechanical efficiency, but his fundamentalistic and vulgarian overtones contributed to its marked decline. At mid-century, the more theologically perceptive William F. ('Billy') Graham gave a chastened revivalism a new lease of life.

Alan Heimert and Perry Miller, eds., *The Great Awakening*, 1967; William G. McLoughlin, Jr, *Modern Revivalism*, 1959; William W. Sweet, *Revivalism in America*, 1944.

ROBERT T. HANDY

Righteousness

Righteousness (Latin: *justitia*, Greek: *dikaiosune*, Hebrew: *tsedaqah*), in Greek thought, was primarily an ethical quality or disposition, conformity to an ethical norm. So also in Catholic theology, which prefers the term 'justice' (q.v.). In the Bible, it is primarily a relational activity, a matter of putting or keeping relationships right (*see* **Justification**). In the OT the righteousness of God can be synonymous with his saving acts (Isa. 46.13; 51.5 f.), and in the NT it is identified with his saving activity in Christ (I Cor. 1.30; Rom. 1.16 f.). Correspondingly, righteousness for man depends on his response to God's activity, his acceptance of the relationship it opens up for him.

We must, however, distinguish between two, and possibly three, kinds of righteousness. Jesus contrasts the righteousness of the scribes and Pharisees with that which belongs to God's kingdom, the righteousness of God (Matt. 5.20; 6.33) – which apparently the publicans and harlots have found (Matt. 21.31). St Paul contrasts the righteousness of the law, or his own righteousness, with that of faith, or righteousness from God (Phil. 3.9) – which the zealous observers of the law have not found (Rom. 10.2). Luther contrasts civil with Christian righteousness. The former is a righteousness of 'works', that is, of legally correct conduct, or dutiful behaviour. It is a good thing as far as it goes, very necessary for the well-being of society, and willed by God; and even sinful men are capable of it. But outward conduct is no guarantee of a man's inner relation to God, and no ground of hope for salvation. For that, only Christian righteousness is of any avail, which is not our own (*propria*) but Another's (*aliena*); i.e. it is not achieved by us and our works, but given to us in Christ and received by faith alone (*see* **Imputation**). That is to say, the right relation of man to God is that which is opened up for him by God's grace, to which the only proper response is faith.

The relationship established by grace through faith, however, results in a third kind of righteousness. For the Spirit of God begins to effect an ethical renewal of man from the moment he enters into it (*see* **Sanctification**). This renewal is not complete in a moment, of course, and there is ample room for growth in grace as long as a man lives; but the fact that it takes place at all is evidence of the reality of the relationship out of which it springs. It must, however, be emphasized that the relationship is not determined by it since God's grace is in no way dependent on it, and it cannot be the ground of faith. To think otherwise is to relapse into legalism (q.v.) and a sinful preoccupation with ourselves and our own condition, which is the surest way to lose the gift of God. *See also* **Original Righteousness**.

A Miller, *The Renewal of Man*, 1952; R. Niebuhr, *Love and Justice*, 1957; A. Nygren, *Commentary on Romans*, 1949; E. G. Rupp, *The Righteousness of God*, 1953; H. Thielicke, *Theological 1954*; P. S. Watson, *Let God be God*, 1947; R. E. Ethics, I, 1966; P. Tillich, *Love, Power and Justice*, C. Browne, 'Righteousness', *DCE*; G. Quell and G. Schrenk, 'Righteousness', *TDNT*, I (also published as a separate title in 1951).

P. S. WATSON

Rigorism

Rigorism has a precise technical meaning in Christian moral theology, but it is also a term used in a wider sense. In technical moral theology rigorism is used of that tradition in ethics which forbids the Christian to take the benefit of the doubt no matter how probable the doubt may be In the wider sense, rigorism is opposed to laxity, to all those attitudes which seem to compromise Christian ethics with the standards of secularism.

K. E. Kirk, *The Vision of God*, 1931.

E. J. TINSLEY

Ritschl, Albrecht

Albrecht Ritschl (1822-1889), German Protestant systematic theologian and founder of the Ritsch-lian school of systematic theology. *See* **Liberal Protestantism; Herrmann, W.; Kaftan, J.; Lotze, H.**

H. R. Mackintosh, *Types of Modern Theology*, 1937 and 1964, ch. v.

JAMES RICHMOND

Ritual

Properly the word 'ritual' signifies the words of a liturgical service and is therefore contrasted with 'ceremonial'. By a strange misuse, however, in popular parlance the distinction has been lost, so that a 'ritualist' is no longer a student of liturgical formularies but a man or woman inordinately addicted to ceremonial of an elaborate kind. The Anglo-Catholics of the nineteenth century were commonly known as 'ritualists'. *See also* **Worship.**

E. L. MASCALL

Ritualism

One of the consequences of the Oxford Movement (q.v.) was a revived interest in liturgy and ceremonial. This was strengthened by the fresh appreciation of the Middle Ages encouraged by the romantic movement and by the more sympathetic study of mediaeval history which began in the mid-nineteenth century. Some disciples of the movement sought to clothe the Prayer Book rite with the ceremonial of mediaeval England, believing that this was what the so-called ornaments rubric legally required when it stated that chancels should remain as they were in times past, and that the ornaments of church and ministers should be retained and in use as they had been in the second year of Edward VI. Others felt it more practicable to borrow from contemporary Roman Catholic practice. The results were seen in many parish churches in the introduction of eucharistic vestments, portable lights, incense and the employment of boys and men as servers. Bitter opposition was aroused and the ritualists were accused of breaking the law and of undoing the work of the Reformation. Their defence was to appeal to the continuity of the Church with the pre-Reformation age and to the positive advantage of a colour-ful ceremonial in commending the religion of the incarnation in a drab and utilitarian age. Their practice brought them into conflict both with the bishops and with the state, and relations were exacerbated when, as an unforeseen result of the Public Worship Regulation Act of 1874, several ritualist priests were imprisoned. In 1888 when the much revered bishop of Lincoln, Edward King, was accused of illegal ritual practices, the archbishop of Canterbury ignored the act and judged the case himself. Since then the act has been a dead letter, but the desire of the church authorities to regulate ritual was an important factor in the attempt to revise the Prayer Book in the 1920s and to revise the canon law in the 1960s. The legalization of vestments by Parliament in 1964 may be regarded as closing this chapter in Anglican history. Meanwhile a wholly new approach to ritual, which begins by asking what is the liturgical act and how it may be most appropriately done is appearing everywhere in Western Christendom.

S. L. Ollard, *A Short History of the Oxford Movement*, 1915; M. Reynolds, *Martyr of Ritualism, A Life of A. H. Mackonochie*, 1965.

R. CANT

Rome, Roman Catholicism

The claim of the Roman Catholic Church to be the only authentic representative of the Church founded by Christ rests partly on Scripture and tradition, partly on history, and partly on other considerations. Christ did not only found his Church, but he founded it upon Peter (not merely on his confession, Matt. 16.18 ff.) and gave Peter primacy over the apostles, thereby assuring to his successors as bishops of Rome a permanent primacy over the whole Church. This primacy was not immediately recognized in its fulness. Like the doctrine of the Trinity it had to be gradually unfolded in the Church's increasing understanding and acceptance of it. But it is clear that the early Church, East and West, from a very early period, certainly as early as that of Irenaeus (c. 180), and perhaps as early as the time of Ignatius (c. 117), accorded a leading position to the bishop of Rome. The Eastern Church always showed the greatest respect for the bishop of Rome, and on significant occasions acknowledged his universal authority. As the centuries advanced this position was more clearly defined and given ampler scope and greater authority. The Church of the early Middle Ages, from Leo the Great (d. 461) to Gregory VII (d. 1087), acknowledged the leadership, the primacy, and in certain significant fields, the jurisdiction of the pope, and did so with virtually no dissentient voices. The see of Rome was very largely responsible for bringing Christianity to northern Europe, and the Church of England no less than the other parts of the Church naturally and simply recognized it as the God-given source of tradition, authority and guidance. The immense increases of formal authority achieved by the popes, largely as a result of the development of canon law, in the later Middle Ages was only a logical development of the earlier position. It was enhanced and buttressed by the successful struggle which many popes of the period made to free the spiritual rights of the Church from lay and secular control, to reform corruption and negligence within the Church and to guard the purity of the Catholic faith. When at the Reformation large bodies of Christians rejected the jurisdiction of the pope, this could only mean that they cut themselves off from the only source of Catholic doctrine and true authority, and thereby rendered the life of their churches defective, their orders invalid and their sacraments ambiguous at best. The majestic development of Roman Catholic dogma since the sixteenth century, the impressive extension of the Roman Catholic Church throughout the world, the remarkable loyalty to their Church usually displayed by the Roman Catholics, the preservation intact of Roman Catholic cult, discipline and religious orders, their enrichment by new forms of devotion and new forms of religious life, the sanctity achieved by thousands of Roman Catholic priests, nuns, monks and laity, and the unique position of leadership in the religious world enjoyed by popes today, all add weightily to the argument that Roman Catholicism is the only true Church and that the claims which it makes for itself are true.

The reply to this argument strikes at that assumption on which everything in the argument depends, that communion with the see of Rome is the definition and touchstone of authentic Christianity. Not only is this proposition not to be found in Scripture, nor to be inferred from it (as the doctrine of the Trinity can be inferred from it), but it has no solid support in the early Church. Christians of other sees in the first six or seven centuries were anxious to be in communion with the see of Rome, of course, as a matter of Christian peace and brotherhood, but they never imagined that this was the touchstone of catholicity. Indeed Cyprian and Firmilian, bishops of Carthage and Cappadocian Caesarea in the third century, expressly deny this conclusion and Basil of Caesarea and John Chrysostom (to name only two authorities), in the fourth century by deriving their orders from those who were out of communion with Rome and pursuing all or most of their careers in the same position deny it in practice even more emphatically. It is impossible to review the history of Eastern Orthodox Christianity from the Council of Chalcedon (451) to the sack of Constantinople (1453) without concluding that the Eastern Church did not regard communion with Rome as a *sine qua non* of orthodoxy. It is certainly true that the Western Church wholeheartedly accepted the authority of the pope for many centuries during the Middle Ages. Historical circumstances combined to make this development almost an irresistible one, and the fine achievements of many popes played their part too; there is no need to deny that this process was providential. But what history confers history can

withdraw, and when by the fifteenth century papal leadership had become papal oppression the doctrine of the pope's authority began rightly to lose its force. Those who guided the Reformed Churches of the next century honestly believed that they were faced with a choice between obeying the demands of the pope and obeying the Word of God, and certainly the popes of the period did little to understand their position or ease their predicament. The Reformed Churches lost catholicity only if catholicity is based upon the questionable assumption that communion with the see of Rome is an essential ingredient in it. The dogmatic development evident in the Roman Church since the sixteenth century only demonstrates how far that body has strayed from sound doctrine since its separation from the rest of Christendom, for this development is based neither on Scripture nor on tradition and calls in question the Roman Church's understanding of the sources of Christian truth. Other Churches can show examples (even though not such impressive ones) of sanctity and richness of spiritual life, and anyway this argument is an invidious one smacking of self-righteousness and incompatible with Christian humility.

The sharpness and bitterness of this 'confrontation' between the Roman Catholic Church and the rest of Christendom has been robbed of much of its force by recent events. Since the pontificate of Pope John XXIII Roman Catholics have been making eirenic advances towards other denominations on a scale quite unknown hitherto. Some concessions have been made in the field of common prayer and common discussion between Roman Catholics and others. Roman Catholic theologians have begun to publish books deeply appreciative of the great men and the great traditions of other churches. The rise of 'biblical theology' affecting Roman Catholics and of the Liturgical Movement influencing Protestants has played its part in bringing both sides nearer to each other. The new attitude of interest and engagement towards the Ecumenical Movement displayed by the Roman Church, though it stops short of full participation, holds promise for the future. It is possible to envisage a new approach to the authority of dogmatic definition in the light of a new understanding of the Bible on the Roman side and a new appreciation of the necessity and the function of tradition by Protestants. This is not to say that the hard facts of difference and discussion do not remain, and that this is not clearly recognized by both sides, but it is clear that a new and decisive stage, much fuller of hope for the future than could have been imagined ten years ago, has been reached in this old controversy.

I. Corbishley, *Roman Catholicism*, 1956; R. A. Knox, *The Belief of Catholics*, 1927; A. de Mendieta, *Rome and Canterbury*, 1962; G. Salmon, *The Infallibility of the Church*, 1923 (last unabridged ed.).

R. P. C. HANSON

Royce, Josiah

Josiah Royce (1855–1916), professor of philosophy at Harvard, was an ingenious defender of absolute idealism. An original argument for the existence of the Absolute was presented in *The Religious Aspect of Philosophy* (1885). He stated that the conditions which determine the logical possibility of error must themselves be absolute truth; the fact that there can be error implies such truth. In his Gifford Lectures, *The World and the Individual* (2 vols., 1900–1), Royce declared that the Absolute is an absolute self which is constituted by the infinity of finite selves in which the Absolute represents itself. In such works as *The Philosophy of Loyalty* (1908), *Sources of Religious Insight* (1912), and the two-volume *The Problem of Christianity* (1913), he discussed Christianity as a religion of loyalty. Loyalty he defined as the willing devotion of a self to a cause which unites many selves in one. His expression 'loyalty to loyalty' meant the rising above narrow, self-centred interests to serve the whole community of mankind. The essence of Christianity is the 'beloved community', the rock on which the church is based. He defended metaphysically the ultimate reality of the actual infinite, God, and of his redeeming power effective in the beloved community. He was widely influential in his day, but the diminishing importance of philosophical idealism restricted his continuing impact.

Stuart G. Brown, ed., *The Religious Philosophy of Josiah Royce*, 1952; John E. Smith, *Royce's Social Infinite*, 1950.

ROBERT T. HANDY

Rule of Faith. *see* Tradition.

Sabbatarianism

A peculiarly British phenomenon, the belief that the Fourth Commandment (Ex. 20.8–11) prohibiting work on the Jewish Sabbath (Saturday) now applies in full rigour to the Christian Sunday. The fact that one of the divine commands of the Decalogue would seem to have no relevance for Christian faith has always created great difficulties for those who interpret the Bible literalistically, and still today evangelical Christians in Britain fight a rearguard action against the forces of secularism. It was, however, in the seventeenth century that controversy was at its height between Anglicans and Puritans. King James I of England published his *Book of Sports* in 1618, prohibiting work but allowing lawful recreations. The Puritans had the book burnt by order of Parliament in 1643. After the Restoration (1660) a less rigorous attitude prevailed, but, even so, the dreariness of 'the Victorian Sunday' remains in popular memory as one of the miseries of a non-permissive society. *See* **Sunday**.

EDITOR

Sabellianism

Sabellianism is an alternative description of modalism (q.v.) derived from Sabellius (early third century) who gave the doctrine its most sophisticated form. He was a native of Libya (though some think of Rome) where his movement gained firm hold. Though the evidence for his opinions may reflect the opinions of later heretics (e.g. Marcellus of Ancyra, q.v.), the following points seem well established. (1) He extended modalism into a threefold form in line with rising interest in the doctrine of the Spirit. He could still, however, describe God as a Son-Father, probably reflecting earlier trends. (2) God is by nature a monad, one *Hypostasis* (q.v.) with three names. Yet he gives a more objective character to the modes as modes of Revelation (*see* **Modes of Being**). He did not, it seems, regard them as simultaneous, but only as successive. The term 'expansion' which might suggest the contrary probably arises from confusion in the sources with Marcellus. (3) He may have used the term *Prosopon* (q.v.) to describe the modalities of the Godhead. This is disputed (Kelly, Prestige) on the ground that this was not the accepted usage of the word. But trinitarian terminology remained fluid for a century after Sabellius and one secular meaning of *Prosopon* could support him. The word drops out of Eastern Trinitarian vocabulary in the late fourth century when Basil in particular feared its Sabellian implications.

H. E. W. TURNER

Sacerdos, Sacerdotal

Sacerdos is the Latin word for 'priest' (Greek: *hiereus*). It does not seem to have been used of Christian ministers until the end of the second century. It was then applied only to bishops, in whom alone the fulness of *sacerdotium* (priesthood) resided. Not until the time of St Cyprian (d. 258) were the presbyters called *sacerdotes*. Even then they could share in the episcopal *sacerdotium* only in the absence of the bishop and with his authorization (e.g. offering the eucharistic sacrifice and receiving a penitent *lapsus*, one who had defected perhaps under threat of persecution). The bishop alone was the proper celebrant of the Eucharist, the offerer of the Christian sacrifice. During the Middle Ages the priests obtained great powers, since now in virtue of their ordination they could celebrate or withhold the sacraments, etc., so that for many Protestants the word 'sacerdotal' is virtually synonymous with perverted magical practices. But the question of the *sacerdotium*, i.e. of the priestly offering of the people (*see* **Laity**) remains. *See also* **Priest**.

EDITOR

Sacerdotalism

Sacerdotalism is the assertion of the existence in the Christian Church of an order of priests (q.v.) charged with sacrificial functions and invested with supernatural powers transmitted to them in ordination. Such a view would be acceptable, for example, to the Roman Church but would be repudiated, for example, by Presbyterians. In a pejorative sense sacerdotalism is sometimes taken to refer to the undue assumption of authority on the part of the priesthood, although this would perhaps be better termed clericalization, that is, an excessive dominance of the Church by its ministry (q.v.) issuing in a reduction of the laity to a condition of passivity.

J. G. DAVIES

Sacrament, Sacramental Theology

Originally Latin *sacramentum* meant a soldier's oath of allegiance, but in Christian usage it became the equivalent of the Greek *musterion*, a mystery (not necessarily in the sense of the 'mystery religions', although it is true that baptism and the eucharist were never celebrated in the presence of non-Christians). Sacraments involve or imply a promise or a commitment, and they are mysteries in the sense that they do not disclose their meaning to unbelieving eyes. As St Augustine and St Thomas Aquinas agreed, they are *signs* of a holy reality, or grace, which sanctifies men. There was wide fluctuation in the varieties of things which could be called 'sacraments', ranging from creeds (*cf.* the soldier's oath) or the Lord's Prayer to baptism and the eucharist. Peter Lombard (c. 1100–1160) enumerated the seven sacraments which have become traditional in Catholicism (and in the Eastern Church): Baptism, Confirmation, the Eucharist, Penance, Unction, Ordination and Matrimony. All these include 'an outward and visible sign of an inward and spiritual grace' (*BCP*, Catechism), e.g. water in baptism, laying on of hands in confirmation and ordination, etc. From ancient times baptism and the eucharist were regarded as being in a class by themselves, because of the NT evidence of their institution by Christ himself ('the dominical sacraments'), and at the Reformation the Church of England and the main Protestant confessions declared that these were the only sacraments 'necessary for salvation'. The Society of Friends and the Salvation Army are the only Christian bodies (they would not call themselves churches) which do not administer the dominical sacraments, though there are doubtless other sects whose practice is ill-defined.

The theology of baptism and the eucharist is discussed under Christian initiation, and eucharistic theology. In general it may be said here that historic Christianity is essentially sacramental in character because through the incarnation of Christ matter has been shown to be, not evil or alien to divine indwelling, but capable of being the vehicle or expression of God's grace and truth (*cf.* John 1.14). For the Christian the whole world is sacramental of the divine glory (though the Society of Friends is probably unique in giving this as an explanation of the non-use of particular sacraments). The Church, which is the body of Christ in the world, is the channel through which

God's sacramental power is given to all members of the body, just as the body of the incarnate Lord was the means through which God's power and grace were communicated to mankind (*cf.* Mark 5.30). Theologians of every principal confession would agree that, though the sacraments are institutional forms within the structures of the Church, the important thing about them is what God does in and through them. The feelings of those who receive the sacraments are subjective and theologically unimportant (however psychologically important that may be to the individual). Nor are the sacraments dependent for their validity as means of grace upon the worthiness of the minister (*see* **Donatism**); Christ himself is the true celebrant of the sacraments. The objectivity of the sacraments is guaranteed by God's covenant and promise. Those who receive in faith and trust God's promise are assured of their union with Christ in the body of his Church. *See* **Initiation, Christian; Eucharist, Eucharistic Theology.**

D. M. Baillie, *The Theology of the Sacraments*, 1957; J. D. Benoit, *Liturgical Renewal*, 1958; P. T. Forsyth, *The Church and the Sacraments*, 1917; B. Leeming, SJ, *Principles of Sacramental Theology*, 1956; E. L. Mascall, *Corpus Christi*, 1965; O. C. Quick, *The Christian Sacraments*, 1927.

EDITOR

Sacramentarians

A name given by Luther to those (such as Zwingli) who denied the real presence of Christ in the consecrated bread and wine of the Eucharist. More recently it has been used of those who hold a high doctrine of the Eucharist (as has also the word 'sacramentalists').

Sacred Heart

Devotion to the Sacred Heart of Jesus represented a new type of affection for the real humanity of Christ which grew up in the Middle Ages under the inspiration of St Bernard of Clairvaux (q.v.). It was a characteristically Western development, introducing a kind of piety unknown to St Athanasius or St Augustine, having a markedly subjective and individualistic character. It survived the Reformation and can be noted in the hymns of evangelicals of the type of Isaac Watts and John Newton.

G. L. Prestige, *Fathers and Heretics*, 1940, pp. 382-420.

EDITOR

Sacrifice. *see* Atonement (3 [b]); Eucharist.

Saint(s). *see* Sanctification.

Salvation

1. *As Deliverance.* The entire story of Israel in the OT is the history of God's activity in saving his chosen people from all their enemies, material and

spiritual. Accordingly all the institutions, practices and ideas of Israel originate in a saving act of God. None of them was imagined or devised by men. In this area, human invention was the characteristic of idolatry, and when met in Israel is the result of heathen or foreign influence. The saving acts of God had been experienced at a known place, from a known danger, at a known time, under a known man of God (Pss. 44.1; 44.26). Abraham is called by God out of his land to a new land (Gen. 12.1). Moses is called by a God who has 'come down to deliver' his people (Ex. 3.7 f.). God led a people that was no people out of captivity into a new and independent life as the people of God. The Israelites were delivered from bondage without a war; delivered from the Red Sea without a boat; delivered from hunger and thirst when there was neither food nor water; delivered from enemies without armed forces. Joyfully the story dilates on 'the mighty acts of God', 'thy wonders in Egypt', 'the multitude of thy mercies', the redeeming power of 'God their saviour' (Ps. 106.2, 7, 21). The whole story of salvation is told in the Bible, as it was always re-told in Israel, to convince men that salvation is only of the Lord, who can save by many or by few.

When God in the course of the centuries had established them as a nation, given them a place, made them a church, they remembered in their great festivals of Passover, Pentecost and Tabernacles, how God had delivered them from slavery, renewed them spiritually with his law, and sustained them through their long journeyings in the wilderness. After they had settled, they developed a deeper awareness of sin, and in course of time their great national fast, the Day of Atonement, took the most prominent place in their calendar. In all this, they were constantly led to recall that their God was a redeeming God, and that the nation lived now by the grace that had been made known to them at the time of the Exodus. The sacrificial system, operated increasingly as time went on by men with a deep awareness of sin, did not mean that by sacrifice a Jew hoped to attain God's grace, but rather that in penitence and faith he sought to retain it and avert its withdrawal. He sought in penitence to recover a favour, a relationship he had once known and had now lost owing to his sin; sin which would earn him wrath and death, if God were not gracious. The whole sacrificial system was an evangelical sacrament of forgiveness and deliverance, and forgiveness and deliverance were entirely God's work, never man's. It was not that man was doing anything to please or propitiate an enigmatic and uncommitted God who had not so far shown his hand. On the contrary, the central element in all Israelite worship was the collective liturgical recollection of all that God had done in their history in visiting and redeeming his people. God had in the past shown himself to Israel as a redeeming and saving God, and men gave thanks for this and prayed that he would contrive so to be still, in their present and in their future.

What distorted this truth, refracted it, and bent it like light through a prism, was man's idolatry. Man scaled God down to his own size. When this happens, as it did to many in OT times, the results are lamentable. At once redemption is dwarfed and diminished. The centre of interest is less the redeeming activity of God for man, and more what man wants from God. He thinks of good crops, salvation in war, material prosperity, freedom from trouble, and beyond that – nothing. He is limited by his own felt needs. His God is now an idol, and if he sacrifices, it is in these idolatrous terms that he understands and explains his action. But it is incontrovertible that in the OT what God was handling through the sacrificial system was precisely man's sin. And the end of the whole story (and the beginning of our own) was that, when he came himself, his name was Jesus, and his mission was to save his people from their sins (Matt. 1.21).

At no point is Christianity more triumphantly realistic than in showing to modern man that the essential evil is his own sin, that man needs saving from the consequences of his sin as well as from his own do-it-yourself cures for his various felt ills, and that only God can deliver and save him from this evil. Man has never shown himself willing to accept this diagnosis, and modern man finds it less acceptable than ever, for his sheer technological Titanism makes it difficult for him to accept his frailty, his finitude, and his creatureliness. There is a feeling abroad that given time, man will master everything. Yet it needs humbly to be stated, and confirmed by adducing all the evidence that reasonable men will heed, that the heart is 'deceitful above all things and desperately corrupt' (Jer. 17.9), and that 'the man who trusts in man, and makes flesh his arm, whose heart turns away from the Lord' is cursed (Jer. 17.5). Our sin is written with a pen of iron and with the point of a diamond. Sin appears in the Bible in many forms. Where the good is thought of as the fulfilment of self, sin is seen as the falling short of that fulfilment. (Saul and David are both examples.) Where the good is thought of as the fulfilment of the Law, or a moral code, sin is thought of as transgression. (Think, for example, of the Pharisees.) The good life includes all these things, but the essential truth of the good life to the biblical writers was that good life means communion or fellowship with God, as the first book in the Bible shows when it speaks of the sweet communion of man 'walking with God' (*see* Gen. 3.8; 5.22–24; 6.9; 17.1; 24.40). Sin breaks this fellowship, alienates us from God, and earns his wrath, the wrath which is the necessary precursor of mercy; for sin burdens the conscience, warps the judgment and darkens the soul. A man knows that he is working against God, and knows the bitterness of the cry, 'Against thee, thee only, have I sinned, and done that which is evil in thy sight' (Ps. 51.4). Such is the man aware of his sin. He knows that, as Augustine put it, he is curved in on himself (*incurvatus in se*), and that at heart he seeks his own concerns in everything (*in omnibus se suaque quaerit*).

Once this diagnosis is made clear to man, he realizes that there is nothing at all that he can do about his plight. Only God can restore this lost fellowship, just as only he could create it. Man cannot draw nearer to God by good works and hard trying; nor can he draw nearer to God by training his intellect; nor can he draw nearer to God by following the path of the mystic. The situation is not that God is far from man and man must strive by discipline and effort to approach him, but it is that man is far from God, who for his part has in Christ done everything that was necessary to meet man's plight: '. . . it is not of him that willeth, nor of him that runneth, but of God that sheweth mercy' (Rom. 9.16 KJV). To sharpen the point still further, the biblical doctrines of election and predestination show that man's salvation is wholly of the mercy of a redeeming God, and that man has no claim on God. The remedy therefore could and can come only from God, and only in a new relationship of forgiveness. Christ speaks only of the grace of God in all his sermons and parables and teaching, just as he shows only the grace of God in his miracles. Here was the righteousness that exceeded the righteousness of the Scribes and Pharisees, for it was not the righteousness of righteous men but the righteousness of Christ dwelling in the heart of penitent and converted men, who live, and yet not they, but Christ lives in them.

This is exactly what the salvation of Christ means. This is the real nature of it. The cross and Passion show the reality of God's forgiveness, and the brutal cost to Christ who, though sinless, and though pronounced sinless by the highest secular court of the day, faced the penalty of the worst sinner in society (death by crucifixion). When the cross and Passion are preached to men the power of this gospel, which is the power of God unto salvation, is generated afresh by the Holy Spirit, for this story awakes the penitence necessary to receive the forgiveness of God in Christ.

2. *As Judgment*. But there are two further dimensions to the biblical doctrine of salvation: the judgment of this present world, and the hope of eternal life. The work of God in the long deliverance of Israel culminating in the message of salvation in Christ is one of great joy and peace in believing, but it has a sombre side. Christ was rejected by Jewry (Matt. 23.37 f.) and the whole of St John's Gospel is written with a deep diapason of rejection and the overtone of judgment (John 1.11; 3.18; 9.39). To reject Christ, or to slight this salvation, incurs the final condemnation of God (Matt. 21.44) Christ came to save but this connotes judgment. He has already condemned the world. In Christ we judge the world in its true colours and know that its sin and evil are condemned, a kind of foretaste of the Last Judgment. The doctrine of judgment belongs to the doctrine of salvation. In Christ a man has a foretaste of his eternal citizenship with Christ, but the corollary of this is the condemnation of the unbelieving world to death. The world passeth away and the lusts thereof, but he that doeth the will of God abideth forever (I John 2.17). It is not fashionable now to speak of this element of salvation, but it is an inescapable concomitant of the doctrine.

3. *As Resurrection*. A complete doctrine of salvation in Christ must speak of the promise of resurrection, for 'if in this life we who are in Christ have only hope, we are of all men most to be pitied' (I Cor. 15.19). The last enemy to be destroyed is death. When in Christ a man finds an answer to the problem of evil and sin, he still faces the real problem of finding a way through pain, suffering and death. The Christian gospel is a gospel of life through death, not a message of deathless life. It is a gospel of resurrection which gives a profound significance to suffering and death, for it takes them and transmutes them into experiences of a wholly other kind. A Christian man faces pain and death, but in Christ he now knows that, though they are frighteningly real, they are not ultimate. These experiences will not destroy him, but will become his gateway to life and joy and peace. The point is worth demonstrating. When the natural man seeks a fuller life, he reaches out for more and deeper experiences of life, to find in these natural experiences (good in themselves) a deeper awareness of his existence. And this he finds. But in so doing he is ministering simply to his own needs and appetites and wants, and thereby renders himself increasingly self-centred and ever in need of more and livelier experiences. This is the man who seeks life and loses it. The man in Christ who seeks the things of Christ will be treated as his master was treated – to rejection, mockery, pain, and suffering. But he will learn in Christ that these experiences – the pain and suffering, the trials and tribulations of life – serve to destroy the real enemy within, the self, and thereby the new man in Christ rises from that death.

Christ triumphed over death, not because he thought death unimportant but because death was, and is, supremely important. His last triumphant call from the cross, 'It is finished!', showed his death as the final act in a life of total, obedient, self-sacrifice. We are now in the realms of mystery too profound to plumb, but it is surely deeply significant that Christ's resurrection body was not the same as his earthly body (for his disciples did not recognize him), yet it bore the marks of his crucifixion, and presumably does so to all eternity. We have a profound truth here – the secret of converting pain, suffering, sorrow, and death into the raw material of a resurrected life. Suffering and death for Christ's sake and the gospel's sake are sacraments conveying eternal life. They are the outward and visible sign of a soul's total self-surrender and self-sacrifice, necessary before this mortal can put on immortality. A man who has grasped this truth sees his whole life as a dying to live, a dying with Christ to live with Christ. And he sees this dying not as a mere death of the body alone, but as a lifelong giving of all that a man has and is in that very secular humdrum life in which he is called to live (II Cor. 6.9). We have indeed wrested heaven's secret out of life when we can say of all our sorrows and sufferings, 'in all these things we are more than conquerors through him who loved us' (Rom. 8.37). In this peculiarly Christian doctrine of resurrection we assert all the dignity and worth and significance of all that is earthly and bodily. There is no dualism here, no Manichaeism, no Gnosticism. It is in our common experience of life in all its earthiness that God meets us, and it is this very life that is resurrected. The doctrine of bodily resurrection also decries the error that man as man can attain heaven or find God. Flesh and blood cannot inherit the kingdom of God, for death has to be swallowed up in victory (I Cor. 15) and mortality swallowed up in life (II Cor. 5.4).

JAMES ATKINSON

Salvation-History. see *Heilsgeschichte.*

Sanctification

Sanctification is making or being made holy. Holiness (or sanctity) is the peculiar and distinctive characteristic of God and of all that is specially associated with God. Thus ancient Israel and the Christian Church the people of God is a 'holy nation' (Ex. 19.6; I Peter 2.9), and all its members are 'saints' (holy ones). They are holy, first of all, in virtue of the fact that God has chosen and called them to be his people, manifesting his presence and activity among them, and not in virtue of any qualities or achievements of their own. At the same time, they are commanded to be holy as he is holy (Lev. 11.44 f.; I Peter 1.16), called to be saints (Rom. 1.7; etc.). They have been chosen to be the people of God in order that they may become the people of God – just as a child adopted into a family both is and has to become a member of it. Holiness is thus both a gift and a goal.

The supreme standard and pattern of holiness is Jesus Christ, the holy one of God (Mark 1.24; Acts 3.14). God intends his people to be conformed to the image of his Son (Rom. 8.29). This is not fully accomplished within the limits of our present life, much less in the first moment of our Christian existence. Nor is it something we can achieve of ourselves. It is the work of God's grace, brought about by the Holy Spirit. Holiness is Christlikeness, which the Spirit effects in us, changing us 'from one degree of glory to another' (II Cor. 3.18). The essential mark of it is love – the divine *agape* of which Christ is the incarnate expression. Love like his, selflessly devoted to the will of his heavenly Father, and poured out in self-sacrificing service towards men, is the essence of Christian holiness.

The chief (though not the only) means which the Spirit employs for his hallowing or sanctifying work are the word and sacraments of the gospel, whereby he manifests his presence and activity among men, and seeks to enter into their hearts and lives. In so far as they are open to his influence

he pours the love of God into their hearts (Rom. 5.5) and produces those graces of character which are the fruit of his working in their lives (Gal. 5.22). When this happens, they know themselves to be children of God (Rom. 8.16), and begin to look on all other men with new eyes, as brothers for whom Christ died (II Cor. 5.14 ff.; Rom. 14.15). They also experience the liberty of the children of God (*see* **Freedom**) and therefore find themselves involved in conflict with all that is hostile to God, both in themselves and in the world around (*cf.* Gal. 5.17; Eph. 6.12).

Those who are specially called saints in the Church (as St Paul, St Francis, etc.), are those in whom the power of the Spirit is outstandingly manifest. They are not flawless paragons of virtue, but men through whom others have become more sure of God and his grace. Even a teacher of entire sanctification like John Wesley, who maintains the possibility of a 'relative perfection' for every Christian, insists that by any absolute standard the entirely sanctified are by no means perfect. They are beset by innumerable 'infirmities' and are liable to all kinds of mistakes, both of judgment and practice, as long as they live, even though they have the love of God filling their hearts and governing their lives.

In Catholic theology, sanctification is the effect of sanctifying grace (*see* **Grace** [2]), which is initially imparted to the soul at baptism. This can be lost through the commission of mortal sin, and then it must be restored through the sacrament of penance (q.v.). It can also be increased, particularly through the use of the sacraments, which contain and convey it. God will also give a further gift of it in answer to our prayers, or we can merit more of it by doing good works (q.v.). In classical Protestantism, sanctification like justification is by grace alone through faith alone. No works of ours contribute anything to it. Yet the difference between the Catholic and Protestant views is not as great as may at first appear. For the Protestant has likewise to avail himself of the means of grace, especially the word and sacraments and prayer. He denies, however, that either these or any good works he may do can be meritorious. A Protestant like Wesley, however, could hold that works of mercy were means of grace hardly less than works of piety, even though they were not meritorious.

D. G. Bloesch, *The Christian Life and Salvation*, 1967; R. N. Flew, *The Idea of Perfection in Christian Theology*, 1934; Paul Hessert, *The Christian Life*, 1967; W. E. Hulme, *The Dynamics of Sanctification*, 1966; Stephen Neill, *Christian Holiness*, 1960. *See also* bibliography under **Justification.**

P. S. WATSON

Sartre, Jean-Paul

Like existentialists in general, Sartre (1905–), French existentialist philosopher and dramatist, sharply distinguishes between the world of material objects and the realm of human existence. Truly to exist means to come out of the former world ·

(the world of speculation and scientific theorizing) and to assume one's freedom in a concrete existence in the world. But Sartre's philosophy is explicitly atheistic (he insists that existentialism is a form of humanism), anti-social (in the sense that he believes that others frustrate and limit my existence) and pessimistic (his writings highlight the *absurdity* and *nonsensicality* of the world and of much worldly intercourse). His theological significance is, first, that he demonstrates dramatically the practical and theoretical implications of atheism, thus undermining much of the optimism complacently thought to be inherent in contemporary atheistic scientific humanism, and, secondly, his brilliant and penetrating analyses of basic human affective attitudes (e.g. of nausea in *La Nausée*) amply demonstrate the cognitive value of these in our attempt to give an account of existence in the world as a whole.

J.-P. Sartre, *Being and Nothingness*, ET, 1957; H. J. Blackham, *Six Existentialist Thinkers*, 1952, ch. V.

JAMES RICHMOND

Satan

In Hebrew the word 'satan' simply means 'adversary' (esp. in law-suits). In the older OT conception 'the Satan' is a member of the heavenly court, whose function is to identify evil persons and to accuse them before God (Job 1 f.). By NT times, however, his character has degenerated and he has become the lord and leader of the evil spirits who oppose God and oppress men. In the Fourth Gospel he retains his role of accuser, and the Holy Spirit appears as counsel for the defence (*see* **Paraclete**). Until the age of Enlightenment (q.v.) belief in an objectivized (q.v.) personal Devil and his minions was all but universal among theologians. Today, however, it is generally recognized that belief in Satan, the leader of the fallen angels, etc. is not a satisfactory answer to the problem of evil: it still leaves us asking the question how evil got into the world which God created and saw was 'very good'. But as a pictorial way of representing the existence of superhuman evil forces in the universe Satan and his hosts call our attention to a very important question for theology. *See also* **Demonic; Powers.**

EDITOR

Savoy Declaration

Savoy Declaration is 'A Declaration of Faith and Order Owned and Practised in the Congregational Churches in England. Agreed upon and consented to by their Elders and Messengers meeting at the Savoy, October 12, 1658.' About 120 representatives attended. The Declaration has a long preface featuring some aspects of the history of the Westminster Assembly. The statement of faith consists of the Westminster Confession with some revisions and insertions. The power of magistrates to call synods is not affirmed as in the earlier document, and they are not authorized to interfere in religious differences between men of good conscience. The visible Catholic Church has no administrative officers for the whole body. There follow thirty articles 'On the Institution of Churches and the Order Appointed in Them'. Christ has given to particular Churches 'all the power and authority which is anyway needful' (v), and has not entrusted with power any Church more extensive or Catholic (vi). The officers appointed by Christ are pastors, teachers, elders and deacons, and these are to be chosen by vote and solemnly set apart with prayer and the imposition of hands by the elders (xi). Like the Cambridge Platform of 1648, the Declaration omits the Westminster statements on synods and councils. The Preface enjoins mutual forbearance among 'saints of all persuasions'. The Savoy Declaration is of doubtful authority for Congregationalism, but holds a respected place.

P. Schaff, *Creeds of Christendom*, I, III (text), 1919; W. Walker, *Creeds and Platforms of Congregationalism*, 1893.

J. T. MCNEILL

Scepticism

'Scepticism' covers a wide variety of attitudes, claims, standpoints, ranging from a general intellectual wariness and caution to a wholesale distrust of reasoning-procedures. It can mean a policy of suspending judgment when evidence is meagre or ambiguous. It can be the rejecting of a limited number of alleged methods of inquiry or argument (*a priori* reasoning about deity, e.g.): or involve a very broad questioning–of knowledge of others' minds, of the past, of value-judgments, of material objects ('all we ever *really* experience are sense-impressions').

Scepticism, therefore, is not the name of a single, distinct philosophical position. Indeed, *every* philosophical investigation ought to involve scepticism in the sense of the serious scrutiny of what is normally taken for granted or held dogmatically. Again, a position may be confidently held (e.g. that the soul is immortal), and yet much room be left for scepticism about the details of its meaning and implications (what it would be *like* to survive death, e.g.).

Historically, however, there have been certain philosophers and movements in philosophy that are labelled 'sceptical' in the history books. Pyrrho (c. 360–270 BC), was disillusioned by the irreconcilable conflicts between rival philosophical systems, and advocated that the quest for such a system be abandoned. Instead, by a suspending of judgment, the more realistic goal of Ataraxia–calmness of mind–should be sought. Other notable Sceptics include a number of Greek philosophers of the fourth to second centuries BC. Abelard and Montaigne should be mentioned, and, nearer our own day, David Hume–though Hume's case is controversial. He certainly was sceptical with regard to many philosophical accounts of the place of reason in e.g. the investigation of causality and moral judgment, but his work on these was not at all a *discrediting* of our claims to knowledge or a showing-up of value-judgment as in any way *illusory*. Rather, he offered a new interpretation of these. On matters of religious belief, however, he was sceptical in a more thorough-going sense. (*See* **Hume, D.**).

No single mid-twentieth-century philosophical doctrine of importance is usefully named 'Scepticism'; though there are clearly sceptical aspects of a number of influential movements. Logical Positivism and some forms of analytical philosophy have been sceptical about any metaphysics which attempts to infer unobservable entities or go beyond experience in any radical way (*see* **Positivism; Metaphysics; Analytical Philosophy**). Scepticism in the field of religious belief can be found also in the naturalistic and materialistic philosophical traditions which have numerous contemporary exponents.

Some philosophers today see scepticism not as a 'position' but as a moment in philosophical argument. To articulate the sceptical option (say, in a problem within theory of knowledge) can draw attention to certain perplexing 'gaps' in our chains of inference – from sense-impressions to material objects, from the overt behaviour of others to their minds, from the finite and temporal data that constitute our 'evidence' to claims about an infinite, eternal deity to whom the evidence allegedly points. Neither deductive nor inductive reasoning can bridge these gaps: we are challenged to discover how they can be bridged, if they can.

Some forms of scepticism can be shown to be untenable on logical grounds. They undermine their own claims – saw off the branch they are sitting upon. For example: one cannot claim to be sceptical about the possibility of making any true statement, or about making any general statement; since even to express these scepticisms involves uttering statements that are intended as true and general. Again, a Christian theologian must not be over-pessimistic about our capacity to make reliable moral judgments, since otherwise he cannot justify what he needs to say about the moral perfection and worship-worthiness of God. Nor can he denigrate human intellect in a general and thoroughgoing way without rendering himself unable to discriminate true claims to revelation from false, a fitting from an unfitting object of faith.

A. J. Ayer, *The Problem of Knowledge*, 1956; R. H. Popkin, 'Skepticism', *The Encyclopedia of Philosophy*, ed. Paul Edwards, 1967.

R. W. HEPBURN

Scheler, Max

Max Scheler (1874–1928), German philosopher and Husserlian phenomenologist, applied the phenomenological method to the religious consciousness, finding the key to consciousness in the concept of *value* (German: *Werth*). Normative and interpretative values, found to be innate by Scheler's use of the phenomenological method, can be arranged in a pyramidical pattern with *religious* values occupying the apex. Rather similarly to Otto, Scheler insisted that man's sense and apprehension of the numinous cannot be reduced, i.e. cannot be explained in inferior non-religious terms. It is this innate sense, according to Scheler, which enables man to seek and relate himself to God, and to participate in the spiritual life. His *On the Eternal in Man* (1921) appeared in an English translation in 1960. *See* **Husserl, E.; Otto, R.; Phenomenology**.

JAMES RICHMOND

Schelling, Friedrich Wilhelm Joseph von

Schelling (1775–1854), German post-Kantian Idealist and Romantic philosopher, was a *pantheistic idealist* in that he formulated a spiritual view of the world, holding, at different stages of his intellectual development, that the finite is the *expression* of the infinite, or that the finite and the infinite are identical, or that the former is but a mode or manifestation of the latter. His thought profoundly influenced nineteenth-century German philosophy and theology. One twentieth-century theologian who has acknowledged a heavy debt to Schelling's thought is Paul Tillich. *See* **Idealism**.

Paul Tillich, *Perspectives on 19th and 20th Century Protestant Theology*, 1967.

JAMES RICHMOND

Schism

The Greek word for schism, of which the English is a transliteration, means a tear or rent, e.g. in a piece of cloth (Mark 2.21) and so a division between two groups of people (John 7.43). It is now generally applied to the Church to refer to a breach in its unity, to the division of the Church into separated and mutually hostile organizations.

Paul used the term of the rival factions at Corinth (I Cor. 1.10). But his question on that occasion – Is Christ divided? – was answered by a universal negative in the period of the early Church. The patristic writers were convinced of two things: first, of the blasphemy and sinful character of schism – hence, according to John Chrysostom, 'nothing angers God so much as the division of the Church; even if we have done ten thousand good deeds, those of us who cut up the fulness of the Church will be punished no less than those who cut his body' (*In Ep.ad Eph.Hom.* xi.5) – and second, that schism is always outside the Church, i.e. of any two bodies at odds with each other and each asserting itself to be the Church only one of them had the right to the claim.

There was, however, not always a clear distinction between schism and heresy, but the former ultimately came to mean, in the words of Optatus, that which 'breaks peace, goes out from the root of mother Church, but retains the faith and the sacraments which they acquired within the Church' (*c.Parm.*1.10–12). Hence Augustine had little to object against the Donatists on the grounds of belief but argued that they were outside the Church since their breach of unity proved their lack of love and therefore of their possession of the Holy Spirit who is its source.

Such a view of schism, that it is outside the Church, is held today by both Roman Catholics and Eastern Orthodox, the former regarding all those out of communion with the pope as in a state of schism. By this means it is possible to assert the unbroken unity of the Church. There are, however, many Christians who would regard this as an oversimplified solution which neglects the evidence of the facts. It is difficult for an outside observer of the Roman and Eastern Orthodox Churches not to hold that each has as good a claim as the other to belong to the Church and that therefore their division must be regarded as internal. Most Anglicans, vis-à-vis these two communions, would also consider their own state of separation to be within the one Church, i.e. schism has not expelled one or other of these bodies from the Church which has instead been internally rent. Such a position, however, would seem to lead to the conclusion that, if oneness is a mark of the Church and if this oneness is no longer apparent because of schism, then the Church itself no longer exists. This statement of an extreme position serves to emphasize the difficulty, if not impossibility, of producing a 'tidy' theology when internal schism is acknowledged, although this seems to be warranted by the observable facts. The alternatives would seem to be either to un-church all Christian bodies save one or to un-church all, for the 'Branch' theory does not seem tenable. This theory was advanced under the inspiration of the Oxford Movement and is to the effect that although the Church has fallen into disunity its several provinces or groups of provinces may yet be branches of the one Church – there being three such main branches: the Roman, the Eastern and the Anglican. This may safeguard the position of the Church of England and its claim, over against Rome, to belong to the Church, but it again conflicts with the data of Christian life and belief provided, e.g. by the Lutherans or Methodists.

Whatever the causes of schism in the past, and it has to be acknowledged that there may be at times an unfortunate conflict between truth and love, it is difficult not to admit that failure to actualize that unity for which Christ prayed, according to the Fourth Gospel (John 17.21), partakes of the nature of sin which is itself divisive.

S. L. Greenslade, *Schism in the Early Church*, 1953 (with valuable chapters on its relevance to modern issues); T. A. Lacey, *Unity and Schism*, 1917.

J. G. DAVIES

Schleiermacher, Friedrich Daniel Ernst

Schleiermacher (1768–1834) is usually regarded as the greatest Protestant theologian since Calvin and as the father of what is vaguely known as 'liberal Protestantism' (q.v.). Born in Breslau (now Wroclaw in Poland), he spent most of his life in Berlin as a preacher and theological professor.

Schleiermacher brought to theological expression influences that had already made themselves felt in Pietism and Romanticism, with their appeal to personal experience and emotion. After the arid debates between Protestant orthodoxy on the one hand and rationalism on the other, Schleiermacher's new approach came like a breath of fresh air.

His well-known early work, *On Religion: Speeches to its Cultured Despisers*, first published in 1799, already introduces some of his leading ideas. The essence of religion is to be sought neither in dogma nor in will, but in inward experience, in man's deepest feelings or intuitions of the divine. 'You must transport yourself into the interior of a pious soul and seek to understand its inspiration.' He declares that 'true religion is sense and taste for the infinite'. Religious beliefs attempt to transcribe into words the content of religious feeling. 'Dogmas are a knowledge about feeling, and in no way an immediate knowledge about the operations of the universe that gave rise to the feeling.'

Schleiermacher's theology finds its fullest expression in *The Christian Faith* (1822). In the introduction to this book, we meet the famous definition of religion as 'the feeling of absolute dependence'. This feeling is universal in human experience and finds expression in all the religions. It is by this feeling that we are convinced of the reality of God, rather than by alleged proofs of his existence. Christianity is the highest form of religion because of the unique place in it of the Redeemer, Jesus Christ. While every man has a 'God-consciousness', this is usually obscured. Only in Jesus Christ was this God-consciousness unimpaired. Because of this, he stood in a unique relation to the Father, and it is through participation in the community which he founded that men are now redeemed through the purging and strengthening of their God-consciousness.

A good deal of debate has gone on concerning the interpretation of Schleiermacher's term 'feeling'. Some have supposed that this feeling is simply subjective emotion, so that Schleiermacher's defence of religion would be at the expense of depriving it of any cognitive content. There can be no doubt that his thought often has been developed into a kind of aestheticism. Yet it is clear that he himself attributed a cognitive dimension to what he called 'feeling', and supposed it to be a genuine insight into the real.

In any case, it should be remembered that Schleiermacher's achievement is by no means exhausted by the notion of the feeling of absolute dependence. He worked on the problem of hermeneutics at a time when this subject was almost totally neglected, and this work in turn inspired the researches of Dilthey (q.v.), who also wrote a noted biographical study of Schleiermacher. He was interested also in history and the historical consciousness. Ethics was another subject that claimed his attention. All of these interests contributed to the total character of his theology.

Schleiermacher's influence was very great in the nineteenth and early twentieth centuries. One might name Ritschl, Harnack, Otto and Tillich (qq.v.) among those who rather obviously show the influence of Schleiermacher in one aspect or another of their thought, but the influence was so widespread that perhaps no Protestant thinking in the past hundred years has been quite free of it. During the ascendancy of Barth and the neo-orthodox school (qq.v.) Schleiermacher came in for a good deal of criticism for exalting individual experience as against the objective criteria for faith supplied by the Bible. More recently, as man has multiplied his power and knowledge, the concept of absolute dependence has been called into question, and with it the supposed universality of the accompanying God-consciousness. On the other hand, there has been re-awakened interest in Schleiermacher's attempts to come to terms with the cultural factor in theology. A knowledge of Schleiermacher is certainly essential to any understanding of Protestant theology today, and it is likely that his views will continue to be debated.

F. D. E. Schleiermacher, *The Christian Faith*, ET, 1928; *On Religion: Speeches to its Cultured Despisers*, ET, 1958; R. R. Niebuhr, *Schleiermacher on Christ and Religion*, 1964; Gerhard Spiegler, *The Eternal Covenant: Schleiermacher's Experiment in Cultural Theology*, 1967.
JOHN MACQUARRIE

Schmucker, Samuel Simon

Samuel Simon Schmucker (1799–1873) was the first professor of theology and head of the Gettysburg Theological Seminary in Pennsylvania. He was involved in the formation (1820) and especially in the preservation of the General Synod, the first national Lutheran body in the USA. He was the principal leader of the 'American Lutheran' movement, which sought to adapt the Lutheran confessional heritage to the American scene. He published the first English text of Lutheran systematic theology, *Elements of Popular Theology* (1834), in which can be discerned influences from scholastic Lutheranism, from pietism, and from the several years of study Schmucker had had at the Calvinistic Princeton Theological Seminary. On such a matter as the mode of the Saviour's presence in the Eucharist, Schmucker presented five classical positions and argued for freedom of interpretation on all matters not clearly determined by the Bible.

Schmucker was a man of irenic spirit, and an ecumenical pioneer; in 1838 he published the *Fraternal Appeal to the American Churches: With a Plan for Catholic Union, on Apostolic Principles*. He envisioned an Apostolic Protestant Church as a federation of denominations with a United Confession encompassing the doctrines common to the major communions. In his latter days, Schmucker's influence was sharply opposed by the resurgence of the confessional emphasis under the leadership of Charles Porterfield Krauth (q.v.). Schmucker issued (anonymously) the *Definite Synodical Platform* (1855), a recension of the Augsburg Confession which omitted some of its 'errors'. The reaction led to the defeat of the American Lutheran movement and the decline of Schmucker's influence.

Vergilius Ferm, *The Christ in American Lutheran Theology*, 1927; Abdel Ross Wentz, *Pioneer in Christian Unity: Samuel Simon Schmucker*, 1967.
ROBERT T. HANDY

Scholasticism, Schoolmen

The words are derived *via* Latin *schola* from Greek *schole*, leisure, discussion, school. Such words as 'scholar', 'scholarship' belong essentially to the ancient and mediaeval tradition of respect for learning. Scholasticism in its broader theological sense is used of the tradition of philosophical and theological study and teaching in the Middle Ages, when philosophers and theologians (as in every age) grouped themselves into differing schools of thought. In the later mediaeval period much time was spent in commenting upon and refining or elaborating the systems of previous thinkers, and it was then that 'scholastic' acquired the pejorative sense in which it is sometimes used today, as denoting unoriginality, triviality and irrelevance. Such usage is quite improper, if it is implied that the great schoolmen (Aquinas and others) spent their time in debating trivialities; they were concerned with the great questions of faith and life, as is living theology in any age. In its narrower sense 'scholasticism' is used with particular reference to the system of Aquinas (*see* **Thomism**) and its developments. At the Reformation the whole scholastic approach was rejected: natural theology (q.v.) tended to be discounted by Protestant theologians, who spoke slightingly of 'the Aristotelian theology', in favour of a purely biblical approach to Christian faith. Nevertheless there grew up in the generations after the Reformers themselves an arid and unoriginal practice of systematizing reformed theology which is now deprecatingly spoken of as 'Protestant scholasticism'.
EDITOR

Science and Religion

This vast subject cannot be adequately treated in a short article. The following points should be noted. Though the phrase 'Greek science' is sometimes used, there was no science in the modern sense of natural or experimental science until the later Middle Ages. It was in fact the domination of European thought by Greek philosophical notions which delayed the rise of modern science until the age of Copernicus, Kepler and Galileo. So long as teleological notions were used as terms of explanation in science (e.g.

the idea that a stone falls because it wants to go home) there could be no science as we know it, and Aristotelianism had to be dethroned before the concept of empirically established laws could be developed. The trial of Galileo (1632), embellished by the legend of his muttered 'And yet it does move', is the paradigm of the struggle of the new scientific outlook against the old but long-established Aristotelianism; it had nothing to do with any clash with Hebraic or biblical thought, but only with the Greek thought which had unhappily become the official orthodoxy of the establishment. In recent years it has been more clearly recognized that modern science could have evolved only within the context of a Christian world-view, with its teaching about a God of order and of rationality, whose created world was under the rule, not of chance, but of regular laws. It is significant that it was in Christendom, not in any other of the world's great civilizations, that modern scientific method was evolved. It is also significant that the leading scientific thinkers of the early age of science were deeply and not merely conventionally Christian men – Francis Bacon, Descartes, Kepler, Galileo, Pascal, Boyle, Ray, Newton and many others. It is true that it took many decades to work the lingering traces of Aristotelianism out of the European mind and to develop 'methodical atheism' (q.v.), i.e. never to resort to God as a term of explanation. Unfortunately many Christians (including some theologians) have still even today not grasped this principle, and believe it necessary to assert that God is to be found at those points at which allegedly scientific explanation is lacking – e.g. the point of emergence of life from the inorganic, or of mind, or of self-consciousness, in the evolutionary process. This kind of God is today often called the 'God of the gaps' and is rightly rejected by thoughtful people. It is essential that philosophical (or religious or theological) explanations be ruled out of scientific thinking. But this does not, of course, involve the view that natural science is atheistic in its conclusions; science as such is not concerned with explanation beyond the range of natural phenomena, and there cannot be any ultimate conflict between religion and natural science. But very often in the past (e.g. at the conflict over Darwin's theory of evolution a century ago) old-fashioned and untenable theological theories about the nature of the biblical revelation have given rise to a widespread assumption, assiduously fostered by the rationalists, that there is an inherent conflict between science and religion. There can be conflict only where false theological theories are held, since natural science itself provides no answer to ultimate questions. But positivistic philosophy endeavours to create an appearance to the contrary by setting itself up as 'the scientific attitude'. In so far as certain psychological theorists claim to evaluate the truth or untruth of religion, psychology in their hands has not yet attained to the status of a science, but is still philosophy masquerading in scientific dress. If

psychology (including the psychology of religion) is, as most psychologists nowadays would claim, a science methodologically akin to the natural sciences, it can make no pronouncement upon the validity of religious or theological statements. See also **Cosmology**; **Methodical Atheism**.

Ian G. Barbour, *Issues in Science and Religion*, 1966; H. Butterfield, *The Origins of Modern Science*, 1950; E. L. Mascall, *Christian Theology and Natural Science*, 1956; Alan Richardson, *The Bible in the Age of Science*, 1961; *History Sacred and Profane*, 1964.

EDITOR

Scripture, Doctrine of Holy

Every theological position involves a doctrine of Holy Scripture, whether explicit or concealed. The very fact that the ancient Church took over the canon of the Jewish Scriptures and proceeded to add to it a canon of Scriptures concerning the new covenant of Jesus Christ implies a definite theological position regarding its own sacred book (Bible: Latin *biblia*, fem. sing., from the Greek *biblia*, neut. plur., 'books'). The theological motive behind this setting apart of The Book from all other books was the recognition that this book contained all the genuine historical witness to Jesus Christ which existed. The whole Bible was a book about Christ, the OT by way of prophecy, the NT by means of proclamation that the expected Redeemer had come. The OT Scriptures are read because their true meaning is understood in the light of Christ's coming; the NT Scriptures have removed the veil which obscures their truth from those who do not know or believe in Christ. The classical Christian doctrine of Holy Scripture, both Catholic and Protestant, has been succinctly formulated by Richard Hooker: 'The general end of both the Old and the New (Testaments) is one; the difference between them consisting in this, that the Old did make wise by teaching salvation through Christ that should come, the New by teaching that Christ the Saviour is come, and that Jesus whom the Jews did crucify, and whom God did raise from the dead, is he' (*Laws of Ecclesiastical Polity*, i. 14).

This, the historic Christian teaching, enables us to answer the question about the authority of Scripture. The Bible is authoritative for Christians because it contains the historical witness of those who were *there* to the mighty acts of God for our salvation. (Incidentally it also answers the question, often asked, why the Christian Scriptures are completed at some date in the second century AD; why should there not be a Bible which contains the witness to Christ of, say, Thomas-à-Kempis, Luther, Wesley, and so on? The answer, of course, is that the Bible contains *historical* witness, the testimony of those whose eyes saw and whose hands handled; the testimony of those who were *there*.) The Bible possesses no authority independently of its prophetic and apostolic interpretation of the events to which it bears witness. Its authority is derived from Christ: if we accept Christ as authoritative for us, we shall accept the authority of the Bible which alone bears historical testimony to him. In this sense the Bible is God's word for us; but we should carefully notice that it is only in a secondary or derivative sense that the Bible is the word of God. God's word in the primary and biblical sense is Christ himself; the Bible may be spoken of as God's word only because it is the means by which the knowledge of God in Christ has been transmitted to us.

The questions about the relation of the authority of the Bible to that of the Church, of tradition and of reason, have been much discussed. The claim that the authority of the Church is superior to that of the Bible, because the Church wrote the Scriptures and authorized them, may be answered by pointing out that in drawing up the canon of Scriptures the Church recognized an authority which she did not confer: authority is to be distinguished from authorization. If by tradition (q.v.) is meant the mind of the Church down the ages as it has received and interpreted the Scriptures, then it is obvious that the guidance of tradition must continually be sought in our attempt to understand the meaning of the Scriptures. But if by tradition is meant some oral or secret knowledge given to the Church in addition to the Scriptures, the evidence is lacking for such a supposition. Aquinas would have agreed with the Reformers that the Scriptures contain all that is necessary for salvation, and that nothing is to be held as *de fide* which cannot be demonstrated from them.

The place of reason in the interpretation of Scripture must nowadays be discussed in terms of scholarly research, of historical knowledge (*see* **Criticism**) and of our contemporary understanding of the world. Since the rise of the modern critical study of the Bible towards the end of the eighteenth century, the Bible has come to be understood as a book (or library of books) with a history, and one which therefore can be understood only in the light of modern critical literary and historical method. The old pre-Enlightenment view of the Bible as having been divinely inspired and guaranteed is no longer tenable and is a hindrance to the proper understanding of the character of revelation as actually having been given in real history (*see* **Revelation; Fundamentalism**). But this does not mean that the Bible is not 'inspired' at all, though it does mean that nineteenth-century liberal views of the Bible as inspired because it is inspiring must be reckoned inadequate. The Bible is not to be commended on the ground that it has been or still is an authentic record of human religious experience. Such views find in Scripture only a human, not a divine, authority, and therefore fall short of the full Christian doctrine of Holy Scripture. (*See* **Witness of the Spirit** for further discussion of the work of the Holy Spirit in the giving and receiving of the Scriptures; *see* **Hermeneutics** for discussion of the exegesis and

preaching of the Bible.)

The Scriptures are the gift of God and are incomprehensible without his gift of faith. This aspect of the Christian doctrine of Holy Scripture has not been understood by nineteenth- and twentieth-century liberal Protestant theology with its over-emphasis upon the complementary truth that God does not intend us to use any of his gifts unintelligently or uncritically. Space does not permit a discussion of the various deviations from the Christian norm in the different types of modern theology. The history-of-religions school in the earlier decades of our century regarded the biblical writings as nothing more than choice specimens in the religious literature of the world. R. Bultmann (whose formative years were spent under the influence of this school) regards the OT as in no sense revelation for us: Israel's history is not our history, Jerusalem is not holier than Athens, and so on. His existentialist philosophy has no place for the Christian doctrine of Holy Scripture. The widespread neglect or repudiation of this doctrine is an unhappy sign of the degeneracy of much Protestant theology in our time.

B. W. Anderson, ed., *The Old Testament and Christian Faith*, 1964 (essays by and about R. Bultmann); S. L. Greenslade, ed., *Cambridge History of the Bible: the West from the Reformation*, 1963; W. Klassen and G. F. Snyder, eds., *Current Issues in New Testament Interpretation*, 1962; Alan Richardson, *Preface to Bible Study*, 9th. imp., 1960 (as an introductory book); James D. Smart, *The Interpretation of Scripture*, 1961; C. Westermann, ed., *Essays on Old Testament Interpretation*, ET, 1963.

EDITOR

Sects

The fissiparous (i.e. having a tendency to break up) character of Protestantism showed itself from the Reformation onwards, and today there are a large number of splinter sects, mostly of an evangelical type, throughout the world. Divisions often arose because of doctrinal disagreement, and thus a concern for truth as it was understood, however narrowly, was one of their causes. But there were also what C. H. Dodd has called 'non-theological factors' at work, i.e. sociological rather than doctrinal incompatibility. Troeltsch (q.v.) divided Christian groupings into the 'church' type and the 'sect' type and adumbrated the time when a developed sociology of religion (q.v.) would throw light upon the social origins of the denominations (*see also* H. R. Niebuhr, *The Social Sources of the Denominations*, 1929). The sect-types remain strong and cohesive in many parts of the world; being generally conservative or perhaps fundamentalist (q.v.) in outlook, they are often quite untouched by the developments in Christian theology since the Enlightenment (q.v.) which could have the effect of making their original doctrinal standpoints seem irrelevant today. Many of the sects stand outside the Ecumenical Movement and are uninfluenced by it or are opposed to it. Their lack of interest in the matter of Christian unity is justified by their belief in the doctrine of the 'invisible church' (q.v.). It is impossible here even to list the names of the many extant sects, which range from the doctrinally orthodox to the marginally Christian. The fissiparous character of Protestantism has long been a strong weapon in the armoury of Roman Catholic polemicists. The altered climate of our times can well be illustrated by comparing J. B. Bossuet's *Histoire des variations des églises protestants* (1688) with H. Daniel-Rops, *Our Brothers in Christ, 1870-1959*, ET, 1967 (History of the Church of Christ, vol. 10), in which will be found a reliable and sympathetic account of all the most notable Christian churches, denominations and sects outside the Roman Catholic Church.

EDITOR

Secular Christianity

This expression has recently come into use in a rather vague way to cover a variety of attitudes towards the theological and social movements of the day. The word 'secular' has become an 'in' word among 'radical' theologians, but they have no agreed usage among themselves. For some the issue is largely a matter of the radical re-interpretation of the Gospel; e.g. Paul van Buren, *Secular Meaning of the Gospel* (1963), for whom the word 'God' is no longer necessary in a secular society; or R. Gregor Smith, *Secular Christianity* (1966), for whom the expression means a radically new version of the Christian faith as demythologized by R. Bultmann, but, with Bultmann, retaining the notion of the divine transcendence. Others who use the terminology of secular Christianity or secular theology have affinities with the 'death-of-God' (q.v.) school. But for most of them the idea of secular Christianity is closely bound up with the loss of a worthwhile role for the Christian minister in the modern technological age (*see* **Secular, Secularization**). To these especially the last words of D. Bonhoeffer make an appeal, and perhaps 'secular' is for them a rough equivalent of his *religionslos* (*see* **Religion**). Christians must stop being 'churchy' and pietistic; they must actively concern themselves with the affairs of secular life. This attitude is often bound up with a denial of the value of corporate worship, prayer and the religious life, and with the passive acceptance of the death of God as a cultural fact. Theologically secular Christianity would seem to signalize the final disintegration of liberal protestantism (q.v.); sociologically it may be regarded as itself a significant cultural fact in Western society in our time, since it represents a radical questioning of the function of the churches and of the role of the minister in social life today. The emphasis upon the need for the participation of Christians in the common life of society is not, of course, new. A succession of Christian leaders (W. Temple, J. H.

Oldham, R. Niebuhr, R. L. Calhoun and many others of a former generation) has called for such participation, and a whole series of ecumenical conferences from Stockholm (1925) to Oxford (1937), Evanston (1954) and New Delhi (1961) has taken up the challenge.

The Churches Survey their Task: Report of the Conference at Oxford, July 1937, on Church, Community and State, with introduction by J. H. Oldham, 1937; R. L. Calhoun, *God and the Common Life,* 1935; Harvey Cox, *The Secular City,* 1965; E. L. Mascall, *The Secularization of Christianity,* 1966; R. Gregor Smith, *Secular Christianity,* 1966; P. van Buren, *Secular Meaning of the Gospel,* 1963.

EDITOR

Secular, Secularization

The word 'secular' is derived from Latin *saecularis,* 'belonging to the particular age' (*cf. saeculum,* an age, era; *in saecula saeculorum,* 'for ever and ever'): thus, the 'secular games' were celebrated every 120 years, and the appropriate 'secular hymns' were sung at them. In mediaeval Latin 'secular' came to be used of 'this present age' (as contrasted with the 'age to come'); thus there were 'the secular arm', 'the secular clergy', as contrasted with the ecclesiastical authority and the 'religious' or 'regular' clergy, who lived according to the *regula* or rule of their order. The civil sphere gradually achieved independence from ecclesiastical control, and after the Reformation many areas of life gradually became autonomous. By the nineteenth century the secular was often thought of as the sphere in which neither the Church nor the Christian conscience had any right to interfere (politics, business, science, etc.). By the twentieth century many more areas of life have been thus 'secularized' (universities, education generally, hospitals, social services, art, etc.). Thus 'sacred' or religious activity has been increasingly confined to a narrow area of ecclesiastical activity and personal piety, and the churches as organizations have lost a great deal of their former significance and influence in modern life. The clergy and ministers of today are thus in many places seeking a new role in society, since their former role has largely been taken over by social service agents, psychiatrists, etc., who possess an expertise which the ordained minister lacks (*see* **Secular Christianity**). Nevertheless the process of secularization has had a certain historical inevitability. When the civilization of Rome collapsed under the pressure of the barbarians, the Church had become willy-nilly the custodian of civilized values and eventually converted the invaders and built the European civilization which was called 'Christendom' (q.v.). The very success of the Church's civilizing mission (education, universities, almshouses, hospitals, parish relief, enforcement of justice, etc.) spelt the inevitable ending of her paternalistic authority. When Renaissance man came of age, such tutelage was found incompatible with his new status. Hence between the sixteenth and twentieth centuries the various departments of human life claimed and took their autonomy. The unwillingness of the Church in many lands to accept the inevitable result of her own civilizing mission (e.g. eighteenth-century France) has been a prime cause of her relegation to the narrow area of ecclesiastical activity and personal devotion. *See also* **Secular Christianity.**

A. MacIntyre, *Secularization and Moral Change,* 1967.

EDITOR

Secularism

The word seems to have been coined in 1851 by G. J. Holyoake (1817–1906) as the name of his philosophical and ethical system, which was designed to interpret and order life without recourse to belief in God, the Bible or a future life. He set up Secular Societies in several English towns. The redoubtable Charles Bradlaugh (1833–1891), who as a Free-thinker (q.v.) conducted a long and eventually successful struggle to enter Parliament, was president of the London Secular Society from 1858 until the year before his death. The bitter anti-religious propaganda and hatred of Christianity of the Secularists has left behind associations which make it difficult for Christians in Britain to understand what certain contemporary 'radical' theologians intend when they speak of 'secular Christianity'. It has also made it difficult to appreciate fully the genuine enthusiasm of the Secularists for social amelioration and reform. The National Secular Society refuses to give the figures of its membership today, but the British Humanist Association (founded in 1963) claims 3,500 members and is now (1967) engaged in a recruiting campaign; the Rationalist Press Association claims 4,000 members, the Progressive League 500, and the South Place Ethical Society 700. The National Secular Society is explicitly atheist, but the British Humanist Association would be better described as agnostic. All these bodies are strongly anti-church and opposed to religious education ('indoctrination' is their word for it). Nevertheless in recent times there has been a willingness on the part of many leading members of these secularist denominations to enter into dialogue with Christians, and churchmen have supported in Parliament and elsewhere certain social projects put forward by them. Their chief problems are how to make their 'gospel' interesting to the public and how to promote morality in a religionless age. *See also* **Humanism.**

Warren Sylvester Smith, *The London Heretics, 1870–1914,* 1967.

EDITOR

Self-Understanding

Self-understanding is a term introduced into contemporary theology by R. Bultmann from the existentialist analysis of M. Heidegger. It is an integral element in the existentialist programme of demythologizing (q.v.), representing in a form which it is claimed is intelligible to the modern man what was formerly understood by such terms as 'salvation'. Acceptance of the *kerygma* (q.v.) brings a change in a man's understanding of himself, releasing him from the fear of nothingness, insignificance and death. Bultmann insists that a change in a man's understanding of himself involves a change in the man himself (conversion). He thereafter lives authentically, whereas formerly his existence was inauthentic. *See* **Bultmann, R.; Existentialism; Openness.**

EDITOR

Semantics

Semantics means the study of meaning in language. It is possible to distinguish between semantics as a department of logic and semantics as a department of linguistics. A primarily logical question, for instance, would be that of the relation of the linguistic sign to that which is signified by it (e.g. between the word *horse* and the entity horse, its 'referent' to which it refers). Statements about this relation are connected with other logical questions, such as the differentiation of different kinds or strata of language (scientific language, ordinary language), the status of signs (like *unicorn*) for which no real referent exists, the relation of individuals to classes (this horse to the class *horse,* this God to the class *gods*), questions of truth and falsehood, and methods of argument, verification and proof. Logic is not primarily concerned with the description of the different natural languages, such as Hebrew, Greek or English.

As a part of linguistics, on the other hand, semantics deals with the identification and description of meaning in the natural human languages. Two approaches can be distinguished. A synchronic approach attempts to describe the meanings with which words (and other linguistic elements) function in a language at one time. In a diachronic approach the linguist tries to stage the ways in which meanings have changed and developed in the history of one or more languages.

Both the logical and the linguistic kinds of semantics are relevant for theology, and perhaps some of the major problems of theology lie in questions of meaning in the logical sense. Nevertheless it is rather in the linguistic sense that the term 'semantics' has been most used in recent theological discussion. It has appeared mainly in questions of the interpretation of Hebrew and Greek linguistic phenomena and their use in the structure of theological argument. The following circumstances are relevant:

1. The massive philological scholarship of the nineteenth century, though rich in the gathering of material and the classification of forms, was often weak and naive in its approach to questions of meaning. The rise of the newer general linguistics in the mid-twentieth century, with its greater emphasis on synchronic description, favoured a closer attention to semantic study.

2. The Judaeo-Christian tradition includes a

long history of fascination with etymology as a means of clarifying obscure expressions and adapting them to use in theological argument. Nineteenth-century comparative philology, by setting etymology on a historical basis, accidentally strengthened this tendency, and it was further supported by the use of etymologies (usually fictitious) in philosophies such as that of Heidegger, which exercised some influence upon theology. The recent semantic discussion involves, among other elements, the re-assertion of function against etymology.

3. The relation between OT and NT language has been a particular centre of concern. Early in the present century many words of biblical Greek, which had previously been supposed to be unique, were identified in the Hellenistic papyri. In reaction against an apparent Hellenizing interpretation of the NT, some argued that the words came from the Greek world but their meanings from the Hebrew background. In turn it has been argued that evidence was distorted in order to fit it into this picture. The matter is part of a larger question, namely, that of the use of the contrast of two ways of thought, the Hebrew and the Greek, to which some currents of theology have assigned positive and negative values respectively.

4. An important issue raised has been the contrast between word-meanings and sentence-meanings. Many attempts to state theological meanings took the form of dictionary articles on words, and gave the impression that characteristics of the Judaeo-Christian revelation were intrinsic to each of the biblical words. Against this it has been argued that theological distinctiveness belongs not to the meanings of words (even biblical words) but to sentences and larger complexes, and that this fact makes possible the translation of theological ideas into other languages, in which all individual words are different.

5. In general, much new analysis is needed in order to penetrate the process by which the modern scholar apprehends and evaluates the indications furnished by an ancient text in Hebrew or Greek. Even the reader of the Bible who does not consider himself a scholar gives only an extremely superficial impression if he says he makes up his mind by looking at a translation, consulting a commentary, or using a dictionary. Among scholars, it may be suspected that the dryness and dullness of many commentaries and exegetical discussions arise from the simplification of a very complex series of semantic indications, and that a greater consciousness of semantics as a discipline may do something to improve the level of exegesis generally.

For modern semantics in general, S. Ullmann, *Semantics, An Introduction to the Science of Meaning,* 1962. For application to biblical problems, J. Barr, *Biblical Words for Time,* 1962; *The Semantics of Biblical Language,* 1961.

JAMES BARR

Sermon. *see* Preaching; Homiletics.

Similitudo Dei

Similitudo Dei means likeness of God. Gen. 1.26 reads 'Let us make man in our image, after our likeness'. Modern scholars are confident that 'image' and 'likeness' (Hebrew: *Tzelem* and *Demuth*) in this verse are used synonymously in a typical example of Hebraic parallelism. Some theologians, however, have interpreted these terms as two different concepts. For example, Irenaeus contrasted the image of God with the likeness of God (Latin: *similitudo*), arguing that the image of God is man's endowment with reason, etc. while the *similitudo* represents the relationship to God for which man was created. Thus in the fall the latter was lost, while the former was retained. *See also* **Man, Doctrine of (2).**

WILLIAM HORDERN

Simul Justus et Peccator

Simul Justus et Peccator (both righteous and a sinner) is a phrase of Luther's describing the Christian as a man justified by grace through faith. Justification, as Luther sees it, means (1) that we are accounted righteous (*reputari justos*) for Christ's sake; (2) that neither sinful acts committed by us in the past, nor the sinfulness still remaining in our nature (original sin) is counted against us (*imputari*); (3) that we are given the firstfruits of the Spirit (*primitiae Spiritus*) and the beginning of a new creature (*initium novae creaturae*); and (4) that we are involved in a battle between the Spirit and the sin that remains in us (*reliquiae peccati in carne*), which sin is both pardoned and conquered through our faith in Christ (*Luthers Werke,* Weimar ed., XXXIX i 83; XL i 364; 408). In other words, justification is a kind of regeneration to newness of life (*ibid.,* XXXIX i 48).

In the light of (1) and (2) above, Luther can say that the Christian is at once wholly sinful and wholly righteous. He is sinful in himself but righteous in Christ; for the righteousness of Christ is reckoned to his credit, completely covering his unrighteousness and (as it were) setting right his account with God (*see* **Imputation).** In the light of (3) and (4), however, Luther can also say that Christians are 'partly righteous and partly sinners'. Although they are not sinless, they are 'in motion or on the way to righteousness'. They are 'sinners in fact, but righteous in hope'; and the hope is already on the way to fulfilment, though it will not be completely fulfilled in this life.

It should be emphasized that when Luther speaks of Christians as sinners, he is not thinking primarily in terms of sinful acts, but rather of the sinful nature from which such acts proceed. Our nature remains sinful as long as we live, and in that sense we cannot be sinless. But we can live without wickedness (i.e. sinful acts), and we ought to do so (*ibid.,* VI 27). For, while it is true that we are not saved by good works, we shall surely be damned if we do not cease from evil works and repent (*ibid.,* XVII i 313; XLVI 467).

As Christian believers, we have, Luther says, 'partly the flesh and partly the Spirit, but in such a way that the Spirit rules and the flesh is subdued, righteousness reigns and sin serves' (*ibid.*, XL ii 93). Hence, as he can also say, we are 'both sinners and saints'.

P. S. WATSON

Sin. *see* Man, Doctrine of.

Social Analogy

The use of a group of human beings as an analogy of the Trinity was first advanced by the Cappadocians (q.v.). Basil cites Peter, James and John in this connection. Its further development as a full-scale analogy belongs, however, to the nineteenth and twentieth centuries in England and America (Illingworth, Thornton, Lowry and Hodgson) under the influence of recent views of personality. While older views had stressed impermeability as its leading characteristic, the modern view emphasized capacity for fellowship as equally important. The Tri-personality of God could, therefore, be interpreted on the analogy of human selves in society. Thus Thornton, arguing against Idealist attempts to find in the universe the necessary counterpart as object to God as Subject finds on the basis of this analogy the subject-object relation adequately embodied within the Godhead itself. Applying this analogy C. C. J. Webb claimed that Christian orthodoxy spoke of Personality *in* God rather than the Personality *of* God as the psychological analogy implies. The motive of the analogy is pluralist, its target a Trinity in Unity and its inherent weakness (without proper qualification) a tendency to tritheism (q.v.). *See* **Psychological Analogy; Thomistic Analogy.**

L. Hodgson, *The Doctrine of the Trinity*, 1943; L. S. Thornton, *The Incarnate Lord*, 1928; C. C. J. Webb, *God and Personality*, 1918; C. Welch, *The Trinity in Contemporary Theology*, 1953, pp. 133–52.

H. E. W. TURNER

Social Gospel Movement

Social Gospel Movement is the name given to the most conspicuous strand of the Christian social movement, especially in the USA in the last several decades of the nineteenth century and the first three of the twentieth. The full impact of the industrial revolution in many countries led to the rise of Christian social movements which addressed themselves to the human problems involved in the unequal distribution of wealth, the rise of the labour movement, and the development of vast cities with teeming slums. The social Christian movement in America developed conservative, progressive and radical wings, but of these the progressive, theologically liberal, moderately reformist, characteristically middle-class strand was the most influential. The 'father of the social gospel' in America was Washington Gladden (1836–1918), a Congregational pastor who

was an important harmonizer of evolutionary thought and biblical criticism with Christian faith as well as a pioneer of liberal social views in Protestantism.

The most conspicuous leader of the social gospel and its ablest theologian was Walter Rauschenbusch (1861–1918). The son of a German-born Baptist minister, he was educated in both Germany and the USA. After graduating from Rochester Theological Seminary, he served (1886–1897) as pastor of a German Baptist Church in New York City, located in a blighted area populated by working men. Disturbed by the evil social conditions amid which he worked, Rauschenbusch began to participate in social reform movements and to read reformist and socialist literature. The central task of his life became that of relating his Christian and his social faiths. He did this by finding inspiration in a 'kingdom of God' theology in the liberal tradition of Ritschl and Harnack.

In 1897 Rauschenbusch was called to teach at Rochester Seminary, soon becoming professor of church history. In many addresses, articles and books he spoke for a social interpretation of Christianity, especially in such major works as *Christianity and the Social Crisis* (1907), *Christtianizing the Social Order* (1912), and *A Theology for the Social Gospel* (1917). In these writings he discussed the kingdom of God as the 'first and most essential dogma of the Christian faith', and the 'lost social ideal of Christendom'. He believed that the kingdom of God would come on earth within history as a nobler though not perfect social order, but one marked by the progressive reign of love in human affairs. Rauschenbusch was typical of most social gospel leaders in stressing the immanence of God though without denying transcendence. He put great stress on the historical Jesus, whom he saw as the incarnation of a new type of human life, the inaugurator of a new humanity. The christology of the social gospel focuses on the way the divine life of Christ can get control of human society. The anthropology of the movement was optimistic; Rauschenbusch was more restrained here than some of his followers. He wrote discerningly of the power of the corporate transmission of sin in human affairs (the kingdom of evil), but saw sin as essentially selfishness which can be overcome individually and socially by Jesus' ethic of love. In discussing specific social ethical patterns, Rauschenbusch drew heavily on the progressive and gradualist socialist thought of the time.

There were other conspicuous leaders of the social gospel, such as Josiah Strong, Richard T. Ely, Frank Mason North and Charles Stelzle. In the northern branches of Congregational, Baptist, Methodist, Presbyterian and Episcopal Churches the social gospel was a highly influential movement, particularly among the clergy, in the early decades of the twentieth century. It was dominant in a number of interdenominational movements, especially the Federal Council of the Churches of Christ in America (1908–1950).

Between the World Wars, social gospel thought tended to become more utopian, humanistic and pacifistic. In the 1930s and 1940s, the rise of realistic and neo-orthodox trends in theology and ethics, especially as represented by Reinhold Niebuhr (q.v.), in part led to the decline of the social gospel, though it has contributed to a lasting interest in social realities within American Protestantism.

Robert T. Handy, ed., *The Social Gospel in America: Gladden, Ely, Rauschenbusch,* 1966; C. Howard Hopkins, *The Rise of the Social Gospel in American Protestantism, 1865–1915,* 1940; Henry F. May, *Protestant Churches and Industrial America,* 1949; Dores R. Sharpe, *Walter Rauschenbusch,* 1942.

ROBERT T. HANDY

Socinianism

The name Socinianism was given in recognition of the influence of Faustus Socinus (1539–1604) of Siena. Having felt the influence of Italian humanism and of his liberal-minded uncle, Laelius Socinus, he made contacts in Lyons and Geneva but returned to Italy, remaining uneasily within the Roman communion. In 1574 he went to Basel and in 1578 removed to Poland where his later life was spent in active effort to organize a church of his persuasion. His principal treatises, *De sacrae scripturae auctoritate* (1571), *De statu primo hominis ante lapsu* (1577), and *De Christo Servatore* (1578) show a complete disregard of Nicene-Chalcedonian orthodoxy, especially on the Person and work of Christ. Christ is true God only in the sense that the Father shared his power with him at the Ascension. His *De baptismo aquae disputatio* (1580), written to refute a Czech treatise against paedobaptism, condemns the re-baptism of those baptized in childhood. Socinus strove to unify the discordant elements in the Minor Reformed Church of Poland, and the Racovian Catechism of 1605 was compiled from writings left by him. This Church was crushed in 1638, but the dispersal of a remnant of Polish Socinians to Transylvania, East Prussia and the Netherlands resulted in the spread of Socinian doctrines in Western Europe. In seventeenth- and eighteenth-century England Socinian influence may be traced in the opinions of Latitudinarians and liberal philosophers and of the so-called Arians of the Church of England.

A. J. McLachlan, *Socinianism in Seventeenth Century England,* 1951; E. M. Wilbur, *A History of Unitarianism: Socinianism and its Antecedents,* 1945; *A History of Unitarianism in Transylvania, England and America,* 1952; G. H. Williams, *The Radical Reformation,* 1962.

J. T. MCNEILL

Sociology of Religion

The sociology of religion received its classical development at the hands of Durkheim and Weber in the late nineteenth and early twentieth centuries.

After that there was a considerable gap until the late 1950s, when there was a revival of interest, particularly in France and America. This revival continues and now includes Eastern European countries, and there is an increasing concern with the role of religion and ideology in the development of countries in the 'Third World'. There has also been renewed interest in England, beginning with B. Wilson's institutional analysis of three sects and J. Highet's more enumerative work on religion in Scotland.

There are some six basic schools of the sociology of religion corresponding to those found in general sociology: empiricist, evolutionary and developmental, functionalist, Marxist, phenomenological and the school of Weber, Troeltsch, etc. They can be briefly surveyed in turn.

The empiricist school tends to be inductivist in approach, concerned with enumeration, and with quantifiable syndromes of opinion, e.g. over such matters as political and religious conservatism, authoritarianism, ethnocentrism. Its earlier manifestations (e.g. the English religious census of 1851, Mudie-Smith's work on religion in London) tended to document and interpret the numerical weakness of institutional religion in the working classes of large industrial towns. This focus still continues, especially in France, with respect both to nineteenth-century and contemporary religion. The work of Le Bras and Boulard emphasizes the varied strength of religion by stratum, area and occupation and indicates the existence of a religious geography.

The evolutionary school has experienced in general the same hiatus as befell the sociology of religion. In its early phase it produced schema suggesting developments from ritual to ethics (Spencer, Hobhouse) or from the theological and metaphysical mode to the positivist mode (Comte). Spencer's formulation of the basic distinction between military and industrial societies included the notion of development from the feudal, aristocratic and priestly style to the democratic, individualistic peaceful style of Free Churches separated from the state. This evolutionary tradition ran parallel to the anthropological school of Tylor, Marrett, Frazer, etc., concerned with the origins of religion, or with such transitions as that from magic to religion to science.

The quest for origins (and conjectural history) fell into abeyance with the rise of functionalism; developmental concerns reappeared only through an emphasis on social differentiation and the compartmentalization of religion attendant on it found in the work of Parsons, Eisenstadt and Bellah.

Functionalism was largely developed by Durkheim and occupied itself in a somewhat static, ahistorical way, with the organic congruences between institutional sectors and their contribution to the maintenance of the overall social fabric. Religion was identified as the mental clothing of this fabric: God equalled Society. The vehicle and expression of society was ritual which therefore displaced belief as the focus of interest. Religion became society's self-awareness, projected either primitively in totems or in symbols like the flag. This emphasis clearly extended the definition of religion to include all kinds of ideological and symbolic material. Will Herberg's important book on contemporary American religion, *Protestant-Catholic-Jew* (1955), is an illustration of how transcendental beliefs may be partly subverted so as to function in Durkheim's terms, in this case as a divine imprimatur for the American way of life.

The Marxist school is generally contrasted with functionalism in terms of its concern with history and its emphasis on social conflict rather than conditions of social harmony. It treats religion as an alienated image and sees it in the period of capitalism as a tool of the bourgeoisie. Yet it also points to a continuity between itself and the unsophisticated religious protest groups of earlier periods. This has led to a great interest in millenarian movements either by Marxists who see them as precursors of genuine political protest (Worsley, Hobsbawm) or by anti-Marxists emphasizing the millenarian and utopian character of Marxism itself. (Hence an increasing use of the term secular religion to describe Marxism.) Of course millenarianism and cargo cults also fascinate those concerned with the effects of contact between cultures at very different levels (e.g. North America, Africa, Melanesia) and with the concomitants of technical development in new nations.

The work of Weber was concerned partly with the varied tensions between religious values and other institutional realms (the economic, aesthetic, erotic, political), partly with the congruence between various religious forms and the lifestyles of particular strata, and above all with religious aspects of the appearance of the modern world: democracy, science, capitalism and industrialism. His thesis concerning the role of Protestantism in the birth of modernity has occasioned enormous debate (Merton, Hagen, Feuer, Samuellson, etc.). So too has the distinction of his friend Troeltsch between the 'church', defined as maintaining the social fabric in the Durkheimian manner, and the 'sect' protesting against it in a proto-Marxist manner.

Those interested in the phenomenological approach should consult P. Berger and T. Luckmann, *The Sacred Canopy*, 1968, and *The Social Construction of Reality*, 1967.

F. Furstenberg, *Religionsoziologie*, 1964; D. A. Martin, *Pacifism*, 1965; *A Sociology of English Religion*, 1967; T. O'Dea, *The Sociology of Religion*, 1966; E. Pin and H. Carrier, *Essais de Sociologie Religieuse*, 1967; W. Stark, *The Sociology of Religion*, 3 vols., 1966-67; E. Wickham, *Church and People in an Industrial City*, 1957; B. Wilson, *Religion in Secular Society*, 1966; S. N. Eisenstadt, 'Protestantism and Capitalism', *Daedalus*, No. 59, 1968.

DAVID A. MARTIN

Sohm, Rudolf

Rudolf Sohm (1841–1917), German Protestant canonist and ecclesiastical historian, drew the conclusion from his studies (published primarily in his two-volume *Kirchenrecht* in 1892) that the development of ecclesiastical canon law was from the point of view of the authentic Christian faith catastrophic, and marked the beginnings of infidelity to primitive spiritual Christianity.

James Luther Adams, 'Rudolf Sohm's Theology of Law and the Spirit', *Religion and Culture: Essays in Honour of Paul Tillich*, ed., W. Leibrecht, 1958, pp. 219–35.

JAMES RICHMOND

Sola Fide, Solifidianism

The doctrine of justification by faith only (*sola fide*) in Christ, apart from any merit or works, is called solifidianism. It was a polemical sharpening of the NT doctrine by Luther, directed against his contemporaries who taught the merit of good works. The word arose when Luther in translating Rom.3.28 added 'alone' to 'faith', as a faithful translation of the text 'apart from any works of Law'. Luther later defended his translation with considerable force in his *On Translating* (1530). Two things may be said. Faith in this context is often interpreted in psychological terms to mean the state of mind a believer contributes to the relationship, and therefore is another 'work' of a more insidious nature. To Luther faith here was wholly and only the creation and gift of God (Eph.2.8). Secondly, faith to Luther meant always and only faith *in Christ*. The force of his word 'alone' was to safeguard the plain meaning of the text that a man was right with God only by virtue of Christ's atoning work and in no sense by his own efforts, works and merits (which was, after all, only another form of Judaism). Luther's position is incontrovertible and is certainly that of the NT as a whole. Melanchthon, partly to win over the Catholic polemists, and partly because he genuinely believed so, sought to modify the stark form of the doctrine taught by Luther into a form which the broad Catholic stream would accept. Many Catholic scholars went along with Melanchthon, and together they produced an eirenic re-statement at Regensburg, 1541, but this hopeful ecumenical stream was immediately dammed at the source by Rome. Roman Catholic scholars are beginning to recognize the truth of the Reformers' protest against justification by merit or works in favour of justification in Christ (*cf.* e.g. Hans Kung, *Justification*, 1967).

JAMES ATKINSON

Solipsism

Suppose I ask, "What evidence have I that other things and other persons exist as well as myself?". The answer will have to be in terms of experiences I myself have, of seeing, handling, hearing, etc. – experiences which, I may argue, are ultimately a matter of my having certain sensations. Then have I any reason to believe that there is anything more in the world than myself and my private sensations? If I am contradicted in this by what appears to be another person asserting his existence in disproof, I may deny that this is *real* contradiction, since the 'other' person is, once again, only a cluster of sensations had by me. If I were to argue in this way with conviction I should have become a solipsist (Latin: *solus,* alone, *ipse,* self).

Whether solipsism is a logically coherent theory is disputable. It is impossible in *practical* terms to act as if it were true; and it is not a theory explicitly held by any philosophers of note. Its chief importance for the theory of knowledge lies in challenging the philosopher to explain how it is that we *do* believe in an external and given world of things and persons, how we do in fact attribute consciousness to other individuals than ourselves and in what ways these beliefs can and cannot be justified by argument. *See also* **Epistemology; Scepticism.**

A. J. Ayer, *The Problem of Knowledge,* 1956, ch.5; G. E. Moore, 'A Defence of Common Sense', 'Proof of an External World', *Philosophical Papers,* 1959; John Wisdom, *Other Minds,* 1953.

R. W. HEPBURN

Soteriology

The word is derived from the Greek *soteria,* salvation. Soteriology is that division of Christian theology which treats of salvation (q.v.). It includes the doctrines of the fall of man and of sin; of God's redemptive work in revelation and its culmination in the atonement; of grace; of man's final destiny. *See* **Atonement; Salvation.**

JAMES ATKINSON

Soul

Greek philosophy (esp. Plato) divided man into two parts, body and soul. In Platonism (q.v.) the soul was both pre-existent and immortal; in this life it was imprisoned or entombed in the body. The Hebrews did not conceive of the soul as existing apart from the body (except perhaps in the unreal and shadowy existence of Sheol, the underworld of departed spirits). A man was a living body. Thus, the ancient Church inherited from Greek thought the notion of a soul-substance which was by nature immortal, and this conception was often intertwined with biblical teaching about resurrection. In the biblical view a man dies and literally ceases to exist: his resurrection (a late OT idea which became normative Pharisaic teaching) was the result of an act of new creation by God. On the Greek view death is merely a change in the manner of existence. (It is, of course, important to realize that generalizations like 'the Greek view' are subject to many qualifications; the Epicureans [*see* **Epicureanism**], for instance, taught the total dissolution of the human personality at bodily death, thus claiming to have released mankind

from superstitious fears of divine vengeance in an after-life.) The idea of 'the resurrection of the body' (*cf.* the Apostles' Creed) was the natural Hebraic manner of speaking about the risen life of Christians with Christ: it is by the body that persons are recognizable as individuals with their own personal identity. Hence 'resurrection of the body' means resurrection after death to a fully personal life with Christ in God, and this is what Christians should understand when they profess the Apostles' Creed. Although in some Pharisaic circles a crudely materialistic conception of physical resurrection was held, involving the notion that all the particles of the dead body will be brought together again, this was not the view of St Paul (himself a convert from Pharisaism), who taught that we shall be raised 'a spiritual body' (I Cor. 15.35–54) and that flesh and blood cannot inherit the Kingdom of God. He means that we shall be raised in our personal individuality, recognizable as those who before their physical death were already 'risen with Christ' (Col.3.1). But St Paul's language about the soul (*psyche*) is not entirely consistent and a unified philosophical view can hardly be constructed from it. The threefold existence of 'body, soul and spirit' appears at I Thess.5.23; but he does not find in human personality an analogy of the Trinity, as later theologians (St Gregory of Nyssa; St Augustine) have done.

In the patristic period Platonic views of the soul were adopted by some theologians, esp. at Alexandria. Origen (q.v.) even speculated about the pre-existence of the soul. There is little agreement about the nature of the soul among theologians in the patristic and earlier mediaeval period. Boethius (q.v.) provided the standard definition of the *person,* used perhaps as equivalent of 'soul' (*anima*): *naturae rationalis individua substantia,* a person is 'an individual substance of a rational nature'. Later St Thomas Aquinas develops the idea in terms of the philosophy of Aristotle (*see* **Thomism**): the soul is an individual spiritual substance which is the 'form' of the body. The soul of men (unlike the angels) is correlative to a body and will be united with a body after the general resurrection of the dead. Post-Reformation theology has no consistent doctrine of the soul, but tends in varying degrees towards a biblical and non-speculative usage. Though the earlier modern philosophers (e.g. Descartes) speculated rather crudely about the soul and its location in or association with the body, it was left to sceptical empiricists like Hume to assert the inutility of traditional conceptions of the soul. Post-Enlightenment philosophy has developed a great variety of theories of the soul and of the priority of matter or mind, but there is no consensus of opinion. Ancient doctrines of an indestructible soul-substance, or of the soul as a 'machine-minder' within the body (Gilbert Ryle's 'ghost in the machine'), have fallen into disfavour. Apart from the teachings of some recent metaphysicians, e.g. J. McT. E. McTaggart (d. 1925), who rejected theism but asserted the existence of an enduring spiritual society of selves (spiritual pluralism), it has become generally recognized that belief in the soul's survival after death can be based only upon belief in a God who so loves mankind that he could no more contemplate the total extinction of the objects of his love than the best of men can view with equanimity the annihilation of their own most cherished children (*cf.* Mark 12.27). *See also* **Creationism; Eschatology.**

EDITOR

Sovereignty of God

'God is the king' (Ps. 47.7); 'the Lord our God the Almighty reigns' (Rev. 19.6). Such statements are common in the Bible; but they demand explanation. Of the questions that fly thick here, three must be considered.

1. Who is the king? Answer: God. That is, the God of the Bible: the Creator and Saviour, the Father, the Son and the Holy Spirit. We are not concerned with some general deity. The very message of the Bible is that only *this* God is king.

2. What does it mean that God is King? Answer: Basically, that he occupies the unique position of lordship, which none can take from him, none can attain to. But he does not hold an empty office. He reigns as king, actively ruling, actively disposing. At this point the danger is to speak of God's kingship in terms of bare power, and so conceive of it as tyrannical or arbitrary. But we must remember our first question. The God of the Bible is king; the God who in Jesus Christ declares himself to be for man. This means that he exercises his power on behalf of man. The Book of Revelation gives us a guarantee of this by saying that the Lamb of God is in the midst of the throne (5.6).

3. What is the sphere of God's sovereignty? Answer: The kingdom of God has no boundaries. There is no territory where the king's writ does not run. Not only heaven, but also earth (Ps. 47.2, 7). Not only one particular group (the Jews, the Church), but all nations (Ps. 47.8). But again we must not speak generally but specifically. The kingdom of God is the kingdom of Christ, the realm in which Jesus is Saviour and Lord. He has put down his usurping opponent and the tyrannical instruments of his rule. The Church believes this and rallies under the victorious banner of Christ. Others do not yet know it and think the falsehood true that something else, or nothing at all, is king. Thus the sovereignty of God receives recognition in the Church; but he is not king over the Church alone but over all (Ps. 103.19).

John Calvin, *Institutes*, ii. 15; W. A. Visser't Hooft, *The Kingship of Christ*, 1948.

T. H. L. PARKER

Spinoza, Benedict de

Benedict de Spinoza (1632–1677) was one of the greatest representatives of the 'Rationalist' tradition in philosophy. At the centre of his thought was a strenuous attempt to give new rigour and consistency to the notion of 'substance'. To think through the idea of substance was to realize that only *one* substance could exist. It must be completely independent, the 'cause of itself', eternal and infinite, and could thus (Spinoza argued) be properly called 'God'. Several factors probably influenced Spinoza in the direction of this monism–dissatisfaction with the dualist thought of Descartes, but perhaps more so certain Jewish mystical, and Renaissance pantheistic, writings.

Spinoza claimed that his infinite substance must be conceived as *Deus sive Natura,* God or Nature. There is hence no room for transcendence: God is not a supernatural being, i.e. *over-against* nature. This pantheistic position was, in his view, required by a consistent reading of God's infinity: an infinity that could not be encroached upon, limited, by the existence of beings *outside* God himself.

If Spinoza sets out to give greater rigour to the ideas and arguments that form the *content* of his philosophy, he sought no less to do the same for philosophical *method*. His *Ethics*, notably, is expounded *more geometrico* (in the geometrical style), the arguments starting from Definitions and Axioms and proceeding to Proofs and Corollaries. Given clear and distinct definitions and processes of strict logical inference, only true conclusions could follow. These conclusions, Spinoza believed, would be not merely 'truths of logic' or tautologies, as the contemporary logician would suspect, but would yield explanations (admittedly in highly abstract and general terms) of the structure of the real world. Spinoza could argue in this way only because of his distinctive rationalist account of causal and logical relations, an account that brackets those two sets of relations together.

Spinoza did not wish to argue that *if* there exists a single, infinite substance, God or Nature, then the world will be of such and such a kind. Since God's essence 'involves absolute perfection, by that very fact it removes all doubt concerning his existence': in other words, Spinoza's system hangs upon a version of the ontological argument.

Of the infinite attributes which Spinoza claimed God must possess, we can know only two— thought and extension. Finite minds like our own are modes of God-or-Nature under the attribute of thought, bodies being likewise modes of God under the attribute of extension. Spinoza wishes thus to admit the difference between mind and body, without making that difference into a reason for bifurcating nature in the manner of Descartes (q.v.). Accounts of events and persons in terms of bodies and accounts in terms of minds are accounts of the same events and the same persons–viewed from different standpoints. It may well be doubted, however, whether this theory really reunites the mind-body split: the difference between the attributes remains no less perplexing than the Cartesian difference of substance. But one interesting implication of Spinoza's theory is that for any mental event there will exist a physical correlate.

God, not being a transcendent or quasi-personal being, does not 'choose' or 'will' to produce the finite modes. Substance *necessarily* produces the modes. This necessitarian strand runs right through Spinoza's thought; and again the causally necessary and the logically necessary are held in the closest rapprochement. None the less, Spinoza attempts to make a distinction, where human beings are concerned, between free and unfree states of being. There are conditions where a person is passive under some emotion (say, hatred). It dominates him, produces a state of 'servitude'. The rational man is the man who seeks to transform emotions from passive to active, by means of increased understanding of his situation. A measure of liberation is thus achieved, and hence of command and initiative. The causes of the free man's acts stem, predominantly, from his own nature. This theory of freedom is of direct and serious relevance to twentieth-century discussions.

Consistently with this pattern, Spinoza's account of 'salvation' is presented again in terms of increase of understanding. The 'intellectual love of God' is his name for the satisfaction yielded in an approach to a synoptic, comprehensive view of nature, a grasp of why things are as they are. Spinoza's idea of salvation could not include individual survival of death, for this was clearly incompatible with his conception of the body-mind relationship.

It is not hard to see why interpreters of Spinoza's philosophy have offered such dramatically divergent accounts of it. Spinoza uses the language of piety, but in conjunction with some very untraditional definitions of his theological terms. Crucially, the word 'God' is throughout interchangeable with the word 'Nature'. Thus the interpreter tends to opt for one of two readings: (1) 'When Spinoza says *God*, all he really means is *Nature*' – there is no supernatural, no transcendence, no worshipful being, no hereafter: instead, an out-and-out deterministic system, anticipating (in certain ways) the scientific naturalisms of our own day.' Or, (2) 'When Spinoza says *Nature*, he means *God*. His is a religious philosophy: the divine pervades all.' This is the 'Romantic' interpretation.

Of the two, the second is somewhat less plausible than the first (in terms of backing by the actual texts), despite its religious and imaginative appeal; since, although Spinoza's concept of God as infinite substance coincides at *some* points with those of Christian theology, it diverges from it radically and misleadingly at others.

Benedict de Spinoza, *Ethics*, Everyman's Library, 1910; *The Correspondence of Spinoza*, ed., A. Wolf, 1929; S. Hampshire, *Spinoza*, 1951; H. H. Joachim, *A Study of Spinoza's Ethics*, 1901.

                                                        R. W. HEPBURN

Spiration

A Scholastic term used in relation to the Spirit.

According to Aquinas there are four immanent relations in the Godhead, Paternity, Sonship, and active and passive Spiration. The first two concern the Father and the Son, the last two relate to the Spirit. Active Spiration describes the activity of the Father and the Son in the procession of the Spirit, passive Spiration to the Spirit as the result of their common operation. Spiration is not a property either of the Father or of the Son but a characteristic of both since both are concerned. Aquinas offers an analogy from human love where the act of attachment by the lover and the response of the beloved are both necessary to lead to a union of the two.

                                                        H. E. W. TURNER

Spirit, Holy Spirit, Spiritism

1. *Difficulties with the Doctrine of the Holy Spirit (a) Transcendence and Immanence of God.* Since the fourth century AD, the Holy Spirit has been acknowledged by the main lines of the Christian churches as the third Person of God the Trinity. In the Constantinopolitan Creed (AD 381), we read, 'We believe . . . in the Holy Spirit, the Lord and Life-giver, who proceeds from the Father [and the Son], Who is worshipped and glorified together with the Father and Son, Who spoke through the prophets . . .' At the time there was hesitation as to whether he should be called 'God' and of the same essence as the Father *(homoousion).* But there was no question among the orthodox that he was a Person of the Godhead and to be worshipped as such. Since that time the churches, Catholic and Protestant, have so worshipped him, as their liturgies make abundantly clear. Priests have begun Mass with *'In nomine Patris, et Filii et Spiritus Sancti'.* Preachers have introduced sermons with the same formula. Children have been baptized 'in the name of the Father, and the Son, and the Holy Spirit', and sinners have been absolved in the name of the same 'Three in One'. Prayers have been offered to the Trinity and hymns have been sung in his praise, or their praise. In the worship of the Church it has been assumed that the Father and the Son and the Holy Spirit are equally God and that the three Persons are Persons in the same sense. The Church has adored and glorified the Three as One, and the One as Three.

On the other hand, the Church's theologians have had much difficulty with the doctrine of the Trinity. They have, with reference to our subject, been unable to find a logical and firm place for the Holy Spirit in the Godhead. Their difficulties have arisen in part from the very language of the trinitarian formula. 'Father' and 'Son' readily function as personal symbols. But 'Spirit' *(Spiritus, Pneuma, Ruach)* which, according to the dictionaries, means breath, or moving air, or wind, or spirit, is not clearly a personal symbol. The Spirit has been spoken of as breathed, or poured; as pervading and filling man and nature, holy things and persons; in connection with wind, fire, water, and oil. He has been represented as a person or as

a dove. His work of sanctification has been regarded as purification by washing, anointing,
burning, or illumination. Given such profusion of
symbols for his Person and action, it has been
difficult to think of him clearly and consistently,
as theologians are called upon to do. Personal
and impersonal language with reference to both
his being and action has produced endless confusion, until he has become an 'oblong blur'.

Besides, since the age of the ancient Church,
there has been a philosophical habit of reflecting
upon God in terms of his transcendence of the
world and his immanence in it. It has been
reasonable to think of God the Father as God
transcendent, as *fons et origo,* as the primordial
Source and Cause of all things. The Son has been
thought of in terms of God's immanence, of
logos, of the principle of intelligibility and creativity in the world. Given the Source and that of
which it is the Source, or the Creator and the
Agent of Creation, or the Revealer and Revelation in its Revealedness, in short, the transcendent and immanent God, as Being and Cause, there
has been no firm, logical place in the Godhead for
a third. Theologians have spoken of the Spirit
as the love of God, or the wisdom of God, or the
power of God, which have also been attributes or
perfections of God; and it has been confusing to
speak of these severally as a Person of the Godhead. The Church's thinking people have wavered
between unitarianism (God as transcendent and
immanent), binitarianism (God as the Father and
the Son), quasi-trinitarianism (God as the Father
and the Son, and the Spirit as the bond between
them), and trinitarianism (God in three Persons,
Father, Son, and Holy Spirit).

(*b*) *God as Person and the Holy Spirit.* In spite
of recent efforts at giving the doctrine of the
Holy Spirit a logical place in Christian theology,
efforts which have been earnest and severally
interesting, this doctrine still remains a puzzle-
ment to the Church. When the Spirit is spoken of
as God in action, the power of God, the presence
of God, and the like, it is hard to think of him
as the third Person of the Trinity. When he is
referred to as the Spirit of Christ, the living Christ,
or again the presence of Christ, the personal influence of Christ, etc., the situation is not
changed. When he is thought of in the analogy of
the human spirit, or spirit in general, we are
hardly nearer to the doctrine of the Trinity. The
more conventional reference to him as the
immanence of God makes him hard to distinguish from God as the Spirit of God. When he is
spoken of in terms of metaphors such as wind or
water, the mind is turned away from the Church's
teaching that he is a Person of the Godhead.
When one tries to put all such designations of the
Holy Spirit into a coherent conception with a
proper referent, the task proves to be extremely
difficult, if not impossible. The Church is left
without a theology of the Holy Spirit as disciplined reflection upon 'the Lord and Life-Giver'
of the Constantinopolitan Creed. There is now
hardly any point in discussing the traditional

topics of the Deity and the Procession and the
Personality of the Holy Spirit.

This situation appears to arise nowadays, so
far as the faith of the Church is concerned, from
the conviction that the word 'Person' commonly refers to the Godhead as such. Since the
orthodox doctrine of the Trinity, with its one
Substance and three Persons, has been largely
replaced by some neo-monarchianism, so that
people speak habitually of 'a personal God', or
of God as a Person, and even of 'Father-God',
it is awkward to speak of the Holy Spirit as the
third Person of the Godhead. It is no better when
people speak of the Spirit of Christ, who is a
person and can hardly have a Spirit who is himself a Person. There may be a personal God and a
personal Christ who is in a sense the Son of God,
but it does not make much sense, given the
unitarianism and the binitarianism common in
the churches, to speak of the Holy Spirit as the
third Person of the Trinity. The best one can do,
according to the mind of the churches and
much theology today, is to say that the Holy
Spirit is personal as the Spirit of God and Jesus
Christ, who are Persons.

The problem is that 'the modern mind'
habitually thinks of a person in psychological
terms. Hence, there is no question that Jesus
Christ was a Person, and Christians believe that
God, whose supreme revelation is Jesus Christ,
also is a Person. Now, there seems to be, to the
modern mind, no reason for conceiving of the
Holy Spirit in this sense, as a third person or
Person. Therefore, theologians prefer to speak of
the Spirit as God in action, the presence of God,
the power or the love of God. In one way or
another, they think of the Spirit as God the
immanent or as the immanence of God.

Now the question arises, how is a Person
transcendent and immanent? One might speak
here of the person in himself and the person as an
agent. Thus, God would be transcendent as he is
in himself, and immanent as he acts. But the
immanence of God understood in this way is
logically incompatible with the incarnation. It is
not adequate to say that Jesus Christ is the action
or love of God. He is a human being who himself
acted and loved and was a person. It is hard to
understand how one person is the immanence of
another. The notions of God as a Person and as
immanent make their contribution to the difficulty of speaking of the Holy Spirit as the third
Person of the Trinity, or indeed of speaking of
him at all except as an abstraction, which becomes his only logical place in the Godhead.

(*c*) *The Spirit and 'Spiritual'.* It has been
suggested that the Spirit characterizes God on
the one hand and Christ on the other. Since
'spirit' means breath, wind, or moving air, it may
be said to characterize God as invisible, powerful,
mysterious, unpredictable, and the like. 'Spirit'
also characterizes Christ in the Church, especially
in the 'means of grace', since he also is invisible
and is apprehended not by the senses but inwardly and 'in the spirit'. Although the presence

of Christ is not like that of wind, the rapture of communion with him suggests a 'spiritual reality'.

However, the Holy Spirit as characterization of God and Christ is binitarian rather than trinitarian and does not present one with the third Person of the Trinity. The deity of God is not a Person in the trinitarian sense, and the presence of Christ risen from the dead is not either the Spirit of God or the Spirit of Christ. A characterization is not a Person as is the Person whose characterization it is. For this reason, the adjective 'spiritual' is often preferred to the noun 'spirit', and God and Christ are characterized as spiritual, and so is the relationship between them and the believer. For this reason also, the Spirit is understood as a quality of divine action and of the effects of that action which are the Christian life.

When Christians insist upon calling upon the Holy Spirit to illumine them, sanctify them, or unite them, they act with the belief that they address themselves to a Spirit who is, with all the reservations due to his deity, a Person and not a quality. They invoke one who is not identical with the Father and the Son, and like them hears prayer. The Holy Spirit is to them a Person in the same way and sense as are the Father and the Son. The theologians who know that the Three are One and the One God is a Spirit, have sought and now seek to correct the apparent tri-theism in Christian piety. But the Christian Church in its faith and worship continues to treat the Holy Spirit as the third Person of the Godhead, and remains unimpressed by, even when not ignorant of, scholarly and theological opinion that the Spirit is a mode of God's or Christ's being or action.

2. The Spirit and Spirits

(a) Spiritism in the Church. One can hardly resist supposing that there is in popular Christian piety an element of what the theologians would recognize as superstition. There apparently is in the Church a deeply-rooted notion that the Spirit is a ghost-like being, not altogether unlike the spirits of 'the invisible world' in which man as it were from the beginning lived, moved, and has had his being. The truth apparently is that besides the 'high gods' of the religions of mankind, who have been objects of public piety, there universally have been lesser gods, and good and evil spirits, which have engaged the attention of people, and elicited from them a lively interest in their comings and goings, and their doings for weal or woe. These spirits have been near, while God or gods have been far. They have been involved in men's private fortunes, in sundry troubles which infest the lives of people upon this earth. The people have had to deal with these spirits as best they could, through diviners and magicians, and witch doctors, either to cajole or force them to desist from their evil doings. There have been good spirits and there have been evil spirits, and both have been companions of the people and powers which have formed their religion.

Such 'superstition' has been universal, and neither Israel nor the Church has been without it. The prophets and priests of the Lord God of Israel fulminated and legislated against it, but their success was partial, and the diviners and magicians remained. The very Spirit of God, both because of and in spite of being *ruach* or wind, acted in ways not unlike a spirit, pouncing upon people, throwing them about, and inducing wild-eyed ecstasy. Official theology contradistinguished the Spirit of God from the other spirits, but he was not without their characteristics and he engaged in divination as well as prophecy. One has only to read the stories about Saul and Samson, Elijah and Elisha and Micaiah, and even the prophesies of Ezekiel and Zechariah, to catch more than a glimpse of spiritism in Israel and its lasting as well as deep fascination for the people. The nearer one comes to NT times, the more spirit-obsessed we find the people of God, and the more air is filled with good and evil spirits. The latter continue to possess people and cause all manner of disease and misfortune. Jesus exorcises them, and so do his disciples in the Church. Wherever the Church goes, the exorcists go with it and vie with the exorcists of the Jews and the Gentiles. Baptism itself becomes in part an exorcism, and so people understand it. In the name of Jesus, in the name of the Father, Son, and Holy Spirit, unclean spirits are cast out and unclean people are washed and purified. Christ battles Satan, angels battle demons, and the warfare of the Church is carried out in heaven as well as on earth. In time, the invisible world of spirits is officially declared God's own creation (the evil spirits having 'fallen' through pride) and God the Father, Son, and Holy Spirit, with his angels, have lined up in the invisible world against Satan and his underlings. So have Christians believed until recently, and in this context they have believed in the Holy Spirit.

The fascination that the doctrine of the Holy Spirit has for the Christian mind, and its meaning in the Christian faith as a whole, cannot be properly understood without an awareness of the spiritism which has always informed the Christian soul. The Holy Spirit belongs in the invisible world filled with angels and demons. Of course, 'Person' in the Trinity is one thing, and 'spirit' is another. But the theologians' insistence upon the unity of God did not hinder the Christian people from carrying over into their faith reverberations of spiritism which we find in the trinitarian utterances of catholic liturgy. Down deep, as it were, in the Christian soul, the Holy Spirit is he who replaces, neither too clearly nor too completely, the spirits, the good spirits, who have been from the beginning man's help in a world where weal and woe are exasperatingly intermixed and unmanageable. The Holy Spirit is the Good Spirit. But still he is mysterious, unpredictable, and all-efficient.

In the mind of the Church, the Holy Spirit is above all, as well as with all, the agent of sanctification. He is holy to make holy, and this is his peculiar function in the Godhead. Even while theologians have agreed that in all the works of God the three Persons act as One, so that there is nothing One does that the Others do not do, yet they have also agreed that making holy is the work of the Holy Spirit. Now, holiness is an especially complex notion and connotes mystery as well as spirit. It is true that in the official theologies of the Church, holiness is realized by the washing away of sin and the introduction of a new principle of goodness into the human heart. Certainly, there is no holiness without righteousness, and sanctification is for love. And yet, the holy is not and has not been in the piety of the Church, as it were, merely ethical. Sanctification is a process in which an evil spirit is displaced by a good spirit; one in which the Holy Spirit strives against 'the flesh', which is possessed by an 'unclean spirit'. In it man has to do with the Spirit, with the Holy Spirit. There is no sanctification without 'spiritual warfare', and in this warfare it is the Holy Spirit that overwhelms unholy spirit and makes peace. The ethical and ritual interpretations of sanctification preferred by theologians partially obscure the work and therefore the reality of the Holy Spirit of the living God as he 'comes upon' the unholy spirit of the flesh with its sin and death, and enacts the mysterious and awesome drama of salvation as sanctification. Thus it is that the Holy Spirit, in spite of the reservations of sober minds in the Church, retains the quality of spirit and is more or less clearly envisaged as a power-full spirit. Thus it appears that spiritism has kept the doctrine of the Holy Spirit alive in the Church and may continue to do so in spite of the seeming exodus of the spirits from 'the secular city'.

(*b*) *Deghostifying the Holy Spirit.* However, it must be recognized that spiritism is hardly a viable alternative to rational discourse. If the theologians may err in doing justice to the dynamics of the Christian life, the pious believers may err in being superstitious. The theologians may be right in refusing to see ghosts. If spiritism is not to be discarded, it must be understood in line with the dynamics of the Christian life. It must be, as it has been, properly demythologized; otherwise, it turns faith into credulity, which is an evil in the Church.

(1) *The Spirit as the Person of God.* The traditional way of deghostifying the Holy Spirit has been to identify him with the power of God. This way, which appears to have begun in the Bible, has considerable merit. The Spirit of God has given prowess to the fighter, competence to the king, utterance to the prophet, and to God's people a 'heart of flesh' with which to keep his covenant of righteousness. He thus has been the enabling spirit or the spirit of power. But since God himself has been regarded as a Spirit, or a Person, the Spirit of God has been identified as the power of God. A Spirit has been replaced by a Power, and superstition has been discouraged.

The Church's theologians have agreed that the Holy Spirit actualizes today in the Church the saving work of Christ on the cross. Since Augustine it has been understood that it is the grace or power of God the Father, Son, and Spirit that converts sinners and makes them holy. In line with this doctrine, the Holy Spirit has represented 'the sovereignty of God in man's redemption'. For this reason, the grace of God, the grace of Jesus Christ, the grace of the Holy Spirit, or simply grace, have been interchangeable expressions; the point being that salvation is the work of God and not the work of man. The Holy Spirit has been identified with grace as the power of God, which in turn has been interpreted either in the analogy of natural causality or in terms of personal influence. The power of God as exercised in the world at large has been viewed as quasi-physical; and as revealed in Christ, it has been regarded as personal. As experienced in the means of grace, it has been spoken of as spiritual, or sacramental, or supernatural. In any case, it has been difficult to distinguish the Holy Spirit from the power of God, and the doctrine of the Spirit has been all but absorbed into the doctrine of grace. Thus the third Person of the Deity has been all but banished from the Godhead, in spite of continued vague noddings in his direction.

(2) *The Spirit as the Spirit of Christ.* A second way of dealing with spiritism has been to identify the Holy Spirit as the Spirit of Christ. For this also there may be biblical precedent, but it has been especially favoured in recent theology. Since in the NT, especially in the Pauline epistles, the several elements in Christian life are said to be alike the work of Christ and the work of the Spirit, the theologians have argued that functionally Christ and the Spirit are the same, or that the Holy Spirit is the Spirit of Christ. There is no unanimity in this matter, since many a passage in Scripture indicates the reality of the Spirit next to the reality of Christ. But there seems to be no binding reason for thinking of the Holy Spirit and the Spirit of Christ, or Christ himself, as distinct Persons. In fact, it appears that the Spirit of Christ is 'the living Christ' who is the Lord and Head of the Church. The logic of this line of thinking suggests that since God and Christ alike are credited with the Christian life, the Spirit of God is the Spirit of Christ, or that God is Christ. Thus the doctrine of God perhaps would have to be deliteralized as well as the doctrine of the Spirit; and there are theologians who have taken this position. However, this extreme is commonly shunned, and the more orthodox theologians hold on to God as well as Christ, and think of the Spirit as the power of both. It is to be noted that here God and Christ are conceived as Persons, and their Spirit is their power as Persons, known by their influence upon persons.

(3) *The Spirit as a Mode of God's Person.* In line with the emphasis upon the Spirit of Christ, or Christ himself, as a person in communion with his people who are persons, there is the interpretation, in the third place, of spirit as the core of personality itself. Here a spirit is a person in the fulness of his powers as a living and

active being. Spirit is understood psychologically and as related to other modes of humanity such as life, soul, heart, or mind. There is precedent for this line of thought in Scripture itself, especially in post-Exilic writings and in the NT. Besides, it is justified by 'personalism' which characterizes much recent theology. Given man in his integrity as a personal being, spirit is a way of characterizing him and there is such a thing in the sense that there is life, soul, or will and mind. Since recent psychology has deghostified the latter, and thinks of them in functional and behavioural terms, it is reasonable that theologians should do the same to the spirit. Thus it appears that the Spirit of God is a characterization of God as Person. As there is no spirit of a person next to a person, there is no Spirit of God next to God. Once again, spiritism is overcome.

3. *The Holy Spirit and the Church*

(a) *The Spirit and Community.* The common characteristic of such ways of demythologizing the doctrines of the Holy Spirit is that they obscure the logic of spiritism in human life.

Spiritism, for all its superstitions, is a way of giving personal relations ontological status. Spiritism may be understood as understanding the world *sub specie humanitatis,* as a realm of willing and acting in the human mode, as a sphere of freedom and responsibility. It is rooted in man himself as a responding being; in human life as transaction, in which the person-ness of 'the other one' is logically entailed and passionately affirmed. Spiritism is an apprehension of reality *sub specie communitatis:* a way of experiencing the world which is met with wherever people are alive to the mystery of man in transaction.

Spiritism has persisted in the Church in spite of all the embarrassments of the theologians with it, because it is integral to the people's awareness of reality as social. The dynamics of human life as such are social, and intensity of life, conscious or unconscious, is a consequence of encounter among agents. A community is a *locus* of agency, and agency both forms and sustains a community. Hence good and evil spirits people a community and maintain it in life, its awesome and mysterious transactions, its actions and passions, its ecstacies and in-stasies. Thus spirits and community belong together, and people remain spiritists, in spite of every criticism, valid or invalid. Spiritism remains in the Church because and in so far as the Church is a people, and it is included in the Church's confession of the Holy Spirit.

The orthodox traditions of Western theology, for certain institutional and philosophical reasons, failed to reflect in a logical way upon the dynamics of the Church as a human community; and because of this failure, they also failed to reflect upon the Holy Spirit as the Spirit of the living God in the Church. They were indeed aware that the locus of the work of the Spirit is the Church, and have written extensively upon this work. Their writings constitute an inexhaustible mine

for the study of the Christian life or the work of the Spirit. On the other hand, they have not left us a viable tradition of thinking on the Person of the Holy Spirit because they have been concerned with establishing the place of the Spirit in the Godhead rather than with the nature of the Church as constituted by the transactions of God's people. Thus they have been slow to discern the logic in the Church's confession of the Holy Spirit as 'Lord and Life-Giver'. They have indeed believed with the Church that the Spirit is the third Person of the Godhead. But it must be said that all in all they have failed to understand and help the people to understand what they have believed.

(b) *St Augustine's 'Social Analogy'.* As Augustine saw, the doctrine of the Trinity demands a social as well as a psychological analogy. In spite of his unitarian predilections, which led him to speak of God in analogy to the human person, he spoke of the Father as the Lover, of the Son as the Beloved, and of the Spirit as the Love between them. Granting that he used this language as analogical, and was no binitarian, his use of it shows that he 'was unwilling to be satisfied with psychological analogies. The very designation of the first two Persons of the Trinity as Father and Son, as well as the language of the Bible as to their relations, together with the common mind and liturgy of the Church, demanded and demands a social analogy to the Godhead. Augustine's social analogy became a permanent element in trinitarian thinking and has perennially counteracted Monarchian tendencies in Western Christianity.

But history and logic alike have shown that Augustine's use of the social analogy was defective for a proper theological statement of the doctrine of the Trinity. The Lover and the Beloved are readily understood as Persons; but not so Love. Even if it be insisted that love is as real as a lover, it is clear that it is not real in the same way that a lover is real. It is no help to say that a divine Person is not a person in the sense that a man is a person. The truth appears to be that the social analogy as used by Augustine left the Church's theologians with the indelible impression that the Spirit, as against the Father and the Son, is an It and not a He. The only way to escape the absurdity of a Trinity with two who are He and one who is It has been to remove the It by identifying It with the God, or Christ, or in a loose way with both at once.

(c) *'Proceeds from the Father and the Son'.* In the long run, the theological tradition has vacillated between Augustine's social and psychological analogies; that means between unitarianism and binitarianism. The teaching of the Western churches that the Spirit proceeds ˙from the Father and the Son, *procedit ex patre filioque,* in spite of the cautions of theologians, has re-enforced both the notion of the unity and the notion of the duality of the Godhead, and worked against both the doctrine of the Spirit as the third Person of the Godhead and the equality of the Spirit with the Father and the Son as God. The word 'procession' as against the word 'generation' (used for the Son), with such other words as 'emanation' and 'infusion' and 'filling', used with regard to the Spirit, have led people to contradistinguish him from the Father and the Son, and to think of him in vague and impersonal terms. By and large, the Spirit has represented a bond or a relation between the Father and the Son, between God and the world, between Christ and the Christians; and a bond or a relation is not a Person as the Persons and things between which It is a bond or relation.

It is true that the notion of the Spirit as a Person has always been in the Church, and people have argued for his 'Personality'. But they have done this latter thing mainly on the basis of the authority of the Scriptures and of the Church. When these authorities have somehow been weakened, the very reality of the Spirit has been questioned and largely repudiated. The 'orthodox' have argued for 'the personal Spirit' on biblical and traditional grounds. The 'liberals', for whom tradition without logic has ceased to be binding, have fallen into unitarianism or binitarian ways of thinking. Whether orthodox or liberal, theologians have been preoccupied, with regard to the Person of the Spirit, with the doctrines of God and Christ. But this preoccupation has led to a 'dead end' where the Holy Spirit has all but vanished from the mind of the Church, having been identified as the immanence of God and as the spirit of Christ.

(d) The Schleiermacher Interlude. Schleiermacher opened a new line of thought on our subject when he approached theology not as the science of God but as the science of the Church's experience of God. This meant that he was concerned not with the question of the deity of the Spirit, but with him as the Holy Spirit of the Church, or as the spirit of and in the Christian community. Schleiermacher's conception of the Spirit as the spirit of a people, or as the ground of the spirit of the Church, did of course confuse the traditional and orthodox doctrine of the Spirit as the third Person of the Trinity, and has led modern theologians to speak of the Spirit as 'It' rather than as 'He'. On the other hand, Schleiermacher's theological method opened the way to a new interest in the theology of the Church, a new inclination to do theology in the light of the Church's experience and piety, and consequently a new approach to the doctrine of the Holy Spirit in the light of the Christian life in the Church. Schleiermacher himself was too one-sidedly impressed with the Church as a unity of spirit to do justice to the work of the Spirit in the mutual communications of Christians one with another. Nevertheless, he broke the hold of orthodox authoritarianism and speculation in the theology of the Spirit, and turned attention to the realities of the Christian community as the proper setting in which the theologian must examine the doctrine of the Holy Spirit.

(e) Evolution and the Spirit. But the seed planted by Schleiermacher was not quickly to grow into a tree and bear good fruit. Attention to Christian experience in his time was largely individualistic and introspective, and lacked his vision of the Christian community as a whole and as one. In the second half of the nineteenth century, 'the warfare of science with religion' all but nullified Schleiermacher's theological accomplishment. Evolutionism led theologians to argue for the immanence of God in the biological process, and even in the cosmos as a whole; and it was now reasonable to identify the Spirit, in a new way, with God's immanence. Schleiermacher's attention to God's peculiar immanence in the Church was not in line with the controversies on science and religion, and the Church itself ceased to be of primary theological concern. Much was said about 'the Creator Spirit' in the universe, and much was also said by pietists about the sanctification of the sinner by the Holy Spirit. But the Church as the place of the Spirit and the setting for a theology of the Spirit was largely ignored, and much theology was done 'in the light of modern science', without the benefit of a doctrine of the Spirit except in general as the doctrine of God's active presence in the world and in man.

At this point one must remember the attempts to interpret traditional trinitarianism in such terms of modern evolutionism. Some theologians have tried to show that the evolutionary process, with its aspects of life, mind, and spirit, suggests a fons et origo which is complex as well as simple, three as well as one; and that a trinitarian conception of God is more in line with reality than one that is unitarian. Especially when one includes Jesus Christ and the Church, the incarnation and history, in one's world view, the doctrine of the Trinity appears quite congenial to a modern mind.

Such evolutionistic understanding of the doctrine of the Spirit has been resisted, especially outside the Anglo-Saxon world, on the ground that it confuses biblical faith with the modern man's common sense. It appears to be exegetically less than rigorous and to make 'interpretation' too easy a task. It works with a principle of continuity between 'revelation' and 'reason', between man and nature, which is debated and debatable. What is at present even more striking, the continuity between theology and metaphysics assumed by such reinterpretations of the Christian faith is disturbed by the questions that have been raised with regard to the enterprise of metaphysics itself.

(f) Depth Psychology and the Spirit. Another approach to our subject has been in terms of 'depth psychology'. Ecstasy traditionally associated with the Spirit appears to emerge from the depths of the human spirit or the realm of the unconscious. When spiritism is demythologized, its phenomena are recognized as psychic, and the spirits are seen as creatures and projections of the subrational processes in the human being. Enthusiasm is understood as the overflow of psychic energy, and demon possession is interpreted in terms of psychic illness. The psychotherapist replaces the exorcist, and enthusiasm is induced by stimulation through suggestion and drugs without waiting for a divine invasion. In short, the Spirit is associated with the non-rational dynamics of the psyche as the Logos had already been associated with the mind in its logical workings. Since the Spirit, like the spirits, has been elusive in his being and potent and unpredictable in his workings, producing extraordinary manifestations of power, it is reasonable that, like the spirits, he should be demythologized into the psyche in its more elusive and potent and unpredictable aspects.

It is, of course, suggestive to the mind, to interpret the doctrine of the Spirit in terms of psychodynamics, as it has been to interpret the doctrine of the Son in terms of *logos,* or logicality. Thus 'the two hands' of God may be understood in terms of reason and power, or form and dynamics, which, like the Persons of the Godhead, are distinct as well as inseparable. In this way we are provided with a psychological and even ontological interpretation of the traditional doctrine of the Son and the Spirit as two Persons of the Trinity. It is a palpable advantage of the psycho-ontological interpretation of the doctrine of the Spirit that it avoids making this doctrine superfluous in theology. As reason and power cannot be identified, so in this way of thinking the Son and the Spirit need to be kept distinct. Thus, binitarianism is avoided, and a place is found for the doctrine of the Spirit in the very conjunction of form and vitality in reality itself. Besides, the interpretation of the Spirit in terms of vitality, dynamics, power, opens the way to the inclusion of natural process, or nature, as such, in a discussion of the doctrine of the Spirit and towards a cosmic view of the work of the Spirit which has always been present in traditional theology as well as in the Bible.

There are certain problems here which need to be faced. The understanding of the Spirit in terms of psychodynamics, although reasonable, creates its own difficulties. It is hard to think of spirit as a modal aspect of the soul as analogous to the Spirit as a Person in the Godhead. The psychological approach to the understanding of the doctrine of the Trinity, whether Augustinian or personalistic, or quasi-Freudian, ends up showing itself incapable of doing justice to the doctrine of the Spirit as the third Person of the Trinity. The whole history of Western theology since Augustine is witness to this difficulty, which is not removed by 'depth psychologies' of our time. Even while the Christian life has its psychodynamics and the working of the Spirit can be understood with new adequacy through a study of the dynamics of the soul, more than an investigation of the individual psyche may be needed for an adequate doctrine of the Spirit.

4. *Towards Understanding the Doctrine of the Holy Spirit*

Following suggestions found in Augustine (the social analogy) and in Schleiermacher (the Holy Spirit as the spirit of the Church), one might suggest that a fruitful approach to the doctrine of the Spirit is through the nature and reality of the Church: the Church as the communion and transactions of its members. In line with Irenaeus' doctrine of 'the two hands of God', one might well say that Jesus Christ is the one and the Church is the other hand of God; that God does his saving work by Christ and the Church.

(a) *'The Two Hands' of God.* This is no new suggestion. It is implied in the traditional Christian conviction that salvation is in the Church, or that there is no salvation without the Church. Our suggestion contains a novel emphasis in that we follow the present-day view of the Church as a people rather than as an institution. Irenaeus' doctrine of 'the two hands' did not bear proper fruit for an adequate doctrine of the Spirit because the work of the Spirit in the Church has been associated with the Word and the sacraments as the principal 'means of grace'. Since the Word was tied to the sacraments, and these two were institutional realities, the presence and work of the Spirit in the communion of God's people with God and one with another failed to lead to fruitful theological reflection upon the doctrine of the Spirit. The Spirit in the 'means of grace' was functionally identified with grace in the Word-with-sacraments, and regarded in the main as an infusion rather than as the third Person. In the Church as constituted by the Word and the sacraments, power rather than spirit became a theological model, and the Person-ness of the Spirit became a conventional if pious notion, without functional or theological justification. Echoes of spiritism were not absent from popular piety, but the theologians favoured an unstable identification of the Spirit with the breath and power or grace of God. Thus, the Spirit was depersonalized in a manner which was not true of the Father or the Son.

(b) *The Communion of Saints as a Means of Grace.* The present-day emphasis upon the Church as the people of God and as constituted by 'the communion of saints' suggests a new understanding not only of the work of the Spirit but also of his Person. We may now take for our model in reflection upon the Trinity the transactions of God's people. It may be that we are to think of the work of the Spirit in connection with the mutual actions of human beings as moral agents who live in the freedom and capability which is theirs as Christ's people and members of his Body. We thus get our clue for the work of the Spirit not only from the efficacy of preaching and the sacraments but also, and inseparably from these, from the efficacy of the transactions of God's people for their mutual work of salvation from death to life. It is now seen that the mutual building-up of God's people, in their very imperfection as 'at once righteous and sinners', is the proper locus of the activity of the Spirit who is holy and makes holy. The doctrine of the Spirit begins to come to its own when the Christian thinker takes seriously the biblical warning that 'if you do not forgive men their trespasses, neither will your Father forgive your trespasses' (Matt.6.15).

Traditional theologies, with their jealousy for the omnificence of God and for the monopoly of the Church as an institution in the distribution of saving grace, have underplayed if not denied the necessity of communion in the Church as a means of grace. They have taken their models for the work of the Spirit from nature or from 'man' rather than from society, and in this way have logically undermined not only the doctrine of the Spirit but also of the Trinity as a unity of three Persons. Even though they have affirmed the Personhood of God and Christ, or of the Father and the Son, they have, by their preoccupation with the institutional means of grace, confused the personal model for the work of the Trinity and impersonalized the work of the Spirit, who has been credited with making the work of Christ effective in the Church. In short, traditional main-line theologies in the Church have taught that the churches as institutions are through their cults the means of grace, and in so teaching they have made the third Person of the Trinity both functionally and the theologically superfluous.

But Scripture and experience alike are against the one-sidedness of tradition in this matter. Moses and Jesus, with prophets, priests, and kings, have been primary means of grace to and in the Church. The incarnation itself, with the total mission of Jesus Christ, once for all established the principle that salvation is by the agency of men. When the humanity of Jesus Christ is not compromised in an explanation of his 'two natures', it becomes evident that his agency as a fellow man is integral to his saving work, and that his communion with his people was and is a prime means of grace. It was in his agency as a fellow man that he was the bearer of the Spirit of God, and it was by the Spirit of God that he did his work as the Christ and Saviour. The very mission of Christ, which is the source of the mission of his people and the model of their lives as well as mission, makes it clear that both the Person and the Work of the Spirit are properly understood in the transactions of fellow men.

(c) *The Holy Spirit and Human Agency*. What is true for the one hand of God is true for the other. The life that came by the ministry of Jesus, is continued and prospers by the ministry of his people who are called to be his vicars and agents, so that to deny their ministry is to deny Christ's own and to deny them is to deny him. Everything in the matter of salvation, according to the tradition, depends upon receiving Jesus as the Christ and Saviour. But if the Church is Christ's Body, everything also depends upon receiving one's fellow men as members of his Body, as his members by whose ministry it is that one is saved and enjoys the Life of the Christian community. There is no grace – faith, and hope, and love – that a man does not receive in the Church and at the hand of his brother. It is true that his brother is saved and sinner, free and in bondage, like himself, imperfect all his days. Still, he may receive life in the Church, that is, in his transactions with his fellow men.

It has as it were always been evident that the mission of Jesus Christ is a mystery. It must now be recognized that the mission of the Church, too, is a mystery. It is quite clear that although salvation is among Christ's people, its efficacy is not their own doing. A man may forgive his neighbour; but his neighbour is not thereby forgiven. Reconciliation between the two occurs as a gift and a surprise. It is recognized by them in the Church as a work of God and not as their own doing. Hence, the biblical and traditional teaching that God alone forgives sin and reconciles sinners to himself and one to another stands as the faith of the Church. It is clear according to the same faith that sanctification and the Christian life as a whole are the work of God in Christ Jesus.

(d) *The Logic of the Doctrine of the Spirit*. The theological question is why the Christian life is credited to the Holy Spirit as well as to God simply considered. The answer to this crucial question may be as follows. With the same logic that the mission of Jesus Christ is attributed both to the Father and to the Son, both to God and to Jesus Christ, so the mission of the Church is attributed both to the Father and the Son, and to the Holy Spirit, or both to God and his Spirit. A distinction between the Father and the Son in the atonement is required by the fact that the man Jesus reconciled us with God. The obedience and faithfulness of Jesus as acts of human agency were integral to the saving work of God, so that it was accomplished by the freedom of the man Jesus for God. Hence the Church has believed that the Son became flesh for our salvation.

Similarly, sanctification and the Christian life are attributed both to God and to the Church as God's people. The Christian life is the work of the Father and the Son by the obedience and faithfulness of the Church who are called to build one another up for maturity as 'children of God'. These people have been baptized in the name of the Father and the Son and the Holy Spirit into the communion of saints, and by their baptism have been designated as the persons and moral agents that they are, and in the Church they have received the freedom to walk as well as live as human beings. Even while without God and Jesus Christ they are 'no people', as beneficiaries of the mission of Jesus they are his people with their mission. As the mission of Jesus required a distinction between the Father and the Son, so the mission of the people of Jesus requires a distinction between the Son and the Spirit. The doctrine of God the Son points to the ground of the mission of Jesus Christ in the Godhead. Similarly, the doctrine of God the Holy Spirit points to the ground of the mission of the Church in the Godhead.

When God is conceived as 'the First Cause', and Jesus and his people as 'second causes', so that the freedom of the latter is obscured and ignored, then there is no theological basis for the doctrine of the Trinity. But when the obedience of Jesus is given its due in *God's* saving work and so is the obedience of God's people, then the distinction between the Father and the Son and the Holy Spirit becomes logical as well as inevitable. In christology the necessity for distinguishing between the Father and the Son has been traditionally recognized and affirmed. The argument here is that the same necessity holds in ecclesiology. A clear view of the agency of the people of God in the sanctifications of the Church requires a distinction between the Son and the Holy Spirit. If Jesus and his people are not one person and one will, so that the monothelite heresy is forbidden in the doctrine of the Church as it was in the doctrine of Christ, then there is an immovable distinction between the Son and the Holy Spirit in the Godhead. Docetism in ecclesiology is no more valid than it is in christology. God does his saving work with 'his two hands', the Son and the Holy Spirit, or Jesus Christ and the Church.

The tradition concerning the doctrine of the Holy Spirit has been greatly confused by the use of certain metaphors such as wind, breath, water, oil, fire, as characterizations of his working in the Church. Correspondingly, certain verbs such as blow, breathe, pour, anoint, purify, or burn, used graphically but uncritically, have given the impression that the Holy Spirit is an invisible fluid of a sort. Then there has been the dove which has been represented as hovering between the Father and the Son. In addition, there have been non-persons such as wisdom, love, power, mystery, which have replaced the third Person of the Godhead. It may not be denied that in every case 'there is something to be said' for these various ways of speaking of the Spirit. Language about the Christian life is necessarily rich and of endless variety. However, the Holy Spirit, 'Lord and Life-Giver', is acknowledged by the Church as the third Person of the Trinity, and Person in the same sense that the Father and the Son are Persons. This teaching of the Church is theologically validated when it is recognized that as God was in Christ, so he is in the Church, sanctifying his people by their mutual ministry in the building up of the body of Christ, so that *mutatis mutandis* the Holy Spirit is to Christ's people as the Son is to Jesus; so that as Christ is the Son, the Church is the bearer of the Holy Spirit, to the glory of God the Father. The Church believes in the Holy Spirit as the third Person of the Godhead because those who are his agents are persons as Jesus is a person.

According to the tradition, the Spirit of God was an agent in creation. He is the principle of life in all living things. He is present not only in the Church, but in all humanity. He is the source of the hope for the final triumph of God and of his kingdom in creation; so that he is an eschatological reality; the bond between the mission of Jesus Christ and its consummation. However, since according to the same tradition, he is all

this as the third Person of the Godhead, this article has been mainly devoted to an understanding of the faith of the Church in him as 'Lord' as well as 'Life-Giver'.

5. *The Work of the Spirit Reconsidered*

This article has been given so far to a discussion of the Person of the Holy Spirit because it is no more feasible to speak of the work of the Spirit unless there is the Spirit whose work it is than to speak of the work of Christ unless there is Christ who 'suffered under Pontius Pilate'. It has been our concern to consider how we may point to the Holy Spirit as the third Person of the Godhead at all.

(a) *The Work of Christ and the Work of the Spirit.* However, now something must be said of the work of the Spirit. The work of the Spirit is the work of Christ, so that the elements of the latter must in the nature of the case appear in the Church. Even while 'we were reconciled to God by the death of his Son' (Rom.5.10), our reconciliation occurs in a human community or a church. Christ does his work in the Church by the agency of his people, and the work is the same that he did on the cross, namely, reconciliation. The work of the Spirit is reconciliation and the same is the work of the Church. This being so, the work of Christ and the work of the Spirit are the same, and this is done by human beings. However, when we consider the work of the Spirit we attend to the dynamics of transaction in a human community, and regard it as integral to God's reconciling act. The doctrine of the Spirit invites us to reflect upon the way or ways in which God, by the agency of his people, fulfils his saving work in the world. It does not so much present us with a work other than that of Christ as with a manner of working by human agency which we seek to understand and to which we respond as moral agents. The logical significance of the doctrine of the Spirit is in the Church's or the people's acknowledging their responsibility to act as a reconciling community. It functions as a criticism of irresponsibility and inaction in the Church, which may be logically justified when 'the communion of saints' as a 'means of grace' is obscured by failure to acknowledge human agency as integral to God's saving work in the world. It follows from the doctrine of the Spirit as presented in this article that the Christian life *in toto,* which is traditionally credited to the Holy Spirit, is the work of the Church; that whether justification or sanctification, whether faith or repentance, whether dying or living, indeed all fruition and hope, are, as rooted and grounded in Christ, from the transaction or communion in the community. As the people may not glorify God without Christ, they may not glorify God and Christ without the Church. But to glorify the Church is to acknowledge the Holy Spirit as 'Lord and Life-Giver'.

(b) *Sanctification as Process of the Church.* Tradition attributes sanctification in particular to the Holy Spirit. We shall understand the reason for the common singling-out of sanctification as the work of the Spirit when we consider that sanctification as against justification is recognized as a process which occurs in the Church and in the Christian life as formed in the Church. Sanctification is co-extensive with the believer's life, and occurs in the continual transactions which constitute his life. In these transactions his fellow men as well as the means of grace as traditionally understood play indispensable roles, and it is through their agency that the believer is sanctified. His life and freedom as a Christian occur by the continued presence and activity of his fellow men, who are to him the bearers of the Holy Spirit, who makes holy, or enables him to participate in the holiness of God in Christ Jesus. The Christian's dependence upon the Church for his sanctification is his help in resisting the temptation to pride which threatens to corrupt his spirit and turn his freedom into bondage. Thus the church acts not only as the means of grace but as the antidote to the lust for autonomy which resists the grace of God while lip service is paid to it. It is in the Spirit of the Church that sanctification becomes real while it remains a gift and is acknowledged as by grace alone. It is in the transactions of the Church that the old paradox of 'grace and free will' appears not as an insoluble problem but as the mystery of the Christian life.

(c) *Worship and the Life of the Church.* When the Spirit is acknowledged as the Spirit of the Church, there emerges a helpful understanding of the way in which worship and life belong together. Worship is an activity of the people being sanctified in the world. There is no worship without thankfulness, and there is no thankfulness without sanctification. But sanctification is a victory over sin and death, which occur in the community. Hence the community assembles to worship God, to acknowledge the struggle of the Spirit against sin and death, and to give thanks for the victory of the Spirit in the Church in the midst of the same struggle. This warfare comprises the ethics of the Church in the total life of the people in the world, and worship is coming to God's presence with it. Thus worship is a prayer as well as a celebration, and so are the preaching and the sacraments. The tradition has commonly acknowledged the presence of the Holy Spirit in these 'means of grace'. Our point here is that the cult of the Church is a means of grace to a people who may celebrate their sanctification in their transactions as members of the Body of Christ in the world.

(d) *'Enthusiasm' in the Church.* The doctrine of the Holy Spirit has traditionally been tied to varieties of 'enthusiasm' which have occurred in the history of the Church. Enthusiasm has been expressed in visions, 'speaking with tongues', energetic behaviour, with sundry extraordinary psychic and physical phenomena, which have rather annoyed the sober people in the Church. Indeed, the identification of the work of the Spirit with enthusiasm is not justified. Faith,

hope, and love, with peace and joy, and every good thing in the Church are also the work of the Spirit. On the other hand, it is not justified to draw a sharp line between the Christian's joy in sanctification and 'enthusiasm'. The work of the Spirit in the Church entails ecstasy and ecstasy will not be contained by convention. Reconsiliation in the Church, the Christians' joy in the presence of the triune God in their midst and in their presence one to another by sanctification, constitute a good which may well move them to extraordinary and unexpected behaviour. Union with God in Christ in the Church is a thing of enthusiasm and is rightly acknowledged as the mark of the Spirit. It constitutes the Church and the existence of the believer. This union, in which God is with man and for man, in which man is with God and for God, in his transactions with Christ and his fellow men, is by enthusiasm and the hope of eternal life. It is the very thing which has kept the doctrine of the Spirit alive in the Church to the knowledge of God and the glory of God. *See also:* **Atonement; Christology; Eschatology; God; Tradition; Trinity; Vision of God; Chrism; Initiation, Christian; Church; Attributes of God; Worship.**

Hendrikus Berkhof, *The Doctrine of the Holy Spirit,* 1964; Arnold B. Come, *Human Spirit and Holy Spirit,* 1959; Lindsay Dewar, *The Holy Spirit and Modern Thought,* 1959; George S. Hendry, *The Holy Spirit in Christian Theology,* 1956; T. Rees, *The Holy Spirit in Thought and Experience,* 1915; Cyril C. Richardson, *The Doctrine of the Trinity,* 1958; H. Wheeler Robinson, *The Christian Experience of the Holy Spirit,* 1928 and 1947; Eduard Schweizer, *et al. The Spirit of God,* 1960; Henry P. van Dusen, *Spirit, Son, and Father,* 1958.

JOSEPH HAROUTUNIAN

Spiritual Gifts

St Paul insists that the Holy Spirit endows Christians with the necessary gifts for the performance of their individual roles or ministries within the Church (I Cor.12). As such they are 'gifts of grace' (*charismata,* 'gracegifts': *see* **Charisma**). In I Cor.12.8–10 he enumerates nine such gifts among church members, ranging from 'wisdom' to the interpretation of 'tongues' (*see* **Glossolalia**). However, in later theology a sevenfold conception of the Spirit and of his gifts was developed under the influence of Isa.11.2 (in the LXX version). This became traditional, particularly in the *Spiritus septiformis* (the sevenfold Spirit) of Latin devotion (*cf.* the hymn *Veni, creator Spiritus,* 'Come, Holy Ghost, our souls inspire' in the translation of Bishop J. Cosin, seventeenth century). The seven spirits of the Apocalypse (Rev.1.4; 3.1; 4.5; 5.6) were also formative of the conception. On the whole subject of the gifts of the Spirit *see* Alan Richardson, *Introduction to the Theology of the New Testament,* 1958, pp. 109–12.

EDITOR

Spiritual Healing

In ancient times religion and healing were intimately connected, though in Greece there had developed a 'scientific' interest in medicine which was intellectual rather than compassionate. The healing ministry of Jesus introduced into the world a new compassion for the sick and it is impossible to overstress the significance of his healing work in the subsequent expansion of Christianity. Since the pagan gods were interested only in the healthy and strong, the preaching of the Saviour-Healer satisfied a need which was largely unmet. It is significant, says Harnack, that Aesculapius, the god of healing, was the pagan god to hold out longest against Christianity: 'Jesus says very little about sickness; he cures it . . . Jesus does not distinguish rigidly between sickness of the body and of the soul; he takes them both as different expressions of one supreme ailment in humanity.' In the apostolic Church the gift of healing was highly regarded as one of the gifts of the Spirit (I Cor.12.9, etc.). The second-century pagan philosopher Celsus derided Christianity for its concern for sick and foolish people. Since that date, however, wherever it has gone, Christianity has established hospitals, asylums, etc., and still today in many parts of the world Christian missions supply the only medical aid that exists. The secularized world has inherited from Christian civilization the concept of the care of the sick and feeble by society as a whole. The bringing together of scientific medicine and humane compassion is undoubtedly one of the supreme achievements of that civilization. It was brought about by a refusal to recognize a distinction between men's spiritual and physical afflictions: both must be healed by medical and 'spiritual' treatment, working together. Whether charismatic or purely spiritual (non-medical, non-psychological) healing is something which Christians today ought to attempt to revive or encourage in our scientific age is a question which will be answered variously by different theologians; but there is evidence to point to 'gifts of healing' in the Church which cannot be ignored. The Roman Catholic Church expects miracles of healing to happen (esp. at certain shrines, notably Lourdes) and points to definite cures. The whole question of spiritual healing has been much discussed in the churches during the present century. Perhaps the consensus of opinion is that, since man is a psychosomatic (q.v.) unity, both spiritual-charismatic means (prayer, unction, the laying on of hands) and medical treatment should be used together, since all healing is ultimately a gift of God. This will for Christians remain true, even if psychotherapeutic treatment by purely 'secular' practitioners becomes more effective than it is today in the present state of our ignorance about the strange psychosomatic existent which is called man.

T. W. Crafer, ed., *The Church and the Ministry of Healing*, 1934; Evelyn Frost, *Christian Healing*, 1940; A. Graham Ikin, *The Background of Spiritual Healing*, 1937; A. Harnack, 'The Gospel of the Saviour and of Salvation', Excursus ii, *The Expansion of Christianity*, ET 1904, I, pp. 121–51; R. A. Lambourne, *Community, Church and Healing*, 1963; Michael Wilson, *The Church is Healing*, 1966. For a Roman Catholic exposition of miraculous healings *see* Louis Monden, *Signs and Wonders*, ET, 1966.

EDITOR

Spiritualism

Spiritualism is the common name of the cult of communication with the spirits of the departed. The Bible has a horror of all such practices (*cf.*I Sam.28; Isa.8.19), and they have no place in Christian belief and practice. The modern cult seems to have spread from America to Europe in the second half of the nineteenth century, although necromancy (q.v.) has been practised in almost all primitive societies. Christians, however, should have no objection to the serious investigation of the subject upon a scientific basis, as (e.g.) under the auspices of the Society for Psychical Research, founded in 1882. The cult is sometimes (and perhaps more accurately) referred to as 'spiritism', but not by its adherents.

EDITOR

Spirituality

The sense in which theologians use this word is not generally accepted by standard English dictionaries, which often give as its first meaning, following mediaeval use, 'the clergy'. Its modern technical use includes piety, the devout life, the interior life of prayer, and yet is not quite covered by these descriptions. It means 'the way a man understands his own ethically and religiously committed existence, and the way he acts and reacts habitually to this understanding' (Urs von Balthasar). There are non-Christian spiritualities, and there are different traditions of spirituality within Christianity. Basically Christian spirituality means the real, effective apprehension of Christian truth in the human consciousness, and its varieties spring as much from the variety of human psychological types as from differences of theology. Although systematic treatment of the spiritual life belongs more to Catholic than to Protestant Christianity, spiritual classics have been produced by all traditions.

L. Bouyer, J. Leclercq, and others, *Histoire de la Spiritualité Chrétiénne*, 1960- , in process of translation; F. P. Harton, *The Elements of the Spiritual Life*, 1932.

R. CANT

Stoicism

The name is derived from Greek *stoa* or 'porch', in which Zeno (335–263 BC), the founder of the movement, taught in Athens. Stoicism, a leading religious philosophy in the NT period (*cf.* Acts 17.18), influenced the language and perhaps the thought of St Paul (*cf.* his use of the terms 'nature' and 'conscience') and exercised a continuing influence upon the development of Christian thought, which eventually incorporated Stoic ideas and language into its system. Two Stoic ideas are especially significant in this connection. The first is that of the *Logos* ('word', 'reason'), or world-soul in which every man coming into the world participates (the so-called 'divine spark' in every man). Was the Fourth Evangelist deliberately using Stoic language so that educated Greeks could understand the significance of Christ in their own thought-forms (*cf.* John 1.1–14: there is nothing in this passage which could not be derived from the language and thought of the OT)? The Logos-conception undoubtedly played the large part which it did in early Christian theology (*see* **Christology**) because of the prevalence of Stoic modes of thought. The second important teaching of the Stoics concerns the identification of nature with reason; the natural is the rational: therefore live according to nature. Man's highest good is to obey the law of his own nature, or reason, thus disregarding ('being Stoical about') the pleasures or sufferings of the moment (and being indifferent to the misfortunes of others as well as to one's own). Stoicism developed a genuinely cosmopolitan attitude; race and nationality were mere accidents which could be disregarded: to be human was the property of no one group or class. Seneca was a slave; Cicero a Roman consul, and Marcus Aurelius the Roman Emperor. Cicero's *De Officiis* (a hand-book for his son on moral conduct), centuries after his death (43 BC), was the model for St Ambrose of Milan's (AD 339–397) most notable work, *De Officiis Ministrorum*, which transmitted the ethic of reason to the Christian Middle Ages. The whole mediaeval conception of natural law (and hence in its turn the possibility of the rise of modern science) would hardly have been developed had it not been for the broad stream of Stoic thought which had flowed into it. *See* **Natural Law**.

Loeb eds. of Cicero, Seneca, Epictetus and Marcus Aurelius; E. V. Arnold, *Roman Stoicism*, 1911; E. R. Bevan, *Stoics and Sceptics*, 1913; R. D. Hicks, *Stoic and Epicurean*, 1911; R. W. Livingstone, *The Mission of Greece*, 1928; P. E. More, *Hellenistic Philosophies*, 1923; R. M. Wenley, *Stoicism and its Influence*, 1924.

EDITOR

Subordinationism

The term signifies the attempt to secure a greater semblance of Divine Unity by positing a difference of status among the three Persons. The use of the Logos concept to clarify the doctrine of the Son led inevitably to this direction. In Greek philosophy the Logos was the intermediary between the Absolute God and the relative universe and therefore tended to slip down towards the universe with which it was deeply involved. The second God (Justin) became in course of time the secondary God (Arius). Greek philosophy was familiar with a hierarchy of Being which had its impact not only on Gnosticism but also on orthodox thought. Origen, although the balance of his thought falls on the side of Co-ordinationist Pluralism, incorporates some strong subordinationist expressions (including perhaps even the term 'creature'). Here he is followed by Origenists like Dionysius of Alexandria and Eusebius of Caesarea. For Arianism it was the leading principle of the system. Ultimately Subordinationism leads either to unitarianism or to polytheism or (in Arianism) to a mixture of both. Subordinationism was excluded by the *Homo-ousios*, the replacement of Logos by Son in Trinitarian theology and the improved theological mapwork of the Cappadocians. Prestige's view that the Double Procession is the last legacy of Subordinationism is very dubious; it is rather an attempt to integrate more closely the three divine Persons under the principle of the divine Monarchy.

There is an orthodox subordinationism in the sense that the Trinity must begin with the Father or lead up to the Father, but this is concerned with order of thought and unity in derivation and does not affect the ontological status of the three Persons.

H. E. W. TURNER

Substance

Substance is the word used in traditional Christian philosophy to indicate the ontological unit, i.e., that which is capable of independent existence. Aquinas used two other words in close connection with substance, namely essence and quiddity. The essence of a substance is *what* it is, i.e., what its exhaustive definition would say that it is; and its quiddity is that which corresponds in the substance to its definition. The substance, however, is more than its essence, although this something more cannot add to its definition, for it consists, not at all in what it is, but precisely in that it is. Accordingly, substance can 'be defined as an essence or quiddity existing by itself in virtue of its own act of being' (É. Gilson, *The Christian Philosophy of St Thomas Aquinas*, 1924, p. 30). Indeed Aquinas distinguished substances according to the three different ways in which they may possess essence, as in the case of God, spiritual substances, and material substances. Thus, in the terminology of traditional Christian theology, the uniqueness of God is represented by reference to the fact that, while like all substances or, as Aquinas sometimes described them, primary realities God is by his own act-of-being, in him alone existence and essence are identical, his essence is his very existing. On the other hand, this clarity of abstract thought remains a *human* ideal, and when taken as regulative for theology it presupposes, as an assumption, the primacy of intellect rather than of will. Accordingly, over a wide area of modern theology the category of substance has played a less important part than its customary one; and it has frequently been assumed, and sometimes argued, that it is too static a concept to provide a reliable characterization of God, and that instead it has been a fruitful source of unreal and insoluble problems in the realms of christology and the Trinity. *See also* **God; Christology; Trinity.**

N. H. G. ROBINSON

Sunday

The name 'Sunday' is older than Christianity: in Greek and Latin the Sun's Day was the weekly festival of the Sun-god. From the earliest Christian times the first day of the week was chosen as the special weekly day of worship (in contrast to the Jewish Sabbath, Saturday) and thus became the weekly festival of the Lord's resurrection; *cf.* Acts 20.7; I Cor.16.2. In Rev.1.10 it is called 'the Lord's Day' and was later known in the West as *Dominica* (*Dies*). It was easy for Christians to retain the name 'Sunday', for was not Christ the Sun of Righteousness arisen with healing in his wings (Mal.4.2)? Since NT times Sunday has been observed throughout Christendom as the day of rest from labour and the day for worship. The weekly holiday was an inestimable boon to generations of workers who had no rest-periods except the holy days of the Church. But the total prohibition of work and recreation on Sunday (*see* **Sabbatarianism**) is neither a possible nor a desirable Christian strategy for today, and in our secular civilization the urgent duty of Christians is to determine and to practise the right use of Sunday by Christians themselves as a day of worship and also of recreation, but they also have a duty to see that those who are compelled by the nature of their occupation to work on Sunday should not be exploited or deprived of their rights in respect of leisure and recreation.

W. Rordorf, *Sunday: the History of the Day of Rest and Worship in the Earliest Centuries of the Church,* ET, 1968; C. H. Cleal, 'Sunday Observance', *DCE.*

EDITOR

Supernatural

Strictly it is a neutral word meaning 'beyond ordinary natural (or human) powers'. In common speech, however, it has come to mean 'uncanny', 'weird', 'ghost-like' (as has also the word 'preternatural', i.e. 'beyond nature'). In theological usage 'supernatural' means *above* nature, i.e., the divine realm; *cf.* John Oman, *The Natural and the Supernatural* (1931).

Syllabus Errorum

Syllabus Errorum was a comprehensive collection of subjects connected with contemporary thought condemned by Pope Pius IX in 1864. It included the right to free speech, the separation of Church from State, the right of non-Catholics in Roman Catholic countries to the free exercise of their worship, religious toleration and liberalism.

R. P. C. HANSON

Symbol, Symbolic Theology

The Greek word *symbolon* meant a sign or token which established identity, e.g. a soldier's badge or watchword which identified his allegiance. In theological usage it came to mean a creed, the expression of a Christian's allegiance. Hence symbolics or symbolic theology is the study of the history and meaning of the Christian creeds.

Symbol, Symbolism

Religion naturally seeks expression through art and symbolism of every kind. It has been conjectured that the Decalogue's prohibition of the making of images of any sort is responsible for the fact that the verbal imagery of both OT and NT is of a kind which does not lend itself to representational art: no one can draw Isaiah's seraphim (Isa.6.2) or the beasts of the Apocalypse 'full of eyes before and behind' (Rev.4.6, etc.). However that may be, both Testaments are full of profound poetic imagery, and it can be argued that without such imagery the transcendent truths of religion cannot be adequately communicated or sustained. The whole history of Christianity is filled with symbolism, from the cross itself or the fish of the catacombs to the glories of mediaeval or baroque architecture and adornment. Protestantism has often been suspicious of symbolism (*cf.* 'puritanism'), but this is doubtless by way of reaction from the excesses of Catholicism, in which it has sometimes been hard to distinguish between a genuinely religious symbolism and a superstitious fetichism and magic. But even within Protestantism distinctions must be drawn, e.g. between Lutheran and Reformed attitudes. The whole subject is complicated and full of pitfalls; it is (e.g.) fatally easy to discuss the place of icons in Eastern Orthodoxy without having any real appreciation of their symbolical significance. But the subject is one which is increasingly recognized to be of great importance and it is today attracting the serious attention of scholars and theologians. What is the difference between religious and secular symbolism? Is there any value at all in religious symbolism in a secular ('religionless') age? What kind of architecture is the appropriate setting for eucharistic worship? Where should the pulpit stand in relation to the altar (or the font in relation to either)? Are the symbols of a long-past age of faith worth preserving (e.g. a Jesse window or a rood screen) in an age which no longer understands their meaning? Should we try to invent entirely new symbols of Christian truth in an 'age of no religion'? To articulate all the questions which are involved in religious symbolism would require a whole dictionary to itself.

Edwyn Bevan, *Symbolism and Belief,* 1938, Fontana, 1962; G. Cope, *Symbolism in the Bible and the Church,* 1959; F. W. Dillistone, *Christianity and Symbolism,* 1956; A. M. Farrer, *The Glass of Vision,* 1948; *A Rebirth of Images,* 1949; P. Hammond, *Liturgy and Architecture,* 1960; J.

Macquarrie, *God-Talk*, 1967, ch. 8; P. Tillich, *Theology of Culture*, 1959.

EDITOR

Synaxis

Synaxis (Greek: assembly), a form of prayer consisting of psalms, Scripture lessons and prayers, probably based on Jewish synagogue worship. By attachment to the original eucharistic rite, which began with the Offertory, the synaxis survives as the first half of the later liturgies, sometimes known as the 'Mass of the Catechumens' or the 'Ministry of the Word'.

E. L. MASCALL

Syncretism

The mingling together of different philosophies or religions, resulting in hybrid forms of philosophy or of religion. It is thus to be distinguished from *eclecticism*, which denotes the choosing of particular elements from different philosophical or religious systems and combining them in a new but not very original system. Both words are from the Greek.

Synergism

Greek, 'working together with': the doctrine, such as that of Melanchthon (q.v.), that the human will has a part to play along with the Holy Spirit (or the grace of God) in the process of conversion.

Systematic Theology

Systematic theology is another name for Dogmatics (q.v.). Before the Enlightenment (q.v.) it was held by Catholics and Protestants alike that the propositions contained in the Scriptures were collectively the total revelation of God to man, given through the Holy Spirit. But these propositions did not present the truth in a systematic form, and thus it was necessary for theologians to systematize the truths contained in the thousands of biblical propositions and so construct a 'system' which should present the whole range of revealed truth from Creation to the Last Things. Aquinas' *Summa Theologica* and Calvin's *Institutes* may be regarded as respectively the principal Catholic and Protestant 'systems' of theology. Since the Enlightenment it has become impossible to regard the task of theology as that of systematizing the biblical propositions regarded as inerrant, but the task of presenting in an orderly fashion the content of Christian truth still remains. Karl Barth's massive *Church Dogmatics* (ET, 1936–) constitutes the most impressive attempt since Calvin to elucidate the content of the Christian revelation, but he does not start from a concept of revealed truth as propositional. Nowadays the expression 'systematics' or 'systematic theology' is generally abandoned in favour of 'dogmatics' for obvious reasons. The notable exception to this statement is Paul Tillich's three-volume *Systematic Theology* (1951, 1957, 1963): but the retention of this title is perhaps not inappropriate, since the whole work retains Christian theological terms in a totally transposed and symbolic form to fit a view of reality which is strictly incompatible with their proper Christian meaning. *See* **Dogmatics.**

EDITOR

Tauler, Johann

Tauler (c.1300–1361) knew well, and was greatly influenced by, the teaching and writings of Meister Eckhart (*see* **Eckhart, Meister**), but in his sermons, which seem to be the only authentic remains of the writings of Tauler which have come down to us, he reveals a caution and pastoral tact which suggests that he was aware of Eckhart's official condemnation. For instance, he avoids using Eckhart's favourite phrase 'the divine spark of the soul' because it was possible to give this phrase a pantheistic interpretation, and he prefers to speak of 'the ground of the soul' and always in such a way as not to obliterate the radical distinction between that which is created and the Creator. There is the same reticence in Tauler, as in Eckhart, in speaking about religious experience, and the same effective impersonal treatment of religion. But when he does speak of his religious experience he does it in such a way as to make quite clear that for him the height of the human awareness of God does not involve anything that could be termed extinction of personality, but on the contrary an enhancement of personal being:

> In as much as the disciples surrendered themselves utterly to the divine will they were in the highest sense in harmony with nature, and their nature did not perish, but was exalted and brought into rightful order; there were no fewer images in their minds than before, but their images did not disturb their inward harmony, or move them out of God. When I said that their minds were to be emptied of images it is to be understood in this sense that it was just as when you set a lighted taper at midday in the sunshine. The taper continues to burn and sheds forth no less light than it did before, but its light is lost in the sunshine, because the greater light prevails over the lesser, and absorbs it, so that it no longer seems to shine with a separate lustre, but is diffused and shed forth in the greater light. Thus I said of images, and of creatures in the case of the disciples that henceforth they performed all their works by means of the divine light, and yet were much more according to nature and their minds as full of images as before.

The basic motivation of the Christian life, for Tauler, is the imitation of Christ. One sets out to copy Christ in his human nature and God himself will 'verily come into him in his superhuman godhead'. In a way that reminds one of St Augustine he speaks of the progress of the Christian life as through Christ-man to Christ-God.

The only English edition of the sermons of Tauler is still that edited by Susanna Winkworth, 1904. This edition reproduces the influential but spurious *History and Life of the Reverend Dr John Tauler*; a good critical edition of the sermons of Tauler is that edited by Hugueny, Théry and Corin, *Sermons de Tauler*, 1928.

E. J. TINSLEY

Taylor, Nathaniel William

Nathaniel William Taylor (1786–1858), Congregational minister and founder of the New Haven theology, graduated from Yale in 1807. After ten years (1812–1822) as pastor of Centre Church in New Haven, Connecticut, he became Dwight Professor of Didactic Theology at the new divinity school at Yale. Taylor, who was influenced philosophically by Scottish common sense realism, claimed to be true to Calvinism, which he interpreted so as to make a larger place for the freedom of man than was generally accorded. He believed that all sin is voluntary in character, and so could affirm that the 'universal depravity of mankind is not inconsistent with the moral perfection of God'. Man's created nature is not the cause but the 'occasion' for his sinning, though the possibility of his not becoming a sinner remains open. It is certain man will sin, Taylor taught, yet he has the power not to do so – 'certainty with power to the contrary' was his favourite theological axiom. These views, repeated in a famous sermon, *Concio ad Clerum* (1828) and in his *Lectures on the Moral Government of God* (1859), had great impact in American Congregational and Presbyterian Churches, and were conspicuous in revival preaching, in which Taylor himself participated. These New Haven views were also highly controversial, contributing to the founding of a new Congregational seminary (Hartford) in reaction, and to the 1837–1838 schism in Presbyterianism.

Sidney E. Mead, *Nathaniel William Taylor, 1786–1858: A Connecticut Liberal*, 1942.

ROBERT T. HANDY

Teilhard de Chardin, Pierre

The stature and the significance of Teilhard's thought have not yet been fully determined. His ideas generate serious perplexities, in particular for the natural scientist and the theologian. To some extent these difficulties may be attributed to the special character of Teilhard's writing. Idiosyncratic and inventive in vocabulary, and with the short essay as his characteristic medium, Teilhard adventured indefatigably with ideas. Balanced assessment is also hindered by the fact that the collected edition of his *Oeuvres* is incomplete and lacks full apparatus. The subtlety, range and movement of his thought defy all but the most careful analysis, internal comparison and exposition. But the ambiguous reaction to

Teilhard's achievement derives in part also from his deliberate intention to raise fundamental questions about our inherited, and often mutually estranged, ways of thought in the different scholarly disciplines. His life-task, in which he was at once most revolutionary and most vulnerable, consisted in structuring (in a provisional but detailed way) a synthetic mode of thought by which man may be seen and understood as a unity, as a child of heaven and of earth. In this intention and hope, namely to believe 'at the same time and wholly in God and the World, the one through the other', are reflected the patterns and preoccupations of Teilhard's own life.

Marie-Joseph-Pierre Teilhard de Chardin (1881–1955), SJ, was born in 1881 in rural Auvergne, was ordained in 1911, and pursued advanced geological and paleontological studies under eminent teachers. After service as a stretcher-bearer in World War I (*see The Making of a Mind*, 1965), Teilhard spent over half the inter-war years in China on active paleontological work, forbidden by his Order from disseminating his experimental ideas in France. He was associated with discoveries of *Pithecanthropus* and *Sinanthropus*, and gained high distinction and widespread professional respect for this and other scientific work (*see The Appearance of Man*, 1965). Confined in China during World War II, Teilhard later returned to Paris and to a measure of open intellectual life. But prohibited from accepting a professorial chair at the Collège de France and from publishing *The Phenomenon of Man* (1959), he was again required to leave France. His later years were spent mainly in the USA working with the Wenner-Gren Foundation for Anthropological Research. Teilhard died in New York on Easter Day 1955.

Teilhard's starting-point is existential, namely that man is trapped inside this 'bubble of the cosmos' and that his taste for life is stifled by the threat that mankind's long history will ultimately founder. Against this, the concept of evolution provides a vital clue to recognizing that man has a special history and, potentially, a remarkable future. Nevertheless it was probably, in the first place, reflection upon the Pauline Christ *in quo omnia constant* as the origin, present centre and goal of the cosmos, that led Teilhard to develop his evolutionary hypothesis. When this biblical insight was combined with the paleontological evidence for the continuity between human and animal evolution, Teilhard felt able to postulate evolution as a universal cosmological law. This led to the notion of a 'hyperphysics' (*see The Phenomenon of Man*), to the suggestion that all matter has a 'within' and a 'without', i.e. possesses 'consciousness' in rudimentary or developed form. Teilhard's intuitions here were influenced by Bergson's account of the inter-relation between matter, spirit and energy. The 'within' and the 'without' are connected by energy operating with two tendencies, 'radial' and 'tangential'. Radial energy draws a unit into greater structures of complexity; tangential energy links units at

the same level of organization. It is through increase in radial energy that decisive 'critical
points' are reached, whether, for example, at the
molecular level or at the leap from instinct to
thought (*see Man's Place in Nature, 1966*). The
two tendencies of energy can be combined under
the 'Law of Complexity-Consciousness'. This
means that in evolution matter becomes more
complex, and that with this rise in complexity
there corresponds a rise in consciousness. In
consequence, evolution, extrapolated backwards
and forwards on an enormous time-scale, and
notwithstanding all its cul-de-sacs, is seen as uni-
directional, as a groping but, at base, coherent
and irreversible ascent (*via* growing complexity)
towards personality. The future prospect for
mankind is only understood aright when we
appreciate that man is now responsible for the
course of this evolution, which must continue at
the spiritual and social level under man's control
and construction (the formation of the no-
osphere). On this basis it is possible to conjecture,
but not to be certain of, a point of human convergence as the goal of evolution.

It is Teilhard's conviction that, if mankind is to
become fully united and fully personal, this can
be achieved only by love as, so to speak, the
highest expression of radial energy (amorization).
Teilhard must therefore be able to postulate an
absolute centre of love in the cosmos, activating
human energy and assuring a successful outcome
for evolution. Thus he seeks to correlate the data
of generalized evolution with the themes of
Christian theology. He concludes that Christ, as
risen, is the present personal centre of the cosmos
and the point of its consummation.

On this view it is impossible to separate
Christian belief from an empirical estimate of the
cosmos, as it is impossible, if there is to be any
authentic human hope, to pursue scientific reflection outside the context of a full-blooded
theistic and christocentric world-view. But Teilhard's ambitious correlation demands sweeping
changes in traditional scientific and theological
self-understanding (*see Science and Christ, 1968*).
Scientifically, it calls for revised attitudes to the
fact of complexity and to the legitimacy of synthesizing work. Theologically, it calls for a radical
recasting of, for example, the doctrines of God,
creation, christology, man, sin, redemption and
eschatology. Creation is that by which the world
follows its creative, convergent evolution in
space-time (cosmogenesis). Christology concerns
not only an historical incarnation, but the evolution of the total Christ (the mystical body) in the
context of human evolution (christogenesis).
Sin, however alarming, is essentially a short-
coming in the ascent of evolution and not a value
in itself. Redemption is above all the work of
Christ in advancing the multi-storied evolution of
mankind (Christ-the-Evolver). Eschatology refers
to the collocation of 'natural' and 'supernatural'
points of convergence for the whole of evolution
(Omega). Christian prayer and spirituality are
related to a doctrine of work and of human

energy (*see Le Milieu Divin, 1960, and L'Activation
de L'Energie, 1963*). Not least, Teilhard's approach
leads to a new shape for Christian theism in
which God, the transcendent personal in 'hierarchical union' with the universe in evolution, is
the agent of creative union out of stubborn
multiplicity. This bears some similarity to process
philosophy (q.v.). All Teilhard's theological concepts presuppose an interlocking of physical and
spiritual energy (noodynamic). For 'he wanted to
be able to pass in a single movement from one
mode of knowledge to another, from the data of
reason on its various levels to the data of Christian revelation, and to do so with ease and without
confusion' (C.F. Mooney).

In a brief summary it is impossible to do justice
to the breadth, detail and acuity of Teilhard's
synoptic vision, or to outline its shortcomings. If
the past revealed to him the construction of the
future (*see The Vision of the Past, 1966*), it is, in
the last resort, from the superior form, from what
is above and beyond, that the shape and direction
of present endeavours are to be prescribed.
Generalized evolution, *pace* Bergson, is essentially
an attraction from above, from Omega. In
Teilhard's view, for man to take upon his own
shoulders the course of evolution as a process of
'collective cerebralization' means that the day-
to-day work of scientific research, technological
development, social and political planning, indeed all efforts of empirical human unification,
are integrally related to the realization of that
mature planetary mankind which is a precondition for Omega. Thus Teilhard's thought
has attracted Marxists, humanists and ecu-
menists, and others ideologically committed to
social change, human progress and inter-mundane
unity (*see The Future of Man, 1964, and Building
the Earth, 1965*).

Teilhard wrote, 'My principal objective is not
to convert you to ideas which are still fluid, but to
open horizons for you . . .' The chief threat to
his inevitably fragile but undeniably barrier-
breaking intellectual edifice will come from those
who wish to tailor his ideas to fit the framework of
delivered Christian orthodoxies, or from those
who over-emphasize one aspect of his work (e.g.
mysticism) at the expense of the carefully balanced
whole. His achievement will only properly be
evaluated if it is allowed freedom to exercise its
own influence, and if his 'style' and method are
related both to new and rapidly changing scientific horizons and to a theological world at once
more open and sensitive than that which Teilhard
knew. 'A conception of this sort is open to attack
on a number of heads; but the crucial point is
whether in its main features it is acceptable and
really does provide the lines on which positive
scientific, philosophical and theological enquiry
can be co-ordinated' (B. Delfgaauw). Many
regard such a co-ordination as an urgent intellectual and human need. At the very least it may be
said that Teilhard personified the challenge in an
imaginative, germinant and, ultimately, optimistic way.

Oeuvres, Editions du Seuil, 1955- , ET, 1955- ;
M. Barthélemy-Madaule, *La Personne et le
Drame humain chez Teilhard de Chardin,* 1967;
C. Cuénot, *Science and Faith in Teilhard de
Chardin,* 1967; *Teilhard de Chardin – A Bio-
graphical Study,* 1965 (includes detailed biblio-
graphy); B. Delfgaauw, *Teilhard de Chardin,*
1968; C. F. Mooney, *Teilhard de Chardin and the
Mystery of Christ,* 1966; C. E. Raven, *Teilhard
de Chardin – Scientist and Seer,* 1962; E. Rideau,
Teilhard de Chardin – A Guide to his Thought,
1967; R. Speaight, *Teilhard de Chardin – A
Biography,* 1967.

A. O. DYSON

Teleology

From Greek *telos,* an end or goal: the study of
final causes or of the purpose for which things are
designed. *See* **Teleological Argument** under **God**
(6).

Temple, William

William Temple (1881–1944) was Archbishop of
Canterbury from 1942 till his death in 1944. At
Oxford he came strongly under the influence of
neo-Hegelian philosophy, and some of his most
notable contributions to theology are an attempt
to express the traditional christology in terms
meaningful to his generation. He had intellectual
difficulties about the creeds which at one time
rendered his ordination unlikely. He contributed
to **Foundations** (q.v.) but in later years moved
steadily to a more orthodox position. His
approach to biblical criticism was always less
radical than his philosophy. He was one of the
leaders in a movement to increase the amount of
self-government in the church, in the cause of
social reform (his speeches and writings helped
to prepare public opinion for the post-war
social reforms) and for fuller participation in the
ecumenical movement.

No church leader of this century has been so
many-sided or so influential in so many different
fields of thought and action. Among his most
famous books are *Nature, Man and God* (1934),
Readings in the Fourth Gospel (1939, 1940) and
Christianity and Social Order (1942).

F. A. Iremonger, *Life and Letters of William
Temple,* 1948; A. M. Ramsey, *From Gore to
Temple,* 1960.

R. CANT

Temptation

Before man sins he must be tempted to sin. Unless
a sinful act entices and motivates a man he will
not commit it. Christian theology always has
tried to locate and explain the source of temptation. The Genesis story of the Garden of Eden
pictures the serpent as tempting Eve to doubt God
and disobey his command. This story symbolizes
man's experience that temptation seems to come
from outside of himself.

The Devil and his demonic cohorts traditionally have been seen as the source of man's temptation. Origen even suggested that, as each man
has a guardian angel to protect him, he has an
evil angel to tempt him. After the age of the
Enlightenment belief grew that all references to
the Devil must be demythologized. On the other
hand, the twentieth century with its history of
totalitarianism, violence, racial disharmony and
war has led a number of thinkers to take seriously
the view that there are suprapersonal forces of
evil that capture men. Regardless of what we
decide about the ontological reality of Satan as a
person, the doctrine of the Devil helps us to express the reality of temptation that meets man
from beyond himself.

Central to the Christian understanding of
temptation is Jesus who was tempted as we are
(Heb.4.15). Because Christ faced temptation in
the ultimate sense and overcame it, the Christian
has the promise that his temptations also may be
overcome by the grace of God.

WILLIAM HORDERN

Tertullian

A lawyer from Carthage converted to Christianity
and later to Montanism, Tertullian (c. 160–220)
was the first theologian to write in Latin and
therefore the founder of the Latin theological
vocabulary. Notwithstanding his lapse into Montanism, he remained influential in Western theology. In many respects the 'phrase-maker' of
the Western Church, he was the first to use the
word *trinitas* and constructed the formula 'One
substance, three persons' (*una substantia, tres
personae*). His treatise *Against Praxeas* (after 213)
is a penetrating critique of Modalism (q.v.).
Despite his opposition to Modalism he adopts a
Monist approach to the doctrine of the Trinity,
and there are indications of strong Economic
Trinitarian tendencies. His conversion to Montanism had, it seems, relatively little effect on his
doctrine of the Spirit and strengthened his disciplinary rigorism rather than his theology. His
terminology is more mature than the thought
which lay behind it. *See* **Trinity, Doctrine of the.**

H. E. W. TURNER

Theism

Theism has been described as a philosophical
theory as distinct from a religious faith, even if
the two are rarely disjoined, and it may be defined
as belief in a single supreme being who is the
source of everything else and who, as A. E.
Taylor would have added (*cf.* A. E. Taylor,
'Theism', *ERE,* XII, pp. 261–87), being himself
complete and perfect, is worthy to be worshipped.
Theism falls to be distinguished, on the one
hand, from deism which affirms the transcendence in theism in divorce from its immanence and which, cutting off the Creator's involvement in his creation, renders the theistic
themes of providence and worship highly ambiguous, and, on the other hand, from pantheism which, affirming immanence at the expense
of transcendence, identifies the divine with the

whole of reality and destroys the distinction between Creator and creation. It also falls to be distinguished from atheism which denies the existence of God, from agnosticism which regards the question of divine existence as unanswerable, and from logical positivism which holds question and answer alike to be strictly meaningless.

N. H. G. ROBINSON

Theocracy

Just as 'democracy' signifies government by the mass of the people in any society or by their duly elected representatives, so 'theocracy' signifies government by God or by his representatives, of which Israel provides the most notable example; but since the will of God is not an empirical reality as is the will of the people, or of any other constitutional group, a theocracy is always more of an ideal than a fact and belongs primarily to the sphere of profession and faith rather than to that of plain practice.

N. H. G. ROBINSON

Theodicy

Theodicy is the name given to that type of theological argumentation which, accepting a basis in theism, seeks by reason to reconcile belief in the goodness, wisdom and power of God with any contrary evidence, such as the existence of evil, and so to 'justify the ways of God to men'. Thus, so far as it goes, a theodicy seeks to supplement faith by sight.

John Hick, *Evil and the God of Love*, 1966.

N. H. G. ROBINSON

Theologia Crucis; Theologia Gloriae

'Theology of the Cross' is Luther's name for the doctrine that our knowledge of God must be drawn from the suffering Christ in his humiliation. He contrasted this with the view of mediaeval scholasticism (q.v.) which maintained that a 'natural' knowledge of God could be obtained by the unaided human reason. He called this view a 'theology of glory'. *See also* **Christology.**

Theology

In classical Greek *theologia* means an account of the gods (or God), whether legendary or philosophical. Stoicism (q.v.) divided theology into three parts: mythical, natural (i.e. rational) and civil (the rites and ceremonies of religion). In patristic Christian usage it meant the biblical account of God's dealings with men, with particular reference to Christ. Hence the late Greek and earlier Latin use of 'theology' for the Scriptures themselves. In the twelfth century Abelard (q.v.) applied the term to the philosophical treatment of Christian doctrines. Though at first deprecated, his usage became current: theology was an academic study of the Scriptures and the Sentences (i.e., select passages from the Fathers: *see* **Lombard, P.**). This was current

English usage by the time of Langland and Chaucer. After the time of St. Thomas Aquinas (*see* **Thomism**), theology, natural and revealed, was regarded as the climax and co-ordinating study of all that is – in fact, 'the Queen of the Sciences'. This attitude continued until the Enlightenment (q.v.): *cf.* Locke (c. 1698): 'Theology, which, containing the knowledge of God and his creatures, our duty to him and our fellow-creatures, and a view of our present and future state, is the comprehension of all other knowledge, directed to its true end'. This statement must today in a sense remain true for Christians, although theology is commonly regarded more narrowly and is often considered an academic subject. As such it is divided into particular branches, e.g., OT and NT theology, dogmatic (or systematic) theology, moral theology, etc. (qq.v.). In short, 'theology' has become a generic term for a number of interrelated disciplines. But there is a widespread feeling abroad that such disciplines should not be regarded merely as an ivory tower for academics: theology must be related to life and is the concern of laymen. But this, after all, is a reaffirmation of what is involved in Locke's definition: theology is the comprehension of all other knowledge, directed to its true end.

EDITOR

Theonomy

An interpretation of man's moral life is theonomous if it finds the ultimate ethical authority in the divine will, as the principle of autonomy finds it in a law which is self-imposed and that of heteronomy in a law which comes from without. It cannot, however, be assumed that the whole truth does not include elements both of autonomy and of heteronomy or, in particular, of theonomy; and if this were the case these might well be regarded, respectively, as immanent and transcendent elements on the ethical side of theism.

N. H. G. ROBINSON

Theotokos. see Christology (4); Mary, The Blessed Virgin.

Thirty-Nine Articles of Religion

Confessions or statements of faith to which assent was demanded appeared in abundance during the Reformation period. In a time of impassioned and often bitter theological debate, when truth itself was believed to be at stake and when the affairs of Church and State were so inextricably mingled, it was frequently necessary to state a doctrinal position with clarity enough for it to be distinct and subtlety enough to allow for varied shades of opinion to be reconciled. The Church of England is peculiar among the reformed Churches in not producing a confession of the scope or authority of those of Augsburg or Westminster. From the beginning the attempts of the English Church to state its position were eirenical in intention. The *Ten Articles* of 1536 were meant 'to establish Christian quietness and unity among us and to

avoid contentious opinions'. They were interpreted in two official handbooks of instruction,
commonly known as the *Bishops' Book* (1537)
and the *King's Book* (1543), which leaned towards
the conservative side. Meanwhile theological discussions had been going on between the English
and continental Reformers, and after the death
of Henry VIII these bore fruit in the Forty-two
Articles which after much revision eventually
appeared in 1553 only a month before the death
of Edward VI. They criticized many parts of
mediaeval teaching and also the more extreme
antinomian and millennarian views of some
Reformers. They were dropped at the accession
of Mary and were further revised during the early
years of Elizabeth I by Convocation and finally
by the Queen herself. In their revised form the
Thirty-nine Articles were passed by Convocation
in 1571 and the text finally determined in 1604;
since when they have remained unchanged. The
present preface dates from 1628, reflecting the
growing sensitiveness to Puritan criticism in its
prohibition of any member of a university from
teaching anything other than the literal and
grammatical sense of the articles. Subscription is
still required from clergymen on their ordination,
and on taking up fresh ecclesiastical appointments,
and until the nineteenth century it was required
from members of universities proceeding to
degrees. In 1865 the form of assent was altered
to an assertion that the doctrine of the Church of
England set forth in the articles was agreeable to
the word of God. Further modification was proposed by the Archbishops' Commission on
Christian Doctrine in 1938.

It is difficult to assess either the permanent
theological value of the Articles or their place in
the life of the Anglican communion today. Both
the language which they employ and the points
of doctrine which they select for emphasis mark
them as belonging to their age. Conservative
evangelicals may regard them as an essential
safeguard and liberal churchmen as a stumbling
block, but it is hardly an exaggeration to say that
the vast majority of Anglicans are hardly aware of
their existence, and that if any is made aware of
them he receives a shock. Some of the more controversial statements of present interest are contained in these articles: I ('God . . . without body,
parts, or passions' – technically orthodox but
difficult to relate to biblical emphasis on the love
of God); XIII ('Works done before the grace of
Christ . . . have the nature of sin' – a case can be
made for this teaching from the Bible, but it is a
harsh message for a church which desires to co-
operate and to do good works with all men of good will);
XXI ('General Councils may not be gathered
together without the commandment and will of
Princes' – it is true as matter of history that in the
past councils have rarely been able to meet without the favour and sometimes the initiative of the
civil power, but few Christians today would want
to regard this as a principle); XXVIII ('Transubstantiation . . . is repugnant to the plain words of
Scripture' – it may be wrong to tie up the doctrine

of Christ's sacramental presence with a particular
philosophy and then impose the theory as a
doctrine, but the notion of 'change' in some sense
can hardly be said to be repugnant to the words
of Jesus as given in the NT. Article XXXVII is
offensive to pacifists, XXXIX to Quakers, and
many phrases allowable perhaps at the time are
now needlessly hurtful to Roman Catholics.

It will probably always be a matter for debate
how far the articles were deliberately ambiguous
in the interests of peace. John Bramhall, a distinguished theologian of the seventeenth century
who ended his career as archbishop of Armagh,
maintained that they were pious opinions fitted
for the preservation of unity. 'Neither do we
oblige any man to believe them, but only not to
contradict them.' Nor is it altogether clear, if they
were meant to describe a *via media*, between what
extremes they were steering. Clearly they repudiate some mediaeval theology, but it is not
certain that they are against the reformed teaching of the Council of Trent whose conclusions
were not finally published till after Convocation
had begun the revision of the articles. Newman in
Tract XC attempted to reconcile them with
Trent, and the task is not altogether impossible.
With equal clarity they dissociate the English
Church from some of the more extreme positions
of the Reformation, and subsequent Puritan
criticism indicates that they fall far short of pure
Calvinism. But Calvin and his own master
Augustine were the tutors of all English theologians of the time, and basically perhaps the
articles are concerned to preserve as many of the
new insights of reformed theology as possible
within a traditional ecclesiastical framework
under strong state control and to interpret them
in the light of the still more authoritative faith of
the early centuries. The same convocation that
approved the articles in 1571 instructed preachers
to teach only what was agreeable to the doctrines
of the OT and NT, and what the Catholic Fathers
and ancient bishops have collected from the same
doctrine.

E. J. Bicknell, *The Thirty-Nine Articles of the
Church of England*, ed., H. J. Carpenter, 3rd ed.
1955; H. E. Symonds, *The Council of Trent and
Anglican Formularies*, 1933.

R. CANT

Thomas Aquinas, St. *see* God (6, 7); Thomism; Averroism; Apologetics; Predestination (1).

Thomism

Thomism is often called Christian Aristotelianism. Provided that this is not understood to the
exclusion of other influences, especially of Proclus, the Pseudo-Dionysius and St Augustine, it
can be accepted. Even so, the system of St
Thomas Aquinas (1226–1274) is too distinctive
to be explained in terms of other outlooks.
Thomism marks a decisive break with previous

thinking in the West above all because St Thomas was the first to act systematically upon the recognition of the difference between the natural and the supernatural, human reason and revelation, the created and the divine. Whereas earlier thinkers, including his own master Albert the Great (c. 1206–1280), had posited two levels of knowledge, that which came through the senses for created things and some kind of divine inner illumination for higher necessary truths, St Thomas treated all human knowledge as sensory in origin: 'Nothing is in the intellect which has not first been in the senses.' By doing so St Thomas changed the foundation of metaphysics and natural theology. He sought to explain both creation and its relation to the creator in terms of categories drawn from experience, and largely taken over from Aristotle. Far from attempting to make the mysteries of faith susceptible to rational demonstration, St Thomas was more aware of the limits of natural knowledge than his predecessors. He was, it need hardly be stressed, a theologian concerned to utilize non-theological knowledge in the service of belief; what could not be known or inferred from natural experience, such as the creation of the world in time, belonged exclusively to faith. Reason was employed to supplement revelation, not to supplant it.

Central to this awareness of the limits of natural knowledge was that it had to start with what was naturally accessible to human experience. Since this world was the result of God's creation this meant that we could only know of it through its effects. In place of divine illumination for the awareness of higher necessary truths, St Thomas took over Aristotle's notion of abstraction as the source of all human knowledge. The mind, by its own natural powers, is able to recognize the intelligible forms and principles inherent in the individual things encountered in the senses. By isolating the universal elements contained within individuals the mind abstracts them from their material setting and restores them to their pure intelligibility, as species and principles, such as the 'humanity' in the individual man Socrates. From its knowledge of these concepts the mind is then able to form judgments about them, affirming, on the basis of its experience, what they are.

Now the most universal of all such concepts is the notion of being; it is the first intelligible by which everything else can be known. From it we are enabled to form a number of axioms which govern all our thinking. These are the principle of contradiction, that 'something cannot be affirmed and denied'; the principle of justification, 'that everything which is has its justification in itself, if it exists in itself, in another it does not exist in itself'; the principle of substance, 'that all that exists as the subject of existence is substance' and is distinguished from its accidents; the principle of efficient causality, that every contingent being, as dependent on another being, has an efficient cause; the principle of finality, that 'everything acts on account of an end', which in terms of ethics means seeking the good and shunning evil.

As for the nature of being itself, St Thomas transformed the traditional notions. These were in greater or lesser degree descended from St Augustine's strongly Platonic interpretation of reality as essence, with truth as the property of the ideas which inhered in the soul and were discovered with the help of divine illumination. It was to put the stress upon the intelligible and the mental order, the stability of whose images was contrasted with flux and uncertainty of sense impressions. St Thomas, however, abolished this dichotomy. Instead he turned to Aristotle's analysis of being as composed of form and matter. With Aristotle, St Thomas distinguished between matter, which was of itself mere potentiality, and form which conferred being upon the matter to which it was joined. The antinomy between non-being and being became the difference between potential being and actual being, it was resolved through the conjunction of matter and form. The effects of this conception were far-reaching. Being became identified with what actually existed as opposed to mere essence. The stone or the man only became such through the combination of form and matter. This meant in turn that, on the one hand, form conferred being: in St Thomas's words 'form gives being to the thing'; and on the other hand, that matter was the principle of individuation, that by which the form realized its own nature.

In the context of the time St Thomas's view of being reversed the accepted order. He dethroned essence for existence; he denied matter its own identity and its own form, and yet at the same time he made it 'the principle of diversity among individuals of the same species'. Above all, he displaced the plurality of forms, which had been commonly taken to constitute any one being, by a single substantial form. By positing being as coming through a single substantial form he was able to eliminate all the other forms which inhered in an individual. Thus in addition to dispensing with an independent form of matter (the so-called form of corporeity), he subsumed all the separate elements that composed an individual under the substantial form by which it was defined as a being, such as the humanity which defined man. In his own words: 'Therefore every created substance is composed of potentiality and act, that is, of that by which it is and being [form] . . . in the way that white is composed of that which is white and whiteness.'

The implications of this approach can be seen in St Thomas's treatment of both God and man. So far as God was concerned, St Thomas applied the same concepts of being to define him and his relation to creatures. Since only that which actually exists is the being, and all created being becomes actual by virtue of its substantial form, God must by definition be pure actuality; for unlike creatures which have to pass from potentiality to actuality, and so need an efficient cause to come into being, God by definition is self-caused. His existence must therefore be given in his essence. As supreme being he is; and whereas the form or essence of man does not entail his existence as the individual Socrates or Plato, in God essence and existence are synonymous. Thus to be God is to be at once first uncaused cause and absolutely simple being without potentiality or composition. This is what ontologically differentiates God from all creatures, including angels who, although they are without matter, are still composed of essence and existence.

To conceive God in these terms is to treat him by way of analogy and causality – as supreme being and first cause. One presupposes the other, since to define God in terms of first cause is to establish what can be said about him from the aspect of his creatures of whom he is the cause. Since this cannot refer directly to God in himself, who is unknowable, it must bear upon the resemblances which can be deduced from what is common to them, namely being and its modes. All things, in so far as they exist, are analogous as beings. Accordingly, from the dependence of a finite contingent being upon an uncaused being, it is possible to define the attributes of God in terms of being. Although there is an infinite gulf between divine and created being, since God is the cause of his creatures' existence, they receive their being from him. In that sense they may be said to participate in God's being, not as sharing his being but in holding their existence from his perfections. Thus the attributes of God's creatures are the results of the archetypes which inhere in him, and enable us to gain a faint glimmering of God's attributes, his omniscience, omnipotence, goodness, wisdom and so on. Although St Thomas rejected Anselm's ontological proof for God's existence, on the grounds that the mind can have no concept of God as infinite being, he adhered to the traditional Augustinian doctrine of divine ideas. They belonged to God's essence as the archetypes of all things. They receive their being only through God's act of willing them to come into existence: 'All things must pre-exist in the Word of God before they exist in their own nature.' They become actual only in so far as they are individuated through the joining of form and matter. Since it is in that condition that we encounter them, we can only establish their analogy with God by working back from individuals to their intelligible principles through abstraction in the way we have earlier described.

In the same way, St Thomas's five proofs for God's existence were drawn from the operations of created being. The first proof rests upon the axiom that 'all that is moved is moved by another': this must mean either an infinite chain of cause and effect or a first uncaused cause. Since there cannot be a regression to infinity there must be such a first cause which is God. The second proof begins from the series of efficient causes, each necessary to the other (e.g., a hand to push a stick); those, too, need a first cause to maintain their order; and this is God. The third proof followed from the distinction between necessary and contingent being, which we have already encountered. Necessary being has no cause but itself; but contingent being is dependent upon an external cause – which as necessary must be God. The fourth proof employs the idea of varying degrees of analogous qualities in things which, to be compared, presuppose an absolute source, which is God. The fifth proof is that of Aristotle's final cause: all things seek an end which actuates them; this can only be God as their author to whom they strive to return. Here, too, the sequence is from imperfect created being to the perfection and fullness of divine being. It is through their community as being that St Thomas was to explain the relation between God as the first cause moving his creatures from potentiality to act. It is here that they are analogous. This was to introduce not only a new conception of being but also a more defined degree of divine determinism in which God was to his creatures as first cause to secondary causes.

In the case of the higher intelligences, we have already indicated that St Thomas conceived angels as pure form, without even the spiritual matter with which many of his predecessors and contemporaries had endowed them. They were distinguished from God in being dependent upon him for their existence and so, being composite, with their essence distinct from their existence. Hence they differed both from him and from all other creatures which are corporeal. For this reason angels were nearer to species than individuals. They also were able to know reality directly, without the aid of discursive reasoning.

It was over his treatment of man that St Thomas reached some of his most controversial positions. To begin with, man can know only through abstraction; that made him rely upon the senses for all his knowledge. In the second place, St Thomas while fully stressing the spiritual nature of the soul, and its immortality as a spiritual being, conceived its relation to the body differently from all previous Christian thinkers. Where they, including Albert the Great, had followed St Augustine in treating it as a spiritual substance inhabiting the body and largely independent of it, St Thomas made the soul the form of the body. As such the soul at once defined man as a substance and give him actuality as a being. 'I say that there is no other substantial form in man than the intellective soul, and that as it contains virtually the sensitive and vegetative souls, so it contains virtually all inferior forms.' This was at one and the same time to cut across two of the most cherished Augustinian principles of the soul's autonomy and the plurality of forms within any being. Not surprisingly it aroused more opposition than any other of his conclusions. To his opponents it appeared that St Thomas had bound the soul to the body, making it dependent upon the senses for its understanding instead of its directing the body. This seemed to be confirmed by St Thomas's denial of divine illumination; man was thereby prevented from any direct contact with intelligible reality or an awareness of the divine truths within the soul. He could, as we have seen, only attain to first principles through sensory knowledge. This enabled St Thomas to dispense with the dualism between body and soul, sensory and intelligible, which had been the accompaniment of nearly all previous Christian thinking. But like all radical departures from tradition it came to be accepted only after widespread initial hostility.

St Thomas also departed from the Augustinian tradition over the primacy which he assigned to the intellect in moral actions. Man as an intelligent being apprehended the objects to which he inclined and so had the capacity to choose between them. In this lay his free will. Now the proper object of man's will was the supreme good. In his natural state, although it was the end to which he strove, he could not apprehend it in itself, but only as particular goods. To discover which of these was most closely related to the supreme good was the ceaseless concern of the intellect. Man's liberty consisted in trying to decide between particular goods and the means appropriate to attaining them. This involved a twofold process, of deliberation by the intellect and consent by the will, before a course of action could be followed. Through repetition of the same choices a moral habit is engendered, which in turn facilitates the performance of the appropriate action: when it is for good it is a virtue, when for evil a vice. The way each is acquired belongs to the history of each individual. Man can only act virtuously by the correct use of his reason which in its speculative aspect is to know the true and in its practical aspect is to know the good. Accordingly every act conforming to reason is good, for it agrees with man's rational nature; and conversely actions which contradict reason are evil. The rules of reason are binding commandments. They spring from the eternal law by which God's providence regulates the whole of creation and which is accessible to man through the natural law which bears its imprint. As man's being is a participation in God's being, so the natural law is a participation in the eternal law. In both cases St Thomas saw the complementarity between the divine and the created. As he expressed it 'grace does not abolish nature but perfects it'.

St Thomas's activities extended to the whole field of theology as well as to biblical exegesis, where he furthered the distinction between the literal and spiritual meaning which had been developed in the twelfth century. The immediate impact of his speculative doctrines, as we have indicated, was to engender controversy. Although he was canonized in 1323 he had to wait until the sixteenth century before his outlook became truly dominant. Since then, it has never been eclipsed. *See also* **God** (6, 7); **Duns Scotus.**

St Thomas wrote commentaries on many of Aristotle's works as well as on those of Proclus and the Pseudo-Dionysius. His three main theological writings are: *Commentary on the Sentences; The Summa against the Gentiles;* and *The Summa Theologica* (uncompleted). Among the many writings on Thomism the following will serve as useful introductions: F. C. Copleston, *Aquinas,* 1955; É Gilson, *Thomism,* 1962.

GORDON LEFF

Thomistic Analogy

The argument underlying Aquinas' discussion of the doctrine of the Trinity is virtually an elaboration of one form of the Psychological Analogy (q.v.) devised by Augustine, *mens, notitia, voluntas.* To establish the conclusion that there are two processions (but no more) in God, Aquinas argues that the procession of the Word resembles the action of the mind which reproduces specific resemblances, since what the intellect conceives is the likeness of what is understood. Since to be and to be understood are identical in God, the Word subsists in the same nature as God. The procession of the Spirit corresponds to another spiritual activity, the will exemplified in the coming forth of love whereby the loved is in the lover just as the thing expressed or understood is in the knower. These two activities are distinct from each other, and in the human self the priority always belongs to the intellect rather than to the will. Nothing can be in the will unless it is previously conceived in the mind (*see* **Procession[s]**). The form of the analogy is one of proportion and therefore intended not as a mere illustration of the Trinity but as something which determines the structure of the doctrine itself.

H. E. W. TURNER

Tillich, Paul

Tillich (1886–1965), Protestant systematic theologian, was born in Germany. He received the degree of Doctor of Philosophy from Breslau in 1911, and the Licentiate in Theology from Halle the next year. After war service as chaplain, he taught theology and philosophy at Berlin, Marburg, Dresden, Leipzig, and Frankfurt. Forced from his post because of his opposition to Hitler, be came to the USA to teach at Union Theological Seminary, New York, becoming Professor of Philosophical Theology. Following retirement, he taught at Harvard and Chicago. He has poured out books and articles over a period of more than half a century. His mature theological position is most fully stated in his *Systematic Theology* (3 vols., 1951, 1957, 1963).

Tillich has insisted that theology must deal honestly with the actual conditions of human existence. His method of correlation 'tries to correlate the questions implied in the situation with the answers implied in the (Christian) message' (*Systematic Theology,* I, p. 8). The world is so created, he has argued, that it embodies certain structures that find their correspondence in the mind of man. Human reason cannot answer the ultimate questions, but it can pose them, and the answers are given through revelation which comes to man through reason. Man's intellectual work cannot bring him to the ultimate, to being itself, or God – there will always be doubt. But just as the Christian concept of justification by grace through faith declares that man is accepted in spite of his unworthiness, so, according to Tillich, is he accepted in spite of his doubt. In the moment of utter separation and despair can come the experience of the paradoxical presence of the ultimate – this has led Tillich to the assertion that there is no truth without doubt and no doubt without truth. There is no realm of life which exists without being related to the unconditional.

Though Tillich has taken existential thought seriously, he presses beyond existential analysis to ontological affirmations, to the point of identity where the infinite reveals itself in the finite, where the split of subject and object is overcome. The search for lost identity in the ultimate union of the separated lies behind Tillich's work and has its philosophical basis in German classical philosophy, especially in F. W. J. von Schelling. Tillich has declared that man's sin is rooted in the estrangement of existence from essence, but he has acknowledged the final union of the ultimate with that from which it has been estranged. Man's separation from the ground of being, the Creator, thrusts him into loneliness and anxiety. But as man recognizes his true helpless and hopeless situation and seeks for the Christ, the 'New Being', there is the promise of salvation.

The picture of Jesus as the Christ in the Bible is that of the new creation, 'New Being' – the pivotal concept of Tillich's system. 'Jesus of Nazareth is the medium of the final revelation because he sacrifices himself completely to Jesus as the Christ' (*ibid.,* p. 136). In the Christ is an uninterrupted transparency to the ground of being so that all separation is overcome. The New Being is the power of salvation that liberates and transforms us so that we participate in new creation. This comes as sheer gift of grace: 'Reconciliation, reunion, resurrection – this is the New Creation, the New Being, the New state of things . . . A New state of things has appeared, it still appears; it is hidden and visible, it is there and it is here. Accept it, enter into it, let it grasp you' (*The New Being,* 1955, p. 24).

Tillich has developed his philosophical-theological system in continuous dialogue with scientists, artists, psychiatrists, and scholars of many disciplines. He has often said that 'religion is the substance of culture, culture is the form of religion' (*Theology of Culture,* 1959, p. 42). He has devoted much attention to myth, symbol and sacrament. His many writings have a penetration and a concern for synthesis that have made him one of the most widely-read and widely-debated thinkers of his time. Among his other better-known books are *The Courage to Be* (1952), *The Shaking of the Foundations* (1955), *Dynamics of Faith* (1957), *The Eternal Now* (1963), and *Christianity and the Encounter of the World Religions* (1963).

James Luther Adams, *Paul Tillich's Philosophy of Culture, Science and Religion,* 1965; K. Hamilton, *The System and the Gospel,* 1963; Charles W. Kegley and Robert W. Bretall, eds., *The Theology of Paul Tillich,* 1952; George H. Tavard, *Paul Tillich and the Christian Message,* 1962; J. Heywood Thomas, *Paul Tillich: An Appraisal,* 1963.

ROBERT T. HANDY

Time and Eternity

Ever since it was born, Christianity has been wrestling with the problem of time. At the centre of the gospel is the assertion that the time is fulfilled: God's unique act of deliverance has been brought about in Jesus Christ. This means that Christian thinkers have always been compelled to look both ways, backwards from the coming of Christ, and forwards to the future. The terms in which they have accomplished this have varied. In the NT itself the Hebrew conception of time greatly predominates; time is meaningful time, not clock time but the time in which God's action can be perceived by faith. Paul exactly expresses it in II Cor.6.2, when, quoting Isa.49.8, he says: 'Behold, now is the acceptable time; behold, now is the day of salvation.' But in at least two places in the NT other conceptions of time make their appearance: the author of the Epistle to the Hebrews, with his background of Alexandrian Neoplatonism, presents a strange amalgam of Moses' time and Plato's time. It is not always easy to tell whether the realm of reality in Hebrews means the eternally existing ideal heaven, or the heaven actually fulfilled and brought near in Christ. Also at the very end of the NT period, the author of II Peter, thinking in terms of clock time, is obviously puzzled at the prolongation of the day of salvation, and can only suggest that God's time is not like ours (*see* II Peter 3.3–10).

Ever since Christianity has had a vested interest in history. The very fact that so many significant books in the long chronicles of Christian theology have been connected with the problem of history would suggest this. Augustine's *The City of God* is primarily concerned with providing a Christian philosophy of history. History is an essential ingredient in Dante's *The Divine Comedy*. When Luther attacked the institutional Church of his day, he attacked in terms drawn from salvation history and called his work 'The Babylonish Captivity of the Church'. One of the most important works of our time, Reinhold Niebuhr's Gifford Lectures, *The Nature and Destiny of Man* (I, 1941 and II, 1943), is concerned with the nature and *destiny* of man. Some people even suggest that without the Hebraic-Christian tradition the very conception of history would never have emerged.

The Platonic tradition had a ready made answer to the problem of time: time is 'the moving image of eternity'; reality consists in having as little to do with movement as possible, therefore time is less real than eternity. Christian thought could not absorb this unmodified, as according to Christian belief God has immersed himself in time by means of the incarnation, or at least has compromised himself with time. But Scholastic thought represented God as knowing and experiencing all points of time simultaneously and thus avoided the great difficulties involved in attributing complete foreknowledge of events to God. This is a solution which is by no means obsolete today.

The post-Hegelian philosophy of the absolute reigned almost unchallenged in Europe until the early years of the twentieth century. It dealt very summarily with time and history. But the rejection of idealism, and the emergence of a vitalist philosophy such as Bergson's, and also of existentialist thought stemming from Kierkegaard, has meant that the problem of time has once more presented itself in an acute form to Christian theologians. In the last forty years Paul Tillich has attempted to do full justice to the Hebrew conception of time by means of his distinction between *kairos* and *chronos*. *Chronos* is clock time, time measured in seconds, minutes, hours, days, and years. But, says Tillich, history does not flow at an even pace: 'History has its ups and downs, its periods of speed and slowness, of extreme creativity and of conservative bondage to tradition' (*Systematic Theology*, III, p. 396). The coming of Jesus was the great *kairos* by which all other *kairoi* are to be judged. But there are other lesser *kairoi;* they occur whenever the prophetic Spirit is active in the churches; they can never be calculated, and can only be apprehended by means of vision, that is, an intuition akin to faith. There can also be false *kairoi,* for example, the period of Nazi supremacy in Germany. Human history is thus from the Christian point of view a series of lesser *kairoi,* all related to, and given power and significance by, the great *kairos* which was the manifestation of the Logos in history. Two other scholars have recently pursued this theme. Oscar Cullmann in *Christ and Time* has taken the extreme view that in Hebrew (and therefore also Christian) thought eternity is only time indefinitely prolonged; he denies any connection whatever with Greek conceptions of eternity. John Marsh quite independently reached a strictly modified version of this view: according to him the biblical writers do not see eternity as time indefinitely prolonged. They understand God's time as being different from our time. What is perhaps most valuable in John Marsh's presentation of the subject is his suggestion that both the biblical doctrine of predestination and the conception of the sacramental life in the NT are means by which we express for ourselves, and experience, the fact that eternity has entered into time. The logical and conceptual difficulties belonging to both these subjects are inevitable for those who believe that eternity and time have in some sense overlapped in the incarnation of the Word of God.

As for the Church's traditional teaching about the end of time, the last judgment, we may well quote John Baillie: 'There can be no complete consummation for the individual until there is a consummation also for society.' This is the significance of the symbol of the last judgment, for the end of time can no more be described in non-symbolic terms than can its beginning, the creation. Before and beyond the last judgment we are promised eternal life; this does not necessarily mean that we shall ultimately possess the same timelessness as God has. What our relation to time will be after this life is a mystery; we may well leave it with a reiteration of the conclusion of the author of II Peter: God's time is not like ours.

O. Cullmann, *Christ and Time*, ET 1951; John Marsh, *The Fulness of Time*, 1952.

A. T. HANSON

Tractarianism. *see* Oxford Movement.

Tradition

The word 'tradition' in ecclesiastical usage can have a number of different meanings. It can stand for the whole of Christianity considered as a complex of doctrines, practices, norms of behaviour, cult and religious experience, handed down from the beginning. It can be used to mean a particular strand of doctrine or of practice (as in 'the tradition of teaching about the Atonement', or 'the tradition of celebrating the Eucharist', or 'Lutheran tradition of preaching'); it can denote a piece or fund of information, whether historical or legendary, about a person or thing (as in 'the tradition that Peter was crucified upside down', or 'the tradition that Christ wrote a letter to Abgar king of Edessa'). But its proper and most widely accepted meaning is the teaching and practice of the Church, formally distinct from the words of Scripture, as this teaching and practice has been carried on continuously from the beginning. In this sense tradition is a necessary part of historical Christianity, and no Christian denomination or communion has existed, or could have existed, without tradition, because all have taught and lived the Christian faith. Even those who have attempted to exist without tradition have only succeeded in establishing a tradition of dispensing with tradition.

The important question is not, whether tradition exists, but what its relation is to other parts of the Christian faith. This question has usually been posed in the form of a decision about the relation of Scripture to tradition. It is impossible to avoid the conclusion that the tradition about Jesus existed in an oral form before the NT was written, and that oral tradition about Jesus continued to circulate in the Church for some time after the NT had been written, side by side with written tradition. Several early Church Fathers during the second half of the second century and the first half of the third appeal to something which they call the *rule of faith* or 'the rule of truth' or some similar name, and there is no doubt that this 'rule of faith' is formally distinct from Scripture, Irenaeus, Clement of Alexandria, Tertullian, Hippolytus, Origen and Novatian, and a few others, give it considerable prominence, and Irenaeus and Tertullian appear sometimes to regard it as in some circumstances a substitute for Scripture. Again, the Creed is another example of very early tradition whose origins were undoubtedly independent of the NT, that is the original, interrogatory, baptismal creed, one example of which ultimately became our 'Apostles'Creed'. The later conciliar creeds (such as our Nicene Creed), composed in the fourth and later centuries, are also, of course, examples of tradition, but not of tradition independent of Scripture, for they all profess to be interpretations of Scripture. Some have professed to find in the sacraments of baptism and of the eucharist, and some even in the Christian ministry, examples of tradition independent of Scripture, inasmuch as they all derive from a period prior to the writing of the NT. Some very ancient customs and practices in the Church have also been claimed by some to constitute original tradition independent of Scripture, such as the custom of turning to the East to pray, the practice of Christians crossing themselves, and the threefold interrogation in baptism.

The Roman Catholic account of tradition has since the formulation of the decrees of the Council of Trent (1545–63) usually taken the form of claiming that unwritten traditions formed a second, independent, original, authentic source of information and doctrine alongside of Scripture, capable of supplementing it, though never contradictory of it. The words used by the relevant part of the decree of Trent appeared to support this view (Session IV, April 1546), 'this truth and this discipline are contained in written books and in unwritten tradition'. Some confirmation of this opinion can be found in the words of some of the Fathers, and notably in the *De Spiritu Sancto* of Basil of Caesarea. But in recent years many theologians in the Roman communion have rejected this account of tradition, and have given a different interpretation both of the doctrine and of the words of the ⌐ouncil of Trent, claiming that the Roman Catholic view of this subject is that Scripture and tradition are identical in content though different in form and that therefore tradition is only formally, but not materially, independent of Scripture, a view which allows much more room for ecumenical discussion of the subject. The question may be said to be an open one in the Roman Catholic Church, because the Dogmatic Constitution on Divine Revelation of the Second Vatican Council (§§ 8 and 9) appears deliberately to have left it so. The Eastern Orthodox view of tradition is difficult to identify and to define, but it can be said with confidence that Orthodoxy would never regard tradition as supplementing Scripture nor as a source of truth of comparable authority to Scripture; it would, however, regard tradition as an immensely important part of the Christian faith, would hold that Scripture could only be understood by tradition, and would conceive of tradition rather in terms of a kind of life than a set doctrine. The Anglican attitude to tradition has from an early period in the history of the Church of England been clear and consistent, and can be identified both in the characteristic Anglican practice of expressing doctrine by means of liturgy and in Articles VI, VIII, XIX-XXI and XXXIV of the Thirty-nine Articles: tradition is to be accepted as a necessary part of the Christian faith, but tradition judged by and found agreeable to Scripture. Tradition is, in this view, the Church's interpretation of Scripture, and therefore cannot be independent of Scripture. Almost all the Churches of the Reformation have in fact accepted this view of tradition, though not all have been as explicit in stating this as has the Church of England. For instance, the Westminster Confession of Faith (1646) professes to reject all traditions of men in preference to Scripture but reproduces with approval the words of the Nicene Creed and the Chalcedonian Formula. Again, the Lutheran Augsburg Confession (1530) is most emphatic in endorsing the traditional dogmas of the undivided Church. On the subject of traditional practice and custom, however, where Scripture for the most part provides little or no light, different churches have differed very widely.

Closely associated with the subject of tradition is that of the *Development of Doctrine* (q.v.). This subject was brought into prominence by J. H. Newman (*Essay on the Development of Christian Doctrine*, 1845) who first realized its importance. He realized that the dogmatic definitions of the Church of the fourth and fifth centuries represented, not merely a logical unfolding of what was there already, but in some sense an addition of something new. He asked, what was to be the criterion of true development? His answer was, the development which took place within that church which could be shown to be the only true one, the Church of Rome. Any development thus guaranteed should be regarded as legitimate, and any such developments must be held to be consistent with Scripture and previous tradition because the Church of Rome said that it was. In this sense tradition could certainly be said to supplement Scripture and only just to fall short of constituting new revelation. Though many Roman Catholic theologians have been attracted by Newman's doctrine and have shown his influence in handling the subject of tradition, his view has never been officially adopted by the Roman Church. Other churches have repudiated Newman's doctrine, but no theologian of a Reformed tradition has yet produced a satisfactory or generally acceptable explanation of the development of doctrine.

In fact, much of what is claimed to be original tradition independent of Scripture can be shown not to be so. Significant, authentic oral tradition had virtually died out by about 250, unable to withstand the influence of the written tradition of the NT. The 'rule of faith' was a summary, in the form of articles, of the Christian faith as preached and taught in the church of the writer who referred to it, in substance the same everywhere but varying a little according to local differences. All the Fathers agree that its content is identical with that of Scripture and all (even Irenaeus and Tertullian) appeal to Scriptural texts to confirm it. The baptismal creed in the early centuries is so meagre and bare in its substance as to constitute no serious rival to or supplement of Scripture. Baptism, the eucharist and the ministry antedate the NT, but without the NT our knowledge of them would be so uncertain and indefinite as to render them useless as vehicles of tradition. As a source of original information independent of Scripture, tradition is useless.

But as a necessary part of living, historical, developing Christianity, tradition is essential and deserves the considerable attention which it is now commanding from theologians of many denominations. In particular, the role of tradition in the interpretation of Scripture is of capital importance for both Catholics and Protestants. That which creates a sense of unity among different churches today in spite of their divisions, and has made possible the Ecumenical Movement, is not the awareness of a common allegiance to Scripture, but the sense of sharing a common tradition deriving from the period of the undivided Church. An appreciation of the necessity, the limits, and the proper function of tradition is essential for all parties in the ecumenical debate.

Y. Congar, *Tradition and Traditions*, 1966; R. P. C. Hanson, *Tradition in the Early Church*, 1962; J. H. Newman, *Essay on the Development of Christian Doctrine*, 1845; G. Salmon, *The Infallibility of the Church*, 1923 (last unabridged ed.); G. Tavard, *Holy Writ and Holy Church*, 1959.

R. P. C. HANSON

Traducianism. *see* Creationism.

Transcendence

This word is derived from the Latin and means to 'go beyond'. Thus, belief in transcendence involves believing that there is a realm of being which exceeds human powers of grasp, save perhaps in mysticism (as in Neoplatonism) or indirectly (as, e.g. by way of analogy, q.v.). Scholastic philosophy would hold (with Aquinas) that human reason can know *that* it is but not *what* it is. Other theologians (e.g. Barth) would assert that we can know nothing of a transcendent Being apart from the gracious self-revelation of that Being. Most Christian philosophers and theologians, while disagreeing with Barth's exclusive definition of revelation in terms of the Word (or Bible) alone, would agree that access to a transcendental realm of being can be gained only through divine assistance: hence the importance of the category of revelation in theological thinking. Certain 'radical' (q.v.) theologians (but not all) would deny the utility of the idea of transcendence for Christian thought and life and would advocate a 'secular Christianity'

(q.v.) which is concerned only with this world and this life; the notion of transcendence is thus repudiated, at least in its traditional forms. Such a repudiation, however, does not imply a belief in the opposite of transcendence, namely, immanence (e.g. pantheism, q.v.); in fact, it would logically seem to dispense with it, since transcendence and immanence are *logical* opposites (like convex and concave). Some contemporary theologians (*see* e.g. **Process Theology**) have attempted new ways of holding the two concepts in balance. It would seem true to say that, if transcendence is denied, Christian theology in its classical forms must be abandoned, since a wholly immanent God, if not a logical absurdity, could not be God in any recognizable sense, but only a force or tendency within the universe itself, or perhaps even only a name we give to our aspirations and ideals. In the current discussion of transcendence it would seem profitable first to look for the experience of transcendence in human life, e.g. the transcendence of our limitations, such as time, in the ability of the mathematician to grasp in one moment of cognition a long and complicated sequence of equations, each of which requires a separate logical thought-process; or the musician's ability to grasp a whole symphony in one transcendental act of cognitive appreciation, and so on. *See also* **Transcendent(al): God** (10).

EDITOR

Transcendent Fall

The transcendent fall is a view, found for example in Platonism and Gnosticism, that sees man's earthly creation itself as a fall from a transcendent state of goodness. The originally pure soul, having fallen from its heavenly realm, is imprisoned in the impure flesh of the human body. There are some hints of this viewpoint in Origen's doctrine of a premundane fall (*see* **Premundane Fall**). When, in modern times, it became impossible to regard the story of Adam and Eve as a history of the first man and woman, some theologians attempted to substitute for it the concept of a transcendent fall. There are hints of it in N. Berdyaev, and E. Brunner once held the view although he later repudiated it. Some critics have charged that P. Tillich had a view of a transcendent fall in his theory that man's coming into being is his fall from his essence into existential estrangement.

The transcendent fall is basically incompatible with the Christian faith. It contradicts the Christian view that God's creation of the material world and man is a good creation. It implies that man's problem is not that he is a sinner but that he is a man. Almost inevitably a view of a transcendent fall must lead to the belief that man is primarily in need of being saved from the material universe and from his body.

WILLIAM HORDERN

Transcendent(al)

In modern philosophical usage 'transcendent' is often used to describe those objects which are beyond the range of human cognition and hence are strictly unknowable. This usage follows Kant's conception of a 'noumenal' realm, the *Ding-an-sich* or thing-in-itself which cannot be perceived or explored by human cognitive faculties. In Scholastic philosophy 'the transcendentals' (*transcendentalia*), so called because they went beyond Aristotle's categories, were held to be the properties common to all objects whatsoever, including God. Aquinas listed six such properties belonging to all objects, though in widely different degrees in the objects which totally make up the Great Chain of Being: *res* (reality), *ens* (being), *verum* (truth), *bonum* (goodness or perfection), *aliquid* (specific character), *unum* (unity or identity). Since these properties are common both to God and to other existences, the *transcendentalia* could be a means of analogical knowledge of God. Many modern theologians would wish to add that holiness, though not a property of all objects as such, is a biblical characteristic of the transcendent being of God and has its analogues in human experience; it is perhaps in the awareness of the holy that our most convincing evidence of transcendence is to be found. *See* **Experience, Religious.**

EDITOR

Transmigration of Souls. *see* Reincarnation.

Transubstantiation

Since the latter part of the twelfth century the word *transsubstantiatio* has been used in the West to denote the conversion of the whole substance of the bread and of the wine in the Eucharist into the whole substance of the body and blood of Christ respectively. At the fourth Lateran Council in 1215 the verb *transsubstantiari* in this context was formally defined (Denzinger 430), and at the Council of Trent in 1551 the noun *transsubstantiatio* (Denz. 877). In the thirteenth century the doctrine had been expressed in terms of Aristotelian philosophy by St Thomas Aquinas (*Summa Theologica*, 3.75–77), according to whom the 'accidents' of the bread and wine remain without the corresponding substances, having as their subject the 'spatial extension' (*quantitas dimensiva*). It is generally agreed that St Thomas avoids any crude 'Capernaite' view of the presence (the reference is to John 6.52 ff.), though the same cannot perhaps be said of all mediaeval theologians and popular expositors; following St Thomas Roman Catholic theologians in general insist strongly that the change (*conversio*) of the bread and wine is not an annihilation. Trent, while emphasizing the change of substance, avoids reference to the 'accidents' altogether and speaks in less technical terms of the 'appearances' (*species*).

The Anglican Article XXVIII rejects 'transubstantiation' as 'overthrowing the nature of a sacrament', an accusation which certainly does not hold against St Thomas and only very doubtfully against Trent. However, it has been argued that the Article was written in the context of late mediaeval nominalist philosophy, for which any distinction between substance and accidents was unintelligible and for which transubstantiation, which was accepted not as a rational doctrine but in sheer obedience to the authority of the Church, could only involve that the appearance of bread and wine was a pure illusion.

The Eastern Orthodox Church copied the West in adopting the term *metousiosis*, and this was formerly defined by the Synod of Jerusalem in 1672. Some writers have tried to distinguish between this term and the Western *transsubstantiatio* and have translated it by 'transessentiation'. It must, however, be admitted that, since the fourth century at latest, *ousia* and *substantia* have been accepted as identical (thus; *mia ousia*= *una substantia* of the Trinity; *homoousios*= *consubstantialis* in the Nicene Creed), so the distinction seems untenable. *See also* **Concomitance; Eucharist.**

H. E. Symonds, *The Council of Trent and Anglican Formularies*, 1933, ch. vi.

E. L. MASCALL

Trent, Council of

The Council was assembled by Pope Paul III and met under the presidency of papal legates. Sessions i to viii were held at Trent from 13 December 1545 to 11 March 1547. Against the Emperor's wish it was then removed to Bologna where sessions ix and x took place from 21 April 1547 to 23 January 1548. It was resumed at Trent on 1 May 1551 in the pontificate of Julius III and to 28 April 1552 held sessions xi to xvi. Its final period, under Pius IV, was from 18 January 1562 to 4 December 1563. Procedures were slowed by disagreements, particularly between prelates representing the papal and the imperial interests. Protestant states sent delegates in 1551, but their demand that the Council, following that of Constance, have superiority to the pope, was dismissed. The chief theological decisions set forth in the Council's Canons and Decrees were specifically framed to combat Protestant statements. The Apocryphal Books, Tobit, Judith, Wisdom, Ecclesiasticus, I and II Maccabees, were included in Holy Scripture, while an equal veneration is professed for 'the unwritten traditions' received by the apostles from Christ or from the Holy Spirit which have been preserved in the Church; and the Vulgate, Latin version of Scripture, alone is held authoritative. The merit of good works, which are the fruit of justification, is strongly affirmed. The seven sacraments are expounded in detail. In the decree on the Eucharist it is taught that 'as much is contained under each species as under both'. Transubstantiation is asserted in Thomist terms and both veneration and reservation of the host are approved. To each of the twenty-five decrees is added a series of canons in which those holding opposing doctrines are anathematized. The decree on Holy Orders, a field of keen debate, makes bishops successors of the Apostles, but they are not said to derive their authority from Christ.

P. Schaff, *Creeds of Christendom*, I, III, 1919; H. Jedin, *History of the Council of Trent*, ET, I, 1957, II, 1961.

J. T. MCNEILL

Tridentine

An adjective meaning 'pertaining to the *Concilium Tridentinum*', i.e. the Council of Trent (q.v.), 1545–63.

Trinity, Doctrine of the

The doctrine of the Trinity is an attempt to draw out the implications of the biblical revelation of God, Father, Son and Holy Spirit. It is not contained formally in Scripture but is both an inference and a construct from the Bible. Its starting-point is salvation-history, the fact of Christ incarnate, crucified and risen and the coming of the Spirit at Pentecost and his continuing impact on the Church and in the world. The structure of the NT is basically triadic and it is verified in the three aspects of the Christian experience of God, dominion, communion and possession. These are closely linked with the decisive moments of revelation, God over us, God with us and God in us, and together exhaust the spiritual possibilities of knowing God. The Essential Trinity (q.v.) of theology proved itself the only adequate framework for these data.

The problem posed for the Church for apologetic and domestic reasons was how to do justice to the new facts and yet retain its status as a monotheistic religion. Could God be both one and many? Could the Church provide both for the unity of God and the divinity of Christ? Could monotheism be expanded without being exploded? Since the fact of Christ made the question inescapable, the problem was first discussed in relation to the Father and the Son. But the impression of binitarianism (q.v.) given by much second- and third-century thought is largely accidental. A theologian may express his doctrine in twofold terms and yet elsewhere use triadic formulae without obvious embarrassment. Accidental binitarianism of this type did not lead to the abandonment of trinitarian baptism. The doctrine of the Spirit awaited later consideration. It developed in the fourth century under the lee of the doctrine of the Son. Two different theological approaches were open. Monist theologians started from the unity of the Godhead and worked tentatively towards divine plurality. Their chief interest lay in the identity of Father and Son in revelation and redemption and they assigned the priority in their assessment to the religious data. Pluralist thinkers, on the other hand, maintained the full co-presence of two (later three) distinct entities within the Godhead and sought a bond of unity strong enough to support their convictions. Unity of derivation from the Father (the Monarchy), harmony of will and finally identity of substance, *Ousia* (*Homoousios*), were

all laid under contribution. Their main concern was to reconcile Christianity and Hellenism and their philosophical background owed much to Middle- and Neoplatonism. Two false trails which they followed had precedents in Greek philosophy; subordinationism (compare the graded hierarchy of Being in Platonism) which sought to provide a greater unity by reducing the status of the Son as compared with the Father, and binitarianism (Greek philosophy had no independent doctrine of the Spirit beside the Logos) which absorbed the functions of the Spirit in the Son, through the medium of the Logos concept. Both terms describe starting-points and pressures of thought. Neither is heretical in itself though each could easily lead to inadequate or ill-balanced formulations.

Some early forms of monism require brief discussion. Modalism (q.v.) spread from Asia Minor to Rome in the second century and made a strong bid to capture the Roman Church. Its aim was to unite within a single theory two facts for which the Church found great difficulty in making simultaneous theological provision, the unity of God and the divinity of Christ. Earlier devotional language had spoken of the sufferings of Christ as 'the passion of God' or 'the passion of my God'. Modalism sought to provide theologically for this by turning solidarity in operation into virtual identity. 'When the Father deigns to be born and to suffer, he is the Son' (Noetus). The status of the divine differentiations was modes or manifestations of the one God. If modalism initially spoke of two modes, this was purely accidental, and later developments extended the theory to cover three modes. It does not seem, however, that at any stage the two or three modes were made simultaneous rather than successive. Modalism provided for the unity but not for the plurality of God and by its failure to provide for the stability of God endangered his essential divinity.

A second monist theory was economic trinitarianism (q.v.). Instead of modes it described the divine differentiations as economies or dispensations extrapolated for the purposes of creation and redemption. Like modalism this theory gave priority to the divine unity but regarded the economies as permanent from the time of their extrapolation. Language of this type is found in Theophilus of Antioch, Irenaeus and Novatian. It played an important part in Tertullian (q.v.) and probably Paul of Samosata (q.v.). It reaches its most sophisticated form in Marcellus of Ancyra (q.v.) with precisely dated extrapolations and the return of the Godhead into monadic isolation at the conclusion of the economy. The last feature is unique to Marcellus. The criticisms which had previously been made of modalism are hardly less relevant here. The economies have greater stability and a slightly improved status but little more. The support given by Marcellus to the *Homoousios* at Nicea was to cause considerable embarrassment to the orthodox party.

From Tertullian to Augustine the West adopted a firmly Monist starting-point. The unity of the Godhead was the touchstone of Western orthodoxy. It is no accident that modalism made a stronger appeal to the West than tritheism, the opposite extreme limit of trinitarian thought. The West even accepted Marcellus into communion after his rejection by the East and refused to modify its verdict even in the interest of Nicene unity. Tertullian (q.v.) was the 'Phrasemaker of the Western Church' whose formula 'One substance, three Persons' has stood the test of time. Yet neither his technical terms nor their theological framework is as mature as has often been thought. More important than the legal (Harnack) or the Aristotelian (E. Evans) background of *substantia* is the Stoic doctrine of substance as the material ground-stuff of existence (Braun) described as spirit in the case of God. This the Father possesses in its totality, but a share (*portio*) is extended to the Son. *Persona* is understood in a less unusual way. It represents the discrete individuality informing the one substance and crystallizes Tertullian's opposition to modalism. Certainly he aims at a balanced formula, yet his own thought verges on economic trinitarianism and has not yet achieved an essential Trinity (q.v.). His key concept is the monarchy of God (both as sole fount of deity and sole ruler). The Father retains the sovereignty but entrusts its administration to the Son. Economy and dispensation are both terms used in this connection. The Son occupies the second, the Spirit the third place in a graded hierarchy of Being, anchored in the unity of substance which both share with the Father, though dependent upon the exigencies of creation and redemption. Tertullian's Trinity is economic and functional, not essential and ontological.

In the East pluralism based upon a Platonic interpretation of Christianity became the dominant tradition. The Logos conception led Justin to the notion of a 'second God in number not in will'. As an intermediary between the transcendent God and the relative universe, the Logos must be distinct and separable from the Father and for the same reason tended to slip imperceptibly towards creation (subordinationism). Partly to economize the *Hypostases*, partly because in Greek thought the Logos absorbed the attributes of the Spirit, a more theologically deliberate binitarianism made itself felt.

This tradition was put into working order by Origen who combined a firm grasp both of Greek philosophy and of church teaching. His trinitarian theology was pluralist in framework. Father and Son were two in *Hypostasis*, one in harmony and identity of will. The Son is different in *Ousia* from the Father where *Ousia* is used in the second Aristotelian sense of the word, the individual member of a class. His principal emphasis is co-ordinationist pluralism, the doctrine of the eternal generation of the Son by the Father understood as an eternally continuous process. A fragment preserved only in Latin uses the *Homoousios* in the sense of the possession both by the Father and the Son of a common generic character (the first Aristotelian sense of the word). The term then occurs in both Aristotelian senses in his writings. He includes the Spirit in his theology but notes that agreement had not been reached about the appropriate technical terms in which the discussion should be conducted. So far Origen's stature as a theologian working within the rule of faith is high. Yet subordinationist expressions also occur. The term 'creature' does not occur in his writings preserved in Greek but is ascribed to him by Justinian. He draws similar conclusions from the titles which Origen applied to the Father and the Son. The Father is Very God, the Son is God. The Father is beyond Being, the Son has his appropriate sphere of operations in Being, the Spirit in the Church, as though in a series of concentric circles of diminishing size. Here we meet Origen the Neoplatonist philosopher. The former strain better represents his real thought, the latter is more sporadic but big with menace for the future. The doctrine of the eternal generation of the Son by the Father is his permanent contribution to theology, yet Origen is the ancestor both of the Cappadocian Fathers and their Arian opponents.

Arius took the subordinationist expressions of Origen as the basis for a complete system. The Father alone is God since he alone is ingenerate (q.v.). Since the Son is generate (q.v.) he could not be fully God. He was different in substance from the Father, not only as a separate concrete particular (Origen) but as lacking a common generic character. On the analogy of human generation Arius argued that 'there was a time when the Son was not'. He was a 'creature but not as one of the creatures', though he enjoyed a special relationship of dependence upon the divine will. The Spirit was on an even lower plane than the Son. If he were God, there would be one grandson or two brothers in the Godhead, which would be absurd. Arius, it seems, extended the category of generation to the Spirit as well as to the Son. His triad, combined within a single formula, left the principle of their inclusion doubtful. Arius claimed to defend monotheism on strict metaphysical premises; the result was an archetypal form of tritheism. The intervention of Constantine turned a theological dispute into high politics. Few churchmen believed the teaching of Arius to be satisfactory. His exclusion from the Church on grounds of truth was inevitable. For the Emperor it was a question not simply of the faith of the Church but the unity of the Empire. The State no less than the Church was involved in the terms of exclusion. The Council of Nicea (325) was the first example of a General (state-sponsored) Council. Its membership came mainly from the East. Some Bishops were confessors who had suffered under but survived the last persecution. Many were Origenists of the right, holding the co-ordinationist pluralism of their master; a handful were Origenists of the left, holding subordinationism in varying degrees.

An important minority like Eustathius and Marcellus were monists with stronger links with Paul of Samosata than with his Origenist opponents. Scriptural terms were proposed for introduction into the Creed but proved too wide to exclude Arianism. With imperial support, and possibly on the suggestion of Ossius of Cordova (the Emperor's ecclesiastical adviser), the term *Homoousios* was finally adopted. It represented the Western phrase *una substantia*, but in the East, owing to the long-standing ambiguity in the term *Ousia*, it could bear one of two meanings. Either it could imply that Father and Son possessed a common generic character (as the term had been used by the Valentinians, by Origen probably and by later Origenists) or that the Father and the Son formed in some sense a single concrete particular. In 268 the Origenist opponents of Paul of Samosata used the word in the first sense, but according to Hilary, Paul himself chose the second meaning. Certainly Marcellus and possibly Eustathius among the monist champions of the term at Nicea understood it in this sense. In either case it would exclude Arius but Origenists who were not Arians might well wonder whether acceptance of the term might involve the rehabilitation of Paul of Samosata, acceptance of Marcellus and the implicit abandonment of Origenism. The term was unpopular even at Nicea but the Emperor, while willing to countenance the exile of its leading supporters (Marcellus and Eustathius, both accused of Sabellianism, and Athanasius), refused to abandon the term. What he wanted was peace, not doctrinal agreement; signatures would serve his turn. Theologically the victory of the *Homoousios* was a surprise attack, not a solid conquest.

Constantine no sooner dead, attempts were made to find an alternative. By 360 new alignments had emerged. The Arians had regrouped into two wings, the Anhomoeans (q.v.) claiming that the Son was 'utterly unlike the Father' and the Homoeans (q.v.), the moderate wing who could accept that 'the Son was like the Father' with the honorific additions 'in all respects' or 'according to the Scriptures'. The former concealed a latent contradiction, the latter begged the question of the implications of the biblical revelation. At the suggestion of Acacius of Caesarea this formula was taken up by the Emperor Constantius as a compromise which might unite the Church. It figures in a series of Creeds adopted by Councils in 359 and 360 with an appended note banning the use of *Ousia* and *Hypostasis*. Of the enforcement of this policy Jerome wrote 'the whole world groaned to find itself Arian'.

The new formula excluded not only extreme Arians and full Nicenes but also the *Homoiousians* (q.v.), a new party under the leadership of Basil of Ancyra, standing nearer to the Nicene than to the Arian position. In their manifesto of 358 they rejected the *Homoousios* partly as a human invention (an objection to which their alternative was equally exposed) and partly because it could

not in their view adequately provide for the divine plurality and proposed the *Homoiousios* (of like substance). Gibbon's jibe on the dispute over a diphthong which divided the orthodox ignores the vital difference between 'the same' (*homos*) and 'like' (*homoios*) when applied to the anchor word for the divine unity.

The way forward lay rather with the Cappadocian Fathers (q.v.) As Origenists they were able to convince the Semi-Nicenes that the *Homoousios* was reconcilable with pluralism and that the answer to their problem lay not in weakening the term but in strengthening the doctrine of the three *Hypostases*. This change of emphasis is misrepresented by Harnack's dictum that they played a practical joke on the Church by securing the universal acceptance of the *Homoousios* but in the sense of the *Homoiousios*. The movement was not of the Nicenes to semi-Nicenism but in the reverse direction. As leaders of the Nicene revival the Cappadocians were the determined foes of Arianism, Sabellianism (q.v.) and Macedonianism (q.v.). Their theology was legitimized by the Council of Constantinople (381).

1. Against the Arians they provided a better mapwork for the doctrine of the Trinity which ousted the Arian dialectic by providing a more adequate substitute. Using the logical distinction between universals and particulars, they defined the universal of the Trinity as uncreatedness and Godhead and the modes of being or differentiating particularities of the three particulars as ingeneracy, generation and procession (qq.v.) respectively. This challenged the Arian premiss that the Father alone was God because he alone was ingenerate and the selection of a new category for the Holy Spirit destroyed the Arian quibble about grandson or brothers in the Godhead. The Arians spoke as if ingeneracy was self-evidently clear, the Cappadocians recognized that all three categories (if indispensable) were equally ineffable.

2. Against the Macedonians or Pneumatomachi they brought the doctrine of the Holy Spirit to a new pitch of development. Gregory of Nazianzus even adopted a theory of development to explain its late emergence. In the OT the Father is revealed, the Son hinted at; in the NT the Son is fully revealed, the Spirit adumbrated. The times of the Church have brought the doctrine of the Spirit to full development. Against the Tropici (of uncertain doctrinal affiliation, possibly Arian) in Egypt Athanasius had argued for the full divinity of the Spirit from his scriptural functions. The Lord and Lifegiver could not be *Homoousios* with those to whom he gives life. Against the Macedonians Basil argues from tradition (the baptismal formula, doxology) that the unity in glory and worship of the Spirit with the Father and the Son must imply his full deity. Gregory of Nazianzus adds the further point, which Basil omits, that he must therefore be *Homoousios*. In harmony with their emphasis on the derivation of the whole Trinity from the Father they speak of the procession of the Spirit as from the Father, though

Gregory of Nyssa outlines two phrasings of the relationship of the Son to the Spirit which will concern us at a later stage.

3. They introduced much-needed clarification into trinitarian terminology restricting *Ousia* to that wherein the Godhead was one, *Hypostasis* to that wherein the Godhead was three. Basil in particular avoided the use of *Prosopon* (q.v.) which he believed to have Sabellian associations. As pluralists in theology they start from the *Hypostases* broadly identical with the modern Person. They are three distinct entities within the one God, and the analogy of three men (Peter, James and John) can be used in this connection (*see* **Social Analogy**). The charge of tritheism (q.v.) has often been raised against them even in their own day but without solid ground. Gregory of Nyssa wrote a reply, *Quod non sint tres dii.* The *Homoousios*, used rather in a qualitative than a quantitative sense, is vital to their system. The three *Hypostases* share one will and activity, one glory and worship. They maintained the unity of derivation (monarchy) and, more significantly, the coinherence (q.v.) of the Trinity. Each *Hypostasis* indwells and reciprocates with the other two.

The Cappadocians are often charged with being logicians and metaphysicians akin to the Arians in their methods though diverse in their conclusions. The real nerve of their theology, however, lies deeper. The Trinity is a worshipful whole of three *Hypostases* related in a single *Ousia*, a vast storehouse of Divine Being and energy in a threefold self-differentiation. A parallel stage in Western theology was reached by Augustine, whose doctrine was almost the exact obverse of the Cappadocian Fathers. Their starting point was pluralist, his (like all Westerners) was monist. Their problematic was, therefore, different. The Cappadocians, starting from the three *Hypostases*, found the need to pay special attention to the divine unity. Augustine, who never lost sight of the unity, found himself in difficulties over the status of the persons. Both reached an essential or immanent Trinity but from different angles and with different pressures. While the Cappadocians made great use of logic and metaphysics, Augustine worked from the mysticism of love. Augustine is rich and profound, the Cappadocians clear and precise. Yet the distinction must not be pressed too hard. Both can use the principle of coinherence, more tightly geared into his total system in Augustine, and both can appeal to the divine mystery of Being, again in Augustine with greater confidence.

The One God is Trinity. He is, therefore, not 'simplex', though Augustine (unlike Victorinus) will not describe him as 'triplex', presumably as implying too great a measure of triplicity. The trinitarian God is one substance, nature, majesty, operation and will. Since the operations of the Trinity are inseparable (*see* opera ad extra) any qualitative differentiation of the Godhead is excluded. The whole Godhead is operative in each Person. Thus the Procession of the Spirit must be from the Father and the Son. Each divine person seen from the side of substance is identical with the others and with the whole divine substance. The comparison with three human persons is, therefore, excluded, and Augustine finds his analogies within the compass of a single human person (*see* **Psychological Analogy**). The *Homoousios*, therefore, raises no problem. Yet Augustine accepts the principle of Appropriation (q.v.) provided that it is balanced by co-operation and coinherence. The first part of the *Quicunque Vult* is unswervingly true to this insight of Augustinian theology.

But three Persons are equally basic to the Church's faith. Here Augustine encounters greater difficulties. The term is used not that a precise statement may be made but lest silence be kept altogether. The Persons are by definition not substance, neither are they accidents (this is excluded by the immutability of God) but relations. They are relative and reciprocal (*ad invicem, ad alterutrum*). Since they are relations of God they must be eternal and immanent. Unlike Tertullian, Augustine maintains an essential Trinity. Thus the One God is never only Father or only Son or only Spirit. These are three mutually reciprocal relations in the One God. Father and Son know each other mutually, the one by begetting, the other by being born. The Spirit is the *communio*, the bond of love (*vinculum amoris*) between the Father and the Son. The principle of Coinherence is not, as with the Cappadocians, an adjunct to a system virtually complete without it; it is the very heart of Augustinian Trinitarianism. Relation plays the same part in Augustinianism as *Hypostasis* in Cappadocian theology. Each proved determinative for the future history of their traditions.

The area of conflict between the two traditions centred in the theology of the procession of the Spirit, whether single (from the Father) or double (from the Father and the Son). The biblical data employed in this connection are mainly drawn from the Fourth Gospel. The Spirit proceeds from the Father (John 15.26) but he also receives from the Son (John 16.14) or is sent by the Son (John 14.16; 15.28; 16.7). Elsewhere in the NT he is described as the Spirit of Christ as well as the Spirit of God. The problem was how to combine these data into a single theological formula. The original text of the Niceno-Constantinopolitan Creed (C) reads 'Who proceedeth from the Father', the form still used universally in the East. The later Western version (our Nicene Creed) adds the words 'and the Son *(Filioque)*'. Between the two lie different theologies and many centuries of tangled and sometimes bitter history.

1. The original clause in C reflects Cappadocian concern for the unity of derivation of the Trinity from the Father, though in his doctrinal writings Gregory of Nyssa in particular attempted to do justice to the other Johannine passages. Later Eastern criticism of the *Filioque* reveals the fear that it might imply a Dyarchy of origin for the Spirit which would endanger the unity of the Godhead on pluralist premisses. This credal con-

servatism or the refusal to insert all that might be believed theologically, to which a later pope called approving attention, has an even more striking parallel in the failure in the same article to repeat the *Homoousios* of the Spirit. Despite the explicit use of the term by Gregory of Nazianzus, the Creed rests content with Basil's formula, 'Who with the Father and the Son is worshipped and glorified', the previous step in the argument. The desire to avoid another Arian controversy on the Holy Spirit is the most likely explanation. An important group of Antiochene thinkers (Theodore of Mopsuestia, Nestorius and Theodoret) refused to go further in their theology than the Article in the Creed, partly for christological reasons, and partly through hostility to Cyril of Alexandria (q.v.).

2. Most Eastern Fathers, however, tried in their theology to combine the doctrine of the single Procession with a phrase indicative of the role of the Son. This was a matter of experiment, and alternative phrasings occur in the writings of the same Father without significant difference of meaning. No attempt to alter the clause in the creed was ever made in the East. Two forms of theological expression were used. The first (which proved rather unhandy) distinguished the respective roles of Father and Son by the use of different verbs. 'Proceed' was reserved for the Father and weaker verbs like 'receive' (Gregory of Nyssa, Didymus, Epiphanius) or 'send' (Athanasius) used of the Son. A neater mode of expression used the single verb 'proceed' and distinguished the respective roles of the Father and the Son by using different prepositions, '*from* the Father *through* the Son' (Basil, Gregory of Nyssa, Cyril of Alexandria and uniformly in the later Eastern tradition). The most complex statement of this kind occurs in Gregory of Nyssa who regards the Son as the intermediary of the Trinity. The Son is caused directly by the Father, the Spirit through the One who was directly from the Father.

3. The West spoke roundly of the Spirit as 'proceeding from the Father and the Son'. The sources of this formula are Hilary and Victorinus but above all, Augustine, for whom it is a necessary corollary of his tightly drawn doctrine of the persons as relations. As a monist (unlike the Cappadocians) he was not preoccupied with safeguarding the divine unity which was never in jeopardy. The only Eastern parallels to this phrase are Epiphanius and Cyril of Alexandria, both of whom also use other formulae as well.

Preference in theological emphasis and language are one thing, alterations in a canonical creed quite another. Since the *Filioque* represents the unanimous tradition in the West, it was inevitably incorporated into local Western Conciliar statements. It first occurs in a series of documents of the fourth and fifth centuries directed against Priscillianism (q.v.), though the text of C used at the first and fourth Councils of Toledo (400, 589) is the unaltered version. While the introduction of the *Filioque* into the version of C used in Spain cannot be precisely dated, it is probably only a matter of time after 589.

For France, the evidence is richer. The *Quicunque Vult,* composed, it seems, between 440 and 520, may be taken as an example of the first type of document. The *Filioque* found its way into the Preface to the Mass. At the Council of Gentilly (787) the term was raised in a general trinitarian context in controversy with the East. More concrete evidence comes in 794 when Charlemagne, who showed a special devotion both to the clause and the theology which it represents, protested against the action of the pope in assenting to the form of the creed of the Second Council of Nicea 'which professes that the Holy Spirit proceeds not from the Father and the Son *according to the faith of the Nicene symbol,* but from the Father through the Son'. This implies that *Filioque* already formed part of the Frankish form of C. The Council of Cividale (796–7) includes the phrase in its text of C with a skilful defence of the insertion added to the Acts of the Council. From this time it is most probable that the expanded text was used in the royal chapel at Aachen and generally in Charlemagne's domains. The papacy was once again drawn into the debate in 808 when a convent of Frankish monks in Jerusalem were threatened with expulsion by their orthodox neighbours for using the creed in this form. They appealed to Pope Leo III asking him to inform the emperor of their plight. Leo first sent them a doctrinal statement containing the clause for use among the Easterns but, despite pressure from Charlemagne, refused to authorize the revised form of the creed and recommended its complete omission from the Mass in France in line with Roman usage. Roman liturgical conservatism and diplomatic skill in avoiding a controversy with the East, in which not the emperor but the pope would have to bear the brunt, emerge from this incident. Leo further set up two silver shields in St Peter's with the unexpanded text of C in Greek and Latin. Thus everywhere in the West the doctrine of the double processions was taught in the ninth century and the creed with the *Filioque* used in Spain, Germany, France but not at Rome. It is a probable guess that it was introduced at Rome during the pontificate of Benedict VIII at the instance of the Emperor Henry II. The East seems justified in charging the West with an uncanonical insertion into a catholic creed but not with doctrinal error in the theology behind the clause.

The doctrine of Aquinas is virtually identical with that of Augustine though set in a scholastic form. If Augustine starts from Scripture, Aquinas moves within the ambit of tradition. His principal contribution to trinitarian theology, the Thomistic analogy (q.v.), is a variant on the psychological analogy of his predecessor with some additional implications for the relation between Son and the Spirit and the doctrine of the double procession. He combines the Augustinian interpretation of person in terms of relation with Boethius' definition of personality as 'the individual substance of a rational nature' (*see* **Person[s]**). Whether he succeeds in harmonizing the two is more arguable. His logical mapwork is more complex than that of the Cappadocians but may not represent an improvement. Questionable points here are the use of the term procession both of the Son and the Spirit, the distinction between active and passive spiration (the latter identical with the narrower meaning of procession), and the concept of the five notions (the four relations of paternity, filiation, the two senses of spiration expanded by the inclusion of ingeneracy). It is significant of his logical *a priorism* that the divine missions, from which an *a posteriori* approach would begin, form the last section of his discussion of the doctrine.

The two classical approaches (described above as monist and pluralist) recur in recent trinitarian theology. The monist accepts the psychological analogy as basic, the pluralist works within the social analogy. The former speaks without difficulty of the personality of God and finds some lesser gloss to put upon the term 'person', the latter prefers to talk about personality in God and finds some different explanation of the concept of the one substance. Of the extreme limits of the doctrine of the Trinity, the former tends to modalism, the latter to tritheism.

Karl Barth may be taken as representative of contemporary monism. For him the Trinity is the immediate implicate of revelation and therefore is expounded first in his *Church Dogmatics*. He can dispense with the use of analogies and must exclude the so-called Vestiges of the Trinity (q.v.). The use of either would imply an alternative route other than revelation to the doctrine. In the Trinity God offers himself as a Thou, not an I or a He. Modalism denies that our God is really God, subordinationism that God is really our God. Against modalism the true doctrine affirms that his modalities of Being are not external to his essence. God is God only as Father, Son and Spirit. Against subordinationism it affirms that God is not less himself as Son and Spirit than as Father and that God is equal to himself in all his modalities. While Barth is willing to concede a distinction between God-in-himself and God-for-us on the ground of his freedom, we cannot stop short of an immanent Trinity since God's freedom is never a freedom to be other than trinitarian. The Act of God involves directly the Being of God. His modalities are modes of Being, not simply modes of revelation. Thus a realism based on revelation replaces Augustine's realism based on relations.

Barth's monism is amply illustrated by his favourable reaction to some elements in the Augustinian and Thomist doctrines, the principle that the external operations of the Trinity are indivisible and the principle of coinherence. On the other hand, he is clearly uneasy about the term Person which he proposes to gloss as Mode of Being (*Seinsweisen*), using a term in Cappadocian theology in a manner foreign to those who first proposed it. Barth's modes are neither temporary

nor merely nominal. They are real and objective styles of Being but they are relations rather than persons. To regard Father, Son and Spirit as three distinct I's is not trinitarianism but tritheism.

Pluralists, on the other hand (C. C. J. Webb, L. Thornton, L. Hodgson), adopt a more empirical approach. The doctrine of the Trinity is an inference from the data of revelation given in event and verified in Christian experience. Trinitarian religion preceded trinitarian theology (Hodgson). The divine missions or operations provide a 'lead in' to the threefold self-differentiation of God. The transition from an economic to an essential Trinity is, therefore, not handled, as by Barth, as a matter of direct revelation, or with Aquinas, as a logical deduction from the nature of relations in God, but as the only adequate supporting inference from the data. The Persons of whom the formula speaks are centres of consciousness and the social analogy is therefore valid. At one level God is akin to ourselves, though even here infinitely richer than ourselves. Human personality is characterized both by impermeability and communicability. A person is a term fulfilled in relations. To speak of the divine relations is, therefore, meaningful provided that they are not used to weaken or as substitutes for the concept of person (Augustine) or as sufficient ground for the differentiation of the persons (Aquinas' deduction of the distinction of persons from the 'opposition of relations'). Pluralists adopt different interpretations of the divine unity. Webb regarded it as a supra-personal hinterland in which the Three are One. This raised the problem whether the Trinity is more strictly a quaternity (the one substance and the three persons) and whether the unity is consubstantial with the three persons. But it can also be regarded as the Three themselves being eternally, ineffably one, not some fourth element in the Godhead which constitutes them One. The doctrine of coinherence is vital to modern pluralism though it is interpreted more in terms of *circumincessio* (*movement*) than of rest (*circuminsessio*). It expresses the mutuality or reciprocity of indwelling whereby the love which is God passes and repasses between Father, Son and Holy Spirit. Such fulness of differentiated personal Being, it is claimed, represents the nearest approach that the human mind can reach to the ineffable mystery of God.

Both approaches are tenable and each can be cogently presented. Both have equal and opposite weaknesses. Neither can exclude the other but synthesis is impossible. Earthed in the biblical revelation and in Christian experience, the doctrine of the Trinity reminds us that 'all things issue in mystery'. Yet it is important for the mind of man, receptive and yet adventurous, to probe as far as it can before retiring baffled. To do otherwise is not the deeper reverence but the greater sloth.

L. Hodgson, *The Doctrine of the Trinity*, 1943; J. N. D. Kelly, *Early Christian Creeds*, 1950;

Early Christian Doctrines, 1958; G. L. Prestige, *God in Patristic Thought*, 1936; A. E. J. Rawlinson, ed., *Essays on the Trinity and the Incarnation*, 1928; C. C. J. Webb, *God and Personality*, 1918; C. Welch, *The Trinity in Contemporary Theology*, 1952.

H. E. W. TURNER

Tritheism

Tritheism is the name applying to one of the extreme limits of the doctrine of the Trinity (*see* **Modalism**) in which the plurality of the persons approximates to belief in three Gods. The clearest form is Arianism which included in a single formula a Father who was fully God, a Son who had the status of a leading creature and a Spirit who was inferior to the Son. In the absence of any stronger principle of association than the will of God which could justify their inclusion within a single formula, this must be deemed a form of Tritheism, even though the divine status of the Son and the Spirit was at best equivocal. The same charge (with less justification) was brought against the Cappadocian Fathers (q.v.) (*see* Gregory of Nyssa, *Quod non tres sint dii*). Karl Barth accuses of tritheism modern pluralist doctrines which appeal to the social analogy: 'To speak of three Divine I's rather than of one Divine I spells Tritheism, to maintain three objects of faith would be three gods. But the so-called three "Persons" in God are never three gods.' While pluralism is always exposed to this danger, many believe that the *Homoousios* and the divine coinherence (q.v.) provide adequate safeguards.

H. E. W. TURNER

Troeltsch, Ernst

Ernst Troeltsch (1865–1923), German philosopher and historian of religion, applied the methods and insights of W. Dilthey's philosophy of history to an analysis of the Christian faith. Insisting that Christianity (like every other religion) can only be investigated in the context of the overall spiritual and religious development of mankind, and that past historical events can only be understood through the sympathetic attempt to 're-live' them, Troeltsch reached the conclusion that *for our Western culture* Christianity marks the highest point in religious development. But, partly in reaction against the christocentric exclusiveness of Ritschlianism, he stressed that this held good only for our own culture, and that it did not preclude at all the possibility of genuine religion and even divine revelation within other non-Western religious traditions. Despite the great contribution that Troeltsch made towards our historical understanding of Christianity and of the evolution of the Western churches, he nevertheless bequeathed several difficult problems to his successors (the first of which received a drastic solution at the hands of the Dialectical theologians, q.v.): first, his apparent denial of the *absoluteness* of the Christian revelation; secondly, his denial of the reliability of the biblical accounts

of the miraculous (and, indeed, of anything at all that transcended our present experience) appeared to constitute a grave difficulty for anyone trying to establish the *historical* basis of the Christian faith. His *Social Teaching of the Christian Churches* (ET, 1931) is a work of deep scholarship and importance. *See also* **Dilthey, W.**

Benjamin A. Reist, *Towards a Theology of Involvement: The Thought of Ernst Troeltsch*, 1966.

JAMES RICHMOND

Tübingen School

The name applies to the German Hegelian school of biblical and historical criticism, whose main members were its founder F. C. Baur, Eduard Zeller and Adolf Hilgenfeld. *See* **Baur, F. C.**

JAMES RICHMOND

Typology, Types. *see* Allegory.

Ubiquity

The divine ubiquity is the divine omnipresence; but the term, technically used in the traditional language of theology, indicates this omnipresence in a certain mode, namely, as applied to the body of the risen Christ in certain forms of sacramental theory.

N. H. G. ROBINSON

Ultramontanism

Ultramontanism is the tendency to support a centralization of power in the pope's hands within the Roman Catholic Church and to grant him absolute control of both administration and doctrine, in contrast to emphasis on the rights of national churches on the one hand and liberalism on the other. Beginning in the eighteenth century, it may be said to have reached its zenith under Pius IX and Pius X.

R. P. C. HANSON

Una Sancta

Una Sancta is a Latin phrase describing the Church when regarded as indivisibly one and holy, in contrast to any theory of the possibility of its being divided.

R. P. C. HANSON

Unction

Though the word itself denotes anointing with oil for any purpose (there is a rite of unction in the Coronation Service), it is normally used to mean extreme unction, a rite used in the Roman Catholic Church for those who are dying. This was not always so: unction was originally a rite used in the Church to assist the recovery of the sick. It is mentioned in Mark 6.13 as being used by the apostles, and its use is recommended in James 5.14 f. For the first seven centuries of the Church's history it continued to be used as a form of strengthening rather than exclusively as a preparation for death. It is still so used in the Eastern Church, particularly as a preparation for the reception of holy communion. In the West, however, from the eighth century onwards it came increasingly to be used as a rite of preparation for death, so that its main purpose came to the remission of venial sin rather than the restoration of health. Unction was defined in accordance with the late mediaeval tradition by the Council of Trent, which also named it as one of the seven sacraments instituted by Christ. In modern times the rite of unction has been revived in Anglicanism and elsewhere as a quasi-sacramental rite for the spiritual and physical benefit of the sick, and various liturgical forms of administration have been authorized both in the Church of England and beyond it. There are some signs that the progress of the Liturgical Movement in the Roman Catholic Church is producing a demand for the restoration of the primitive use of the rite of unction.

A. T. HANSON

Unipersonality (of God)

Unipersonality (of God) is the view that the Godhead consists in one person only, as in Unitarianism (q.v.).

Unitarianism

The view that God is one person only and which therefore denies the doctrines of the divinity of Christ and of the Holy Spirit (as distinct from the person of God), and therefore also the doctrine of the Trinity. Both philosophically and theologically Unitarianism creates more problems than it solves; e.g. what was a lonely God doing in infinite ages before he created a world to love? The love of God becomes an impossible conception, and Unitarianism knows nothing of a God who so loved the world that he himself became incarnate for the sake of our salvation. Though unitarian ideas were not unknown in the early Church, as in some forms of Monarchianism (see **Christology** [4]), the main developments of the doctrine occurred after the Reformation. In the eighteenth century in England Unitarianism was widely prevalent among Dissenters (esp. Presbyterians) and in the nineteenth century a strongly rationalist form of Unitarianism was advocated by such leaders as J. Martineau (1805–1900). From the end of the eighteenth century a strongly ethical form of the doctrine found a home in Boston, Massachusetts, and contributed to the distinctive culture of New England in the nineteenth century. Unitarians do not profess any formal creed or confessional statement. See also **Trinity**.

J. E. Carpenter, *Unitarianism*, 1921; H. McLachlan, *The Unitarian Movement*, 1934; E. M. Wilbur, *Our Unitarian Heritage*, 1925.

EDITOR

Universalism

1. The view, emphasized by some of the later anti-nationalist prophets (e.g. Second Isaiah and Jonah), that God's purposes were not to be limited to the Jewish race but embraced other (or all) nations. The idea can also be traced back quite clearly to the first call of the patriarchs, Abraham (Gen. 12.3, etc.), Isaac (Gen. 26.4), Jacob (Gen. 28.14), and is to be found in the first writing prophet (Amos 9.7). The idea does not controvert utterly biblical particularism, in that such universalism has its roots in the particularist, elective call of Israel out of all nations: 'You only have I known' (Amos 3.2). The special call of Israel was not a favour and privilege but rather a responsibility which Paul (Rom. 9–11) envisaged as a re-integration of all mankind in Christ (*see* **Atonement** [5]; **Recapitulation**).

2. The doctrine (more properly known as *Apocatastasis* and not to be confused with (1) above, which holds that hell is temporal and purgative and that in the end all beings will be saved, arguing that all free moral creatures – angels, men, devils – will share in the grace of God's salvation ultimately. The doctrine is to be found in certain of the liberal Greek Fathers, Clement of Alexandria (c. 150–c. 215), Gregory of Nyssa (c. 330–c. 395) and Origen (c. 185–c. 254), who actually taught that the Devil himself would be converted in the end. The doctrine was strongly opposed by Augustine and was condemned at Constantinople in AD 543. The Reformers followed Augustine here, and neither Catholic nor Protestant holds these views, though they continue to be defended by certain Anabaptists, Moravians and Christadelphians, and during the last century and a half have often been taught by theologians of a liberal tendency.

JAMES ATKINSON

Universals. *see* Nominalism-Realism.

Utilitarianism

Utilitarianism is a moral theory which claims that the goal of moral endeavour is the general good, that the rightness of actions is to be measured by their production of good consequences and the reduction of evil. 'Good' has often, though not always, been conceived *hedonistically* by utilitarians; 'the greatest happiness of the greatest number' being the moral ideal. A utilitarian may argue (1) that individual moral acts are to be evaluated by reference to the 'greatest happiness principle', or (2) that normally the individual act should be referred only to a 'secondary moral rule' (such as the rules against stealing, cheating or lying). The secondary rules, he may claim, are referred for evaluation to the primary principle: individual acts are referred to it only in cases of conflict between rules. The non-hedonistic form of utilitarianism is called 'ideal utilitarianism'. According to it, there is a plurality of irreducible goods – knowledge, aesthetic experience, human relationships like love and friendship, for instance. Institutions, moral rules, dispositions of character are again to be evaluated in terms of their utility in bringing about these intrinsically desirable objectives.

Utilitarianism has been, and is, a valuable element in moral thinking – in its down-to-earth empiricism, its hostility to all obscurantism, and its humane insistence upon the question 'What effect will this proposed law, or this rule, this political policy . . . have upon the happiness or unhappiness of the human beings affected by it?' It is doubtful, however, whether utilitarianism can offer a *comprehensive* account of morality: in particular, there are difficulties in its treatment of justice, the notions of desert, guilt and punishment.

Historically: a large number of writers in modern British philosophy have been utilitarians or have had utilitarian strands in their moral thought. Utility was the basis of Hobbes' civil society. There was a hedonistic utilitarian side to Locke's ethics. Francis Hutcheson stated that 'that action is best which procures the greatest happiness for the greatest numbers, and that worst which . . . occasions misery'. In Paley's version of theological utilitarianism, virtue is 'the doing good to mankind, in obedience to the will of God, and for the sake of everlasting happiness'. Hume's (untheological) utilitarian theory was much more carefully developed and philosophically attractive. In the *Enquiry* he wrote, 'Everything which contributes to the happiness of society recommends itself directly to our approbation and goodwill.' Benevolence is not simply a veiled form of self-love. There is a close relationship between the utilitarianism of Hume and that of Bentham and the Mills, though emphases and details vary. Bentham (1748–1832) made notable applications of the principle of utility to the reform of law; but as a moral *theorist* he was less subtle than J. S. Mill (1806–1873). Mill introduced modifications, e.g. qualitative differences between forms of pleasure and happiness. These, however, with his emphasis on liberty and individuality, really prevent his theory from being classified as 'hedonistic utilitarianism' in any strict sense. A very detailed attempt was made by H. Sidgwick to present a consistent hedonistic theory: and G. E. Moore produced the best-known example of ideal utilitarianism. The tradition is by no means at an end in the mid-twentieth century.

Karl Britton, *John Stuart Mill*, 1953; J. S. Mill, *Utilitarianism* . . . , ed. Mary Warnock, Fontana Library of Philosophy Series, 1962; J. J. C. Smart, *An Outline of a System of Utilitarian Ethics*, 1961; Leslie Stephen, *The English Utilitarians*, 1900.

R. W. HEPBURN

Validity

Validity is a term applied to a sacrament of which

the divinely appointed sign has been duly performed and to which therefore is necessarily attached the divinely promised gift. Hence the notion of validity arises from the belief that sacramental reality is present when there is a particular outward sign specially appointed by divine authority to be the instrument and expression of some inward and spiritual good. This means that when the sign is performed spiritual good is conveyed through it, although it has to be acknowledged that it can only be effective for salvation to those who are spiritually fitted to receive it. This concept, which is common to Roman Catholics and many Anglicans, plays an important part in discussions about the sacraments, in so far as for a sacrament to be a sacrament it has to be valid, i.e. the divinely appointed sign must be duly performed. So, e.g. if one holds that the only proper minister at the Eucharist is one who has been ordained by a bishop in the apostolic succession, one would also maintain that a Eucharist celebrated by any other person not so ordained would be invalid. It is important to note further that this concept of validity is to be distinguished from that of efficacy. The spiritual gift is present in every valid sacrament, but the valid sacrament may not be efficacious for good if the recipient is unworthy. Conversely, the gift which is present in the valid sacrament may be conveyed efficaciously apart from it in certain conditions. So, to apply the term, a Roman Catholic would contend that a Methodist Eucharist was invalid, since the minister was not episcopally ordained, but he would not thereby be arguing that it was inefficacious, since the spiritual good conveyed by the sacrament is not always restricted by its validity.

J. G. DAVIES

Vatican

Vatican is the name of the hill in Rome on which is the site of the martyrdom of St Peter, the *martyrium* or memorial church built on the spot, now known as St Peter's, the papal residence, and the headquarters of the papal government, which have been situated there since 1377. St Peter's is not the cathedral of the see of Rome, but St John Lateran. Two councils have been held there, reckoned as General by the Roman Church, in 1869–70, the Council which promulgated the dogma of the infallibility of the pope and the council which was convened by Pope John XXIII and finished its work under his successor, Pope Paul VI, sitting from 1962 to 1965 (*see* **Vatican Council II**).

R. P. C. HANSON

Vatican Council I. *see* Vatican; Infallibility.

Vatican Council II

The Second Vatican Council was convoked by John XXIII on 25 December 1961. It met in four successive autumns, beginning on 11 October

1962, and ending on 8 December 1965. John XXIII died on 3 June 1963, and it fell to his successor, Paul VI (elected 21 June 1963) to continue the Council and promulgate its Acts.

The Acts of the Second Vatican Council consist of sixteen documents of three different types: Constitutions, Decrees and Declarations. Of the four Constitutions, two (on the Church and on divine revelation) are entitled 'dogmatic', and it is therefore in these two documents primarily that we can discover the doctrinal teaching of the Council. But doctrinal or theological issues arise in many of the other documents, in particular in the Constitutions on the Divine Liturgy and on the Church in the World of Today, and in the Declaration on Religious Liberty.

The Constitution on the Church (*Lumen Gentium*) was promulgated on 21 November 1964, during the third year of the Council. It consists of eight chapters: The mystery of the Church; The people of God; The hierarchical constitution of the Church, especially the episcopate; The lay-people; The universal vocation to holiness in the Church; Religious; The eschatological character of the pilgrim Church and its union with the heavenly Church; the Blessed Virgin Mary who gave birth to God, in the mystery of Christ and the Church.

The title of the seventh chapter, in which the Church on earth is designated as 'the pilgrim Church' serves to indicate that the subject of the Constitution as a whole is the Church as a whole, not merely the Church in her earthly existence. The Church is a 'mystery' (ch. 1), indeed 'Christ and the Church' can be described as a (single) mystery (title of ch. 7). The word suggests that it is impossible to give a complete rational account of the Church; it transcends our human understanding though of course, like God, it can be made the subject of rational discourse. The first chapter, after describing the foundation of the Church as a part of the 'story of salvation', enumerates various biblical images (n.6) by which it is not defined but inadequately described. N.7 concentrates attention on one of these images, that of 'the body of Christ': 'the Son of God . . . redeemed man and transformed him into a new creature. By communicating his Holy Spirit he constituted his brethren, called together from all nations, as his mystical body.' They are sacramentally united with him, and the whole body, with its diversity of functions and organs, is animated by the one Spirit of Christ, bound together in the bond of charity. Christ is the head of this body, and the exemplar of those who belong to it.

Christ established his Church on earth as a visible structure (*compaginem*); as such it is 'a community of faith, hope and charity'. The Church has thus two aspects: it is an interior reality springing from the presence and operation of the spirit of Christ in believers; and it is also a visible and identifiable factor in public history. These are the descriptions of two aspects of one reality, not of two distinct realities. There is an analogy between the relation of these two aspects of the Church (on earth) and the relation of the divine and human natures of Christ in the indissoluble unity of his person; and as, according to traditional theology, Christ's human nature is a living organ and instrument of the divine Word, so the visible aspect of the Church serves 'for the increase of the body' of Christ. It should be noted that, while affirming the single identity of the Church as 'mystical' and at the same time 'visible', this passage does not affirm the material co-extensiveness of the two aspects. Even the visibility of the Church is not necessarily confined, *de facto*, to the unique structured communion which is the Roman Catholic Church: 'The Church, established and organized in this world as a society, *subsists in* the catholic church, governed by the successor of Peter and the bishops in communion with him' (n.8). The words italicized are a deliberate substitution for the word *is*. We have here a delicately nuanced doctrine, a challenge to a renewed theology of the Church. The *de jure* claim that the Roman Catholic Church with its hierarchical structure is the visible reality to which all men are called to belong is no wit abated: the (Roman) Catholic Church was founded by God through Christ as 'necessary', and 'they could not be saved who, aware (of that necessity), yet refused to enter it or persevere in it' (n.14). But the remotely conditional form of the sentence just cited indicates a desire to recognize that an indefinite number of people, Christians and non-Christians, are not aware of this necessity and consequent obligation. Such men, if they 'fear God and do justice' (n.9) – or, to state it differently, are 'men of good will' – can be living, even unaware, by the spirit of Christ; in which case they too belong to his mystical Body. And groups of such God-fearers, joined together on the basis of gospel principles, have a positive role to play in the actual working-out of the divine purpose of redemption (*De Ecumenismo*, n.3). The Council's total fidelity to the traditional assertion that the Roman Catholic Church is objectively right in her essential claims goes hand in hand with a new emphasis on the possible co-existence of objective error or defect with subjective recitude, as also with an implicit priority accorded to subjective rectitude over objective correctness.

The third chapter is noteworthy for its treatment of the episcopate, a subject neglected by the First Vatican Council. Vatican II here teaches that bishops possess, by virtue of their consecration, 'the fullness of the priesthood', including the threefold role of sanctifying, teaching and governing. By their consecration they are called to membership of the episcopal 'college', in which the apostolic college lives on, and which is headed by the successor of Peter, the bishop of Rome. This college has supreme authority over the whole Church, just as its head, the pope, has. The Council regards presbyters and deacons as sharing in part of the fullness of the sacrament of Order; it does not commit itself to the assertion that these two ranks of the 'ministry' were immediately instituted by Christ.

In the last chapter of the Constitution the Blessed Virgin Mary is presented as closely associated with her Son in the history of salvation, and as the exemplar of the Church. Immaculately conceived, and assumed into heaven, she is at once our model and the object of our devotion. It is strongly emphasized that nothing which the Church affirms about her in any way derogates from the incomparable status of Christ as the unique and divine Redeemer.

The short Constitution on Divine Revelation begins with a fresh approach to the whole theme of revelation, too often presented in modern manuals of theology in an abstract fashion and with 'apologetic' interest. It takes as its subject the actual 'economy of revelation', the nexus of historical events (with their interpretation) culminating in the incarnation. Christ himself is both the mediator and the fullness of revelation, a divine intervention on the human scene calling for the act of faith by which man 'freely commits himself fully' to God thus self-revealed.

The question of the transmission of revelation, through the mediation of the Church, is the subject of the second chapter. The first chapter had rescued the notion of revelation from the exclusively conceptualist view, that revelation is the communication to man of truths capable of exhaustive propositional expression; on the contrary, it teaches, revelation is given in a human life and a divine person, and the truth which it communicates is not primarily knowledge about but acquaintance and communion with him. The second chapter, however, reverts in the main to the more ordinary modern view: revelation is a set of truths once conveyed to the apostles and now still available through a twofold mode of transmission: Holy Writ and Sacred Tradition. These two are inter-related, and combine to provide 'as it were a mirror' in which the believer contemplates God. We are told that Sacred Tradition develops through the intellectual, spiritual and apostolic action of the Church and its leaders, and that the episcopal college with its head is empowered to interpret authentically both Scripture and Tradition, though completely subservient to the 'word of God' transmitted by them.

The reason for this relapse into a preconciliar mode of thought is the influence within the Council of theologians dedicated to the outlook of the Council of Trent. This Counter-Reformation Council had insisted, against the Protestants, that the gospel was transmitted not only by Scripture but by 'traditions'. In post-Tridentine theology it was usually assumed (1) that Trent implied the 'material insufficiency' of Scripture, (2) that the 'traditions' in question were, though unwritten, essentially similar (in other respects) to Scripture – though not, like Scripture, inspired. There was a strong and, in the main, successful effort on the part of the 'new theologians' to avoid committing the Council to the material in-

sufficiency of Scripture, but in the course of the long-drawn-out struggle it seems to have been overlooked that ch. 2 was slipping into the old 'conceptualist' language about tradition and, by implication, about revelation. However, the chapter does manage to say that what the Church transmits is 'all that she is and all that she believes'. Since the Constitution on the Church teaches that the Church is the mystical Body of Christ, it is thus possible to hold that it is Christ himself who is sacramentally transmitted in and by the totality of the Church's supernatural reality and endowments. Among these endowments is of course inspired Scripture, which, despite the language of this chapter, should be considered part of Sacred Tradition. It is in virtue of this 'sacramental' transmission of Christ that the individual believer is able to make that act of faith in the present content of revelation (sc. Christ in his living presence) without which man is not justified.

As already suggested, the books of the Bible are, from one point of view, a collection of documents from antiquity like the plays of the Greek tragedians or the Annals of Tacitus. They provide data for historical reconstruction and some at least of them purport, or may be taken as purporting, to be historical in intention. The Church's claim on man's conscience is bound up with the affirmation of some of the alleged historical events recorded in these documents. It has always claimed, and this claim is reaffirmed by the Second Vatican Council, that, with reference to these events, these documents, and in particular the four Gospels, are veridical. The claim is part of its *kerygma* rather than of its *didache*. It should, however, be borne in mind that it does not involve a claim that the documents are the work of scientific historians, nor therefore that their affirmations are intended to have the precision of scientific history. As the Constitution on Revelation states: Truth is set forth in varying modes in texts which are in various ways historical, or prophetic, or poetic, or of other literary types (n.12).

But the truth of Scripture is something to which the Church is committed also on another level. It teaches that the books of the Bible are inspired by the Holy Spirit; and he cannot be the author of lies. Hence the Constitution teaches that these books 'teach without error the truth which God, for the purpose of our salvation, willed to be consigned to Holy Writ'. Here it must be observed that the truth in question is not any kind of truth but a limited kind: that which God willed to be written down *for the purpose of our salvation*. Salvation-truth is not co-extensive with scientific truth. The Constitution here refers, in a footnote, to passages of St Augustine and St Thomas Aquinas which emphasize this limitation. The former urges that God did not will, in Scripture, to satisfy our natural curiosity about scientific cosmogony. The argument may be widened out: God did not will by Scripture to satisfy our historical curiosity about the near East – except in so far as historical events occurring in that context contain or are strictly relevant to the economy of salvation and revelation. Biblical and Christian 'truth' is not scientific but religious truth. Yet the actual life, ministry, passion and resurrection of Christ are, in their broad substance, integral to religious truth. Hence the Council (n.19) 'unhesitatingly affirms the historicity' of the four Gospels in particular; the word historicity here should be understood in the light of the earlier quotation referring to various modes of historicity; and this qualification is perhaps ratified by the subsequent reference (n.9) to the kerygmatic character of the Gospels and the modes of composition employed by their authors. We may, in general, say that, just as the episcopal college and its head have full authority over our intellect to the extent that they propound what belongs to divine revelation or is intrinsically connected with it, so the Bible, in its apparently historical affirmations, has that full authority over our intellects in so far as it leads us on to the apprehension of Christ, the mediator and fullness of divine revelation.

Theology, in the concrete, is to be defined not only by the theses which it takes up and the solutions which it propounds, but by the principles which it utilizes and the spirit which animates it. The theology of Vatican II in its most creative aspects gives expression to a fresh orientation of the Roman Catholic mind. It shows a shift, some have suggested, from an 'essentialist' to an 'existentialist' standpoint. Perhaps one could say, more deeply, that it shows a new appreciation of the basic significance of history in a religion of incarnation, that is to say realized eschatology. And since history is what man creates by the use of his freedom and responsibility, it could be further said that the Council shifted the Church's emphasis from the objectively true to the subjectively right. Perhaps one should point out that, in each case, the shift is a matter of emphasis, not of exclusion of the complementary point of view. Nevertheless, such a shift of emphasis is pregnant with the possibility of hitherto unsuspected novelty in the development of the Christian Church and the exposition and application of the gospel.

What authority does the theology of Vatican II possess for a Roman Catholic? It was an ecumenical council, and as such could have promulgated new irreformable definitions of doctrine. In fact it did not. Perhaps its closest approach to doing so is its presentation of the once disputed doctrine of episcopal consecration: 'The Holy Synod *teaches* (*docet*) that by episcopal consecration the fullness of the sacrament of Order is conferred.' The historian of the Council will note the omission of the adverb 'solemnly' before 'teaches'; and the theologian will distinguish 'teaches' from 'defines' (*cf.* and contrast the introduction to Vatican I's definition of papal infallibility: '... we teach and define to be a dogma divinely revealed: . . .'). But there can be no question that the doctrine of Vatican II possesses

very high authority, particularly in those elements of it in which it is obvious that the Council's mind was deeply engaged. Its teaching on revelation, inspiration and the nature and extension of the Church will be normative for further theological progress.

W. M. Abbott, ed., *The Documents of Vatican II*, 1966; B. C. Butler, *The Theology of Vatican II*, 1967; B. Leeming, *The Vatican Council and Christian Unity*, 1967; J. H. Miller, ed., *Vatican II: an Inter-Faith Appraisal*, 1967; John Moorman, *Vatican Observed*, 1967; B. C. Pawley, ed., *The Second Vatican Council*, 1967; E. Schillebeeckx, *Vatican II: the Real Achievement*, 1967; H. Vorgrimler, ed., *Commentary on the Documents of Vatican II*, I, 1967, II, 1968.

B. C. BUTLER

Vestigia Trinitatis

The term applies to illustrations of or analogies to the Trinity drawn from within the created order. They may be of different levels of profundity. There is the three-leaved shamrock and the triads, root, tree and fruit; source, stream and river; sun, apex and ray (Tertullian – but really twofold analogies artificially extended to include a third term), and spring, stream and lake (Anselm). Other examples are weight, number and measure; solid, fluid and gaseous; the three dimensions of solids, and the three primary colours. But these can serve only as subjective confirmations of what is believed on other grounds. More penetrating is the threefold structure of the human self (*see* **Psychological Analogy**) and Aquinas held that it has value in determining the shape of the doctrine (*see* **Thomistic Analogy**). On the principle of the *analogia entis* it is claimed that there is an objective bond between Creator and creature resulting in a similitude of being between them. Karl Barth dismisses the 'vestigia' on the ground that the doctrine of the Trinity rests upon revelation alone and admits of no parallel or supplementary source. This is in keeping with his rejection of analogy as claiming the existence of an objective bond between Creator and creature other than grace.

H. E. W. TURNER

Via Eminentiae. see Language, Religious.

Via Negativa

Historically, the *via negativa* refers to a method of speculative theology associated particularly with the Neoplatonists, in the first instance Proclus (AD 410–485), and developed in a way most important for its influence on Christian theology by Pseudo-Dionysius (c.500) in his *Mystical Theology*. In essence the *via negativa* is a way of using language about God which keeps constantly before the attention of its user the fact that human language is hopelessly inadequate to use of the ineffable God. The method begins by trying to reduce, as far as possible, the effects of the necessarily anthropomorphic character of human theological language. The stripping away process begins by removing from consideration those human creaturely qualities which are inappropriate when applied to God. The *via negativa* is therefore a method of theological speech which is a constant reminder that speech originated and developed to deal with human relationships and is not equipped to deal adequately with the divine human encounter.

The *via negativa* has been regarded as a necessary first exercise for the theologian in both Western and Eastern traditions. St Thomas Aquinas regards it as a necessary preliminary to the *via positiva* (*see* **Via Positiva**). In the tradition of the Eastern Orthodox Church the *via negativa* is specially stressed and is known as the apophatic way.

The *via negativa* has been criticized by W. R. Inge because he believed that it led necessarily to a Buddhistic self-annihilating cult of *apatheia*. Other theologians have felt that it inevitably involves a turning of one's back on finite existence and a despising of it. Here it needs to be remembered that the *via negativa* is a way of theological speech which is determined by a profound sense of the utter transcendence of God. It has a right place, therefore, as a religious ascesis, but it is inadequate as a theological method if used in isolation. It needs to be balanced, as it is balanced in the theology of St Thomas Aquinas, by a use of the *via positiva*. The relation of the two methods has perhaps never been better described than by Charles Williams when he wrote: 'Both methods, the affirmative way and the negative way, were to co-exist, one might almost say to co-inhere, since each was to be the key to the other' (*The Descent of the Dove*, 1939, p. 57).

E. J. TINSLEY

Via Positiva

Like the *via negativa* (*see* **Via Negativa**) this is a theological method taken over into the Christian tradition from Pseudo-Dionysius. He explains what he means by the *via positiva* in his book *The Divine Names*. The *via positiva* is a method which theologically relies on the doctrine of creation, with its implication that marks of the Creator are necessarily discernible to a greater or lesser extent in his work of creation, and more particularly on the doctrine of man as made in the image of God. The highest human qualities are pointers which can be confidently taken as signs of the perfection of God. But the method emphasizes that while it is possible to take certain human qualities as pointers to God, and therefore to use them of God, it is necessary to emphasize that these things are true of God only in a pre-eminent way. This is the reason why the *via positiva* is sometimes referred to as the *via eminentiae*. *See also* **Language, Religious.**

E. J. TINSLEY

Virgin Birth

The doctrine that Christ was miraculously born of the Virgin Mary by the power of the Holy Spirit, having no human father. In the NT the only unambiguous statements of this birth as an historical event are to be found in Matt. 1.18–25 and Luke 1.34 ff. The historical evidence for it is thus quite incomparable with the NT evidence for the resurrection of Christ and should not be placed on the same level of credibility: every part of the NT states or implies the historical reality of Christ's resurrection. Since the rise of modern historical science theologians who uphold the historicity of the Virgin Birth have done so chiefly on the grounds that it is 'congruous' with the belief in Christ's divinity. Two frequently alleged objections to the belief may be discounted at once. First, it is said that virgin-births are common in all pagan religions and that it was inevitable that when Christ came to be supposed divine, he should be deemed to born of a virgin. This statement, however, is false: pagan mythology is full of legends of a superhuman hero born of intercourse between a god and a human woman. But this is scarcely *virgin* birth, and there is no real parallel to the story of the birth of Christ in pagan literature. The Jewish mind (and Matt. 1 and Luke 1 are intensely Jewish) would have been revolted by the idea of physical intercourse between a divine being and a woman. Secondly, it is alleged that the belief in the Virgin Birth of Christ arose from a morbid notion of sexual intercourse as sinful and therefore unacceptable as the means of the incarnation of the holy God. But again this morbid notion of sexuality is totally absent from the Jewish mind in general and from the birth narratives of the Gospels in particular. If we are looking for motives which would account for the 'invention' of a legend of the Virgin Birth, it could more plausibly be found in the desire of the Gospel-writers to stress the reality of Christ's humanity as one who was truly born of a woman, like other men, as over against incipient adoptianist (q.v.) and Gnostic (q.v.) notions that he was not really a man at all but only a play-acting divine manifestation.

Though it must be admitted that belief in the Virgin Birth plays no obvious part in NT proclamation (apart from the two passages cited: John 1.13 is too ambiguous), it may be claimed that the doctrine is significantly *congruous* with the whole biblical outlook. Both Matthew and Luke place great emphasis upon the eschatological character of Christ's birth through the Holy Spirit of the 'last times'. They assert the truth that God has set in motion the train of events which will inaugurate the new age of messianic salvation and judgment: the birth of Christ is an eschatological event ushering in the promised day of the Lord. They do not regard it as merely a sign that Christ is one of the 'divine men' of pagan religion. It is unique, because the once-only event of the coming of the Saviour is an essential element in the apostolic witness to the truth of that which had been fulfilled among men.

The Catholic teaching down the ages has stressed the work of the Holy Spirit in guiding the Church into all truth, of which the doctrine of the Virgin Birth of Christ has been regarded as an essential element. On the other hand, liberal protestant theology, with its general tendency to question miracle (q.v.), has often regarded the Virgin Birth as a legendary accretion to the original preaching and as possessing little significance for Christian faith; even some neo-orthodox theologians have acquiesced in this verdict (see, e.g., E. Brunner, *The Mediator*, ET, 1934, pp. 322 ff.). Today many theologians who would not themselves deny the doctrine would assert that it should not be equated with belief in the incarnation as such, but that it should be left to the judgment of the individual believer to accept it as an historical event or 'sign', or to regard it as a symbolic way of representing the unique figure of Christ, in much the same manner as they might accept symbolically the truth of Christ's descent into hell or ascension into heaven, both of which affirmations are made, like that of the Virgin Birth, in the Apostles' Creed. It may perhaps be added that radical biblical criticism which has not compromised its independence through submission to historical positivism (q.v.) does not necessarily reject the historicity of the Virgin Birth. Such questions are in the last resort answered by judgments based upon personal faith rather than by principles derived from criticism itself. The incarnation remains a mystery of faith and the doctrine of the Virgin Birth should not be regarded as an attempt to give a biological explanation of it. *See also* **Mary, the Blessed Virgin.**

T. Boslooper, *The Virgin Birth*, 1962 (in which a full bibliography is given). For the NT materials see C. K. Barrett, *The Holy Spirit and the Gospel Tradition*, 1947, pp. 6–10; Alan Richardson, *Introduction to the Theology of the New Testament*, 1958, pp. 169–78; V. Taylor, *The Historical Evidence for the Virgin Birth*, 1920; G. H. Box, *The Virgin Birth of Christ*, 1916; D. Edwards, *The Virgin Birth in History and Faith*, 1943; J. G. Machen, *The Virgin Birth of Christ*, 1930; J. Orr, *The Virgin Birth of Christ*, 1907.

EDITOR

Vision of God

To be aware of God in the perfection of his being, in Christian tradition, has always been closely associated with the beatitude of Christ: 'Blessed are the pure in heart, for they shall see God.' In the biblical tradition, the vision of God is an eschatological reality only possible to man in the life beyond death. In general, the OT, for example, uses the metaphor of the vision of God reluctantly as far as human experience in this life is concerned. 'No man shall see God and live' is an OT refrain. The only people who see God in the OT are exceptional persons like Moses, for example, and even he is spoken of as being granted a vision only of the 'back parts' of God. Nevertheless, it would not be true to say that in the OT the human experience of God is described exclusively in terms of the hearing of God. Frequently enough the prophet sees the word of God as well as hears it (see **Mysticism**).

In the NT also the vision of God is an eschatological reality. But again significantly in the records of the mission of Christ the imagery of seeing is very frequent indeed in relation to the responsibility which is laid upon disciples for the way they interpret Jesus ('having eyes do you not yet see?', 'blessed are the eyes that see the things that ye see').

In mysticism (see **Mysticism**) the vision of God is regarded as the apex of the whole process of ascetical discipline (see **Asceticism; Ascetical Theology**). Similarly in the Christian monastic tradition the vision of God was awaited as the crown of monks' discipline. And there are instances where Christian mystics speak of the vision of God in an extravagant way which, strictly speaking, would make it incompatible with Christian eschatology. That is to say, they identify their experience of ecstasy (see **Ecstasy**) with the beatific vision. It is for this reason that the Protestant tradition of Christianity has been generally suspicious of the whole notion of the vision of God. In it there inevitably lies concealed, Protestants have insisted, the idea of a ladder which a man is able to scale by his own endeavour and achieve the beatific vision, independent of the work of grace. Inevitably, it was believed to involve a side-tracking of the central place of the humanity of Christ and the historical incarnation and atonement.

But if the vision of God is seen to be an inadequate metaphor for the profoundly personal reciprocal character of the human communion with God in its perfection, the inadequacy of the metaphor of hearing God must be realized also. Both are required for expressing the transcendental and immanental aspects of religious experience. To isolate one metaphor and concentrate on audition, word, speech, which has been a feature of Protestantism, often leads to a denigration of art and aesthetic experience which a close hold on the necessity of retaining the metaphor of vision would have avoided.

John Baillie, *Our Knowledge of God*, 1939; John Burnaby, *Amor Dei*, 1938; K. E. Kirk, *The Vision of God*, 1931; Ray Petry, ed., *Late Mediaeval Mysticism*, 1957.

E. J. TINSLEY

Vocation

In the NT 'vocation' (Greek *klesis*) always refers to God's call to men through Christ to the life of faith within the body of the 'called' (*ekkletoi*). The Church is the *ekklesia*, called out of 'the world'. The word never refers to a Christian's worldly trade, profession, etc. Paul was called to be an apostle, not a tent-maker (Acts 18.3). All the 'called' were expected to serve God in their daily lives (cf. the so-called 'house-tables', Col. 3. 22–4.1; Eph. 6. 5–9; I Tim. 6.1 f.; Titus 2.9 f.; I Peter 2.18–25); they were to work as unto their

Master in heaven. Thus, daily work is sanctified, but it is not to be confused with God's calling into the fellowship of the saints. During the Middle Ages the word *vocatio* came to be used solely of the call to the religious (monastic) life. In protest against this 'double standard' (the religious and the workaday) Luther and Calvin began to use the words *Beruf* (German, 'calling') and *vocatio* of men's everyday tasks and stations. Calvin's teaching had particular relevance to the age of the bourgeoisie and the rise of capitalism, as has been noted by Weber and Tawney. In doing this the Reformers were only developing the truth taught by the fourteenth and fifteenth century mystics, Eckhardt and Tauler, that the vision of God was accessible to the humblest labourer as well as to the monk. But in the period of secularization (q.v.) after the Reformation the idea of vocation was itself secularized, so that today people speak readily about someone having a 'vocation' to be a schoolmaster or doctor (though hardly a dustman or a bus-conductor) without any reference to the call of God in Christ. The whole question of *Christian* vocation deserves and has received careful attention in our own time. *See* **Lay, Laity.**

Alan Richardson, *The Biblical Doctrine of Work*, 1952; R. H. Tawney, *Religion and the Rise of Capitalism*, 1963; Max Weber, *The Protestant Ethic and the Spirit of Capitalism*, 1930; G. Wingren, *The Christian's Calling: Luther on Vocation*, 1958.

EDITOR

Voluntaryism

Voluntaryism is the view that the Church should be independent of control by the state and of state aid or establishment.

Waldenses

The origin of the Waldenses has been erroneously traced to Claudius, a ninth-century bishop of Turin who opposed the use of images in worship, but the founder was certainly Peter Waldo of Lyons, who at his conversion (c.1176) entered on a life of poverty and preaching. Waldo induced two priests to translate the Bible from the Vulgate into the French of the Lyons area. He was excommunicated, but continued with his followers to spread and expound the vernacular Scriptures, often reciting the sacred writings from memory. The early Waldenses offended the church authorities not so much by their doctrines as through unauthorized preaching and by an independent biblicism using unauthorized texts; but they were denounced and persecuted as heretics. They later became irreconcilably hostile to Rome, as shown by the *Noble Lesson*, a fifteenth-century document which rejects auricular confession, the mass, and papal claims. Surviving many attempts

to exterminate them, they occupied at the time of the Reformation chiefly the Piedmont valleys and the neighbouring French region of the upper Durance. In the 1520s they sought relationships with the Lutheran and Zwinglian reformed leaders. A notable convention held at Chanforan in 1532, attended by William Farel and other Protestants, produced a declaration which states briefly the doctrine of predestination, rejects auricular confession and prohibition of clerical marriage, prescribes Sunday rest and approves two sacraments only. Christians are never to take revenge, but they may become magistrates. From the same synod came the plan by which Pierre Robert Olivétan was employed to prepare a scholarly French translation of the Bible (1535). Calvin took a great interest in the Waldenses and was instrumental in training a number of their missionary preachers. During the last hundred years the Waldenses have shown new energy and, aided by British and American sympathizers and by the recent liberalizing of the laws, have expanded to about 200 centres in Italy, and formed numerous colonies in the Americas.

J. Jalla, *Les Vaudois des Alpes*, 1934; A. Javanel, *The Waldenses and the Reformation*, 1961.

J. T. MCNEILL

Warfield, Benjamin Breckinridge

B. B. Warfield (1851–1921), American Calvinist theologian, was a native of Lexington, Kentucky. He was educated at both the college and seminary at Princeton, and studied at Leipzig. After serving as Professor of NT at Western Theological Seminary (1879–87), he became Professor of Didactic and Polemic Theology at Princeton Theological Seminary (1887–1921).

Warfield was a conspicuous defender of the 'Princeton theology' so long championed by Charles Hodge (q.v.) and by his son, A. A. Hodge. A man of impressive learning, schooled in conservative, scholastic Calvinism, Warfield stated the doctrine of the inerrancy of the Bible in a full, carefully-defined way, limiting inerrancy to the 'original autograph' manuscripts of the Bible. He declared that the doctrine of scriptural inerrancy could be overthrown only by proving that error existed in the original (and now lost) autographs. On this basis he resisted critical approaches to the Scriptures. His immense labours in the field of systematic theology were predicated on the view that the sole source of theology is revelation, especially as given in God's written word, 'incomparably superior to all other manifestations of Him in the fullness, richness, and clearness of its communications' (*Studies in Theology*, p. 60). During his lifetime, Warfield wrote many articles and treatises on a wide range of theological subjects, many of which were posthumously collected and published. His views, especially on biblical inerrancy, were for a time dominant in American Presbyterianism. He was a vigorous opponent of liberal theology and credal revision.

B. B. Warfield, *Calvin and Calvinism*, 1931;
Perfectionism, 2 vols., 1931; *Studies in Theology*,
1932.

ROBERT T. HANDY

Wellhausen, Julius

Julius Wellhausen (1844–1918), distinguished
German OT scholar, was best known for his
epoch-making researches on the structure of the
Pentateuch (with special reference to the book of
Genesis). He was the first to analyse those docu-
ments now known within OT scholarship as
J, E and *P*.

JAMES RICHMOND

Wesley, John. *see* Methodism.

Westminster Catechisms and Confession

The Westminster Assembly of Divines, 1 July
1643 to 25 March 1652, was called by the English
Parliament, then at war with Charles I, to bring
the Church of England into nearer agreement with
the reformed Churches. Its 151 members included many distinguished for learning and piety.
but Episcopalians, obeying the King's command,
did not attend. The majority, including the
Scottish commissioners sent under the Solemn
League and Covenant, were Presbyterians, but a
few learned Erastians concerned to maintain
parliamentary control of the Church and the
highly vocal 'Five Dissenting Brethren' who
maintained the principles of Independency, kept
up protracted debates. The Westminster Confession and the Larger and Shorter Catechisms were
all issued in 1647. The Confession bears no
structural relationship with any continental document but is in large degree an amplified revision
of Archbishop Usher's Irish Articles of 1615. It
is firmly Calvinistic, including with the doctrine of
election that of reprobation in the modified form
of preterition. The covenant of works made with
Adam has been superseded by the covenant of
grace, and the latter is conceived as having two
dispensations, the OT promises and types, and the
gospel. The Shorter Catechism is a brief and
explicit handbook of indoctrination, while the
Larger Catechism is rather a directory for the
use of teachers. The Westminster Assembly
documents present a condensed, comprehensive,
and extraordinarily precise statement of seventeenth-century Calvinism.

Texts in P. Schaff, *Creeds of Christendom*, III,
1919 and in T. F. Torrance, *The School of Faith*,
1959; *see also* G. S. Hendry, *The Westminster
Confession for Today*, 1960; W. M. Hetherington,
History of the Westminster Assembly, 5th ed.,
1890; E. D. Morris, *Theology of the Westminster
Symbols*, 1901.

J. T. MCNEILL

Whitehead, Alfred North. *see* Process Theology.

Whitsunday. *see* Pentecost.

Witness of the Spirit

The doctrine of the witness of the Holy Spirit
(*testimonium Sancti Spiritus internum*) in the
reading, preaching or hearing of the Scriptures is
a doctrine of the whole Church. The Spirit
breathes life into what would otherwise be the
dead letter of the written words, so that we know
that they are addressed to us personally: they are
'brought home' to us. St Luke's story of the walk
to Emmaus shows how the risen Lord, not to be
distinguished from the Spirit of Christ and of
God, causes the hearts of faithful disciples to
'burn within us' as he is in the way with us,
expounding to us the Scriptures (Luke 24.25–32;
cf. also II Cor. 3.14–18). Calvin (q.v.) has given
this universal Christian insight its classical formulation: 'For as God alone can properly bear witness to his own words, so these words will not
obtain full credit in the hearts of men until they
are sealed by the inward testimony of the Spirit
(*testimonium Spiritus intus*). The same Spirit,
therefore, who spoke by the mouth of the prophets, must penetrate our hearts in order to convince us that they faithfully delivered the message
with which they were divinely entrusted.' Or
again, Scripture 'deigns not to submit to proofs
and arguments, but owes the full conviction with
which we ought to receive it to the testimony of
the Spirit' (*Institutes*, i.7.4–5). The opening article
of the Westminster Confession (1643) likewise
speaks of 'the inward work of the Holy Spirit
bearing witness by and with the word in our
hearts'. But though the doctrine was thus clearly
defined and emphasized by the Reformed theologians, it was no new Reformation doctrine: the
mediaeval view, both Augustinian and Thomistic,
laid stress upon the divine work in the reception
of the scriptural truth in the hearts of the faithful.
See further, Alan Richardson, *Christian Apologetics*, 1947, pp. 211–20, where evidence is cited.
See also **Scripture, Doctrine of Holy; Inspiration.**

EDITOR

Work. *see* Lay, Laity; Vocation.

Works

It is classical Protestant teaching that men are
saved (i.e. justified and sanctified) by grace alone
through faith alone, quite apart from any 'works'
of theirs. For the gospel does not say: If you do
this or that, God will be gracious to you and reward you with salvation. That is the way of the
law and salvation by works. But the gospel says:
God *is* gracious and freely gives you salvation in
Christ – have faith in him! only believe! (*cf.*
Mark 5.36). Admittedly, believing or having faith
is something we do, but it is not a 'work' by which
we move God to be gracious to us; it is rather a

response to which we are moved by his grace. The Protestant slogan 'by faith alone' sometimes obscures this fact, since faith can be subtly misconstrued as a work. This happens when, e.g. the suggestion is made that because the way of the law and its works has proved too difficult, God has graciously provided something easier for us to do – quite ignoring the fact that it is often much easier to be busy doing things than to have faith in God. More frequently, faith is misconstrued as an inward disposition or subjective mood, which qualifies us in God's sight as recipients of his grace – an idea which can only lead to unhealthy preoccupation with ourselves, resulting either in self-righteous pride when we think we have faith enough and of the right sort, or hopeless despair when we fear we have not. Moreover, the idea of faith as a purely inward state often leads to disparagement of the outward means of grace, particularly the sacraments, as encouraging 'work-righteousness'. It is true, of course, that our use of the means of grace can be misconstrued as a meritorious work by which we gain favour with God. But the means of grace themselves are not our works, but God's gifts, and there is no merit in our use of them. We use them (i.e. receive them) rightly, only as we respond 'by faith alone' to the grace that is manifested in them; but the neglect or refusal to use them is no demonstration of true faith. *See also* **Good Works.**

P. S. WATSON

Worship

The word is derived from Anglo-Saxon *weorth-scipe*, honour. In older English usage worship can be rendered to men of excellence (*cf.* in England, 'the Worshipful the Mayor'): so KJV, Matt. 8.2, not necessarily implying divinity. Except in archaic forms (e.g., the *Book of Common Prayer,* 1662, Solemnization of Matrimony: 'with my body I thee worship') or in extravagant speech, the word is nowadays used only in religious language. In the Bible God alone is supremely the object of worship and adoration; no one and nothing is to be worshipped beside him.

The word 'worship' is very useful in the English religious vocabulary, and other languages (e.g. German) which have no precise equivalent are the poorer for their lack of it. Though God is to be worshipped in life as well as in word, 'worship' in its normal usage refers to the expression in in corporate gatherings of adoration, praise and thanksgiving to God through Christ. From the earliest times and down all the Christian centuries Christians have gathered, whether in churches specially built for the purpose or in improvised surroundings, to worship God in this way, for this is their spontaneous (though it may become formalized and conventional) response to God's revelation of his saving acts. Worship is thus essentially thanksgiving (*cf.* Greek *eucharistia*) and praise. It may be offered formally according to fixed rites: *ritual* is the fixed form of words ordered by authority for specified days or times

(though the word is commonly misused to denote ceremonial). Or it may be offered in 'free' worship, i.e., without fixed forms, and perhaps with *extempore* prayer, in which individuals in the congregation may participate. It may be offered with full and rich *ceremonial,* i.e. accompanying actions, processions, vestments, genuflexions, etc., and with choirs and music, as in a High Mass or Sung Eucharist. Or it may be offered with a minimum of ceremonial, or in corporate silence as in a Quaker meeting. But the purpose of all worship is the same: to offer praise to God for his grace and glory.

In most corporate acts of Christian worship certain elements are usually found: a preparation, consisting of a general confession of sin, followed perhaps by a declaration of absolution by an authorized minister; the ministry of the word – the reading of scriptural 'lessons' and the sermon which expounds the truth and relevance of the Scriptures; the singing of psalms or hymns; and the prayers or intercessions (*see* **Prayer, Theology of**). In many Christian Confessions these acts of devotion are followed by the celebration of the Lord's Supper (by whatever name it is called – Holy Communion, Mass, Eucharist, etc.). The intention of all such acts of worship is to declare the saving power of God and to make this power a reality in the hearts and lives of those who participate in them. However diverse may be the forms which Christian worship may take, there is a common intention underlying them all. This truth is perceived in our own ecumenical age, as it has not always been perceived in previous times. The *Directory of Public Worship,* compiled by the Westminster Assembly (1645), abolished the *Book of Common Prayer,* and indeed there are significant differences between the two works; yet the basic elements of Christian worship may be seen to be present in both.

Forms of worship designed for special occasions (e.g. baptism, marriage, sickness, burial) are to be found in almost all Christian denominations. It is appropriate that special occasions in the lives of Christian families or congregations should thus be solemnized in an act of worship. In comparatively recent times it has become common to compile special services or acts of worship for specific occasions (e.g. Harvest Festivals) or for specific vocational groups or interests (e.g. Hospital Services). Whatever defects these improvised occasional services may have, they are a means of witnessing to the relevance of the Christian faith in particular areas of life and of reminding people of their duty of Christian worship, if they profess the name of Christ.

A matter of great theological importance is the recognition of the priority of worship over doctrinal formulation. The normal order of things is that worship precedes credal formulation and theology. The earliest Christians found themselves worshipping Christ before they had reached any formal theological definitions of his person and nature. To make the point in another way: the earliest Christian confessions of faith would seem to have had their origin in worship, as (e.g.) in the Christ-hymn in Phil. 2.5–11, which in the opinion of many scholars was not composed by St Paul but was quoted by him from a familiar act of Christian worship. It was only long after Christ had been worshipped as the divine Lord and Saviour that the Church's theologians began to work out an intellectual *rationale* of Christ's nature as the God-man. Thus, *lex adorandi est lex credendi:* we believe according as we worship. Worship is primary; theology is secondary – a point frequently overlooked in academic circles. Theology is often incredible because worship is neglected. On the other hand, it should be emphasized that theology has a most important function to fulfil in relation to worship. Theology must prune worship of all that is foreign to Christian truth, constantly bring it under the critique of rational judgment, and articulate its essential meaning so that those who worship with their hearts may worship with their understanding also. But the truth remains that worship is the *raison d'être* of theology, not vice-versa. *See also* **Office, Divine; Prayer, Theology of; Liturgical Worship.**

W. K. Lowther Clarke, ed., *Liturgy and Worship,* 1932, and subsequent editions; P. Dearmer, *The Art of Public Worship,* 1919; J. O. Dobson, *Worship,* 1941; L. Duchesne, *Christian Worship: its Origin and Evolution,* ET, 1903; R. Otto, *The Idea of the Holy,* ET, 1923; Evelyn Underhill, *Worship,* 1936.

EDITOR

Wrath of God

Wrath, like judgment, is an element in the NT writers' account of God's dealings with man which cannot be ignored without misunderstanding the NT message as a whole. Paul is the writer who makes most use of the concept; his term is *orge* (*thumos* only once, Rom. 2.8), and it has a markedly impersonal sense, so much so that it can be used absolutely as 'the wrath'. It does not describe an affection of God, but a condition of man. It is the description of man in his state of alienation from God, and it belongs to the sphere of law, curse, sin, and death. Essentially the same idea is found in the Fourth Gospel (*see* John 3.36; *cf.* 3.17–19). God is never described as angry in the NT, nor is any verb meaning 'to feel or express anger' used of him. In the Apocalypse, the vivid OT figure of the cup of God's wrath is employed (the history of this figure can probably be traced back as far as the Ras Shamra tablets), and many scholars have suggested that God's wrath in the Apocalypse is viewed in OT rather than NT terms. But even here the wrath is closely connected with the cross, and the interpretation of the symbolism would seem to favour the impersonal conception on the whole. A. Feuillet has recently argued that the cup which Jesus accepts in Gethsemane is intended to be the cup of God's wrath (*RB*, 74 [1967], pp. 356–391). But

NT writers carefully avoid saying that Jesus experienced the wrath of God or that God's wrath had to be appeased.

This profound and well-balanced account of God's wrath was not, of course, always appreciated or adhered to by later theologians. Very soon we find a simple moralistic view of God's wrath prevailing. Either it is said that God is angry with sinners but loves the pious. Or else God is described as very loving, and as showing very great long-suffering towards sinners, but there comes a point where he lets his wrath take its course against the obstinate. The fact that the church has always been tempted to give the OT equal authority with the NT meant that it was much more difficult to distinguish the NT doctrine of the wrath of God. Both the earliest OT conception of a God of capricious wrath, and the much deeper conception exemplified in Hosea of God's wrath as his generous indignation against disobedience, have influenced Christian thought on the subject. The wrath also came into play in connection with the doctrine of the atonement (q.v.). Theologians have described Christ as appeasing the Father's wrath (though Calvin does maintain that one should not describe God as being angry with Christ). By the nineteenth century the wrath of God was an indispensable feature of orthodox Protestant theology, so that William Cowper could write in his last years of religious melancholia:

Me miserable! How shall I escape
Infinite wrath and infinite despair?

The first reaction of liberal theology (q.v.) was to dispense with the wrath of God altogether. This is well illustrated in Ritschl's work: he considers that the wrath of God should find no place in a scheme of Christian theology. Later theologians rightly rejected the idea that Christ propitiated the Father's wrath, but often sought to find a place for the personal wrath of God. Notable among these is P. T. Forsyth, who disliked the notion of an impersonal wrath, on the grounds that God in the Scriptures is always revealed as personal. C. H. Dodd in his commentary on Romans mainly emphasizes the impersonal nature of the wrath. Karl Barth tends to use language of a personal kind about the wrath, though a reading of his *Commentary on Romans* leaves one doubtful as to whether he regards it as actually personal. In the *Doctrine of the Word of God* he leans more to the thought of wrath as God's personal reaction to sin.

The doctrine of the wrath of God is an area in which the NT might be said to have done its own demythologizing, and modern theologians would do well to accept this thankfully, instead of making forays into the OT material which has already been screened and purified by the revelation in Christ. The wrath of God is a descriptive term for the consequences of sin working themselves out in society through the ages. It should not be taken to indicate an emotion, attitude, or affection of God. It is essentially impersonal, and it is no more derogatory to the personal conception of God to regard the wrath as impersonal than it is to regard the law as impersonal, the law which was, after all, itself ordained by God according to Paul. The wrath therefore belongs to the realm of sin, death, curse, and law. This is why judgment in the NT is so often described in legal terms (e.g. the 'uttermost farthing' of the parable). However, the Christian conception of God's wrath is distinguished from a mere idea of moral retribution, as found for instance, in the Hindu doctrine of karma, by two features: it is God's wrath, i.e. this is a moral universe and God has ordained that sin brings consequences, and wrath can be changed into redemptive suffering by the power of Christ. It is not inexorable. The wrath can therefore find a significant place in a Christian doctrine of God, if we are careful to observe the limits observed by the NT writers. The alternative is to regard God's wrath as his personal reaction to sin or to the sinner. This always leads to a fatal dichotomy; either God is depicted as loving and angry by turns, or, still worse, the Father is depicted as just and angry and the Son as merciful and loving. (Counter-Reformation piety and some Orthodox thought found a variant of this by depicting Christ as the stern judge and the Blessed Virgin as the one who shows mercy.) If we are to take 'God is love' in I John 4.8 seriously, we must follow the NT writers in regarding the wrath as impersonal.

Karl Barth, *Church Dogmatics*, I: *Doctrine of the Word of God*, 1, ET, 1936, pp. 204 f., 268 f.; P. T. Forsyth, *The Work of Christ*, 1910, pp. 236 ff.; A. T. Hanson, *The Wrath of the Lamb*, 1957; R. V. G. Tasker, *The Biblical Doctrine of the Wrath of God*, 1951; H. Kleinknecht, J. Fichtner, G. Stählin, *et al*, 'Wrath' *TDNT* (also published as a separate title in 1964).

A. T. HANSON

Wyclif, John

Wyclif (c. 1328–1384), English pre-Reformer, earned three degrees at Oxford although his studies were interrupted by clerical appointments and by the Black Death (1349) and much time was given to teaching. About 1370 he began to put forth somewhat original and disturbing theological treatises and to criticize the papacy. In *De dominio divino* (1375) he declared that lordship is held from God and cannot truly belong to one in mortal sin. In *De civili dominio* (1376) this doctrine was given revolutionary application in matters of Church and State, and was employed to justify the deprivation of unworthy clerics, including popes. In *De benedicta Incarnatione* (1370) he argued, with philosophical realism, that Christ took on the 'common humanity' of all men, a theory tending, in Workman's view, to 'the exaltation of humanity at large'. But his purpose is to combat the nominalist view of *singularis humanitas*, not to affirm the excellence of man apart from grace. While appealing, like Luther, to the authority of Scripture against the

usages and abuses of the time, he followed the scholastic methods of argument in which he had been trained. No point of doctrine received from Wyclif more attention than the eucharist. His *De Eucharistia* (1379) rejects the adoration of the bread as Christ's body: Christ is 'insensibly hidden' in the sacrament. The annihilation of the substance with the survival of the accidents is for him a logical absurdity. 'This is my body' is equivalent to 'This figures forth (*figurat*) my body'. Wyclif's late years were spent in the rectory at Lutterworth. Many of his earlier opinions were uncompromisingly restated in his *Trialogus* (1382) and in numerous late controversial tracts against popes, clergy, monks and friars.

J. A. Robson, *Wyclif and the Oxford Schools: the Relation of the* Summa de ente *to Scholastic Debates at Oxford*, 1961; M. Spinka, ed., *Advocates of Reform: From Wyclif to Erasmus*, 1953; H. B. Workman, *John Wyclif: A Study of the English Medieval Church*, 2 vols., 1926; J. T. McNeill, 'Some Emphases in Wyclif's Teaching', *JR*, VII (1927), 447–56.

J. T. MCNEILL

Zinzendorf, Nicholas Lewis, Count von

Nurtured in the home of a devout grandmother, and at the age of four blessed by the Pietist leader, Spener, Zinzendorf (1700–1760) had intense religious experiences in childhood. At the Halle grammar school headed by A. H. Francke he became in his teens deeply concerned for the heathen and with schoolboy adherents organized the Order of the Grain of Mustard Seed for missions. Later at Wittenberg and Utrecht his piety deepened, and at Paris he made friends among Roman Catholic dignitaries including the archbishop, Cardinal Noailles. He entered the service of the elector of Saxony, and having married settled on his estate at Berthelsdorf. In 1722 he made contact with a company of exiled Moravian Brethren who had begun a settlement on the Hutberg. Thereafter he gave his energies largely to the expansion and spiritual stimulation of this community, called Herrnhut, and to the extensive missions its members undertook at his prompting. He was ordained at Lutheran hands, and became a bishop of the Moravians (1737). His interests were world-wide; he felt deeply a fraternal bond with all Christians, and entertained somewhat grandiose schemes of Church unity. His well-meant but too hasty efforts in this direction during a visit to Pennsylvania evoked antagonism. He published in London an interchurch hymnal and liturgy with intercessions for many churches by name.

F. Blanke, *Zinzendorf und die Einheit der Kinder Gottes,* 1950; E. Langton, *History of the Moravian Church,* 1956; A. J. Lewis, *Zinzendorf the Ecumenical Pioneer,* 1962; A. G. Spangenberg, *Leben des Grafen von Zinzendorf,* 3 vols., 1722–5, abr. English ed., 1838; J. R. Weinlich, *Count Zinzendorf,* 1956.

J. T. MCNEILL

Zwingli, Huldreich

The son of a village official aided by a clerical uncle, Zwingli (1484–1531), Reformer of German Switzerland, obtained a good education, chiefly at Basel (MA 1506) where he felt the influence of Thomas Wyttenbach, an able biblical scholar with reforming interests. While pastor in Glarus, 1506–16, he pursued the study of Greek, read the works of Erasmus, and cultivated his musical talents. His writings against the mercenary traffic, which he saw in operation during two excursions as chaplain to troops in Italy, marked him as a Swiss patriot. Having removed to Einsiedeln, he denounced abuses connected with indulgences. His rising fame as a preacher led to his call to Zurich as 'People's Priest' in the Great Minster, where his duties began at the opening of the year 1519. The Reformation in Zurich grew out of Zwingli's scriptural preaching and the civic decisions induced by it. In his twelve-year ministry there he imparted his spirit to the city, the canton, and the Confederacy. A challenging early formulation of his theology is the *Sixty-seven Conclusions* which he prepared for the First Disputation of Zurich, 29 January 1523. Here he denies that the gospel is subject to the approval of the Church and declares the sum of the gospel to be the reconciliation and redemption wrought by Christ. Christ is the head of all believers who are his body and constitute the Catholic Church, the communion of saints. All Christians are brothers of Christ and of each other, and none is to be called 'father'. Other works are: *On the Clarity and Certainty of the Word of God* (1522), a theme which he handles with enthusiasm; *Commentary on True and False Religion* (1523), on the nature of the Holy Catholic Church of true saints and its distinction from the visible Church of professed Christians; *The Shepherd* (1524), an expanded sermon on the duties of pastors, and the two short confessions which he addressed respectively to Charles V, 1530, and to Francis I, 1531. He defended infant baptism against the Zurich Anabaptists, affirming on inference from statements of the early Fathers that it was practised in the early Church and that it took the place of circumcision. His adoption of an old interpretation of I Cor. 11.24. 'This is my body', by which 'is' means 'signifies' led to a controversial exchange with Luther (q.v.). At the Conference of Marburg, 1529 (q.v.), in disagreement with Luther, he denied the corporeal presence, arguing that Christ's body remains in heaven. Zwingli was obliged to do his writing rapidly amid crises and did not live to present a theological system.

Huldreich Zwinglis sämmtliche Werke, ed., E. Egli *et al,* I–XIII, 1905 (*Corpus Reformatorum* ed.); G. W. Bromiley, *Zwingli and Bullinger,* 1953 (selections); J. Courvoisier, *Zwingli,* 1953; O. Farner, *Huldrych Zwingli,* 4 vols., 1943–60; S. M. Jackson, ed., *The Latin Works and Correspondence of Huldreich Zwingli,* 3 vols., 1912–29; J. Rilliet, *Zwingli, Third Man of the Reformation,* ET, 1964.

J. T. MCNEILL